THE LAW OF REAL PROPERTY

THE LAW
of
REAL PROPERTY

BY

The Hon. Sir ROBERT MEGARRY,
M.A., LL.D.(Cantab.), Hon.LL.D.(Hull), F.B.A.

Hon. Fellow of Trinity Hall, Cambridge;
a Justice of the Chancery Division of the High Court

AND

H. W. R. WADE,
Q.C., LL.D., D.C.L., F.B.A.

an Honorary Bencher of Lincoln's Inn;
Professor of English Law in the University of Oxford

FOURTH EDITION

LONDON
STEVENS & SONS LIMITED
1975

First Edition	-	-	1957
Second Impression	-		1958
Second Edition	-	-	1959
Second Impression	-		1964
Third Edition	-	-	1966
Second Impression	-		1971
Fourth Edition	-	-	1975

Published in 1975 by
Stevens & Sons Limited
of 11 New Fetter Lane
London — Law Publishers
and printed in Great Britain
by The Eastern Press
Limited of London and
Reading.

S.B.N. 420 44310 X

PREFACE

OVER eight years have elapsed since the last edition of this book appeared; and in that time there have been many developments of the law. There has been no new statute with the fundamental import of the Perpetuities and Accumulations Act 1964, though the Law of Property Act 1969 made some significant changes. The main activity has been in the courts. They have provided us with a bountiful harvest which has left few sections of the book untouched. The main crop of consequent new or rewritten passages will be found in Chapters 12, 13 and 17 (Covenants and Licences affecting Land; Incorporeal Hereditaments; and Registration); and, as might be expected, by far the greater part of Chapter 18 (Social Control of Land), where Parliament has indeed been active, has had to be recast or rewritten. The space needed for the new matter has in the main been found by pruning historical material, mostly in the first six chapters, and so continuing the process applied to the last edition. Our regrets at having to make these excisions have been tempered by the thought that the passages in question will continue to be available in surviving copies of the two previous editions; and where possible we have inserted much shortened indications of the gist of what has gone. The upshot is that the net increase in length of this edition has been limited to 36 pages, or some three per cent. We only wish that the increase in price could have been proportionate; but book publishers face formidable difficulties these days, and we have joined with them in doing what was possible to minimise an increase that otherwise would have been even more daunting.

Certain of the changes perhaps invite further and better particulars. Some decisions have not fitted easily into the established principles, and two cases in the House of Lords (*Steadman* v. *Steadman*, p. 566; *Beswick* v. *Beswick*, p. 746) may prove to have generated more problems than they have resolved. Radical changes in matrimonial law have had their impact (pp. 446, 785), and restrictive covenants, where we have somewhat reorganised the material, are showing welcome signs of shedding some of their less necessary technicalities (pp. 760–772). We are not alone in regretting that our law of covenants is falling behind that of some other countries as a result of the failure to resolve the problems of positive covenants, discussed in the Wilberforce Report (p. 755).

Despite the disappearance of registration of deeds, the length of the chapter on Registration (Chapter 17) has increased by a quarter.

This is due partly to the insertion or expansion of a number of passages, and partly to the increased volume of case law. In the past
eight years, many more problems on the subject have been coming
before the courts, both on registration of charges and on registration
of title; and disturbing defects in the law have been emerging. Some
of the shortcomings of the law of registration of land charges have
long been notorious, but they are of diminishing seriousness as registration of title more and more takes over. The defects of registration
of title are far more grave. One of the main objects of the reform of
property law during this century has been to pave the way for
universal registration of title (p. 1158). Yet it is becoming increasingly
clear that the Land Registration Act 1925 received far less than its
fair share of the loving care that was lavished on the other property
statutes of 1925. On many matters the moment when the clock of
Lincoln's Inn struck midnight on December 31, 1925, has justly been
regarded as being the hour of fate; but only more recently has it
been becoming clear that it was the Land Registration Act 1925 that
was Cinderella. (The metaphor, we hasten to add, is not to be
pressed too far). Now that half the conveyancing in the country falls
within the Act, there are compelling reasons for subjecting the Act
and the Rules to a thorough overhaul. As they stand, they house too
many provisions which cannot be made to work satisfactorily by even
the wisest of administrations.

In preparing this edition we have been greatly assisted by many
helpful suggestions. We warmly thank those who have taken the time
and trouble to make them, both for ourselves and for the readers who
will benefit from the consequent improvements. We cannot mention
them all by name, but we must express our special gratitude to Dr.
J. H. C. Morris and Mrs. E. H. M. Thorneycroft for their lists of
constructive suggestions. We are also greatly indebted to Mr. P. V.
Baker, Q.C., for reading the proofs and detecting many frailties. Our
thanks are due to the publishers, both for preparing the tables and
the index and for many other matters, and to the printers, who, faced
by the many difficulties of the past year, nevertheless triumphantly
surmounted them all. Although it was over a year ago that we sent
them the first half of the manuscript, they have incorporated our
alterations to the proofs down to the last moment. Subject to the
decencies of proof correction, the law stated is, we hope, as it stood at
the date of this preface.

Finally, we would add that, as should be obvious, the book
derives no added authority from the fact that one of us is a judge of
the Chancery Division. As was pointed out in *Cordell* v. *Second Clanfield Properties Ltd.* [1969] 2 Ch. 9 at 16 (in a passage repeated in

the preface to the current edition of *Snell's Principles of Equity*), authorship and judicial determination are two entirely different processes. Each may learn from the other; but they remain discrete.

LINCOLN'S INN,

Candlemas, 1975.

R. E. M.

H. W. R. W.

PREFACE TO THE FIRST EDITION

THIS is a book in which we have attempted to state the English law of real property within a reasonable compass and in a form which will be both intelligible to students and helpful to practitioners. In some other spheres, the claims of student and practitioner are barely reconcilable, but here we are fortunate in our subject. In the main, the English law of real property rests on the logical development of clear principles, and it is these principles that throughout we have sought to emphasise. There are, indeed, certain passages in this book which are addressed solely or mainly to the student, and a number of details which, though important to the practitioner, need trouble none save the more zealous students; but for the most part it is our hope to have achieved a work of dual utility.

The book is founded on a pre-war manuscript from which *A Manual of the Law of Real Property* has already been drawn. As first conceived, the task was to revise and bring the manuscript up to date; in the outcome most, but by no means all, of that manuscript has found its way into this book, while at the same time much new material has been interwoven with it. For unlike the manuscript and the *Manual*, this is a work of joint authorship, with all the mutual aid that flows from the application of a second mind to what was conceived and in the main executed as a complete entity. Instead of dividing up the subject-matter and each writing the text of part, nearly all of this book has been covered by each of us in close detail, often more than once. It would be too much to hope that even this time-consuming process has extirpated all error, but we hope that the result will be thought to have justified the effort. In addition to this, other factors have combined to delay publication, including our geographical separation, the press of other claims upon our time, difficulties in resolving how much of the original manuscript to omit, and the troubles of the printing industry in 1956. The printers' skill has, however, enabled us to keep the text under constant revision, and although the vicissitudes of publication have made it difficult to ensure that the whole of the text has been brought up to the same date, we hope that in general the law will be found to have been accurately stated down to the beginning of 1957, with such later additions as the state of the proofs admitted.

The publication of this work completes the original scheme for two books of a common design but different scope. Those who in student days have become familiar with the *Manual* should be able to turn with ease to the greater amplitude of this book; and the similarity of design will, we hope, not only assist teachers of law in their tasks, but also make it possible for future editions of the *Manual* to become a little slimmer.

Finally, we have the pleasure of giving thanks where thanks are due. Some of our obligations are general and distributed; we are grateful to many of those whom we have severally sought to teach, for they have themselves taught us more than they are ever likely to realise. Other gratitude is more specific. The publishers and printers have earned more praise than even they are accustomed to; it would be wrong if we did not mention specifically the printers' skill and publishers' generosity which made it possible for the work to proceed when the manuscript and galley proofs had reached a condition more deplorable than any we had seen before. Mr. I. Goldsmith also gave invaluable help with the manuscript at that stage, Mr. P. V. Baker read the proofs, and Mr. R. Higgins prepared the table of cases and table of statutes. To all of them we are grateful.

LINCOLN'S INN,   R. E. M.
New Year's Day, 1957   H. W. R. W.

CONTENTS

APPENDIX

TABLE OF CASES

xvii

TABLE OF STATUTES

COMMONWEALTH STATUTES

ALPHABETICAL LIST OF STATUTES

This list will enable any statute to be found in the chronological Table of Statutes, ante, p. lxvii.

TABLE OF STATUTORY INSTRUMENTS

ABBREVIATIONS

STATUTES, ORDERS AND CASES

A.E.A. - -	Administration of Estates Act.
A.H.A. - -	Agricultural Holdings Act.
B.S. - -	Building Society.
C.A. - -	Conveyancing Act.
F.R.A. - -	Fines and Recoveries Act.
I.E.A. - -	Intestates' Estates Act.
In b. - -	(In bonis) In the Goods of, In the Estate of.
I.R.C. - -	Inland Revenue Commissioners.
J.A. - -	Judicature Act.
L. & T. A. -	Landlord and Tenant Act.
L.C.A. - -	Land Charges Act.
L.P.A. - -	Law of Property Act.
L.P.Am.A. -	Law of Property (Amendment) Act.
L.R.A. - -	Land Registration Act.
L.R. & L.C.A.	Land Registration and Land Charges Act.
L.R.R. - -	Land Registration Rules.
L.T.A. - -	Land Transfer Act.
R.P.A. - -	Real Property Act.
R.S.C. - -	Rules of the Supreme Court.
S.E. - -	Settled Estate(s).
S.T. - -	Settlement Trusts.
S.I. - -	Statutory Instrument.
S.L.A. - -	Settled Land Act.
S.R. & O. -	Statutory Rules and Orders.
T.A. - -	Trustee Act.
W.T. - -	Will Trusts.

BOOKS AND PERIODICALS

Bailey, *Wills*: S. J. Bailey, The Law of Wills, 7th ed., 1973.

Bl.Comm.: Sir William Blackstone, Commentaries on the Laws of England, 15th ed., by E. Christian, 1809 (first ed. published, 1765).

Blount, Frag.: Thomas Blount, Fragmenta Antiquitatis, or Antient Tenures, 2nd ed., 1784.

Bracton: Henry de Bracton, De Legibus et Consuetudinibus Angliae, Rolls ed. by T. Twiss, 1879; G. E. Woodbine's ed., 1915–1942. "Bracton" is thought to have been written in the years prior to 1257.

Challis: H. W. Challis, The Law of Real Property, 3rd ed. by C. Sweet, 1911.

C.L.J.: Cambridge Law Journal.

C.L.Y.: Current Law Year Book.

Cole, *Ejectment*: W. R. Cole, The Law of Ejectment, 1857.

Col.L.R.: Columbia Law Review.

Co.Litt.: Coke upon Littleton, 19th ed., with notes by F. Hargrave and C. Butler, 1832 (Littleton's Tenures was first printed in or about 1481; Sir Edward Coke's commentary was first published in 1628).

Conv.(N.S.): The Conveyancer, new series, 1936–

Conv.(O.S.): The Conveyancer, old series, 1916–1936.

Conv.Y.B.: Conveyancers' Year Book.

Coote, *Mortgages*: Coote's Law of Mortgages, 9th ed. by R. L. Ramsbotham, 1927.

C.P.L.: Current Property Law.

Cru.Dig.: William Cruise, A Digest of the Laws of England, 4th ed. by H. H. White, 1835.

Curtis & Ruoff: *see* Ruoff & Roper.
Dart, V. & P.: Dart's Vendors and Purchasers of Real Estate, 8th ed. by
    E. P. Hewitt and M. R. C. Overton, 1929.
Digby: K. E. Digby, Introduction to the History of the Law of Real Property,
    5th ed. by K. E. Digby and W. M. Harrison, 1897.
E.H.R.: English Historical Review.
Elphinstone, *Covenants*: Sir L. H. Elphinstone, Covenants Affecting Land,
    1946.
Emmet: Emmet on Title, 15th ed. by J. Gilchrist Smith and J. T. Farrand,
    1967. A 16th edition 1974, by J. T. Farrand, has now appeared.
Farrand, Contract and Conveyance: J. T. Farrand, Contract and Conveyance,
    2nd. ed., 1973.
Farwell, *Powers*: Sir G. Farwell, Powers, 3rd ed. by C. J. W. Farwell and
    F. K. Archer, 1916.
Fearne: Charles Fearne, Essay on the Learning of Contingent Remainders and
    Executory Devises, 10th ed., with C. Butler's notes, 1844 (1st ed. published,
    1772). The second volume of the 10th edition is Josiah W. Smith's
    Original View of Executory Interests.
Fisher and Lightwood, *Mortgage*: Fisher and Lightwood's Law of Mortgage,
    8th. ed., by E. L. G. Tyler, 1969.
Fletcher: E. W. S. Fletcher, Contingent and Executory Interests in Land, 1915.
Foa, L. & T.: Edgar Foa, Law of Landlord and Tenant, 8th ed. by H.
    Heathcote Williams, 1957.
Fry, S. P.: Sir E. Fry, Specific Performance, 6th ed. by G. R. Northcote, 1921.
Gale: C. J. Gale, Law of Easements, 14th ed., by S. G. Maurice and R. Wake-
    field, 1972 (1st ed. published 1839).
Gilb. *Uses*: Gilbert on Uses and Trusts, 3rd ed. by E. B. Sugden, 1811.
Gray: J. C. Gray, Perpetuities, 4th ed. by R. Gray, 1942.
Halsb.: Halsbury's Laws of England, 3rd ed., 1952–1963. References to the
    fourth edition, now in course of publication (1973–   ), are distinguished
    by the addition " 4th ed.".
Hanbury, *Modern Equity*: H. G. Hanbury, Modern Equity, 9th ed., by R. H.
    Maudsley, 1969.
Harv.L.R.: Harvard Law Review.
Hawkins and Ryder: Hawkins and Ryder's The Construction of Wills, by
    E. C. Ryder, 1965 (based on Hawkins on the Construction of Wills,
    3rd ed. 1925).
Hayes: William Hayes, An Introduction to Conveyancing, 5th ed. 1840.
        Limitations: William Hayes, Limitations to Heirs of the Body in
            Devises, 1824.
H.E.L.: Sir W. S. Holdsworth, A History of English Law, 1903–1952; latest
    editions as in 61 L.Q.R. 346 (1945); also vol. i, 7th ed., 1956; vol. xiii,
    1952; vol. xiv, 1964; vol. xv, 1965; vol. xvi, 1966.
Hill & Redman, L. & T.: Hill and Redman's Landlord and Tenant, 15th ed.,
    by M. Barnes, 1970.
Hood and Challis: Hood and Challis' Property Acts, 8th ed., by J. H. Boraston,
    1938.
Jarman: Thomas Jarman, A Treatise on Wills, 8th ed. by R. W. Jennings and
    J. C. Harper, 1951 (1st ed. published 1841–1843).
Jurid.Soc.Papers: Juridical Society's Papers, 1858–1874.
K. & E.: Key and Elphinstone's Precedents in Conveyancing, 15th ed. by
    various editors, 1953–1954.
Lewin: Lewin on Trusts, 16th ed. by W. J. Mowbray, 1964 (1st ed. published
    1837).
Lewis, *Perpetuity*: W. D. Lewis, The Law of Perpetuity, 1843.
Littleton: see Co.Litt.
L.J.News.: Law Journal (the weekly periodical).
L.Q.R.: Law Quarterly Review.
Maitland, *Coll. Pp.*: F. W. Maitland, Collected Papers, ed. by H. A. L. Fisher,
    1911.
        Equity: F. W. Maitland, Equity, revised ed. by J. W. Brunyate,
            1936.
        Forms of Action: F. W. Maitland, Forms of Action at Common
            Law, ed. by A. H. Chaytor and W. J. Whittaker, 1936 (first
            printed with *Equity*, 1909).
Marsden: R. G. Marsden, Perpetuities, 1883.

Millard, *Tithes*: P. W. Millard, Tithes, 3rd ed., 1938.
Mod.L.R.: Modern Law Review.
Morris and Leach: J. H. C. Morris and W. B. Leach, The Rule against
    Perpetuities, 2nd ed., 1962, with Supplement, 1964.
Norton, *Deeds*: R. F. Norton, Deeds, 2nd ed. by R. J. A. Morrison and H. J.
    Goolden, 1928.
O.E.D.: Oxford English Dictionary.
Perk.: Perkins' Profitable Book Touching the Laws of England, 15th ed. by
    R. J. Greening, 1827 (first ed. published 1530).
Platt on *Leases*: Thomas Platt, Law of Leases, 1847.
P. & M.: Sir F. Pollock and F. W. Maitland, History of English Law before
    the time of Edward I, 2nd ed., 1898.
Preston: Richard Preston, An Elementary Treatise on Estates, 2nd ed., 1820–
    1827.
    Abstracts: Richard Preston, Essay on Abstracts of Title, 2nd ed.,
    1823–1824.
    Conveyancing: Richard Preston, A Treatise on Conveyancing, 3rd
    ed., 1819–1829.
Prideaux: Prideaux's Forms and Precedents in Conveyancing, 25th ed.,
    1958–1959. Vol. 1 by T. K. Wigan and I. M. Phillips; Vol. 2 by V. G. H.
    Hallett, A. P. McNabb and T. A. Blanco White; Vol. 3 by I. M. Phillips,
    E. H. Scammell and V. G. H. Hallett (1st ed. published 1853).
Rob.Gav.: Thomas Robinson, The Common Law of Kent, or the Custom of
    Gavelkind, 3rd ed. by J. Wilson, 1822 (this edition is usually referred to;
    the latest is 5th ed. by C. J. Elton and H. J. H. Mackay, 1897).
Ruoff & Roper: T. B. F. Ruoff and R. B. Roper, The Law and Practice of
    Registered Conveyancing, 3rd ed., 1972 (formerly Curtis & Ruoff).
Sanders, *Uses*: F. W. Sanders, Uses and Trusts, 5th ed. by G. W. Sanders and
    J. Warner, 1844.
Scriven: J. Scriven, A Treatise on the Law of Copyholds, 7th ed. by A. Brown,
    1896.
Shep.Touch.: Sheppard's Touchstone of Common Assurances, 8th ed. by E. G.
    Atherley, 1826 (7th ed. (1st ed. published 1641) by R. Preston, 1820, is,
    however, not superseded).
Smith, *Executory Interests*: see Fearne.
Smith's L.C.: J. W. Smith, Leading Cases, 13th ed. by T. W. Chitty, A. T.
    Denning and C. P. Harvey, 1929.
Snell, *Equity*: Snell's Principles of Equity, 27th ed. by R. E. Megarry and
    P. V. Baker, 1973 (1st ed. published 1868).
S.J.: Solicitors' Journal.
S.S.: Selden Society's Publications.
Sugden, *Powers*: E. B. Sugden, A Practical Treatise on Powers, 8th ed., 1861.
    V. & P.: E. B. Sugden, The Law of Vendors and Purchasers, 14th
    ed., 1862.
Tudor L.C.: Tudor's Leading Cases on Real Property, 4th ed. by T. H. Carson
    and H. B. Bompas, 1898.
Vin.Abr.: Viner's Abridgment of Law and Equity, 2nd ed., 1791–1806.
Waldock, *Mortgages*: C. H. M. Waldock, Mortgages, 2nd ed., 1950.
Wh. & T.: White and Tudor's Leading Cases in Equity, 9th ed. by E. P.
    Hewitt and J. B. Richardson, 1928.
Williams, *Executors*: Williams and Mortimer on Executors, Administrators
    and Probate (which includes the 15th edition of Williams on Executors),
    by J. H. G. Sunnucks, 1970.
Williams, *Statute of Frauds, Section IV*: James Williams, The Statute of
    Frauds, Section Four, 1932.
Williams, R.P.: Joshua Williams, Principles of the Law of Real Property,
    23rd ed. by T. C. Williams, 1920. (This is cited in preference to
    24th ed. by R. A. Eastwood, 1926, since Williams is a classic
    work on the pre-1926 law.)
    Seisin: Joshua Williams, The Seisin of the Freehold, 1878.
Williams, V. & P.: T. C. Williams, A Treatise on the Law of Vendor and
    Purchaser, 4th ed. by T. C. Williams and J. M. Lightwood, 1936.
Wolst. & C.: Wolstenholme and Cherry's Conveyancing Statutes, 13th ed. by
    J. T. Farrand, 1972.
Woodfall, L. & T.: William Woodfall, Landlord and Tenant, 27th ed. by
    L. A. Blundell and V. G. Wellings, 1968 (1st ed. published 1802).

GLOSSARY

[The object of this glossary is to provide a ready source of reference to the meanings of some of the more troublesome technical expressions used in the text. For the most part, brief but not necessarily exhaustive definitions have been given, with references by means of numerals in brackets to the pages of the text where further information can be obtained and the terms may be seen in their context; references which are essential to a proper understanding of the terms are in heavy type. Where the text contains a convenient collection and explanation of a number of contrasting terms, a simple reference to the appropriate pages is given instead of setting out the definitions. See also the entries in the index under WORDS AND PHRASES.]

Absolute: not conditional or determinable (in relation to an estate) (137).
Abstract of title: an epitome of documents and facts showing ownership (**597**).
Ad hoc settlement or trust for sale: one with special overreaching powers (**379**).
Ademption: failure of a testamentary gift, *e.g.*, by the testator ceasing to own the property (500).
Administrators: persons authorised to administer the estate of an intestate (534); compare Executors.
Advancement: gift by parent or husband to provide for child or wife (445).
Advowson: a right of presenting a clergyman to a vacant benefice (800).
Alienation: the act of disposing of or transferring.
Ante-nuptial: before marriage.
Appendant: attached to land by operation of law (823); compare Appurtenant.
Approvement: appropriation of portion of manorial waste free from rights of common.
Appurtenant: attached to land by act of parties (823); compare Appendant.
Assent: an assurance by personal representatives vesting property in the person entitled (536).
Assignment: a disposition or transfer, usually of a lease.
Assurance: a disposition or transfer.
Attorney, power of: authority to another person to execute deeds or carry out transactions (462).

Bargain and sale: contract for sale (165).
Base fee: a fee simple produced by partially barring an entail (88).
Beneficial owner: a person entitled for his own benefit and not, *e.g.*, as trustee.
Beneficiaries: those entitled to benefit under a trust or will.
Betterment levy: a tax on the realisation of development value (1105).
Bona vacantia: goods without an owner.

Caution: an entry protecting an interest in registered land (1070).
Cestui que trust: a beneficiary under a trust.
„   „   *use*: a person to whose use property was conveyed (152).
„   „   *vie*: a person for whose life an estate *pur autre vie* lasts (100).
Charge: an incumbrance securing the payment of money.
Collaterals: blood relations who are neither ancestors nor descendants.
Commorientes: persons dying at the same time (492).
Condition precedent: a condition which must be fulfilled before a disposition can take effect (75).
Condition subsequent: a condition which may defeat a gift after it has taken effect (75).
Consolidation: a requirement that a mortgagor shall not redeem one mortgage without another (926).
Constructive: inferred or implied (121, 442).
Contingent: operative only upon an uncertain event (**173**): compare Vested.
Contractual tenancy: a tenancy under a lease or agreement which is still in force; contrast Statutory tenant.

cxii

Controlled tenancy: a tenancy protected by the older system of rent restriction (1126).

Conversion: a change in the nature of property, either actually or notionally (**286**).

Conveyance: an instrument (other than a will) transferring property.

Co-parceners: persons together constituting the heir (**429**).

Copyhold: a form of tenure peculiar to manors (26).

Corporeal: admitting of physical possession (788).

Covenant: a promise contained in a deed.

Coverture: the continuance of a marriage.

Cross-remainders: remainders, on death without issue, to survivors of a class (386).

Curtesy: a widower's life estate in his wife's realty (514).

Customary heir: the heir according to a local custom.

Cy-près: as nearly as possible (205).

Deed: a document signed, sealed and delivered.

Deed poll: a deed with only one party (601); compare Indenture.

Defeasance: the determination of an interest on a specified event.

Demise: a transfer, usually by the grant of a lease.

Determine: terminate, come to an end.

Development: altering land or the use of it (1089).

Development charge: a payment to the State for the right to develop land (1099).

Development gains tax: a tax on the disposal of land (1106).

Devise: a gift of real property by will.

Disentail: to bar an entail (90).

Disseisin: dispossession; see Seisin.

Distrain, distress: the lawful extrajudicial seizure of chattels to enforce a right, *e.g.*, to the payment of rent (691).

Dominant tenement: land to which the benefit of a right is attached (806); compare Servient tenement.

Dower: a widow's life estate in one-third of her husband's realty (516).

Durante viduitate: during widowhood.

Easement: a right over land, such as a right of way (806).

Emblements: growing crops which an outgoing tenant may take (109).

En ventre sa mère: conceived but not born.

Enceinte: pregnant.

Enfranchise: the statutory right of certain tenants to purchase the fee simple (1151).

Entail: an estate or interest descending only to issue of the grantee.

Entireties: joint ownership between husband and wife (432).

Equities: equitable rights.

Equity of redemption: the sum of a mortgagor's rights in the mortgaged property (**891**).

Escheat: a lord's right to ownerless realty (18).

Escrow: a document which upon delivery will become a deed (601).

Estate: 1. the *quantum* of an interest in land (14).
2. an area of land (15).
3. the whole of the property owned by a deceased person (533).

Estoppel: prohibition of a party from denying facts which he has led another to assume to be true (645).

Estovers: wood which a tenant may take for domestic and other purposes (106).

Execute: 1. to perform or complete, *e.g.*, a deed.
2. to convert, *e.g.*, to transform the equitable interest under a use into a legal estate (156).

Executors: persons appointed by a testator to administer his estate (533); compare Administrators.

Executory: not yet completed (contrasted with " executed ") (162, 447).

Executory instrument: an instrument not yet fully carried into effect.

Executory interest: a valid future interest not complying with the legal remainder rules (**188**).

Executory limitation: a limitation creating an executory interest (189).

Executory trust: a trust the details of which remain to be set out in some further document (447).

Fee: base (88), conditional (75), determinable (74), simple (41), tail (42).
Feme covert: married woman.
Feme sole: unmarried woman.
Feoffee to uses: a person holding property to the use of another (152).
Feoffment: a conveyance by livery [delivery] of seisin (50).
Fine: 1. a collusive action partially barring an entail (87); compare Recovery.
    2. a premium or a lump sum payment, *e.g.*, for the grant of a lease.
Foreclosure: preceedings by a mortgagee which free mortgaged property from the equity of redemption (905).
Freebench: dower (of copyhold lands).
Freehold: 1. free tenure (19, 33).
      2. an estate of uncertain maximum duration (**41**).

Gavelkind: a special customary tenure, formerly common in Kent (20).
General equitable charge: an equitable charge of a legal estate not protected by a deposit of title deeds (1040).
Good consideration: natural love and affection for near relatives (116, 165).

Heirlooms: 1. inheritable chattels (522).
      2. settled chattels (342).
Hereditaments: inheritable rights in property (787).
Heriot: the best beast of a deceased tenant, to which the lord of the manor was entitled (25).
Heritable issue: descendants capable of inheriting (515).
Hotchpot: the bringing into account of benefits already received before sharing in property (528).

In capite: in chief, holding immediately of the Crown (14).
In esse: in existence (opposed to *in posse*, not in existence) (731).
In gross: existing independently of a dominant tenement (806).
Incorporeal: not admitting of physical possession (787).
Incumbrance: a liability burdening property.
Indenture: a deed between two or more parties (601); compare Deed poll.
Infant: a person under 18 years of age.
Injunction: an order of a court restraining a breach of obligation, or commanding performance.
Instrument: a legal document.
Interesse termini: the rights of a lessee before entry (**632**).
Intestacy: the failure to dispose of property by will.
Issue: descendants of any generation (59).

Jointure: provision by a husband for his widow, usually under a settlement (385).
Jus accrescendi: right of survivorship (391).
Jus tertii: a third party's title (1004).

Lapse: the failure of a gift, especially by the beneficiary predeceasing the testator (489).
Legal memory: any time later than the accession of Richard I, 1189 (847).
Letters of administration: an authorisation to persons to administer the estate of a deceased person (534).
Licence: a permission, *e.g.*, to enter on land (776).
Lien: a form of security for unpaid money (885).
Limitation of actions: statutory barring of rights of action after a period of years (1010, 1011).
Limitation, words of: words delimiting the estate granted to some person previously mentioned (**52, 61**); compare Purchase, words of.
Limited owner: an owner with an estate less than a fee simple.
Lis pendens: a pending action (1037).

Marriage articles: the preliminary agreement for a marriage settlement (403).
Merger: the fusion of two or more estates or interests (193).

Mesne: intermediate, middle (14).
Minor interest: an interest in registered land which requires protection by an
    entry on the register (1067).
Minority: the state of being an infant.
Mortmain: the holding of land by a corporation (1000, 1001).

Next-of-kin: the nearest blood relations (519).
Notice: knowledge or imputed knowledge (114, 121).
Nuncupative: oral (of wills) (488).

Occupancy: occupation of land held *pur autre vie* (101).
Overreach: to transfer rights from land to the purchase-money paid therefor
    (148, 149).
Override: to render rights void, *e.g.*, against a purchaser (149).
Overriding interest: an interest in registered land which binds the proprietor
    without being entered on the register (1064).

Parol: word of mouth.
Partibility: divisibility of inheritance among children (as opposed to primo-
    geniture).
Particular estate: an estate less than a fee simple (179).
Per capita: by heads; one share for each person (521); compare *Per stirpes*.
Per stirpes: by stocks of descent; one share for each line of descendants (520);
    compare *Per capita*.
Periodic tenancy: tenancy from year to year, month to month, etc. (633, 637).
Perpetuity: undue remoteness of a future gift; excessive inalienability (**200**).
Personal representatives: executors or administrators (533).
Portions: provisions for children, especially lump sums for the younger
    children under a settlement (385).
Possibility of reverter: the grantor's right to the land if a determinable fee
    determines (74).
Post-nuptial: after marriage.
Powers: appendant (461); appurtenant (461), collateral (461), in gross (461),
    general (253), special (253).
Prescription: the acquisition of easements or profits by long user (841, 1003).
Privity of contract: the relation between parties to a contract (721).
Privity of estate: the relation of landlord and tenant (721).
Probate: the formal confirmation of a will, granted by the court to an
    executor (533).
Procreation, words of: words confining the persons mentioned to issue of a
    particular person (57).
Protector of settlement: the person able to control the barring of an entail (91).
Puisne mortgage: a legal mortgage not protected by a deposit of title deeds
    (969, 1039).
Pur autre vie: for the life of another person (100).
Purchase, words of: words conferring an interest on the person they mention
    (52); compare Limitation, words of.
Purchaser: a person who takes land by act of parties and not by operation of
    law (509).

Que estate: dominant tenement (846).

Recovery: a collective action completely barring an entail (85); compare
    Fine, 1.
Regulated tenancy: a tenancy protected by the newer form of rent restriction
    (1126).
Release: waiver of some right or interest without transfer of possession (428).
Remainder: the interest of a grantee subject to a prior particular estate
    (178, 181).
Rent: chief rent (800), fee farm rent (138, 800), ground rent (572), quit rent
    (800), rack rent (572), rent of assize (800), rentcharge (792), rent seck
    (793), rent service (792).
Restraint on anticipation: a restriction on a married woman disposing of
    capital or future income (995, 996).
Restrictive covenant: a covenant restricting the use of land (133, 751).

Resulting: returning to the grantor, or remaining in him, by implication of law or equity (156, 442).

Reversion: the interest remaining in a grantor after granting a particular estate (178).

Riparian owner: the owner of land adjoining a watercourse (72).

Root of title: a document from which ownership is traced (580).

Satisfied term: a term of years created for a purpose since fulfilled (387).

Scintilla juris: a spark (or remnant) of title (188).

Seignory: the rights of a feudal lord.

Seisin: the possession of land by a freeholder (**48**).

Servient tenement: land burdened by a right such as an easement (806); compare Dominant tenement.

Settlement: provisions for persons in succession (or the instruments making such provisions) (300, 314).

Severance: the conversion of a joint tenancy into a tenancy in common (403).

Severance, words of: words showing that property is to pass in distinct shares (399).

Specialty: a contract by deed.

Spes successionis: a possibility of succeeding to property (67).

Squatter: a person wrongfully occupying land and claiming title to it (1004).

Statutory owner: persons with the powers of a tenant for life (297).

Statutory tenant: a person holding over under the Rent Restriction Acts (1134); compare Contractual tenancy.

Statutory trusts: certain trusts imposed by statute (439), especially—
1. the trust for sale under co-ownership (410).
2. the trusts for issue on intestacy (527).

Subinfeudation: alienation by creating a new tenure (30).

Sub-mortgage: a mortgage of a mortgage (956).

Sui juris: " of his own right," *i.e.*, subject to no disability.

Surrender: the transfer of an interest (*e.g.*, for life, or for years) to the person next entitled to the property (193, 667).

Survivorship: a surviving joint tenant's right to the whole land (391).

Tabula in naufragio: " a plank in a shipwreck " (a form of tacking mortgages) (979).

Tacking: extension of a mortgagee's security to cover a later loan (978).

Tenement: property held by a tenant.

Tenure: the set of conditions upon which a tenant holds land (14); compare Estate, 1.

Term of years: a period with a defined minimum for which a tenant holds land (140).

Time immemorial: the time of the accession of Richard I, 1189 (847).

Title: the evidence of a person's right to property.

Trust: bare (438), completely constituted (447, 448), constructive (442), executed (447), executory (447), express (440), implied (441), incompletely constituted (447), precatory (440), resulting (440), secret (451).

Trust corporation: one of certain companies with a large paid-up capital, or one of certain officials (376).

Trust for sale: a trust requiring the trustees to sell the property.

Undivided share: the interest of a tenant in common or co-parcener (396, 431).

Use: active (158), resulting (156), shifting (162), springing (162).

User: use, enjoyment (Note: *not* the person who uses).

Vested: unconditionally owned (**173**); compare Contingent.

Vesting assent (301), declaration (458), deed (300), instrument (299).

Voluntary conveyance: a conveyance not made for valuable consideration.

Volunteer: a person who takes under a disposition without having given valuable consideration.

Waiver: abandonment of a legal right.

Waste: ameliorating (104), equitable (105), permissive (104), voluntary (104),

CHAPTER 1

INTRODUCTION

Sect. 1. Prefatory

THE English law of real property has never achieved that simplicity which, according to Lord Bryce, distinguishes the laws of the more civilised ages. Cromwell, in blunter style, is alleged to have called it " a tortuous and ungodly jumble." Its reputation has not wholly been redeemed by the reforming legislation of modern times; but it can at least be said that the path of the student is much smoother today than it was a century ago. Until about 1880 it was almost obligatory to begin any discourse on this branch of the law with apologies for many rules both intricate and uncouth. A great authority, Joshua Williams, lectured in 1878 with this preface: " Some of the most remarkable of these laws, viewed by themselves, apart from their history, and judged only by the benefits which now result from them, appear to me to be absolutely worthless. Others are more than worthless, they are absurd and injurious." [1] " Now," said Maitland, " when those who are set to teach the youth hold such language as this, there are but two courses open to us—to silence the professors, or to reform the laws." [2]

Reforming the laws was the more practical of these remedies. With the Conveyancing Act, 1881, there began the great modern period of statutory reform which culminated in the comprehensive property legislation of 1925. These Acts have simplified both practice and study in a multitude of ways. Obsolete and incongruous rules have been cleared away, new and beneficent principles have been invented. In a great many matters it is now unnecessary to go behind these Acts. But they are not a code: as was said in 1922, they represent evolution rather than revolution.[3] They proceed by patchwork, often adapting old ideas to new problems in much the same manner as led the old law into some of its tangles. But, on the whole, they have done much to infuse simplicity and reason.

[1] Williams, *The Seisin of the Freehold*, 1.
[2] Maitland, Coll.Pp., i, 165.
[3] See *post*, p. 1123.

1

Despite all this reform, the first thing that the student must understand is that the basis of the subject remains the " old " law, and that the elements of this must be mastered before the new statutes can be understood. The approach to this subject, especially in the early stages, is still bound to be historical. But so many refinements of the old learning have now been made obsolete that its outlines emerge more clearly than before. The fundamental rules, with their new statutory superstructure, can now be presented without apology as one system, and as a branch of the law which has at last received its full share of reform. The system is certainly still complex, partly as the result of its continuous growth through so many centuries, and partly because of the social need for a highly developed scheme of private property in land.

The student will quickly feel that one of the primary difficulties of the subject is the way in which its various parts interlock. Such topics as can be studied more or less in isolation have been relegated to the later chapters of this book. But the main principles (mostly to be found in Chapters 1–7) must in the first place be studied as a whole, for they constantly interact, unlike (for example) the various torts or crimes, which are more or less independent branches of their subjects. At first it is best to read fast and often, until an understanding of the main scheme of rules begins to dawn. In the early stages it is not necessary to linger over difficulties, for often what is incomprehensible at first will seem plain on a second reading, and perhaps obvious on a third. Technicality of language is another stumbling-block for the beginner, and he should make a free use of the glossary of terms which precedes this chapter.

Objects of learning the subject. The objects of learning the law of real property are—

    (i) to acquire a knowledge of the rights and liabilities attached to interests in land; and

    (ii) to lay a foundation for the study of conveyancing.

It is not easy to distinguish accurately between real property and conveyancing. In general it can be said that the former is static, the latter dynamic; real property deals with the rights and liabilities of landowners, conveyancing with the art of creating and transferring rights in land. Yet inevitably the two overlap, and often the exact place at which to draw the line is mainly a matter of taste. But although this is a book on the law of real property, it is built upon a conveyancing foundation. In deciding what to include and what to exclude, conveyancing has played a large part.

The reader's knowledge of land law has to be carried to the point when it will be possible for him to embark with profit on a study of conveyancing; the joints must be true and the overlapping restrained within due limits. It is, indeed, best to regard real property and conveyancing not as two separate though closely related subjects, but as two parts of the one subject of land law; it is convenience rather than necessity that dictates the division.

Conveyancing influences any book on real property in another way, namely, by making it essential to include a substantial historical element. A conveyancer acting for a client who is purchasing property must frequently investigate the title to the land, both as to ownership and as to incumbrances, over a substantial period of time; those who are engaged in this work must consequently know the law not only as it is but also as it was. The story of the Statute of Uses, 1535, explains far more vividly than any generalisation what human ingenuity can make of a statute; the Statute remained in operation until 1926, and its effects can still be seen in many places.[3a] The mode of conveyance known as the lease and release forcefully illustrates the possible advantages of using two deeds to do the work of one,[4] and he who knows the expedients of yesterday is the better able to forge the devices of today, *e.g.*, to circumvent the Rent Acts.[5] But these are not the only uses of history. The truth is that although much can be learnt, little can be understood without knowledge of the reasons which moulded the law into its present forms. In this department of the law, more perhaps than in any other, history is the key to knowledge; it is indeed mistaken to suppose that it is of little or no use in practice.

Scope of the subject. There are many possible ways of arranging a book on real property, each with its merits. In this book the first consideration throughout has been to assist the reader by adopting an order which minimises the amount of repetition and preliminary explanation which is so often necessary.

The book falls into three divisions. The first deals with a man's rights over his own land, the second with his rights over his neighbour's land, and the third with provisions ancillary to these rights, such as the registration of rights in land. A brief survey of these divisions follows, partly to give an idea of the stuff real property is made of and partly to introduce some of the most important technical terms.

[3a] *Post*, pp. 155 *et seq.*
[4] *Post*, p. 164.
[5] See *White* v. *Richmond Court Ltd.* [1944] K.B. 576.

After some introductory passages, the first division, comprising Chapters 1 to 12, gives an account of tenures and estates. *Tenure* means the holding of land on certain terms and conditions; in other words it refers to the *manner* in which the law allows a person to hold land. Points of tenure are rare in practice today; but tenure is still the fundamental doctrine of the law of land, and logically it must come first. *Estates* are fundamental in both theory and practice. The term " estate " has reference to the size, in the sense of the duration, of a landowner's interest: he may hold his land, for example, in fee simple, which means that he is virtually an absolute owner; or he may hold it for a limited period of time, for example, for his life or under a lease for seven years. He will then be said to have an estate in fee simple, or for life, or for a term of years, as the case may be.

Next comes the very heart of the subject, *Law and Equity*. These are technical terms, corresponding to the two systems of justice, " common law " and " equity," which were separately administered in England until 1875, and which have each made great contributions to the law of property. Nowadays their administration is unified, but interests in land are still classed as " legal " or " equitable " interests, with consequences of great importance. This is a typical example of a distinction which can be understood only with the aid of history, but which has been taken over by the Acts of 1925 as one of the cornerstones of the reformed land law. In this chapter, therefore, an account of doctrines originating in medieval times has to be interwoven with the story of changes effected by Parliament at several different periods of history.

Future Interests follow, being also of central importance. If A gives land to B for life and after B's death to C in fee simple, during the period of B's life C has a future interest. There are limits to the future interests which the law allows; and in particular the period of time during which they can take effect is limited by the " rule against perpetuities," now radically reformed by statute. When land has been made subject to successive (*i.e.*, partly future) interests it is said to be subject to a " settlement," and the problems connected with the sale and management of such land are dealt with in the following chapter.

The book then turns from successive to concurrent interests, and deals with *Co-ownership*. This arises, for example, where X and Y are entitled to some piece of land in equal shares, but the share of each is merely a part interest in the whole.

At this point it may perhaps be said that the worst is over; the central complex of rules has been expounded, and what remains is a series of more distinct topics which can more easily be studied one by one. Some of the rules of *Trusts* are of special importance and are here included, together with *Powers*. A power may be described as a right to dispose of someone else's property, as where A leaves property by will to such of B's children as B may appoint.

The chapter on *Wills and Intestacy* describes the legal machinery for succession at death, generally but inaccurately known as inheritance. This is followed by a chapter on the transfer of land between living people, *Contracts and Conveyancing*. An attempt has here been made to deal with some elements of conveyancing which readers of more technical works on the subject are often assumed to know. Then follows the law of landlord and tenant, a subject which today has two main aspects: general principles, and the various forms of statutory control, especially the Rent Acts. These statutes are treated separately in the chapter on *Social Control of Land*, since they are a modern statutory system of their own and really demand a book to themselves; nor can they be explained without presupposing a knowledge of general principles. This group of chapters ends with *Covenants and Licences Affecting Land*. A covenant is a promise contained in a deed; and a *restrictive* covenant, such as a covenant not to use a house for business purposes, can be made binding on the property even though it subsequently changes hands. This is a branch of the law of contract which has developed into a doctrine of property. Sometimes a *licence* which is a mere permission, may have a similar effect.

Chapters 13 and 14 comprise the second main division of the book, dealing with certain rights over the land of other people. The most important of these are *Rentcharges, Easements and Profits*, and *Mortgages*. A rentcharge is a right over land created as security for a periodical payment, such as £100 a year. An easement is a right over a neighbour's land, such as a right of way or a right to light; and a profit is similar, save that it comprises the right to remove something, such as a right to work gravel or to take game. A mortgage is a conveyance of land for the purpose of securing a loan of money, under which the lender obtains power to sell the land or to take other steps if the debt or the interest upon it are not duly paid. This group of interests, together with restrictive covenants, are collectively called " incumbrances," since they are burdens on the ownership of land.

The third and last main division contains miscellaneous subjects: *Disabilities*, such as affect infants and lunatics and make them less able to dispose of land than other people; *Adverse Possession and Limitation*, under which an interloper can become the owner of land by twelve years' occupation of it; and *Registration*. Registration is a system of recording either the ownership of land or transactions affecting land, so as to make them more easily discoverable than if they were kept private. The former type, registration of title, has revolutionised the technique of conveyancing; but it applies only in certain parts of the country. The latter type, registration of charges, applies generally. Finally, there is *Social Control of Land*, which collects the modern statutory restrictions on an owner's right to do as he wishes with his land; and last, the legislation of 1925 is summarised.

The law in action. It may help the beginner to give a short account of a typical transaction, introducing some of the commoner interests in land. As good an example as any is the sale of a house.

Let us suppose that V (the vendor) has agreed to sell his house to P (the purchaser) and that their solicitors proceed to make the legal arrangements. The agreement is a contract, and since it concerns land it must be evidenced in writing. But a mere contract will not transfer the full legal ownership from V to P: V must execute a deed of conveyance in P's favour. The contract is the first binding step in the proceedings and the conveyance is the last; the final exchange of the conveyance for the purchase money is called completion. But between contract and completion much will have happened. P will not wish to part with his money without first making sure that he will get what V has agreed to sell him, and so he will investigate V's title. P must make sure that V is not merely a tenant for years, who has only a leasehold interest to sell, or a life-tenant under a family settlement, who cannot effectively sell the land unless a special procedure is used. Similarly, if V should be an infant, or one of several joint owners, the sale can only be made subject to special statutory safeguards, and it will partly be P's responsibility to see that they are complied with.

Even if V is the sole and absolute owner, as P will probably have assumed, there may be other obstacles. Normally V will have to prove his title by showing the deeds under which the land has changed hands in the recent past, *i.e.*, the period of not less than fifteen years prior to the sale. This is a somewhat arbitrary period, but it is long enough to raise a strong presumption that V is owner, provided of course that the deeds show a series of transactions which appear to be in order and to end with some disposition in favour of V. But it is always possible that P's solicitor may detect some fault or gap in V's title which may imply that the true owner is not V but someone else: there may have been a mistake in the interpretation of some document, or some uncertainty as to the identity of the property conveyed, which throws doubt on the title. It might even happen that V's title had been barred by lapse of time, if a " squatter " had been in effective adverse possession of the land for twelve years or more.

A more common source of trouble is incumbrances. V's property may be subject to easements, such as rights to light or rights of way acquired by neighbours, or to restrictive covenants preventing any occupant from using it, for instance, as a shop or for business. V may have mortgaged it as security for a loan, so that the creditor has rights in the land which must be protected. Various official registers may be inspected as a precaution against some of these incumbrances, while others must be guarded against by other inquiries. The appearance of any incumbrance will enable P to rescind the contract, unless he has agreed to accept it, as a purchaser will often do, if due allowance is made in the price. Perhaps P has not the purchase money ready to hand, and has arranged to borrow most of it on a mortgage of the house, as a purchaser can usually do with the assistance of a building society or other lender. In that case P will, immediately after receiving the conveyance from V, make a further conveyance by way of mortgage for the loan; P will then be able to occupy the house so long as he keeps up the payments due under the loan, while the creditor is given an immediate and indefeasible interest in the land as security against non-payment. Until he has repaid the loan P's position is not unlike that of a tenant who pays mortgage interest instead of rent.

The common law basis of the subject. The law of real property has been deeply marked by the course of its history. Its original elements, some of which still survive, were part of the common law of England. "Common law " means the law applied to the whole country in common by the King's ordinary courts, as contrasted with the ancient customary laws which varied from place to place and were administered in each locality free of central control. The centralised judicial system established in the two centuries after the Norman Conquest resulted in a body of new and uniform rules, although some of the old customs survived in the form of local variations of common law.

The new rules were laid down and developed by the decisions of the judges in particular cases. Centralised records were kept and a systematic body of doctrine began to develop. When the old local jurisdictions were forgotten, the " common law " came to mean the ordinary judge-made law of the royal courts. This was then contrasted with statute. Statutory reform of the land law was hardly less familiar in medieval than in modern times, as witness the Acts of Edward I. As these statutes in their turn receded into history, they came to be looked upon as of a piece with the judge-made rules, and "the common law" might, in a suitable context, include these ancient statutes, for the purposes of contrast with modern parliamentary reforms.

A third force entered the field in the form of equity. As will be seen in due course,[6] certain interests in land were not protected by the courts of common law but were later protected by the Chancellor, the royal officer who dispensed the Crown's residuary powers of redressing wrong. It was the Chancellor who first compelled trustees to carry out their trusts, and devised remedies for cases where, owing to non-compliance with some formality, the result at common law would not have been equitable. In this aspect "common law" came to be contrasted with "equity" as well as with statute. Rights which the common law courts would recognise and enforce were known as rights at common law, or simply as "legal rights." Rights enforced by the Chancellor, but not at common law, were called rights in equity, or "equitable rights." As the name implies, the Chancellor proceeded on grounds of equity or good conscience, and would grant special remedies where the justice of the case required some tempering of the rigour of common law. In the course of time equity developed into a separate branch of the legal system. It profoundly modified the common law of real property, and the special characteristics of equitable rights led to the fundamental distinction between legal and equitable interests in land which was adopted as the foundation of the reforms of 1925. Although law and equity are now both administered in the same courts, and the Chancellor's independent powers have vanished, common law and equity are still quite different concepts.

The expression "common law" will, therefore, often be found bearing different senses, but the context will usually make it plain whether the contrast is with equity, with statute or with local customary law. The law of real property still rests upon its common law foundations, whatever the sense given to the term.

Sect. 2. Historical Outline

The history of the law of property in land can broadly be divided into five periods.

1. Formulation of principles. This was the early period, extending from the Norman Conquest to the end of the fourteenth century, during which the common law courts formulated many of

---

[6] *Post*, pp. 110 *et seq.*

the fundamental rules of land law. A number of important statutes were passed during this period, particularly in the reign of Edward I (1272–1307).

2. Growth of equity. This was the period from about 1400 to 1535, when the jurisdiction of the Chancellor to give relief in cases not covered by the common law rules was firmly established' and developed.

3. The Statute of Uses. This was the period from 1535 to the middle of the seventeenth century, when the great changes made by the Statute of Uses, 1535, were being worked out.

4. Development of the modern law. This encompassed the end of the seventeenth century and the eighteenth century, when trusts, which had been considerably restricted by the Statute of Uses, 1535, were once more enforced. The modern form of a strict settlement of land, by which land was " kept in the family " from one generation to another, was fully developed during this period. So was the modern form of mortgage.

5. Statutory reforms. This period consists of the nineteenth and twentieth centuries, when far-reaching reforms were made by Parliament, culminating in the 1925 legislation. Although many reforms were made at intervals during the nineteenth century, particularly in the periods 1832–45 and 1881–90, none rivalled the complex and sweeping alterations of 1922–25. There were two stages in this legislation. First, by the Law of Property Act, 1922, and the Law of Property (Amendment) Act, 1924, the necessary changes in the law were made. Secondly, these Acts were then in the main, before they came into force, repealed and replaced by a series of Acts passed in 1925. In the Acts of 1925 the changes made by the Acts of 1922 and 1924 were consolidated with much of the law laid down by earlier statutes (particularly those of 1881–90), which were likewise repealed and replaced by the new legislation; and the resulting body of law was distributed among the Acts of 1925 according to subject-matter. These consolidating Acts, together with the unrepealed portions of the Acts of 1922 and 1924, constitute " the 1925 property legislation." They are—

The Settled Land Act, 1925.
The Trustee Act, 1925.
The Law of Property Act, 1925.
The Land Registration Act, 1925.
The Land Charges Act, 1925.
The Administration of Estates Act, 1925.

All this legislation (including the surviving portions of the Acts of 1922 and 1924) came into force on the same date, namely, January 1, 1926.

The form of this legislation sometimes affects its construction. The Acts of 1925 are all consolidation Acts, and so they are presumed not to alter the pre-existing law more than necessarily appears. Where the Acts of 1922 and 1924 left the old law unchanged, then the presumption is against the Acts of 1925 having changed that old law.[6a] But where the Act of 1922 or 1924 made some change in the old law, then the presumption is merely against the Acts of 1925 having changed that change.[7] The repealed parts of the Acts of 1922 and 1924 may thus be needed to resolve obscurities in the Acts of 1925.

Since 1925 there has been piecemeal legislation for carrying out particular reforms. The main statutes are the Law of Property (Amendment) Act, 1926, the Law of Property (Entailed Interests) Act, 1932, the Perpetuities and Accumulations Act 1964, the Law of Property (Joint Tenants) Act 1964 and the Law of Property Act 1969. The Land Charges Act 1972 is another consolidating Act, replacing the Land Charges Act, 1925.

Sect. 3. Meaning of " Real Property "

As is the case with so many expressions in English law, the explanation of the term " real property " is historical.

In early law, property was deemed " real " if the courts would restore to a dispossessed owner the thing itself, the " *res*," and not merely give compensation for the loss. Thus, if X forcibly evicted Y from his freehold land, Y could bring a " real " action whereby he could obtain an order from the court that X should return the land to him. But if X took Y's sword or glove from him, he could bring only a personal action which gave X the choice of either returning the article or paying the value thereof. Consequently, a distinction was made between real property (or " realty "), which could be specifically recovered, and personal property (or " personalty "), which was not thus recoverable. Nature has provided one division of property, namely into immovables (*i.e.*, land) and movables; the English division into real and personal property is similar with one important exception. In general, all interests in land are real property, with the exception of leaseholds (or " terms of years "), which are classified as personalty.

6a See, *e.g.*, *Beswick* v. *Beswick* [1968] A.C. 58 (L.P.A., 1925, s. 56); and see *Re Eichholz* [1959] Ch. 708 (esp. at pp. 726, 727), where the presumption was stated but misapplied: see (1960) 76 L.Q.R. 197 (R.E.M.); *Lloyds Bank Ltd.* v. *Marcan* [1973] 1 W.L.R. 339 at 344 (affirmed at p. 1387).

7 See *Grey* v. *I.R.C.* [1960] A.C. 1 (L.P.A., 1925, s. 53); *Re Turner's W.T.* [1937] Ch. 15 (T.A., 1925, s. 31).

This peculiar exception was first of all due to the fact that leases were foreign to the feudal system of landholding by tenure, under which, in its earliest form, the social and economic status of every member of society was fixed. Originally leases were rather regarded as personal business arrangements under which one party allowed the other the use of his land in return for a rent.[8] They were, in other words, personal contracts, operating *in personam* between the parties and not creating or transferring any rights *in rem, i.e.,* rights in the land itself which could affect feudal status. Leases helped to supply a useful form of investment for a society which knew nothing of stocks and shares. Money might be employed in buying land and letting it out on lease in order to obtain an income from the capital, or in buying a lease for a lump sum which would be recovered with interest out of the produce of the land. These were commercial transactions, more in the sphere of money than of land, as land-owning was then understood. Once leaseholds were classed with personal property it was discovered that the position was not without its advantages. Not only were leases then immune from feudal burdens and the intricate legal procedure required for freeholds: they could be bequeathed by will in times when wills of other land were still not allowed.[9] Thus the illogical position continued until it became too well settled to alter.

Leaseholds are still, therefore, personalty in law. But having now for so long been recognised as interests in land and not merely contractual rights,[10] they have been classed under the paradoxical heading of " chattels real." The first word indicates their personal nature (cattle were the most important chattels in early days, hence the name), the second shows their connection with land.[11] The three types of property may, therefore, be classified thus:

$$
\begin{array}{l}
\textit{Land} \\
\textit{Personalty}
\end{array}
\left\{
\begin{array}{l}
\text{(i) Realty.} \\
\left\{
\begin{array}{l}
\text{(ii) Chattels real.} \\
\text{(iii) Pure personalty.}
\end{array}
\right.
\end{array}
\right.
$$

Although strictly speaking a book on real property should exclude leaseholds, it has long been both customary and convenient to include them, and this course is adopted here.

The legislation of 1925 abolished many of the remaining differences between the law governing realty and that governing

---

8 *Post,* p. 43.
9 *Post,* p. 44.
10 *Post,* p. 45.
11 See *Smith* v. *Baker* (1737) 1 Atk. 385 at 386; *Ridout* v. *Pain* (1747) 3 Atk 486 at 492, *per* Lord Hardwicke L.C. (" *extractions* out of the real ").

personalty.[12]   For example, before 1926, if a person died intestate (*i.e.*, without a will), all his realty passed to his heir, while his personalty was divided between certain of his relatives; again, realty could be entailed and personalty could not. After 1925, however, realty and personalty both pass on intestacy to certain relatives, and both kinds of property can be entailed. Nevertheless, the distinction still remains of importance.

Real property itself comprises two distinct genera, called corporeal and incorporeal hereditaments. " Hereditament " indicates property which descended to the heir on intestacy before 1926, *i.e.*, realty as opposed to personalty. Corporeal hereditaments are lands, buildings, minerals, trees and all other things which are part of or affixed to land—in other words, the physical matter over which ownership is exercised. Incorporeal hereditaments, on the other hand, are not things at all, but rights. Certain rights were classified as real property, so that on intestacy before 1926 they also descended to the heir, rather than to the relatives entitled to personalty. The most important incorporeal hereditaments are easements, profits and rentcharges,[13] but there are others also.[14] This classification is better discussed in a later place.[15] It has little practical importance, but despite the changes made in 1925 the terms corporeal and incorporeal hereditaments are still sometimes useful.

---

[12] There were other chattels real than leaseholds: see *post*, p. 17. Coke mentions " Wardships, the interest of tenant by statute staple, by statute merchant, by elegit and such like ": Co.Litt. 118b. But leaseholds are the only chattels real of any importance today. For wardships, see *post*, p. 17.
[13] See *ante*, p. 5, and *post*, pp. 789, 792, 805.
[14] *Post*, p. 789.
[15] *Post*, p. 787.

CHAPTER 2

TENURES

Part 1

TENURES AND ESTATES

1. Crown ownership. The basis of English land law is that all land in England is owned by the Crown. A small part is in the Crown's actual occupation; the rest is occupied by tenants holding either directly or indirectly from the Crown. "*Nulle terre sans seigneur*" (no land without a lord): no land in England is allodial, *i.e.*, owned by a subject and not "held of" some lord.[1]

2. Feudal structure. This unusually perfect feudal structure was imposed after the Norman Conquest. William I regarded the whole of England as his by conquest. To reward his followers and those of the English who submitted to him, he granted and confirmed certain lands to be held of him as overlord.[2] These lands were granted not by way of an out-and-out transfer, but to be held from the Crown upon certain conditions. Thus, Blackacre might have been granted to X on the terms that he did homage and swore fealty, that he provided five armed horsemen to fight for the Crown for forty days in each year, and the like. Whiteacre might have been granted to Y on condition that he supported the King's train in his coronation. X and Y might each in turn grant land to other persons to hold of them in return for services, and these others might repeat the process.

3. Services. In this way the feudal pyramid was constructed from the top downwards, with the King at the apex and the actual occupants of the land at the base. In the middle were persons who both rendered and received services, much in the same way as a modern leasehold tenant who has sublet the property. In days when land and its produce constituted nearly the whole tangible wealth of a country, it was more usual to secure the performance of services by

---

[1] P. & M. i, 232; H.E.L. ii, 183; Co.Litt. 1b; *Doe d. Hayne* v. *Redfern* (1810) 12 East 96 at 103; *Att.-Gen. of Ontario* v. *Mercer* (1883) 8 App.Cas. 767 at 772.
[2] Williams R.P. 12.

the grant of land in return for those services than it was to secure them by payment. The whole social organisation was based on landholding in return for service, and for most purposes, such as military service and taxation, government was carried on by devolving upon each lord the control of his immediate tenants. The King need look only to his " tenants in chief," they in their turn to their immediate dependants, and so on downwards if there were further steps in the scale.

Tenants in chief were those who held directly of the King; there were about 1,500 of them in 1086, at the time of Domesday Book. Those who in fact occupied the land were called tenants in demesne. Those who stood between the King and tenants in demesne were called mesne lords or mesnes (mesne, meaning intermediate). The King was lord paramount. The status of lordship, including the right to receive the tenant's services, was called seignory.

4. Tenure. Feudal services became to a certain extent standardised. Thus there was one set of services (which included the provision of armed horsemen for battle) which became known as knight's service, and there was another set (which included the performance of some honourable service for the King in person) which was known as grand sergeanty. Each of these sets of services was known as a *tenure*, for it showed upon what terms the land was held (*tenere*, to hold).[3] The commonest type of tenure was that known as socage.[4]

5. Estates. Whatever the tenure, the land might be held for different periods of time. It might be granted for life (for so long as the tenant lived), in tail (for so long as the tenant or any of his descendants lived), or in fee simple (for so long as the tenant or any of his heirs, whether descendants or not, were alive).[5] Each of these interests was known as an *estate*, a word derived from *status*.[6] Thus the Crown might grant land to A for an estate in fee simple, and A in turn might grant it to B for life. Both the Crown and A thus retained interests in the land. A man might hold land for one or more estates, yet this was only a qualified form of ownership.

The largest estate in land, the fee simple, has come more and more to resemble absolute ownership, and its proprietor is commonly called the owner of the land. This is because the tenurial relationship

3 Co.Litt. 1a.
4 *Post*, p. 19.
5 Leaseholds (which are now estates: *post*, p. 45) fell outside the feudal system, since in early times they were not considered to be estates but merely personal contracts. See Challis 63, 64, *ante*, p. 10 and *post*, p. 43.
6 H.E.L. ii, 351, 352; Williams R.P. 7, 8.

is now so slender that it can in practice be ignored. But even today it is in one sense true to say that all land in England is vested in the Crown; a subject can hold it only as tenant. When we say " X owns Blackacre in fee simple " we really mean " X holds Blackacre of Y (his lord) by the tenure of free and common socage for an estate in fee simple." But the difference in practice is negligible and the full formula is, therefore, not used. It should be noted that both in popular speech and in legal parlance the word " estate " is often used in other senses, for example, as a description of an area of land (as in " The Blank estate is to be sold "), or as a general term meaning property (as in " the deceased's net estate "). The context will usually leave little doubt about which sense is intended.

6. Fundamental doctrines. There are thus two fundamental doctrines in the law of real property—

(i) the doctrine of tenures: all land is held of the Crown, either directly or indirectly, in one or other of the various tenures; and

(ii) the doctrine of estates: land held in tenure is also held for an estate, that is to say for some period of time.

In short, the tenure answers the question " upon what terms is it held?", the estate the question " for how long?"

These two doctrines of tenures and estates are considered in greater detail in this chapter and the next.

Part 2

TYPES OF TENURE

The main tenures which existed at common law may be classified as follows:

1. Free tenures: A. Tenures in Chivalry (or Military Tenures).
                      B. Tenures in Socage.
                      C. Spiritual Tenures.
2. Unfree tenures.
3. Miscellaneous tenures.

Sect. 1. Free Tenures

A. Tenures in Chivalry

There were two tenures in chivalry, grand sergeanty and knight's service.

1. Grand sergeanty. By tenure in grand sergeanty the King provided for his principal servants, holders of high offices and places of honour. The tenant was bound to perform in person some service for the King of an honourable nature, such as carrying his banner, leading his army, or being his chamberlain.[7] There were many grand sergeanties in connection with the coronation.[8] " Honorary services " might extend even to the duties of the royal carver or butler, or to " cornage," alleged to be the duty to guard the Scottish border and " winde a horn " to give warning if " the Scots or other enemies " entered the country.[9] Such services were regarded as personal to the King, and this tenure was ultimately [10] (though not originally [11]) confined to tenants in chief. It followed from this that land could be held in grand sergeanty only by a tenant in chief.

2. Knight's service. By tenure in knight's service the lord provided himself with an army. The lord in question was, of course, most commonly the King, but land could be held in knight's service of a mesne lord.[12] Originally the distinguishing feature of this tenure was the obligation of the tenant to provide his lord with a fixed number of fully armed horsemen for forty days in each year,[13] but by the middle of the twelfth century this obligation had in most cases been commuted for a money payment known as escuage or scutage,[14] and by the fourteenth century the levy of scutage had ceased.[15]

Tenures in chivalry were subject to an elaborate catalogue of " incidents," some of which remained important until modern times. The list may be summarised as follows: —

(1) THE HONOURABLE OR MILITARY SERVICE, mentioned above.

(2) HOMAGE, FEALTY AND SUIT OF COURT. Homage was the spiritual bond created by the tenant swearing to be his lord's man,[16] fealty the temporal link arising from the tenant's oath to perform

---

[7] Litt. 153 ; Challis 9.
[8] Blount, Frag., 25, 26. In this work are collected many curious conditions of tenure, not all of which are honourable by modern standards (*e.g.*, at p. 60); Some of the more remarkable are recounted in Megarry, *Miscellany-at-Law*, 154–157.
[9] Litt. 156. But much more probably cornage was a payment for the right to pasture horned cattle: Maitland, Coll.Pp., ii, 98–100.
[10] Litt. 161.
[11] Bracton 35b ; P. & M. i, 285.
[12] *Ante*, p. 14, for this term.
[13] P. & M. i, 252 *et seq.* ; H.E.L. iii, 37 *et seq.* The last summons of the feudal levy was in 1385: (1958) 73 E.H.R. 1 (N. B. Lewis).
[14] P. & M. i, 266.
[15] H.E.L. iii, 44, 45.
[16] Litt. 85 ; Co.Litt. 64b, 65a.

his feudal obligations faithfully,[17] and suit of court the tenant's obligation to attend his lord's court and assist in its deliberations.[18]

(3) WARDSHIP AND MARRIAGE. These affected only infant heirs. Wardship was the lord's right to manage for his own profit [19] the lands of a tenant who left as his heir a male under twenty-one or a female under fourteen (or sixteen, if not married before the land descended to her).[20] The lord was in this way compensated for his tenant's incapacity for service. At the end of the wardship, the lord was entitled to a further half-year's profits of the land as the price of its surrender to the heir ("suing out livery," [21] or "ouster-le-main" [22] (removing his hand)); but the right to levy this additional impost was confined to the King by Magna Carta, 1215.[23] Marriage was the lord's right to select a. spouse for any tenant whom he had in wardship, and to fine the ward for declining a suitable spouse or for marrying under age without the lord's licence.[24] These rights were often of considerable value; they could be bought, sold, and bequeathed, and came to be classed as chattels real.[25]

(4) RELIEF AND PRIMER SEISIN. These affected only heirs of full age,[26] and represented the price paid by the heir for the right to succeed as tenant.[27] Relief was the lord's right to a payment, often of one year's value of the land,[28] when an heir of full age succeeded to the land on the death of the tenant. Where the King was the lord he enjoyed also the prerogative right called primer seisin (first seisin), the right to take possession until homage and relief were rendered. This in practice entitled the Crown to a further year's profits in addition to the relief.[29]

(5) AIDS. These were payments which a lord could demand from his tenants on certain occasions involving the lord in expense. Magna Carta, 1215, limited these occasions to three: the ransom of

---

17 Litt. 91; Co.Litt. 67b.
18 Williams R.P. 49.
19 But he could not commit waste: Magna Carta, 1215, cc. 4, 5; P. & M. i, 319. A lord who wasted the land forfeited the wardship: *ibid.* For waste, see *post*, p. 103.
20 Litt. 103.
21 Bl.Comm. ii, 76; Co.Litt. 77a; H.E.L. iii, 64.
22 *Anon.* (1559) 2 Dy. 168a.
23 c. 3; but see *Anon.* (1559) 2 Dy. 168a.
24 Litt. 103–110; Statute of Merton, 1235; Statute of Westminster I, 1275, c. 22. The lord might not tender a disparaging marriage (for a catalogue of disparagements, see Co.Litt. 80a, b, and *cf.* Litt. 107–109); but if the ward refused a " covenable " [suitable] marriage, he or she was liable to pay to the lord " the value of the marriage." If the ward married against the lord's consent, this fine was doubled: Litt. 110.
25 P. & M. i, 322; ii, 116.
26 Magna Carta, 1215, c. 3.
27 H.E.L. iii, 57.
28 H.E.L. iii, 60.
29 Bl.Comm. ii, 66; Cru.Dig. i, 25–26; Statute of Marlbridge, 1267, c. 16.

the lord, the knighting of his eldest son, and the marriage of his eldest daughter.[30] The last two aids did not, however, apply to grand sergeanty.[31]

(6) ESCHEAT AND FORFEITURE. Unlike the previous incidents, escheat and forfeiture retained their importance until comparatively recent years. One was an essential part of the feudal structure, the other was valuable to the State. Escheat occurred on the extinction of a tenancy: the immediate lord became tenant in demesne [32] and entitled to occupy the land. Thus was preserved the principle that some person must always be in possession (or " seised "). Escheat always took place when a tenancy came to an end, for whatever cause,[33] but only two types of escheat were common—

(i) *propter defectum sanguinis* (for failure of blood): if a tenant died without heirs, the land escheated to the lord from whom he held it [34]; and

(ii) *propter delictum tenentis* (for the tenant's crime).[35] If a tenant was attainted for felony [36] (*i.e.*, convicted and sentenced to death, and not merely convicted [37]), his land escheated to his lord subject to the Crown's right to " year, day and waste," which was a right to hold the land for a year and a day and commit waste (such as cutting down trees).[38] The attainder related back to the time when the felony was committed, and so invalidated intermediate dealings.[39]

Forfeiture was a right of the Crown, dependent upon the Royal Prerogative and not upon tenure, to seize and keep the lands of any person attainted of high treason, whether he held of the Crown or some mesne lord.[40] For while felony was, in its earliest sense, a breach of homage, treason was a breach of allegiance. As with felony, the attainder related back to the time when the treason was

---

[30] Magna Carta, 1215, cc. 12, 15; the amounts leviable for the last two were fixed by the Statute of Westminster I, 1275, c. 36, and 25 Edw. 3, st. 5, c. 11, 1351: H.E.L. iii, 66.

[31] Co.Litt. 105b.

[32] For this term, see *ante*, p. 14.

[33] See, *e.g.*, *British General Insurance Co. Ltd.* v. *Att.-Gen.* [1945] L.J. N.C.C.R. 113; *post*, p. 36, n. 1.

[34] Co.Litt. 13a; Williams R.P. 49.

[35] Co.Litt. 13a.

[36] Felony included certain serious crimes such as murder, suicide, arson, robbery, and many kinds of larceny. Many other felonies were created by statute. Almost all felonies were punishable with death until the law was reformed in the first half of the nineteenth century. See Radzinowicz, *History of English Criminal Law*, i, 3–5, 578–607.

[37] See *R.* v. *Wilks* (1820) 3 B. & Ald. 510; and see *R.* v. *Kelly* [1950] 1 K.B. 164.

[38] Challis R.P. 34, 35; Williams R.P. 49. For waste, see *post*, p. 103. The usual practice was for the lord to compound with the Exchequer for year, day and waste, and take the land at once.

[39] H.E.L. iii, 69; see Co.Litt. 390b, 391a.

[40] P. & M. i, 351; H.E.L. iii, 70.

committed.[41] A tenant might also forfeit his land to his lord if he failed to perform his feudal services, either by virtue of an express right for forfeiture reserved by the lord,[42] or under statute. The primary remedy for default in services was distress, *i.e.*, the lord's right to seize chattels on the land and hold them until the services were performed. This, however, was often unsatisfactory, and the Statute of Gloucester, 1278,[43] gave the lord an action for forfeiture if services were two years in arrear and there were no distrainable goods on the land; and this action was made effective against third parties who acquired the land.[44]

B. *Tenures in Socage*

There were other tenures, less exalted than tenures in chivalry, where the tenants were nevertheless free tenants. We must now consider Petty Sergeanty and Socage. Each is, strictly speaking, a distinct variety of tenure, but they are much alike and can both be correctly classed as socage.[45] In general, these socage tenures were subject to all the incidents of tenures in chivalry except homage,[46] the honourable or military service, wardship and marriage.[47] Relief, however, was normally one year's rent (not one year's profits), and so was payable only where an annual money rent was reserved.[48] Nor was there any legal necessity for any incident but fealty.[49]

1. Petty sergeanty. The tenant was bound to perform for the King some service of a non-personal nature, such as supplying him with footmen, arrows, or straw for his bed.[50] After the fifteenth century it could exist only as a tenure in chief.[51]

2. Socage. This was the commonest form of socage tenure and ultimately became the commonest tenure of all. All free tenure was common socage [52] unless proved to be one of the others, and it is

---

[41] *Pimbs Case* (1585) Moo.K.B. 196; P. & M. i, 352–355; H.E.L. iii, 70.
[42] P. & M. i, 352.
[43] c. 4. The writ employed was the writ *cessavit per biennium.*
[44] Statute of Westminster II, 1285, c. 21.
[45] Litt. 118, 160, 162.
[46] Litt. 118, 131.
[47] In socage tenure the place of wardship and marriage was taken by guardianship. The lord had no right to be guardian and the guardian's rights and duties were fiduciary: P. & M. i, 321; H.E.L. iii, 65.
[48] Co.Litt. 93a, Hargrave's note.
[49] Litt. 131.
[50] Blount, Frag., 73–184. The dividing line between sergeanty and other tenures, and between grand and petty sergeanty, was shadowy: P. & M. i, 287, 323. *Cf.* Litt. 159, 160.
[51] Litt. 161.
[52] The word " socage " is probably derived from the Saxon " soc," meaning " seek," for the tenant had to seek his lord's " soke " or court: H.E.L. iii, 51; formerly it was thought to be derived from the French " soc," a ploughshare, on account of the usual agricultural service: *ibid.*; Litt. 119.

defined not by what it is but by what it is not. Any type of service might be reserved,[53] though generally it was some agricultural service which was fixed both as to nature and amount, *e.g.*, so many days' ploughing each year.[54] By the end of the fifteenth century most of these services had been commuted for money payments, often known as " quit rents," for the tenant thereby went quit, or free, from his services.

The conditions of socage tenure might vary from place to place according to local custom.[55] In contrast to " common socage " (the ordinary type) there were two customary variations which were particularly important, gavelkind and borough English. Their peculiarities relate more to the law of inheritance [56] and alienation than to the law of tenure, but it is convenient to collect them together here.

(*a*) *Gavelkind.*[57] The custom of gavelkind (from the Saxon " gafol," or " gavel," a rent [57]) applied to all land in Kent unless the contrary was shown.[58] It could apply to land outside Kent (there were variants in Wales and Ireland, for example [59]), but in that case the burden of proof was on the person who alleged that it applied.[59] The chief feature of the custom was *partibility*, whereby on intestacy the land descended to all males of the same degree equally, instead of to the eldest male in accordance with the ordinary rule.[60] Thus if a tenant died leaving five sons, the five took in equal shares if the land was gavelkind, but the eldest took to the exclusion of the others if the land was held in common socage. This rule was not confined to descendants, but applied also to collaterals,[61] such as brothers,[62] cousins [63] or great nephews [64]; and it applied to entails as well as to fees simple.[65]

In the case of gavelkind land in Kent, certain other peculiarities were attached by immemorial custom. Even where a statute had

---

[53] *e.g.*, to be a hangman, " the worst tenure that I have read of ": Co.Litt. 86a. The question whether the services must be certain in amount, or whether they might be variable at the lord's discretion, was raised but not decided in *Att.-Gen. for Alberta* v. *Huggard Assets Ltd.* [1953] A.C. 420.

[54] H.E.L. iii, 52.

[55] For the principle that ancient custom can produce local variations in the common law, see *post*, p. 821.

[56] *Post*, p. 508. Customary variations in conditions of tenure were often called " tenures ": see P. & M. i, 239, 240, 293, 294.

[57] Rob.Gav. 3.

[58] *Ibid.* 48 ; Bl.Comm. ii, 84 ; H.E.L. iii, 262.

[59] Rob.Gav. 22 ; Co.Litt. 176a, note 1.

[60] For the ordinary rule of primogeniture, see *post*, p. 511.

[61] *Re Chenoweth* [1902] 2 Ch. 488.

[62] Co.Litt. 140a.

[63] *Re Fullager* (1812) Rob.Gav. 117.

[64] *Hook* v. *Hook* (1862) 1 H. & M. 43.

[65] See, *e.g.*, *Doe* d. *Bosnall* v. *Harvey* (1825) 4 B. & C. 610.

disgavelled land (*i.e.*, converted the tenure into common socage and so abolished partibility),[66] these other peculiarities usually continued.[67] They were as follows—

(1) DEVISES. From the earliest times, the land might be devised (*i.e.*, disposed of by will),[68] whereas by the end of the thirteenth century it had been settled that other land was not devisable.[69]

(2) NO ESCHEAT. Upon the tenant being attainted of felony, the land did not escheat to the lord, nor was the Crown entitled to year, day and waste: " The father to the bough, the son to the plough." [70] But gavelkind land was subject to forfeiture for high treason.[71]

(3) INFANT'S CONVEYANCE. An infant of fifteen years of age or more could make a binding conveyance of his land if the conveyance was made for full value and was in the form known as a feoffment (pronounced feffment).[72] The parties to a feoffment were called the feoffor and the feoffee, the former being the person making the conveyance and the latter the recipient. In the case of other land, any feoffment made by an infant was liable to be set aside by him at or soon after his majority.[73]

(4) DOWER. When a tenant died leaving a widow, she was entitled to dower, which in common socage land was a life interest in one-third of her husband's realty.[74] But dower in gavelkind was in one half of the realty,[75] though it only lasted *dum casta et sola, i.e.*, while she remained chaste and unmarried.[76] It was benevolently held that for this purpose unchastity could be established only by the birth of a child [77]; but the widow could not waive her right to one half of gavelkind land *dum casta et sola* and choose to take one third without these restrictions.[78]

(5) CURTESY. When a tenant died leaving a widower, he was entitled to curtesy, which in common socage land was a life interest in all his wife's realty, but could be claimed only if issue capable of inheriting the land had been born of the marriage.[79] Curtesy in gavelkind land, however, was in only one half and lasted only until remarriage, although it could be claimed even if no issue was born.[80]

These five collateral customs were primarily customs annexed to gavelkind land in Kent, but some or all of them might apply to

---

[66] *e.g.*, Statute of Wales, 1543, which disgavelled all land in Wales.
[67] *Wiseman* v. *Cotten* (1663) 1 Sid. 135.
[68] Rob.Gav. 298 *et seq.*
[69] *Post*, p. 68.
[70] *Brook* v. *Ward* (1572) 3 Dy. 310b.
[71] *Case of Tanistry* (1608) Dav.Ir. 28 at 37.
[72] *Re Maskell & Goldfinch's Contract* [1895] 2 Ch. 525; Rob.Gav. 248, 249; for feoffment, see *post*, p. 163.
[73] *Post*, p. 991.
[74] *Post*, p. 516.
[75] *e.g.*, *Re Wilson* [1916] 1 Ch. 220.
[76] *Cobham* v. *Tomlinson* (1672) T.Jo. 6.
[77] Rob.Gav. (5th ed.) 142–144.
[78] *Davies* v. *Selby* (1601) Cro.Eliz. 825.
[79] *Post*, p. 514.
[80] Rob.Gav. 183–201.

land elsewhere if their existence could be proved. Unlike partibility, they were not essential to the existence of gavelkind.[81]

(*b*) *Borough English.* This was a custom existing in many parts of the country, principally Sussex and Surrey,[82] whereby land descended on intestacy to the youngest son instead of the eldest.[83] The custom applied only to sons; thus if a tenant died leaving only brothers, the elder brother was preferred to the younger unless a special custom extending to remoter relatives could be proved.[84] The name "borough English" seems to have originated in Nottingham, where the custom applied in the English part of the town but not in the French,[85] though it was mainly a rural custom and originally more widespread in villein tenure than in socage.[86] Its origins are obscure and few of the suggested explanations are neither lame nor fanciful.[87] The least improbable perhaps is that which links the custom with "that pastoral state of our British and German ancestors, which. Caesar and Tacitus describe."[88] In such times, it is said, the elder sons might be endowed out of their father's flocks and migrate, while the youngest would remain at home to help his father, and so naturally inherited his house.

Other customs attaching to socage land were sometimes called tenures, as if they were distinct. An example is tenure in burgage,[89] which was "only a kind of town socage."[90] In boroughs where this prevailed there were usually special local customs, such as the power to devise the land, or the widow's dower being in the whole of the land; and money rents generally took the place of all other services.

C. *Spiritual Tenures*

In ancient times much monastic and ecclesiastical land was held in spiritual tenure.[91] The two spiritual tenures were frankalmoign and

---

[81] Rob.Gav. 51–53.   [82] Kenny, *Primogeniture*, 30; Rob.Gav. (5th ed.) 238.
[83] *Weeks* v. *Carvel* (1602) Noy 106; *Lutwyche* v. *Lutwyche* (1735) Ca.t.Talb. 276. Maitland calls this custom "ultimogeniture": P. & M. ii, 279.
[84] Rob.Gav. 390, 391; *Re Smart* (1881) 18 Ch.D. 165.
[85] Y.B. 1 Edw. 3, f. 12, pl. 38 (1327).
[86] P. & M. ii, 279.
[87] *e.g.,* Litt. 211; and the imaginative association with the *jus primae noctis*: Bl.Comm. ii, 82.
[88] Bl.Comm. ii, 83; *cf.* P. & M. ii, 280–283. A similar custom was certainly widespread in Germany.
[89] Litt. 162–167. For borough customs generally, see H.E.L. iii, 269–275. For an example, see *Busher* v. *Thompson* (1846) 4 C.B. 47.
[90] Bl.Comm. ii, 82; *cf.* P. & M. i, 295.
[91] But Magna Carta, 1217, c. 43, and the Statutes of Mortmain, 1279 and 1290, forbade the conveyance of land to religious bodies, since this led to loss of feudal dues. If land was conveyed "into mortmain," the "dead hand" of the corporation meant that there would be no reliefs, wardships, marriages or escheats: Williams R.P. 54. For the mortmain legislation, now repealed, see *post*, p. 1001.

divine service. If land was granted to an ecclesiastical corporation, whether a corporation sole such as a bishop, or a corporation aggregate such as a monastery,[92] tenure in frankalmoign (" free alms ") arose if no fealty was demanded and no specific services were reserved.[93] In that case the tenant's sole obligation was to pray for the repose of the grantor's soul, and even this could be enforced only by complaint to the ecclesiastical powers.[94] Tenure in divine service, on the other hand, was tenure subject to definite spiritual services, such as singing mass every Friday or giving a certain sum of money to the poor.[95] Fealty was then due, and the lord could enforce the service in the ordinary way by distraint or forfeiture.[96]

Spiritual tenures could exist only between the grantor (or his heirs) and the grantee; if the tenant disposed of the land or there was an escheat of the lord's seignory (*i.e.*, his right to the feudal services)[97] such tenures usually became socage subject to the sole incident of fealty.[98]

Sect.-2. Unfree Tenures

The great unfree tenure was villeinage, later called copyhold. There was also a variety known as customary freehold. Generally speaking, one may say that free tenure was the tenure of landed proprietors and independent farmers, while unfree tenure was the tenure of common labourers. In law they were contrasted as follows.

(1) NO SEISIN. In the case of free tenures, the tenant had seisin, which meant that for feudal purposes he was deemed to be the lawful tenant of the land, and the King's courts would protect him against ejectment, even by his lord.[99] In the case of unfree tenure, the seisin was deemed to be in the lord and the tenant merely occupied on his behalf; the King's courts originally would not recognise any claim by the tenant, whose only recourse was to the court of his lord.[1] At first, therefore, the villein had no place in the feudal scale.

(2) UNCERTAIN SERVICES. The services of a freeholder were fixed both as to quantity and quality, whereas the services of an unfree tenant, although fixed as to quantity, were unfixed as to quality, and often more onerous. The freeholder might have to do so much ploughing or so much reaping for his lord each year, but these were

---

[92] For corporations sole and aggregate, see *post*, p. 54.
[93] H.E.L. iii, 35.
[94] Litt. 135, 136; *R.* v. *Brockham* (1628) Litt.R. 105 at 109.
[95] Litt. 137.
[96] *Ante*, p. 19, Litt. 137. There was a writ *cessavit de cantaria*: P. & M. i, 240.
[97] *Ante*, p. 14.
[98] Litt. 139, 141.
[99] H.E.L. iii, 30. For seisin, see *post*, p. 48.   [1] P. & M. i, 361.

" certain services." [2] The villein would have to work so many days
a week at whatever his lord required. When villeins " go to bed on
Sunday night they do not know what Monday's work will be " [3]; it
might be ditching, it might be threshing, it might be driving a cart.
A free tenant, on the other hand, was less a servant and more an
independent contractor [4]; either he had a set task which he carried
out in the way he thought best, or he merely paid a fixed rent in
money or in kind.

(3) SERVILE STATUS. All land held in free tenure was held by
tenants who were personally free. Until the fourteenth and fifteenth
centuries, however, many but not all tenants of land held in unfree
tenure were themselves personally unfree. Villein status must thus
be distinguished from villein tenure [5]; if a man of villein status held
land, the tenure was necessarily villein tenure, whereas land of villein
tenure might be held by a free man.

1. Villeinage

(*a*) *Origin.* A large proportion of England after the Conquest
was held in villein tenure, and most agricultural labour was done by
villein tenants.[6] This tenure was closely connected with that
important feudal unit, the manor. A manor usually consisted of—

   (i) the lord's demesne, comprising the manor house and the
        cultivable land which the lord himself occupied;
  (ii) the land held by tenants, in either free or unfree tenure; and
 (iii) the waste, on which the tenants could pasture their beasts.[7]

The cultivation of the lord's demesne was ensured by the services
owed by the tenants. Each manor had its own courts in which
disputes were settled and land transferred. There was a Court
Baron for the free tenants, and a Customary Court for the unfree
tenants.[8]

---

[2] Litt. 117; P. & M. i, 364.   [3] P. & M. i, 371.
[4] H.E.L. iii, 31.
[5] See P. & M. i, 414–420; H.E.L. iii, 491 *et seq.* The villein was protected in
life and limb, but had few other rights against his lord. He could be sold,
leased or recovered, but gained his freedom if not captured within four days.
Against third parties he had all the rights of a free man, so that his status
was not that of slavery (P. & M. i, 415). Villeins were later classified as either
" in gross " or " regardant to a manor," *i.e.*, either as separate property or
as part of a manor; unless sold separately villeins would pass with a conveyance of the manor: see Litt. 181; P. & M. i, 413; H.E.L. iii, 509. Villeins
were corporeal hereditaments: *post,* p. 788. In many colonies statutes declared
slaves to be real property: see Burton's *Compendium* (8th ed., 1856), Appendix.
[6] H.E.L. iii, 198; *Heydon's Case* (1584) 3 Co.Rep. 7a at 8b.
[7] For the manor, see P. & M. i, 594 *et seq.*; H.E.L. ii, 375 *et seq.*; iii, 32, 33,
491, 492.
[8] Co.Litt. 58a. If the number of free tenants fell below two, the Court Baron
ceased to exist (*Tonkin* v. *Croker* (1700) 2 Ld.Raym. 860 at 864), and the
manor became a " reputed manor " (Scriven 3).

The dependence of the villein tenants upon the manor is shown by the development of villein tenure. At first, the villein tenant was literally a tenant "at the will of the lord," [9] who could at any time evict him: the King's courts would not protect him, and he could not sue his lord in the manor court.[10] Yet his tenure, precarious in theory, came in practice to be well enough protected, for customs arose in each manor that tenants should not lose their lands unless they had done some act which was recognised as meriting forfeiture. The "custom of the manor" became the recognised "law" of the manor court, and although there was no means of enforcing it against the lord, he normally (as was natural) observed it.[11] The villein was therefore said to hold "at the will of the lord and according to the custom of the manor." In practice the second condition counted for most, though only the first was admitted by the common law.

(b) *Incidents.* The principal incidents of villein tenure were:

    (i) Agricultural services. These have been mentioned above. During the fourteenth and fifteenth centuries, as we shall see,[12] most of them were commuted for money payments.

    (ii) Fealty and suit of court.[13]

    (iii) Reliefs in some cases.[14]

    (iv) Escheat and forfeiture. Since the villein had no tenure recognised outside the manor, these were always in favour of the lord; the Crown had no claim even in the case of treason.[15]

    (v) Heriots.[16] By a very general custom, which occasionally applied even to freehold land,[17] the lord was entitled to take the tenant's best beast or other chattel on the tenant's death.[18] This was a relic of times when the lord furnished each new villein tenant with cattle and farming implements, and on the tenant's death took back his own.

    (vi) Fines, payable to the lord on alienation of the land. Originally these were at the discretion of the lord; but ultimately two years' improved value of the land (*i.e.*, the annual value of the land together with all increases in its value due to improvements) was regarded as the ordinary maximum.[19]

---

9 P. & M. i, 360.
10 *Ibid.* And see at pp. 377, 379–382.
11 *Ibid.* 361, 376, 377.
12 *Post*, p. 26.
13 Williams R.P. 519.
14 *Ibid.*
15 *Ibid.*
16 For derivation, see P. & M. i, 312–314, 316, 317.
17 See, *e.g.*, *Copestake* v. *Hoper* [1908] 2 Ch. 10.
18 See, *e.g.*, *Western* v. *Bailey* [1897] 1 Q.B. 86 (immaterial that beast had never been in the manor).
19 Scriven 182.

(c) *Transition from villein tenure to copyhold.* Great changes were wrought in villein tenure in the fourteenth and fifteenth centuries and they were accelerated by the Black Death of 1349 and 1361, and the Peasants' Revolt of 1381.[22] The Black Death greatly reduced·the number of labourers and strengthened their bargaining power. It became common to commute villein services for fixed money rents. Just as in the twelfth and thirteenth centuries the feudal levy was turned into a paid army, and military service into scutage,[23] so in the fourteenth and fifteenth centuries was labour service replaced by hired labour, and the serf by a rent-paying, wage-earning tenant. This process in turn hastened the disappearance of villein status; and in 1618 the last case on villein status was fought and decided against the lord.[24]

Meanwhile, as the old system of manorial agriculture changed, and as public policy demanded better control over feudal powers, the royal courts took the important step of protecting tenants of villein land against their lords.[25] The Chancery made the first move in 1439, and by the end of the fifteenth century, it seems, the common law courts were ready to assist any tenant ejected by his lord otherwise than in accordance with the custom of the manor.[26] No change, however, was made in the rule that the lord, not the tenant, had the legal seisin of the land.

At law, therefore, as well as by custom, the villein tenant held " at the will of the lord according to the custom of the manor," [27] with the emphasis upon the latter words. Everything was regulated by the custom of the particular manor in question, which, when proved, would be enforceable at common law. This change was marked by a change in name: " tenure in villeinage " became known as " tenure by copy of the court roll " or " copyhold," and the term " villein " was reserved for the few remaining persons whose status was still unfree.[28]

(d) Copyhold

(1) CONVEYANCE. The name " copyhold " is derived from the way in which such land was conveyed. In the case of free tenures (after 1290) a conveyance could be made without reference to the lord [29]; copyholds, however, could be transferred only by a surrender and admittance made in the lord's court. The transferor surrendered his land to the lord, who then admitted as tenant the person

[22] H.E.L. iii, 203–205.
[23] *Ante,* p. 16.
[24] *Pigg* v. *Caley* (1618) Noy 27; H.E.L. iii, 508 (" sixty " in line 1 of the note on p. 509 is a slip for " six ").   [25] H.E.L. iii, 206–209.
[26] Litt. 77, 82; H.E.L. iii, 208, 209. The remedy was by the action of ejectment (*post*, p. 1170): H.E.L. vii, 9.   [27] *Brown's Case* (1581) 4 Co.Rep. 21a.
[28] H.E.L. iii, 206.   [29] *Post*, p. 31.

nominated by the transferor. In practice, the lord's steward or bailiff conducted the business of the manor court for the lord; and sometimes there was a symbolic surrender and delivery of a small rod or verge, whence the term " tenant by the verge." [30] In the days of villeinage the lord had some discretion in controlling such transfers. After the transition to copyhold he had none; he was merely " custom's instrument." [31] The transaction was recorded on the court rolls and the transferee had a copy of the entry to prove his title; he thus held " by copy of the court roll."

(2) SURRENDER AND ADMITTANCE. Surrenders could be made in or out of court; if made out of court, due " presentment " (*i.e.*, mention) of this at the next court was necessary.[32] Admittances could be made only in court [33] unless made by the lord himself.[34] But after the Copyhold Act, 1841, presentment became unnecessary and admittances could be made out of court even by the steward.[35] The substantial part of a transfer was the surrender; the admittance was a mere form.[36] Nevertheless, until admittance the legal estate remained in the transferor, and the transferee's title was incomplete. But the admittance, when made, related back to the time of the surrender as against all save the lord,[37] and so invalidated any intermediate dealings inconsistent with the surrender.[38]

(3) CUSTOM. By the end of the sixteenth century the legal position of the copyholder had become substantially settled. But, of course, the custom of the manor in which the land lay was all-important; " the custom of the manor is the soul and life of copyhold." [39] Yet all customs were required to be reasonable.[40] Gavelkind and borough English might be found among copyhold customs, as well as in free tenure.[41] Copyhold lost its taint of servility, and became merely a form—indeed, one of the commonest forms—of tenure. Since rents could not be increased as the value of money fell, copyhold lands became valuable inheritances to their tenants, and permanently ceased to be a source of much profit to their lords.[42]

(4) RIGHTS OF THE LORD. History, nevertheless, left enduring

---

[30] Litt. 78.
[31] H.E.L. iii, 247, 248.
[32] Williams R.P. 527.
[33] *Doe* d. *Gutteridge* v. *Sowerby* (1860) 7 C.B.(N.S.) 599.
[34] *Melwich* v. *Luter* (1588) 4 Co.Rep. 26a.
[35] ss. 88, 90.
[36] *Baddeley* v. *Leppingwell* (1764) 3 Burr. 1533 at 1543.
[37] *Holdfast* d. *Woollams* v. *Clapham* (1787) 1 T.R. 600.
[38] Scriven 97, 130; Williams R.P. 529; see, *e.g.*, *Doe* d. *Wheeler* v. *Gibbons* (1835) 7 C. & P. 161.
[39] *Brown's Case* (1581) 4 Co.Rep 21a.   [40] Scriven 313.
[41] Scriven 19–20, 172–174; H.E.L. vii, 300. For gavelkind and borough English, see *ante*, p. 20.   [42] H.E.L. iii, 212.

marks on this tenure. First, despite the loosening of the communal bonds within the manor, the method of conveyance prevented the lord from losing touch with his tenants, and so preserved the feudal incidents. Fines, reliefs and heriots, for example, were taken as before. Freehold tenants, on the other hand, could convey their land without reference to their lords, who sooner or later found it hardly worth while to trace their tenants in order to collect feudal dues which had greatly diminished in value. Secondly, the lord had valuable timber and mineral rights, the rules for which were the same.[43] The ownership of all timber and minerals was vested in the lord,[44] but as they were in the possession of the tenant, it was a trespass for the lord to enter to take them without the tenant's consent.[45] Both these rules were subject to any custom to the contrary, but in the absence of any such custom, the trees and minerals could not be dealt with except by agreement between lord and tenant.[46] Copyhold tenants therefore rarely thought it worth while to cultivate timber; " the oak scorns to grow except on free land." [47] Further, the lord had no right to use the space left by minerals which had been extracted (*e.g.*, for transporting minerals from another mine), for the space belonged to the tenant.[48]

2. Customary freehold. " Customary freehold " was the name given to copyhold where the tenant was expressed to hold " according to the custom of the manor," but not " at the will of the lord." [49] A conveyance of such land might be made by surrender and admittance, by an ordinary conveyance followed by admittance, or by an ordinary conveyance coupled with surrender and admittance. In other respects, customary freehold was no different from ordinary copyhold, so that its title was misleading. Seisin was in the lord,[50] and the lord was entitled to the timber and minerals.[51] A more apt name for customary freehold was " privileged copyhold." [52]

Sect. 3. Miscellaneous Tenures

The law constantly aimed at classifying tenures, and so achieved (in Maitland's opinion) " a simplicity that is truly marvellous." [53]

---

[43] *Lewis* v. *Branthwaite* (1831) 2 B. & Ad. 437 at 443.
[44] *Eardley* v. *Earl Granville* (1876) 3 Ch.D. 826 at 832.
[45] *Bourne* v. *Taylor* (1808) 10 East 189 (minerals); *Whitechurch* v. *Holworthy* (1815) 4 M. & S. 340 (trees).
[46] *Commissioners of Inland Revenue* v. *Joicey* (*No. 2*) [1913] 2 K.B. 580 at 586.
[47] Williams R.P. 506.   [48] *Eardley* v. *Earl Granville* (1876) 3 Ch.D. 826.
[49] Scriven 14–19. Distinguish " ancient freeholds " (*ibid*. 19), which were a species of free tenure subject to manorial customs: see *Passingham* v. *Pitty* (1855) 17 C.B. 299.
[50] *Doe* d. *Cook* v. *Danvers* (1806) 7 East 299; *Thompson* v. *Hardinge* (1845) 1 C.B. 940.
[51] *Bishop of Winchester* v. *Knight* (1717) 1 P.Wms. 406.
[52] *Duke of Portland* v. *Hill* (1866) L.R. 2 Eq. 765 at 776.   [53] P. & M. i, 406.

The scheme did not always fit the facts, and there were several ancient types of tenure which were not easy to classify. Of these we must mention two.

1. Homage Ancestral. This was sometimes treated as if it were a tenure by itself, but in reality it was a name given to either knight's service or socage when homage was due and neither the tenement nor the seignory had been alienated within legal memory, *i.e.*, since 1189.[54] It was, for obvious reasons, probably obsolete by the seventeenth century.[55] It had the same peculiarity as frankalmoign, being able to exist only between the original grantor and grantee and their respective heirs, and becoming common socage upon alienation.

2. Ancient demesne. Manors which belonged to the Crown in 1066 were known as " manors of ancient demesne." [56] These ancient manors had a peculiar status, and they retained it even when granted by the King to a subject. They might contain the usual types of free and unfree tenants.[57] But there was a third class, called " tenants in ancient demesne," who did villein services and had to defend their holdings in the manorial court, but who could, if necessary, enforce the custom of the manor by invoking the aid of the royal court. Eventually it had to be decided whether or not they were freeholders.[58] The doctrine in the end adopted was that those who could convey their holdings independently of the lord's court were free tenants, whereas those who had to convey by manorial machinery were unfree (in effect, therefore, copyholders). Both classes were barred from bringing actions for their land directly in the royal courts until the Common Law Procedure Act. 1852.[59]

Part 3
REDUCTION IN THE NUMBER OF TENURES
Sect. 1.   Prohibition of New Tenures After 1290

1. Before 1290. In early times there was no theoretical limit to the number of intervening tenures between the King and the tenant in occupation of the land. A new rung could always be

---

[54] Litt. 143–152; Challis 13. For 1189 as the limit of legal memory, see *post*, p. 847.   [55] Co.Litt. 105 (*a*), n. 1.
[56] P. & M. i, 383 *et seq.*; H.E.L. iii, 263 *et seq.*; Williams R.P. 61, 62. There has been much confusion over " ancient demesne " as a class of tenure. The Report of the Real Property Commissioners adopted in *Merttens* v. *Hill* [1901] 1 Ch. 842 at 853 really relates to socage tenure.
[57] All classes of tenants on the ancient demesne had a group of special privileges and liabilities in public law: H.E.L. iii, 264. *Iveagh* v. *Martin* [1961] 1 Q.B. 232 deals with liability to tolls in a manor of ancient demesne.
[58] The point at issue was the parliamentary franchise, which was confined to freeholders: H.E.L. iii, 269.   [59] Williams R.P. 62.

added at the bottom of the feudal ladder by the creation of a further tenure. This process was called subinfeudation. It was popular in an age where land was almost the only form of capital wealth, for then the seller of land preferred to take payment in the form of a continuing right to rent or services charged on the land. For example, the King might grant to A, A might grant to B and B might grant to C. A and B would then be mesne lords,[60] and if A (for example) was not rendered his services by B, he could proceed against the land, *i.e.*, distrain on C. C in turn had a remedy against B, the writ of mesne.[61] But for obvious reasons this system was excessively cumbrous and inconvenient, particularly as the value of seignories came to lie in incidents rather than in services.[62] " Suppose that A enfeoffed B to hold by knight's service, and that B enfeoffed C to hold at a rent of a pound of pepper; B dies leaving an heir within age; A is entitled to a wardship; but it will be worth very little : instead of being entitled to enjoy the land itself until the heir is of age, he will get a few annual pounds of pepper. And so in case of an escheat, instead of enjoying the land for ever he may have but a trifling rent." [63] Further, if B disappeared, A would be ignorant of the occasions on which the benefits of escheat, marriage and wardship arose.

The alternative to subinfeudation was substitution. B might grant to C not by creating a new tenure but by letting C step into his shoes so that C became, and B ceased to be, tenant of A. But could A be compelled to take C for his tenant at B's instance? " If a new is substituted for an old tenant, a poor may take the place of a rich, a dishonest that of an honest man, a foe that of a friend, and the solemn bond of homage will be feeble if the vassal has a free power of putting another man in his room." [64] There was a further objection if B alienated only a part of his land by substitution : the lord would have to look to two tenants instead of one for the services. Nevertheless, and despite the personal character of the feudal bond, it appears to have become the general rule in the thirteenth century that tenants could alienate by substitution without their lords' consent. In that period freedom of alienation was in the ascendant as a principle of public policy.[65]

2. The Statute Quia Emptores, 1290

(*a*) *The statute.* Magna Carta, 1217, c. 39, had attempted to meet the lords' objections by prohibiting alienations which left

---

[60] See *ante*, p. 14.
[61] P. & M. i, 238.
[62] H.E.L. ii, 348, 349; iii, 80.
[63] P. & M. i, 330.
[64] *Ibid*.
[65] P. & M. i, 344.

insufficient security for the services. But dissatisfaction continued until a revolutionary settlement was made by the statute *Quia Emptores*, 1290.[66] The effect of this was as follows:

(i) Alienation by subinfeudation was prohibited (c. 1).

(ii) All free tenants were authorised to alienate the whole or part of their land by substitution, without the lord's consent, the new tenant to hold by the same services as the old (c. 1).

(iii) On alienation of part of the land by substitution, the feudal services were to be apportioned (c. 2).

(iv) The statute applied only to grants in fee simple (c. 3).

(*b*) *Effect of the statute.* *Quia Emptores* marked the victory of the modern concept of land as alienable property over the more restrictive principles of feudalism. For no new tenures in fee simple could thenceforth be created except by the Crown. Existing tenures could be freely transferred from hand to hand, and they could be extinguished as before by escheat or forfeiture. The network of tenures could therefore no longer grow; it could only contract. Every conveyance of land in fee simple by a subject after 1290 was bound to be an out-and-out transfer and could not create the relationship of lord and tenant between the parties. On such a conveyance no services could be reserved; any rights reserved, such as a rent, must be rights existing independently of the relationship of lord and tenant. Nor could any fines for alienation be lawfully demanded by any subject.[67]

(*c*) *Limits of statute.* Since the statute was expressly confined to alienations in fee simple, it did not prevent a tenant in fee simple from granting a life estate or a fee tail to another to hold of him as lord.[68] Further, as it did not mention the Crown either expressly or by necessary implication, the Crown was not bound by it.[69] Consequently the statute conferred no right of free alienation upon tenants in chief, and an Ordinance of 1256 forbidding them to alienate without a royal licence remained effective. However, in 1327 tenants in chief were given a right of free alienation, subject only to the

---

[66] An abbreviated version of the first chapter may be given as follows: " Whereas purchasers of lands and tenements have many times heretofore entered into their fees, to be holden in fee of their feoffors and not of the chief lords of the fees, whereby the said chief lords have many times lost their escheats, marriages and wardships; which things seemed very hard and extreme unto those lords and other great men: our lord the king has granted, provided and ordained that henceforth it shall be lawful for every freeman to sell at his own pleasure his lands and tenements, or part of them; so nevertheless that the feoffee shall hold the same lands or tenements of the chief lord of the same fee, by such service and customs as his feoffor held before."

[67] See, *e.g.*, *Merttens* v. *Hill* [1901] 1 Ch. 842.   [68] Challis 22.

[69] Litt. 140. See H.E.L. iii, 84, i, 473. But tenants in chief were prevented from subinfeudating: *Re Holliday* [1922] 2 Ch. 698.

payment of a reasonable fine in some cases,[70] and the Tenures Abolition Act, 1660, abolished this fine.[71] Nor did the Statute prevent the Crown from granting land to be held of the Crown; but the Tenures Abolition Act, 1660, provided that such grants could be made only in common socage.[72]

(*d*) *Effect today.* *Quia Emptores*, 1290, is still in force today and may be regarded as one of the pillars of the law of real property. It operates every time that a conveyance in fee simple is executed, automatically shifting the status of tenant from grantor to grantee and fulfilling the rule that all land held by a subject shall be held in tenure of the Crown either mediately or immediately. The lord of the fee is the successor in title to the person who was lord in 1290, for there can have been no change in the tenure since then.[73] But it is rare for records of a mesne lordship to have been preserved for so long, except in the case of manors where mesne tenure remained of importance until 1925 and later.[74] Other cases are governed by the presumption that, if no mesne lord appears, the land is held immediately of the Crown.[75] Innumerable mesne lordships came to be forgotten as, with the passage of time and the inflation of the currency, the ancient services or commutation rents ceased to be worth collecting. After 1290 the feudal pyramid began to crumble. The number of mesne lordships could not be increased, evidence of existing mesne lordships gradually disappeared with the passing of time, and so most land came to be held directly from the Crown.

Sect. 2. The Tenures Abolition Act, 1660

1. Tenures. The system of landholding in return for services fell into decay long before the most onerous incidents of tenure were legally abolished. In particular, the incidents of military tenure, such as wardships, marriages and aids, were zealously preserved by the Crown for the sake of revenue.[76] The King, who was always lord and never tenant, was the only proprietor who had all to gain and nothing to lose by preserving these feudal imposts. But, like certain other items of unparliamentary revenue, they were swept away in the seventeenth century. The Tenures Abolition Act, 1660, confirming

---

[70] 1 Edw. 3, st. 2, cc. 12, 13, 1327; *cf.* 34 Edw. 3, c. 15, 1360, confirming alienations made before 1272.
[71] s. 1. For this statute, see below.
[72] s. 4.
[73] But it is possible that a subinfeudation in fee simple can be brought about (since 1881) by the enlargement of a long lease: see *post*, p. 670.
[74] See *post*, p. 34.
[75] Williams R.P. 58; Challis 33; and see *Re Lowe's W.T.* [1973] 1 W.L.R. 882.
[76] Bl.Comm. ii, 69, 76. There was also the lucrative prerogative right to compel military tenants in chief to assume knighthood: *ibid.*

a resolution of the Long Parliament of 1646, converted all tenures into free and common socage with the exceptions of frankalmoign and copyhold.[77]

2. Incidents. The statute also abolished many burdensome incidents, including aids for the knighting of the lord's eldest son and the marriage of his eldest daughter, wardships, marriages, primer seisin, *ouster le main*, and most fines for alienation; and it abolished the Court of Wards and Liveries which the Crown had set up to enforce some of these incidents against tenants *in capite*. The Crown was compensated for its loss of revenue by the imposition of a tax on beer and other beverages. Fixed rents, heriots and suit of court were expressly saved, and reliefs were restricted to those payable for land of socage tenure, *i.e.*, one year's rent. Since it was uncommon for military tenure to be subject to rent, relief in effect disappeared with the other incidents.

3. Summary. The principal results of the Act may be summarised thus:

(a) Nearly all burdensome incidents were abolished for all land of free tenure. Escheat and forfeiture survived as the only important incidents of free tenure. Fealty survived, but was of no importance.

(b) All free tenures were converted into free and common socage and no other type of tenure might be created in future. But the Act preserved, *inter alia*, (i) copyhold, (ii) frankalmoign, (iii) the honorary incidents of grand sergeanty, and (iv) services incident to socage (*e.g.*, those of petty sergeanty [78]). Customs such as gavelkind and borough English, and the peculiarities of ancient demesne, continued unaltered.

Sect. 3. The 1925 Legislation

A. Tenures

1. Before 1926. From 1645 until 1926 the two surviving tenures held the field: socage (often called freehold) and copyhold. Frankalmoign, since it could not survive alienation at any time after 1290, had become obsolete.[79] This dual system of tenure was an impediment to conveyancing. Copyhold had the great merit that the books

---

[77] For animadversions on the drafting of this statute, see Co.Litt. 108a, note 1, and Challis 23.
[78] Despite the sweeping words of the statute, it has been asserted that the actual tenure of petty sergeanty continued in being, and not merely the incidents: see Co.Litt. 108a, n. 1; Cru.Dig. i, 41.   [79] *Ante*, p. 31.

of the manor were a register of title,[80] while freehold titles had to be proved in the traditional way by investigating past transactions recorded in the title deeds.[81] But copyhold had disadvantages. Its peculiar mode of conveyance (surrender and admittance) made it impossible to convey freeholds and copyholds by a single deed. It was subject both to customary incidents which might vary from manor to manor and also to the lord's rights to timber and minerals. Accordingly provision was made by statute for the enfranchisement of copyholds, *i.e.*, the conversion of land of copyhold tenure into socage. The Copyhold Acts of 1841, 1843 and 1844 provided for voluntary enfranchisement, *i.e.*, enfranchisement where both lord and tenant agreed. The Copyhold Acts of 1852, 1858 and 1887 (consolidated in the Copyhold Act, 1894) enabled either lord or tenant to secure compulsory enfranchisement. But apart from any proceedings taken under these Acts, tenures remained substantially unaltered until the legislation of 1922–25 came into force.

2. After 1925. By the Law of Property Act, 1922 (which took effect at the beginning of 1926), all copyhold land was enfranchised, *i.e.*, made land of freehold (socage) tenure.[82] Freehold and copyhold incidents were dealt with as explained below. At the same time frankalmoign was formally abolished.[83] A new system of intestate succession was introduced whereby all special customs of descent, including gavelkind and borough English, were superseded.[84] The only remaining traces of special types of freehold tenure are now the services incident to grand and petty sergeanty, which were left untouched by the Acts.[85] The result was that as from the beginning of 1926 (when these provisions all took effect) all land has been held in freehold, the modern name for free and common socage.[86]

B. Incidents

1. Freehold. Quit rents, reliefs, fealty, suit of court and occasional escheats were the only feudal incidents ordinarily existing in freehold land in 1925. Most of the money payments had ceased

---

[80] Williams, *Seisin*, 41.   [81] *Ante*, p. 6, *post*, p. 578.
[82] s. 128 and 12th Sched., para. (1). A.E.A., 1925, 2nd Sched., Pt. I, also repealed the saving words of s. 7 of the Tenures Abolition Act, 1660.
[83] A.E.A., 1925, 2nd Sched., Pt. I. This repeals the words in the Tenures Abolition Act, 1660, s. 7, which saved frankalmoign from destruction by s. 1 of that Act, whereby all tenures as from February 24, 1646, "and for ever thereafter" were to be "turned into free and common socage." In the face of these words and s. 7, the suggestion that frankalmoign still survives because it is not mentioned in s. 1 seems unsound. See, however, Co.Litt. 100b, n. 1.
[84] A.E.A., 1925, s. 45 (1), 2nd Sched., Pt. I; *post*, p. 523. Infants' power to convey gavelkind land was abolished by L.P.A., 1925, ss. 1 (6), 51 (1).
[85] L.P.A., 1922, s. 136.
[86] There is some doubt whether the tenure of ancient demesne has been abolished: see *Iveagh* v. *Martin* [1961] 1 Q.B. 232 at 241.

to be payable; the value of money had fallen so much that the payments were not worth collecting, and after non-payment for twelve years they were barred by statute.[87] Manorial incidents affecting freeholds (*e.g.*, freehold within manors or enfranchised copyholds) were dealt with in the same way as copyhold incidents.[88] Fealty and suit of court, although abolished in the case of copyholds, have been left in existence in the case of freeholds. This is probably accidental but quite unimportant.

Escheat *propter defectum sanguinis* (on death of the tenant intestate and without heirs) was often the one valuable right of the lord still in existence in 1925. In most cases it was impossible for the mesne lord to prove his lordship, for freeholders could alienate their land without reference to the lord and thus for many years no act to mark the lordship might occur.[89] The Administration of Estates Act, 1925, abolished this form of escheat and provided that if a person died leaving property not disposed of by will, that property should pass to the Crown [90] in default of any of the limited class of relatives set out in the Act.[91] Escheat *propter delictum tenentis* (for felony) no longer existed in 1925. The Corruption of Blood Act, 1814, had restricted it to cases of *petit* treason and murder, and the Forfeiture Act, 1870, completely abolished it, together with the Crown's prerogative right of forfeiture for high treason. No longer, therefore, can there be an escheat of either of the two principal kinds.

Nevertheless, in certain cases, the possibility of escheat remains. Escheat is a principle inseparable from tenure which ensures that land will never be without an owner, for if there is no tenant and no mesne lord it will return to the Crown.[92] There may still today be escheat if the trustee in bankruptcy of a landowner exercises his statutory power [93] to disclaim the land [94]; and although on the dissolution of a company governed by the Companies Acts special provision is made for its property to vest in the Crown,[95] there will be an escheat of the real property of any other corporation that is

---

[87] *Post*, pp. 792, 1018. *De Beauvoir* v. *Owen* (1850) 5 Exch. 166 (freehold); *Howitt* v. *Harrington* [1893] 2 Ch. 497 (copyhold).
[88] L.P.A., 1922, s. 138 (1); and see *post*, p. 37. Any remaining privileges of tenants in ancient demesne seem to have survived: *Iveagh* v. *Martin* [1961] 1 Q.B. 232.
[89] *Ante*, p. 31.
[90] Or Duchy of Lancaster or Duke of Cornwall.
[91] ss. 45, 46; and see Crown Estate Act, 1961, s. 8 (3).
[92] But awkward questions can arise if the Crown disclaims: see (1954) 70 L.Q.R. 25 (D. W. Elliott).
[93] Bankruptcy Act, 1914, s. 54.
[94] *British General Insurance Co. Ltd.* v. *Att.-Gen.* [1945] L.J.N.C.C.R. 113, discussed (1946) 62 L.Q.R. 223 (R.E.M.); see also (1931) 75 S.J. 843 (T. C. Williams).
[95] Companies Act, 1948, s. 354.

dissolved.[96] Leases owned by such a corporation, on the other hand, will pass to the Crown under the Crown's prerogative right to *bona vacantia, i.e.,* personal property without an owner.[97]

2. Copyhold. In the case of copyholds, the incidents were in most cases still fully effective in 1925. The Law of Property Act, 1922, divided them into three classes:

(*a*) *Those abolished forthwith.*[98] As soon as the Act came into force (on January 1, 1926), the following incidents were abolished subject to a single payment of compensation.[99]

(i) Forfeiture for alienation in freehold (*i.e.,* for purporting to convey the land as freehold) or without licence.

(ii) Fealty and customary suits and services.

(iii) Escheat for want of heirs.[1]

(iv) Special customs of descent (*e.g.,* gavelkind and borough English), dower, freebench (the usual name for dower in copyhold land) and curtesy.

(*b*) *Those preserved until* 1936.[2] This class automatically disappeared after December 31, 1935, unless previously extinguished either voluntarily or compulsorily. Until 1936 the parties could extinguish them at any time voluntarily, or either party could serve a notice on the other requiring the amount of compensation to be ascertained.[3] Immediately on service of the notice the incidents ceased, and compensation became payable as fixed by the Minister of Agriculture according to a scale. If the compensation was £20 or less it was payable by the tenant as a debt. If it was more than £20 it took the form of a rentcharge running with the land and spread over twenty years.[4]

So long as any incidents in this class existed, no conveyance of the land would pass the legal estate unless it was produced to the

---

[96] *Re Wells* [1933] Ch. 29 at 54, approving Challis 467; *Re Strathblaine Estates Ltd.* [1948] Ch. 228. Previously it had been doubtful whether there was escheat, or reverter to the donor: Co.Litt. 13b; Preston ii, 50; Challis 65, 66, 226; (1933) 49 L.Q.R. 160 (Holdsworth), 240 (Farrer); (1935) 51 L.Q.R. 347 (Hughes), 361 (Farrer). See also *post,* p. 245.

[97] *Re Wells* [1933] Ch. 29 (equitable interest in leaseholds).

[98] 12th Sched., para. (1).

[99] 13th Sched., Pt. II, para. 13, as amended by L.P.Am.A., 1924, 2nd Sched., para. 4 (3), and L.P.Am.A., 1926, Sched. (usually 20 per cent. of the annual value of the land).

[1] In *British General Insurance Co. Ltd.* v. *Att.-Gen.* [1945] L.J.N.C.C.R. 113 at 125 it was said that all kinds of escheat were abolished for enfranchised land by L.P.A., 1922, 12th Sched., para. (1) (*c*). But the more natural interpretation is that escheat is excluded only where the Crown takes as *bona vacantia* under the A.E.A., 1925 (replacing Part VIII of the L.P.A., 1922).

[2] ss. 128, 129, 138, 140, 13th Sched., Pt. II.

[3] In order to give the tenant time to raise the money the lord was prohibited from serving a notice until 1931: L.P.A., 1922, s. 138 (1) (*b*).   [4] s. 139 (1) (v).

steward of the manor within six months and indorsed by him with a certificate that all payments due on the transfer had been duly made. This provision was necessary since the land, being freehold, became transferable without reference to the lord, and thus the lord might not know that there had been a conveyance entitling him to a fine or some other payment.

Even though the incidents ceased at the end of 1935 (and thus production of a conveyance made after 1935 was unnecessary), the lord was enabled to claim compensation, originally up to 1941, and later, by a war-time extension, up to the end of October, 1950.[5]

The incidents in this class are as follows.

(i) Quit rents, chief rents and other similar payments.

(ii) Fines, reliefs, heriots and dues (including fees payable to stewards).

(iii) Forfeitures other than for alienation in freehold or without licence.

(iv) Timber rights.

As mentioned above,[6] these provisions for extinguishment apply also to the few cases where incidents of manorial origin were attached to freehold land.

(c) *Those preserved indefinitely.*[7] The rights which continue indefinitely unless abolished by written agreement between lord and tenant are as follows.

(i) Any rights of the lord or tenant to mines [8] and minerals.

(ii) Any rights of the lord in respect of fairs, markets and sporting.

(iii) Any tenant's rights of common (*e.g.*, to pasture beasts on the waste land of the manor).

(iv) Any liability of lord or tenant for the upkeep of dykes, ditches, sea walls, bridges, and the like.

Only by the existence of these rights and duties is land which was formally copyhold now distinguishable from other land as regards the conditions of tenure.

---

5 Postponement of Enactments (Miscellaneous Provisions) Act, 1939, s. 3; S.I. 1949, No. 836.

6 *Ante*, p. 35.

7 ss. 128 (2), 138, 12th Sched., paras. (4)–(6).

8 " Mines " is a more comprehensive term than " minerals," for it relates not only to the minerals but also to the passages in the mine: *Batten Pooll* v. *Kennedy* [1907] 1 Ch. 256.

Part 4

TENURE AND OWNERSHIP TODAY

There is only one feudal tenure left today, namely socage, now called freehold. Feudal incidents have in practice disappeared,[9] except for land formerly held in grand sergeanty, petty sergeanty or copyhold, where some traces of the former tenure remain. Except in the case of land formerly copyhold, mesne lordships are nearly all untraceable, for it is many years since there were any enforceable rights to preserve evidence of the relationship of lord and tenant; consequently the courts are ready to act on the presumption that the land is held directly of the Crown, *e.g.*, for the purposes of escheat.[9a]

Yet despite the sweeping changes made by statute, " the fundamental principles of the law of ownership of land remain the same as before the legislation of 1925. Land is still the object of feudal tenure; the Sovereign remains the lord paramount of all the land within the realm; every parcel of land is still held of some lord . . . and the greatest interest which any subject can have in land is still an estate in fee simple and no more." [10] The title " tenant in fee simple " is still the technically correct description of the person who is popularly regarded as the owner of land, and every conveyance in fee simple substitutes the new tenant for the old as provided by the statute *Quia Emptores*, 1290. Nevertheless, as will be seen, for all practical purposes ownership in fee simple " differs from the absolute dominion of a chattel in nothing except the physical indestructibility of its subject." [11] Our law has preferred to suppress one by one the practical consequences of tenure rather than to strike at the root of the theory of tenure itself. It remains possible, therefore, that in rare cases not covered by the statutory reforms recourse may have to be had to the feudal principles which still underlie our land law.[12]

There is one field where rules derived from tenure are still of importance, as its name implies: that of landlord and tenant. But leasehold tenure lay outside the feudal system, and will be treated independently.[13]

---

[9] For a Crown grant in 1913 of Canadian land in socage in fee simple subject to rent service (a royalty), see *Att.-Gen. for Alberta* v. *Huggard Assets Ltd.* [1953] A.C. 420. In principle there is nothing to prevent the Crown reserving services upon such grants.

[9a] See, *e.g.*, *Re Lowe's W.T.* [1973] 1 W.L.R. 882 at 886.

[10] Cyprian Williams, 75 S.J. 848 (" The fundamental principles of the present law of ownership of land," 1931).

[11] Challis 218; and see *post*, p. 66; but compare *post*, p. 40, n. 2.

[12] *e.g.*, in the still possible cases of escheat: *ante*, p. 35.   [13] *Post*, Chap. 11

For practical purposes, therefore, the law of tenure is no longer of assistance in solving problems about rights over land. The owner in fee simple is regarded as absolute owner, and the fundamentals of his title depend on principles which have nothing to do with tenure. Two of the most important principles are that title depends ultimately upon possession, and that an owner can transfer no greater interest than he himself has (*nemo dat quod non habet*). The latter principle will be seen in operation throughout this book,[14] but the former can suitably be explained only at a later stage.[15]

---

14 Except where the land has registered title: *post*, pp. 1054, 1063. There used also to be an exception at common law, since by using a feoffment a tenant with a limited estate could convey a fee simple: see Litt. 596, 611 and Co.Litt. 330b, note by Butler. But such " tortious feoffments," once the subject of much intricate law, were abolished by R.P.A., 1845, s. 4. Since then all conveyances are " innocent," *i.e.*, they can transmit no more than the grantor himself has.
15 *Post*, p. 1004 and Appendix I.

Chapter 3

ESTATES

Part 1

CLASSIFICATION

THE term "estate," as we have seen,[1] indicates an interest in land of some particular duration. It is now necessary to consider the different kinds of estate, *i.e.*, the various possible interests in land classified according to their duration.

It is the doctrine of estates, coupled with the permanence of land as opposed to destructible chattels, which makes the law relating to land so much more complex than the law governing chattels.[2] At common law it can in general be said that only two distinct legal rights can exist at the same time in chattels, namely, possession and ownership. If A lends his watch to B, the ownership of the watch remains vested in A, while B has possession of it. But in the case of land, a large number of legal rights could and still can exist at the same time. Thus the position of Blackacre in 1920 might have been that A was entitled to the land for life, B to a life estate in remainder (*i.e.*, after A's death), and C to the fee simple remainder. At the same time, D might own a lease for 99 years, subject to a sub-lease in favour of E for 21 years, and the land might be subject to a mortgage in favour of F, a rentcharge in favour of G, easements such as rights of way in favour of H, J, and K, and so on indefinitely. Before 1926 all these estates and interests could exist as legal rights, and most, but not all, can exist as legal rights today.

It may thus be said that in the case of a chattel, ownership will be absolute ownership; it is either owned outright by one person (or several persons jointly or in common with each other) or it is not owned at all. In the case of land, however, the law in theory knows no absolute ownership. The land is held in tenure of the Crown or of a subject.[3] It may so be held for various different

---

[1] *Ante*, p. 14.
[2] Land is not always indestructible, *e.g.*, an upper floor of a house (*cf.* Co.Litt. 48b). Thus there have for long been "flying freeholds" in New Square, Lincoln's Inn, which statute has regulated: Lincoln's Inn Act, 1860. In recent years freehold flats have become increasingly popular, *e.g.*, in order to avoid the Rent Acts: see generally (1950) 14 Conv.(N.S.) 350 (S. M. Tolson); George & George, *The Sale of Flats* (3rd. ed. 1970). See *post*, p. 675.   [3] *Ante*, Chap. 2.

estates, *i.e.*, for a greater or less period of time. In popular speech one may refer to X's ownership of Blackacre; but technically, one should speak of X holding Blackacre in fee simple or for a term of years, and subject perhaps to easements, mortgages, and the like, which give other people limited rights of property in the land. Land law, therefore, has to concern itself with many varieties of qualified ownership.

The system of estates is of vital importance, but since it was radically amended in 1925, the past tense will be used in much of the discussion. The new law can be understood only by reference to the old.

Estates were divided into two classes:
1. Freehold estates.
2. Leasehold estates.

It should be noted that "freehold" here has nothing to do with freehold (or socage) tenure; it is merely that the same word is used sometimes to express the quality of the tenure, and sometimes the quantity of the estate. "Freehold" is normally used by the man in the street as combining these senses; thus when a house agent advertises "a desirable freehold residence," he may be taken to refer to a fee simple estate in land of freehold tenure.

Sect. 1. Estates of Freehold

1. The three estates. There were three estates of freehold:
  (i) fee simple;
  (ii) fee tail; and
  (iii) life estate.[4]

The fee simple and the life estate have always existed in English law. The fee tail was introduced by statute in 1285. Before considering the estates in any detail a brief account of each must be given.

(a) *Fee simple.* Originally this was an estate which endured for so long as the original tenant or any of his heirs (blood relations, and their heirs, and so on)[5] survived. Thus at first a fee simple would terminate if the original tenant died without leaving any descendants or collateral blood relations (*e.g.*, brothers or cousins), even if before his death the land had been conveyed to another tenant who was still alive.[6] But by 1306 it was settled that where

---

[4] Co.Litt. 43b.
[5] The exact meaning of "heir" is explained later: see *post*, pp. 509 *et seq.*
[6] H.E.L. iii, 106; P. & M. ii, 14.

a tenant in fee simple alienated the land, the fee simple would continue as long as there were heirs of the new tenant, and so on, irrespective of any failure of the original tenant's heirs.[7] Thenceforward a fee simple was virtually eternal, subject only to escheat if the tenant for the time being died leaving no heir.[8]

(*b*) *Fee tail.* This was an estate which continued for so long as the original tenant or any of his lineal descendants survived. Thus if the original tenant died leaving no relatives except a brother, a fee simple would continue, but a fee tail would come to an end. The terms " fee tail," " estate tail," " entail " and " entailed interest " are often used interchangeably; but " fee tail " is the correct expression for a legal entail,[9] and " entailed interest " is usually reserved for an equitable entail.[10]

(*c*) *Life estate.* As its name indicates, this lasted for life only. The name " life estate " usually denoted that the measuring life was that of the tenant himself, *e.g.*, when the grant was to A for life. The form of life estate where the measuring life was that of some other person was known as an estate " *pur autre vie* " (for the life of another), *e.g.*, to A for so long as B lives.

2. " Freehold." A common feature of all estates of freehold was that the duration of the estate, though limited, was uncertain. Nobody could say when the death would occur of a man and all his future heirs, or a man and all his descendants, or a man alone. But the duration was in no case certain to be perpetual; the estate was always liable to determine if some event occurred. In the case of the fee simple and the fee tail, the word " fee " denoted (i) that the estate was an estate of inheritance, *i.e.*, an estate which, on the death of the tenant, was capable of descending to his heir[11]; and (ii) that the estate was one which might continue for ever.[12] The words " simple " and " tail " distinguished the classes of heirs who could inherit. A fee simple descended to the heirs general, including collaterals.[13] A fee tail descended to heirs special, *i.e.*, to lineal descendants only.

A life estate, on the other hand, was not a fee. It was not an estate of inheritance and it could not continue for ever. On the death

---

7 Y.B. 33–35 Edw. 1 (R.S.) 362; H.E.L. iii, 106, 107.
8 *Ante*, p. 18; and see T. C. Williams, 69 L.J.News. 369, 385; 70 L.J.News. 4, 20; 75 S.J. 847.
9 Challis 60.
10 *Post*, p. 137
11 Litt. 1, 9; Preston i, 262; Challis 218.
12 Preston i, 419, 480.
13 Preston i, 428. Formerly the word " simple " also signified " absolute," as opposed to " conditional "; Co.Litt. 1b; Challis 218; *post*, p. 74, n. 16.

of the tenant an ordinary life estate determined, and an estate *pur autre vie* did not descend to the tenant's heir, but passed under the special rules of occupancy.[14] Life estates were sometimes called "mere freeholds" or simply "freeholds," as opposed to "freeholds of inheritance." [15]

Each estate of freehold could exist in a number of varied forms which will be considered in due course.

Sect. 2. Leaseholds

1. Nature of leases. At first the three estates of freehold were the sole estates recognised by law; the only other lawful right to the possession of land was known as a tenancy at will, under which the tenant could be ejected at any time, and which therefore gave him no estate at all.[16] Terms of years grew up outside this system of estates. Originally they were regarded not as property (an object of ownership) but as personal contracts binding only on the parties. The leaseholder was not fully protected against other persons until the end of the fifteenth century, and the nature of the remedy (the action of ejectment) marked off leaseholds from the other estates.[17] When they became fully protected by the law of property they became estates,[18] but it was too late for them to be classified with the others.

2. "Less than freehold." Leaseholds have long been denominated "estates less than freehold," and in theory they are inferior. "In law the duration of a term is immaterial, and a term for twenty-one years is as great an estate as one for 21,000 years. The distinction is between a chattel interest, which is a term for years, and a freehold interest. A freehold interest of the smallest duration is greater in the contemplation of law than the longest term." [19] Nevertheless, their inferiority exists only in history and in theory. A rent-free lease for 3,000 years may be as secure and as valuable as any freehold estate.[20] It is true that the early attitude towards leases led to their being classified as personal and not as real property, and that this distinction, which is still law, remains of some importance even after 1925.[21] It is also true that before 1926 leasehold property could not be entailed or granted by deed for life.[22] On the other

---

14 *Post*, p. 101.
15 Co.Litt. 266b, note 1; Preston i, 214; Challis 99.
16 *Post*, p. 45.
17 *Post*, p. 1170; H.E.L. iii, 213–217; iv, 486.
18 Litt. 58.
19 *Re Russell Road Purchase-Moneys* (1871) L.R. 12 Eq. 78 at 84, *per* Malins V.-C.
20 *Cf. post*, p. 892, in regard to mortgages.
21 *Ante*, p. 11.
22 *Post*, pp. 94, 161, 787.

hand, leases in early times had the important advantage that since they were personalty they could be devised, while wills of freehold land were not allowed before 1540.[23]

3. Categories of leaseholds. Today, the various forms of leasehold estates are of the first importance. Their distinguishing characteristic, by contrast with freehold estates, is that their maximum duration is fixed in time. The principal categories are as follows; they are dealt with more fully later.[24]

(*a*) *Fixed term of certain duration.* The tenant may hold the land for a fixed term of certain duration,[25] as under a lease for 99 years. The possibility of the term being curtailed (*e.g.*, by forfeiture for non-payment of rent) under some provision to this effect in the lease does not affect the basic conception, which is one of certainty of duration in the absence of steps being taken for extension or curtailment. A lease for " 99 years if X so long lives " also fell under this head; it was not an estate of freehold,[26] for although X might well die before the 99 years had run, the maximum duration of the lease was fixed. Even if there was no chance of X outliving the 99 years, so that the duration of the lease would be the same as an estate granted " to X for life," yet in law the former was leasehold and the latter freehold. Partly as a result of the intervention of statute, such leases are comparatively rare today.[27]

(*b*) *Fixed term with duration capable of being rendered certain.* A lease of land " to A from year to year," with no other provision as to its duration, will continue indefinitely unless either landlord or tenant takes some step to determine it. But either party can give half a year's notice to determine it at the end of a year of the tenancy, and thus ensure its determination on a fixed date. It consists, furthermore, of an initial term for one year supplemented by automatic yearly extensions of one year each.[28] At any given moment, therefore, the tenant's estate has a fixed term set to it, though it may later be extended if no notice is given. The same applies to quarterly, monthly, weekly and other periodical tenancies. A term of years accompanied by an option for either party to renew the lease is, on similar principles, regarded as a lease for a term certain.

(*c*) *Tenancies at will and at sufferance.* Tenancies at will and tenancies at sufferance,[29] which are generally treated as part of the

[23] *Post*, p. 68.
[25] Bracton Bk. iv, c. 28, f. 207 ; Preston i, 203.
[27] *Post*, p. 642.
[29] For these interests, see *post*, p. 638.

[24] *Post*, pp. 630 *et seq.*
[26] Cru.Dig. i, 47.
[28] *Post*, p. 633.

law relating to leasehold estates,[30] require special explanation,[31] as they are "unlike any other tenancy." [32] A tenancy at will is a tenancy which may continue indefinitely or may be determined by either party at any time.[33] This involves tenure [34] (*i.e.*, a relationship of landlord and tenant) but no definite estate,[35] for there is no defined duration of the interest. The tenant has nothing which he can alienate.[36] T holds of L, but not for any appointed period. This resembles the earliest type of precarious tenure (*precarium*), which perhaps existed before estates were granted at all.[37]

A tenancy at sufferance arises where a tenancy has terminated but the tenant "holds over" (*i.e.*, remains in possession) without the landlord's assent or dissent.[38] Such a tenant differs from a trespasser only in that his original entry was not wrongful and the landlord must re-enter before he can sue for trespass.[39] His "estate" in the land [40] is no true estate, and there is no real tenure [41]; the "tenancy" seems to have originated as a pretext for preventing the occupation being regarded as "adverse possession," which in time could bar the landlord's title altogether.[42] The old rules as to adverse possession have long disappeared,[43] and this "tenancy" might be permitted to go with them. Neither tenancies at will nor tenancies at sufferance, therefore, need be classified as additions to the catalogue of estates. If they are excluded, the classification can be simplified into freeholds and leaseholds.

4. Leasehold tenure and estates. In early times, when leaseholds were regarded as mere contractual rights to occupy land,[44] they were hardly estates at all. But in time, when the law came to give them full protection as proprietary interests,[45] they were added to the list of recognised legal estates. They always remained outside the feudal system of landholding, but when they became a new type

---

30 Preston i, 25, 28, 29, etc., speaks of an " estate at will." *Cf.* Co.Litt. 55a, note 3 ; Bl.Comm. ii, 144 ; Cru.Dig. i, 242 ; Tudor L.C. 11.
31 And see *post*, pp. 638 *et seq.*
32 *Wheeler* v. *Mercer* [1957] A.C. 416 at 427, *per* Viscount Simonds.
33 *Post*, p. 638.
34 Litt. 460 ; Co.Litt. 270b, note 1. Despite the tenure, a tenant at will was absolved from fealty because he had no estate: Litt. 132, Co.Litt. 63a.
35 Litt. 68 (" no certain nor sure estate ") ; *cf.* Litt. 132.
36 Bl.Comm. ii, 144.
37 Bracton Bk. ii, c. 9, f. 27 (Digby, 178) ; Co.Litt. 55a, 266b, n. 1 ; Bl.Comm. ii, 55.
38 See *post*, p. 640.
39 See Co.Litt. 57b, 270b, n. 1.
40 So called : Cru.Dig. i, 249 ; Tudor L.C. 7.
41 See Co.Litt. 270b, n. 1.
42 *Remon* v. *City of London Real Property Co. Ltd.* [1921] 1 K.B. 49 at 58 : Tudor L.C. 9.
43 *Post*, p. 1013.
44 *Ante*, p. 43.
45 *Post*, p. 1170.

of estate it was impossible to deny that they were also a new type of tenure; for every tenant must hold by tenure of some sort if he is to hold an estate at all.[46]

This position has been recognised since the time of Littleton [47] (c. 1480), and is still recognised today; tenure is essential between landlord and tenant,[48] and leaseholds are within the statutory term [49] " land of any tenure." [50] By a paradox of history the relationship of landlord and tenant, originally no tenure at all, is now the only tenure which has any practical importance. It is a non-feudal tenure and is not, of course, touched by the statute *Quia Emptores*, 1290, which applies only to fees simple,[51] and so does not prevent the grant of sub-leases. The one remaining feudal tenure, socage, has been shorn of all the incidents of any consequence, whereas in the case of leaseholds a valuable rent (called rent-*service* because of the tenure [52]) is nearly always payable, and the lord, in addition to his tenurial remedy of distress,[53] usually has power to determine the lease if the tenant does not fulfil his obligations. In all these ways it appears that leases imply tenure. A lease is still personalty, as opposed to realty, but the most important differences to which this technicality gave rise have now been abolished.[54]

5. Interests in leaseholds. At common law a freehold estate could not be created out of a leasehold estate, for the obvious reason that a disposition by a leaseholder was only a disposition of personalty and he could give no seisin. The estates of freehold were peculiar to the land law and there was no corresponding system for personalty. But when other methods of conveyance not dependent upon seisin were introduced (for example, wills and trusts), these technical difficulties were overcome. Thus if A held Blackacre for a term of 200 years, at common law he could not effectively assign the lease to X for life with remainder to Y absolutely. This would merely give the whole lease to X outright [55]; since limited estates in personalty could

[46] *Ante*, p. 14.
[47] Litt. 132, saying that a tenant for years owes fealty to his landlord because of the tenure subsisting between them. Challis (65, 424–427) was unwilling to admit that terms of years were held in tenure; but his criticisms cannot be reconciled with the authorities (*ante*, p. 45, n. 34).
[48] *Milmo* v. *Carreras* [1946] K.B. 306 at 310, 311.
[49] L.P.A., 1925, s. 205 (1) (ix).
[50] *Re Brooker* [1926] W.N. 93; *Re Berton* [1939] Ch. 200 at 203; *cf.* Hood & Challis 333; *post*, p. 613.
[51] *Ante*, p. 30.
[52] *Post*, p. 689.
[53] *Post*, p. 691.
[54] *Post*, p. 509.
[55] *Woodcock* v. *Woodcock* (1600) Cro.Eliz. 795; *Anon* (1552) 1 Dy. 74a; *North* v. *Butts* (1557) 2 Dy. 139b at 140b; " The gift of a term (like any other chattel) for an hour, was good for ever "; *Wright* d. *Plowden* v. *Cartwright* (1757) 1 Burr. 282 at 284, *per* Lord Mansfield C.J.

not be created, a limited gift was an absolute gift. But when, in due course, wills and settlements by way of trust were invented, A could carry out his design by employing one or other of the new kinds of disposition. The account of these belongs to a later chapter.[56] It must also be mentioned that even the new methods of transfer were ineffective to create an entailed interest in personalty: only since 1925 has it been possible to limit leasehold property in tail.[57]

Sect. 3. Remainders and Reversions

An estate in land may exist in one of three different ways: in possession, in remainder or in reversion.[58] An estate in possession gives an immediate right to possession and enjoyment of the land. Estates in remainder or reversion, on the other hand, are future interests, and meanwhile some other person is usually entitled in possession. "Remainder" signifies a future gift to some person not previously entitled to the land. "Reversion" signifies the residue of an owner's interest after he has granted away some lesser estate in possession to some other person.[59]

Reversions and remainders are fully treated in the chapter on Future Interests,[60] but at this point the general meaning of the terms may be made clear by examples. If A owns land in fee simple, and makes a grant " to B for life and thereafter to C in fee simple," B has a life estate in possession and so long as that estate continues C has a fee simple estate in remainder. When B dies, C has the fee simple in possession. A, having granted away his whole interest, has nothing. But if A had granted the land " to B for life and thereafter to C for life (or in tail)," B would have had a life estate in possession, C would have had a life estate (or estate tail) in remainder, and A would have retained the fee simple in reversion. So too if A had merely granted the land " to B for life," A would have had the fee simple in reversion while B had his life estate in possession. A reversion will thus be found in every case where the owner has made a grant which does not exhaust the whole of his own interest.[61]

Similarly, if A wishes to grant his land to B for life and thereafter to C in fee simple, and does so by single deed, C's estate is a remainder. But if the transaction is carried out in two steps by two successive grants, C's estate is a reversion, for he has acquired the reversion which was left in A after his initial grant to B. If A grants

[56] *Post*, p. 160 (wills), p. 167 (trusts).
[57] *Post*, p. 94.
[58] Bl.Comm. ii, 163.
[59] " Reversion, reversio, commeth of the Latine word *revertor*, and signifieth a returning againe ": Co.Litt. 142b.
[60] *Post*, p. 173.
[61] See *post*, p. 178.

to B a lease, A is likewise said to retain the reversion; and if B grants a sub-lease to C both A and B have reversions. In the eye of the law a lease is always a lesser estate than a freehold,[62] so that if a tenant for life grants a lease for 100 years (for example) he retains a life estate in reversion expectant upon the lease.

Sect. 4. Seisin

1. Meaning of seisin. One very important distinction between freeholders and leaseholders was that only a freeholder had seisin. Seisin has nothing to do with the word "seizing," with its implication of violence. To medieval lawyers, as Maitland said, it suggested the very opposite—peace and quiet.[63] A man who was put in seisin of land was " set " there and continued to " sit " there.[63] Seisin thus denotes quiet possession of land,[64] but of a particular kind. Although at first the term was applied to the possession of a leaseholder as well as that of a freeholder,[65] during the fifteenth century it became confined to those who held an estate of freehold.[66] A leaseholder merely had possession; his landlord, as the freeholder, was seised.[67] And since, as we shall see, it was essential that someone should always have seisin, it followed that a freeholder remained seised even after he had granted a term of years and given up physical possession of the land. Receipt of rent was evidence of seisin,[68] but a mere right to recover possession was not by itself seisin.[69] Further, only land of freehold tenure carried seisin with it. A copyholder could not be seised, even if he held a fee simple [70]; seisin in that case was in the lord of the manor.

2. Elements of seisin. From this it will seen that a person was seised if—

(i) he held an estate of freehold,
(ii) in land of freehold tenure, and
(iii) either he had physical possession of the land, or a leaseholder or copyholder held the land from him.

Seisin, therefore, was a word which reflected the historical differences between the two main types of tenures and estates. It

---

[62] *Ante*, p. 43.
[63] P. & M. ii, 30.
[64] Co.Litt. 153a ; *Brediman's Case* (1607) 6 Co.Rep. 56b at 57b.
[65] Williams, *Seisin*, 4.
[66] Maitland, Coll.Pp. i, 359 ; Challis 99.
[67] Litt. 324 ; Co.Litt. 17a, 200b.
[68] See *De Grey* v. *Richardson* (1747) 3 Atk. 469 at 472.
[69] *Leach* v. *Jay* (1878) 9 Ch.D. 42.
[70] Preston i, 212, 213. But occasionally copyholders were said to be seised : *e.g.*, *Chudleigh's Case* (1595) 1 Co.Rep. 113b at 117a, explained in *Wade* v. *Bache* (1668) 1 Wms.Saund. 144 at 147.

meant possession of land, disregarding those interests (leaseholds and copyholds) which the King's courts did not at first protect as property.[71] But the attribution of seisin to lords of manors and landlords, who had not possession, made it difficult to define seisin concisely. " Possession by a freeholder " embodies the fundamental idea.

3. Nature of seisin. Seisin was a characteristic product of the feudal system, and the three following rules help to explain its nature :

(i) Someone must always be seised. The person seised was the person against whom any default of feudal services had to be enforced,[72] and if seisin could be in abeyance the feudal system could not work. The common law abhorred an abeyance of seisin.[73]

(ii) The person seised must be a person with a status in the feudal scale, *i.e.*, a person who held in free tenure for an estate of freehold. The person at the bottom of the scale was seised of the land. A mesne lord was seised of a seignory, *i.e.*, the right to the tenant's services.[74]

(iii) Seisin was a fact, not a right. If A, a freeholder, was dispossessed by B, B acquired seisin and A was disseised. A could, of course, recover the land from B, and be put back into seisin. But until he did so B claimed the freehold and, having actual possession, was seised in the eye of the law.

4. Importance of seisin. Seisin is no longer of importance, for the distinctions which gave it its peculiar meaning no longer exist. But it was the key to many of the mysteries of our land law before the statutory reforms of the 1830s and later. For example—

(i) Feudal services could be enforced only against the tenant seised of the land.[75] If distress was levied on him for services due from a mesne lord, he could claim indemnity by writ of mesne.

(ii) A real action (originally the only type of action in which the land itself could be recovered and not merely damages [76]) could be brought only against the tenant seised.[77]

---

[71] See *post*, p. 1170. [72] *Ante*, p. 30.
[73] For this principle and for exceptional cases, some common law and some statutory, see Challis 100, 101 ; C.A., 1881, s. 30 ; *Re Pilling's Trusts* (1884) 26 Ch.D. 432 at 433.
[74] P. & M. ii, 38, 39.
[75] Challis 100.
[76] H.E.L. iii, 3, 4; *post*, p. 1167.
[77] *Freeman* d. *Vernon* v. *West* (1763) 2 Wils.K.B. 165 at 166.

(iii) Curtesy and dower could not be claimed if the deceased had been disseised.[78]

(iv) Conveyances of freehold land could originally be made only by a feoffment with livery of seisin. This was a solemn ceremony carried out by the parties entering on the land, and the feoffor, in the presence of witnesses, delivering the seisin to the feoffee either by some symbolic act, such as handing him a twig or sod of earth, or by uttering some words such as "Enter into this land and God give you joy" and leaving him in possession of the land.[79]

In general it was the person seised—and he alone—who could exercise an owner's rights over the land. It did not matter whether his seisin was rightful or wrongful, or subject to the right of some other person to recover the land. Only the person seised could convey, for only he could give livery of seisin. Only the heir of the person seised could succeed to the land at that person's death. The fact of seisin, irrespective of the strength of the title of the person seised, used to be of greater technical importance than it is today.[80] Possession is still, of course, of great importance, but it is usually no longer necessary to distinguish it from seisin.

Part 2

ESTATES OF FREEHOLD

The two main branches of the law concerning estates of freehold relate to—

(1) the words required to create each of the estates, and

(2) the characteristics of each estate.

Sect. 1. Words of Limitation

1. Meaning. "Words of limitation" is the phrase used to describe the words which limit (*i.e.*, delimit, or mark out) the estate to be taken. Thus in a conveyance today "to A in fee simple," the words "in fee simple" are words of limitation, for they "measure out the quantity of estate"[81] that A is to have. The distinction between "words of limitation" and "words of purchase" is explained below.[82]

---

[78] *Post*, p. 514.
[79] *Post*, p. 163.
[80] H.E.L. iii, 91, 92. For discussion of seisin, possession and ownership, see *post*, pp. 1004 *et seq.*
[81] *Goodright* v. *Wright* (1717) 1 P.Wms. 397, *per* Parker C.J.
[82] *Post*, p. 52.

2. Inter vivos. The rule at common law was that a freehold estate of inheritance could be created in a conveyance *inter vivos* (*i.e.*, a transfer of land between living persons) only by a phrase which included the word "heirs."[83] In no other way could a fee simple or fee tail be created. Any attempted grant of a freehold estate in other terms (as "to A," or "to A in fee simple") gave A merely a life estate.[84] This rule was perhaps a relic of ancient times when grants were normally made at will or for life and could be extended only by using appropriate words.[85] Despite its incongruity, it survived until 1925, with only a minor mitigation in 1881. It is important to note that no other word would do in place of "heirs": "relatives," "issue," "descendants," "assigns," "for ever," "in fee simple," "in tail" and so on were all ineffective.[85a] "Heirs" was the sacred word of limitation, and had a magic which no other word possessed.

3. In wills. In the case of gifts by will, the attitude of the courts was different. A conveyance *inter vivos* was originally a solemn ceremony in which considerable importance was attached to the exact form of words. Later, the nature of a conveyance changed and became more complex, so that professional assistance was usually sought. Further, if there was any flaw in the transaction, the grantor would usually still be alive to put things right. Consequently conveyances *inter vivos* were construed strictly by the courts. Most wills of land, however, were first enforced by the Court of Chancery, which looked to the intent of any transaction rather than the form. When the Statute of Wills, 1540, compelled common law courts to give effect to wills, both the words of the Statute, which authorised any person to dispose of land "at his free will and pleasure," and the former practice of the Court of Chancery encouraged the courts to interpret wills liberally.[86] Wills were often home-made, and since they were inoperative until the testator's death, mistakes would usually lie hidden until it was impossible to put them right.[87] The result was that strict words of limitation were not required in wills. Provided the intention of the testator was clear, it would be effectuated.[88]

The detailed rules will now be considered, taking the fee simple, fee tail and life estate in turn and dealing separately under each head with conveyances *inter vivos* and wills.

---

[83] Litt. 1; Co.Litt. 20a.
[84] *Ibid.*
[85] *Cf.* Co.Litt. 266b, n. 1.
[85a] Litt. 1; Co.Litt. 20a.
[86] *Post*, p. 495.
[87] Testators' "ignorance and simplicity demands a favourable interpretation of their words": *Paramour* v. *Yardley* (1579) 2 Plowd. 539 at 540, in argument; *cf. Newis* v. *Lark* (1571) 2 Plowd. 403 at 413.
[88] *Throckmerton* v. *Tracy* (1555) 1 Plowd. 145 at 162, 163; Perkins, s. 555.

A. Words of Limitation for a Fee Simple

I. CONVEYANCES INTER VIVOS

1. At common law

(a) Natural persons

(1) " HEIRS." At common law the proper expression to employ was " and his heirs " following the grantee's name, *e.g.*, " to A and his heirs." [89] " Heir " in the singular would not suffice,[90] and the word " and " could not be replaced by " or ": " to A or his heirs " gave A a mere life estate,[91] and so did expressions not containing the word " heirs," *e.g.*, " to A for ever," or " to A in fee simple." [92]

(2) LIMITATION NOT PURCHASE. It is important to note that the words " and his heirs " gave no estate in the land to the heirs. They were words of limitation, as opposed to words of purchase. This means that they limited (in the sense of " defined ") an estate to be given to a person already named (A), as opposed to conferring any interest on any other person.[93] " To A " is an example of words of purchase. " And his heirs " are words of limitation.[94] In this technical sense a " purchaser " is a person who takes property by grant (*e.g.*, by gift or sale) and not by mere operation of law (*e.g.*, by intestacy).[95]

The distinction is important in the case of the word " heirs " because it can be used in both senses. In the grant " to A's heir and his heirs," considered below, " heir " is a word of purchase and " heirs " is a word of limitation. Similarly, in a grant " to A and his heirs," if A had a son at the time of the conveyance, the son acquired no estate by it, but had merely a *spes successionis, i.e.*, a hope of succeeding to the fee simple if A died without having disposed of it.[96] Although A's eldest son is his " heir " in the popular sense, the legal maxim is " *nemo est heres viventis* " (a living person has no heir).[97] A living person may have an heir apparent, *i.e.*, a person who, if he survives A, will be A's heir, such as his eldest son; or he may have an heir presumptive, *i.e.*, a person who, if he

---

[89] Preston ii, 1. For a solemn consideration of the apt words for monsters and hermaphrodites, see Co.Litt. 8a.

[90] Co.Litt. 8b; Preston ii, 397; Challis 221, 222; *cf. Re Davison's Settlement* [1913] 2 Ch. 498.

[91] Co.Litt. 8b; Preston ii, 11; *Mallory's Case* (1601) 5 Co.Rep. 111b at 112a; contrast *Wright* v. *Wright* (1750) 1 Ves.Sen. 409 at 411.

[92] Litt. 1.

[93] For this distinction, see Fearne 79, 80.

[94] *Doe* d. *Long* v. *Laming* (1760) 2 Burr. 1100 at 1106.

[95] *Post*, p. 509.

[96] *Re Parsons* (1890) 45 Ch.D. 51 at 55.

[97] Co.Litt. 8b; (1308) Y.B. 2 Edw. 2, Mich. (S.S.) 70.

outlives A and no person with a better claim comes into existence, will be A's heir, such as his daughter: but not until A's death can A's heir be ascertained.[98]

(3) SPECIAL RULES. Two special rules should be noticed. First, a fee simple could not be restricted to heirs of any particular sex; a conveyance " to A and his heirs male " gave A the fee simple, the word " male " being rejected as repugnant thereto.[99]

Secondly, a conveyance " to the heirs of A," A being dead at the time of the conveyance, gave a fee simple to the person who was A's heir. Strictly, perhaps, the phrase should have been " to A's heir and his heirs," but it was held that " to the heirs of A " had the same effect.[1] If A was alive at the time of the conveyance, it failed utterly, for (as mentioned above) neither A's heir apparent nor heir presumptive was yet A's " heir," and since the conveyance sought forthwith to divest the grantor of the seisin and there was nobody in whom it could vest, the conveyance was void.[2]

(4) EXCEPTIONS. There were a few unimportant exceptions to the rule that the words " and his heirs " were essential to every grant in fee simple to an individual. Thus these words might be incorporated by reference to another document, as where a father granted to his son and his heirs and the son granted back to the father " as fully as the father granted to him." [3] Further, they were not required in releases made between joint tenants,[4] or in fines and recoveries, those long obsolete modes of conveyance which were nominally proceedings in court.[5]

(b) Corporations

(1) TYPES. Different rules governed conveyances to **corporations**, which are themselves legal persons, distinct from the individuals who represent them. This artificial personality may be created by royal charter,[6] by statute, or by some rule of law. Corporations are usually classified as of two kinds, aggregate and sole. A corporation aggregate is made up of two or more individuals acting under a corporate

---

[98] See *Re Parsons, supra,* at p. 63.
[99] Litt. 31; Co.Litt. 13a; Preston i, 472; *Idle* v. *Cook* (1705) 1 P.Wms. 70 at 77. But contrast wills (*post*, p. 59); and as to " to A and the heirs of his father," see *post*, p. 58, n. 47.
[1] *Marshall* v. *Peascod* (1861) 2 J. & H. 73. See further, *post*, p. 58, n. 48. At p. 75 it is said that " to the heir of A " would have the same effect; but see *Re Davison's Settlement* [1913] 2 Ch. 498.
[2] See *Else* v. *Osborn* (1717) 1 P.Wms. 387; *Re Midleton's W.T.* [1969] 1 Ch. 600; and see *post*, p. 183.
[3] Co.Litt. 9b; Challis 222, 223; *Grant* v. *Edmondson* [1930] 2 Ch. 245; [1931] 1 Ch. 1, is an example of this principle applied to a grant of a rentcharge.
[4] Or coparceners; or in the grant of a rentcharge for equality of partition between them: Co.Litt. 9b; Challis 222, 223.
[5] *Ibid.* For these see *post*, pp. 85, 163.
[6] The Crown has the prerogative power of incorporation.

name, *e.g.*, the mayor and corporation of a borough, a dean and chapter, or a limited company. A corporation sole consists of a single individual holding an office which has a perpetual succession. Few corporations sole are known to the law: examples are (at common law) the Crown, a bishop, a parson; and (by statute) the Treasury Solicitor and the Secretary of State for Defence.[7]

(2) CORPORATIONS AGGREGATE. A conveyance of land to a corporation aggregate by its corporate name has always given it a fee simple without any special words of limitation.[8] For, since such a corporation neither died nor had heirs, it could take no other estate, apart from a lease.

(3) CORPORATIONS SOLE. Corporations sole, on the other hand, were mortal men, and died.[9] The rule at common law for corporations sole was that except in the case of grants in frankalmoign [10] or in favour of the Crown,[11] land would pass with the office only if limited to the holder "" and his successors." [12] A conveyance in fee simple to the See of Ely would therefore have to be phrased " to the Bishop of Ely and his successors."

At common law (as also by statute) ecclesiastical corporations had restricted powers of alienation.[13] A parson could not prejudice the rights of his successors, so that any rights which he attempted to grant in the church lands, except as empowered by statute,[14] would terminate at his death.[15] It was sometimes said therefore that he had only a life interest and that the fee was in abeyance.[16] But it seems more probable that the corporation sole possessed a qualified fee [17]

---

[7] C. T. Carr, *Corporations*, 15, 23–25; Defence of (Transfer of Functions) Act 1964, s. 2 (1).

[8] *Re Woking U. D. C. (Basingstoke Canal) Act, 1911* [1914] 1 Ch. 300 at 312; Co.Litt. 94b.

[9] Maitland, Coll.Pp., iii, 240. In his essay " The Corporation Sole " (*ibid.*, 210; (1900) 16 L.Q.R. 335) Maitland demonstrated that a corporation sole was never a true legal person at all, since it lacked immortality; it was either " natural man or juristic abortion." A corporation sole could not convey to himself as an individual (*Salter* v. *Grosvenor* (1724) 8 Mod. 303; and see *Howley* v. *Knight* (1849) 14 Q.B. 240); but he could be tenant in common with himself as individual (Co.Litt. 190a) which implies two distinct legal persons. Probably no explanation will fit all the facts.

[10] Such grants have been impossible since 1290: see *ante*, p. 31.

[11] Co.Litt. 9b; Preston ii, 50. This may reflect the theory that the King never died; but the position of the Crown was unique and not amenable to the ordinary law of persons. See Maitland, " The Crown as Corporation," Coll.Pp. iii, 244.

[12] Co.Litt. 8b, 94b; *Ex p. Vicar of Castle Bytham* [1895] 1 Ch. 348 at 354; but consider *Bentley* v. *Bishop of Ely* (1732) Fitz. 305; Co.Litt. 94b, n. 5.

[13] Co.Litt. 44a, 341b; Challis 225.

[14] See Halsb. xiii, 429.

[15] See note 13, *supra*.

[16] *St. Gabriel, Fenchurch Street (Rector)* v. *City of London Real Property Co. Ltd.* [1896] P. 95 at 101; *Re St. Paul's, Covent Garden* [1973] 1 W.L.R. 464 at 466; *cf.* Litt. 648.

[17] Co.Litt. 341b. Co.Litt. 44a says that with the consent of the patron and ordinary a parson could make a grant in fee at common law. See also Cru.Dig. i, 114.

to which special restrictions attached, and which was in abeyance only when the office was vacant.[18] Where the vacancy exists at the time of the conveyance, statute has retrospectively provided that the property is to vest in the successor as soon as the vacancy is filled, without prejudice to his right to disclaim the property.[19]

A conveyance to a corporation sole without any words of limitation would give the incumbent merely a life estate. But a conveyance to him "and his heirs" would give him a fee simple in his private capacity, under the ordinary rule,[20] for the person of the grantee was clearly described[21] and the proper words of limitation were used.

2. By statute

(a) *After* 1881. It has been seen that at common law a conveyance "to A in fee simple" would not create a fee simple, but only a life estate. This was remedied by the Conveyancing Act, 1881,[22] which enacted that in deeds executed after 1881 the words "in fee simple" would suffice to pass the fee simple, without the word "heirs." The expressions available at common law still remained effective; the Act merely supplied an alternative, and this alternative had to be employed as strictly as the older expression. Thus a conveyance "to A in fee" passed only a life estate[23]; but if it could be shown that "simple" had been specifically intended, but was omitted by accident, the court might in a proper case rectify the conveyance by inserting the missing word.[24]

Since the Act's intention was evidently to make the words "in fee simple" an alternative to the words "and his heirs," it has been suggested that it did not extend to grants to corporations sole in their official capacity, for there the necessary words were "and

---

[18] Litt. 647; Challis 101; and see *St. Edmundsbury and Ipswich Diocesan Board of Finance* v. *Clark (No. 2)* [1973] 1 W.L.R. 1572 at 1580.

[19] L.P.A., 1925, s. 180 (2).

[20] See Shep.Touch. 237; *contra*, Norton on *Deeds* 333, and Emmet 290, who say that these words created only a life interest. But their authorities do not support them. The source of this opinion appears to be Y.B. 9 Hen. 5, Mich., pl. 2, 8 at 9 (1421), where it was held that a conveyance to an abbot "and his heirs" gave him only a life estate. But an abbot, as an individual, became "dead in law" when he took final solemn vows in his monastery, and could have no heir as regards property acquired later. The Y.B. significantly adds that the case of a bishop was said to be different. A bishop, not being under monastic vows, did not suffer civil death and could have an heir.

[21] It would seem from the discussion of the *Chantry Priest's Case* in Co.Litt. 9a, and from Preston ii, 48, 49, that it did not matter whether the private or official title of the grantee was used; but contrast Co.Litt. 94b, n. 5. Normally, both would be used together, *e.g.*, to A, Bishop of Ely. If the grant was to him, "his heirs and successors," the title used might help to resolve the ambiguity: Co.Litt. 9a.

[22] s. 51.   [23] *Re Ethel and Mitchells and Butlers' Contract* [1901] 1 Ch. 945.

[24] *Ibid.* at p. 948; *Banks* v. *Ripley* [1940] Ch. 719. For rectification, see *post*, p. 595.

his successors." [25] If this were so, a conveyance after 1881 to " the Vicar of Bray in fee simple " would presumably give him a fee simple in his personal capacity, just like a conveyance to him " and his heirs."

(*b*) *After* 1925. By the Law of Property Act, 1925,[26] the necessity for words of limitation in creating a fee simple was abolished in the case of all deeds executed after 1925, for the grantee takes " the fee simple or other the whole interest which the grantor had power to convey in such land, unless a contrary intention appears in the conveyance." The same is provided for conveyances to a corporation sole, and the proof of the grant being intended for the corporation rather than the individual is now the use of the " corporate designation " in the grant.[27] The principle which for so long ruled grants by deed has now been exactly reversed: a conveyance without words of limitation passes the largest, not the smallest, of the possible freehold estates. In practice, the words " in fee simple " are always inserted to make it clear that there is no contrary intention; and this is preferable to " and his heirs," since heirs are now obsolete.[28]

II. GIFTS BY WILL

1. Before 1838. Before 1838 no formal words of limitation were required in a will, but it was necessary for the will to show an intent to pass the fee simple.[29] Thus " to A for ever," or " to A and his heir," or " to A to dispose at will and pleasure " all sufficed to pass the fee simple.[30] But it was for the devisee to show from the terms of the will (read as a whole) that a fee simple was intended to pass; a devise " to A " prima facie passed merely a life estate.[31]

2. After 1837. By the Wills Act, 1837,[32] the fee simple or other the whole interest of which the testator has power to dispose passes in a gift of real property by any will made or confirmed after 1837 unless a contrary intention is shown. The effect is to reverse the onus of proof; a devise " to A " passes the fee simple unless a

[25] Challis 225.
[26] s. 60 (1). As to rentcharges, see *post*, p. 795. As to easements, see *post*, p. 827.
[27] s. 60 (2). But a conveyance by both personal and corporate designations, *e.g.*, " to A, Bishop of Ely," is presumably no less ambiguous than before. Indeed, it is even more ambiguous, since in most cases under the previous law the necessary words of limitation made the matter plain.
[28] *Post*, p. 523.
[29] Preston ii, 68; *ante*, p. 51.
[30] *Chamberlayne* v. *Turner* (1628) Cro.Car. 129; *Countess of Bridgwater* v. *Duke of Bolton* (1704) 6 Mod. 106 at 111; Gilb. *Uses*, 24. For other examples, see Cru.Dig. vi, Chap. 11.
[31] Preston ii, 78; Cru.Dig. vi, 259–274.
[32] ss. 28, 34.

contrary intention is shown. But the rule applies only to the disposition of an existing interest, as opposed to the creation of a new interest.[33] Thus if the testator owns a perpetual rentcharge and leaves it by will " to A," A takes it in fee simple; but if the will creates a new rentcharge in a gift " to A," A will take it only for life, subject, in each example, to any contrary intention shown.[34]

As the same rule was extended to deeds in 1925 (as mentioned above), there is now no longer any difference between the rule for deeds and the rule for wills.

B. *Words of Limitation for a Fee Tail*

I. CONVEYANCES INTER VIVOS

1. At common law

(a) *" Heirs " with words of procreation.* The expression required to create a fee tail was the word " heirs " followed by some words of procreation, *i.e.*, words which confined " heirs " to descendants of the original grantee.[35] An example is " to X and the heirs of his body." The word " heirs " was essential, but any words of procreation sufficed. Thus " to A and the heirs of his flesh " or " to A and the heirs from him proceeding " sufficed to create entails.[36] But expressions such as " to A and his issue " or " to A and his seed " would not create a fee tail in a deed, for the vital word " heirs " was missing,[37] and A and any issue then alive would probably have taken joint life estates.[38] There were some qualifications of these rules in special cases, so that in certain contexts " heir " instead of " heirs " would suffice,[39] words of procreation might be dispensed with,[40] and " heirs " might confer a fee tail in one part of a deed and a fee simple in another [41]; yet in general the rules were strictly enforced.

The reason why words of procreation were required was that " heirs " extended to all the " heirs general," including relatives other than descendants of the grantee, such as his brothers, uncles or cousins. An entail, however, was an interest which could pass only to lineal descendants of the original grantee (heirs special) and so " heirs " had to be restricted by the addition of words of procreation.[41a]

[33] *Nichols* v. *Hawkes* (1853) 10 Hare 342.   [34] *Ibid.*
[35] Preston ii, 477, 478.
[36] *Idle* v. *Cook* (1705) 1 P.Wms. 70 at 73 ; 2 Ld.Raym. 1144 at 1153 ; *Beresford's Case* (1607) 7 Co.Rep. 41a at 42a.
[37] *Wheeler* v. *Duke* (1832) 1 Cr. & M. 210 ; Co.Litt. 20b.
[38] See (1936) 6 C.L.J. 81 (S. J. Bailey).
[39] See *Re Davidson's Settlement* [1913] 2 Ch. 498 at 505, discussing the authorities.
[40] *Wall* v. *Wright* (1837) 1 Dr. & Wal. 1.
[41] See *Doe* d. *Littledale* v. *Smeddle* (1818) 2 B. & Ald. 126 ; *Galley* v. *Barrington* (1824) 2 Bing. 387.   [41a] *Ibid.*

(*b*) *Restricted entails.* By the addition of suitable words an entail could be further restricted so that it descended only to a particular class of descendants.[42] There were thus the following types of entail:

(i) a tail general, *e.g.*, " to A and the heirs of his body," where any descendants of A, male or female, could inherit;

(ii) a tail male, *e.g.*, " to A and the heirs male of his body," in which case only male descendants of A who could trace an unbroken descent from him through males could inherit, and not, *e.g.*, a son of A's daughter [43];

(iii) a tail female, *e.g.*, " to A and the heirs female of his body," where corresponding rules applied.[44]

In addition, a " special tail " could be created, confining the heirs entitled to those' descended from a specified spouse, such as " to A and the heirs of his body begotten upon Mary," when only issue of A and Mary could inherit; Mary, of course, took nothing.[45] A special tail could exist in any of the three above forms: special tail general, special tail male, special tail female. The unrestricted types of entail could by contrast be called " general tail ": general tail, general tail male, general tail female.

(*c*) *Limitation not purchase.* As in the case of a fee simple, the words following A's name were mere words of limitation. " To A and the heirs of his body " gave A a fee tail; it gave his heir apparent or heir presumptive no estate but only a *spes successionis.* But a conveyance " to the heirs of the body of A," A being dead,[46] gave a fee tail to the heir of A's body,[47] although a conveyance " to the heir of the body of A " passed a mere life estate to such heir.[48] The former phrase could be expanded into " to the heir of the body of A and the heirs of the body of A," while the latter could not. The entail created by the former phrase is peculiar in that it continues so long as there is any heir of the body of A, even though the heirs of the body of the first taker (*i.e.*, of A's eldest son or other first heir of the body) die out.[49] Such an entail could be created expressly, *e.g.*, by a gift to B and the heirs of A's body, where B was A's heir of the body.[50] Probably a corresponding type of fee simple [51] lacked this peculiarity.[52]

---

[42] See Challis 294.
[43] Litt. 21, 24. See also *post*, p. 65 (" doctrine of very heir ").
[44] Litt. 22.   [45] Litt. 29; Preston ii, 488.
[46] If A was alive, the conveyance was void: *ante*, p. 53.
[47] *Mandeville's Case* (1328) Y.B. 2 Edw. 3, Hil. pl. 1 and 2; Co.Litt. 26b.
[48] *Chambers* v. *Taylor* (1837) 2 My. & Cr. 376; but see *Marshall* v. *Peascod* (1861) 2 J. & H. 73 at 75 (*ante*, p. 53).
[49] *Allgood* v. *Blake* (1872) L.R. 7 Ex. 339; Fearne 82; Challis 298.
[50] Litt. 30; *cf. Re Mountgarret* [1919] 2 Ch. 294 at 303, 304.
[51] *Ante*, p. 53.   [52] Challis 281, 282; *Moore* v. *Simpkin* (1885) 31 Ch.D. 95.

2. By statute

(a) *After* 1881. In the case of deeds executed after 1881, the Conveyancing Act, 1881,[53] made provisions for entails similar to those made for a fee simple. In addition to the expressions which sufficed to create an entail at common law, the words "in tail" following the name of the grantee (*e.g.*, "to X in tail") would create a fee tail; it will be noted that the phrase is not "in fee tail," though doubtless this would suffice, "fee" being treated as surplusage. If it was desired to restrict the entail to a particular class of descendants, apt words could be added, *e.g.*, "to A in tail male."

(b) *After* 1925. These rules still apply after 1925, the provisions of the Conveyancing Act, 1881, being now replaced by the Law of Property Act, 1925.[54] The policy of the Act of 1925 was to maintain the strict rules for the limitation of entails, so that entails should occur only where the proper technical words were deliberately used. As will be seen later, entails have many peculiarities and are no longer so popular as they were. Expressions intended to create entails which would not have created them before 1926 will not therefore create them after 1925. Such expressions now take effect subject to the special provisions of section 130 (2), which are discussed below.[55] Whatever their effect may be, words like "to A and his issue" cannot create an entail today.

II. GIFTS BY WILL

1. Before 1926. The rule before 1926 was that any words showing an intent to create an entail sufficed in a will, even if no technical expressions were used. Thus "to A and his seed,"[56] "to A and his heirs male"[57] (where the court supplied "of his body"[58]), "to A and his descendants,"[59] "to A and his issue,"[60] and "to A or his issue"[61] all usually sufficed to create entails.[62] A devise "to A and his children" was governed by a special rule which sometimes gave A an entail and sometimes gave the property to A and his children jointly; this is considered later.[63] "Children" prima facie meant descendants of the first generation only, and so was less apt to create an entail than words such as "issue," which prima facie included descendants of any generation and were thus

---

[53] s. 51.
[54] ss. 60 (4), 130 (1).
[55] *Post*, p. 60.
[56] Co.Litt. 9b.
[57] *Wood* v. *Ingersole* (1610) 1 Bulstr. 61 at 63 ; *Baker* v. *Wall* (1697) 1 Ld.Raym. 185.
[58] *Roberts* v. *Roberts* (1613) 2 Bulstr. 123 at 129 ; contrast *ante*, p. 52.
[59] *Re Sleeman* [1929] W.N. 16.
[60] *Slater* v. *Dangerfield* (1846) 15 M. & W. 263 at 272.
[61] *Re Clerke* [1915] 2 Ch. 301 ; *Re Hayden* [1931] 2 Ch. 333.
[62] Preston ii, 534 *et seq.*
[63] *Post*, p. 506.

the informal equivalent of "heirs of his body." [64] In a suitable context, even "to A and his heirs" could suffice. [65]

2. After 1925. The Law of Property Act, 1925, [66] made the rules for the creation of entails by will more rigid than before. It laid down that informal expressions should no longer suffice to create an entail in a will, but that expressions which would have been effective to create an entail in a deed before 1926 must be employed. This reflects the policy already mentioned and makes the creation of an entail by will a matter of technical words rather than a matter of intention. It also establishes the same rules for both deeds and wills, not (as in the case of fee simple) by extending the liberal rules for wills so as to cover deeds but by applying the restrictive rules for deeds to wills as well. Thus in deeds and wills alike either the word "heirs" followed by words of procreation or the words "in tail" must now be used.

Special provision is made for expressions like "to A and his issue," which could formerly create an entail in a will but can now no longer do so. [67] Such expressions, in both deeds and wills, and for both realty and personalty alike, now operate to create "absolute, fee simple or other interests corresponding to those which, if the property affected had been personal estate, would have been created therein by similar expressions before [1926]." [67] This provision may well prove difficult to apply, [68] but at least it is clear that no entail can arise from it because personalty could not be entailed before 1926. [69] For example, "To A and his issue" will either give an absolute interest to A jointly with such of his issue as are living when the gift takes effect, or else give an absolute interest to A alone; perhaps the latter is the better view. If no issue are living at that time A will take absolutely, *i.e.*, in fee simple.

C. The Rule in Shelley's Case

1. The Rule. The Rule in *Shelley's Case* [70] was one of the classic pitfalls of the old conveyancing. It was an important common law rule of medieval invention, [71] though it took its name from the case of 1581 in which it was precisely formulated. It applied before 1926 to both deeds and wills. It has been abolished in respect of all instruments coming into operation after 1925. [72]

---

[64] Jarman 1581, 1651.　　　　　　　　　　[65] *Re Waugh* [1903] 1 Ch. 744.
[66] s. 130 (1).　　　　　　　　　　　　　　　[67] L.P.A., 1925, s. 130 (2).
[68] For a full discussion of various possibilities, see (1936) 6 C.L.J. 67; (1946) 9 C.L.J. 185 (S. J. Bailey), and contrast (1945) 9 C.L.J. 46 (R.E.M.).
[69] *Post*, p. 94.
[70] (1581) 1 Co.Rep. 88b. An account of the case is given by Challis 154 *et seq.*
[71] H.E.L. iii, 107 *et seq.* See, *e.g.*, *Abel's Case* (1324) Y.B. 18 Edw. 2, fo. 577 (translated 7 Man. & G. 941).　　　　　　[72] *Post*, p. 65.

The essence of the Rule lies in the following two examples. If land was limited before 1926

" to A for life, remainder to his heirs," or
" to B for life and to the heirs of his body," [73]

under the Rule A took an immediate fee simple and B took an immediate fee tail, although the natural meaning of the words was that A and B should each take life estates, and that at their deaths A's heir should take a fee simple and B's heir a fee tail. The Rule in *Shelley's Case* required that these remainders in fee simple and fee tail should vest at once in A and B, and not in the persons who would be their heirs when they died. The words " remainder to his heirs " or " and to the heirs of his body " were thus treated as words of limitation, marking out the estates taken by A and B, and not as words of purchase conferring any interest on the persons they mentioned, namely, the heirs of A and B. As A also took a life estate under the first part of the gift that life estate merged with his fee simple remainder so as to give him an immediate fee simple in possession. " To A for life, remainder to his heirs " thus produced the same effect as " to A and his heirs." B's limitation was likewise equivalent to " to B and the heirs of his body."

In abstract and technical terms the Rule could be stated as follows:

It is a rule of law that when an estate of freehold is given to a person, and by the same disposition an estate is limited either mediately or immediately to his heirs or to the heirs of his body, the words " heirs " or " heirs of his body " are words of limitation and not words of purchase.

2. Origin of the Rule. The origin of the Rule is mysterious, and many different conjectures have been made.[74] Probably it was a branch of the old rule of common law which forbad a person's heir to take by purchase from his own ancestor.[75] For example, if A granted land to B for life with remainder to A's heirs, the remainder was void and A himself had the reversion.[76] Similarly if a person could take either by descent or by purchase, the law rejected the title by purchase and preferred the title by descent.[77] Thus if X devised land to the person who was in fact his heir, that person took by descent, for " the estate of the heir by inheritance so far over-

---

[73] *Sheppard* v. *Gibbons* (1742) 2 Atk. 441 at 444.
[74] See Co.Litt. 22b; Fearne 83 *et seq.*; Challis 166; *Trevor* v. *Trevor* (1719) 1 Eq. Ca.Abr. 387 at 390; *Van Grutten* v. *Foxwell* [1897] A.C. 658 at 668; A. D. Hargreaves (1938) 54 L.Q.R. 75.
[75] Hargrave, *Law Tracts* i, 564–573; Fearne 84, citing opinion of Gilbert C.B.; Challis 167n. For " purchase," see *ante*, p. 52.
[76] Co.Litt. 22b.
[77] Challis 239.

powered the devise of the testator as that the devise was inoperative." [78] These rules may in turn have owed their origin to the fact that feudal liabilities, such as relief and wardship, fell upon those who took by descent but not upon those who took by purchase. But the theories of the feudal origin of the Rule in *Shelley's Case* which became current in the eighteenth century should possibly be regarded with some suspicion.[79]

It is important to realise that the Rule arose independently of, and subsequently to, the ordinary forms of grant " to A and his heirs " and " to A and the heirs of his body "; those forms of grant therefore owed nothing to the Rule.[80] The Rule applied only where two independent gifts were attempted, first to the ancestor and secondly by way of remainder to his heirs. Had a gift " to A and his heirs " been an example of the Rule, there would have been curious consequences when the Rule was abolished in 1925.[81]

3. Operation of the Rule. A mass of technical doctrine accumulated round the Rule in former times.[82] The following were some of its salient features:

(*a*) "*It is a rule of law.*" The Rule was not a rule of construction, designed to carry out the intention of the grantor or testator as far as possible, but a rigid rule of law which applied notwithstanding any contrary intention.[83] Thus the Rule was not ousted even by an express declaration that A was to hold the land for his life and no longer,[84] or that he should have no power to bar the entail.[85]

(*b*) "*Either mediately or immediately.*" The Rule applied whether or not there was some estate or interest between the estate of freehold and the remainder.[86] The examples considered hitherto have been cases where the remainder has been limited immediately,

---

[78] *Owen* v. *Gibbons* [1902] 1 Ch. 636 at 638, *per* Farwell J. This doctrine of " worthier title," as it is called, was abolished by the Inheritance Act, 1833, s. 3 (*cf.* L.P.A., 1925, s. 132), but traces of it remain in American law, *e.g.*, where A grants land to B for life with remainder to A's heirs, and A is held to take the fee simple reversion and the heirs nothing. See *Powell on Real Property*, s. 381 ; J. W. Morris (1956) 54 Mich.L.R. 451.

[79] *Cf.* H.E.L. iii, 107, citing *The Provost of Beverley's Case* (1366) Y.B. 40 Edw. 3, Hil. pl. 18. The emphasis on relief here was because the action was for relief, which seems a sufficient explanation.

[80] *Re McElligott* [1944] Ch. 216 at 218.

[81] See F. E. Farrer (1937) 53 L.Q.R. 371 ; (1945) 10 Conv.(N.S.) 7 ; *contra*, A. D. Hargreaves (1938) 54 L.Q.R. 70.

[82] A fuller account was given in previous editions of this book.

[83] *Jesson* v. *Doe* d. *Wright* (1820) 2 Bli. 1 ; *Roddy* v. *Fitzgerald* (1858) 6 H.L.C. 823, ending the controversy started by *Perrin* v. *Blake* (1770) 1 Wm.Bl. 672, for an account of which see *Van Grutten* v. *Foxwell* [1897] A.C. 658 at 668–677. And see *Foxwell* v. *Van Grutten* (1900) 82 L.T. 272 at 276.

[84] *Robinson* v. *Robinson* (1756) 1 Burr. 38 ; 3 Bro.P.C. 180.

[85] *Perrin* v. *Blake*, *supra*.

[86] Challis 153, 163 ; Preston i, 266, 267.

i.e., where there has been no intervening estate. Where this was the case, the estate in possession and that in remainder merged.[87] But the commonest type of case to which the Rule applied was where the remainder was limited mediately, *e.g.*, " to A for life, remainder to X for life, remainder to the heirs of A." The result was that A took a life estate in possession, X took a life estate in remainder, and A took the fee simple remainder, a vested interest which he could dispose of in his lifetime or by will.[88] X's vested estate of freehold prevented A's two estates merging together.[89]

Where the intermediate limitation did not create a present vested estate of freehold but merely a contingent interest (*i.e.*, an interest which would become vested only if some condition was fulfilled [90]), merger occurred, but the two estates separated to let in the intervening interest as soon as it vested.[91] Thus if land was given · " to A for life, remainder to his eldest son in tail, remainder to the heirs of A," the Rule gave A a fee simple in possession until he had a son; upon birth of a son, A's life estate in possession and fee simple in remainder separated and allowed the son's vested remainder in tail to fall into its proper place.[92] But if the final remainder to A's heirs was contingent (*e.g.*, " remainder to the heirs of A if A shall survive B "), A's life estate and his contingent remainder in fee simple remained unmerged.[1]

It was in cases like these that the Rule might bring disaster upon family settlements. Land was very frequently settled on a tenant for life with numerous other successive limitations for other members of his family, born on unborn.[2] In case these limitations failed, the draftsman might incautiously add an ultimate remainder to the heirs of the tenant for life. The effect was to give the tenant for life a fee simple and the heirs nothing, thus often frustrating the settlor's intention to keep the land in the family

(c) " To his heirs or to the heirs of his body "

(1) CONVEYANCE. In a conveyance *inter vivos* the only words to attract the Rule were " heirs," or " heirs " followed by words of procreation.[3] The Rule did not apply to " heir " in the singular, for

---

[87] *Ibid.*
[88] For " vested," see *post*, p. 173.
[89] *Ambrose* v. *Hodgson* (1781) 3 Bro.P.C. 416; but an intervening term of years did not prevent merger: *Bates* v. *Bates* (1697) 1 Ld.Raym. 326.
[90] For " contingent," see *post*, p. 173.
[91] Fearne 36; Challis 137, 138. This was achieved by a modification of the law of merger, explained *post*, p. 193. In effect the estate of inheritance resulting from the merger was a conditional fee (*post*, p. 75) which was subject to the contingent remainderman's rights.
[92] *Lewis Bowles's Case* (1615) 11 Co.Rep. 79b.
[1] Hayes i, 544: Challis 163.
[2] See *post*, p. 384.   [3] *Walker* v. *Snow* (1621) Palm. 359; Norton 360.

" heir " was not an apt word of limitation for an estate of inheritance.[4]

(2) WILL. In a will the testator's intentions were regarded to this extent, that it was a question of construction whether the remainder was intended to be given to the heirs generally or to a *persona designata, i.e.*, one specific person.[5] In the former case the Rule applied, irrespective of the testator's other intentions; in the latter it did not, and the specified person was allowed to take by purchase.[6] Not only the word " heirs " but also any *nomen collectivum* (collective name) would be governed by the Rule if the context showed that it meant " the whole succession of inheritable blood." [7] Difficult questions of construction might thus arise. Even words such as " son " or " child " might be held to be *nomen collectivum*, while on the other hand even such words as " heirs of the body " might be held to denote children as *personae designatae* and so exclude the Rule.[8]

In a will (unlike a deed) the Rule could apply even if the remainder was to the " heir " in the singular.[9] But in this case it was easier for the court to find an intention that the testator did not mean thereby to refer to the whole line of heirs but referred only to an individual.[10] In particular, unlike the Rule in *Archer's Case*,[11] if " heir " was followed by any words of limitation the Rule in *Shelley's Case* did not apply. Thus if land was devised " to A for life, remainder to his heir and his heirs," A took a life estate and his heir a fee simple.

(3) EQUITY. As we shall see, equity followed the law with regard to words of limitation, including the Rule in *Shelley's Case* [12] But the Rule was followed only where both limitations were equitable. If one limitation was legal and the other equitable the Rule was

---

[4] *Ante*, p. 52. The heir thus took a life estate. As to superadded words of limitation after " heirs," see n. 11, *infra*.

[5] See Jarman (7th ed.), Chap. 49.

[6] *Van Grutten* v. *Foxwell* [1897] A.C. 658 at 668, 685.

[7] *Ibid.* at 668. See *Re Routledge* [1942] Ch. 457 (testator died in 1874), discussed in (1943) 59 L.Q.R. 272 (R.E.M.).

[8] *Goodtitle* d. *Sweet* v. *Herring* (1801) 1 East 264; Jarman (7th ed.), Chap. 49.

[9] *Whiting* v. *Wilkins* (1612) 1 Bulstr. 219; *Blackburn* v. *Stables* (1814) 2 V. & B. 367 at 371; *Re Hack* [1925] Ch. 633.

[10] *Silcocks* v. *Silcocks* [1916] 2 Ch. 161 at 166.

[11] (1597) 1 Co.Rep. 63b. Later there accumulated many refinements of learning as to the effect in wills of such " superadded words of limitation " in various different cases, the latest of which was *Re Routledge, supra*, as reported in [1942] 2 All E.R. 418. See Fearne 178–184; Preston i, 367 *et seq.*; Challis 164, 165; Jarman (7th ed.), Chap. 49. The principle lurking in this dark jungle of authorities is that the superaddition of words of limitation after " heir " or " heirs " may make it impossible to construe that word itself as a word of limitation.

[12] *Post*, p. 130; Lewin 53; *Cooper* v. *Kynock* (1872) 7 Ch.App. 398; *Re White and Hindle's Contract* (1877) 7 Ch.D. 201. There was an exception in favour of executory trusts which required some further disposition: Lewin 54; Challis 166; *post*, p. 131.

inapplicable.[13] Thus if land was given to trustees to hold on trust for A during A's life, so that his estate was equitable, with a legal remainder to the heirs of his body, the Rule did not apply.[14]

4. Abolition of the Rule

(a) *Abolition.* By the Law of Property Act, 1925,[15] the Rule was abolished for all instruments coming into operation after 1925. Accordingly in a limitation " to A for life, remainder to his heirs " the word " heirs " is now a word of purchase and not a word of limitation. The section provides that the " same person or persons shall take as would in the case of freehold land have answered that description " [*i.e.*, " heirs," " heirs of the body," etc.] " under the general law in force before the commencement of this Act." The heir or heir of the body, as the case may be, ascertained according to the general law in force before 1926 (and not under special customs such as gavelkind), now takes the remainder.

(b) *" Very heir."* Where the remainder is " to the heirs [or heir] male of A's body," the obscure and controversial " doctrine of very heir " becomes relevant. Under this, the limitation was treated as if it were " to the heir (being male) of A's body," so that a person could take if (but only if) he satisfied the double condition of being A's heir general of the body and also being a male. This excluded both the daughter of the eldest son (as not being male) and the son of a younger son (as not being heir general), though it let in the son of an only daughter. Similar rules applied to a limitation " to A's heir male." [16]

(c) *The heir's estate.* The estate taken by the heir is governed by any further words of limitation according to the ordinary rules. Thus in a limitation " to A for life, remainder to his heirs," A will take a mere life interest, while his heir takes the remainder in fee simple. Had the remainder been " to the heirs of his body," probably the heir of A's body would take an entail [17]; had it been " to the heir of his body," he would take a fee simple.[18]

13 Challis 165.
14 *Viscount Say and Seal* v. *Lady Jones* (1729) 3 Bro.P.C. 113; *Shapland* v. *Smith* (1780) 1 Bro.C.C. 75; *Silvester* d. *Law* v. *Wilson* (1788) 2 T.R. 444.
15 s. 131.
16 See generally Co.Litt. 24b; Jarman 1547 *et seq.*; *Re Routledge* [1942] Ch. 457; (1943) 59 L.Q.R. 272 (R.E.M.); (1973) 37 Conv.(N.S.) 113 (J. Adams).
17 See *Mandeville's Case, ante*, p. 58, n. 47. There seems no reason why the peculiarity of that kind of entail should not still attach to it.
18 *Ante*, p. 58.

D. *Words of Limitation for a Life Estate*

I. CONVEYANCES INTER VIVOS

A life estate was created before 1926 either by words showing an intention to create a life estate, such as " to A for life," or by using expressions insufficient to create a fee simple or fee tail, such as " to A," or " to A for ever." The rule that a life estate was created by such imperfect expressions has already been explained.[31] A tenancy for an indefinite period more than from year to year was usually construed as a tenancy for life.[32]

After 1925, a fee simple (or the whole of the interest the grantor has power to convey, if it is less than a fee simple) passes unless a contrary intention is shown.[33] Thus in order to create a life interest words showing an intention to do so must normally be used, *e.g.*, " to A for life."

II. WILLS

Before the Wills Act, 1837, a devise passed only a life estate unless an intention to create a fee simple or fee tail was shown.[34] Section 28 of the Act provided, as has already been noticed,[35] that the fee simple passes unless a contrary intention is shown. The rule for wills therefore anticipated the modern rule for deeds, and they are now the same. Some words of limitation are therefore equally necessary in order to create a life interest by will.

Sect. 2. Nature of the Estates of Freehold

A. *The Fee Simple*

The fee simple is the most ample estate which can exist in land.[36] Although strictly speaking it is still held in tenure and therefore falls short of absolute ownership, in practice it is absolute ownership,[37] for nearly all traces of the old feudal burdens have disappeared. " A tenant in fee simple enjoys all the advantages of absolute ownership, except the form." [38] His powers of " enjoying,

---

[31] *Ante*, p. 51.
[32] *Re Coleman's Estate* [1907] 1 I.R. 488 at 492; and see *post*, p. 630.
[33] *Ante*, p. 56.
[34] *Ante*, p. 56.
[35] *Ante*, p. 56.
[36] Litt. 11; Williams R.P. 6.
[37] See Challis 218; and as to the possible effect of the 1925 legislation, see 70 L.J.News. 4, 20 (T. C. Williams).
[38] 75 S.J. 843 (T. C. Williams). To Joshua Williams' statement that " the first thing the student has to do is to get rid of the idea of absolute ownership," Maitland added " and the next thing the student has to do is painfully to reacquire it " (*ibid.*).

using and abusing" his land are indeed limited in many ways by statute and by the rights of his neighbours, but they are not limited by any inherent narrowness in the concept of property in land.[39]

Pre-eminent among a fee simple owner's rights are his right of alienation (the right to transfer to another the whole or any part of his interest in the land) and his right to everything in, on, or over the land. These will be considered in turn, and will be followed by a discussion of the various types of fee simple.

I. RIGHT OF ALIENATION

Today a tenant in fee simple may dispose of his estate in whatever way he thinks fit, either by will[40] or *inter vivos*.[40a] This has not always been so. Before the Norman Conquest much land seems to have been freely alienable,[41] but under the universal feudalism of the Normans the tendency at first was to restrict alienation.[42] Two people might suffer if a tenant was able to dispose of his land: his heir and his lord.

1. Rights of the heir. In early law the heir apparent or heir presumptive was regarded as having a definite interest in the land, so that the tenant could not dispose of the land without his consent; and as subsequent events might show that the prospective heir was not the person who would have succeeded to the land had it not been alienated, it was not unusual to get the consent of as many near relatives as possible.[43]

By about 1200 this doctrine had disappeared, and a tenant in fee simple was able to alienate his land *inter vivos* so as to defeat all claims by his heirs.[44] Thereafter the prospective heir was regarded as having no estate or interest in the land but only a mere hope of succeeding to it, a *spes successionis*.[45] And it was then clear that the words " and his heirs " in a conveyance were words of limitation, not words of purchase.[46] By the beginning of the fourteenth century the existence of a fee simple had ceased to be in any way dependent upon the existence of heirs of the original owner. Strictly, if land

---

[39] There are still a few instances of movable estates in land, *e.g.*, a fee simple in such part of a specified area as may be allocated in an annual drawing of lots (the " lot meadows " at Yarnton, Oxfordshire): see (1936) 1 Conv.(N.S.) 53 (F. E. Farrer); 1 Preston 258.

[40] Subject to proper provision being made for near relatives in certain cases: *post*, p. 472.

[40a] Subject to the law against racial discrimination in dispositions of land: Race Relations Act 1968, ss. 5, 7.

[41] H.E.L. ii, 68, iii, 73.

[42] Williams R.P. 68; Cru.Dig. iv, 3. [43] P. & M. ii, 309, 310.

[44] *Ibid.* 311, 313.

[45] This was not an assignable interest at common law, but " an absolutely bare possibility ": Challis 76.

[46] *Ante*, p. 52.

were given " to A and his heirs," the fee simple should have determined as soon as A and all his heirs were dead, even if A had
alienated the land. But a fee simple became potentially eternal
when the courts decided that if a' fee simple was alienated it continued to exist so long as there was no failure of heirs of the owner
for the time being.[47]

Although after the twelfth century a tenant in fee simple could
alienate his land *inter vivos* and so defeat the expectations of his
relatives, he could not dispose of it by will. In some cases devises
were permitted as late as the latter half of the thirteenth century,
but from the end of that century the rule was settled that land was
not devisable. Any land not disposed of before death must descend
to the heir and to no one else: for, said Glanville, " only God can
make an heir." [48] This remained law until wills of land were made
possible by uses [49] and later by the Statute of Wills, 1540.[50]

2. Rights of the lord. The feudal aspects of alienation, the two
methods of subinfeudation and substitution, and the final prohibition of the former by the Statute *Quia Emptores*, 1290, have already
been discussed.[51] Both methods of alienation could work to the
disadvantage of the lord. By *Quia Emptores* all land held in fee
simple became freely alienable by substitution but by substitution
only: the grantee became tenant of the grantor's lord, not of the
grantor. From this time onwards no feudal restrictions hampered
the alienability of the fee simple, except that fines were sometimes
payable on alienation of land held directly of the Crown until
1660,[52] and of copyhold land until 1926.[53]

II. RIGHT TO EVERYTHING IN, ON OR OVER THE LAND

1. General rule. The maxim is *cujus est solum, ejus est usque
ad coelum et ad inferos* [54] : the owner of the soil is presumed to own
everything " up to the sky and down to the centre of the earth," [55]
though these have been described as fanciful phrases.[56] Prima facie
the owner in fee simple is in possession of, and therefore entitled to,

---

[47] Y.B. 33–35 Edw. 1 (R.S.) 362 (1306); H.E.L. iii, 106, 107.
[48] P. & M. ii, 325; H.E.L. iii, 75, 76. But customs to devise were admitted,
e.g., under the customs of gavelkind or burgage, *ante*, pp. 20, 22.
[49] *Post*, p. 154.
[50] *Post*, p. 160.　　　　　　　　　　　　　　　　　　　[51] *Ante*, p. 31.
[52] *Ante*, p. 33. In other cases fines upon alienation were illegal, as being contrary
to *Quia Emptores*: *Merttens* v. *Hill* [1901] 1 Ch. 842.　　[53] *Ante*, p. 37.
[54] *Mitchell* v. *Moseley* [1914] 1 Ch. 438 at 450. For discussion of " this brocard "
see *Commissioner for Railways* v. *Valuer-General* [1974] A.C. 328.
[55] *Corbett* v. *Hill* (1870) L.R. 9 Eq. 671 at 673, *per* James V.-C.
[56] *Wandsworth Board of Works* v. *United Telephone Co.* (1884) 13 Q.B.D. 904 at
915, *per* Brett M.R.

any chattel not the property of any known person which is found under or attached to his land,[57] *e.g.*, in the bed of a canal.[58] This rule also applies to chattels not under or attached to the land,[59] unless the circumstances indicate the contrary, in which case the finder is prima facie entitled to possession.[60]

The owner is also entitled to land added by gradual accretion from the sea.[61] Sudden accretions of substantial size belong to the Crown, which also owns the foreshore (the land between high and low water) unless it has parted with its rights in any particular place.[62]

An owner can, if he wishes, divide his land horizontally or in any other way. He can dispose of minerals under the surface, or the top floor of a building,[63] so as to make them separate properties. But unless some contrary intention is shown [64] a grant will normally pass the owner's whole interest in the space above and below the land, so that, for example, a lease will give the tenant the right to the air-space above the land let.[65] Again, he may in general use his property in the natural course of user in any way he thinks fit.[66] He may waste or despoil the land as he pleases and he is not normally liable merely because he neglects it.[67]

2. Qualifications. The absolute freedom of the tenant is qualified in many ways.

(*a*) *Other rights over his land.* He is naturally subject to such rights as others have over his land, such as rights of way, the rights of tenants under leases, and the rights of mortgagees.

(*b*) *Statute.* In the last century, and particularly during the last sixty years, there has been much legislation imposing on landowners restrictions and liabilities in the public interest and subjecting them to interference by public authorities. Indeed, it has been said that " the fundamental assumption of modern statute law is that the land-owner holds his land for the public good." [68]

---

[57] *Elwes* v. *Brigg Gas Co.* (1886) 33 Ch.D. 562; *South Staffordshire Water Co.* v. *Sharman* [1896] 2 Q.B. 44.

[58] *R.* v. *Rowe* (1859) 28 L.J.M.C. 128.   [59] See *Re Cohen* [1953] Ch. 88.

[60] *Bridges* v. *Hawkesworth* (1851) 15 Jur. 1079; *Hannah* v. *Peel* [1945] K.B. 509; see Goodhart, *Essays in Jurisprudence and the Common Law*, 75–90.

[61] *Gifford* v. *Lord Yarborough* (1828) 5 Bing. 163; Bl.Comm. ii, 262; Halsb. xxxix, 560.

[62] Halsb. xxxix, 559.

[63] Co.Litt. 48b; Challis 54; and see 106 S.J. 345; L.P.A. 1925, s. 205 (1) (ix).

[64] *Truckell* v. *Stock* [1957] 1 W.L.R. 161.

[65] *Kelsen* v. *Imperial Tobacco Co.* (*of Great Britain and Ireland*) *Ltd.* [1957] 2 Q.B. 334; *Grigsby* v. *Melville* [1974] 1 W.L.R. 80.

[66] *Wilson* v. *Waddell* (1876) 2 App.Cas. 95 at 99; (1895) 11 L.Q.R. 225 (T. C. Williams).

[67] *Giles* v. *Walker* (1890) 24 Q.B.D. 656 (thistles); *Brady* v. *Warren* [1900] 2 I.R. 632 (rabbits). But see *Davey* v. *Harrow Corporation* [1958] 1 Q.B. 60.

[68] (1936) 49 Harv.L.R. 426 at 436 (W. I. Jennings).

These statutes are of great importance but they do not, generally speaking, affect the principles of the law of real property. They restrict the liberties of great numbers of landowners and so may affect, among other things, the prices at which they can sell their land and the terms of sale. But the substance of the various possible transactions in land is not thereby altered: sales, settlements, leases, mortgages, and so on, continue as before. These statutes form a body of regulatory or administrative law which stands apart from property law. The Town and Country Planning Acts [1] and the Rent Acts [2] are treated concisely in this book. But the Housing Acts [3] and the Public Health Acts [4] are not, since they lie outside the subject. The same applies to the law about compulsory purchase of land and compensation,[5] under which many public authorities have power to acquire land for public purposes, subject to compensation. The Leasehold Reform Act 1967 is in a class by itself: it expropriates certain landlords of property let on long leases in favour of their tenants, though neither for public purposes nor subject to compensation. This remarkable statute is explained alongside the Rent Acts.[6]

(c) *Liability in tort.* A landowner may be liable in tort for injuries caused to third parties by his acts and omissions, *e.g.*, if he withdraws support to which his neighbour is entitled,[7] or if water in a reservoir escapes,[8] or if a lamp projecting over a highway gets into a dangerous state of repair and injures a passer-by.[9] In the same way he may be liable for nuisance, *e.g.*, if he makes an unusual and excessive collection of manure which attracts flies and causes a smell.[10]

(d) *Air-space.* Intrusion into the air-space above land is a trespass and often also a nuisance. The owner can therefore take proceedings if his air-space is invaded by a tree, a crane, a cornice or telephone wires,[11] or if projectiles are fired over it.[12] Damages

---

[1] *Post*, p. 1086.
[2] *Post*, p. 1124.
[3] Housing Acts, 1957 to 1974.
[4] Public Health Acts, 1875 to 1961.
[5] The principal statutes are the Acquisition of Land (Authorisation Procedure) Act, 1946, Compulsory Purchase Act 1965, and the Land Compensation Acts, 1961 and 1973.
[6] *Post*, p. 1149.
[7] See *post*, p. 814.
[8] *Rylands* v. *Fletcher* (1868) L.R. 3 H.L. 330.
[9] *Tarry* v. *Ashton* (1876) 1 Q.B.D. 314.
[10] *Bland* v. *Yates* (1914) 58 S.J. 612.
[11] *Fay* v. *Prentice* (1845) 1 C.B. 828 at 835; *Lemmon* v. *Webb* [1895] A.C. 1; *Gifford* v. *Dent* [1926] W.N. 336; 71 S.J. 83; *Kelsen* v. *Imperial Tobacco Co. (of Great Britain and Ireland) Ltd.* [1957] 2 Q.B. 334. But see McNair, *Law of the Air* (3rd ed.), Chap. 3.
[12] *Clifton* v. *Viscount Bury* (1887) 4 T.L.R. 8.

may be claimed for any injury, but the most important remedy is an injunction to prevent the wrong continuing. In a proper case, the court may as always refuse or defer an injunction, *e.g.*, for trespass by a crane where the neighbouring work is far advanced and fair compensation is offered [13]; but in principle an injunction is available even where there is no danger.[14]

Aircraft enjoy a wide dispensation under the Civil Aviation Act, 1949,[15] which provides that no action shall lie in respect of trespass or nuisance by reason only of the flight of aircraft over property at a height which is reasonable under the circumstances, provided the proper regulations are observed.

(*e*) *Minerals.* Although prima facie a tenant in fee simple is entitled to all mines and minerals under his land,[16] this is subject to some exceptions. Thus at common law, as modified by statute, the Crown is entitled to all gold and silver in gold and silver mines [17]; and under the Pertoleum (Production) Act, 1934, petroleum existing in its natural condition in strata is vested in the Crown. Under the Coal Act, 1938, all interests in coal (except interests arising under a coal-mining lease) were vested in the Coal Commission in return for compensation; and these interests (including coal-mining leases) have now vested in the National Coal Board.[18]

(*f*) *Treasure trove.* The Crown is at common law entitled to all treasure trove.[19] For objects to amount to treasure trove—

(i) they must consist of gold or silver, whether in bullion, coin or some manufactured object;

(ii) they must have been hidden in or on the land deliberately, and not merely lost; and

(iii) the true owner must be unknown.[20]

(*g*) *Wild animals.* Wild animals are not the subject of ownership.[21] But a landowner has what is sometimes called a " qualified property " in them, consisting of the exclusive right to catch, kill and appropriate the animals on his land; and as soon as the animals are killed, they fall into the ownership of the landowner, even if killed by a trespasser.[22]

---

[13] *Woollerton & Wilson Ltd.* v. *Richard Costain Ltd.* [1970] 1 W.L.R. 411 ; but see *Charrington* v. *Simons & Co. Ltd.* [1971] 1 W.L.R. 598 at 603.
[14] *Ibid.*   [15] s. 40, replacing Air Navigation Act, 1920, s. 9.
[16] *Mitchell* v. *Mosley* [1914] 1 Ch. 438 at 450.
[17] *The Case of Mines* (1568) 1 Plowd. 310 ; Royal Mines Acts, 1688, 1693 ; and see *Att.-Gen.* v. *Morgan* [1891] 1 Ch. 432.
[18] Coal Industry Nationalisation Act, 1946.   [19] 3 Co.Inst. 132.
[20] See *Att.-Gen.* v. *Moore* [1893] 1 Ch. 676 at 683 ; *Att.-Gen.* v. *Trustees of the British Museum* [1903] 2 Ch. 598 at 608–611 ; Halsb. ii, 101 (m).
[21] *The Case of Swans* (1592) 7 Co.Rep. 15b at 17b.
[22] *Blades* v. *Higgs* (1865) 11 H.L.C. 621 ; *R.* v. *Townley* (1871) L.R. 1 C.C.R. 315.

(*h*) *Water*. A landowner has no property in water which either percolates through his land [23] or flows through it in a defined channel.[24] In the case of percolating water, at common law the landowner could draw any or all of it off without regard to the claims of neighbouring owners [25]; but now, by statute, he normally cannot do so without a licence granted by a river authority unless the water is taken for the domestic purposes of his household.[26]

In the case of water flowing through a defined channel, even at common law the riparian owner (the owner of the land through which the water flows) could not always take all the water [27]; but he has certain valuable rights.

(1) FISHING. As part of his natural right of ownership,[28] he has the sole right to fish in the water.[29] Except in tidal waters,[30] the public has no right of fishing even if there is a public right of navigation.[31] For although a public right of navigation on a river may be acquired in much the same way as a public right of way over land can be acquired,[32] this no more entitles the public to fish in the stream than a right of way entitles the public to shoot on the highway [33]: the public's right is merely a right of passage.

(2) FLOW. He is entitled to the flow of water through the land unaltered in volume or quality, subject to ordinary and reasonable use by the upper riparian owners,[34] and he is bound by a corresponding obligation to the lower riparian owners.

(3) ABSTRACTION. The ordinary and reasonable use which at common law a riparian owner was entitled to make of the water flowing through his land was—

> (i) the right to take and use all water necessary for ordinary purposes [35] connected with his riparian tenement (such as for watering his cattle [1] or for domestic purposes,[2] or,

---

[23] *Ballard* v. *Tomlinson* (1885) 29 Ch.D. 115 at 121.
[24] *Mason* v. *Hill* (1833) 5 B. & Ad. 1 at 24.
[25] *Chasemore* v. *Richards* (1859) 7 H.L.C. 349; *Langbrook Properties Ltd.* v. *Surrey C.C.* [1970] 1 W.L.R. 161; and see *Bradford Corpn.* v. *Pickles* [1895] A.C. 587.
[26] Water Resources Act 1963, ss. 23, 24 (3).
[27] See *post*, p. 815. As to the right to divert water, see (1958) 74 L.Q.R. 361 (D. P. Derham).
[28] See *Cooper* v. *Phibbs* (1867) L.R. 2 H.L. 149 at 165
[29] *Eckroyd* v. *Coulthard* [1898] 2 Ch. 358 at 366.
[30] *Malcolmson* v. *O'Dea* (1863) 10 H.L.C. 593; *Alfred F. Beckett Ltd.* v. *Lyons* [1967] Ch. 449 (coal on sea shore).
[31] *Pearce* v. *Scotcher* (1882) 9 Q.B.D. 162; *Blount* v. *Layard* [1891] 2 Ch. 681 at 689, 690.
[32] *Post*, p. 815.
[33] *Smith* v. *Andrews* [1891] 2 Ch. 678 at 695, 696. But local inhabitants may sometimes acquire fishing rights: *post*, p. 821.
[34] See *John Young & Co.* v. *The Bankier Distillery Co.* [1893] A.C. 691 at 698.
[35] *Miner* v. *Gilmour* (1858) 12 Moo.P.C. 131 at 156.
[1] *McCartney* v. *Londonderry and Lough Swilly Ry.* [1904] A.C. 301 at 306.
[2] *Kensit* v. *Great Eastern Ry.* (1883) 23 Ch.D. 566 at 574.

possibly, in some manufacturing districts, for manufacturing purposes [3]), even though this completely exhausted the stream [4]; and

(ii) the right to use the water for extraordinary purposes connected with his riparian tenement, provided the use was reasonable [5] and the water was restored substantially undiminished in volume and unaltered in character.[6] Such purposes included irrigation [7] and (in all districts [8]) manufacturing purposes,[9] such as for cooling apparatus.[10] The amount by which the flow might be diminished was a question of degree in each case.[11]

Statute has now severely curtailed these rights, so that in most cases a riparian owner cannot take any water without a licence granted by a water authority. The two main exceptions are where the water is taken for use on a holding comprising the riparian land and any other land held therewith, and the use is for either—

(i) the domestic purposes of the occupier's household, or

(ii) agricultural purposes other than " spray irrigation " (*i.e.*, watering land by jets or sprays from hoses and the like).

If a licence is granted, it constitutes a defence to any action (*e.g.*, by a lower riparian owner) in respect of the abstraction of any water in accordance with it.[12]

Apart from these rights a riparian owner cannot take water from a stream at all; thus without statutory authority a waterworks company owning land on the bank of a stream cannot take water to supply a neighbouring town.[13] The owner of only one bank of a non-tidal stream is prima facie entitled to exercise riparian rights up to the middle of the stream.[14] But when the waters are tidal,

---

[3] See *Ormerod* v. *Todmorton Joint Stock Mill Co. Ltd.* (1883) 11 Q.B.D. 155 at 168. *Sed quaere*: such a rule would enable an upper riparian owner, by starting a factory on his land, to take all the water previously enjoyed by factories lower down; and compare *McIndoe* v. *Jutland Flat (Waipori) Gold Mining Co. Ltd.* (1893) 12 N.Z.L.R. 226 at 238. See generally (1959) 22 M.L.R. 35 (A. H. Hudson).

[4] *McCartney* v. *Londonderry and Lough Swilly Ry.*, *supra*, at p. 307.

[5] See *Sharp* v. *Wilson, Rotheray & Co.* (1905) 93 L.T. 155.

[6] *McCartney* v. *Londonderry and Lough Swilly Ry.*, *supra*, at p. 307; *Rugby Joint Water Board* v. *Walters* [1967] Ch. 397 (spray irrigation).

[7] See *Embrey* v. *Owen* (1851) 6 Exch. 353; *Rugby Joint Water Board* v. *Walters*, *supra*.

[8] *Semble*, despite the language in *Elmhurst* v. *Spencer* (1849) 2 Mac. & G. 45 at 50.

[9] *Swindon Waterworks Co. Ltd.* v. *Wilts and Berks Canal Navigation Co.* (1875) L.R. 7 H.L. 697 at 704.

[10] *Kensit* v. *Great Eastern Ry.* (1883) 23 Ch.D. 566.

[11] *Embrey* v. *Owen*, *supra*, at p. 372.

[12] Water Resources Act 1963, ss. 23, 24 (2), 31, 135 (1), as amended by Water Act 1973, s. 9.

[13] See the *Swindon* case, *supra*.

[14] *Micklethwait* v. *Newlay Bridge Co.* (1886) 33 Ch.D. 133.

prima facie the Crown is entitled to the foreshore (*i.e.*, the land between high and low water marks), and there are no private riparian rights.[15]

III. TYPES OF FEE SIMPLE

A fee simple may be absolute or modified; a modified fee simple (often called a modified fee) is any fee simple except a fee simple absolute. There are four types of fee simple.[16]

1. Fee simple absolute. This is the type most frequently encountered in practice, and is an estate which continues indefinitely. " Fee " and " simple " have already been explained. " Absolute " means perpetual, *i.e.*, not determinable by any special event.[17]

2. Determinable fee. A determinable fee is a fee simple which will automatically determine on the occurrence of some specified event which may never occur.[18] If the event is bound to happen at some time, the estate created is not a determinable fee; for it is said to be an essential characteristic of every fee that it may possibly last for ever.[19] Thus a grant before 1926 " to A and his heirs until B dies " gave A an estate *pur autre vie*, and a grant " to C and his heirs " for a fixed term of years (or until any inevitable event) gave C a mere lease for a term of years.[20] A grant to X and his heirs until a specified lease was made, or to Y and his heirs " as long as the church of St. Paul shall stand," [21] however, created determinable fees. The estates of X and Y might continue for ever, but if the specified state of affairs came about, the fee determined and the land reverted to the original grantor or his heirs. The grantor's interest was called a possibility of reverter, *i.e.*, a possibility of having an estate at a future time.[22] If the occurrence of the determining event became impossible, the possibility of reverter was destroyed and the fee simple became absolute, *e.g.*, if land was given " to A and his heirs until B marries " and B died a bachelor.[23]

15 *Gann* v. *Free Fishers of Whitstable* (1865) 11 H.L.C. 192.
16 " Fee simple " has sometimes been used to mean " fee simple absolute " only: Co.Litt. 1b; Preston i, 428–431; Challis 438; but here the term is used in its wider and more usual sense. And " fee," by itself, is sometimes used for " fee simple absolute ": see Litt. 293; Challis 438.
17 See *post*, p. 137.
18 Preston i, 419, 431, 479; Challis 251.
19 Challis 251.
20 Challis 252; Litt. 740; compare *Vernon* v. *Gatacre* (1564) 3 Dy. 253a; *Gawen* v. *Ramtes* (1600) Cro.Eliz. 804.
21 *Walsingham's Case* (1573) 2 Plowd. 547 at 557; and see *Idle* v. *Cook* (1705) 1 P.Wms. 70 at 75 (" as long as such a tree stands "); see also the catalogue of examples given by Challis, 255–260.
22 Preston i, 441; Fearne 381; Challis 83.
23 Preston i, 440; Challis 254; and see *Re Leach* [1912] 2 Ch. 422 at 429.

It has been suggested that the Statute *Quia Emptores*, 1290, made it impossible to create determinable fees at common law [24] but there are dicta,[25] assumptions [26] and a decision [27] to the contrary, and the suggestion seems unsound in principle.[28] In any case, whatever doubts there may be about determinable fees created by direct grant (which are rarely encountered in practice), it has long been generally accepted that such fees could be created by means of trusts and (before 1926 [29]) uses,[30] as in the usual provision of a marriage settlement whereby the settlor grants land to himself until the solemnisation of the marriage.[31]

3. A fee simple upon condition.[32] Akin to but distinct from a determinable fee is a fee simple which has some condition attached to it by which the estate given to the grantee may be cut short. A grant of land " to X in fee simple on condition that he does not marry Y," for example, will give X a fee simple, which is liable to forfeiture if the forbidden marriage takes place. This type of condition is sometimes called a condition subsequent, in order to distinguish it from a condition precedent relating to the beginning

---

[24] See the authorities cited in *Hopper* v. *Corporation of Liverpool* (1944) 88 S.J. 213 and *Third Report of Real Property Commissions* (1832) 36; Marsden, *Perpetuities*, 71; Sweet's note in Challis 439.

[25] See Challis 251–262, 437–439; R. R. B. Powell, 23 Col.L.R. 207 *et seq.*

[26] See *Re Leach* [1912] 2 Ch. 422; contrast *Re Chardon* [1928] Ch. 464 at 469, treating the question as open.

[27] *Hopper* v. *Corporation of Liverpool, supra*, analysed in 1945 Conv.Y.B. 203 and noted at (1946) 62 L.Q.R. 222 (R.E.M.).

[28] See Morris and Leach, 209, 210. Gray, *Perpetuities*, ss. 31 *et seq.*, 774 *et seq.*, is the chief proponent of the suggestion. His theory amounted to treating a possibility of reverter as a form of escheat (*ante*, p. 18) with tenure between grantor and grantee. Challis, 437–439, seems to accept this, but treats *Quia Emptores* as confined to grants in fee simple absolute. Neither explains why a possibility of reverter must depend on tenure, or why, if it is merely escheat, it is not so called. In fact it belongs to the law not of tenures but of estates, and is classified as a possibility: see Challis 76n. It need no more depend on tenure than contingent remainders or rights of entry. In 1467 Choke J. laid down that reverter and escheat are distinct (Y.B. 7 Edw. 4, Trin., fo. 12, pl. 2), and this is plain from the authorities generally, *e.g.*, Challis 35, 36 (though as to the early use of the term, see *Burgess* v. *Wheate* (1759) 1 Eden. 177 at 191). The books contain little about possibilities of reverter between 1290 and the sixteenth century; probably, like contingent remainders, they became recognised when the system of estates was transcending certain feudal limitations. The rule that there could be no remainder or reversion after a fee simple offers the only obstacle to classifying them with remainders or reversions. For the contingent character of a possibility of reverter for the purposes of the perpetuity rule, see *post*, p. 244. Gray's contention (at s. 37) that *Collier* v. *Walters* (1873) L.R. 17 Eq. 252 is " strong authority that determinable fees do not now exist " ignores the fact that the question there was merely one of construction.

[29] See *post*, p. 171.

[30] See *post*, pp. 167–171, 187.

[31] *Post*, p. 385.

[32] Commonly called a conditional fee. But there has been much confusion of language over determinable and conditional fees. " Conditional fee " was often used for both (see, *e.g.*, Challis 261, 262), and " determinable fee " may cover both: S.L.A., 1925, s. 117 (1) (iv).

of the estate, *e.g.*, " to X in fee simple when he reaches 21."
Conditions precedent are dealt with under future interests.[33]

The difference between a determinable fee and a fee simple
defeasible by condition subsequent is not always easy to discern.[34]
The essential distinction is that the determining event in a determinable fee itself sets the limit for the estate first granted. A
condition subsequent, on the other hand, is an independent clause
added to a limitation of a complete fee simple absolute which
operates so as to defeat it. Thus a devise to a school in fee simple
" until it ceases to publish its accounts " creates a determinable
fee, whereas a devise to the school in fee simple " on condition that
the accounts are published annually " creates a fee simple defeasible
by condition subsequent.[35] Words such as " while," " during,"
" as long as," " until " and so on are apt for the creation of a
determinable fee,[36] whereas words which form a separate clause of
defeasance, such as " provided that," " on condition that," " but
if," or " if it happen that," operate as a condition subsequent.[37]

Descriptive phrases could operate as words of limitation: a grant
" to X and his heirs tenants of the manor of Dale " would create a
determinable fee limited to the duration of the tenure of that
manor.[38] It will be seen that the difference is really one of words [39];
the determining event may be worked into the limitation in such a
way as to create either a determinable fee, or a fee simple defeasible
by condition subsequent, whichever the grantor wishes. The question is whether the words limit the utmost time of continuance of the
estate, or whether they mark an event which, if it takes place in
the course of that time, will defeat an estate already granted; in
the first case the words take effect as a limitation, in the second as
a condition. A limitation marks the bounds or compass of the
estate, a condition defeats the estate before it attains its boundary.[40]

The distinction has been called " little short of disgraceful to our
jurisprudence." [41] It is sometimes fine, but it is important, since
there are differences between the two forms of fee. These are here

---

[33] *Post*, p. 174.
[34] See *Re Moore* (1888) 39 Ch.D. 116.
[35] *Re Da Costa* [1912] 1 Ch. 337.
[36] *Newis* v. *Lark* (1571) 2 Plowd. 403 at 413; *Mary Portington's Case* (1613) 10
Co.Rep. 35b at 41b; Challis 252.
[37] *Mary Portington's Case, supra*, at p. 42a; Litt. 328–330; Shep. 121; and see
Sifton v. *Sifton* [1938] A.C. 656 at 677. Technically such words reserve a right
of entry (*post*, p. 138) to the grantor. This is a reservation out of the grant,
which is quite distinct from a limitation. *Cf. Brandon* v. *Robinson* (1811) 18
Ves. 429 at 432, 433.
[38] Co.Litt. 27a; Challis 255, 256.
[39] *Dean* v. *Dean* [1891] 3 Ch. 150 at 155.
[40] Preston i, 49; see *Re Moore, supra*.
[41] *Re King's Trusts* (1892) 29 L.R.Ir. 401 at 410, *per* Porter M.R.

enumerated, although this requires a number of references to later parts of the book.

(*a*) *Determination*: a determinable fee automatically determines when the specified event occurs,[42] for the natural limits of its existence have been reached and the land reverts to the grantor or, if the grantor is dead, to the person entitled under his will or intestacy.[43] A fee simple upon condition merely gives the grantor (or whoever is entitled to his interest in the land, if the grantor is dead)[43] a right to enter and determine the estate when the event occurs[44]; unless and until entry is made, the fee simple continues.[45] The *possibility of reverter* after a determinable fee therefore operates automatically. The *right of entry* arising on a breach of condition is exercisable at the option of the grantor or his successor. These two special rights must be carefully distinguished.[46]

As a condition subsequent thus gives rise to a right of forfeiture, the courts construe it strictly, and require precise wording; such a condition is void unless it can be seen precisely and distinctly from the moment of its creation what events will cause a forfeiture.[47] Thus conditions subsequent requiring a donee to " continue to reside in Canada," [48] or prohibiting marriage with a person " not of Jewish parentage and of the Jewish faith," [49] have been held insufficiently precise, and so void. The question, however, is one of certainty of concept and not ease of application, so that a sufficiently certain condition is not invalidated merely by possible difficulties in ascertaining whether events have occurred which give rise to a forfeiture.[50]

These strict rules do not, however, apply to a condition precedent : in order to qualify, the claimant need only show that, whatever its possible uncertainty in other cases, he at least has complied with it.[51] A condition against marriage with " a person professing the Jewish faith " may thus be valid as a condition of entitlement but void as a condition of forfeiture.[52]

---

[42] Co.Litt. 214b; Challis 252; *Newis* v. *Lark, supra*; *Mary Portington's Case, supra*, at p. 42a.

[43] As to the transferability of possibilities of reverter and rights of entry, see *post*, p. 81.

[44] Litt. 331; Co.Litt. 214b; Challis 208, 261.

[45] *Matthew Manning's Case* (1609) 8 Co.Rep. 94b at 95b; Challis 219; *Re Evans's Contract* [1920] 2 Ch. 469 at 472.

[46] Here again, however, there is confusion of terminology. Challis (76 note, 228) uses " possibility of reverter " as meaning " right of entry."

[47] *Clavering* v. *Ellison* (1859) 7 H.L.C. 707.

[48] *Sifton* v. *Sifton* [1938] A.C. 656; *cf. Re Coghlan* [1963] I.R. 246.

[49] *Clayton* v. *Ramsden* [1943] A.C. 320; *Re Tarnpolsk* [1958] 1 W.L.R. 1157; *Re Krawitz* [1959] 1 W.L.R. 1192.

[50] *Re Gape* [1952] Ch. 743.

[51] *Re Allen* [1953] Ch. 810; *Re Abrahams' W. T.* [1969] 1 Ch. 463.

[52] *Re Abrahams' W. T., supra*.

The court may grant relief against forfeiture where the object of a condition subsequent is to secure the payment of money or the performance of covenants, provided that the breach is not wilful and the default is made good.[53] This equitable jurisdiction, well established in the fields of leases [54] and mortgages,[55] may occasionally be invoked in other cases.

(*b*) *Remoteness*: under the rules against remoteness a right of entry was void at common law if it might possibly arise at too distant a date. It follows that in such a case a condition subsequent had no effect and the fee simple became absolute.[56] But a determinable limitation could not last beyond the limiting event, no matter how far in the future that event might lie; and this was so even if the possibility of reverter was void for remoteness.[57] Statute has now modified this rule.[58]

(*c*) *Existence at law*: it is probable that a determinable fee cannot exist as a legal estate after 1925, but that a fee simple subject to a condition subsequent can.[59]

(*d*) *Flexibility*: determinable fees are less hampered by restrictions on the events on which they may be made to determine. Conditions subsequent are more jealously regarded by the law and are more readily held to be void (so making the fee simple absolute) as being contrary to public policy. The law of conditions is a large subject and its rules apply to all kinds of dispositions, including trusts, and not only to the rights of entry at common law with which we are here concerned. Taking the authorities together, we find the following general rules.

(1) ALIENATION. The condition must not take away the power of alienation. One of the incidents of ownership is the right to sell or otherwise dispose of the property.[60] A condition [61] against alienation is said to be repugnant to this right, and contrary to public policy,[62] if it substantially takes away the tenant's power of alienation; and such conditions are void. Examples are conditions prohibiting—

alienation at any time,[63]

---

[53] See *Shiloh Spinners Ltd.* v. *Harding* [1973] A.C. 691.
[54] *Post*, p. 659.
[55] *Post*, p. 889.
[56] *Sifton* v. *Sifton* [1938] A.C. 656.
[57] *Post*, p. 244.
[58] *Post*, p. 246.
[59] *Post*, p. 138.
[60] Litt. 360. *Ante*, p. 31 (Statute *Quia Emptores*, 1290).
[61] But not a mere contract or covenant, where breach gives rise to a claim for damages but not to forfeiture of the estate: *Caldy Manor Estate Ltd.* v. *Farrell* [1974] 1 W.L.R. 1303; *post*, p. 755.
[62] (1917) 33 L.Q.R. 11 (E. Jenks).
[63] Co.Litt. 223a; *Hood* v. *Oglander* (1865) 34 Beav. 513 at 522. An important exception was the "restraint upon anticipation" (now abolished) which was a valid restriction in a trust affecting the property of a married woman: see *post*, p. 995.

alienation during some person's life,[64]
alienation to anyone except X,[65]
alienation to anyone except a brother of the donee,[66] or
alienation by mortgage [67] or by will.[68]

The question is, however, one of degree, and it is possible for some kinds of " partial restraint " to be valid. An example, well known but much criticised, is given by a case where land was devised to A " on the condition that he never sells it out of the family." The condition was held valid on the grounds that it did not prohibit any form of any alienation except sale, it did not prohibit sales to members of the family, and it bound only A and not subsequent owners of the land.[69] And a condition that land should not be disposed of except to four sisters or their children has been upheld.[70] But it would not be safe to treat these decisions as examples of the court's normal attitude to restraints on alienation.

It may be mentioned that entails [71] and life interests [72] are in principle equally protected against such restraints. But in the case of life interests the court is much readier to find that what appears to be a conditional limitation is intended to be determinable,[73] which makes an important difference.[74] Thus provisos for forfeiture of a life interest upon any attempt at alienation, or upon bankruptcy, are generally upheld.[75]

(2) COURSE OF LAW. The condition must not be directed against a course of devolution prescribed by law. A condition rendering a fee simple liable to be defeated if the tenant dies intestate,[76] becomes

---

[64] *Re Rosher* (1884) 26 Ch.D. 801 ; *Corbett* v. *Corbett* (1888) 14 P.D. 7.
[65] *Re Cockerill* [1929] 2 Ch. 131 ; *Attwater* v. *Attwater* (1853) 18 Beav. 330 ; *cf.* *Re Elliott* [1896] 2 Ch. 353 (condition that part of proceeds of sale should be paid to X held void).
[66] *Re Brown* [1954] Ch. 39 (holding that the doctrine extends to personalty, *e.g.*, to a share under a trust for sale).
[67] *Ware* v. *Cann* (1830) 10 B. & C. 433.
[68] *Re Jones* [1898] 1 Ch. 438 ; *Re Dunstan* [1918] 2 Ch. 304.
[69] *Re Macleay* (1875) L.R. 20 Eq. 186 (Jessel M.R.). Contrast *Re Rosher, supra*; *Re McDonnell* [1965] I.R. 354 ; Gray, *Restraints on the Alienation of Property*, 2nd ed., 28, 43 ; Jarman 1480. And see discussion by Harman J. in *Re Brown*, *supra*. *Re Macleay* was distinguished in *Re Brown* by the fact that in the latter case the permitted class was small and was bound to diminish. See also (1917) 33 L.Q.R. 236, 342 (Sweet) ; (1954) 70 L.Q.R. 15 (R.E.M.) ; and see *Petrofina (Gt. Britain) Ltd.* v. *Martin* [1965] Ch. 1073 at 1097 (not raised on appeal, [1966] Ch. 146).
[70] *Doe* d. *Gill* v. *Pearson* (1805) 6 East 173.
[71] See *post*, p. 89.
[72] *Brandon* v. *Robinson* (1811) 18 Ves. 429 ; *Rochford* v. *Hackman* (1852) 9 Hare 475 at 480.
[73] *Rochford* v. *Hackman, supra*, at pp. 480, 482 ; *Hurst* v. *Hurst* (1882) 21 Ch.D. 278 at 283.
[74] This is explained *ante*, p. 77.
[75] See Jarman, 1485, 1496 ; Lewin 99. The common " protective trusts " set out in T.A., 1925, s. 33 include a determinable life interest.
[76] *Re Dixon* [1903] 2 Ch. 458.

bankrupt,[77] or has the estate seized in execution,[78] is void; for on each of these events the law prescribes that a fee simple shall devolve in a particular way, and this course of devolution cannot be altered by condition.[79]

(3) PUBLIC POLICY. The condition must not be illegal, immoral or otherwise contrary to public policy. The condition most frequently encountered under this head is a condition in restraint of marriage. Partial restraints, for example, prohibiting marriage with a Papist,[80] or a Scotsman,[81] or a person who had been a domestic servant,[82] have been held good.[83] But total restraints (or restraints which are virtually total, *e.g.*, against marrying a person who has not freehold property worth £500 per annum [84]) are void unless the intent is not primarily to restrain marriage but simply to provide for the donee until marriage,[85] or unless the donee has already been married once.[86] A condition giving a wife an incentive to cease to cohabit with her husband is bad.[87]

Other conditions which are contrary to public policy, and therefore void, are conditions requiring the donee to acquire a dukedom [88] (as being a title carrying with it legislative rights), or forbidding entry into the naval or military services,[89] or the undertaking of any public office.[90] A donee may be forbidden to dispute a will, but such a condition is void if drawn so widely as to disable the donee from protecting his rights.[91] A condition may forbid a change of religion,[92] but only in the case of an adult: for otherwise it conflicts with the parent's duty to provide proper religious instruction for his child.[93] A condition that X should not be allowed to set foot on the property has been held good.[94]

---

[77] *Re Machu* (1882) 21 Ch.D. 838.   [78] *Re Dugdale* (1888) 38 Ch.D. 176 at 182.
[79] *Holmes* v. *Godson* (1856) 8 De G.M. & G. 152.
[80] *Duggan* v. *Kelly* (1847) 10 Ir.Eq.R. 295.
[81] *Perrin* v. *Lyon* (1807) 9 East 170.
[82] *Jenner* v. *Turner* (1880) 16 Ch.D. 188.
[83] And see *Greene* v. *Kirkwood* [1895] 1 I.R. 130; but such gifts should be closely scrutinised for sufficient certainty: see *ante*, p. 77.
[84] *Keily* v. *Monck* (1795) 3 Ridg.P.C. 205.
[85] See *Jones* v. *Jones* (1876) 1 Q.B.D. 279; *Re Hewett* [1918] 1 Ch. 458 (personalty). The rules as to personalty are " proverbially difficult " (*ibid.*); partial restraints are treated as intended merely *in terrorem* (and so void in law) unless enforced by a gift over or a clear clause of revocation. See *Re Whiting* [1905] 1 Ch. 96; *Re Hanlon* [1933] Ch. 254.
[86] *Newton* v. *Marsden* (1862) 2 J. & H. 356 (woman); *Allan* v. *Jackson* (1875) 1 Ch.D. 399 (man).
[87] *Wilkinson* v. *Wilkinson* (1871) L.R. 12 Eq. 604 (life estate); *Re Johnson's W. T.* [1967] Ch. 387.
[88] *Egerton* v. *Brownlow* (1853) 4 H.L.C. 1 (fee tail); contrast *Re Wallace* [1920] 2 Ch. 274 (the " barren title " of baronet).
[89] See *Re Beard* [1908] 1 Ch. 383.   [90] *Re Edgar* [1939] 1 All E.R. 635.
[91] *Cooke* v. *Turner* (1846) 15 M. & W. 727; *Re Boulter* [1922] 1 Ch. 75.
[92] *Hodgson* v. *Halford* (1879) 11 Ch.D. 959 (life estate).
[93] *Re Borwick* [1933] Ch. 657 (personalty); *Re Tegg* [1936] 2 All E.R. 878 (personalty).   [94] *Re Talbot-Ponsonby* [1937] 4 All E.R. 309.

(4) DETERMINABLE FEES. A determinable fee, on the other hand, is not so strictly confined [95]; " if the gift is until marriage, and no longer, there is nothing to carry the gift beyond the marriage." [96] A devise of freeholds on trust for X " until he shall assign charge or otherwise dispose of the same or some part thereof or become bankrupt . . . or do something whereby the said annual income or some part thereof would become payable to or vested in some other person " has been held to give X a determinable fee.[97] On any of the events occurring X's estate would determine; if he died before any of them occurred, the fee simple would become absolute, for it ceases to be possible for any of them to occur.[98] But although a fee may thus be made determinable on alienation or on bankruptcy or on similar events, a limitation would probably be void if it were contrary to public policy for the fee to be determinable on the stated event, *e.g.*, if the event were the return to her husband of a wife who was separated from him.[99] In such a case the whole gift fails, for there is no proper limitation; whereas a corresponding conditional gift would become absolute, since the fee is properly limited even though the condition fails.[1]

(*e*) *Alienability of the expectancy.* At common law a right of entry and a possibility of reverter were descendible but not alienable *inter vivos*, for they were not themselves estates but merely special rights incident to other estates.[2] Nor did they become devisable by the Statute of Wills, 1540. But rights of entry for condition broken were made devisable in 1837 [3] and alienable *inter vivos* in 1845.[4] They may also now be made exercisable by any person,[5] not merely by the grantor or his successors in title, so that they may now be given to some other person at the moment of their creation. It is not

---

[95] *Brandon* v. *Robinson* (1811) 18 Ves. 429 at 432, 433; *Re Wilkinson* [1926] Ch. 842 at 847.

[96] *Morley* v. *Rennoldson* (1843) 2 Hare 570 at 580, *per* Wigram V.-C.; and see *Leong* v. *Chye* [1955] A.C. 648 at 660.

[97] *Re Leach* [1912] 2 Ch. 422; Jenks (1917) 33 L.Q.R. 14. *Re Machu* (1882) 21 Ch.D. 838 does not conflict with this, since there the fee simple was subject to a condition, and was not a determinable fee: Challis 261.

[98] *Re Leach* [1912] 2 Ch. 422 at 429.

[99] *Cf. Re Moore* (1888) 39 Ch.D. 116 (life interest in personalty determinable on wife returning to husband: held void).

[1] Co.Litt. 206a, b; *Re Greenwood* [1903] 1 Ch. 749; *cf. Sifton* v. *Sifton* [1938] A.C. 656.

[2] Co.Litt. 201a, n. 1; Challis 76n. For the unsettled state of the law in the twelfth and thirteenth centuries, see Maitland, " Remainders after Conditional Fees," Coll. Pp. ii, 174; Challis 428.

[3] Wills Act, 1837, s. 3; *Pemberton* v. *Barnes* [1899] 1 Ch. 544.

[4] R.P.A., 1845, s. 6; L.P.A., 1925, s. 4 (2); Wolst. & C. i, 60.

[5] L.P.A., 1925, s. 4 (3). This is subject to the perpetuity rule: *post*, p. 244.

quite so clear that a possibility of reverter is devisable [6] or assignable, but it seems highly probable that it is, at least after 1925.[7]

4. A base fee. A base fee is a particular kind of determinable fee.[8] The two essentials of a base fee are: (*a*) it continues only so long as the original grantor or any heirs of his body are alive; and (*b*) there is a remainder or reversion after it. Such estates are more fully dealt with below.[9]

Nature of modified fees. The owner of a modified fee has the same rights over the land as the owner of a fee simple absolute: thus the common law refused to restrain him from committing acts of waste,[10] such as opening and working mines. Equity, on the other hand, intervened to prevent the commission of equitable waste, *i.e.*, acts of wanton destruction,[11] although the owner of a fee simple absolute is under no such restraint; for where there is a modified fee, there is some other person interested in expectancy whose interest may need protecting.

At common law the owner of a modified fee could not convey a fee simple absolute but merely a fee liable to determination, for a man cannot convey more than he has.[12] But these interests now fall within the statute law dealing with settlements, so that they are now subject to the statutory powers of making sales and other dispositions.[13] A modified fee may, moreover, become enlarged into a fee simple absolute, *e.g.*, by the determining event becoming impossible [14]; and there are special rules for the enlargement of base fees.[15]

B. The Fee Tail

I. HISTORY

1. Before the Statute De Donis, 1285: fees conditional on the birth of issue. The hall-mark of a fee tail is a limitation to a person and the heirs *of his body*, restricting inheritance to his lineal descendants, as opposed to a fee simple which could pass to collateral

---

[6] Challis 228, 229, where "possibility of reverter" is apparently used to mean "right of entry."

[7] As a "future equitable interest" under L.P.A., 1925, s. 4 (2), which in any case is not exclusive of any interest of any kind. Only if "interest" is made synonymous with "estate" is there any difficulty in fitting possibilities into it. The only possibility specifically included is "a possibility coupled with an interest," which does not include a possibility of reverter: Challis 76n.

[8] Challis 325 *et seq.*

[9] *Post*, pp. 96–97. For the controversial but unimportant "qualified fee" (*e.g.*, "to A and the heirs of his father") see Co.Litt. 220b; Challis 269 *et seq.*; and *cf. ante*, pp. 53, 58.

[10] Challis 262; *Lewis Bowles's Case* (1615) 11 Co.Rep. 79b at 81a. For waste, see *post*, p. 103.

[11] Williams R.P. 414; *Re Hanbury's S. E.* [1913] 2 Ch. 357 at 365.

[12] Preston i. 435, 436.
[13] *Post*, pp. 314, 315.
[14] *Ante*, p. 77.
[15] *Post*, p. 96.

relations if there were no issue.[16] The fee tail is a creature of statute. Before the Statute *De Donis Conditionalibus*, 1285,[17] no such estate existed [18]; the common law recognised only two estates of freehold, the fee simple and the life estate, each existing in varying forms. The fee tail was created as a substitute for certain varieties of fee simple.[19] The learning relating to these has long been obsolete and only a short account of them will be given here.

(*a*) *Maritagium.* Perhaps the earliest variant of the fee simple was the *maritagium.* This was a gift of land, usually made by a father on the marriage of his daughter, whereby the land was conveyed to the daughter and her husband or one of them, and the heirs of their bodies. Such provisions existed in a variety of forms.[20]

(*b*) *Conditional fee.* By 1272 the courts had adopted a fixed construction of all gifts to a man and the heirs of his body, based on the differing forms of *maritagium.* The words " heirs of the body " seem to have been read as if they imposed a condition that issue should be born, the donee taking a fee simple conditional upon birth of issue, or, more shortly, a conditional fee. On the birth of issue, the donee was as free to alienate the land as if he had a fee simple.[21] But subject to any alienation the estate reverted to the donor when the donee and all his issue were dead. These rules fulfilled the common law's long favoured policy of making land more easily alienable,[22] but they were unpopular with landowners on account of the power of alienation, which frustrated the intentions of settlors. To remedy this the Statute *De Donis Conditionalibus* was made in 1285.

2. 1285–1834 : fee tail barrable by recovery or fine.

(*a*) *The new estate.* Strictly speaking, the Statute *De Donis Conditionalibus,* 1285, did not create any new estate but merely modified the rules relating to conditional fees [23] : the statute " is called the nurse, and not the mother, of estates-tail." [24] Nevertheless this modification was so important that the estate was thenceforward renamed " fee tail " or " estate tail," and for all practical purposes it

---

16 *Ante*, p. 41; *post*, p. 508.
17 Statute of Westminster II, 1285, c. 1.
18 Litt. 13. For the early history of entails, see H.E.L. iii, 111.
19 See Challis 60, 263.
20 See the 3rd edition of this book at p. 84, and the authorities there cited.
21 *Nevil's Case* (1605) 7 Co.Rep. 33a at 35.
22 Its practical wisdom now has statutory recognition: see L.P.A., 1925, s. 134, *post*, p. 506.
23 *Nevil's Case, supra,* at p. 35; *Newcomen* v. *Barkham* (1716) 2 Vern. 729 at 733; Challis 60, 287, 288.
24 *Goodright* v. *Wright* (1717) 1 P. Wms. 397 at 398, *per* Parker C.J.

may be regarded as a new estate.[25] The Statute provided that in the case of these conditional gifts, the will of the donor should be observed *secundum formam in carta doni expressam* (according to the form expressed in the deed of gift) and that notwithstanding any alienation by the donee, the land should descend to his issue on his death and revert to the donor when the donee and all his issue were dead.[26] Each heir of the body was ascertained according to the ordinary principles of inheritance.[27] Thus if the donee died leaving several sons, the eldest would inherit, except that if the customs of gavelkind or borough English applied, the land would pass to the heir of the donee's body according to the custom.[28] Any heir of the body of the original donee could inherit an estate tail, even though he was not heir of the body of the person last in possession.[29] This special rule of descent is still in force today.[30]

It should be observed that every fee tail, unlike a fee simple, had a reversion or remainder following it.[31] For on failure of the donee's lineal issue the land would still belong to the original donor in fee simple: the fee tail was a lesser estate which did not exhaust his interest. Alternatively he could also alienate this reversionary interest and thereby make someone entitled by way of remainder.

(*b*) *Inalienability.* The name " fee tail " indicated that the fee was *talliatum* or *taillé, i.e.,* cut down [32]; unlike the fee simple, which could descend to any class of heirs, a fee tail could descend only to a restricted class, namely, those who were issue of the original donee.[33] The Statute did not prevent a tenant in tail or his issue from alienating the land, but the estate so created could be defeated after their death by the heirs to the fee tail or by the reversioner or remainderman, as the case might be.[34] For purposes of disposition they had in effect only a life interest.[35] Nor could the rights of the issue be prejudiced by the tenant levying a fine [36] (a fine being a collusive action in which

[25] See *Willion* v. *Berkley* (1561) 1 Plowd. 223 at 248; H.E.L. ii, 350.
[26] The statute provided for a writ of " formedon in the descender " to enable the donee's issue to claim the land. Reversioners and remaindermen were already protected by writs of formedon in the reverter and formedon in the remainder: H.E.L. iii, 18; P. & M. ii, 28; (1940) 7 C.L.J. 238 (W. H. Humphreys); (1944) 8 C.L.J. 275, note 9 (S. J. Bailey); and occasionally a formedon in the descender had been used before the statute in cases where a tenant in tail died seised and the heir entitled under the entail was not also the heir general: (1956) 72 L.Q.R. 391 (S. F. C. Milsom). " Formedon " is from " forma doni."
[27] *Post*, p. 508.
[28] Rob.Gav. 119, 120.
[29] Williams R.P. 245.
[30] *Post*, p. 531.
[31] Challis, 298.
[32] Co.Litt. 18b.
[33] Co.Litt. 1b; Preston i, 420, 428.
[34] See note 26, *supra*.
[35] Strictly speaking, he could create a base fee: *post*, p. 88; Challis 322.
[36] Statute *De Donis*, 1285, s. 4.

the tenant agreed to judgment being entered against him [37]) or by any act of escheat or forfeiture.[38] The Statute therefore conceded to landowners what the common law would not allow them: the power to create a virtually inalienable estate. It "established a general perpetuity by Act of Parliament." [39]

(c) *Unbreakable settlements.* The Statute opened the door to elaborate settlements, and to all the mischiefs which attend settlements when there is no power of alienation. Since the rights of the issue could not be defeated by sale or gift, nor affected indirectly by any more limited transactions, such as leases or rentcharges, of a previous tenant in tail, it followed that the owner of entailed property lacked many of the most necessary powers of management. Nevertheless the entail provided what very many landed proprietors wanted: a means of tying their descendants to the family property, and of preserving it from forfeiture (a practical consideration in troubled times). "As the nobility were always fond of this statute, because it preserved their family estates from forfeiture, there was little hope of procuring repeal by the legislature." [40]

(d) *Fictitious actions.* For some two hundred years this " common grievance of the realm " [41] continued. But in the fifteenth century the courts, hostile as always to restraints upon alienation, began to countenance devices by which the Statute *De Donis Conditionalibus* could be frustrated.[42] The two successful devices were the common recovery and the fine. These were products of legal ingenuity, contrived and perfected in a period notable for formalism and fictitious processes. Each involved the use, or rather the abuse, of an action at law, and each took advantage of the binding effect of a judgment of the court. In their details they were highly complex and strongly flavoured with antiquity; but it is only their final effects which need now be understood.

(e) *The common recovery*

(1) THE ACTION. It seems clear from *Taltarum's Case*,[43] decided in 1472, that by then it was recognised that it was possible for a

[37] *Post*, p. 86.
[38] The escheat or forfeiture lasted only for the lifetime of the tenant in tail: Co.Litt. 392b; Challis 37. Entails became forfeitable for treason by 28 Hen. 8, c. 13, 1534, s. 5, and the Crown took a base fee (*post*, p. 88); Challis 328; Williams R.P. 115n.
[39] *Mildmay's Case* (1605) 6 Co.Rep. 40a.
[40] Bl.Comm. ii, 116, where the many inconveniences of entails are bewailed. But see n. 38, *supra*.
[41] Bl.Comm. ii, 116.   [42] H.E.L. iii, 118, 119.
[43] Y.B. 12 Edw. 4, Mich., fo. 14b, pl. 16, fo. 19a, pl. 25; 13 Edw. 4, Mich., fo. 1a, pl. 1. A full translation of the record and reports is in Kiralfy, *Source Book of English Law* (1957), pp. 86–99 (where the name of the case appears as *Talcarn's Case*, or in the modern style *Hunt* v. *Smith*); and there is an account of the case in Challis 309.

tenant in tail in possession to " bar " the entail by means of a recently invented process known as a common recovery. This was a collusive action in which the tenant in tail offered no defence to a claim to the land by a stranger. In effect the tenant in tail admitted that his title was bad, that he had no right to the land at all, and that the stranger should " recover " it. He was thus said to " suffer a recovery." The stranger brought an action and, there being no dispute, the court gave judgment in his favour.

(2) VOUCHER TO WARRANTY. A judgment, however, normally binds only the parties and persons claiming through them, *i.e.* (in our case) the tenant in tail and his issue.[44] In order to bar the claims of any reversioners and remaindermen a further artifice was needed, for their interests were not derived from the tenant in tail. This was achieved under the old law of warranty, whereby a grantor had to recompense the grantee with lands of equal value if the grantor's title turned out to be bad.[45] The tenant in tail " vouched to warranty " a collaborator who admitted (falsely) that he had granted the land with warranty to the tenant in tail, and suffered judgment for recompense to be given against him. Since this recompense was to be land, which would pass on to all concerned, it followed that reversioners and remaindermen were barred, for otherwise they would take twice over.[46] The fictitious element was that the court allowed this judgment on the warranty to be given against anyone nominated by the parties, without further investigation. Consequently a " man of straw " could be used, and when recoveries had become standardised the common crier of the court would obligingly fill this position for a small fee.[47]

(3) EFFECT. In the final result the stranger emerged as owner in fee simple[48]; all other claimants were barred and left to console themselves with a valueless judgment.[49] It then only remained for the stranger, the collusive claimant, to reconvey the land to the tenant

---

[44] Perhaps not even the issue in this case, since they claimed *per formam doni*: Cru.Dig. v, 375.

[45] *Post*, p. 602. Contrast the modern system of covenants for title: *ibid.*

[46] Challis 311. In the fully developed form of the common recovery the practice was to employ " double voucher " or even " treble voucher." An example of double voucher is given in Bl.Comm. ii, Appendix V; and see 3rd edition of this book, p. 88.

[47] Challis 311. For this purpose he was called " the common vouchee."

[48] *Martin* d. *Tregonwell* v. *Strachan* (1743) 5 T.R. 107n.; affd. Willes 444.

[49] *Capel's Case* (1593) 1 Co.Rep. 61b; *Cholmley's Case* (1597) 2 Co.Rep. 50a at 52a. There were certain limits to the operation of recoveries. They did not defeat incumbrances: Challis 314; Preston, *Conveyancing*, i, 16. Tenants holding under leases were in any case protected against fictitious recoveries by the statute for falsification of recoveries (21 Hen. 8, c. 15, 1529); other incumbrancers were protected, it seems, by a concession to expediency. Nor were tenants in fee simple allowed to suffer recoveries, *e.g.*, so as to bar rights of entry or possibilities of reverter: Shep.Touch. 40, nn. (*m*) and (*n*). Nor did recoveries bar the Crown, until 1833: F.R.A., 1833, s. 15.

in tail [50] or to pay the purchase-money if he was himself to buy it. In this way the entail was turned into a fee simple.

This triumphant device had one most important limitation. Since actions for land had to be brought against the person seised,[51] recoveries could not be suffered by a tenant in tail in remainder unless the freeholder in possession would collaborate [52]: if land was given " to A for life, remainder to B and the heirs of his body," B could not suffer a recovery during A's lifetime without the assistance of A. It was this limitation that the second device, the fine, was designed to circumvent.

(f) *The fine*

(1) THE ACTION. A fine was a " final " compromise (*finalis concordia*), a formal agreement which was entered in the court records to show the terms on which, with the court's leave, the action was discontinued.[53] The practice of " levying a fine " was of earlier origin than the common recovery, and was much used in early times as a mode of conveyance owing to its sanctity as a compromise approved by the court and registered in the records.[53] But as the Statute *De Donis Conditionalibus* expressly prohibited the barring of entails by fines,[54] legislation was necessary for this purpose. The Statute of Fines, 1489, which dealt with fines generally, provided a pretext for holding that a fine would thenceforth bar the issue in tail [55]; and an Act of 1540 confirmed this construction, so that the fine was immediately effective to bar the issue.[56]

(2) EFFECT OF FINE. A fine had the advantage that it could be levied without the concurrence of the tenant in possession.[57] But it

---

50 After the Statute of Uses, 1535 (*post*, p. 155), this step was automatic if a use was declared on the recovery: Challis 395.
51 *Ante*, p. 49; *post*, p. 1|169. The action used was a writ of entry in the post (for which see *post*, p. 1169); Bl.Comm. ii, Appendix V.
52 Challis 310; Cru.Dig. v, 274; Williams R.P. 106.
53 Williams R.P. 73n.; H.E.L. iii, 236 *et seq.* Originally a title acquired by fine was impregnable if not contested within a year and a day. This was modified by legislation, especially by the Statute of Fines, 1489, which made fines binding immediately on the parties " and their privies," and allowed other persons five years in which to make their claims: *ibid.* For " privies," see Challis 306, 307.
54 *Ante*, p. 85.
55 See Cru.Dig. v, 155, 156. Blackstone (Comm. ii, 354) says: " It seems to have been the intention of that politic prince, king Henry VII, to have covertly by this statute extended fines to have been a bar of estates-tail, in order to unfetter the more easily the estates of his powerful nobility, and lay them more open to alienations; being well aware that power will always accompany property."
56 32 Hen. 8, c. 36; Williams R.P. 103, 104; Challis 306, 307.
57 This was because a fine was the compromise of a personal action (an action of covenant: H.E.L. iii, 236) which could be brought against anyone. But one of the parties to a fine was required to have some interest, even though future, otherwise it could be set aside; Challis 393. *Cf. post*, p. 92.

was not so effective as a common recovery, for although it barred the rights of the issue in tail, it did not bar the owner of the subsequent remainder, reversion or other estate,[58] that is to say, the person who would be entitled to the land on failure of the heir of the body of the original tenant in tail. There was always some such person, either the donor or his successors (by way of reversion) or some designated stranger (by way of remainder). The estate produced by a fine was known as a " base fee." In effect a base fee was a determinable fee simple: it endured for as long as the entail would have continued if it had not been barred, and determined when the entail would have ended.[59] Thus if land was limited to A for life, remainder to B in tail, remainder to C in fee simple, and during A's lifetime B barred his entail by a fine in favour of X, X took a base fee. X and his successors in title remained entitled to the land for as long as B or any of his issue lived, but when they were all dead, C became entitled to the land. A base fee was therefore an unattractive interest in the eyes of a purchaser, and accordingly a tenant in tail in remainder would scarcely be able to sell his expectancy on favourable terms without the co-operation of the tenant in possession.

(3) POWER TO LEVY FINE. Though less effective, fines had a much wider scope than recoveries. A fine could be levied by one who had no entail but merely a hope of being the heir (*spes successionis*)[60] or who had a merely contingent or executory interest[61] in tail,[62] *i.e.*, an entail to which he would be entitled only if some specified event occurred. For example, a fine could be levied in B's lifetime by one of his children and this would be effective to bar the entail if it descended to that child or his issue in tail; and B could bar his entail even if it was given to him conditionally upon his outliving X, and X was still alive. Only the person seised could suffer a recovery; and if he would not collaborate, a fine was the only device available for barring an entail which had not yet fallen into possession.

It should, of course, be observed that not even a recovery barred estates *prior* to the entail. Thus in the above example a recovery suffered by B with A's consent would not affect A's life estate.[63]

---

58 *Margaret Podger's Case* (1613) 9 Co.Rep. 104a.
59 On base fees see Challis 325 *et seq.* A base fee was a fee simple, *i.e.*, it descended to the heirs general on intestacy, but (unlike any other fee simple: *ante*, p. 82; *post*, p. 184) it had a reversion or remainder expectant upon it.
60 Preston, *Conveyancing*, i, 219; Cru.Dig. v, 160; Shep.Touch. i, 25, 26n., where the decisions to this effect are criticised.
61 For such interests, see *post*, Chap. 5.
62 *Johnson* v. *Gabriel* (1593) Cro.Eliz. 122. The fine " operated by estoppel," and when the estate vested, it " fed the estoppel ": *Doe* d. *Christmas* v. *Oliver* (1829) 10 B. & C. 181 at 187. For " feeding the estoppel," see *post*, p. 646.
63 *Pledgard* v. *Lake* (1599) Cro.Eliz. 718; *Cuppledike's Case* (1602) 3 Co.Rep. 5b; and see *ante*, p. 86, n. 49.

(g) *Differences between fines and recoveries.* The main differences between fines and recoveries may be summarised as follows:

FINE	RECOVERY
(i) Action compromised.	(i) Action proceeded to judgment.
(ii) Consent of freehold tenant in possession not required.	(ii) Consent of freehold tenant in possession essential.
(iii) Available to all, including owners of future or contingent entails, and to expectant issue.	(iii) Available only to owners of vested entails.
(iv) Produced a base fee.	(iv) Produced a fee simple absolute.

Both these methods of barring entails became purely formal; all that a tenant had to do was to instruct his lawyers to take the necessary steps.[64] It may seem strange that by means of a recovery the rights of any remainderman or reversioner could be completely defeated, but the courts were prepared to sacrifice him upon the altar of free alienability of land.[65]

(h) *No unbarrable entails.* So far did the judges go to suppress the inconveniences of the Statute *De Donis Conditionalibus* that they created a rule that the power to suffer recoveries and levy fines was an inseparable incident of every entail, and that any attempt to hamper this power in any way was void, whether the attempt was made by way of proviso,[66] condition,[67] covenant,[68] limitation,[69] custom,[70] or otherwise.[71] Thus a condition that the tenant should not suffer a recovery was treated as repugnant to the entail and void,[72] so that the tenant could bar it with impunity. The interests of issue in tail, remaindermen and reversioners were by these means made entirely precarious, precisely contrary to the provisions of the statute. To revert to the above example, C's fee simple was safe during A's life-

---

64 For examples of the forms in use in the eighteenth century, see Bl.Comm. ii, Appendix V.
65 No technical rationalisation is possible. Willes C.J. said in 1744 that "when men attempt to give reasons for common recoveries they run into absurdities, and the whole of what they say is unintelligible jargon and learned nonsense": *Martin* d. *Tregonwell* v. *Strachan* (1744) 1 Wils.K.B. 66 at 73.
66 *Corbet's Case* (1600) 1 Co.Rep. 77b.
67 *Sonday's Case* (1611) 9 Co.Rep. 127b.
68 *Collins* v. *Plummer* (1708) 1 P.Wms. 104.
69 *Foy* v. *Hynde* (1620) Cro.Jac. 697.
70 *Taylor* v. *Shaw* (1665) Carter 6, 22.
71 *Mary Portington's Case* (1613) 10 Co.Rep. 35b; Fearne 256 *et seq.*; Cru.Dig. v, 381. See, however, *Hunt* v. *Bancroft* (1622) Ritchie 65.
72 *Mildmay's Case* (1605) 6 Co.Rep. 40a. The rule was not affected by F.R.A., 1833: see *Dawkins* v. *Lord Penrhyn* (1878) 4 App.Cas. 51 at 64.

time if A refused to co-operate with B in barring the entail; but if A consented to this, or died, C was completely at B's mercy.

3. The Fines and Recoveries Act, 1833. By the eighteenth century fines and recoveries had become purely formal, but no less dilatory, complicated and expensive.[73] But the barring of entails played a vital part in the mechanism of family settlements, representing as it did the law's fundamental compromise between restriction and alienability.[74] Simpler methods of forming entails were therefore provided by the Fines and Recoveries Act, 1833. This Act, recognised as a masterpiece of Parliamentary draftsmanship,[75] was designed to produce almost exactly the same results as the earlier law. It is still in force to-day.

(*a*) *Disentailing assurance.* In the first place the Act provided that an entail [76] could be barred by any assurance (*i.e.*, any conveyance or other transfer) which a fee simple owner could employ, except a will. Normally disentailing under the Act was effected by a conveyance in fee simple.[77] Unlike a common recovery, a disentailing assurance under the Act passed to the grantee a legal estate derived from the grantor, but enlarged from an entail into a fee simple.[78] It was necessary that the disentailing assurance should be either made or evidenced by a deed [79]; a mere declaration that the entail was barred was not enough, for an assurance was what the Act required. A declaration of trust sufficed,[80] but not a grant to trustees rendered ineffective by their disclaimer.[81] If the tenant barring the entail wished to retain the land himself, he conveyed it to some trustee for him [82]; if he wished to dispose of it, he made the disentailing assurance in favour of the grantee. It was necessary for every disentailing assurance to be enrolled within six calendar months of execution, formerly in the Court of Chancery, and later in the Central Office of the Supreme Court.[83] A conveyance which

---

[73] For the forms then in use see Bl.Comm. ii, Appendix V.
[74] See *post*, p. 283. *Cf.* Hayes i, 131 *et seq.*
[75] See Hayes i, 217, 218; H.E.L. xi, 380. The draftsman was the eminent conveyancer Brodie, who was also one of the Real Property Commissioners. But the Act was not without blemish: see *Re Wainwright* (1843) 1 Ph. 258 at 261, 262.
[76] Legal or equitable (s. 1 defines " estate " to include both). Equitable interests are dealt with in Chap. 4.
[77] A temporary disentailment could be effected by lease under ss. 15, 41. As to the disentailing effect of mortgages, see s. 21 and Challis 322, 323.
[78] *Lord Lilford* v. *Att.-Gen.* (1867) L.R. 2 H.L. 63.
[79] F.R.A., 1833, ss. 15, 40.
[80] *Carter* v. *Carter* [1896] 1 Ch. 62.
[81] *Peacock* v. *Eastland* (1870) L.R. 10 Eq. 17.
[82] Until 1926 he would convey to his own use under the Statute of Uses, 1535 (*post*, p. 162). Since 1925 he can convey to himself under L.P.A., 1925, s. 72 (3).
[83] F.R.A., 1883, s. 41; the former R.S.C., Ord. 61, r. 9, has now been replaced by Ord. 63, r. 10. Certain leases were excepted.

did not comply with the provisions of the Act did not bar the issue or the reversioner or remainderman; it produced a base fee liable to determination after the death of the tenant in tail, *e.g.*, by entry of the issue in tail.[84]

(*b*) *Protector of the settlement.* The effect of a disentailing assurance varied in a way modelled on the earlier law. The person whose consent would formerly have been necessary to a recovery was represented by the " protector of the settlement," whose status and powers were set forth in the Act. Accordingly if the tenant in tail was entitled in possession to the land, there was no protectorship. But if he was not entitled in possession under the instrument creating the entail, and some prior estate in possession existed (as where land was held by A for life with remainder to B in tail), then there was a protectorship. The protector of a settlement was normally the person in possession, *i.e.* (more precisely) the beneficial [85] owner of the first estate subsisting for the time being under the settlement, excluding a mere lease for years, but including a lease for years determinable on life [86]; and if there was no such person who was capable of acting, the court was the protector.[87] A protector remained such even though he parted with his own estate.[88]

(*c*) *Special protectors.* The settlor was, however, allowed to nominate a special protector, if he preferred, in the settlement creating the entail. Not more than three living persons might be appointed to this office, and subject to any contrary intention in the settlement, on the death of any of them the survivors were protector [89]; but the settlor could confer a power to fill up vacancies if he so wished.[90] Special protectors, however, were rarities.

The usual form of settlement gave the land to one person for life with remainder to other persons in tail, with an ultimate remainder in fee simple, *e.g.*, to A for life, remainder to B in tail, remainder to C in fee simple. In such a case there was a protectorship for so long as A lived. If no special protector had been appointed, A was the natural protector. But as soon as B's entail ceased to be in remainder and vested in possession (as on A's death) the protectorship, whether special or natural, ceased.[91]

---

[84] Challis 322.
[85] Contrast *Re Dudson's Contract* (1878) 8 Ch.D. 628 with *Re Blandy Jenkins' Estate, infra.*
[86] F.R.A., 1833, s. 22.
[87] *Ibid.* s. 33, apparently overlooked in *Re Blandy Jenkins' Estate* [1917] 1 Ch. 46: see *Re Darnley's W. T.* [1970] 1 W.L.R. 405.
[88] F.R.A., 1833, ss. 22, 27; Hayes i, 181.
[89] *Bell* v. *Holtby* (1873) L.R. 15 Eq. 178; *Cohen* v. *Bayley Worthington* [1908] A.C. 97.
[90] F.R.A., 1833, s. 32.
[91] *Ibid.*, ss. 22, 32, 34.

(*d*) *Effect of disentailing.* The importance of the protectorship was that a disentailing assurance executed without the protector's consent produced only a base fee.[92] But if there was no protectorship, or if there was a protector but he concurred in the disposition (whether by executing the disposition[93] or by executing a separate deed even after the disposition[94]), a disentailing assurance conveyed a fee simple absolute, free from all subsequent limitations and provisions, including any which would defeat[95] or postpone[96] the entail in specified events.[97] This in effect preserved the distinction between fines and recoveries: the protector was absolutely unfettered in exercising his discretion whether or not to concur in the disentailment,[98] and although an agreement to withhold consent was void,[99] he could refuse to consent unless he was given a bribe.[1]

Although disentailment enlarged the estate barred into a fee simple, it could not expand the property in which the entail existed. Thus if a rentcharge had been created in favour of X in tail, he could obtain only a base fee in it by barring the entail; for the duration of the rentcharge was limited to that of the entail.[2] But if the rentcharge had been given to X in tail with remainder to Y in fee simple, X would have obtained a fee simple in it.[3]

(*e*) *Power to disentail.* Before 1834 a person entitled to a mere *spes successionis* could levy a fine,[4] but the Act provided that such a person could no longer effect a bar.[5] Any other future interest in tail, even though merely a contingent or executory interest, could be barred under the Act, subject to the provisions already explained.[6] Thus if an entail is limited to whoever succeeds to a specified dukedom, any person capable of succeeding to it may bar his contingent interest,[7] even though the contingency involves a *spes successionis*.

---

92 *Ibid.*, s. 34.
93 *Re Wilmer's Trusts* [1910] 2 Ch. 111.
94 F.R.A., 1833, ss. 42–47; *Whitmore-Searle* v. *Whitmore-Searle* [1907] 2 Ch. 332.
95 *Re Knox* [1912] 1 I.R. 288.
96 *Milbank* v. *Vane* [1893] 3 Ch. 79.
97 F.R.A. 1833, ss. 15, 22, 34.
98 *Ibid.*, ss. 36, 37.
99 *Ibid.*, s. 36.
1 *Bankes* v. *Le Despencer* (1843) 11 Sim. 508 at 527.
2 *Pinkerton* v. *Pratt* [1915] 1 I.R. 406.
3 *Re Franks's Estate* [1915] 1 I.R. 383.
4 *Ante*, p. 88.
5 F.R.A., 1833, s. 20.
6 *Ibid.*, s. 15; Hayes i, 194, 195; *Re St. Albans' W. T.*, *infra*. As to barring of equitable entails, see *post*, p. 94. Equity adopted fines and recoveries (Cru.Dig. v, 181, 384–389), and the Act of 1833 extended to trusts.
7 *Re St. Albans' W. T.* [1963] Ch. 365; yet see *Re Midleton's W. T.* [1969] 1 Ch. 600.

II. RIGHTS OF A TENANT IN TAIL

Apart from the peculiar law about alienation a tenant in tail had all the rights of enjoyment of a fee simple owner. He was not liable for waste of any kind, and he could therefore cut timber, open mines or pull down buildings as he pleased,[8] even if some statute restrained him from barring the entail.[9] A statute of 1540 empowered him to grant leases binding on his issue (but not remaindermen or reversioners) for terms of not more than twenty-one years or a period of three lives.[10] This power remained until superseded by the new law of settlements in the nineteenth century.[11]

III. ENTAILS OF COPYHOLD

The Statute *De Donis*, 1285, did not extend to copyholds, so that even in 1925 a conveyance of copyhold land " to X and the heirs of his body " gave X a conditional fee.[12] But many manors had a custom that copyholds might be entailed, and this custom was allowed to be valid despite the theoretical difficulty that customs must be deemed to have originated before 1189 [13] and entails were unknown until 1285.[14] These customary entails were generally subject to the same principles as those arising under the statute. They could therefore be barred, but the proceedings had to take place in the manorial court and the formalities varied. Recoveries, surrenders, forfeitures and regrants were all in use before 1834.[15] The Fines and Recoveries Act, 1833, made a surrender (*i.e.*, the normal form of conveyance of copyhold land) the only effective disentailing assurance for copyholds.[16] The Act applied generally to entailed copyholds, and accordingly introduced the protector of the settlement in the same manner as for lands of freehold tenure.[17]

At the beginning of 1926 all copyhold tenure was converted into freehold,[18] so that no further conditional fees can be created by grants limited to heirs of the body in manors where there was no custom of entail.

---

8 Williams R.P. 114, 198; *Lord Glenorchy* v. *Bosvilie* (1733) Ca.t.Talb. 3 at 16 (not liable for equitable waste).

9 *Att.-Gen.* v. *Duke of Marlborough* (1813) 3 Madd. 498.

10 32 Hen. 8, c. 28; and see *Att.-Gen.* v. *Duke of Marlborough, supra*, at p. 532.

11 *Post*, Chap. 6. As to leases by disentailing assurance, see *ante*, p. 90, n. 77.

12 Scriven 46, 56.

13 *Post*, p. 821.

14 Challis 263–268; Williams R.P. 511–514. Many eminent real property lawyers exercised their imaginations in attempting to justify this paradox.

15 Scriven 46, 47.

16 F.R.A., 1833, s. 50. But as to equitable entails see ss. 50, 53.

17 F.R.A., 1833, ss. 50–52.

18 *Ante*, p. 33.

IV. TYPES OF ENTAIL

The various types of entail, such as special tail or tail male, have already been considered.[19] Entails may be made determinable, or subject to conditions, in the same way as a fee simple or any other estate.[20]

V. PRESENT LAW

The Law of Property Act, 1925, has made some important amendments to the law of entails, but the general principles remain as before 1926. The following are the principal changes.

1. **Existence only in equity.** It is now no longer possible for a fee tail to exist as a legal estate.[21] The significance of this will appear in Chapter 4. After 1925 all entails must exist as equitable interests behind a trust. This means that the legal estate in fee simple must be vested in some trustees or trustee (who may be the tenant in tail himself) on trust for the person entitled in tail and everyone else interested in the land. This does not alter anyone's rights of enjoyment: only the bare legal ownership is affected. Since an entail is no longer the legal estate for which the land itself is held, but only an interest under a trust, the proper title for an entail is no longer " estate tail " or " fee tail," but " entailed interest." Similarly a " base fee " can no longer be a legal estate but exists only as an equitable interest in the nature of a base fee. The Fines and Recoveries Act, 1833, still applies to these equitable interests in the same way as before 1926.[22]

2. **Personalty entailable.** Any property, real or personal, may be entailed after 1925.[23] This was not so before 1926, for the Statute *De Donis*, 1285, applied only to " tenements," *i.e.*, property held in tenure, real property.[24] Nor could an entail subsist in any property which was not a hereditament (*i.e.*, inheritable), for otherwise the heirs of the body would have nothing to take. Thus the land itself, and inheritable rights in realty such as perpetual rent-charges[25] (*e.g.*, £100 per annum charged on Blackacre), could be entailed, but life estates (which were not inheritable) and leaseholds and other personalty could not be entailed.[26] Before 1926

---

19 *Ante*, p. 57.
20 Litt. 326; Challis 253; Preston ii, 361, 362: *Stanhope* v. *Thacker* (1716) Prec. Ch. 435; and see *ante*, p. 74.
21 L.P.A., 1925, s. 1; *post*, p. 134.
22 It is continued in force by L.P.Am.A., 1924, 9th Sched.
23 L.P.A., 1925, s. 130 (1).
24 Challis 43, 47, 61.
25 For such hereditaments see *post*, p. 787.
26 *Leventhorpe* v. *Ashbie* (1635) 1 Roll.Abr. 831, pl. 1; *Leonard Lovie's Case* (1614) 10 Co.Rep. 78a; Co.Litt. 20a, n. (5). But as to life estates, see *post*, p. 102.

a gift of personalty " to A and the heirs of his body " or " to A in tail " gave A the absolute ownership of the personalty, whether the gift was by deed or will.[27] Informal words such as " to A and his issue " or " to A and his descendants " usually gave the property to A and such of his issue or descendants as were alive at the relevant date.[28]

Since 1925 entails can be created in personalty, and all the rules applying to entails of realty (*e.g.,* as to words of limitation, barring, interests equivalent to a base fee, and the like) apply to entails of personalty.[29] But it is expressly provided that if after 1925 personalty is directed " to be enjoyed or held with, or upon trusts corresponding to trusts affecting " land which is already held in tail, this will be sufficient to entail the personalty,[30] provided this exact wording is used.[31]

3. No special customs of descent. The old law of inheritance still applies to entails, for they could not exist if it did not.[32] But on a death after 1925 an entail (if unbarred) descends according to the *general* law in force before 1926, so that special customs such as gavelkind are excluded.[33]

4. No new special protectors. Although any special protector appointed before 1926 continues in office, no special protector can be appointed after 1925.[34]

5. No enrolment. A disentailing assurance made after 1925 need not be enrolled.[35]

6. Barring by will. By virtue of section 176 of the Law of Property Act, 1925, a tenant in tail can now bar his entail by will, and thus dispose of the fee simple or any other estate. This power is subject to a number of limitations:

(*a*) It applies only to entails in possession: there is no power to bar an entail in remainder by will, even if the protector consents.

(*b*) The tenant in tail must be of full age.

---

27 Norton, *Deeds*, 376 (deed); *Dawson* v. *Small* (1874) 9 Ch.App. 651 (will); and see *Portman* v. *Viscount Portman* [1922] 2 A.C. 473.
28 *Re Hammond* [1924] 2 Ch. 276; see *ante*, p. 59. As to the " relevant date," when the class closes, see *post*, p. 501.
29 L.P.A., 1925, s. 130 (1).
30 *Ibid.*, s. 130 (3).
31 *Re Jones* [1934] Ch. 315 at 321. *Quaere* why the rule should be so strict: *cf. ante*, p. 53 for referential limitations of a fee simple before 1926.
32 A.E.A., 1925, s. 45 (2); *post*, p. 531.
33 L.P.A., 1925, s. 130 (4); *Re Higham* [1937] 2 All E.R. 17 (land disgavelled by A.E.A., 1925, s. 51 (2)). For gavelkind, see *ante*, p. 20.
34 L.P.A., 1925, 7th Sched., repealing F.R.A., 1833, s. 32.
35 L.P.A., 1925, s. 133.

(c) The will must be either executed after 1925 or confirmed by a codicil executed after 1925.

(d) The will must refer specifically either to—

    (i) the property (*e.g.*, " Blackacre "),[36] or

    (ii) the instrument under which it was acquired (*e.g.*, " all the property to which I succeeded under Uncle Harry's will "), or

    (iii) entails generally (*e.g.*, " all property to which I am entitled in tail ").

This power extends to all entailed property, whether real or personal, whenever the entail was created. Further, it allows the owner of a base fee in possession to enlarge it by a disposition by will, provided that he complies with the above conditions, and provided that he is capable of enlarging it into a fee simple absolute without the consent of anyone else.[37] But the section does not apply to a tenant in tail after possibility or to a tenant in tail restrained by statute from barring his entail.[38] Except so far as is necessary to give effect to the will, the entail or base fee is unaffected[39]; thus if instead of disposing of the fee simple in the entailed land the testator merely devises a life interest, the entail will resume its natural devolution when the life interest ceases.

VI. BASE FEES

The nature and mode of creation of base fees have already been considered.[40] Base fees have always been unsatisfactory interests in land since they determine on failure of the heirs of the body of the persons creating them. Nowadays they are rarely met. A base fee in possession could, however, be enlarged into a fee simple absolute in the same way as a fee tail, *i.e.*, by the former tenant in tail (and not the owner of the base fee) suffering a recovery.[41] Recoveries were abolished in 1833,[42] and the rules as to enlargement are now statutory. If land is given to A for life, remainder to B in tail, remainder to C in fee simple, a base fee created by B can be enlarged as follows.

(a) *New disentailment*: by the former tenant in tail (*i.e.*, B) executing a fresh disentailing assurance with the consent of the protector (A), or after the protectorship has ceased (*e.g.*, after A's

---

[36] See *Acheson* v. *Russell* [1951] Ch. 67 (" all other my estate and interest " in the property held sufficiently specific).   [37] As to enlargement, see below.
[38] For these see *post*, pp. 97, 98.
[39] L.P.A., 1925, ss. 130 (4), 176 (1).
[40] *Ante*, pp. 88, 91.
[41] Challis 335 ; Cru.Dig. v, 373 ; Shep.Touch. 37n.
[42] *Ante*, p. 89.

death).[43] This can be done by B even after the base fee has been conveyed to a purchaser; and if B is dead, his eldest son (or whoever would have succeeded to the entail) can do it.[44] But the purchaser himself, it seems, has no power of enlargement.[45]

(*b*) *Acquisition of reversion*: by the owner of the base fee acquiring the immediate remainder or reversion in fee simple (*i.e.*, by B, or any person to whom he has conveyed the base fee, acquiring C's fee simple). By statute [46] this does not merge the base fee in the remainder or reversion and so subject the owner of the base fee to any burdens attached to the remainder or reversion, such as a mortgage, but enlarges the base fee into a fee simple absolute free from any incumbrances on the remainder or reversion.

(*c*) *Long possession*: by the owner of the base fee (*i.e.*, B or anyone to whom he has conveyed it) remaining in possession of the land for twelve years after the protectorship has ceased.[47] This prospect of automatic enlargement in twelve years after obtaining possession makes a base fee a somewhat less unattractive proposition to a purchaser.

(*d*) *Devise*: by a gift by will complying with section 176 of the Law of Property Act, 1925.[48] This power is exercisable only by a person who is entitled to a base fee in possession and who could enlarge it without the concurrence of any person. Thus B can enlarge his base fee by will if the protectorship has ceased before he dies. But if B has conveyed the base fee to some other person, neither B nor that person can enlarge it by will, for B is not in possession, and the person to whom he conveyed is not within the section.[49]

VII. INTERESTS IN TAIL AFTER POSSIBILITY

A tenant in special tail loses all possibility of having inheritable issue if the specified spouse predeceases him (or her) without leaving issue. He then becomes "a tenant in tail after possibility of issue extinct," or, for brevity, "a tenant in tail after possibility." [50] For example, if land is given "to A and the heirs of his body begotten

---

[43] F.R.A., 1833, ss. 19, 35.
[44] *Ibid.*, s. 19.
[45] *Bankes* v. *Small* (1887) 36 Ch.D. 716; Williams R.P. 109, n. (*c*).
[46] F.R.A., 1833, s. 39; Challis 336. It was otherwise before 1834: *Earl of Shelburne* v. *Biddulph* (1748) 6 Bro.P.C. 356.
[47] Limitation Act, 1939, s. 11, replacing Real Property Limitation Acts, 1833, s. 23, and 1874, s. 6. These Acts are dealt with *post*, Chap. 16.
[48] *Ante*, p. 95.
[49] L.P.A., 1925, s. 176 (3).
[50] Litt. 32, 33.

on Mary," and Mary dies without leaving issue, A is a tenant in tail after possibility. Such a tenant is in a peculiar position,[51] for—

(i) unlike an ordinary tenant in tail, he cannot bar the entail[52]; the reversion or remainder is therefore bound to take effect after his death; and

(ii) although like other tenants in tail he is not liable for voluntary waste,[53] he is liable for equitable waste (wanton destruction).[54] Since the reversion or remainder is certain to fall in, the property is to this extent protected by the rule of equity.

A tenant in tail after possibility is therefore in some respects[55] in the position of a tenant for life. This interest can arise only on the death of the spouse specified in the limitation, *i.e.*, out of a special tail; for even if a tenant in general tail is unmarried and of a great age, it is always deemed possible that he or she will marry and have issue.[56]

VIII. UNBARRABLE ENTAILS

1. The rule. It became a rule, as has been seen, that it was impossible to create an unbarrable entail, and that any attempt to restrain the tenant from barring was ineffective.[57] Thus a limitation or condition requiring that the tenant should not suffer a common recovery was repugnant to the entail and so void. This rule was not affected by the Fines and Recoveries Act, 1833.[58]

2. Exceptions. Despite this general rule there are certain entails which cannot be barred. These are:

(i) An interest in tail after possibility (as explained above).

(ii) Entails created by the Crown for services rendered to the Crown, the reversion being in the Crown.[59]

(iii) Entails made unbarrable by special Acts of Parliament, such as the entails given to reward the first Duke of Marlborough[60] and the first Duke of Wellington.[61]

3. Persons who cannot bar entails. Certain persons are unable to bar an entail, even if the entail is one which can be barred.

---

51 More fully investigated in Co.Litt. 28a.
52 32 Hen. 8, c. 31, 1540; 14 Eliz. 1, c. 8, 1572; F.R.A., 1833, s. 18 (inadvertently repealed by L.P.(Am.)A., 1924, 10th Sched. and revived by Expiring Laws Act, 1925).   53 *Williams* v. *Williams* (1810) 12 East 209.
54 *Cooke* v. *Whaley* (1701) 1 Eq.Ca.Abr. 400; *Anon.* (1704) Free.Ch. 278; and see *post*, p. 105.   55 See *Lewis Bowles's Case* (1615) 11 Co.Rep. 79b at 80a.
56 Co.Litt. 28a.   57 *Ante*, p. 89.
58 See *Dawkins* v. *Lord Penrhyn* (1878) 4 App.Cas. 51 at 64.
59 34 & 35 Hen. 8, c. 20, 1543; F.R.A., 1833, s. 18 (as to which see n. 52, *supra*); *Robinson* v. *Giffard* [1903] 1 Ch. 865.
60 6 Anne, c. 6, 1706, s. 5; 6 Anne, c. 7, 1706, s. 4.
61 54 Geo. 3, c. 161, 1814, s. 28.

(a) *Infants*. Before 1833, for technical reasons, infants could not bar entails [62]; but although it is sometimes said that they cannot do so now, there is nothing in the Fines and Recoveries Act, 1833, to prevent this.[63] However, infants cannot make irrevocable grants,[64] and the possibility of revocation means that no entail barred by an infant is a marketable interest until the infant has come of age and confirmed the disentailment. But an infant's disentailing assurance seems to be valid until revoked, so that if no steps are taken to revoke it at eighteen (or by the personal representative in case of death during infancy) it will ripen into an effective disposition. An infant may disentail in his own favour so as to bar the interests of those in remainder or reversion; but, owing to a special provision of the Administration of Estates Act, 1925, this will be an effective bar only if the infant reaches full age or marries.[65] The court also has power to appoint a person to bar an infant's entail where this is for his maintenance, education or benefit.[66]

(b) *Some married women*. Certain married women and widows could not bar entails but these disabilities have long been repealed.[67]

(c) *Lunatics*. Mental patients cannot bar entails. But although the mental patient cannot bar the entail, this can be done under an order of the judge or the Court of Protection, *e.g.*, by his receiver.[68]

(d) *Bankrupts*. A bankrupt cannot bar his entails; this can be done only by his trustee in bankruptcy.[69]

C. The Life Estate

After 1925 an interest in land for life can no longer exist as a legal estate but only as an equitable interest.[70] In general, the law of life estates set out below appears to apply equally to the corresponding life interests after 1925; at all events, this is assumed in practice.[71]

---

[62] Cru.Dig. v, 127 (fine), 348–350 (recovery); and see *Porter* v. *Bradley* (1789) 3 T.R. 143 at 146.

[63] There is no direct authority on the point since 1833. The courts have ordered or authorised infants to disentail or make binding dispositions under certain statutes, *e.g.*, 11 Geo. 4 & 1 Will. 4, c. 47, 1830, s. 11; see *Radcliffe* v. *Eccles* (1836) 1 Keen 130; Sugden, *New Statutes relating to Real Property* (2nd ed., 1862), pp. 205, 209, 414.

[64] *Post*, p. 991.

[65] A.E.A., 1925, s. 51 (3); *post*, p. 991.

[66] T.A., 1925, s. 53: *Re Meux* [1958] Ch. 154; *Re Lansdowne's W. T.* [1967] Ch. 603.

[67] See 3rd edition of this book, p. 101.

[68] Mental Health Act, 1959, Part VIII. The Act repeals L.P.A., 1925, s. 171; *post*, p. 997.

[69] Bankruptcy Act, 1914, s. 55 (5).

[70] L.P.A., 1925, s. 1; *post*, p. 134.

[71] See, *e.g.*, *Re Harker's W. T.* [1938] Ch. 323.

I. TYPES OF LIFE ESTATE

The two types of life estate were the ordinary life estate for the life of the tenant and the estate *pur autre vie*.

1. Estate for the life of the tenant. This arose either—

  (i) by express limitation, as by a grant "to A for life"[72]; or

  (ii) by operation of law, as in the case of curtesy and dower.[73]

2. Estate pur autre vie. An estate *pur autre vie*[74] was an estate which was granted for the life of someone other than the tenant. The person whose life measured the duration of the estate was called the "*cestui que vie*."[75] More than one *cestui que vie* could be named, and the estate could be limited either for the longest or for the shortest (*i.e.*, for the joint lives) of such persons.[76] An estate *pur autre vie* could arise either—

  (i) by the owner of a life estate (or an entail after possibility[77]) assigning it to another. *Nemo dat quod non habet* (nobody can give what he has not got): the assignor could create no interest which would last for longer than his own life; or

  (ii) by express grant, *e.g.*, "to A for the life of X."

  (*a*) *Nature of the estates.* Both types of life estate were estates of freehold,[78] but neither was a freehold of inheritance, for neither could descend to the tenant's heir. This was self-evident in the case of an ordinary life estate. But if A held for the life of B and predeceased B, what was to happen to the residue of A's estate? It had not yet ceased,[79] but A's heir could not inherit as such. This problem was solved by the special rules of occupancy set out below. If A had alienated before his death the same problem would present itself on the death of the alienee (not of A) before that of the *cestui que vie*.[80]

---

[72] *Ante*, p. 42.

[73] *Post*, p. 514.

[74] More correctly, but less commonly, "*pur auter vie*": Challis 356. Much of the learning about this estate will be found in *Doe* d. *Jeff* v. *Robinson* (1828) 2 Man. & Ry. 249, and the notes thereon.

[75] Difficulties in proving the existence of a *cestui que vie* were dealt with by Acts of 1666 (18 & 19 Car. 2, c. 11, as to presumption of death after seven years' absence from the realm) and 1707 (6 Anne, c. 72, as to production of a *cestui que vie* to prevent concealment of death): see, *e.g.*, *Re Owen* (1878) 10 Ch.D. 166).

[76] Challis 356.

[77] Challis 357; for such entails, see *ante*, p. 97.

[78] Litt. 57.

[79] *Utty Dale's Case* (1590) Cro.Eliz. 182.

[80] Challis 362.

Both types of life estate could be made determinable or subject
to conditions subsequent.[81] Limitations of this kind were often found
in settlements, for example, where a life interest was given to a wife,
if she should survive her husband, " during her widowhood " or to
a man " until he may become bankrupt." The principles governing
such determinable or conditional life interests were probably [82] the
same as those governing the corresponding types of fee simple.[83]

(b) *Occupancy.* At common law a tenant *pur autre vie* could
not devise his estate,[84] and it always devolved on his death according
to the rules of occupancy. " Occupancy " was invented to explain
the title to land which was neither inheritable nor devisable, and
which therefore would belong to the first occupier (as the first person
to get seisin) after the death of the tenant *pur autre vie.*[85] " He that
can first hap it, shall enjoy out the term." [86]

(1) SPECIAL OCCUPANCY. If an estate *pur autre vie* was granted
" to A and his heirs," on A's death the land passed to A's heir (*e.g.,*
the youngest son in the case of borough English [87]) as special
occupant for the rest of the life of the *cestui que vie.*[88] The heir was
allowed this special right to occupy the land by reason of the mention
of " heirs " in the grant; the heir did not take by descent from A,
and the land in his hands was not liable for A's debts.[89]

(2) GENERAL OCCUPANCY. If the estate *pur autre vie* was merely
granted " to A " without any mention of his heirs, A's heir had no
special claim to the land,[90] for it was not inheritable. The first
person to enter the land after A's death was therefore entitled to it
as " general occupant " for the rest of the life of the *cestui que vie,*[91]
free from liability for A's debts.[92]

(3) STATUTE OF FRAUDS. This unsatisfactory position was
changed by the Statute of Frauds, 1677.[93] By this—

(i) a tenant *pur autre vie* was enabled to dispose of his interest
by will;

---

[81] Co.Litt. 42a; *Brandon* v. *Robinson* (1811) 18 Ves. 429; and see *Re Evans's Contract* [1920] 2 Ch. 469. See also *ante,* p. 78.
[82] In *Re Machu* (1882) 21 Ch.D. 838 at 842 the possibility of determinable interests being subject to special rules was raised but not decided.
[83] *Ante,* pp. 74 *et seq.*
[84] Challis 362. The Statute of Wills, 1540 (*post,* p. 160) did not apply: *ibid.* And see *Re Inman* [1903] 2 Ch. 241 at 246.
[85] As to titles based on seisin and possession, see *post,* p. 1004.
[86] Finch, *Law* (ed. of 1678), 115, quoted by Challis 359n.; Bl.Comm. ii, 258.
[87] *Baxter* v. *Doudswell* (1675) 2 Lev. 138.
[88] Challis 358, and notes.
[89] *Doe* d. *Blake* v. *Luxton* (1795) 6 T.R. 289 at 291.
[90] *Re Sheppard* [1897] 2 Ch. 67.   [91] Co.Litt. 41b; Preston i, 259; Challis 359.
[92] Halsb., 2nd ed., Vol. 27, p. 704.   [93] s. 12.

(ii) if he failed to do so and there was no special occupant, the estate devolved on the tenant's personal representatives on trust (as was later provided) for the next-of-kin, so that it was distributable in the same way as personal property [94];

(iii) whether it passed to the heir or personal representatives, it was made available for the payment of the debts of the deceased.

No new general occupancy could thereafter arise [95]; but special occupancy remained [96] until the new law of intestacy came into force in 1926.[97] Thenceforth the tenant's interest passes like any other property to his personal representatives, who hold it in trust for the persons entitled under his will or intestacy.

(4) COPYHOLDS. In the case of copyholds seisin was in the lord, so that he was invariably entitled in lieu of a general occupant unless there was a custom to the contrary.[98] But special occupancy was recognised in copyhold lands as elsewhere,[99] since it was founded on a right of entry in the heir rather than the fact of seisin. It also, of course, was abolished in 1925.[1]

(c) *Quasi-entails.* An estate *pur autre vie,* not being an estate of inheritance, could not be entailed under the Statute *De Donis,* 1285.[2] But if an estate for the life of X was granted " to Z and the heirs of his body," an estate known as a quasi-entail was created.[2] Until terminated by X's death this estate devolved on the heirs of Z's body successively in the same way as an entail, but it was not a true entail because the heirs took not by descent but as special occupants.[3] Even before the Fines and Recoveries Act, 1833, it could be barred by an ordinary deed of conveyance, and that Act did not make it necessary for the deed to be enrolled.[4] Such a conveyance could bar not only the rights of the heirs of the body, which were merely rights of occupancy, but also the rights of any remainder-man.[5] But, as in the case of entails proper, a quasi-tenant in tail

---

[94] For the legislation of 1740 and 1837 see Williams R.P. 138; Challis 362: *Witter* v. *Witter* (1730) 3 P.Wms. 99.   [95] Statute of Frauds, 1677, s. 12.

[96] See, *e.g., Doe* d. *Jeff* v. *Robinson* (1828) 8 B. & C. 296.

[97] See A.E.A., 1925, s. 45 (1) (a).

[98] *Doe* d. *Foster* v. *Scott* (1825) 4 B. & C. 706 at 714; *Smartle* v. *Penhallow* (1703) 2 Ld.Raym. 994 at 1000. The legislation of 1677 and 1740 did not apply to copyholds, but corresponding provisions were applied to them by the Wills Act, 1837, ss. 3, 6: Challis 362; *Zouch* d. *Forse* v. *Forse* (1806) 7 East 186.

[99] *Doe* d. *Lempriere* v. *Martin* (1777) 2 Wm.Bl. 1148.

[1] *Ante,* p. 33.   [2] Challis 362, 363; Williams R.P. 139, 140.

[3] *Ibid.*; *Low* v. *Burron* (1734) 3 P.Wms. 262; *Ex p. Sterne* (1801) 6 Ves. 156 at 158.

[4] Fearne 499; Tudor L.C. 102 (listing the dealings that would bar a quasi-entail); Williams R.P. 140.

[5] *Re Michell* [1892] 2 Ch. 87; Challis 360n., 363; Fearne 498, 499; Tudor L.C. 102.

in remainder could bar a later remainderman only with the consent of the tenant in possession.[6] The analogy between estates created out of a fee simple and those created out of a life estate was developed as far as possible.[7]

II. POSITION OF A TENANT FOR LIFE AT COMMON LAW

A tenant for life at common law was subject to important restrictions imposed by the law of waste (particularly as to timber and minerals), and by the rules relating to emblements and fixtures. These rules still apply to the modern equitable life interests.[8]

Waste

1. Function. Although the law of waste is of importance in other connections, notably in the law of landlord and tenant, it is most suitably considered in relation to life interests, where it is applicable both to ordinary life interests and to interests *pur autre vie*.[9] Its object is to prevent a limited owner, such as a tenant for life or years, despoiling the land to the prejudice of those in reversion or remainder. Their remedy is to bring an action for damages or to apply for an injunction[10]; and if the tenant for life has profited from the waste (*e.g.*, by cutting timber), he may be made liable for the money received from the sale, or an account.[11]

There was an ancient writ of waste which gave treble damages and recovery of the place wasted[12]; but as it had serious defects, and could be used only by the owner of a vested estate of inheritance immediately expectant on the estate in possession,[13] it was superseded by the remedies just mentioned,[14] and abolished in 1833.[15]

2. Nature. Technically, waste consists of any act which alters the nature of the land, whether for the better or for the worse, *e.g.*,

---

[6] *Forster* v. *Forster* (1741) 2 Atk. 259; *Slade* v. *Pattison* (1835) 5 L.J.Ch. 51; Challis 363.

[7] See *Re Barber* (1881) 18 Ch.D. 624 at 629.

[8] This was assumed in *Re Harker's W. T.* [1938] Ch. 323, but criticised at (1938) 2 Conv.(N.S.) 233 (H. Potter).

[9] See *Edward Seymor's Case* (1612) 10 Co.Rep. 95b at 98a.

[10] *Woodhouse* v. *Walker* (1880) 5 Q.B.D. 404 (damages); *Lowndes* v. *Norton* (1864) 33 L.J.Ch. 583 (injunction).

[11] *Seagram* v. *Knight* (1867) 2 Ch.App. 628 at 632; *Dashwood* v. *Magniac* [1891] 3 Ch. 306.

[12] Statute of Gloucester, 1278.

[13] But see *Bacon* v. *Smith* (1841) 1 Q.B. 345.

[14] For the common law, see notes to *Greene* v. *Cole* (1682) 2 Wms.Saund. 252; for equity, see *Garth* v. *Cotton* (1750) 1 Ves.Sen. 546; Wh. & T. ii, 927, 962; J.A., 1925, s. 45 (3); and see generally Tudor L.C. 147–157.

[15] Along with the real actions: *post*, p. 1172.

the conversion of arable land into a woodland or vice versa.[16] Four types of waste must be considered: ameliorating, permissive, voluntary and equitable.[17]

(a) *Ameliorating waste.* Alterations which improve the land, such as converting dilapidated store buildings into dwellings [18] or a farm into a market-garden,[19] constitute what is paradoxically termed ameliorating waste. Claims for this type of waste find little favour in the courts unless the whole character of the property has been changed. Where improvements have been made, an action for damages will fail because no damage has been suffered, and an injunction will be awarded only if the court thinks fit.[20]

(b) *Permissive waste.* This is failure to do that which ought to be done, as by the non-repair of buildings [21] or sea or river walls,[22] or the failure to clean out a ditch or moat so as to prevent foundations becoming rotten.[23] But mere non-cultivation of land is not permissive waste.[24] A tenant for life is not liable for permissive waste unless an obligation to repair is imposed upon him by the terms of the limitation under which he holds.[25] This obligation is as rare in life tenancies as it is common in tenancies for years.

(c) *Voluntary waste.* This is doing that which ought not to be done. " The committing of any spoil or destruction in houses, lands, etc., by tenants, to the damage of the heir, or of him in reversion or remainder " [26] is voluntary waste. Examples are opening and working a mine in the land [27] (but not merely working a mine already open [28]), or cutting timber.[29] Timber consists of oak, ash and elm trees which are at least twenty years old and not too old to have a reasonable quantity of usable wood in them.[30] Other trees may rank as timber by local custom, e.g., beech in Buckinghamshire, willow in Hampshire and birch in Yorkshire and Cumber-

---

16 Co.Litt. 53a, b; *Lord Darcy* v. *Askwith* (1618) Hob. 234; but see *Jones* v. *Chappell* (1875) L.R. 20 Eq. 539.
17 For the common law rules about waste, see (1950) 13 Conv.(N.S.) 278 (M. E. Bathurst).
18 *Doherty* v. *Allman* (1878) 3 App.Cas. 709; and see *Hyman* v. *Rose* [1912] A.C. 623 (chapel into cinema).
19 *Meux* v. *Cobley* [1892] 2 Ch. 253; *cf. Jones* v. *Chappell* (1875) L.R. 20 Eq. 539 (erection of buildings).
20 *Doherty* v. *Allman, supra*; *Re McIntosh and Pontypridd Improvements Co. Ltd.* (1891) 61 L.J.Q.B. 164.
21 Co.Litt. 53a; *Powys* v. *Blagrave* (1854) 4 De G.M. & G. 448.
22 *Anon.* (1564) Moo.K.B. 62; *Griffith's Case* (1564) Moo.K.B. 69.
23 *Sticklehorne* v. *Hatchman* (1586) Owen 43.
24 *Hutton* v. *Warren* (1836) 1 M. & W. 466 at 472.
25 *Re Cartwright* (1889) 41 Ch.D. 532.
26 Bacon's *Abridgment*, 7th ed., viii, 379.
27 *Saunders's Case* (1599) 5 Co.Rep. 12a; *Campbell* v. *Wardlaw* (1883) 8 App.Cas. 641.
28 *Dashwood* v. *Magniac* [1891] 3 Ch. 306 at 360.
29 *Honywood* v. *Honywood* (1874) L.R. 18 Eq. 306.
30 *Ibid.*, at p. 309.

land [31]; and custom may also prescribe some qualification other than an age of twenty years for the trees to be considered timber, *e.g.*, an age of twenty-four years or a specified girth.[31a]

A tenant for life is liable for voluntary waste [32] unless his interest was granted to him by an instrument [33] exempting him from liability for voluntary waste, *e.g.*, a grant "without impeachment of waste." [34] Where there is such an exemption the tenant is said to be "unimpeachable of waste"; otherwise he is said to be "impeachable of waste." Thus if nothing is said about waste, the tenant is impeachable; in practice, however, he is often made unimpeachable.

(*d*) *Equitable waste.* Even where a tenant for life was unimpeachable for waste it was held inequitable to allow him to ruin the property by acts of wanton destruction. To prevent these the equitable remedy of an injunction [35] would be granted. "Equitable waste is that which a prudent man would not do in the management of his own property." [36] The term applies to acts such as stripping a house of all its lead, iron, glass, doors, boards, etc., to the value of £3,000,[37] or pulling down houses,[38] or cutting timber planted with the object of providing ornament or shelter [39] (whether or not in fact it does provide it [40]), unless this is necessary for the preservation of part of the timber.[41] These acts are, of course, also voluntary waste, but are not relevant as such where the tenant is unimpeachable. Equitable waste therefore is a peculiarly flagrant branch of voluntary waste, which the ordinary dispensation from waste will not excuse.

A tenant for life is liable for equitable waste unless the document conferring his interest upon him shows an intention to allow him to commit it. It is not enough that his interest has been given to him without impeachment of waste; he must show that it is intended that he should be allowed to commit equitable as well as voluntary waste.[42]

[31] *Aubrey* v. *Fisher* (1809) 10 East 446 (Bucks); Cru.Dig. i, 117 (Hants.); *Countess of Cumberland's Case* (1610) Moo.K.B. 812 (Yorks.); *Pinder* v. *Spencer* (——) Noy 30 (Cumb.).
[31a] *Honywood* v. *Honywood*, *supra*, at p. 309.
[32] *Pardoe* v. *Pardoe* (1900) 82 L.T. 547; *Re Ridge* (1885) 31 Ch.D. 504 at 507; H.E.L. iii, 121, 122. As to a tenant for life of leaseholds, see *Re Parry and Hopkin* [1900] 1 Ch. 160; *Re Field* [1925] Ch. 636.
[33] See *Dowman's Case* (1583) 9 Co.Rep. 1a at 10b.
[34] *Lewis Bowles's Case* (1616) 11 Co.Rep. 79b at 82b; *Waldo* v. *Waldo* (1841) 12 Sim. 107.
[35] *Post*, p. 112.   [36] *Turner* v. *Wright* (1860) 2 De G.F. & J. 234 at 243.
[37] *Vane* v. *Lord Barnard* (1716) 2 Vern. 738.
[38] *Williams* v. *Day* (1680) 2 Ch.Ca. 32.   [39] *Marker* v. *Marker* (1851) 9 Hare 1.
[40] *Weld-Blundell* v. *Wolseley* [1903] 2 Ch. 664.
[41] *Baker* v. *Sebright* (1879) 13 Ch.D. 179.
[42] L.P.A., 1925, s. 135, replacing J.A., 1873, s. 25 (3); *Micklethwait* v. *Micklethwait* (1857) 1 De G. & J. 504 at 524.

Timber and Minerals

Although largely governed by the general law of waste, the rights of a tenant for life with regard to timber and minerals are so important as to merit separate treatment.

1. Timber

(*a*) *Estovers.* Whether impeachable of waste or not, a tenant for life can take reasonable estovers (or botes) from the land. These consist of wood and timber taken as—

    (i) house-bote, for repairing the house or burning in it;
    (ii) plough-bote, for making and repairing agricultural implements; and
    (iii) hay-bote, for repairing fences.[43]

The tenant's right to house-bote does not entitle him to cut down timber in excess of his present needs in order to use it for any repairs which become necessary in the future, nor does it authorise him to sell the timber, even if he employs the proceeds in repairs, or the timber proves unfit for repairs.[44]

(*b*) *Timber estate.* If the land is a timber estate (an estate cultivated mainly for the produce of saleable timber which is cut periodically [45]), the tenant can cut and sell timber according to the rules of proper estate management even if he is impeachable of waste. The reason for this rule is that the timber properly cut on such an estate is part of the annual fruits of the land rather than part of the inheritance.[46]

(*c*) *Timber planted for ornament or shelter.* As has been seen,[47] it is equitable waste to cut timber planted for ornament or shelter, and only a tenant unimpeachable of equitable waste is permitted to do this.

(*d*) *Trees.* A tenant for life, even if he is impeachable of waste, may cut dotards (dead trees not fit for use as timber) and all trees which are not timber, *e.g.,* in most cases larches or willows.[48] But there are a number of exceptions to this. It is voluntary waste to

---

43 Co.Litt. 41b, 53b; Tudor L.C. 147.
44 *Gorges* v. *Stanfield* (1597) Cro.Eliz. 593; *Simmons* v. *Norton* (1831) 7 Bing. 640; Co.Litt. 53b.
45 *Honywood* v. *Honywood* (1874) L.R. 18 Eq. 306 at 309, 310, where " merely " is used in place of " mainly."
46 *Honywood* v. *Honywood* (1874) L.R. 18 Eq. 306 at 309, 310; *Dashwood* v. *Magniac* [1891] 3 Ch. 306; *Re Trevor-Batye* [1912] 2 Ch. 339.
47 *Ante,* p. 105.
48 *Herlakenden's Case* (1589) 4 Co.Rep. 62a at 63b; *Phillipps* v. *Smith* (1845) 14 M. & W. 589; *Honywood* v. *Honywood, supra*; *Re Harker's W. T.* [1938] Ch. 323.

cut trees which would be timber but for their immaturity (unless the cutting is necessary to thin them out and so allow proper development) [49] or to cut fruit trees in a garden or orchard.[50] Further, it is voluntary waste to cut wood which a prudent man would not cut, such as willows which help to hold a river bank together [51]; and it may be equitable waste to cut trees planted for ornament or shelter, or to grub up an entire wood.[52]

(e) *Normal rules.* Subject to the above special rules, the position is that a tenant for life who is unimpeachable of waste may cut and sell timber and keep all the proceeds.[53] But if the tenant is impeachable of waste, his only right to cut timber is that given to him by statute.[54] This authorises him to cut and sell timber ripe and fit for cutting, provided—

(i) the consent of the trustees of the settlement under which he holds his life interest, or an order of the court, is obtained; and

(ii) three-quarters of the proceeds are set aside as capital money. This means that the trustees hold this portion of the price on trust for all persons having any interest in the land, paying only the interest to the tenant for life. The remaining quarter of the proceeds is paid to the tenant for life as income.

(f) *Ownership of severed timber.* Standing trees are part of the land and do not belong to the tenant for life until properly cut by him. Therefore if the land is sold with the trees standing, the life tenant cannot claim any share of the price even though he could lawfully have cut them.[55] Once severed, at common law the trees belonged to the life tenant if he was entitled to cut them, whether the severance was effected by himself, a stranger, or an act of God, such as a storm.[56] If he was not entitled to sever them, they belonged not to him but to the owner of the next vested estate or interest of inheritance.[57] This was so, it seems, even if there was an

---

49 *Phillipps* v. *Smith, supra,* at p. 594; *Bagot* v. *Bagot* (1863) 32 Beav. 509 at 518; *Earl Cowley* v. *Wellesley* (1866) L.R. 1 Eq. 656.
50 Co.Litt. 53a; *Kaye* v. *Banks* (1770) Dick. 431.
51 *Stripping's Case* (1621) Winch 15.
52 *Lord Tamworth* v. *Lord Ferrers* (1801) 6 Ves. 419; *Aston* v. *Aston* (1749) 1 Ves.Sen. 264 at 265.
53 *Lewis Bowles's Case* (1615) 11 Co.Rep. 79b; Cru.Dig. i, 127.
54 S.L.A., 1925, s. 66, replacing S.L.A., 1882, s. 35; *post,* p. 342. This is one of the many statutory powers of a tenant for life under the settled land legislation. See notes in Wolst. & C. iii, 145.
55 *Re Llewellin* (1887) 37 Ch.D. 317; *Re Londesborough* [1923] 1 Ch. 500.
56 *Anon.* (1729) Mos. 237 at 238; *Lewis Bowles's Case, supra,* at p. 84a.
57 *Paget's Case* (1593) 5 Co.Rep. 76b; *Bewick* v. *Whitfield* (1734) 3 P.Wms. 267; *Honywood* v. *Honywood* (1874) L.R. 18 Eq. 306 (for exceptions see at p. 311); but see *Tooker* v. *Annesley* (1832) 5 Sim. 235 at 240.

intervening tenant for life unimpeachable for waste,[58] for a tenant for life could claim timber only if it was severed during his possession of the land[59]; and in such cases the life tenant did not even get the income. But where settlements were made by way of a trust, as they are today, equity would sometimes modify the common law rules by declaring the proceeds of timber wrongfully cut to be part of the settled property, to be held for the benefit of all parties other than the wrongdoer.[60] The tenant for life might also be allowed to take the income if the court would have authorised the cutting.[61]

2. Minerals. The mineral rights of a tenant for life depend on two factors, namely, whether the mine was already open when his tenancy began, and whether he is impeachable of waste.

(*a*) *Right to work mines.* A tenant for life may work a mine and take all the proceeds unless—

(i) he is impeachable of waste, and

(ii) the mine was not open when his tenancy began.

Where both these conditions are satisfied, he cannot work the mine at all, for to open and work an unopened mine is voluntary waste.[62] But it is not waste to continue working a mine already open[63] even if new pits are made on different parts of the same plot of land to pursue the same or a new vein, for the grantor, by opening or allowing the opening of the mines, has shown an intent that the minerals should be treated as part of the profits of the land.[64] Minerals improperly got are dealt with in the same way as timber wrongfully cut.[65]

(*b*) *Right to lease mines.* The Settled Land Act, 1925,[66] authorises a tenant for life to grant mining leases for one hundred years or less, whether the mine is open or not and whether or not the tenant is impeachable of waste. Leases granted under this

---

[58] See *Gent* v. *Harrison* (1859) Johns. 517 at 524.
[59] *Pigot* v. *Bullock* (1792) 1 Ves.Jun. 479 at 484.
[60] *Lushington* v. *Boldero* (1851) 15 Beav. 1; *Honywood* v. *Honywood, supra*; Tudor L.C. 155.
[61] *Tooker* v. *Annesley* (1832) 5 Sim. 235; *Waldo* v. *Waldo* (1835) 7 Sim. 261; (1841) 12 Sim. 107; *Bateman* v. *Hotchkin* (*No. 2*) (1862) 31 Beav. 486; compare *Re Harrison's Trusts* (1884) 28 Ch.D. 220 at 228 (larches: trust for sale).
[62] *Ante*, p. 104. As to the meaning of " open," see *Greville-Nugent* v. *Mackenzie* [1900] A.C. 83; *Re Morgan* [1914] 1 Ch. 910 at 919, 920; *Elias* v. *Snowdon Slate Quarries Co.* (1879) 4 App.Cas. 454 at 465.
[63] *Viner* v. *Vaughan* (1840) 2 Beav. 466 at 469.
[64] *Re Hall* [1916] 2 Ch. 448 at 493; *Spencer* v. *Scurr* (1862) 31 Beav. 334; *cf. Re Ridge* (1885) 31 Ch.D. 504 at 508 and contrast *Re Maynard* [1899] 2 Ch. 347.
[65] *Re Barrington* (1886) 33 Ch.D. 523 at 527; *supra*.
[66] ss. 41, 42, 45–47, replacing and extending S.L.A., 1882, ss. 6, 9–11, and S.L.A. 1890, s. 8.

power are binding on those in remainder or reversion. In each case the tenant for life is entitled to three-quarters of the rent, except that if he is impeachable of waste and the mine is unopened, he is entitled to only one-quarter of the rent under any lease granted by him and not by any previous owner or tenant for life.[67] The balance of rent is capital money and held for the benefit of all those interested under the settlement. But the whole of the rent will be paid to the tenant for life if the settlement shows such an intention. The powers conferred upon tenants for life by the settled land legislation are treated more fully later.[68]

Emblements and fixtures

A tenant for life cannot foresee the date on which his estate will determine. In order to encourage him to cultivate his land by assuring him of the fruits of his labour, the law gives him a right to emblements.[69] This means that the tenant's personal representatives, or in the case of an estate *pur autre vie* the tenant himself,[70] may enter the land after the life estate has determined and reap the crops which the tenant has sown.[71] This applies only to cultivated crops such as corn, hemp, and flax, and not to things such as fruit trees and timber; and it extends only to the crops actually sown by the tenant for life [72] and growing at the determination of the tenancy.[73] Where the end of the tenancy is brought about by the tenant's own act (*e.g.*, where a life estate is granted to a widow until remarriage and she remarries) there is no right to emblements.[74]

Prima facie any fixtures attached to the land by a tenant for life must be left after his death for the person next entitled to the land; but trade fixtures and ornamental and domestic fixtures are excepted. This is explained in greater detail later.[75]

[67] S.L.A., 1925, s. 47; *Re Fitzwalter* [1943] Ch. 285.
[68] *Post*, p. 338.
[69] *Graves* v. *Weld* (1833) 5 B. & Ad. 105 at 107.
[70] *Kelly* v. *Webber* (1860) 3 L.T. 124.
[71] Co.Litt. 55b.
[72] *Grantham* v. *Hawley* (1615) Hob. 132.
[73] *Graves* v. *Weld*, *supra*, at p. 119.
[74] *Oland's Case* (1602) 5 Co.Rep. 116a; Williams R.P. 135.
[75] *Post*, p. 711.

CHAPTER 4

LAW AND EQUITY

Part 1

GENERAL PRINCIPLES

THE most fundamental distinction in the law of real property is that between legal and equitable interests in land. This was a product of the history of the courts, the ordinary judges in the courts of common law being concerned with legal interests and the Chancellor in his Court of Chancery being concerned with equitable interests. Although these rival jurisdictions have now been amalgamated for a century, the dual system which they produced remains firmly embedded in the law.[1]

Sect. 1. The Historical Basis of Equity

1. Common law: the writ system

(a) *The writs.* In order to commence an action in any of the common law courts (King's Bench, Common Pleas and Exchequer) normally a writ had first to be issued under the seal of the Chancellor, the keeper of the Great Seal. Each different kind of action had its own writ, often with its own special procedure.[2] If an heir was claiming land from a dispossessor after his father's death, the action had to be started by a writ of *mort d'ancestor*; if he was the grandfather of the heir, a writ of *aiel* had to be used; or if he was the great-grandfather, a writ of *besaiel*.[3] No action could succeed unless the correct writ was chosen.[4] There was, therefore, a strictly *formulary* legal system: a plaintiff would succeed only if some writ provided a formula to fit his case. England was no exception to the rule that in early law justice was dominated by procedure.[5]

(b) *New writs.* At first new writs were invented with comparative freedom for cases not covered by existing writs, though some were

---

[1] This is a shortened version of the text in the 3rd edition of this book, pp. 113–116.
[2] Maitland, *Forms of Action*, 2. For a discussion of actions for the recovery of land, see *post*, pp. 1167 *et seq.*
[3] Maitland, *Forms of Action*, 31.
[4] *Ibid.* 4; H.E.L ix, 245.
[5] Maine, *Early Law and Custom*, 389; Maitland, *Forms of Action*, 1, 6.

110

disallowed by the courts.[6] They were severely restricted by the Provisions of Oxford, 1258, in which the Chancellor swore that he would seal no new form of writ without the command of the King and his Council.[7] But the Statute of Westminster II, 1285, provided in the famous Chapter 24, *In Consimili Casu*, that the clerks in Chancery should have a limited power to invent new writs. If there already existed one writ and in a like case (*in consimili casu*), falling under like law and requiring like remedy, there was none, the clerks in Chancery might make a suitable writ, or else refer the matter to the next Parliament. The result, nevertheless, was to stunt the growth of the writ system,[8] and to leave many cases without remedy.

2. Petitions to the King and Chancellor. Suitors therefore turned to the King, as the fountain of justice. Their petitions were heard by the King's Council, of which the Chancellor was an important member.[9] After the reign of Edward III petitions were often addressed to the Chancellor alone, and in this way he acquired a regular and expanding judicial business. At first the decisions upon the petitions were made either in the name of the King's Council or else with the advice of the serjeants and judges. In 1474 the Chancellor made his first known decree on his own authority, and after that date his decrees became frequent.[10]

3. The Court of Chancery

(*a*) *The Chancellor.* In this way there gradually came into existence a Court of Chancery in which the Chancellor, acting independently of the King's Council, sat as a judge administering a system of justice called equity. After the end of the seventeenth century only lawyers were appointed to the office.[11] Equity, which had varied with the ideas of each Chancellor, began with Lord Ellesmere (1596–1617) to develop into a code of principles, and the work of Lord Nottingham (1673–82) in systematising the rules earned him the title of the Father of Equity.[12] When Lord Eldon retired in 1827 the rules of equity were as well settled as those of the common law; a "*rigor aequitatis*" had developed, and he could safely say "nothing would inflict on me greater pain, in quitting this place, than the recollection that I had done anything to justify the reproach

---

[6] Maitland, *Forms of Action*, 41.
[7] *Ibid.* 41, 46, 51; H.E.L. i, 398.
[8] The relation of the statute to the later forms of action is controversial: Maitland, *Forms of Action*, 51; 31 Columbia L.R. 778; (1931) 47 L.Q.R. 334; (1936) 52 L.Q.R. 68, 220; 46 Yale L.J. 1142; [1954] C.L.J. 105; Kiralfy, *The Action on the Case*.
[9] H.E.L., i, 400.
[10] *Ibid.*, 402–404.
[11] *Ibid.* 411.　　　　　　　　　　[12] *Kemp* v. *Kemp* (1801) 5 Ves. 849 at 858.

that the equity of this court varies like the Chancellor's foot." [26]
But equity, although it followed the inevitable course towards fixity
and dogma, remained in general a more modern and flexible system
than the common law. Originally it provided the means, needed in
every legal system, of adapting general rules to particular cases, and
this character was never entirely lost.

(b) *A court of conscience.* In the course of time various subsidiary officials were appointed to assist the Chancellor, a system of
appeals grew up, and finally in 1875 the Chancery system was merged
with the common law courts to form the present Supreme Court of
Judicature. [27] In short, the practice of petitioning the King for justice
in exceptional cases gradually opened the way to a supplementary
system of law administered regularly by a court, but by a court quite
different and separate from the courts of common law. The latter
decided cases according to the strict common law rules, and with
much fondness for technicality. Chancery, on the other hand,
deliberately mitigated the rigour of the common law, tempering its
rules to the needs of particular cases on principles which seemed just
and equitable to generations of Chancellors, and technical pleas were
usually unsuccessful. The common law courts were mainly concerned with enforcing the strict rights of the parties regardless of
their merits, whereas Chancery was a court of conscience where
remedies would be withheld from a party guilty of sharp practice or
any kind of unconscionable conduct.

(c) *Conflict.* The decrees of the Chancellor would often, therefore, conflict with judgments obtained at common law. A party who
had lost his case because of some trickery or accident, for example,
could obtain in Chancery an injunction forbidding his opponent to
execute the common law judgment. This power to interrupt the
common law process was used so often that this type of injunction
was called a " common injunction." The Chancellor's jurisdiction
to issue it was clearly established after the decision of James I in the
celebrated dispute between Coke C.J. and Lord Ellesmere L.C. [28]

(d) *Equity acts in personam.* A peculiarity of equity was that it
acted *in personam,* " on the person." The Chancellor's ultimate
sanction was to imprison for contempt anyone who disobeyed his

---

[26] *Gee* v. *Pritchard* (1818) 2 Swans. 402 at 414. Selden had complained (*Table
Talk*, 31b) that equity varied with the conscience of each Chancellor, and that
this was as absurd as making the measurement known as a foot vary with each
Chancellor's foot.

[27] *Post,* p. 128. For the reorganisation of the Court of Chancery in the nineteenth
century, see H.E.L. i, 442 *et seq.*

[28] *Earl of Oxford's Case* (1615) 1 Ch.Rep. 1; H.E.L. iii, 460–465.

decree. He could not, as could the common law courts, award damages enforceable by a sheriff's execution against the defendant's property. But he could decree that the defendant should pay a sum of money, and imprison him if he would not, or that he should do or abstain from doing something on pain of imprisonment for disobedience.[29]

Sect. 2. The Nature of Equitable Rights

A. Distinction Between Legal and Equitable Rights

1. Legal and equitable ownership. The essential difference between legal and equitable rights is best understood by comparing absolute ownership with trusts. The history of trusts is explained below,[30] and at this point it is only necessary to appreciate that trusts were unenforceable at common law. If land was conveyed to A in fee simple upon trust for B in fee simple, the common law courts regarded A as absolute owner and would not recognise any rights in B. But the Chancellor would enforce trusts, as matters of conscience, and compel A to hold the land on B's behalf and to allow B to enjoy it. In such a case A is the " legal owner," B is the " equitable owner." The land is vested in A, but since he is trustee of it he is not the beneficial owner: he has only the " bare legal estate," and the beneficial interest belongs to B.

Now legal ownership confers rights *in rem*, rights of property in the land itself, which can be enforced against anyone. Equitable ownership conferred at first only a right *in personam*, a right to compel the trustee personally to perform his trust. But what should happen if the trustee died or disposed of the land? Trusts would have been hopelessly insecure if means had not been found to protect them from such events.

2. Extent of enforcement. The Chancellors solved this problem by extending the categories of persons upon whom performance of the trust would be enjoined. As case followed case the extensions became very wide. In 1465 it was laid down that a trust would be enforced against anyone who took a conveyance of the land *with notice of the trust*.[31] In 1483 the Chancellor said that he would enforce a trust against the trustee's heir.[32] In 1522 it was said that a trust would be enforced against anyone to whom the land had been conveyed as a gift.[33] It was later decided that others such as the

---

[29] Maitland, *Equity*, 9; H.E.L. i, 458. [30] *Post*, p. 152.
[31] Y.B. 5 Edw. 4, Mich. pl. 16. [32] Y.B. 22 Edw. 4, Pasch. pl. 18.
[33] Y.B. 14 Hen. 8, Mich. pl. 5, fo. 7. See *Chudleigh's Case* (1595) 1 Co.Rep. 113b at 122b.

executors and execution creditors of the trustees would be bound by the trust.[34]

3. The purchaser without notice. Two equitable principles explain these developments. First, a person who takes the land without giving value in exchange (such as an heir, executor or donee) must take it with all its burdens, equitable as well as legal: trusts bind volunteers. Secondly, even a person who has given value will be bound if before he obtained the land he knew of the trust: trusts bind all who take with notice. Both these principles are summed up in the cardinal maxim in which is expressed the true difference between legal and equitable rights:

Legal rights are good against all the world; equitable rights are good against all persons except a bona fide purchaser of a legal estate for value without notice, and those claiming under such a purchaser.[35]

4. Equitable interests. This rule runs right through the law of property; it has been called "the polar star of equity." [36] Its detailed anatomy will be investigated below. Its general meaning is that equitable rights advanced almost to the status of legal rights, but not quite. Equity always stopped short of enforcing a trust against a person who had bought the land from the legal owner in genuine ignorance of the existence of the trust. An equitable owner was therefore never quite in the impregnable position of a legal owner: he never had an absolutely indefeasible title. But the rules relating to notice and the system of conveyancing founded upon them protected equitable interests, as we shall see, for nearly all practical purposes, so that for the sake of their other advantages they were very much used. They became much more than rights *in personam* against trustees: they were a new species of property right, really rights *in rem*,[37] but exceptional because of their peculiar infirmity, that they would be lost if the legal title came to a bona fide purchaser without notice. They are therefore commonly called "equitable interests" (*sc.* in property); for "equity has modelled them into the shape and quality of real estates." [38]

---

34 Maitland, *Equity*, 112, where an account is given of these successive steps.
35 *Ibid.* 114, 115; *cf.* L.P.A., 1925, s. 2 (5).
36 *Stanhope* v. *Earl Verney* (1761) 2 Eden 81 at 85, *per* Lord Henley L.C.
37 Maitland laid stress on the personal nature of equitable rights, for historical and other good reasons: *Equity*, 23, 29, 107, 117. If by rights *in rem* is meant (as normally) rights enforceable against third parties generally, as opposed to rights *in personam* which are enforceable only against specified persons (*e.g.*, contractual rights), then equitable rights to property are unquestionably rights *in rem*, though somewhat different from legal rights to property.
38 *Burgess* v. *Wheate* (1759) 1 Eden 177 at 249, *per* Henley L.K.

5. Persons bound. The wide, proprietary character of equitable interests is shown by the modern form of the fundamental rule. Instead of enumerating all the classes of persons bound in addition to trustees themselves, the rule lays down in the first place that equities bind *all* persons, and then gives a single but very important exception. This change of form marks an increase in scope. In 1905 the question arose whether a squatter (a person who obtained title to land by long occupation uncontested by the previous owner [39]) was bound by an equitable interest created by the previous owner. A squatter was not among the classes of persons held liable in the line of cases which led to the rule. But he was not a purchaser for value; and the rule was so well established in its wide form that there was no difficulty in deciding that the squatter was bound.[40]

This special characteristic of equitable rights may be made clearer by an illustration. Suppose that in 1920 [41] A was legal owner of Blackacre, holding it upon trust for B absolutely, and that Blackacre was subject to a legal lease to a tenant T, to a legal right of way owned by R, to a legal mortgage in favour of L and an equitable mortgage [41a] in favour of E. If in 1921 A succeeded in selling Blackacre to a purchaser P who had no notice of any of the other interests, P's position would be as follows. On taking a conveyance of the legal estate he would still be bound by T's lease, R's right of way and L's legal mortgage, since these belong to the class of legal estates and interests which bind all comers. But B's trust and E's equitable mortgage would be defeated by the purchase of the legal estate without notice: B and E would lose their rights over the land, and their only remedies would be against A personally.

B. *The Purchaser Without Notice*

The plea of a purchase of a legal estate for value without notice is " an absolute, unqualified, unanswerable defence " [42] against the claims of any prior equitable owner. The onus of proof lies on the

---

[39] *Post*, p. 1003.

[40] *Re Nisbet and Potts' Contract* [1906] 1 Ch. 386 (squatter held liable to restrictive covenant); followed in *Ashe* v. *Hogan* [1920] 1 I.R. 159. Contrast *Bolling* v. *Hobday* (1882) 31 W.R. 9 (squatter held free from trust for sale) and see 51 S.J. 141, 155 (T. C. Williams). Account must now be taken of the Limitation Act, 1939, s. 7, dealt with *post*, p. 1020; this contains provisions for land held upon trust which alter the principle of *Bolling* v. *Hobday*. The difficulty which was felt was that a squatter acquired a new legal estate (*post*, p. 1028), and not the legal estate which was subject to the trust. But in reality it is the land, not the estate, which is affected.

[41] This date is chosen because if created after 1925, the equitable mortgage would probably have been registrable: see *post*, p. 969.

[41a] A less formal type of mortgage: *post*, p. 900.

[42] *Pilcher* v. *Rawlins* (1872) 7 Ch.App. 259 at 269, *per* James L.J.

person setting it up[43]: it is a single plea, and is not sufficiently made out by proving purchase for value and leaving it to the plaintiff to prove notice if he can.[44] The principal points of detail are as follows.

1. Bona fide. The purchaser must act in good faith. Any fraud or sharp practice will forfeit the privileges of a purchaser in the eyes of equity. But this requirement of good faith mainly serves to emphasise that the purchaser must be innocent as to notice,[45] and this is considered in detail below.

2. Purchaser for value. The words " for value " are included to show that value must have been given, because " purchaser " in its technical sense does not necessarily imply this.[46] " Value " does not necessarily mean full value.[47] It means any consideration in money, money's worth (*e.g.*, other land, or stocks and shares, or services) or marriage.[48] " Money's worth " extends to all forms of non-monetary consideration in the sense used in the law of contract, but it also includes the satisfaction of an existing debt.[49] " Marriage," however, extends only to a future marriage: an ante-nuptial agreement (*i.e.*, a promise made in consideration of future marriage) is deemed to have been made for value as regards both the spouses and the issue of the marriage[50]; but a promise made in respect of a past marriage (a post-nuptial agreement) is not.[51] " Good consideration " (the natural love and affection which a person has for his near relatives) is of small importance and does not amount to value.[52] " Purchaser " is not confined to someone who acquires a fee simple; it includes, for example, mortgagees and lessees, who are purchasers *pro tanto* (to the extent of their interests).[53]

If the purchase is for money consideration, the purchaser must actually pay all the money before receiving notice of the equitable interest; and if such notice is received before the money is paid, no obligation or security for its payment will be enforceable.[54] The

---

[43] *Re Nisbet and Potts' Contract* [1906] 1 Ch. 386 at 404, 409, 410; but see *Shears* v. *Wells* [1936] 1 All E.R. 832.

[44] *Re Nisbet and Potts' Contract* [1905] 1 Ch. 391 at 402 (on appeal, [1906] 1 Ch. 386); *Wilkes* v. *Spooner* [1911] 2 K.B. 473 at 486.

[45] See *Le Neve* v. *Le Neve* (1747) 1 Ves.Sen. 64; Wh. & T. ii, 157; *Willoughby* v. *Willoughby* (1756) 1 T.R. 763.   [46] *Cf. ante*, p. 52, and *post*, p. 509.

[47] *Basset* v. *Nosworthy* (1673) Rep.t.Finch 102; Wh. & T. ii, 138, 140.

[48] See, *e.g.*, *Wormald* v. *Maitland* (1866) 35 L.J.Ch. 69 at 73; *Salih* v. *Atchi* [1961] A.C. 778.

[49] *Thorndike* v. *Hunt* (1859) 3 De G. & J. 563; Maitland, *Equity*, 134; (1943) 59 L.Q.R. 208 (R.E.M.).

[50] *Att.-Gen.* v. *Jacobs Smith* [1895] 2 Q.B. 341.   [51] Wh. & T. ii, 791.

[52] *Goodright* d. *Humphreys* v. *Moses* (1774) 2 Wm.Bl. 1019.

[53] *Ibid.*; *Brace* v. *Duchess of Marlborough* (1728) 2 P.Wms. 491; *Re King's Leasehold Estates* (1873) L.R. 16 Eq. 521 at 525.

[54] *Tourville* v. *Naish* (1734) 3 P.Wms. 307; Wh. & T. ii, 140.

mere execution of a conveyance of a legal estate before notice is received, without payment of the money, will not suffice.[55]

3. Of a legal estate. This element is most important. The immunity from equities enjoyed by the purchaser without notice is founded on equity's deference to the legal estate. " As courts of equity break in upon the common law, when necessity and conscience require it, still they allow superior force and strength to a legal title to estates." [56] Unless he is a volunteer or has notice the legal owner cannot be interfered with by merely equitable claimants.

A purchaser of an equitable interest, even without notice, is in an entirely different position.[57] If A and B hold land on trust for X, and X sells his equitable interest to Y, Y takes subject to any other prior equitable interests there may be in the land, whether or not he has notice of them. The owner of an equitable interest can prima facie convey only what is vested in him, so that if part of his equitable interest has already been conveyed away, a subsequent purchaser can take only so much of it as remains.[58] The rule is thus that " where the equities are equal, the first in time prevails." [59] It is only acquisition of the legal estate for value and without notice which will reverse the natural order of priority. A neat illustration is provided by a case where land held upon trust was fraudulently mortgaged first to legal and later to equitable mortgagees, none of whom had notice of the trust. It was held that the legal mortgagee took priority over the beneficiaries under the trust, but that the equitable mortgagees did not.[60]

The purchaser must have the legal estate properly vested in him (*e.g.*, by a conveyance [61]) before he will be safe. If he has paid the purchase-money, but then gets notice of a prior equitable interest before the purchase is completed by the conveyance of the legal estate, he will take subject to the equity.[62] But this does not apply to a subsequent equitable interest. A purchaser who takes a con-

---

[55] *Story* v. *Windsor* (1743) 2 Atk. 630. For the converse case, see below.
[56] *Wortley* v. *Birkhead* (1754) 2 Ves.Sen. 571 at 574, *per* Lord Hardwicke L.C.; and see *Pilcher* v. *Rawlins* (1872) 7 Ch.App. 259 at 268, 269; *L. & S. W. Ry.* v. *Gomm* (1882) 20 Ch.D. 562 at 586.
[57] *Phillips* v. *Phillips* (1862) 4 De G.F. & J. 208. The rule (abolished since 1925) allowing a later equitable incumbrancer to defeat a prior equitable incumbrancer by getting in a paramount legal estate is considered later under tacking of mortgages, *post*, p. 978.
[58] See *Phillips* v. *Phillips, supra*, at p. 215. [59] Snell, *Equity*, 45.
[60] *Cave* v. *Cave* (1880) 15 Ch.D. 639. And see *post*, p. 119, n. 76.
[61] But an imperfect conveyance operating by estoppel may suffice: *Sharpe* v. *Foy* (1868) 4 Ch.App. 35.
[62] *Wigg* v. *Wigg* (1739) 1 Atk. 382 at 384. For this rule as applied to mortgages, see *Saunders* v. *Dehew* (1692) 2 Vern. 271; *Allen* v. *Knight* (1846) 5 Hare 272, affirmed 16 L.J.Ch. 370; *Mumford* v. *Stohwasser* (1874) L.R. 18 Eq. 556; *cf. McCarthy & Stone, Ltd.* v. *Julian S. Hodge & Co., Ltd.* [1971] 1 W.L.R. 1547 (equity registered before legal estate vested in mortgagee). In *Mumford* v. *Stohwasser* the *obiter dicta* of Jessel M.R. at pp. 562–563 are not clear.

veyance of the legal estate with notice of an equitable interest created after he contracted to buy the land takes free from it; for his equitable interest under the contract [63] has priority over the later equity, and the conveyance merely carries out the contract.[64]

The rule that the purchaser must take a legal estate before receiving notice is subject to two qualifications, or perhaps three.

(a) *Superior right to legal estate.* A purchaser without notice who acquires only an equitable interest can defeat a prior equity if his equitable interest gives him a superior right to the legal estate. This rule is thus consistent with the principle that the legal estate must prevail. The simplest example is where the purchaser procures a conveyance not to himself but to some person who is trustee for him, and neither purchaser nor trustee has notice of the equity at the time of the conveyance.[65] An analogous but less obvious case could arise before 1926 where the legal estate was outstanding, *i.e.,* was held by some third person who had no knowledge of the equity and who, before having notice of it, declared himself trustee for a purchaser who also had no notice.[66] This situation rarely occurred, but when it did the later purchaser took precedence. Since 1925 the priority of equitable claimants to an outstanding legal estate is governed by different rules which must be explained later, in connection with mortgages.[67]

This exception does not alter the general rule that a purchaser of an equitable interest who purchases it from the owner of the legal estate, but does not obtain the legal estate, is bound by all previous equitable interests affecting the land, whether or not he has notice of them. Nor is a superior right to a legal estate any shield against the legal estate itself; a purchaser of a legal estate without notice of a prior equitable interest takes free from it in accordance with the basic rule even though the equitable interest conferred an equitable right to call for a legal estate.[68] Thus if A holds land upon trust to convey the legal estate to B, but then wrongfully conveys it to C, a purchaser without notice, C's title, of course, prevails.

[63] See *post*, p. 132.
[64] An example similar in principle is *Barclays Bank, Ltd.* v. *Bird* [1954] Ch. 274.
[65] *Stanhope* v. *Earl Verney* (1761) 2 Eden 81 ; " the *cestuy que trust* and trustees are one " : *ibid.,* at p. 85, *per* Lord Henley L.C.
[66] *Wilkes* v. *Bodington* (1707) 2 Vern. 599; *Wilmot* v. *Pike* (1845) 5 Hare 14 at 21, 22; *Rooper* v. *Harrison* (1855) 2 K. & J. 86; *Taylor* v. *London & County Banking Co.* [1901] 2 Ch. 231 at 262, 263; *Assaf* v. *Fuwa* [1955] A.C. 215, noted in [1955] C.L.J. 32 (H.W.R.W.). These examples (except the last) are complicated, and are best studied as part of the law of priority of mortgages, *post*, pp. 958 *et seq.* (esp. p. 963, n. 68).
[67] *Post*, pp. 964–965, 976. The rule since 1925 is that the first interest of which the trustees get notice prevails.
[68] *Garnham* v. *Skipper* (1885) 55 L.J.Ch. 263 ; 53 L.T. 940 (contract to grant legal mortgage to A followed by grant of legal mortgage to B. B, having no notice, prevailed).

(*b*) *Mere equities.* A purchaser without notice does not have to take a legal estate in order to take free from a " mere equity," *i.e.,* an equitable right which falls short of an equitable interest in land.[69] There are a number of such " equities," arising out of special forms of equitable relief which the court will normally enforce against successors in title. Examples are the right of a party to a deed to have the deed set aside on account of fraud [70] or undue influence [71] and the right to have a document rectified for mutual mistake,[72] as where a lease stated the rent to be £130 but £230 was the figure to which the parties had in fact agreed.[73] The right of a mortgagor to reopen a foreclosure is probably in the same category [74]; and so, it has been held, are the possessory rights of a contractual licensee,[75] in so far as they are capable of running with land. On the other hand the rights of beneficiaries under a trust,[76] and a vendor's lien for unpaid purchase-money,[77] are equitable interests in land as opposed to mere equities; thus they will obey the general rule and bind a purchaser without notice unless he obtains the legal estate.

---

[69] *Phillips* v. *Phillips* (1862) 4 De G.F. & J. 208 at 218; *Westminster Bank, Ltd.* v. *Lee* [1956] Ch. 7.

[70] *Bowen* v. *Evans* (1844) 1 Jo. & Lat. 178 at 263, 264; *Phillips* v. *Phillips, supra*; *Ernest* v. *Vivian* (1863) 33 L.J.Ch. 513; *Latec Investments, Ltd.* v. *Hotel Terrigal Pty, Ltd.* (1965) 113 C.L.R. 265; and see *Cloutte* v. *Storey* [1911] 1 Ch. 18 at 24, 25. For setting aside conveyances, see *post,* p. 611.

[71] *Bainbrigge* v. *Browne* (1881) 18 Ch.D. 188 (charge of equitable interest, executed under undue influence, held binding only upon volunteers and purchasers with notice, and so not upon chargee who took without notice; but the case contains no mention of " mere equities " or of the importance of the legal estate).

[72] For rectification, see *post,* p. 595.

[73] *Garrard* v. *Frankel* (1862) 30 Beav. 445 (see *post,* p. 595). *Smith* v. *Jones* [1954] 2 All E.R. 823 is evidently a case of a purchase of a *legal* estate without notice; the report in [1954] 1 W.L.R. 1089 is not clear on the point.

[74] For this right, see *post,* p. 907.

[75] *Westminster Bank, Ltd.* v. *Lee* [1956] Ch. 7 at p. 20, *obiter.* But the whole doctrine of licences as interests in land may be unsound, as was the doctrine of the " deserted wife's equity," also said to be a mere equity (*ibid.*). See *post,* pp. 783 *et seq.*

[76] *Cave* v. *Cave* (1880) 15 Ch.D. 639; *cf. Re Vernon, Ewens & Co.* (1886) 33 Ch.D. 402. But *Cave* v. *Cave* has not been followed in Ireland: *Re Ffrench's Estate* (1887) 21 L.R.Ir. 283; *Re Sloane's Estate* [1895] 1 I.R. 146; and see (1958) 21 Conv.(N.S.) 195 (V. T. H. Delany). In the Irish cases it was held that beneficiaries under a trust had " mere equities " which would not bind a later equitable mortgagee who had no notice; and *Scott* v. *Scott* [1924] 1 I.R. 141 applied the same doctrine to assets improperly applied by an administrator. These decisions are strongly tinged with the old idea that equitable interests under trusts are primarily rights *in personam* against the trustee, and that any right " to follow the trust property " is less substantial and a mere equity: see especially *Scott* v. *Scott, supra,* at pp. 150, 151. But in England the courts have tended rather to treat equitable interests as fully developed rights *in rem* (*ante,* p. 113) and rights under trusts should really be the equitable interests *par excellence.* The English doctrine is both simpler and more consistent with the paramount necessity of making the trust a secure form of property.

[77] *Mackreth* v. *Symmons* (1808) 15 Ves. 329; *Rice* v. *Rice* (1853) 2 Drew. 73; *Kettlewell* v. *Watson* (1882) 21 Ch.D. 685 at 711 (on appeal, 26 Ch.D. 501); *Cave* v. *Cave* (1880) 15 Ch.D. 639 at 648, 649. For this lien, see *post,* pp. 575, 886.

The same is presumably true of estate contracts and restrictive covenants.[78]

The courts have not explained precisely where the dividing line between equitable interests and mere equities lies. All that can be said is that mere equities which may affect a purchaser are essentially rights which are ancillary to or dependent upon some interest in the land which that purchaser takes.[79] There is thus a parallel with the ordinary rule relating to the purchaser of a legal estate without notice. Just as that purchaser takes the estate free from the equitable interests which affect it (and *a fortiori* any mere equities), so a purchaser of an equitable interest takes it entire and free from any mere equities affecting it of which he has no notice.[80]

Underlying the whole subject is the principle that it is only *where the equities are equal* that the first in time prevails [81]; and sometimes the balance between competing equities may be too delicate to be settled by rigid rules. Even an equitable interest may lose priority to a later equity if there has been negligence or fraud on the part of the equitable owner.[82] A " mere equity " has the additional weakness that it is more at the discretion of the court; and the court may naturally be loth to exercise its discretion against an innocent purchaser without notice, even though he is not clad in the armour of the legal estate, and even though the person entitled to the earlier equity cannot be accused of misconduct.[83]

(c) *Subsequent acquisition of legal estates.* A purchaser of an equitable interest who pays the purchase-money without notice of a prior equity has been held to be protected if he later acquires a legal estate, even with notice, provided it is not conveyed to him in breach of trust.[84] Yet this supposed exception may be merely a corollary

---

[78] *National Provincial Bank, Ltd.* v. *Ainsworth* [1965] A.C. 1175 at 1238, *per* Lord Upjohn. [79] *Ibid.*

[80] See (1955) 71 L.Q.R. 481, 482, approved in *National Provincial Bank, Ltd.* v. *Ainsworth, supra*, at p. 1238, *per* Lord Upjohn.

[81] *Rice* v. *Rice, supra*, contains a classic discussion of this principle by Kindersley V.-C.

[82] *Rice* v. *Rice, supra* (lien of unpaid vendor postponed to equitable mortgage because vendor had signed receipt for the purchase-money); *Re King's Settlement* [1931] 2 Ch. 294. And even a legal estate may lose its priority for similar reasons: see the cases on mortgages cited *post*, p. 960.

[83] See [1955] C.L.J. at p. 160 (H.W.R.W.); (1955) 19 Conv.(N.S.) 343 (F. R. Crane); (1957) 21 Conv.(N.S.) at p. 201 (V. T. H. Delany).

[84] *Bailey* v. *Barnes* [1894] 1 Ch. 25 at 36; *cf. Powell* v. *London & Provincial Bank* [1893] 1 Ch. 610, affirmed [1893] 2 Ch. 555. In *Bailey* v. *Barnes* property subject to equitable claims by creditors was first mortgaged to A (legal estate) and then sold to B (equity of redemption). Neither A (it seems) nor B had notice. B later got notice, paid off A and acquired the legal estate. *Held*, the equity did not bind B. As A, it seems, had no notice himself, B, as a successor in title to A, would not in any case have been bound: *post*, p. 125. But the Court of Appeal invoked the principle of tacking mortgages (*post*, p. 978), though this seems inapplicable to the facts since the legal estate was from the first

of the general rule. For if the legal estate is subject to a prior equity inconsistent with the purchaser's title, it will necessarily be a breach of trust to convey it to him,[85] whether or not the facts are known to the person conveying it. If the prior equity is consistent with the purchaser's title, as where it is a mere incumbrance such as a restrictive covenant, the " breach of trust " exception probably does not apply at all; for it is founded on rules devised for competing mortgages,[86] which are wholly inapplicable to consistent titles. Those rules were abolished as regards mortgages in 1925,[87] being " technical and not satisfactory." [88] They would be best abandoned altogether.

4. Without notice. There are three kinds of notice.

(*a*) *Actual notice.* A person has actual notice of all facts of which he has (or has had) actual knowledge, however that knowledge was acquired [89]; but he is not regarded as having actual notice of facts which have come to his ears only in the form of vague rumours.[90] By statute a number of rights have become registrable in the Land Charges Register, and it has been provided that registration of such rights constitutes actual notice; this subject is dealt with below.[91]

(*b*) *Constructive notice*

(1) DUTY OF DILIGENCE. Equitable interests would have been entirely insecure if it had been made easy for purchasers to acquire the legal estate without notice, as by merely asking no questions. Accordingly the Court of Chancery insisted that purchasers should inquire about equitable interests with no less diligence than about legal interests, which they could ignore only at their own peril. The motto of English conveyancing is *caveat emptor* [92]: the risk of incumbrances is on the purchaser, who must satisfy himself by a full investigation of title before completing his purchase.

(2) STANDARD REQUIRED. By the doctrine of constructive notice equity adopted a similar principle and adapted itself to the ordinary

subject to the equity and not paramount to it, as was requisite for tacking: *post*, p. 981. The same difficulty arises in *McCarthy & Stone, Ltd.* v. *Julian S. Hodge & Co., Ltd.* [1971] 1 W.L.R. 1547, although there the purchaser had constructive notice at the outset and therefore failed.
[85] See *Mumford* v. *Stohwasser* (1874) L.R. 18 Eq. 566; *McCarthy & Stone, Ltd.* v. *Julian S. Hodge & Co., Ltd., supra* (breach of trust to mortgage land already subject to contract of sale).   [86] Explained *post*, p. 978.
[87] L.P.A., 1925, s. 94 (3); *post*, p. 983. Apparently the provision applies only to mortgages: *McCarthy & Stone, Ltd.* v. *Julian S. Hodge & Co., Ltd., supra,* at p. 1556; contrast (1957) 21 Conv.(N.S.) at p. 196 (V. T. H. Delany).
[88] *Bailey* v. *Barnes, supra,* at p. 36.
[89] *Lloyd* v. *Banks* (1868) 3 Ch.App. 488.
[90] *Barnhart* v. *Greenshields* (1853) 9 Moo.P.C. 18 at 36, explained in *Reeves* v. *Pope* [1914] 2 K.B. 284.
[91] *Post*, p. 144.   [92] Let a purchaser beware.

conveyancing practice. A purchaser would be able to plead absence of notice only if he had made all usual and proper inquiries, and had still found nothing to indicate the equitable interest.[93] If he fell short of this standard he could not plead that he had no notice of rights which proper diligence would have discovered. Of these he was said to have " constructive notice." A purchaser accordingly has constructive notice of a fact if he—

(i) had actual notice that there was some incumbrance and a proper inquiry would have revealed what it was, or

(ii) deliberately abstained from inquiry in an attempt to avoid having notice, or

(iii) omitted by carelessness or for any other reason to make an inquiry which a purchaser acting on skilled advice ought to make and which would have revealed the incumbrance.[94]

A purchaser's ordinary duties fall into two main categories: inspection of the land, and investigation of the vendor's title.

(3) INSPECTION OF LAND. A purchaser is expected to inspect the land and make inquiry as to anything which appears inconsistent with the title offered by the vendor. If the vendor is in occupation, the purchaser need not make inquiry merely because the vendor's spouse or other members of his family also live there, since this involves no inconsistency.[95] But occupation by some other person will usually amount to notice of that person's right.[96] Thus occupation by a tenant is notice of the interest of the tenant,[97] the terms of his tenancy[98] and his other rights,[99] though not of any right not apparent from the lease, such as a right to have it rectified[1] on account of a mistake. But a purchaser is under no duty to find out to whom a tenant pays rent or otherwise to investigate the tenant's title, so that failure to make such inquiries does not give him constructive notice of any rights of the tenant's landlord, who may be a different person from the vendor.[2] Yet notice that property is subject to certain trusts is notice of all the trusts to which it is subject in

---

[93] *Bailey* v. *Barnes* [1894] 1 Ch. 25 at 35; C.A., 1882, s. 3 (1) (i), replaced by L.P.A., 1925, s. 199 (1) (ii).
[94] See *Jones* v. *Smith* (1841) 1 Hare 43 at 55; Snell, *Equity*, 50–53; Maitland, *Equity*, 118, 119.
[95] *Caunce* v. *Caunce* [1969] 1 W.L.R. 286 (*post*, p. 447); but see *Hodgson* v. *Marks* [1971] Ch. 892 at 934.
[96] See *Hodgson* v. *Marks* [1971] Ch. 892 (occupier entitled under trust). This extends to " all the equities " which the occupier may have in the land: *Jones* v. *Smith*, *supra*; *Barnhart* v. *Greenshields*, *infra*.
[97] *Daniels* v. *Davison* (1809) 16 Ves. 249; *Allen* v. *Anthony* (1816) 1 Mer. 282; *Mumford* v. *Stohwasser* (1874) L.R. 18 Eq. 556; *Hunt* v. *Luck* [1902] 1 Ch. 428.
[98] *Taylor* v. *Stibbert* (1794) 2 Ves.Jun. 437.
[99] *Barnhart* v. *Greenshields* (1853) 9 Moo.P.C. 18.
[1] *Smith* v. *Jones* [1954] 1 W.L.R. 1089.   [2] *Hunt* v. *Luck*, *supra*.

the hands of the trustees,[3] and notice of the existence of a document that might be expected to be relevant [4] is notice of its contents.[5]

(4) INVESTIGATION OF TITLE. A purchaser has constructive notice of all rights which he would have discovered [6] had he investigated the vendor's title to the land for the period allowed by law in ordinary cases where the parties make no special agreement as to length of title. Investigation of title means the examination of documents relating to transactions in the land during the period immediately prior to the purchase.[7] This period used by convention to be at least sixty years, but by the Vendor and Purchaser Act, 1874, it was reduced to at least forty years, and by the Law of Property Act, 1925, to at least thirty years. Under the Law of Property Act 1969 it is now at least fifteen years.[8] The period is " at least " fifteen years, for the purchaser can call for a good root of title which is at least fifteen years old, and see all subsequent documents which trace the dealing with the property.[9] A good root of title may be, for example, a conveyance or a mortgage, provided that it offers a clear starting point for the title. To do this it must be a document which deals with the whole legal and equitable interest in the land, describes the property adequately, and contains nóthing to throw any doubt on the title.[9]

For example, if the title consists of a series of conveyances respectively 5, 14, 25 and 48 years old, as well as older deeds, a purchaser is entitled to production of the conveyance 25 years old and all subsequent conveyances. If in fact he fails to investigate the title at all,[10] or else investigates it for only part of this period (*e.g.* because he has agreed to accept a shorter title, or to make no objection to some dubious transaction),[11] he is fixed with constructive notice of everything that he would have discovered had he investigated the whole title for the full statutory period. With transactions prior to the root of title a purchaser need have no concern. He may be affected by notice if he actually investigates them or inquires about them, but not otherwise.[12] A purchaser who, having notice of relevant title deeds, inquires for them, and is met with a reasonable excuse for their non-production is (by an exceptional rule) free from notice of

---

[3] *Perham* v. *Kempster* [1907] 1 Ch. 373.
[4] *Re Valletort Sanitary Steam Laundry Co.* [1903] 2 Ch. 654; Snell, *Equity*, 51.
[5] *Bisco* v. *Earl of Banbury* [1676] 1 Ch.Ca. 287.
[6] See *Carter* v. *Williams* (1870) L.R. 9 Eq. 678.
[7] For a fuller account of proof of title, see *post*, p. 578.
[8] L.P.A. 1969, s. 23. See *post*, p. 578, for these periods.
[9] *Post*, p. 579.
[10] *Worthington* v. *Morgan* (1849) 16 Sim. 547.
[11] *Re Cox & Neve's Contract* [1891] 2 Ch. 109 at 117, 118; *Re Nisbet and Potts' Contract* [1906] 1 Ch. 386.
[12] *Post*, p. 581.

their contents.[13] But this does not alter the rule as to notice by failing to inquire at all [14] even if an inquiry would probably have been met by some false but apparently reasonable excuse.[15]

(c) *Imputed notice.* If a purchaser employs an agent, such as a solicitor, any actual or constructive [16] notice which the agent receives is imputed to the purchaser. The basis of this doctrine is that a man who empowers an agent to act for him is not allowed to plead ignorance of his agent's dealings.[17] Thus where a solicitor discovered an equitable mortgage on the title and was deceived by a forged receipt into believing that the mortgage had been discharged, the purchaser had imputed notice of the mortgage and was bound by it.[18] Since solicitors are usually employed to investigate title this branch of the doctrine of notice is essential. But, in order to check its extension, it is now confined by statute to notice which the agent acquires acting as such and in the same transaction.[19] Before the Conveyancing Act, 1882, notice received by an agent in a previous transaction was occasionally imputed to a purchaser, but this discouraged the employment of local solicitors with knowledge of local affairs.[20]

Since imputed notice rests upon a man's presumed knowledge of his agent's dealings an exception arises where the agent deliberately defrauds the principal.[21] Where the same solicitor acts for both parties, any notice he acquires is ordinarily imputed to both parties [22]; but if he enters into a conspiracy with one to conceal something from the other, that other may plead that he purchased without notice.[23] The same applies if the purchaser employed the solicitor not generally but merely to draw up the conveyance.[24]

(d) *Extent of doctrine of notice.* The tendency of the Court of Chancery was constantly to extend and refine the doctrines of constructive and imputed notice. So much property was held under

---

13 *Hewitt* v. *Loosemore* (1851) 9 Hare 449 at 458; *Espin* v. *Pemberton* (1859) 3 De G. & J. 547; Williams V. & P. 309; criticised *post,* p. 964.
14 *Peto* v. *Hammond* (1861) 30 Beav. 495.
15 *Jones* v. *Williams* (1857) 24 Beav. 47.
16 *Re The Alms Corn Charity* [1901] 2 Ch. 750.
17 Williams V. & P. 306.
18 *Jared* v. *Clements* [1903] 1 Ch. 428.
19 L.P.A., 1925, s. 199 (1) (ii), (b), replacing C.A., 1882, s. 3 (1) (ii); *Thorne* v. *Marsh* [1895] A.C. 495 at 501.
20 See *Re Cousins* (1886) 31 Ch.D. 671; for the previous law, see Williams V. & P., 3rd ed., 235–239.
21 Williams V. & P., 306, 307.
22 *Dryden* v. *Frost* (1838) 3 My. & Cr. 670; *Meyer* v. *Chartres* (1918) 34 T.L.R. 589; and see *Kennedy* v. *Green* (1834) 3 My. & K. 699; *Lloyds Bank, Ltd.* v. *Marcan* [1973] 1 W.L.R. 339 at 348 (affirmed [1973] 1 W.L.R. 1387); but see *Bateman* v. *Hunt* [1904] 2 K.B. 530.
23 *Sharpe* v. *Foy* (1868) 4 Ch.App. 35; *Cave* v. *Cave* (1880) 15 Ch.D. 639.
24 *Kettlewell* v. *Watson* (1882) 21 Ch.D. 685; (1884) 26 Ch.D. 501.

trusts and other equitable dispositions that the frequent appearance of the bona fide purchaser of the legal estate without notice would have been intolerable. Equity's ambition was to eliminate him, so far as possible, by ensuring that it should be almost impossible to escape notice of any equity properly created and recorded. In so far as he could be excluded, equitable rights were as secure as legal rights. Equity's policy was in the main successful, as may be judged from the rarity and abstruseness of the cases in which the defence of purchaser without notice has been made out. But the fundamental danger to which equitable interests are exposed by the doctrine must never be forgotten, and from time to time the danger materialises.[25] Legal policy requires the acceptance of some degree of risk in order that land may be a freely marketable commodity. Even though purchasers without notice rarely appear, much conveyancing law is founded upon the doctrine of notice and will be understood only when that doctrine and its refinements have been mastered.

The Conveyancing Act, 1882, is regarded as closing the period in which the rules relating to notice were widely extended. Apart from the change in the law about imputed notice, mentioned above, the Act merely stated that a purchaser should not be affected by notice unless he had failed to make " such inquiries and inspections as ought reasonably to have been made by him." [26] This, it has been said, " really does no more than state the law as it was before, but its negative form shows that a restriction rather than an extension of the doctrine of notice was intended by the legislature." [27]

5. Successors in title. The protection of the doctrine of purchaser without notice also extends to any purchaser claiming through such a purchaser,[28] even though he took with notice of the equity.[29] Similarly, a mere volunteer, if he claims through a purchaser without notice, can presumably claim freedom from the equity, for the principle is that once a legal estate has passed into the hands of a purchaser without notice of the equity, that equity ceases to be enforceable against that estate, and cannot be revived.[30] Unless this were so, the owner of the equity could, by widely advertising his claim, make it difficult for the purchaser without notice to dispose of the land for the price that he gave for it.[30]

---

[25] A striking instance is that of equitable interests of husbands and wives: see *post*, p. 447.
[26] s. 3 (1) (i), replaced by L.P.A., 1925, s. 199 (1) (ii). See Maitland, *Equity*, 120, 121.
[27] *Bailey* v. *Barnes* [1894] 1 Ch. 25 at 35, *per* Lindley L.J.; and see *Caunce* v. *Caunce* [1969] 1 W.L.R. 286.
[28] *Sweet* v. *Southcote* (1786) 2 Bro.C.C. 66; *Wilkes* v. *Spooner* [1911] 2 K.B. 473; Wh. & T. ii, 110.
[29] See, *e.g.*, *Harrison* v. *Forth* (1695) Prec.Ch. 51; *Wilkes* v. *Spooner, supra.*
[30] Maitland, *Equity*, 117.

The only qualification to this rule is based on the principle that a man cannot take advantage of his own wrong. If a trustee disposes of trust property to a purchaser without notice, and later reacquires the property, he will again hold it subject to the trusts, and not free from them.[31]

Sect. 3. Equitable Remedies

1. Discretionary nature of equitable remedies. A further distinction between law and equity lay in the matter of remedies. In general, if a legal right was infringed, the person injured was entitled as of right to a legal remedy, either an order for the recovery of his land or damages. Thus if A trespassed on X's land, X had a legal right to sue him for damages and, on proving his case, he was entitled to damages as of right. If the trespass was trivial the damages might be nominal (*e.g.*, forty shillings) or contemptuous (*e.g.*, one farthing) and X might be ordered to pay the costs; but he had a right to judgment. A plaintiff seeking an equitable remedy, on the other hand, had no right to anything at all; equitable remedies were discretionary, and even if the plaintiff proved his case, equity might refuse to give him any assistance if, for example, his claim was trivial or it would be inconvenient or unconscionable to grant an equitable remedy. This discretion was exercised not arbitrarily according to the whim of the judge but " judicially," according to settled principles, so that a plaintiff could succeed in equity only if, in addition to a right having been infringed, there was no equitable principle which prevented him from being granted a remedy.[32]

2. The remedies. The principal remedies given by equity were specific performance (an order to a person to carry out his obligations) and injunction (an order to a person to refrain from doing some act in the future or, more rarely, to put right something already done). These remedies were evolved from the forms of decree acting *in personam.* Equity would also make orders for money payments where no remedy existed at law, as, for example, where a trustee had dissipated trust moneys. But equity would not award damages for breach of contract and did not acquire jurisdiction to do so until the Chancery Amendment Act, 1858. This Act provided that in any case where the Chancery had power to entertain an application for an injunction or specific performance, it could award damages either in addition to or in substitution for such

---

[31] *Re Stapleford Colliery Co.* (1880) 14 Ch.D. 432 at 445; *Gordon* v. *Holland* (1913) 82 L.J.P.C. 81; and contrast *Piggott* v. *Stratton* (1859) 1 De G.F. & J. 33 with *Wilkes* v. *Spooner, supra.*

[32] Snell, *Equity*, 630–633.

injunction or specific performance. This did not alter the rule that equitable remedies were discretionary, neither did it enable courts of equity to award damages in all cases; if the case was one where the Chancery had no jurisdiction to grant specific performance or an injunction, it could award no damages under the Act. In other words, the Act allowed the Chancery to award damages only in cases where an equitable remedy might be available; it did not give the Chancery jurisdiction in cases where it had no jurisdiction before.[33]

In the same way that the Chancery was originally unable to give the legal remedy of damages, the common law courts were unable to give the equitable remedies of specific performance and injunction. Consequently a plaintiff who wanted, say, damages for past trespasses, and an injunction to restrain future trespasses, formerly had to take proceedings both in one of the common law courts and in Chancery.

3. Relationship with law. The manner in which the courts of common law and of Chancery used to operate side by side, with mutually exclusive but complementary jurisdictions, cannot here be explained at length.[34] But it may be illustrated by the fourfold classification of the jurisdiction in equity. This comprised—

   (i) the exclusive jurisdiction, dealing with matters which the common law totally ignored, such as trusts;

  (ii) the concurrent jurisdiction, where equity offered remedies better suited to some cases than damages at common law, as, for example, specific performance of contracts for the sale of land, and injunctions against trespass or breach of covenant;

 (iii) the auxiliary jurisdiction, where equity assisted common law procedure, for example, by decrees for discovery of documents; and

 (iv) the overriding jurisdiction, interrupting common law process in the manner already explained.[35]

In all these ways equity supplied or corrected deficiencies of the common law. But until 1875 equity was administered in its own

---

[33] *Lavery* v. *Pursell* (1888) 39 Ch.D. 508; *Proctor* v. *Bayley* (1889) 42 Ch.D. 390; *Wroth* v. *Tyler* [1974] Ch. 30, holding that the scale of damages may be different from that at common law: *post,* p. 594; Wh. & T. ii, 399 *et seq.*

[34] Maitland, *Equity,* 17–19; Ashburner, *Equity,* 2nd ed., 10 *et seq.*; Snell, *Equity,* 11 *et seq.*

[35] *Ante,* p. 112. This classification of equitable jurisdictions was rendered obsolete by the Judicature Act, 1873.

separate court. To put an end to multiplicity of proceedings where both legal and equitable issues arose in the same case was one of the principal objects of the Judicature Acts, 1873 and 1875.

Sect. 4. The Judicature Acts: Union of the Courts of Law and Equity

1. Union of courts. By the Judicature Act, 1873,[36] the superior courts of law and equity were united into one Supreme Court, divided into a High Court and Court of Appeal. All parts of the Supreme Court were given full jurisdiction both in law and in equity without any distinction of subject-matter. For convenience the High Court was divided into five Divisions, each of which had certain matters assigned to it. In 1880 [37] the Common Pleas Division and Exchequer Division were merged into the Queen's Bench Division, and in 1972 the Probate, Divorce and Admiralty Division was re-named the Family Division,[38] with some adjustments of jurisdiction. There are now three Divisions:

> the Chancery Division
> the Queen's Bench Division, and
> the Family Division.

2. Jurisdiction of Divisions. It is important to notice that these are only divisions of one court, the High Court, and not separate courts having distinct jurisdictions [39]; each Division of the High Court has the same jurisdiction and can enforce both legal and equitable rights and give both legal and equitable remedies. This means that it is no longer necessary to go to two separate courts to enforce legal and equitable rights or to obtain legal and equitable remedies. If a point of equity arises in an action in the Queen's Bench Division, for example, the court can deal with it; and it will not be fatal to an action if it is started in the wrong Division, for the case may be transferred to the proper Division if it is not decided in the Division in which it was started.[40] The allocation of business between the three Divisions cannot therefore affect any question of law: it is so arranged merely for administrative convenience.

---

[36] This came into force on November 1, 1875 (Supreme Court of Judicature (Commencement) Act, 1874, s. 2). The Judicature Acts, 1873 and 1875, are now replaced by the J.A., 1925.

[37] Order in Council of December 16, 1880, made under J.A., 1873, s. 32.

[38] Administration of Justice Act 1970.

[39] *Serrao* v. *Noel* (1885) 15 Q.B.D. 549 at 558.

[40] J.A., 1925, ss. 58, 59; R.S.C., Ord. 4, r. 3; Practice Direction [1973] 1 W.L.R. 627, which would have saved much difficulty in *Wroth* v. *Tyler, supra*, if it had been in force then.

3. Law and equity still distinct. Law and equity nevertheless remain distinct.[41] The two bodies of law have not been altered, although they are now both administered by the same court.[42] A legal right is still enforceable against a purchaser of a legal estate without notice, while an equitable right is not. Equitable rights are still enforceable only by equitable remedies, subject to the jurisdiction conferred by the Chancery Amendment Act, 1858, a jurisdiction which has survived the repeal of the Act.[43] The so-called " fusion of law and equity " has not in fact altered the substance of any person's rights, duties or remedies: it has altered only the courts which enforce them. The reform was therefore primarily a reform of procedure, providing new judicial machinery for the enforcement of the settled rules of law and equity.[44]

4. Conflict. The continuing distinction between the two systems is emphasised by the provision that where there is any conflict between the rules of law and those of equity, the rules of equity shall prevail.[45] This effectively preserves the established relationship between law and equity, by which equitable principles can modify common law rules. Before the Judicature Acts equity asserted itself, when in conflict with common law, by the overriding jurisdiction and the common injunction.[46] The Judicature Acts abolished both this special machinery and the need for it. In practice, of course, these cases of conflict were not fought out because of equity's acknowledged right to the last word. Common law and equity have been harmoniously administered side by side for centuries.

Much therefore still depends upon the division between legal and equitable interests. Our property law is as much founded upon it now as it was before the Judicature Acts. The Court of Chancery is a ghost, but like many other English legal ghosts, its influence can be felt on every side.

Part 2

EQUITABLE RIGHTS BEFORE 1926

Equitable rights may be divided into two classes: those modelled upon common law rights; and those invented by equity independently.

---

41 *Salt* v. *Cooper* (1880) 16 Ch.D. 544, 549.
42 *Clements* v. *Matthews* (1883) 11 Q.B.D. 808 at 814.
43 *Leeds Industrial Co-operative Society Ltd.* v. *Slack* [1924] A.C. 851.
44 See " Reflections on the Fusion of Law and Equity after 75 years," Sir R. Evershed (1954) 70 L.Q.R. 326 at 327.
45 J.A., 1873, s. 25 (11), now J.A., 1925, s. 44. For a leading illustration, see *post*, p. 625; and see generally Snell, *Equity*, 15–17.
46 *Ante*, p. 112.

1. " Equity follows the law." The device of the trust [47] brought into being a large family of equitable interests closely corresponding to the analogous legal estates. The legal fee simple could, for example, be held by trustees upon trust for A for life with remainder to B in tail with remainder to C in fee simple; or upon trust for A for 99 years; or upon trust for A until he should die or become bankrupt. Equitable life interests, entails, leases, reversions and remainders, and any other interest corresponding to an interest recognised at common law, could thus be created under trusts. The maxim was " Equity follows the law." [48]

This was carried to great lengths. An equitable fee simple, for example, descended on intestacy to the heirs general, an equitable entail descended to the heirs of the body. Even the common law's mysterious methods of barring entails [49] were adopted in due course, so that there were equitable fines and recoveries.[50] And for the creation of this type of equitable interest equity adopted many of the common law rules as to words of limitation. A conveyance in trust " for A " would give A only a life interest [51]; and the rule in *Shelley's Case* [52] was espoused with all its refinements. It is true that there were exceptions, as mentioned below. " But," as a great authority wrote, " the cases, where the analogy fails, are not numerous; and there scarcely is a rule of law or equity, of a more ancient origin, or which admits of fewer exceptions, than the rule, that equity followeth the law." [53]

2. Equity corrects the law. Equity did not, of course, follow the law in matters where it was concerned to amend it. The maxim means rather that equity was content to adopt much common law doctrine without modification for the purpose of developing the trust. In particular the fundamental rules as to the possible estates, devolution on intestacy and words of limitation were followed respectfully. But even in these regions there were exceptions, as will be found in later parts of this book. It may be convenient to collect the leading exceptions here.

(i) Equity gave curtesy but not dower.[54] Dower out of equitable interests was given by statute in 1833.[55]

---

[47] For the history of trusts, see *post*, pp. 152 *et seq.*
[48] Snell, *Equity*, 29.
[49] *Ante*, pp. 85 *et seq.*
[50] *Kirkham* v. *Smith* (1749) Amb. 518; Lewin, *Trusts*, 15th ed., 631, 632; Bayley, *Fines and Recoveries* (1828) pp. 254–265.
[51] *Post*, p. 131.
[52] *Ante*, p. 60.
[53] Co.Litt. 290b, n. 1 (xvi) by Butler.
[54] *Post*, pp. 514, 516.
[55] *Post*, p. 518.

(ii) Certain types of future interest (known as executory interests) could be created in equity but not at common law.[56]

(iii) Equitable remainders were not liable to destruction in the same way as legal remainders.[57]

(iv) Equitable interests did not escheat [58] until 1884, when statute made them do so on intestacy.[59] Equity did not in general follow the law derived from feudal tenure.

(v) Equity allowed special restraints on alienation for the protection of married women.[60]

(vi) In trusts, informal expressions were allowed to operate as words of limitation, if clearly intended as such, even though they would have been ineffective at common law. A formal declaration of trust " for A absolutely " would give A an equitable fee simple, for the word " absolutely " showed that limitation by language other than strict conveyancing language was intended.[61] But a similar trust " for A " would be construed as giving A only a life interest.[62] This was so even if the document elsewhere made it plain that the donor intended an absolute gift, for equity followed the law; but if the court was asked to rectify the document, and not merely construe it, the court could carry out the donor's intention.[63] In construing the document the donor's intention in effect prevailed only when he had used words which were ineffective as words of limitation at common law.[64]

Under documents executed after 1925, equity will doubtless follow the new rule of law [65] that a fee simple or other absolute interest will pass unless a contrary intention appears. Further, strict words of limitation have never been required in executory trusts [66]; but this was not a true exception, for under executory trusts the issue is not the legal effect of the words used but the intention lying behind them; and apt words for carrying out that intention will be inserted in the formal instrument which gives effect to such trusts.[67]

[56] *Post*, p. 188. [57] *Post*, p. 187.
[58] *Burgess* v. *Wheate* (1759) 1 Eden 177.
[59] I.E.A., 1884, s. 4. Since 1925 escheat for want of heirs is abolished: *ante*, p. 35.
[60] *Post*, p. 995.
[61] *Re Arden* [1935] Ch. 326; *cf. Re du Cros' S. T.* [1961] 1 W.L.R. 1252 (males descended through females are " male descendants " but not " male issue ").
[62] *Re Arden, supra*, at p. 332; *Re Bostock's Settlement* [1921] 2 Ch. 469 at 483; and see cases there considered. The law was previously confused: see the history traced in *Jameson* v. *McGovern* [1934] I.R. 758.
[63] *Banks* v. *Ripley* [1940] Ch. 719; *post*, p. 595.
[64] There is a distinct affinity between two quite different and apparently perverse rules: the rule stated in the text, and the rule in *Purefoy* v. *Rogers, post*, p. 194.
[65] See *ante*, p. 56. [66] *Post*, p. 447.
[67] *Jervoise* v. *Duke of Northumberland* (1820) 1 Jac. & W. 559; *Re Oliver's Settlement* [1905] 1 Ch. 191; and see *ante*, p. 64, n. 12.

3. New equitable interests. Quite apart from those equitable interests which corresponded in a general way with the comparable common law estates, equity devised certain interests in land which had no common law equivalents. These were therefore additions made by equity to the limited number of interests in land which the law permits.[68] They are few in number, for the law is slow to extend the species of property rights (rights *in rem*) which can be created by private transactions. Personal rights and duties of almost any kind can be created by contract as rights *in personam*. But rights *in rem*, binding not only the parties but other persons generally, can exist only in the form approved by the law and not in any fancy form desired by the parties creating them. Yet equity did make possible dispositions of property which were impossible at common law. Some of these could exist only under trusts, where the interests affected were equitable in any case; these included executory interests [69] (which by statute became capable of existing at law [70]), the restraint of a married woman from anticipating her income,[71] and life interests, remainders and reversions (but not entails) in lease-holds and other personalty.[72] But apart from trusts of the ordinary kind, equity introduced three important new interests in property: estate contracts, restrictive covenants, and the mortgagor's equity of redemption. These property rights, which are distinct from " mere equities," [73] require brief explanation.

(*a*) *Estate contracts.* Equity would decree specific performance of certain contracts which were remediable only by damages at common law. Of these the most important were contracts for the sale or lease of land, now called estate contracts.[74] A purchaser under contract to buy land had therefore at common law only a right to damages if his vendor broke the contract. But in equity he had a right to compel his vendor to convey the land itself. This right to specific performance created a right in the land, a species of equitable property right. Therefore, if A agreed to sell land to B, but instead later sold and conveyed it to C, B could recover the land from C if C had notice of B's contract when he obtained the land. B was equitable owner from the time of the contract, and could enforce his equitable right to the land against anyone except a bona fide purchaser of a legal estate without notice of the contract.

---

68 Called " nondescript equities " by Challis, 183.
69 *Ante*, p. 131 ; *post*, p. 188.
70 *Post*, p. 188.
71 *Post*, p. 995.
72 *Ante*, p. 46 ; *post*, pp. 161, 789.
73 See *ante*, p. 110.
74 For a fuller explanation, see *post*, pp. 575, 1040.

(*b*) *Restrictive covenants.* A landowner selling a plot of land will often wish to restrict its use if he has other land adjoining. He may make his purchaser contract accordingly, but a simple contract will bind only the parties and not other future owners. Equity allowed covenants restrictive of the use of land (for example, covenants not to build, or not to use the property otherwise than as a private dwelling) to run with the land [75] so as to bind all future owners except a bona fide purchaser of a legal estate without notice of the covenant. The benefit of such a covenant, belonging to the original vendor, was thus a new kind of property right created by equity.

(*c*) *Mortgagor's equity of redemption.* If A conveyed his land to B as security for a loan, equity would allow A at any time, after repayment of the loan fell due, and despite any contrary provisions in the mortgage, to recover his land by paying to B what was due to him under the loan. This was the equitable right to redeem. Taken together with the other rights of the mortgagor, the mortgagor thus had an " equity of redemption," which was in effect ownership of the property subject to the rights of the mortgagee.[76] A could so recover the land not only from B but from anyone to whom B had conveyed it, saving only a bona fide purchaser of a legal estate without notice of the mortgage. Equity thus gave the mortgagor a right of property which was valuable if, as is usual, the land was worth more than the amount of the debt.

4. Separation of legal and equitable interests. Often the legal estate in land carries with it the beneficial interest, and no separate equitable interest exists.[77] But if Blackacre is merely conveyed to X in fee simple, X takes it beneficially, for his own enjoyment.[78] But although in the case of a beneficial legal owner there is no need to consider separately the legal and equitable estate in land, in other cases this is the only way to arrive at a proper understanding of the law. The ability of the beneficial owner of a legal estate to separate the equitable from the legal interest, so that the legal owner becomes a mere trustee for the equitable owner, is one of the fundamentals of English law.[79] The history of the trust will be considered further on,[80] and so will the way in which equity sometimes protects a person's rights in property without conferring any equitable interest in it upon him.[81]

[75] For a fuller explanation, see *post*, p. 750.
[76] For a fuller explanation, see *post*, p. 889.
[77] See *Selby* v. *Aston* (1797) 3 Ves. 339.
[78] See *Sammes's Case* (1609) 13 Co.Rep. 54 at 56; Co.Litt. 23a; *Commissioner of Stamp Duties (Queensland)* v. *Livingston* [1965] A.C. 694 at 712.
[79] See *Abbot* v. *Burton* (1708) 11 Mod. 181 at 182; Challis 385. For the later history of the trust, see *post*, p. 167.
[80] *Post*, p. 167.   [81] *Post*, p. 539.

Part 3

THE 1925 LEGISLATION

Sect. 1. Policy of the Legislation

It has been seen that a purchaser who buys without notice of some adverse right is bound by that right if it is legal and takes free from it if it is equitable. Consequently the fewer legal estates and interests which can exist in land, the less precarious is the position of a purchaser. But conversely, the more equitable interests which can exist in land the more precarious are rights in real property generally, for all such equitable interests lie open to the risk that the legal estate may be bought without notice. The property legislation of 1925 radically altered the system of legal and equitable interests in order to simplify the law, to protect purchasers from interests of which they had no notice, and at the same time to protect equitable owners. Two prime measures of this policy must now be described—

   (i) The reduction of legal estates to two; and

   (ii) The protection of certain equitable interests by registration in the register of land charges.

Sect. 2. Reduction of Legal Estates to Two

A. The General Scheme

1. Two estates. The scheme of the Acts is to provide that after 1925 only two kinds of legal estate can exist, the fee simple absolute in possession and the lease. Apart from leases, therefore, all interests derived out of the fee simple must now be equitable: life interests, entails, and the remainders or reversions (even though in fee simple) expectant upon them, determinable fees, base fees, and so on, must all now be mere equitable interests. That is to say, in any such case the fee simple absolute in possession, the legal estate, is held upon trust to give effect to the lesser interest in equity. By transitional provisions this scheme was applied to all such interests existing at January 1, 1926,[82] as well as to all future cases.

2. The indivisible fee. Conveyancing is materially assisted by this uniform system of allowing life interests and the like to exist only behind trusts of the legal estate. Before 1926 it was always possible for a fee simple owner to make a settlement (for example, on A for life with remainder to B in fee simple) by which the legal estate was

---

[82] L.P.A., 1925, 1st Sched.

split up into portions. In the above example there would be no immediate fee simple owner during A's life: the absolute owner had temporarily disappeared. The new scheme ensures that he can never disappear. The legal estate, the fee simple absolute in possession, cannot be split up into derivative interests: derivative interests can be created only as trusts of the fee simple, which itself remains inviolate. Therefore in conveyancing the title to the fee simple will now always have a continuous history. It cannot be lost among the fragments of life or other lesser interests.

3. Leases. Leases may still exist as legal estates, but they stand on a different footing from the interests mentioned above. A lease is generally a business transaction for which the mechanism of trusts is inapposite. Leases as legal estates were no serious danger to purchasers since the possession of the tenant was usually self-evident. Leases therefore may, and ordinarily do, still take effect as legal estates.

4. " Family " and " commercial " interests. The key to the new arrangement of legal and equitable interests is the distinction which may roughly be expressed as that between " family " and " commercial " transactions. Life interests, entails, and determinable fees, for example, are typically found in family settlements made by deed or will. To these the machinery of a trust is natural and convenient. The design is therefore to make all such interests equitable, under the trusts of the legal estate. On the other hand, leases, rentcharges, easements, profits and similar interests (often generically called incumbrances) are generally granted for money or other valuable consideration on a commercial basis. For these the machinery of a trust is out of place. The purchaser expects a legal estate and, as will be seen, the scheme of the Act ensures that he may still get one.

5. Section 1. Section 1 of the Law of Property Act, 1925, must now be looked at more closely. The terms of the first three subsections of this section are as follows:

" 1.—(1) The only estates in land which are capable of subsisting or of being conveyed or created at law are—

(*a*) An estate in fee simple absolute in possession;

(*b*) A term of years absolute.

" (2) The only interests or charges in or over land which are capable of subsisting or of being conveyed or created at law are—

(*a*) An easement, right, or privilege in or over land for an interest equivalent to an estate in fee simple absolute in possession or a term of years absolute;

(*b*) A rentcharge in possession issuing out of or charged on land being either perpetual or for a term of years absolute;

(*c*) A charge by way of legal mortgage;

(*d*) Land tax, tithe rentcharge,[83] and any other similar charge on land which is not created by an instrument;

(*e*) Rights of entry exercisable over or in respect of a legal term of years absolute, or annexed, for any purpose, to a legal rentcharge.

" (3) All other estates, interests, and charges in or over land take effect as equitable interests."

6. Existence at law. It should first be noted that the section does not provide that the estates and interests mentioned in subsections (1) and (2) are *necessarily* legal, but merely that they alone *can* be legal. For example, a life interest or an entail cannot be legal estates after 1925, for they are not included in section 1; on the other hand, a lease for a term of years is included in section 1 and so may exist either as a legal estate, as it normally does, or as an equitable interest under a trust. A leasehold is " land " for the purposes of the Act.[84] This means that an interest for life or in tail in leasehold land must be equitable, for it is governed by section 1 (1). Previously it was possible to create a legal life interest in leasehold land by will, but no entail in leasehold could be created at all.[85]

7. Incidents. The incidents of equitable interests are in general similar to those attaching to corresponding legal estates before 1926; thus the position of a tenant for life as regards waste seems to have remained unchanged despite the conversion of his legal life estate into an equitable life interest at the beginning of 1926. There is no express provision on this point but " equity follows the law." [86]

8. Rights over other land. The general scheme of the section is to deal with the legal rights of ownership in the land itself in subsection (1), and with legal rights over the land of another in subsection (2). Subsection (2) contains an important list of charges or incumbrances which can still be legal and of which purchasers must therefore still beware. This list is modelled on the traditional definition of real property,[87] which includes not only physical land (corporeal hereditaments) but also certain rights over land such as easements, profits (covered by subsection (2) (*a*)) and rentcharges (incorporeal heredita-

---

83 These four words have been repealed: see *post*, p. 142.
84 *Ante*, p. 46.
85 *Ante*, pp. 46, 94.
86 *Ante*, pp. 103, 130.
87 See *ante*, p. 11.

ments).[88] Any of these, being real property, can be held for any estate or interest known to the law.[89] For this reason they are included within the meaning of "land" for the purposes of the Law of Property Act, 1925.[90] A rentcharge, for example, can be held in fee simple, for a term of years, or for life. In the first two cases, but not in the third, it may still be a legal incumbrance, either under subsection (1) as "land" held for a permissible legal estate, or in its own right under subsection (2) (*b*). There are other incorporeal hereditaments which rank as real property in our law and which may be held for either of the two possible legal estates although they are not mentioned in subsection (2), such as an advowson (the right to present a clergyman to a living).[91] These curiously assorted interests all fall within the above-mentioned statutory definition of "land."

9. Estates and interests. It will be noted that the rights mentioned in subsection (1) are called legal estates and those mentioned in subsection (2) are called legal interests or charges. This is a convenient distinction between rights over a person's own land and rights over the land of another, but both types of right are referred to in the Act as "legal estates," and have the same incidents attached to them as attached to legal estates before 1926.[92] The title of "estate owner" is given to the owner of a legal estate.[92] Before 1926 equitable rights in land were frequently and properly called equitable estates, but they should now be called equitable interests and the name "estate" reserved for legal rights.

The various legal estates and interests must now be examined more closely.

B. *The Estates and Interests*

1 (a). "Fee simple absolute in possession." The meaning of "*fee simple*" has already been considered.[93]

"*Absolute*" is used in its accustomed sense to distinguish a fee simple which will continue for ever [94] from a modified fee, such as a determinable fee or a base fee.[95] The policy of the Act requires that any such interest, being less than a fee simple absolute, should

---

[88] For incorporeal hereditaments, see *ante*, p. 12, *post*, p. 787.
[89] *Post*, p. 787. It will be remembered that only a "tenement" could be held in tail before 1926: *ante*, p. 94, *post*, p. 787.
[90] L.P.A., 1925, s. 205 (1) (ix).
[91] *Post*, p. 800.
[92] s. 1 (4).
[93] *Ante*, p. 41.
[94] See *Edward Seymor's Case* (1612) 10 Co.Rep. 95b at 97b.
[95] *Ante*, p. 74.

take effect only in equity, under a trust of the legal estate. A fee simple defeasible by condition subsequent would also necessarily be equitable but for the Law of Property (Amendment) Act, 1926.[96] By this Act an amendment was made to meet an unforeseen difficulty connected with rentcharges. In some parts of the country, particularly Manchester and the north, it is a common practice to sell a fee simple not for a capital sum, but for an income in the form of a perpetual rentcharge (an annual sum charged on the land).[97] Rentcharges of this kind are commonly called "fee farm rents."

Now the remedies for non-payment of a rentcharge include a right to enter on the land temporarily to collect the rents and profits [98]; further, in a number of cases an express right of re-entry is reserved by the conveyance, entitling the grantor to enter and determine the fee simple and thus regain his old estate if any payment is a specified number of days in arrear. The reservation of a right of re-entry clearly made the fee simple less than absolute, and it was thought by some that even a temporary right of entry might have this effect.[99] This meant that those who had purchased land in this way before 1926 and had obtained legal estates suddenly found that their estates might no longer be legal and that it was doubtful who had the legal estate. Further, the complicated provisions of the Settled Land Act, 1925, probably applied.[1]

To remedy these difficulties the Schedule to the Law of Property (Amendment) Act, 1926, added a clause to the Law of Property Act, 1925, s. 7 (1), providing that " a fee simple subject to a legal or equitable right of entry or re-entry is for the purposes of this Act a fee simple absolute." This amendment thus allows a fee simple to remain a legal estate even though it is subject to a right of entry, and rules out any possible complication with the Settled Land Act, 1925, where land is subject to a legal rentcharge such as a fee farm rent. But the exception is so widely drawn that it affects all conditional fees; for the effect of a condition subsequent annexed to the fee simple is to give rise to a right of re-entry exercisable on breach of the condition, and until this right of re-entry is exercised, the fee simple continues.[2] Consequently, by virtue of the Amendment Act any fee simple defeasible by condition subsequent appears able to rank as a legal estate if limited to take effect as such, even though it is far from being " absolute " in the ordinary sense of the

---

[96] Sched.
[97] For rentcharges, see *post*, pp. 141, 792.
[98] *Post*, p. 797.
[99] See 61 L.J.News. 50, 145, 167, 501.
[1] *Post*, p. 314.
[2] *Ante*, p. 76.

word. Yet in cases which do not arise out of rentcharges it seems possible that the Settled Land Act, 1925, may still apply, as it was originally intended to do. This will be discussed later.[3]

Two other statutory exceptions to the meaning of *absolute* are to be found in the Law of Property Act, 1925, s. 7. These relate to fees simple liable to be divested by statute, and the property of corporations. By subsection (1) a fee simple may be absolute for the purposes of the Act although liable to be divested by statute, *e.g.*, by the Lands Clauses Acts or the School Sites Acts.[4] Such Acts provide that land acquired for various public purposes shall re-vest in the grantor or some other person if the purpose is not carried out, or if use for that purpose ceases in the future. Thus a highway authority, in which the surface of the highway is vested until the land ceases to be used as a highway, has a legal estate.[5] By subsection (2) similar provision is made for a fee simple vested in a corporation, so that even if it were argued that a corporation's fee simple is determinable on its dissolution,[6] the fee would not be less than absolute.

The three exceptions made by section 7 (as amended) are, of course, exceptions only for the purposes of the Act, that is to say, for the purpose of allowing those interests to be legal estates. Section 7 in no way alters the conditions attached to them.

" *In possession* " means that the estate must be immediate, and not in remainder or reversion.[7] Remainders and reversions are now equitable interests, taking effect behind a trust of the legal estate. But, in order to prevent temporary interests such as leases from disturbing the legal ownership, " possession " is defined so as to include not only physical possession of the land but also the receipt of rents and profits or the right to receive them, if any.[8] Thus a fee simple is still " in possession " even though the owner has granted a lease, for he is entitled to the rent reserved by the lease, and even if the land has also been mortgaged, for he is entitled to the rents and profits, if any, in excess of any interest payable to the mort-gagee.[9] But if land has been granted " to A for life, remainder to B in fee simple," the interests of both A and B are necessarily equitable, for a life interest cannot now be legal and B's fee simple is

---

[3] See *post*, p. 315.
[4] See, *e.g.*, *Re Cawston's Conveyance* [1904] Ch. 27; *Pickin* v. *British Railways Board* [1974] A.C. 765.
[5] *Tithe Redemption Commission* v. *Runcorn U. D. C.* [1954] Ch. 383.
[6] A view rejected in *Re Strathblaine Estates Ltd.* [1948] Ch. 228; and see *ante*, p. 74.
[7] See *District Bank, Ltd.* v. *Webb* [1958] 1 W.L.R. 148.
[8] L.P.A., 1925, s. 205 (1) (xix); and see s. 95 (4).
[9] *Post*, p. 914.

not in possession. These words therefore signify that future estates
of freehold cannot be legal after 1925.[10]

1 (b). " Term of years absolute." *" Term of years "* is defined as
including a term of less than a year, or for a year or years and a
fraction of a year, or from year to year.[11] In effect, " term of years "
seems to mean any term for any period having a fixed and certain
duration as a minimum. Thus in addition to a tenancy for a specified
number of years (*e.g.*, " to X for 99 years "), such tenancies as a
yearly tenancy or a weekly tenancy are " terms of years " within
the definition, for there is a minimum duration of a year or a week
respectively. But a lease " for the life of X " cannot exist as a legal
estate, for it is limited by the uncertain duration of X's life and not
by a term of years.[12]

Tenancies at will and at sufferance are perhaps best regarded
as not being estates or interests within the meaning of the Act, but
as being bare tenure and mere occupation respectively.[13] If this
view is legitimate it avoids the absurdity of turning these special
types of tenancy into equitable interests. It would be strange if a
fee simple owner became trustee for a tenant for years holding over
after expiry of the lease, and stranger still if he became trustee for
his tenant at sufferance, holding over without his consent.

" Absolute." This word is here used in no intelligible sense, for
it is provided that a term of years is not prevented from being
absolute merely by being " liable to determination by notice, re-entry,
operation of law, or by a provision for cesser on redemption, or in
any other event (other than the dropping of a life, or the determination of a determinable life interest)." [13a] This means that a term
of years may be absolute even if it contains a clause enabling either
party to determine it by giving notice,[14] or if it provides (as is almost
always the case) that the landlord may recover the land if the rent
is not paid or a covenant is broken.[15] " Operation of law " is
illustrated by the doctrine of satisfied terms,[16] and a proviso for cesser
on redemption by the law of mortgages.[17]

It will be seen from this that by the express provisions of the
Act a term of years absolute may consist of a tenancy which is

---

[10] For a very limited exception, see Welsh Church (Burial Grounds) Act, 1945,
s. 1 (2).
[11] L.P.A., 1925, s. 205 (1) (xxvii); *post*, p. 615; for an analogy *cf.* Litt. 67. See
also *Re Land and Premises at Liss, Hants.* [1971] Ch. 986 at 990.
[12] For terms of years determinable on life, see *post*, p. 642.
[13] *Ante*, p. 45, *post*, p. 638.
[13a] L.P.A., 1925, s. 205 (1) (xxvii).
[14] Consider *Simons* v. *Associated Furnishers, Ltd.* [1931] 1 Ch. 379.
[15] See *post*, p. 654.
[16] *Post*, p. 387.   [17] *Post*, p. 892.

neither a " term of years " nor " absolute " according to the natural meaning of the words, *e.g.*, a monthly tenancy liable to be forfeited for non-payment of rent.

It should be noted that, unlike a fee simple absolute, a term of years absolute may be a legal estate even though not " in possession." A lease granted now but to commence in five years' time may thus be legal, although there is now a limit to the length of time which may elapse between the grant of a lease and the commencement of the term.[18] There is no limit to the length of a term of years absolute: terms of three thousand years are common in the case of mortgages.[19] But there is no such thing as a lease in perpetuity, for that is not a " term " at all.[20]

2 (a). " An easement, right, or privilege in or over land for an interest equivalent to an estate in fee simple absolute in possession or a term of years absolute." This head includes both easements and profits *à prendre*.[21] An easement confers the right to use the land of another in some way, or to prevent it from being used for certain purposes. Thus rights of way, rights of water and rights of light may exist as easements. A profit *à prendre* gives the right to take something from the land of another, *e.g.*, peat, fish or wood. " Right or privilege " means only rights in property known to the law, such as profits or other incorporeal hereditaments [22] (not being rentcharges, which are separately dealt with next). Rights such as a franchise to wrecks [23] or treasure trove [24] can thus apparently still exist at law. Under this head rights can be legal only if they are held for interests equivalent to one of the two legal estates; thus a right of way for 21 years may be legal but a right of way for life must be equitable.

2 (b). " A rentcharge in possession issuing out of or charged on land being either perpetual or for a term of years absolute." " *A rentcharge* " is a right which, independently of any lease or mortgage, gives the owner the right to a periodical sum of money secured on land, as where the fee simple owner of Blackacre charges the land with a payment of £50 per annum to X.[25] The rentcharge is a burden on the land since the freeholder is personally liable to pay it, and if payment is in arrear the beneficiary has a right of entry on the land.[26]

---

18 *Post*, p. 631.   19 *Post*, p. 892.
20 *Post*, p. 630.
21 For these interests, see *post*, pp. 805 *et seq*.
22 See *post*, p. 789.
23 *R. v. Forty-Nine Casks of Brandy* (1836) 3 Hagg.Adm. 257.
24 *Att.-Gen.* v. *Trustees of the British Museum* [1903] 2 Ch. 598 at 612. For franchises, see *post*, p. 790.
25 For rentcharges, see *post*, p. 792.
26 *Post*, p. 797.

"*In possession.*" Under the subsection a rentcharge to start at a date subsequent to that on which it is granted cannot be legal, whether it is perpetual or for a term of years absolute. But the Law of Property (Entailed Interests) Act, 1932,[27] provides that a rentcharge is "in possession" notwithstanding that the payments are limited to commence or accrue at a date subsequent to its creation, unless the rentcharge is limited to take effect in remainder after or expectant on the failure or determination of some other interest. Thus if X conveys land to Y in consideration of a perpetual rentcharge becoming payable one year after the conveyance (a practice common in some parts of the country for building land [28]), the rentcharge may nevertheless be legal; but if a perpetual rentcharge is granted "to A for life, remainder to B absolutely," B's interest cannot be legal until it is duly vested in him in possession after A's death.[29]

"*Issuing out of or charged on land.*" "Land" includes another rentcharge.[30] Thus if P charges his fee simple estate in Blackacre with the payment to Q of £100 per annum in perpetuity, Q can create a legal rentcharge of £50 per annum in favour of R, charged on his rentcharge of £100.

"*Being either perpetual or for a term of years absolute.*" "Perpetual" is used here in place of "fee simple absolute" used in 2 (a) above. But there seems to be no practical importance in this difference of wording.

2 (c). "A charge by way of legal mortgage." This must be explained later.[31] It is one of the ways of creating a legal mortgage after 1925, and is similar in effect to the ordinary form of mortgage made by grant of a long term of years. It may be mentioned here that this is a new interest in land created by the Law of Property Act, 1925.

2 (d). "Land tax, tithe rentcharge, and any other similar charge on land which is not created by an instrument." This group comprises periodical payments with which land is burdened by law and not by some conveyance or other voluntary act of parties. "Instrument" is so defined as to exclude statute [32] and the charges covered in this group are statutory. In fact, both land tax and tithe rentcharge have been abolished, and the first four words of this provision have been

---

[27] s. 2. The Act takes its name from another matter: *post*, p. 417.
[28] See 73 L.J.News. 321 (J.M.L.).
[29] The rentcharge is "settled land," and devolves as such: see *post*, p. 308.
[30] L.P.A., 1925, ss. 122, 205 (1) (ix); *post*, p. 793.
[31] *Post*, p. 897.
[32] L.P.A., 1925, s. 205 (1) (viii).

repealed.[33] The unrepealed remnant still has some effect, even though no longer grammatical and without any point of reference for " similar."

Land tax was a small annual tax on land first imposed in 1692, made perpetual in 1798, and administered under the Land Tax Redemption Act, 1802.[34] Many landowners redeemed their land from the tax by lump sum payments.[35] It was finally abolished in 1963.[36]

Tithe rentcharge was abolished by the Tithe Act, 1936.[37] It was a peculiar type of rentcharge imposed by statute in lieu of the former right of parsons and others to one-tenth of the produce of land. Land formerly burdened with tithe rentcharge is now subject to a tithe redemption annuity,[38] and although this is not expressly stated to be a legal interest, it clearly falls within that category as being a " similar charge on land which is not created by an instrument."

2 (e). " Rights of entry exercisable over or in respect of a legal term of years absolute, or annexed, for any purpose, to a legal rentcharge." As already mentioned,[39] a legal term of years absolute is usually made subject to the right of the landlord to re-enter if the tenant fails to pay rent or comply with the covenants. A right of entry is itself an interest in land[40] and in the cases mentioned it may still be a legal right. The statutory language seems wide enough to cover any right of entry affecting a legal lease. But it has been held that the scheme of the Act requires the right to be merely equitable if it is created on the assignment (rather than, as normally, on the grant) of the lease, and it is limited to an uncertain period instead of being perpetual or for a term of years.[41]

A right of entry or re-entry is often attached to a legal rentcharge in order to secure the due payment of the rent.

Concurrent legal estates. Any number of legal estates may exist concurrently in the same piece of land.[42] Thus A may have the legal

---

[33] Tithe Act, 1936, s. 48, 9th Sched. (tithe rentcharge); Finance Act 1963, s. 73, 14th Sched. (land tax).
[34] For the history and nature of Land Tax, see *R.* v. *Commissioners of Land Tax for the Tower Division, Middlesex* (1853) 2 E. & B. 694; *Mayor of Westminster* v. *Johnson* [1904] 2 K.B. 737, 746.
[35] Redemption was compulsory in certain cases under Finance Act, 1949, Part V.
[36] Finance Act 1963, Part V, 14th Sched.
[37] s. 1, taking effect on October 2, 1936. But see *post*, p. 803.
[38] Tithe Act, 1936, s. 3; *post*, p. 804.
[39] *Ante*, p. 140.
[40] For its alienability, see *ante*, p. 81.
[41] *Shiloh Spinners, Ltd.* v. *Harding* [1973] A.C. 691. The exercise of such a right will not put an end to the lease, but there is no reason in principle or in the language of the Act why this should matter.
[42] L.P.A., 1925, s. 1 (5).

fee simple in Blackacre, subject to a legal mortgage in favour of B, a legal rentcharge in favour of C, a legal lease in favour of D, and so on. The legal fee simple is often referred to as *the* legal estate because of its paramount importance. Legal leases, mortgages, rentcharges, easements and the like are regarded as incumbrances upon it.

Sect. 3. Extension of System of Registration of Charges

1. Registration. The greatest risk of disaster in transactions in land is the possibility that some interest may not be discovered at the proper time. If the interest is legal an innocent purchaser will find himself bound by it; if it is equitable, its owner may lose it to a purchaser without notice. Registration of interests, particularly of such as are least likely to appear in a routine investigation of title, is one obvious solution to such problems. It was in use before 1926, but it was greatly extended by the 1925 legislation. Registration of pending actions relating to land was introduced in 1839,[43] and was extended to certain annuities and rentcharges in 1855.[44] The system was further extended by the Land Charges Registration and Searches Act, 1888, and the Land Charges Act, 1900. But even then the interests which were registrable were comparatively few and unimportant. By the Land Charges Act, 1925 (now replaced by the Land Charges Act 1972), a large body of important interests became registrable, and for the first time registration became a fundamental part of the general system of conveyancing.[45]

At the same time the Land Registration Act, 1925, provided for the extension of registered title. This is a wholly new system of conveyancing which over the last century has come to cover a large part of the country and which will in time supersede the old system completely. The new system has its own machinery and rules for the registration of titles and third parties' rights; it is separately considered later.[46]

Under both these systems of registration the doctrine of notice has been profoundly changed; indeed, in substance it has been abandoned. If the right in issue is registrable, the question is whether it is registered rather than whether the purchaser knows or should have known of it. This is a sharp departure from equity in the sense of fairness, but a gain in practical convenience

The elements of the system of registration of land charges, which for many years has formed part of the traditional system of conveyancing, must now be briefly examined.

[43] Judgments Act, 1839.   [44] Judgments Act, 1855.
[45] All kinds of registration are dealt with later at greater length, *post*, Chap. 17.
[46] *Post*, p. 1054.

2. Principles of registration. The two cardinal principles of the registration of land charges are—

(i) Failure to register makes the interest *void against a purchaser.*[47]

(ii) Registration is deemed to constitute *actual notice to all persons for all purposes* connected with the land.[48]

It is a corollary of (i) that if an interest is registrable but unregistered a purchaser is unaffected by notice obtained through other channels: even though he knew of the interest, he will take free from it.[49] The doctrine of notice thus exists in name only. It has been mechanised by statute; the test is now the state of the register, not the state of the purchaser's mind. It is therefore best not to try to translate this system of registration into terms of the equitable rules about a purchaser without notice, but to treat it as a separate system. There are two reasons for this.

(i) Certain legal rights[50] are registrable, and if not registered are void against a purchaser. Registration thus deprives these legal rights of some of the security against purchasers which they formerly enjoyed. This cannot be explained by reference to the doctrine of notice, which had no application to legal rights.

(ii) Under the rules of equity a purchaser without notice took free from equities if he gave *value* and acquired a *legal estate.* An unregistered right is sometimes void against a purchaser if he gave *value* and acquired *any estate, legal or equitable,* and sometimes void against a purchaser only if he gave *money or money's worth* and acquired a *legal estate.*[51]

3. Unregistrable interests. In cases not covered by the provisions as to registration the ordinary legal and equitable rules still apply. An equitable interest, for example, even though registrable and unregistered, will still bind anyone who is not a purchaser protected by the Land Charges Act, *e.g.,* a person who takes the land as a gift. The legislation is concerned only with the protection of purchasers, and registrable interests remain valid for all other purposes despite non-registration.

4. Summary. The position created by the extension of registration is therefore best described as follows.

[47] See L.C.A., 1972, s. 4; *post,* p. 1047.
[48] L.P.A., 1925, s. 198.
[49] By L.P.A., 1925, s. 199 (1) (i), a purchaser is not to be prejudicially affected by notice of any registrable land charge which is void against him for want of registration.
[50] *Post,* pp. 1037, 1038.
[51] L.C.A. 1972, s. 4; *post,* p. 1047.

(i) Most legal rights are not registrable; these continue to be good against the whole world.

(ii) Some equitable rights are not registrable; these continue to be good against the whole world except a bona fide purchaser for value of a legal estate without notice or someone claiming through such a person.

(iii) A few legal rights and many equitable rights are registrable. If these are not registered, they will be void for non-registration against certain purchasers, irrespective of any question of notice. If they are registered, they bind every purchaser, again irrespective of notice. Whether they are legal or equitable no longer makes any difference.

5. Classification of rights. The following is a summary of the most important rights which are registrable after 1925. They will not explain themselves at first sight, and they must be dealt with in detail later.[52]

(a) Legal interests

(i) A charge on land imposed by certain statutes such as the Agricultural Holdings Act, 1948.

(ii) A puisne (pronounced " puny ") mortgage, defined as a legal mortgage not protected by a deposit of title deeds. This covers most second, third or later legal mortgages.

(iii) A charge for death duties, if arising after 1925.

(b) Equitable interests

(i) A limited owner's charge. This includes a charge on land acquired by some limited owner, such as a tenant for life, who pays out of his pocket estate duty (which is a death duty payable on the death of the previous owner) which should have been borne by the estate. Security for the debt from the estate to the tenant for life is provided by the charge.

(ii) A general equitable charge, defined as an equitable charge which affects a legal estate in land but does not arise under a trust and is not secured by a deposit of title deeds. This class covers many equitable mortgages and annuities. It is the residuary class into which equitable interests may fall if not registrable under other heads.

[52] *Post*, p. 1036.

(iii) An estate contract,[53] defined as a contract to convey or create a legal estate. This includes every contract for the sale or lease of a legal estate.

(iv) A restrictive covenant,[54] provided that it is made after 1925 and is not made between lessor and lessee.

(v) An equitable easement, or similar right, provided that it is created after 1925. An easement held for life would be an example, but in practice this class is narrowly confined.

6. Operation of the system. The heterogeneous nature of this catalogue makes it difficult to describe the registration machinery in simple terms. The design of the Land Charges Acts can be perceived only after study of a multitude of different interests. But four clues may be given in advance.

(i) Registration is not applicable to trusts, that is, to interests of the " family " type found in settlements. These are sufficiently protected by the elaborate provisions of the Settled Land Act, 1925, briefly described in the next section.

(ii) Mortgages have special peculiarities, in particular the device of protection by deposit of title deeds. This protection makes registration unnecessary and explains the reservations as to title deeds in (a) (ii) and (b) (ii) above.

(iii) It will be noticed that two of the interests invented by equity [55] outside trusts appear in the list, namely, estate contracts and restrictive covenants (there are special reasons for excluding the mortgagor's equity of redemption). These are the best examples to observe and bear in mind as registrable interests. They are the commonest of the interests which became registrable in 1926 and represent the most important extension of the field of registration.

(iv) Registrable interests are a miscellaneous collection because they comprise only such interests as are not sufficiently protected by other means. Registration has been introduced only where it was thought necessary to strengthen the weak points of the existing system of conveyancing, not as a comprehensive system. Thus there is no presumption that equitable interests which cannot be overreached (as explained next) are registrable.[56] The machinery set up in 1925, moreover, has many weak points of its own.[57]

---

53 *Ante*, p. 132.
54 *Ante*, p. 133.
55 *Ante*, pp. 132, 133.
56 *Shiloh Spinners, Ltd.* v. *Harding* [1973] A.C. 691. Examples which fall into neither category are interests under bare trusts (*post*, p. 438); certain equitable rights based on estoppel and acquiescence (*post*, p. 777); and equitable rights of entry (*post*, p. 1045). Parts of the 1925 legislation appear to assume that no such rights can exist; but this assumption was erroneous: see *post*, p. 383.
57 *Post*, p. 1165.

Sect. 4. Extension of Overreaching Provisions

1. Settlements. A settlement, in its general sense, is any arrangement creating successive interests in property.[58] Such arrangements are of course very common. For example, if a person by his will leaves his property to his widow for life and after her death to his children, this is a settlement. Any disposition of a life interest, entail or other limited interest necessarily creates a settlement since after the limited interest someone else will be entitled in succession. Settlements of land fall into two classes, " strict settlements " (as they may generally be called)[59] and trusts for sale. In a strict settlement the land itself is given to the beneficiaries, *e.g.,* " to A for life with remainder to B in fee simple." In a trust for sale the land is given to trustees who are instructed to sell it, invest the purchase-money, and hold it as a trust fund, perhaps again for A for life with remainder to B absolutely.

2. Trusts for sale. When land is held upon trust for sale, any purchaser will have notice of the trusts from the title deeds. But since sale by the trustees is the very thing the trust commands, the purchaser will not be concerned with the equitable interests. From the moment of sale these attach, by the terms of the trust itself, not to the land but to the purchase-money. They are, it is said, *over-reached,*[60] that is shifted from the land to the purchase-money. The land, originally held upon trust for sale, is freed from all trusts by the sale and the purchaser takes the full beneficial interest in the land.

3. Strict settlements. Where the settlor desired that the land should be kept in the family, and consequently employed a strict settlement, there was no way in which the land could be sold without the purchaser being bound by the settlement. But to prevent land being made temporarily inalienable by this kind of settlement (for which the terms " settlement " and " settled land " are often used by themselves), the Settled Land Acts, 1882 and 1925, have enabled settled land to be sold in all cases so as to shift all the equitable interests to the purchase-money in the same way as under a trust for sale. This legislation will be fully explained in due course.

[58] For settlements, see *post,* Chap. 6.
[59] The term " strict settlement " primarily means a marriage settlement in the usual form (see *post,* pp. 283, 384); but for want of a better term it is often used to comprehend any settlement, in whatever form, that falls within the Settled Land Acts.
[60] But see *post,* p. 377.

4. Overreaching. The important element which must be noticed here is the device of overreaching, which allows land held upon trust to be sold to a purchaser free from the trust, even though he has notice of it. Although the beneficiaries lose any prospect of enjoying the land itself, they are not defrauded in any way, for they have corresponding interests in the purchase-money. This distinguishes overreaching from an interest being overridden, *i.e.*, being void against a purchaser of a legal estate without notice, or for want of registration: if an interest is overreached, it is transferred from the land to money in the hands of trustees; if an interest is overridden, it ceases to be an interest in any property.

Overreaching is therefore a valuable means of preventing certain equitable interests from inconveniencing purchasers. It is eminently suited to interests of the "family" type. In general, of course, interests arising under settlements which can be overreached are not registrable, since purchasers are not concerned with them. Registration is the alternative mode of protection used where an interest is valuable because of the specific property to which it applies (as in the case of estate contracts and restrictive covenants) and cannot fitly be overreached and so be converted into an interest in money.

5. Extent of overreaching. Overreaching, like registration, can be applied, and has been applied, to some legal as well as to many equitable interests. Before 1926 the rights of the beneficiaries under a settlement might be either legal or equitable, according as the legal estate had been conveyed to the beneficiaries or had been given to trustees on trust for them. But whether their rights were legal or equitable, they could equally be overreached under the Settled Land Act, 1882. Since 1925 no legal life estate or legal entail or legal remainder is possible. Statutory overreaching of legal estates under settlements is therefore now no longer necessary under the new scheme of estates and interests. But that does not imply that overreaching is less used than before. On the contrary, it still applies to all settlements; and moreover it has been usefully employed in certain fields to which it did not previously extend. The chief extensions may be briefly mentioned:

(i) Trusts for sale are imposed by statute in certain cases where they did not exist before, *e.g.*, under an intestacy, or in the case of concurrent interests (joint tenancy or tenancy in common).[61] These are all cases where a number of different interests will probably have to be satisfied out of the land,

[61] See *post*, pp. 408 (concurrent interests), 523 (intestacy).

and where it may be desirable to sell the land as a whole and satisfy those interests out of the purchase-money.

(ii) Under certain special trusts for sale or settlements (usually called "*ad hoc*" trusts for sale or settlements) it is possible to overreach several equitable rights which could not be thus overreached before 1926.[62]

The first of these provisions means that there are now more cases in which a conveyance will overreach equitable rights, the second means that some conveyances now have a wider overreaching effect than before.

6. Other overreaching conveyances. Although settlements and trusts for sale are most important sources of overreaching conveyances, they are not the only sources. Thus if X has mortgaged his land to M, and then fails to pay the interest, M has a statutory power to sell the land free from X's equitable right to redeem it. X's rights will then be transferred to the purchase-money in M's hands, for M is a trustee for X of any surplus after paying off the mortgage debt.[63] Again, a conveyance by the personal representatives of a deceased person will overreach the claims of the beneficiaries under the will or intestacy; the purchaser gets a clear title, and the beneficiaries are satisfied out of the purchase-money.[64] A list of overreaching conveyances is to be found in section 2 (1) of the Law of Property Act, 1925.

In general, only equitable rights can now be overreached; with few exceptions (such as a mortgagee's power to overreach the legal estate which a mortgagor retains) there is no power to overreach legal rights.[65]

Sect. 5.   Effect of a Sale on Legal and Equitable Rights

The operation of the foregoing provisions on a sale of land subject to legal and equitable rights may be summarised and illustrated as follows.

1. Summary

(1) The purchaser takes subject to all legal rights.

Exceptions: He takes free from—

(i) the few legal rights which are void against him for want of registration; and

---

62 *Post*, pp. 379 *et seq.*
63 *Post*, p. 913.
64 *Post*, p. 538.
65 *Post*, p. 373.

(ii) the few legal rights which are overreached.

(2) The purchaser takes subject to all equitable rights.
Exceptions: He takes free from—

(i) equitable rights which are void against him for want of registration: notice is irrelevant;

(ii) the many equitable rights which are overreached, *e.g.*, under a settlement or trust for sale: notice is irrelevant; and

(iii) unregistrable and non-overreachable equitable rights in respect of which he can show either that he is a bona fide purchaser of a legal estate for value without notice, or else that he claims through such a person.

2. Example. An example may help towards an understanding of the above summary. A has bought land from trustees for sale, and at the time of the sale the land was subject to—

(i) the rights of the beneficiaries under the trust for sale,

(ii) a restrictive covenant imposed before 1926,

(iii) a binding contract of sale made by the trustees with X shortly before they offered the land to A (an estate contract), and

(iv) a lease to Y (a legal estate).

A's position is as follows:

(i) he is not bound by the rights of the beneficiaries (class (2) (ii) above);

(ii) he is bound by the pre-1926 restrictive covenant only if he had notice of it at the time of completing his purchase (class (2) (iii) above);

(iii) he is bound to give up the land to X, the earlier purchaser, only if X registered his estate contract before A completed his purchase (class (2) (i) above); and

(iv) he is in any event bound by the lease.

The classical doctrine that legal rights bind all the world while equitable rights do not bind a bona fide purchaser of a legal estate without notice is therefore now subject to many important exceptions. The doctrines relating to (i) legal estates, (ii) notice, (iii) registration, and (iv) overreaching, are all fundamental to the position of a purchaser; and the two latter can cut across the two former. The classical doctrine by itself could not solve all the problems satisfactorily, and since 1925 the practical importance of the purchaser without notice has been very much reduced. The present more elaborate system prescribes the appropriate way for disposing of each individual type of charge on a sale of the legal estate.

Part 4

USES AND TRUSTS

Sect. 1. Before the Statute of Uses, 1535

A. Development of Uses

1. Origin. Everyone today is familiar with the nature of trusts, whereby the ownership of property is vested in one or more persons (the trustees) who hold it for the benefit of others (the beneficiaries). The ancestor of the trust is the use, which had substantially the same character. Uses deeply influenced the development of our law of real property and their nature and utility must be understood in outline. The word "use" was derived not from the Latin. "*usus*" but from the Latin "*opus*" in the phrase "*ad opus*" (on his behalf), via the Old French "*al oes*" or "*al ues*," and hence "to the use of it"[66]: thus land might be conveyed to A and his heirs "to the use of" B and his heirs, where nowadays we should say "in trust for" B.

Although there are records of uses having been created even before the Norman Conquest,[67] the only uses found for some time after the Conquest appear to have been merely temporary uses, *e.g.*, dispositions to the use of a man's wife or dependants while he went on a crusade.[68] In about 1225 the Franciscan friars came to England. The rules of their Order prevented their owning property, but by ecclesiastical interpretation there was held to be no objection to land being conveyed, for example, to some town to the use of the friars.[69] Thereafter uses of a permanent nature became more common, and by the middle of the fourteenth century they were in constant use.[70]

2. Enforcement. After early hesitations[71] the common law courts refused to recognise uses. If land was conveyed by A "to B and his heirs to the use of C and his heirs" the common law courts refused to compel the feoffee[72] to uses, B, to hold the land for the benefit of C,[73] who was called the *cestui que use* (a shortened form, it seems,

---

[66] Maitland, *Equity*, 24. [67] P. & M. ii, 229, 234; H.E.L. iv, 412.
[68] P. & M. ii, 231.
[69] *Ibid.*, 237, 238.
[70] Maitland, *Equity*, 25; Sanders, *Uses*, i. 12. Strictly speaking, a "use," as distinct from a "trust" or "confidence," was a permanent as opposed to a temporary or limited arrangement: Sanders, *Uses*, i, 2 *et seq.*; 1 Co.Rep. 122a, n. (U). But this distinction was not generally observed: see *post*, p. 169.
[71] H.E.L., iv, 414, 415.
[72] For feoffment, see *ante*, p. 50.
[73] Maitland, *Equity*, 27, 28; H.E.L. iv, 416, 430; but see *Select Essays in Anglo-American Legal History*, ii, 713.

of "*cestui a qui oes le feffment fut fait*" [74]). B was the person seised, the legal owner, and the common law would take notice of his rights alone; C had no interest which the law would recognise,[75] for "uses were but imaginations." [76] Nevertheless many uses were created in reliance on the honour and good faith of the feoffees to uses, even though there was no legal remedy for breaches of trust. Towards the end of the fourteenth century the Chancellor's aid was sought and although there is no record of a decree in favour of a *cestui que use* until 1446, equitable relief was probably given early in the fifteenth century.[77] Uses were peculiarly matters of good faith and trust, and were therefore suitable subjects for the Chancellor's equitable jurisdiction.[78] Moreover the Chancery procedure was much better adapted to discovering informal or secret trusts by compelling the feoffee himself to make answer on oath. At common law the parties to an action were not competent witnesses. Therefore uses became enforceable in Chancery only, and the great cleavage between legal and equitable interests was made.

3. Rights in equity. The duties of the feoffees to uses towards their *cestui que use* were threefold: they were bound—
  (i) to permit him to take the profits of the land;
  (ii) to dispose of the land in accordance with his instructions; and
  (iii) to take all necessary proceedings to protect or recover the land.[79]

Although at first the *cestui que use* was regarded as merely having a right to compel the feoffees to uses to carry out their duties, the rights of the *cestui que use* were so extensive that it was soon recognised that he had an estate in the land.[80] The legal estate (the bare legal ownership) was in the feoffees to uses, the equitable estate (the beneficial right of enjoyment) in the *cestui que use*: the former had the husk, the latter the kernel. With some qualifications it could be said in Chancery that "equity is the land." [81]

B. Advantages of Uses

The advantages of the Chancellor's system of equity were so great that by the time of the Wars of the Roses, it was said, the greater

---

[74] H.E.L. iv, 411.
[75] Y.B. 4 Edw. 4, Pasch, pl. 9 (1464); Preston i, 144–146.
[76] *Chudleigh's Case* (1595) 1 Co.Rep. 113b at 140a, *per* Anderson C.J. A Papal Bull of 1279 had declared that a use was not property within the meaning of a vow of poverty: H.E.L. iv, 416, 417.
[77] See Ames, *Lectures on Legal History*, 237.   [78] H.E.L. iv, 418.
[79] *Delamere* v. *Barnard* (1657) 1 Plowd. 346 at 352; Sanders, *Uses*, i. 2; Challis 385.   [80] *Brent's Case* (1583) 2 Leon. 14 at 18.
[81] See Hayes, i, 98–101.

part of the lands in England were held in use.[82] The advantages, which were both substantial and technical, were principally as follows.

1. Evasion of feudal burdens. . As the feudal liabilities fell only upon the person or persons who were seised of land,[83] many feudal liabilities could be avoided by keeping the land vested in two or more joint feoffees to uses of full age. This protected it against the onerous incidents of inheritance [84] and infancy, and was also a safe-guard against forfeiture for treason and escheat for felony. The chief loser, of course, was the king—always lord and never tenant—and after 1485 the Tudor kings set about repairing their exchequer by attaching feudal incidents to uses.[85] This legislation culminated in the Statute of Uses, 1535, which until 1926 was one of the great pillars of English land law.

2. Power to devise. The common law prohibition against devises of land which had become established by the end of the thirteenth century [86] could be evaded by the would-be testator conveying land to the uses of his last will. Until the testator died, the feoffees held the land to his use; thereafter they held it to such uses as he had declared by his will.[87] This testamentary power was perhaps the main reason for the popularity of uses.[88]

3. Avoidance of curtesy and dower.[89] At common law a husband could not dispose of his land free of his wife's prospective right to dower if she survived him. This was such a serious fetter on alien-ability that equity refused to follow the law so as to give dower out of equitable interests.[90] Lands held in use were therefore free from it. Originally the husband's own right to curtesy could be avoided in the same way,[91] but later curtesy (though not dower) was allowed out of equitable interests.[92]

---

[82] Y.B. 15 Hen. 7, Mich., pl. 1 (1499), *per* Frowicke C.J.; Co.Litt. 272a; Sanders *Uses*, i, 17. For further details, see 3rd ed. of this book, pp. 158–173.
[83] *Ante*, p. 50.
[84] If one died, the land vested in the survivors by survivorship (*post*, p. 391), not by inheritance.
[85] See Co.Litt. 76b; Sanders, *Uses*, i, 49–51. 4 Hen. 7, c. 17, 1489, applied wardship and relief to uses of land held in knight's service, with a consequent risk of double wardship (Co.Litt. 76b); by 19 Hen. 7, c. 15, 1504, uses of socage land were subjected to socage incidents; and 26 Hen. 8, c. 13, 1534, s. 4, rendered uses forfeitable for high treason.
[86] *Ante*, p. 67.
[87] H.E.L. iv, 420–423; Litt. 363.
[88] Maitland, *Equity*, 25.
[89] For curtesy and dower, see *post*, pp. 514, 516.
[90] *Ante*, p. 130; *post*, p. 516.
[91] See *Chudleigh's Case* (1595) 1 Co.Rep. 113b at 123b.
[92] *Ante*, p. 130, *post* p. 514.

4. Conveyance into mortmain. If land was conveyed to a corporation, such as a monastery, the lord lost his profitable feudal dues, for the land was held by a tenant which was never under age, never died and could never be attainted of treason or felony. *Magna Carta*, 1217,[93] and the Statutes of Mortmain, 1279 and 1290, prevented the conveyance of land to religious bodies without licence from the Crown.[94] This was evaded by conveying land to feoffees to the use of the religious body. But a statute of 1391 stopped this evasion and, further, brought municipal corporations within the Statutes of Mortmain.[95] This was extended to unincorporated bodies in 1531,[96] and the courts prevented evasions by the grant of long leases by drawing a somewhat uncertain line at about 80 or 100 years.[97]

5. Technical advantages. Uses facilitated conveyancing and settlements in a number of other ways. They enabled a husband to convey land (via feoffees to uses) to himself and his wife or to his wife alone. They made possible the creation of powers of revocation and appointment, so as to revoke existing uses and appoint new ones. Most important of all, they brought into being new varieties of future interests known as executory interests, as explained below.[98] In all these ways the system of uses broke through the boundaries of the common law.

Sect. 2. The Statute of Uses, 1535

A. Provisions of the Statute

1. The statute. The king was the person most affected by the evasion of feudal dues. It was he alone who was always lord and never tenant: he was the one person who had all to gain and nothing to lose by the abolition of uses.[99] After various manoeuvres, " the Statute of Uses was forced upon an extremely unwilling parliament by an extremely strong-willed king." [1] The object of this famous and far-reaching statute was to turn uses into legal estates which

---

[93] c. 43.   [94] *Post*, p. 1000, for the mortmain legislation.
[95] 15 Ric. 2, c. 5; Sanders, *Uses*, i, 16, 17.
[96] 23 Hen. 8, c. 10: Sanders, *Uses*, i, 51.
[97] See, *e.g.*, Y.B. 4 Hen. 6, Hil., pl. 1 (1426) (80 years bad); *Anon.* (1537) B.N.C. 134 at 135 (100 years good); Bro.Abr., tit.Mortmain, 39 (1538) (99 or 100 years good); *Hemming* v. *Brabason* (1660) O.Bridg 1 at 7 (81 years bad). And see *post*, p. 1000, for the modern law.   [98] *Post*, pp. 162, 188.
[99] But the extreme informality and flexibility of the system of uses had created many private grievances long before 1535. Legislation of 1377–1504 was passed to prevent frauds on creditors; and in 1483 Parliament attempted to remedy the plight of purchasers who discovered later that the legal estate was lodged in feoffees to uses. But in the latter case the remedy proved worse than the disease. See H.E.L. iv, 443–446; Sanders, *Uses*, i, 21, 22; Gilbert, *Uses*, 66.
[1] Maitland, *Equity*, 34. For the political causes of the statute, see H.E.L. iv, 450–461.

would be subject to all the usual incidents. It remained in force, and of fundamental importance, until 1926.

The Statute is long and verbose, not only in the preamble which catalogues the supposed evils of uses, but also in the substantive provisions. Section 1 may be summarised thus:

> Where any person or persons are seised of any lands or other hereditaments to the use, confidence or trust of any other person or persons or any body politic [*i.e.*, corporation], the latter person or persons or body politic shall be deemed and adjudged in lawful seisin, estate and possession of the hereditaments for the like estates as they had in the use, confidence or trust.[2]

2. Execution of uses. The effect of this was to " execute "[3] all uses to which it applied by taking the legal estate out of the feoffees to uses and converting the equitable interests of the *cestui que use* into corresponding legal estates. For example, if freehold land was conveyed " to A and his heirs to the use of B and his heirs," the Statute executed the use, with the result that A was divested of all interest in the land,[4] and B's equitable fee simple became legal. A's seisin was momentary and theoretical, and so did not, *e.g.*, give rise to any rights to curtesy or dower.[5] B was by statute deemed to be in actual possession of the land even though he had never entered upon it or seen it.[6] The Statute applied both to uses existing when it was passed and to those created afterwards.

3. Resulting uses. Resulting uses as well as express uses were executed.[7] For example, if before 1535 land had been conveyed by X " to A and his heirs to the use of B for life," X would have disposed of the whole legal estate, which vested in A, but would have disposed of only part of the equitable interest, namely, an estate for B's life. The residue of the equitable interest (*i.e.*, the equitable fee simple subject to B's life interest) would remain vested

---

[2] The full text is printed in Digby, 347 *et seq.* Sect. 2 made similar provision for cases where two or more persons were seised to the use of one or more of themselves.

[3] " Executed " means effected or perfected, as opposed to " executory " (*e.g.*, executory interests) which means not perfected. A conveyance executes an estate in the grantee; a contract to convey gives the intended grantee an interest which is executory until perfected by conveyance.

[4] Sanders, *Uses*, i. 117.

[5] *Ibid.*

[6] *Anon.* (1586) Cro.Eliz. 46; Hayes, i, 79; Williams R.P. 185; *Hadfield's Case* (1873) L.R. 8 C.P. 306, where the limits of this doctrine are discussed.

[7] Sanders, *Uses*, i, 97, 101.

in X, " for that which a man has in him, and does not dispose from him, remains still in him." [8] The effect of the Statute on such a transaction was to deprive A of his legal estate, and give B a legal life estate and X a legal fee simple subject thereto; B's express use and X's resulting use were alike executed by the Statute.

A resulting use also usually arose on a voluntary conveyance (*i.e.*, a conveyance for no consideration) if it was made in fee simple to a stranger and if no use was expressed. In such a case equity deemed it improbable that the grantee was intended to take a free gift beneficially, and so presumed a resulting use of the whole estate granted. The Statute executed this use, so that the grantor's legal estate returned to him and the conveyance was wholly ineffective. [9]

4. No enlargement of estates. It will be seen from this that the Statute did not enlarge the interests of the *cestuis que use* but merely made legal what was formerly equitable. [10] If land was held by A in fee simple to the use of X for life, the Statute did not give X the fee simple but transformed his life interest from one valid only in equity to one valid at law. Conversely, no greater estate could be executed in the *cestuis que use* than was given to the feoffees to uses; the estate of the feoffees limited the duration of the use declared upon it. [11] Thus after 1535 a conveyance " to A for life to the use of B for life " gave B a legal life estate determinable by the death of A; and a conveyance " to A for life to the use of B and his heirs " gave B an estate *pur autre vie* which would last until A died. [12] The duration of the estate taken by the *cestui que use* could not therefore exceed either that of the estate given to him or that of the estate given to the feoffee to uses.

B. Uses Not Executed by the Statute

1. The Statute applied only where a person was *seised* of land. Seisin was a term peculiar to freehold estates of freehold tenure. [13] Thus if freehold land was given " to A and his heirs to the use of B for 21 years," the Statute gave B a legal term of years and the grantor the legal reversion in fee simple. [14] But if an existing lease-hold was assigned to uses, the Statute had no application, for it

---

[8] *Ayres* v. *Falkland* (1697) 1 Ld.Raym. 325 at 326; and see Co.Litt. 23a, 271b.
[9] See *post*, p. 443.
[10] *Beckwith's Case* (1589) 2 Co.Rep. 56b at 57b.
[11] Preston i, 181; Sanders, *Uses*, i, 107.
[12] *Anon.* (1560) 2 Dy. 186a; *Crawley's Case* (1599) 2 And. 130 (rent); *Dixon* v. *Harrison* (1670) Vaugh. 36 at 49; Gilbert, *Uses*, 127, 430; Sanders, *Uses*, i, 107; contrast *Meredith* v. *Joans* (1630) Cro.Car. 244.
[13] *Ante*, p. 48.
[14] See Cru.Dig. i, 350; Gilbert, *Uses*, 182.

used the word " seised," and a leaseholder could have no seisin.[15]
Thus an assignment of a lease for 99 years " to A to the use of B
for 21 years " was not affected by the Statute, and the use took effect
in equity just as before.[16] Similarly, uses of copyholds were not
executed by the Statute, for the seisin was in the lord of the manor.[17]

Seisin of any kind of land, in its broadest legal sense,[18] would
fall within the Statute. But it did not apply where incorporeal
hereditaments,[19] such as easements or profits, were created for the
first time. For unless they existed before the feoffment to uses,
the feoffee to uses could not be seised of them to another's use.[20]
The Conveyancing Act, 1881,[21] abolished this anomaly, and so made
it possible for all incorporeal hereditaments to be both created and
transferred at law by means of uses.

2. The Statute did not apply where a corporation was seised to uses.
Before 1535 a use would not be enforced against a corporation, which
as such lacked a conscience to which the Chancellor could appeal
or a body which he could imprison.[22] Although this rule disappeared
soon after the Statute,[23] the Statute did not apply where a corporation
was seised to uses, for it applied only where " any person or persons "
were seised to the use " of any other person or persons or of any
body politic," and this showed that " person or persons " was not
intended to include bodies politic.[24] But for the same reason a
corporation could be a *cestui que use*.

3. The Statute did not execute active uses. If the feoffee had some
active duty to perform, the uses were not executed, for otherwise
the feoffee would have been unable to carry out his duties.[25] Thus
if land was conveyed " to A and his heirs to the use that he should
collect the rents and profits and pay them to B and his heirs," the
legal fee simple remained in A, and B merely took the equitable fee
simple which was implied by the absolute right to rents and
profits.[26] The same applied if the duty imposed on A was to convey

---

[15] Sanders, *Uses*, i, 87, 275.
[16] Maitland, *Equity*, 37.
[17] *Ante*, p. 48; *Rowden* v. *Maltster* (1626) Cro.Car. 42 at 44; Scriven 55.
[18] *Ante*, p. 48.
[19] *Post*, p. 805.
[20] *Beaudely* v. *Brook* (1607) Cro.Jac. 189; Sanders, *Uses*, i, 105–107.
[21] s. 62.
[22] *Croft* v. *Howel* (1578) 2 Plowd. 530 at 538; Challis 389.
[23] Sanders, *Uses*, i, 87; *Mayor, etc., of Coventry* v. *Att.-Gen.* (1720) 7 Bro.P.C.
    235; *Green* v. *Rutherforth* (1750) 1 Ves.Sen. 462 at 468; H.E.L. ix, 52, 58.
    Chancery process could be, and was, used against the corporation's servants,
    through whom it had to act.
[24] Sanders, *Uses*, i, 87; ii, 28.
[25] *Anon.* (1544) B.N.C. 94; *Symson* v. *Turner* (1700) 1 Eq.Ca.Abr. 383; Sanders,
    Uses, i, 253, 254.
[26] *Silvester* d. *Law* v. *Wilson* (1788) 2 T.R. 444.

or sell the land.[27] The common formula " to the use that he should pay the rents and profits to B or permit him to receive them " was held to be an active use (unexecuted) in a deed but a passive use (executed) in a will [28]; for the rule was that in a deed the former of two inconsistent directions prevails, but in a will the latter.[29] If the active duties existed during a limited period only, *e.g.*, while X lived, the feoffee to uses ceased to hold the legal estate when the period ended,[30] for " the trustees are to take only so much of the legal estate as the purposes of the trust require " [31]; but if the active duties were recurrent and there were no other provisions which enabled the trustees to perform them, the trustees retained the legal estate throughout.[32]

4. The Statute did not apply where a person was seised to his own use. The words of the Statute required that one person should be seised to the use of another, not of himself, before the use would be executed.[33] If land was conveyed " to A and his heirs to the use of A and his heirs " A was said to be " in by the common law and not by the Statute " [34]; it was by virtue of the common law and not the Statute that A held his estate, the expression of a use in his favour merely serving to show that the use was also vested in him.[35]

5. The Statute did not execute a use upon a use. This was by far the most important technicality decided under the Statute. It had been resolved before 1535 that a use upon a use was entirely void; a conveyance " to A and his heirs to the use of B and his heirs to the use of C and his heirs " gave C no interest either at law or in equity.[36] It was comprehensible that A should have the legal estate and B the equitable interest, but the use in favour of C was repugnant to B's interest and so void.[37] " The use is only a liberty

---

[27] *Roberts* v. *Dixwell* (1738) 1 Atk. 607; and see *Bagshaw* v. *Spencer* (1743) 2 Atk. 570; Sanders, *Uses*, i, 253, 254.

[28] *Sir Moyl Finch's Case* (1600) 4 Co.Inst. 85; Preston i, 185; Sanders, *Uses*, i, 253, 254.

[29] See *Doe* d. *Leicester* v. *Biggs* (1809) 2 Taunt. 109 at 113; *Baker* v. *White* (1875) L.R. 20 Eq. 166; *Re Adams and Perry's Contract* [1899] 1 Ch. 554; Maitland, *Equity*, 38–41.

[30] *Adams* v. *Adams* (1845) 6 Q.B. 860; Sanders, *Uses*, i, 258–275.

[31] *Barker* v. *Greenwood* (1838) 4 M. & W. 421 at 429, *per* Parke B.

[32] *Van Grutten* v. *Foxwell* [1897] A.C. 658 at 683.

[33] *Sammes's Case* (1609) 13 Co.Rep. 54 at 56; *Peacock* v. *Eastland* (1870) L.R. 10 Eq. 17; *Orme's Case* (1872) L.R. 8 C.P. 281.

[34] See, *e.g.*, *Jenkins* v. *Young* (1630) Cro.Car. 230 at 231; *Long* v. *Buckeridge* (1718) 1 Stra. 106 at 111; and see Hayes, i, 460, 461.

[35] *Doe* d. *Lloyd* v. *Passingham* (1827) 6 B. & C. 305 at 314–316.

[36] Bro.Abr. Feff.al.Uses, 40 (1532); Sanders, *Uses*, i, 42, 43.

[37] *Dillam* v. *Frain* (1595) 1 And. 309 at 313; *Corbet's Case* (1600) 2 And. 134 at 136.

or authority to take the profits, but two cannot severally take the profits of the same land, therefore there cannot be an use upon an use." [38]

After 1535 there was some hesitation but ultimately this doctrine was confirmed. In *Tyrrel's Case*,[39] 1557, a use upon a use was held to be void notwithstanding the Statute. For if, taking the above example, there was no use in favour of C before 1535, there was no use which the Statute could execute in him afterwards. And, on a strict interpretation, it could not be said that B's use was a hereditament of which he was in the first place seised. In such a case, therefore, the new law vested the whole legal and equitable interest in B, leaving nothing for A or C.[40] But great changes impended a century later; for, as will be seen shortly,[41] the Chancery then began to modify this doctrine in a way which made it once more possible to create equitable interests whenever desired.

C. Consequences of the Statute

The consequences of the Statute were many and important.

1. The evasion of feudal dues was partially stopped. The Statute revived the Crown's feudal revenue considerably. But, as its loopholes were discovered, various methods of avoiding feudal dues were seen to remain, for example, active uses and uses of long terms of years.[42]

2. The Statute of Wills, 1540, was passed. The Statute of Uses, 1535, was intended to abolish the power to devise land [43] and was generally believed to have done so.[44] In fact, it increased the power of testators by making it possible for them to devise legal estates instead of mere equitable interests, by means of executed

---

[38] *Daw* v. *Newborough* (1716) 1 Com. 242 at 243, *per* King C.J.

[39] 2 Dy. 155a. See H.E.L. iv, 469–473; Ames, *Lectures on Legal History*, 242–247. The facts of the case were that Jane Tyrrel bargained and sold (by deed enrolled) land to her son to the use of herself for her life and then to the use of her son in tail. It was held that the use raised by the bargain and sale was executed but all subsequent uses were void, so that the son took the fee simple both at law and in equity.

[40] For arguments in favour of C taking a legal estate, see Gilbert, *Uses*, 348, 349.

[41] *Post*, p. 167.

[42] H.E.L. iv, 465, 472; v, 304.

[43] See the preamble, reciting (in characteristic vein) wills made " by such persons as be visited with sickness, in their extreme agonies and pains, or at such time as they have scantly had any good memory or remembrance; at which time they being provoked by greedy and covetous persons lying in wait about them, do many times dispose indiscreetly and unadvisedly their lands and inheritances."

[44] As from May 1, 1536 (s. 11).

uses.[45] This, however, was not realised at the time, and the supposed abolition of the power to devise was so unpopular that it became one of the causes of the rebellion known as the Pilgrimage of Grace, 1536.[46] As a concession the Statute of Wills [47] was passed in 1540. By this Statute a testator was allowed to devise " at his free will and pleasure," notwithstanding any former law or custom to the contrary, all land held by him in socage and two-thirds of his land held in knight service. Thus for the first time did land become generally devisable at law.

A much-debated question was whether the Statute of Uses, 1535, executed uses contained in wills made under the Statute of Wills, 1540.[48] Whether it did or not, it was settled that, by following the presumed intention of the testator, the same result should be produced as if the Statute had applied, unless the will gave sufficient indication of contrary intention. Thus if land was devised " to A and his heirs to the use of B and his heirs," B took a legal fee simple in the absence of any indication to the contrary [49]; a direction that A should pay the testator's debts [50] or that he should receive the rent and pay them to B might amount to a contrary indication.[51]

The wide language of the Statute of Wills was held to override the rule that a freehold estate could not be created in a chattel interest in land.[52] Consequently, it became possible to give a life interest in leasehold land by will,[53] though not by conveyance *inter vivos*.[52]

3. Legal estates could be conveyed by a man to himself or his wife.

At common law a conveyance by A " to A and B and their heirs "

---

45 This appeared in *Sir Edward Clere's Case* (1599) 6 Co.Rep. 17b; see (1941) 7 C.L.J. 354 (R.E.M.). This was in fact the use of a testamentary power of appointment of the type made possible by the statute: *post*, p. 162.
46 H.E.L. iv, 464, 465.
47 32 Hen. 8, c. 1; text in Digby, 387.
48 Sanders, *Uses*, i, 250–253; Gilbert, *Uses*, 356; Co.Litt. 271a, n. 1 (viii); Sugden, *Powers*, 146–148; Challis 387, 388.
49 See *Baker* v. *White* (1875) L.R. 20 Eq. 166 at 171.
50 *Re Brooke* [1894] 1 Ch. 43.
51 *Doe* d. *Gratrex* v. *Homfray* (1837) 6 A. & E. 206; *cf. Gregory* v. *Henderson* (1813) 4 Taunt. 772; *Barker* v. *Greenwood* (1838) 4 M. & W. 421; *Cunliffe* v. *Brancker* (1876) 3 Ch.D. 393; *Van Grutten* v. *Foxwell* [1897] A.C. 658 at 683; *Re Adams and Perry's Contract* [1899] 1 Ch. 554 at 561.
52 *Ante*, p. 47.
53 *Matthew Manning's Case* (1609) 8 Co.Rep. 94b; *Lampet's Cases* (1612) 10 Co.Rep. 46b; *Howard* v. *Duke of Norfolk* (1681) 2 Swans. 454 at 464, 465, where an historical sketch is given; Fearne 401–404; Williams, *Personal Property*, 18th ed., 439. A remainder could also be limited after the life interest, and this took effect by way of executory devise: *Manning's Case*, *ante*; for executory devises, see *post*, p. 183. A life interest in leaseholds created under the Statute of Wills, 1540, was the only form of life interest in personalty which could exist *at law*. Equity allowed personalty to be held on trust for life, but not in tail (*ante*, p. 94). Since 1925 personalty may be entailed in equity (*ante*, p. 94), or given for life in equity, but a legal life interest in leaseholds can no longer be created (*ante*, p. 134).

vested the whole estate in B.[54]   This was particularly inconvenient
where A was the sole surviving trustee and wished to vest the trust
property in himself and B, a new trustee, jointly.   After 1535 this
rule could be evaded by conveying the property to feoffees to the
use of A and B and their heirs and thus letting the Statute vest it
in A and B.[55]   A man could convey property to his wife in a similar
way.[56]   He could also disentail in his own favour, so dispensing
with a reconveyance by a collaborator; for uses could be declared on
fines, recoveries and (after 1833) disentailing assurances, and a tenant
in tail suffering a recovery (for example) to his own use would
acquire the fee simple under the Statute.[57]   These devices were much
used until statute made it possible for a man to convey property to
himself by an ordinary conveyance.[58]

4. Legal powers of revocation and appointment could be created.
After 1535 the powers of revocation and appointment mentioned
above [59] became effective under the Statute to revoke or effect the
grant or conveyance of legal estates.[60]   Thus a conveyance " to X
and his heirs to the use of A for life and thereafter to such uses
as A should appoint " gave a legal power of appointment to A;
on the power being exercised in favour of " C and his heirs," C took
a fee simple which was legal and not merely equitable.[61]

5. Legal executory interests could be created.   The main features
of this complicated subject [62] must be mentioned here.   At common
law future interests by way of remainder were hedged about by many
technical restrictions, derived mainly from feudal law.   It was
impossible to create an estate which might cut short another estate,
or spring up in the future without any estate being granted to anyone
in the meantime.   A conveyance " to A when he marries," for
example, was entirely ineffective if A was unmarried.   But these rules
were not followed by equity, and before 1535 such interests could
be created in equity by means of uses, known as shifting and
springing uses.   By a shifting use a preceding interest could be cut
short, as in a grant " to A and his heirs to the use of B for life (or
in fee) but if B inherits Blackacre then to the use of C for life (or in
fee)."   By a springing use a grant could be made, for example, " to

---

[54] *Perkins*, s. 203 ; *ante*, p. 155.   [55] Sanders, *Uses*, i. 135.
[56] Co.Litt. 112a.
[57] Cru.Dig. i, 367.
[58] L.P.Am.A., 1859, s. 21 (personalty, including leaseholds); C.A., 1881, s. 50
(freehold land), replaced and extended by L.P.A., 1925, s. 72.
[59] *Ante*, p. 155.
[60] Sanders, *Uses*, i, 160–200.
[61] Williams R.P. 417.
[62] Explained more fully *post*, p. 188.

A and his heirs to the use of B when he marries," or " to the use of B at 21." After 1535 the courts of law were in a difficulty. The Statute of Uses, 1535, provided that the *cestui que use* should have legal estates similar to those which they had in the use, yet the estates which existed in the use in many cases infringed the common law rules. Ultimately, with one important qualification,[63] the same liberty was allowed at law to executed uses as equity allowed to unexecuted uses.[64]

In this way the scope of legal conveyances was greatly extended by the addition of this new group of legal future interests. By the employment of uses more elaborate settlements became possible. These future interests created by way of uses were called " executory interests " because they remained executory (*i.e.*, not executed)[65] until the prescribed time arrived; thereupon the feoffee became seised to the use of the beneficiary, the Statute executed the use, and the beneficiary took a legal estate. " Instead of the land stifling the activity of uses, the latter have imparted their mercurial properties to the land."[66] The common law judges were thus forced to inquire what the rules of equity were, for so far as concerned executed uses, the rules of equity became the rules of the law also.[67]

6. New forms of conveyance became possible. Enough has already been said to show that the Statute of Uses brought many unforeseen advantages in its train, and that " conveyancers soon began to make a servant of the Statute."[68] Such were its powers, when fully understood, that conveyances themselves were refashioned in more convenient if not in simpler form. The principal forms of conveyance at common law were the feoffment with livery of seisin and the grant by deed. Fines and recoveries were also in use as conveyances, but they were expensive and slow, and useful only where no other form would serve.[69] An estate in possession could not be conveyed by simple grant until 1845,[70] so that the best form of conveyance for ordinary purposes was a feoffment with livery of seisin,[71] which was usually evidenced by a charter of feoffment; not until 1677 was written evidence of a feoffment made essential,[72] and in 1845 a deed was required.[73]

---

[63] The rule in *Purefoy* v. *Rogers*; *post*, p. 190.
[64] H.E.L. iv, 440, 474.   [65] *Ante*, p. 156, n. 6.
[66] Challis 387. *Cf. Brent's Case* (1583) 2 Leon. 14 at 16, *per* Manwood J.: the use in the hands of the grantor is " as clay is in the hands of the potter."
[67] See *Darlington* v. *Pulteney* (1775) 1 Cowp. 260 at 266.
[68] Williams R.P. 189.
[69] *e.g.*, for disentailing (*ante*, p. 86) or disposing of a married woman's land (*post*, pp. 993, 994). See H.E.L. iii, 236, 246 for their use in earlier times.
[70] *Post*, p. 167.   [71] *Ante*, p. 50.
[72] Statute of Frauds, 1677, s. ll.   [73] R.P.A., 1845, s. 3; *post*, p. 167.

A feoffment had the disadvantages that it was public,[74] and that it demanded actual entry on the land by both parties, or their attorneys.[75] This was often inconvenient. For example, where both parties were at York and the land lay in Cornwall, long journeys would be necessary or else the appointment of attorneys; in the latter case the parties would not know at what precise time the transfer took effect.[76] And feoffments were often impeached for some failure in the formalities of livery. Professional ingenuity was therefore applied in searching for some means of conveying land which should be private and which should operate merely by the execution of a deed.

(a) *Before* 1535: *Lease and Release at common law.* Before the Statute of Uses, 1535,[77] a means of avoiding publicity had been found. If V wished to convey land to P, he granted a lease to P for, say, one year; the lease, not being real property, would be granted without feoffment.[78] V's fee simple reversion could then be conveyed to P a day or two later by a deed of release, thereby enlarging P's estate into a fee simple in possession.[79] For a reversion, not being an estate in possession, could be conveyed by a grant without livery of seisin.[80]

The disadvantage of this device was that it required entry on the land by P between the grant of the lease and the making of the release. For the tenant could take no legal estate until he took possession by making entry; until then he had a mere *interesse termini* (an interest of a term [81]), and a release of a freehold could be made only to a legal tenant in possession.[1]

(b) *After* 1535. The Statute of Uses, 1535, unwittingly removed this last difficulty, for it provided that the *cestui que use* should be " deemed and adjudged in lawful seisin, estate *and possession* " for the equivalent legal estate. Therefore if matters were so arranged that V became seised to the use of P, the legal estate would be vested in P forthwith by virtue of the Statute. The Statute was clearly a powerful engine for transferring legal estates, and the following new forms of conveyance came into use.

---

74 Preston, *Conveyancing,* ii. 219. But the publicity incident to feoffments (*Perryman's Case* (1599) 5 Co.Rep. 84a at 84b) is probably something of a myth, for private witnesses could be used : see Co.Litt. 330b, n. 1 by Butler.
75 In order to effect " livery of seisin," *ante,* p. 50.
76 Preston, *Conveyancing,* ii, 218, 219.
77 This form of conveyance was known by the beginning of the fifteenth century : see Y.B. 11 Hen. 4, Mich., pl. 61 (1409).
78 *Post,* p. 620; Litt. 59.
79 Shep.Touch 207; Co.Litt. 48b.
80 Cru.Dig. iv, 113. See also Sanders, *Uses,* ii, 74, 75; Williams R.P. 212, 213.
81 *Post,* p. 632, where this is explained.
1 Litt. 459; Co.Litt. 270a.

(1) BARGAIN AND SALE. If V contracted to sell land to P, and P paid the price (which at first had to be the full value,[2] but later might be nominal, *e.g.*, twelve pence [3] or a peppercorn [4]), V was said to have " bargained and sold " the land to P. Equity deemed V to be seised to the use of P,[5] much as today V is said to be trustee for P until the land is duly conveyed in accordance with the contract.[6] The use was then executed and P took the legal estate both secretly and without entry on the land. This possibility was foreseen by the authors of the Statute of Uses and in the same session the Statute of Enrolments, 1535,[7] was passed. This provided that from July 31, 1536, no bargain and sale of freeholds was to be effective unless in writing indented (*i.e.*, made by indenture [8]), sealed and within six months enrolled in one of the King's Courts of Record at Westminster or in the county where the land was situated.[9] Thereafter entry on the land but not publicity could be avoided by a bargain and sale enrolled. But as a form of conveyance it suffered from the great disadvantage that no uses could be validly declared upon it; since it involved a use in itself, any further uses would be uses upon uses and so void at law.[10] *Tyrrel's Case* [11] shows the disastrous results of employing this form of conveyance in a family settlement.

(2) COVENANT TO STAND SEISED. After some hesitation it was settled in 1565 that if a tenant in fee simple covenanted to stand seised of his land in favour of some near relative, the " good consideration " of natural love and affection sufficed to raise a use in favour of the relative; the use was then executed and the legal estate vested in the relative.[12] This type of conveyance was of limited application as it could not be employed to convey land to strangers [13]; and, like the bargain and sale enrolled, it could not carry any further uses under the Statute.[13a] But where it could be used it had the advantage of not requiring enrolment.[14]

(3) LEASE AND RELEASE UNDER THE STATUTE OF USES, 1535. The defects of the above two forms of conveyance were eventually

---

2 See Sanders, *Uses*, ii, 53.
3 *The Case of Sutton's Hospital* (1612) 10 Co.Rep. 1a at 34a.
4 *Barker* v. *Keate* (1680) 2 Vent. 35.
5 Sanders, *Uses*, ii, 53 ; H.E.L. iv, 424, 425.
6 *Ante*, p. 132, *post*, p. 575. Under the old doctrine the use arose upon payment; under the modern doctrine it arises upon contract.
7 27 Hen. 8, c. 16. See Sanders, *Uses*, ii, 65–68.
8 *Post*, p. 601.   9 s. 2 exempted certain boroughs.
10 *Ante*, p. 159; Challis 421. Possibly active trusts were exempt from this handicap: *Sir Moyl Finch's Case* (1600) 4 Co.Inst. 85; [1957] C.L.J. at 77 (D. E. C. Yale).
11 *Ante*, p. 160.
12 H.E.L. iv, 425, 426; vii, 356; Challis 392; *Sharington* v. *Strotton* (1565) 1 Plowd. 298.   13 Sanders, *Uses*, ii, 98–100.   13a *Ibid.*
14 Sanders, *Uses*, ii. 96: but a deed was necessary: *Tallarde* v. *Tallarde* (1596) 2 And. 64.

avoided by an ingenious combination of the lease and release at common law with the bargain and sale. This was invented early in the seventeenth century, and by the end of the century was rapidly becoming the normal method of conveyance.[15] It was substantially a lease and release, though the initial lease was created by bargain and sale under the Statute. It gave the tenant, without entry, a legal lease which did not require enrolment; and further uses could be declared on the release.[16]

The conveyance was made as follows: V bargained and sold the land to P for one year, in consideration of a nominal payment of, say, five shillings. By the Statute of Uses, 1535, P was then deemed to be in actual possession of the land, neither enrolment nor entry being necessary. The next day[17] (or even, it seems, by the same document[18]) V conveyed the reversion to P by a release, and the balance of the price was paid. Although usually called "a lease and release under the Statute," it should be noted that the lease alone operated under the Statute; the release took effect at common law.[19] This gave it the further advantage over the forms depending solely on the Statute, that uses declared on the release would be duly executed by the Statute at the proper time; so that legal executory interests, powers, and all the refinements of an elaborate settlement could be incorporated in the deed of release.[20]

This strange transaction was the classical form of assurance for all kinds of ordinary grants and settlements in the eighteenth and early nineteenth centuries. It was also employed for remainders and reversions, for although these could be conveyed by an ordinary deed of grant, it was essential to such a conveyance to be able to show that the prior life or other particular estate was in existence.[21] After the Statute of Frauds, 1677,[22] it was necessary for the lease to be in writing, signed by the vendor or his agent authorised in writing; in practice it was usually made by deed.

The lease and release did not render feoffments, "the most venerable of assurances,"[23] entirely obsolete. A feoffment was still required for a conveyance of gavelkind land by an infant,[24] or for the conveyance of any land by a corporation[25] (which could not be seised to uses within the Statute[26]), unless it used a lease and release at common law.

---

[15] H.E.L. vii, 360, 361.   [16] See 3rd edition of this book, p. 173.
[17] See Sanders, *Uses*, ii. 76.
[18] *Barker* v. *Keete* (1678) Freem.K.B. 249 at 251.   [19] Challis 380.
[20] A full-length example is given in Bl.Comm. ii, Appendix ii, 2.
[21] Preston, *Abstracts*, ii, 85, *Conveyancing*, ii, 235; Challis 382.
[22] ss. 1, 3; *post*, p. 621.
[23] Challis 397.   [24] *Ante*, p. 21; Challis 402.
[25] Challis 381; 397; Preston, *Conveyancing*, ii, 234; Co.Litt. 272a, n. (1), vi, 2.
[26] *Ante*, p. 158; the use of the lease could therefore not be executed.

(c) *Modern reforms.* Lease and release operated undisturbed by statute for over two centuries. By the Conveyance by Release Act, 1841, however, a release was made sufficient by itself, enabling land to be conveyed by the curious method of the release of a reversion upon a non-existent lease. The Real Property Act, 1845, put matters on a more rational basis by providing that all corporeal hereditaments should be deemed to lie in grant as well as in livery.[27] Lease and release thereupon became obsolete, and a simple deed of grant became the common form of conveyance, as it is today. Corporations could employ a deed of grant, though in some cases feoffments lingered on[28]; but an infant conveying land under a custom such as gavelkind still had to employ a feoffment, and except in the case of such conveyances by infants the Act required every feoffment to be evidenced by deed.[29]

Finally the Law of Property Act, 1925,[30] abolished conveyance " by livery or livery and seisin, or by feoffment, or by bargain and sale " and provided that all lands and all interests therein should lie in grant. It also provided, following in substance the Act of 1845 [31] and subject to certain exceptions,[32] that " all conveyances of land or of any interest therein are void for the purpose of conveying or creating a legal estate unless made by deed." [33] Conveyance by deed alone then became in law as well as in practice the only mode of transfer of legal estates and interests. A conveyance by lease and release will still operate, if the release is by deed, but not under the Statute of Uses, 1535, for the Statute was repealed in 1925.[34]

Sect. 3. Development of the Trust

1. Use upon a use void. It had been firmly laid down in *Tyrrel's Case* that a use upon a use was void,[34a] so that a conveyance " to A and his heirs to the use of B and his heirs to the use of C and his heirs " gave the whole legal and equitable interest to B and nothing to A or C. This became a dogma of the common law courts in their operation of the Statute of Uses. But clearly there could be

---

[27] s. 2, replacing the Transfer of Property Act, 1844, ss. 2, 13. See Challis 415–418.
[28] Challis 397.
[29] R.P.A., 1845, s. 3.
[30] s. 51.
[31] R.P.A., 1845, s. 3.
[32] s. 52 (2). The exceptions are: assents by personal representatives (*post*, p. 537); certain bankruptcy disclaimers; surrenders by operation of law, including those not required to be in writing (*post*, p. 668); informal leases (*post*, p. 620); certain receipts; vesting orders; and conveyances taking effect by operation of law (*post*, p. 651).
[33] s. 52 (1).
[34] *Post*, p. 171.
[34a] *Ante*, p. 160.

cases where it might be unconscionable to deprive C of an interest intended for him. *Tyrrel's Case* provides just such an example, though at a time when the Chancellor was not prepared with any remedy. But in the course of time, as it became axiomatic that the first *cestui que use* took the legal estate, it came to be forgotten that there was any objection to a further equitable use declared in favour of a second *cestui que use*. It was settled that any such second use was void for the purposes of the Statute of Uses.

2. Use upon a use enforced. About a century after the Statute, however, the Chancellor began to enforce second uses in equity, where the justice of the case required it. The reports of the mid-seventeenth century are poor, and the precise origins of this revolutionary change are unknown. It now seems clear that, contrary to long tradition, *Sambach* v. *Dalston* (or more properly *Daston*),[35] decided in 1635, is not the first reported case in which this was done; for there the court, in apparently granting relief against mistake, decreed that the land should be conveyed, and not held upon a passive trust.[36] But it is plain that the enforcement of second uses by the Chancellor grew into a general practice during the second half of the century,[37] and was well established by 1700.[38] Political events favoured it, for after the Tenures Abolition Act, 1660,[39] the King and his servant the Chancellor had no longer any pecuniary interest in the Statute of Uses.

By this great step uses were brought back to life. The combination of the doctrine of *Tyrrel's Case*, which prevented the Statute from executing a use upon a use, and the Chancery's reversal of its own decision not to enforce a use upon a use, thus enabled purely equitable interests to be created as freely as before 1535. If it was desired to vest the legal estate in B for the benefit of C, the form adopted before 1535 was " to B and his heirs to the use of C and his heirs." After the middle of the seventeenth century it was " to A and his heirs to the use of B and his heirs in trust for C and his heirs," for a grantee to uses (in this case A) had to be inserted in order to exhaust the effect of the Statute of Uses. A conveyance " to B in trust for C " or " to B to the use of C " of course still gave the legal estate to C under the Statute, and this remained true until the repeal of the Statute in 1925.

---

[35] Tot. 188, more fully reported *sub nom. Morris* v. *Darston* (1635) Nels. 30; see (1958) 74 L.Q.R. 550 (J. E. Strathdene). See also [1957] C.L.J. 72 at 78 (D. E. C. Yale); (1966) 82 L.Q.R. 215 (J. L. Barton); H.E.L. v, 307–309, vi, 641.

[36] [1957] C.L.J. 72 at 78 (D. E. C. Yale); (1958) 74 L.Q.R. 550 (J. E. Strathdene).

[37] See *Grubb* v. *Gwillim* (1676) Lord Nottingham's Chancery Cases, 73 S.S. 347.

[38] *Symson* v. *Turner* (1700) 1 Eq.Ca.Abr. 383.

[39] *Ante*, p. 32.

3. Trusts. It will be seen that in the new formula the expression denoting C's interest was the word " trust " instead of " use." This by itself would not have prevented the Statute from executing it, for the Statute applied to any " use confidence or trust." What did preserve it from the Statute was the use in favour of B. But it was convenient to have a word which indicated that the person whose name followed it had a mere equitable interest, so that " use " was in practice reserved for uses executed by the Statute, and " trust " used for interests which remained equitable.[40] In law the two terms were synonymous, as the above examples show.[41]

4. " Unto and to the use of." A further refinement increasingly employed as time went on was the formula " unto and to the use of B and his heirs in trust for C and his heirs," which was a compressed version of " unto B and his heirs to the use of B and his heirs in trust for C and his heirs.[42] In this case, since B was seised to his own use, the Statute did not execute the first use, and B was in at common law. Nevertheless, the trust in favour of C was not executed by the Statute, for it was a use upon a use; " when we speak of ' a use upon a use,' we do not [necessarily] mean a use upon a use *executed* by the Statute, but a use upon a use *declared* by the instrument." [43] Consequently trusts could be created as easily as uses had been before 1535. All that was required was that instead of conveying the land " to " the trustee, it should be conveyed " unto and to the use of " the trustee, or more shortly " to the use " of the trustee.

In this way was established a construction which " mocked the reason and spirit of the statute, if indeed it did not militate against the plainest principles of interpretation." [44] Lord Hardwicke, the celebrated Lord Chancellor, even said, by way of hyperbole, that " by this means a statute made upon great consideration, introduced in a solemn and pompous manner, by this strict construction, has had no other effect than to add at most three words to a conveyance." [45] Strictly this was neither precise nor true. The " three words " were in fact five (" and to the use of ") [46]; the Statute had many important and unexpected consequences, as has been seen;

---

[40] See Cru.Dig. i, 381 ; and see Sanders, *Uses,* i, 2, 3.
[41] See *ante,* p. 152, n. 70, for an obsolete distinction. The important point is that " use " and " trust " had exactly the same effect (i) under the Statute of Uses, 1535, and (ii) in equity; and see *post,* p. 170.
[42] See Preston, *Abstracts,* i, 101, and compare Preston, *Estates,* i, 182, *Abstracts,* iii, 52, 123.
[43] Hayes (4th ed.) 357; see *Doe* d. *Lloyd* v. *Passingham* (1827) 6 B. & C. 305.
[44] Hayes, i, 54.
[45] *Hopkins* v. *Hopkins* (1738) 1 Atk. 581 at 591.
[46] " Three " may have been used not arithmetically but " vaguely for a small or trifling number ": O.E.D. xi, 354.

and no additional words were needed in a conveyance made for either good or valuable consideration and not seeking to create a trust, such as an ordinary sale.

5. Developments in trusts. The ancient use is thus the ancestor of the modern trust. There was no technical difference between them, and both terms could be used interchangeably at least from 1535 onwards. But after the invention of the trust, which led as has been seen to the term " use " being confined to interests executed by the Statute, great developments took place in " trusts." The Court of Chancery developed and settled the many new questions which were presented by the resurrection of purely equitable interests. As Lord Mansfield observed, " An use and a trust may essentially be looked upon as two names for the same thing; but the opposition consists in the difference of the practice of the Court of Chancery." [47]

Equitable interests, after their rebirth under the name of trusts, went through a second phase of growth which made the modern trust a more flexible, useful and complex device than the older use.[48] The trust was of course developed with different objectives, for evasion of feudal incidents was no longer the dominating purpose. Several of the old limitations attached to uses were abandoned in the case of trusts (or second uses). For example, a trust was enforceable against a corporation but a use originally was not [49]; trusts could be attached to any interest in any kind of property, but uses at first could attach only to a legal fee simple in land [50]; a surviving husband was entitled to curtesy out of his wife's trust estate, although curtesy had not been given out of uses [51]; and equity followed the law in allowing the barring of entails.[52] On the other hand equity adopted stricter rules with regard to words of limitation.[53] Trusts were, in short, freely adapted to the needs of more modern times, with important and beneficial results to our law of property.

But it must not be forgotten that the Statute of Uses remained in full vigour until repealed in 1925.[54] An executed use was an essential first step in the creation of a trust. A conveyance " to A and his heirs in trust for B and his heirs " would give B the legal estate by the Statute. " To the use of A and his heirs . . ." was vital if A was to be made trustee for B. Apart from such technicalities, which were traps for the unwary, legal executory interests

---

[47] *Burgess* v. *Wheate* (1759) 1 Eden 177 at 217.
[48] See Challis 386.
[49] *Ante*, p. 158.
[50] Sanders, *Uses*, i, 28 *et seq.*; H.E.L. iv, 429, 430.
[51] *Ante*, p. 130; Sanders, *Uses*, i, 293.
[52] *Ante*, p. 130.
[53] *Ante*, p. 130.
[54] *Infra*.

and powers created by way of an executed use were still important interests which could be created only under the Statute. Since the repeal of the Statute in 1925 and the reduction in the number of legal estates these interests must now be equitable.

Sect. 4. Effect of the 1925 Legislation

1. Repeal of the Statute of Uses, 1535. The Statute of Uses, 1535, was from the first out of touch with the needs of society, yet it had become a fundamental part of our modern land law. Not until 1925 was it extricated and repealed. In 1879 Maitland, in a mood of frivolity, had called it " that marvellous monument of legislative futility . . . through which not mere coaches and four, but whole judicial processions with javelinmen and trumpeters have passed and re-passed in triumph. . . . It is not a mere Statute of Uselessness but a Statute of Abuses." [55] The many unexpected consequences of the Statute, although harnessed with great ingenuity, were more profitable to lawyers than serviceable to the community. The Statute was at last repealed by the Law of Property Act, 1925,[56] but so as not to affect dealings taking effect before 1926.

2. Consequences. The following are the principal changes associated with the repeal of the Statute.

(i) Trusts of land are no longer created by the formula " unto and to the use of X and his heirs in trust for . . . . . ."; instead, the land is conveyed " to X and his heirs in trust for . . . . . ." or, in more modern language, " to X in fee simple in trust for . . . . . ."

(ii) Where a use arose under the previous law, it can now take effect in equity only, as a trust; for equitable interests can no longer be executed so as to become legal estates. But it is now provided that a voluntary conveyance shall no longer give rise to a resulting use [57] merely because the property is not conveyed " to the use of " the grantee.[58] In other words, in a gift by deed the words " to A in fee simple " now have the same effect as the words " unto and to the use of A in fee simple " had in 1925.

(iii) Legal executory interests can no longer exist.

(iv) Legal powers of appointment can no longer exist.

---

55 Coll.Pp. i, 191.
56 7th Sched.
57 *Ante*, p. 156.
58 L.P.A., s. 60 (3); see *post*, p. 444, for discussion of this provision.

(v) The forms of conveyance made possible by the Statute can no longer be employed.

(vi) A conveyance by a person to himself or his spouse can no longer be made under the Statute; but it may now be made by virtue of the Law of Property Act, 1925, which allows a person to " convey land to or vest land in himself." [59] But this provision does not enable a man to grant a lease to himself; for the difficulties in the concept of a man being both landlord and tenant, and enforcing covenants against himself,[60] are too great.[61]

---

[59] L.P.A., 1925, s. 72 (3).
[60] L.P.A., 1925, s. 82 (1), does not overcome this difficulty.
[61] *Rye* v. *Rye* [1962] A.C. 496, where the subsection was also held not to apply to oral tenancies.

CHAPTER 5

FUTURE INTERESTS

Part 1

INTRODUCTION : VESTED AND CONTINGENT INTERESTS

1. Meaning of "vested" and "contingent." A future interest
in land is an interest which confers a right to the enjoyment of the
land at a future time, such as a right to land by way of remainder
after the death of a living person. A future interest may be either
vested or contingent, and vested interests may be either "vested in
interest" or "vested in possession." An interest is "vested in
possession" when it gives the right of present enjoyment [1]; but of
course it is not then a future interest. If it is vested in interest but
not in possession (for which situation the term "vested" is ordinarily
used by itself) it is a "future interest," since the right of enjoyment
is postponed, yet it is also an already subsisting right in property
vested in its owner: it is a present right to future enjoyment.[1a] By
contrast with a vested interest, a contingent interest is one which
will give no right at all unless or until some future event happens. So
if land is settled on A, B and C, all living persons, as follows—

> "to A for life, remainder to B for life, remainder to C in
> fee simple if he survives B,"

then A's interest is vested in possession, B's is vested in interest but
not in possession (a vested remainder) and C's is contingent. If B
dies first, C's remainder will vest; and on A's death it will fall into
possession.

2. Conditions of vesting. The distinction between vested and
contingent remainders is of fundamental importance, both in the
old and in the modern law.[2] A remainder is vested if two conditions
are satisfied:

(i) the person or persons entitled to it must be ascertained [3];
and

(ii) it must be ready to take effect in possession forthwith, and

---

[1] See Fearne, *Contingent Remainders*, 2. Fearne's treatise (10th ed., 1844,
with notes by Butler) is the classic work on the whole subject of future interests.
The other leading works are *Gray on Perpetuities* (4th ed., 1942) and Morris and
Leach, *The Rule against Perpetuities* (2nd ed., 1962; supp. 1964).

[1a] Fearne 2.

[2] Its modern importance will appear in connection with the rules against
remoteness, *post*, p. 209.

[3] Fearne 9: *Re Legh's S. T.* [1938] Ch. 39 at 52.

173

be prevented from doing so only by the existence of some prior interest or interests.[4]

If either condition is not satisfied, the remainder is contingent.

To return to the example—

" to A for life, remainder to B for life, remainder to C in fee simple if he survives B,"

it has been seen that B's interest is vested and C's is contingent. Neither is vested in possession, for A has the only interest which is vested both in interest and in possession. And C's interest is bound to remain contingent during B's life, even if A is already dead, since it depends not only upon the determination of B's life interest but upon the further contingency of C outliving B. B's interest is vested because, if A's life interest were to terminate forthwith, an ascertained person, B, is already entitled to the land, subject only to A's prior interest. Even if A is aged 23 and B 97, so that it is improbable that B's interest will ever vest in possession, B nevertheless has a vested interest[5]; for an interest may be vested even if there is no certainty of it taking effect in possession at any time[6]: otherwise no future life interest or entail could be vested.[6a] If land is given to X in tail, remainder to Y in fee simple, Y's remainder is vested, not because X's entail is bound to determine at some time (for this is not the case[7]) but because Y has been at once *invested* with the fee simple, subject only to X's entail.[8] On the other hand, an interest is not necessarily vested because it is bound to take effect at some time. For example, if property is given—

" to A and B for their joint lives, with remainder to the survivor,"

the death of one before the other is bound to occur at some time[9]; yet since it is uncertain which will be the survivor, the remainder is contingent, whether the remainder is in fee simple[10] or for life.[11]

Other examples of contingent interests occur where there is a gift to the heir of a living person (for until that person dies, his heir cannot be ascertained),[12] or where although the gift is in favour of a specified person, it is made contingent upon some event

---

[4] *Cf.* Fearne 3–9, 216; Gray, ss. 101, 108; Tiffany (1913) 29 L.Q.R. 290 *et seq.*
[5] Fearne 216.
[6] *Smith d. Dormer* v. *Packhurst* (1740) 3 Atk. 135.　　　　　　6a Fearne 216.
[7] *Contra*, Smith, *Executory Interests*, 67 (this work forms Vol. ii of the 10th edition of Fearne, *Contingent Remainders, supra*).
[8] Hawkins & Ryder 282.
[9] See *post*, p. 592, as to L.P.A., 1925, s. 184, which deals with the ascertainment of the survivor in doubtful cases.
[10] *Biggot* v. *Smyth* (1628) Cro.Car. 102; *Quarm* v. *Quarm* [1892] 1 Q.B. 184.
[11] *Whitby* v. *Von Luedecke* [1906] 1 Ch. 783; *Re Legh's S. T.* [1938] Ch. 39.
[12] Challis 75.

occurring, *e.g.*—

> " to A upon attaining 25 or marrying," [13] or
> " to B if he returns to England." [14]

In such cases, the interests of A and B are contingent until the event occurs, whereupon they become vested.[15]

3. Concealed vestings and contingencies. It is in most cases obvious whether or not a remainder is made subject to a contingency; but there are some apparently conditional phrases which do not create legal contingencies, and some apparently unconditional remainders which are nevertheless contingent. For example, a limitation—

> " To A in tail, but if A's issue should at any time fail then to B in fee simple "

gives B a vested remainder, for the phrase beginning " but if " adds no contingency other than the inevitable possibility that A's entail may come to its natural end[16]; it can be read as being merely the equivalent of " subject to the prior interest." [16a] The limitation in effect is simply to A in tail with remainder to B in fee simple, giving B a vested remainder. Similarly a limitation—

> " To A (a bachelor) for life, remainder to his eldest son for life, but in default of such issue then to B in fee simple "

gives B a vested remainder, for the contingency expressed is merely the non-existence of a preceding life interest on the failure of which B stands ready to take.[17]   But if the gift had been—

> " To A (a bachelor) for life, remainder to his eldest son (if any) in fee simple, remainder to B in fee simple,"

B's remainder would have been contingent, for there was a rule that no interest which followed a contingent fee simple could be vested.[18] This was because although a grantor can create any number of successive life interests or entails (limited interests) and vest them in living persons, he can part with the fee simple (an absolute interest) only once; so that any two limitations of the fee simple are not successive but alternative, and if one is contingent the other must

---

13 *Leake* v. *Robinson* (1817) 2 Mer. 363.
14 *Re Arbib and Class's Contract* [1891] 1 Ch. 601.   15 Preston i, 88.
16 *Cf. Smith* d. *Dormer* v. *Packhurst* (1740) 3 Atk. 135, *post*, p. 195.
16a See *Maddison* v. *Chapman* (1858) 4 K. & J. 709 at 719 (affd. (1859) 3 De
   G. & J. 536); *Permanent Trustee Co. of New South Wales Ltd.* v *d'Apice*
   (1968) 118 C.L.R. 105.
17 For the effect of expressions such as " in default of such issue," see *White* v.
   Summers [1908] 2 Ch. 256 at 271 *et seq.*
18 *Loddington* v. *Kime* (1697) 1 Ld.Raym. 203; 1 Salk. 199; Fearne 225, 374–377;
   Gray, s. 112, who is hesitant.   The rule is disputed by Hayes, *Limitations*, 81
   et seq.; Tiffany (1913) 29 L.Q.R. 296.   But the authorities in favour of the rule
   seem sufficient, and its principle seems sound.

depend on the converse contingency.[19]   For somewhat similar reasons
a gift which follows a determinable or conditional fee simple is
regarded as contingent, as for example B's interest in a limitation—

> "to A in fee simple until he ceases to reside in the family
> home, remainder to B in fee simple." [20]

4. Size of beneficiary's interest.   An interest may be vested
although the size of the beneficiary's interest is not finally ascertained.
For example, where land is devised—

> "to A for life, remainder to all his children who shall attain
> the age of 21 years,"

each child obtains a vested interest on attaining his majority [21];
but these vested interests are liable to open to let in each child
who subsequently attains full age.[22]   Thus if X and Y are the only
children who have attained their majority, they each have a vested
interest in one-half of the property, but that interest may later be
partially divested in favour of subsequent children [23]; the divesting
affects only the *quantum* of the interest vested in each beneficiary.[24]
When Z becomes 21, the shares of X and Y each fall to one-third
and Z has the other third; and so on for the other children.[25]   X and
Y can dispose of their vested shares either *inter vivos* or by will,[26]
although even in the hands of the transferee the shares will be liable
to be diminished by other children attaining full age.   But any child
of A who dies under 21 has no interest in the property at all [27]; for
the contingent interest which he had while alive has failed to vest.

5. Vested interest subject to divesting.   A remainder may also be
vested and yet subject to a possibility of its being divested, not only
partially but completely.   For example, if land is settled on A for
life, remainder to such of A's issue as A shall appoint, and in default
of appointment among all A's children in equal shares, the remainders
to the children in equal shares are vested, subject to being divested

---

[19] See 1 Ld.Raym. at p. 208.
[20] Gray, s. 114, n. 3.
[21] *Brackenbury* v. *Gibbons* (1876) 2 Ch.D. 417 at 419; *Randoll* v. *Doe* d. *Roake*
(1817) 5 Dow 202.
[22] *Re Lechmere and Lloyd* (1881) 18 Ch.D. 524 at 529; *Baldwin* v. *Rogers* (1853)
3 De G.M. & G. 649 at 657.
[23] *Cattlin* v. *Brown* (1853) 11 Hare 372 at 379; *Holmes* v. *Prescott* (1864) 10
Jur.(N.S.) 507 at 510.
[24] *Matthews* v. *Temple* (1699) Comb. 467; *Stanley* v. *Wise* (1788) 1 Cox Eq.
432 at 433.
[25] *Doe* d. *Comberbach* v. *Perryn* (1789) 3 T.R. 484 at 493, 495.
[26] *Oppenheim* v. *Henry* (1853) 10 Hare 441.   For the alienability of contingent
interests, see *post,* p. 177.
[27] *Rhodes* v. *Whitehead* (1865) 2 Dr. & Sm. 532.

to the extent of any appointment made by A.[28]   In cases of doubt
the law favours early vesting, and every interest is construed as being
vested forthwith if that is possible; if not, it is treated as becoming
vested as soon as possible.[29]

6. Assignability. It is in reference to futurity of possession that
vested and contingent remainders are classed as future interests. In
one sense a vested remainder is an existing interest, and therefore
not future. And in one sense a contingent remainder is future, but
is not an interest: it is only a possibility that an interest may arise
if some contingency happens. Contingent remainders were so
regarded by the common law,[30] and were therefore inalienable by
conveyance[31]; for there was no subsisting estate which could be
granted. But, exceptionally, they were able to pass by inheritance,[32]
e.g., where land was limited to A in tail, but in case A inherited
Blackacre then to B and his heirs. If B died and then A inherited
Blackacre, B's heir would take the land.[33] But equity would enforce
assignments of contingent remainders[34] by compelling the assignor
to convey the property to the assignee when it fell into possession[35];
and in this way contingent remainders could in practice be sold.

Statute of Wills, 1540,[36] it was held that contingent interests could
    Statutes gave further assistance. By a liberal interpretation of the
be devised[37]; and this was confirmed by the Wills Act, 1837.[38]
Finally, by the Real Property Act, 1845,[39] they became fully alienable
at law. Although a right does not necessarily become an interest
in land merely because statute has made it alienable, it now seems
proper to regard such contingent interests as interests in land rather
than mere possibilities; but the difference between vested and contingent interests is of course unaffected. Further, where the

---

[28] *Cunningham* v. *Moody* (1748) 1 Ves.Sen. 174; *Doe* d. *Willis* v. *Martin* (1790)
4 T.R. 39; *Lambert* v. *Thwaites* (1866) L.R. 2 Eq. 151; *Re Master's Settlement*
[1911] 1 Ch. 321; Fearne 226 *et seq.*; Farwell, *Powers*, 310 *et seq.*; Challis 75.
For a classification of vested remainders, see Restatement of the Law of Property,
§ 157.
[29] Smith, *Executory Interests*, 73; Hawkins & Ryder 302; Jarman 1365 *et seq.*
[30] Challis 76, 77; Williams R.P. 398, 400.
[31] *Lampet's Case* (1612) 10 Co.Rep. 46b. But they could be released, *i.e.*, waived
in favour of the holder of a prior vested estate (*ibid.*); and until the F.R.A.,
1833, they could to some extent be alienated by fine or recovery operating by
estoppel: Fearne 365, 366; Cru.Dig. ii, 333; Williams R.P. 398.
[32] *Weale* v. *Lower* (1672) Pollexf. 54; *Goodright* d. *Larmer* v. *Searle* (1756) 2
Wils.K.B. 29.
[33] Fearne 364 *et seq.*; Challis 76n.
[34] *Wright* v. *Wright* (1750) 1 Ves.Sen. 409; *Crofts* v. *Middleton* (1856) 8 De G.M.
& G. 192.
[35] Fearne 548 *et seq.*
[36] *Ante*, p. 160.
[37] *Jones* v. *Roe* d. *Perry* (1789) 3 T.R. 88; Fearne 368 (discussing earlier authorities
to the contrary, *e.g.*, *Bishop* v. *Fountaine* (1695) 3 Lev. 427).
[38] s. 3.
[39] s. 6, now replaced by L.P.A., 1925, s. 4 (2).

contingency is as to the person entitled, as in the case of a limitation to the heir of a living person,[40] or the survivor of two living persons,[41] there is still no transmissible interest vested in anyone.[42]

The principal categories into which future interests fall are reversions, remainders and executory interests; these will be considered in turn.

Part 2

REVERSIONS

1. Nature of reversions. So far the nature of reversions and remainders has been only briefly explained.[43]   A reversion is such part of a grantor's interest as is not disposed of by his grant; a remainder is such part as is disposed of, provided that it is postponed to some estate in possession created at the same time. Thus if a tenant in fee simple grants a life interest, the fee simple which he retains is a reversion. His estate in fee simple in possession has become a fee simple in reversion. If, on the other hand, he creates a lesser estate and by the same instrument disposes of some or all of the residue of his estate to one or more other persons, the interests of those other persons are not reversions but remainders.   In the case of a reversion, the land reverts to the grantor when the lesser estate determines; in the case of a remainder, it remains away from him for the benefit of some third party.[44]   It follows that while there may be many remainders created out of one estate, there can be but one reversion.   Thus if X, a tenant in fee simple, grants land—

"to A for life, remainder to B for life, remainder to C in tail,"

he retains the reversion in fee simple, and yet has created two remainders, namely, those of B and C.   It will be seen that a reversion arises by operation of law, a remainder by act of parties.[45] If the estate in possession was created at some earlier time, the grantee takes no remainder but a transfer of the grantor's reversion or some estate derived out of it.   A reversion therefore need not necessarily be owned by the person who created the antecedent estate.

---

[40] Fearne 371.
[41] *Doe* d. *Calkin* v. *Tomkinson* (1813) 2 M. & S. 165.
[42] *Re Cresswell* (1883) 24 Ch.D. 102 at 107.
[43] *Ante*, p. 47.
[44] See the discussions by Maitland at (1890) 6 L.Q.R. 25 and S.S., Vol. 17, pp. xxxviii. In the text, " reversion " is always employed in its correct sense, although in practice the terms " reversions " or " reversionary interests " are often loosely applied to remainders as well as reversions.
[45] Williams R.P. 362.

Estates less than a fee simple, and upon which therefore remainders or reversions (or both) are expectant, are called " particular estates," [46] for such an estate is given for a particular portion of time,[47] and is only a part (or *particula* [48]) of the fee simple. But no fee simple could be a particular estate, even if it was a determinable fee.[49] Future interests expectant on a conditional or determinable fee simple, such as a right of entry or a possibility of reverter, are neither reversions nor remainders, for they exist independently of any estate in their owners. The fee simple has been disposed of, and so there is nothing left of the grantor's estate, even though the fee simple granted is made determinable or subject to conditions. These special interests are best treated in connection with the special types of fee simple to which they attach,[50] and they may here be left out of account.

2. All reversions are vested. From its very nature it follows that a reversion is a vested interest [51]; for it is the remnant of an estate which has never passed away from the grantor, and he or (if he is dead) his representatives stand ready to receive the land as soon as the particular estate determines. According to feudal principles, moreover, a freehold reversioner on a term of years has an estate which is vested not only in interest but also in possession, for the grant of a lease does not deprive a grantor of seisin,[52] and he therefore has what is properly called a freehold in possession subject to the term.[53] From this point of view a reversion on a lease is not a reversion or, indeed, a future interest at all.[54] This technicality is a relic of the ancient doctrine that leases were not even estates and were to be disregarded for feudal purposes.[55] But, as has been seen, leases have long since achieved the status of estates, and it is therefore common and correct to speak of a landlord's reversion.[56] Although seisin as such is no longer important, a landlord's reversion is still an ambiguous interest, for as explained above, it is regarded as being an estate in possession for the purposes of the Law of Property Act, 1925.[57]

3. Reservations of services. The Statute *Quia Emptores*, 1290, forbade subinfeudation, so that no man could grant a fee simple

---

[46] Preston, *Conveyancing*, iii, 169. [47] *Ibid.*
[48] Williams R.P. 361.
[49] Preston, i, 91.
[50] *Ante*, p. 74; *post*, p. 244.
[51] Cru.Dig. ii, 336; Challis 67.
[52] Challis 233; see *De Grey* v. *Richardson* (1747) 3 Atk. 469 at 472.
[53] Challis 100.
[54] *Wakefield & Barnsley Union Bank Ltd.* v. *Yates* [1916] 1 Ch. 452 at 460.
[55] *Ante*, p. 43.
[56] Challis 80. [57] *Ante*, p. 139; and see *post*, p. 616.

to be held of him as lord.[58]   But this did not apply to the grant of a particular estate,[59] and on the grant of a legal fee tail, life estate or term of years, the relationship of lord and tenant would still arise between the parties.[60]   It was therefore possible for services to be reserved on such a grant.   This has of course long been unusual in the case of life interests and entails, for in family settlements there is no desire to reserve services[61]; and all such interests must now be equitable, so that the beneficiaries no longer hold in tenure but under trusts.   But legal terms of years are usually granted at a rent and such a rent is rent-service (as opposed to rentcharge) because of the tenure subsisting between landlord and tenant.[62]   For this reason the landlord still has the ancient feudal remedy of distress (the right to seize and sell chattels on the land[63]) if the rent is unpaid.[64]

4. Reversions after 1925.   Before 1926 a reversion might be legal or equitable, depending on the estate out of which it was created. After 1925 a reversion upon an entail or life estate is necessarily equitable,[65] for even if it is a fee simple absolute it is not in possession; the land will be settled land and in accordance with the Settled Land Act, 1925, the legal estate will be vested in the tenant for life or statutory owner.[66]   A reversion upon a term of years, however, can still exist as a legal estate because—

(i) if the owner of a legal fee simple absolute in possession grants a lease, his estate remains a legal estate, for " possession " for this purpose is defined by statute so as to include the right to receive the rents and profits, if any[67]; and

(ii) if the owner of a legal term of years absolute grants a sub-lease, there is nothing in this to render his estate any the less legal; any number of legal estates can exist concurrently in the same land.[68]

---

58 *Ante*, p. 31.
59 *Quia Emptores*, 1290, c. 3; Cru.Dig. i, 72; *ante*, p. 30.
60 This was inevitable if the estate was created *de novo*: Challis 22. If an existing entail or life estate was to be transferred, either subinfeudation or substitution was possible.
61 Leases for lives at a rent were at one time popular, however: see *post*, p. 615.
62 *Ante*, p. 46, *post*, p. 689.
63 *Post*, p. 691; and the lessee owes fealty to the reversioner: Co.Litt. 23a, *post*, p. 613.
64 Litt. 214; Perkins, s. 693; Williams R.P. 364.
65 L.P.A., 1925, s. 1 (1), (3).
66 *Post*, p. 296.
67 L.P.A., 1925, s. 205 (1) (xix); *ante*, p. 139.
68 *Ibid.*, s. 1 (5); *ante*, p. 143.

Part 3

FUTURE INTERESTS OTHER THAN REVERSIONS

In addition to reversions, there were two main types of future interests before 1926, namely, remainders and executory interests. These existed in both legal and equitable forms, which must be treated separately. Equitable remainders and executory interests can however be considered together under the heading " future trusts." Legal executory interests came into being only after the Statute of Uses, 1535. The most convenient order of explanation is therefore as follows,

(1) Legal remainders.

(2) Future trusts.

(3) Legal executory interests.

Executory interests may shortly be described as a special class of future interests which derived from the Statute of Uses, 1535, and the Statute of Wills, 1540, and which were not governed by the common law rules for legal remainders. By the use of executory interests it was possible to make contingent grants which could take effect in ways not permitted by the older common law.

This was a region of the law noted, in the words of its acknowledged master, for " much intricate and abstruse learning." [69] Today nearly all this learning is obsolete. It represents a primitive system for restricting future interests in land which was effectively superseded for the last two centuries by the modern rule against perpetuities.[70] But it was allowed to linger on and complicate the law, though to a diminishing extent, until 1925. A brief account of it must be given here in order to supply the background to the modern law. Those who require more detail and illustrations will find them in the earlier editions of this book.[71] The history of contingent remainders sheds light at many points on the older principles of our land law. Many of these principles were still operative until 1926, and may operate even today where titles depend upon the effect of pre-1926 transactions.

Sect. 1. Legal Remainders

A. Nature of Legal Remainders

A remainder is the estate created when a grantor who, having granted away a particular estate, by the same instrument grants to another person an estate in the same land limited to commence after the

[69] Fearne, Preface to 4th ed.   [70] *Post*, p. 207.
[71] The best detailed account for modern readers is that given by Holdsworth, H.E.L. vii, 81–149.

particular estate,[72] *e.g.,* " to A for life, remainder to B in fee simple." The particular estate and any remainders are all derived out of the grantor's original estate. Together with any reversion they amount to the whole original estate,[73] which is often, though perhaps inaccurately, regarded as having been split up into portions.[74]

Even before 1066 it was allowed that vested remainders could be created.[75] Early lawyers saw comparatively little difficulty in the owner of a fee simple carving it up into a number of successive vested interests, for the whole interest in the land was immediately transferred to ascertained persons. But contingent remainders presented far more difficulty. Thus if land was conveyed to A for life, remainder to the heirs of B (a living person), it was difficult to say where the grantor's fee simple was. The grantor had tried to convey the whole of his estate, yet until B's death it could not be said who was the heir to whom the remainder was given. As late as 1410 it was said that such a remainder was void,[76] but in 1431 it was said to be good [77] and in 1453 this was confirmed by the whole court.[78] After this the courts no longer required that all the estates should be vested forthwith, but were satisfied if there was an immediate transfer of the seisin to the tenant of the particular estate. Nevertheless, it was not finally admitted until the middle of the sixteenth century that contingent remainders which depended on some contingency other than the ascertainment of the remainderman (such as a remainder to X " when he marries ") were valid.[79] The courts then turned to the framing of strict rules to which contingent remainders were required to conform.

Even after the validity of contingent remainders had become firmly established, the ownership of the inheritance remained an unsettled question. Some said that under the above remainder to the heirs of B, the fee simple was in abeyance,[80] or *in nubibus* (in the clouds) [81] or *in gremio legis* (in the bosom of the law) [82]; others

---

[72] Co.Litt. 49a, 143a ; Cru.Dig. ii, 202 ; Preston, i, 91 ; Challis 77–79 ; Gray, § 8.

[73] Co.Litt. 143a ; Fearne 308 ; Challis 78.

[74] For the orthodox view, see Co.Litt. 22b ; Preston i, 120 ; Challis 83. For a criticism, see Tiffany (1913) 29 L.Q.R. 291, who maintains that the fee simple always remained intact, whatever other estates were derived out of it.

[75] P. & M. ii, 21.

[76] Y.B. 11 Hen. 4, Trin., fo. 74, pl. 14, *per* Hankford J. ; and see Litt. 721.

[77] 9 Hen. 6, Trin., fo. 23, pl. 19, at fo. 24, *per* Martin J.

[78] Fitzherbert's *Abridgment*, Feffements et Faits, pl. 99 ; H.E.L. iii, 134–136.

[79] H.E.L. vii, 88.

[80] *Colthirst* v. *Bejushin* (1550) 1 Plowd. 21 at 35 ; *Vick* v. *Edwards* (1735) 3 P.Wms. 372 ; Perkins, s. 708.   [81] Y.B. 11 Hen. 4, Trin., fo. 74, p. 14 (1410).

[82] *Carter* v. *Barnardiston* (1718) 1 P.Wms. 505 at 516 ; Williams R.P. 389. See also *Chudleigh's Case* (1595) 1 Co.Rep. 113b at 137b (" And Baron Clarke said, some have supposed these future uses were preserved in the bowels of the land, and that the land should be charged with them in whose hands soever it should come ; and some have supposed they were preserved *in nubibus*, and in the custody of the law, but he said, in our case, be they below in the land,

argued on the principle that what the grantor had not conveyed away he still had in him,[83] and so said that the fee simple remained vested in the grantor,[84] or, if he was dead, his devisee [85] or heir.[86] The question was never finally settled, but the latter view more nearly corresponds with modern ideas.[87]

Remainders could be legal only if the grantor had power to dispose of a legal estate. Naturally no legal estate could be created by anyone who had a mere equitable interest vested in him, although he could create equitable remainders. Unlike equitable remainders (which are dealt with under the head of future trusts), legal remainders were subjected to inflexible rules largely based on the sanctity of seisin, and these must now be set forth.

B. Rules Governing Legal Remainders

There were four main rules governing legal remainders.

1. A remainder was void unless when it was created it was supported by a particular estate of freehold created by the same instrument.[88]

It was impossible at common law to create a freehold estate which would spring up in the future by itself.[89] Thus if a grant of land was made—

" to A's first son and the heirs of his body,"

and A had no son at the time of the grant, the grant was void.[90] The reason was that the common law required that the seisin should pass out of the grantor into the grantee at the moment when the estate of freehold was created [91]: there must never be an abeyance of seisin. Had the conveyance been—

there they should be perpetually buried, and should never rise again, and be they above *in nubibus*, in the clouds, there they should always remain, and should never descend." The remainders in question had failed to vest in due time: see *post*, p. 186). The supporters of such theories said that the grantor retained no reversion, but a mere possibility of reverter: Preston, *Abstracts*, ii, 100–107.

[83] See *Carter* v. *Barnardiston* (1718) 1 P.Wms. 505 at 516, 517; *Hopkins* v. *Hopkins* (1734) Ca.t.Talb. 44 at 52.
[84] Fearne 351–364; *Davis* v. *Speed* (1692) Carth. 262.
[85] *Egerton* v. *Massey* (1857) 3 C.B.(N.S.) 338 at 356.
[86] *Plunkett* v. *Holmes* (1661) T.Raym. 28. See also n. 82 above.
[87] See Cru.Dig. i, 55; Williams R.P. 389; Gray, § 11, citing authorities.
[88] Fearne 280, 281, 301; Preston, *Abstracts*, ii, 90; Challis 104.
[89] *Goodtitle* d. *Dodwell* v. *Gibbs* (1826) 5 B. & C. 709 at 716; *Boddington* v. *Robinson* (1875) L.R. 10 Ex. 270 at 273.
[90] See *Goodright* v. *Cornish* (1694) 1 Salk. 226; *Scatterwood* v. *Edge* (1697) 1 Salk. 229.
[91] Fearne 281; Smith, *Executory Interests*, 441; Challis R.P. 105; Fletcher 52.

> " to X for life, remainder to A's first son and the heirs of
> his body,"

the gift to A's son would not have infringed this rule, for X would
take an estate of freehold and thus could receive the seisin forthwith. Put technically, the difference was that X's particular estate
supported the contingent remainder to A's son. Similarly, a
conveyance—

> " to A and the heirs of his body after my death," [92] or
> " to B for life from June 24th next," [93]

created no estate at all.

It was essential that the particular estate should be an estate of
freehold; a particular estate for years would not support a freehold
contingent remainder, for the term of years carried no seisin with
it.[94] A conveyance—

> " to A for 21 years and then to B's (unborn) son in fee
> simple "

gave A a valid lease, but created no other estate or interest,[95] the
grantor retaining the fee simple reversion.[96] But for the same reason
a conveyance—

> " to A for 21 years and then to B in fee simple "

took effect as an immediate conveyance to B in fee simple subject
to the lease in favour of A [97]; B had a vested estate of freehold, and
there was no objection to the seisin passing to him, A taking livery
of seisin on his behalf.[98]

The rule also required that the remainder should be created by
the same instrument as the particular estate.[99]

2. A remainder after a fee simple was void.

A grant in fee simple exhausted the grantor's powers, and he
could create no further estate.[1] "There is not in the law a clearer
rule than this, that there can be no remainders limited after a fee
simple." [2] Accordingly if land was given—

> " to A and his heirs, remainder to B and his heirs,"

---

[92] *Hogg* v. *Cross* (1591) Cro.Eliz. 254.
[93] *Buckler's Case* (1597) 2 Co.Rep. 55a.
[94] *Ante*, p. 48.
[95] Smith, *Executory Interests*, 114; see *Goodright* v. *Cornish* (1694) 1 Salk. 226;
cf. Elie v. *Osborne* (1717) 2 Vern. 754.
[96] See Burton, *Compendium*, 10.
[97] *Boraston's Case* (1587) 3 Co.Rep. 19a; Smith, *Executory Interests*, 112; Challis
99, 100.
[98] Litt. 60; Co.Litt. 49a.
[99] *Key* v. *Gamble* (1678) T.Jo. 123; *Moore* v. *Parker* (1695) 1 Ld.Raym. 37;
Fearne 302.
[1] Fearne 12, 372 *et seq.*; Sanders, *Uses*, i, 149; Preston, *Abstracts*, ii, 90; see
Nottingham v. *Jennings* (1700) 1 P.Wms. 23 at 24, 25.
[2] *Duke of Norfolk's Case* (1681) 3 Ch.Ca. 1 at 31, *per* Lord Nottingham L.C.

the limitation to B was void, for A's fee simple absolute comprised the maximum possible interest in the land and left nothing for B. But the rule was not confined to a fee simple absolute; it applied equally to a fee simple defeasible by condition subsequent or to a determinable fee.[3]

To this rule there was one exception. Although a base fee was a species of fee simple, a remainder (and also a reversion) could exist after a base fee.[4] This could arise only where land had been given in tail with remainders over; in such a case, the Statute *De Donis*, 1285,[5] enabled the remainder to exist after the fee tail, and the subsequent conversion of the fee tail into a base fee did not affect the remainders. A base fee can accordingly be defined as " a fee descendible to the heirs general, upon which subsists a remainder or reversion in fee simple." [6] Yet such a remainder or reversion must necessarily have been created before the base fee.

3. A remainder was void if it was designed to take effect in possession by defeating the particular estate.[7]

A remainder was a limitation so framed as to be immediately expectant on the *natural* determination of a particular estate of freehold, and the rule was that a future limitation which might cut short the particular estate could not be a valid remainder.[7] Thus if a conveyance was made—

> " to A for life, but if he becomes bankrupt, to his children immediately," [8]

or—

> " to A for life, but if B has a son five years old, A's estate shall cease and the land pass to that son," [9]

the last gift in each limitation was void and the condition was ineffective: A took a full life estate in each case, and the grantor the reversion. This is a consequence of the common law rule that if a condition was broken, only the grantor or his heirs could take advantage of it and recover the land [10]: the condition could not be made to benefit the remainderman. But if the breach of condition occurred and the grantor failed to re-enter, A's estate continued, and

---

[3] Fearne 373; Smith, *Executory Interests*, 57; Challis 83, 84; *Earl of Stafford* v. *Buckley* (1750) 2 Ves.Sen. 170 at 180.
[4] *Ante*, p. 82; Challis 325.
[5] *Ante*, p. 83.
[6] Challis 325.
[7] Fearne 261; Challis 81; Sanders, *Uses*, i, 155; Preston, *Abstracts*, i, 91.
[8] *Blackman* v. *Fysh* [1892] 3 Ch. 209.
[9] *Cogan* v. *Cogan* (1596) Cro.Eliz. 360; Fearne 263.
[10] *Ante*, p. 77.

at its natural termination B's remainder took effect.[11] B's remainder was therefore not void *ab initio*: it was potentially valid, but liable to destruction.

Conditional gifts must here again be distinguished from determinable limitations.[12] In the above examples the remainder would have been valid if the estate had been limited in the first place to determine naturally on the event prescribed,[13] as could be done merely by using different words, such as—

" to A for life or until he becomes bankrupt." [14]

4. A remainder was void if it did not in fact vest during the continuance of the particular estate or at the moment of its determination.

This rule reflected the common law's abhorrence of an abeyance of seisin,[15] which made it impossible to tolerate a gap between the determination of the particular estate and the vesting of the remainder. If there was bound to be such a gap, the remainder was void from the outset. If there might or might not be such a gap, its validity remained in suspense, awaiting the event.[16]

The following are examples of contingent remainders which were void under this rule:

(i) " to A for life and one day-after his death to B and his heirs " [17];

(ii) " to A for life, remainder to such child or children of his as shall attain the age of 21 after his death " [18];

(iii) " to A for life, remainder to his first son to attain the age of 21 " [19]; and

(iv) " to A for life, remainder to B if B marries."

It will be seen that (i) and (ii) were cases where the remainder was void from the outset, whereas in cases (iii) and (iv) it would be void

---

[11] Challis 82, distinguishing the class of cases where the remainder did not refer to the condition; contrast Fearne, 263, 264.

[12] For this distinction, see *ante*, p. 75.

[13] As in the case of determinable fees: *ante*, p. 74.

[14] *Brandon* v. *Robinson* (1811) 18 Ves. 429; *Rochford* v. *Hackman* (1852) 9 Hare 475.

[15] See *ante*, p. 183.

[16] Fearne 307, 308; *Cunliffe* v. *Brancker* (1876) 3 Ch.D. 393.

[17] *Colthirst* v. *Bejushin* (1550) 1 Plow. 21 at 25; *Corbet* v. *Stone* (1653) T.Raym. 140 at 144.

[18] See *Re Lechmere and Lloyd* (1881) 18 Ch.D. 524; *Miles* v. *Jarvis* (1883) 24 Ch.D. 633; *Dean* v. *Dean* [1891] 3 Ch. 150 at 151.

[19] *Cf. White* v. *Summers* [1908] 2 Ch. 256. Had the remainder been to A's sons as a class, only those who attained 21 before A's death could benefit: *Festing* v. *Allen* (1843) 12 M. & W. 279.

only if events turned out unfavourably, *i.e.*, if A died before a son reached 21 or B married. If the contingency occurred in A's lifetime, the remainder vested at once and was good. If A died first, the remainder failed.[20]

THE "WAIT AND SEE" RULE

It will be noticed that with one exception all the legal remainder rules could be applied as soon as the limitation was made. It could be determined forthwith whether a remainder was supported by a particular estate of freehold, whether it was so worded that it could cut short the particular estate and so on. But whether or not a limitation complied with rule 4 could be determined only by waiting to see what the future brought, unless the facts of the case predicted for certain either that the rule would be infringed or that it would not. In short, there was no "wait and see" about rules 1, 2 and 3; rule 4 alone might be a "wait and see" rule, and continue to threaten the validity of a contingent remainder which was not invalid upon its face. Rule 4 was therefore of particular importance, as will shortly be seen.

Sect. 2. Future Trusts

The strict common law rules relating to remainders did not apply to equitable interests. If the whole legal estate was vested in trustees, the common law was satisfied, for it took no cognisance of equitable interests at all.[21] Nor did equity see any reason for applying to equitable interests the rigid common law rules founded largely on a feudal view of the sanctity of seisin; in this respect, equity refused to follow the law.[22] For example, land could be given—

> " to X and his heirs to the use of A and his heirs until B
>   marries and then to the use of B and his heirs," [23] or
> " to Y and his heirs to the use of B's heir and his heirs."

Before 1535 the limitations in such cases were valid gifts in equity. After the Statute of Uses, 1535, they became legal executory interests, as explained below.

---

[20] There was an exception in favour of posthumously born children, the interval between A's death and his child's birth being ignored: *Reeve* v. *Long* (1694) 1 Salk. 227. 10 Will. 3, c. 22, 1698 (Ruff. 10 & 11 Will. 3, c. 16) extended this rule to deeds as well as wills.

[21] *Corbet's Case* (1600) 2 And. 134 at 147 (a use is " solement imaginacion "); *Abbot of Bury* v. *Bokenham* (1536) 1 Dy. 7b at 12a (" L'use n'est rien en ley "); and see *ante*, p. 152.

[22] See *Re Finch* (1881) 17 Ch.D. 211 at 229.

[23] Selden Society, Vol. 10, pp. 43 (no. 40—after 1389), 48 (no. 45—1393), 114 (no. 117—1417-1424); Brooke's *Abridgement*, Feffments al Uses, 30 (1552).

Sect. 3. Legal Executory Interests

A. *Springing and Shifting Uses and Devises*

1. New legal interests. Before the Statute of Uses, 1535, apart from reversions, the only future interests which could be created were (i) legal remainders, which were subject to the strict legal remainder rules but gave the security of a legal estate; and (ii) future trusts (then called uses), which were free from the legal remainder rules but gave the beneficiaries mere equitable interests. The effect of the Statute of Uses, 1535, was to make it possible to create future interests which had the best of both worlds, giving the owners legal estates and yet being free from the legal remainder rules. This was quickly recognised,[24] and the validity of such interests at law was generally accepted by the end of the sixteenth century.[25] The two categories, shifting uses and springing uses, have already been considered briefly.[26]

2. Shifting uses. An example of a shifting use was a conveyance—

> " to T and his heirs to the use of A and his heirs, but to the use of B and his heirs as soon as B is called to the Bar."

Before 1535 T took the legal fee simple on trust for A and B, A taking an equitable fee simple subject in equity to a gift over to B in fee simple. After 1535 the effect of T being seised to the use of A and B was that the use was executed, T dropped out and the equitable interests of A and B became exactly corresponding legal estates, notwithstanding the rule of common law that there could be no fee upon a fee. B, on being called to the Bar, obtained a legal fee simple.[27] The legal remainder rules could not prevail against the express provision of the Statute that the *cestuis que use* should be seised and possessed of the like estates as they had in the use.

---

[24] The earliest cases seem to be *Anon.* (1538) Brooke Abr. Tit. Feoff. al Use, pl. 50 (shifting use), and *Mutton's Case* (1568) 3 Dy. 274b (springing use).

[25] See *Woodliff* v. *Drury* (1596) Cro.Eliz. 439.   [26] See *ante*, p. 162.

[27] How this actually operated was the subject of a great controversy. It was objected that X could never be seised to the use of B since the execution of the use in A deprived X of the legal estate. Therefore it was suggested that X retained a *scintilla juris* (a spark of title) on which the Statute could operate a second time: *Brent's Case* (1575) 3 Dy. 339b at 340b, *per* Dyer C.J. and Manwood J. The *scintilla* theory was greatly criticised (see *Chudleigh's Case* (1595) 1 Co.Rep. 113b at 132b), and finally Lord St. Leonards succeeded in bringing about its formal condemnation by L.P.Am.A., 1860, s. 7. The anti-*scintilla* school contended that all the uses were executed in the first place, and that thereafter the parties had legal interests under the Statute to which, by force of the Statute, the mercurial properties of uses adhered. For the subject generally, see H.E.L. vii, 138 *et seq.*; Gilbert, *Uses*, 292 *et seq.*; Cru.Dig. ii, 260, 282 *et seq.*; Fearne 289 *et seq.*, notes by Butler, and Appendix II; Preston i, 156 *et seq.*; Sanders, *Uses*, i, 112; and for various theories, see Tudor L.C. 298.

3. Springing uses. An example of a springing use was a conveyance—

> " to X and his heirs to the use of Y and his heirs after my death." [28]

Before 1535, as in the case of the previous example, Y's interest was equitable only. But after 1535 it became a legal fee simple as soon as the donor died. Meanwhile, as happened whenever there was a gap in the beneficial interests specified, equity implied a resulting use in favour of the grantor, which the Statute then executed,[29] so that until the donor's death the legal estate was vested in him rather than in X.

4. Conveyances. The result was that all that was required to validate a limitation *inter vivos* which infringed the legal remainder rules was the insertion of the formula—

> " to X and his heirs to the use of . . ."

before the desired limitations; the Statute of Uses, 1535, did the rest. But in assurances *inter vivos* the insertion of some phrase such as this was essential; the court would not supply it if it was omitted.

5. Wills. In the case of wills a more lenient rule was adopted. Even if no use was inserted, the court gave the same treatment to a devise as if a use had been inserted.[29a] This was probably due to the wording of the Statute of Wills, 1540,[30] which gave a testator power to dispose of land " at his free will and pleasure." [31] Consequently an " executory devise " such as a shifting devise [32]—

> " to A and his heirs, but if A fails to convey Blackacre to my executors, to B and his heirs," [33]

or a springing devise [33a]—

> " to the child of which my wife is now enceinte," [34]

was fully effective, although if contained in a deed the first would have given no interest to B and the second would have been totally void. Any interest of which the will did not dispose descended to

---

[28] *Roe d. Wilkinson* v. *Tranmer* (1757) 2 Wils.K.B. 75.
[29] Cru.Dig. ii, 326; Challis 172.
[29a] " One may devise an estate by his last will in such manner, as he cannot do by any grant or conveyance in his life ": *Matthew Manning's Case* (1609) 8 Co.Rep. 94b at 95a, *per* Coke C.J.
[30] H.E.L. iv, 466, 467, vii, 117; Challis 169. See, however, Lewis, *Perpetuity*, 75–79, Suppt. 127.
[31] ss. 1, 2. See Challis 169; *ante*, p. 161. *Pells* v. *Brown* (1620) Cro.Jac. 590 (" the Magna Charta of this branch of the law ": *Porter* v. *Bradley* (1789) 3 T.R. 143 at 146, *per* Lord Kenyon C.J.) set the final seal of approval on such interests: see Lewis, *Perpetuity*, 80, 81; Gray, § 138.
[32] Challis 174.
[33] *Fulmerston* v. *Steward* (1596), cited Cro.Jac. 592.   [33a] Challis 174.
[34] *Taylor* v. *Bydall* (1677) 1 Freem.K.B. 243 at 244; *Gulliver* v. *Wickett* (1745) 1 Wils.K.B. 105 at 106.

the testator's heir,[35] so that in the latter example the heir was entitled in fee simple unless and until the child was born.[36]

6. Consequences. This group of interests (springing and shifting uses, and the corresponding executory devises) were collectively known as legal executory interests. They revolutionised the subject of settlements, since they allowed new kinds of legal estates to be created in defiance of the rules of common law.

B. *The Rule in Purefoy* v. *Rogers*

1. The rule. It might be thought from the foregoing passages that if a limitation was contained in a grant to uses or in a will, the legal remainder rules were completely ousted. This was often so, but not always; for the notorious rule in *Purefoy* v. *Rogers*[37] deprived one class of future interests of the protection which a grant to uses or a will could give. The class in question was that to which, had there been no grant to uses or will, the " wait and see " rule would have applied, *i.e.*, such interests as would have been of uncertain validity under rule 4[38]; and the rule in *Purefoy* v. *Rogers* demanded that rule 4 should be applied to them, irrespective of any grant to uses or will, just as if they had been limited as contingent remainders at common law.[39]

2. A rule of law. This rule probably originated as a rule of construction,[40] but it became a sanctified dogma of the law, to be applied without exception[41] and without regard to the grantor's intentions.[42] " Now, if there be one rule of law more sacred than another, it is this, that no limitation shall be construed to be an executory or shifting use, which can by possibility take effect by way of remainder." [43] This meant that if any limitation, even though contained in a grant to uses or a will, was by any possibility *capable* of complying with the legal remainder rules, it was to be treated as a legal contingent remainder and not as an executory interest.

3. Scope of the rule. There were three possibilities. A contingent interest in a grant to uses or a will, when scrutinised as at the moment of its creation, might either—

---

35 Fearne 537, 538; *Clarke* v. *Smith* (1698) 1 Lut. 793 at 798.
36 *Cf. Pay's Case* (1602) Cro.Eliz. 878.
37 (1671) 2 Wms.Saund. 380. This extended to wills the doctrine established for grants *inter vivos* in *Chudleigh's Case* (1595) 1 Co.Rep. 113b at 137b, 138a.
38 *Ante*, p. 186.
39 Lewis, *Perpetuity*, 75; Preston, *Abstracts*, ii, 153, 154.
40 See H.E.L. vii, 126, 127.
41 *Doe* d. *Mussell* v. *Morgan* (1790) 3 T.R. 763 at 765.
42 *White* v. *Summers* [1908] 2 Ch. 256 at 267.
43 *Cole* v. *Sewell* (1843) 4 Dr. & War. 1 at 27, *per* Sugden L.C.; 2 H.L.C. 186.

(i) defy the legal rules from the outset, and be certain to infringe them if it took effect at all, as did springing and shifting interests; or

(ii) comply with them from the outset, and be certain to vest (if at all) within the limits and in the way required at common law; or

(iii) be capable of complying with them, but not certain to do so unless events turned out favourably.

Interests in class (i) were unaffected by the rule in *Purefoy* v. *Rogers*; they remained legal executory interests, and were free from the common law rules. But interests in classes (ii) and (iii) were required to conform to the common law rules and became legal contingent remainders. This could in no way injure class (ii). But class (iii) was exposed to the danger that if events turned out adversely the interest would be invalidated under the " wait and see " rule at some time in the future. The danger was that the particular estate might determine before the remainder had vested, thus leaving the fatal gap which the common law rules would not tolerate.

4. Operation of the rule. Many common forms of gift were endangered by this unreasonable rule, as, for example, a devise—

" to A for life, remainder in tail to the first of A's sons to attain the age of 21 years," A having no son of full age at the testator's death.[44]

There was nothing in this limitation as it stood which made it impossible for the legal remainder rules to be complied with; it is true that the gift to the son might fail to vest in A's lifetime, but this was not bound to happen. The rule in *Purefoy* v. *Rogers* therefore applied and the limitation to the son had to be treated as a legal remainder. Consequently if no son had reached full age at A's death, the remainder failed. Had the life estate been omitted, leaving a gift " to the first of A's sons to attain the age of 21 years," the limitation would have been incapable of complying with the common law rules, since it would necessarily violate rule 1. Therefore it would have been a valid executory devise, *Purefoy* v. *Rogers* would not have applied, and the land would have gone to the first son to attain his majority, even if he did so some time after A's death.[45]

By the same reasoning (if reasoning it can be called) a devise " to A for life with remainder to all his children who shall attain 21 "

---

[44] *White* v. *Summers* [1908] 2 Ch. 256.
[45] *White* v. *Summers, supra,* at p. 262; and see *Weale* v. *Lower* (1672) Pollexf. 54 at 65 (a feoffment to the use of A for life, and after the death of A and B to the use of C in fee, produces a contingent remainder, *Purefoy* v. *Rogers* applying; but a feoffment to the use of C and his heirs after the death of A and B is not a remainder but a springing use).

could benefit only such of the children as attained 21 before A's death.[46] But if the last words had been " shall attain 21 either before or after his death," so making it clear that rule 4 was to be violated if necessary, the whole class gift was a valid executory devise.[47]

5. Trusts. The rule in *Purefoy* v. *Rogers* had no application to future trusts, *i.e.*, to cases where equitable interests were given under trusts which the Statute of Uses would not execute.[48] All its perils could therefore be avoided by vesting the legal estate firmly in trustees, as, for example, by a conveyance—

> " unto and to the use of T and his heirs upon trust for A for life, with remainder upon trust for the first son of A who shall attain 21 and his heirs,"

or by a devise to trustees. upon similar trusts. A's son could then take even though he attained 21 after A's death. In the interim there was a resulting trust for the grantor.[49]

Sect. 4. Destruction of Contingent Remainders

The combined effect of the " wait and see " rule (rule 4) and the rule in *Purefoy* v. *Rogers* would, as we have seen, frequently be fatal to the validity of a remainder. If it did not vest in time, and therefore failed, it suffered natural destruction owing to the normal operation of these rules.

But this was not the only danger: a remainder might suffer artificial destruction. By certain devices derived from medieval law it was possible to bring about the premature determination of the particular estate; and if this was done before the remainder vested the remainder would from that moment be destroyed. In other words, the fatal gap could be created artificially. The devices used for this purpose were tolerated, and indeed favoured, by the courts because they countered the tendency to perpetuities (*i.e.*, restraints upon alienation) which all settlements involved.[50] They were as follows.[51]

1. Disseisin with loss of right of entry. A contingent remainder could be supported by a right of entry but not by a mere right of

---

[46] *Festing* v. *Allen* (1843) 12 M. & W. 279.
[47] *Re Lechmere and Lloyd* (1881) 18 Ch.D. 524 at 528, 529; *Miles* v. *Jarvis* (1883) 24 Ch.D. 633; *Re Bourne* (1887) 56 L.T. 388; *Dean* v. *Dean* [1891] 3 Ch. 150.
[48] *Berry* v. *Berry* (1878) 7 Ch.D. 657; *Astley* v. *Micklethwait* (1880) 15 Ch.D. 59 (limitation saved because legal estate was outstanding in mortgagee and remainders were therefore equitable); *Re Finch* (1881) 17 Ch.D. 211; Gray, § 116.
[49] *Re Eddels' Trusts* (1871) L.R. 11 Eq. 559.
[50] See H.E.L. vii, 217, 218.
[51] For a fuller account, see earlier editions of this book.

action.[52] These were technically distinguished under the ancient law. If a tenant for life was disseised (*i.e.*, dispossessed) by an interloper who held the land peaceably for five years and then, on his death, the land devolved on his heir, the tenant for life's right of entry against the interloper was converted into a mere right of action against his heir.[53] Any contingent remainder expectant upon the life estate thereupon failed.[54]

2. Forfeiture. If the particular estate was forfeited, any contingent remainders which it supported were also destroyed.[55] Forfeiture might occur in a number of ways.[56] The commonest device for deliberately destroying contingent remainders was what was called a *tortious conveyance, i.e.*, a conveyance by which a tenant for life or in tail conveyed a fee simple.[57] It was possible to do this by the three most ancient modes of conveyance (feoffment, fine and recovery[58]), for they operated in such cases as if the grantor had formally repudiated his limited interest, claimed a fee simple as a disseisor,[59] and then alienated it. As the estate so acquired was a totally new estate and the grantor's old estate was automatically destroyed by forfeiture, any contingent remainders dependent on the grantor's estate at once failed.[60] A vested remainderman, however, had a valid right of entry[61]; this in time provided the basis for a useful counter-device.[62]

3. Surrender. If a tenant for life surrendered his life estate to a vested remainderman, the life estate coalesced with the vested remainder and so ceased to exist as a particular estate.[63] A tenant for life and a vested remainderman could thus conspire together and destroy intermediate contingent remainders. For example, under a settlement upon A for life, with remainder to his eldest son in tail, with remainder to B in fee simple, A and B could defeat the interest of an unborn son of A.

4. Merger. The principle is the same as in surrender. If a particular estate of freehold (other than a fee tail, which could not

---

[52] Fearne 286, 287.
[53] This was called a " descent cast," which " tolled the right of entry "; *i.e.*, the law cast the land on the heir by descent and this tolled (took away) the right of entry: see Litt. 385; Co.Litt. 237b. As to the five years, see 32 Hen. 8, c. 33, 1540; H.E.L. iv, 483; Co.Litt. 238a. The ousted tenant, having lost his right of entry, could no longer use the action of ejectment but must have recourse to one of the old real actions: *post*, p. 1171.
[54] *Thompson* v. *Leach* (1697) 1 Ld.Raym. 313 at 316.   [55] Challis 135.
[56] For forfeiture for treason, see *ante*, p. 18; for forfeiture by denial of title, see *post*, p. 654; Co.Litt. 251b; Challis 135.
[57] For the classic account of tortious conveyances, see Co.Litt. 330b, n. 1, by Butler.
[58] Challis 138; see, *e.g.*, *Noel* v. *Bewley* (1829) 3 Sim. 103.
[59] For a disseisor's fee simple estate, see *post*, p. 1007.
[60] Challis 138, 139; *Chudleigh's Case* (1595) 1 Co.Rep. 113b; *Archer's Case* (1597) 1 Co.Rep. 63b.
[61] Litt. 415, 416.   [62] *Post*, p. 194.   [63] Fearne 318, 322; Challis 136.

merge in a fee simple or another fee tail [64]) and the fee simple remainder or reversion became vested in the same person in the same right, any intermediate contingent remainders were destroyed.[65] Thus in the last example if B conveyed his remainder to A,[66] or A and B both conveyed their interests to X,[67] the son's contingent remainder was destroyed.[68]

5. Disclaimer. A person to whom an estate was conveyed without his consent could disclaim it if he wished,[69] whereupon it revested in the grantor,[70] and any contingent remainders supported by it were destroyed.[71]

Copyholds. In the case of copyholds, seisin was in the lord. The rule was, nevertheless, that contingent remainders of copyholds could fail through the natural determination of the particular estate,[72] though not through the artificial determination of the particular estate,[73] *e.g.*, by surrender.[74] The reason for this distinction is not clear.[75]

Sect. 5. Preservation of Contingent Remainders

A. Trustees to Preserve Contingent Remainders

By a conveyancing device invented in the seventeenth century it became possible to protect contingent remainders against artificial destruction.[76] This was done by interposing a vested remainder which took the place of the particular estate if it were prematurely destroyed. If land was settled on—

---

[64] *Wiscot's Case* (1599) 2 Co.Rep. 60b at 61a; *Roe* d. *Crow* v. *Baldwere* (1793) 5 T.R. 104 at 110, 111; this was due to the statutory rights of the issue in tail under *De Donis*, 1285, and did not therefore apply to a tenant in tail after possibility: Co.Litt. 28a. See also Preston, *Conveyancing*, iii, 246, 343.

[65] Fearne 324.

[66] *Purefoy* v. *Rogers* (1671) 2 Wms.Saund. 380.

[67] *Egerton* v. *Massey* (1857) 3 C.B.(N.S.) 338.

[68] This had to be distinguished from situations under the rule in *Shelley's Case* where the merged estates would open to let in the remainder when it vested: *ante*, p. 63.

[69] "The law certainly is not so absurd as to force a man to take an estate against his will": *Townson* v. *Tickell* (1819) 3 B. & Ald. 31 at 36, *per* Abbott C.J. On the nature of disclaimer, see *Re Stratton's Disclaimer* [1957] Ch. 132; *Re Hatfeild's W. T.* [1958] Ch. 469.

[70] *Nicloson* v. *Wordsworth* (1818) 2 Swans. 365 at 372; *Mallott* v. *Wilson* [1903] 2 Ch. 494.

[71] *Re Sir Walter Scott* [1911] 2 Ch. 374 at 378.

[72] *Ante*, p. 186.

[73] *Pickersgill* v. *Grey* (1862) 30 Beav. 352.

[74] *Lane* v. *Pannell* (1617) 1 Rolle R. 238, 317, 438; *Mildmay* v. *Hungerford* (1691) 2 Vern. 243.

[75] Fearne 319, 320; Smith, *Executory Interests*, 450 (a somewhat unconvincing explanation); Scriven 65.

[76] H.E.L. vii, 112. For examples, see Williams R.P. 405n.; Bl.Comm. ii, appendix II, 2.

"A for life, remainder to his first-born son and the heirs of
his body, remainder to B and his heirs,"

the entail given to the son was contingent until his birth and so
liable to artificial destruction. Consequently the settlor inserted
a remainder to trustees between A's life estate and the entail,
providing that if A's life estate should determine in his lifetime by
forfeiture or otherwise, the land should pass to trustees and their
heirs during the life of A, in trust for him and to preserve contingent
remainders. The result of this was that if A's life estate determined
naturally on his death, the remainder to the trustees never took effect.
But if A's life estate was artificially determined (*i.e.*, in his lifetime)
the trustees, as the owners of the next vested interest, took the land
for an estate *pur autre vie* on trust for A until his death, when the
entail took effect if it had then become vested.

This device of appointing "trustees to preserve contingent
remainders" became almost common form in settlements until, as
will be seen, the Real Property Act, 1845, rendered it unnecessary.
After much controversy it was settled that the remainder to the
trustees was vested,[77] and that the device was accordingly effective.
This result seems quite consistent with principle if it is remembered
that the remainder to the trustees was simply a remainder *pur autre
vie*, in which the words of contingency added nothing to the sense.[78]

The limitations of this device were that not all settlors were
prudent enough to use it, and that it did nothing to preserve
contingent remainders from natural destruction.[79]

B.   Statutory Reforms

1. Artificial destruction abolished. The five methods of destroying contingent remainders artificially [80] were successively abolished
as follows.

(*a*) *The Real Property Limitation Act, 1833*,[81] put an end to the
first method by abolishing the distinction between a right of entry
and a right of action; it also prevented the death of a disseisor from
destroying a right of entry.

(*b*) *The Real Property Act, 1845*,[82] abolished the second, third

---

[77] *Duncomb* v. *Duncomb* (1695) 3 Lev. 437; *Smith* d. *Dormer* v. *Packhurst* (1740)
3 Atk. 135. The latter case, a decision of the House of Lords, settled the
controversy.
[78] For otiose contingencies, see *ante*, p. 175.
[79] Remainders could, of course, be saved from destruction by natural or artificial
means if the legal estate was vested in trustees (*ante*, p. 192); but this meant
that the beneficiaries took mere equitable interests.
[80] *Ante*, pp. 192–194.   [81] ss. 4, 5, 39.
[82] s. 8. The Transfer of Property Act, 1844, s. 8, had provided that all contingent
remainders should take effect as executory interests, but this was retrospectively
repealed by R.P.A., 1845, s. 1.

and fourth methods by providing that after 1844 a contingent remainder should take effect notwithstanding the determination by forfeiture, merger or surrender of any preceding estate of freehold, in the same manner as if such determination had not happened. The Act also completed the abolition of tortious conveyances. Fines and recoveries had been abolished at the end of 1833,[83] and the Real Property Act, 1845,[84] provided that no feoffment made after October 1, 1845, should have any tortious operation. Thenceforward there was no exception to the principle that a man cannot convey a greater estate than he has, unless indeed he is empowered to do so by the owner of the greater estate or by statute.

(*c*) *The Contingent Remainders Act*, 1877, substantially abolished the fifth method by saving most contingent remainders from destruction by disclaimer.[85] This Act is explained below.

2. Natural destruction abolished

(*a*) *Abolition of "wait and see" rule.* Finally, the Contingent Remainders Act, 1877, abolished the "wait and see" rule. It had for centuries been a senseless and useless trap, an "arbitrary feudal rule" which "ought to have been abolished long ago."[86] The Act in effect provided that every contingent remainder created by an instrument executed after August 2, 1877 (including a will confirmed after that date), should, if the particular estate determined before the remainder vested, take effect as an executory limitation, if it was capable of being valid as such.[87] Thus the rule in *Purefoy* v. *Rogers*[88] was reversed, and an interval of time between the end of the particular estate and the vesting of the remainder was no longer fatal.

(*b*) *Remainders outside the Act.* The Act deliberately excluded remainders which would be void if treated as executory interests. For example, if land was given—

> "to A [a bachelor] for life, remainder to his first grandchild to marry,"

the remainder would be void if treated as an executory interest, since

---

83 F.R.A., 1833, s. 2; *ante*, p. 90.   84 s. 4.
85 *Re Sir Walter Scott* [1911] 2 Ch. 374 at 380.
86 *Cunliffe* v. *Brancker* (1876) 3 Ch.D. 393 at 399, *per* Jessel M.R.
87 The main operative words are: "Every contingent remainder . . . which would have been valid as a springing or shifting use or executory devise or other limitation had it not had a sufficient estate to support it as a contingent remainder, shall, in the event of the particular estate determining before the contingent remainder vests, be capable of taking effect in all respects as if the contingent remainder had originally been created as a springing or shifting use or executory devise or other executory limitation."
88 *Ante*, p. 190.

it might then vest at a remote time in the future and was void under the rule against perpetuities.[89] But so long as it was required to vest, if at all, not later than A's death, it was valid, and had at least a chance of taking effect. The old law therefore continued to govern it.

(c) *Other rules.* The old law also remained unchanged except as regards the " wait and see " rule. Thus in 1925 it was still impossible to create a remainder after a fee simple, or to create an interest unsupported by a particular estate, unless the limitation was contained in a will or conveyance to uses.

(d) *Defects.* The Act had a number of drafting defects. Its main provision[90] did not seem to fit the obvious case where no use or will was employed, *e.g.*, a grant by deed to A for life, remainder to his first son to attain 21; for in such a case, if there had been no particular estate, the remainder could never have been valid. Yet this type of case must surely have been intended to be within the benefit of the Act.[91] Nor did the Act provide clearly for class gifts: if, for example, some but not all of a class of children had vested interests at the time when the particular estate determined, it was uncertain whether those who qualified later could take or not.[92]

(e) *No acceleration.* The Act did not accelerate the vesting of remainders. If the particular estate determined before the remainder vested, the land reverted to the grantor or, if the remainder was created by will, to the devisee or heir of the testator, until the remainder either vested or became incapable of vesting.[93]

3. Land Transfer Act, 1897

(a) *Vesting in personal representatives.* The Land Transfer Act, 1897, provided that when a person died after 1897, all his realty[94] should vest in his personal representatives in the same way as his personalty.[95] The result was that all the deceased's property passed in the first place to his personal representatives, who became trustees for its distribution according to the will (if any) or the rules of intestacy. The rights of the beneficiaries were thus necessarily equitable, unless and until the personal representatives, in discharge of their duties, conveyed the legal estate to them. This is the meaning of the modern maxim that " wills operate in equity only."

---

[89] *Post*, p. 208.
[90] See note 87, *supra.*
[91] *Cf.* Williams R.P. 394, 444.
[92] See *Re Robson* [1916] 1 Ch. 116 at 121, 122; *Williams on Seisin*, 205 *et seq.*
[93] Halsb. (2nd ed.), Vol. 27, p. 737.
[94] This did not include copyholds: s. 1 (4).
[95] s. 1 (1), (5); and see *post*, pp. 535, 536.

(*b*) *All devises equitable.* An important but incidental consequence of this alteration in the law of devolution was that it became
impossible for a legal remainder or legal executory interest to be
created by the will of a testator dying after 1897; the only future
interests which could arise under such a will were future trusts, to
which the old contingent remainder rules did not apply. Thus if
land was given by will—

> " to A for life, remainder to all his children who shall attain
> the age of 21 years,"

and the testator died after 1897, the children who were still infants
at the time of A's death would have been entitled to share equally
with those of full age [96]; the legal estate in the personal representatives freed the interests of the children from any dependence upon a
particular estate. This position was not affected by the personal
representatives conveying the legal estate to the beneficiaries after
completing the administration of the testator's property, for that was
merely performance of the trust and could not retrospectively alter
the character of the equitable interest which was the primary interest
conferred by the will.[97]

C. Legislation of 1925

The long history of the contingent remainder rules was at last brought
to an end by the fundamental reforms of 1925, which abolished all
legal remainders and thus altered the whole basis of the law.

1. The reforms. The two decisive reforms are the following :
   (i) the Statute of Uses, 1535, has been repealed [98]; and
   (ii) no future estate can now be legal (apart from reversions
        expectant on leases [99]), for the only legal estate of freehold
        now possible is the fee simple absolute in possession.[1]

2. Effect. The result is therefore that—
   (i) legal remainders can no longer exist, for the second reason
       above, and
   (ii) legal executory interests can no longer exist, for both
        reasons; but
   (iii) future trusts can still exist, and all remainders must fall into
         this class.

3. Consequences. After 1925, therefore, all future interests in
realty must necessarily be equitable, the legal estate (fee simple

---

[96] *Re Robson* [1916] 1 Ch. 116, criticised (1920) 6 Conv.(o.s.) 44; and contrast *ante*,
p. 197.
[97] See *Re Freme* [1891] 3 Ch. 167.
[98] L.P.A., 1925, 7th Sched.; *ante*, p. 171.
[99] Because the right to the rents and profits is deemed to be " possession ";
ante, p. 139.
[1] *Ante*, p. 135.

absolute in possession) being vested in some person as trustee. Neither the legal remainder rules nor *Purefoy* v. *Rogers* [2] can apply; the Real Property Act, 1845, s. 8, and the Contingent Remainders Act, 1877, are repealed.[3] Legal remainders and legal executory interests existing before 1926 were automatically converted into equitable interests.[4] Thus the comparatively simple law of future trusts, free from feudal rules and statutory modifications, now applies to all future interests [5]; but the old rules may not yet be entirely forgotten, for upon them may depend many titles which still have to be proved from dates prior to 1926. In particular the distinction between vested and contingent interests remains of vital importance in the application of the modern rule against perpetuities, dealt with below. In all cases, the land will either be settled land and subject to the code laid down by the Settled Land Act, 1925, or else be subject to a trust for sale.[6]

Part 4

RULES AGAINST REMOTENESS

Sect. 1.   Introduction

1. Power to control the devolution of land. It has commonly been the ambition of landowners to dictate to posterity how their land is to devolve in the future, and so to fetter the powers of alienation of those to whom they may give it [7]; and it has always been the purpose of the courts, as a matter of public policy, to confine such settlements within narrow limits and to frustrate them when they attempt to reach too far into the future. We have already seen how the courts in time circumvented the designs of the barons who had obtained by the Statute *De Donis*, 1285, the power to create an inalienable estate tail.[8] For similar reasons the courts later laid down that all unduly remote future interests were void as " perpetuities "; for, as Lord Nottingham L.C. observed in 1681, " the law hath so long laboured to defeat perpetuities, that now it is become a sufficient reason of itself against any settlement to say it tends to a perpetuity . . . such perpetuities fight against God, by affecting a stability which human providence can never attain to, and are utterly against the reason and policy of the common law." [9]

---

[2] *Ante*, p. 190.
[3] L.P.(Am.)A., 1924, 10th Sched. [4] L.P.A., 1925, 1st Sched., Pt. I.
[5] Except, of course, reversions, dealt with *ante*, p. 178.
[6] *Post*, p. 282.
[7] " *Te teneam moriens* is the dying lord's apostrophe to his manor, for which he is forging these fetters, that seem, by restricting the dominion of others, to extend his own ": Jarman, *Wills*, 1st ed., i, 196. [8] *Ante*, p. 85.
[9] *Duke of Norfolk's Case* (1681) 2 Swans. 454 at 460.

2. Rules restricting the power. All types of future interests have therefore been made subject to important rules limiting the period for which a settlor can exercise control over property. Thus a settlor cannot render property for ever inalienable, nor can he settle it so that it may vest an inordinate number of years in the future. The following rules must be distinguished:

    (i) The rule in *Whitby* v. *Mitchell*,[10] sometimes called the old rule against perpetuities, or the rule against double possibilities.

    (ii) The rule against perpetuities. This is sometimes referred to as the modern rule against perpetuities to distinguish it from the rule in *Whitby* v. *Mitchell*.

    (iii) The rule against inalienability or perpetual trusts.

    (iv) The rule against accumulations.

3. Origin of the rules. *Whitby* v. *Mitchell* was a rule dating from the sixteenth century. It applied only to legal (and, later, equitable [11]) remainders, and so when executory interests became more and more popular, some other restraint had to be devised to keep them within bounds. The rule which was eventually evolved became known as the modern rule against perpetuities. Its general outline first emerged in 1685, when the House of Lords settled the great legal controversy which arose in the *Duke of Norfolk's Case*.[12] The new principle was that the vesting of an interest must not be capable of exceeding a period based upon an existing lifetime. It was developed step by step [13] until it reached its final form in 1833.[14] It is far wider than *Whitby* v. *Mitchell*, for it extends to all interests in all property. The rule against inalienability is also based on decided cases of respectable antiquity. The rule against accumulations, on the other hand, has a statutory and comparatively modern origin, the Accumulations Act, 1800. All the rules except the rule in *Whitby* v. *Mitchell* are still in force.

Sect. 2. The Rule in Whitby v. Mitchell

A. The Rule and its History

1. The rule. Although this rule is now known by the name of a case decided in 1890 [15] in which it was thoroughly discussed, it

---

[10] (1890) 44 Ch.D. 85.   [11] *Re Nash* [1910] 1 Ch. 1.
[12] (1681) 2 Swans. 454; (1685) 3 Ch.Ca. 1; H.E.L. vii, 223–225. The development of the modern rule is well explained in H.E.L. vii, 215–238.
[13] H.E.L., vii, 226, 227; *post*, p. 207.
[14] *Cadell* v. *Palmer* (1833) 1 Cl. & F. 372 (also a decision of the House of Lords).
[15] (1890) 44 Ch.D. 85.

seems to be of considerable but uncertain age.[16] Stated in its simplest form, the rule was as follows:

> If an interest in realty is given to an unborn person, any remainder to his issue is void,[17] together with all subsequent limitations.[18]

Thus if land was limited—

> "to A for life, remainder to his daughter for life, remainder to her children and their heirs" (A having no daughter at the time of the gift),

the life estates of A and his daughter were valid, but the remainder to the daughter's children was void.[19] If the children had instead been given mere life estates, followed by a fee simple in favour of B (a living person), the gift to B was held to be void as well as the gift to the children.[20] Even a vested gift might thus fail under the rule.

2. Similar rules. The rule is sometimes referred to as "the rule against double possibilities" or "the rule that a possibility upon a possibility is void," but these descriptions are unsuitable.[21] At one time there were no less than three supposed rules which tended to become confused with each other.[22] Two of these so-called rules never became accepted as law. The third was the rule in *Whitby* v. *Mitchell*. The two abortive rules were as follows.

(a) *The rule against remote possibilities* was a rule which postulated that a limitation to take effect upon a remote or unlikely contingency was void and that the law permitted only common or likely possibilities.[23] The rule seems to have started with *Cholmley's Case* in 1597,[24] and a decision seems to have been based on it in 1623 [25]; but the difficulty of drawing any line between common and remote contingencies made its application a matter of great uncertainty. The supposed rule never had any real vitality and soon became discredited. At most it can be regarded as authority for the

---

[16] *Re Nash* [1910] 1 Ch. 1 at 7; H.E.L. vii, 209 *et seq.* The rule appears in *Perrot's Case* (1594) Moo.K.B. 368, but was not clearly laid down until *Duke of Marlborough* v. *Earl Godolphin* (1759) 1 Eden 404 at 415, 416.

[17] *Whitby* v. *Mitchell* (1889) 42 Ch.D. 494 at 500; affirmed, 44 Ch.D. 85.

[18] *Brudenell* v. *Elwes* (1801) 1 East 442; *Re Mortimer* [1905] 2 Ch. 502; Jarman 366, 367. Even a vested interest would fail if it followed a gift made void by the rule. See the example next given.

[19] *Whitby* v. *Mitchell* (1890) 44 Ch.D. 85.

[20] *Re Mortimer* [1905] 2 Ch. 502. See Gray, § 251, withdrawing previous criticism.

[21] *Re Nash* [1910] 1 Ch. 1 at 10.

[22] See Bordwell, 25 Iowa L.R. 1–22, where references are given to most of the literature on the subject.

[23] *Sir Hugh Cholmley's Case* (1597) 2 Co.Rep. 50a at 51a, b.

[24] 2 Co.Rep. 50a. *Cf. Lampet's Case* (1612) 10 Co.Rep. 46b at 50b. The "rule" was repudiated in *Cole* v. *Sewell* (1843) 4 Dr. & War. 1 at 28; 2 H.L.C. 186.

[25] *Child* v. *Baylie* (1623) Cro.Jac. 459.

propositions that limitations to the heirs of an unborn person or to a corporation not in existence were void.[26]

(b) *The rule against double possibilities* was a rule which appears to have been first suggested in the *Rector of Chedington's Case* in 1598,[27] when Popham C.J. said that a lease was void because " it could not commence upon a contingent which depended upon another contingent." [27] The principle seems to have been that a limitation which depended upon more than one possibility was void. But a gift to A for life with remainder to the eldest grandson of B (a bachelor) involved at least two possibilities, namely, that B might have no child, and that even if he had a child, the child might have no son; yet the remainder was valid,[28] and the same applied to a remainder to the first son of Z to be 21.[29]

In the face of cases such as these, and others where valid remainders contained treble[30] or quadruple[31] possibilities, it was difficult to maintain that there was any real rule against double possibilities. Since the time of Coke[32] it has been rejected by the best authority,[33] and although it made a fleeting appearance in the eighteenth century,[34] one is justified in concluding that it " never had any real existence; it perished almost as soon as it drew breath." [35] Apart from the rule in *Whitby* v. *Mitchell*, there was no rule against double possibilities,[36] nor does the rule in *Whitby* v. *Mitchell* appear to be descended from any rule against double possibilities.[37]

3. Effect of the rule. The rule in *Whitby* v. *Mitchell* met the ingenuity of settlors who wished to keep land in their families indefinitely. Ever since *Taltarum's Case* in 1472[38] it has been possible to bar an entail,[39] and so a limitation—

" to X and the heirs of his body "

gave no assurance that the land would descend from father to son

---

[26] See Challis 116, 117.
[27] 1 Co.Rep. 148b at 156b. It was subsequently repeated: *Lord Stafford's Case* (1609) 8 Co.Rep. 73a at 75a; *Mayor and Commonalty of London* v. *Alford* (1640) Cro.Car. 576; Co.Litt. 184a.
[28] Challis 118, note by Sweet.
[29] Fearne 251; Lewis, *Perpetuity*, 602.
[30] Preston, *Abstracts*, i, 128, 129.
[31] *Routledge* v. *Dorril* (1794) 2 Ves.Jun. 357; Fearne 251.
[32] *Blandford* v. *Blandford* (1616) 1 Rolle 318 at 321 (" *si l'opinion de Popham serroit estre ley ceo violet shaker les common assurances del' terre* ").
[33] See Lord Nottingham's repudiation of it in the *Duke of Norfolk's Case* (1681) 3 Cha.Ca. 1 at 29.
[34] *Chapman* d. *Oliver* v. *Brown* (1765) 3 Burr. 1626 at 1634, 1635.
[35] Sweet, 12 Columbia L.R. 216.
[36] See *Whitby* v. *Mitchell* (1890) 44 Ch.D. 85 at 92; *Re Ashforth* [1905] 1 Ch. 535 at 543.
[37] See Gray, § 133n., Appendix K; Challis 206.
[38] Y.B. 12 Edw. 4, Mich., pl. 25, fo. 19a; *ante*, p. 85.
[39] As to the impossibility of creating an unbarrable entail, see *ante*, p. 89.

for any length of time. A settlor might consequently attempt to create what was known as a " perpetual freehold " by giving the land—

> " to X for life, remainder to his son for life, remainder to the son's son for life "

and so on *ad infinitum*,[40] thus creating a series of life estates closely resembling an unbarrable entail. Many such attempts were made in the sixteenth and early seventeenth centuries, but the courts resolutely declared any limitations savouring of unbarrable entails to be invalid.[41] At this period the modern rule against perpetuities was only beginning to emerge,[42] and the device of successive life interests was kept within bounds by the rule in *Whitby* v. *Mitchell*.[43] The rule against unbarrable entails and the rule against successive life interests were thus complementary to one another. It is not therefore surprising to find traces of the latter rule in 1594.[44] But not until 1759 was it laid down in clear terms,[45] and it was still possible to challenge it in *Whitby* v. *Mitchell* in 1889.

B. *Scope of the Rule*

1. Property within the rule. The rule applied to both legal and equitable remainders in realty,[46] so that it governed future trusts as well as legal contingent remainders.[47] Although it also seems to have applied to trusts for sale,[48] it did not apply to other interests in personalty,[49] nor does it seem to have applied to legal or equitable executory interests in realty.[50]

2. Limitations within the rule. It was a rule against possibilities (as is also the modern rule against perpetuities): if there was any possibility of the rule being infringed, the gift was void *ab initio*; there was therefore no " wait and see." [51] But subject to this it was

---

40 See *Manning and Andrews Case* (1576) 1 Leon. 256; *Humberston* v. *Humberston* (1716) 1 P.Wms. 332.
41 *Ante*, p. 89.
42 See *post*, p. 207.
43 See *Perrot's Case* (1594) Moo.K.B. 368 at 371, 372, *per* Coke *arg.*; *Chudleigh's Case* (1595) 1 Co.Rep. 113b at 138a.
44 See *Perrot's Case* (1594) Moo.K.B. 368 at 371 *et seq.* The rule seems to have been unknown in 1576: see *Manning and Andrews Case* (1576) 1 Leon. 256 at 258.
45 *Duke of Marlborough* v. *Earl Godolphin* (1759) 1 Eden 404 at 415, 416.
46 *Re Nash* [1910] 1 Ch. 1.
47 Including interests within the rule in *Purefoy* v. *Rogers* (*ante*, p. 190).
48 *Re Bullock's W. T.* [1915] 1 Ch. 493; *Re Garnham* [1916] 2 Ch. 413; interests under such trusts are personalty for many purposes: see *post*, pp. 286, 287.
49 *Re Bowles* [1902] 2 Ch. 650.
50 See Williams 452. But this was doubtful: Sweet (1911) 27 L.Q.R. 171; Gray, § 947n.
51 This was assumed in the cases cited in n. 48, *supra*.

closely confined to cases falling within the strict letter of the rule. Thus in a limitation to trustees—

> on trust for X for life, remainder on trust for the first-born son of A [a bachelor] for life, remainder on trust for that son's first-born child,

the second remainder infringed the rule and was void; for after a gift to an unborn person there was remainder to his issue. The rule would not have been infringed had the gift been to trustees—

> on trust for X for life, remainder on trust for the first-born grandson of A [a bachelor],

for although there was a limitation to the issue of an unborn person, that limitation was not preceded by a gift to the unborn person.[52] The rule was directed against a series of gifts to persons lineally related, and not against isolated gifts, even to those remotely unborn; the rule is not a rule that a gift to the issue of an unborn person is void, nor a rule that " all remainders after an estate for life to an unborn person are void." [53] As will be seen shortly,[54] however, the last gift would have infringed the modern rule against perpetuities and thus be void. But if it had been expressly confined within the perpetuity period, *e.g.*, to trustees—

> on trust for X for life, remainder on trust for the first-born grandson of A [a bachelor], *provided he is born within* 21 *years of A's death*,

it would have been valid; the italicised words would have prevented the gift from infringing the perpetuity rule, the rule in *Whitby* v. *Mitchell* would not have applied, and so the gift would have been good.[55]

3. Limitations outside the rule. The rule did not invalidate a gift to the issue of two life-tenants, one born and one unborn. This position often arose in settlements where, for example, land was devised to A (a bachelor) for life, with remainder for life to any wife he might marry, with remainder in fee simple to the eldest son of the marriage. A might marry someone not alive at the testator's death, and that person might survive him; but that possibility did not destroy the remainder to the son even though the immediately preceding gift was one to his (possibly) unborn mother.[56]

---

[52] See *Ward* v. *Van der Loeff* [1924] A.C. 653; Jarman 294; (1909) 25 L.Q.R. at p. 385.

[53] See *Re Mountgarret* [1919] 2 Ch. 294 at 300; *post*, p. 206, n. 69.

[54] See *post*, p. 208.

[55] *Whitby* v. *Mitchell* (1889) 42 Ch.D. 494 at 501; affirmed, 44 Ch.D. 85.

[56] *Re Bullock's W. T.* [1915] 1 Ch. 493; *Re Garnham* [1916] 2 Ch. 413; Williams 451. The earlier authorities to the contrary (*e.g., Re Park's Settlement* [1914] 1 Ch. 595) are to be regarded as wrong on this point: see also Sweet in 27 Yale L.J. 978.

4. Powers. The rule in *Whitby* v. *Mitchell* applied to remainders created under powers of appointment in the same manner as does the modern rule against perpetuities.[57]

C. The Cy-près Doctrine

1. The doctrine. The doctrine of *cy-près* was introduced by the courts to mitigate the severity of the rule in *Whitby* v. *Mitchell* in certain cases. It may be stated thus:

> Where there is a limitation of realty by will to an unborn person for life, with remainder to his children successively in tail, then since the remainders are void for remoteness, the court will give effect to the testator's intention as nearly as possible (*cy-près*) and construe the devise as a gift to the unborn person in tail.[58] The same would be done where there was a perpetual series of life estates to the issue of the unborn person.[59]

For example, if land was devised—

> " to A [a bachelor] for life, remainder to his eldest son for life, remainder to the first and other sons of A's eldest son successively in tail male,"

A's eldest son would take an estate in tail male; the ultimate remainder infringed the rule in *Whitby* v. *Mitchell*, and so the court, instead of merely striking it out and leaving A and his eldest son with mere life estates, adopted the *cy-près* rule of construction and gave A's eldest son an estate in tail male,[60] A, of course, taking a life estate. This approximated to the testator's intention, for if A's eldest son did not bar the entail, the property would descend to just those persons whom the testator intended to benefit.[61]

2. Limits of the doctrine. As will be seen from the statement of the doctrine, it did not extend to deeds,[62] nor to personalty (which before 1926 could not be entailed),[63] nor when the remainder was in fee simple, so that the unborn person would be free to defeat the testator's intentions.[64] Further, the doctrine was not applied if the result would have been to exclude some person whom the testator

---

[57] *Whitby* v. *Mitchell* (1890) 44 Ch.D. 85; *post*, p. 252.
[58] *Nicholl* v. *Nicholl* (1777) 2 Wm.Bl. 1159; *East* v. *Twyford* (1853) 4 H.L.C. 517.
[59] *Humberston* v. *Humberston* (1716) 1 P.Wms. 332; *Parfitt* v. *Hember* (1867) L.R. 4 Eq. 443.   [60] *Parfitt* v. *Hember, supra*, at p. 446.
[61] If he barred the entail he could dispose of the property as he liked; but it was always probable that he would resettle the property on his descendants in some way, and so approach the testator's intention more nearly than would a construction that gave him a mere life estate: see *Parfitt* v. *Hember* (1867) L.R. 4 Eq. 443 at 446; and *post*, p. 283.
[62] *Brudenell* v. *Elwes* (1802) 7 Ves. 382.
[63] *Routledge* v. *Dorril* (1794) 2 Ves.Jun. 357 at 364, 365; *ante*, p. 94.
[64] *Hale* v. *Pew* (1858) 25 Beav. 335.

intended to take,[65] or to include a person whom the testator did not intend to benefit.[66] Thus a devise to an unborn person for life, with remainder to his first son in tail male, could not be construed *cy-près* into a tail male for the unborn person, since that would let in his second and other sons.[67] Again, a devise to an unborn person for life, with remainder to his sons successively in tail general, could not be construed as giving a tail general to the unborn person, for that would include his daughters; nor could it be construed as giving a tail male to the unborn person, for that would exclude the daughters of his sons.[68] It will be seen that the remainder had to be to the issue in tail general, the sons in tail male, or the daughters in tail female, if the doctrine was to be applicable.

D. The Rule after 1925

In modern times the rule in *Whitby* v. *Mitchell* was at best a useless survival. The perpetuity rule formed a uniform and satisfactory guard against any real mischief of remoteness, and the somewhat narrow and technical rule in *Whitby* v. *Mitchell*, by sometimes invalidating gifts despite their compliance with the perpetuity rule, was a purposeless trap for unwary draftsmen. Accordingly the rule in *Whitby* v. *Mitchell* was abolished for all instruments coming into operation after 1925.[69] No express provision has been made for the *cy-près* doctrine. Where it operated before 1926, it saved the limitation from the destructive effect of both the rule in *Whitby* v. *Mitchell* and the modern perpetuity rule [70]; and although one view is that the doctrine can no longer apply, it seems probable that the courts would still employ it to rescue such gifts from the perpetuity

---

65 *Re Rising* [1904] 1 Ch. 533.
66 *Re Mortimer* [1905] 2 Ch. 502.
67 *Monypenny* v. *Dering* (1852) 2 De G.M. & G. 145.
68 *Re Rising* [1904] 1 Ch. 533.
69 L.P.A., 1925, s. 161; *cf. Re Leigh's Marriage Settlement* [1952] 2 All E.R. 57. S. 161 is widely worded, and abolishes the rule " prohibiting the limitation, after a life interest to an unborn person, of an interest in land to the unborn child or other issue of an unborn person." This covers the possibility considered, but not decided, in *Honeywood* v. *Honeywood* (1905) 92 L.T. 814 at 815, 816, that a remainder to the unborn issue of an unborn person would be void even if it followed a life interest to an unborn person who was not lineally related to the issue (*e.g.*, " to A's son for life, remainder to B's grandchildren in fee simple," A and B both being bachelors). Probably the rule did not extend to cases such as this: *ante*, p. 204.
70 A remainder which infringed the rule in *Whitby* v. *Mitchell* did not necessarily infringe the perpetuity rule: *e.g.*, " to A [a bachelor] for life, remainder to his firstborn son for life, remainder to the firstborn son of that son *to be born within twenty-one years of A's death* ": the italicised words prevented the perpetuity rule from being infringed, but the remainder still failed under the independent rule in *Whitby* v. *Mitchell*: *Whitby* v. *Mitchell* (1889) 42 Ch.D. 494 at 500, 501 (in C.A., 44 Ch.D. 85). But a remainder to which the *cy-près* doctrine could apply could not avoid this: see (1939) 55 L.Q.R. 427 (R.E.M.).

rule where the necessary strict words of limitation [71] for an entail have been used.[72]

Sect. 3. The Rule against Perpetuities

A. History

1. Origin. The requirement that a legal remainder must vest during the continuance of the particular estate or at its end normally made it impossible so to limit land at common law that its devolution would still be controlled in the remote future. The only particular estate which could support remainders for more than one lifetime was the entail, but then the remainders were quite precarious since they could be barred by the tenant in tail.[73] But by means of springing and shifting uses, estates could be made to spring up or shift at remote future dates, so that the ultimate ownership and right of alienation of the fee simple absolute might be put into abeyance for a long time. A rule was invented which kept such interests within due limits: settlors were allowed to leave the ultimate ownership uncertain for a maximum period of one subsisting lifetime and a further 21 years. This rule was modelled upon the period for which the power of alienation could normally be restrained in settlements operating at common law [74]: land could be settled upon A for life with remainder to his son in tail, so that the maximum period which could elapse before the entail could be barred was A's lifetime plus the son's minority, *i.e.*, 21 years.

2. Development. It was many years before the rule was finally settled.[75] In 1662 the limitation of a term of years to several living persons in succession was held good [76]; and so in 1678 was an executory devise which might not have vested until the expiration of a lifetime plus 21 years.[77] But the rule became firmly established only by later stages. The *Duke of Norfolk's Case* [78] in 1685 settled beyond doubt that a shifting use bound to take effect, if at all, during a life in being was valid. In 1697 a life in being plus one year was held valid [79]; and in 1736 this was extended to a life in being plus a minority, *i.e.*, plus a maximum period of 21 years.[80]

[71] L.P.A., 1925, s. 130; *ante*, p. 59.
[72] See (1939) 55 L.Q.R. 422 (R.E.M.).
[73] *Ante*, p. 89.
[74] See *Long* v. *Blackall* (1797) 7 T.R. 100 at 102; Hargrave, *Law Tracts*, 518; Butler's notes to Co.Litt. 20 (a), note (5); Fearne 444, 566.
[75] See H.E.L. vii, 215 *et seq.*; Morris & Leach, Chap. 1 (dealing both with the history of the rule and its general place in the legal system).
[76] *Goring* v. *Bickerstaffe*, Pollexf. 31.
[77] *Taylor* d. *Smith* v. *Biddall* 2 Mod. 289.
[78] 3 Ch.Ca. 1.
[79] *Lloyd* v. *Carew*, Show.P.C. 137.   [80] *Stephens* v. *Stephens*, Ca.t.Talb. 228.

In 1797 it was settled that a child *en ventre sa mère* (conceived but not born) might be treated as a life in being,[81] thus extending the period by a possible further nine months; and by then it had also become accepted that the period of 21 years after the life in being also might be extended to cover a further period of gestation if it existed.[82] In 1805 it was finally settled that the lives in being might be chosen at random and be unconnected with the property[83]; and in 1833 the rule was completed by the decision of the House of Lords in *Cadell* v. *Palmer*[84] that the period of 21 years was an absolute period without reference to any minority, but that the periods of gestation could be added only if in fact gestation existed. These two last decisions show that the analogy with common law limitations was not followed very far.

3. Reform. The invention of this rule provided a general solution to the problem of perpetuity. Subject to a few exceptions the courts applied it to all contingent interests in property, whether legal or equitable, whether in realty or personalty and whether created by deed, will, contract or otherwise. It is a striking example of wholly new law created judicially. It was amended in minor respects by the Law of Property Act, 1925, and it has now suffered major alterations under the Perpetuities and Accumulations Act 1964.[85] Statutory reform, however, has proceeded as usual by building on the old law. An understanding of the old law is still the first essential, both because it still governs future interests taking effect under past dispositions, and also because the new law applies for the most part only where a disposition would fail under the old law. It is a typical case of reform by supplementation rather than by replacement.

B. Statement of the Rule

The rule in its classical form, as it existed before the reforms of 1964, may be epitomised in two propositions[86]:

(i) Any future interest in any property, real or personal,[87] is void from the outset if it may possibly vest after the perpetuity period has expired.

---

[81] *Long* v. *Blackall*, 7 T.R. 100.
[82] Lewis, *Perpetuity*, 149. These extensions were assisted by a statute of 1698 (10 Will. 3, c. 22; Ruff. 10 & 11 Will. 3, c. 16) which enacted that a child born after the father's death should be deemed to be born in his lifetime for purposes of succession: *ibid.*
[83] *Thellusson* v. *Woodford*, 11 Ves. 112.
[84] 1 Cl. & F. 372.
[85] For the Act of 1964 see Elphinstone, *Perpetuities and Accumulations Act 1964*; Morris & Leach, 1964 Supp.
[86] For the classical definitions, see *Re Thompson* [1906] 2 Ch. 199 at 202; Gray, § 201; Morris & Leach, 1; Lewis, *Perpetuity*, 164.
[87] Marsden, *Perpetuities*, 4; Morris & Leach, 12.

(ii) The perpetuity period consists of any life or lives in being [89] together with a further period of 21 years [90] and any period of gestation.

The Perpetuities and Accumulations Act 1964 [91] has introduced two important modifications:

(i) Instead of being void because it may possibly vest outside the perpetuity period, the interest is void only where it must so vest, if it is to vest at all.

(ii) The perpetuity period may, alternatively, be a fixed period not exceeding 80 years.

The first of these modifications alters the character and application of the rule fundamentally. The Act of 1964 (as it will be called) applies, however, only to interests arising under instruments [92] taking effect after July 15, 1964. Great care must therefore be taken for many years to come to ascertain whether or not the Act of 1964 applies. The following discussion accordingly deals separately with—

(i) the rule at common law,[93] and

(ii) the rule as amended by statute;

but in discussing the elements of the rule the corresponding common law and statutory principles will be treated together so far as possible.

1. The meaning of " vest "

(a) *Vest in interest.* The rule does not require that an interest should be incapable of vesting *in possession* after the period has run, but only that it should be incapable of becoming vested *in interest* outside the period.[94] This distinction has already been explained.[95] Thus if land is devised on trust for X for life with remainder to his first and other sons successively for life, the limitations are valid even if X was a bachelor at the time of the gift. Each of X's sons obtains a vested interest at birth, and these interests are not invalidated by the fact that some of the sons may not be entitled to possession of the property until after the period has run. It is thus immaterial that if X was a bachelor at the time of the gift and his eldest son outlives him by 50 years, the interest of the second son will not vest in possession until 29 years after the perpetuity period has expired.[96]

---

[89] *Lord Dungannon* v. *Smith* (1846) 12 Cl. & F. 546 at 563.

[90] This is unaffected by the reduction of the age of majority to 18 under the Family Law Reform Act 1969 (*post*, p. 988).

[91] The Act is based on the Fourth Report of the Law Reform Committee, Cmnd. 18 (1956), which was first acted on in Western Australia: see the Law Reform (Property, Perpetuities and Succession) Act, 1962, of that State. The Perpetuities Act (Northern Ireland) 1966 avoids some of the drafting defects of the English Act.   [92] See *Re Holt's Settlement* [1969] 1 Ch. 100 (order of court).

[93] And also, of course, in equity: for brevity, the phrase " at common law " is used for the rule as unamended by statute.

[94] *Evans* v. *Walker* (1876) 3 Ch.D. 211.

[95] *Ante*, p. 173.   [96] *Re Hargreaves* (1890) 43 Ch.D. 401.

(b) Test. For the purposes of the perpetuity rule, however, an interest will rank as vested only if it satisfies a particularly stringent test. The two usual conditions [97] must be satisfied:

(i) the person or persons entitled must be ascertained; and
(ii) the interest must be ready to take effect in possession forthwith, subject only to any prior interests.

But there is also a third requirement:

(iii) the size of the benefit must be known.

The importance of this third requirement will be seen in connection with class gifts, discussed below. If there is any possibility that a person's share of the property given may vary according to some future event, the whole gift will fail for remoteness if that event might possibly happen outside the perpetuity period.[98] Thus in a gift " to such of A's grandchildren as attain 21," where A is alive at the date of the gift and none of his grandchildren have yet come of age, the whole gift must fail under the perpetuity rule at common law, even as regards any grandchildren of X who were alive at the date of the gift, and so were bound to attain 21 (if at all) during their own lifetimes.[99] Until it is known exactly how many grandchildren will ultimately attain 21, the size of each grandchild's interest will necessarily remain uncertain, and its final determination may well occur outside the perpetuity period. In other words, the possibility that the size of a person's share may vary is treated as a contingency (as indeed it is [1]) for perpetuity purposes.

If the size of a person's interest is known, it matters not that its amount or value may fluctuate. Thus an annuity or rentcharge is not void for perpetuity merely because it is made to vary with the total rent and outgoings of a house [2] or its rating assessment,[3] and this may occur outside the period. But it is otherwise if the annuity or rentcharge may not arise until the period has run.[4]

(c) Leaning towards vesting. In doubtful cases the court, as already explained,[5] leans in favour of vesting. A natural inclination to save gifts from the perpetuity rule sometimes leads to fine dis-

---

[97] *Ante*, p. 173.
[98] *Jee* v. *Audley* (1787) 1 Cox Eq. 324; *Leake* v. *Robinson* (1817) 2 Mer. 363; *Cattlin* v. *Brown* (1853) 11 Hare 372; *Pearks* v. *Moseley* (1880) 5 App.Cas. 714; *Re Whiteford* [1915] 1 Ch. 347 at 352. See Morris & Leach, 38.
[99] *Cf. Boreham* v. *Bignall* (1850) 8 Hare 131.
[1] Gray, § 110.1, and note. *Cf.* the expression " absolute vesting " in L.P.A., 1925, s. 163, dealt with *post*, p. 235.
[2] *Re Cassel* [1926] Ch. 358.
[3] *Beachway Management Ltd.* v. *Wisewell* [1971] Ch. 610.
[4] *Re Whiteford* [1915] 1 Ch. 347; *Re Johnson's S. T.* [1943] Ch. 341 (trust to make up unborn beneficiary's income to a given amount). A discretionary trust will similarly fail: *post*, p. 247.
[5] *Ante*, p. 177. See *Duffield* v. *Duffield* (1829) 3 Bli.(N.S.) 260 at 331; *Re Petrie* [1962] Ch. 355 (realisation of estate: executor's year taken).

tinctions. For example, a bequest to an unborn person " at 21," or " when he attains 21," is clearly contingent.[6] But it may be held that " to B, to be paid at 21 " gives B an immediately vested interest, with a postponed right of enjoyment.[7] It may also be held that " to A at 21, but if A dies under that age, to B " gives A a vested interest, subject to being divested in favour of B if the contingency occurs.[8] In this class of case the words of contingency are treated as governing the gift to B but not the gift to A.

(*d*) *Interests within the rule.* The rule applies to all types of proprietary interests. Thus an easement in fee simple to use all drains " hereafter to pass " under the grantor's adjacent land is void for perpetuity for it might first arise in favour of a successor in title to the grant at an indefinitely future date.[9]

2. No " wait and see " at common law

(*a*) *Possibilities.* The cardinal doctrine of the rule at common law is that everything depends upon possibilities, not probabilities or actual events.[10] Every interest must be considered at the time when the instrument creating it takes effect. Thus a deed must be considered at the time when it is executed, while a will must be considered at the moment of the testator's death.[11] If at the relevant moment there is the slightest possibility that the perpetuity period may be exceeded,[11a] the limitation is void *ab initio*, even if it is most improbable that this in fact will happen and even if, as events turn out, it does not.[12] For example, if property is given—

" to the first son of A who may marry,"
the gift must fail at common law if A is alive and has no married son at the time of the gift. For all existing sons of A may die unmarried, then A may have another son (not a life in being at the time of the gift), then A may die, and finally the last-born son may marry more than 21 years after the death of A, the last surviving life in being. This possibility may be exceedingly remote, as where

---

[6] *Stapleton* v. *Cheales* (1711) Prec.Ch. 317; *Hanson* v. *Graham* (1801) 6 Ves. 239; *cf. Re Blackwell* [1926] Ch. 223 (" upon attaining 21 ").

[7] *Re Couturier* [1907] 1 Ch. 470.

[8] *Phipps* v. *Ackers* (1842) 9 Cl. & F. 583; *Re Heath* [1936] Ch. 259; *Re Mallinson's Trusts* [1974] 1 W.L.R. 1120. See Jarman 1388 *et seq.* for a variety of special cases, in particular as to the effect of an ultimate gift over on the construction of the prior gift. See also Morris & Leach, 44.

[9] *Dunn* v. *Blackdown Properties Ltd.* [1961] Ch. 433. *Cf. S.E. Ry.* v. *Associated Portland Cement Manufacturers (1900) Ltd.* [1910] 1 Ch. 12; *Sharpe* v. *Durrant* (1911) 55 S.J. 423: *Smith* v. *Colbourne* [1914] 2 Ch. 533.

[10] Morris & Leach, 70.

[11] *Vanderplank* v. *King* (1843) 3 Hare 1 at 17; *Re Mervin* [1891] 3 Ch. 197 at 204: Lewis, *Perpetuity*, 171, Suppt. 64; Gray, § 231; Morris & Leach, 56.

[11a] Ambiguity may be resolved in favour of validity: see *Re Deeley's Settlement* [1974] Ch. 454.

[12] This sentence was approved in *Re Watson's S. T.* [1959] 1 W.L.R. 732 at 739.

a son of A is to be married within the next week, or where A is a woman past the age of child-bearing. But the degree of improbability is immaterial.[13]

Similarly, in the case of a gift—

" to A (a bachelor) for life, remainder to his widow for life, remainder to the eldest of his brothers living at the widow's death,"

the remainder to the brother is bad if A's parents are alive. Even if A already has brothers living, they may predecease him, and another brother may be born later. It is then just possible that A will marry someone who was not alive at the time of the gift, so that if A's wife survived him for more than 21 years, the property might become vested outside the period in a brother born after the date of the gift. This possibility renders the gift to the brother void, even if A is old and unlikely to marry or in fact later marries someone alive at the time of the gift,[14] and even if A's parents are so old that they are most unlikely to have more children.[15]

(b) *Impossibility*. Even where it can be proved that the birth of further children is a physical impossibility, the rule at common law maintains the same stubborn disregard for the facts of life.[16] But it respects the legal proprieties, and so will disregard what can only be done in breach of trust.[16a] In one case [17] the gift was made—

to such of the grandchildren of G, living at the testatrix's death or born within five years thereafter, who should attain 21 or being female marry under that age.

The perpetuity period could have been exceeded only if a child of G born after the testatrix's death (and so not a life in being) had had a child within the prescribed period of five years after the testatrix's death. This was rejected as being not merely physically but legally impossible, for no legitimate child can be born to a person under the age of sixteen [18]; and so the gift was good.

---

13 See notes 14 and 15 below.
14 See *Hodson* v. *Ball* (1845) 14 Sim. 558; *Lett* v. *Randall* (1855) 3 Sm. & Giff. 83; Gray, § 214; Morris & Leach, 72.
15 *Ward* v. *Van de Loeff* [1924] A.C. 653 (persons aged 66); *Jee* v. *Audley* (1787) 1 Cox Eq. 324 (persons aged 70); *cf.* Co.Litt. 40a.
16 *Jee* v. *Audley, supra*; *Re Dawson* (1888) 39 Ch.D. 155; *Re Deloitte* [1926] Ch. 56. For reforms made by the Act of 1964, see *post*, p. 217. In Eire the courts have rejected the doctrine as absurd: *Exham* v. *Beamish* [1939] I.R. 336.
16a *Re Atkins' W. T.* [1974] 1 W.L.R. 761 (postponing sale).
17 *Re Gaite's W. T.* [1949] 1 All E.R. 459.
18 Marriage Act, 1949, s. 2 (replacing Age of Marriage Act, 1929, s. 1), invalidating any marriage by a person under the age of 16. Had the gift extended to illegitimate grandchildren (*post*, p. 495), it might have been void. And in any case it is arguable that legitimate grandchildren might have qualified outside the perpetuity period under foreign law: see Morris & Leach, 85, 86; J. H. C. Morris (1949) 13 Conv.(N.S.) 289; W. B. Leach (1952) 68 L.Q.R. 35, 46. Professor Leach's article is an entertaining attack on many developments of

Much care is therefore necessary to detect any possibility, however remote and in whatever improbable circumstances, that a gift may transgress the rule. A gift " to the first son of A to be called to the Bar " is similarly void if A is alive, however old A may be, and even if he has a son who is due to be called to the Bar the next day; for it is possible that this son may never be called, and A may have another son (not a life in being at the time of the gift) who may be called to the Bar more than 21 years after the death of his father and his elder brothers.

Similarly, a gift of property to certain persons " if the minerals under the said farm should be worked " offends the perpetuity rule and is void because of the possibility that the minerals will first be worked outside the perpetuity period.[19]

(c) *Gifts which may never vest.* It is immaterial that the gift may never vest at all; the question is whether, if it does vest, it is capable of vesting outside the period. A gift to the first son of X, a bachelor, may never vest at all, for X may never have a son. But this possibility does not render the gift void for perpetuity. The gift is incapable of vesting outside the perpetuity period, for if X does have a son, the son must be born or conceived during X's lifetime and X is a life in being. The rule requires, therefore, that the gift shall be bound to vest, *if it vests at all*, within the perpetuity period. Again, a gift by will—

" to the first of my daughters to marry after my death "
is valid, even though no daughter may marry; for if any daughter does marry, she must do so in her own lifetime, and since the testator is dead when the gift takes effect, no further daughters can be born and all those who are alive or *en ventre sa mère* rank as lives in being. Had the gift been made by deed, it would have been void, for the donor might have had further daughters after the date of the gift (who would not have been lives in being) and one of these might have been the first to qualify for the gift by marrying more than 21 years after the death of the donor and all his other daughters.

To this rule against " wait and see " there are two special exceptions, which are considered below under the respective headings of " alternative contingencies " and " powers of appointment." [20]

the perpetuity rule, particularly on the " fertile octogenarian " cases, and foreshadows the reforms of 1964. The law admits the physical impossibility of child-bearing for other purposes: see, *e.g.*, *Re Widdow's Trusts* (1871) L.R. 11 Eq. 408; *Re Millner's Estate* (1872) L.R. 14 Eq. 245; *Re White* [1901] 1 Ch. 570; *Re Tennant's Settlement* [1959] Ir.Jur.Rep. 76; *Re Westminster Bank, Ltd.'s Declaration of Trusts* [1963] 1 W.L.R. 820; *Re Pettifor's W. T.* [1966] 1 W.L.R. 778; and contrast *Croxton* v. *May* (1878) 9 Ch.D. 388.
[19] *Thomas* v. *Thomas* (1902) 87 L.T. 58.
[20] *Post*, pp. 242, 256.

(*d*) *Express clauses.* A gift which would otherwise be too remote may be validated by the insertion of an express clause confining its vesting to the proper period. Thus a gift by a testator to such of his issue as shall be living when certain gravel pits become exhausted is void as it stands, even if it is highly probable that the pits will be worked out in 5 or 6 years.[21] The gift would have been valid, however, if worded " to such of my issue as shall be living 21 years after my death or when the gravel pits are exhausted, whichever first happens," [22] or " to such of my children and grandchildren as shall be living when the gravel pits are exhausted, provided that no grandchild aged 21 or over shall participate." But a clause seeking to confine the vesting within the period must do so sufficiently explicitly; the addition of words providing that the vesting shall be postponed only " so far as the rules of law and equity will permit " will not validate a void gift,[23] though " within the limitations prescribed by law " may suffice.[24]

3. " Wait and see " under the Act of 1964

(*a*) *Operation of the new rule.* The absolute certainty required by the rule at common law was convenient in that it enabled the validity of contingent gifts to be determined at the outset. But this convenience was bought at too high a price : the rule defeated many gifts which might well have vested within the permitted period, and which in any case could have been validated by an express clause of the kind mentioned in the previous paragraph. In order to stop this " slaughter of the innocents " [25] the Act of 1964 has now introduced the principle of " wait and see." The Act provides that a gift is to fail only if and when " it becomes established that the vesting must occur, if at all, after the end of the perpetuity period "; and until that time arrives the Act requires the disposition to be treated as if it were not subject to the rule.[26] Corresponding provision is made for powers and rights (for example, an option [27])

---

[21] *Re Wood* [1894] 3 Ch. 381.
[22] See (1938) 51 Harv.L.R. 638 at 645 (W. B. Leach).
[23] *Portman* v. *Viscount Portman* [1922] 2 A.C. 473. But such words may be effective in a contract or in an executory trust (*ante*, p. 131, *post*, p. 447) where the settlor has not " been his own conveyancer " and set out all the trusts explicitly, but has merely given a general indication of how the settlement is to be made. In such cases the trusts will be " moulded so as to carry out the intentions of the testator so far as the rules of law permit " (*Christie* v. *Gosling* (1866) L.R. 1 H.L. 279 at 290, *per* Lord Chelmsford L.C.), so confining the limitations within the permitted boundaries, unless the settlor has clearly intended them to be exceeded : *Lyddon* v. *Ellison* (1854) 19 Beav. 565. See also *Re Hooper* [1932] 1 Ch. 38.
[24] *Re Vaux* [1939] Ch. 465, on which see *I.R.C.* v. *Williams* [1969] 1 W.L.R. 1197; and contrast *Re Abrahams'* *W. T.* [1969] 1 Ch. 463.
[25] Leach in (1952) 68 L.Q.R. 35.
[26] s. 3 (1).
[27] For options, etc., see *post*, p. 258.

which do not so much "vest" as become exercisable in the future, and accordingly any power, option or other right is to be void for perpetuity only if and so far as it is not fully exercised within the period.[28] Thus the new principle extends to all classes of proprietary interests, powers and rights. But it has two most important limitations:

(i) it applies only to instruments taking effect after July 15, 1964; and

(ii) it applies only to dispositions which would be void at common law.

Even where the gift is made after July 15, 1964, therefore, the first step must always be to apply the old rule, *i.e.*, the rule at common law. For only if the gift fails to satisfy the rule at common law will it fall within the scope of the Act. Instead of replacing the old rule, the Act merely supplements it by coming to the rescue when needed, but not otherwise.

(*b*) *Impossibility of vesting in time.* A gift which would be void for perpetuity at common law, therefore, is now to be void only if and when circumstances make it clear that it can only vest outside the perpetuity period. If circumstances make this clear at the outset, the gift is void from the beginning. In other cases its validity depends on later events which actually happen, as opposed to depending on events which might happen, as at common law. Thus where land is devised—

"to A's first son to marry,"

and A is a bachelor at the testator's death, it is clear that the gift would be void at common law, and equally clear that the first son to marry might be a son who marries in A's lifetime or within 21 years of A's death. The Act therefore allows us to wait and see whether this happens; and if it does, the gift is good. But if A dies before any of his sons has married, and none of them marry during the next 21 years, it then "becomes established" that the gift is incapable of vesting within the perpetuity period, and thereupon it fails. In effect, it operates like a gift "to A's first son to marry before the expiration of 21 years from A's death," which of course is valid at common law, and involves a similar period of waiting to see whether any son of A becomes entitled. Had A died before the testator, the gift would in any case have been valid at common law, and the Act would have no application.

As another illustration we may take a devise—

---

[28] Act of 1964, s. 3 (2), (3).

" to A for life, remainder to his eldest son for life, remainder to the eldest of A's issue living at the son's death."

At common law the final remainder would be void. But under the Act we may wait and see whether in fact it vests (a) in a person who was alive at the date of the gift or (b) in a person born later, where not more than 21 years have elapsed since the death of the last survivor of A and any of his issue who were alive at the date of the gift (why these are the lives in being is explained below [29]). If (a) or (b) in fact occurs, the final remainder is good; but as soon as the facts show that neither (a) nor (b) can occur, it fails.

Similarly, in the case of a gift to such of the testator's issue as are alive when certain gravel pits become exhausted, [30] the gift will be valid if the pits are exhausted within 21 years of the death of the survivor of those of the issue who were alive at the testator's death. In the case of a grant of the right to use all drains " hereafter to pass " under certain land, the grant will be valid in respect of all drains constructed within 21 years of the death of the survivor of the grantor and the grantee. [31]

In all these cases it will be seen that the perpetuity periods made available by the Act of 1964 are such as the donor could himself have validly used at common law, had he been well advised. Although, therefore, the change to " wait and see " is in one sense revolutionary, in another sense it is merely a reframing of the gift so as to give it the best possible chance of satisfying the rule at common law.

(c) *Relation to other rules.* Where other provisions of the Act of 1964 (explained later) may save a gift by reducing an excessive age, or by excluding members of a class, or by accelerating vesting during the life of a surviving spouse, the Act requires the " wait and see " rule to be applied first. [32] Only if and when it becomes apparent that " wait and see " by itself will not save the gift will these other provisions come into play. It is important to observe that this is the order of priority of these various gift-saving provisions. In applying them the motto is " first wait and see." This embodies the policy that the gift should be given every opportunity to take effect as the donor intended, and that only as a last resort should his dispositions be modified by statute.

(d) *Maintenance and advancement.* While the validity of a gift remains in suspense under the " wait and see " provisions trustees

---

[29] *Cf. post,* p. 221.
[30] *Cf. ante,* p. 214.
[31] This is under s. 3 (3). *Cf. ante,* p. 211. For explanation of the choice of lives in being, which is governed by the Act of 1964, see *post,* p. 228.
[32] This is the effect of the opening words of s. 3, excluding ss. 4 and 5.

have their usual powers of maintenance and advancement, which enable them to use income and capital for the benefit of contingent beneficiaries, subject to certain restrictions.[33] If it turns out that a contingent beneficiary who has been assisted in this way fails to qualify for the gift, *e.g.*, by failing to attain 21 or marry, the validity of the trustees' action is unaffected.[34] It is thus possible for a substantial part of a gift to be used for the benefit of someone who never becomes entitled to take, at the expense of the one who does become entitled.

(*e*) *Future parenthood.* Statutory presumptions as to "future parenthood" have also been enacted, in order to remedy the absurdities which can occur under the rule at common law.[35] Where the gift is made after July 15, 1964, the Act of 1964 requires it to be presumed that—

  (i) a male can have a child at the age of fourteen years or over, but not under that age; and

  (ii) a female can have a child at the age of twelve years or over, but not under that age, or over the age of fifty-five years.[36]

But these presumptions are rebuttable; evidence may be given to show that a living person will or will not be able to have a child at the time in question.[37] Thus medical evidence of a person's incapacity may be given, and may be contradicted by evidence of capacity.

The above provisions apply only where a perpetuity question arises " in any proceedings," meaning legal proceedings[38]; if necessary, a declaratory judgment can be sought.[39] Once the question is decided, the decision will govern any future proceedings concerning the same gift for perpetuity purposes.[40]

For the purposes of the Act, " having a child " extends not only to natural birth but to " adoption, legitimation or other means."[41] It is obviously possible that a child may be legitimated or adopted after the date of the gift by a woman over fifty-five, thus falsifying the statutory presumption. To deal with this, and also with any cases of freak births inconsistent with the statutory ages or evidence of incapacity, the High Court is given discretion to make such order as it thinks fit for placing the persons interested in the property, so far as may be just, in the position they would have held had the statutory

---

[33] Trustee Act, 1925, ss. 31, 32.
[34] Act of 1964, s. 3 (1). See (1964) 80 L.Q.R. 454.
[35] *Ante*, p. 212.
[36] s. 2 (1) (*a*).
[37] s. 2 (1) (*b*).
[38] s. 2 (1).
[39] Under R.S.C., Ord. 15, r. 16.
[40] s. 2 (3).
[41] s. 2 (4). For the right to such children to take, see *post*, p. 495

provisions not been applied.[42] The Act therefore contemplates the possibility that it may not be right to order full restitution by those who had previously taken the property, or expected to take it.

4. Lives in being at common law

(a) *Relevant lives.* Any living person or persons may be used as lives in being, since for a gift to be valid at common law it is only necessary to demonstrate that it must necessarily vest, if at all, within the period of a (meaning " any ") life in being plus 21 years. In the literal sense, everyone alive at the time of the gift is a life in being.[43] Nevertheless the only lives in being which can be of assistance for the purposes of the perpetuity rule are those which in some way or other can govern the time when the gift is to vest.   The only lives worth considering are thus those which are implicated in the contingency upon which the vesting has been made to depend.[44]

(b) *Lives mentioned in gift.* It follows that the life or lives in being must be mentioned in the gift either expressly or by implication. In the great majority of cases the only lives which can possibly be of use are those of the persons expressly mentioned in the gift. Any or all of them may be used to demonstrate, if possible, that the gift must vest, if at all, within the permitted period.   There is therefore no difficulty in ascertaining the relevant lives.   But sometimes lives which are relevant to the period of vesting are brought in by implication, without express mention.   If a testator gives property to such of his grandchildren as attain the age of 21, his children's lives clearly help to confine the period of time within which the gift can vest; therefore his children can be taken as lives in being. They are all bound to have been born [45] by the time of the testator's death, and a gift to grandchildren presupposes the existence of children. The gift is therefore good,[46] for no grandchild can take longer than 21 years from its parent's death to reach the age of 21. But a gift to the grandchildren of a living person is of course bad,[47] unless the class is restricted in some way, *e.g.*, to those living at the death of a life in being [48]; for the living person might have another child after the date of the gift and then, more than 21 years after all those alive at the date of the gift had died, that child might have a child.

42 Act of 1964, s. 2 (2).
43 See *Pownall* v. *Graham* (1863) 33 Beav. 242 at 246, 247.
44 *Cf.* Morris & Leach, 62.
45 Or about to be born: see *post*, p. 226; Morris & Leach, 65.
46 Gray, § § 220, 370; *cf. Blagrove* v. *Hancock* (1848) 16 Sim. 371 (where, however, the excessive age of 25 was specified); *Re Lodwig* [1916] 2 Ch. 26.
47 *Seaman* v. *Wood* (1856) 22 Beav. 591 at 594.
48 *Wetherell* v. *Wetherell* (1863) 1 De G.J. & S. 134 at 139, 140.

Consequently it can be said that everyone who—

(i) is alive at the time of the gift, and

(ii) is mentioned in it either expressly or by implication,

should be considered as a possible life in being. But it does not follow that everyone so mentioned will be an effective life in being, for the life of the person in question may have no connection with the contingency which governs the vesting and thus set no limit to the time within which it must occur. If A grants to B the right in fee simple " to use all drains hereafter to pass under Blackacre," both A and B are mentioned in the gift, but neither of their lives has any bearing on the fact that no such drain may be built until long after the perpetuity period, when some successor of B might claim to use it; and so the gift is void.[49] For similar reasons all persons not mentioned in the gift must be ignored, since the length or shortness of their lives can have no bearing on the vesting of the gift.

(c) *Time for ascertaining lives.* In the case of gifts made *inter vivos,* the date of the instrument, and, in the case of wills, the date of the testator's death, is the time when the period starts running and the facts must be ascertained; to be a life in being a person must be alive at that moment.[50]

(d) *Choice of lives.* For a person to be a life in being for the purposes of the rule, it is unnecessary that he should receive any benefit from the gift or that he should be related in any special way to the beneficiaries.[51] Nor is there any restriction upon the number of lives selected, provided that it is reasonably possible to ascertain who they are, " for let the lives be never so many, there must be a survivor, and so it is but the length of that life." [52] " If a term be limited to one for life, with twenty several remainders for lives to other persons successively, who are all alive and in being, so that all the candles are lighted together, this is good enough." [53]

For example, gifts by a testator to such of his descendants as

---

49 *Dunn* v. *Blackdown Properties Ltd.* [1961] Ch. 433; *ante,* p. 211. It is otherwise under the Act of 1964; *post,* p. 225.

50 See *ante,* p. 211.

51 *Cadell* v. *Palmer* (1833) 1 Cl. & F. 372. This was said to be a mistaken doctrine (*Cole* v. *Sewell* (1848) 2 H.L.C. 186 at 233), and Lewis, *Perpetuity,* 167, calls it " a flagrant abuse of the spirit of the Rule." But the law had generally been supposed to be thus for some time (see, *e.g., Goodman* v. *Goodright* (1759) 2 Burr. 873 at 879); and it was settled beyond question by the House of Lords' decision first cited.

52 *Scatterwood* v. *Edge* (1697) 1 Salk. 229.

53 *Howard* v. *Duke of Norfolk* (1681) 2 Swans. 454 at 458, *per* Lord Nottingham L.C. And see *Low* v. *Burron* (1734) 3 P.Wms. 262 at 265; *Robinson* v. *Hardcastle* (1786) 2 Bro.C.C. 22 at 30; *Thellusson* v. *Woodford* (1805) 11 Ves. 112 at 136.

are living 21 years after the death of the last survivor of the members
of a given school living at the testator's death,[54] or 20 years after
the death of the last survivor of all the lineal descendants of Queen
Victoria living at the testator's death,[55] have been held valid. In
the latter case the testator died in 1926, when there were 120 lives
in being and it was reasonably possible to follow the duration of their
lives; a similar limitation today might well be void for uncertainty,
and so should preferably be made by reference to a smaller class,
such as the descendants of King George V.[56] The clearest possible
case of uncertainty occurred where a testatrix chose the period " until
21 years from the death of the last survivor of all persons who shall
be living at my death." [57]

The lives must be human lives, and not the lives of animals.[58]

5. Alternative fixed period under the Act of 1964. " Royal lives
clauses," of the type just discussed, have been much used as a draftsman's device for providing a long perpetuity period when required
for any purpose under the rule at common law.[59] In order to provide
a more straightforward substitute the Act of 1964 has made
available an alternative perpetuity period consisting of a fixed period
of years not exceeding eighty.[60] Although this period is to be
" specified in that behalf " in the instrument,[61] it probably suffices if,
without expressly stating it to be the perpetuity period, the limitation
specifies a period of years within which vesting must occur. Thus
a gift by will " to my first descendant to marry within eighty years
of my death" seems to fall within the provision. Yet it would be
safer to specify the perpetuity period in terms, as by framing gifts
by will—

> (i) " To A's first son to marry within eighty years of my death,
> which period I hereby specify as the perpetuity period for
> this gift "; or
>
> (ii) " To A's first son to marry. I hereby specify the period of
> eighty years from my death as the perpetuity period for this
> gift."

---

[54] *Pownall* v. *Graham* (1863) 33 Beav. 242 at 245, 247.
[55] *Re Villar* [1929] 1 Ch. 243.
[56] See *Re Leverhulme (No. 2)* [1943] 2 All E.R. 274.
[57] *Re Moore* [1901] 1 Ch. 936.
[58] For remarks on this, see *Re Kelly* [1932] I.R. 255 at 260, 261. *Re Dean* (1889)
41 Ch.D. 552 is probably incorrect on this point. See Gray, § 896, and *post*,
p. 269, n. 91. See also *post*, p. 267, as to the necessity for a beneficiary able
to enforce the trust.
[59] *e.g.*, to confine a discretionary trust within legal limits. See Fourth Report of
the Law Reform Committee, 1956, Cmnd. 18, p. 6.
[60] s. 1.
[61] *Ibid.*

The difference in effect should be noticed. Example (i) is a straight-forward case of a valid gift, which is bound to vest, if at all, within the specified statutory period. The gift in example (ii) is not so confined, and it may or may not vest within that period (assuming A to be alive and without a married son at the testator's death); the " wait and see " provisions therefore apply, and the period of waiting in such a case is the specified statutory period.[62]

Nothing in the Act of 1964 affects the validity of an ordinary " royal lives clause " or similar perpetuity clause where the gift must vest, if at all, within the specified period.

6. Lives in being under the Act of 1964

(a) *Effect of the introduction of " wait and see."* It is a con-troversial question whether the introduction of the " wait and see " principle called for any special provisions for restricting the persons who could be used as lives in being. The policy of the " wait and see " provisions of the Act of 1964 is not to alter the length of the perpetuity period,[63] but to provide that gifts shall be valid if they do in fact vest within it rather than be void if they might by possibility vest outside it. The perpetuity period itself remains unchanged, and the lives in being which determine the period in any given case ought likewise to remain unchanged. But, according to the school of thought which the Act has followed, an unconfined " wait and see " provision would enable a contingent gift to remain in suspense for 21 years beyond the life of anyone in the world who could be shown to have been alive at the date of the gift.[64] The weakness of this theory is that it disregards the fact, already explained, that the only lives in being which are significant under the rule at common law are those which in some way restrict the time within which the gift can vest, and which are expressly or impliedly connected with the gift by the donor's directions. No other lives can affect the available perpetuity period, which must necessarily be ascertained before it can be said whether the gift succeeds or fails. The most that was required, therefore, was to enact that no extension

---

[62] See Act of 1964, s. 3 (4).
[63] Except by introducing the alternative fixed period under s. 1 (*ante*, p. 220).
[64] Allan (1963) 6 U. of W.A.L.Rev. 27, 43–46; Allan (1965) 81 L.Q.R. 106; Maudsley (1970) 86 L.Q.R. 357; *cf*. Simes (1963) 6 U. of W.A.L.Rev. 21, 22–25. The argu-ment is founded on the fallacy that the common law rule identifies only lives which validate a gift, so that it gives no help in the case of gifts not valid at common law. In reality the conditions (including lives) designed by the donor to govern the time of vesting remain equally ascertainable, whether the gift succeeds or fails. Thus in the examples under the Act discussed above, pp. 215–216, the common law perpetuity period is equally obvious in each case. The question is simply whether the vesting is or is not bound to occur within it. If this were not so, the statutes of several other countries (see next note) would be unworkable.

of this category of lives should be implied from the enactment of the
" wait and see " principle.[65]

Unfortunately the Act of 1964 has enacted a detailed definition
of the lives in being which are to be used for the purposes of its
" wait and see " provisions. It is both more complex and less
rational in operation than the reforming statutes of other countries,
which have followed simpler and sounder principles.[66] The definition
is a fertile source of difficulties and obscurities. As compared with the
rule at common law, it sometimes allows different lives in being to be
used, and is sometimes more indulgent than the common law and
sometimes less so. Although in many cases there will be no discrepancy and little difficulty, this cannot be taken for granted.

(*b*) *Conditions for the use of statutory lives in being.* It is only
for the purpose of its " wait and see " provisions that the Act of 1964
defines the lives in being.[67] A gift which is valid at common law
(*e.g.*, one confined by a conventional " royal lives clause ") is
unaffected, as also is a gift made before July 16, 1964. Where the
donor has chosen the alternative of appointing a fixed statutory
perpetuity period, of course no lives in being can be used.[68]

In all other cases where " wait and see " applies, the Act provides
that the perpetuity period shall be determined by reference to the
lives of certain categories of persons and no others. The definition
is therefore both imperative and exclusive. The persons concerned
must, of course, be in being at the relevant time. In addition,
they must satisfy two requirements—

(i) they must be ascertainable at the commencement of the
    perpetuity period, and
(ii) if a " description of persons," they must not be so numerous
    as to render it impracticable to ascertain the date of death
    of the survivor.[69]

The second of these requirements is in conformity with the rule at
common law, as already explained.[70] The first requirement is new,

---

[65] For fuller discussions see Morris and Wade (1964) 80 L.Q.R. 486, 495–501 ; *cf.*
Elphinstone, *Perpetuities and Accumulations Act 1964*, 14. For examples of such
provisions, see Law Reform (Property, Perpetuities and Succession) Act, 1962, s. 7
(3) (Western Australia); Perpetuities Act 1966, s. 6 (Ontario); Perpetuities and
Accumulations Act 1968, s. 6 (4) (Victoria). The Victorian statute is especially
interesting, since its " wait and see " provision initially follows the wording of
the U.K. Act but rejects its definition of lives in being in favour of a simple
and accurate formula indicating the same lives as at common law. New Zealand,
however, adopted the definition : Perpetuities Act 1964.
[66] See previous note.
[67] s. 3 (4).
[68] *Ibid.*
[69] s. 3 (4) ; see *Re Thomas Meadows & Co. Ltd.* [1971] Ch. 278.
[70] *Ante*, p. 220.

and is a restriction of the rule at common law. For example, in a gift by will—

> " to A's first grandchild to marry a woman born before my death " (A being alive at the testator's death),

the gift is presumably valid at common law because it must vest during the lifetime of the potential wife, who is by definition a life in being. It does not matter that the wife is not ascertainable at the commencement of the perpetuity period, *i.e.*, at the testator's death. But in cases where the " wait and see " provisions of the Act apply, such a life may not be used, for it is unascertainable at the outset.

(*c*) *Statutory categories of lives in being.* Where the above-mentioned conditions are satisfied, the Act of 1964 provides that four categories of lives in being are to be used.[71] If none of these are in fact available, the perpetuity period for " wait and see " purposes is 21 years only.[72] The four statutory categories are as follows.[73]

(a) THE DONOR : " the person by whom the disposition was made."

(b) A DONEE : " a person to whom or in whose favour the disposition was made, that is to say—
   (i) in the case of a disposition to a class of persons, any member or potential member of the class;
   (ii) in the case of an individual disposition to a person taking only on certain conditions being satisfied, any person as to whom some of the conditions are satisfied and the remainder may in time be satisfied ";
   (iii) and (iv) (these concern special powers of appointment, discussed separately below);
   (v) " in the case of any power, option or other right, the person on whom the right is conferred."

(c) A DONEE'S PARENT OR GRANDPARENT : " a person having a child or grandchild within sub-paragraphs (i) to (iv) of paragraph (b) above, or any of whose children or grandchildren, if subsequently born, would by virtue of his or her descent fall within those sub-paragraphs."

(d) THE OWNER OF A PRIOR INTEREST : " any person on the failure or determination of whose prior interest the disposition is limited to take effect." [74]

---

[71] s. 3 (5).
[72] s. 3 (4) (*b*).
[73] s. 3 (5).
[74] See *Re Thomas Meadows & Co., Ltd.* [1971] Ch. 278.

(*d*) "*The disposition.*" Each of these categories, it will be noticed, is defined in relation to " the disposition " [75]; and it is plain from the Act that each distinct gift counts as a distinct disposition. Thus in a gift by will—

> " To A's first son to marry, and, in default of any son of A marrying, then to B's first son to marry " (A and B being alive and without married sons at the testator's death),

there are two separate dispositions. Any son of A alive at the testator's death is a life in being under (b) for the purposes of the first gift, and under (d) for the purposes of the second gift. Any such son of B is a life in being under (b) for the purposes of the second gift, but not a life in being at all for the purposes of the first gift. A is also a life in being under (c) for the purposes of the first gift, but not the second; and B is a life in being under (c) for the purposes of the second gift, but not the first. The scheme is thus both more complicated and more restrictive than that under the rule at common law. At common law royal lives, or any other lives, may be specified by the settlor. But such lives are now useless for statutory " wait and see " purposes.

A class gift is a single " disposition " to which the Act applies as explained below.[76]

(*e*) *Examples.* Some further examples will illustrate the operation of the statutory rules, and what seems to be their pointless divergence from the principle of the rule at common law.

Suppose that a settlement made *inter vivos* in 1965 gives property " to A's first grandson to attain 21 " and that A is then alive and without such a grandson. The gift would be void at common law, and therefore " wait and see " applies. The possible lives in being are the settlor (under (a)), A and any existing children of A (under (c)), any existing grandsons of A (under (b) (ii)), and also, it seems A's spouse, the spouses of A's children, and the parents of the latter spouses.[77] The validity of the gift may therefore remain in suspense until 21 years after the death of the last of these persons who was alive at the date of the settlement. Here the Act goes much further than the rule at common law: for the life of the settlor has nothing to do with the conditions for vesting, nor has the life of an existing child of A as regards anyone but that child's own son or sons; nor has the life of an existing grandson of A, except as regards himself; nor have the lives

---

[75] Registration of a member of a pension scheme may be " the disposition ": *Re Thomas Meadows & Co., Ltd., supra.*
[76] *Post*, p. 233.
[77] Unless excluded by the words " by virtue of his or her descent." For this and other obscurities see [1969] C.L.J. 284 (M. J. Prichard).

of the above-mentioned spouses and parents. A grandson may thus be allowed to " wait and see " for the duration of several lives which are irrelevant to his interest and so operate fortuitously. If, for example, he happens to have an uncle or a cousin born before the settlement, his chances of taking may be greatly extended. The complexity of this new law is evident.

Suppose that a testator dying in 1965 leaves property " to A's first son to marry, but if there is no such son, to B." Here the eligible lives are, for the first disposition, A and A's spouse (under (c)) and any existing sons of A (under (b) (ii)); but for the second disposition, the only available lives are any existing sons of A (under (d)) and perhaps [78] B himself (under (b) (ii)): A's life will not count. Here the Act is more restrictive than the common law, for plainly the life of A may affect the period of time within which the gift to B may vest. If A has no son and survives B for more than 21 years, B's gift will therefore fail to vest within the statutory perpetuity period, and B's estate will take nothing, although, in fact, the period is not extended beyond the lifetime of a living person, namely, A.

Suppose, finally, that A grants to B the right to use " all drains hereafter to be constructed under Blackacre." Here the Act allows the use of A (under (a)) and B (under (b) (v)) as lives in being, so that B or his successors in title will be entitled to use all such drains in fact constructed within 21 years of the death of the survivor of A and B. Here the Act goes further than the rule at common law, for the lives of A and B have no necessary effect on the time within which the right may become exercisable: A and B might die or sell their interests long before that time, yet their lives will continue to be important to their successors. If A and B are both corporations, the period is 21 years only.

(f) *Comparison with common law lives.* It will be observed that, as a general rule, the Act allows a greater number of lives in being to be used than could be used at common law. But the Act is more restrictive than the common law in two situations—

(i) where a life in being is not an ascertainable person at the time of the gift; and

(ii) where there is a gift over and the donee dies more than 21 years before the gift is to vest.

---

[78] Is B a person "as to whom some of the conditions are satisfied "? His mere identity can hardly count, since an immediate gift " to B " is vested and not conditional at all. Benevolent construction may solve this problem.

7. Perpetuity period without lives in being. If no lives in being are available, the perpetuity period is 21 years only. This is equally true at common law [79] and under the Act of 1964,[80] unless, of course, the alternative statutory perpetuity period (not exceeding 80 years) [80a] has been used.

At common law, for example, a gift by a testator to all his issue living 50 years after his death,[81] or to all the children of X (who is alive) living 28 years after the testator's death,[82] is void. The difficulty is that neither the lives of the testator's children in the first case nor X's life in the second case have any bearing on the time of vesting: it is a period of years quite unconnected with any lifetimes, so that all available lives might fail more than 21 years before its termination. There are therefore no effective lives in being and the perpetuity period is 21 years only. This is sometimes called a period in gross. A gift to all the children of X living 30 years after the testator's death is of course good if X is dead, for all the beneficiaries are lives in being.[83]

The Act of 1964, as explained above, has abandoned the principle that lives in being must be connected with the time of vesting. All the persons mentioned in the above two examples of void gifts would, if the Act of 1964 applied, be within the new statutory categories of lives in being, and " wait and see " would operate during the period of their lives plus 21 years. An example of a gift without lives in being under the Act of 1964 is a devise to the first woman to land on the moon. Here " wait and see " will operate, but only during the period of 21 years.

8. Children en ventre sa mère. For the purposes of the perpetuity rule, a child *en ventre sa mère* is treated as if it had been born.[84] even if the child does not benefit from the gift.[85] Two cases can arise:

> (i) A child may be *en ventre sa mère* at the beginning of the period, *i.e.*, at the time of the gift. In this case the child is treated as a life in being.[86] Thus if a testator gives property for life to the child with which his wife is enceinte, with a remainder contingent upon certain circumstances existing at

[79] Marsden 34.
[80] s. 3 (4) (*b*). This applies only in cases of " wait and see." In other cases the Act leaves the common law unchanged.
[80a] *Ante*, p. 220.
[81] *Speakman* v. *Speakman* (1850) 8 Hare 180.
[82] *Palmer* v. *Holford* (1828) 4 Russ. 403.
[83] *Lachlan* v. *Reynolds* (1852) 9 Hare 796.
[84] *Thellusson* v. *Woodford* (1805) 11 Ves. 112 at 141.
[85] *Re Wilmer's Trusts* [1903] 2 Ch. 411; contrast *post*, p. 490.
[86] *Thellusson* v. *Woodford, supra,* at p. 143; *Re Wilmer's Trusts, supra,* at p. 421.

that child's death, or bound to occur within 21 years thereof, the remainder is good, for the contingency must be resolved within the permissible period.[87]

(ii) A child may be *en ventre sa mère* during the period. In this case the period is extended so far as is necessary to include the period of gestation.[88] Thus if property is given to the first of A's sons to reach 21 years, the gift is valid even if A's only son was unborn at A's death; the perpetuity period in such a case is A's lifetime plus the period of gestation and 21 years.

It will be seen from this that two periods of gestation may arise in the same case; both are then allowed.[89] If property is given to Jane's eldest child for life, with remainder to the first son of that child to be 21 and Jane is pregnant with her first child at the time of the gift, the remainder does not infringe the perpetuity rule even though Jane's child may be a son who dies leaving his wife enceinte of an only son. Jane's child is treated as a life in being, and the perpetuity period will be extended to cover the period of gestation of the child's son.[90] In exceptional cases, there may even be three periods of gestation.[91]

These rules do not allow the addition of any period or periods of nine months or so for all cases; they apply only where gestation actually exists, and where the date of the subsequent birth affects the period chosen.[92]

The Act of 1964 makes no change in these rules.

9. "Surviving spouse" conditions. Donors often made gifts to such children as might be living at the death of their last-surviving parent. Such gifts often failed at common law where one parent was not a life in being, and so the Act of 1964 has made special provision for preventing this particular disaster. Where a gift is made by will—

> "to A (a bachelor) for life, with remainder to any wife of A for life, with remainder to such of their children as survive them both,"

the remainder to the children is, as we have seen, void at common law if A is alive at the same time of the gift.[93] But if the gift is made after July 15, 1964, the Act of 1964 now saves the remainder to the

---

[87] *Long* v. *Blackall* (1797) 7 T.R. 100.
[88] *Gray*, § 221; Morris and Leach, 65; Jarman 305, 306.
[89] *Thellusson* v. *Woodford* (1805) 11 Ves. 112 at 143, 149, 150.
[90] See *Gulliver* v. *Wickett* (1745) 1 Wils.K.B. 105; *Thellusson* v. *Woodford, supra,* at pp. 149, 150.
[91] *Smith* v. *Farr* (1838) 3 Y. & C. Ex. 328; *Gray*, § 222.
[92] *Cadell* v. *Palmer* (1833) 1 Cl. & F. 372 at 421, 422.
[93] *Ante,* p. 212.

children. This it does by providing that, subject to the "wait and see" rule, "where a disposition is limited by reference to the time of death of the survivor of a person in being at the commencement of the perpetuity period and any spouse of that person, and that time has not arrived at the end of the perpetuity period, the disposition shall be treated for all purposes, where to do so would save it from being void for remoteness, as if it had instead been limited by reference to the time immediately before the end of that period." [93a] In such cases, therefore, under the "wait and see" rule no change in the time of vesting is required if the survivor of the parents in fact dies within the perpetuity period (A's lifetime plus 21 years). But if A's widow survives him for 21 years, the "wait and see" rule can do no more, and the Act then converts the gift into a gift to the children then living, even if some of them predecease the widow and so fall outside the class which the testator intended to benefit.

10. Class gifts

(a) At common law

(1) NATURE OF CLASS GIFTS. A class gift is a gift of property to all who come within some description, the property being divisible in shares varying according to the number of persons in the class.[94] Thus gifts of property—

> "to my children who shall live to be 25," [95] or

> "to all the nephews and nieces of my late husband who were living at his death, except A and B," [96] or

> "to my children A, B, C, D, and E and such of my children hereafter to be born as shall attain the age of 21 years or marry," [97] or

> "to A. B. C. D and E if living." [98]

are class gifts. The essence of the matter in each case is the intention that if one member of the class is subtracted the shares of the others will be increased. But gifts of property to be equally divided between—

> "the five daughters of X," [99] or

> "my nine children," [1]

or a gift of £2,000—

> "to each of my daughters," [2]

[93a] s. 5.
[94] See Gray, § 369n.; *Pearks* v. *Moseley* (1880) 5 App.Cas. 714 at 723; *Kingsbury* v. *Walter* [1901] A.C. 187 at 192; Jarman 341, 348.
[95] *Boreham* v. *Bignall* (1850) 8 Hare 131.
[96] *Dimond* v. *Bostock* (1875) 10 Ch.App. 358.
[97] *Re Jackson* (1883) 25 Ch.D. 162.   [98] *Re Hornby* (1859) 7 W.R. 729.
[99] *Re Smith's Trusts* (1878) 9 Ch.D. 117.
[1] *Re Stansfield* (1880) 15 Ch.D. 84.
[2] *Wilkinson* v. *Duncan* (1861) 30 Beav. 111; *Rogers* v. *Mutch* (1878) 10 Ch.D. 25.

are not class gifts, for a distinct one-fifth or one-ninth share or the sum of £2,000 is given to each child, exactly as if he or she had been named [2a]; and these shares cannot vary according to the number of the recipients. It is therefore necessary to distinguish class gifts, where the ultimate shares are at first uncertain in amount, from groups of independent gifts, where the shares are quantified from the beginning.

(2) APPLICATION OF RULE. At common law the perpetuity rule applies to class gifts in the following way. If a single member of the class might possibly take a vested interest outside the period, the whole gift fails, even as regards those members of the class who have already satisfied any required contingency.[3] A class gift cannot be good as to part and void as to the rest: " the vice of remoteness affects the class as a whole, if it may affect an unascertained number of its members." [4] Until the total number of members of the class has been ascertained, it cannot be said what share any member of the class will take, and this state of affairs will continue so long as it is possible for any alteration in the number to be made. Commonly the offending possibility is that the number may be increased; but the possibility that it may be decreased is equally fatal. Even though in such a case the minimum amount of each share is fixed within the period, the whole gift is void if the shares could be augmented by an event which is too remote.[5]

Thus if before 1926 [6] personalty was given—

" to A for life and after her death to be equally divided between all her children who shall attain the age of 25,"

an intent being shown to include every child of A, the remainder was void even as regards children alive at the time of the gift, who were thus lives in being.[7] This was so even if A was in fact many years past the age of child-bearing, for in theory other children might be born [8]; and since one of these might not be 25 until more

---

[2a] Similarly, a gift to " each child that may be born to either of the children of either of my brothers ": *Storrs* v. *Benbow* (1853) 3 De G.M. & G. 390.

[3] Thus even a vested share can fail for perpetuity, for although vested in the ordinary sense it is not vested in the special perpetuity sense (*ante*, p. 210): *Leake* v. *Robinson* (1817) 2 Mer. 363. See criticism of this rule by Leach in (1938) 51 Harv.L.R. 1328 and (1952) 68 L.Q.R. 35 at 50; Morris & Leach, 125.

[4] *Pearks* v. *Moseley* (1880) 5 App.Cas. 714 at 723, *per* Lord Selborne L.C.; and see *Re Lord's Settlement* [1947] 2 All E.R. 685; *Re Hooper's S. T.* [1948] Ch. 586.

[5] *Smith* v. *Smith* (1870) 5 Ch.App. 342; *Hale* v. *Hale* (1876) 3 Ch.D. 643; *Re Hooper's S. T.* [1948] Ch. 586.

[6] After 1925 the gift will be saved by L.P.A., 1925, s. 163; and see the Act of 1964: *post*, p. 236.

[7] *Leake* v. *Robinson* (1817) 2 Mer. 363.

[8] *Ante*, p. 212.

than 21 years after the death of all lives in being at the time of the gift, the period might be exceeded. However, a gift to a class as joint tenants, if otherwise complying with the rule, is not invalidated merely because the joint tenancy gives a right of survivorship [9] which may operate outside the period.[10]

(3) GIFTS NOT SEVERABLE. At common law class gifts are not, of course, severable, since it is the essence of the rule that any taint of remoteness affects the whole class. But what appears at first sight to be a gift to a class may in truth be two gifts to separate classes, so that the first may be valid even if the second is void. The usual test must be applied: if the size of the shares given to members of a class cannot be affected by some further contingent gift which is too remote, the class gift may stand although the further gift cannot. For example, suppose land to be settled on A (a bachelor) for life, remainder for life to any wife he may marry, remainder in fee simple to their children in equal shares, with a proviso that if any such child dies before A or his wife, leaving children who survive A and his wife, these children shall take their parent's share. In this case each child's share vests at birth, subject to being divested by the proviso if the contingency occurs. And if a child of A dies before A or his wife and leaves no children who survive A and his wife, that child's vested share passes under his will or intestacy. Whatever happens, therefore, the size of the shares given to A's children is unaffected, and their vested interests are not invalidated by the proviso, which is a separate gift and void for perpetuity at common law.[11]

Contrast with this the all too common form of gift " to all the children of A who attain 21, provided that if any child of A dies under 21 leaving children who attain 21 such children shall take the share which their parent would have taken had he attained 21." If A is alive, this is wholly void at common law, since the size of all the shares may possibly be varied according to the age attained by some grandchild of A outside the perpetuity period.[12] If the gift were instead " to the children of A, provided that " (etc.), at least the gift

---

[9] For joint tenancy and survivorship, see *post*, p. 391.

[10] See *Re Roberts* (1881) 19 Ch.D. 520; Gray, § 232.1.

[11] See *Goodier* v. *Johnson* (1881) 18 Ch.D. 441 (a somewhat tangled case).

[12] *Pearks* v. *Moseley* (1880) 5 App.Cas. 714; *Re Lord's Settlement* [1947] 2 All E.R. 685; *Re Hooper's S. T.* [1948] Ch. 586. The question has been thought to be one of construction, the question being whether the final gift was or was not "substitutional": Jarman 344, 345; Gray, §§ 386–388. But it is submitted that the question is really one of law, as stated in the text, depending not upon the testator's supposed intention of making one gift or two, but upon the possible effect of his directions on the size of the individual shares: see especially *Re Hooper's S. T., supra*, at pp. 590, 591; *cf.* Morris & Leach, 104–106.

to the children would be valid, since their interests would vest at birth and the provision for a possible divesting at an unduly remote time would be void for perpetuity.[13]

(4) ACT OF 1964. The Act of 1964 has mitigated the severity of the common law rule as applied to class gifts. But before the Act is explained it is necessary to notice the judge-made rules which govern the closing of classes. These rules are an essential part of the common law as to class gifts, and have to be applied before it can be determined whether the Act is applicable.

(b) Rules of construction as to closing of classes

(1) THE RULE IN *Andrews* v. *Partington.* For the sake of convenience the courts have laid down the rule, often called the Rule in *Andrews* v. *Partington*,[14] that a numerically uncertain class of beneficiaries normally closes when the first member becomes entitled to claim his share.[15] If this were not so, it would be impossible to give him his portion without waiting until there could be no more members of the class. Therefore the settlor is presumed to have intended that the class should close as soon as the first share vests in possession [16]; no one born subsequently can enter the class, but any potential member of it already born is included. Thus by closing the class against those born later, the maximum number of shares is fixed and the first taker can receive his share.[17]

(2) OPERATION. If the gift is contingent, *e.g.*, upon the members of the class attaining 21, the class will close when the first member attains 21, if he is then entitled in possession. Any others who are then in existence but under age will take their shares if they attain 21; but any not yet born will be excluded, in order that the minimum size of the shares may be fixed. If such a gift is preceded by a life interest, the class will not close until the death of the tenant for life at the earliest, since not before then can any share vest in possession; and if there is then no member aged 21, the class will remain open until there is such a member, whereupon it will close,

---

[13] *Cf. Re Hooper's S. T., supra,* at pp. 590, 591.
[14] (1791) 3 Bro.C.C. 401.
[15] See *post,* p. 501, where this rule is further explained. For valuable accounts of it for the purposes of the perpetuity rule, see Morris & Leach, 109 *et seq.*; (1954) 70 L.Q.R. 61 (J. H. C. Morris, dealing especially with the perpetuity rule); [1958] C.L.J. 39 (S. J. Bailey, dealing especially with the rule against accumulations). See also the discussion by the Court of Appeal in *Re Bleckly* [1951] Ch. 740 (not a perpetuity case).
[16] *Barrington* v. *Tristram* (1801) 6 Ves. 345 at 348; Jarman 1660, 1671.
[17] If any other potential member of the class dies without having become entitled, those who do become entitled will receive accrued shares in addition.

so as to exclude any person then unborn.[18] For no obvious reason there is an exception where the members of the class are to take vested interests at birth and no member exists at the time when the property is available for distribution: in such cases the class remains open indefinitely, *i.e.,* no special rule applies.[19]

(3) EXAMPLES. This doctrine is important here because by limiting a class it may save a gift which at common law would otherwise be void for perpetuity.[20] Some examples will explain its operation.

(i) Devise " to all A's grandchildren," where A is living at the testator's death and has a living grandchild. The class closes at once, since one share is already vested in possession, and includes only grandchildren who are already lives in being.[21] Therefore the gift, which would otherwise be void for perpetuity, is saved. But if A had no grandchildren living at the testator's death, the gift would fail,[22] for the class might remain open beyond the perpetuity period.

(ii) Devise " to A for life, with remainder to all the grandchildren of B in equal shares," where B is living at the testator's death. Here the class will close at A's death, if a grandchild is born to B before that moment.[23] But the perpetuity rule at common law will not allow us to wait and see whether this happens: the matter must be settled on the facts as they stand at the *testator's* death. Therefore if B has a grandchild living at the testator's death, the remainder is saved; for one share has vested, and even if that grandchild dies before A, someone will be entitled (by succession) to call for that share at A's death.[24] But if B has no grandchild living at the testator's death, the remainder fails; for there is then no certainty that the class will close at A's death, since no grandchild will necessarily be born in A's lifetime.

(iii) If the gifts to the grandchildren in the above examples had been contingent on some further event (*e.g.,* on attaining 21 or previously marrying), it would have been necessary for a grandchild to have fulfilled the condition before the testator's

---

[18] *Post,* p. 502; *Re Bleckly* [1951] Ch. 740.
[19] *Shepherd* v. *Ingram* (1764) Amb. 448; (1954) 70 L.Q.R. 66, 67 (J. H. C. Morris).
[20] See *Picken* v. *Matthews* (1878) 10 Ch.D. 264.
[21] *Cf. Warren* v. *Johnson* (1673) 2 Rep.Ch. 69.
[22] Jarman 1683; (1954) 70 L.Q.R. 66 (J. H. C. Morris); *Shepherd* v. *Ingram* (1764) Amb. 448. This would be the exceptional case where the special rule does not apply. But even if it did, the gift would be equally void for perpetuity.
[23] *Ayton* v. *Ayton* (1787) 1 Cox Eq. 327; (1954) 70 L.Q.R. at p. 67 (J. H. C. Morris).
[24] *Re Chartres* [1927] 1 Ch. 466.

death in order to save the class gift. This again follows from the requirements of the perpetuity rule at common law. Were it not for the perpetuity rule the class could remain open until the first grandchild reached 21 or married, or (in example (ii)) until the life tenant died, whichever was the later.

(4) INTENTION. The doctrine applies both to deeds [25] and wills, but is most commonly met with in construing wills. In connection with wills it is explained more generally below.[26] Being a rule of construction, it will yield to any expression of contrary intention. But expressions like "all or any," and "born or to be born," may not by themselves prevent the class being prematurely closed for the sake of convenience, at least where the gift is by way of remainder.[27] Where the language is ambiguous and one interpretation makes the gift void for perpetuity, the court may prefer the interpretation which will save the gift [28]; and there are certain other class gifts which, even though outside the rule of construction, have been construed as confining the gift to those living at the testator's death.[29]

(c) *Class-reduction under the Act of* 1964. Even where a class gift is made after July 15, 1964, and so is subject to the Act of 1964, the first necessity is to construe it, taking account of the class-closing rules where applicable, and then to determine whether it is valid or void at common law. If it is valid, the Act will not apply. But if it would be void the Act will save some or all of it, if that can be done by eliminating offending members of the class. The principle that a class gift cannot be partially good and partially bad has been abandoned, and it is thus no longer true that any taint of remoteness affects the whole class.

The Act provides that where the inclusion of potential members of a class would cause the disposition to fail for remoteness, those persons shall, unless their exclusion would exhaust the class, be deemed for all the purposes of the disposition to be excluded.[30] This

---

[25] *Re Knapp's Settlement* [1895] 1 Ch. 91.
[26] *Post*, p. 501.
[27] See *post*, p. 502.
[28] *Pearks* v. *Moseley* (1880) 5 App.Cas. 714 at 719; *Re Mortimer* [1905] 2 Ch. 502 at 506; *Re Hume* [1912] 1 Ch. 693; *Re Deeley's Settlement* [1974] Ch. 454.
[29] See, *e.g., Elliott* v. *Elliott* (1841) 12 Sim. 276 (to the children of A at 22); *Re Coppard's Estate* (1887) 35 Ch.D. 350 (similar, but at 25); see also *Re Barker* (1905) 92 L.T. 831 at 834; *Wetherell* v. *Wetherell* (1863) 1 De G.J. & S. 134; *Re Powell* [1898] 1 Ch. 227 (gift to grandchildren of a living person held valid). In principle these decisions are doubtful: see Jarman 1676; Gray, §§ 634–642; Morris & Leach, 113, 250.
[30] s. 4 (4).

provision comes into play whenever it "becomes apparent" that inclusion of the potential members would be fatal.[31] But, following its policy of allowing the donor's intentions to take effect if possible, the Act requires the "wait and see" rule to be applied first. Only if that fails to save the gift will the question of class-reduction arise.[32]

For example, take the case of a gift by will—

"to all the children of A who marry."

If A has predeceased the testator, the gift is valid at common law and the Act does not apply. If A survives the testator, so that the gift would be void at common law, the "wait and see" rule protects the whole class so long as any member may marry within the perpetuity period (the lifetimes of A, and of any children of A born before the testator's death, plus 21 years). If all A's children marry within this period, there is no question of excluding members of the class. But if at the end of the period unmarried children of A are living, it then becomes apparent that the whole class gift would be void at common law, even as modified by "wait and see." Thereupon the Act excludes those unmarried children, provided that they are not the only members of the class, thus saving the gift to the other members. The practical effect of these two rules ("wait and see" and class-reduction) is that the Act treats a class gift as a gift to those members of the class who do in fact comply with the perpetuity rule.

The Act makes special provision for cases where class-reduction has to be combined with age-reduction.[33] This is explained below.[34]

11. Reduction of excessive ages. At common law gifts frequently failed because they were made contingent upon the beneficiary attaining an age greater than 21. Thus property might be given—

"to the first of A's children to attain the age of 25."

In certain circumstances the gift would be good: if A was dead at the time of the gift, he could have no further children and since every possible claimant was a life in being, the gift would be valid.[35] Even if A was then alive, the gift would be valid if one of his children was already aged 25 or over, so that the gift would vest at once.[36] But if A was alive and no child had attained the age of 25, the gift was bad.[37] This was so even if a child had attained the age of 24, for there was no certainty that he would not die before his twenty-fifth

---

[31] s. 4 (4).
[32] *Ante*, p. 216.
[33] s. 4 (3).
[34] *Post*, p. 238.
[35] *Southern* v. *Wollaston* (No. 2) (1852) 16 Beav. 276; *ante*, p. 226.
[36] *Picken* v. *Matthews* (1878) 10 Ch.D. 264.
[37] *Merlin* v. *Blagrave* (1858) 25 Beav. 125.

birthday, so that a child born after the date of the gift and shortly before the death of A might be the first child to reach the age of 25.[38]

Both the Law of Property Act, 1925, and the Perpetuities and Accumulations Act 1964 contain provisions for substituting lower ages in such cases, so that the gift may comply with the perpetuity rule. These are respectively as follows.

(*a*) *Under the Law of Property Act*, 1925

(1) SUBSTITUTING 21. The Act of 1925, s. 163, introduced the principle that in certain circumstances the age of 21 may be substituted for the offending age.[39] This may be done only if—

(i) the limitation is contained in an instrument executed after 1925, or in the will of a testator dying after 1925 [40]; and
(ii) the limitation would otherwise be void [41]; and
(iii) the excess is in the age of the beneficiary or class of beneficiaries.[42]

The first point needs no illustration; the second may be illustrated by considering the limitation mentioned above, namely, " to the first of A's children to attain the age of 25." Before 1926, if A was alive and no child had reached the age of 25, the gift failed; if made after 1925, section 163 substitutes " 21 " for " 25 " and the gift is good, the first child to attain the age of 21 taking the property at that age. If the section applies, therefore, it not only saves but accelerates the gift. But if A had been dead, the gift would have been valid without the aid of section 163 and so " 25 " would be left undisturbed. In the result, if A's eldest child is aged 19 at the time of the gift, he must wait either two years or six before becoming entitled, according to whether A is alive or dead.

(2) ACCELERATION. Where section 163 applies it can both save and accelerate a remainder or gift over limited to take effect upon the failure of the gift to the first beneficiary. For example, in a gift " to the first of A's children to attain 25, but if no such child attains 25 then to the eldest of B's children living at the date of B's death," the section will validate the first part of the gift and thereby also save the gift over in case all A's children die in infancy.[43] Furthermore, the section will operate equally well where there are several contingencies, as for example in a gift " to the first of A's children to

---

[38] See, *e.g.*, *Re Finch* (1881) 17 Ch.D. 211, where the child was nineteen.
[39] As suggested by the Third Report of the Real Property Commissioners, 1832, p. 41. But no action was taken until 1925.
[40] L.P.A., 1925, s. 163 (2). [41] *Ibid.*, subs. (1).
[42] See previous note.
[43] This is a " dependent " limitation as explained below.

attain 25 or marry under that age." The condition as to marriage is unaffected, so that a child who marries at 20 takes immediately.[44]

The third point may be illustrated by cases where vesting is postponed for a fixed period of years. A gift to the testator's issue living 50 years after his death was void before 1926 and is equally void under section 163; for the " 50 " is not the age of a beneficiary.

(b) *Under the Act of* 1964. The Act of 1964, where it applies, has replaced the Law of Property Act, 1925, s. 163, by an amended provision. Section 163 is repealed but only as regards instruments taking effect after July 15, 1964.[45] Where the instrument took effect after 1925 but before July 16, 1964, section 163 still applies.

(1) CONDITIONS. The Act of 1964 provides for age-reduction where the following conditions are all satisfied:

(i) The instrument takes effect after July 15, 1964;

(ii) the disposition is not saved by the " wait and see " rule [46];

(iii) " the disposition is limited by reference to the attainment by any person or persons of a specified age exceeding 21 years "; and

(iv) it is apparent when the disposition is made, or becomes apparent later—

(1) that the disposition would otherwise be void for remoteness, but

(2) that it would not be thus void if the specified age had been 21 years.

In such cases the disposition is treated for all purposes as if in place of the age specified there had been specified the nearest age which would prevent the disposition from being void for remoteness.[47] The Act thus differs from section 163 both in that the reduction in age is not necessarily to 21 years, and also in that it applies even if the offending age is not that of a beneficiary, as when the gift is to A's eldest descendant living when B's first son attains 25 years.

(2) EXAMPLES. Thus in the case of a gift by will—

" to the first of A's children to attain the age of 25,"

where A is alive and unmarried at the testator's death, the first necessity is to wait and see whether a child of A in fact attains 25 during A's lifetime or within 21 years of A's death. If so, the child will take at 25. But if at A's death his only child is aged 3, it is apparent that the child cannot take at age 25 within the perpetuity period. The qualifying age is therefore reduced to 24, being

---

[44] s. 163 (3).
[45] Act of 1964, ss. 4 (6), 15 (5); see *post,* p. 257.
[46] For this principle, see *ante,* p. 216.
[47] s. 4 (1).

the nearest age at which the gift could be good. If A left three children aged 3, 2 and 1 at A's death, the problem is more difficult. Is the qualifying age first to be reduced to 24, and then successively to 23 and 22 in case the two elder children die prematurely? Or is there to be a single reduction to 22, so as to eliminate perpetuity trouble once and for all? Since the Act requires reduction to the *nearest* age which prevents the gift being void, and since it intends that " wait and see " shall continue to operate, the former solution may be right. In that case no reduction is required if the eldest child is aged 6 or more at A's death, unless and until that child dies under 25. A case can, however, be made for a once-for-all reduction to an age which will protect all the children.[48]

The same dilemma presents itself where the gift is to a class, as in a gift by will—

" to all A's children who attain the age of 25."

Suppose that A is alive at the testator's death but dies 10 years later leaving children aged 3, 2 and 1. Here there is a stronger case for once-for-all reduction to 22. Although 24 would be the *nearest* age at which " wait and see " could continue, it would require the assumption that the younger children might die, leaving only the eldest child to take. But the gift is to the children as a class, and to preserve it as such requires reduction to an age which will protect them all. Here again a case can be made for the alternative solution, *i.e.*, for age-reduction by stages.[49] The departure from the sound 1925 policy of reducing excessive ages uniformly to 21 has produced a crop of doubts and difficulties.

(3) DEFECTIVE REPEAL OF SECTION 163. The evident intention of the Act of 1964, as explained above, is that the " wait and see " rule shall operate before age-reduction comes into play. But an awkward flaw in the drafting may frustrate this policy.[50] The " wait and see " rule is contained in section 3, which operates where a gift would be void " apart from the provisions of this section and of sections 4 and 5 of this Act." [51] Section 4 contains the provisions for age-reduction. But it also contains the repeal of section 163 of the Law of Property Act, 1925,[52] so that in applying section 3 it must apparently be assumed that section 163 remains unrepealed. On this hypothesis a gift made in 1965 to A's first child to attain 25 (for example) would not be void, because the imaginary section 163 would save it and thus " wait and see " will not operate. Turning then to section 4, we must ask whether the gift would, " apart from this section," be void.

---

[48] See [1969] C.L.J. 286 (M. J. Prichard).
[49] *Ibid.*, 290.
[50] See (1965) 81 L.Q.R. 346 (J. D. Davies).
[51] s. 3 (1).
[52] s. 5 (4).

For this purpose we are again required to ignore the repeal of section 163, so that on that hypothesis the gift would be valid and section 4 will accordingly not save it. Yet section 163 is in fact repealed, so that the ultimate fate of the gift is that it must fail, being merely a gift at common law. It may be hoped, however, that judicial construction will be guided by the evident intention of the Act rather than by its literal provisions.

(4) DIFFERENTIAL AGES. The Act of 1964 (unlike section 163) also makes provision for differential ages, as, for example, in a gift—

> " to all the children of A who being sons attain 25 or being daughters attain 30."

Where the above-mentioned conditions for the application of the Act are satisfied the effect is to reduce each such age so far as is necessary to save the gift.[53]

(5) CLASS-REDUCTION. The Act allows age-reduction to be combined with class-reduction, where this would save a gift which neither form of reduction would by itself suffice to save. An example is a gift by will—

> " to such of A's children as attain 25 together with such children as attain 25 of any children of A who may die under 25." [54]

If A is unmarried at the time of the gift, and at his death his only two children are aged 3 and 1, it is plain that no grandchildren can attain 25 within the perpetuity period, even if their qualifying age is reduced to 21. The grandchildren are therefore excluded from the class, and the qualifying age for A's children is then reduced as already explained.[55]

The effect of age-reduction under the Act of 1964 in saving and accelerating a remainder or gift over is the same as under section 163, explained above.

12. Gifts which follow void gifts. The general rule is that where there are successive limitations in one instrument of gift, the perpetuity rule must be applied to each limitation separately. Thus if there is a gift—

> " to A for life, remainder to his eldest son for life, remainder to B's eldest grandson in fee simple,"

there are three distinct gifts, each of which must by itself pass the test of the rule. Where all the gifts are valid, no difficulty arises. But where one of the gifts is void, this may sometimes invalidate another gift. The rules are as follows.

---

[53] s. 4 (2).
[54] For this form of gift, see *ante*, p. 230.   [55] s. 4 (3).

(*a*) *No limitation is void merely because it is followed by a void limitation.*[56] A gift " to A for life " standing by itself is clearly good, and it is not invalidated merely because a limitation which infringes the rule is added, *e.g.*, " to A for life, remainder to the first of his descendants to marry a Latvian." In such a case A takes a life interest and after his death the property reverts to the grantor or, if the grantor is dead, passes under his will or intestacy.[57]

(*b*) *At common law a limitation which is subsequent to and dependent upon a void limitation is itself void, even though it must itself vest (if at all) within the perpetuity period.*[58]

(1) THE RULE. It will be noticed that a limitation is not void merely because it follows a void limitation; it is invalidated by the rule only if in addition to following the void limitation it is also dependent upon it. A " dependent " limitation for this purpose is one intended to take effect only if the prior gift does, or (as the case may be) does not, itself take effect. By contrast, an independent limitation is one intended to take effect in any case, whether the prior gift takes effect or not.[59] The vesting of a dependent limitation therefore remains uncertain until the fate of the prior gift can be seen; an independent limitation vests (in interest) at its own separate time, and the fate of the prior gift, to which it is subject, affects only the date at which it finally takes effect in possession. It follows that a gift made " subject to " a prior void gift will often nevertheless be independent of it as regards the all-important moment of vesting,[60] and, on the other hand, that where the prior void gift is a gift in fee simple, the subsequent gift will always be dependent, since it must be contingent upon the prior gift failing.[61]

If, for example, a testator devises property in fee simple—
> " to the first of X's sons to become a clergyman, but if X
> has no such son, to Y for life,"

and when the testator dies X is alive, the first part of the gift is clearly void at common law since the required event might occur more than 21 years after the death of lives in being. The gift to Y is, equally clearly, subsequent to and dependent upon this void limita-

---

[56] *Garland* v. *Brown* (1864) 10 L.T. 292. But see *Re Abraham's W. T.* [1969] 1 Ch. 463, where valid and void limitations were so intermixed as to vitiate the whole settlement.
[57] *Stuart* v. *Cockerell* (1870) 5 Ch.App. 713.
[58] *Proctor* v. *Bishop of Bath and Wells* (1794) 2 Hy.Bl. 358; *Re Abbott* [1893] 1 Ch. 54 at 57; *Re Hubbard's W. T.* [1963] Ch. 275; *Re Leek* [1967] Ch. 1061.
[59] J. H. C. Morris in (1950) 10 C.L.J. 392 criticises the rule about " dependent " gifts as meaningless. But its principle seems clear from the authorities next cited and from the initial classification of contingent remainders by Fearne 5. See also Morris & Leach, 173 ; A. K. R. Kiralfy (1950) 14 Conv.(N.S.) 148.
[60] *See Re Canning's W. T.* [1936] Ch. 309.
[61] As explained *ante*, p. 175.

tion; for its vesting depends entirely upon the gift to X's son not taking effect. It therefore makes no difference that it is itself bound to vest (if at all) within Y's lifetime and so within the perpetuity period.[62]

(2) CLASSES OF LIMITATION. Limitations which follow void limitations can accordingly be divided into three classes for the purposes of the rule at common law.

    (i) Vested. These are always safe from the perpetuity rule.[63] Example: gift to A for life, remainder for life to A's first son to marry, remainder to B in fee simple. If A is alive and has no married son at the time of the gift, the second gift is void; but the remainder to B is valid, for since it is ready to take effect in possession at any time, whether the prior interests determine naturally or fail, it must be vested from the beginning.[64]

    (ii) Contingent, but independent. This class will be valid if its own contingency does not infringe the perpetuity rule, and it will make no difference that some prior gift fails for perpetuity.[65] Example: gift to A for life, remainder for life to A's first son to marry, remainder in fee simple to B (an infant) at 21. Here again, unless A already has a married son, the first remainder will be void. But B's remainder is still valid, for the only contingency is that B shall attain 21, an event which has nothing to do with the possible events which make the prior gift void.

    (iii) Contingent, but dependent. In this case the ulterior gift fails, even though itself bound to vest (if at all) within the perpetuity period.[66] Example: gift to A for life, remainder in fee simple to A's first son to marry, but if there is no such son then remainder to B for life. Here, unless A already has a married son, both remainders are void. B's remainder, although itself confined to the period of a life in being (B),

---

[62] *Proctor* v. *Bishop of Bath and Wells* (1794) 2 Hy.Bl. 358. See also *Re Hubbard's W. T.* [1963] Ch. 275; *Re Buckton's S. T.* [1964] Ch. 497 (good examples of the settled rules); contrast *Re Robinson* [1963] 1 W.L.R. 628; and see (1964) 80 L.Q.R. 323 (R.E.M.).

[63] See *Re Allan* [1958] 1 W.L.R. 220. So far as *Re Backhouse* [1921] 2 Ch. 51 invalidates vested interests, it is probably wrong in principle and contrary to authorities cited under the next class: see Morris & Leach, 175–179.

[64] *Lewis* v. *Waters* (1805) 6 East 336; *Re Hubbard's W. T.* [1963] Ch. 275; Fearne 222; Jarman 366. To the same class belong cases where there is a void appointment and a vested gift in default of appointment: Jarman 364. *Cf.* (1944) 60 L.Q.R. 297, 298 (R.E.M.).

[65] *Re Abbott* [1893] 1 Ch. 54; *Re Canning's W. T.* [1936] Ch. 309; *Re Coleman* [1936] Ch. 528; *Re Hubbard's W. T.*, *supra*.

[66] *Re Thatcher* (1859) 26 Beav. 365 at 369; *Re Hewitt's Settlement* [1915] 1 Ch. 810; *Re Ramadge* [1919] 1 I.R. 205; *Re Hubbard's W. T.*, *supra*.

is a contingent interest, for it follows a gift in fee simple [67]; and the contingency is that no son of A shall marry. Since B's remainder depends upon precisely the converse contingency to that which invalidates the prior gift, it is dependent upon that gift not taking effect and is therefore void. It would make no difference if the words " but if there is no such son " were omitted, since the contingency which they express is inherent in any gift which follows a gift in fee simple.[68] If the final remainder had been to B in fee simple, it would have failed on its own account, quite apart from its dependence on the prior gift, for there would have been nothing to confine it within the perpetuity period: the contingency itself is unduly remote, since some successor in title to B could have taken at a distant time in the future.[69]

(3) CONSTRUCTION. The dependence or independence of a gift is a question of construction, for it is governed by the donor's intention so far as it can be collected from the terms of the gift. In one much criticised line of decisions [70] the courts appear to have forsaken their usual presumption in favour of early vesting, and to have held cases of the type of class (i) to belong to class (iii). The argument runs that " the persons entitled under the subsequent limitation are not intended to take unless and until the prior limitation is exhausted; and as the prior limitation which is void for remoteness can never come into operation, much less be exhausted, it is impossible to give effect to the intentions of the settlor in favour of the beneficiaries under the subsequent limitation." [71] This reasoning could perhaps apply to cases where the only prior interest is void, *e.g.*, to a devise for life to A's first son to marry, remainder to B in fee simple; for there B is evidently not intended to take at once, and the

---

[67] As explained *ante*, p. 175.
[68] *Proctor* v. *Bishop of Bath and Wells* (1794) 2 Hy.Bl. 358; *Palmer* v. *Holford* (1828) 4 Russ. 403 (decided on this ground alone without mention of " dependence "); *cf.* the remarks of Jessel M.R. in *Miles* v. *Harford* (1879) 12 Ch.D. 691 at 703. *Re Mill's Declaration of Trust* [1950] 1 All E.R. 789; [1950] 2 All E.R. 292 is a case of this type, although the judgments proceed upon the alternative (but logically posterior) ground that the ultimate gift was dependent. For the rule under which B's successors can take, see Jarman 1342.
[69] See previous note.
[70] *Robinson* v. *Hardcastle* (1788) 2 T.R. 241 at 251; *Brudenell* v. *Elwes* (1801) 1 East 442 at 454; *Beard* v. *Westcott* (1822) 5 B. & Ald. 801, as explained by Lord St. Leonards in *Monypenny* v. *Dering* (1852) 2 De G.M. & G. 145 at 182 (though see Jarman 368, n. (*q*)). For criticism, see Gray, § 254; Jarman 365, 366; J. H. C. Morris (1950) 10 C.L.J. at p. 396; Morris & Leach, 179–181.
[71] *Re Abbott* [1893] 1 Ch. 54 at 57, *per* Stirling J.; he also cites *Routledge* v. *Dorril* (1794) 2 Ves.Jun. 357, but that case was apparently within class (iii) for other reasons (see at p. 363).

remainder cannot, in Lord St. Leonards' words, "dovetail in and accord with previous limitations which are valid." [72] But even in that kind of case the construction put upon the gift seems to be hostile to the testator's wishes [73]; and in some of the cases it seems to be directly contrary to the principle which requires gifts to be construed as vested wherever possible.[74]

(c) *Where the Act of 1964 applies, a gift cannot fail merely because it is dependent upon a prior void gift.* If the gift is made after July 15, 1964, so that it is governed by the Perpetuities and Accumulations Act 1964, it will no longer fail merely because it is "ulterior to and dependent upon" another gift which is void.[75] Where the Act applies, therefore, all the complications of the law about dependent gifts disappear: each distinct gift must stand or fall by itself, and the perpetuity rule must be applied to each in isolation.

It is also provided that the vesting of an interest shall not be prevented from being accelerated on the failure of a prior interest merely because the failure is caused by remoteness.[76] This eliminates the questionable reasoning mentioned in the last-but-one paragraph above, and removes any obstacle to the acceleration of the ulterior gift, if valid, to fill the vacuum left by the failure of the preceding gift. But any contingency specifically applicable to the ulterior gift must, of course, be fulfilled before it can vest.[77] These rules under the Act of 1964 operate *ab initio,* and are not dependent upon the "wait and see" rule.

13. Alternative contingencies

(a) *"Wait and see" at common law.* Where a gift expresses two alternative contingencies upon which the property may vest, and one contingency is too remote and one is not, the gift is good at common law if in fact the valid contingency occurs.[78] This is one of the rare occasions when even the common law will allow "wait and see." [79] Thus in one case [80] a testator gave property to his grandchildren and issue of his grandchildren living—

> "on the decease of my last surviving child or on the death of the last surviving widow or widower of my children as the case may be whichever shall last happen."

[72] *Monypenny* v. *Dering* (1852) 2 De G.M. & G. 145 at 182.
[73] Nor is it assisted by words such as "and after his death" before the remainder: J. H. C. Morris (1950) 10 C.L.J. at p. 396.
[74] *Ante,* p. 177.   [75] s. 6.
[76] *Ibid.*
[77] See *Re Edwards' W. T.* [1948] Ch. 440; *Re Allan* [1958] 1 W.L.R. 220; *Re Hubbard's W. T.* [1963] Ch. 275.
[78] *Longhead* d. *Hopkins* v. *Phelps* (1770) 2 Wm.Bl. 704; *Hodgson* v. *Halford* (1879) 11 Ch.D. 959.
[79] For the other case, see *post,* p. 256 (powers of appointment).
[80] *Re Curryer's W. T.* [1938] Ch. 952.

It was held that this gift did not necessarily infringe the perpetuity rule as it stood, and that if in fact one of the testator's children outlived all the other children and their spouses, the gift would be valid. There were two alternatives:

(i) that one of the testator's children (a life in being) would be the last survivor, or

(ii) that the spouse of one of the testator's children (not necessarily a life in being) would be the last survivor.

If the former alternative actually occurred, the gift did not infringe the rule. If the latter in fact occurred, it did, and must fail. Whether it was to fail or not could only be told by events.

(b) *Implicit alternatives.* This benignant principle applies only if the two alternative contingencies are expressed in the gift.[81] If only one contingency is expressed in the gift and that may be too remote, the gift fails even if there are in fact two contingencies. Thus in *Proctor* v. *Bishop of Bath and Wells* [82] only one contingency was expressed, namely, that if no son of A became a clergyman, B should be entitled. In fact, two contingencies were implicit in the gift, namely,

(i) A might leave no son; this must be known at A's death, which would be within the period;

(ii) A might leave one or more sons, who might become clergymen more than 21 years after A's death, which would be outside the period.

Nevertheless, the gift to B was void *ab initio*, for the only contingency expressed was a void one. Had the gift over been worded—

"but if no son of A shall become a clergyman, or if A shall leave no son, to B in fee simple,"

the gift to B would have been valid if A had died leaving no son, *i.e.*, if the valid contingency had occurred.[83]

(c) *Act of* 1964. The Act of 1964 has made no change in this rule. But where the Act applies, the "wait and see" rule will now operate in its normal way if the unduly remote contingency occurs or if only one contingency is expressed. In the example in (a), above, the "surviving spouse" rule [84] may also assist.

---

[81] *Re Harvey* (1888) 39 Ch.D. 289 ; *Re Bence* [1891] 3 Ch. 242.
[82] See *ante*, p. 239.
[83] *Miles* v. *Harford* (1879) 12 Ch.D. 691 at 703.
[84] *Ante*, p. 227.

14. Determinable and conditional interests

(a) Determinable interests [85]

(1) THE RULE AT COMMON LAW. " The rule against perpetuities is not dealing with the duration of interests but with their commencement, and so long as the interest vests within lives in being and twenty-one years it does not matter how long that interest lasts." [86] That is to say, the perpetuity rule does not invalidate a limitation merely because it provides that an interest shall cease at some future date outside the perpetuity period. Accordingly where property is given to an unborn person—

> for life or until she becomes a member of the Roman Catholic Church,[87]

or—

> for life or until marriage,[88]

the specified event may occur outside the perpetuity period but at common law the limitation is nevertheless valid. The better view is that it is immaterial that the determinable interest is a fee simple and the event on which it will determine may not happen for centuries,[89] *e.g.*, where property is conveyed to the X Co., Ltd., in fee simple until the premises are used otherwise than as a biscuit factory, or to trustees " for so long as the premises are used for the purpose of a public library." [90] In certain circumstances these interests may cease at any time in the future, and the perpetuity rule will not prolong them.

(2) POSSIBILITY OF REVERTER. The grantor's possibility of reverter is, it seems, exempt from the perpetuity rule at common law, and so always able to take effect. On the face of it this is anomalous. A possibility of reverter was not a reversion (and so vested) but a " bare possibility " that an interest might vest in the future,[91] and so necessarily contingent.[92] Being a potential fetter on property, such

---

[85] For these, see *ante*, p. 74.

[86] *Re Chardon* [1928] Ch. 464 at 468, *per* Romer J.; see Gray, §§ 41, 603.9.

[87] *Wainwright* v. *Miller* [1897] 2 Ch. 255.

[88] *Re Gage* [1898] 1 Ch. 498. And see *Re Randell* (1888) 38 Ch.D. 213; *Re Blunt's Trusts* [1904] 2 Ch. 767.

[89] See *Att.-Gen.* v. *Pyle* (1738) 1 Atk. 435; *Boughton* v. *James* (1844) 1 Coll.C.C. 26 at 46; Tiffany, *Real Property*, 603.

[90] *Hopper* v. *Corporation of Liverpool* (1944) 88 S.J. 213; *ante*, p. 75.

[91] *Ante*, p. 74.

[92] Jarman 289; Tudor L.C. 702; *cf.* Challis 76n, classifying possibilities as one degree more remote than contingent remainders, since there is merely a chance that upon a certain contingency an interest may arise; and *cf. ante*, p. 74. Gray, §§ 113, 312, maintains that they are vested interests, though a " vested possibility " seems a contradiction in terms.

an interest ought to be subject to the perpetuity rule,[93] and in one modern case (of a conveyance *inter vivos* before 1926) it has been held that it is.[94] But weightier authorities indicate that there can be a valid reverter or resulting trust [95] after an interest which terminates, even where an express gift after that interest would be void for perpetuity.

Thus on a direct devise of land to a school " so long as it shall continue to be endowed with charity " Lord Hardwicke L.C. held that the testator's heir had a valid possibility of reverter.[96] In a similar modern case land was conveyed to trustees in fee simple upon trust for an orphans' home, and upon failure of that trust then upon trust for other purposes. The latter trust was clearly void for perpetuity; nevertheless it was held not only that the trust for the orphans' home duly determined in accordance with the donor's intention,[97] but also that there was a valid resulting trust for the donor's estate.[98]

(3) RESULTING TRUSTS. The equitable doctrine is that any beneficial interest of which the settlor fails to dispose remains in him under a resulting trust,[99] and that this interest is vested *ab initio* even if it is uncertain when, if ever, it will become effective.[1] Even if before 1926 the perpetuity rule applied to legal possibilities of reverter, such interests are necessarily equitable after 1925,[2] and as

[93] See Fourth Report of the Law Reform Committee (1956, Cmnd. 18), para. 39; Morris & Leach, 213; and the Real Property Commissioners (Third Report (1832), p. 36) would have been of the same view had they not supposed possibilities of reverter to be extinct at law: *ante*, p. 75. The view that the perpetuity rule was inapplicable for historical reasons (powerfully championed by Palles C.B. in *Att.-Gen.* v. *Cummins* (1895) [1906] 1 I.R. 406) has been rejected in England: *post*, p. 247, n. 13.

[94] *Hopper* v. *Corporation of Liverpool* (1944) 88 S.J. 213 (Vice-Chancellor of Lancaster); see (1946) 62 L.Q.R. 222 (R.E.M.); 1945 Conv.Y.B. 203; (1957) 21 Conv.(N.S.) 213 (P. H. Pettit).

[95] For resulting trusts, see *post*, p. 443.

[96] *Att.-Gen.* v. *Pyle* (1738) 1 Atk. 435; *sub nom. Att.-Gen.* v. *Montague* (1738) West t.Hard. 587 (an authority merely *sub silentio*: the brief reports disclose no express consideration of the rule against perpetuities); *Re Tilbury West Public School Board and Hastie* (1966) 55 D.L.R. (2d) 407, considering the rule and holding it inapplicable to possibilities of reverter.

[97] Had no such intention appeared, the limitation would have created a fee simple absolute.

[98] *Re Cooper's Conveyance Trusts* [1956] 1 W.L.R. 1096; *cf. Gibson* v. *South American Stores (Gath and Chaves) Ltd.* [1950] Ch. 177. See also similar decisions on bequests of personalty: *Re Randell* (1888) 38 Ch.D. 213; *Re Blunt's Trusts* [1904] 2 Ch. 767; *Re Chardon* [1928] Ch. 464. These three cases also appear to hold that property can fall into residue and so benefit a residuary legatee at any future time, even though a remainder to that legatee would be void for perpetuity; and consider n. 96, *supra*. But this distinction is difficult to analyse satisfactorily. On the problematical case of *Re Chardon* and the use of " vested " therein, see (1938) 54 L.Q.R. 264 (M. J. Albery) and contrast *Re Wightwick's W. T.* [1950] Ch. 260 at 265, 266.

[99] *Post*, p. 443.

[1] See cases in n. 98, *supra*.

[2] Under L.P.A., 1925, s. 1; *ante*, pp. 134 *et seq.*

such should be free from any difficulty arising from the common law objection to any vested interest following a determinable fee.[3] There is also the problem of finding an owner for the land if the right of reverter is void. The determinable interest will not become absolute. for the problem arises only when that interest has first terminated independently for reasons of its own. An equitable interest in land does not escheat,[4] nor does it pass to the Crown as bona vacantia since that prerogative right appears to apply only to personalty [5]; and it would ill accord with modern equitable principles to allow the trustees to take beneficially. The only solutions left are to make the determinable interest absolute, as the Act of 1964 has now done, or to allow a resulting trust for the grantor, which may be said to correspond with the escheat of legal estates (where the seignory is vested) and to be equally outside the perpetuity rule.

(4) THE ACT OF 1964. In cases of dispositions made after July 15, 1964, the Act of 1964 has applied the perpetuity rule to possibilities of reverter and resulting trusts arising on the termination of any other determinable interest in property.[6] The anomaly of their exemption at common law is thus removed. And, as is logically necessary, the preceding determinable interest is made absolute in cases where the possibility of reverter or resulting trust fails.[7] If today a testator leaves property to an orphans' home for so long as it exists, with a gift over to A in case the prior gift terminates, the first step is to apply the " wait and see " rule : if the orphans' home ceases to exist within 21 years (there are no lives in being), A can take. But after the 21 years neither A nor the testator's successors can take, and the property belongs to the home absolutely.

The Act of 1964 achieves this result by requiring the possibility of reverter or resulting trust to be treated as if it were a condition subsequent created by a separate disposition.[8] Conditions subsequent are discussed below. The rules for determinable and conditional interests have thus been assimilated.

(*b*) *Conditional interests.* A condition may be either precedent or subsequent.[9]

(1) CONDITIONS PRECEDENT. A condition precedent is one which must be fulfilled before the beneficiary is entitled to a vested interest.

---

[3] See *ante*, pp. 74, 184.
[4] *Ante*, p. 131.
[5] See *Re Wells* [1933] Ch. 29 at 57, 58, discussed in B. V. Ing, *Bona Vacantia* (1971) pp. 172–179, contending for the Crown's right to an equitable interest in freeholds as bona vacantia.
[6] s. 12. [7] *Ibid.*
[8] *Ibid.* [9] *Ante*, p. 78.

It is of course to conditions of this type that the perpetuity rule most commonly applies, and many examples have already been given, such as "to A at 21," and "to A if he survives B." A less obvious but similar type of case is a discretionary trust, as where land is given to trustees upon trust to apply the rents and profits for the benefit of an unborn person in the trustees' absolute discretion. Since the trustees need not necessarily pay the beneficiary any particular sum within the perpetuity period, at common law the whole gift fails [10]; no ascertainable interest ever vests at all, even though the beneficiary must be born within the period. Some decision by the trustees is a condition precedent to every payment.

(2) ACT OF 1964. Where the Act of 1964 applies, conditions precedent are now of course subject to the "wait and see" principle. For the purposes of the Act discretionary trusts rank as powers of appointment,[11] which are discussed below.

(3) CONDITIONS SUBSEQUENT. A condition subsequent, as already explained,[12] is one which authorises the grantor or his representatives to determine an existing interest. It will be remembered that a gift of land to trustees in fee simple—

> "on condition that it shall always be used for the purposes of a hospital only"

gives the grantor and his successors in title a right of re-entry if the condition is broken. If such a condition infringes the perpetuity rule the right of re-entry, being of course contingent, is void.[13] The interest which it was intended to defeat is not invalidated [14]; rather, it becomes an absolute interest, since the condition subsequent can defeat it only if re-entry is actually made,[15] and the right of re-entry is void. A determinable interest, on the other hand, determines automatically at common law, as explained above, whether the possibility of reverter is void or not.[16]

Thus if there is a valid gift by a testator to his grandchildren followed by a provision for the forfeiture of the interest of any

---

10 *Re Blew* [1906] 1 Ch. 624; *Re Coleman* [1936] Ch. 528; *Re Leek* [1967] Ch. 1061; *ante*, p. 210, n. 1; and see, *e.g.*, *Pickford* v. *Brown* (1856) 2 K. & J. 426.
11 s. 15 (2). See *post*, p. 254.
12 *Ante*, p. 75.
13 *Re the Trustees of Hollis' Hospital and Hague's Contract* [1899] 2 Ch. 440 (criticised, Challis 207; not followed, *Walsh* v. *Wightman* [1927] N.I. 1); *Re Da Costa* [1912] 1 Ch. 337; *Re Macleay* (1875) L.R. 20 Eq. 186; *Dunn* v. *Flood* (1883) 25 Ch.D. 629; 28 Ch.D. 586 at 592; *Imperial Tobacco Co., Ltd.* v. *Wilmott* [1964] 1 W.L.R. 902. See now L.P.A., 1925, s. 4 (3). For general comment, see *post*, p. 249.
14 *Blease* v. *Burgh* (1840) 2 Beav. 221; *Ring* v. *Hardwick* (1840) 2 Beav. 352.
15 *Ante*, p. 77.
16 For this distinction generally, see *ante*, p. 76; for its application here, see *Re Talbot* [1933] Ch. 895 and cases there cited.

grandchild who forsakes the Jewish faith or marries outside that faith, the provision might not take effect until the perpetuity period had run. It is accordingly void, and can neither carry the property to any other person [17] nor determine the interests of the grandchildren, despite any intention to do so [18]; the grandchildren accordingly take absolute interests.

(4) ACT OF 1964. Apart from applying the " wait and see " principle, no change in these rules has been made by the Act of 1964. As already explained,[19] the Act has extended the law governing conditions subsequent so that it now also governs possibilities of reverter and resulting trusts.

15. Legal contingent remainders

(a) *Application of the rule.* After much controversy among the authorities,[20] it was finally settled that the perpetuity rule applied to legal contingent remainders in the same way as to other future interests.[21]

At common law, as explained already,[22] a legal contingent remainder failed altogether unless it vested during the continuance, or at the determination, of the preceding particular estate. A single legal contingent remainder was accordingly bound to vest, if at all, during or at the end of a life in being, and so could not offend the perpetuity rule.[23] But if there were two or more of such interests in succession, the second and subsequent remainders might be invalidated. For example, if land was given—

> " to A for life, remainder for life to any husband she may marry, remainder to all A's children living at the death of the survivor of A and her husband," [24] or

---

[17] *Re Brown and Sibly's Contract* (1876) 3 Ch.D. 156; *Re Spitzel's W. T.* [1939] 2 All E.R. 266; *Re Pratt's S. T.* [1943] Ch. 356.

[18] *Re Pratt's S. T.* [1943] Ch. 356, confirming Jarman (now p. 1425); and see *Harding* v. *Nott* (1857) 7 E. & B. 650. If a gift over is void not for perpetuity but for some other reason, then if such an intention appears the condition may defeat the first gift even though the gift over is void: *Doe* d. *Blomfield* v. *Eyre* (1848) 5 C.B. 713.   [19] *Ante*, p. 246.

[20] See Morris & Leach, 203; Lewis, *Perpetuity*, Suppt. (1849), pp. 97 *et seq.*, claiming Fearne, Preston and Jarman as supporters of the view that the perpetuity rule applied. In fact, their statements related merely to the rule in *Whitby* v. *Mitchell* (*ante*, p. 200) which plainly did apply. Challis (200, 213 *et seq.*) and Williams (12th ed., 269 *et seq.*, 318 *et seq.*) strongly criticised the application of the perpetuity rule. See also H.E.L. vii, 234–238; Gray, § § 284–298; (1935) 51 L.Q.R. 668. A good account of the later stages of the controversy will be found in Jarman 383–388. For general comment, see *post*, p. 249.

[21] *Re Frost* (1889) 43 Ch. 246 at 254; *Re Ashford* [1905] 1 Ch. 535; *Monypenny* v. *Dering* (1852) 2 De G.M. & G. 145 at 168, explaining *Cole* v. *Sewell* (1843) 4 Dr. & War. 1 at 28 (on appeal, 2 H.L.C. 186); *Att.-Gen.* v. *Cummins* (1895) [1906] 1 I.R. 406.

[22] *Ante*, p. 186. After 1897 no legal remainder could be created by will, since wills operated by way of trust under L.T.A., 1897: *ante*, p. 197.

[23] Thus the rule in *Purefoy* v. *Rogers* (*ante*, p. 190) could save a gift by requiring it to vest as a contingent remainder.   [24] *Re Frost* (1889) 43 Ch.D. 246.

" to B for life, remainder to all B's children for life, remainder to the surviving child in tail," [25]

the second remainder in each case was void for perpetuity. In the first example, the legal remainder rules merely required that the ultimate remainder should vest during the lifetime of the survivor, who might be a husband not born at the date of the gift. In the second example, the survivor might not be ascertained until more than 21 years after the death of B and all his children living at the time of the gift.

(b) *Conversion to equitable interests.* Legal remainders which were safe from the perpetuity rule before 1926, because of the rule requiring them to vest during the continuance of the particular estate, were not destroyed by the perpetuity rule when they became converted into equitable interests at the beginning of 1926.[26] Conversely, it may be that having been created before 1926, they are still liable to fail if they do not vest at or before the determination of the particular estate. They can hardly have it both ways: if they may vest at any time, the perpetuity rule must apply; if it does not, they must vest within the period of the particular estate.[27] The Act of 1964 can, of course, have no bearing on interests created before 1926.

(c) *Attitude of the courts.* Some general comment should perhaps be made upon the controversy which was provoked by the application of the perpetuity rule to common law interests, such as legal contingent remainders [28] and rights expectant upon conditional [29] fees. The arguments are not entirely obsolete, and they shed light on the judicial attitude to the perpetuity rule. The central criticism was simply that contingent remainders, rights of re-entry and possibilities of reverter were well known at common law long before the perpetuity rule began to emerge in the late seventeenth century [30]; that the courts were not free to alter the common law; and that interests which were valid in the time of Coke must still have been valid in the reign of Queen Victoria.[31] This view commended itself to the rigorous minds of the most learned conveyancers; but it was less acceptable to the judges,[32] who seem instead to have appreciated

---

[25] *Re Ashford* [1905] 1 Ch. 535. [26] L.P.A., 1925, 1st Sched., Pt. 1.

[27] See Wolst. & C. (12th ed.) i, 517, taking the example of a pre-1926 grant " to A for life, remainder to his first son to attain 25." This passage is omitted from the 13th edition.

[28] *Ante,* p. 248, n. 20.

[29] *Ante,* p. 247, n. 13.

[30] *Ante,* p. 207.

[31] See Sweet's notes in Challis 207 *et seq.*; H.E.L. vii, 234, 235. Gray, § 296, reprehends " the vulgar error that judges cannot make law."

[32] Thus the Real Property Commissioners in their Third Report (1832) at p. 29 significantly said: " The ancient common law did not restrain the creation of future interests to a given period. The time allowed for re-entries, under

that the perfection of the wide modern perpetuity rule, after various false starts, was a comprehensive solution to the perpetuity problem as a whole, both in equity and at law. All interests therefore had to submit to it, whether or not they had enjoyed an earlier state of freedom. It is hard to understand what is illegitimate about this, or why the medieval common law should alone be sacrosanct against the movements of history.

16. Powers and duties

(a) *Powers, duties and trusts generally*

(1) PERPETUITY RULE APPLIES. Settlements often authorise persons to do things which they would otherwise have no legal ability to do. Such provisions create *powers*.[33]

The exercise of a power creates or alters an interest, and accordingly it is the general rule at common law that a power which is exercisable outside the perpetuity period is void. A power given to trustees to lease[34] or to sell[35] which may be exercisable during the lifetime of an unborn person is therefore void *ab initio* at common law. The same principle applies *a fortiori* to duties, for a duty to do something of course includes a power to do it: thus a trust for sale which may be exercised outside the perpetuity period will be void, even though it may be for the benefit of living persons whose equitable interests in the property vest at once and so are valid.[36] But it is unnecessary to set a separate time-limit to trusts and powers if they are incidental to an interest which will keep them within due bounds,[37] as for example where powers are given to a tenant for life who is a life in being. Where a power of sale is limited to come into existence at the end of a life in being, the court may find an intention in the will or settlement that the power should be exercised, if at all, within a reasonable period, and since 21 years is more than a reasonable period for this purpose, the power will be held valid[38];

---

conditions broken, . . . was indefinite, however courts of justice may at present be disposed to consider them within that policy of the law which restrains perpetuities." But the Commissioners appreciated that as a matter of policy these interests ought to be subject to the rule (at p. 36) and recommended legislation (at p. 43). See also Gray, § 298.

[33] For powers, see *post*, p. 461.

[34] *Re Allott* [1924] 2 Ch. 498 (power exercisable during the lifetime of an unborn person and so void).

[35] *Re Daveron* [1893] 3 Ch. 421 (trust to sell in 49 years' time held void); *Goodier* v. *Johnson* (1881) 18 Ch.D. 441 at 446 (trust to sell during the lifetime of an unborn person held void); *Re Wood* [1894] 3 Ch. 381 (trust to sell gravel pits when they were worked out held void).

[36] *Goodier* v. *Edmunds* [1893] 3 Ch. 455 at 461; and see preceding note.

[37] *Peters* v. *Lewes & East Grinstead Ry.* (1881) 18 Ch.D. 429 at 433, 434; *Re Wills' W. T.* [1959] Ch. 1; *cf. Pilkington* v. *I.R.C.* [1964] A.C. 612.

[38] See *Peters* v. *Lewes & East Grinstead Ry.*, *supra*, at p. 434; *Re Lord Sudeley and Baines & Co.* [1894] 1 Ch. 334; and as to construction of powers, Jarman 319–326.

and a trust to sell at the " expiration " of a term of 21 years arises *eo instanti* with the expiration of the term, and so does not exceed the period.[39]

(2) STATUTORY POWERS. The perpetuity rule may also apply to statutory powers. Many powers which used to be conferred on trustees and beneficiaries by lengthy clauses in settlements are now, for the sake of convenience, embodied in statutes. For example, trustees have statutory power to advance capital to a potential beneficiary [40]; and if they do so by making a settlement on him and his children, this is analogous to a power of appointment and therefore subject to the special perpetuity rules discussed below.[41] Statutory powers of sale, leasing and management, on the other hand, which Parliament intends all owners to have as a matter of policy and which themselves create no beneficial interest, are in a different category: thus it is assumed that the various powers given to tenants for life by the Settled Land Act, 1925, can be exercised at any time,[42] as where land is settled on A (a bachelor) for life with remainder to his widow for life. The same is presumably true of statutory trusts for sale.

(3) ACT OF 1964. The Act of 1964 has extended its " wait and see " principle to powers, provided that the instrument creating the power takes effect after July 15, 1964. A power is no longer void, in a case governed by the Act, merely because it might be exercised outside the perpetuity period: it will be void only if and so far as it is not in fact fully exercised during the period.[43] The person on whom the power is conferred counts as a life in being.[44] These new rules have already been explained.[45] Similarly, other provisions of the Act, for example for reducing excessive ages, may apply to grants of powers in the same way as to other grants. Presumably all these provisions extend also to duties, for the reasons given in the previous paragraph, although duties do not so easily fit within the statutory words " any power, option or other right."

(4) ADMINISTRATIVE POWERS. Further indulgence towards special classes of powers is shown by the Act of 1964. It is provided that the perpetuity rule shall not invalidate a power conferred on trustees or other persons to dispose of property for full consideration or to

---

[39] *English* v. *Cliff* [1914] 2 Ch. 376.
[40] T.A., 1925, s. 32. This power does not extend to land (unless held on trust for sale) or to trust property representing land.
[41] *Pilkington* v. *I.R.C.* [1964] A.C. 612; *Re Abraham's W. T.* [1969] 1 Ch. 463.
[42] Wolst. & C. iii, 1; *post*, p. 291.
[43] s. 3 (3).
[44] s. 3 (5) (*b*) (v).
[45] *Ante*, pp. 214, 223, 224.

do any other act in the administration (as opposed to the distribution) of any property.[46] The Act thus makes a distinction between administrative (or ancillary) powers and beneficial powers. A power to sell or let for full value, or to make or vary investments, is accordingly exempted from the perpetuity rule, but a power to sell at an undervalue is not, because it contains an element of gift. The Act also protects powers to pay reasonable remuneration for services, *e.g.*, those of trustees or agents.[47] Furthermore, and exceptionally, the Act protects these various powers if they are exercised after July 15, 1964, even if the instrument conferring them took effect before that date.[48] This reflects the opinion that the application of the perpetuity rule to such powers was a mistake.[49]

(b) Powers of appointment and analogous powers

(1) CLASSIFICATION. The powers which most frequently have to be considered in relation to the perpetuity rule are powers of appointment.[50] A power of appointment is a power for the person to whom it is given (" the donee of the power ") to appoint property to such persons (" the objects of the power ") as he may select. The power is known as a " special power " if the donee's choice is restricted to a limited class of objects, such as X's children, and as a " general power " if his choice is unrestricted. Special powers are very common in settlements, as where land is given " to A for life, and after his death to his surviving children in such shares as he may by deed or will appoint." The distinction between general and special powers is important here because special powers to some extent restrict disposal of the property, so that the rule applies to their exercise, whereas general powers do not, and are therefore unobjectionable.

The rules now to be explained also apply in principle to powers which are analogous to powers of appointment, such as a trustee's power of advancement, even if statutory,[51] and a discretionary trust.[52] Any power to create or alter a beneficial interest deriving from a settlor by way of gift will fall within these rules.

(2) GENERAL OR SPECIAL. For the purposes of the perpetuity rule, a power to appoint with the consent of X is a special power,[53] unless the court can find grounds for holding that the donee was in sub-

---

[46] s. 8 (1).
[47] s. 8 (1).
[48] ss. 8 (2), 15 (5).
[49] See Fourth Report of the Law Reform Committee, Cmnd. 18, 1956, para. 34, comparing the rule to an unruly dog wandering into the wrong places.
[50] Considered *post*, p. 463.
[51] *Pilkington* v. *I.R.C.*, *supra*.
[52] *Ante*, p. 247.
[53] *Re Watts* [1931] 2 Ch. 302.

stance the owner of the property and free to deal with it at will.[54] A power exercisable jointly by two or more persons has also been held to be special,[55] and probably a power for the donee to appoint to anyone except himself would also be held to be special.[56] On the other hand, a power for the donee to appoint to himself or anyone else except X[57] or to a class of people including himself,[58] would probably be held to be general. For where the donee may at once appoint to himself he can, by doing so, obtain unfettered powers of disposition. An unrestricted power to appoint by will only is the subject of a distinction. It has been held to be special for the purpose of deciding the validity of the power,[59] but general for the purpose of determining the validity of the appointment[60]; for such a power fetters the property during the donee's life but leaves him an unrestricted choice in his will.

(3) ACT OF 1964. The Act of 1964 in effect confirms the above distinctions in cases where it applies, and provides for the resolution of doubtful cases. For the purposes of the rule against perpetuities a power of appointment is to be treated as a special power unless it satisfies two conditions:

(i) it is expressed to be exercisable by one person only; and
(ii) it empowers the donee to transfer the whole property to himself immediately at all times when he is himself of full age and capacity without the consent of any other person or compliance with any other condition (not being a mere formal condition as to its mode of exercise).[61]

It will be seen that these conditions determine the character of the power from the outset. If a power is exercisable by A and B jointly, or by A with the consent of B, the subsequent death of B will not make it a general power for the purposes of the Act. As regards powers exercisable by will only, the Act confirms the previous case-law by providing that for the purpose of applying the perpetuity rule to an appointment made under such a power, the power shall

---

[54] *Re Dilke* [1921] 1 Ch. 34; *Re Phillips* [1931] 1 Ch. 347.
[55] *Re Churston S. E.* [1954] Ch. 334 (criticised at (1955) 71 L.Q.R. 242 (A. H. Droop); supported by Morris & Leach 137); *Re Earl of Coventry's Indentures* [1974] Ch. 77. *Sed quaere*: like an estate held jointly, any restriction flows not from the power or estate itself but merely from the form of ownership of it.
[56] See *Re Park* [1932] 1 Ch. 500; (1937) 1 Conv.(N.S.) 198 (F. E. Farrer).
[57] Consider *Platt* v. *Routh* (1841) 3 Beav. 257; affirmed *sub nom. Drake* v. *Att.-Gen.* (1843) 10 Cl. & F. 257; and see (1932) 48 L.Q.R. 475 (H.P.). Compare *Re Triffitt's Settlement* [1958] Ch. 852 at 860, 861 (exclusion of two persons, and requirement of consent of trustees: a special power for perpetuity purposes).
[58] *Cf. Re Penrose* [1933] Ch. 793.
[59] *Wollaston* v. *King* (1868) L.R. 8 Eq. 165; *Morgan* v. *Gronow* (1873) L.R. 16 Eq. 1.
[60] *Rous* v. *Jackson* (1885) 29 Ch.D. 521; *Re Flower* (1885) 55 L.J.Ch. 200.
[61] s. 7.

be treated as general if it would have been so treated had it been exercisable by deed.[62]

(4) EXERCISE OF SPECIAL POWERS. In general, the Act of 1964 applies to powers of appointment (including for this purpose discretionary trusts[63]) in the same way as it applies to other transactions. The conferring of a power and the exercise of a power are both " dispositions " within the meaning of the Act.[64] The " wait and see " principle applies, and both the donee and the objects or potential objects of the power may count as lives in being.[65] But there are two special provisions:

(i) In the case of a special power (as determined according to the foregoing rules, whenever it was created), the Act applies only when both the creation and the exercise of the power were under instruments taking effect after July 15, 1964.[66] Thus the governing date is the date of the original settlement, not the date of the exercise of the special power.

(ii) The alternative fixed perpetuity period (not exceeding 80 years) cannot be used in the *exercise* of a special power.[67] But it can be used in the *creation* of a special power, and in that case it will of course govern the exercise of the power also. In other words, the alternative fixed period can apply to a special power only if it is specified in the original settlement. If it is not so specified, the donee of the power cannot prolong the perpetuity period by invoking it.

(c) *Application of the rule to powers of appointment.* The application of the perpetuity rule to powers of appointment can be clarified by dealing separately with the two questions:

(i) Does the power itself infringe the rule?

(ii) If it does not, does the appointment made under the power infringe the rule?

(1) VALIDITY OF THE POWER

(i) A special power. A special power of appointment is subject to the ordinary rule relating to powers and is thus void at common law if it could be exercised outside the period. Time runs from the date when the instrument creating the power took effect.[68] Thus

---

[62] *Ibid.*
[63] s. 15 (2) includes any discretionary power to transfer a beneficial interest without valuable consideration.
[64] s. 15 (2).
[65] s. 3 (2), (3), (5) (*b*) (iii)–(v).
[66] s. 15 (5).
[67] s. 1 (2).
[68] *Re De Sommery* [1912] 2 Ch. 622 ; *Re Watson's S. T.* [1959] 1 W.L.R. 732.

if the donee of the power will not necessarily be ascertained within the period (if at all) [69] or is capable of exercising the power when the period has expired,[70] it is bad. But a power given exclusively to a person living when it was created can never be void for remoteness,[71] unless it allows only appointments that would necessarily be void.[72]

If a power complies with these conditions, it is not void merely because an appointment which offends the rule might be made under it.[73] For example, where a living person is given the power to appoint to his issue, he might make an appointment to his great-great-grandchildren; but this possibility does not invalidate the power itself or an appointment which in fact complies with the rule.[74]

If the power is created by an instrument taking effect after July 15, 1964, it will no longer be void *ab initio* merely because it could be exercised outside the perpetuity period. The "wait and see" principle of the Act of 1964 will apply, and the power will be void only in so far as it is not in fact fully exercised within the period.[75] If, for example, property is given by will—

> "to A for life, with remainder for life to any widow A may leave, with remainder to such of their issue as the survivor of them may appoint,"

and A is unmarried at the testator's death, the power is valid during A's lifetime and for 21 years thereafter (assuming A's widow to be still living) but then becomes void.

If a power is void for remoteness, a gift in default of appointment (*e.g.*, "but if no appointment shall be made, to X and Y equally ") is not thereby invalidated; provided it does not itself infringe the rule, it is valid.[76]

(ii) A general power. For the purposes of the perpetuity rule, a general power to appoint by deed or will is so nearly akin to absolute ownership that the time and manner of its exercise are irrelevant [77]: the perpetuity rule is satisfied if the power must be acquired (if at all) within the period.[78] But if the power is exercisable by will only, it ranks for this purpose as a special power, as already explained, and is subject to the rules stated above.

---

[69] See *Re Hargreaves* (1890) 43 Ch.D. 401.
[70] *Re Abbott* [1893] 1 Ch. 54 (power exercisable by the survivor of X and her husband: X might have married someone not born when the power was given, and so it was void).
[71] Jarman 329.
[72] *Bristow* v. *Boothby* (1826) 2 Sim. & St. 465; Gray, § 476.
[73] *Slark* v. *Dakyns* (1874) 10 Ch.App. 35.
[74] See *Routledge* v. *Dorrill* (1794) 2 Ves.Jun. 357.
[75] s. 3 (3).
[76] *Re Abbott* [1893] 1 Ch. 54. Such gifts may be vested: *ante*, p. 176.
[77] See *Re Fane* [1913] 1 Ch. 404 at 413.
[78] *Bray* v. *Hammersley* (1830) 3 Sim. 513; 2 Cl. & F. 453.

The Act of 1964 applies its " wait and see " principle in the usual way, so that a general power created by an instrument taking effect after July 15, 1964, is not void merely because it might be acquired at too remote a time: it is valid unless and until it becomes established that it will not be exercisable within the perpetuity period.[79]

(2) VALIDITY OF APPOINTMENTS MADE UNDER A VALID POWER. If the power itself is void, clearly no valid appointment can be made under it. But even if the power itself is valid, an appointment made under it may nevertheless be too remote.

(i) A special power. In the case of a special power of appointment, the property is fettered from the moment the power is created. If an appointment is made, it will carry the property to one or more of a class of persons designated by the original settlor who is the true donor. The perpetuity period therefore starts to run from the creation of the power.[80] But, as has been seen,[81] the mere fact that the power authorises the making of an appointment which may be too remote does not invalidate it, and until the appointment is in fact made, it cannot be said whether it is too remote. Even at common law, therefore, " the principle seems to be to wait and see." [82] The rule at common law is that when the appointment is ultimately made, it must be examined to see whether the interests appointed are bound to vest (if at all) within 21 years of the dropping of lives which were in being (or *en ventre sa mère* [83]) *when the power was created* and ascertainable from the instrument creating it. Facts existing at the time of the *appointment*, although irrelevant for ascertaining the perpetuity period, must be taken into account in order to find the true nature of the appointment itself, before it can be referred back to the date of the original instrument and tested by the facts existing at that time.[84]

Some examples may make this clearer.

(i) Devise to A for life with power to appoint to his children: A appoints to his son B " when he is 23 ": B was unborn at the testator's death (in 1950) but aged 3 at the time of the appointment. A is the only life in being, but since the property is bound to vest (if at all) within 20 years of his

[79] s. 3 (2).
[80] *Re Brown and Sibly's Contract* (1876) 3 Ch.D. 156; *Re Thompson* [1906] 2 Ch. 199.
[81] *Ante*, p. 255.
[82] *Re Witty* [1913] 2 Ch. 666 at 673, *per* Cozens-Hardy M.R.
[83] *Re Stern* [1962] Ch. 732.
[84] It is therefore inaccurate to say (see *Duke of Marlborough* v. *Lord Godolphin* (1750) 2 Ves.Sen. 61 at 78; *Harvey* v. *Stracey* (1852) 1 Drew. 73 at 134) that the appointment must be looked at as if it were contained in the instrument creating the power: see *Re Thompson* [1906] 2 Ch. 199 at 205; Gray, § 515.

death, the appointment is good.[85] The facts existing at the
time of the appointment show that it is really an appointment
" to B in 20 years' time, if he is then living." That is to say,
the maximum possible postponement of vesting is, in truth,
20 years from A's death. Had B been aged 1 at the time of
the appointment, then if it had been made before 1926 it
would have been void; if it had been made after 1925, B
would have taken when he was 21,[86] unless the testator died
after July 15, 1964, in which case B would have taken when
he was 23 if in fact he attained that age within the perpetuity
period, and if he could not do so he would take at 22.[87]

(ii) Marriage settlement, made in 1930, upon C for life, remainder
as he should appoint among his issue: C appoints in favour
of his daughter D, postponing the vesting of her interest until
her marriage; D is unmarried at the date of the appointment.
The appointment is void.[88] A few years later D marries and
C then executes a document confirming the void appointment.
D is entitled to the property, since the confirmation operates
as a fresh appointment, and in the light of the facts existing
at the time of the appointment the property can be said to
have vested during the lifetime of a person alive at the date
of the settlement, namely, C.[89] Had the settlement been
made in 1965, the first appointment would have been valid
unless and until it appeared that D would not marry within
the perpetuity period,[90] which runs from the date of the
settlement.

(iii) Deed, made in 1940, giving property to F for life with power
to appoint to his issue: F appoints by his will in favour of
his grandchildren G and H (neither of whom was alive at
the date of the gift) for their joint lives as tenants in common,
with remainder to the survivor. The interest for their joint
lives is valid but the remainder is void.[91] Had the deed
been made in 1965, the remainder would be valid if in fact
it vested within the perpetuity period. The period would
run from the date of the deed and the lives in being would

---

[85] This example is suggested by *Peard* v. *Kekewich* (1852) 15 Beav. 166.
[86] L.P.A., 1925, s. 163; *ante*, p. 235. The statements in Wolst. & C. i, 293, ii, 141,
that neither s. 163 nor the Act of 1964 applies if the appointment but not the
settlement is made after July 15, 1964, appears to overlook s. 15 (5) of the Act
of 1964, which leaves s. 163 unrepealed in such a case.
[87] Perpetuities and Accumulations Act 1964, s. 4 (1); *ante*, p. 236. This is subject
to the difficulty mentioned on p. 237 (defective repeal of s. 163).
[88] This example is based on *Morgan* v. *Gronow* (1873) L.R. 16 Eq. 1.
[89] See previous note.
[90] Perpetuities and Accumulations Act 1964, s. 3 (1); *ante*, p. 214.
[91] *Re Legh's S. T.* [1938] Ch. 39.

be the donor, F, and any of F's issue living at the date of the deed.[92]

As will be evident from these examples, the provisions of the Act of 1964 (*e.g.*, the provisions for " wait and see," age-reduction and class-reduction) apply to an appointment made under a special power in the same way as they apply to gifts generally, provided only that the instrument creating the power took effect after July 15, 1964.[93]

(ii) A general power. Since the property is unfettered until the appointment has been made and the donee of the power is able to deal with it as he wishes, the perpetuity period does not begin to run until the date of the appointment[94]; and this is so even if the power is exercisable by deed only[95] or by will only.[96] Thus for the purposes of the perpetuity rule there is no difference between the exercise of a general power and a conveyance by an absolute owner.

The difference between appointments under general and special powers may be summarised thus. In both cases, the relevant facts are those existing at the time of the appointment; but the time from which the perpetuity period runs, and at which the lives in being must be ascertained, is the creation of the power in the case of a special power, and the exercise of the power in the case of a general power.

17. Contractual interests, obligations, covenants and options. The perpetuity rule was devised in order to control interests in property, not mere personal obligations. Here we reach the boundary between property and contract. Here, also, the Act of 1964 has made important changes.

(*a*) *Personal obligations* (*at common law*)

(1) CONTRAST WITH PROPRIETARY INTERESTS. The perpetuity rule was never applied to mere personal obligations created by contract, *e.g.*, to pay money,[97] or to buy stone exclusively from a particular quarry.[98] The rule is directed against the tying up of property by

---

[92] *Ante*, p. 223.
[93] s. 15 (5).
[94] *Re Thompson* [1906] 2 Ch. 199 at 202.
[95] Consider *Re Phillips* [1931] 1 Ch. 347.
[96] *Ante*, p. 253. Contrast the rule as to the power itself, *ante*, p. 255.
[97] *Walsh* v. *H.M. Sec. of State for India* (1863) 10 H.L.C. 367; *Witham* v. *Vane* (1883) reported in Challis 440; *Borland's Trustee* v. *Steel Brothers & Co. Ltd.* [1901] 1 Ch. 279; see Challis 440.
[98] *Keppell* v. *Bailey* (1834) 2 My. & K. 517 at 527; *South Eastern Ry.* v. *Associated Portland Cement Manufacturers (1900), Ltd.* [1910] 1 Ch. 12 (allowing landowner to make a tunnel under adjoining land); see 54 S.J. 471, 501; *Sharpe* v. *Durrant* (1911) 55 S.J. 423; [1911] W.N. 158 (allowing landowner to make crossings over a tramway); (1911) 27 L.Q.R. 151; Challis 184.

granting interests in it which may vest at too remote a date. By
" interests " is meant rights *in rem*, rights of property, enforceable
against other persons generally according to the principles governing
legal and equitable interests.[99] Contracts, on the other hand,
primarily create personal obligations between the contracting parties;
and therefore between the parties themselves (and their respective
personal representatives, who can sue and be sued on a deceased
person's contract) the rule against perpetuities, in its classical common law form has no application[1]: a contracting party may be
made liable on any contingency, however remote, so that, *e.g.*, an
option given by one corporation to another in (say) 1800 or 1950
may remain enforceable for ever.[2]

(2) SPECIFIC PERFORMANCE. It makes no difference that the
contract is specifically enforceable (as for example a contract for
the sale of land), and thus gives one party a right to obtain specific
property; for the rights of the parties *inter se* are personal as well as
proprietary, and " specific performance is merely an equitable mode
of enforcing a personal obligation with which the rule against
perpetuities has nothing to do." [3] If the vendor, for instance, has
parted with the land contracted to be sold, it is useless to decree
specific performance against him when he can no longer perform
his obligations. The property itself, therefore, is not fettered by the
vendor's obligations in so far as they are personal to him. " The
real answer to the argument founded on the inconvenience of tying
up land is that the action upon the covenant sounds in damages only
unless the defendant has still got the land to which the covenant
relates." [4]

(3) ASSIGNMENT. Since it is the general rule that the benefit, but
not the burden, of a contract is assignable,[5] an assignee of a contractual right can enforce it against the original promisor personally,
or his estate if he is dead, at any time regardless of the perpetuity
rule.[6] But the assignment itself, which is proprietary in nature and
so resembles a conveyance rather than a contract, must take effect
within the period, running from the date when it is made.[7]

[99] The true character of equitable interests as rights *in rem* clearly emerges here:
see *ante*, p. 114.
[1] Challis 184n. But restrictive covenants create property rights: see *ante*, p. 133.
[2] Challis 184n.
[3] *Hutton* v. *Watling* [1948] Ch. 26 at 36, per Jenkins J.
[4] *South Eastern Ry.* v. *Associated Portland Cement Manufacturers (1900), Ltd.*
[1910] 1 Ch. 12 at 34, *per* Farwell L.J.
[5] *Cf. post*, p. 628.
[6] *South Eastern Ry.* v. *Associated Portland Cement Manufacturers (1900), Ltd.*
[1910] 1 Ch. 12.
[7] Gray, § 329, n. 1.

(b) Proprietary interests (at common law)

(1) PERSONAL AND PROPRIETARY RIGHTS. Many contracts create not only personal obligations but interests in property as well. Contracts for the sale or lease of land, if specifically enforceable, are binding as equitable interests (estate contracts) not only upon the original promisor but also upon his successors in title, subject to the reservations which must always be remembered.[8] Against such successors in title, who are not parties to the contract, the contract can be enforced only in so far as it creates an interest in land, a right *in rem*; and to this element of it the perpetuity rule naturally applies.[9] At common law, therefore, although a contract creating an interest in property which may arise outside the perpetuity period is valid as against the original promisor, or his estate, at the suit of anyone entitled to the benefit of it, it is void as against third parties. Probably a firm contract (as opposed to a mere option) for sale " in twenty-five years' time " would also be void against a third party, for the purchaser's equitable interest, though it arises at once,[10] cannot be truly vested until the time has expired.[11]

(2) OPTIONS. The contracts which most commonly produce contingent interests in property, capable of arising after an extended period of time, are options. At common law these must obey the above rules, and since the time for exercising the option usually has no connection with lives in being (unless, for example, a " royal lives clause " is used), the perpetuity period is normally 21 years only. Options occur particularly commonly in leases, both in the form of options to purchase the reversion (*i.e.*, the freehold, or some superior lease) and in the form of options for the renewal of the lease. Options *to purchase the reversion* are likewise subject to the above rules at common law.[12] But options *to renew a lease* enjoy a special exemption from the perpetuity rule.[13] This is because options to renew a lease, unlike options to purchase a freehold, are among the recognised leasehold covenants which " run with the land," [14] and if long leases are to be allowed this class of covenant must, in general, be allowed to run with them. But statute now provides that a contract

---

[8] *Ante*, p. 113. As to estate contracts, see *ante*, p. 132; *post*, p. 575.

[9] *L. & S.W. Ry.* v. *Gomm* (1882) 20 Ch.D. 562; *Woodall* v. *Clifton* [1905] 2 Ch. 257; *Worthing Corpn.* v. *Heather* [1906] 2 Ch. 532. And see the illuminating judgment of Jenkins J. in *Hutton* v. *Watling* [1948] Ch. 26, not challenged on this point on appeal: [1948] Ch. 398.

[10] *Post*, p. 575.

[11] See Gray, § 330, n. 2. Ordinary contracts for sale are safe because even if no date is fixed for completion there is an implied term that completion shall take place within a reasonable time.

[12] *Woodall* v. *Clifton* [1905] 2 Ch. 257.

[13] *L. & S.W. Ry.* v. *Gomm* (1882) 20 Ch.D. 562 at 579; *Woodall* v. *Clifton, supra,* at pp. 265, 268; *Weg Motors, Ltd.* v. *Hales* [1962] Ch. 49; Gray, § 230.

[14] *Post*, p. 727; *Muller* v. *Trafford* [1901] 1 Ch. 54 at 61. This in itself is somewhat anomalous.

to renew a lease for more than 60 years is void if made after 1925.[15] Even covenants which made leases perpetually renewable were exempt from the perpetuity rule [16]; but now perpetually renewable leases can no longer exist.[17]

(c) *Statutory changes.* The Act of 1964 has made three changes in the law in the case of instruments taking effect after July 15, 1964.

(i) An option to acquire for value any interest in land is subject to a perpetuity period of 21 years only.[18] No period based on lives in being and no alternative fixed statutory period may be used. (An exception is made in favour of certain rights of pre-emption conferred on public or local authorities in respect of land devoted to religious use which ceases to be used thus.[19]) The "wait and see" principle also applies.[20] As against a successor in title of the person who gave the option, therefore, the option is valid for 21 years from the date of the instrument creating it (assuming that it was duly registered) and thereafter is void.

(ii) A contract or other disposition *inter vivos* which creates an interest in property is void even between the original contracting parties wherever it would have been void for remoteness as against a third party.[21]

(iii) The perpetuity rule does not apply to an option for a lessee (whether under a lease or an agreement for a lease) to purchase the freehold or a superior leasehold reversion, provided that it is exercisable only by the lessee or his successors in title and that it ceases to be exercisable not later than one year after the end of the lease.[22]

The reason underlying (iii) is that an option for a tenant to purchase the reversion is not an objectionable fetter on the property, for it encourages the tenant to maintain the property and make improvements. It is, in fact, merely a means of prolonging the ownership which he already has. Options unconnected with leases (options in gross) have the opposite effect, for they put it into the power of a stranger to take the benefit of any increase in the value of the land. This is the reason underlying (ii), although this goes beyond the subject of perpetuity and represents an interference with freedom of contract.[23]

---

[15] *Post*, p. 645.   [16] *Hare* v. *Burges* (1857) 4 K. & J. 45 at 57.
[17] *Post*, p. 644.
[18] s. 9 (2).   [19] *Ibid.*
[20] s. 3 (1), (3).
[21] s. 10. The language of this provision is curious. See (1964) 80 L.Q.R. 486 at 525.
[22] s. 9 (1).
[23] See Fourth Report of the Law Reform Committee, Cmnd. 18, 1956, paras. 35–38.

Changes (i) and (ii) above do not, as will be seen, fit together neatly, since (i) is confined to options relating to land whereas (ii) operates more widely. This difference will be brought out in the examples which follow, in which it must also be remembered that the option or contract may need to be registered as an estate contract if it is to be valid against a later purchaser from the grantor.[24]

(*d*) *Examples* (*common law and statute*). The effect of the common law rules and of the Act of 1964 may be seen from the following examples.

(i) Contract made between A and B giving B the option to purchase Blackacre from A for £1,000 " at any future date." If the contract was made before July 16, 1964, the option is enforceable by B (and also by B's personal representatives and assignees from B) against A and A's personal representatives. If they still have the land, specific performance or damages may be awarded against them.[25] If A sold the land to C, A may also be liable in damages for non-performance of the contract.[26] But as against C the option is void for perpetuity because it might be exercised more than 21 years after its creation. It would be equally void against C if he had taken the land under A's will.

If the contract was made after July 15, 1964, it will be valid for 21 years both against A and against any of A's successors in title. But if not in fact exercised within that time it becomes equally void against all of them.

(ii) Contract made between A and B by which A is to sell Blackacre to B for £1,000 if and when it is possible to obtain planning permission to build on the land. If the contract was made before July 16, 1964, the common law rules apply as in example (i) above. If the contract was made on or after that date, it will apparently be valid (both against A and against A's successors in title) if in fact permission is obtainable within 21 years of the death of the survivor of A and B,[27] but otherwise the contract will be void (against all of them). The difference between this and example (i) is that the special 21-year perpetuity period applies only to an " option," meaning presumably a contract which only one party can insist upon enforcing.

(iii) Lease for 99 years made in 1910 between L and T giving to T (the tenant) the option to purchase the freehold at a stated price at any time during the term. During the term L assigns the reversion to X and T assigns the lease to Y. If Y or his successor in title wishes to

---

[24] *Post*, p. 1040.
[25] *Hutton* v. *Watling* [1948] Ch. 26.
[26] See *post*, pp. 1049, 1050.
[27] They are lives in being under s. 3 (5) (*a*) and (*b*) respectively: *ante*, p. 223.

exercise the option, he can recover damages from L's personal representatives if any of L's assets remain unadministered. But he cannot obtain either the property or damages from X or his successors in title,[28] for the option is void except in its purely contractual aspect.

If the lease had been made in 1965, the option would be valid against X and his successors in title as well as against L.[29]

(iv) Lease for 50 years made in 1930 between L and T giving to T (the tenant) the option to renew the lease, at its expiry, for a further 50 years. This option is valid at common law both against L and against L's successors in title to the reversion. It would be equally valid if the lease had been made in 1965.

C. Exceptions from the Perpetuity Rule

1. Certain limitations after entails

(a) *Power to bar.* Remainders following upon entails have been recognised as valid since early times.[30] As a consequence of the Statute *De Donis*, 1285,[31] they became indefeasible interests; but when entails later became barrable [32] they were left in a precarious state, and thenceforth were liable to be destroyed if at any time the entail was barred. When, later still, the modern rule against perpetuities was devised, the courts did not apply it to these well-recognised interests,[33] since the prior tenant in tail was potentially an absolute owner and his power to alienate the land was in no way fettered by any remainder.[34]

(b) *Vesting before entail determines.* Interests limited to take effect after entails may be either vested or contingent. If contingent, they will be exempt from the perpetuity rule only if they are certain to vest, if at all, during the continuance of the entail or at the moment of its determination.[35] Thus a gift to X in tail, with remainder to such of Y's issue as are alive when the entail determines, is valid, even though the persons entitled to take the remainder may not be ascertained for several hundred years.[36] Similarly a devise to Y in tail, with a gift over to other persons if Y or the heirs of his body should become seised of certain land, is valid; for this event could

---

[28] *Wooodall* v. *Clifton* [1905] 2 Ch. 257. On this case, see (1955) 19 Conv.(N.S.) 255–257.
[29] See *post*, p. 742.
[30] *Ante*, p. 84.
[31] *Ante*, p. 83.
[32] *Ante*, pp. 85, 86.
[33] *Nicholls* v. *Sheffield* (1787) 2 Bro.C.C. 215.
[34] See, *e.g., Newell* v. *Crayford Cottage Society* [1922] 1 K.B. 656 at 663.
[35] *Morris & Leach,* 195.
[36] See *Heaseman* v. *Pearse* (1871) 7 Ch.App. 275 at 282, 283.

occur only while Y or an heir of his body was alive, *i.e.*, during the period for which the entail, if unbarred, would endure.

(*c*) *Possible vesting later.* This exception, however, does not protect limitations which might possibly vest at some time later than the moment of the natural determination of the entail.[37] If property is given to trustees in trust for A in tail, remainder to the first son of B to marry, A's entail is valid but the remainder is void at common law, for it might vest after the period had run and the entail determined.[38] Again, in a limitation in trust for X in tail male with a gift over to Y's oldest descendant living when all X's issue fail, the gift over is void at common law, since the existence of female issue of X might postpone its vesting until some date later than the end of the tail male.[39]

(*d*) *Act of* 1964. The Act of 1964 makes no change in the above rules, since its " wait and see " provisions operate only by reference to the regular perpetuity periods [40] and the Act does not allow " wait and see " during the continuance of an entail. But, of course, gifts following entails which do in fact vest during the regular perpetuity periods will be saved by the Act, where it applies, in the normal way.

2. Certain gifts to charities. The general rule is that a gift to a charity [41] is subject to the rule in the same way as any other gift.[42] If there is a gift to a private person with a gift over to a charity, the gift over is void for perpetuity if it is capable of vesting outside the period.[43] Similarly a charitable gift which is to take effect on the appointment of the next lieutenant-colonel of a volunteer corps is void.[44] But if there is a gift to one charity followed by a gift over to another charity on a certain event, the gift over is not void merely because the event may occur outside the perpetuity period.[45] Thus if property is given to Charity A with a proviso that it shall go to Charity B if Charity A fails to keep the testator's tomb in repair,

---

[37] Morris & Leach, 195.
[38] See Marsden, 147; and see authorities quoted in Halsb. xxix, 302.
[39] See *Bristow* v. *Boothby* (1826) 2 Sim.. & St. 465.
[40] *i.e.*, lives in being plus 21 years; or 21 years only; or a fixed term not exceeding 80 years: s. 3 (4); *ante*, pp. 221, 226.
[41] For charities, see *post*, p. 1001.
[42] *Chamberlayne* v. *Brockett* (1872) 8 Ch.App. 206 at 211; *Re Bowen* [1893] 2 Ch. 491 at 494; dicta to the contrary (*e.g.*, *Goodman* v. *The Mayor and Free Burgesses of the Borough of Saltash* (1882) 7 App.Cas. 633 at 650; *Re St. Stephen, Coleman Street* (1888) 39 Ch.D. 492 at 501; *Re Rymer* [1895] 1 Ch. 19 at 25) are concerned with " inalienability " (*post*, p. 267) rather than " perpetuity."
[43] *Att.-Gen.* v. *Gill* (1726) 2 P.Wms. 369; *Re Johnson's Trusts* (1866) L.R. 2 Eq. 716.
[44] *Re Lord Stratheden & Campbell* [1894] 3 Ch. 265.
[45] *Christ's Hospital* v. *Grainger* (1849) 1 Mac. & G. 460.

the gift over is valid.[46] To this extent alone are charities exempted from the rule against perpetuities [47]; thus a gift to a natural person is not validated merely because it is preceded by a gift to charity.[48]

3. Certain contracts and covenants

(a) *Personal obligations.* The exemption of personal obligations created by contract or covenant, and the changes made by the Act of 1964, have already been explained.[49]

(b) *Options in leases.* The exemptions allowed for options to renew leases (at common law) and for options to acquire the reversion (under the Act of 1964) have also already been explained.[50]

(c) *Restrictive covenants.* A restrictive covenant (whether affecting freehold or leasehold land) creates an equitable interest in the land [51] which is enforceable against future occupiers at any distance in time. It is not subject to the perpetuity rule, because a future breach of the covenant does not bring about the vesting of any interest in the land.[52] This is not, therefore, a genuine exception.

4. Forfeiture of leases and enforcement of rentcharges.

Leases often contain a forfeiture clause, by which the tenant agrees that if at any time he breaks the terms of the lease the landlord may re-enter and put an end to the lease.[53] This contingent liability to re-entry runs with the land demised and is a proprietary interest.[54] But since it is a recognised incident of leases it is exempt from the perpetuity rule.[55] For similar reasons statutory exemption was given in 1925 to certain rights of entry reserved to secure payment of rentcharges, whether such rights were given by contract or by statute [56]; and for rentcharges created after July 15, 1964, the exemption has now been extended to all powers and remedies for enforcing rentcharges.[57] A

---

[46] *Re Tyler* [1891] 3 Ch. 252 (doubted in *R.S.P.C.A. of N.S.W.* v. *Benevolent Society of N.S.W.* (1960) 102 C.L.R. 629); contrast *Re Dalziel* [1943] Ch. 277. This is so even if the maintenance of the tomb will leave no surplus for Charity A: *Re Davies* [1915] 1 Ch. 543. The gift to Charity A is also valid, even though it may continue indefinitely: see *ante*, p. 243.

[47] But for their exception from the rule against inalienability, see *post*, p. 271.

[48] *Re Bowen* [1893] 2 Ch. 491.

[49] *Ante*, p. 258.   [50] *Ibid.*

[51] *Ante*, p. 133, *post*, pp. 750 *et seq.*

[52] *Mackenzie* v. *Childers* (1889) 43 Ch.D. 265 at 279; *Marten* v. *Flight Refuelling Ltd.* [1962] Ch. 115 at 136; Gray, § 280. Contrast *Halsall* v. *Brizell* [1957] Ch. 169 (positive covenant).

[53] See *post*, p. 654.   [54] L.P.A., 1925, s. 1 (2) (*e*);*ante*, p. 136.

[55] *Re Tyrrell's Estate* [1907] 1 I.R. 292 at 298; Gray, § 303; Challis 186 and see *Re Garde Browne* [1911] 1 I.R. 205 at 210; *Woodall* v. *Clifton* [1905] 2 Ch. 257 at 279.

[56] L.P.A., 1925, s. 121 (6) (contrast s. 4 (3)), replacing C.A., 1911, s. 6 (1); *post*, p. 797.

[57] Perpetuities and Accumulations Act 1964, ss. 11 (1), 15 (5); see (1964) 80 L.Q.R. 486 at 528.

right to redeem a rentcharge for, *e.g.*, 500 years, on payment of a fixed sum at any time, is not invalidated by the perpetuity rule.[58] It will be remembered, on the other hand, that rights of entry or re-entry reserved on the grant of a conditional fee simple in corporeal land are subject to the perpetuity rule[59]; they are contingent rights to substantial ownership, not rights incidental to some other legitimately vested interest such as is conferred by a lease or a rentcharge.

5. Resulting trusts. The exception permitted by the common law and abolished by the Act of 1964 has been explained above.[60]

6. Mortgages. "The rule has never been applied to mortgages," and thus a clause postponing the mortgagor's right to redeem the property is not invalid merely because the right is postponed for longer than the perpetuity period.[61]

7. Right of survivorship. As already mentioned,[62] a joint tenant's right of survivorship[63] is exempt from the rule.[64] Since it can always be destroyed by severance by the other joint tenant,[65] it is no more objectionable than a remainder after an entail.[66]

8. Miscellaneous. The Law of Property Act, 1925,[67] sets out a list of certain special rights exempted from the rule both for the future and retrospectively. These rights relate to rentcharges,[68] minerals, timber, and repair or maintenance of land, buildings, sewers, and other things. The general effect of the exemptions is to enable rights which are merely ancillary to other valid interests to be exercised outside the perpetuity period.[69] Registered pension funds for employees have also been given exemption by statute, subject to certain conditions.[70]

---

[58] *Switzer & Co. Ltd.* v. *Rochford* [1906] 1 I.R. 399.
[59] *Ante*, p. 247.
[60] See *ante*, p. 245.
[61] *Knightsbridge Estates Trust Ltd.* v. *Byrne* [1939] Ch. 441 at 463, *per* Greene M.R. (affirmed on another ground, [1940] A.C. 613).
[62] *Ante*, p. 230.
[63] *Post*, p. 391.
[64] *Re Roberts* (1881) 19 Ch.D. 520; Gray, § 232.1.
[65] *Post*, p. 403.
[66] *Ante*, p. 263.
[67] s. 162.
[68] See also *ante*, p. 265.
[69] *Dunn* v. *Blackdown Properties Ltd.* [1961] Ch. 433. *Cf. ante*, p. 211.
[70] Superannuation and other Trust Funds (Validation) Act, 1927.

Sect. 4. The Rule against Inalienability

1. " Perpetual trusts "

(a) *The principle.* It is a fundamental principle of English law that property must not be rendered inalienable.[71] It is therefore necessary to prohibit not only indefeasible future interests which are unduly remote, but immediate gifts which are subject to some permanent restraint upon alienation. The two principles are often confused, but need to be considered separately. Restraints upon alienation attached to direct gifts of property are generally invalid on their face, as repugnant to the interest granted.[72] But if a trust is employed the donor's intention may be that the capital shall be held indefinitely, or that some beneficial interest given to a club or other permanent institution shall continue indefinitely so that it is, in effect, inalienable. The rule now to be explained is therefore sometimes also called " the rule against perpetual trusts," [73] although the rule against such trusts is only part of a wider rule against inalienability.

(b) *Purpose trusts.* The trusts in question are sometimes called " purpose trusts," meaning that the trust property is to be used to promote some particular purpose (as in the examples given in the next paragraph) rather than to benefit some particular individual or class. In such cases the ordinary perpetuity rule cannot prevent the property from being tied up indefinitely, since there are no individual beneficiaries in whom successive interests are to vest. It seems probable that " purpose trusts " are valid only in certain anomalous cases,[74] for the general rule is that a trust is void if there is no person able to enforce it, *i.e.*, no *cestui que trust*.[75]

(c) *Void gifts.* A gift is void if effect can be given to it only by holding property indefinitely and applying it or its income for specified purposes.[76] Thus a devise of land to be retained in perpetuity for use as a family burial ground is void.[77] The question in every case is whether there is some provision preventing the disposition of the property or the beneficial interest in it. Either the terms of the gift,[78] or, in the case of trusts for an association or club,

---

71 *Cf. ante*, p. 78 (conditions in restraint of alienation); and see *Carne* v. *Long* (1860) 2 De G.F. & J. 75 at 80.
72 *Ibid.*
73 See Gray, § 909.1.
74 Such as maintenance of a grave (*Re Hooper* [1932] 1 Ch. 38) or of animals (*Re Dean* (1889) 41 Ch.D. 552).
75 *Re Astor's S. T.* [1952] Ch. 534; *Re Shaw* [1957] 1 W.L.R. 729; *Re Endacot* [1960] Ch. 232; contrast *Re Denley's Trust Deed* [1969] 1 Ch. 373 (indirect interest of individuals suffices). See Morris & Leach, 307 *et seq.*
76 See *Cocks* v. *Manners* (1871) L.R. 12 Eq. 574 at 585, 586.
77 *Yeap Cheah Neo* v. *Ong Cheng Neo* (1875) L.R. 6 P.C. 381.
78 *Re Patten* [1929] 2 Ch. 276.

the rules of the society,[79] may make the property inalienable.[80]
Further examples of gifts void for inalienability are the following:

> bequest to trustees upon trust to maintain a tomb [81];
>
> bequest to trustees for the provision of an annual cup for the most successful yacht of the season [82]; and
>
> bequest to trustees upon trust to pay the income to a company as a contribution to the holiday expenses of its workpeople.[83]

(*d*) *Valid gifts.* The foregoing gifts must be distinguished from absolute gifts which impose no restraint, such as—

> on trust for an old boys' club to be used as a committee thought best,[84] or
>
> to the trustees of the London Library for general purposes,[85] or
>
> to a convent to be paid to the superior.[86]

Unless under the constitution of the recipient society all its property is effectually made inalienable, such gifts are valid, for there is nothing to prevent the capital being alienated. A gift to the Athenaeum Club, for example, may be so expressed as to make the capital inalienable and the income earmarked in perpetuity for the use of the Club; or it may simply be an outright gift to the Club which the present members can dispose of as they wish. The former gift will be void but the latter (which is the prima facie construction) will be valid.[87]

(*e*) *Restriction for perpetuity period.* Although property cannot be rendered inalienable for ever, or for a period to which no clear and definite limit is set,[88] it seems that alienation may be validly restricted for a period which cannot exceed a life or lives in being at the time of the gift, and a further 21 years.[89] This period is

---

79 *Re Dutton* (1878) 4 Ex.D. 54; and see *Re Clarke* [1901] 2 Ch. 110; *Re Recher's W. T.* [1972] Ch. 526. Unless there is some trust or statutory provision to prevent the members from distributing the property, mere rules of the club which prevent this may not create perpetuity, for the members may be able to change the rules: see *Re Clarke, supra*; and see the discussion in *Leahy* v. *Att.-Gen. for New South Wales* [1959] A.C. 547; *cf. Carne* v. *Long* (1860) 2 De G.F. & J. 75 at 80.

80 *Re Patten, supra*; *Re Gwyon* [1930] 1 Ch. 255 (provision that income was to be used to provide knickers each year for boys resident in certain parts of Surrey).

81 *Rickard* v. *Robson* (1862) 31 Beav. 244.

82 *Re Nottage* [1895] 2 Ch. 649.

83 *Re Drummond* [1914] 2 Ch. 90.

84 *Ibid.*

85 *Re Prevost* [1930] 2 Ch. 383.

86 *Cocks* v. *Manners* (1871) L.R. 12 Eq. 574.

87 See *Re Ray's W. T.* [1936] 2 All E.R. 93 at 97, 98; *Re Turkington* [1937] 4 All E.R. 501; *Leahy* v. *Att.-Gen. for New South Wales* [1959] A.C. 457 at 478.

88 *Kennedy* v. *Kennedy* [1914] A.C. 215; *Re Wightwick's W. T.* [1950] Ch. 260.

89 See *Thellusson* v. *Woodford* (1805) 11 Ves. 112 at 135, 146; *Carne* v. *Long* (1860) 2 De G.F. & J. 75 at 80; *Re Dean* (1889) 41 Ch.D. 552 at 557.

borrowed from the rule against perpetuities,[90] and as under that rule, probably the lives must be human lives.[91]

(f) *The Act of* 1964. The Act of 1964 expressly refrains from making any change in the law where property is to be applied for purposes other than the benefit of any person or class of persons.[92] " Purpose trusts " are thus unaffected by the Act.

2. Other restraints on alienability

(a) *Restraint on anticipation.* Another restrictive provision which could offend against the rule was the restraint upon anticipation, a restraint which formerly was allowable for the purpose of preventing a married woman from disposing of property or anticipating the future income in any way (this is dealt with more fully later).[93] A restraint upon anticipation imposed upon a living woman did not infringe the rule against inalienability, for alienation was restrained only while she was married, *i.e.,* during her lifetime.[94] But restraint imposed upon property given to an unborn female was void, for she might have married, and so brought the restraint into operation, more than 21 years after the death of all persons alive at the date of the gift [95]; in such a case, the donee took the property free from the restraint,[96] although if the restraint had been worded so as to be operative only during the proper period, it would have been valid.

(b) *Protective trusts.* A rather different type of limitation, now used as a substitute for the restraint on anticipation, is the protective trust.[97] This may be created by directing any life or lesser interest to be held " on protective trusts," thus incorporating statutory forms of trust,[98] or by setting out express trusts. Such trusts provide for the income to be paid to the principal beneficiary during his life (or lesser period) under a determinable limitation, *i.e.,* until he attempts any alienation, or any other event occurs whereby he might be deprived of any of the income; and thereafter the property is held on discretionary trusts for a number of persons, including the principal beneficiary.

---

[90] *Ante,* p. 209.
[91] *Re Dean* (1889) 41 Ch.D. 552 (upholding a trust for dogs and horses for their lives) is probably wrong; see *ante,* p. 220.
[92] s. 15 (4).
[93] *Post,* p. 995.
[94] *Herbert* v. *Webster* (1880) 15 Ch.D. 610 ; *Cooper* v. *Laroche* (1881) 17 Ch.D. 368.
[95] *Re Cunninghame's Settlement* (1871) L.R. 11 Eq. 324.
[96] *Fry* v. *Capper* (1853) Kay 163 ; *Re Teague's Settlement* (1870) L.R. 10 Eq. 564 ; and see *Re Game* [1907] 1 Ch. 276 as to applying the rule to classes.
[97] See generally Snell, *Equity,* pp. 135–138.
[98] See Trustee Act, 1925, s. 33 ; Family Law Reform Act 1969, s. 14 (3); *post,* p. 997.

If such a trust is created in favour of, for example, an unborn child of a living person, to vest at birth, it seems that at common law it is partly valid and partly void. On the principle that the perpetuity rule is not concerned with the determination of interests,[99] the determinable interest will duly terminate whenever the specified event occurs, even if it is outside the perpetuity period; but the discretionary trust, which may arise at too remote a date, is plainly void.[1] Where the Act of 1964 applies, the result will be different: if the determinable interest in fact outlasts the perpetuity period, it will become absolute and the discretionary trust will be void[2]; but otherwise the discretionary trust will be valid up to the end of the perpetuity period, and thereafter void.[3]

3. Capital and income

(a) *Inalienable capital.* If the beneficial interest, *i.e.*, the right to the income, is itself free from any trust or restraint and so is freely assignable, it does not matter that the capital may be vested inalienably in trustees. Thus a life interest in a trust fund may be given to an unborn person, provided of course that it must vest within the perpetuity period, even though the capital of the fund must be held by the trustees until the beneficiary's death, which may be more than 21 years from the end of lives in being at the date of the gift.[4] The same principle has been applied even to the case of a determinable interest in the income of a trust fund,[5] analogous to a determinable fee in real property, where the capital might have remained in the hands of the trustees for ever.

(b) *Alienable income.* If this is correct it would seem that a gift to trustees upon trust " to apply the income to the upkeep of my grave " is bad, since both capital and income are tied up indefinitely by the trust[6]; but a trust " to pay the income to X during such time as my grave is properly tended " is good, for X can dispose of his determinable interest in the income without any breach of trust;

---

[99] *Ante,* p. 244.
[1] And see *ante,* p. 247.
[2] *Ante,* p. 247.
[3] s. 3 (3). S. 15 (2) treats discretionary trusts as powers of appointment: *ante,* p. 247.
[4] *Wainwright* v. *Miller* [1897] 2 Ch. 255; *Re Gage* [1898] 1 Ch. 498.
[5] *Re Chardon* [1928] Ch. 464, followed in *Re Chambers' W. T.* [1950] Ch. 267. The criticisms excited by *Re Chardon* (*ante,* p. 245, n. 98) mainly relate to the gift over, not to the determinable interest: see (1937) 53 L.Q.R. 24; (1938) 54 L.Q.R. 258; Tudor, *Charities* (5th ed.), 701; Jarman 288. But if the determining event is so vague that the time of its happening could never be proved by evidence, the capital is perpetually tied up and the gift is void: *Re Wightwick's W. T.* [1950] Ch. 260 (abolition of vivisection by law " in the United Kingdom of Great Britain and Ireland, on the continent of Europe and elsewhere ").
[6] See, *e.g.*, *Re Dalziel* [1943] Ch. 277.

and the fact that the capital is to be held upon trust meanwhile is held to be immaterial, for the person able to dispose of the income and the persons entitled on the determination of the interest [7] could at any time combine and put an end to the trust.[8]

(c) *Settled land.* Since land held upon trust for limited interests has been alienable since 1882 under the powers conferred by the Settled Land Acts,[9] it is only a beneficial interest in land which can now be made inalienable, as for example where a life interest is made subject to protective trusts. This explains why the rule against inalienability must be illustrated chiefly by trusts of personalty. When settled land is sold, the purchase-money is in fact personalty, but by statute it is treated as land for all purposes of disposition, transmission and devolution.[10]

4. Exemption of charities. Charities are exempt from the rule against inalienability; no gift for charitable purposes is void merely because it renders property inalienable in perpetuity.[11] Were this not so it would be virtually impossible to make gifts to charity, since the income, if not also the capital, would almost always be confined by some trust for use for the purposes of the charity only.

Sect. 5. The Rule against Accumulations

This rule resembles the rule against inalienability in that it is directed against remoteness of control over property, whether or not vested in a beneficiary, rather than against remoteness of vesting. The principle at common law was that accumulations of income could validly be directed only for so long as property might validly be rendered inalienable.[12] These two restrictions therefore originally went hand in hand. But they parted company when the Accumulations Act, 1800, drastically cut down the period allowed for accumulation, without affecting the rest of the law about inalienability. The Act was the sequel to the famous case of *Thellusson* v. *Woodford*.[13] The "Thellusson Act," as it was often called, bore the stigma of being "one perhaps of the most ill-drawn Acts to be

---

[7] Probably only residuary legatees may be so entitled (*ante*, p. 245, n. 98); and the Perpetuities and Accumulations Act 1964, where it applies, may affect their interests: *ante*, p. 246.

[8] *Re Chardon* [1928] Ch. 464 at 470; *Re Wightwick's W. T.* [1950] Ch. 260 at 264, 265; *Re Chambers' W. T.* [1950] Ch. 267.

[9] *Post*, p. 288.   [10] *Post*, p. 350.

[11] *Chamberlayne* v. *Brockett* (1872) 8 Ch.App. 206 at 211. A charitable trust established in 1585 was upheld in *Att.-Gen.* v. *Webster* (1875) L.R. 20 Eq. 483.

[12] See *Thellusson* v. *Woodford* (1799) 4 Ves. 227 at 317, 318, 338, 339; (1805) 11 Ves. 112 at 146, 147.

[13] (1799) 4 Ves. 227; (1805) 11 Ves. 112. See the discussion of Thellusson and his will at (1974) 118 S.J. 544, 560.

found in our statute book." [14] Mr. Thellusson had by his will directed that the income of his property should be accumulated at compound interest during the lives of his sons, grandsons and great-grandchildren living at his death, and that on the death of the survivor the accumulated fund should be divided among certain of his descendants. This direction, being confined to lives in being, was held valid, but as it was calculated that the accumulated fund would probably amount to many millions of pounds,[15] Parliament intervened to prevent other testators or settlors afflicting their successors with compulsory hoarding upon this scale.[16]

The common law rule was that a direction to accumulate was valid if it was confined to the perpetuity period,[17] so that in theory Mr. Thellusson might have effectively directed accumulation for a further 21 years; but at that time the principle that an extra 21 years is always available had not been firmly settled.[18] The normal perpetuity period was therefore excessively long in the case of accumulations, and the statutory rules cut it down severely.

A. The Statutory Periods

1. The periods. The present law is contained in the Law of Property Act, 1925,[19] and the Perpetuities and Accumulations Act 1964. If the disposition took effect before July 16, 1964, so that only the Act of 1925 applies, accumulation of income may not be directed, either expressly or impliedly,[20] for longer than one (not more [21]) of the following periods.

(i) The life of the grantor or settlor.

(ii) 21 years from the death of the grantor, settlor or testator.

(iii) The minority or respective minorities of any person or persons living or *en ventre sa mère* at the death of the grantor, settlor or testator.

(iv) The minority or respective minorities only of any person or

---

[14] *Tench* v. *Cheese* (1855) 6 De G.M. & G. 453 at 460, *per* Lord Cranworth L.C.; and see *Edwards* v. *Tuck* (1853) 3 De G.M. & G. 40 at 55 (" Lord Loughborough's Act ").

[15] Challis 201; Marsden 321. Under favourable circumstances less than £750,000 might have produced over £100,000,000 by the end of the period. In fact, owing to mismanagement and the costs of litigation, the fund actually accumulated was comparatively small: H.E.L. vii, 230; and see (1965) 62 Law Society's Gazette 613.

[16] See *Re Earl of Berkeley* [1968] Ch. 744 at 780, approving this statement.

[17] *Harrison* v. *Harrison* (1786) cited 4 Ves. 338; *Wilson* v. *Wilson* (1851) 1 Sim.(N.S.) 288 at 298; Marsden 314; Challis 201.

[18] *Ante*, p. 208; Challis 201.

[19] ss. 164–166, replacing with amendments the Accumulations Acts, 1800 and 1892.

[20] See *Re Rochford's S. T.* [1965] Ch. 111.

[21] *Re Errington* (1897) 76 L.T. 616.

persons who under the limitations of the instrument directing accumulation would for the time being, if of full age, be entitled to the income directed to be accumulated.[22]

The Act of 1964 has now added two further periods in the case of dispositions taking effect after July 15, 1964:

(v) 21 years from the making of the disposition.

(vi) The minority or respective minorities of any person or persons in being at that date.[23]

In other words, where the Act of 1964 applies, it allows periods (ii) and (iii) to run from the date of a settlement *inter vivos*, as well as from the death of the settlor. Previously it appeared arbitrary that those periods could run only from the date of death.[24]

2. Choice of periods. The question which period has been chosen in any particular case is one of construction.[25] The first two periods cause little difficulty. Of the first it should be noted that it is the only period of a life available for accumulation, and that it must be the life of the grantor or settlor himself and not of some other person.[26] The second period is a fixed term of years which starts to run at the beginning of the day after the testator's death and expires at the end of the twenty-first anniversary of his death.[27] Thus if a testator directs accumulation to start at the end of an interval after his death and continue for 21 years, he has exceeded the second period.[28]

3. The periods of minorities. The third, fourth and sixth periods are all minorities. Minority now ends at the age of 18.[29] But this does not affect the validity of directions for accumulation in dispositions made before 1970 with reference to the earlier period of minority ending at 21.[30]

The third period and (where it applies) the sixth period differ from the fourth period in the following respects.

[22] L.P.A., 1925, s. 164 (1).
[23] s. 13.
[24] See, *e.g.*, *Re Bourne's S. T.* [1946] 1 All E.R. 411 at 415, 416; *Jagger* v. *Jagger* (1883) 25 Ch.D. 729 at 733.
[25] *Jagger* v. *Jagger* (1883) 25 Ch.D. 729; see, *e.g.*, *Re Watt's W. T.* [1936] 2 All E.R. 1555.
[26] *Re Lady Rosslyn's Trust* (1848) 16 Sim. 391.
[27] *Gorst* v. *Lowndes* (1841) 11 Sim. 434; *Att.-Gen.* v. *Poulden* (1844) 3 Hare 555.
[28] *Webb* v. *Webb* (1840) 2 Beav. 493.
[29] Family Law Reform Act 1969, s. 1. The Act does not change the second and fifth periods of 21 years but only the meaning of " minority," " infancy," " full age " and similar expressions.
[30] *Ibid.*, 3rd Sched., para. 7; S.I. 1969 No. 1140.

(*a*) *Living infants.* The third and sixth periods are confined to the minorities of persons alive or *en ventre sa mère* at the death of the settlor or at the date of the settlement, as the case may be. The fourth period is not so confined.[31]

(*b*) *Beneficiaries.* The third and sixth periods are not confined to the minorities of those who are prospectively entitled to any benefit under the gift, whereas the fourth period is confined to the minorities of those who can say "but for my infancy I should be entitled to the income which is being accumulated." [32]

(*c*) *Successive minorities.* The third and sixth periods can never exceed a single minority; for even if accumulation is directed during a large number of minorities, the period is in effect merely the longest of these minorities. Nor can any accumulation continue under them for longer than the second period, except where a child is *en ventre sa mère* at the relevant time. Under the fourth period, on the other hand, accumulation is possible during the minorities of persons unborn at the time of the gift [33]; and these minorities may be successive, for any beneficiary's interest may be made subject to accumulation during his own minority. For example, before 1970 property could be settled upon A for life with remainder to his eldest son at 21, with a direction to accumulate income meanwhile if A dies leaving such son under age. If the settlement was made after 1969, accumulation could continue only until the son was 18.

Successive accumulations may be illustrated by the following example.[34] A testator devises the residue of his property to all the children of his sons, whether born before or after his death, the income of their shares to be accumulated during their respective minorities. At the testator's death there is only one child of his sons alive, and she is an infant named D. The whole of the income must be accumulated during this minority, the direction to accumulate falling within the fourth period; for if she was of full age she would for the time being be entitled to the whole of the income. After D attains her majority, a child C is born to one of the testator's sons. C becomes entitled to one-half of the estate, subject to the same liability, *i.e.*, that his share may be partially divested by the birth of other children. During the minority of C, the income from his share must be accumulated, even though the income from the whole of the residuary estate has already been accumulated once.

[31] See *Sidney* v. *Wilmer* (1863) 4 De G.J. & S. 84.
[32] See *Jagger* v. *Jagger* (1883) 25 Ch.D. 729 at 733, as corrected in *Re Cattell* [1914] 1 Ch. 177 at 189.   [33] See *Re Cattell, supra,* at p. 189.
[34] See *Re Cattell* [1914] 1 Ch. 177.

If D had not been born until after the testator's death, there could have been no accumulation under the fourth period until her birth, for not until then would her minority have begun.[35]

(*d*) *Purchase of land.* Where accumulation is directed for the sole [36] purpose of purchasing land, only the fourth period may be selected.[37] But this restriction does not apply to accumulations to be held as capital money under the Settled Land Act, 1925, or any of the Acts which it replaces.[38]

4. Application of rules. These rules apply whether the limitations are contained in a deed or a will,[39] whether the accumulation is at simple or compound interest,[40] whether there is a positive direction or a mere power to accumulate,[41] and whether the whole or any part of the income of a fund is to be accumulated.[42]

B. Excessive Accumulation

1. Exceeding perpetuity period. If the period for which accumulation is directed may possibly exceed the perpetuity period, the direction to accumulate is totally void.[43] This is the original common law rule, and it still operates. Thus where accumulation was directed until a lease with over 60 years to run had "nearly expired," no accumulation at all was permissible.[44] This applies even to accumulations for the benefit of charities.[45]

The Act of 1964 appears to leave this rule of common law unaltered. One might expect that the "wait and see" principle would be applied, but the Act apparently makes no such provision.[46] It is possible that the "wait and see" provisions governing "any

---

[35] *Ellis* v. *Maxwell* (1841) 3 Beav. 587 at 596. The income meanwhile would have fallen into residue or (if there was no residuary gift) would have gone as on intestacy: *post*, p. 508.

[36] *Re Knapp* [1929] 1 Ch. 341.

[37] L.P.A., 1925, s. 166, replacing Accumulations Act, 1892, which introduced this rule for accumulations directed after June 27, 1892; *e.g.*, where a testator dying after that date directs accumulation by a will made before that date: *Re Baroness Llanover (No. 2)* [1903] 2 Ch. 330.

[38] *Supra.*   [39] *Re Lady Rosslyn's Trust* (1848) 16 Sim. 391.

[40] *Re Hawkins* [1916] 2 Ch. 570 at 577; *Re Garside* [1919] 1 Ch. 132 at 137; Marsden 325; *contra*, *Re Pope* [1901] 1 Ch. 64 at 69, 70 and authorities there cited (and see *Union Bank of Scotland* v. *Campbell*, 1929 S.C. 143) for the opinion that only accumulations at compound interest are prohibited. There would seem to be little justification in principle for this opinion. The Perpetuities and Accumulations Act 1964, where it applies, rejects it: s. 13 (2).

[41] *Re Robb* [1953] Ch. 459; Perpetuities and Accumulations Act 1964, s. 13 (2).

[42] *Re Travis* [1900] 2 Ch. 541 (surplus income).

[43] *Marshall* v. *Holloway* (1820) 2 Swans. 432; *Boughton* v. *James* (1844) 1 Coll.C.C. 26 at 45.

[44] *Curtis* v. *Lukin* (1842) 5 Beav. 147.

[45] *Martin* v. *Maugham* (1844) 14 Sim. 230.

[46] S. 3 (1) applies only where an interest may vest too remotely, and remote vesting is not the basis of the rule against accumulations: *ante*, p. 271.

power, option or other right [47] might extend to accumulations, on the reasoning (explained above) that duties are subject to the same rules as apply to powers.[48] This would be straining the language of the Act; but it would perhaps best fulfil its general policy, and may therefore possibly find favour.

2. Exceeding accumulation period

(a) *Excess void.* If the period for which accumulation is directed cannot exceed the perpetuity period but exceeds the relevant accumulation period, the direction to accumulate is good *pro tanto* and only the excess over the appropriate accumulation period is void [49]; for the statutory provisions merely cut down the wider powers permitted by common law.[50]

(b) *Appropriate period.* In determining the appropriate period, the starting point is to ascertain which of the periods the testator or settlor seemingly had in mind,[51] if, indeed, he had any in mind.[52] Thus where accumulation is directed by a deed made *inter vivos* for the lifetime of someone other than the settlor, accumulation takes place during the first of the periods, *i.e.*, during the period common to the lives of the settlor and the named person.[53] But the first period is clearly inapplicable to accumulations directed by will, and in a case such as the above arising under a will, the second period is the most appropriate; accumulation will thus take place for 21 years from the testator's death if the named person so long lives.[54] The second period is also the most appropriate where a will directs accumulation for a period of years,[55] or, until X is 25,[56] or from the time Y remarries until her death,[57] or from the death of either A or B until the death of the survivor,[58] or, in some cases, during an inappropriate minority.[59] In each of these cases, if accumulation is still continuing 21 years after the death of the settlor or testator, it must cease forthwith even if it has been proceeding for only a short period, *e.g.*, two years.[60]

---

[47] s. 3 (3).
[48] *Ante*, p. 250. *Cf*. Act of 1964, s. 13 (2).
[49] Challis 202, 203; *Griffiths* v. *Vere* (1803) 9 Ves. 127; *Eyre* v. *Marsden* (1838) 2 Keen 564 (affirmed, 4 My. & Cr. 231).
[50] *Leake* v. *Robinson* (1817) 2 Mer. 363 at 389.
[51] *Re Watt's W. T.* [1936] 2 All E.R. 1555 at 1562.
[52] See *Re Ransome* [1957] Ch. 348 at 361.
[53] *Re Lady Rosslyn's Trust* (1848) 16 Sim. 391.
[54] *Griffiths* v. *Vere* (1803) 9 Ves. 127; *Talbot* v. *Jevers* (1875) L.R. 20 Eq. 255 (for A's life or such portion of it as the rules of law will permit).
[55] *Longdon* v. *Simson* (1806) 12 Ves. 295 at 298.
[56] *Crawley* v. *Crawley* (1835) 7 Sim. 427; and see *Carey's Trustees* v. *Rose*, 1957 S.C. 252 (trust for unborn person on attaining full age).
[57] *Weatherall* v. *Thornburgh* (1878) 8 Ch.D. 261.
[58] *Webb* v. *Webb* (1840) 2 Beav. 493.
[59] *Re Ransome* [1957] Ch. 348.
[60] *Shaw* v. *Rhodes* (1836) 1 My. & Cr. 135.

(c) *Minorities.* If property is given by will to all the children of X (a living person) who attain their majority, and accumulation of the whole fund is directed while any child of X is an infant, the first two periods are clearly not intended and the fourth is not appropriate, for the accumulation is directed to continue for as long as *any* child is an infant even if some of the children are of full age; even though the latter children are of full age, they are not entitled to the income to be accumulated within the wording of the fourth period. Consequently the third period is the most appropriate, and so far as it is exceeded the direction is void; accumulation will therefore cease as soon as all children living at the testator's death are of full age.[61]

(d) *The Act of* 1964. In the case of settlements made *inter vivos* after July 15, 1964, the fifth or sixth periods may be appropriate.

C. Surplus Income

1. Person entitled. Where a direction to accumulate is void, either wholly or partially, the income so released passes to the persons who would have been entitled had no such accumulation been directed.[62] Thus if a beneficiary is entitled in possession to the enjoyment of the property or to its income, subject only to an excessive trust for accumulation, that beneficiary will be entitled to any income not validly accumulated.[63] For example, where property is given by will to X, subject to a direction that the income exceeding a certain figure is to be accumulated during X's life for the benefit of Y, the accumulation must cease 21 years after the testator's death and the surplus income will go to X.[64] But if there is no such person, as, for example, if X is given a mere annuity of a certain sum and excessive accumulation of the surplus is directed, the surplus after 21 years reverts to the settlor or his estate,[65] or in the case of a will may pass under a residuary gift,[66] or, in default, go to the persons entitled on intestacy.[67]

2. No acceleration. There is no acceleration of subsequent interests.[68] Thus a remainderman whose interest is not to fall into possession until the death of a life annuitant cannot claim surplus

---

[61] *Re Watt's W. T.* [1936] 2 All E.R. 1555.
[62] L.P.A., 1925, s. 164 (1); *Green* v. *Gascoyne* (1865) 4 De G.J. & S. 565.
[63] *Combe* v. *Hughes* (1865) 2 De G.J. & S. 657.
[64] *Trickey* v. *Trickey* (1832) 3 My. & K. 560.   [65] *Re O'Hagen* [1932] W.N. 188.
[66] *O'Neill* v. *Lucas* (1838) 2 Keen 313; *Ellis* v. *Maxwell* (1841) 3 Beav. 587; *Re Ransome* [1957] Ch. 348. The income is treated as income of the residue, not as capital, as between tenant for life and remainderman: *Morgan* v. *Morgan* (1851) 4 De G. & Sm. 164; *Re Garside* [1919] 1 Ch. 132.
[67] *Mathews* v. *Keble* (1868) 3 Ch.App. 691; *Re Walpole* [1933] Ch. 431.
[68] *Green* v. *Gascoyne* (1865) 4 De G.J. & S. 565 at 569; see *Re Parry* (1889) 60 L.T. 489.

income arising before the annuitant's death.[69] The statutory rules do not alter any disposition made by the testator except his direction to accumulate.[70]

D. The Rule in Saunders v. Vautier [71]

1. The rule. Under this rule a beneficiary of full age who has an absolute, vested and indefeasible interest in property may at any time, notwithstanding any direction to accumulate, require the transfer of the property to him and terminate any accumulation. A man may do as he likes with his own, and the court will not enforce a mere restraint on his enjoyment of the property if that restraint cannot benefit any other person.[72] Thus if property is given absolutely to A, aged 10, with a direction to accumulate the income for his benefit until he is 24, A can demand payment of both the original property and the accumulations as soon as he is of full age.[73]

2. Operation. The rule applies equally where a number of adult beneficiaries seeking to put an end to an accumulation together comprise every person who has any vested or contingent interest in the property [74]; and it applies to charities.[75] But it will not apply if there is a gift to a class of persons [76] or charities [77] not yet determined. This remains true, at common law, even if an increase in the class is most improbable, *e.g.*, dependent on a woman of 65 having another child.[78] But the Act of 1964 applies its presumptions as to "future parenthood," already explained,[79] in cases where the disposition took effect after July 15, 1964.[80] An accumulation cannot be terminated at the sole request of a beneficiary whose interest is future, contingent or in any way limited, for in all such cases there are bound to be other persons interested in the accumulation, either actually or potentially.[81] It will be seen that the rule, where it does

---

[69] See *Weatherall* v. *Thornburgh* (1878) 8 Ch.D. 261 at 269, 271, 272; *Berry* v. *Geen* [1938] A.C. 575; *Re Robb* [1953] Ch. 459.
[70] *Eyre* v. *Marsden* (1838) 2 Keen 564 at 574, affirmed 4 My & Cr. 231.
[71] (1841) 4 Beav. 115, affirmed Cr. & Ph. 240.
[72] See *Gosling* v. *Gosling* (1859) Johns. 265 at 272.
[73] *Josselyn* v. *Josselyn* (1837) 9 Sim. 63.
[74] See *Berry* v. *Geen* [1938] A.C. 575 at 582.
[75] *Wharton* v. *Masterman* [1895] A.C. 186.
[76] *Green* v. *Gascoyne* (1865) 4 De G.J. & S. 565.
[77] *Re Jefferies* [1936] 2 All E.R. 626; there is no such entity as "charity": *ibid.*
[78] *Re Deloitte* [1926] Ch. 56. This may one day be reconsidered by the House of Lords: *Berry* v. *Geen* [1938] A.C. 575 at 584.
[79] *Ante*, p. 217.   [80] s. 14.
[81] See *Eyre* v. *Marsden* (1839) 4 My. & Cr. 231; *M'Donald* v. *Bryce* (1838) 2 Keen 276. As to determination of an accumulation of surplus income subject to an annuity (which may raise difficult questions as to the precise rights of the annuitant, who may have an interest in the accumulation if a deficiency of income in any year may be made up out of the accumulated fund), see *Re Travis* [1900] 2 Ch. 541 at 548; *Wharton* v. *Masterman* [1895] A.C. 186; *Harbin* v. *Masterman* [1896] 1 Ch. 351; *Berry* v. *Geen* [1938] A.C. 575; *Re Coller's Deed Trusts* [1939] Ch. 277.

apply, makes the trust for accumulation precarious whether or not it is confined to one of the permitted periods.[82]

E. Exceptions from the Rule against Accumulations

There are the following exceptions from the rule against accumulations.

1. Payment of debts : a provision for accumulation for the payment of the debts of any person.[83] By the terms of the Act this exception includes an accumulation directed for the payment of any debts, whether of the settlor or testator, or any other person.[84] Indeed, an accumulation for the payment of the debts of the settlor or testator is valid even if it may exceed the perpetuity period [85]; such a direction can cause little mischief, for the creditors may terminate the accumulation at any time by demanding payment.[86] But an accumulation to pay the debts of any other person (though not the National Debt [87]) must be confined within the perpetuity period.[88]

The exception extends only to debts deriving from an existing source of obligation [89]; and the accumulation must be directed bona fide for their payment.[90] Subject to this, it may extend both to existing and to contingent debts,[91] as where the object of the accumulation is to discharge a mortgage [92] or to provide for liability under a leasehold covenant not yet broken.[93]

2. Portions : a provision for accumulation for raising portions for any legitimate [94] issue (even if unborn [95]) of the grantor, settlor or testator or any person to whom an interest is limited under the settlement.[96] This is a statutory exception from the rule against accumulations only; such accumulations must be confined to the

---

[82] *Wharton* v. *Masterman* [1895] A.C. 186 at 200.

[83] L.P.A., 1925, s. 164 (2) (i).

[84] *Viscount Barrington* v. *Liddell* (1852) 2 De G.M. & G. 480 at 497, 498.

[85] *Lord Southampton* v. *Marquis of Hertford* (1813) 2 V. & B. 54 at 65; *Bateman* v. *Hotchkin* (1847) 10 Beav. 426.

[86] Gray, § 676.

[87] Superannuation and other Trust Funds (Validation) Act, 1927, s. 9.

[88] See *Viscount Barrington* v. *Liddell* (1852) 2 De G.M. & G. 480 at 498; Marsden 344.

[89] *Re Rochford's S. T.* [1965] Ch. 111 (accumulation for paying estate duty on deaths of living persons not exempted).

[90] *Mathews* v. *Keble* (1868) 3 Ch.App. 691 at 697.

[91] *Varlo* v. *Faden* (1859) 1 De G.F. & J. 211 at 224, 225.

[92] *Bateman* v. *Hotchkin* (1847) 10 Beav. 426 at 433.

[93] *Re Hurlbatt* [1910] 2 Ch. 553.

[94] *Shaw* v. *Rhodes* (1836) 1 My. & Cr. 135 at 159 (on appeal *sub nom. Evans* v. *Hellier* (1837) 5 Cl. & F. 114). But see now Family Law Reform Act 1969, s. 15.

[95] *Beech* v. *Lord St. Vincent* (1850) 3 De G. & Sm. 678.

[96] L.P.A., 1925, s. 164 (2) (ii).

perpetuity period. The meaning of " portions " here is not clear.[97] It is not confined to sums raised out of real estate,[98] nor to provisions for the benefit of the younger children of a marriage [99]; and it applies equally to portions created by the instrument directing accumulation [1] or any other instrument.[2] It does not, however, extend to a direction to accumulate the income from the whole of,[3] or the bulk of,[4] a testator's estate, for " it is not raising a portion at all, it is giving everything." [5] An accumulation for raising portions for the unborn children of X, a beneficiary, and in default of such children for Y, depends upon the event; if X has children it is within the exception, otherwise it is not.[6]

3. Timber or wood : a provision for accumulation of the produce of timber or wood.[7] Although expressly excepted from the statutory accumulation rules, such a direction will be void if it can exceed the perpetuity period.[8]

4. Minority : accumulations made during a minority under the general law or any statutory power.[9] While the person entitled to any trust property is an infant, a statutory power is given to the trustees to apply the income for his maintenance; subject thereto, they are bound to accumulate the residue of the income.[10] Since 1925 it is expressly provided that the period of such accumulation is to be disregarded when determining the period for which accumulations are permitted.[11] Thus if a testator directs accumulation for 21 years after his death and the beneficiary at the end of

---

[97] See *Watt* v. *Wood* (1862) 2 Dr. & Sm. 56 at 60. As to " portions " in their ordinary context, see *post*, p. 385.

[98] *Re Elliott* [1918] 2 Ch. 150 at 153.

[99] *Re Stephens* [1904] 1 Ch. 322.

[1] *Beech* v. *Lord St. Vincent* (1850) 3 De G. & Sm. 678.

[2] *Halford* v. *Stains* (1849) 16 Sim. 488 at 496.

[3] *Wildes* v. *Davies* (1853) 1 Sm. & G. 475.

[4] *Bourne* v. *Buckton* (1851) 2 Sim.(N.S.) 91.

[5] *Edwards* v. *Tuck* (1853) 3 De G.M. & G. 40 at 58, *per* Lord Cranworth L.C.; but see the next sentence in his judgment.

[6] *Re Clulow's Trust* (1859) 1 J. & H. 639.

[7] L.P.A., 1925, s. 164 (2) (iii). This exception is said to be due to the need for naval timber in 1800: Marsden, *Perpetuities*, 346, who also cites Pepys's dictum that " timber is an excrescence of the earth, provided by God for the payment of debts."

[8] *Ferrand* v. *Wilson* (1845) 4 Hare 344.

[9] L.P.A., 1925, s. 165. This is new, but applies whenever the trust was created or the accumulations made.

[10] T.A., 1925, s. 31, replacing C.A., 1881, s. 43. They had to do so in any case, unless otherwise empowered, owing to the inability of an infant to give a binding receipt (as to infants' disabilities, see *post*, p. 988). A *married* infant may now give a valid receipt under L.P.A., 1925, s. 21; but this does not, it seems, apply to an infant who is a widow or a widower.

[11] See note 9, *supra*.

this period is an infant, the accumulations both for the 21 years and during the minority are valid.[12]

5. Maintenance of property : a provision for maintaining property at its present value.[13] If the property is of a wasting nature, it may be kept up out of income; this is not " accumulation " within the meaning of the Act, for the property is never augmented, even though income is added to capital.[14] This head is accordingly not a true exception to the rule but merely a case in which there is no real accumulation. Thus directions to devote surplus income to main-taining buildings in a proper state of repair [15] (as distinct from building new houses [16]), or to apply a fixed annual sum to keep up a " sinking fund " insurance policy to replace the capital lost by the expiry of leaseholds,[17] are outside the statutory rules against accumulations.[18] But an accumulation for replacing the capital lost in payment of estate duty is not within this exception, at any rate if it extends to more than a reasonable proportion of the income.[19]

Dispositions falling within this exception must be confined to the perpetuity period.[20]

6. Certain commercial contracts : transactions which cannot fairly be described as settlements or dispositions. The Act merely provides that no person may " settle or dispose " [21] of property in breach of the restrictions against accumulations, and there are many commercial transactions involving accumulation which are not pro-perly within these terms, *e.g.*, partnership agreements providing for the accumulation of certain profits,[22] certain policies of life insurance,[23] and investment trusts which capitalise part of their income.[24] Such transactions, and provisions for making payments (*e.g.*, of premiums) in respect of them, are accordingly outside the rule; and most of them also fall outside the perpetuity rule as being mere personal obligations sounding in contract.[25]

---

[12] *Re Maber* [1928] Ch. 88.
[13] *Re Gardiner* [1901] 1 Ch. 697 at 699, 700.
[14] *Re Gardiner, supra,* at pp. 699, 700. *A fortiori* if surplus income is not added to capital but is merely retained to meet possible future deficiencies of income for paying annuities: *Re Earl of Berkeley* [1968] Ch. 744.
[15] *Vine* v. *Raleigh* [1891] 2 Ch. 13 ; *Re Mason* [1891] 3 Ch. 467.
[16] *Vine* v. *Raleigh, supra,* at p. 26.
[17] *Re Gardiner* [1901] 1 Ch. 697.
[18] For other examples, see *Bassil* v. *Lister* (1851) 9 Hare 177 at 184.
[19] *Re Rochford's S. T.* [1965] Ch. 111.
[20] *Curtis* v. *Lukin* (1842) 5 Beav. 147.
[21] L.P.A., 1925, s. 164 (1).
[22] See *Bassil* v. *Lister, supra,* at p. 184.
[23] *Ibid.*
[24] *Re A. E. G. Unit Trust (Managers) Ltd.'s Deed* [1957] Ch. 415.
[25] See *ante,* p. 258.

CHAPTER 6

SETTLED LAND AND TRUSTS FOR SALE

Part 1

BEFORE 1883

Sect. 1. Introductory

THE word " settlement " is used in a general sense for all kinds of arrangements whereby property is given to particular persons in succession. If A by his will leaves property to B for life with remainder to C in fee simple, that is a simple type of settlement. Whenever a donor creates a limited interest (an interest less than a fee simple absolute) there will usually be a settlement, since someone will or may be entitled in succession after the limited interest.[1] The essence of a settlement is a series of interests created by a single gift, whether by deed or will. Almost all the examples given in the preceding chapter on future interests are also examples of settlements. Under the title of future interests the question was whether certain remainders and other rights could exist at all. Under the title of settlements must be considered the rights and powers of all the various people having interests in the land, assuming their interests to be valid; and this subject is particularly concerned with the position of the person actually in possession, usually a tenant for life.

The more elaborate types of settlement, such as the old-fashioned marriage settlement,[2] are the product of the settlor's desire to keep his land in the family and to provide carefully for the family's various members. But these transactions have become generally disadvantageous for family properties owing to modern fiscal legislation, particularly death duties. The best policy today is to leave every successive owner as free as possible, so that he can make the most advantageous dispositions from time to time. Nevertheless many family settlements of the old type still exist; and many simple transactions are still governed by the law of settled land, which, as already indicated, applies whenever a testator leaves his house to his widow for her life.

---

[1] Leases are an exception, and do not normally give rise to settlements: *post*, p. 304.
[2] See *post*, p. 384.

282

In the course of time two distinct methods of settling land came into general use; the strict settlement and the trust for sale. The epithet " strict " applies most aptly to the complicated restrictive type of family settlement which flourished before the period of statutory reform. So " settlement " by itself is nowadays used also in a special sense, meaning any settlement which is not made by way of trust for sale. In practice this ambiguity causes no trouble,[3] and " settlement " does double duty both for the genus and for a species.

Sect. 2. The Strict Settlement

1. Evils of settlements

(a) *Form of settlement.* The strict settlement was the classical type of landed settlement, devised with the object of preserving a family estate intact through succeeding generations. In its simplest form it might be, for example, a gift by will to the testator's eldest son for life with remainder to that son's eldest son in tail. A life interest followed by an entail was the most effective limitation for tying up the land, since anything more restrictive would violate the perpetuity rules.[4] The settlement would commonly contain many other provisions to provide for other members of the family, *e.g.,* annuities for widows (known as jointures) and lump sums (known as portions) for younger children, often to be raised by mortgaging the land.[5] The property might thus become burdened with debt, which aggravated the problem of its inalienability.

(b) *Inalienability.* In such cases the land was substantially inalienable until the eldest son became able to bar the entail on attaining his majority. Even then he could create no more than a base fee without the consent of his father, if still alive; and by that time his father would, in his turn, probably regard himself as in duty bound to preserve the property for the sake of yet more distant generations. What often happened was that the son, when he came of age, felt the need of ready money and wished to bar the entail and sell or mortgage his estate in remainder. But his father, instead of consenting to this, would agree to give him some immediate share (perhaps an annual income) in the property if he would join in a resettlement. Father and son would then in collaboration bar the entail, but resettle the property, subject to any outstanding jointure and to the son's annuity, upon the father for life, remainder to the son for life, remainder to the son's eldest son in tail.[6] The land was thus tied up for another generation.

(c) *Sterilisation.* This process of settlement and resettlement had

---

3 Though see, as an example, *Re Leigh's S. E.* (*No.* 1) [1926] Ch. 852 at 857.
4 *Ante,* p. 263.   5 For details see *post,* p. 385.
6 For a more detailed explanation, see 3rd ed. of this book, p. 395.

therefore a self-perpetuating tendency. So long as it continued it
prevented any person of full age from having more than a life estate;
and the tenant in possession of the land was always a tenant for life.
The tenant for life could alienate his life estate, but that was all;
no matter how desirable or necessary it was, he had no power to
sell the fee simple in any part of the land or to grant leases which
would be binding after his death. If improvements to the property
were required, he could effect them only if he paid for them out of
his own pocket. He could not grant long building or mining leases
with adequate security of tenure for the lessee. For many purposes
of management and development the land was sterilised. Settlors
could, and often did, provide extensive powers of management and
even of sale, though the purchase money would have to be paid to
trustees who would hold it for the benefit of all concerned. But often
no such powers were conferred, and then the land was subjected to a
new species of perpetuity, contrary to the public interest which
requires land to be marketable.

(*d*) *The legal estate.* Under the pre-1926 law the legal estate
in settled land might either be split up between the beneficiaries
or vested in trustees, according to the way in which the settlement
was made. For example a conveyance

> " unto and to the use of A for life, remainder to the use of B
> and the heirs of his body, remainder to the use of C and
> his heirs "

gave A a legal life estate, B a legal fee tail and C a legal fee simple.
If the conveyance had been worded

> " unto and to the use of T and his heirs in trust for . . ."

the legal fee simple would have been in T, and A, B and C would
have had merely equitable interests. In the first case, the settlement could confer any desired powers upon A by means of legal
powers operating under the Statute of Uses, 1535 [7]; the settlement
took effect as if the land had been given to A for life and then,
subject to such sales, leases and other authorised dealings as A
made, to B in tail with remainder to C in fee simple.[8] In the
second case, the powers conferred upon A would be merely equitable,
but T was bound to give effect to any authorised disposition made
by A, and the court would compel him to create or transfer the
necessary legal estate.[9]

[7] For such powers, see *ante*, p. 162. Uses were an essential part of the mechanism
of settlements, since legal powers could not be created otherwise: Sanders,
Uses, i, 170.
[8] By the middle of the nineteenth century the power of sale had become " a
somewhat complex and elaborate piece of mechanism ": Davidson, *Precedents
in Conveyancing*, 3rd ed., III, 556.
[9] See *Re Brown* (1886) 32 Ch.D. 597 at 601.

2. Statutory reform. The fetters were gradually removed from settled land by statutes passed in the nineteenth century. Limited powers to charge the cost of improvements on the land were given by the Settled Estates Drainage Acts, 1840 and 1845, the Improvement of Land Act, 1864, and the Limited Owners Residences Acts, 1870 and 1871. More generally, the Settled Estates Acts of 1856 and 1877 empowered the court to authorise certain dealings with settled land, such as sales and certain leases; and they empowered the tenant for life by himself to grant leases for not more than twenty-one years on specified conditions. The latter Act, though in force until 1926, was largely superseded by the Settled Land Act, 1882, drafted by Mr. Wolstenholme and piloted through Parliament by Lord Cairns.[10] This was a comprehensive piece of legal reform, much of which is still in substance operative today. But before it can be explained it is necessary to consider briefly the other kind of settlement, the trust for sale.

Sect. 3. Trusts for Sale

1. Objects of trusts for sale. A trust for sale is a trust which directs the trustees to sell the trust property, invest the proceeds, and hold the resulting fund upon the trusts declared by the settlor. Its objects and operation are therefore quite different from those of a strict settlement. Instead of aiming to preserve a family estate against sales, mortgages, or other vicissitudes, as did the old type of strict settlement, the trust for sale set out by treating the property as so much potential money. Dividing it among the family was therefore easy, and there was the convenience that a mixed fund of land and personalty could be disposed of under the same set of trusts. This form of settlement was ideal for settling fortunes made in commerce, and for this reason trusts for sale were sometimes called " traders' settlements."

2. Origin of trusts for sale. It is therefore not surprising that, compared with strict settlements, settlements by way of trust for sale are of comparatively recent origin. It is true that trusts for sale created by will can be traced back for some 500 years, but most of the earliest of these trusts seem to have been designed to raise sums of money, *e.g.*, for the payment of debts, rather than to provide for persons by way of succession. Trusts for sale created *inter vivos* are more recent in origin; not until about a century ago do marriage settlements by way of trust for sale appear to have become at all common.[11]

---

[10] For an excellent account of the changes in the law of settled land, see Underhill's lecture, printed in *A Century of Law Reform* (1901), 281–297, and *Select Essays in Anglo-American Legal History* (1909) III, 674–686.

[11] See J. M. Lightwood, (1927) 3 C.L.J. 62.

3. Position pending sale.   In a trust for sale the legal estate was vested in the trustees upon trust to sell the land and hold the income until sale and the proceeds thereafter upon specified trusts for the beneficiaries.   The trustees were usually given power to postpone sale in their discretion, and to manage the land until sale.   Thus the trustees did not have to sell until market conditions were suitable. Often the consent of the beneficiaries entitled in possession was made requisite to a sale, so that they could, if they wished, enjoy the property specifically, as by living in a house, or enjoying the rents if the land was let.   The purchase-money arising on a sale was usually directed to be invested in stocks, shares and other securities,[12] and then held upon trusts for the members of the family.   These trusts would often provide for life interests, widows' annuities, remainders to children, and so on, much after the style of a strict settlement.[13] But there was one important difference: until 1926 no entail could be created under a trust for sale, for the reasons given in the next paragraph.

4. The doctrine of conversion.   The effect of creating a trust for sale is that even before sale the rights of the beneficiaries are for certain purposes deemed to be rights in personalty.   This is a case of equity treating that as done which ought to be done.[14]   As soon as there is a binding obligation to sell (including the making of any necessary request, where the trust is to sell on request[15]), the interests of the beneficiaries are notionally converted into the money into which the land is destined to be converted.[16]   Even if there is a power to invest the proceeds of sale in the purchase of other land, that land will, unless there is some provision to the contrary, be held on trust for sale[17] and so be treated as money.   Correspondingly, if money is directed to be laid out in the purchase of land, it is forthwith treated as land[18]; and a trust to sell land and purchase other land with the proceeds of sale works a double conversion, so that the interests of the beneficiaries remain land throughout.[19]

This is the equitable doctrine of conversion.[20]   It rests on the principle that it would be wrong that the precise moment at which the trustees carried out their administrative duty of selling should

---

[12] See Davidson's *Precedents in Conveyancing*, 3rd ed., III, 711, 712, 868.
[13] For details, see *post*, p. 384.
[14] See, *e.g.*, *Lechmere* v. *Earl of Carlisle* (1733) 3 P.Wms. 211 at 215; *Guidot* v. *Guidot* (1745) 3 Atk. 254 at 256.
[15] See *Re Goswell's Trusts* [1915] 2 Ch. 106; Wh. & T. i, 308.
[16] *Fletcher* v. *Ashburner* (1779) 1 Bro.C.C. 497; *cf. Re Walker* [1908] 2 Ch. 705; *Stevens* v. *Hutchinson* [1953] Ch. 299.
[17] L.P.A., 1925, s. 32.
[18] Wh. & T. i, 301; *Re Scarth* (1879) 10 Ch.D. 499.
[19] See Wh. & T. i, 309.
[20] See generally, Snell, *Equity*, 467.

determine whether the rights of the beneficiaries were realty or personalty, especially where a delay in selling might be due to a breach of trust.[21] For important rights can depend on the character of the property: before 1926, for example, realty and personalty descended to different persons on intestacy, and a testator may still give his realty to one person and his personalty to another. A devise of " all my realty to R and all my personalty to P " by a person having a vested remainder under a trust for sale gives his interest to P, even though the property is land which has not yet been sold by the trustees.[22] It is more equitable that the interests of the beneficiaries should be treated as personalty from the start, as the settlor contemplated, so that they would not be affected by the exercise of the trust for sale.

The consequences of the doctrine have in general been followed out logically: thus there could be no entail under a trust for sale made before 1926,[23] since personalty was not entailable.[24] This explains why trusts for sale were sometimes called " personalty settlements " even when they comprised land. However, when one or more beneficiaries are absolutely entitled to the whole beneficial interest under a trust for sale, he or they can elect to treat the property as land and so put an end to the fiction that it is personalty[25]; and if for any reason a trust for sale comes to an end before the land is sold, the beneficial interest in it is reconverted into an interest in land.[26]

The doctrine of conversion does not therefore alter the fact that the primary rights of the beneficiaries are that the land shall be held and sold for their benefit. Without owning " land," they are " interested in land," [27] and they own an " interest in land " within certain statutory provisions [28]; and unless duly overreached,[29] their rights prevail against all save a purchaser of a legal estate without notice.[30] But the individual interest of one of several beneficiaries is not an " interest in land " for the purpose of making a charging order on it,[31] though the collective interests of those who own the entire legal and beneficial interest are within this term.[32]

---

21 Maitland, *Equity*, 277.
22 *Re Kempthorne* [1930] 1 Ch. 268; *post*, p. 415; Wh. & T. i, 359.
23 *Cf. post*, p. 417.   24 *Ante*, p. 94.
25 *Re Lord Grimthorpe* [1908] 1 Ch. 666 ; [1908] 2 Ch. 675; Wh. & T. i, 316.
26 For an example, see *Re Cook* [1948] Ch. 212, *post*, p. 415.
27 *Elias* v. *Mitchell* [1972] Ch. 652 (L.R.A., 1925, ss. 3, 54).
28 *Cooper* v. *Critchley* [1955] Ch. 431 (L.P.A., 1925, s. 40: *obiter*); *post*, pp. 416, 549. For the statutes, see Snell, *Equity*, 468. Contrast cases such as *Barclay* v. *Barclay* [1970] 2 Q.B. 677 at 684, 685 (" no interest in " the land; " simply an interest in personal estate ").
29 *Ante*, p. 149.   30 *Post*, p. 378.
31 *Irani Finance Ltd.* v. *Singh* [1971] Ch. 59.
32 *National Westminster Bank Ltd.* v. *Allan* [1971] 2 Q.B. 718.

The practice of making trusts for sale *inter vivos* by two separate documents is explained later.[33]

Part 2

THE SETTLED LAND ACT, 1882

The Settled Land Act, 1882, which was passed as the result of a period of agricultural depression, had as its paramount object the liberation of settled land from legal restrictions which often made good management impossible.[34] " The leading purpose of the legislature was to prevent the decay of agricultural and other interests occasioned by the deterioration of lands and buildings in the possession of impecunious life-tenants," [35] and to " strike off the fetters against alienation which in process of time had become attached to land." [36] The general scheme of the Act was to give the tenant for life under the settlement wide powers of dealing with the land free from the trusts of the settlement without the consent of the other beneficiaries, or application to the court, just as if he were owner in fee simple; the rights of the beneficiaries were protected in the case of a sale by shifting the settlement from the land to the purchase-money, which had to be paid into court or into the hands of the trustees. The purchaser would have no concern with the trusts of the settlement. The effect was therefore not very different from that of a trust for sale. " Keeping the land in the family " was gone for ever.

A brief account of the main framework of the Act of 1882 will serve as an introduction to the Act of 1925.

Sect. 1. Settled Land

A. Definition of Settled Land

The key to the definition of settled land is a succession of interests. The definition covered any land, or any estate or interest in land, which under any document stood for the time being limited to, or in trust for, any persons by way of succession.[37] The term " settlement " in the Act meant the document itself rather than the state of

---

[33] *Post,* pp. 298, 363.
[34] See *Re Mundy & Roper's Contract* [1899] 1 Ch. 275 at 288.
[35] *Lord Henry Bruce* v. *Marquess of Ailesbury* [1892] A.C. 356 at 363, *per* Lord Watson.
[36] *Cardigan* v. *Curzon-Howe* (1885) 30 Ch.D. 531 at 537, *per* Chitty J.
[37] S.L.A., 1882, s. 2.

affairs produced by it. Thus if freehold or leasehold [38] land was conveyed by deed or given by will

> "unto and to the use of A and his heirs in trust for X for
> life, remainder in trust for Y and his heirs"

or freehold land was conveyed

> "to A for life remainder to B and his heirs," or
> "to X and his heirs to the use of Y and the heirs of his
> body"

in each case the land was settled land. In the third case the requirement that there should be an element of succession was satisfied by the resulting use in fee simple to the grantor subject to Y's entail. Thus every grant or devise of a limited interest (*e.g.*, for life, in tail, or for a conditional or determinable [39] fee) created a succession, and therefore a settlement. It made no difference whether the interests were legal or equitable.

The Act also extended to land held by, or in trust for, infants [40]; and this was so even where there was no succession, as for example where a testator devised land to his infant son in fee simple. This was in order to make an infant's land marketable notwithstanding his legal privilege of revoking any transaction when he came of age, a privilege which naturally discouraged purchasers. [41] The Act enabled an infant's land to be sold irrevocably by the trustees of the settlement acting on his behalf, [42] without the consent of his parents or guardians, [43] with the usual safeguard that the purchase-money had to be held by the trustees until the infant came of age. Similarly the Act conferred full powers of management.

B. Powers of the Tenant for Life

1. The powers. The object of the Act was to give to one person wide powers of sale, [44] exchange, [45] leasing, [46] mortgaging [47] and otherwise dealing with the land. That person was the tenant for life [48] or other limited owner in possession, [49] such as a tenant in tail, tenant in fee simple subject to a gift over, or person entitled to a

---

[38] *Re Mundy & Roper's Contract* [1899] 1 Ch. 275 at 291.
[39] It is perhaps not quite clear that a determinable fee fell within s. 58 (1) (ii).
[40] S.L.A., 1882, s. 59.
[41] *Post*, p. 988.
[42] S.L.A., 1882, s. 60.
[43] See *Re Duke of Newcastle's Estate* (1883) 24 Ch.D. 129 at 142.
[44] S.L.A., 1882, s. 3 (i).
[45] *Ibid.*, s. 3 (iii).
[46] *Ibid.*, s. 6.
[47] *Ibid.*, s. 18.
[48] *Ibid.*, s. 2 (5).
[49] "Possession" included receipt of income: *ibid.*, s. 2 (10) (i).

base fee.[50] For convenience, the phrase " tenant for life " is used to include not only those who had an actual life estate, but any other person who had the powers of a tenant for life; the Act drew no distinction between them.[51] If the tenant for life was an infant, the trustees of the settlement could exercise the statutory powers on the infant's behalf,[52] and give any necessary approval *qua* trustees.[53]

2. Powers fiduciary. These extensive powers were given in the interests of the settled estate as a whole, and not merely for the personal benefit of the tenant for life. He could exercise them as he thought best, but in so doing the Act required him to have regard to the interests of the other beneficiaries: in relation to the exercise of the powers by him, he was deemed to be a trustee for all parties,[54] including himself, so that his was " a highly interested trusteeship." [55] The court could therefore intervene if he sought to sell at a price well below the value of the property,[56] or to make an investment which, although not outside his powers, was undesirable,[57] or to effect any transaction which, though within his powers, would prejudice other beneficiaries.[58] In one case a tenant for life who was a total abstainer was restrained from leasing a public-house on the terms that no intoxicating liquor should be sold there, for that would have reduced the value of settled property.[59] But the court would not intervene on speculative evidence as to prospective value, *e.g.*, as to an increase in value if a Bill for the construction of a railway which might run through the estate were passed by Parliament.[60]

3. Exercise of discretion. Even if there would be no pecuniary loss, an exercise of the powers not made bona fide would be restrained. Thus although a lease was not necessarily bad because it was granted to the spouse of the tenant for life,[61] if the interest of

---

[50] *Ibid.*, s. 58 (1).
[51] *Re Jones* (1883) 24 Ch.D. 583 at 586.
[52] S.L.A., 1882, s. 60.
[53] *Re Greys Court Estate* [1901] W.N. 60.
[54] S.L.A., 1882, s. 53. The cases on this section are collected in Carson's *Real Property Statutes*, 3rd ed., 966, 967.
[55] *Re Earl of Stamford and Warrington* [1916] 1 Ch. 404 at 420, *per* Younger J.
[56] *Wheelwright* v. *Walker (No.* 1) (1883) 23 Ch.D. 752 at 762.
[57] *Re Hunt's S. E.* [1905] 2 Ch. 418 ; [1906] 2 Ch. 11.
[58] See *Hampden* v. *Earl of Buckinghamshire* [1893] 2 Ch. 531 at 544.
[59] *Re Earl Somers, deceased* (1895) 11 T.L.R. 567. The main purpose of the Act was to secure " the welfare of the land itself, and all interested therein, including the tenants, and not merely of the persons taking under the settlement ": *Re Mundy & Roper's Contract* [1899] 1 Ch. 275 at 288, *per* Lindley M.R. and Chitty L.J.
[60] *Thomas* v. *Williams* (1883) 24 Ch.D. 558.
[61] *Gilbey* v. *Rush* [1906] 1 Ch. 11 at 16–20.

the tenant for life would cease on remarriage she would not be allowed to lease the property to her intended husband in order that she might continue to live in the house, since this was merely a device for giving herself longer enjoyment than the settlement intended.[62] A tenant for life must " exercise his discretion as if he were an independent trustee for himself and all the other members of the family—that is, he is to exercise his discretion as a fair and honest and careful trustee would under the circumstances." [63] Nevertheless, provided a transaction was otherwise a proper one, it would not be invalidated merely because the tenant for life was motivated by selfishness or even malice, *e.g.*, that " he is selling out of ill will or caprice, or because he does not like the remainderman, because he desires to be relieved from the trouble of attending to the management of land, or from any other such object, or with any such motive." [64]

4. Powers unfettered. Subject to this restriction, the tenant for life was in general unfettered in the exercise of his powers. They could not be taken away or cut down either directly or indirectly,[65] nor could he curtail or divest himself of them or effectively contract not to exercise them.[66] Additional or larger powers could be conferred by the settlor on the tenant for life or the trustees,[67] and the Act in no way restricted such powers.[68] Indeed, it assisted them, for it provided that they should operate as if conferred by the Act [69]; and thus they were safeguarded against the perpetuity rule,[70] just like the purely statutory powers conferred upon all tenants for life.[71]

Where, however, powers which the Act already conferred on the tenant for life were conferred on the trustees by the settlement (as distinct, for example, from a private Act which merely conferred powers without forming part of the settlement [72]), the terms of the Act prevailed,[73] and the trustees were unable to exercise such powers

---

[62] *Middlemas* v. *Stevens* [1901] 1 Ch. 574; and see *Dowager Duchess of Sutherland* v. *Duke of Sutherland* [1893] 3 Ch. 169.

[63] *Re The Earl of Radnor's W. T.* (1890) 45 Ch.D. 402 at 417, *per* Lord Esher M.R.

[64] *Cardigan* v. *Curzon-Howe* (1885) 30 Ch.D. 531 at 540, *per* Chitty J.

[65] S.L.A., 1882, ss. 51, 52; for illustrations of the effect of this provision, see *post*, p. 351.

[66] S.L.A., 1882, s. 50; but the rights of an assignee for value of the tenant for life's interest were protected: see *post*, p. 355.

[67] S.L.A., 1882, s. 57.

[68] *Ibid.*, s. 56 (1).

[69] *Ibid.*, s. 57.

[70] *Ante*, p. 251.

[71] See Wolst. & C. iii, 1.

[72] *Talbot* v. *Scarisbrick* [1908] 1 Ch. 812.

[73] See *Earl of Lonsdale* v. *Lowther* [1900] 2 Ch. 687.

without the consent of the tenant for life,[74] though this need not be in writing.[75] Furthermore, the trusteeship imposed upon him did not affect his exercise of powers vested in him not by the Act but by virtue of his beneficial interest in the land. Thus if a tenant for life received payment for accepting a surrender of a lease and had power to do this by virtue of the life estate vested in him, he could retain it, whether the lease had been granted under a power in the settlement [76] or a power in the Act.[77] Again, a tenant for life unimpeachable of waste could exercise his common law right to sue for and retain damages for dilapidations by a lessee, even though the lease was granted under statutory powers.[78]

The tenant for life was thus normally in complete control of the land, even if he was " a spendthrift, who has ruined himself by his own extravagance and folly, who has brought disgrace on the family name, and who has exposed the family estate to destruction for the rest of his life." [79]

C. The Trustees of the Settlement

The Act contained an elaborate definition of the persons who were the trustees of the settlement,[80] but in any settlement made after 1882 they normally consisted of those persons expressly appointed as trustees of the settlement for the purposes of the Act. It is important to note that whether or not the legal estate was vested in the trustees,[81] they had no real control over the land. Their main function was to receive and hold any capital money, *e.g.*, when land was sold; and for certain transactions the tenant for life had to give them prior notice or, in a few cases, obtain their consent.[82]

D. Effect of a Sale or Other Dealing

The effect of a dealing with the settled land such as a sale was that the rights of the beneficiaries under the settlement were over-reached (*i.e.*, removed from the land and transferred to the purchase-

---

74 S.L.A., 1882, s. 56 (2). See, *e.g.*, *Re Osborne & Bright's Ltd.* [1902] 1 Ch. 335.
75 *Re Pope's Contract* [1911] 2 Ch. 442.
76 *Re Hunloke's S. E.* [1902] 1 Ch. 941. But see *contra, Re Rodes* [1909] 1 Ch. 815, where an equitable tenant for life was held to accept the surrender as trustee. In principle there should have been no difference between the position of legal and equitable tenants for life.
77 *Re Penrhyn's Settlement* [1922] 1 Ch. 500. See now S.L.A., 1925, ss. 52 (7), 81; *post*, p. 350.
78 *Re Lacon's Settlement* [1911] 2 Ch. 17; compare *Re Pyke* [1912] 1 Ch. 770, and see now S.L.A., 1925, s. 80.
79 *Re Marquis of Ailesbury's S. E.* [1892] 1 Ch. 506 at 535, *per* Lindley L.J.
80 S.L.A., 1882, s. 2 (8); S.L.A., 1890, s. 16. The present definition of Settled Land Act trustees is substantially the same: see *post*, p. 324.
81 This depended on the way in which the settlement was made: see *ante*, p. 284.
82 As under the Act of 1925: *post*, pp. 331, 340, 357.

money) provided that the money was paid to the trustees, being not less than two in number, or into court.[1] This was so whether the legal estate was vested in trustees or split up between the beneficiaries. A tenant for life had a statutory power to convey something not vested in him, namely, the whole legal estate. The capital money in the hands of the trustees, which had to be invested in accordance with the Act,[2] was treated as if it were the land " for the purposes of disposition, transmission, and devolution." [3] " The effect of a sale under the Settled Land Act is merely to substitute money for land, and whatever rights persons had in the land are preserved to them in the money produced in its sale." [4]

For example, if land was settled on " A for life, remainder to B for life, remainder to C and his heirs," the effect of a sale by A was to vest the legal fee simple in the purchaser, free from the legal rights of A, B and C, who took corresponding rights in the capital money. Thus C had a fee simple in remainder in the capital money, which on his death would pass with the rest of his realty under his will or, if he was intestate, to his heir.[5] Had his remainder been in tail, it would (if unbarred) have passed to his heir of the body, so that in this way there could be produced an entail of personalty even before 1926.[6] This statutory fiction (which, however, did not extend so far as to make words of limitation necessary to pass more than a life interest in the money [7]) continued until the money finally came into the hands of someone absolutely entitled.[8] If the land was conveyed " unto and to the use of " trustees on trust for the beneficiaries, the position was exactly the same: A's statutory power of sale enabled him to transfer to the purchaser the legal estate vested in the trustees.

It made no difference, of course, that the purchaser had notice of the beneficial interests. For whether they were legal or equitable, they were overreached because it was so ordained by statute,[9] and not for any other reason.

Sect. 2. Trusts for Sale

1. The Acts of 1882 and 1884. The original draft of the Act of 1882 did not apply to land held on trust for sale,[10] but " the

---

[1] S.L.A., 1882, ss. 20, 22 (5), 39 (1).   [2] *Ibid.*, s. 22.
[3] *Ibid.*, s. 22 (5); and see *post*, p. 376.
[4] *Hampden* v. *Earl of Buckinghamshire* [1893] 2 Ch. 531 at 544, *per* Lindley L.J.
[5] See *Re Bond* [1901] 1 Ch. 15.
[6] *Cf. ante*, p. 94.
[7] *Re Monckton's Settlement* [1913] 2 Ch. 636; *Re Nutt's Settlement* [1915] 2 Ch. 431.
[8] S.L.A., 1882, s. 21 (ix).
[9] *Ibid.*, s. 20 (2).
[10] See 27 S.J. 113; 28 S.J. 703; *Re Harding's Estate* [1891] 1 Ch. 60 at 63.

unprompted wisdom of Parliament "[11] added a section (s. 63), "drafted in a fine style of perplexed verbiage," [12] which provided that such land was to be deemed settled land, and thus within the Act, if the proceeds of sale or income were to be applied or disposed of for any person or persons for life or any other limited period. The apparent effect of this was that all the powers, including that of sale, belonged to the life beneficiary and not to the trustees. Consternation among conveyancers resulted in the Settled Land Act, 1884,[13] which provided that in the case of trusts for sale the tenant for life should be unable to exercise the powers of the Act of 1882 without an order of the court, and that until such an order was made, the trustees could sell without the consent of the tenant for life.[14] A purchaser could safely deal with the trustees for sale unless such an order had been registered as a *lis pendens* (pending action).[15]

Although the Act of 1884 restored the trustees' power of sale it did nothing to equip them with other powers of management (*e.g.*, of leasing) which they might need if sale was postponed. This therefore became a disadvantage of the trust for sale.

2. Trust for sale or power of sale. After the Act of 1884 it became a matter of vital importance, especially to a purchaser of the settled land, to know whether a trust for sale existed or not. If it did, and no order of the court had been made, a purchaser could get a good title only from the trustees. In any other case he could get a good title only from the tenant for life. For conveyancing purposes, therefore, it was essential to keep trusts for sale sharply distinguished from other settlements. But this was not always a simple matter, for the settlement itself might not be clearly drawn. A mere *power* of sale given to trustees [16] was not a *trust* for sale: there had to be some obligation upon the trustees to sell, in the sense (familiar in the law of trusts) of an imperative *trust* as opposed to a discretionary *power*. But trusts and powers often shade into one another, and a *trust* to sell with a *power* to postpone sale had to be distinguished from a *trust* to retain with a *power* to sell; even words such as "upon trust to sell" might not create a trust for sale if the context showed that a mere power was intended.[17]

A power to postpone sale indefinitely was consistent with, and commonly found in, a trust for sale.[18] Thus a trust to sell with the

---

[11] 27 S.J. 113.
[12] 28 S.J. 322.
[13] s. 7.
[14] S.L.A., 1884, s. 6 (1).
[15] *Ibid.*, s. 7 (vi); *post*, p. 1037.
[16] As in *Re Clitheroe Estate* (1885) 31 Ch.D. 135.
[17] *Re Hotchkys* (1886) 32 Ch.D. 408; *Re Newbould* (1913) 110 L.T. 6.
[18] *Re Johnson* [1915] 1 Ch. 435.

consent of X, or at his request, was nonetheless an immediately effective trust for sale,[19] for X had no more than a discretionary power to postpone sale. But if the trust was merely to sell at the request of a person who was also empowered to give a binding direction to the trustees never to sell, there was no effective trust for sale,[20] at all events until that person had requested a sale. Again, if a trust for sale was exercisable only at some future date,[21] or only on a few very limited contingencies,[22] it was not a trust for sale within the meaning of the Act. A trust " to retain or sell the land " was a borderline case: it might or might not be construed as a trust for sale, depending upon whether the general intention of the settlement was that the land should be sold [23] or that it should be retained as land.[24]

3. Bare trusts. It should be noted that the Settled Land Acts never applied to a trust where one or more persons of full age were entitled in possession absolutely, *i.e.*, where there was no element of succession and no infancy, whether there was a trust for sale or not.[25] Thus a conveyance " unto and to the use of A and his heirs in trust for B and C and their heirs " created a bare or simple trust which was not within the Acts.[26] The position is the same today.

Part 3

THE SETTLED LAND ACT, 1925

The Settled Land Act, 1925, continued the policy of the Act of 1882, making certain extensions and alterations of the statutory powers. In substance the position of a tenant for life is little changed; although the Act of 1882 is repealed, the powers (as amended) are set out again in the Act of 1925. But, as part of the wider design of the 1925 legislation to improve the system of conveyancing, important changes have been made in the legal machinery by which settlements are made and settled land is disposed of. In the following account of the Act of 1925 these new principles will be considered first.

---

[19] *Re Childs' Settlement* [1907] 2 Ch. 348 (request); *Re Wagstaff's S. E.* [1909] 2 Ch. 201 (request or consent); *Re Ffennell's Settlement* [1918] 1 Ch. 91 (consent). *Quaere* how far *Re Childs' Settlement, supra,* is reconcilable with *Re Goodall's Settlement, infra.*
[20] *Re Goodall's Settlement* [1909] 1 Ch. 440 and see *Re Wagstaff's S. E., supra,* at p. 205.
[21] *Re Horne's S. E.* (1888) 39 Ch.D. 84.
[22] *Re Smith and Lonsdale's Contract* (1934) 78 S.J. 173.
[23] *Re Johnson* [1915] 1 Ch. 435; and see *Re Crips* (1907) 95 L.T. 865.
[24] *Re White's Settlement* [1930] 1 Ch. 179.
[25] See, *e.g., Re Earle and Webster's Contract* (1883) 24 Ch.D. 144.
[26] See, *e.g., Re British Land Co. and Allen's Contract* (1900) 44 S.J. 593; for these trusts, see *post,* p. 438.

Sect. 1.   Principal Alterations Made by the Act of 1925

A.   *Trusts for Sale are Excluded from the Act*

Land subject to " an immediate binding trust for sale " [27] is expressly excluded from the definition of settled land.[28]   Trusts for sale are now governed by the Law of Property Act, 1925, and are considered later under a separate head.[29]   If a trust for sale arises the Settled Land Act cannot apply, even if the land was previously settled. Thus under a settlement upon A for life with remainder to trustees for sale the Settled Land Act applies during A's life but ceases to apply at his death.[30]

B.   *The Legal Estate is Normally in the Tenant for Life*

Before 1926 the legal estate in settled land was either vested in trustees or split up between the beneficiaries, depending upon how the settlement was made [31]; in either case, the tenant for life was enabled to deal with it by his statutory powers.   After 1925 the settlor has no choice: apart from the exceptions stated below, the whole legal estate is always vested in the tenant for life; and this legal estate will usually be a fee simple absolute in possession.[32] This is given to the tenant for life not for his personal benefit (for he is trustee of it, as of the other statutory privileges [33]) but in order to make the system of conveyancing more logical.   Instead of being endowed with a power to sell or administer a legal fee simple which he had not got, the tenant for life is now actually invested with the legal fee simple itself.   But since he must still be prevented from taking advantage of it except for proper purposes, his powers as fee simple owner are still artificially restricted,[34] so that the new system represents primarily a change of forms.   By this means, tracing title to the legal estate has been made a somewhat simpler task and the position of a purchaser has been improved.   This is explained below.[35]

---

[27] S.L.A., 1925, s. 117 (1) (xxx), referring to L.P.A., 1925, s. 205 (1) (xxix); the meaning of this phrase is discussed *post*, p. 359.
[28] S.L.A., 1925, s. 1 (7), added by L.P.(Am.)A., 1926, Sched.
[29] *Post*, p. 358.
[30] *Post*, p. 358.
[31] *Ante*, p. 284.
[32] *Ante*, p. 137.   Other interests in land (*e.g.*, leaseholds) may also be settled, but they are less common.
[33] *Post*, p. 350.
[34] *Post*, p. 313.
[35] *Post*, p. 306.

Where a settlement is made after 1925, the legal estate must be conveyed to the tenant for life, unless, of course, it is already vested in him,[36] as is the case where the owner of property settles it upon himself as tenant for life, with remainders over (" with remainders over " is a concise way of referring to the remainders following the life interest without setting them out in detail). In the case of a settlement made before 1926, the legal estate was automatically vested in the tenant for life at the first moment of 1926.[37]

Thus today the tenant for life is not only a trustee of the statutory powers, as he was before 1926, but he is also (and this is new) a trustee of the legal estate; both the powers[38] and the estate[39] are vested in him on trust for himself and the other beneficiaries under the settlement. This demonstrates the dual capacity of a tenant for life: he holds two interests in the land, the legal estate as trustee and his own interest beneficially.[40] In the usual case where his beneficial interest is a life or other limited interest, this must now of course be equitable, *i.e.*, he is trustee for himself to this extent.

In two cases, however, the legal estate and statutory powers are vested, not in a tenant for life, but in the " statutory owner." These two cases are as follows.

1. Tenant for life an infant. A legal estate cannot be vested in an infant after 1925[41] and it would be undesirable to give him the statutory powers. Consequently where the person who would otherwise be the tenant for life is an infant, the legal estate and the statutory powers are vested in the statutory owner, who is—

(i) any personal representative in whom the land is vested, provided no vesting instrument[42] has been executed, *e.g.*, where the settlement has been made by the will of a testator who has just died; but otherwise,

(ii) the trustees of the settlement.[43]

---

[36] S.L.A., 1925, s. 4 (2).

[37] L.P.A., 1925, 1st Sched., Pt. II, para. 6 (*c*).

[38] S.L.A., 1925, s. 107 (1), replacing S.L.A., 1882, s. 53; the former decisions (*ante*, p. 290) thus still apply.

[39] S.L.A., 1925, s. 16 (1); see *Re Boston's W. T.* [1956] Ch. 395 (esp. at p. 405); (1956) 72 L.Q.R. 328 (R.E.M.). For the power of a tenant for life to acquire the settled land or part of it, see *post*, p. 350.

[40] See *Re Liberty's W. T.* [1937] Ch. 176.

[41] L.P.A., 1925, s. 1 (6); *post*, p. 988.

[42] *Post*, p. 300.

[43] S.L.A., 1925, ss. 26 (powers) and 117 (1) (xxvi) (definition); *ibid.*, s. 4 (2), and L.P.A., 1925, 1st Sched., Pt. II, paras. 3, 5, 6 (*c*) (legal estate). Where a personal representative is the statutory owner, he must follow the directions of the trustees of the settlement: S.L.A., 1925, s. 26 (2).

2. No tenant for life. Where under a settlement there is no tenant for life,[44] the legal estate and statutory powers are vested in the statutory owner, who is—

(i) any person of full age upon whom the settlement [45] expressly confers the powers [46]; if none,

(ii) the trustees of the settlement.[47]

The question who is a tenant for life and the cases where there is no tenant for life are dealt with below.[48] For the present it is sufficient to say that there usually is a tenant for life but that in some cases there is not, *e.g.*, where the first life interest is not to begin until marriage, or until after a period of accumulation. In such cases the Act of 1925 has effected a considerable improvement, for before 1926 the land could often not be dealt with at all.[49] And in all cases it preserves the principle that the legal estate and the managerial powers should not be separated.

It should be noted, however, that the legal estate is never vested in the trustees of the settlement as such: they may hold it only in some other capacity, such as statutory owner [50] or special personal representatives.[51]

C. All Settlements Must be Made by Two Documents

Before 1926 a settlement was usually made by one document. If the settlement was made by will, the will constituted the settlement; a settlement *inter vivos* was made by deed. The result was that if the land was sold, the purchaser had to examine the lengthy, and, for this purpose, mainly irrelevant, provisions of the settlement in order to discover the principal facts essential to his obtaining a good title; these were normally—

(i) that the land he had agreed to buy was included in the settlement;

(ii) that the person who had agreed to sell to him was the duly constituted tenant for life; and

(iii) that the persons to whom he was proposing to pay the purchase-money were the duly appointed trustees of the settlement.

---

41 See *post*, p. 324.
45 This includes the last document of a compound settlement: S.L.A., 1925, s. 1 (1); *Re Beaumont S. E.* [1937] 2 All E.R. 353.
46 See, *e.g.*, *Re Craven S. E.* [1926] Ch. 985; *Re Norton* [1929] 1 Ch. 84.
47 S.L.A., 1925, ss. 23 (powers) and 117 (1) (xxvi) (definition); *ibid.*, s. 4 (2), and L.P.A., 1925, 1st Sched., Pt. II, paras. 3, 5 and 6 (*c*) (legal estate). For a further case of a statutory owner, see S.L.A., 1925, s. 23 (2), *post*, p. 321, n. 19.
48 *Post*, p. 320.
49 See, *e.g.*, *Re Horne's S. E.* (1888) 39 Ch.D. 84; *Re Astor* [1922] 1 Ch. 364.
50 *Supra*.   51 *Post*, p. 309.

To discover these facts was often a tedious task, for the settlement was a long document setting out the trusts in full and a purchaser often had to waste time in reading clauses which were of no interest to him in order to ascertain a few simple facts. There were corresponding inconveniences to the beneficiaries and trustees. Not only were the details of the family's interests exposed to a stranger's eye,[52] but the document containing them would either belong to the purchaser as one of his title deeds, or would be subject to inspection at his or his successor's demand whenever there was occasion to prove title in future.[53]

The Act meets these difficulties by adopting what has long been the practice of conveyancers in the case of trusts for sale made *inter vivos*.[54] There also the instrument setting out the trusts was one which the trustees would wish to retain, while the conveyance to the trustees was an essential link in the purchaser's title. Since, from the moment of sale, the beneficial interests were to be interests in money only and no longer bound the land, there was no need for a purchaser to investigate them.[55] The practice was, therefore, to draw two separate deeds (each referring to the other), a *conveyance* to the trustees upon trust to sell, and a *trust instrument* declaring the trusts of the proceeds of sale. When the land was sold, the purchaser took the conveyance and the trustees retained the trust instrument. This convenient practice still continues.[56]

Similar machinery might have been introduced for settlements made *inter vivos* after 1882, except that a purchaser would sometimes have had to investigate the trust instrument in order to find out who was the tenant for life with power of sale. But in practice such settlements continued to be made by one document until the Act of 1925 made the use of two documents compulsory in all cases, even where the settlement was made by will and even where it was made before 1926.

The two documents now made necessary are a vesting instrument and a trust instrument.[57] The vesting instrument contains all the information to which a purchaser is entitled. The trust instrument sets out the details of the settlement and the purchaser is normally

---

[52] He was, of course, not prejudiced by notice of the beneficial interests; see *ante*, p. 293.
[53] See *post*, p. 598.
[54] See J. M. Lightwood (1927) 3 C.L.J. 62, 63 ; S. J. Bailey (1942) 8 C.L.J. 43, 44.
[55] The question whether the purchaser should nevertheless inspect the trust instrument in order to make sure that it contains nothing inconsistent with the trustees' authority to sell (*e.g.*, a requirement that X should consent to the sale, or a power of revocation) is discussed by S. J. Bailey in (1942) 8 C.L.J. 43–49; a negative answer is suggested.
[56] *Post*, pp. 598, 599.
[57] S.L.A., 1925, ss. 4 (1), 6, 8 (1).

not concerned with them. The trusts are said to be " behind the curtain " formed by the vesting instrument, and the purchaser is not entitled to look behind the curtain.[58] Wills, and settlements made before 1926, are brought into line by the provision that the document creating the settlement is to be treated as the trust instrument, and that before the land can be dealt with a vesting instrument must be executed.[59] These provisions must now be examined in greater detail.

1. Settlements made after 1925

(a) *Settlements made inter vivos.* Every settlement of a legal estate in land made *inter vivos* after 1925 must be made by two deeds: a principal vesting deed and a trust instrument.[60] The contents of these deeds are as follows:

This [61]—   TRUST INSTRUMENT
   (i) Declares the trusts affecting the settled land.
  (ii) Bears any *ad valorem* stamp duty payable in respect of the settlement.
 (iii) Appoints trustees of the settlement.
  (iv) Contains the power, if any, to appoint new trustees of the settlement.
   (v) Sets out, either expressly or by reference, any powers intended to be conferred by the settlement in extension of those conferred by the Act.

This [62]—   PRINCIPAL VESTING DEED
   (i) Describes the settled land, either specifically or generally.[63]
  (ii) Declares that the settled land is vested in the person or persons to whom it is conveyed or in whom it is declared to be vested upon the trusts from time to time affecting the settled land.
 (iii) States the names of the trustees of the settlement.
  (iv) States the names of any persons empowered to appoint new trustees of the settlement.
   (v) States any additional or larger powers conferred by the trust instrument.

---

[58] *Ibid.*, s. 110 (2); but in four cases a purchaser *is* concerned to see the trust instrument: see *post*, pp. 302, 305, 308.
[59] S.L.A., 1925, ss. 9, 13.   [60] *Ibid.*, s. 4 (1).
[61] *Ibid.*, s. 4 (3).   [62] *Ibid.*, s. 5 (1).
[63] The description may be by reference to another document, but not by reference to a trust instrument except in the case of a settlement made before 1926: s. 5 (2). The reason for the exception is that a pre-1926 settlement concerns a purchaser: *post*, p. 302.

It will be noticed that the last three particulars [64] in both vesting deed and trust instrument are similar, the only difference being that whereas the trust instrument actually makes the appointment and confers the powers, the vesting deed merely recites what has been done by the trust instrument. The vesting deed here acts as a précis of those parts of the trust instrument which are of concern to a purchaser, so that he need inquire no further. The operative parts of the vesting deed are the first and second, which have no counterparts in the trust instrument. It is by these provisions that the legal estate is duly vested in the tenant for life. The main operative part (the second) is worded so as to cover two cases: (i) where the vesting deed acts as a conveyance from the settlor to the tenant for life or statutory owner, as where X settles property on A for life with remainders over; and (ii) where the same person is both settlor and tenant for life, so that there is no transfer of the legal estate, as where Z on his marriage settles property on himself for life with remainders over.

A vesting deed is not invalidated merely because of some mistake in the statutory particulars.[65] But it will of course be inoperative if it has some fundamental defect, *e.g.*, if the wrong person executes it.[66]

(*b*) *Settlements made by will.* Where land is settled by the will of a testator dying after 1925, the will is treated as the trust instrument.[67] The legal estate, by the ordinary law, vests immediately in the testator's personal representatives.[68] Upon them, therefore, falls the duty of transmitting the legal estate (after providing for death duties [69]) to the tenant for life by means of a proper vesting instrument, and the Act imposes a trust to this effect.[70] Since personal representatives can convey land to beneficiaries by a simple assent in writing,[71] a vesting assent can be employed instead of a vesting deed. This saves the cost (fifty pence) of a deed stamp.[72] But a vesting assent must contain the same particulars as a vesting deed.[73]

2. Settlements made before 1926. A deed or will creating a settlement existing at the beginning of 1926 is treated as a trust instrument.[74] The Act provided that as soon as was practicable

---

[64] The order adopted by the Act, which seems to have no special significance, has been varied so as to place the similarities side by side.

[65] S.L.A., 1925, s. 5 (3).

[66] *Re Cayley and Evans Contract* [1930] 2 Ch. 143; *cf. Re Curwen* [1931] 2 Ch. 341.

[67] S.L.A., 1925, s. 6 (*a*).   [68] *Post*, p. 537.

[69] L.P.A., 1925, s. 16 (1); S.L.A., 1925, s. 8 (3).

[70] S.L.A., 1925, ss. 6 (*b*), 8 (4).   [71] *Post*, p. 538.

[72] S.L.A., 1925, s. 14 (2); Wolst. & C. iii, 36.

[73] S.L.A., 1925, s. 8 (1), (4).

[74] *Ibid.*, 2nd Sched., para. 1 (1).

the trustees of the settlement might, and at the request of the tenant for life or statutory owner must, execute a vesting deed [75]; more than one deed might be used if it was desired to provide separate titles for different parts of the estate.[76] Normally the Law of Property Act, 1925, automatically vested the legal estate in the tenant for life or statutory owner at the beginning of 1926 [77]; a subsequent vesting deed therefore conveyed no estate in such cases, but its function was to provide documentary evidence of the location of the legal estate and to bring the settlement into conformity with settlements made under the new procedure. Where the legal estate was outstanding in personal representatives, *e.g.*, because they were still in the course of administering the testator's estate at the beginning of 1926,[78] they held it upon trust to convey it to the tenant for life or statutory owner by a vesting assent or vesting deed.[79] Although capital money is for most purposes treated as land,[80] no vesting deed was required in respect of capital money.[81]

Pre-1926 settlements were thus equipped with vesting deeds and brought into line with others; nevertheless, it was thought necessary to provide for confirming the accuracy of such vesting deeds executed merely for the sake of conformity with the Act. A purchaser is therefore required to verify from the trust instrument, if it took effect before 1926, that the settlement includes the land described in the vesting deed and that the proper persons are named as tenant for life and trustees of the settlement.[82] This is one of the two important cases where the trust instrument is not kept behind the curtain and it is not considered safe to allow a purchaser to rely on the vesting instrument alone, as in principle, of course, he ought to be allowed to do.[83]

3. Section 13. Some provision had to be made to prevent evasion of the requirement that there should be a vesting instrument. The policy of the Act is therefore to make it impossible to deal with the land in any case where a vesting instrument ought to exist but does not. First, a settlement of a legal estate in land made by a single

---

[75] *Ibid.*, para. 1 (2).
[76] *Re Clayton's S. E.* [1926] Ch. 279.
[77] L.P.A., 1925, 1st Sched., Pt. II, paras. 3, 5, 6 (c); see, *e.g.*, *Re Dalley* (1926) 136 L.T. 223.
[78] *i.e.*, who had not yet assented to the vesting of the legal estate; see L.P.A., 1925, 1st Sched., Pt. II, paras. 3, 5, 6 (c); S.L.A., 1925, 2nd Sched., para. 2. This is the only important case where this occurred.
[79] S.L.A., 1925, 2nd Sched., para. 2.
[80] S.L.A., 1925, s. 75 (5); *post*, p. 376.
[81] *Re Clayton's S. E.* [1926] Ch. 279.
[82] S.L.A., 1925, s. 110 (2).
[83] For the other important case, see *post*, p. 305.

document cannot transfer or create a legal estate [84]; the tenant for life or statutory owner, however, can require the trustees of the settlement (not the settlor) to put matters right by executing a vesting deed.[85] Secondly, section 13 of the Settled Land Act, 1925 [86] (sometimes called the "paralysing section"), in effect provides that where a tenant for life or statutory owner has become entitled to have a vesting instrument executed in his favour, no disposition of a legal estate can be made until a vesting instrument has been executed in accordance with the Act; until this has been done, any purported disposition of the land *inter vivos* by any person operates only as a contract for valuable consideration [87] to carry out the transaction after the requisite vesting instrument has been executed. The object is to force the tenant for life to obtain a proper vesting instrument before he can exercise his powers under the Act of selling, leasing or otherwise disposing of the land. The section does not appear to affect any disposition not made under the Act,[88] and by express provision it does not prevent the tenant for life from disposing of his equitable interest (*e.g.*, his beneficial life interest) or exercising any equitable powers given to him by the trust instrument.

To this rule against premature disposal of a legal estate there are certain exceptions.

(*a*) *Disposition by personal representative.* The section does not apply where the disposition is made by a personal representative.[89] Thus if a settlement took effect before 1926 and the tenant for life subsequently died without a vesting deed having been executed, the legal estate (which was nevertheless automatically vested in the tenant for life at the beginning of 1926) duly passed to his personal representatives, who could dispose of the land without a vesting instrument being executed,[90] *e.g.*, if part of the land was sold by them to raise money for death duties. This preserved the usual powers of personal representatives to deal freely with the land in the due course of administering the estate and to make title to a purchaser by virtue of their office.[91]

(*b*) *Purchaser without notice of the settlement.* The section does not apply where the disposition is made to a purchaser of a

---

[84] S.L.A., 1925, ss. 4 (1), 6.
[85] *Ibid.*, ss. 4, 9.
[86] As amended by L.P.(Am.)A., 1926, s. 6 and Sched.
[87] Registrable as an estate contract, and, if not registered, void against a purchaser of a legal estate for money or money's worth: *post*, p. 1047.
[88] S.L.A., 1925, s. 112 (2); *Re Alefounder's W. T.* [1927] 1 Ch. 360; but consider Wolst. & C. iii, 55; *Weston* v. *Henshaw* [1950] Ch. 510 (on s. 18: see *post*, p. 313).
[89] S.L.A., 1925, s. 13.
[90] Wolst. & C. iii, 56.
[91] See *post*, p. 538.

legal estate without notice of the tenant for life or statutory owner having become entitled to a vesting instrument.[92] For example, if before 1926 [93] A by deed settled land on himself for life with remainders over, and after 1925, suppressing the deed, sold the land to a purchaser who was ignorant of the settlement, the purchaser would get a good title even though no vesting deed had been executed.[94] But the purchaser's title would of course be subject to any third party rights which are binding upon him. Thus if before the sale A had leased the land to B, who knew of the settlement, but B had registered his interest as an estate contract (which is what section 13 makes it [95]), the purchaser would take subject to B's right to a legal lease.

(c) *Settlement at an end.* The section does not apply where the settlement has come to an end before a vesting instrument has been executed.[96] The settlement ends when one person becomes solely and absolutely entitled, and the trusts of the trust instrument are otherwise exhausted. Thus a tenant in tail in possession, whose interest is "settled" only because of the ultimate remainder or reversion, can bar the entail and so become absolutely entitled. There is then no longer a succession of interests, so that the settlement terminates and there is no need for a vesting instrument to be executed [97] before the land can be conveyed to a purchaser.[97a] When the land ceases to be settled, the fetters of section 13 drop off.

(d) *Section 1 of the Amendment Act.* Section 13 does not apply where advantage is taken of section 1 of the Law of Property (Amendment) Act, 1926. In a limited class of cases this allows settled land to be dealt with as if it were not settled; the section is dealt with below.[98]

An illustration of the operation of these provisions is given by the case of a settlor who attempts to make a settlement *inter vivos* today in favour of his son and family by a single document. This is an imperfect settlement, and—

(i) The document is ineffective to transfer or create any legal estate, which thus remains vested in the settlor.[99]

---

[92] S.L.A., 1925, s. 13, as amended by L.P.(Am.)A., 1926, Sched.

[93] If made after 1925, such a settlement would normally be made by a vesting deed in the first place: *ante*, p. 300.

[94] See Wolst. & C. iii, 55–56.   [95] *Ante*, p. 303, n. 87.

[96] *Re Alefounder's W. T.* [1927] 1 Ch. 360, applying S.L.A., 1925, s. 112 (2). "This interesting question is considerably complicated by the simplifications introduced by the new property legislation": *ibid.*, at p. 363, *per* Astbury J. But if the legal estate is not already vested in the owner he must of course obtain a conveyance of it (see s. 7 (5)) before he can make title to a purchaser.

[97] Nor can it be done: for after the settlement has ended there is no longer any "settled land" within the meaning of s. 5.

[97a] *Re Alefounder's W. T., supra.*

[98] *Post*, p. 319.   [99] S.L.A., 1925, s. 4 (1).

(ii) The document is treated as a trust instrument.[1]

(iii) As soon as is practicable the trustees of the settlement may, and at the request of the tenant for life or statutory owner must, execute a principal vesting deed; this will operate to take the legal estate out of the settlor and vest it in the tenant for life or statutory owner.[2] If the legal estate is already so vested (*e.g.*, where the same person is both settlor and tenant for life), the vesting deed is merely declaratory.

(iv) Until the trustees have duly executed the vesting deed, section 13 operates to prevent any disposition of the land being made. It will be noticed that the section prevents the settlor from rectifying his mistake by executing a vesting deed himself; it is the trustees of the settlement, and they alone, who can execute the vesting deed. If there are no trustees and no persons able and willing to appoint trustees, an application must be made to the court for the appointment of trustees.[3]

(v) Even after a vesting deed has been executed the settlement is not as convenient as one made in the proper manner, for the document creating the settlement, although treated as the trust instrument, is not behind the curtain.[4] This is the other of the two important exceptions to the rule that a purchaser is not concerned with the trust instrument: a settlement *inter vivos* which is wrongly made in the first place, just like a settlement made before 1926 (which is the other important exception [5]), must be investigated by any purchaser in order to make sure that the vesting deed, executed at a later date, really contains the true particulars about the land, the tenant for life, and the trustees. The penalty for making an imperfect settlement falls therefore mainly upon the head of any purchaser from the tenant for life.

4. Subsidiary vesting deed. Where land is brought into an existing settlement, it must be conveyed to the tenant for life or statutory owner by a vesting deed.[6] If at the time no other land is held under the settlement, but only capital money, a principal vesting

---

[1] *Ibid.*, s. 9 (1) (iii).
[2] *Ibid.*, s. 9 (2).
[3] *Ibid.*, s. 9 (3).
[4] *Ibid.*, s. 110 (2).
[5] *Ante*, p. 302. For the other (less important) exceptions, see s. 110 (2) and *post.* p. 308.
[6] S.L.A., 1925, s. 10 (1).

deed is required [7]; in other cases a subsidiary vesting deed must be executed.[8] This must be done in the following cases:

(i) Where land is acquired with capital money or in exchange for settled land.[9]

(ii) Where settled land is sold and a rentcharge is reserved. In this case the property to be vested is the rentcharge.[10]

(iii) Where capital money has been lent on mortgage and the mortgagor's right to redeem the property has become barred (*e.g.*, by foreclosure). In this case the trustees at first hold the land on trust for sale, but at the request of the tenant for life or statutory owner they must execute a subsidiary vesting deed.[11]

A subsidiary vesting deed, in addition to conveying the land to the tenant for life or statutory owner (if it is not already vested in him), must contain the following statements and particulars [12]—

(i) particulars of the last or only principal vesting deed affecting land subject to the settlement;

(ii) a statement that the land conveyed is to be held upon and subject to the same trusts and powers as the land comprised in the principal vesting deed;

(iii) the names of the trustees of the settlement;

(iv) the name of any person entitled to appoint new trustees of the settlement.

It is unnecessary to refer to the trust instrument or to any additional powers conferred thereby.[13]

D. A Purchaser May Not Go Behind the Vesting Deed

The objects of the separate vesting deed are, as already explained, to vest the fee simple in the tenant for life; to provide in a concise form a means of proving title to the legal estate without reference to the trust instrument; and to keep the trust instrument off the title, so as to facilitate still further the sale of settled land. The vesting deed is, as it is said, a curtain: the trusts of the settlement are kept behind it, out of sight of any purchaser, who is allowed to trace only the course of the legal estate as shown by the vesting deed. Such a purchaser then takes free from the trusts of the settlement, because they are overreached according to the provisions of the

---

[7] S.L.A., 1925, s. 10 (1), proviso.
[8] *Ibid.*, s. 10 (1).
[9] *Ibid.*
[10] *Ibid.*
[11] L.P.A., 1925, s. 31.
[12] S.L.A., 1925, s. 10 (2).
[13] Wolst. & C. iii, 51.

Act.[14] Overreaching operates in much the same manner as under the Act of 1882; the precise effect of the present overreaching provisions is considered later.[15] We must here notice certain other rules which govern the working of the system of documents introduced in 1925.

In the first place, a purchaser is not entitled to see the trust instrument.[16] On ordinary principles it would be a document relating to the title which a purchaser would wish to inspect. But it is expressly taken off the title by the Act. Secondly, a vesting deed is not invalidated by any mistake in the particulars required to be contained in it.[17] Thirdly, section 110 (2) provides that a purchaser of a legal estate in settled land shall be bound and entitled to assume that the particulars required to be stated in the vesting deed are correct as to the persons who are the tenant for life and the trustees. What happens if any of these matters are in fact wrongly stated in the vesting deed is a question to which the Act gives no obvious answer; for although it both permits and compels the purchaser to take the vesting deed at its face value, it does not provide that it shall be deemed to be correct against anyone other than the purchaser. It does not, therefore, guarantee his title, which must to some extent depend on the new practice being properly observed and the vesting deed being correctly drawn up.

Suppose, for example, that a testator leaves his land by his will to his widow, W, for life or until remarriage, with remainder to X in fee simple; and that the widow remarries, and then nevertheless purports (as tenant for life) to sell the land to P, P duly paying the purchase-money to the trustees. If P had been allowed to inspect the trust instrument he would have discovered that W was no longer tenant for life and consequently had no power to sell to him. But he cannot discover it from the vesting deed or assent, which is all he is allowed to see. He must assume what is untrue, that W is still tenant for life. He probably obtains the legal estate, for that was vested in W and should pass by her conveyance.[18] But it seems unlikely that P can rely upon section 110 (2), mentioned

---

14 See also M. J. Albery in (1939) 4 Conv.(N.S.) 203, suggesting that the purchaser has no notice of the trusts since he is not allowed (s. 110 (2)) to see the trust instrument. But the vesting deed itself tells him that there are trusts, and his inability to see the documents may not necessarily protect him: see *Patman* v. *Harland* (1881) 17 Ch.D. 353, discussed *post*, p. 706.

15 *Post*, pp. 371 *et seq.*

16 S.L.A., 1925, s. 110 (2); nor may he see any deed appointing trustees, if curtained off by a deed of declaration: *post*, p. 357.

17 S.L.A., 1925, s. 5 (3). But a vesting deed executed by the wrong person is inoperative: *ante*, p. 300.

18 Notwithstanding s. 18 (discussed *post*, p. 313), for that applies only to a conveyance by a tenant for life, and W ceased to be tenant for life when she remarried.

above, for on W's remarriage the settlement came to an end, and P is not " a purchaser of a legal estate in settled land." P is a purchaser with constructive notice of the trust in favour of X, which W (not being tenant for life) has no power to overreach.[19] P therefore takes a bad title. This disaster would be avoided only if " settled land " could be held to mean " land which appears to be settled land but is not." [20] If that were possible, P could plead purchase of a legal estate without notice that W was not still tenant for life and so empowered to sell.

In order to minimise the risks of the new practice, a purchaser is allowed to look behind the curtain (*i.e.*, see the trust instrument) in certain cases where there is a chance that the vesting instrument may not have been correctly executed. The two most important cases have already been encountered, *i.e.*, pre-1926 settlements, whether made by deed or will, and imperfect settlements made *inter vivos* after 1925.[21] Two other cases must be mentioned: these are [22] instruments which by the Act are, for special reasons, " deemed to be settlements," [23] and settlements which are similarly " deemed to have been made by any person." [24] All four cases are abnormal in that no proper vesting instrument is provided in the normal course of constituting the settlement, and therefore the accuracy of a vesting deed executed at a later stage may be checked by reference to the trust instrument.[25] Vesting assents or deeds executed in order to perfect settlements made by will after 1926 are in no way abnormal, and therefore form impenetrable curtains.

E. The Legal Estate Must be Transferred in Due Form

1. Title to legal estate. It is a principle of the new system of documents that the title to the legal estate shall be independent of the trust instrument. The legal estate will therefore remain in the tenant for life until he disposes of it or dies. If he sells it under his statutory power, it of course passes by his conveyance. If his

---

[19] S.L.A., 1925, s. 72 (discussed *post*, p. 371): *cf.* ss. 7 (4), 19. In Wolst. & C. iii, 44 it is said that " title can be made by the *de facto* estate owner," but no such general rule is laid down in the Act. See A. H. Withers in 83 S.J. 45, and (1946) 62 L.Q.R. 168, 169 ; (1958) 22 Conv.(N.S.) at 78 (F. R. Crane).

[20] For a somewhat similar interpretation of another section of the Act, see *post*, p. 425.

[21] S.L.A., 1925, s. 110 (2); *ante*, pp. 302, 305.

[22] *Ibid.*, s. 110 (2).

[23] *e.g.*, under s. 29 (1), requiring land held on trust for charitable, ecclesiastical or public purposes to be deemed to be settled land, and the instruments creating such trusts to be deemed to be settlements.

[24] *e.g.*, under ss. 1 (2) (infant entitled under intestacy), 1 (3) (dower assigned by metes and bounds), 20 (3) (curtesy). See *post*, p. 319.

[25] *Cf. ante*, p. 302.

interest determines before his death, he must forthwith convey the land to the new owner by an appropriate form of deed.[26] For example, land is settled on A for life or until he succeeds to Blackacre, remainder to B for life, remainder to C in fee simple. If A succeeds to Blackacre during B's lifetime, A is bound by statute to convey the legal estate to B by a further vesting deed, since the land remains settled land.[27] In this way an independent title to the legal estate is kept up, so that B may, if he wishes, sell it without reference to the trust instrument. But if B dies and then A succeeds to Blackacre, A must convey the land to C by an ordinary conveyance, for C is absolutely entitled and the settlement is at an end.[28] If any necessary document is not executed, the court may make a vesting order instead of it.[29]

2. Death of tenant for life. Similar principles apply where the tenant for life dies, except that they are complicated by special rules for devolution on death. If, in the above example, A never succeeds to Blackacre but survives B, on A's death the land ceases to be settled unless any rights such as voluntary rentcharges still exist under the settlement [30] or C has previously settled his fee simple.[31] Then, as the settlement is at an end,[32] under the ordinary rules the legal estate vests in A's personal representatives who must transmit it to C by an ordinary assent or conveyance [33]; and similarly if instead of C being absolutely entitled the land ceased to be settled because it became subject to a trust for sale.[34] If, on the other hand, B is living at A's death, or for any other reason the land remains settled,[35] it vests in the trustees of the settlement [36] in the capacity of " special personal representatives " [37]; and the special and general personal representatives can each deal with the land under their

---

[26] S.L.A., 1925, s. 7 (4). If a paramount right to the legal estate arises (*e.g.*, by condition broken and re-entry) the tenant for life must convey accordingly: *ibid.*, s. 16 (1) (ii).

[27] S.L.A., 1925, s. 8 (4) (*a*).

[28] *Ibid.*, s. 7 (5).

[29] *Ibid.*, s. 12. See, *e.g.*, *Re Shawdon Estates Settlement* [1930] 2 Ch. 1.

[30] *Re Norton* [1929] 1 Ch. 84.

[31] *In b. Taylor* [1929] P. 260.

[32] See *Re Dalley* (1926) 136 L.T. 223; *In b. Bordass* [1929] P. 107; *In b. Birch* [1929] P. 164.

[33] *Re Bridgett and Hayes' Contract* [1928] Ch. 163. If A dies intestate his administrator succeeds to the legal estate: see Wolst. & C. v, 26.

[34] *Re Thomas* [1939] Ch. 513.

[35] See *Re Egton S. E.* [1931] 2 Ch. 180.

[36] A.E.A., 1925, s. 22 (1) (will), J.A., 1925, s. 162 (1) (intestacy), as amended by the Administration of Justice Act, 1928, s. 9.

[37] A.E.A., 1925, s. 22 (1) (will); J.A., 1925, s. 162 (intestacy). And see *Re Rawlinson* (1934) 78 S.J. 602 (special personal representatives held beneficially entitled); *Re Mortifee* [1948] P. 274.

control independently of each other.[38] Accordingly, if the land remains settled, it follows a different course of devolution through special personal representatives.

This reveals a flaw in the operation of the curtain: whether or not the land remains settled can be ascertained only from the trust instrument, which no later purchaser is allowed to see. Where the deceased's estate consists partly of land which remains settled and partly of land which does not, there may be separate grants of probate to different persons, to some as " special personal representatives " as to settled land and to others as ordinary personal representatives for other land. A later purchaser must then take the risk that the legal estate did not in fact vest in the particular personal representatives, either ordinary or special, through whom his title is derived.[39] But where an unqualified [40] grant of probate is made to ordinary personal representatives, the purchaser is protected by the statutory provision that purchasers can rely upon orders of the court.[41] Such a grant may be made where there are no Settled Land Act trustees, or where the trustees are unwilling to take a grant,[42] in which case the general personal representatives deal with the land as if they were special personal representatives.[43]

3. Effectiveness of curtain. This new conveyancing machinery has therefore smoothed the path of purchasers only at some risk to their titles. " The ' curtain provisions ' relating to assents and settled land are not working as satisfactorily as was hoped . . . the system is artificial, and its rules are not always observed." [44] The artificiality derives from the numerous restrictions on the tenant for life's power to dispose of the legal estate. An ordinary trustee can dispose of a legal estate subject only to the doctrine of notice as to the trusts, which are on the title. In the case of settled land the trusts are taken off the title, but the doctrine of notice is replaced by other restrictions which are neither legal nor equitable, but statutory; and their implications have not yet been worked out. The fundamental

---

[38] A.E.A., 1925, s. 24.

[39] See A. H. Withers (1946) 62 L.Q.R. at 168. It is assumed that nothing in A.E.A., 1925, s. 36 (*post*, p. 538), enables the personal representatives to transfer a legal estate which they have never had. Some strength may be lent to the title by a declaration by the trustees that the land was, or was not, settled: Wolst. & C. iii, 64.

[40] That is to say, where the grant does not contain words such as " save and except settled land." The purchaser can of course see this from the grant of probate.

[41] L.P.A., 1925, s. 204 (replacing C.A., 1881, s. 70), as applied in *Re Bridgett and Hayes' Contract* [1928] Ch. 163.

[42] See *In b. Powell* [1935] P. 114.

[43] See also Wolst. & C. v, 36, 37; *post*, p. 538.

[44] A. H. Withers (1946) 62 L.Q.R. 167, 168. See also (1946) 10 Conv.(N.S.) 135, (1946) 11 Conv.(N.S.) 91 and (1947) *ibid*. 159 for other dubious questions.

difficulty is that "settlement," "tenant for life," "trustees" and the like are defined in terms of facts which lie behind the curtain and beyond a purchaser's ken; even if he knows that the vendor has, or once had, the legal estate under a vesting instrument, there is no guarantee that some change of events behind the curtain may not have deprived him of his power to dispose of it. It might have been more satisfactory if the tenant for life's powers had been made exercisable at any time while he retained the legal estate. This would at least be more in accordance with ordinary principles.

F. *The End of the Settlement Must Sometimes be Evidenced by a Deed of Discharge*

1. Need for deed of discharge. A deed of discharge is the instrument designed by the Act to cancel the effects of the vesting deed when its work has been done. If the land eventually devolves upon someone who is absolutely entitled, he must have some means of proving this to a purchaser without showing him the trust instrument. It is therefore laid down that when the legal estate is held free from all the limitations of a trust instrument, the trustees of the settlement must execute a deed declaring that they are discharged from their duties.[45] In case of difficulty, the court may make an order to the same effect.[46] The deed or order of discharge entitles (and compels [47]) a purchaser to assume that the trusts mentioned in the vesting deed no longer exist. He may then safely pay the money to the vendor, for his notice of the trusts is cancelled by the deed of discharge.

If, for example, the settled land becomes vested (by a vesting deed) in A, as tenant in tail of full age in possession, and A then disentails, so becoming absolute owner, he will require a deed of discharge before he can sell the land and take the purchase-money himself.[48] For otherwise a purchaser, having seen the vesting deed but not the trust instrument creating A's entail, will have no proof that A is now the sole beneficial owner. A has, in fact, a perfectly good title, but without the deed of discharge he cannot prove it.

2. Deed of discharge not required. There are two cases where no deed of discharge is required.

(a) *No vesting instrument executed.* The object of a deed of discharge is to neutralise the vesting deed, and so no deed of discharge

---

[45] S.L.A., 1925, s. 17; but there is a proviso for securing interests created by any derivative settlement, *e.g.*, where a beneficial interest has itself been settled.
[46] *Ibid.*, s. 17 (2).
[47] *Ibid.*, s. 110 (2) (*e*).
[48] This follows from the terms of S.L.A., 1925, ss. 17 (1), 18 (1).

is needed if the land ceases to be settled before any vesting instrument has been executed. For there is then no tenant for life or statutory owner, and the land must be dealt with outside the Settled Land Act. If, in the above example, A had been the first beneficiary under the settlement and had disentailed before any vesting instrument had been executed, the settlor or his personal representatives would have had to convey to him by an ordinary conveyance or assent, and this would prove his title to any purchaser.[49]

(b) *Disposition under ordinary conveyance or assent on the title.* No deed of discharge is required if, after a vesting instrument has been executed, there appears on the title a simple assent or conveyance not referring to the trustees of the settlement. This follows from a provision that if a vesting instrument has been executed, but there is a subsequent conveyance or assent on the title which does not contain a statement of the names of the Settled Land Act trustees, a bona fide purchaser of a legal estate for value[50] is both entitled and bound to assume that every statement in the assent or conveyance is correct and that the person in whom the land was thereby vested holds it free from all rights under the settlement.[51] Thus if land is settled on A for life with remainder to B in fee simple, the simple assent executed by A's personal representatives in favour of B shows on the face of it that the land is no longer settled land; for if the land had remained settled (*e.g.*, because a voluntary annuity in favour of X still existed), the assent in favour of B would have been a *vesting* assent, stating, *inter alia*, who were the trustees of the settlement. The events which determine whether the settlement continues or not are thus kept behind the curtain formed by the documents of title.

G. *Duration of Settlements*

Once a settlement has been made (even if before 1926[52]), it is deemed to continue for the purposes of the Act so long as—

  (i) any limitation, charge or power of charging under the settlement still subsists or is capable of being exercised, or

  (ii) the person beneficially entitled in possession is an infant,[53]

unless in either case the land is held on trust for sale.[54] Thus a

---

[49] *Cf. Re Alefounder's W. T.* [1927] 1 Ch. 360, where the legal estate was vested in the tenant in tail by the transitional provisions of the L.P.A., 1925 (*ante*, p. 304).

[50] S.L.A., 1925, ss. 110 (5), 117 (1) (xxi): as usual, this includes a lessee or mortgagee (*ibid.*).

[51] S.L.A., 1925, s. 110 (5).

[52] *Re Lord Alington and the L.C.C.'s Contract* [1927] 2 Ch. 253.

[53] S.L.A., 1925, s. 3.

[54] L.P.(Am.)A., 1926, Sched. See *post*, p. 360, for the effect of a trust for sale arising.

settlement is no longer deemed to continue when the only subsisting limitation is an absolute interest vested in a person of full age; and even if a trust for such a person still exists, as where the land is still vested in the personal representatives of the last tenant for life on trust for the absolute owner under the final limitation of the settlement, it is generally assumed that the settlement is nevertheless at an end.[55] Nor will part of a compound settlement under which all rights have ceased be kept alive by this provision.[56]

H. While the Settlement Continues, the Land can be Dealt With Only Under the Act

We have already seen how section 13 paralyses dealings in the land until there is a vesting instrument.[57] After the vesting instrument has been executed, and for so long as the settlement continues, it avails the tenant for life or statutory owner nothing that he has the legal estate; for he can deal with it only as allowed by the Act, or any other Act,[58] or by any larger powers in the settlement. He can of course dispose of his beneficial interest, if any. But by section 18 any irregular disposition by the tenant for life or statutory owner is void,[59] except for the purpose of binding the tenant for life's own beneficial interest while it continues. In one case [60] a father sold land to his son and later bought it back again; on his death he settled the land by will upon his son for life with remainder to a grandson. The son mortgaged the land, not under his Settled Land Act powers but for his own personal needs, showing to the mortgagee only his original title by purchase from his father. Since he was in fact tenant for life and his father's executors had made a vesting assent in his favour, his improper mortgages were held void against the grandson, so that the mortgagee lost his security.

Sect. 2.   Other Provisions Relating to Settled Land

The other provisions relating to settled land in the main correspond to similar provisions in the Act of 1882, although in a number of cases important extensions and additions have been made.

---

[55] Wolst. & C. iii, 34; and see *Re Bridgett and Hayes' Contract* [1928] Ch. 163, *ante*, p. 309; *cf*. S.L.A., 1925, s. 7 (5).

[56] *Re Draycott S. E.* [1928] Ch. 371.

[57] *Ante*, p. 302.

[58] *e.g.*, L.P.(Am.)A., 1926, s. 1.

[59] But see the example discussed above, p. 307, as to the effect of a disposition by a person who has ceased to be tenant for life. S. 18 ceases to apply when the settlement ends, even though no deed of discharge has been executed: see s. 18 (1) (*a*), (*b*), (*c*) (once the settlement is at an end no " tenant for life " or " capital money " can exist: ss. 19, 20, 117 (1) (ii)).

[60] *Weston* v. *Henshaw* [1950] Ch. 510. The argument that the scope of s. 18 was restricted by s. 112 (2) was rejected: *ante*, p. 303, n. 88. For a doubt on this case, see *post*, p. 334.

A. Essentials of Settled Land

Land is settled land if "it is or is deemed to be the subject of a settlement." [61] There are three questions of primary importance—

(1) whether the land is the subject of a settlement;

(2) who is the tenant for life; and

(3) who are the trustees.

I. DEFINITION OF SETTLEMENT

1. "Settlement." The policy of the Act of 1925, like that of its predecessor, was to give full powers of management to all limited owners. In general, therefore, any limited interest (*e.g.*, for life, in tail, or for a determinable fee) indicates a settlement. " Settlement " thus covers both obvious cases, as where a testator leaves a life interest to his widow, and also any situation where a life interest results, *e.g.*, where a person acquires a right to occupy a house during his life rent free under a contract or trust.[61a] The precise terms of the Act are important. By section 1 (1) a settlement is created by any document (including a deed, will, agreement or Act of Parliament [62]) or documents [63] whereby one of the following conditions is satisfied.

(*a*) *Succession*: where land " stands for the time being limited in trust for any persons by way of succession." [64]

In addition to cases such as limitations " to A for life, remainder to B in fee simple," this definition seems to be wide enough to cover the following cases, which are somewhat superfluously set out in the section as independent heads: namely, where land is limited in trust for any person in possession—

(i) for an entailed interest, whether or not capable of being barred or defeated;

(ii) for an estate in fee simple or for a term of years absolute subject to an executory gift over (*e.g.*, a devise to trustees in trust for " A in fee simple but for B in fee simple when B marries ");

---

[61] S.L.A., 1925, s. 2.

[61a] *Bannister* v. *Bannister* [1948] 2 All E.R. 133 ; *Binions* v. *Evans* [1972] Ch. 359, Lord Denning M.R. dissenting on this point; and see *post*, p. 779.

[62] S.L.A., 1925, s. 1 (1); see, *e.g.*, *Vine* v. *Raleigh* [1896] 1 Ch. 37 (settlement composed of a will and a public Act of Parliament (the Accumulations Act, 1800)); *cf. Talbot* v. *Scarisbrick* [1908] 1 Ch. 812, where a private Act merely conferred powers and did not directly or indirectly create or incorporate any of the limitations.

[63] *e.g.*, *Re Lord Hereford's S. E.* [1932] W.N. 34 (one private Act of Parliament and three conveyances).

[64] This substantially repeats the definition given by S.L.A., 1882, s. 2: *ante*, p. 288.

(iii) for a base or determinable fee, including a fee determinable by condition,[65] or any corresponding interest in leasehold land.

In all these cases there is an element of succession sufficient to satisfy the definition in (a). Thus if S settles land upon trust for X in tail, the land stands limited in trust for persons by way of succession, since (i) there must be some reversion or remainder to take effect after the entail, even if it is only the grantor's own reversion; and (ii) both the entail and the reversion or remainder are equitable interests, so that someone must hold the legal estate upon trust to give effect to them.[65a] If the entail is barred, the legal estate then becomes held upon trust for X absolutely, and the settlement ends. Furthermore, all the interests are to be treated as subsisting under the settlement,[66] so that they can all be overreached by a sale under the statutory power.[67]

(b) *Springing interests*: where land is limited in trust for an estate in fee simple or for a term of years absolute contingently on the happening of any event (*e.g.*, a devise to trustees in trust for X in fee simple if his brothers die under the age of 21 years [68]). Here too there will usually be an element of succession, although sometimes there may not; for it is possible for the settlor to direct that the rents and profits shall meanwhile be accumulated for the eventual beneficiary,[69] within the limits allowed by the rule against accumulations.[70]

(c) *Infant*: where land stands limited in trust for an infant in possession for an estate in fee simple or for a term of years absolute.[71]

(d) *Restraint*: before the abolition of restraints upon anticipation in 1949, where land stood limited to or in trust for a married woman of full age in possession for an estate in fee simple or a term of years absolute or any other interest with a restraint upon anticipation.

---

[65] S.L.A., 1925, s. 117 (1) (iv).

[65a] A minority opinion to the contrary is expressed by Lord Denning M.R. in *Binions* v. *Evans* [1972] Ch. 359 at 366.

[66] S.L.A., 1925, s. 1 (4); and see *Re Hunter & Hewlett's Contract* [1907] 1 Ch. 46 on the corresponding section of the S.L.A., 1882 (s. 2 (2)) (conveyance before 1926 without words of limitation: held, the grantor's reversion in fee simple arose under the settlement and so could be overreached under a conveyance by the tenant for life).

[67] For overreaching, see *post*, p. 371.

[68] See *Re Bird* [1927] 1 Ch. 210; and see *Re Walmsley's S. E.* (1911) 105 L.T. 332.

[69] Under a will, this happens in any case, in default of other directions: L.P.A., 1925, s. 175.

[70] *Ante*, p. 271.

[71] This merely repeats S.L.A., 1882, s. 59: *ante*, p. 289.

(e) *Family charges*: where land stands charged, whether voluntarily or in consideration of marriage or by way of family arrangement, with the payment of any sums for the benefit of any persons.

2. " Limited in trust." It will be noted that under heads (a) (succession), (b) (springing interests) and (c) (infants), but not (d) (married women subject to a restraint) or (e) (family charges), it is necessary for the land to be " limited in trust " if it is to fall within the definition; if there is no trust, the land is not settled land. But this requirement is satisfied automatically, since none of the beneficial interests mentioned under heads (a), (b) and (c) can exist as a legal estate.[72] Either the interest is a limited one (*i.e.*, less than a fee simple absolute), or it is not yet in possession, or it is held by an infant who since 1925 cannot hold a legal estate.[73] Consequently, on the principle that there is a trust if the legal estate is in one person and the equitable interest in another,[74] the land must be held upon trust in these cases.[75]

But one exception is possible: a fee simple defeasible by condition subsequent may, if so limited, still exist as a legal estate; and the intention of this arrangement is to free certain kinds of conditional fees from the Settled Land Act.[76] This clearly happens in the cases intended, where the conditional right of entry is given to secure payment of a legal rentcharge,[76] for such a right of entry may also be a legal interest[77] and there is then no trust. But if given for any other purpose (*e.g.*, as a beneficial gift over) the right of entry must be equitable, and the legal estate might then be said to be held upon a contingent trust for a future beneficiary, and so be " settled " within head (b) above. In any case, if a trust is employed the land must be settled land, as for example where there is a devise " to A in fee simple, but if A succeeds to Blackacre then to B " (for every will automatically creates a trust[78]) or a grant by deed " to T and his heirs upon trust for A . . . "[79] for a similar interest.

---

[72] L.P.A., 1925, s. 1 (1), (2); *ante*, p. 135; and as to wills, see L.P.(Am.)A., 1924, 9th Sched., para. 3.   [73] L.P.A., 1925, s. 1 (6): *post*, p. 988.

[74] See *Rayner* v. *Preston* (1881) 18 Ch.D. 1 at 13; *Hardoon* v. *Belilios* [1901] A.C. 118 at 123.

[75] Yet *quaere* whether land is " limited " in trust if the trust arises by operation of law and not by limitation: contrast a devise " to A in tail " with one " to my trustees in trust for A in tail." Contrast also the wording of S.L.A., 1882, s. 2 (1). In *Binions* v. *Evans* [1972] Ch. 359 at 366 Lord Denning M.R. expressed a minority opinion that " limited " meant " expressly limited."

[76] *Ante*, p. 138.

[77] L.P.A., 1925, s. 1 (2) (e).   [78] *Ante*, p. 198; *post*, p. 535.

[79] A devise in fee simple absolute by the owner of land subject to a fee farm rent (*ante*, p. 138) presumably creates no settlement, since the condition is a legal right attaching to the legal estate itself and is not part of the trusts upon which it is held; *cf.* Wolst. & C. iii, 24.

Under heads (*d*) and (*e*) no limitation by way of trust is required. Whether the estate which was made subject to the restraint on anticipation or to the family charges was conveyed directly to the beneficiary or whether it was held in trust for the beneficiary, the land is nevertheless settled land.

3. New provisions. Although heads (*a*) and (*c*) substantially repeated the provisions of the Settled Land Act, 1882, there were four cases in which land which was not settled land before 1926 became settled land after 1925. These are—

(i) *Head* (*b*): *springing interests.* Only where there were also successive interests would the land have been settled before 1926. But even where there is only one possible beneficiary (as under a devise to the testator's first son to attain 21, where the intermediate rents and profits are to be accumulated and added to the gift) it is equally necessary to give full powers of management during the period while the gift is in suspense.

(ii) *Head* (*d*): *restraint on anticipation.* The restraint on anticipation (now abolished)[80] was a special kind of limitation, enforceable only in equity, by which a married woman could be prevented from disposing of her interest in property. It is explained more fully later.[81] Since a restraint could be attached to an absolute interest (as in a grant to X's wife in fee simple without power of anticipation), alienation might thus be fettered even though there was no succession of interests and the land was not, therefore, settled land under the Act of 1882.[82] In order to confer full powers of sale and management on all married women the Act of 1925 extended the definition of settled land to cover all such cases; but, of course, any restraint on anticipation attached to the purchase-money if the land was sold.

(iii) *Head* (*e*): *family charges.* Before 1926, a settlement of the traditional type usually came to an end[83] when the land vested in fee simple in a person absolutely entitled,[84] even if the land was still subject to charges under the settlement, *e.g.*, for a jointure for a widow, or portions for children[85]: for in such a case the land no longer stood limited to persons by way of succession.[86] Only if the

---

[80] *Post*, p. 996.
[81] *Post*, p. 995.
[82] *Bates* v. *Kesterton* [1896] 1 Ch. 159.
[83] See, *e.g.*, *Re Gordon & Adams' Contract* [1914] 1 Ch. 110.
[84] See *Re Marshall's Settlement* [1905] 2 Ch. 325; *Re Monckton's Settlement* [1917] 1 Ch. 224.   [85] See *ante*, p. 283, and *post*, p. 385.
[86] See *Re Mundy and Roper's Contract* [1899] 1 Ch. 275 at 298; *Re Trafford's S. E.* [1915] 1 Ch. 9; *Re Earl of Carnarvon's Chesterfield S. E.* [1927] 1 Ch. 138 at 152, 155; *Re Ogle's S. E.* [1927] 1 Ch. 229 at 235, 236; *Re Austen* [1929] 2 Ch. 155 at 159, 160.

charges were for sums not presently payable but to arise in the future (whether or not secured by any trust or term of years [87]) was there a " succession " which would make the land settled land [88]; accordingly it was only in these cases that the charges could be overreached.

In order to make it possible to sell such land free from the charges even if they contained no element of futurity, the Act of 1925 eliminated any requirement of succession under this head by extending the definition of a settlement to all cases where land stands for the time being charged with the payment of any sums " voluntarily or in consideration of marriage or by way of family arrangement." [89] These words do not confine this head to charges such as portions, advancement and maintenance [90]; but they exclude charges of a business character where the security is part of the bargain. Thus there is no settlement if the charge was created for money or money's worth, as where a tenant in fee simple sells his land and takes a charge on it as part of the price. Further, it must be proved that the charge was created in one of these ways, even if, for example, it appears probable that it was created voluntarily, or where there is a rentcharge for charitable or ecclesiastical purposes.[91] But subject to these limitations, it is immaterial whether the charge is present or future, whether it is for capital or annual sums,[92] or whether it is for a limited period (*e.g.*, for life) [93] or in perpetuity.[94] Thus if a testator devises land to trustees on trust to pay a perpetual annuity to X, and subject thereto on trust for A in fee simple, the land becomes settled land.[94]

The effect of this provision was that at the beginning of 1926 much land which had previously not been settled land was forth-with converted into settled land.[95] In a number of cases this caused hardship to those who had purchased such land before 1926. The practice had been that unless the land could be freed from the charges, as by the owners of the charges all releasing them in return for a share of the purchase-money, or by paying a sufficient sum into court,[96] the vendor conveyed the land to the purchaser subject to the charges but with an indemnity against them, *i.e.*, the vendor agreed to pay the charges himself and so ensure that

[87] *Re Trafford's S. E., supra*; but see *Re Collis's Estate* [1911] 1 I.R. 267 at 270.
[88] *Re Earl of Carnarvon's Chesterfield S. E., supra.*
[89] S.L.A., 1925, s. 1 (1) (v).
[90] *Re Bird* [1927] 1 Ch. 210 at 215, 216.
[91] *Re Braby and Newman's Contract* (1926) Wolst. & C. iii, 25, v, 71, cited [1929] 2 Ch. 163–165.
[92] *Re Bird* [1927] 1 Ch. 210; *Re Lindsley's Estate* (1927) 63 L.J.News. 375.
[93] *Re Bird, supra.*
[94] *Re Austen* [1929] 2 Ch. 155.
[95] See, *e.g.*, *Re Ogle's S. E.* [1927] 1 Ch. 229; *Re Austen, supra.*
[96] C.A., 1881, s. 5, now replaced by L.P.A., 1925, s. 50.

they would not be enforced against the land.[97]　In cases where this had been done, the purchaser found to his surprise (if, indeed, he could understand the matter at all) that at the beginning of 1926 his land had become settled land and that it could be sold only after compliance with the troublesome Settled Land Act procedure, *e.g.*, as to the appointing of trustees and the execution of a vesting deed.

To meet this situation the Law of Property (Amendment) Act, 1926,[98] provided that where a person of full age is beneficially entitled in possession to land in fee simple or for a term of years absolute subject to charges of this kind, he can nevertheless create or convey a legal estate subject to the charges in the same way as if the land were not settled land.　This applies whether the charges arose before 1926 or after 1925, and whether the person entitled to the land is the tenant under the settlement [99] or a purchaser from him,[1] and whether or not such a purchaser bought with the benefit of an indemnity.[2] But it applies only if the sole reason for the land being deemed settled land is that it is subject to the charges and not, for example, when it is also entailed.　Where the Amendment Act applies, a vendor may thus sell the land either (i) free from the charges, by making use of the Settled Land Act procedure, or payment into court, or (ii) subject to the charges, by virtue of the Amendment Act. He may also sell with the concurrence of the owners of the charges, but a purchaser is entitled to refuse to accept a title made in this way.[3]

(iv) *Dower assigned by metes and bounds.*　The position of dower must be distinguished from that of curtesy.　Dower and curtesy are now very rare,[4] but when they exist there will in most cases be a settlement.　For the effect of both is to confer some kind of life interest, and the doweress or tenant by curtesy needs the statutory powers as much as any other tenant for life.　Before 1926, where a married woman died and her husband took curtesy, the element of succession required to make the land settled land was satisfied by the fact that he took a mere life estate and that subject thereto the land passed to his wife's heir.　Nevertheless, the land was not settled land within the meaning of the Settled Land Act, 1882, since the husband's interest arose by operation of law and not under any document.[5]　The Settled Land Act, 1884,[6] accordingly

---

[97] See, *e.g.*, *Re Ogle's S. E.* [1927] 1 Ch. 229; *Re Ossemsley Estates Ltd.* [1937] 3 All E.R. 774.
[98] s. 1.　　　　　　　　　　　　　　　　[99] L.P.(Am.)A., 1926, s. 1 (1).
[1] *Ibid.*, s. 1 (2).
[2] *Ibid.*
[3] See *post*, p. 587.
[4] *Post*, p. 532.
[5] See *ante*, p. 288; *Re Pocock and Prankerd's Contract* [1896] 1 Ch. 302 at 306.
[6] s. 8.

declared that in such a case the husband was deemed to take under a settlement made by the wife (and so, presumably, was the wife's heir, at least for the purpose of his interest being overreached [7]), and so the land was settled land; but this did not apply if the wife was still alive so that the husband's right of curtesy was merely prospective.[8] This provision of the Act of 1884 was repeated in the Act of 1925 [9] and so the existence of curtesy made the land settled land under head (a) above.

A similar notional settlement was likewise introduced [10] for the case of dower assigned by metes and bounds, where a similar difficulty arose. The mode in which dower was enjoyed was either that the widow received one-third of the income of the land or else that she had her dower " assigned by metes and bounds," i.e., had a distinct one-third part of the land marked out for her exclusive occupation for the rest of her life.[11] The former method did not create a settlement before 1926 and still does not do so,[12] for the dower is simply a money charge [13] and the doweress has no right to hold or manage the land. The latter method did not create a settlement before 1926, for although the requisite element of succession was present, the wife claimed her third under the general law and not under any document, and there was no provision that dower should be deemed to arise under a settlement as there was in the case of curtesy. But since the doweress actually occupied her assigned part of the land as tenant for life, she needed the statutory powers. It is therefore now provided that the letters of administration or probate of the husband's estate shall be deemed to be a settlement made by the husband,[14] so that the widow's one-third is settled land and she will be the tenant for life.[15]

II. DEFINITION OF TENANT FOR LIFE

1. Tenant for life

(a) Definition. The Settled Land Act, 1925, defines " tenant for life " as including any person (other than a statutory owner [16]) who has the statutory powers.[17] As these statutory powers are conferred

---

[7] See Mogridge v. Clapp [1892] 3 Ch. 382.

[8] Bates v. Kesterton [1896] 1 Ch. 159.

[9] S.L.A., 1925, s. 20 (3).

[10] Ibid., s. 1 (3).

[11] Post, p. 518; Williams v. Thomas [1909] 1 Ch. 713. Dower can no longer arise, but dower which arose before 1926 may still continue: post, p. 532.

[12] Wolst. & C. iii, 30. For the way in which land can be freed from dower in such a case, see 3rd ed. of this book, p. 391.

[13] Not arising in any of the three ways which would create a settlement under the head " family charges," ante, p. 317.

[14] S.L.A., 1925, s. 1 (3).

[15] See Wolst. & C. iii, 30.

[16] Ante, p. 298.   [17] S.L.A., 1925, s. 117 (1) (xxviii).

not only on those who have life interests (by s. 19), but also on many other persons (under s. 20), "tenant for life" has for this purpose an artificially extended meaning. Generally speaking, every limited owner who is of full age and beneficially entitled in possession under the settlement [18] is thus a "tenant for life," so that the definition of tenant for life is complementary to the definition of settled land. A "tenant for life" may thus be a person entitled to a life interest, a tenant in tail, [19] a tenant in fee simple subject to a gift over or to family charges, a tenant for years terminable on life, [20] a tenant *pur autre vie*, a person entitled to the income of land for his own or any other life, (formerly) a married woman entitled subject to a restraint on anticipation, and others. As explained later, [20a] two or more persons entitled jointly may also constitute the tenant for life.

(*b*) *Special cases.* Although it is essential that the person claiming to have the powers of tenant for life should fit precisely into one or other of the specified classes, there is usually little difficulty in ascertaining him. But the following cases require special mention.

(1) TENANTS FOR YEARS. Here a line has to be drawn between "family" and "commercial" leases; the Settled Land Act is concerned only with the former. [21] It is usually only in the case of "commercial" leases that rent is payable. Therefore the definition of "tenant for life" extends to tenants for years determinable on life, [22] and tenants *pur autre vie*, provided in both cases that they do not hold "merely under a lease at a rent." [23] In one case, where a testator gave his widow the right to take a yearly tenancy at a rent of £1 per annum, it was decided that the widow had not the powers of a tenant for life [24]; the powers probably belonged to the remainderman under case (3) below. [25]

(2) INCOME: persons entitled to the income of the land. If the settlement gives the land to trustees upon trust to pay the income to

---

[18] See *post*, p. 322.
[19] Even if unable to bar his entail, unless the property was purchased with money provided by Parliament and statute prohibits barring the entail: S.L.A., 1925, s. 20 (1) (i). But see *Re Duke of Marlborough's Parliamentary Estates* (1891) 8 T.L.R. 179; *Re Duke of Marlborough's Blenheim Estates* (1892) 8 T.L.R. 582; and see S.L.A., 1925, s. 23 (2).
[20] And see S.L.A., 1925, s. 20 (1) (vi) (determinable interests); *Re Boyer's S. E.* [1916] 2 Ch. 404.   [20a] *Post*, p. 424.
[21] *Cf. ante*, p. 317.
[22] *Re Mundy & Roper's Contract* [1899] 1 Ch. 275 at 298.
[23] s. 20 (1) (iv), (v). Determinable leases (*e.g.*, to the use of A for 99 years if he should so long live) were sometimes used in settlements before 1833 in order to prevent the barring of a subsequent entail, for there was then no freehold tenant in possession who could consent to the bar; but F.R.A., 1833, made such a tenant the protector of the settlement (*ante*, p. 91); see *Bell* v. *Holtby* (1873) L.R. 15 Eq. 178 at 189.
[24] *Re Catling* [1931] 2 Ch. 359. See also *Re Hazle's S. E.* (1885) 29 Ch.D. 78.
[25] Had he not been so entitled, they would have belonged to the trustees as statutory owner: *ante*, p. 298.

A for life, A has, and the trustees have not,[26] all the statutory powers.[27] A can therefore call for a vesting deed in his own favour, and so obtain the right to occupy the land, even though before 1926 he would have had no right to possession unless the court had thought it proper to give it to him.[28] It makes no difference that A is entitled only to the net income, after payment of outgoings, expenses of management, or incumbrances,[29] or that there is a trust for accumulation, *e.g.*, to pay off mortgages,[30] or that prior charges, such as annuities, in fact exhaust the income from the land.[31] But it is essential that there should be a right to the whole surplus of income, however much or little it may be: a right merely to two-thirds of the income,[32] or a discretionary trust which gives not a right to the income but a mere hope that it will be paid,[33] will not give a beneficiary the powers of a tenant for life. And the right must be for the life of the beneficiary (including a right for 99 years if he so long lives[34]) or for some other life, or until sale of the land or determination of his interest, and not for any other period.[35]

(3) ENTITLED SUBJECT TO CHARGES: persons beneficially entitled to a legal estate, in fee simple or for a term of years absolute, but subject to interests created by a settlement. If, for example, X becomes entitled to land in fee simple, subject to a widow's jointure rentcharge, the land is settled land because of the family charge. Although X can deal with it freely (despite sections 13 and 18) under the Law of Property (Amendment) Act, 1926,[36] he may wish to sell under the Settled Land Act, 1925, so as to overreach the rentcharge. He is therefore given the powers of a tenant for life.[37] His legal estate need not necessarily have arisen under a settlement, provided that the interest to which it is subject did so arise.[38]

(c) *Beneficially entitled in possession.* In addition to falling within the above-mentioned provisions a tenant for life must also be of full age and beneficially entitled in possession under the settlement.[39] " Of full age " merely means " not being an infant," so that

---

26 *Post*, p. 351.   27 s. 20 (1) (viii).
28 *Re Bagot's Settlement* [1894] 1 Ch. 177; *Re Earl of Stamford & Warrington* [1925] 1 Ch. 162 at 171, 172; Wolst. & C. iii, 77. Since 1925, being trustee of the land for himself (*ante*, p. 297), he may occupy the land if he wishes, and it is arguable that he falls within s. 19 as well as within s. 20.
29 *Clarke* v. *Thornton* (1887) 35 Ch.D. 307.
30 *Re Stevens and Dunsby's Contract* [1928] W.N. 187.
31 *Re Jones* (1884) 26 Ch.D. 736; *Re Cooke's S. E.* [1885] W.N. 177; and see *Re Bennett* [1903] 2 Ch. 136.   32 *Re Frewen* [1926] Ch. 580.
33 *Re Atkinson* (1886) 31 Ch.D. 577; *Re Gallenga W. T.* [1938] 1 All E.R. 106; Wolst. & C. iii, 78, 79.
34 *Re Waleran S. E.* [1927] 1 Ch. 522.   35 *Re Astor* [1922] 1 Ch. 364.
36 *Ante*, p. 319.   37 s. 20 (1) (ix).
38 *Re Earl of Carnarvon's Chesterfield S. E.* [1927] 1 Ch. 138 at 156; *cf. Re Ogle's S. E.* [1927] 1 Ch. 229; Wolst. & C. iii, 80, 210.
39 S.L.A., 1925, ss. 19 (1), 20 (1). The *Carnarvon* case (n. 38 above) is an exception.

a corporation may be a tenant for life under the Act.[40] " In possession " means " not in remainder or reversion," [41] and so excludes a person with only a future interest in the land. The terms " beneficially entitled " and " under the settlement " both create difficulties, for they appear in the Act only in section 19, in relation to a tenant with an actual life interest, and not in section 20, in relation to those with other interests such as an entail or a fee simple subject to family charges.[42] However, it was held before 1926 that there was an implied requirement of a beneficial interest in all cases,[43] and the relatively minor changes in drafting do not appear to have disturbed this conclusion.[44] Somewhat exceptionally, an executor of a person beneficially entitled (*e.g.*, a tenant in tail or a tenant *pur autre vie*) is regarded as satisfying the words " beneficially entitled " [45]; such a person, although not entitled for his own benefit, at least represents the deceased's beneficial interest as against others. The words " under the settlement " exclude an assignee of a life interest, for he holds under the assignment and not under the settlement [46]; in such a case the assignor, though no longer beneficially entitled, remains tenant for life for the purposes of the Act.[47]

(*d*) *Effect of definition*. The practical effect of the definition is that where there is some person of full age beneficially entitled to either the possession of some specific settled land [48] or the whole of the income from it, that person will have the statutory powers. A mere right for a person, *e.g.*, to occupy such one of fourteen houses as he should from time to time choose is not enough [49]; but the exercise of an option to reside in a specified house suffices.[50]

The position where two or more persons are entitled jointly or in common in this way is dealt with later.[51]

[40] *Re Earl of Carnarvon's Chesterfield S. E.* [1927] 1 Ch. 138 (limited company).
[41] *Re Morgan* (1883) 24 Ch.D. 114 at 116; and see *Re Strangways* (1886) 34 Ch.D. 423; *Re Martyn* (1900) 69 L.J.Ch. 733; *Re Beauchamp's W. T.* [1914] 1 Ch. 676.
[42] See *Re Earl of Carnarvon's Chesterfield S. E.* [1927] 1 Ch. 138 at 156; Radcliffe, *Real Property*, 2nd ed., 273, 274.
[43] *Re Jemmett & Guest's Contract* [1907] 1 Ch. 629.
[44] Compare S.L.A., 1925, ss. 19 (1), 20 (1), with S.L.A., 1882, ss. 2 (5), 58 (1); and the definition of " tenant for life " in S.L.A., 1925, s. 117 (1) (xxviii) may have some unifying effect.
[45] See *Vine* v. *Raleigh* [1896] 1 Ch. 37; *Re Johnson* [1914] 2 Ch. 134.
[46] *Re Earl of Carnarvon's Chesterfield S. E.* [1927] 1 Ch. 138, also holding that under a pre-1926 assignment of land subject to family charges which did not become settled land until 1926 the assignee had the powers of a tenant for life under S.L.A., 1925, s. 20 (1) (ix).
[47] *Re Earl of Carnarvon's Chesterfield S. E., supra.* This is also the result of S.L.A., 1925, s. 104, explained *post*, p. 356.
[48] See *Re Carne's S. E.* [1899] 1 Ch. 324; *Re Baroness Llanover's Will* [1903] 2 Ch. 16; but see *Re Trenchard* (1900) 16 T.L.R. 525.
[49] *Re Bond* (1904) 48 S.J. 192.
[50] *Re Anderson* [1920] 1 Ch. 175; *Re Gibbons* [1920] 1 Ch. 372.
[51] *Post*, p. 424.

2. Cases where there is no tenant for life. In some cases there may be a settlement, but no person entitled as tenant for life. Examples are [52]—

(i) Where the person entitled is an infant.[53]

(ii) Where no person is entitled to the whole residue of income, *e.g.*, where there is a trust to pay to X a fixed annuity,[54] or a definite fraction of the income,[55] with a direction to accumulate the balance.

(iii) Where no person is entitled to the income at all. This state of affairs is produced by a discretionary trust, *e.g.*, a direction to trustees to pay the income to such person or persons as they think fit. No recipient is then entitled as of right to any income[56]; and the same applies even if X is entitled to all the income (if any) not distributed by the trustees under such a trust.[57]

(iv) Where trustees are directed to accumulate the income for a future contingent beneficiary, without any other limitations which would create successive interests.[58]

In all such cases, as already explained,[59] the legal estate and statutory powers are in the statutory owner. But a statutory owner is not subject to all the duties and restrictions imposed upon tenants for life, unless they are expressed to apply; for the definition of " tenant for life " specifically excludes statutory owners.[60]

III.　DEFINITION OF TRUSTEES OF THE SETTLEMENT

1. The definition. The trustees of the settlement are defined by section 30 of the Settled Land Act, 1925. There are five heads, which must be applied in turn; thus if there are any trustees under one head, they will exclude any trustees under a subsequent head.[61] The definition is as follows.

---

[52] *Cf.* Wolst. & C. iii, 86.

[53] See *ante*, p. 297 and (for special powers of statutory owners) S.L.A., 1925, s. 102.

[54] *Re Jefferys (No. 2)* [1939] Ch. 205.　　　　[55] *Re Frewen* [1926] Ch. 580.

[56] *Re Atkinson* (1886) 31 Ch.D. 577; *Re Horne's S. E.* (1888) 39 Ch.D. 84; *Re Gallenga W. T.* [1938] 1 All E.R. 106.

[57] *Re Alston-Roberts-West's S. E.* [1928] W.N. 41.

[58] *i.e.*, where there is to be a springing absolute interest within S.L.A., 1925, s. 1 (1) (iii). In this case also special powers of interim management are conferred by s. 102.

[59] *Ante*, p. 297.

[60] S.L.A., 1925, s. 117 (1) (xxviii); *Re Craven S. E.* [1926] Ch. 985.

[61] For a list of the trustees' duties and an explanation of the documents used in case of a change of trustees see *post*, p 357.

(i) The persons who, under the settlement, are trustees with power to sell the land (even if this power is subject to the consent of anyone, *e.g.*, the tenant for life [63]) or .with power of consenting to or approving the exercise of a power of sale.[64]

For example, if in a settlement on A for life, with remainders over, there is a provision giving X and Y power to sell the land, this will make them trustees of the settlement, in preference even to any other persons expressly appointed Settled Land Act trustees. X and Y will in fact have no power to sell the land, for, as will be seen,[65] this power is taken away from them and given to the tenant for life [66]; nevertheless, the attempt to give them the power suffices to make them trustees of the settlement.[67] A mere power to " vary securities " may be a sufficient power to sell,[68] and where trustees of personalty have a power to sell and vary the investments, the settlement of land upon the same trusts as the personalty makes the trustees Settled Land Act trustees under this head.[69] But the power of sale must be a general power, and not a power limited to special purposes [70] such as payment of debts.[71]

(ii) The persons declared by the settlement to be trustees thereof for the purposes of the Settled Land Acts, 1882 to 1890, or 1925, or any of them.[72]

This is the head under which the trustees of the settlement will usually be found, for cases under head (i) are rare. It should be noted that it is not sufficient to appoint X and Y " trustees of the settlement," or " trustees ": the appointment will be ineffective unless words such as " for the purposes of the Settled Land Act, 1925 " are added.[73]

(iii) Persons who, under the settlement, are trustees with power of sale or of consenting to or approving of a sale, or upon trust for sale, of *other* land held under the same settlement and upon the same trusts.[74]

(iv) Persons who, under the settlement, are trustees with a *future* power of sale, or under a *future* trust for sale, or with a

---

[63] *Constable* v. *Constable* (1886) 32 Ch.D. 233.
[64] S.L.A., 1925, s. 30 (1) (i).
[65] *Post*, p. 351.
[66] S.L.A., 1925, s. 108 (2).
[67] *Ibid.*, s. 30 (2).
[68] *Re Tapp and London and India Dock Co.'s Contract* (1905) 74 L.J.Ch. 523.
[69] *Re Garnett Orme & Hargreaves' Contract* (1883) 25 Ch.D. 595.
[70] *Re Coull's S. E.* [1905] 1 Ch. 712.
[71] *Re Carne's S. E.* [1899] 1 Ch. 324; and see *Re Morgan* (1883) 24 Ch.D. 114.
[72] S.L.A., 1925, s. 30 (1) (ii).
[73] See, *e.g.*, *Re Bentley* (1885) 54 L.J.Ch. 782 (" trustees ").
[74] S.L.A., 1925, s. 30 (1) (iii).

power of consenting to or approving the exercise of such a future power of sale, even if the power or trust does not take effect in all events.[75]

Thus if there is a settlement of Blackacre and Whiteacre which attempts to give to trustees (albeit ineffectively) a power of sale over Blackacre alone, clause (iii) makes those trustees Settled Land Act trustees of both properties.[76] Again, if Greenacre is settled on A for life with remainder to X and Y upon trust for sale, clause (iv) makes X and Y Settled Land Act trustees,[77] unless, indeed, the trust for sale is void for perpetuity.[78] Under both clauses it is immaterial that the powers given by the settlement are, under the Act, not exercisable by the trustees.[79]

(v) The persons appointed by deed by those able to dispose of the whole equitable interest in the settled land.[80]

For example if land is settled on A for life, remainder to B in tail, A and B can appoint trustees of the settlement; for B could bar the entail with A's consent, and thus between them they could dispose of the whole equitable interest in the land.[81]

It is noteworthy that nothing in the Act prevents the tenant for life himself from being one of the trustees, or even two or more joint tenants for life from being the sole trustees,[82] although of course the primary duty of the trustees is to protect the interests of future beneficiaries against abuse of the tenant for life's powers.

2. Personal representatives. Where a settlement arises under a will or intestacy and there are no trustees under any other provisions, the personal representatives of the deceased are trustees of the settlement until other trustees are appointed.[83] This useful provision is new. It rarely applies to intestacies, for an intestacy after 1925 normally creates a trust for sale.[84] But it operates even where

---

[75] *Ibid.,* s. 30 (1) (iv).
[76] *Re Moore* [1906] 1 Ch. 789, where Blackacre had been sold and other land brought into the settlement.
[77] *Re Johnson's S. E.* [1913] W.N. 222.
[78] *Re Davies and Kent's Contract* [1910] 2 Ch. 35 at 45; for the perpetuity rule, see *ante,* p. 208.
[79] S.L.A., 1925, s. 30 (2); *post,* p. 351.
[80] *Ibid.,* s. 30 (1) (v).
[81] *Re Spearman S. E.* [1906] 2 Ch. 502; *cf. Re Spencer's S. E.* [1903] 1 Ch. 75 (appointment executed by some only of the beneficiaries held invalid).
[82] See *Re Jackson's S. E.* [1902] 1 Ch. 258; *Re Davies and Kent's Contract* [1910] 2 Ch. 35 at 50, 51; *Re Pennant's W. T.* [1970] Ch. 75; and see S.L.A., 1925, s. 68 (3). But a sole trustee can no longer give a good receipt for capital money by himself: *post,* p. 376.
[83] S.L.A., 1925, s. 30 (3). If there is only one personal representative, and he is not a trust corporation, he is bound to appoint another trustee to act with him: *ibid.* The section does not empower the personal representatives to retire and appoint new trustees, but they may do so under T.A., 1925, ss. 64 (1), 68 (5): *Re Dark* [1954] Ch. 291.   [84] See *post,* p. 253.

the settlor died before 1926 [85] and his personal representatives had completed their administration of his estate.[86] It deals with the most frequent cause of a lack of trustees, namely, a will made without proper legal advice. Where even this provision fails (*e.g.*, where there is a home-made settlement created *inter vivos*) the court has power to appoint trustees on the application of any person interested under the settlement.[87] Once persons have became trustees, whether by order of the court or otherwise, they or their successors in office remain trustees as long as the settlement subsists.[88]

3. Referential settlements. Special provision is made [89] for referential settlements, that is to say, settlements incorporating by reference the terms of earlier settlements, with or without variations,[90] *e.g.*, a settlement of Blackacre directing it to be held on the same trusts as Whiteacre, which is already settled.[91] Unless trustees are separately appointed under head (ii) above, the trustees of the earlier settlement become trustees of the later settlement which refers to it.[92] Such settlements are dangerous, for they sometimes give rise to difficult questions of construction [93]; in one case, settlement B was made by reference to settlement A, and when on a divorce the court varied settlement A, it was held that the variation did not apply to settlement B.[94]

B. Compound Settlements

1. Compound settlements. Before 1926 difficulties sometimes arose in the case of compound settlements. " Compound settlement " is the term used to describe the state of affairs when the trusts affecting the land are created by two or more instruments, as where a settlement is followed by a resettlement. Occasionally it is used to describe a referential settlement [95]; but it is best confined to two or more sets of trusts applying to one parcel of land rather than two or more parcels of land governed by similar trusts.[96] For example, suppose that land has been settled on A for life with remainder

---

[85] See, *e.g.*, *Re Shelton's S. E.* [1928] W.N. 27 (settlor died in 1898).
[86] See 62 L.J.News. 436.
[87] S.L.A., 1925, s. 34.
[88] S.L.A., 1925, s. 33 (1). See the example in Wolst. & C. iii, 101. As to appointment, replacement and removal of trustees, see *post*, pp. 451, 454, 456.
[89] S.L.A., 1925, s. 32, which operates retrospectively (*ibid.*, subs. (2)).
[90] *Ibid.*, s. 32 (3).
[91] See, *e.g.*, *Re Shelton's S. E.* [1928] W.N. 27.
[92] S.L.A., 1925, s. 32 (1); see, *e.g.*, *Re Adair* (1927) 71 S.J. 844.
[93] See *Re Arnell* [1924] 1 Ch. 473 at 478.
[94] *Re Gooch* [1929] 1 Ch. 740.
[95] See, *e.g.*, *Re Byng's S. E.* [1892] 2 Ch. 219; for such settlements, see the text above.
[96] See *Re Adair* (1927) 71 S.J. 844.

(subject to provisions for other members of the family) to his son in tail, and that on the son attaining his majority, A and the son bar the entail and resettle the property on A for life, with remainder to the son for life and remainders over.[97] Since a settlement may consist of a single instrument or any number of instruments,[98] there are then three distinct settlements to consider—

(1) the original settlement;

(2) the resettlement; and

(3) the compound settlement, which is a separate entity.[99]

2. Position of tenant for life. Formerly the position of a tenant for life under a compound settlement was as follows.

(i) Provided there were trustees of the original settlement,[1] he could exercise his powers as tenant for life under that settlement, and so, if he sold the land, overreach the rights of the beneficiaries under both the settlement and the resettlement.[2] This was so provided his estate arose under the original settlement, whether he was the original[3] or a subsequent[4] tenant for life. But while acting under the settlement he could not avail himself of any additional powers conferred by the resettlement.

(ii) He could act as tenant for life under the resettlement, availing himself of any additional powers conferred by it,[5] but in this case he could not overreach the rights of beneficiaries under the original settlement[6]; for rights under the original settlement had priority over the resettlement and could not be overreached by powers subsequently created.

(iii) He could act as tenant for life under the compound settlement, and so exercise any additional powers conferred by either settlement, and also overreach the rights of the beneficiaries under both the settlement and the resettlement.[7]

3. Trustees of the compound settlement. The third method combined the advantages of the first two methods, but it could be employed only if there were trustees of the compound settlement,

---

[97] See 3rd ed. of this book, p. 395.

[98] S.L.A., 1925, s. 1 (1).

[99] See *Re Coull's S. E.* [1905] 1 Ch. 712 at 720.

[1] *Re Cornwallis-West and Munro's Contract* [1903] 2 Ch. 150.

[2] *Re Lord Wimborne and Browne's Contract* [1904] 1 Ch. 537; *Re Curwen and Frames' Contract* [1924] 1 Ch. 581; and see *Re Knowles' S. E.* (1884) 27 Ch.D. 707.

[3] *Re Cope and Wadland's Contract* [1919] 2 Ch. 376.

[4] *Re Keck and Hart's Contract* [1898] 1 Ch. 617.

[5] *Re Constable's S. E.* [1919] 1 Ch. 178.

[6] See *Re Mundy and Roper's Contract* [1899] 1 Ch. 275 at 295.

[7] See *Re Cowley S. E.* [1926] Ch. 725.

who could receive any purchase-money on behalf of all the various interested parties.[8] Such trustees were rarely to be found. Except where they were appointed by the persons together able to dispose of the whole equitable interest,[9] they could be appointed only by the court [10]; for on making a settlement, the settlor probably had no power to declare who should be the trustees of any resettlement,[11] and on a resettlement being made, an appointment of trustees thereof could not bind the beneficiaries under the original settlement.[12]

4. Tenant for life. As regards the tenant for life, it was settled law that where one person was tenant for life under both settlements,[13] or under the resettlement alone,[14] he could act as tenant for life under the compound settlement. In the example given above, A could exercise the powers of a tenant for life under either settlement or under the compound settlement; it was immaterial whether or not the life estate conferred on him by the resettlement was expressed to be " in restoration and confirmation " of his life estate under the settlement.[15] Such a phrase was used in order to show an intention to keep alive the powers conferred by the original settlement,[16] and this was effective even if in fact the life estate was not restored.[17] Not until December 18, 1925, was it finally settled that giving a life estate expressly " in restoration and confirmation " of that conferred by the original settlement gave the tenant for life not only the powers (as had previously been thought) but also an actual life estate under the original settlement.[18]

5. Need for trustees of compound settlement. In most cases the comparative rarity of trustees of the compound settlement caused no difficulty, as, for example, where the tenant for life wished to sell free from the rights of the beneficiaries under both settlements, and

---

[8] *Re Marquis of Ailesbury and Lord Iveagh* [1893] 2 Ch. 345; *Re Phillimore's Estate* [1904] 2 Ch. 460.

[9] *Re Spearman S. E.* [1906] 2 Ch. 502.

[10] As in *Re Marquis of Ailesbury and Lord Iveagh, supra,* and *Re Tibbits' S. E.* [1897] 2 Ch. 149.

[11] See 51 S.J. 95.

[12] *Re Spencer's S. E.* [1903] 1 Ch. 75. A possible solution was to appoint the original trustees as trustees of the resettlement, especially if the original settlement had purported to appoint them trustees of the compound settlement: see 51 S.J. 79, 95, 96.

[13] *Re Mundy & Roper's Contract* [1899] 1 Ch. 275.

[14] *Re Phillimore's Estate* [1904] 2 Ch. 460.

[15] *Re Wright's Trustees & Marshall* (1884) 28 Ch.D. 93; *Re Mundy & Roper's Contract, supra;* *Re Constable's S. E.* [1919] 1 Ch. 178; S.L.A., 1925, ss. 22 (2), 50.

[16] *Re Constable's S. E., supra,* at p. 194.

[17] *Ibid.;* *Alexander* v. *Mills* (1870) 6 Ch.App. 124.

[18] *Parr* v. *Att.-Gen.* [1926] A.C. 239, overruling *Re Constable's S. E., supra,* to this extent, and retrospectively confirmed by S.L.A., 1925, s. 22 and 4th Sched., para. 8: see *Re Cradock's S. E.* [1926] Ch. 944.

he held under the original settlement of which there were properly appointed trustees,[19] or where he held under the resettlement and merely wished to exercise additional powers conferred thereby.[20] But in one case trustees of the compound settlement were needed in order to achieve the desired object: this was where there was no tenant for life under the original settlement and the tenant for life under the resettlement wished to overreach the rights of beneficiaries under the original settlement.[21]   In this case, if no such trustees existed, it was impossible to avoid the expense of an application to the court, either to appoint such trustees, or for leave to make a payment into court where this would discharge the incumbrances [22]; the tenant for life's option to have purchase-money paid into court was not exercisable if there were no trustees.[23]

6. After 1925. After 1925 this difficulty no longer exists. Where before 1926 the court had appointed trustees of the compound settlement, they continue in office.[23]   In other cases it has been provided in effect that even in the case of settlements made before 1926,[24] the trustees of the original settlement (provided it is still subsisting [25]), or, in default,[26] the trustees of the resettlement, shall be trustees of the compound settlement.[27]

C. Powers and Position of a Tenant for Life

The powers and position of a tenant for life remain substantially the same as under the Act of 1882. But in matters of detail a number of changes have been made, mostly tending to widen the powers of the tenant for life. A general account of the powers must now be given. In general, what follows applies to statutory owners as well as to tenants for life.

---

[19] *Re Du Cane & Nettlefold's Contract* [1898] 2 Ch. 96 ; *Re Lord Wimborne & Browne's Contract* [1904] 1 Ch. 537 ; *Re Cope & Wadland's Contract* [1919] 2 Ch. 376 ; *Re Curwen & Frames' Contract* [1924] 1 Ch. 581. If there were no trustees under the original settlement, the court sometimes appointed trustees of the compound settlement (see, *e.g.*, *Re Tibbits' S. E.* [1897] 2 Ch. 149) although it would have sufficed to appoint trustees of the original settlement : Wolstenholme's *Conveyancing Acts*, 10th ed., 363.

[20] *Re Constable's S. E.* [1919] 1 Ch. 178.

[21] *Re Trafford's S. E.* [1915] 1 Ch. 9 ; see Williams, V. & P., 365, 366 ; Wolstenholme's *Conveyancing Acts*, 10th ed., 363.

[22] Under C.A., 1881, s. 5 ; see *Re Cornwallis-West & Munro's Contract* [1903] 2 Ch. 150 at 155.

[23] *Re Fisher and Grazebrook's Contract* [1898] 2 Ch. 660.

[24] S.L.A., 1925, s. 31 (2).

[25] *Re Gordon and Adams' Contract* [1914] 1 Ch. 110 ; compare *Re Lord Alington and the L.C.C.'s Contract* [1927] 2 Ch. 253 ; S.L.A., 1925, ss. 3, 33.

[26] *Re Cayley and Evans' Contract* [1930] 2 Ch. 143.

[27] S.L.A., 1925, s. 31 (1), as amended by L.P.(Am.)A., 1926, Sched. See *e.g.*, *Re Symons* [1927] 1 Ch. 344.

I. POWERS OF A TENANT FOR LIFE

A tenant for life can of course deal with his limited interest in the land as he likes, subject only to the law of waste.[28]   Therefore he may lease it rent-free, or give away valuable rights over it such as easements; but these transactions will not bind his successors since they can take effect only out of his own interest.[29]   But his successors will be bound by transactions authorised by the Act or by any additional powers given by the settlement,[30] and it is therefore important that the extent of the statutory powers should be understood.   It is also important to remember that although he has the legal estate vested in him, he cannot dispose of any legal estate or interest except as permitted by the Act.[31]

As was the case under the Act of 1882, a tenant for life is normally subject to no control in the exercise of his statutory powers.[31a] The chief safeguards against abuse are—

(1) his position as a trustee for the beneficiaries;
(2) the provision that in the case of the most important powers he must give notice to the trustees of his intention to exercise them; and
(3) the provision that in a few exceptional cases he must not exercise his powers without the leave of the trustees or an order of the court.

1. His position as trustee.   This fundamental safeguard has already been explained.[32]

2. Powers exercisable upon giving notice.   If the tenant for life intends to make a sale, exchange, lease, mortgage or charge, or to grant an option, he must give written notice to the trustees of the settlement, and, if known, to the solicitor for the trustees.[33]   Trustees who are also the statutory owner need not, however, go through the " idle ceremony " of giving notice to themselves.[34]   The notice must be given by registered letter posted at least one calendar [35] month before the transaction or the contract therefor [36]; this provision is cast in an alternative form which seems to be satisfied by a notice given at least a month before the transaction, even

---

[28] *Ante*, p. 103.   [29] S.L.A., 1925, s. 18 (1).
[30] *Ante*, p. 297.
[31] S.L.A., 1925, s. 18; *ante*, p. 313.   But if the disposition complies with the Act, it need not be intended to be an exercise of the statutory power: *Re Pennant's W. T.* [1970] Ch. 75.
[31a] One joint tenant for life cannot force the other to sell: *Re 90 Thornhill Road, Tolworth* [1970] Ch. 261.   *Cf. post*, p. 365.
[32] *Ante*, p. 290; and see further *post*, p. 350.
[33] S.L.A., 1925, s. 101 (1).
[34] See *Re Countess of Dudley's Contract* (1887) 35 Ch.D. 338 at 342.
[35] Interpretation Act, 1889, s. 3.   [36] S.L.A., 1925, s. 101 (1).

if less than a month before the contract.[37] The notice is invalid unless when it is given the trustees consist of two or more persons or a trust corporation[38]; thus if there are no trustees, a tenant for life is not entitled to exercise these powers,[39] and an injunction may be granted to restrain him from doing so.[40]

The object of this provision for giving notice seems to be to enable the trustees to prevent any improper dealing[41] by applying to the court for an injunction.[42] The tenant for life may also be handicapped, if he has failed to give notice, by being refused the equitable remedy of specific performance against a purchaser.[43] But for general purposes the requirement of notice gives little protection, for—

(i) the trustees are apparently under no obligation to interfere with an improper transaction,[44] although they may, if they wish, bring the matter before the court[45];

(ii) except in the case of a mortgage or charge, a general notice suffices,[46] *e.g.*, " take notice that I intend from time to time to exercise any or all of my powers under the Settled Land Act, 1925." [47] In such cases, however, the tenant for life must, at the request of a trustee of the settlement, give reasonable information as to any sales, exchanges or leases effected, in progress or immediately intended[48];

(iii) any trustee may by writing accept less than one month's notice, or waive it altogether,[49] even if the contract was made before any trustees had been appointed[50]; and

(iv) a person dealing in good faith with the tenant for life is not concerned to inquire whether notice has been given.[51] Even if there are no trustees, a bona fide purchaser for value of a legal estate gets a good title if the transaction is one on which no capital money is payable,[52] *e.g.*, the grant of a lease without a premium.[53]

---

37 *Duke of Marlborough* v. *Sartoris* (1886) 32 Ch.D. 616; *sed quaere.*
38 S.L.A., 1925, s. 101 (1).
39 *Re Bentley* (1885) 54 L.J.Ch. 782.
40 *Wheelwright* v. *Walker (No.* 1) (1883) 23 Ch.D. 752.
41 See *Re Lord Monson's S.E.* [1898] 1 Ch. 427 at 432.
42 See *Hampden* v. *Earl of Buckinghamshire* [1893] 2 Ch. 531, where some of the beneficiaries obtained an injunction.
43 Wolst. & C. iii, 204. For a vendor's right to specific performance, see *post*, p. 593.
44 S.L.A., 1925, s. 97, replacing S.L.A., 1882, s. 42; the dictum to the contrary in *Wheelwright* v. *Walker (No.* 1) (1883) 23 Ch.D. 752 at 762 seems unsound as it was apparently uttered without reference to s. 42 of the S.L.A., 1882.
45 S.L.A., 1925, s. 93.
46 *Ibid.*, s. 101 (2).
47 See *Re Ray's S. E.* (1884) 25 Ch.D. 464.
48 S.L.A., 1925, s. 101 (3).
50 *Hatten* v. *Russell* (1888) 38 Ch.D. 334.
52 S.L.A., 1925, ss. 110 (4), 117 (1) (xxi).
53 See *Mogridge* v. *Clapp* [1892] 3 Ch. 382.
49 S.L.A., 1925, s. 101 (4).
51 S.L.A., 1925, s. 101 (5).

Each of the powers in respect of which notice is normally required must now be examined.

(a) *Power to sell.* A tenant for life may sell the settled land or any part thereof, or any easement, right or privilege of any kind over the land.[54] He may, for example, sell rights in the subsoil needed for making a railway tunnel.[55] But he cannot, so as to bind his successors, give away the land or any rights over it, except in certain special cases,[56] such as water rights,[57] the dedication of highways or open spaces,[58] or small grants of land for public or charitable purposes [59] when this is for the general benefit of the settled land. In all other cases the rule is that he must obtain the best consideration in money [60] that can reasonably be obtained.[61]

In one case [62] a tenant for life was made an offer by another beneficiary, but being unwilling to sell to him, proposed to sell to a third party for a lower price; the court restrained the tenant for life from selling for less than the price offered by the beneficiary, or from selling at all without informing the beneficiary of the proposed price and giving him two days in which to increase his offer.[63] But there is no need for the sale to be by auction; and it may be made in one lot or several lots, and free from or subject to stipulations as to title or otherwise [64]; and if the property is auctioned, the tenant for life may fix a reserve and buy it in.[65]

A purchaser is also protected by a provision that if he deals in good faith with the tenant for life or statutory owner, he is to be conclusively taken, as against all the beneficiaries, to have given the best consideration reasonably obtainable and to have complied with all the requirements of the Act; he is thus protected against the operation of section 18,[66] which invalidates irregular transactions.

[54] S.L.A., 1925, s. 38 (i).
[55] *Re Pearson's Will* (1900) 83 L.T. 626.
[56] See S.L.A., 1925, s. 39 (2)–(4), which allows a sale in consideration of a rent-charge (which may be nominal for the first five years) to be apportioned between capital and income; and s. 39 (5), which allows the price to be composed wholly or in part of fully paid securities in a statutory company (not an ordinary limited company).
[57] S.L.A., 1925, s. 54.
[58] *Ibid.*, 1925, s. 56; *post*, p. 349.
[59] *Ibid.*, 1925, ss. 55, 57 (2); *e.g.*, a town hall, a hospital or land for allotments or working class dwellings.
[60] On the ground that Consols were " as good as cash," payment in Consols was held to satisfy the requirement of the best " price " in S.L.A., 1882, s. 4 (1): *Re Sutton's Contract* [1921] W.N. 9 at 10. The present wording (" in money ") probably excludes this decision.
[61] S.L.A., 1925, s. 39 (1).
[62] *Wheelwright* v. *Walker (No.* 2) (1883) 31 W.R. 912.
[63] *Cf. Buttle* v. *Saunders* [1950] 2 All E.R. 193.
[64] S.L.A., 1925, s. 39 (6).
[65] *Ibid.*, s. 39 (7).
[66] *Ante*, p. 313.

This applies both to sales and to other dealings such as leases [67] and mortgages.[68] In one case a purchaser who made a good bargain and bought for £2,000 property which he forthwith resold for £3,000 was held to be protected.[69] It is essential that the purchaser should act in good faith,[70] but he need not be aware that he is dealing with a tenant for life.[70a]

(b) *Power to exchange.* Settled land, or any part of it, or any easement, right or privilege over it, may be exchanged for other land or any easement, right or privilege.[71] For "equality of exchange" (*i.e.*, to adjust any difference in value) capital money may be paid or received [72] and every exchange must be for the best consideration obtainable.[73] But settled land in England and Wales may not be given in exchange for land outside England and Wales.[74]

(c) *Power to lease*

(1) THE POWER. The settled land, or any part of it, or any easement, right or privilege over it (*e.g.*, for shooting or fishing, or to let down the surface by mining [75]), may be leased for any period not exceeding—

(i) 999 years for building or forestry;
(ii) 100 years for mining;
(iii) 50 years for any other purpose.[76]

Before 1926 the periods were 99, 60 and 21 years, respectively, and there was no special provision for forestry leases. After 1925, however, the new periods apply even if the settlement was made before 1926.

A building lease is defined as one made partly in consideration of erecting, improving, adding to or repairing buildings or an agreement to do this [77]; the advantage to the settled land is that in return for a reduced rent the lessee must leave on the land at the end of his lease the new or improved buildings. The wording is very wide, but it probably does not include an ordinary repairing lease,[78] nor does it include a lease made at a low rent in return for repairs, additions

---

[67] *Mogridge* v. *Clapp* [1892] 3 Ch. 382; *Re Morgan's Lease* [1972] Ch. 1. See L.P.A., 1925, s. 152, explained *post*, p. 337.   [68] S.L.A., 1925, s. 110 (1).
[69] *Hurrell* v. *Littlejohn* [1904] 1 Ch. 689.
[70] *Re Handman and Wilcox's Contract* [1902] 1 Ch. 599. As to leases, see *post*, p. 337.
[70a] *Re Morgan's Lease*, *supra*, doubting *Weston* v. *Henshaw* [1950] Ch. 510.
[71] S.L.A., 1925, s. 38 (iii). For an exchange of easements, see *Re Bracken's Settlement* [1903] 1 Ch. 265; *cf. Re Brotherton* (1908) 77 L.J.Ch. 373.
[72] S.L.A., 1925, ss. 38 (iii), 73 (1) (v).
[73] *Ibid.*, s. 40 (1).   [74] *Ibid.*, s. 40 (3).
[75] *Sitwell* v. *Earl of Londesborough* [1905] 1 Ch. 460.
[76] S.L.A., 1925, s. 41. The court may extend the periods (*post*, p. 337) and the limits do not apply to mortgage terms: see *post*, p. 339.
[77] S.L.A., 1925, ss. 44 (1), 117 (1) (i).
[78] See Wolst. & C. iii, 235; Hood and Challis, 561.

and improvements previously made voluntarily by the tenant.[79] But it includes a lease which requires the tenant to spend a substantial fixed sum on repairs [80]; and although it is usual to stipulate that some agreed sum must be expended within a fixed time, *e.g.*, two years,[81] this is not essential.[82] Where the land is to be leased in lots there are certain restrictions to ensure an even apportionment of the rent [83]; and the tenant for life has no power to lease settled land together with land of his own unless the rent is apportioned between the two.[84] A forestry lease means a lease to the Minister of Agriculture, Fisheries and Food for purposes authorised by the Forestry Act, 1945.[85] Mines and minerals may be disposed of separately from the surface, and *vice versa*.[86]

" Lease " includes an agreement for a lease (as it does throughout the Act [87]), but in this context it has been held to include only such tenancy agreements as take effect either in law or in equity as demises.[88] Contracts for the grant of future leases are the subject of different provisions.[89]

(2) CONDITIONS OF LEASE. Every lease of settled land must comply with the following conditions.

(i) It must be made by deed.[90]

(ii) It must be made to take effect in possession not more than one year after its date, or in reversion after an existing lease with not more than 7 years to run at the date of the new lease.[90] Thus if a tenant for life grants a lease to commence in 14 months' time, it is invalid [91] unless it is to commence after the determination of an existing lease.[92] But a *contract* to grant a lease in, say, ten years' time is valid.[93]

(iii) It must reserve the best rent reasonably obtainable in the circumstances, regard being had to any fine taken, and to any money laid out or to be laid out for the benefit of the land.[94] " Fine " is widely defined as including any premium

---

[79] *Re Chawner's S. E.* [1892] 2 Ch. 192.   [80] *Re Daniell's S. E.* [1894] 3 Ch. 503.
[81] *Re Earl of Ellesmere* [1898] W.N. 18.
[82] *Re Grosvenor S. E.* [1933] Ch. 97 (lease for 999 years with covenant to rebuild premises when necessary and, in particular, when required to do so by the lessor's surveyor).
[83] S.L.A., 1925, s. 44 (3); *Re Rycroft's Settlement* [1962] Ch. 263.
[84] *Re Rycroft's Settlement, supra.*
[85] S.L.A., 1925, s. 117 (1) (x); Forestry Act, 1967, Sched. 6 (5); and see Sched. 2.
[86] S.L.A., 1925, s. 50; see *Re Gladstone* [1900] 2 Ch. 101 ; *Re Duke of Rutland's S. E.* [1900] 2 Ch. 206.   [87] S.L.A., 1925, s. 117 (1) (x).
[88] *Re Rycroft's Settlement, supra* ; but see *Re Morgan's Lease* [1972] Ch. 1, holding that an executory contract is included. For this distinction, see *post*, p. 624.
[89] *Post*, p. 350.   [90] S.L.A., 1925, s. 42 (1) (i).
[91] See *Kisch* v. *Hawes Bros. Ltd.* [1935] Ch. 102 ; but see also L.P.A., 1925, s. 152, explained *post*, p. 337.
[92] For the general rules about reversionary leases, see *post*, p. 631.
[93] See preceding paragraph.   [94] S.L.A., 1925, s. 42 (1) (ii).

or fore-gift, and any payment, condition or benefit in the nature of a fine, premium or fore-gift,[95] so that although it usually means a lump sum paid for the grant of the lease, it is not confined to such payments.[96] Any fine is capital money.[97] A lease granted by a tenant for life at a reduced rent in return for a bribe[98] or the release from a claim for damages against him personally[99] has accordingly been held ineffective, as not complying with the statutory requirements. A nominal or reduced rent may be reserved for not longer than the first five years of a building lease[1] or the first ten years of a forestry lease,[2] and in the case of mining[3] or forestry[4] leases, there are wide powers to vary the rent, *e.g.*, according to the value of the minerals or trees taken.

(iv) It must contain a covenant by the lessee for payment of rent and a condition of re-entry (*i.e.*, a provision for forfeiture of the lease) on rent not being paid within a specified time not exceeding 30 days.[5]

(v) A counterpart (*i.e.*, copy) of the lease must be executed by the lessee and delivered to the tenant for life; it is sufficient evidence that this has been done if the tenant for life duly executes the lease.[6]

It will be seen that normally a lease must be by deed, and notice must be given to the trustees. In certain cases, however, these requirements are relaxed. A lease at the best rent reasonably obtainable without a fine and not exempting the lessee from liability for waste has two advantages:

(i) If it is for not more than 21 years, it may be made without giving notice to the trustees; and

(ii) if it is for not more than 3 years (and this appears to include a weekly or other periodic tenancy, even though it may last more than 3 years[7]), it may also be made merely in writing and not by deed, with an agreement, instead of a covenant, to pay the rent.[8]

---

95 S.L.A., 1925, s. 117 (1) (xxii).
96 *Lloyd-Jones* v. *Clark-Lloyd* [1919] 1 Ch. 424 at 438; and see *Waite* v. *Jennings* [1906] 2 K.B. 11; *Comber* v. *Fleet Electrics Ltd.* [1955] 1 W.L.R. 566.
97 S.L.A., 1925, s. 42 (4); see *Pumford* v. *W. Butler & Co. Ltd.* [1914] 2 Ch. 353.
98 *Chandler* v. *Bradley* [1897] 1 Ch. 315.
99 *Re Handman and Wilcox's Contract* [1902] 1 Ch. 599.
1 S.L.A., 1925, s. 44 (1).
2 *Ibid.*, s. 48 (1) (i).
3 *Ibid.*, s. 45 (1); and see *Re Aldam's S. E.* [1902] 2 Ch. 46.
4 S.L.A., 1925, s. 48 (1).
5 *Ibid.*, s. 42 (1) (iii).
6 *Ibid.*, s. 42 (2).
7 See *Davies* v. *Hall* [1954] 1 W.L.R. 855.
8 S.L.A., 1925, s. 42 (5).

In the case of building and mining leases the court may relax the statutory requirements, including the maximum term, if these conflict with what is customary in the district or make it difficult to grant such leases.[9]

(3) DEFECTIVE LEASES. A lease which does not comply with the requirements of the Act is void, except so far as it binds the beneficial interest of the tenant for life.[10] But under statutory provisions dating from 1849,[11] and now contained in the Law of Property Act, 1925,[12] leases which are invalid because they fail to comply with the terms of a power may nevertheless be effective in equity at the lessee's option as contracts for leases,[13] subject to such variations as are necessary in order to comply with the power. This saving enactment applies only if the lease was made in good faith and the lessee has taken possession,[12] so that only sitting tenants are benefited; and by judicial construction its operation is confined, it seems, to the curing of minor irregularities only, such as the omission of some restriction or condition, or a mistake in form.[14]

Furthermore the Settled Land Act, 1925,[15] gives special protection, as already noticed,[16] to a purchaser (including a tenant) who deals in good faith with the tenant for life: he is conclusively presumed, as against those entitled under the settlement, to have given the best consideration reasonably obtainable and to have complied with the other requirements of the Act. If the consideration is insufficient, therefore, the title of such a tenant is none the worse, and the point can only be disputed as between the beneficiaries under the settlement. If, however, the lease on its face violates the requirements of the Act, the tenant will not be taken to have dealt in good faith and he may have to be prepared to prove that he gave the best consideration reasonably obtainable, or complied with any of the other statutory conditions which is alleged to have been violated.[17]

---

[9] *Ibid.*, s. 46.
[10] *Ibid.*, s. 18 (1) (*ante*, pp. 313, 333), in effect resolving the doubt whether the lease was void or voidable: see *Re Handman and Wilcox's Contract* [1902] 1 Ch. 599.
[11] Leases Acts, 1849, 1850.   [12] s. 152 (retrospective: s. 154).
[13] Registrable as estate contracts (Wolst. & C. i, 281), but in any case remaindermen or revisioners will be bound since they are not purchasers: see L.C.A. 1972, s. 4, *post*, p. 1047. But it is arguable that registration is not required, since L.P.A., 1925, s. 152 (1), provides that the contract "shall take effect" against successors in title.
[14] *Hallett to Martin* (1883) 24 Ch.D. 624; *Brown* v. *Peto* [1900] 1 Q.B. 346; *Re Newell* [1900] 1 Ch. 90; Foa 30; Halsb. xxiii, 423.
[15] s. 110 (1).   [16] *Ante*, p. 333.
[17] *Davies* v. *Hall* [1954] 1 W.L.R. 855, explaining the dictum of Farwell J. in *Kisch* v. *Hawes Bros. Ltd.* [1935] Ch. 102 at 109, 110; and see *Re Morgan's Lease* [1972] Ch. 1, holding that the protection extends to an option to renew a lease. See generally (1971) 87 L.Q.R. 338 (D. W. Elliott).

As a corollary to his power to grant leases, a tenant for life has wide powers of accepting surrenders of leases [18] and of varying or waiving the terms of any lease.[19] These powers are exercisable without notice to the trustees.

(4) RENT FROM LEASES. The normal rule is that the tenant for life is entitled to the whole of the rent from leases of the settled land.[20] But as seen above,[21] this does not apply to mining leases, where the capital value of the land is being diminished. The general rule as to rent from mining leases granted under the Act is that, subject to any contrary intention in the settlement,[22] the tenant for life is entitled to three-quarters of the rent; but if he is impeachable of waste [23] and the mine is an unopened one, he is entitled to only one-quarter of the rent payable under any lease granted by him (and not by some previous owner or tenant for life): in each case the balance of the rent is capital.[24] A direction to apply all the rent under a mining lease as income is a sufficient contrary intention,[25] but not a direction to pay the " rent and annual income " to the tenant for life,[26] nor the mere fact that the person with the powers of a tenant for life has been given a fee simple defeasible by condition.[27]

These provisions for apportioning the rent are confined to rent from leases granted under the Act, so that if the lease is granted under an express power in the settlement,[28] or if the lease [29] or a contract therefor [30] was made before the land was settled under the existing settlement (as where it was granted under a previous settlement),[31] the tenant for life is entitled to the whole of the income; and this is not affected by the tenant for life extending the term of the lease by virtue of his powers under the existing settlement.[32] Further, the rules as to the tenant for life working the minerals himself [33] are different from the rules as to leases. Again, where

---

[18] S.L.A., 1925, s. 52.
[19] *Ibid.*, s. 59. See *Re Savile S. E.* [1931] 2 Ch. 210 (mining lease for 60 years extended to 100 years).
[20] See, *e.g.*, *Re Wix* [1916] 1 Ch. 279.
[21] *Ante*, p. 108.
[22] See, *e.g.*, *Re Duke of Newcastle's Estate* (1883) 24 Ch.D. 129; *Re Bagot's Settlement* [1894] 1 Ch. 177.
[23] *Ante*, p. 105.
[24] S.L.A., 1925, s. 47; *Re Chaytor* [1900] 2 Ch. 804; *Re Fitzwalter* [1943] Ch. 285.
[25] *Re Rayner* [1913] 2 Ch. 210.
[26] *Re Daniels* [1912] 2 Ch. 90.
[27] *Re Hanbury's S. E.* [1913] 2 Ch. 357.
[28] *Earl of Lonsdale* v. *Lowther* [1900] 2 Ch. 687.
[29] *Re Hall* [1916] 2 Ch. 488 at 494; *Re Bruce* [1932] 1 Ch. 316.
[30] *Re Kemeys-Tynte* [1892] 2 Ch. 211.
[31] *Re Arkwright's Settlement* [1945] Ch. 195 (see 1946 Conv.Y.B. 176).
[32] *Ibid.*
[33] *Ante*, p. 108: he can keep all the profits unless he is impeachable of waste and the mine is unopened, in which case he may not work it at all.

the tenant for life has not a life interest but some other interest, such as a fee simple subject to a gift over,[34] he is unimpeachable of waste even if the settlement is silent on the subject[35]; the owner of a mere life interest, on the other hand, is impeachable unless the settlement exempts him from liability for waste.[36]

(d) *Power to mortgage.* In the absence of a contrary provision in the settlement,[37] a tenant for life has no power to mortgage or charge the legal estate for his own benefit. If he wishes to raise money for his own use, he can of course do so by mortgaging his beneficial interest, consisting of his life interest, entail or whatever interest he has. The legal estate, on the other hand, can be mortgaged or charged for the following purposes only:

(i) To provide money which is required to be raised under the provisions of the settlement,[38] e.g., portions.[39]

(ii) To provide money where it is reasonably required[40] for certain specified purposes.[41] These are all cases connected with the well-being of the land, and include—[41]

(a) discharging an incumbrance of a permanent nature (and not, e.g., annual sums payable for a life or term of years[42]) on all or part of the land, including such matters as charges for making up streets.[43] Thus it may be possible to pay off two or more mortgages on which interest at 5 per cent. is payable by raising money on a new mortgage with interest at 3¾ per cent.,[44] and the whole of the land may be mortgaged in order to pay off a mortgage on part[45];

(b) paying for authorised improvements[46];

(c) equality of exchange[47];

(d) extinguishing manorial incidents;

(e) payment of the costs of the above and certain other transactions, e.g., the costs of discharging mortgages.[48]

---

[34] See, e.g., *Re Hanbury's S. E.* [1913] 2 Ch. 357.   [35] *Ante*, p. 69.
[36] *Ante*, p. 105.   [37] See *Re Egerton's S. E.* [1926] Ch. 574.
[38] S.L.A., 1925, s. 16 (1); if such sums have already been raised by means of an equitable charge affecting the whole of the land, the tenant for life can replace this charge by a legal mortgage or charge: *ibid.* Whether the money has been already raised or not, on being requested in writing the tenant for life is bound to create the requisite legal mortgage or charge: *ibid.*
[39] For these, see *ante*, p. 283 and *post*, p. 385.
[40] *Re Clifford* [1902] 1 Ch. 87; *Re Bruce* [1905] 2 Ch. 372 at 376.
[41] S.L.A., 1925, s. 71 (1).   [42] S.L.A., 1925, s. 71 (2).
[43] *Re Smith's S. E.* [1901] 1 Ch. 689; and see *Re Pizzi* [1907] 1 Ch. 67.
[44] *More* v. *More* (1889) 37 W.R. 414.
[45] *Re Lord Monson's S. E.* [1898] 1 Ch. 427.
[46] See *post*, p. 344.   [47] *Ante*, p. 333
[48] *More* v. *More* (1889) 37 W.R. 414; and see *Re Maryon-Wilson's S. E.* [1915] 1 Ch. 29.

Since a mortgage overrides the beneficiaries' interests under the settlement,[49] and they do not automatically attach to the money raised by the mortgage, the court will intervene to prevent the power of mortgaging being used so as to prejudice beneficiaries, and will treat any such inequitable mortgage as a breach of trust.[50]

A mortgage of the legal estate is required to be a legal mortgage or a charge by way of legal mortgage.[51] But since an equitable mortgage is really a contract to create a legal mortgage,[52] and a tenant for life can make such a contract,[53] it seems probable that an equitable mortgage would be effective, provided that it was made for one of the permitted purposes.

(*e*) *Power to grant options.* A tenant for life may grant an option in writing to purchase or take a lease of all or any part of the settled land or of any easement, right or privilege over it.[54] But—

> (i) the price or rent must be the best reasonably obtainable[55] and must be fixed at the time of granting the option[55a]; a tenant for life thus has no power to agree to sell at a price to be fixed by arbitration[56];
>
> (ii) the option must be made exercisable within an agreed number of years not exceeding ten[57];
>
> (iii) the option may be granted with or without any consideration being paid,[57a] but if any is paid, it is capital money.[58]

3. Powers exercisable with consent of the trustees or under an order of the court. In the following cases, the tenant for life can exercise his powers only with the consent of the trustees of the settlement or under an order of the court.

---

[49] *See post*, p. 373.
[50] *Hampden* v. *Earl of Buckinghamshire* [1893] 2 Ch. 531; this is the case " in which the court has gone the furthest in controlling the discretion of the tenant for life ": *Re Richardson* [1900] 2 Ch. 778 at 790, *per* Stirling J.
[51] S.L.A., 1925, ss. 16 (1), 71 (1), 117 (1) (xi). S. 71 (3) expressly empowers the tenant for life to grant the long term of years (*e.g.*, 3,000 years) by which legal mortgages are now made (*post*, p. 896), despite the restrictions on the length of leases imposed in other cases by the Act (*ante*, p. 334).
[52] *Post*, p. 899.
[53] S.L.A., 1925, s. 90 (1) (i).
[54] *Ibid.*, s. 51 (1). Before 1926 options could be granted only in building leases under S.L.A., 1889, ss. 2 and 3, which were in similar terms.
[55] S.L.A., 1925, s. 51 (3).   [55a] *Ibid.*, s. 51 (1).
[56] *Re Earl of Wilton's S. E.* [1907] 1 Ch. 50 at 55; but where the total price or rent is fixed and only part of the land is taken the sums payable may be apportioned by any method, including arbitration: S.L.A., 1925, s. 51 (3).
[57] S.L.A., 1925, s. 51 (2).   [57a] *Ibid.*, s. 51 (1).
[58] *Ibid.*, s. 51 (5).

(a) Power to dispose of the principal mansion house

(1) THE POWER. If the tenant for life wishes to make a disposition of the principal mansion house, if any, and the pleasure-grounds and park (whether or not usually occupied therewith [59]) and land, if any, usually occupied therewith, the consent of the trustees or an order of the court is required—

    (i) if the settlement was made before 1926 and does not expressly provide to the contrary; or

    (ii) if the settlement was made after 1925 and expressly requires such consent or order to be obtained.[60]

In other cases, no consent is required, but the usual notice must be given. " Disposition " includes sales, leases, mortgages, exchanges and every other assurance of property by any instrument except a will,[61] whether of the land itself or of rights over it, such as easements.[62]

(2) PRINCIPAL MANSION HOUSE. If a house is usually occupied as a farmhouse, or if the site of a house and the pleasure-grounds and park and lands, if any, usually occupied therewith do not together exceed 25 acres, the house is not deemed a principal mansion house.[63] In other cases it is a question of fact whether at any given moment a house is a principal mansion house.[64] Where two separate establishments are comprised in the same settlement, there may be two principal mansion houses, or one may be subsidiary to the other,[65] as where one is used as the main residence and the other as a shooting-box.[66] A house may cease to be a principal mansion house, as where it is let as a school [67]; and if the tenant for life then uses a smaller house on the estate as his home, that may become a principal mansion house.[68]

(3) CONSENT. The trustees' consent must be given before the transaction is effected, though it need not be formal or in writing.[69]

---

[59] *Pease* v. *Courtney* [1904] 2 Ch. 503, holding that " usually occupied therewith " governs " lands " only. *Sed quaere* ; to support such a construction the wording should have been " the pleasure grounds and park and *the* lands, if any usually occupied therewith," whereas in fact the italicised word is missing.

[60] S.L.A., 1925, s. 65 (1).

[61] *Ibid.*, s. 117 (1) (v).

[62] *Dowager Duchess of Sutherland* v. *Duke of Sutherland* [1893] 3 Ch. 169; *Pease* v. *Courtney* [1904] 2 Ch. 503.

[63] S.L.A., 1925, s. 65 (2).

[64] *Re Feversham S. E.* [1938] 2 All E.R. 210 at 212, 213.

[65] *Re Wythes' S. E.* [1908] 1 Ch. 593 at 598.

[66] *Gilbey* v. *Rush* [1906] 1 Ch. 11 at 21.

[67] *Re Wythes' S. E.* [1908] 1 Ch. 593 (two estates, each with a principal mansion house, comprised in same settlement, one let as a school); *Re Feversham S. E.* [1938] 2 All E.R. 210 (single estate, sole principal mansion house let as a school).

[68] *Re Feversham S. E., supra.*

[69] *Gilbey* v. *Rush* [1906] 1 Ch. 11.

Where the consent of the court is sought, the court considers all the circumstances of the case,[70] such as whether the property is an old family estate [71] and the effect of a sale will be to " strip from an ancient, noble, and landed family the last acre of land which is attached to the title," [72] whether the price offered is good,[73] whether there is an alternative estate on which the family can live,[73] and, if pictures and other chattels have been settled to devolve with the house as heirlooms, what provision is to be made for them.[74]

(*b*) *Power to cut and sell timber.* This has already been dealt with.[75]   It is only if the tenant for life is impeachable of waste that he requires the consent of the trustees or an order of the court,[76] and then three-quarters of the proceeds are capital money [77]; if he is unimpeachable, he needs no consent or order and may keep all the proceeds.[75]

(*c*) *Power to compromise claims.*   Subject to the consent in writing of the trustees, the tenant for life has a wide power to compromise and settle disputes relating to the settled land or any part thereof.[78]   He has a similar power by deed or writing to release, waive or modify rights over other land which benefit the settled land, *e.g.*, easements and restrictive covenants, whether or not consideration is given.[79]

(*d*) *Power to sell settled chattels*

(1) SETTLED CHATTELS.   The Settled Land Acts are not in general concerned with chattels,[80] but they have made special provision for personal chattels settled so as to devolve with, or as nearly as possible with, settled land (including, it has been held, a baronetcy [81]), and for personal chattels settled together with land or on trusts declared by reference to trusts affecting land.[82]   Thus furniture, pictures,

---

[70] Thus the application may be directed to stand over until further information is produced : *Re Sebright's S. E.* (1886) 33 Ch.D. 429.
[71] *Re Wortham's S. E.* (1896) 75 L.T. 293.
[72] *Re Marquis of Ailesbury's S. E.* [1892] 1 Ch. 506 at 546, *per* Fry L.J.
[73] *Marquis of Camden* v. *Murray* (1883) Hood and Challis, *Conveyancing Acts,* 7th ed., 582 (the 8th ed., p. 479, omits this report).
[74] *Re Brown's Will* (1884) 27 Ch.D. 179.
[75] *Ante,* p. 107.
[76] S.L.A., 1925, s. 66 (1).
[77] *Ibid.*, s. 66 (2).
[78] *Ibid.*, s. 58 (1).
[79] *Ibid.*, s. 58 (2).
[80] The Act of course applies to leasehold land (*ante,* pp. 314, 315) but not to personal chattels as such.
[81] As being an incorporeal hereditament, and so " land " within S.L.A., 1925, s. 117 (1) (ix): *Re Sir J. Rivett-Carnac's Will* (1885) 30 Ch.D. 136.   *Sed quaere* : see Challis 45, 471 ; Hood and Challis 485.
[82] S.L.A., 1925, s. 67 (1), replacing S.L.A., 1882, s. 37.

armour and other family possessions, if settled along with land, are now governed by the Act of 1925. Such things are often, though inaccurately,[83] called " heirlooms."

(2) POWER OF SALE. Before the Act of 1882 the court had no power to order a sale merely because it would benefit all concerned,[84] and the tenant for life could dispose of no more than his right to enjoy the chattels for his life. But now the tenant for life is empowered to sell chattels [85] (though not to lease them [86]), provided he first obtains an order of the court [87]; there is no provision enabling him to sell with the consent of the trustees. The purchase-money (though not any damages paid in respect of the chattels [88]) is treated as capital money,[89] and thus may, *e.g.*, be used for effecting improvements,[90] paying off mortgages [91] or repairing other chattels [92]; and under an order of the court [93] it may be used to buy other chattels to be held on the same trusts.[94] The land and the chattels are treated as if they were settled by the same instrument,[95] even if the land is settled by deed and the chattels by will.[96]

(3) CIRCUMSTANCES FOR SALE. In deciding whether to authorise a sale the court considers all the circumstances,[97] the onus of making out a case for sale being on the applicant.[98] The interests of the other beneficiaries will be considered, the greater weight being given to the interests of those more nearly entitled.[99] Circumstances which have influenced the court against a sale include: that the tenant for life's only reason was that he required a larger income [1]; that the fact that there was no house for the valuable pictures in question was

---

83 See *post*, p. 523.
84 *D'Eyncourt* v. *Gregory* (1876) 3 Ch.D. 635; but see *Fane* v. *Fane* (1876) 2 Ch.D. 711.
85 S.L.A., 1925, s. 67 (1).
86 See *Re Lacon's Settlement* [1911] 1 Ch. 351 at 353, 354; [1911] 2 Ch. 17 at 19.
87 S.L.A., 1925, s. 67 (3).
88 *Re Walton* (1900) 44 S.J. 645.
89 S.L.A., 1925, s. 67 (2).
90 *Re Houghton Estate* (1885) 30 Ch.D. 102.
91 *Re Lord John Thynne* (1884) 77 L.T.News. 195.
92 *Re Waldegrave* (1899) 81 L.T. 632.
93 S.L.A., 1925, s. 67 (3).
94 *Ibid.*, s. 67 (2).
95 *Re Earl of Egmont's S. E.* [1912] 1 Ch. 251.
96 *Re Lord Stafford's Settlement and Will* [1904] 2 Ch. 72.
97 *Re The Earl of Radnor's W. T.* (1890) 45 Ch.D. 402.
98 *Re Hope's Settlement* (1893) 9 T.L.R. 506.
99 *Re The Earl of Radnor's W. T.* (1890) 45 Ch.D. 402; *Re Hope's S. E.* (1910) 26 T.L.R. 413.
1 *Re Fetherstonhaugh's Settlement* (1898) 42 S.J. 198; *Re Sebright, deceased* (1912) 28 T.L.R. 191 (where, on a change of circumstances being shown, the court later ordered a sale: *Re Sebright* (1914) 31 T.L.R. 25). If the tenant for life has got himself into difficulties by his own extravagance, he cannot expect this to commend his application to the court: *Re Hope* [1899] 2 Ch. 679.

the result of the applicant's own act in selling the house[2]; that the chattel is of unique character and historical repute which the remaindermen regard as an object of pride[3]; and that the chattels are pictures which are characteristic features of the mansion house.[4] Circumstances which have influenced the court in favour of a sale include: that all except possible unborn beneficiaries agree to a sale[5]; that, without any fault on his part, the tenant for life will be too poor to marry unless something is sold, and the opposition is raised by a remainderman unlikely to succeed to the property and for whom the chattels have no special value[6]; that only 3 out of 279 pictures are to be sold[7]; that the chattels to be sold are those unsuitable for removal to a new residence of the tenant for life[8]; and that the chattels are portraits which include no portraits of famous ancestors.[9]

(4) ENTAILED CHATTELS. If the chattels are entailed, as is possible since 1925, the entail can be barred in the same way as an entail of land,[10] and this may provide a means of avoiding an application to the court; but the trusts of a strict settlement will often ensure that the entail can be barred only if the tenant for life's consent is obtained.[11]

(e) *Power to do anything proper with the court's consent.* The court has a statutory jurisdiction to authorise the tenant for life to effect any transaction not otherwise authorised by the Act or the settlement[12] if it affects the settled land, is for the benefit of the land or the beneficiaries,[13] and is a transaction which an absolute owner could validly effect.[14] "Transaction" is widely defined, and includes the application of capital money.[15] The court has, for example, authorised a tenant for life to mortgage the land, and so save himself

[2] *Re Hope's Settlement* (1893) 9 T.L.R. 506.
[3] *Re Hope* [1899] 2 Ch. 679 (the Hope diamond: leave refused. A sale was ordered in 1910: see *Re Hope's S. E.* (1910) 26 T.L.R. 413).
[4] *Re Beaumont's S. E.* (1888) 58 L.T. 916.
[5] *Re Lord Bateman's Settled Heirlooms* (1926) 70 S.J. 810.
[6] *Re Townshend's Settlement* (1903) 89 L.T. 691.
[7] *Re The Earl of Radnor's W. T.* (1890) 45 Ch.D. 402.
[8] *Browne* v. *Collins* (1890) 62 L.T. 566.
[9] *Re Hope's S. E.* (1910) 26 T.L.R. 413.
[10] L.P.A., 1925, s. 130 (1); *ante*, p. 95.
[11] See *ante*, pp. 90, 91, *post*, p. 374. For the sale of chattels settled so as to devolve independently of land, see Snell, *Equity*, pp. 250, 251.
[12] See *Re Symons* [1927] 1 Ch. 344 at 354.
[13] See, *e.g.*, *Re Cleveland Literary and Philosophical Society's Land* [1931] 2 Ch. 247.
[14] S.L.A., 1925, s. 64, as amended by Settled Land and Trustee Acts (Court's General Powers) Act, 1943, s. 2. See also s. 1 of the latter Act (amended and made permanent by Emergency Laws (Miscellaneous Provisions) Act, 1953, s. 9), giving power to authorise expenses of management to be treated as capital outgoings.
[15] S.L.A., 1925, s. 64 (2), as amended: see preceding note.

from bankruptcy, where his debts arose from the expenses of maintaining the land.[16] Further, this jurisdiction allows the court to authorise, on behalf of those who cannot consent (such as infants and unborn persons), a scheme which alters the beneficial interests under the settlement,[17] which before the Variation of Trusts Act, 1958, could not normally be done under the general law.[18]

4. Other powers of a tenant for life

(a) *Power to effect improvements*

(1) IMPROVEMENTS. Improvements have to be distinguished in principle from current repairs. The former are special operations of a capital nature, the latter are ordinary outgoings and must be paid for out of income. A tenant for life may of course effect both improvements and repairs at his own expense, and often in the case of repairs it is only at his own expense that he can effect them at all.[19] But in the case of improvements he may be entitled [20] to have the cost borne either temporarily or permanently by capital money, or raised by a mortgage or charge of the settled land.

(2) SCHEMES. Under the Act of 1882 the tenant for life had to submit in advance to the trustees or the court a detailed scheme,[21] though the trustees were not concerned with his general policy in making improvements, but had only to see whether, acting in good faith and on proper advice, he was submitting a proper scheme for improvements within the Act.[22] Under the Act of 1925, no prior scheme is required.[23] Indeed, there is power for the court to authorise the application of capital money for improvements made before 1926 without the prior submission of a scheme,[24] though the fact that the tenant for life must have expected to bear the cost himself is a strong reason for the court not exercising this discretionary power.[25]

---

[16] *Re White-Popham S. E.* [1936] Ch. 725.

[17] *Re Simmons* [1956] Ch. 125, holding that L.P.A., 1925, s. 28 (1) (*post*, p. 365), incorporates this rule into trusts for sale of land.

[18] See *Chapman* v. *Chapman* [1954] A.C. 429, decided on the different wording of T.A., 1925, s. 57; (1954) 70 L.Q.R. 473 (R.E.M.). For the Act of 1958, see Snell, *Equity*, 231–235.

[19] See, however, *post*, p. 348.

[20] See *Re Hotchkin's S. E.* (1887) 35 Ch.D. 41; *Re Ormrod's S. E.* [1892] 2 Ch. 318: cf. *Rowley* v. *Ginnever* [1897] 2 Ch. 503.

[21] S.L.A., 1882, s. 26.

[22] See *Re Earl of Egmont's S. E.* [1906] 2 Ch. 151.

[23] S.L.A., 1925, s. 84 (1).

[24] *Ibid.*, s. 87.

[25] See *Re Tucker's S. E.* [1895] 2 Ch. 468; *Re Lord Sherborne's S. E.* [1929] 1 Ch. 345; *Re Jacques S. E.* [1930] 2 Ch. 418; *Re Borough Court Estate* [1932] 2 Ch. 39.

(3) IMPROVEMENTS AFTER 1925. For improvements effected after 1925 the tenant for life must first ascertain that the proposed improvements are within the list of those authorised by the Act. He may then carry out the work. But it must be done to the satisfaction of a surveyor or engineer: for capital money can only be paid out in the following circumstances.

(i) If the money is in the hands of the trustees, there must be—

(a) a certificate furnished by a competent engineer or able practical surveyor employed independently of the tenant for life, certifying—

(i) that the work or some specific part thereof has been properly executed; and

(ii) the amount properly payable in respect thereof; or

(b) an order of the court directing payment [26]; and such an order will be made only if there is sufficient evidence to satisfy the court that the scheme is proper.[27]

(ii) If the money is in court, there must be—

(a) a report or certificate of the Minister of Agriculture, Fisheries and Food [28]; or

(b) a report of a competent engineer or able practical surveyor approved by the court; or

(c) such other evidence as the court thinks fit.[29]

(4) REPAYMENT. When the improvements are paid for out of capital, the question arises whether or not the tenant for life must repay the money. This depends on the nature of the improvements. A long list is set out in the Third Schedule to the Act,[30] which is divided into three parts:

(i) If the improvement is authorised by the settlement [31] or falls within the twenty-five heads of Part I, repayment cannot be ordered. These heads include drainage (e.g., the straightening, widening or deepening of drains, streams and watercourses [32]), bridges, labourers' cottages (including a cottage for a gardener [33] but not a house for an estate

---

[26] S.L.A., 1925, s. 84 (2).
[27] *Re Keck's Settlement* [1904] 2 Ch. 22.
[28] S.L.A., 1925, ss. 84 (3), 117 (1) (xvi).
[29] *Ibid.*, s. 84 (3).
[30] For notes and authorities on the various branches of this list, see Wolst. & C. iii, 261 *et seq.* For the special provisions as to agricultural land made by the Agricultural Holdings Act, 1948, see *post*, p. 348, n. 53.
[31] See, however, *Re Sudbury and Poynton Estates* [1893] 3 Ch. 74.
[32] See, *e.g.*, *Re Lord Leconfield's S. E.* [1907] 2 Ch. 340.
[33] *Re Earl of Lisburne's S. E.* [1910] W.N. 91.

agent [34]), and additions or alterations to buildings reasonably necessary or proper to enable them to be let. This last head applies whether or not the additions or alterations are structural,[35] and includes the substitution of a new roof for one worn out,[36] and the conversion of a dwelling-house, cottage and shop into residential flats and shops,[37] but not the erection of an entirely new building in place of an old one.[38] It applies only if there is a present intention of letting,[39] or if the tenant has threatened to leave unless the improvements are made and it would be difficult to find another tenant.[40] The test whether the works are necessary or proper is whether a reasonable and prudent person would effect them if he were absolute owner.[41]

(ii) If the improvement falls within the six heads of Part II, the trustees or the court have a discretion to order repayment by instalments out of the income of the settled land.[42] These heads include houses for employees, restoration of damage by dry-rot,[43] and structural additions to or alterations in buildings reasonably required, whether or not let or to be let; and this last head has been held to extend to the erection of a garage, workshop, tool-shed and similar buildings close to the principal mansion house with which they formed a unit.[44]

(iii) If the improvement falls within the three heads of Part III (*e.g.*, the installation of heating apparatus or artificial light in a building), the trustees or the court must order repayment by instalments out of the income of the settled land.[45]

(5) INSTALMENTS. The number of the instalments is within the discretion of the court or the trustees, except that trustees may not order more than fifty half-yearly instalments [46]; the court is unfettered as to the number of instalments.[47] There are provisions for securing

---

[34] *Re Lord Gerard's S. E.* [1893] 3 Ch. 252; but this is included in Part II, para. (i).
[35] *Re Lindsay's Settlement* (*No.* 2) [1941] Ch. 119, criticised (1941) 57 L.Q.R. 312 (R.E.M.). Formerly they had to be structural: *Re Blagrave's S. E.* [1903] 1 Ch. 560, decided on S.L.A., 1890, s. 13 (ii).
[36] *Re Gaskell's S. E.* [1894] 1 Ch. 485.
[37] *Re Swanwick House, Prestbury* [1939] 3 All E.R. 531.
[38] *Re Leveson-Gower's S. E.* [1905] 2 Ch. 95.
[39] *Re De Teissier's S. E.* [1893] 1 Ch. 153.
[40] *Re Calverley's S. E.* [1904] 1 Ch. 150.
[41] *Stanford* v. *Roberts* [1910] 1 Ch. 440.   [42] S.L.A., 1925, s. 84 (4).
[43] This meets the difficulties disclosed by *Re Legh's S. E.* [1902] 2 Ch. 274.
[44] *Re Insole's S. E.* [1938] Ch. 812.
[45] S.L.A., 1925, s. 84 (2), (4).
[46] *Ibid.*, s. 84 (2).
[47] *Ibid.*, s. 84 (4). *In Re Jacques S. E.* [1930] 2 Ch. 418 the court ordered 20 half-yearly instalments.

payment by a rentcharge created by the tenant for life [48] or by an
order of the court, which automatically operates as a rentcharge
sufficient to pay the instalments, taking effect in priority to the
estate of the tenant for life.[49]   Any such rentcharge, being a
charge on income, may not be redeemed out of capital money; but
while it lasts it may be overreached in the usual way by a sale.[50]

(6) POLICY OF THE ACT.   The general purpose of these rules is to
secure that capital money shall be expended only for permanent
improvements which will benefit the remainderman as much as the
tenant for life.   Various improvements of a temporary character may
be financed with capital money, but subject to the provisions for
repayment by instalments.   The policy of the Act is to keep the
accounts straight as between the tenant for life and remainderman,[51]
but subject to this to make it possible for capital money to be usefully
employed on the land.

(7) AGRICULTURAL LAND.   An important breach was made in this
scheme by the Agricultural Holdings Act, 1948, which quite
anomalously allows the cost of current repairs (as distinct from
improvements) to agricultural land [52] to be met from capital money [53]
without replacement.[54]   This means that the tenant for life may throw
the cost of any repairs effected after April 30, 1948,[55] on to the
remainderman, even where a tenant to whom the land was let had
covenanted in his lease that he would do such repairs himself.[56]   The
tenant for life cannot be reimbursed out of capital for compensation
which under the same Act he has had to pay to outgoing tenants for
their improvements, for such payments are not within the power to
pay for improvements under the Act of 1925.[56a]   As improvements are
a proper charge to capital but repairs are not, the result is to wreck the
correct system of accounting which was so carefully safeguarded by
the Settled Land Acts.

[48] S.L.A., 1925, s. 85 (1).   [49] *Ibid.*, s. 85 (2).
[50] *Ibid.*, s. 85 (3).   It endures only while the land remains settled land (*ibid.*).
[51] But see *post*, p. 350, n. 78.
[52] Whether or not an "agricultural holding" as defined by s. 1 of the Act:
  Re Duke of Northumberland [1951] Ch. 202.
[53] Agricultural Holdings Act, 1948, s. 96 and 3rd Sched., Pt. II, para. 23 (" Repairs
  to fixed equipment, being equipment reasonably required for the proper farming
  of the holding, other than repairs which the tenant is under an obligation to
  carry out "), to which S.L.A., 1925, s. 73 (1) (iv), must now be taken to refer:
  Re Duke of Northumberland [1951] Ch. 202; see (1951) 67 L.Q.R. 167 (R.E.M.);
  [1954] C.L.J. 63 (H.W.R.W.); *post*, p. 349.
[54] Agricultural Holdings Act, 1948, s. 81 (1).
[55] *Re Sutherland S. T.* [1953] Ch. 792; compare *Re Wynn (No.* 2) [1955] 1
  W.L.R. 940, *post*, p. 366.
[56] *Re Lord Brougham and Vaux's S. E.* [1954] Ch. 24.   This decision eliminates
  the distinction between landlord's and tenant's repairs made by the Agricultural
  Holdings Act, 1948 (see n. 53, above).
[56a] *Re Duke of Wellington's Parliamentary Estates* [1972] Ch. 374.   But the judgment
  indicates a way of escape.

(8) MATERIALS FROM THE LAND. Apart from these rules, stone, timber (unless planted for ornament or shelter) and other substances from the land may be used to make any authorised improvement by any tenant for life, even if he is impeachable of waste.[57]

(b) *Power to select investments for capital money.* Capital money must be applied in one or more of the twenty-one methods specified in the Act.[58] These include investments in trustee securities,[59] discharge of incumbrances,[60] paying for authorised improvements, the purchase of land held in fee simple or on a lease with 60 or more years unexpired,[61] and any other method authorised by the settlement. The tenant for life may select which of these methods of application shall be employed (though not which broker [62]), in default of which the trustees make the choice.[63] If the tenant for life chooses the mode of application, he must of course in so doing act as a trustee.[64]

(c) *Power to dedicate highways and open spaces.* For the general benefit of the residents on the settled land or any part thereof, the tenant for life has wide powers of dedicating land for use as streets, paths, squares, gardens or other open spaces.[65]

(d) *Power to take a lease of other land.* There may be practical advantage to the settled land in taking on lease other land, mines, easements, rights or privileges which can conveniently be held or worked with it, and in such cases the lease should devolve with the settled land after the tenant for life's death. A tenant for life is therefore empowered to take such leases [66]; the lease is deemed to be a subsidiary vesting deed and the requisite particulars may be

---

[57] S.L.A., 1925, s. 89.
[58] S.L.A., 1925, s. 73 (1). In general the permitted objects are all of a capital nature, *i.e.*, including improvements but excluding repairs. But they include payment of the costs of exercising any of the powers (s. 73 (1) (xx)), and although it has been held that this would not cover the costs of granting a short occupation lease (for 14 years, determinable in certain events : *Re Leveson-Gower's S. E.* [1905] 2 Ch. 95), it is not clear how the line is to be drawn.
[59] *i.e.*, those specified in the Trustee Investments Act, 1961, which greatly extends the categories previously allowed by the T.A., 1925. Securities authorised by the settlement are also included.
[60] S.L.A., 1925, s. 73 (1) (ii) (incumbrances generally); (vii) and (viii) (manorial incidents); (xiii) (improvement rentcharges); (xvi) (tithe redemption annuities). As to these two last items, see *Re Sandbach* [1951] Ch. 791.
[61] See *Re Wellsted's W. T.* [1949] Ch. 296. Since leases of this nature are authorised investments, they are not subject to the rule in *Howe* v. *Lord Dartmouth* (1802) 7 Ves. 137, which governs other wasting assets: *Re Gough* [1957] Ch. 323; and see *post*, p. 366.
[62] *Re Duke of Cleveland's S. E.* [1902] 2 Ch. 350.
[63] S.L.A., 1925, s. 75 (2).
[64] *Re Sir Robert Peel's S. E.* [1910] 1 Ch. 389; *Re Gladwin's Trust* [1919] 1 Ch. 232; *cf. Re Lord Coleridge's Settlement* [1895] 2 Ch. 704; *Re Hotham* [1902] 2 Ch. 575.
[65] S.L.A., 1925, s. 56; and see *ante*, p. 333.   [66] *Ibid.*, s. 53 (1).

either inserted in it or indorsed on it [67]; but no fine may be paid out of capital money.[68]

(e) *Power to contract.* Detailed powers are conferred on tenants for life to enter into contracts for sales, leases, mortgages and other dispositions authorised by the Act.[69] Such contracts are enforceable by and against the tenant for life's successors in title,[70] and are subject to any directions by the court.[71] The transaction must be authorised by the Act at the time when the contract comes to be performed, so that in the case of a contract for a lease the rent must be the best rent reasonably obtainable when the lease is finally granted, and the other statutory conditions must also be satisfied then.[72] The powers extend also to the variation and rescission of contracts.

II. POSITION OF TENANT FOR LIFE

1. The tenant for life is trustee both of the land and of his powers. This has already been generally explained.[73] Two special aspects of this trusteeship need mention here.

(a) *Capital money.* All receipts of a capital nature must be treated as capital money and paid to the trustees of the settlement or into court.[74] " Capital money " includes not only the proceeds of sale or mortgage, fines upon the grant of leases, and part of the proceeds of mining and timber transactions, but also money (not being rent) paid by a tenant as compensation for breach of covenant,[75] or as the price of being allowed to surrender his lease [76] (unless in either case the court otherwise directs), insurance money receivable under a policy of insurance kept up under a requirement of the settlement or of the Act, or by a tenant for life impeachable for waste,[77] any money arising outside the Act "which ought to be capital money," [78] and various other specified receipts.[79] Even so, tenants for life have been held to be entitled to retain compensation for damage done to the property while under requisition,[80] and also income tax allowances resulting from improvements effected with capital money.[81]

(b) *Acquisitions by tenant for life.* The tenant for life is given a special power to acquire any or all of the settled land for himself. It

---

[67] *Ibid.*, s. 53 (2).
[68] *Ibid.*, s. 53 (1).
[69] *Ibid.*, s. 90.
[70] *Ibid.*, s. 90 (2).
[71] *Ibid.*, s. 90 (3).
[72] *Re Rycroft's Settlement* [1962] Ch. 263. For the conditions, see *ante*, p. 335.
[73] *Ante*, pp. 290, 297.
[74] See *post*, p. 375.
[75] S.L.A., 1925, s. 80 (1).
[76] *Ibid.*, s. 52 (7).
[77] T.A., 1925, s. 20. See, *e.g.*, *Re Scholfield's Trusts* [1949] Ch. 341.
[78] S.L.A., 1925, s. 81; see Wolst. & C. iii, 180, giving examples.
[79] For a list, see Wolst. & C. iii, 156.
[80] *Re Pomfret's Settlement* [1952] Ch. 48; contrast *Re Thompson* [1949] Ch. 1.
[81] *Re Pelly's W. T.* [1957] Ch. 1.

is a settled rule of equity that no trustee may acquire the trust property for himself either directly or indirectly, no matter how fair the transaction may be,[82] for " the court will not permit a party to place himself in a situation in which his interest conflicts with his duty." [83] To avoid this difficulty, the Settled Land Act, 1925,[84] authorises the trustees of the settlement to exercise all the powers of a tenant for life in carrying out any transaction whereby the tenant for life acquires any interest in the settled land. The trustees are empowered to act in the name and on behalf of the tenant for life even if he is one of them, in which case he should join in the transaction as one of them [85]; but they may not have dealings with a body of persons which includes one of the trustees, not being the tenant for life, unless the court approves the transaction.[86] There is a similar power to carry out certain other transactions, such as a purchase from the tenant for life of land to be brought into the settlement.[87]

2. No powers can be given to anyone except the tenant for life. Any power, other than a power of revocation or appointment, which the settlement purports to give to anyone except the tenant for life, is exercisable not by that person but by the tenant for life as if it were an additional power conferred by the settlement.[88] This is so whether or not the tenant for life already has such a power under the Act.[88] Thus if land is devised " to X and Y in fee simple with power to sell, on trust for A for life and then for B absolutely " the power of sale purported to be given to X and Y is divested out of them and given to A despite the statutory power of sale which A already has. But the abortive attempt to give a power of sale to X and Y may not be wholly without effect, for it may make them Settled Land Act trustees.[89]

3. The statutory powers cannot be ousted, curtailed or hampered.

(a) *The Act prevails.* The settlor may confer additional powers on the tenant for life and such powers are exercisable in the same

---

[82] *Fox* v. *Mackreth* (1791) 2 Cox Eq. 320; *Ex p. Hughes* (1802) 6 Ves. 617; *Ex p. Lacey* (1802) 6 Ves. 625; *Ex p. James* (1803) 8 Ves. 337; *Sanderson* v. *Walker* (1807) 13 Ves. 601; *Whitcomb* v. *Minchin* (1820) 5 Madd. 91.

[83] *Re Bloye's Trust* (1849) 1 Mac. & G. 488 at 495, *per* Lord Cottenham L.C.; affirmed *sub nom. Lewis* v. *Hillman* (1852) 3 H.L.C. 607.

[84] s. 68, replacing and greatly extending S.L.A., 1890, s. 12.

[85] *Re Pennant's W. T.* [1970] Ch. 75; and see *ante*, p. 326.

[86] S.L.A., 1925, s. 68 (3).

[87] S.L.A., 1925, s. 68 (1).

[88] S.L.A., 1925, s. 108 (2).

[89] *Ante*, p. 324. Had the words " with power " been " on trust," there would have been a trust for sale, and the Settled Land Act, 1925, would not have applied; the legal estate and statutory powers would then have been vested in X and Y: see *post*, p. 364.

way as if they were conferred by the Act.[90] Further, nothing in the
Act in any way restricts powers which the settlement gives to the
tenant for life or purports to give to the trustees [91] to be exercised
with the approval of the tenant for life; the powers given by the
Act and the settlement are cumulative.[92] But in other respects, so far
as the settlement and the Act conflict in relation to powers exercisable
under the Act, the Act prevails.[93] Thus if the settlement provides
that no sale shall be made without the consent of some specified
person, this provision is inconsistent with the unfettered power of
sale given by the Act and the latter prevails,[94] even if the provision
was contained, for example, in a settlement created before 1882 by
a private Act of Parliament.[95]

(b) *Void provisions.* In particular, there is a sweeping section [96]
which makes void any provision in any document (*e.g.*, another
settlement [97]) " as far as it purports, or attempts, or tends, or is
intended to have, or would or might have " the effect of preventing
or discouraging the tenant for life from exercising his statutory
powers or from requiring the land to be vested in him. This applies
even when the attempt to restrain the exercise of the powers is made
by way of determinable limitation [98]; a settlement on " Y for life
until he attempts to alienate the land " gives Y a life interest which
continues despite any alienation by him.[99] Nevertheless, there must
be a limitation which, but for the attempted prohibition, would
constitute a tenant for life under the Act [1]; for the section does
nothing to enlarge the beneficiary's estate.[2] Finally, it is provided
that notwithstanding anything in a settlement, the exercise of a
statutory power can never cause a forfeiture.[3]

(c) *Extent of invalidity.* Provisions for the curtailment or forfeiture of the interest of a tenant for life are not automatically
invalidated by these rules; they are affected only so far as they in
fact tend to fetter the statutory powers of the tenant for life or

---

[90] S.L.A., 1925, s. 109: see, *e.g.*, *Re The Earl of Egmont's S. E.* (1900) 16
T.L.R. 360; *Re Duke of Westminster's S. E.* (*No.* 2) [1921] 1 Ch. 585; *Re
Cowley S. E.* [1926] Ch. 725. The wording of S.L.A., 1925, s. 108 (2) seems
to have reversed the law laid down in *Re Duke of Westminster's S. E.* (*No.* 1)
[1920] 2 Ch. 445.
[91] Such powers are exercisable by the tenant for life: see above.
[92] S.L.A., 1925, s. 108 (1); see *Re Jefferys* (*No.* 2) [1939] Ch. 205.
[93] S.L.A., 1925, s. 108 (2).
[94] *Re Jefferys* (*No.* 2), *supra.*
[95] *Re Chaytor's S. E. Act* (1884) 25 Ch.D. 651.
[96] S.L.A., 1925, s. 106 (1), replacing S.L.A., 1882, s. 51.
[97] *Re Smith* [1899] 1 Ch. 331; *Re Burden* [1948] Ch. 160.
[98] S.L.A., 1925, s. 106 (2).
[99] *Ibid.*
[1] *Re Atkinson* (1886) 31 Ch.D. 577 at 581.
[2] *Re Hazle's S. E.* (1885) 29 Ch.D. 78 at 84.
[3] S.L.A., 1925, s. 106 (3).

statutory owner. This may be illustrated by a condition of residence, *e.g.*, a provision in the settlement that the tenant for life shall forfeit his interest on ceasing to reside on the settled land. In such cases, if the tenant for life ceases to reside for some reason other than the exercise of his statutory powers (as where he prefers to live elsewhere) the proviso for forfeiture is operative and he loses his interest.[4] But if the reason for his ceasing to reside is that he has exercised his statutory powers, as by leasing [5] or selling [6] the land, or both,[7] there is no forfeiture,[8] and he continues to be entitled as tenant for life, receiving the rent from the lease [9] or the income from the purchase-money.[10] Another example to which the same distinction applies is a condition that the tenant for life should provide a home for X on the settled land.[11]

(*d*) *Inoperative fetters.* One result of these rules is that a provision which attempts to fetter the powers may actually encourage their exercise: if the tenant for life is subject to a condition of residence but wishes to reside elsewhere, he can protect his life interest from the condition by first selling or letting the land. Further, quite apart from these rules, provisions of this nature are sometimes wholly void under the doctrine that conditions subsequent will be construed strictly and held ineffective unless it can be seen precisely upon what counts a forfeiture will be incurred [12]; and an infant who cannot control his place of residence cannot be said to " refuse or neglect " to reside on the property so as to incur a forfeiture.[13]

(*e*) *Upkeep of property.* Difficulty sometimes arises over funds provided by the settlor for the payment of rates, taxes and other such outgoings during the tenant for life's personal occupation. Here the settlor's object is to enable the tenant for life to live on the property free from the expenses of its upkeep. It has been held that the tenant for life can still claim such payments after letting the land,[14] but not after selling it.[15] There has been some difference of

---

4 *Re Haynes* (1887) 37 Ch.D. 306; *Re Trenchard* [1902] 1 Ch. 378. As to " residence " contrast *Re Moir* (1884) 25 Ch.D. 605 (residence) with *Re Wright* [1907] 1 Ch. 231 (non-residence).   5 *Re Gibbons* [1920] 1 Ch. 372.
6 *Re Paget's S. E.* (1885) 30 Ch.D. 161.
7 *Re Acklom* [1929] 1 Ch. 195.
8 *Re Orlebar* [1936] Ch. 147; *cf. Re Ames* [1893] 2 Ch. 479.
9 *Re T. J. Freme* (1912) 56 S.J. 362.
10 *Re Sarah Dalrymple* (1901) 49 W.R. 627.
11 *Re Richardson* [1904] 2 Ch. 777.
12 *Ante*, p. 77. Contrast *Sifton* v. *Sifton* [1938] A.C. 656 (" so long as she shall continue to reside in Canada " held too vague) with *Re Gape* [1952] Ch. 743 (condition requiring " permanent residence " in England held effective).
13 *Partridge* v. *Partridge* [1894] 1 Ch. 351.
14 *Re Patten* [1929] 2 Ch. 276.
15 *Re Simpson* [1913] 1 Ch. 277, not following *Re Trenchard* (1900) 16 T.L.R. 525; *Re Burden* [1948] Ch. 160; *Re Aberconway's S. T.* [1953] Ch. 647. Contrast *Re Ames* [1893] 2 Ch. 479; and *cf. Re Eastman's S. E.* (1898) 68 L.J.Ch. 122 (provision for reduction of annuity).

judicial opinion on this difficult subject, which has been fully reviewed by the Court of Appeal.[16] Further, where the Act gives special powers to the trustees (for example, the powers of management during a minority [17]), they are made subject to any contrary intention and are not, therefore, protected like the powers of a tenant for life.

4. The tenant for life cannot assign, release or contract not to exercise his powers.[18]

(a) *Exercise of powers.* A statutory owner can release his powers,[19] but a tenant for life cannot. Once a person has become a tenant for life, he is incapable of divesting himself of his powers, even if he parts with his entire beneficial interest,[20] as he is entitled to do [21]; it is he, and not the assignee of his beneficial interest, who alone can exercise the statutory powers,[22] and this is so whether the disposition was voluntary or involuntary (*e.g.*, on bankruptcy), and even if it was made while the life interest was still in remainder.[23] But in three exceptional cases [24] the statutory powers may become exercisable by someone other than the tenant for life.

(1) EXTINGUISHMENT OF INTEREST. Where the interest of the tenant for life has been assured, with intent to extinguish it, to the person next entitled under the settlement, the statutory powers cease to be exercisable by the tenant for life and become exercisable as if he were dead.[25] For this purpose an " assurance " is any surrender, conveyance, assignment or appointment which operates in equity to extinguish the interest.[26] A partial surrender is insufficient,[27] and so is a surrender to a later remainderman where some intermediate gift remains capable of taking effect, even though contingently.[27a] But it is immaterial that a term of years or charge intervenes between the interest surrendered and that of the person next entitled, or that the latter interest is defeasible, or that the interest surrendered was in remainder at the time.[28]

---

16 *Re Aberconway's S. T., supra*; see [1954] C.L.J. 60 (R. N. Gooderson).
17 S.L.A., 1925, s. 102; *ante*, p. 289; Wolst. & C. iii, 208.
18 S.L.A., 1925, s. 104 (1), (2); and see s. 19 (4).
19 *Re Craven S. E.* [1926] Ch. 985.
20 *Re Mundy and Roper's Contract* [1899] 1 Ch. 275; *Re Cope and Wadland's Contract* [1919] 2 Ch. 376.
21 *Re Trenchard* [1902] 1 Ch. 378 at 384, 385.
22 *Re Earl of Carnarvon's Chesterfield S. E.* [1927] 1 Ch. 138 at 145, 146; see, *e.g.*, *Earl of Lonsdale* v. *Lowther* [1900] 2 Ch. 687.
23 S.L.A., 1925, s. 104 (1).
24 See also *ante*, p. 350 (acquisition of the settled land).
25 S.L.A., 1925, s. 105 (1).
26 *Ibid.*, s. 105 (2).
27 *Re Barlow's Contract* [1903] 1 Ch. 382.
27a *Re Maryon-Wilson's Instruments* [1971] Ch. 789.
28 S.L.A., 1925, s. 105 (1).

This provision may be illustrated by a settlement of land on A for life, remainder to B for life, remainder to C in fee simple. The effect of A surrendering his life interest to B is to make the statutory powers exercisable by B instead of A, and A must forthwith convey the legal estate to B by a vesting deed.[29] If A is bankrupt, his trustee in bankruptcy can surrender A's interest, with like effect[30]; and if A refuses to execute the requisite vesting deed, the court can instead make a vesting order.[31] If after the surrender of A's interest B then surrenders his life interest to C, he must convey the legal estate to C,[32] but by an ordinary conveyance, for the land ceases to be settled land.[33]

(2) ORDER OF COURT. If the tenant for life—

(i) has ceased to have a substantial interest in the land, whether by bankruptcy, assignment or otherwise, and

(ii) either consents to an order being made or else has unreasonably refused to exercise his statutory powers,

any person interested in the land may apply to the court for an order authorising the trustees to exercise any or all of the statutory powers in the name and on behalf of the tenant for life.[34] Such an order prevents the tenant for life from exercising any of the powers affected by the order, but until it has been registered[35] the order does not affect persons dealing with the tenant for life.[36] It should be noticed that such an order vests neither the legal estate nor the statutory powers in the trustees, who do not become the statutory owner; the order merely authorises the trustees to exercise the powers on behalf of the tenant for life and in his name. Further, the provision is confined to tenants for life, and does not apply to statutory owners.[37]

(3) LUNATIC. Where the tenant for life is a mental patient, his statutory powers may be exercised under an order of the judge or Court of Protection, *e.g.*, by his receiver.[38]

(b) *Position of assignees.* A voluntary assignee of the beneficial interest of a tenant for life has ordinarily no control over the exercise of the tenant for life's powers; nor has his trustee in bankruptcy,

---

[29] S.L.A., 1925, ss. 7 (4), 8 (4).
[30] *Re Shawdon Estates Settlement* [1930] 2 Ch. 1.
[31] S.L.A., 1925, s. 12 (1); see, *e.g.*, *Re Shawdon Estates Settlement, supra.*
[32] S.L.A., 1925, s. 7 (5).
[33] Wolst. & C. iii, 43; *cf. ante*, p. 308.
[34] S.L.A., 1925, s. 24 (1); see, *e.g.*, *Re Cecil's S. E.* [1926] W.N. 262.
[35] As an " order affecting land ": *post*, p. 1038.
[36] S.L.A., 1925, s. 24 (2).
[37] *Re Craven S. E.* [1926] Ch. 985.
[38] Mental Health Act, 1959, Part VIII. The Act repeals S.L.A., 1925, s. 28; and see *post*, p. 997.

who is an assignee by operation of law.[39] But an assignee for
money or money's worth has certain rights of control, though they
were cut down by the Act of 1925. Since it would not have
been just to have altered the law to the detriment of assignees who
had parted with their money before 1926 on the strength of the law
as it then was, it is necessary to treat pre-1926 and post-1925
assignments separately.

(1) ASSIGNMENT MADE BEFORE 1926. If the assignment was made
for money or money's worth,[40] the tenant for life can exercise his
powers so as to affect the assignee only if the assignee consents.[41]
This is so whether the assignment was absolute or not, *e.g.*, if it was
by way of mortgage.[42] The assignee need not be a party to the
transaction, provided his consent has been given [43]; and this may
be implied from conduct.[44] Further, a purchaser is not concerned
to see that the consent has been obtained,[45] and no consent is
required—

    (i) for the grant of leases authorised by the Act at the best rent
        without a fine, unless the assignee is actually in possession
        of the land, or

    (ii) for the investment of capital money in trustee securities.[46]

If the land is sold, the rights of the assignee are transferred to
the capital money which represents it.[47]

(2) ASSIGNMENT MADE AFTER 1925. Even if the assignment was
made for money or money's worth, the consent of the assignee is not
required for the exercise of the statutory powers.[48] But for the
application of capital money affected by the assignment for any
purpose other than for investment in trustee securities, the consent
of the assignee is necessary if the assignment so provides or takes
effect by operation of the law of bankruptcy, and the trustees have
notice of this.[49] Further, unless the assignment otherwise provides,
notice of any intended transaction must be given to the assignee.[50] No

---

[39] See S.L.A., 1925, s. 104 (4), (10).
[40] *Ibid.*, s. 104 (11), *q.v.* for details.
[41] *Ibid.*, s. 104 (3).
[42] *Ibid.*, s. 104 (12).
[43] *Re Dickin & Kelsall's Contract* [1908] 2 Ch. 213 ; *Re Davies & Kent's Contract*
    [1910] 2 Ch. 35 at 55.
[44] *Re Kingsley & Holder's Contract* (1903) 115 L.J.News. 201 (bidding at an
    auction and requiring the sale to be made under the Act). As to infants, who
    cannot consent, see s. 104 (8).
[45] S.L.A., 1925, s. 104 (5).
[46] *Ibid.*, s. 104 (3). For trustee securities, see Trustee Investments Act, 1961 ; Snell,
    Equity, 207–215. If the interest assigned has itself been settled, see S.L.A., 1925,
    s. 104 (6), (7), (9), and *Re Mountgarret & Moore's Contract* [1915] 1 Ch. 443.
[47] S.L.A., 1925, s. 104 (4), (5).
[48] *Ibid.*, s. 104 (4); and see subss. (10), (11).
[49] *Ibid.*, s. 104 (4).
[50] *Ibid.*

period of notice is specified, and a purchaser is not concerned to see or inquire whether notice has been given.[51]

As before, if the land is sold the rights of the assignee are transferred to the capital money which represents the land,[52] and provision is made for obtaining consents in any cases of difficulty.[53]

NOTE ON SETTLED LAND ACT TRUSTEES

(a) *Their appointment.* We have already dealt with the question of finding the initial trustees of the settlement.[54] New trustees may thereafter be appointed, and old trustees may retire, in the ordinary way,[55] provided that their number does not rise above four or fall below two, or one, if it is a trust corporation.[56]

The curtain principle now extends to the appointment and discharge of Settled Land Act trustees, in order that a purchaser may be exempted from investigating such matters. The Act of 1925 provides for the execution of a " deed of declaration " stating who are the trustees of the settlement after any appointment or discharge,[57] and in favour of a purchaser this is conclusive evidence of the matters stated in it.[58] This deed is made supplemental to the principal vesting deed, on which the names of the new trustees are also indorsed.[59] The actual deed of appointment or discharge is kept by the trustees and is not seen by the purchaser. The deed of declaration provides the necessary link in his title between the old and the new trustees.

(b) *Their functions.* It may perhaps be useful to collect together the principal functions of the Settled Land Act trustees. They are as follows.

    (i) To receive and hold capital money.[60]

    (ii) To receive notice from the tenant for life of his intention to effect certain transactions.[61]

    (iii) To give consent to certain transactions.[62]

    (iv) To act as special personal representatives on the death of a tenant for life.[63]

---

[51] *Ibid.*
[53] *Ante*, p. 355.
[55] *Post*, p. 456.
[52] *Post*, p. 376.
[54] *Ante*, p. 314.
[56] T.A., 1925, ss. 34, 39.
[57] S.L.A., 1925, s. 35 (1). This adopts a practice often used voluntarily before 1926 (much as a trust for sale was usually made by two documents: *ante*, p. 299): Vaizey, *Settlements*, i, 293.
[58] S.L.A., 1925, s. 35 (3).
[59] *Ibid.*, s. 35 (1); T.A., 1925, s. 35 (2). For how to appoint trustees if there is no vesting instrument, see (1949) 13 Conv.(N.S.) 347–349.
[60] S.L.A., 1925, ss. 18 (1) (b), 75 (1); *ante*, p. 350.
[61] *Ante*, p. 331.
[62] *Ante*, p. 340.
[63] *Ante*, p. 309.

(v) To act as statutory owner if the tenant for life is an infant or there is no tenant for life.[64]

(vi) To execute the principal vesting deed in cases where it is not provided in the ordinary course.[65]

(vii) To execute a deed of discharge, when that is necessary, on the determination of the settlement.[66]

(viii) To exercise the powers of the tenant for life if he wishes to acquire the settled land for his own benefit.[67]

(ix) To exercise the powers of the tenant for life where he has no substantial beneficial interest and either consents to such exercise or unreasonably refuses to exercise his powers.[68]

(x) To exercise a general supervision over the well-being of the settled land.[69] Thus they will be parties to all litigation concerning the land; yet where they have nothing to say against a transaction for which the tenant for life is seeking the authority of the court, their duty is " to hold an even hand " and refrain from supporting the application.[70]

Part 4

TRUSTS FOR SALE AFTER 1925

1. What is a trust for sale. We have already touched upon the vital importance of differentiating trusts for sale from other settlements. Since 1925 trusts for sale are the only type of settlement which fall outside the Settled Land Act. This is because they are expressly excluded, and are dealt with separately in the Law of Property Act, 1925. Every settlement, therefore, is governed by the Settled Land Act unless and until a trust for sale arises. But once a trust for sale appears the Settled Land Act can no longer apply.[71] A conveyance " to X and Y upon trust to sell the land and hold the proceeds upon trust for A for life with remainder to B absolutely " falls entirely outside the Settled Land Act. A conveyance " to A for life with remainder to X and Y upon trust to sell the land and hold the proceeds upon trust for B for life with

---

[64] *Ante*, p. 297.
[65] *Ante*, pp. 301, 305.
[66] *Ante*, p. 311.
[67] *Ante*, p. 350.
[68] *Ante*, p. 355.
[69] *Ante*, p. 290: and see *Re Boston's W. T.* [1956] Ch. 395 at 405.
[70] See *Re Hotchkin's S. E.* (1887) 35 Ch.D. 41 at 43; *cf. Re Marquis of Ailesbury's S. E.* [1892] 1 Ch. 506 at 526.
[71] S.L.A., 1925, s. 1 (7), added by L.P.(Am.)A., 1926, Sched.; *ante*, p. 296.

remainder to C absolutely " is subject to the Settled Land Act while A's life interest continues, but thereafter the Settled Land Act stands excluded by the trust for sale.

The broad distinction between trusts for sale and settlements is plain: under a trust for sale, all powers of dealing with the land rest with the trustees; under a settlement, they rest with the tenant for life. But, as we have already seen, there are borderline cases which may cause difficulty. The Law of Property Act, 1925, now provides a statutory definition: only an " immediate binding trust for sale," as further defined by the definition section, now ranks as a trust for sale.[72] The Settled Land Act, 1925, uses the same definition,[73] so that only an " immediate binding trust for sale " falls outside it.

The meaning of this phrase is thus of great importance and must be examined carefully. A mistake will be fatal to a purchaser's title, as where he takes a conveyance from trustees purporting to be trustees for sale, but it turns out that the land is settled land, so that the only person competent to dispose of it is the tenant for life.

(a) *There must be a trust for sale.* As before 1926, there must be a true trust to sell and not a mere power of sale.[74] Thus a conveyance to trustees on trust for persons in succession, giving the trustees a power of sale, makes the land settled land; the conveyance operates as an imperfect settlement[75] and the trustees cannot sell.[76] Some of the difficulties which arose from trusts " to retain or sell the land "[77] are solved by the provision that in a disposition or settlement coming into operation after 1925 such a trust shall be construed as a trust for sale with power to postpone sale[78]; this solution is only partial, since it does not alter the position if the disposition or settlement took effect before 1926.[79]

(b) *The trust for sale must be " immediate."* Here again, the position is in most respects the same as before 1926[80]; a trust to sell at some future date, *e.g.*, when X attains the age of 25, does not prevent land from being settled land for the time being.[81] But if there is a trust for sale which is immediately operative, this takes the land out of the Settled Land Act, even if the trustees have

[72] L.P.A., 1925, s. 205 (1) (xxix).
[73] S.L.A., 1925 s. 117 (1) (xxx).
[74] For this distinction, see *ante*, p. 294.
[75] *Ante*, p. 304.
[76] *Ante*, p. 351.
[77] *Ante*, p. 295.
[78] L.P.A., 1925, s. 25 (4).
[79] *Re White's Settlement* [1930] 1 Ch. 179.
[80] *Ante*, p. 295.
[81] *Re Hanson* [1928] Ch. 96.

power to postpone the sale and even if a sale cannot be made without the request or consent of some person.[82] There is therefore one change from the former law: a trust for sale does not cease to be such merely because it is exercisable only at some person's request.[83]

(c) *There must be a " binding trust for sale."* A strange fate has befallen this apparently guileless expression. Anyone asked to construe it on January 1, 1926, would probably have said that "binding" indicated the familiar distinction between a binding trust and a discretionary power, and so emphasised the meaning of "trust" as explained in (a) above.[84] In this sense it would cause no difficulty. The objection that on this view the word is mere surplusage [85] is met by treating it as being explanatory language, natural in a definition section.

In a series of cases, however, the expression "binding trust for sale" has been made to serve an entirely different purpose, *i.e.*, to determine the moment when the Settled Land Act, 1925, gives way to the Law of Property Act, 1925, in cases where there is first a settlement, and a trust for sale then arises before all the limitations of the settlement are exhausted. Suppose, for example, that land is settled upon A for life, with a jointure for his widow and portions for his younger children,[86] and remainder to trustees for sale for the benefit of his eldest child absolutely. If A dies leaving a widow and children, is the land settled land or not? Should it be vested in the eldest child by a vesting assent, or in the trustees for sale by a simple assent? There is clearly some kind of trust for sale, but it is subject to the jointure rentcharge (an equitable interest for the life of the widow) and, if the portions have been raised, to one or more legal mortgages (comprising legal terms of years) in favour of outside creditors.

Now the apparent intention of the 1925 legislation was, as we have seen,[87] that so soon as an effective trust for sale arose, it should displace the Settled Land Act. It might have been provided that the Settled Land Act should continue to apply so long as any limitation of the settlement continued. But this was plainly not intended, for by the Law of Property (Amendment) Act, 1926,[88] settled land was confined to land "not held upon trust for sale."

---

[82] L.P.A., 1925, s. 205 (1) (xxix); *Re Herklot's W. T.* [1964] 1 W.L.R. 583 (trust for sale subject to A's right to occupy house for life: held, immediate trust for sale subject to A's consent).

[83] Contrast *ante*, p. 295, and *Re Goodall's Settlement* [1909] 1 Ch. 440.

[84] See *Re Parker's S. E.* [1928] Ch. 247 at 261, where this interpretation was favoured.   [85] *Re Leigh's S. E. (No.* 1) [1926] Ch. 852 at 859.

[86] For further details of jointure and portions, see *post*, p. 385.

[87] *Ante*, p. 358.

[88] Sched., amending S.L.A., 1925, s. 3; *ante*, p. 296.

Nevertheless there is some judicial reluctance to hold that a later trust for sale of the legal estate [89] will displace a settlement so long as any interests created by the settlement are still outstanding. Perhaps it is thought wrong that the prior beneficiaries should lose the protection of their own Settled Land Act trustees if the land should be sold.[90] The trustees for sale would of course be bound by the prior interests (*e.g.*, that of a jointress), but there might possibly be some danger that they would overlook them; at any rate, they have not quite the same special responsibilities as the trustees of the settlement. The courts therefore strive to preserve the machinery of the antecedent settlement, and this can only be done by denying that the trust for sale is an " immediate binding trust for sale " within the meaning of section 1 (7) of the Settled Land Act, 1925, as amended.

For this purpose the word " binding " was first seized upon, and given the unusual meaning of " overreaching." It was held that any prior equitable interest which the trustees for sale could not overreach prevented the trust for sale from being " binding " [91]; and so the settlement continued. If, for example, there was a jointure rentcharge outstanding under the prior settlement, the trust for sale would be " binding " only if the trustees were approved by the court or a trust corporation [92]; and in this way the jointress would get the protection of special trustees. But this reasoning met with much criticism [93] and was rejected in later cases.[94] Yet much the same result was achieved by holding that a " trust for sale," within the meaning of the Settled Land Act, 1925, s. 1 (7), was only such a trust for sale as would embrace " the whole legal estate which is the subject-matter of the settlement." [95] Thus an outstanding legal portions term would disqualify the ensuing trust for sale, and it would be *a fortiori* if the settlor had vested no legal estate in the trustees, *e.g.*, because he had none,[96] or because the conveyance

---

[89] A trust for sale of an equitable interest is ineffective to oust the Settled Land Act (though as to tenancies in common, see *post*, p. 423 *et seq.*): *Re Sharpe's Deed of Release* [1939] Ch. 51; *cf.* S.L.A., 1925, s. 17 (1) proviso.

[90] But see *post*, p. 362, n. 1.

[91] *Re Leigh's S. E. (No.* 1) [1926] Ch. 852 (Tomlin J.).

[92] For this means of overreaching prior equities, see *post*, p. 379. For its application in a case like that put in the text, see *Re Leigh's S. E. (No.* 2) [1927] 2 Ch. 13 (Tomlin J.); *cf. Re Lindsley's Estate* (1927) 63 L.J.News. 375.

[93] See 61 L.J.News. 554, 555; 62 *ibid.* 391; 63 *ibid.* 23, 374, 375; 70 S.J. 750, 769; 71 S.J. 444, 798, 985; 84 S.J. 71.

[94] *Re Parker's S. E.* [1928] Ch. 247; *Re Norton* [1929] 1 Ch. 84; *cf. Re Ryder and Steadman's Contract* [1927] 2 Ch. 62; (1927) 43 L.Q.R. 443; 64 L.J.News. 292, 293, 310.

[95] *Re Parker's S. E.* [1928] Ch. 247 at 262, *per* Romer J. This decision concerns the meaning not of " binding " (though see n. 94 above) but of " trust for sale " for the purpose of S.L.A., 1925, s. 1 (7).

[96] *Re Sharpe's Deed of Release* [1939] Ch. 51.

purported to carry none.[97]   A " binding " trust for sale is thus one
which is capable of binding the whole legal estate that has been
settled, and not merely part of it.[98]   Further, the existence of even
an equitable interest under a settlement (*e.g.*, a jointure rentcharge)
may prevent the legal estate from vesting in the trustees for sale,[99]
and so inhibit the trust for sale from taking effect, since " the
intention of the legislature was that trustees for the purposes of the
Act are not to be discharged so long as there is any equitable interest
remaining outstanding which it is their duty to protect." [1]

If these decisions are followed the result would appear to be
that a settlement can never be displaced by a trust for sale,[2] even
in a case where the trustees for sale are a trust corporation or
approved by the court and so able to overreach a prior equitable
interest.[3]   A final disposition upon trust for sale may therefore be
prevented from taking effect as such for a long period merely because
portions have been raised, or because a jointress or some other
annuitant is still alive.   Meanwhile the land is settled land and the
first beneficiary under the trust for sale will generally have the
powers of a tenant for life.[4]   No beneficial interest can be prejudiced,
but the difficulty lies in advising a purchaser whether he should take
a conveyance from a beneficiary (as tenant for life) or from the
trustees (as trustees for sale).   A solution which is inelegant, but
which can hardly be censured in the present state of the authorities,
is to take a conveyance from both.

It is clearly desirable that there should be an end to " what is
in fact perfectly useless litigation. . . . In all these cases there is
clearly a power of sale.   The only question is, who is to exercise it.
This may be of importance to the solicitors of the parties.   To the
parties themselves it is [usually] a matter of entire indifference." [5]

2. Species of trusts for sale.   A trust for sale may arise—

(*a*) expressly, by land being deliberately limited on trust for
   sale,[6] or

(*b*) by operation of statute.

---

97 *Re Beaumont S. E.* [1937] 2 All E.R. 353 ; and see 65 L.J.News. 248, 272, 293.
98 *Re Parker's S. E., supra*, at p. 262 ; *Re Norton, supra*, at p. 88.
99 See S.L.A., 1925, s. 7 (5); but on the difficulties of reading this subsection with
   S.L.A., 1925, s. 3, see 65 L.J.News. 294 ; 67 L.J.News. 24, 44.
1 *Re Norton* [1929] 1 Ch. 84 at 91, *per* Romer J., referring to S.L.A., 1925, s. 17
   (*ante*, p. 311). The difficulty here is that the L.P.(Am.)A., 1926, plainly
   intended that when a trust for sale arose the whole of the S.L.A., 1925, should
   be excluded, s. 17 equally with the rest.
2 Except in case of a tenancy in common, under s. 36; *post*, p. 424.
3 *Post*, p. 379.   4 Under S.L.A., 1925, s. 20 (1) (viii) or (ix), *ante*, p. 321.
5 J.M.L., 67 L.J.News. 24.
6 As to the history and development of the trust for sale, see J. M. Lightwood
   (1927) 3 C.L.J. 59–61 ; Davidson, *Precedents in Conveyancing*, 3rd ed., III, 58, 59 ;
   Elphinstone, *Introduction to Conveyancing*, 7th ed., 403.

(a) *Express trusts for sale.* Mention has already been made of the long-standing practice of making trusts for sale by means of two separate documents,[7] namely, a conveyance on trust for sale and a trust instrument [8]; for it was this analogy which suggested the vesting deed and trust instrument of the Settled Land Act, 1925.[9] The practice of using two documents enabled the trustees, when they sold the land, to keep the original instrument which declared the trusts of the money. The purchaser had no concern with these trusts, not because he had no notice of them (for the conveyance would expressly refer to the trust instrument) but because from the time of the sale they attached to the proceeds of sale and not to the land at all [10]; and since 1860 purchasers have been exonerated by statute from seeing that the money paid to the trustees is properly applied.[11] There is now a provision to the same effect in the Law of Property Act, 1925, which is merely declaratory of the previously established law.[12]

Although today two documents are almost invariably employed to create a trust for sale *inter vivos,* there is nothing in the nature of a trust for sale or in the 1925 legislation to make this legally necessary. In the case of testamentary trusts for sale, the usual position before 1926 was that the will was the sole document. After 1925 a written assent is required to vest the legal estate in the trustees for sale,[13] so that now there will usually be two documents in such cases; and since the assent has become a necessary link in the title to the legal estate, and a purchaser is no longer concerned with the terms of the will,[14] the assent does the work of the conveyance and the will that of the trust instrument. Even if the trustees for sale are the same persons as the personal representatives, it is necessary for them, as personal representatives, to make a written assent in favour of themselves, as trustees for sale,[15] so that the usual two documents will be provided; and a purchaser may be entitled to require production of such an assent to prove that they had ceased to act as personal representatives if they sell as trustees for sale,[16] though not if they sell as personal representatives.[17]

---

[7] *Ante,* p. 299.
[8] J. M. Lightwood (1927) 3 C.L.J. 63.
[9] *Ibid.* 65.
[10] *Ante,* p. 295.
[11] T.A., 1860, s. 29; C.A., 1881, s. 36; T.A., 1893, s. 20; T.A., 1925, s. 14. For the earlier law see Wh. & T. ii, 837–839.
[12] L.P.A., 1925, s. 27 (1).
[13] A.E.A., 1925, s. 36 (4).
[14] *Ibid.,* s. 36 (7); *post,* p. 538.
[15] *Re Yerburgh* [1928] W.N. 208; *Re King's W. T.* [1964] Ch. 542; *post,* p. 539; *cf. Re Cugny's W. T.* [1931] 1 Ch. 305.
[16] See *Re Hodge* [1940] Ch. 260 at 264; *cf. Re King's W. T., supra.*
[17] See A.E.A., 1925, s. 36 (4); *Eaton* v. *Daines* [1894] W.N. 32; *Re Ponder* [1921] 2 Ch. 59; *Re Pitt* (1928) 44 T.L.R. 371; J.M.L., 87 L.J.News. 372.

Where a trust for sale was created before 1926, the legal estate remains vested in the trustees for sale if it was already vested in them; if it was not, it automatically vested in them at the beginning of 1926.[18]

(b) *Statutory trusts for sale.* A trust for sale is a convenient device for liquidating and distributing property, and is employed by statute in a number of cases. Four examples may be given.

(i) If two or more persons are entitled to land as joint tenants or tenants in common, a trust for sale is normally imposed by the Law of Property Act, 1925.[19]

(ii) The Administration of Estates Act, 1925, imposes a trust for sale on the property of a person dying intestate.[20]

(iii) If trustees lend money on mortgage and the property becomes vested in them free from the right of repayment (*e.g.*, by foreclosure[21]) they hold it upon trust for sale.[22] This preserves the character of the trust property: the money was pure personalty, and under the doctrine of conversion[23] the rights of the beneficiaries under a trust for sale are treated as interests in pure personalty, even if the subject-matter of the trust is land.[24]

(iv) If trustees of a settlement of personalty, made after 1911,[25] or trustees for sale of land, invest the trust funds in the purchase of land,[26] that land is to be held upon trust for sale unless the settlement otherwise provides.[27] This, again, preserves the character of the property as personalty; and it prevents it being caught in the meshes of the Settled Land Act, 1925.

The Law of Property Act, 1925, introduced a number of convenient powers and provisions covering both express and statutory trusts for sale, which will now be explained. In other respects these trusts continue as before. The doctrine of conversion, for example, operates unchanged.[27a]

---

[18] L.P.A., 1925, 1st Sched., Pt. II, paras. 3, 6 (*b*).
[19] *Post*, pp. 423–425.　　　　　　　　　　　　　　　[20] *Post*, p. 523.
[21] *Post*, p. 905.　　　　　　　　[22] L.P.A., 1925, s. 31, replacing C.A., 1911, s. 9.
[23] *Ante*, p. 286.
[24] If the money was Settled Land Act capital money, the tenant for life can require the land to be vested in him and until this is done the land is held on trust for sale: *ante*, p. 305. Nevertheless, it is possible that S.L.A., 1925, s. 75 (5) preserves the character of the property, and that the beneficiaries will be treated as having interests in land.
[25] L.P.A., 1925, s. 32 (2).　　　　　　　　　　　　　[26] See *post*, p. 366.
[27] L.P.A., 1925, s. 32 (1). See also *ibid.*, s. 28 (1), imposing a trust for sale in all cases where trustees for sale acquire land in the exercise of the powers thereby conferred on them, *e.g.*, by exchange.
[27a] *Ante*, p. 286.

3. Position of trustees for sale

(a) *Power to postpone sale.* Unless a contrary intention appears (*e.g.*, where the vesting of a gift depends upon the time of sale [28]), a power to postpone sale is implied after 1925 in every trust for sale of land,[29] even if it was created before 1926.[30] In such cases, in the absence of an express provision to the contrary, the trustees are not liable in any way if they postpone sale indefinitely in the exercise of their discretion,[31] nor is a purchaser of the legal estate concerned with directions respecting the postponement of sale.[32] The court has power to order a sale at the instance of any person interested [33]; but it will normally not interfere with trustees who, having considered the circumstances, exercise their discretion one way or the other.[34] Where there is no power to postpone, a year is usually considered a reasonable period in which to effect a sale.[35]

If the trustees cannot agree whether or not to postpone sale, the land must be sold, even though the majority wish to retain it.[36] For the rule is that any trustee can compel his co-trustees to do their *duty* (*i.e.*, to sell), but that they must be unanimous if they wish to exercise a *power* (*e.g.*, to postpone sale); thus the power of postponement is exercisable only if all trustees concur. Nevertheless, many trusts for sale are created with the intention that the land shall be retained for a long time before being sold, and on the assumption that the trustees will duly concur in exercising their power to postpone the sale. As a means of making a settlement, the trust for sale has become recognised as a useful alternative to settled land.[37]

(b) *Other powers of trustees for sale.* The powers of trustees for sale were considerably extended by the Law of Property Act, 1925. Before 1926 they had no powers of leasing, mortgaging or otherwise dealing with the land except by way of sale.[38] After 1925 they have all the powers both of a tenant for life of settled land and of Settled Land Act trustees, including the powers of management which the Settled Land Act, 1925, confers during a minority,[39] even if no

---

[28] *Re Atkins' W. T.* [1974] 1 W.L.R. 761.
[29] L.P.A., 1925, s. 25 (1). This is a new provision.
[30] *Ibid.*, s. 25 (3).
[31] *Ibid.*, s. 25 (2).
[32] *Ibid.*
[33] *Ibid.*, s. 30; *Re Solomon* [1967] Ch. 573; but see *Re Buchanan-Wollaston's Conveyance* [1939] Ch. 738; *post*, p. 415.
[34] See *Re Blake* (1885) 29 Ch.D. 913; *Re Horsnaill* [1909] 1 Ch. 631; *Re Kipping* [1914] 1 Ch. 62; *cf. Re Marshall* [1914] 1 Ch. 192.
[35] *Vickers* v. *Scott* (1834) 3 My. & K. 500; *Re Atkins' W. T., supra.*
[36] *Re Mayo* [1943] Ch. 302. For cases where the position is governed by some trust or contract, see *post*, p. 414.
[37] For the relative advantages and disadvantages of each method, see *post*, p. 384.
[38] *Ante*, p. 285.
[39] L.P.A., 1925, s. 28 (1); for these powers, see S.L.A., 1925, s. 102; *ante*, p. 289.

minority in fact exists.[40] Thus trustees for sale are invested with full powers of management pending sale. They can therefore lease or mortgage the land subject to the same restrictions which govern a tenant for life,[41] or they can use capital money to pay for improvements permitted by the Settled Land Act, 1925 [42]; and provided that they have not, by parting with all their land, ceased to be trustees for sale of land,[43] they may purchase land with the proceeds of sale in their hands.[44] Further, where settled land becomes vested in the Settled Land Act trustees on the form of trusts for sale known as the " statutory trusts," [45] the trustees have all the additional powers (if any) conferred by the settlement on the tenant for life, statutory owner or trustees of the settlement. But in all these cases the powers are subject to the consent of anyone whose consent would be necessary to a sale; for example, if the trustees are to sell only with the consent of X, X's consent is equally necessary to a lease or mortgage.[46]

(c) *Application of income.* Unless there is contrary provision in the trust for sale, the income from the land until sale is to be applied in the same way as the income from the investments which represent the proceeds of sale would be applied.[47] This, however, is subject to keeping down the cost of repairs and insurance and other outgoings, and also subject to setting aside as capital money any part of the income which the Settled Land Act, 1925, requires to be set aside (*e.g.,* three-quarters of the rent of a lease of an unopened mine [48]) unless the trust for sale shows a contrary intention.[49] Thus the whole of the income from leaseholds held on trust for sale is payable to the person entitled to the income from the proceeds of sale,[50] even though the value of the leaseholds gradually diminishes as the terms run out in a way that would not happen with the investments that could be bought if the leaseholds were sold. If the property is in need of repair, the trustees may pay for the repairs out of income,[51] or, if the work falls within the list of improvements in the Settled Land Act, 1925,[52] out of capital.[53] Where

---

[40] *Re Gray* [1927] 1 Ch. 242 (on the meaning of " repairs ").
[41] *Ante,* pp. 334, 339.
[42] *Ante,* p. 345, and see *infra.*
[43] L.P.A., 1925, s. 205 (1) (xxix); *Re Wakeman* [1945] Ch. 177.
[44] L.P.A., 1925, s. 28 (1); S.L.A., 1925, s. 73 (1) (xi); *Re Wellsted's W. T.* [1949] Ch. 296.
[45] See *post,* pp. 423–425. This arises out of a tenancy in common.
[46] L.P.A., 1925, s. 28 (1), as amended by L.P.(Am.)A., 1926, Sched.
[47] L.P.A., 1925, s. 28 (2), following the ordinary rule of equity: *Hutcheon* v. *Mannington* (1791) 1 Ves.Jun. 366; *Re Laing's Trusts* (1866) L.R. 1 Eq. 416.
[48] *Re Ridge* (1885) 31 Ch.D. 504.
[49] L.P.A., 1925, s. 28 (2); *Re Bagot's Settlement* [1894] 1 Ch. 177.
[50] *Re Brooker* [1926] W.N. 93; *Re Berton* [1939] Ch. 200; and see *ante,* p. 348.
[51] L.P.A., 1925, s. 28 (1); S.L.A., 1925, s. 102 (2) (*b*), (3).
[52] *Ante,* p. 346.
[53] L.P.A., 1925, s. 28 (1); S.L.A., 1925, ss. 73 (1) (iii), 83, 3rd Sched.

repairs include such improvements, the trustees thus have a discretion to pay for them out of either capital or income. If the trustees
ask the court for directions, the court will tell them to pay for ordinary
current repairs out of income and to pay for improvements [54] out
of capital [55]; but if the trustees do not consult the court, and in the
exercise of their discretion use income to pay for repairs which
could instead have been paid for out of capital, the court will not
intervene.[56]

(d) Curtailment of the statutory powers

(1) CURTAILMENT. The extent to which it is possible for the
powers of trustees for sale to be curtailed by the settlement is
uncertain. The powers of management derived from section 102 of
the Settled Land Act, 1925, are ordinarily subject to any contrary
intention,[57] and the same presumably is true under trusts for sale.
But it is less easy to say whether the powers borrowed from tenants
for life, which in settlements are made indefeasible,[58] remain
indefeasible when transferred to trusts for sale.

(2) CONSENTS. It is clear that the Law of Property Act, 1925,
contemplates the exercise of any of these powers being made subject
to the requirement that the consent of specified persons should be
first obtained, for it is provided that they shall be exercised with
such consents (if any) as would have been required on a sale under
the trust for sale.[59] It is common to impose a condition that a sale
shall be made only with the consent of a beneficiary, so that he can
enjoy the property as land if he prefers; and such a condition may be
implied, *e.g.*, so as to give effect to a direction that a beneficiary may
occupy the property during his life.[60] If the consent of more than
two persons is required, the Act provides that a bona fide
purchaser for value [61] is protected if the consent of any two of such
persons is obtained,[62] and further, that he need not concern himself
with the consents of any persons under disability.[63] But this pro-

---

[54] *i.e.*, improvements within Parts I and II of the 3rd Sched. of S.L.A., 1925, or
other works in the nature of permanent improvements of the trust property
(*Re Smith* [1930] 1 Ch. 88 at 100, 101). See criticism of this by R. L.
Robinson (1937) 19 *Bell Yard* 22. As to agricultural repairs, see *Re Boston's W.*
T. [1956] Ch. 395; and *ante*, p. 348.
[55] *Re Robins* [1928] Ch. 721: *Re Whitaker* [1929] 1 Ch. 662; *Re Smith* [1930]
1 Ch. 88. The trustees should be guided by the principles laid down in *Re*
Hotchkys (1886) 32 Ch.D. 408 (*Re Conquest* [1929] 2 Ch. 353 at 360).
[56] *Re Gray* [1927] 1 Ch. 242; *Re Robins* [1928] Ch. 721 at 736; *Re Wynn* (*No. 2*)
[1955] 1 W.L.R. 940.
[57] S.L.A., 1925, s. 102 (6); *ante*, p. 354.
[58] *Ante*, p. 351.
[59] L.P.A., 1925, s. 28 (1); and see s. 205 (1) (xxix); J.M.L., 72 L.J.News. 247, 283.
[60] *Re Herklots' W. T.* [1964] 1 W.L.R. 583; *ante*, p. 360.
[61] L.P.A., 1925, s. 205 (1) (xxi).
[62] *Ibid.*, s. 26 (1).
[63] *Ibid.*, s. 26 (2).

vision applies only in favour of a purchaser: the trustees will be guilty of a breach of trust if they do not obtain the full number of consents stipulated. Any consent required from an infant, however, may be given by his parent or guardian, and that of a mental patient under an order of the judge or Court of Protection, *e.g.*, by his receiver [64]; and on the application of any person interested (in the sense of owning some right of property [65]) the court has power to dispense with consents which cannot be obtained,[66] as where the person whose consent is necessary refuses to give it.[67]

(3) INALIENABILITY. It is obviously contrary to the essence of a trust for sale that the trustees' duty to sell should be so hedged about with conditions as to be ineffective; if this were done, the transaction might be held not to be a trust for sale at all, so that the Settled Land Act would apply. But one case has occurred where the court assumed that a testator had succeeded in making his land inalienable under the guise (paradoxically) of a trust for sale: this was where the trustees were directed to sell only with the consent of X, and X was a contingent remainderman who was to benefit only if the land was unsold at the death of the life beneficiary.[68] X's consent to a sale was unobtainable for obvious reasons; and the question whether the court would dispense with it, or what would happen to X's interest if it did, was not raised.

(4) EXCLUSION OF POWERS. Apart from the question of consents, it seems probable that the powers of the trustees cannot be cut down by the instrument creating the trust, except in cases (for example, the power to postpone under section 25) where the power is expressly subjected to a contrary intention. Section 28 (1) states that the trustees " shall have all " [69] the Settled Land Act powers, and it seems unlikely that the settlor can take them away. It is, of course, the policy of the 1925 legislation that all limited owners shall have indefeasible powers of management. Whether a determinable limitation (*e.g.*, " to A for life or until the property is sold ") or a forfeiture clause will be effective if designed so as to operate on an exercise of the powers is uncertain.[70] There is no provision corresponding to section 106 of the Settled Land Act, 1925; but it is

---

[64] Mental Health Act, 1959, Part VIII, superseding L.P.A., 1925, s. 26 (2); and see *post*, p. 997.
[65] *Stevens* v. *Hutchinson* [1953] Ch. 299.
[66] L.P.A., 1925, s. 30; *cf.* T.A., 1925, s. 57.
[67] *Re Beale's S. T.* [1932] 2 Ch. 15.
[68] *Re Inns* [1947] Ch. 576 at 582. *Quaere* whether this was in substance a " trust for sale," since its effect was exactly the opposite.
[69] See *Re Wellsted's W. T.* [1949] Ch. 296 at 312; *Re Simmons* [1956] Ch. 125.
[70] In *Re Davies' W. T.* [1932] 1 Ch. 530 it was held that there could be no forfeiture in the case of land held upon " the statutory trusts " arising out of co-ownership (*post*, p. 410); but this seems to be a decision on s. 35, not s. 28.

arguable that that section is imported along with the Settled Land
Act powers by section 28 of the Law of Property Act, 1925, *i.e.*, that
the Settled Land Act powers are indefeasible powers as thereby
provided.[71]

4. Position of the beneficiaries

(a) *Powers in trustees.* Although normally the net income is
paid to the beneficiary or beneficiaries entitled,[72] a person with an
immediate life interest in the whole property may be permitted by
the trustees to occupy it himself if he wishes, and trusts for sale are
often created with the intention that this shall be done. But such
a person has none of the powers of a tenant for life of settled land,
for all the powers are vested in the trustees for sale.

(b) *Qualifications.* This rule is nevertheless subject to two
qualifications.

(1) DELEGATION. The trustees may revocably and in writing
delegate certain powers to the person of full age (not being merely
an annuitant) who for the time being is beneficially entitled in
possession to the net rents and profits of the land for his life or any
less period.[73] The powers which may be so delegated are the
powers of, and incidental to, leasing, accepting surrenders of leases
and management; and production of the writing is sufficient evidence,
unless the contrary appears, both that the person named is a proper
delegate and that the delegation has not been revoked.[74] The powers
thus delegated must be exercised in the names and on behalf of the
trustees [75]; but if they are misused, the liability rests not on the
trustees, but on the person exercising the powers, who is deemed to
be in the position of a trustee.[76] If the trustees refuse to delegate
these powers, the court may, if it thinks fit, compel them to do so.[77]

(2) ORDER OF COURT. Where at the end of 1925 an order under
section 7 of the Settled Land Act, 1884, was in force, authorising the
person entitled to the income to exercise any of the powers under
the Settled Land Act, 1882,[78] such powers are exercisable by that
person in the same way as if they had been delegated to him by the

---

[71] See the argument in *Re Davies' W. T., supra,* at pp. 532, 533.
[72] *Ante,* p. 366.
[73] L.P.A., 1925, s. 29 (1).
[74] *Ibid.,* s. 29 (1). As to management, see *ante,* p. 365.
[75] L.P.A., 1925, s. 29 (2). See *Stratford* v. *Syrett* [1958] 1 Q.B. 107.
[76] L.P.A., 1925, s. 29 (3).
[77] *Ibid.,* s. 30.
[78] See *ante,* p. 294.

trustees under the foregoing provisions,[79] even if they are powers which in fact could not thus be delegated, *e.g.*, a power [80] of sale.[81]

(c) *Consultation.* Although all the powers belong to the trustees, they must in some cases be exercised in accordance with the wishes of the beneficiaries: in relation to the exercise of all their powers (and not merely their power of sale [82]) the trustees must, so far as is practicable, consult the persons of full age for the time being beneficially interested in possession in the rents and profits of the land until sale (including annuitants [83]) and must, so far as is consistent with the general interests of the trust, give effect to their wishes, or to the wishes of the majority in terms of value.[84] But by the Law of Property (Amendment) Act, 1926, this provision is confined to trusts for sale which either are created by statute or show an intention that this provision is to apply. The majority of express trusts for sale are thereby excluded. In any case, a purchaser is not concerned to see that the trustees have complied with this requirement,[85] though a beneficiary may restrain a trustee who seeks to sell in breach of it.[86]

5. Protection of purchasers. For the protection of any purchaser thereunder, a trust for sale, once created, is deemed to subsist until the land has been conveyed either to the beneficiaries themselves or to some other person under their direction.[87] This meets the difficulty that if all the possible beneficiaries were of full age and subject to no disability, they could put an end to the trust for sale by electing to have the land retained, thus perhaps turning it into settled land. Formerly this difficulty was overcome by requiring one of the beneficiaries to concur in the conveyance, thus showing that there had not been a unanimous election to terminate the trust for sale.[88] Under the present law a purchaser is entitled to insist on a conveyance from the trustees for sale unless they can show that the trust for sale has been discharged.[89] The burden of proof of termination for the trust is thus put upon the trustees, much as in the case of settlements

---

[79] L.P.A., 1925, s. 29 (4).
[80] Strictly, a *duty* to sell: *ante*, p. 359.
[81] *Re Lady Francis Cecil's S. T.* [1926] W.N. 138; *Re Leigh's S. E. (No.* 1) [1926] Ch. 852 at 862; *(No.* 2) [1927] 2 Ch. 13.
[82] *Re Jones* [1931] 1 Ch. 375.
[83] *Re House* [1929] 2 Ch. 166.
[84] L.P.A., 1925, s. 26 (3), as amended by L.P.(Am.)A., 1926, Sched.
[85] *Ibid.*
[86] *Waller* v. *Waller* [1967] 1 W.L.R. 451.
[87] L.P.A., 1925, s. 23, replacing C.A., 1911, s. 10 (3).
[88] See *Re Jenkins & H. E. Randall & Co.'s Contract* [1903] 2 Ch. 362.
[89] L.P.A., 1925, s. 23.

the trustees of the settlement are required to provide a deed of discharge.[90]

The purchaser's position when the sale is irregular is considered below in connection with overreaching.[91]

Part 5

OVERREACHING EFFECT OF DISPOSITIONS

The general principle of overreaching has already been explained.[92] The machinery of settlements and trusts for sale is designed to make land freely marketable even though it is subject to trusts of which purchasers have notice. This machinery can work only if the beneficial interests are overreached, *i.e.*, transferred from the land to the purchase-money on a sale or other disposition being made. The overreaching effect of trusts for sale was automatic, and needed no assistance by statute.[93] Under the Settled Land Acts, on the other hand, overreaching could operate only under the provisions of the Acts. The device of overreaching is so useful that it was somewhat extended by the legislation of 1925, and it is now necessary to study not only the Settled Land Act, 1925, but also some provisions of the Law of Property Act, 1925, which extend to certain trusts for sale. The law relating to settled land will be considered first.

Sect. 1. Under the Settled Land Act, 1925

The Settled Land Act, 1925, in section 72, after first authorising a tenant for life to effect a sale or other transaction by deed, goes on to state the overreaching effect of such a deed (a term which here includes any lease authorised by the Act to be made merely in writing [94]). In its general provisions it follows the Settled Land Act, 1882 [1]; but in a number of details it is adapted to other innovations of 1925. It is a somewhat formidable section, perhaps not very happily drawn. The key to its policy is that a line has to be drawn between the beneficial interests of the family, which ought to be overreached on a sale, and commercial interests, which ought not to be overreached. For example, the beneficial interest of a tenant for life is overreachable; but a lease or mortgage created by the

---

[90] *Ante*, p. 311.
[91] *Post*, p. 377.
[92] *Ante*, p. 148.
[93] *Ante*, p. 148.
[94] S.L.A., 1925, s. 72 (4); see *ante*, p. 337.
[1] s. 20.

tenant for life, in the exercise of his managerial powers, obviously ought not to be overreachable: it is an interest in land obtained for value, which cannot be translated into money without breaking a business arrangement with an outside party which stands on an entirely different footing from the settlement. If the land is sold, it must (like any other land) be sold subject to such leases and other interests as have been validly created.

A second complication is that interests (both family and commercial) which arise under the settlement must be distinguished from interests which affected the land before it was settled, and which therefore have priority to the settlement. The overreaching principle has been extended even to some prior interests, but here also it has to be confined to those of a family character.

A third obstacle is that section 72 draws a number of its terms from the catalogue of registrable interests set out in the Land Charges Act, 1925. These interests have already been briefly noticed, and something has been said of the difficulty of explaining them side by side.[2] But if the policy of section 72 is kept clearly in mind its provisions will be found to be less obscure than they appear. The overreaching of two different classes of rights must be treated separately.

1. Rights under the settlement

(a) *Rights overreached.* The deed is effectual to pass the land or other interests concerned " discharged from all the limitations, powers, and provisions of the settlement, and from all estates, interests, and charges subsisting or to arise thereunder "[3]; it is immaterial whether or not a purchaser has notice of these rights.[4] In short, the purchaser takes the land free from all the rights under the settlement, and from all other rights created out of them (*e.g.,* mortgages of beneficial interests).[5]

(b) *Exceptions.* This provision, however, is obviously too sweeping, for it does not distinguish between family and commercial interests. The Act therefore makes certain qualifications to the rule: certain rights which are prior to the settlement, and numerous commercial interests which may have been created under the settlement by exercising the Settled Land Act powers, are excepted. The land is to pass to the purchaser discharged from the above

---

[2] *Ante,* p. 146. For details, see *post,* p. 1035.
[3] S.L.A., 1925, s. 72 (2).
[4] L.P.A., 1925, s. 2 (1).
[5] *Re Dickin and Kelsall's Contract* [1908] 1 Ch. 213; *Re Davies and Kent's Contract* [1910] 2 Ch. 35.

estates, interests and charges, " but subject to and with the exception of " the following categories.

(1) PRIOR LEGAL ESTATES: " all legal estates and charges by way of legal mortgage having priority to the settlement." [6] This provision is normally mere surplusage,[7] for no power is given under this head to overreach rights prior to the settlement, and so the qualification is unnecessary.[8] If X makes a legal mortgage of land and later settles the land, the tenant for life has no power to overreach the mortgage, which continues to bind the land.

(2) EXISTING LEGAL ESTATES: " all legal estates and charges by way of legal mortgage which have been conveyed or created for securing money actually raised at the date of the deed." [9] This is a true exception, for it excludes a commercial interest arising under the settlement which otherwise would have been included in the overreaching provision.[10] Thus if a tenant for life creates a legal mortgage to pay for improvements [11] or raise portions,[12] and the mortgagee has actually paid the money, the mortgage cannot be overreached.[13] If the money has not in fact been paid [14] (*e.g.*, where a legal term of years has been created in favour of " portions term trustees " [15] to secure portions which have not been raised [16]) the right is overreached; for the term itself is merely a family interest, and it becomes commercial only after it has been mortgaged to some outside investor. Equitable mortgages are not mentioned, because a tenant for life is empowered to make legal mortgages only.[17]

---

6 S.L.A., 1925, s. 72 (2) (i).

7 *Re Davies and Kent's Contract* [1910] 2 Ch. 35 at 54, 57; for a possible case where this provision may have some effect see J.M.L., 77 L.J.News. 39.

8 Probably " subject to " applies to clause (1), and " with the exception of " to clauses (2) and (3): *Re Dickin & Kelsall's Contract* [1908] 1 Ch. 213 at 220, 221. Clause (1) seems to have been inserted for caution: *Re Davies & Kent's Contract* [1910] 2 Ch. 35 at 54; but the wording of the Act of 1925 differs a little from the wording of the Act of 1882; see J.M.L., 77 L.J.News. 21; *post*, p. 383.

9 S.L.A., 1925, s. 72 (2) (ii).

10 *Re Dickin and Kelsall's Contract* [1908] 1 Ch. 213 at 221.

11 *Ante*, p. 339.

12 *Post*, p. 385.

13 See *Re Keck and Hart's Contract* [1898] 1 Ch. 617 at 624.

14 See *Re Du Cane and Nettlefold's Contract* [1898] 2 Ch. 96 at 108; *Re Mundy and Roper's Contract* [1899] 1 Ch. 275 at 290.

15 See *post*, p. 387.

16 See *post*, p. 387; J.M.L., 77 L.J.News. 57. Since 1925 this situation is unusual, since portions terms are now normally equitable in the first place (*post*, p. 388), and although the tenant for life is bound to create the necessary legal term on being required to do so (S.L.A., 1925, s. 16 (1); L.P.A., 1925, s. 3 (1)), no legal estate is created until the money is advanced.

17 *Ante*, p. 339; but see the mention there of equitable mortgages as possibly effective as contracts; if so, they will be protected from overreaching under para. (3) next following.

(3) BINDING RIGHTS CREATED UNDER THE SETTLEMENT: all leases and grants of other rights which at the date of the deed were—

(i) created for money or money's worth (or agreed so to be) under the settlement or any statutory power, or otherwise made binding on the successors in title of the tenant for life; and

(ii) duly registered, if capable of registration.[18]

This also is a true exception,[19] for it takes out of the general rule the whole body of commercial interests which can be created under the settlement either in accordance with the directions of the settlor or under the Settled Land Act powers. Leases, easements, and other rights properly granted by the tenant for life are thus preserved, as they ought to be, against overreaching. So are equitable rights of the commercial sort, for example, contracts for sale or for a lease not yet executed, or restrictive covenants[20]; but these, if created since 1925, must be registered as estate contracts and restrictive covenants respectively.[21] Lastly, the exception protects such "non-family" dispositions as the tenant for life is allowed to make voluntarily (*e.g.*, gifts of land for public purposes[22]). For these, if duly made under a power, are binding on his successors in title; that is to say, they bind the legal estate.[23]

2. Rights prior to the settlement. Having dealt with the exceptions to the rule that all rights arising under the settlement can be overreached, the Act proceeds to lay down that certain rights, even though prior to the settlement, will always be overreached. Rights in this group are therefore equally overreachable whether they exist under the settlement or take priority to it. The Act provides that—

(i) an annuity,[24]

(ii) a limited owner's charge,[25] and

(iii) a general equitable charge[26]

shall be overreached on a disposition under the Act even if they have been duly protected by registration. These rights are treated as if they had been created by the settlement even if in fact they

---

[18] S.L.A., 1925, s. 72 (2) (iii).
[19] See *Re Dickin & Kelsall's Contract* [1908] 1 Ch. 213 at 221.
[20] See J.M.L., 77 L.J.News. 57.
[21] *Ante*, p. 147 (outline); *post*, p. 1040 (detail).
[22] *Ante*, p. 333.
[23] There is probably a logical difficulty here. What gifts are not overreachable? Those which bind successors in title. What gifts bind successors in title? Those which are not overreached. But the sense is plain.
[24] *Post*, p. 1037.
[25] *Post*, p. 1039.
[26] *Post*, p. 1040. A general equitable charge must be prior to the settlement, for by definition it cannot exist under the settlement: *ibid*.

arose before it came into existence.[27] Although not exclusively family rights,[28] these are all rights which represent merely claims to money and so will not suffer from being transferred to the purchase-money. It is therefore convenient to take the opportunity of clearing them off the title when an overreaching disposition is being made.

3. Summary. For those who wish to have a bird's eye view of the general results of these provisions (necessarily at the expense of some accuracy) they may be sketched as follows:

(i) There is in general no power to overreach the rights of persons who are not beneficiaries under the settlement. Three exceptions to this principle are set out above. Another exception, mentioned below, is that the interests of assignees of the equitable interests of beneficiaries are overreached together with those of the beneficiaries.

(ii) There is power to overreach all the equitable rights of the beneficiaries under the settlement, including derivative rights, *e.g.*, the rights of a mortgagee of the beneficial interest of a tenant for life [29] or remainderman.[30]

(iii) These principles make no distinction between legal and equitable interests. But in practice nearly all legal rights today are of a commercial kind, and therefore not overreachable.[31]

4. Payment of capital money

(*a*) *Payment.* There is one important condition which must be observed if a deed is to take effect under the Act and so have an overreaching effect.[32] This is the rule that any capital money [33] payable in respect of the transaction must be paid either—

---

[27] S.L.A., 1925, s. 72 (3).

[28] The fate of an equitable mortgage not protected by deposit of title deeds (a commercial interest) depends on whether it is regarded as a general equitable charge (overreached) or as an estate contract (not overreachable). For this question, see *post*, p. 971.

[29] See, *e.g.*, *Re Dickin & Kelsall's Contract* [1908] 1 Ch. 213.

[30] See, *e.g.*, *Re Davies & Kent's Contract* [1910] 2 Ch. 35.

[31] See, however, *ante*, p. 150, Wolst. & C. iii, 25, and S.L.A., 1925, s. 85 (3) for comparatively unimportant exceptions to this. Before 1926 the interests of the beneficiaries were often legal (*ante*, p. 284), so that legal interests were often overreached. Since 1925 this can occur only in rare cases, *e.g.*, if the legal fee simple owner creates a legal rentcharge voluntarily and then sells the land; *cf. Re Austen* [1929] 2 Ch. 155, where the perpetual rentcharges were equitable: see *ibid.*, at p. 162. Before 1926, too, there was no provision corresponding to S.L.A., 1925, s. 72 (3), which made it possible to overreach rights having priority to the settlement. Otherwise the overreaching provisions (see S.L.A., 1882, s. 20 (2)) were in general similar.

[32] S.L.A., 1925, s. 18 (1) (*b*); L.P.A., 1925, s. 2 (1) (i).

[33] As to what is capital money, see *ante*, p. 350.

> (i) to, or by the direction of, all the trustees of the settlement,[34] who must be either two or more in number [35] or a trust corporation, or
>
> (ii) into court.[36]

This rule applies notwithstanding anything to the contrary in the settlement,[37] so that a provision authorising the tenant for life as sole trustee to give a receipt for capital money is no longer effective.[38] A "trust corporation" is elaborately defined, and includes the Public Trustee, Treasury Solicitor, the Official Solicitor, and companies incorporated in the United Kingdom under the Companies Acts to undertake trust business if they have an issued capital of at least £250,000 of which not less than £100,000 has been paid up in cash.[39]

(b) *Failure.* If a purchaser fails to pay his money in accordance with these provisions and pays it, for example, to the tenant for life, he will not get a good discharge, will not take the land free from the beneficial interests,[40] and will be unable to make a good title to a subsequent purchaser.[41] It lies with the tenant for life to decide which of the two methods of payment is to be adopted [42]; but if there are no trustees he cannot direct payment into court,[43] although if he does so, a purchaser unaware that there are no trustees will get a good discharge.[44] Where no capital money arises on a transaction (as where a lease is granted without taking a fine), a disposition in favour of a bona fide purchaser for value of a legal estate [45] takes effect under the Act and thus has an overreaching effect even though there are no trustees.[46]

(c) *Capital money as land.* As under the Act of 1882,[47] capital money and any investments representing it are for all purposes of disposition, transmission and devolution treated as land, and are held for and go to the same persons, in the same manner and for

---

34 S.L.A., 1925, s. 18 (1) (b).
35 *Ibid.*, s. 18 (1) (c).
36 *Ibid.*, s. 18 (1) (b).
37 *Ibid.*, s. 18 (1) (c). This was not so under S.L.A., 1882: see s. 39 (1).
38 As occurred in *Re Johnson's S. E.* [1913] W.N. 222. There can now be no need for the court to intervene in such cases to protect the other beneficiaries: see *Re Davies & Kent's Contract* [1910] 2 Ch. 35.
39 Public Trustee (Custodian Trustee) Rules, 1926 (S.R. & O., 1926, 1423/L. 37); L.P.(Am.)A., 1926, s. 3; L.P.A., 1925, s. 205 (1) (xxviii); S.L.A., 1925, s. 117 (1) (xxx). For details, see Lewin 462 *et seq.*
40 S.L.A., 1925, s. 18 (1) (b); *ante*, p. 313.
41 *Re Norton & Las Casas' Contract* [1909] 2 Ch. 59.
42 S.L.A., 1925, s. 75 (1).
43 *Hatten* v. *Russell* (1888) 38 Ch.D. 334 at 345.
44 *Re Fisher & Grazebrook's Contract* [1898] 2 Ch. 660 at 662.
45 S.L.A., 1925, s. 117 (1) (xxi).
46 *Ibid.*, s. 110 (4).
47 *Ante*, p. 293.

the same estates, interests and trusts, as the land wherefrom they arise would have been held and have gone under the settlement.[48] The object of this provision is " to preserve the legal character of settled land notwithstanding its conversion into capital money. . . . Where you are dealing with a settled freehold which is sold, the capital money would be treated as freehold, and, where you have a settled leasehold which is sold, the capital money would be treated as leasehold." [49] Thus an absolute interest in the capital money representing settled freeholds cannot be disposed of by a will that only disposes of personalty,[50] and before 1926 the money would have passed to the heir and not the next-of-kin [51]; yet for fiscal purposes the money is not treated as land.[52] Nevertheless, in general the state in which the settled property happens to be at any given moment, whether it is land, investments or money, cannot affect the rights of the beneficiaries or those claiming under them.

Sect. 2. Under a Trust for Sale

1. Overreaching. In one sense, a trust for sale has no overreaching effect: under the doctrine of conversion the rights of the beneficiaries are from the first rights not in land but in money.[53] There is a trust, for their benefit, that the land shall be sold; but that trust is of course discharged by a proper sale, so that no purchaser will be bound by it if he buys without notice of any irregularity. Nevertheless, it is convenient to use the term " overreaching " as including the process by which the beneficiaries have their rights in what is money in theory but land in fact transferred to what is money both in theory and in fact.[54]

2. Position of purchaser. A proper disposition under a trust for sale is automatically effective to overreach the rights of the beneficiaries thereunder, so that the purchaser has no concern with them. These rights are necessarily equitable; there is no power to overreach legal estates,[55] nor to overreach rights already existing when the trust for sale was created.[56] The purchaser's immunity from the rights of

---

[48] S.L.A., 1925, s. 75 (5).
[49] *Re Cartwright* [1939] Ch. 90 at 103, 104, *per* Greene M.R.
[50] *Re Cartwright* [1939] Ch. 90.
[51] *Re Cutcliffe's W. T.* [1940] Ch. 565; on deaths after 1925, realty and personalty devolve on the same person: see *post*, p. 523.
[52] *Earl of Midleton* v. *Baron Cottesloe* [1949] A.C. 418.
[53] J.M.L., 77 L.J.News. 57; *ante*, p. 286.
[54] See J. M. Lightwood (1927) C.L.J. 65; 61 L.J.News. 214; 77 L.J.News. 73. There is legislative authority for this: L.P.A., 1925, s. 2 (1) (ii) refers to interests " capable of being overreached " by trustees for sale: and see s. 28 (1).
[55] J.M.L., 77 L.J.News. 57.
[56] Except in the special case of an *ad hoc* trust for sale: *post*, p. 381. The argument that trustees for sale have all the S.L.A. powers (*ante*, p. 365) including power to overreach certain prior equities (*ante*, p. 374) was rejected in *Re Ryder and Steadman's Contract* [1927] 2 Ch. 62 at 82. The reasoning is not very clear but the result is satisfactory.

the beneficiaries depends, however, upon the sale being made in accordance with the law and the terms of the trust: a purchaser with notice that the sale is irregular (e.g., where the purchase-money is not duly paid to the trustees) will take subject to the trust for sale. In this important respect the beneficiaries have an equitable interest in the land itself, i.e., the right to require that it shall be sold for their benefit; and only a proper sale can overreach this right.

The Law of Property Act, 1925, requires that the proceeds of sale or other capital money, notwithstanding anything to the contrary in the trust for sale,[57] " shall not be paid to or applied by the direction of fewer than two persons as trustees for sale, except where the trustee is a trust corporation." [58] There is no provision for payment into court. Where no capital money arises (e.g., on the grant of a lease without a fine [59]) it is unnecessary to have more than one trustee [60]; and a sole personal representative, acting as such, may still give a valid receipt even for capital money.[61]

The Act omits to say what will happen if these directions are not obeyed. The existence of a trust for sale will not always appear from the title deeds, as where a house stands in the husband's name but was bought partly with the wife's money, so that she owns a share under a statutory trust for sale.[62] In that case there is nothing to displace the principle that, except in the case of registered land,[63] a bona fide purchaser of the legal estate without notice of the trust will take free from it.[64] In this instance, furthermore, a purchase without notice may easily occur.[65] There is thus a sharp contrast with the drastic provisions of the Settled Land Act, 1925, which purchasers must obey at their peril.[66]

3. Capital money. Subject to any express trust to the contrary, any capital money arising from the exercise of the statutory powers (e.g., a fine paid for the grant of a lease, but not mere compensation paid under other statutes [67]) must either be paid or applied in the same way as capital money arising from settled land, or else be applied as if it represented proceeds of sale.[68] These provisions do

---

[57] But see *Re Wight & Best's Brewery Co. Ltd.'s Contract* [1929] W.N. 11.
[58] L.P.A., 1925, ss. 2 (1) (ii), 27 (2), as amended by L.P.(Am.)A., 1926, Sched.
[59] See *Re Myhill* [1928] Ch. 100.
[60] L.P.A., 1925, s. 27 (2), as amended by L.P.(Am.)A., 1926, Sched.
[61] *Ibid.*
[62] See *post*, p. 447.
[63] The question then is whether a minor interest is registered: *post*, p. 1068.
[64] *Caunce* v. *Caunce* [1969] 1 W.L.R. 286 (statutory trust for sale for joint tenants defeated by legal mortgage without notice); and see (1969) 33 Conv.(N.S.) 240 (J. F. Garner).
[65] See *post*, p. 447.   [66] *Ante*, p. 313.
[67] *Re Meux* [1958] Ch. 154 (Town and Country Planning Act, 1954: see *post*, p. 1102).
[68] L.P.A., 1925, s. 28 (1); see *ante*, p. 349.

not, however, effect a conversion into realty, and as before 1926 [69] the rights of the beneficiaries remain rights in personalty.[70] Any land acquired under this provision must be conveyed to the trustees for sale on trust for sale.[71]

Sect. 3. Under Ad Hoc Settlements and Trusts for Sale

1. Overreaching prior interests. The original intention of the 1925 legislation was that a conveyance under a settlement or trust for sale should overreach not only the interests of the beneficiaries but also prior equities of the kind which are translatable into money and can conveniently be cleared off the title to the legal estate.[72] It has been seen how this policy is carried out by dispositions under the Settled Land Act, 1925.[73] But in the case of trusts for sale it was confined, after attacks in Parliament,[74] to cases where the trust had " guaranteed " trustees, *i.e.*, either trustees appointed or approved by the court, or a trust corporation. In such cases the trust is called an " *ad hoc* " trust for sale, and the overreaching of certain prior equities is allowed. The idea is that the special trustees are likely to be particularly trustworthy and that this will console those whose interests, being overreached, lose the security of the land which was previously charged with the payments. That is the theory; in practice, little use is made of such trusts for sale, for the additional overreaching powers conferred are meagre and, indeed, inappropriate.

An even rarer phenomenon, said to be " hardly worth the ingenuity spent on it," [75] is the *ad hoc* settlement under the Settled Land Act, 1925.[76] This corresponds to the *ad hoc* trust for sale; there is the same requirement of special trustees, and the special overreaching powers are the same.[77]

The object of these two devices is to enable the owners of legal estates, where they are subject to some prior equitable interest which is of an overreachable kind, to dispose of the land free from that interest. Where this can be done, it must be done if the purchaser so requires.[78] The owner is given a choice between setting up *ad hoc* (*i.e.*, for the purpose of overreaching the prior equity) either a special settlement or a special trust for sale. In practice an *ad hoc* trust for sale will probably be chosen.[79]

---

[69] S.L.A., 1882, s. 63 (2) (iii).
[70] *Ante*, p. 387; *Re Kempthorne* [1930] 1 Ch. 268.
[71] L.P.A., 1925, s. 28 (1); *ante*, p. 364.
[72] J. M. Lightwood (1927) 3 C.L.J. 67, 68.
[73] *Ante*, p. 374.
[74] See 61 L.J.News. 468 (J.M.L.).
[75] 77 L.J.News. 73 (J.M.L.).
[76] 71 L.J.News. 341 (J.M.L.).
[77] *Ibid.*
[78] L.P.A., 1925, s. 42 (1); *post*, p. 587.
[79] See Wolst. & C. iii, 82.

2. Need for ad hoc machinery. If the land is already subject to a settlement, there will generally [80] be no need to use the special machinery; for, as has been seen, an ordinary settlement confers power to overreach certain prior equities.[81] But an ordinary trust for sale does not; and therefore if the land is already subject to a trust for sale, it will be necessary for the trustees to be approved by the court, or for special trustees to be appointed, in order to sell land which is subject to some prior equity of an overreachable kind.

Since most overreachable equities are family charges, and most land subject to family charges is settled land, it is very rarely that the special *ad hoc* machinery need be used.[82] Land charged with a life annuity created for money or money's worth (and not by way of family arrangement) would be an example; another would be land subject to a limited owner's charge, *e.g.*, where land is devised to A for life with remainder to B in fee simple, and A then dies having paid death duties on the testator's death out of his own pocket.[83] If it had been held that a settlement came to an end as soon as a trust for sale arose, despite the continued existence of rights under the settlement such as a jointure, there would have been some utility in the *ad hoc* machinery; for the rights under the settlement would have been overreached only if the trustees for sale were thus " guaranteed." But by holding that a settlement continues so long as any interest under it subsists,[84] despite any trust for sale, the courts have left the *ad hoc* machinery little scope.

Ad hoc settlements and trusts for sale may be said, in general, to be both complicated and ineffective. But their details must be described. They are as follows.

3. Creation

(*a*) *Ad hoc settlements.* If a person of full age is beneficially entitled in possession to a legal estate subject to any equitable interests or powers, then for the purpose of overreaching these rights he may by deed declare that the legal estate is vested in him on trust to give effect to all equitable interests and powers affecting the legal estate.[85] Such a deed is treated as a vesting deed and must also be executed either by two or more individuals approved or appointed by the court, or by a trust corporation, who must be

---

[80] For the rare exceptions, see *post*, p. 383.
[81] *Ante*, p. 374.
[82] See 71 L.J.News. 341 (J.M.L.): " a special trust for sale or special settlement is hardly, I imagine, to be found in practice."
[83] For other examples, see Wolst. & C. iii, 82.
[84] See *ante*, p. 360.
[85] S.L.A., 1925, s. 21 (1).

stated to be Settled Land Act trustees.[85a] Thereupon the land is deemed to be settled land and the estate owner becomes a tenant for life [85b]; the instruments creating his estate and the equitable interests or powers are deemed to be the trust instrument, in default of which a trust instrument must be executed contemporaneously with the vesting deed.[85c] It will be noticed that these provisions are inappropriate to land which is already settled, for normally there will be no person *beneficially* entitled in possession to a *legal* estate [86]; the provisions contemplate only settlements set up *ad hoc* (expressly for the purpose).

(*b*) *Ad hoc trusts for sale.* If a legal estate is subject to a trust for sale and the trustees thereof are either—

(i) two or more individuals approved or appointed by the court, or their successors in office, or

(ii) a trust corporation,

then the effect of a conveyance is to overreach certain equities having priority to the trust for sale.[87] This provision is not confined to trusts for sale created *ad hoc* but can apply to any trust for sale, whether already in existence [88] or set up expressly for the purpose of overreaching equities [89]; provided the conditions as to trustees are satisfied, the wider overreaching powers exist.[90] The provision including successors of the trustees appointed or approved by the court (which has no counterpart for *ad hoc* settlements [90]) is an important breach in the theory of " guaranteed " trustees; "largely the guaranteed trust is a myth." [91] Further, approval by the court may be inferred from approval of the trustees for some other purpose, such as an infant's marriage settlement.[92]

4. Overreaching effect of dispositions

(*a*) *Extent.* For both *ad hoc* settlements [93] and *ad hoc* trusts for sale [94] the overreaching provisions are in similar terms. Equitable rights having priority to the settlement or trust for sale are overreached with the exception of—

(*a*) equitable interests protected by a deposit of documents relating to the legal estate affected: in practice, this means

---

85a *Ibid.*   85b *Ibid.*
85c *Ibid.*
86 This is not an absolute rule: see *e.g.*, head (*e*), *ante*, p. 317.
87 L.P.A., 1925, s. 2 (2), as amended by L.P.(Am.)A., 1926, Sched.
88 See *Re Leigh's S. E.* (*No.* 2) [1927] 2 Ch. 13. This was not so before the amendment made by L.P.(Am.)A., 1926: 63 L.J.News. 374.
89 J. M. Lightwood (1927) 3 C.L.J. 69.
90 But see T.A., 1925, s. 36 (7).   91 77 L.J.News. 73 (J.M.L.).
92 *Re Leigh's S. E.* (*No.* 2) [1927] 2 Ch. 13; see *post*, p. 991.
93 S.L.A., 1925, s. 21 (1), (2).   94 L.P.A., 1925, s. 2 (2), (3).

equitable mortgages or charges protected by a deposit of title deeds;

(*b*) restrictive covenants;

(*c*) equitable easements;

(*d*) estate contracts;

(*e*) equitable interests protected by registration under the Land Charges Act 1972, other than—

　　　(i) annuities,

　　　(ii) limited owner's charges, and

　　　(iii) general equitable charges.[95]

(*b*) *Additional ad hoc powers.* It will be seen from this that the last three rights can always be overreached under an *ad hoc* settlement or an *ad hoc* trust for sale. Such rights can, indeed, be overreached under an ordinary settlement,[96] so that no wider powers are given in this case; indeed, an ordinary settlement may even do what an *ad hoc* settlement or trust for sale cannot, namely, overreach a legal right.[97] But the three rights mentioned cannot be overreached under an ordinary trust for sale, so that in this respect an *ad hoc* trust for sale has a clear advantage over an ordinary trust for sale. The other exceptions are all rights of a commercial kind, which cannot in any case be overreached without being destroyed. Head (*e*) really adds nothing to the previous heads, for the only rights it includes are included under (*b*), (*c*) and (*d*).[98] These rights are, in general, capable of registration only if created after 1925,[99] so that, for example, a restrictive covenant is protected by head (*b*) if created in 1920 and by heads (*b*) and (*e*) if created in 1930.

(*c*) *Unregistrable equities.* The drafting of the various over-reaching provisions gives rise to one difference between an ordinary settlement on the one hand and an *ad hoc* settlement (or *ad hoc* trust for sale) on the other. This springs from the fact that the Settled Land Act, 1925, follows the model of the Act of 1882 [1] in section 72 (overreaching effect of an ordinary settlement) but follows a different model [2] in section 21 (overreaching effect of an *ad hoc* settlement). Both aim at the same result: the overreaching of prior equitable annuities, limited owner's charges and general equitable

---

[95] *Ibid.*, s. 2 (3); S.L.A., 1925, s. 21 (2).

[96] *Ante*, p. 374.

[97] See *ante*, pp. 374, 375; 77 L.J.News 39 (J.M.L.).

[98] See *post*, p. 1040, for their various definitions.

[99] *Post*, p. 1050; estate contracts created before 1926 are registrable if transferred (*i.e.*, assigned) after 1925: *post*, p. 1051; restrictive covenants made between lessor and lessee are not registrable at all: *post*, p. 1042.

[1] s. 20.

[2] L.P.A., 1925, s. 2.

charges. Section 72 states simply that these are overreached. Section 21 states that all prior equities are overreached except (*inter alia*) registered land charges other than these three. It follows that any prior equity which is not in the catalogue of registrable land charges cannot be overreached under an ordinary settlement but can, if not within the list of exceptions, be overreached by using the *ad hoc* machinery.

In fact the only examples of such equities likely to occur are commercial (as opposed to family) interests, which it is absurd to speak of overreaching.[3] Two instances are an equitable right of way which is yet not an equitable easement,[4] and an equitable right of entry to secure performance of a covenant,[5] and there are probably others. To overreach such interests is to destroy them, and it cannot be supposed that even the *ad hoc* provisions intend this. These provisions are founded on the faulty assumption that the catalogue of registrable land charges included the whole residue of equitable interests in land, an assumption which the House of Lords has rejected.[6] They seem to be an example of over-confident drafting.[7]

Sect. 4. Summary of Overreaching Provisions

In broad outline, the position may be said to be as follows:

(*a*) A conveyance under an ordinary trust for sale overreaches the rights of the beneficiaries thereunder.

(*b*) A conveyance under an ordinary settlement overreaches—

    (i) the rights of the beneficiaries thereunder, and

    (ii) annuities, limited owner's charges and general equitable charges.

(*c*) A conveyance under an *ad hoc* settlement or trust for sale overreaches—

    (i) the rights of the beneficiaries thereunder;

    (ii) annuities, limited owner's charges and general equitable charges; and

    (iii) certain other equities, though the provisions for this seem misconceived.

---

[3] Some pre-1926 family interests might have qualified, *e.g.*, dower not assigned by metes and bounds (for which see *ante*, p. 319, *post*, p. 516): Wolst. & C. iii, 30.

[4] As in *E. R. Ives Investment Ltd.* v. *High* [1967] 2 Q.B. 379; *post*, p. 1043.

[5] As in *Shiloh Spinners Ltd.* v. *Harding* [1973] A.C. 80; *post*, p. 1043.

[6] *Shiloh Spinners Ltd.* v. *Harding, supra.*

[7] It is also a mistake to assume that new equitable interests will not arise. As Harman J. once said, " Equity is not to be presumed to be of an age past childbearing ": Megarry, *Miscellany-at-Law* (1955) p. 142; *A Second Miscellany-at-Law* (1973) p. 293.

Part 6

METHODS OF SETTLING LAND

Sect. 1.   Comparison of Settled Land with Trusts for Sale

Although the settlement and the trust for sale remain sharply distinct in law, the available powers of disposition and management have to a large extent been assimilated.[8] From the standpoint of an owner considering which form to employ, the principal difference is that a settlement puts these powers into the hands of the tenant for life, while a trust for sale gives them to the trustees. Where the intention is not to " make an eldest son " but to share out the property among all the children, a trust for sale is much more convenient. For most purposes a trust for sale is simpler, cheaper and more suitable generally. It may even offer better prospects of keeping the land in the family, since sale may be made subject to consent in a way which cannot be done with settled land.[9] In this respect settlements and trusts for sale have changed places since the middle of the last century.

Sect. 2.   Traditional Forms of Settlement

Settlements and trusts for sale often arise under wills, in which case the trusts depend entirely upon the testator's wishes. The trusts of settlements and trusts for sale created *inter vivos* may also be in any form. But settlements made on marriage acquired a traditional form which was evolved over the centuries while settlors and their advisers were seeking to tie up the land for successive generations and Parliament and the courts were frustrating these efforts and making the land freely alienable.[10] After the Settled Land Act, 1882, the land itself was always alienable, and the settlement could do no more than ensure that either the land or the proceeds of sale remained settled. Today, for fiscal reasons,[11] the traditional form of settlement has fallen out of favour; but many such settlements still exist, and they illustrate the former practice.

A.   A Strict Settlement Made upon Marriage

Within the limits imposed by the rule against perpetuities, the best arrangement for keeping property in the family was the old method of settlement and resettlement, explained earlier.[12] The technicalities

---

[8] *Ante*, p. 365.
[9] *Ante*, p. 367.
[10] For a sketch of this development, see 3rd edition of this book, pp. 394–396.
[11] *Ante*, p. 282.
[12] *Ante*, p. 283.

of fines and recoveries were thereby moulded into a basic law of family property which in substance remains in full force,[13] though in practice it is less and less used. The core of the conventional settlement and resettlement, which date from the end of the seventeenth century,[14] was —

SETTLEMENT	RESETTLEMENT
(1) H for life	(1) H for life
(2) Son in tail	(2) Son for life
	(3) Son's son in tail

Round this core was built a complex structure which made provision for H's wife and the younger children of the marriage. The trusts are best illustrated by the provisions usually made where H, a tenant in fee simple, was settling his land on the occasion of his marriage with W. Such a settlement was normally made a few days before the marriage. The trusts were as follows.[15]

1. The trusts

(*a*) *Determinable fee*: For H in fee simple until the celebration of the marriage. This is to guard against the marriage not taking place. H takes a determinable fee which becomes a fee simple absolute if either party dies prematurely.[16]

(*b*) *Pin money*: Thereafter, a rentcharge of £*x* per annum to W during the joint lives of H and W, by way of pin money. This provides W with an income for her personal expenses.

(*c*) *Life interest*: Subject thereto, to H for life. This would usually be granted without impeachment of waste.

(*d*) *Jointure*: Subject thereto, a rentcharge of £*y* per annum to W for life if she survives H, by way of jointure. This will be for a larger amount than the pin money, since it is intended to support W completely after H's death.

(*e*) *Portions*: Subject thereto, a trust for portions for the younger children of the marriage. This provision gives a capital sum to each child of the marriage other than the child who takes the land, so that all of them are provided for. The machinery by which this is done is explained below.[17]

---

13 *Ante*, p. 90.
14 H.E.L. vii, 376–380; Scrutton, *Land in Fetters*, 118–120.
15 See Prideaux iii, 246 *et seq.*
16 Challis 257.
17 *Post*, pp. 387, 388.

(*f*) *Entails*:

    (i) Subject thereto, for the first and other sons successively in tail male.

    (ii) Subject thereto, for the first and other sons successively in tail general.

    (iii) Subject thereto, for all the daughters in equal shares as tenants in common in tail general with cross remainders.

The effect of these provisions is best shown by an example. Suppose that H and W have had two sons and two daughters, and that each son has had a son and a daughter, thus:

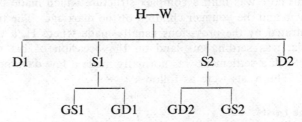

Assuming that no entail is barred, S1 takes under (i) and on his death GS1 becomes entitled under the same provision. On the death of GS1 without male issue (or on failure of the male line of his issue at any future time [18]) the tail male given to S1 determines and S2 becomes entitled under (i). On his death, GS2 succeeds to the land and on his death without male issue (or on failure of his male issue) the provisions of (i) are exhausted. GD1 therefore becomes entitled under the tail general given to S1 by (ii), but if her issue fail GD2 becomes similarly entitled under S2's tail general. On failure of her issue, (ii) is exhausted and D1 and D2 become entitled under (iii). Each has a distinct half share which will be inherited by her issue, but if, say, D2 dies without issue, the cross remainder will carry her half share to D1.[19]

(*g*) *Reversion*: Subject thereto, for H in fee simple. Thus on failure of the entails, the land reverts to H and will pass under his will or intestacy.

(*h*) *Miscellaneous provisions.* The details of the portions are usually included here, and provision is made for the wife and issue of any future marriage of H, *e.g.*, if W dies and H remarries. The

---

[18] The perpetuity rule has no application to such remainders after entails (*ante*, p. 263) and these remainders are in any case vested.

[19] For the further intricacies of cross remainders in tail, see Challis 370–373. Each daughter has in the aggregate a vested remainder in the whole of the lands, but it is composed of a number of separate remainders of different degrees of remoteness.

provisions which the Settled Land Act, 1925, requires to be inserted in a trust instrument [20] (*e.g.*, the appointment of trustees of the settlement) are also set out.

2. Operation of the trusts

All these interests are of a familiar kind except pin money, jointure and portions.

(*a*) *Pin money and jointure.* As an annual income is required for the pin money and jointure, these can be secured by rentcharges. Adequate remedies are given by statute for enforcing payment of rentcharges,[21] so that W is properly protected.

(*b*) *Portions.* Portions cannot be secured by rentcharges because capital and not annual sums are required.

(1) PORTIONS TERMS. The traditional device employed to secure payment of portions is for the settlement to create a long term of years (*e.g.*, a thousand years) in favour of " portions term trustees " (usually distinct from the trustees of the settlement) on trust to raise the sums specified. As the provision for portions precedes the entails, the eldest son takes the land subject to a burden which he cannot shake off by barring his entail. The trustees can raise the money by sale or mortgage of the term of years,[22] which, being granted them without impeachment of waste and without any rent being reserved, really represents the full value of the land. If the portions are raised in this way, the effect is that the eldest son takes it burdened with the mortgages made for the benefit of his younger brothers. Usually, however, the money is paid either out of capital or by the eldest son out of his own pocket so as to clear the estate.[23] On payment of the money, the term of years becomes a " satisfied term " and automatically ceases.[24] This has not always been the position, but the complicated situation which formerly existed [25] need not be examined here.

---

[20] *Ante*, p. 300.
[21] *Post*, p. 796.
[22] *Kelly* v. *Lord Bellew* (1707) 4 Bro.P.C. 495.
[23] See *Burrell* v. *The Earl of Egremont* (1844) 7 Beav. 205 ; 77 L.J.News. 57 (J.M.L.).
[24] L.P.A., 1925, s. 5.
[25] See Williams, R.P. 584–594. At common law, unless the lease contained a " proviso for cesser," the term remained outstanding until it was reconveyed to the owner in fee and so merged in it. It often happened that a tenant in tail, on coming into possession, barred the entail and sold the estate, arranging to redeem an outstanding portions term out of the purchase-money. In such cases the practice was for the purchaser to keep the term alive by requiring it to be assigned to trustees (so preventing merger: *post*, p. 669) " in trust to attend the inheritance." This protected him against any incumbrances created by the tenant in tail, who had no power to incumber the

(2) PORTIONS TRUST. In modern settlements the cumbersome device of creating portions terms was normally avoided by inserting a trust to raise portions which could be effectuated by the creation of a legal mortgage if necessary. There seems to be no advantage in a portions term, for if there is merely a declaration that the portions are to be raised on the security of the settled land, the tenant for life can be compelled to make a legal mortgage of the land for the purpose of raising them.[26]

(3) " ELDEST SON." A curious problem arises in drafting provisions for portions. It is usually desired to endow the children with their portions so soon as they reach 21, but to give no portion to the eldest son, who will succeed to the estate. But a younger child who has received a portion at 21 may later turn out to be entitled to the estate as well; and if his elder brothers die without issue (and with their entails unbarred) in the lifetime of H, he will himself be the " eldest son " for the purposes of the settlement. In practice this risk is generally taken. Portions are given to all " younger children," and this term is defined so as to include all the children except a son who during his minority (or at its termination) has become entitled to an entail in possession or in remainder immediately expectant on the death of H.[27] A child who escapes these words of exception and so takes a portion does not lose it if he succeeds to the land.

3. Settled chattels

(a) *Deferred vesting.* Before 1926 there were several difficulties in settling chattels along with land: only in rare cases could they descend with it as " heirlooms," [28] and any attempt to give personalty in tail resulted in the donee obtaining absolute ownership.[29] Therefore as soon as the eldest son was born he took an absolute interest in the chattels [30] and could dispose of them as he thought fit; and his father had not the same power to induce him to resettle them as he had in the case of land. If the eldest son died childless before he had resettled the land his entail in the land determined and the land

---

paramount portions term though he could of course incumber his own estate tail. (See also *post,* p. 981.) The Satisfied Terms Act, 1845, stopped this cumbrous practice by providing that without prejudice to existing rights all existing satisfied terms attending the inheritance should cease at the end of 1845, and that all such terms becoming satisfied thereafter should similarly cease. L.P.A., 1925, s. 5, replaced and extended this provision by making it immaterial whether or not the term attended the inheritance.

[26] S.L.A., 1925, s. 16 (1) (iii), (7); L.P.A., 1925, s. 3 (1) (a).
[27] For the form of definition used, see Prideaux iii, 286; and see, *e.g., Collingwood* v. *Stanhope* (1869) L.R. 4 H.L. 43; *Re Wrottesley's Settlement* [1911] 1 Ch. 708; *Re Wise's Settlement* [1913] 1 Ch. 41; *Re Leeke's S. T.* [1937] Ch. 600.
[28] *Ante,* p. 343; *post,* p. 522.
[29] *Ante,* p. 95.
[30] *Foley* v. *Burnell* (1785) 4 Bro.P.C. 319.

would pass to his younger brother; but the chattels would pass to those entitled under the elder son's will or intestacy.[31] To avoid these defects as far as possible, the chattels would be settled on the same trusts as the land, with the proviso that they should not vest absolutely in an unborn person who took an entail by purchase until he or she should attain full age.[32]

(b) *Effect.* This proviso meant that none of the children got a vested interest until he or she was of full age. Further, its operation was confined to the children by the words " by purchase," so that the children's children, who could take entails only by descent and not by purchase, were not affected by it; otherwise it would have been void as infringing the perpetuity rule.[33] The effect of this proviso was that until there was a child capable of executing a resettlement, the chattels did not become the absolute property of anyone, and so when that child was persuaded to resettle the land, he could probably be persuaded to resettle the chattels also.[34]

(c) *Vesting contingent on possession.* Even this proviso did not exclude a child who attained full age but predeceased his father, and so vesting was sometimes made to depend upon the child also obtaining "actual possession" of the land.[35] Yet this made it impossible for the eldest son on attaining full age to join with his father in resettling the chattels, for *ex hypothesi* he had no vested interest in them.[36] Oddly enough, the entail that would have avoided all these difficulties appeared if the chattels were sold under an order of the court [37]; for the proceeds of sale were treated as capital money of the settled land, and so the child took an entail in the money in place of absolute ownership of the chattels.[38]

(d) *Entails after 1925.* After 1925 the provision that personalty can be entailed avoids these complications, and chattels can now be settled on the same trusts as land.

B. A Trust for Sale Made upon Marriage

If H is marrying W and settling land upon trust for sale, the usual trusts are as follows [39]:

---

31 See, *e.g.*, *Re Coote* [1940] Ch. 549.
32 *Hill (Viscount)* v. *Hill (Dowager Viscountess)* [1897] 1 Q.B. 483 at 495; see, *e.g.*, *Re Lewis* [1918] 2 Ch. 308; *Re Coote, supra.*
33 *Ante*, p. 208; and see *Portman* v. *Viscount Portman* [1922] 2 A.C. 473.
34 In the case of executory trusts, the court would insert such a provision so as to carry out the settlor's wishes: see, *e.g.*, *Shelley* v. *Shelley* (1868) L.R. 4 Eq. 540; *Re Beresford-Hope* [1917] 1 Ch. 287; *cf. Pole* v. *Pole* [1924] 1 Ch. 156.
35 The principles are summarised in *Re Morrison's Settlement* [1974] Ch. 326.
36 See *Re Parker* [1910] 1 Ch. 581 at 585.
37 See *ante*, p. 343.
38 See *Re Duke of Marlborough's Settlement* (1886) 32 Ch.D. 1; *Re Lord Stafford's Settlement and Will* [1904] 2 Ch. 72.   39 See Prideaux iii, 308 *et seq.*

(a) for H until the marriage; thereafter
(b) for H for life; then
(c) for W for life; then
(d) for the children or remoter issue of the marriage in such shares—

    (i) as H and W jointly by deed appoint; in default,
    (ii) as the survivor may by deed or will appoint; in default,

(e) for such of the children of the marriage as attain the age of 21 years or being females marry under that age; in default,
(f) for H absolutely.

It will be noted—

    (i) that no pin money is provided for W;

    (ii) that if W survives H, she is entitled to the whole income from the property and not merely a jointure;

    (iii) that subject to the life interests of H and W, the issue are entitled absolutely and not in tail;

    (iv) that H and W are able to choose which of their issue shall benefit; they are not confined to their children, but can, for example, appoint to their grandchildren and exclude their children. If they fail to make an appointment, however, it is the children who share equally to the exclusion of the remoter issue.

CHAPTER 7

CO-OWNERSHIP

HITHERTO no consideration has been given to cases where two or more persons have been entitled to the simultaneous enjoyment of land. Four types of such ownership must be considered:

(1) Joint tenancy.
(2) Tenancy in common.
(3) Coparcenary.
(4) Tenancy by entireties.

In these titles " tenancy " means simply ownership, and has nothing to do with leases. The terms " co-ownership," " concurrent interests " and " estates and interests in community " may each be used to include all four forms of co-ownership. Of the four types, the first two are far more important than the others and they will be considered together.

Part 1

JOINT TENANCY AND TENANCY IN COMMON

Sect. 1. Nature of the Tenancies

A. *Joint Tenancy*

" A gift of lands to two or more persons in joint tenancy is such a gift as imparts to them, with respect to all other persons than themselves, the properties of one single owner." [1] Although as between themselves joint tenants have separate rights, as against everyone else they are in the position of a single owner.[2] The intimate nature of joint tenancy is shown by its two principal features, the right of survivorship and the " four unities."

1. The right of survivorship. This is, above all others, the distinguishing feature of a joint tenancy.[3] On the death of one joint tenant, his interest in the land passes to the other joint tenants by the right of survivorship (*jus accrescendi*), and this process continues

---

[1] Williams R.P. 143.
[2] *Ibid.* 145.
[3] Preston, *Abstracts*, ii, 57.

until there is but one survivor, who then holds the land as sole owner.[4] This right of survivorship takes precedence over any disposition made by a joint tenant's will[5]: *jus accrescendi praefertur ultimae voluntati.*[6] The same principle applies if a joint tenant dies intestate; a joint tenancy cannot pass under a will or intestacy. For this reason, among others, joint tenants were said to be seised "*per my et per tout,*"[7] "*my*" apparently meaning "not in the least"[8]: each joint tenant holds nothing by himself and yet holds the whole together with his fellows.[8a] Or again, a joint tenant may become entitled to nothing or to all, according to whether or not he is the last survivor. Where it was doubtful who had survived, as where joint tenants perished in a common disaster, their respective heirs held in joint tenancy, so that there was 'no survivorship[9]; but today statute usually resolves the question who is deemed to be the survivor.[10]

If there could be no right of survivorship there could be no joint tenancy. This is shown in the common law rule that as a corporation could never die, it could not be a joint tenant.[11] Therefore a conveyance to A and the X Co. Ltd. jointly, or to the X Co. Ltd. and the Y Co. Ltd. jointly, made the grantees tenants in common.[12] After a tentative half measure of reform[13] Parliament provided in 1899 that a corporation should be able to acquire and hold any property in joint tenancy in the same manner as if it were an individual.[14] This provision became necessary when banks and other corporations took up the work of acting as trustees. Trustees are always made joint tenants because of the convenience of the trust property passing automatically by the right of survivorship to the other trustees when one trustee dies; if trustees were made tenants

---

[4] Litt. 280; Co.Litt. 181a; Preston, *Abstracts*, ii, 57.

[5] Litt. 287; Co.Litt. 185b; *Swift* d. *Neale* v. *Roberts* (1764) 3 Burr. 1488; *Gould* v. *Kemp* (1834) 2 My. & K. 304 at 309.

[6] Co.Litt. 185b. But before 1815 copyholds were an exception: see *post*, p. 472.

[7] Litt. 288.

[8] Co.Litt. 186a. But the word has been variously said to mean (i) everything (Litt. 288), (ii) nothing (Co.Litt. 186a), (iii) a moiety, *i.e.*, half (Bl.Comm. ii, 182). Challis 367 appears to use senses (ii) and (iii) in the same paragraph, following first Littleton and then Blackstone. For further discussion, see *Daniel* v. *Camplin* (1845) 7 Man. & G. 167, 172n.; *Murray* v. *Hall* (1849) 7 C.B. 441, 455n.; and see *post*, p. 433. Kelham's *Law-French Dictionary* (1779) gives " mi " as " half," and " mie " as " not."						[8a] Co.Litt. 186a.

[9] *Bradshaw* v. *Toulmin* (1784) Dick. 633.

[10] L.P.A., 1925, s. 184; *post*, p. 492.

[11] Litt. 297; Bl.Comm. ii, 184; Williams R.P. 331; *Bennet* v. *Holbech* (1671) 2 Wms.Saund. 317, 319; *Law Guarantee & Trust Society Ltd.* v. *Bank of England* (1890) 24 Q.B.D. 406 at 411.

[12] *Fisher* v. *Wigg* (1700) 1 Ld.Raym. 622 at 627; Litt. 296; Co.Litt. 189b; Cru.Dig. ii, 372.

[13] National Debt (Stockholders Relief) Act, 1892, s. 6.

[14] Bodies Corporate (Joint Tenancy) Act, 1899; see *In b. Martin* (1904) 90 L.T. 264; *Re Thompson's S. T.* [1905] 1 Ch. 229.

in common, a conveyance of the trust property to the surviving trustees by the personal representatives of the deceased trustee would be necessary. The right of survivorship of a joint tenancy is often unsuitable for beneficial owners because it introduces an element of chance; but it is ideal for trustees.

The right of survivorship does not mean that a joint tenant cannot dispose of an interest in the land independently. He has full power of alienation *inter vivos*, though if, for example, he conveys his interest, he destroys the joint tenancy by severance and turns his interest into a tenancy in common. But he must act in his lifetime, for a joint tenancy cannot be severed by will. These rules are explained later.[15]

2. The four unities must be present. The four unities of a joint tenancy are the unities of possession, interest, title and time.[16]

(*a*) *Unity of possession.* Unity of possession is common to all forms of co-ownership. Each co-owner is as much entitled to possession of any part of the land as the others.[17] He cannot point to any part of the land as his own to the exclusion of the others; if he could, there would be separate ownership and not co-ownership. This doctrine led to difficulties where one joint tenant (for example) occupied the whole property, or took the whole of the rents and profits, to the exclusion of the others. No one co-owner had a better right than another, so that an action for trespass or for money had and received or an account would not normally lie [18]: only actual eviction of one by the other [19] or the destruction of part of the subject-matter (*e.g.*, by removing soil) [20] would ground an action at common law. But an Act of 1705 [21] gave an action of account against a co-owner who received more than his share, so that there

---

[15] *Post*, pp. 403 *et seq.*
[16] This analysis appears to have been first made by Blackstone, Comm. ii, 180–182, but it is disparaged by Challis 367, as having a " captivating appearance of symmetry and exactness " rather than any practical utility; yet see Preston, *Abstracts*, ii, 62.
[17] Litt. 288; Bl.Comm. ii, 182. In the case of co-ownership in remainder (*e.g.*, where land was limited to A for life with remainder to B and C in fee simple) there was a *potential* unity of possession.
[18] *Thomas* v. *Thomas* (1850) 5 Exch. 28; Co.Litt. 200b. Similarly time would not at first run under the Statutes of Limitation: see *post*, p. 1012.
[19] *Murray* v. *Hall* (1849) 7 C.B. 441; *Stedman* v. *Smith* (1857) 8 E. & B. 1; *Jacobs* v. *Seward* (1872) L.R. 5 H.L. 464; *cf. Reading* v. *Royston* (1703) 2 Salk. 423.
[20] *Wilkinson* v. *Haygarth* (1847) 12 Q.B. 837; and see *Martyn* v. *Knowllys* (1799) 8 T.R. 145 (cutting trees).
[21] 4 & 5 Anne, c. 3, repealed by L.P.(Am.)A., 1924, 10th Sched. Since 1925 joint tenants are trustees for one another if the legal estate is vested in themselves (*post*, p. 408); if it is vested in others (*e.g.*, a testator's personal representatives), the court may hold the joint tenants accountable *inter se* in administering the trust. For the old equity practice, see *Pulteney* v. *Warren* (1801) 6 Ves. 73 at 77, 78 (equitable liability to account as between tenants in common).

was an effective remedy if the land or its profits had been converted into money.[22] If the land was still held under the joint tenancy, the remedy of a joint tenant excluded from possession was to enforce partition.[23]

(b) *Unity of interest.* The interest of each joint tenant is the same in extent, nature and duration, for in theory of law they hold but one estate. This has important consequences.

(i) Although in theory of law each joint tenant has the whole of the property, the rents and profits of the land are to be divided equally between them.

(ii) There can be no joint tenancy between those with interests of a different nature, *e.g.*, a freeholder and a tenant for years, a tenant in possession and a tenant in remainder, or a tenant with a vested interest and a tenant with a contingent interest.[24] But personal disability (*e.g.*, lunacy, infancy, or restraint on anticipation) is not inconsistent with a joint tenancy.[25]

(iii) There can be no joint tenancy between those whose interests are similar but of different duration. Thus before 1926 a tenant in fee simple and a tenant in tail both owned freeholds but the differing durations of the estates prevented them from being held in joint tenancy.[26]

(iv) Any legal act, *e.g.*, a conveyance or lease of the land, or a surrender of a lease [27] requires the participation of all the joint tenants; one cannot dispose of it by himself, for he by himself has not the whole estate in it.[28] But exceptions to this rule are found in the cases of personal representatives [29] and of the determination of periodic tenancies (*e.g.*, weekly or monthly tenancies), which are determinable on the usual notice [30] given by one of joint landlords [31] or one of joint

---

[22] See *Jacobs* v. *Seward* (1872) L.R. 5 H.L. 464.
[23] *Post*, p. 427.
[24] *Kenworthy* v. *Ward* (1853) 11 Hare 196 at 198, 199; *M'Gregor* v. *M'Gregor* (1859) 1 De G.F. & J. 63 at 74; *Ruck* v. *Barwise* (1865) 2 Dr. & Sm. 510 at 512. See, *e.g.*, *Woodgate* v. *Unwin* (1831) 4 Sim. 129 (gift to class on attaining twenty-one cannot create joint tenancy, for some interests would be vested and some contingent: *Ruck* v. *Barwise*, *supra*, at p. 512); *cf. M'Gregor* v. *M'Gregor*, *supra*, at p. 74, showing that the interpretation put on *Woodgate* v. *Unwin*, *supra*, in *Booth* v. *Alington* (1857) 3 Jur.(N.S.) 835 at 837 is unsound. See also Tudor L.C., 275.
[25] *Re Gardner* [1924] 2 Ch. 243 at 251.
[26] Bl.Comm. ii, 181.
[27] *Leek and Moorlands B. S.* v. *Clark* [1952] 2 Q.B. 788.
[28] Bl.Comm. ii, 183.
[29] See *post*, pp. 540, 541.
[30] See *post*, p. 637.
[31] *Doe* d. *Aslin* v. *Summersett* (1830) 1 B. & Ad. 135.

tenants,[32] since unanimity is required to continue such a tenancy. Yet for one co-owner to give such a notice without the consent of all persons beneficially entitled will, after 1925, usually be a breach of the trusts now existing in cases of co-ownership.[33]

Unity of interest must apply to the estate which is held jointly; but if that requirement is satisfied, it does not matter that one joint tenant has a further and separate interest in the same property.[34] A conveyance " to A and B as joint tenants for lives, remainder to B in fee simple " would make A and B joint tenants for life despite the remainder to B.[35]

(c) *Unity of title.* Each joint tenant must claim his title to the land under the same act or document.[36] This requirement is satisfied if all the tenants acquired their rights by the same conveyance[37] or if they simultaneously took possession of land and acquired title to it by adverse possession.[38]

(d) *Unity of time.* The interest of each tenant must vest at the same time.[39] This does not necessarily follow from the existence of unity of title. For example, if land was conveyed " to A for life, remainder to the heirs of B and C," and B and C died at different times in A's lifetime, B's heir and C's heir took the fee simple remainder as tenants in common; the heirs could not take as joint tenants, for although there was unity of title there was no unity of time.[40]

Two exceptions to the necessity for unity of time grew up: neither in a conveyance to uses nor in a gift by will was the rule applied.[41] Thus if a bachelor conveyed land to the use of himself and any wife he might marry, when he married he held as a joint tenant with his wife.[42] Again, if land was devised[43] or conveyed to

---

[32] *Leek and Moorlands B. S.* v. *Clark* [1952] 2 Q.B. 788 at 793.
[33] See *post,* p. 408.
[34] Burton's *Compendium,* 245.
[35] Co.Litt. 182a, b, 184a; *Wiscot's Case* (1599) 2 Co.Rep. 60b; *Quarm* v. *Quarm* [1892] 1 Q.B. 184. Litt. 285 and Co.Litt. 188a, which speak of joint tenants, one for life and one in fee, must be understood to refer to this situation.
[36] Litt. 278; Co.Litt. 189a, 299b; Bl.Comm. ii, 181.
[37] Cru.Dig. ii, 367.
[38] Litt. 278; *Ward* v. *Ward* (1871) 6 Ch.App. 789; *post,* p. 1022.
[39] Bl.Comm. ii, 181. For " vest " (in interest), see *ante,* p. 173.
[40] Co.Litt. 188a; Bl.Comm. ii, 181.
[41] *Blamford* v. *Blamford* (1615) 3 Bulstr. 98 at 101; *Kenworthy* v. *Ward* (1853) 11 Hare 196; *M'Gregor* v. *M'Gregor* (1859) 1 De G.F. & J. 63 at 73; Sanders, *Uses,* i, 141; Jarman 1791; and see *Wats* v. *Ognell* (—) Noy 124.
[42] *Mutton's Case* (1568) 3 Dy. 274b; *Sammes's Case* (1609) 13 Co.Rep. 54 at 56; and see *Shelley's Case* (1581) 1 Co.Rep. 88b at 101a, n. Q. 3; Gilbert, *Uses,* 135n.
[43] *Ruck* v. *Barwise* (1865) 2 Dr. & Sm. 510; and see *Oates* d. *Hatterley* v. *Jackson* (1742) 2 Stra. 1172.

the use [44] of A for life with remainder to the use of the children of B, each child of B born in A's lifetime acquired a vested interest at birth, yet the disparity of time did not prevent them from taking as joint tenants.

B. Tenancy in Common

A tenancy in common differs greatly from a joint tenancy.

1. The tenants hold in undivided shares. Unlike joint tenants, tenants in common hold in undivided shares: each tenant in common has a distinct share in property which has not yet been divided among the co-tenants.[45] Thus tenants in common have quite separate interests; the only fact which brings them into co-ownership is that they both have shares in a single property which has not yet been divided among them. While the tenancy in common lasts, no one can say which of them owns any particular parcel of land.

2. There is no right of survivorship. The size of each tenant's share is fixed once and for all and is not affected by the death of one of his companions. When a tenant in common dies, his interest passes under his will or intestacy, for his undivided share is his to dispose of as he wishes.[46] But rights equivalent to survivorship may be given by express limitation.[47]

3. Only the unity of possession is essential. Although the four unities of a joint tenancy may be present in a tenancy in common, the only unity which is essential is the unity of possession.[48] In particular, it should be noted that the unity of interest may be absent and the tenants may hold unequal interests, so that one tenant in common may be entitled to a one-fifth share and the other to four-fifths, or one may be entitled for life and the other in fee simple.[49]

---

[44] *Hales* v. *Risley* (1673) Pollex. 369 at 373; *Earl of Sussex* v. *Temple* (1697) 1 Ld.Raym. 310; *Doe* d. *Hallen* v. *Ironmonger* (1803) 3 East 533.

[45] *Fisher* v. *Wiggs* (1700) 12 Mod. 296 at 302; *cf. Re King's Theatre, Sunderland* [1929] 1 Ch. 483 at 488.

[46] Challis 368.

[47] See *Doe* d. *Borwell* v. *Abey* (1813) 1 M. & S. 428; *Haddelsey* v. *Adams* (1856) 22 Beav. 266; *Taaffe* v. *Conmee* (1862) 10 H.L.C. 64; and see *ante*, p. 386, for tenants in common with cross remainders.

[48] Co.Litt. 189a; Cru.Dig. ii, 399. Tenants in common were said to be entitled " *per my et per tout* ": Litt. 323; *Murray* v. *Hall* (1849) 7 C.B. 441 at 455n. But the more normal use of the phrase is peculiar to joint tenancy; *ante*, p. 392, n. 8. In America tenants in common have been said to be seised " *per my et non per tout* ": Corpus Juris 62, 409. *Cf. ante*, p. 392, *post*, pp. 431, 433.

[49] Challis 370; Williams R.P. 148; Bl.Comm. ii, 191; and see *Sturton* v. *Richardson* (1844) 10 M. & W. 17.

Sect. 2. Estates in which the Tenancies Could Exist

In general, before 1926 joint tenancies and tenancies in common could exist at law or in equity (*i.e.*, as legal estates or as equitable interests), and in possession or in remainder, in any of the estates of freehold or in leaseholds.[50] Thus if land was given to A and B as joint tenants for their lives, they enjoyed it jointly for their joint lives, and the survivor enjoyed the whole for the rest of his life,[51] whereas an interest given for their *joint* lives would end as soon as one died.[52] If A and B were made tenants for life, the survivor would retain his original share and no more,[53] the non-survivor's share having passed to the remainderman. Where X and Y were joint tenants for the life of X, if X survived he became sole tenant of the whole for the rest of his life, whereas if Y were the survivor he took nothing, for the estate which he acquired by survivorship was one which determined at the moment he received it.[54]

In the case of entails, however, exceptions arose from the difficulty of reconciling the provisions of the Statute *De Donis*, 1285,[55] with the principle of survivorship. The only possible joint tenancy in tail was where the estate was limited to two persons capable of intermarrying and the heirs of their two bodies.[56] A limitation to two men and the heirs of their two bodies made them joint tenants for life with remainders in common in tail.[57]

After 1925 the position is substantially the same except that a tenancy in common can no longer exist at law; this is dealt with below.[58] Further, since life estates and entails can exist only in equity,[59] even a joint tenancy in these interests must also now be equitable.

Sect. 3. Creation of the Tenancies

The key to a proper understanding of joint tenancies and tenancies in common is always to consider the legal estate separately from the equitable interest. Thus it may be found that at law A and B are joint tenants, while in equity they are tenants in common; that is

---

[50] Williams R.P. 143. As to periodic tenancies, see *ante*, p. 394.
[51] *Moffat* v. *Burnie* (1853) 18 Beav. 211; *Jones* v. *Jones* (1881) 44 L.T. 642 at 644.
[52] *Re Legh's S. T.* [1938] Ch. 39.
[53] Co.Litt. 191a; Preston, *Abstracts*, ii, 63.
[54] Challis 366.
[55] *Ante*, p. 83.
[56] Litt. 16, 283, 284; Co.Litt. 20b, 25b; Williams R.P. 143, 144; Challis 365.
[57] *Huntley's Case* (1573) 3 Dy. 326a; *Cook* v. *Cook* (1706) 2 Vern. 545; *Re Tiverton Market Act* (1855) 20 Beav. 374; and see authorities in n. 56 *supra*. *Quaere* whether either can disentail his share: see Jenks' *English Civil Law* (4th ed.), 943.
[58] *Post*, p. 408.
[59] *Ante*, p. 134.

to say, A and B hold the legal estate jointly as trustees upon trust
for themselves as tenants in common.[61] Their rights of enjoyment,
therefore, are the rights of tenants in common, not the rights of
joint tenants. The effect of A's death on the legal joint tenancy is
that B is solely entitled; but A's equitable interest (his undivided
share) passes under his will or intestacy. In the result, B holds the
legal estate on trust for himself as to his share, and for A's personal
representatives as to A's share.

It must also be understood that it is always possible, as explained
later,[62] for a joint tenant to turn his beneficial interest into a tenancy
in common by effecting a severance.

The modes of creating joint tenancies and tenancies in common
must now be considered. These are the primary rules of common
law and equity, on which the statutory reforms of 1925 were later
superimposed.

I. AT LAW

In early times a joint tenancy was preferable to a tenancy in common
for various reasons: to feudal lords, because the operation of the
doctrine of survivorship made it more likely that the land would
ultimately vest in a single tenant from whom the feudal services
could more conveniently be exacted than from a number sharing the
burden; to feudal tenants, because a tenancy in common, but not a
joint tenancy, rendered certain feudal services due separately from
each tenant, thus increasing the burden on the land [63]; and to conveyancers who had to investigate title, because joint tenants held by
a single title, whereas the title of every tenant in common had to be
separately examined.[64] If a joint tenant died, there was merely one
tenant the less, and still but one title, whereas if a tenant in common
died, it might be found that his share had been left equally between
his twelve children, thus increasing by eleven the titles to be
investigated before the property could be sold as a whole.

Accordingly the presumption at law was in favour of a joint

---

[61] *Contra, Re Selous* [1901] 1 Ch. 921 where it was held that the equitable interest
merged in the legal estate. Leasehold land had been bequeathed to T upon
trust for A and B as tenants in common. T later assigned the lease to A and
B as joint tenants, A and B joining as parties and giving covenants. Held: A
and B took as beneficial joint tenants. Perhaps the decision can be justified
because A and B concurred in the assignment. But the statement that the
merger operates in the case of co-owners just as in the case of a sole beneficial
owner can hardly be right. See Williams V. & P. 501, 502. The question cannot
arise after 1925 owing to the statutory trust for sale: *post*, p. 408.

[62] *Post*, p. 403.

[63] *Attree* v. *Scutt* (1805) 6 East 476.

[64] See *Bruerton's Case* (1594) 6 Co.Rep. 1a; *Fisher* v. *Wigg* (1700) 1 P.Wms. 14
at 21; *Garland* v. *Jekyll* (1824) 2 Bing. 273.

tenancy.[65] " The law loves not fractions of estates, nor to divide and multiply tenures." [66] If land was conveyed to two or more persons a joint tenancy of the legal estate was created unless either—

(i) one of the unities was absent; or

(ii) words of severance were employed.

1. Absence of unities. The four unities have already been considered. If there was unity of possession but one or more of the other unities were missing, the parties took as tenants in common; if there was no unity of possession, the parties took as separate owners.

2. Words of severance

(*a*) *Express words.* Any words in the grant showing that the tenants were each to take a distinct share in the property amounted to words of severance and thus created a tenancy in common.[67] Words which have been held to have this effect include—

" in equal shares " [68]

" share and share alike " [69]

" to be divided between " [70]

" to be distributed amongst them in joint and equal proportions " [71]

" equally " [72]

" between " [73]

" amongst " [74]

" respectively." [75]

---

[65] *Campbell* v. *Campbell* (1792) 4 Bro.C.C. 15; *Morley* v. *Bird* (1798) 3 Ves. 628; *Corbett* d. *Clymer* v. *Nicholls* (1851) 2 L.M. & P. 87 at 89.

[66] *Fisher* v. *Wigg* (1700) 1 Salk. 391 at 392, *per* Holt C.J.

[67] See *Robertson* v. *Fraser* (1871) 6 Ch.App. 696 at 699. Decisions on particular expressions (other than those given in the text) are *Marryat* v. *Townley* (1748) 1 Ves.Sen. 102 (" respective ages "); *Sutcliffe* v. *Howard* (1869) 38 L.J.Ch. 472 (" respective lives "); *Re Atkinson* [1892] 3 Ch. 52 (" respective heirs "); *Sheppard* v. *Gibbons* (1742) 2 Atk. 441 (" severally "); *Halton* v. *Finch* (1841) 4 Beav. 186 (" each "); *Liddard* v. *Liddard* (1860) 28 Beav. 266 and *Robertson* v. *Fraser* (1871) 6 Ch.App. 696 (" participate "). At one time stronger words were required in deeds than in wills, and in law than in equity, but these differences gradually decreased: see Sanders, *Uses*, i, 130.

[68] *Payne* v. *Webb* (1874) L.R. 19 Eq. 26.

[69] *Heathe* v. *Heathe* (1740) 2 Atk. 121; and see *James* v. *Collins* (1627) Het. 29 (" part and part alike "). Contrast *Re Schofield* [1918] 2 Ch. 64 (mere reference to " share " insufficient).

[70] *Peat* v. *Chapman* (1750) 1 Ves.Sen. 542; *cf.* *Askeman* v. *Burrows* (1814) 3 V. & B. 54 (personalty). For similar expressions, see *Fisher* v. *Wigg* (1700) 1 P.Wms. 14; *Goodtitle* d. *Hood* v. *Stokes* (1753) 1 Wils.K.B. 341; *Bridge* v. *Yates* (1842) 12 Sim. 645; *Lucas* v. *Goldsmid* (1861) 29 Beav. 657.

[71] *Ettricke* v. *Ettricke* (1767) Amb. 656.

[72] *Lewen* v. *Dodd* (1595) Cro.Eli. 443; *Lewen* v. *Cox* (1599) Cro.Eliz. 695; *Denn* d. *Gaskin* v. *Gaskin* (1777) 2 Cowp. 657; *Right* d. *Compton* v. *Compton* (1808) 9 East 267 at 276.

[73]-[75] For footnotes, see p. 400.

(b) *Other provisions.* Even if there were no clear words of severance, the gift taken as a whole might show that a tenancy in common was intended.[76] Thus provisions for the use of capital or income or both for the maintenance and advancement of those concerned created a tenancy in common.[77] For example, if under a settlement on children containing such provisions an advance was made to one child, it would have to be debited against that child's share and this could not be done unless the child was a tenant in common and so had a distinct share.[78] Similarly a bequest to A and B on condition that they should pay the testator's widow an annuity " in equal shares " was held to create a tenancy in common, since the testator was presumed to have intended that the gift should correspond to the obligation.[79]

(c) *Words negating severance.* On the other hand, expressions which by themselves might have created a tenancy in common could be negatived by words showing a clear intention to create a joint tenancy.[80] The contradictory expression " jointly and severally " was solved by the quaint rule that the first word prevailed in a deed, but the last in a will.[81]

(d) *Special cases.* Mention may be made of two special situations. First, under a testamentary gift to a vague class, such as the testator's " relations," the court could sometimes save the gift from uncertainty by restricting the class to those who would take on an intestacy[82]; the class would then take as joint tenants, not as tenants in common in the statutory shares, unless by an express reference to the statutes governing intestacy or otherwise the testator had

---

[73] *Lashbrook* v. *Cock* (1816) 2 Mer. 70. But " all and every " (introducing members of a class, *e.g.*, children) were not normally words of severance: *Stratton* v. *Best* (1787) 2 Bro.C.C. 233 ; *Binning* v. *Binning* (1895) 13 R. 654 ; but contrast *Re Grove's Trusts* (1862) 3 Giff. 575.

[74] *Richardson* v. *Richardson* (1845) 14 Sim. 526.

[75] *Stephens* v. *Hide* (1734) Ca.t.Talb. 27.

[76] See *e.g., Ryves* v. *Ryves* (1871) L.R. 11 Eq. 539; *Surtees* v. *Surtees* (1871) L.R. 12 Eq. 400.

[77] *Re Ward* [1920] 1 Ch. 334; *Bennett* v. *Houldsworth* (1911) 104 L.T. 304; *Re Dunn* [1916] 1 Ch. 97.

[78] *L'Estrange* v. *L'Estrange* [1902] 1 I.R. 467; *cf. Twigg* v. *Twigg* [1933] I.R. 65.

[79] *Re North* [1952] Ch. 397.

[80] See cases collected in Halsb. xxxix, 1104.

[81] *Slingsby's Case* (1587) 5 Co.Rep. 18b at 19a (deed); *Perkins* v. *Baynton* (1781) 1 Bro.C.C. 118 (will); contrast *Cookson* v. *Bingham* (1853) 17 Beav. 262, 3 De G.M. & G. 668 (will: contrary intention). For this rule, see *ante*, p. 159. and *post*, pp. 498, 499.

[82] See *post*, pp. 496–497.

shown a contrary intention.[83] Secondly, under a substitutionary gift, as where a gift to children in equal shares provided that children of a deceased child were to take that child's share, prima facie those substituted would take as joint tenants unless there were further words of severance; for in a gift to a compound class, compound words of severance are usually required.[84]

II. IN EQUITY

Unlike the common law, equity did not favour joint tenancy[85]; for equity often did not follow the law where it was merely feudal in character, and equity in this case was more concerned to achieve fairness than to simplify the tasks of conveyancers. Equity therefore preferred the certainty and equality of a tenancy in common to the chance of " all or nothing " which arose from the right of survivorship.[86] Equity leans against joint tenancy. This maxim meant that a tenancy in common would exist in equity not only in those cases where it would have existed at law, but also in certain other cases where an intention to create a tenancy in common ought to be presumed. There were three such special cases, in all of which persons who were joint tenants at law were compelled by equity to hold the legal estate upon trust for themselves as equitable tenants in common.

1. Purchase-money provided in unequal shares. If two or more persons together purchased property and provided the money in unequal shares, the purchasers were presumed to take beneficially as tenants in common in shares proportionate to the sums advanced[87]; thus if A found one-third and B two-thirds of the price, they were presumed to be equitable tenants in common as to one-third and two-thirds respectively. If, on the other hand, the purchasers provided the money in equal shares, they were presumed joint tenants. This distinction has been criticised,[88] but it has long been accepted as sound.[89] The presumptions could be rebutted by

---

83 *Re Gansloser's W. T.* [1952] Ch. 30; and see *Re Kilvert* [1957] Ch. 388; contrast *Bullock* v. *Downes* (1860) 9 H.L.C. 1.
84 *Re Brooke* [1953] 1 W.L.R. 439; Jarman 1792, 1797; but see *Re Froy* [1938] Ch. 566.
85 *Gould* v. *Kemp* (1834) 2 My. & K. 304 at 309.
86 " Survivorship is looked upon as odious in equity ": *R.* v. *Williams* (1735) Bunb. 342 at 343, *per cur.*; and see *Re Woolley* [1903] 2 Ch. 206 at 211.
87 *Lake* v. *Gibson* (1729) 1 Eq.Ca.Abr. 290, 291; *Robinson* v. *Preston* (1858) 4 K. & J. 505 at 510; *Bull* v. *Bull* [1955] 1 Q.B. 234.
88 *Jackson* v. *Jackson* (1804) 9 Ves. 591 at 604n.
89 See Lewin 131. *Sed quaere* in the case of husband and wife: see *Gissing* v. *Gissing* [1971] A.C. 886.

evidence of circumstances showing that those providing the purchase-money equally intended to take as tenants in common [90] or *vice versa*.[91] These rules are equally applicable as between husband and wife,[92] save that in such cases there may be implied or resulting trusts giving effect to some agreement or understanding under which the property was acquired.[93]

2. Loan on mortgage. Where two or more persons advanced money on mortgage, whether in equal or unequal shares, equity presumed a tenancy in common in the land between the mortgagees.[94] " If two people join in lending money upon a mortgage, equity says, it could not be the intention, that the interest in that should survive. Though they take a joint security, each means to lend his own and take back his own." [95] " It is obvious, however, that this proposition cannot be put higher than a presumption capable of being rebutted." [96] Yet it should be noted that the " joint account clause " which was normally inserted in mortgages to make the mortgagees figure as joint tenants to the outside world, and so simplify the mechanism of discharging the mortgage,[97] does not affect this presumption of a tenancy in common in the relationship of the mortgagees *inter se*.[98]

3. Partnership assets. Where partners acquired land as part of their partnership assets, they were presumed to hold it as beneficial tenants in common.[1] " *Jus accrescendi inter mercatores locum non habet* " [2]: *pro beneficio commercii*,[3] the right of survivorship has no place in business. The rule extended to any joint undertaking carried on with a view to profit, even if there was no formal partnership

---

[90] *Edwards* v. *Fashion* (1712) Prec.Ch. 332 (where the purchase by mortgagees was " founded on the mortgage ": *Aveling* v. *Knipe* (1815) 19 Ves. 441 at 444); *Harrison* v. *Barton* (1860) 1 J. & H. 287.

[91] See *Harris* v. *Fergusson* (1848) 16 Sim. 308, as explained in *Robinson* v. *Preston* (1858) 4 K. & J. 505 at 515, 516 (initial joint tenancy held to extend to addition to it made with purchase-money provided unequally); *Garrick* v. *Taylor* (1860) 29 Beav. 79.

[92] *Waller* v. *Waller* [1967] 1 .W.L.R. 451.

[93] See *post*, p. 447.

[94] *Petty* v. *Styward* (1632) 1 Ch.Rep. 57; *Rigden* v. *Vallier* (1751) 2 Ves.Sen 252 at 258; *Vickers* v. *Cowell* (1839) 1 Beav. 529.

[95] *Morley* v. *Bird* (1798) 3 Ves. 628 at 631, *per* Arden M.R.

[96] *Steeds* v. *Steeds* (1889) 22 Q.B.D. 537 at 541, *per* Wills J.

[97] See *post*, p. 953.

[98] *Re Jackson* (1887) 34 Ch.D. 732.

[1] *Jeffereys* v. *Small* (1683) 1 Vern. 217; *Lake* v. *Gibson* (1729) 1 Eq.Ca.Abr. 290 : *Lake* v. *Craddock* (1732) 3 P.Wms. 158; Sugd., V. & P. 698.

[2] *Hamond* v. *Jethro* (1611) 2 Brownl. & Golds. 97 at 99; *Buckley* v. *Barber* (1851) 6 Exch. 164 at 179.

[3] Co.Litt. 182a.

between the parties,[4] and even if the property had not been purchased but had been devised to persons who used it for trade.[5] The legal estate might be held on a joint tenancy, but in equity the partners were presumed to be entitled in undivided shares,[6] so that the surviving partners (or whoever held the legal estate) would be compelled to hold the legal estate on trust for those entitled to the property of a deceased partner as to his share.[7]

Contracts and executory trusts. It often happened that a preliminary contract or declaration of trust required to be perfected by the execution of a proper deed of settlement. Marriage articles, for example, are a contract to execute a marriage settlement upon certain terms. In construing marriage articles and other executory transactions [8] the court would readily find that gifts to classes, *e.g.,* to the children of the marriage, were intended to give each child a separate share for his own family, even though the appropriate words of severance were absent, and decree accordingly; " joint tenancy as a provision for the children of a marriage, is an inconvenient mode of settlement, because during their minorities, no use can be made of their portions for their advancement, as the joint tenancy cannot be severed." [9] This was not a case where equity enforced a tenancy in common on persons who were joint tenants at law: it was simply an example of the rule that contracts are construed so as to give effect to the true intention of the parties. But the question would normally fall to the Chancery side since the remedy sought would be a decree for the execution of a proper settlement by deed, *i.e.,* a decree for specific performance.[10]

Sect. 4. The Right of Severance

The common law mitigated the uncertainty of the *jus accrescendi* by enabling a joint tenant to destroy the joint tenancy by severance, which had the result of turning it into a tenancy in common. " The

---

[4] *Lake* v. *Gibson* (1729) 1 Eq.Ca.Abr. 290; *Lyster* v. *Dolland* (1792) 1 Ves.Jun. 431; *Dale* v. *Hamilton* (1846) 5 Hare 369; (1847) 2 Ph. 266; *Darby* v. *Darby* (1856) 3 Drew. 495; *Re Hulton* (1890) 62 L.T. 200; *cf. Brown* v. *Dale* (1878) 9 Ch.D. 78. Contrast *Ward* v. *Ward* (1871) 6 Ch.App. 789 (farming jointly but not as partners).

[5] *Jackson* v. *Jackson* (1804) 9 Ves. 591; *cf. Morris* v. *Barrett* (1829) 3 Y. & J. 384.

[6] *Re Fuller's Contract* [1933] Ch. 652. As to the nature of this equitable interest see *Ashworth* v. *Munn* (1880) 15 Ch.D. 363 at 369; Tudor L.C. 286; (1930) 46 L.Q.R. 77 (1934) 50 L.Q.R. 19; Lindley, *Partnership,* 13th ed., 266.

[7] *Elliott* v. *Brown* (1791) 3 Swans. 489; *Re Ryan* (1868) 3 Ir.R.Eq. 222 at 232; *Wray* v. *Wray* [1905] 2 Ch. 349; Partnership Act, 1890, s. 20 (2).

[8] See, *e.g., Synge* v. *Hales* (1814) 2 Ball & B. 499; *Mayn* v. *Mayn* (1867) L.R. 5 Eq. 150; compare *Re Bellasis' Trust* (1871) L.R. 12 Eq. 218.

[9] *Taggart* v. *Taggart* (1803) 1 Sch. & Lef. 84 at 88, *per* Lord Redesdale L.C. But consider now T.A., 1925, s. 32.

[10] For this remedy, see *post,* p. 593.

duration of all lives being uncertain, if either party has an ill opinion
of his own life, he may sever the jointenancy by a deed granting
over a moiety [*i.e.*, conveying one-half] in trust for himself; so that
survivorship can be no hardship, where either side may at pleasure
prevent it." [12] " Severance " strictly includes partition, but the word
is normally used to describe the process whereby a joint tenancy is
converted into a tenancy in common, and it is used in this sense
here. Although no joint tenant owned any distinct share in the land,
yet each had a potential share equal in size to that of his companions,[13] and so depending upon the number of joint tenants at the
time in question. Thus if there were five joint tenants, each had
the right to sever his joint tenancy and become tenant in common of
one undivided fifth share; if one joint tenant died before the
severance, each of the survivors had a potential quarter share and
so on.

Before 1926 a joint tenancy could be severed both at law and in
equity, though after 1925, as will be seen later, no severance at law
is possible.[14] Severance was effected by destroying one of the unities.
Unity of time could not be severed, and severance of the unity of
possession meant partition, but severance of the unity either of title
or of interest converted a joint tenancy into a tenancy in common.
A joint tenancy could be severed in the following ways.

1. By alienation

(*a*) *Total alienation.* If a joint tenant alienated his interest *inter
vivos*,[15] his joint tenancy was severed and the person to whom the
interest was conveyed took it as a tenant in common with the other
joint tenants, for he had no unity of title with them [16]: *alienatio
rei praefertur juri accrescendi.*[17] Such a severance did not affect the
other joint tenants, who remained joint tenants *inter se*.[18] Thus
if A, B and C were joint tenants, and A sold his interest to X, X
became tenant in common as to one-third with B and C as to two-
thirds, but B and C remained joint tenants of those two-thirds as
between themselves. If B then died, C alone profited by the *jus
accrescendi*, X and C being left as tenants in common as to one-
third and two-thirds respectively.[19] Involuntary alienation would
also effect severance, as where a joint tenant went bankrupt and

---

[12] *Cray* v. *Willis* (1729) 2 P.Wms. 529, *per* Jekyll M.R.
[13] Preston, *Abstracts*, ii, 62.
[14] *Post*, p. 408.
[15] A will can effect no severance: *post*, p. 406.
[16] Litt. 292; Williams R.P. 147.
[17] Co.Litt. 185a; *Partriche* v. *Powlet* (1740) 2 Atk. 54.
[18] Litt. 294.
[19] See *Philpott* v. *Dobbinson* (1829) 3 Moo. & P. 320 at 330; *Denne d. Bowyer* v.
Judge (1809) 11 East 288; *Williams* v. *Hensman* (1861) 1 J. & H. 546.

under the bankruptcy law his property became vested in his trustee in bankruptcy.[20] But although before 1883 a husband acquired important rights of control over his wife's property,[21] marriage did not sever any joint tenancy of the wife's,[22] for the property did not *vest* in her husband.[23]

(b) *Partial alienation.* Severance also resulted from a partial alienation by one joint tenant, *e.g.*, if he created a mortgage[24] or life interest[25] out of his individual share, but not from the creation of a mere incumbrance, such as a rentcharge.[26] The distinction here appears to lie between acts which are inconsistent with holding " *per my et per tout* "[27] and with the right of survivorship, and acts which are not. A rentcharge can be satisfied out of one joint tenant's share of the rents and profits[28] without disturbing the joint tenancy; it confers no right of occupation, "and the tenements are in the same plight as they were before."[29] A lease for years, on the other hand, confers a right to possession of some particular share of the land for a fixed period, and this right arises by a separate title. Although the point was not accepted as free from doubt, both principle and judicial opinion inclined to the conclusion that a lease for years granted by one or more (but not all[30]) of the joint tenants effected a severance of the whole estate, *i.e.*, after the lease expired as well as beforehand[31]; certainly it did so where a joint tenant of a lease granted an under-lease, whether to a stranger[32] or to one of his fellow joint tenants.[33] In any case the lessee's rights were unaffected by the

---

20 *Morgan* v. *Marquis* (1853) 9 Exch. 145 at 147, 148.
21 See *post*, p. 993.
22 *Bracebridge* v. *Cook* (1572) 2 Plowd. 416 at 418; *Palmer* v. *Rich* [1897] 1 Ch. 134.
23 See *Re Butler's Trusts* (1888) 38 Ch.D. 286.
24 *York* v. *Stone* (1709) 1 Salk. 158; *Re Pollard's Estate* (1863) 3 De G.J. & S. 541 at 558; *Re Sharer* (1912) 57 S.J. 60. *Quaere* whether since 1925 this is subject to the doubt as regards leases, *infra*, since mortgages are now made by demise: *post*, p. 896.
25 Litt. 302 and Coke's comment.
26 Litt. 286.
27 *Ante*, p. 392.
28 *Ante*, p. 393.
29 Litt. 289.
30 See *Palmer* v. *Rich* [1897] 1 Ch. 134.
31 *Clerk* v. *Clerk* (1694) 2 Vern. 323; *Gould* v. *Kemp* (1834) 2 My. & K. 304 at 310; *Cowper* v. *Fletcher* (1865) 6 B. & S. 464 at 472; *Re Armstrong* [1920] 1 I.R. 239. *Contra, Harbin* v. *Loby* (1629) Noy 157 at 158; Co.Litt. 185a; Preston, *Abstracts*, ii, 58; Challis 367n. Coke's doctrine was that during the lease the right to receive rent, etc., was an interest held in common, but that the reversion went by survivorship to the surviving joint tenant: Co.Litt. 185a, 318a. But Littleton's distinction between incumbrances and rights of occupation (s. 289) and his treatment of the comparable case of a lease for life (s. 302) point to severance of the reversion in the case of a lease for years. Another weight in the balance is the settled doctrine that a sub-lease by one joint tenant of a lease severed the leasehold reversion: see the text above.
32 *Sym's Case* (1584) Cro.Eliz. 33; *Connolly* v. *Connolly* (1866) 17 Ir.Ch.R. 208 at 223.
33 *Pleadal's Case* (1579) 2 Leon. 159; and see Co.Litt. 192a.

death of the lessor,[34] whereas a mere incumbrance such as a rent-charge could take effect only subject to the right of survivorship: *jus accrescendi praefertur oneribus*.[35]

(c) *Alienation in equity.* In equity, as we have seen,[36] a specifically enforceable contract to alienate creates an equitable interest in the property even though the legal act of alienation has not taken place. If, therefore, one joint tenant contracted to sell his interest to X, this worked a severance in equity so that the original joint tenants held the legal estate subject to X's equitable right to one share as tenant in common.[37] Severance was therefore brought about by a covenant in marriage articles or a marriage settlement to the effect that property held in joint tenancy would be settled,[38] or by a contract between joint tenants that they would thenceforward hold as tenants in common[39]; and such a contract might be inferred from conduct,[40] even if the tenants were unaware of their joint tenancy[41] Recent decisions have gone still further, and it seems that the court will accept a unilateral declaration or course of conduct as a severance in equity, if it indicates an intention to terminate the joint tenancy.[42]

A joint tenancy could never be severed by will: *jus accrescendi praefertur ultimae voluntati*.[43] But there may be a severance by the making of mutual wills.[43a]

2. By acquisition of another estate in the land. Although it was not fatal to a joint tenancy that one of the tenants was initially given some further estate in the land than his joint tenancy,[44] the subsequent acquisition of some further estate in the land destroyed

---

[34] *Anon.* (1560) 2 Dy. 187a; *Harbin* v. *Barton* (1595) Moo.K.B. 395; *Whitlock* v. *Horton* (1605) Cro.Jac. 91; *Lampit* v. *Starkey* (1612) 2 Brownl. & Golds. 172 at 175; *Smallman* v. *Agborow* (1617) Cro.Jac. 417; Litt. 289.

[35] Litt. 286; Co.Litt. 185a.   [36] *Ante,* p. 132.

[37] *Brown* v. *Raindle* (1796) 3 Ves. 256; *Goddard* v. *Lewis* (1909) 101 L.T. 528. *Secus* if the contract was made by all the joint tenants: *Re Hayes' Estate* [1920] 1 I.R. 207.

[38] *Caldwell* v. *Fellowes* (1870) L.R. 9 Eq. 410; *Baillie* v. *Treherne* (1881) 17 Ch.D. 388; *Burnaby* v. *Equitable Reversionary Interest Society* (1885) 28 Ch.D. 416 (but as to the effect of infancy, discussed in that case, and supported by Co.Litt. 337b and Preston, *Abstracts*, ii, 59, see to the contrary *Re Wilks* [1891] 3 Ch. 59 at 62). In *Re Hewett* [1894] 1 Ch. 362 it was held that an aptly worded covenant would sever a joint tenancy in property subsequently acquired.

[39] *Frewen* v. *Relfe* (1787) 2 Bro.C.C. 220 at 224; *Gould* v. *Kemp* (1834) 2 My. & K. 304; *Kingsford* v. *Ball* (1852) 2 Giff.App. i; *Re Wilford's Estate* (1879) 11 Ch.D. 267; *In b. Heys* [1914] P. 192 at 195, 196; Cru.Dig. ii, 389.

[40] *Jackson* v. *Jackson* (1804) 9 Ves. 591; *Wilson* v. *Bell* (1843) 5 Ir.Eq.R. 501.

[41] *Williams* v. *Hensman* (1861) 1 J. & H. 546.

[42] *Hawkesley* v. *May* [1956] 1 Q.B. 304; *Re Draper's Conveyance* [1969] 1 Ch. 486 (application to court for order for sale), not citing *Re Wilks* [1891] 3 Ch. 59 and earlier authorities to the contrary; and see *Jackson* v. *Jackson* (1804) 9 Ves. 591 (trading in partnership). *Contra, Nielson-Jones* v. *Fedden* [1974] 3 W.L.R. 583; and see *post,* p. 409.   [43] *Ante,* p. 393.

[43a] *Re Wilford's Estate, supra; In b. Heys, supra; post,* p. 441.

[44] *Ante,* p. 395.

the unity of interest and severed the joint tenancy.[45] Thus if land was limited to A, B and C as joint tenants for life, with remainder to C in fee simple, the mere existence of C's fee simple remainder did not destroy his joint tenancy for life; but if A acquired C's fee simple, A's life estate merged in the fee simple and severed his joint tenancy for life.[45a] So also if land was held by X for life with remainder to Y and Z in fee simple as joint tenants, and X conveyed his life estate to Y, the joint tenancy was severed.[46] If X had instead *surrendered* his life estate to Y, this would have extinguished it,[47] and so both Y and Z would have benefited from their joint tenancy taking effect in possession.[48]

There was no severance by the acquisition of another estate in the land unless that estate differed from the estate held in joint tenancy. Thus if A, B and C were joint tenants in fee simple, and A conveyed his interest to B, B took A's one-third share as tenant in common,[49] but his joint tenancy with C in the remaining two-thirds was not affected; B therefore held one-third as tenant in common with himself and C as to two-thirds, but those two-thirds were still held by B and C in joint tenancy.[50]

3. By homicide. The rule that no one may benefit in law from his own crime[51] requires that, if one joint tenant criminally kills another, the killer cannot take any beneficial interest by survivorship, so that there is necessarily a severance. If A and B are joint tenants in law upon trust for themselves jointly, and A murders B, the legal estate will vest by survivorship in A alone, but upon trust for A and B's estate as equitable tenants in common in equal shares.[52] If there had been a third joint tenant, C, the legal estate would vest in A and C jointly upon trust for C as to one-third and for A and C as joint tenants as to the remaining two-thirds.[53]

Sect. 5. The 1925 Legislation

Under the law as it stood before 1926, tenancy in common was clearly the most desirable kind of co-ownership for beneficial owners. But it was a great inconvenience in conveyancing, for whether it was

---

[45] *Morgan's Case* (t. Eliz. 1) 2 And. 202; *Wiscot's Case* (1599) 2 Co.Rep. 60b; *ante*, p. 395.   [45a] *Ibid.*

[46] Co.Litt. 183a, 192a; Preston, *Conveyancing*, iii, 24.

[47] See *post*, p. 668.

[48] Co.Litt. 192a; Preston, *Conveyancing*, iii, 24, 25; Perkins, s. 615.

[49] This share was severed by alienation: see above.   [50] Litt. 304, 312.

[51] *e.g.*, *In b. Hall* [1914] P. 1. See the general survey by *T. G. Youdan* (1973) 89 L.Q.R. 235; and see *post*, p. 494.

[52] *Schobelt* v. *Barber* [1967] 1 O.R. 349; *Rasmanis* v. *Jurewitsch* (1969) 70 S.R. (N.S.W.) 407; *Re Pechar* [1969] N.Z.L.R. 574; *Re Gore* [1972] 1 O.R. 550.

[53] *Rasmanis* v. *Jurewitsch, supra*, holding (at p. 412) that the severance of the one-third is effected by imposing on A a constructive trust (*post*, p. 442) for C where that is necessary to prevent A from profiting from his crime.

legal or equitable a purchaser who bought the land as a whole was compelled to investigate the titles of all the co-owners. Since there was no unity of title, the titles to all the separate shares had to be scrutinised and pieced together. If, for example, out of four original tenants in common one had sold his share to a partnership, another had made a settlement, another had made several mortgages of his share, and another had died intestate leaving numerous relatives, there might then be the titles of thirty or more owners to investigate, some of whom might own a sixty-eighth share worth just over £10, and who might be so scattered about the world that it took six months to get their signatures to a conveyance.[54] In order to eliminate such difficulties substantial changes in the law have been made by the Law of Property Act, 1925. The new principles have already been met in other fields: the reduction in the varieties of legal estates,[55] and the extension of the system of overreaching equitable interests.[56]

1. A legal tenancy in common cannot exist after 1925. Even if there are clear words of severance, after 1925 the legal estate cannot be held by tenancy in common.[57] A tenancy in common can now exist only in equity; at law the only form of co-ownership possible after 1925 is a joint tenancy. Thus a conveyance today " to A, B and C in fee simple as tenants in common " (all being of full age) will vest the legal estate in A, B and C as joint tenants, although in equity they will be tenants in common.[58] If any of the co-owners is an infant, it has to be remembered that since 1925 an infant cannot hold a legal estate in land.[59] Therefore if A is an infant, he can be a co-owner in equity but the legal estate will vest in B and C alone [60] : B and C will be trustees for A, B and C. If A, B and C are all infants, it is clear that the legal estate remains in the grantor,[61] but uncertain whether he holds the land on trust for the infants or whether the transaction is wholly void.[62]

2. A legal joint tenancy cannot be severed after 1925.[63] This rule is the obvious counterpart of the preceding rule, for there can now be no method of creating a legal tenancy in common. It does not

---

[54] See Cosway (1929) 15 Conv.(o.s.) 83.   [55] *Ante*, p. 134.
[56] *Ante*, p. 148.
[57] L.P.A., 1925, ss. 1 (6), 34 (1), 36 (2) ; S.L.A., 1925, s. 36 (4).
[58] L.P.A., 1925, s. 34 (2).   [59] *Ibid.*, s. 1 (6) ; S.L.A., 1925, s. 27 (1).
[60] This is plainly the intention of the legislation, but no provision covers it precisely. There must be a trust on behalf of the infant and perhaps S.L.A., 1925, s. 36 (4), makes this a trust for sale. L.P.A., 1925, s. 19 (2), (5), do not appear to meet the case. See (1944) 9 Conv.(N.S.) 39.   [61] L.P.A., 1925, ss. 1 (6), 34 (1).
[62] See Emmet 310. L.P.A., 1925, s. 19 (1), and S.L.A., 1925, s. 27 (1), clearly provide for this situation in the case of joint tenants (see *post*, 988) and possibly these provisions could also be held to cover tenants in common on the ground that the legal estate must pass to them as joint tenants if at all.
[63] L.P.A., 1925, s. 36 (2). It is immaterial that the legal estate is vested in trustees.

prevent one joint tenant from releasing his interest to the others, nor does it affect the right to sever a joint tenancy in equity.[64] It is this latter right which is now important.

3. An equitable joint tenancy can be severed as before, or by notice in writing.

(a) *Power to sever.* It is provided that " where a legal estate (not being settled land) is vested in joint tenants beneficially, and any tenant desires to sever the joint tenancy in equity, he shall give ' to the other joint tenants a notice in writing [65] of such desire, or do such other acts or things as would, in the case of personal estate, have been effectual to sever the joint tenancy in equity," whereupon the parties concerned are to be treated in equity as if there had been an actual severance.[66] The effect of a severance is, of course, limited to the tenants' interests in equity in the proceeds of sale. A joint tenant may therefore now sever the joint tenancy in equity either in one of the ways available under the old law, or else by the new and convenient device of notice in writing.

(b) *Effect of power.* In general, the rules for personalty before 1926 were the same as the rules for realty explained above; in particular, a severance would be effected by a common course of conduct indicating that all the joint tenants intended to treat the property as held in common.[67] It is difficult to see why this statutory provision excludes settled land and also, apparently, cases where the legal estate is held not by all the joint tenants beneficially but by some of them on trust for all, or by trustees for them all. In such cases no severance by written notice seems possible, so that any severance must be effected by one of the modes applicable to real property before 1926.[68] But it might be possible to construe the statutory words " vested in joint tenants beneficially " so as to give them a wider meaning than normally.

(c) *Legal estate.* A co-owner who alienates his share does not cease to be joint tenant and trustee of the legal estate, if that was his position before he alienated. He can divest himself of the legal estate only by retiring from the trust, or by releasing his interest in the legal estate to the other joint tenants of it. But unless he is a

---

64 L.P.A., 1925, s. 36 (2).
65 See L.P.A., 1925, s. 196; *Re 88 Berkeley Road, N.W.9* [1971] Ch. 648 (notice duly posted in accordance with s. 196 but not received held effective).
63 L.P.A., 1925, s. 36 (2), proviso; and see *ante*, p. 406, n. 42. Once they have contracted to sell the land it is said that no severance by notice is possible because the legal estate is no longer vested in them beneficially: see *Nielson-Jones* v. *Fedden* [1974] 3 W.L.R. 583 at 589. *Sed quaere*: see (1974) 93 L.N. 303.
67 See *Williams* v. *Hensman* (1861) 1 J. & H. 546 at 557; *Re Wilks* [1891] 3 Ch. 59 at 61, 62; *Re Denny* [1947] L.J.R. 1029. 68 See L.P.A., 1925, s. 36 (2).

joint tenant and trustee of the legal estate he should now have a memorandum of severance indorsed on or annexed to the conveyance which vested the legal estate in the joint tenants so as to protect his interest if there is a conveyance of the legal estate by a sole surviving joint tenant; this is explained later.[69]

(d) *Husband and wife.* It has been said that where a dwelling-house is conveyed to a husband and wife as joint tenants at law and in equity for use as a matrimonial home, neither can sever the joint tenancy or dispose separately of his or her equitable interest.[70] But it is difficult to perceive the basis for this view [71]; and the contrary opinion, clearly based upon the Act, seems preferable.[72]

4. The legal estate is held upon trust for sale

(a) *The imposition of a statutory trust for sale.* The turning of tenancies in common into equitable interests would not by itself simplify the investigation of title, for a purchaser would have notice of the trusts. It was therefore essential to provide overreaching machinery, so that the purchaser need only investigate the title to the legal estate. This was done by imposing a statutory trust for sale upon land conveyed to or held by or on behalf of two or more persons beneficially, whether as tenants in common or joint tenants,[73] whether given interests in the land itself or in the income from it, and whether immediately or in the future. In all the following cases, therefore, the legal estate is now subject to a statutory trust for sale [74]:

    (i) a conveyance or devise to A and B jointly (*i.e.*, as beneficial joint tenants);

    (ii) a conveyance [75] or devise [76] to A and B as tenants in common;

    (iii) a conveyance or devise to X and Y jointly upon trust for A and B either jointly or in common (or upon trust to pay the income to A and B jointly or in common).[77]

---

[69] See *post*, p. 414.
[70] *Bedson* v. *Bedson* [1965] 2 Q.B. 666 at 678, *per* Lord Denning M.R.; *Ulrich* v. *Ulrich* [1968] 1 W.L.R. 180 at 186.
[71] Apparently based on L.P.A., 1925, s. 36 (1), (3). But the subsections seem to provide no support: see (1966) 82 L.Q.R. 31 (R.E.M.).
[72] *Bedson* v. *Bedson, supra*, at p. 690, *per* Russell L.J., based on L.P.A., 1925, s. 36 (2); followed in *Re Draper's Conveyance* [1969] 1 Ch. 486; and see *Radziej* v. *Radziej* [1967] 1 W.L.R. 659.
[73] This states the combined effect of L.P.A., 1925, ss. 34 and 36, which deal with the various cases. The machinery is described more particularly below.
[74] L.P.A., 1925, s. 36 (1).
[75] *Ibid.*, s. 34 (2).
[76] *Ibid.*, s. 34 (3).
[77] *Re House* [1929] 2 Ch. 166 (devise upon trust for tenants in common held to fall within s. 34 (3)). The same presumably applies to a conveyance, which will then fall within s. 34 (2), but it is not clear whether the legal estate then vests

In the case of a devise it should be noted that the legal estate vests not in any of the persons named but in the testator's personal representatives,[78] who therefore become the trustees for sale. Since they automatically hold the deceased's property upon trust to give effect to the will, there is no point in creating another set of trustees. There are special provisions for settled land, which will be treated later.[79]

The scheme of the Act was evidently to impose a trust for sale in all cases of beneficial co-ownership. In the case of joint beneficial interests this is effected in a straightforward way [80] by section 36 (1). In the case of beneficial interests held in common there are several cases which do not appear to be covered by any of the miscellaneous provisions of section 34. The difficulty about a case which falls outside these various provisions is that not only is there no trust for sale but the very existence of the beneficial interests is forbidden by section 34 (1).[1] The chief cases in question are the following [2]:

(i) a conveyance to A (an infant) and B (an adult) as tenants in common [3];

(ii) a conveyance to A and B as joint tenants, where equity requires them to take as beneficial tenants in common, *e.g.*, because they are partners, or contribute purchase-money in unequal shares [4];

(iii) a conveyance to X, purchasing as trustee for A and B who are equitable owners in common of the purchase-money; and

(iv) a declaration by A, as sole owner, that he holds on trust for himself and B in equal shares.[4a]

in X and Y or in A and B. The case is even more difficult, on the wording of s. 34 (2), where there is a conveyance to X (alone) upon trust for A and B in common. Beneficial joint tenancy is clearly dealt with by s. 36: the legal estate vests in the trustee or trustees.

[78] L.P.A., 1925, s. 34 (3).

[79] *Post*, p. 423.

[80] See, however, 62 L.J.News. 437; 64 *ibid.* 66.

[1] *Cf.* S.L.A., 1925, s. 36 (4), to the like effect.

[2] See (1944) 9 Conv.(N.S.) 37 *et seq.* There are other possible cases, *e.g.*, a residuary devise to X and Y in equal shares where X predeceases the testator and his share lapses, and there is an intestacy as to it. Y and some other person are then entitled as tenants in common, but the case does not seem to be covered by L.P.A., 1925, s. 34 (3).

[3] If they are joint tenants, L.P.A., 1925, s. 19 (2) covers the case.

[4] *Ante*, p. 401. In two such cases (of purchasers contributing unequally) two different solutions have been found: that the case falls within L.P.A., 1925, s. 36 (1), which governs beneficial joint tenancy (*Re Buchanan-Wollaston's Conveyance* [1939] Ch. 217 at 222; [1939] Ch. 738 at 744); and that S.L.A., 1925, s. 36 (4) governs any case of tenancy in common not otherwise provided for (*Bull* v. *Bull* [1955] 1 Q.B. 234).

[4a] Examples are *Re Hind* [1933] Ch. 208; *Jones* v. *Jones* [1972] 1 W.L.R. 1269. Another case is that of a husband's or wife's share acquired under the Matrimonial Proceedings and Property Act 1970; see *post*, p. 446.

Cases (ii) and (iii) arise because section 34 (2) applies only where
land is *expressed* to be conveyed to persons in undivided shares,
and seems to exclude cases where the undivided shares arise only
by implication of law or by some other instrument.[5] The true
intention is perhaps that this subsection should apply to all cases
where undivided shares (either legal or equitable) would have arisen
from an express disposition under the previous law. It would require
some fortitude to construe it in this sense, but if it could be done it
would avoid difficulties. The Court of Appeal has found a way of
escape in section 36 (4) of the Settled Land Act, 1925,[6] which
provides that an undivided share in land cannot be created "except
under a trust instrument or under the Law of Property Act, 1925,
and shall then only take effect behind a trust for sale." Plainly
this provision is not well framed to remedy the deficiencies of the
Law of Property Act, 1925. But to employ it for that purpose is
probably a better course than to extend the incomplete provisions
of that Act by straining their language.[7]

(*b*) "*The statutory trusts.*" The statutory trust for sale is, in
all these cases, referred to in the Act as " the statutory trusts." The
definition of " the statutory trusts "[8] may be summarised thus:

> upon trust to sell the land, and stand possessed of the net
> proceeds of sale and of the net rents and profits until sale upon
> such trusts and subject to such powers and provisions as may
> be requisite for giving effect to the rights of those interested
> in the land.

By this device the beneficial interests of the co-owners are kept
off the title: a purchaser is concerned not with the beneficial interests
in the land but only with the legal estate vested in the trustees for
sale. Provided he pays his purchase-money to trustees for sale who
are either two or more in number or a trust corporation, he takes
free from the rights of the beneficiaries.[9] To a purchaser who does
this, it is immaterial whether in equity there are three or thirty people
entitled, or whether they are joint tenants or tenants in common.
The statutory machinery has to apply to a joint tenancy because,
as will shortly be seen, a joint tenancy may often be turned into a
tenancy in common, which must be equitable; and a purchaser must
be absolved from inquiring whether this has happened or not.

---

[5] Possibly " expressed " may be construed to include " implied "; see *Re Royal Victoria Pavilion, Ramsgate* [1961] Ch. 581.
[6] *Bull* v. *Bull, supra.*
[7] The solution adopted in *Re Buchanan-Wollaston's Conveyance, supra,* is at the expense of the word " beneficially " in L.P.A., 1925, s. 36 (1).
[8] L.P.A., 1925, s. 35.
[9] For this machinery, see *ante,* pp. 375, 376.

(c) Determination of the statutory trusts

(1) UNION IN SOLE TENANT. Once all the legal and equitable interests in the property have finally vested in one person (*e.g.*, where A, B and C were beneficial joint tenants in fee simple and B and C have died), there can no longer be an effective trust and the statutory trust for sale therefore ceases.[10] In the example given, A can sell as sole owner and take the purchase-money. Furthermore, in such a case the purchaser is deprived of his right to insist on a conveyance from trustees for sale,[11] for by the Law of Property (Amendment) Act, 1926, it was provided that nothing in the Law of Property Act, 1925, affects the right of a survivor of joint tenants who is solely and beneficially interested to deal with his legal estate as if it were not held on trust for sale. The object of this was to save A going through the pointless procedure of appointing another trustee of a trust under which he was the sole beneficiary.

(2) INVESTIGATION OF TITLE. The purchaser, however, could not tell whether the vendor was solely *and beneficially* interested unless he investigated the beneficial interests. A beneficial joint tenancy, for example, might have been turned into a tenancy in common [12] by some act or event not shown in the title to the legal estate, and perhaps not even known to the vendor, so that A, in the above example, might turn out to be trustee for sale for himself and some other person claiming through B or C. Even in this case the purchaser, if he had made all due inquiries and found no evidence of a tenancy in common, could probably plead that he was a bona fide purchaser of the legal estate for value without notice of the outstanding equitable interest.[13] But no purchaser wishes to be driven to that plea; and there was the practical problem of what proof of a negative (non-severance) could be given.

(3) STATEMENTS UNDER THE ACT OF 1964. This situation was a constant nuisance in conveyancing. It violated the principle of the 1925 legislation that the purchaser should not be concerned with the beneficial interests; and purchasers often had to be advised to obtain the appointment of another trustee to join the vendor in receiving the purchase-money, in case by some mischance the statutory trusts were

---

[10] *Re Cook* [1948] Ch. 212. This may have important results on beneficial interests affected by the doctrine of conversion: *ante* p. 287.

[11] Under L.P.A., 1925, 23; *ante*, p. 365.

[12] *i.e.*, severed, *e.g.*, by a sale of a share: *ante*, p. 408.

[13] L.P.A., 1925, s. 27 (2), which requires payment of capital money to two trustees or a trust corporation where there is a trust for sale, appears to contain nothing to weaken this fundamental rule.

not extinct.[14] The Law of Property (Joint Tenants) Act 1964 has now supplied a remedy. This short statute provides that, in favour of a purchaser of the legal estate, a survivor of two or more joint tenants shall " be deemed to be solely and beneficially interested if he conveys as beneficial owner [as he will normally do [15]] or the conveyance includes a statement that he is so interested." [16] Thus the purchaser of the legal estate will take it without notice of any severance, and will defeat the equitable title of any owner of a severed share. Where the survivor has himself died, his personal representatives are given corresponding powers. The new legislation is retrospective: it is deemed to have come into force on January 1, 1926, and vendors and their personal representatives are empowered to make statements in respect of conveyances made before the Act.[17]

(4) EXCLUSION OF THE ACT. The Act of 1964 does not apply if before the date of the conveyance by the survivor a memorandum of severance is indorsed on or annexed to the conveyance which vested the legal estate in the joint tenants; the memorandum must be signed by one or all of them and record the severance on a specified date.[18] Nor does the Act apply where, before the same date, a bankruptcy petition or receiving order has been registered [19] so as to affect the purchaser with notice of it,[20] or where the title to the land is registered.[1]

(5) SEVERANCE. The Act of 1964 will provide more convenient conveyancing machinery in the normal case where there has been no severance. But where there has been a severance, which may be unknown to the survivor, the title of the owner of the severed share will be imperilled unless he attaches a memorandum of severance to the document of title. The Act gives him no power to insist upon this, but his powers as co-owner probably suffice.[2] Nor does the Act say what is to happen where the vendor conveys as beneficial owner but the purchaser has notice that there has been a severance. On its face, the Act even then protects the purchaser. But the court

---

[14] See 219 L.T.News. 217; *Encyclopaedia of Forms and Precedents*, 1958 Supp., 716. A statutory declaration by the vendor was often obtained: see Emmet, 334. The burden of proof of severance is normally on the person alleging it: *Leak v. Macdowall* (1862) 32 Beav. 28 at 30. See, further, 62 L.J.News. 459; 63 *ibid.* 268; 64 *ibid.* 66; 78 *ibid.* 57, 335, 353, 375; (1944) 9 Conv.(N.S.) 73–75; (1947) 12 Conv.(N.S.) 137; 219 L.T.News. 217.
[15] See *post*, p. 602.
[16] s. 1.
[17] s. 2.
[18] s. 1.
[19] Under L.C.A. 1972: *post*, pp. 1036, 1038.
[20] s. 1.
[1] s. 3: see *post*, p. 1054.
[2] See *post*, p. 601.

is sometimes unwilling to allow purchasers to take advantage of such provisions inequitably.[3]

(d) Operation of the statutory trusts

(1) CONTROL BY BENEFICIARIES. The statutory trust for sale is subject to the ordinary rules, both statutory and otherwise, which govern trusts for sale.[4] One result of this is to enable a majority of the beneficiaries, according to the value of their interests, to give directions to the trustees so far as may be consistent with the general interest of the trust.[5] Thus if, as will often be the case, the same persons are both trustees and beneficiaries, one of them cannot compel the others to sell if the majority (by value) favour postponing sale.[6] Orders of the court will be made only in accordance with the rules of equity, and with due regard to any contract or trust. Therefore a trustee-beneficiary who has covenanted to sell only with another co-owner's consent will not be assisted to break his contract by forcing a sale against the wish of the other co-owner.[7] Nor will a sale be ordered where two persons become co-owners for some particular purpose, *e.g.*, for joint occupation of a house, and that purpose still exists.[8] But if the purpose no longer exists, *e.g.*, because of breakdown of a marriage, the court will order a sale.[9]

(2) CONVERSION. Another result of imposing a statutory trust for sale is to import the principle of conversion.[10] Before 1926 the beneficial interests of co-owners were interests in land; since 1925 they are interests in personalty (the proceeds of sale), even while the land remains unsold. For example, a testator who owned a share in freehold land made a will before 1926 leaving all his freehold property to F and all his personal estate to P. He died in 1928, and as the land had become subject to the statutory trusts on January 1, 1926, his interest, instead of passing to F, passed to P.[11] The result

---

[3] *Cf.* the judicial restriction of the provision protecting purchasers from mortgagees: *post*, p. 910.

[4] Explained *ante*, p. 358.

[5] L.P.A., 1925, s. 26 (3), as amended by L.P.(Am.)A., 1926, Sched.: *ante*, p. 370; and see *Bull* v. *Bull* [1955] 1 Q.B. 234 at 238; *Barclay* v. *Barclay* [1970] 2 Q.B. 677. See also [1955] C.L.J. 156 (H.W.R.W.); (1955) 18 M.L.R. 303 (V. Latham), 408 (H. R. Gray); (1956) 19 M.L.R. 312 (G. A. Forrest).

[6] Contrast cases where s. 26 (3) does not apply: *ante*, p. 370.

[7] *Re Buchanan-Wollaston's Conveyance* [1939] Ch. 738. An agreement to sell only with another person's consent is consistent with a trust for sale: *ante*, p. 360.

[8] *Bull* v. *Bull* [1955] 1 Q.B. 234 (mother and son), as interpreted in *Jones* v. *Challenger* [1961] 1 Q.B. 176; and see *Bedson* v. *Bedson* [1965] 2 Q.B. 666 (no sale at behest of deserting spouse).

[9] *Jones* v. *Challenger, supra*; *Rawlings* v. *Rawlings* [1964] P. 398; *Jackson* v. *Jackson* [1971] 1 W.L.R. 1539; *Re Turner* [1974] 1 W.L.R. 1556 (husband bankrupt).   [10] *Ante*, p. 286.

[11] *Re Kempthorne* [1930] 1 Ch. 268. *Cf. Edwards* v. *Hall* [1949] 1 All E.R. 352 (share of tenant in common in a farm not an " agricultural holding "); *Taylor* v. *Taylor* [1968] 1 W.L.R. 378 (claim to interest not registrable as pending action).

would have been the same if he had made a specific gift to F of his share in the land,[12] unless it could be construed as a gift of all the testator's interest in the property, whatever its state,[13] or the will had been expressly [14] or impliedly [15] confirmed by a codicil made after 1925.

Yet although in general the shares of the beneficiaries are personalty, for some purposes they have an interest in land [16] in the sense that the land, while unsold, is impressed with a trust for their benefit; thus the sale of a share is the sale of an interest in land which should be evidenced in writing.[17] But if a single person becomes solely entitled both at law and in equity, there is no longer a trust for sale and the doctrine of conversion ceases to apply. Accordingly where a husband and wife were beneficial joint tenants of a house, and the wife survived the husband and left all her personal estate to P, the house passed not to P but as on intestacy.[18]

(e) *The overriding effect of the statutory trusts.* Problems may arise where the instrument creating the concurrent interests contains provisions which are inconsistent with the statutory trusts. It has been held that the statutory trusts are paramount, so as to authorise a sale despite an administration action commenced before 1926,[19] and rendering inoperative a beneficiary's right of pre-emption,[20] restrictions on sale,[21] and a power to partition the land.[22] But there are indications that this interpretation is open to question in the Court of Appeal,[23] and it is subject to the criticism that the conveyancing machinery introduced in 1925 should so far as possible be operated so as not to affect beneficial interests.[24] Further, a provision applicable to express trusts may apply also to the statutory trusts that supersede them, *e.g.,* a provision as to the persons to be trustees [25] or enabling a solicitor-trustee to charge for work done.[26]

---

12 *Re Newman* [1930] 2 Ch. 409.
13 *Re Mellish* (1927) [1929] 2 K.B. 82n.
14 *Re Warren* [1932] 1 Ch. 42.
15 *Re Harvey* [1947] Ch. 285; but see *Re Galway's W. T.* [1950] Ch. 1.
16 See *Re Bradshaw* [1950] Ch. 78 at 82; *ante,* p. 287.
17 *Cooper* v. *Critchley* [1955] Ch. 431; *post,* p. 549.
18 *Re Cook* [1948] Ch. 212.
19 *Bernhardt* v. *Galsworthy* [1929] 1 Ch. 549.
20 *Re Flint* [1927] 1 Ch. 570 (" a most iniquitous decision ": 75 S.J. 668).
21 *Re House* [1929] 2 Ch. 166, 172.
22 *Re Thomas* [1930] 1 Ch. 194.
23 *Re Buchanan-Wollaston's Conveyance* [1939] Ch. 738 at 747. *Jones* v. *Chalenger* [1961] 1 Q.B. 176 shows the court's present inclination to make the statutory trusts subject to the intention of the parties. They are " not the steam roller " that at first they seemed to be: see J.M.L., 88 L.J.News. 4.
24 See J.M.L., 73 L.J.News, 41, 57, 75, 93, 111 (the " bull in the china shop " rule: 73 L.J.News. 58); and see *Re Davies' W. T.* [1932] 1 Ch. 530 at 536.
25 *Re Wilson* (1929) 67 L.J.News. 137; 72 L.J.News. 105; see 72 L.J.News. 191; 88 L.J.News. 80; 75 S.J. 694.
26 *Re Pedley* [1927] 2 Ch. 168.

On the other hand, it has been held that a sale or lease under the statutory trusts will not put an end to a determinable interest, so that a life's tenant's share which was limited to last " so long as he shall reside upon and assist in the management of my said farm " was thus released from the restriction so far as necessary to make way for the new statutory powers.[27]

(*f*) *Entails.* Another unforeseen result was that if at the end of 1925 two or more persons were entitled to land as tenants in common in tail [28] their interests became absolute interests at the beginning of 1926 [29]; for by the doctrine of conversion the beneficial interests became interests in personalty, and personalty could not be entailed under instruments which took effect before 1926.[30] The Law of Property (Entailed Interests) Act, 1932,[31] amended the definition of the statutory trusts so as to make it clear that entails should instead exist in the proceeds of sale under the trusts. The amendment was retrospective to the beginning of 1926, save as regards orders of the court made or titles acquired for money or money's worth before June 16, 1932, when the Act was passed.

5. The legal estate cannot be vested in more than four persons. The various provisions which impose the statutory trusts also limit the number of the trustees in accordance with the new principle that in settlements and trusts for sale of land there shall not be more than four trustees. For tenancies created after 1925 [32] the rules are as follows.

(*a*) *Tenancies in common.* A conveyance of land to trustees for sale on trust for tenants in common is subject to the general rule which limits the number of trustees of land to four.[33] If the conveyance is made to the tenants in common themselves, and they are of full age, it operates as a conveyance " to the grantees, or, if there are more than four grantees, to the first four named in the conveyance, as joint tenants upon the statutory trusts." [34] A gift of land by will to, or in trust for,[35] tenants in common operates as a gift to the

---

[27] *Re Davies' W. T.* [1932] 1 Ch. 530; *cf. ante,* p. 375.
[28] Often found in settlements among daughters : *ante,* p. 386.
[29] *Re Price* [1928] Ch. 579, said by Wolst. & C. (12th ed.) i, 450, to be wrongly decided. The decision would have frustrated many cross-remainders of the kind usual in settlements (*ante,* p. 386).
[30] *Ante,* p. 95.
[31] s. 1.
[32] Under tenancies created before 1926 it is still sometimes possible for there to be more than four trustees if they were appointed before 1926: *post,* p. 420.
[33] T.A., 1925, s. 34 (2); *post,* p. 453.
[34] L.P.A., 1925, s. 34 (2).
[35] *Re House* [1929] 2 Ch. 166.

Settled Land Act trustees of the will, or, if none, to the testator's personal representatives, upon the statutory trusts [36]; and the number of Settled Land Act trustees [37] or personal representatives [38] cannot exceed four.

(*b*) *Joint tenancies.* There are no provisions dealing expressly with the number of persons in whom the legal estate can be vested when two or more persons are beneficially entitled as joint tenants. But the trust for sale arising in such cases is subject to the general provision that in a disposition of land on trust for sale made or coming into operation after 1925 the number of trustees shall not exceed four, and " where more than four persons are named as such trustees, the first four named (who are able and willing to act) shall alone be the trustees." [39]   In the case of a devise to joint tenants, the general rules against more than four personal representatives [40] or trustees for sale [41] of land prevent the legal estate from vesting in or being conveyed to more than four persons.

6. Operation of the present law.   An example illustrating the present position may be useful.   In 1960 X purported to convey land to A, B, C, D and E in fee simple; all were of full age.   The legal estate vested in A, B, C and D on the statutory trusts; in equity, A, B, C, D and E were tenants in common if there were words of severance or if it was one of equity's special cases, but otherwise joint tenants.   If they were joint tenants and A died, B, C and D would then hold the legal estate on the statutory trusts for B, C, D and E as joint tenants; E would not automatically fill the vacancy at law, but could, of course, be appointed a new trustee in place of A.   If B afterwards sold his interest to P, then B, C and D would continue to hold the legal estate, but the statutory trusts would be for P as tenant in common of a quarter and C, D and E as joint tenants of three-quarters.   If C then effected a severance of his share by agreement [42] with D and E, the legal estate would remain in B, C and D as before, on the statutory trusts for P and C as tenants in common of one-quarter each, and D and E as joint tenants of half. On D's death, B and C would hold on the statutory trusts for P, C

---

[36] L.P.A., 1925, s. 34 (3).   This at times introduces an apparently needless complication: see J.M.L., 65 L.J.News. 332.

[37] *Ante*, p. 324.

[38] *Post*, p. 533.

[39] T.A., 1925, s. 34: the language is obviously designed to fit express trusts for sale and is not very apt for statutory trusts, where no persons are " named as . . . trustees "; but it seems probable that it would be held applicable; and see (1926) 42 L.Q.R. 480 (R. R. Formoy).

[40] *Post*, p. 541.

[41] T.A., 1925, s. 34 (2); *post*, p. 453.

[42] Severance by notice seems impossible, for the legal estate is not vested in all the joint tenants beneficially: see *ante*, p. 408.

and E as tenants in common as to one-quarter, one-quarter and one-half respectively.

It will be noticed that the three main changes introduced by the 1925 legislation all assist the purchaser. The prohibition of a legal tenancy in common and the limitation of the number of tenants of the legal estate to four means that purchasers are no longer exposed to the burden of having to investigate the titles of each of a large number of tenants in common. Further, the overreaching effect of a trust for sale enables a purchaser to ignore the equitable rights of the beneficiaries. These benefits may be thought to have been dearly purchased in view of the complexity of the new provisions, particularly since draftsmanship in this part of the 1925 legislation was not at its best. But the abolition of the conveyancing problems formerly common under legal tenancies in common is undeniably an improvement in the law.

7. Transitional provisions. The following provisions apply to tenancies created before 1926.

(a) *Tenancies in common.* Elaborate transitional provisions[43] were enacted with the objects of imposing the statutory trusts in all cases where undivided shares were already vested in possession, and of ensuring that the legal estate should vest in suitable persons at the first moment of 1926. In the transition from the old system to the new, it was necessary to provide machinery for finding a safe home for the legal estate, which could no longer remain in tenants in common as such. There were four separate heads which had to be taken in order[44]; if a case fell under both Head 1 and Head 3, for example, the operative provisions were those of Head 1.[45] The provisions applied to any land which at the end of 1925 was held at law or in equity in undivided shares vested in possession.[46] Thus they applied where there were life interests in possession,[47] or where there was an immediate trust to divide the income between a class of persons,[48] but not where there were life interests which carried the income only after certain debts were paid,[49] or which did not arise until certain mortgages had been discharged.[50]

---

[43] L.P.A., 1925, 1st Sched., Pt. IV. A fuller account of these provisions was given in the 1st and 2nd editions of this book. See Emmet 327 *et seq.* As to undivided shares vested in the Crown, see Crown Estate Act, 1961, s. 8 (2).

[44] See *Re Dawson's S. E.* [1928] Ch. 421; *Re Barrat* [1929] 1 Ch. 336. The contrary was assumed in *Re Flint* [1927] 1 Ch. 570, *Re Colyer's Farningham Estate* [1927] 1 Ch. 677 and *Re Higgs' and May's Contract* [1927] 2 Ch. 249.

[45] *Re Dawson's S. E., supra.*

[46] L.P.A., 1925, 1st Sched., Pt. IV, para. 1.

[47] *Re Dawson's S. E., supra.*

[48] *Re Robins* [1928] Ch. 721.

[49] *Re Earl of Stamford & Warrington* [1927] 2 Ch. 217.

[50] *Re Stevens & Dunsby's Contract* [1928] W.N. 187.

HEAD 1: TRUSTEES OR PERSONAL REPRESENTATIVES. If the entirety of the land was vested in trustees or personal representatives [51] in trust for persons entitled in undivided shares,[52] it remained vested in them (even if they numbered more than four), to be held on the statutory trusts.[53]

HEAD 2: BENEFICIAL OWNERS. If the entirety of the land (not being settled land) was " vested absolutely and beneficially in not more than four persons of full age entitled thereto in undivided shares free from incumbrances affecting undivided shares, but subject or not to incumbrances affecting the entirety," it vested in them as joint tenants upon the statutory trusts.[54]

HEAD 3: SETTLED LAND. If the entirety of the land was settled land held under one settlement, it vested in the trustees (if any) of the settlement as joint tenants [55] on the statutory trusts.[56] If, however, there were no such trustees, the legal estate vested (free as aforesaid) in the Public Trustee upon the statutory trusts,[57] although he could not act in the trust or charge any fee until he was requested in writing to act by or on behalf of persons interested in more than an undivided half of the land or the income thereof.[58]

There is one case where, although Head 3 is prima facie applicable, special provisions have been made, and there is not even a trust for sale: this is dealt with below.[59]

HEAD 4: ANY OTHER CASE. In any case not covered by the foregoing heads, the land vested in the Public Trustee in the same way as under Head 3.[60]

(b) *Joint tenancies.* The complex transitional provisions about tenancies in common did not apply to joint tenancies.[61] The section imposing the statutory trusts in all cases " where a legal estate (not being settled land) is beneficially limited to or held in trust for any

---

[51] Including a sole trustee (*Re Dawson's S. E.* [1928] Ch. 421) or sole personal representative: *Re Myhill* [1928] Ch. 100; *Re Collins* [1929] 1 Ch. 201.

[52] Where the legal estate was vested in the personal representatives of a testator who had devised the land to trustees on trust for tenants in common, it vested in the personal representatives (and not the trustees) on the statutory trusts: *Re Foster* [1929] 1 Ch. 146.

[53] L.P.A., 1925, 1st Sched., Pt. IV, para. 1 (1).

[54] *Ibid.*, para. 1 (2). See, *e.g.*, *Re Fuller's Contract* [1933] Ch. 652.

[55] This can apply only if there were two or more trustees of the settlement, for the legal estate could not have vested in one trustee " as joint tenants ": *Re Price* [1929] 2 Ch. 400.

[56] L.P.A., 1925, 1st Sched., Pt. IV, para. 1 (3).

[57] *Ibid.*, para. 1 (3) (i).

[58] *Ibid.*, para. 1 (3) (ii).

[59] *Post*, pp. 423–426.

[60] L.P.A., 1925, 1st Sched., Pt. IV, para. 1 (4).

[61] See *Re Gaul & Houlston's Contract* [1928] Ch. 689 at 698; J.M.L., 62 L.J.News. 437; 64 *ibid.* 66.

persons as joint tenants "[62] applied irrespective of the date when
the beneficial joint tenancy arose, and the only specifically transitional provision in point is that where land is subjected to a trust
for sale at the beginning of 1926, the legal estate is to vest in the
trustees for sale.[63]   Unless the land was settled land, it remained
vested in the persons in whom it was vested before 1926, even if
they exceeded four in number; this was so whether it was vested in
beneficial joint tenants or in trustees on trust for joint tenants.[64]
There appears to be no restriction upon the numbers in such a case
except the general provision that until the number of trustees is
reduced below four no new trustees can be appointed.[65]

Where the land was settled land within the meaning of the
Settled Land Act, 1925,[66] the above provisions did not apply and the
legal estate automatically vested in the two or more persons of
full age (without limit as to number) who were the joint tenants for
life.   Thus the land remained subject to the Settled Land Act and
there was no trust for sale.   The rules as to settled land are explained
separately below.[67]

Sect. 6. Special Rules for Husband and Wife

A. *Before* 1926

1. One person.   For many purposes the common law treated
husband and wife as one person.[68]   As will be seen shortly,[69] a
conveyance to a husband and wife without words of severance
formerly created a tenancy by entireties, which was virtually an
unseverable joint tenancy; but the Married Women's Property Act,
1882, prevented the creation of such tenancies after 1882.[70]

2. One share.   This Act, however, did not affect[71] another special
rule based upon the unity of husband and wife, namely, the rule
of construction[72] that in the absence of a contrary intention,[73] a
conveyance to a husband and wife and third parties, whether as joint

---

[62] L.P.A., 1925, s. 36 (1).
[63] L.P.A., 1925, 1st Sched., Pt. II, para. 6 (*b*).
[64] See *Re Gaul & Houlston's Contract* [1928] Ch. 689 at 699, 700; (1926) 42
    L.Q.R. 480 (R. R. Formoy).
[65] T.A., 1925, s. 34 (1); J.M.L., 62 L.J.News. 437; 64 *ibid.* 66; *post*, p. 456.
[66] *Re Gaul & Houlston's Contract, supra,* at p. 698.
[67] *Post*, p. 423.
[68] Litt. 291; Co.Litt. 187b.
[69] *Post*, p. 432.
[70] See *post*, p. 434.
[71] *Re Jupp* (1888) 39 Ch.D. 148.
[72] *Re March* (1884) 27 Ch.D. 166 at 170; *Re Jeffery* [1914] 1 Ch. 375.
[73] *Re Wylde's Estate* (1852) 2 De G.M. & G. 724; *Re March, supra,* at p. 170.

tenants [74] or tenants in common,[75] gave the husband and wife only one actual or potential share between them. For example, a limitation before 1926 to

" H and W and X in equal shares "

created a tenancy in common under which X took one half and H and W (the husband and wife) the other.[76] Had the words " in equal shares " been omitted, there would have been a joint tenancy in which X held one potential half share and H and W the other half as joint tenants *inter se* [77] (or, before 1883, as tenants by entireties [78]). The requisite unity of interest could theoretically be preserved by treating husband and wife as one.

3. Contrary intention. The rule limiting husband and wife to one share between them yielded to any contrary indication, however slight,[79] and the astuteness of the courts in detecting a contrary intention in the form of the gift led to distinctions of great nicety. Mere words of severance, such as " in equal shares " were not enough,[80] for they merely showed that the interest taken by the unit consisting of husband-and-wife was to be held under a tenancy in common and not a joint tenancy. But the rule was often excluded merely by the way in which copulatives were used. For example, the form of the limitations in the first column below has been held sufficient to exclude the rule and give H and W one share each, whereas the form of the limitations in the second column did not oust the rule, and H and W took one share between them.

RULE EXCLUDED	RULE APPLIED
to " H W and X " [81]	to " H and W, and X " [82]
to " A, B, H and W " [83]	to " A B and H and W " [84]
to " H1, W1, X, Y, Z, H2 and W2 " [85]	to " A, and H, and W " [86]

---

[74] Litt. 291; *Gordon* v. *Whieldon* (1848) 11 Beav. 170; *Re Wylde's Estate, supra*; *Re March* (1884) 27 Ch.D. 166.

[75] *Bricker* v. *Whatley* (1684) 1 Vern. 233; *Anon.* (1684) Skin. 182; *Warrington* v. *Warrington* (1842) 2 Hare 54; *Re Wylde's Estate, supra.* The dicta on this point in *Lewin* v. *Cox* (1599) Moo.K.B. 558 and *Marchant* v. *Cragg* (1862) 31 Beav. 398 appear unsound, although the actual decision in the latter case can perhaps be supported on other grounds: see n. 87, *infra.*

[76] *Re Wylde's Estate, supra.*   [77] *Re March* (1884) 27 Ch.D. 166 at 170.

[78] *Back* v. *Andrew* (1690) 2 Vern. 120; Preston, *Abstracts,* ii, 40.

[79] *Dias* v. *De Livera* (1879) 5 App.Cas. 123 at 136; *Re March* (1884) 27 Ch.D. 166 at 170; *Re Dixon* (1889) 42 Ch.D. 306.

[80] *Bricker* v. *Whatley, supra*; *Re Wylde's Estate, supra.* Dicta to the contrary in *Marchant* v. *Cragg, supra,* are unsound.

[81] *Re Jeffery* [1914] 1 Ch. 375, not following *Re Jupp* (1888) 39 Ch.D. 148.

[82] *Back* v. *Andrew* (1690) 2 Vern. 120; *Re Wylde's Estate, supra.*

[83] *Warrington* v. *Warrington, supra*; and see *Re Dixon, supra,* at p. 309.

[84] *Bricker* v. *Whatley* (1684) 1 Vern. 233; *cf. Marchant* v. *Cragg* (1862) 31 Beav. 398.

[85] *Re Dixon, supra.*   [86] *Re March, supra.*

The distinction between these turns upon the use of the copulative " and." It is perhaps best explained by saying that if " H and W " were enclosed in a bracket, or replaced by a single symbol such as " Q," the limitations in the second column would still read smoothly and naturally, whereas those in the first column would not. Thus

" A, B, (H-and-W)," or
" A, B, Q "

from column 1 should be contrasted with

" A B and (H-and-W)," or
" A B and Q "

from column 2. " Though a man may devise to ten persons, and add an (*and*) betwixt every person's name, yet it is not natural or usual to add an (*and*) till you come to the last person."[87] If the donor " couples the husband and wife together in such a way as to refer to them jointly as husband and wife, then the ordinary rule applies."[88]

The rule had no application to persons who were unmarried when the limitation took effect but who intermarried afterwards,[89] nor did it apply to class gifts,[90] *e.g.*, a gift to the grantor's nephews and nieces, two of whom were married to each other.[91]

B. *After* 1925

By the Law of Property Act, 1925,[92] a husband and wife are to be treated as two persons for all purposes of acquisition of any interest in property under a disposition made or coming into operation after 1925, so that the rule has disappeared except in respect of limitations which took effect before 1926. But the relationship of husband and wife may affect the operation of joint tenancies and tenancies in common of the matrimonial home.[93]

Sect. 7. **Position of Settled Land**

Before 1926, where land fell within the definition of settled land but two or more persons were together entitled in possession, they

---

[87] *Bricker* v. *Whatley* (1684) 1 Vern. 233, *per* Lord Guilford L.K. Perhaps where there were two or more donees in addition to H and W, and an " and " was inserted between each name, the rule was excluded: see *Marchant* v. *Cragg* (1862) 31 Beav. 398.

[88] *Re Jeffery* [1914] 1 Ch. 375 at 380, *per* Warrington J. *Gordon* v. *Whieldon* (1848) 11 Beav. 170 and *Atcheson* v. *Atcheson* (1849) 11 Beav. 485 are perhaps unsound on this point.

[89] Co.Litt. 187b.

[90] *Ante*, p. 228.

[91] *Re Gue* (1892) 61 L.J.Ch. 510; *Re Smith* [1892] W.N. 106.

[92] s. 37.

[93] See *ante*, pp. 413, 417, 418; *post*, p. 997.

together formed a composite tenant for life, whether they held as
joint tenants, tenants in common or otherwise.[94] Since 1925 this is
true only in the case of joint tenants, so that joint tenancy must
now be treated separately from tenancy in common.

A. Joint Tenancy

If two or more persons of full age are entitled to settled land as
joint tenants, they together constitute the tenant for life,[95] even,
it seems, if they are more than four in number. If any of them are
infants, such one or more of them as for the time being is or are of
full age constitute the tenant for life [96]; if they are all infants, the
legal estate and statutory powers are vested in the statutory owner [97]
until one of them is of full age.[98] The land thus remains settled land
and there is no trust for sale.[99]

B. Tenancy in Common

1. Trust for sale. The scheme of the 1925 legislation is that
whenever two or more tenants in common or coparceners become
entitled in possession, the land cannot be settled land and must be
held upon trust for sale.[1] Therefore if A and B are tenants in common
for life, the land cannot be settled land and the statutory trust for
sale takes effect.[2] Similarly in the common case of a devise to A
for life and after his death to his children in equal shares: during
A's life the land is settled land, but on his death it must cease to be so.

In these situations the person or persons, whoever they may be,
in whom the legal estate is vested will forthwith hold it upon the
statutory trusts.[3] Any former Settled Land Act trustees are empowered to require the legal estate to be conveyed to them if it is not
already vested in them; for although the settlement is superseded
by the statutory trust for sale, it is appropriate that the same trustees
should be able to act, if they wish, in the new trust. If they do, they
will hold the land on the statutory trusts, namely, on trust for sale,

---

[94] S.L.A., 1882, s. 2 (6).
[95] S.L.A., 1925, s. 19 (2). For the position in case of disagreement, see *ante,* pp. 331, 365.
[96] S.L.A., 1925, s. 19 (3).
[97] *Ante,* p. 297.
[98] L.P.A., 1925, s. 26 (4), (5).
[99] *Ibid.,* s. 36 (1); *Re Gaul and Houlston's Contract* [1928] Ch. 689.
[1] *Cf.* the case where land is given to three persons upon their attaining full age, and only one is of full age: there is then a settlement for the time being: *Re Bird* [1927] 1 Ch. 210.
[2] S.L.A., 1925, s. 36 (1); L.P.A., 1925, 1st Sched., Pt. IV, para. 2; *Re Thomas* [1939] Ch. 513. As to pre-1926 settlements see L.P.A., 1925, 1st Sched., Pt. IV, para. 1 (3), *Re Ryder and Steadman's Contract* [1927] 2 Ch. 62 and *Re Catchpool* [1928] Ch. 429.
[3] S.L.A., 1925, s. 36 (1), (2).

with power to postpone sale, holding the income until sale and the proceeds thereafter upon such trusts and subject to such provisions as are requisite for giving effect to the rights of the persons interested in the land.[4]

The principal provision for carrying out this plan is section 36 of the Settled Land Act, 1925. At the outset it presents a problem of construction, for it applies where " settled land is held in trust for persons entitled in possession under a trust instrument [5] in undivided shares," [6] and it goes on to say that such land is to be held upon the statutory trusts. Of course, land held upon the statutory trusts cannot be settled land, for the trust for sale ousts the Settled Land Act.[7] In order to give the section the meaning which it is obviously intended to bear, its reference to " settled land " must be taken to mean " land which would otherwise be settled land " or " land which was previously settled land " [8]; for this purpose, apparently, " the effect of the trust for sale in putting an end to the settlement is to be ignored." [9]

2. Devolution on death. A consequential difficulty arises in tracing the devolution of the legal estate on death. We have seen how, in a settlement in due form upon A for life with remainder to B in fee simple, the legal estate devolves at A's death upon A's ordinary personal representatives, since the settlement no longer exists.[10] In a settlement upon A for life with remainder to his children in equal shares the same rule applies in the first instance. But then (paradoxical as it may seem [11]) section 36 of the Settled Land Act is also held to apply, so that the trustees of the settlement (which *ex hypothesi* no longer exists) may call upon A's personal representatives to convey the land to them; and if they are the same persons, they should assent in favour of themselves as trustees for sale.[12] In any case, of course, the land is held upon the statutory trusts, and is not settled land for any purpose other than the interpretation of section 36.

A similar procedure should presumably be followed in cases where the land would, apart from the section, continue to be settled,

---

[4] S.L.A., 1925, s. 36 (2), (6).
[5] See *Re Hind* [1933] Ch. 208 at 222, surmounting the difficulty where the shares arise by some disposition subsequent to the trust instrument.
[6] S.L.A., 1925, s. 36 (1).
[7] *Ante*, p. 360.
[8] *Cf.* Wolst. & C. iii, 106.
[9] Wolst. & C. i, 369, approved in *Re Cugny's W. T.* [1931] 1 Ch. 305 at 309; see also *Re Thomas* [1939] Ch. 513 at 519, *per* Bennett J.: the land " is still notionally for the purposes of the Act to be regarded as settled land."
[10] *Ante*, p. 309.
[11] See 71 L.J.News. 179.
[12] *Re Cugny's W. T., supra.* Despite the dictum at p. 309, this should be an ordinary assent, and not a vesting assent; and see *ante*, p. 312.

e.g., where the limitations are to A for life, remainder to his children as tenants in common for life, remainder to B in fee simple. On A's death, if he leaves children, the land becomes subject to the statutory trusts, and the former trustees of the settlement will have to call for the legal estate since it will have vested in A's ordinary personal representatives.[13]

3. Land devolving as a whole. There was one exception to these provisions, and that was where at the end of 1925 there were two or more tenants for life of full age entitled under some settlement in undivided shares and the whole of the land was limited to devolve together (not in undivided shares) after the cesser of all their interests in the income; in such a case, there was no trust for sale and the persons entitled held the legal estate as joint tenants and formed a composite tenant for life, without, of course, affecting their rights in equity.[14] For example, if land was settled on A and B as tenants in common for life with remainder to C for life, remainder to D in fee simple, this provision would apply, for after the cesser of the interests of A and B the land was limited to devolve as an undivided whole; thus A and B formed a composite tenant for life and there was no trust for sale. Had the land been limited after the death of A and B to their respective children, the ordinary rule would have applied and the Settled Land Act trustees would have held the land on trust for sale. The exception was purely transitional and had no application to settlements made after 1925. It received a narrow interpretation.[15]

4. Overreaching powers. Where the normal rule applies, the former Settled Land Act trustees hold on a special form of trust for sale which enables them to overreach not only the rights under the trust for sale but also any other rights existing under the former settlement and not protected by a legal mortgage.[16] For example, if land is settled on A for life, subject to an equitable rentcharge for B, with remainder to C and D as tenants in common, on the death of A the Settled Land Act trustees hold on trust for sale with power to overreach B's rentcharge even though it has priority to the trust for sale. This is therefore a case where trustees for sale can over-reach certain prior interests without having to resort to the " *ad hoc* " procedure.[17]

---

[13] *Ante*, p. 309.
[14] L.P.A., 1925, 1st Sched., Pt. IV, para. 4, added by L.P.(Am.)A., 1926, Sched.
[15] See *Re Colyer's Farningham Estate* [1927] 1 Ch. 677; *Re Higgs' and May's Contract* [1927] 2 Ch. 249; *Re Barrat* [1929] 1 Ch. 336.
[16] S.L.A., 1925, s. 36 (2); L.P.A., 1925, 1st Sched., Pt. IV, para. 1 (3), as amended by L.P.(Am.)A., 1926, Sched.; see *Re Flint* [1927] 1 Ch. 570.
[17] *Ante*, p. 379.

Sect. 8. Determination of Joint Tenancies and Tenancies in Common

Joint tenancies and tenancies in common may be determined by partition or by union in a sole tenant. As already explained, joint tenancies may also be determined by severance, which converts them into tenancies in common.

A. Partition

1. Voluntary partition. Joint tenants and tenants in common can always make a voluntary partition of the land concerned if all agree [18]; their co-ownership thus comes to an end by each of them becoming sole tenant of the piece of land allotted to him. This voluntary partition must be effected by deed.[19]

2. Compulsory partition. At common law there was no right to compel a partition.[20] Coparceners, who took their land by descent from the former owner,[21] were allowed to insist upon partition,[22] for as their co-ownership was " cast on them by the act of the law, and not by their own agreement, it was thought right that the perverseness of one should not prevent the others from obtaining a more beneficial method of enjoying the property." [23] This argument, however, was not applied to joint tenancy or tenancy in common, which necessarily arose by act of parties [24]; but by the Partition Acts, 1539 and 1540,[25] a statutory right to compel partition was conferred upon joint tenants and tenants in common,[26] one tenant being entitled to insist upon a partition [27] however inconvenient it might be.[28]

3. Sale. It was not until the Partition Act, 1868,[29] that the court was empowered to decree a sale instead of partition, an order which might be highly desirable where, for example, the cost of partition proceedings would exceed the value of the property,[30] or where a

---

[18] Litt. 290, 318.
[19] L.P.A., 1925, ss. 52 (1), 205 (1) (ii), replacing R.P.A., 1845, s. 3. For the previous law, see Co.Litt. 169a, 187a.
[20] Litt. 290, 318.
[21] See *post*, p. 429.
[22] Litt. 241.
[23] Williams R.P., 243, 244.
[24] *Ibid.*, 149; Bl.Comm. ii, 180.
[25] 31 Hen. 8, c. 1 (estates of inheritance); 32 Hen. 8, c. 32 (estates for life or years). The procedure was improved by the Partition Act, 1697 (8 & 9 Will. 3, c. 31).
[26] See note (2) to Co.Litt. 169a.
[27] *Parker* v. *Gerard* (1754) Amb. 236.
[28] *Warner* v. *Baynes* (1750) Amb. 589; *Baring* v. *Nash* (1813) 1 V. & B. 551 at 554.
[29] As amended by the Partition Act, 1876. See *Pemberton* v. *Barnes* (1871) 6 Ch.App. 685; *Powell* v. *Powell* (1874) 10 Ch.App. 130; *Drinkwater* v. *Ratcliffe* (1875) L.R. 20 Eq. 528.
[30] See *Griffies* v. *Griffies* (1863) 11 W.R. 943.

single house had to be partitioned into thirds, and the owner of two-thirds was given all the chimneys and fireplaces and the only stairs[31]; but if there were three houses, each share would have consisted of one house, and not a third of each house.[32]

The Partition Acts have now been repealed.[33] Instead, subject to certain qualifications, a power is given to the trustees for sale in whom the legal estate is vested to effect a partition with the consent of the beneficiaries, and convey the land to them.[34] If the trustees or any of the beneficiaries refuse to agree to a partition, any person interested[35] may apply to the court, which may make such order as it thinks fit,[36] such as an order for sale.

B. Union in a Sole Tenant

1. Union. Joint tenancies and tenancies in common may be determined by the entirety of the land becoming vested in a single beneficial owner. Thus where one of two surviving joint tenants dies, the other becomes sole tenant and the joint tenancy is at an end. Similarly if one joint tenant or tenant in common acquires the interests of all his fellows, as by purchase, the co-ownership is at an end.

2. Release. Because in theory each joint tenant is seised of the whole of the land, the appropriate way for one joint tenant[37] to transfer his rights to another joint tenant before 1926 was by a deed of release[38]; and this, which operated to extinguish rather than to convey, required no words of limitation.[39] Although it has now been retrospectively provided that one co-owner can convey to another by grant,[40] the power of a joint tenant to release his interest has been preserved,[41] so that a joint tenant may still release his legal estate or equitable interest (or both) to his fellow joint tenants. A release resembles a conveyance (and differs from a surrender[42]) in that it benefits only the person in whose favour it is made. Thus, subject

---

[31] See *Turner* v. *Morgan* (1803) 8 Ves. 143, 11 Ves. 157n.
[32] *Earl of Clarendon* v. *Hornby* (1718) 1 P.Wms. 446.
[33] L.P.(Am.)A., 1924, ss. 10, 12 (3), 10th Sched.; L.P.A., 1925, 7th Sched.
[34] L.P.A., 1925, s. 28 (3).
[35] For the meaning of " person interested," see *Stevens* v. *Hutchinson* [1953] Ch. 299.
[36] L.P.A., 1925, s. 30.
[37] Or coparcener (*post*, p. 430): Co.Litt. 193b.
[38] Co.Litt. 9b, 200b; Preston, *Abstracts*, ii, 61; Cru.Dig. ii, 382.
[39] *Estost's Case* (1597) 3 Dy. 263a; Co.Litt. 193b.
[40] L.P.A., 1925, s. 72 (4).
[41] *Ibid.*, s. 36 (2).
[42] See *ante*, p. 407.

to the rule that after 1925 a legal joint tenancy can never be severed,[43] if A, B and C are joint tenants and A releases his interest to B, B alone acquires A's one-third share, remaining joint tenant with C as to the other two-thirds.[44] Any purported conveyance will be construed as a release,[45] and so will a disclaimer to which the other joint tenants are parties.[46] A tenant in common, on the other hand, cannot release his share to his fellows, for "a release supposes the party to have the thing in demand;"[47] he has to convey it by some assurance by which a sole tenant can convey his land.[48]

3. Sale. Co-ownership in land is also extinguished if the land is duly sold to a purchaser under the statutory trusts; for the co-ownership is transferred from the land to the proceeds of sale, in which in theory of law it has always existed.

Part 2

COPARCENARY

Sect. 1. Before 1926

A. *Origin of Coparcenary*

When a person died intestate before 1926 his real property descended to his heir, who in most cases was a single person; thus if the intestate died leaving sons, normally the eldest son was the heir.[49] But sometimes two or more persons together constituted the heir, and in this case they took the land as "parceners" or "coparceners," the latter expression being the more common. This occurred [50]—

(i) At common law, where the intestate's nearest relatives were two or more females; thus where a man died leaving three daughters and no sons, the three daughters took as coparceners.[51]

---

[43] See *ante*, p. 408.
[44] *Ante*, p. 408; Litt. 304, 305, and Coke's comment. A release (like a grant) in such a case " doth enure by way of mitter l'estate, and not by way of extinguishment ": Co.Litt. 193a.
[45] *Eustace* v. *Scawen* (1624) Cro.Jac. 696; *Chester* v. *Willan* (1670) 2 Wms. Saund. 96.
[46] *Re Schär* [1951] Ch. 280.
[47] Co.Litt. 193a, n. (1).
[48] Preston, *Abstracts*, ii, 77; Challis 368.
[49] For details, see *post*, p. 508.
[50] See Litt. 241–276.
[51] See *post*, p. 510. A man might be a coparcener in certain cases by representing his mother, *e.g.*, if she predeceased her father (the intestate) but her son and one or more of the intestate's daughters survived him and took as coparceners: *ibid.*

(ii) By the custom of gavelkind,[52] where the intestate's nearest
relatives were two or more males; thus where a man died
leaving several sons, they took as coparceners.

In theory of law coparceners together constituted a single heir[53] :
" they be but one heire, and yet severall persons." [54]   They were
called parceners because, as already seen,[55] every coparcener had a
common law right to have a partition made.[56]

B. Nature of Coparcenary

Coparcenary bore resemblances both to joint tenancy and tenancy
in common. It resembled joint tenancy in two respects.

1. The four unities were normally present. Coparcenary could
arise only by operation of law[57]; a devise[58] or conveyance[59] to the
heirs of a person who had, say, two daughters and no sons made
those daughters joint tenants and not coparceners.[60]   As coparcenary
could thus arise only by descent on intestacy, the four unities were
usually present.[61]   But this was not always the case. Thus if X died
intestate leaving two daughters, and one of these subsequently died
intestate leaving three granddaughters, the three granddaughters
and the surviving daughter would be coparceners (for coparcenary
could continue as long as the land continued to descend on
intestacy[62]), yet the daughter would have a half share and each
granddaughter a one-sixth share, the half and the sixths having been
acquired at different times and being held by different titles.[63]

2. Coparceners were jointly seised for some purposes.[64]   Thus
a statute which applied to persons who were " seised . . . jointly "
has been held to apply to coparceners.[65]   Again, each coparcener
was sufficiently seised of the whole of the land for her (or him) to be
able to transfer his interest to the others by release.[66]

52 *Ante,* p. 20.
53 *Evans* v. *Evans* [1892] 2 Ch. 173 at 185; *Owen* v. *Gibbons* [1902] 1 Ch. 636
   at 648 ; Litt. 241 ; Co.Litt. 163b ; Preston, *Abstracts,* ii, 69.
54 Co.Litt. 164a.
55 *Ante,* p. 427.
56 Litt. 241 ; Co.Litt. 164b.
57 Williams R.P. 243.
58 *Re Baker* (1898) 79 L.T. 343.
59 *Berens* v. *Fellowes* (1887) 56 L.T. 391.
60 *Owen* v. *Gibbons* [1902] 1 Ch. 636.
61 See Bl.Comm. ii, 187, 188 ; Cru.Dig. ii, 391.
62 Litt. 313 ; Bl.Comm. ii, 188.
63 *Ibid.*; Co.Litt. 164b; Preston, *Abstracts,* ii, 68, 69; and see *post,* pp. 510, 511.
64 Preston, *Abstracts,* ii, 70.
65 *Re Templer's Trusts* (1864) 4 N.R. 494; *Re Greenwood's Trusts* (1884) 27
   Ch.D. 359 (T.A., 1850, s. 10); *cf. McMurray* v. *Spicer* (1868) L.R. 5 Eq. 527.
66 Co.Litt. 9b, 200b; Preston, *Abstracts,* ii, 69; and see *ibid.,* 70, 430, where
   coparceners are said to be seised *per my et per tout* (*cf. Murray* v. *Hall* (1849)
   7 C.B. 441 at 455n.). But see *ante,* p. 396, n. 48; also p. 392, n. 8.

On the other hand, coparcenary resembled tenancy in common in two other respects.

3. There was no jus accrescendi. The estate of a deceased coparcener passed under his will or intestacy in the same way as the estate of a tenant in common [67]; thus it was subject to curtesy or dower.[68]

4. Coparceners held in undivided shares. Each coparcener held a distinct but undivided share which might be equal or unequal in size to the shares of the others.[69] Thus the shares might be initially equal and subsequently become unequal, as in the example above, or they might be initially unequal, *e.g.*, where a man had two daughters and one predeceased him leaving two daughters, in which case the surviving daughter would take a half and the granddaughters a quarter each.[70] For the purpose of alienation *inter vivos* or on death, each coparcener was solely seised of his or her share.[71]

It will be seen that although it is possible to say that coparcenary is intermediate in its nature between joint tenancy and tenancy in common,[72] the rights of the coparceners *inter se* resemble in general those of tenants in common. Coparcenary is best regarded as " not a joint tenancy, but a tenancy in common of a peculiar nature, having some of the incidents of a joint tenancy." [73]

C. Determination of Coparcenary

Coparcenary might come to an end—

    (i) by partition [74];

    (ii) by union in a sole tenant [74];

    (iii) by alienation [74]; if a coparcener alienated his share, it was forthwith held under a tenancy in common,[75] the other tenants remaining coparceners *inter se*.[76]

---

[67] *Paterson* v. *Mills* (1850) 19 L.J.Ch. 310; *Cooper* v. *Frame* (1850) 19 L.J.Ch. 313; *Re Matson* [1897] 2 Ch. 509; Preston, *Abstracts*, ii, 70; Bl.Comm. ii, 188.

[68] Cru.Dig. ii, 394.

[69] Preston, *Abstracts*, ii, 68, 69; iii, 463; but see ii, 430, 431.

[70] *Ibid.*, ii, 68, 69.

[71] See Co.Litt. 164a; *McMurray* v. *Spicer* (1868) L.R. 5 Eq. 527 at 539.

[72] Burton's *Compendium* 112; Challis 374.

[73] *McMurray* v. *Spicer* (1868) L.R. 5 Eq. 527 at 538, *per* Malins V.-C.

[74] Bl.Comm. ii, 189–191.

[75] Litt. 309; *Doe* d. *Crosthwaite* v. *Dixon* (1836) 5 A. & E. 834 at 839. Thus at common law the remaining coparceners or coparcener could enforce a partition, but the purchaser, being a tenant in common, could not: see *Ballard* v. *Ballard* (1556) 2 Dy. 128a; Co.Litt. 175a.

[76] Tudor L.C. 267.

Sect. 2. After 1925

A. Transitional Provisions

Any coparcenaries existing at the end of 1925 were dealt with by the transitional provisions in the same way as tenancies in common, for these provisions applied to all cases of undivided shares.[77] The land thus became subject to a trust for sale and the coparcenary existed only as an equitable interest in the proceeds of sale.

B. Deaths after 1925

Descent to the heir has, in general, been abolished in the case of deaths after 1925, so that coparcenary normally cannot arise after 1925. The only possible occasions for it are the two exceptional cases[78] where, despite the new law of succession, real property still descends to the heir according to the general law in force before 1926. These are:

(i) where the deceased was a lunatic of full age at the end of 1925 and dies intestate in respect of the land without having recovered his testamentary capacity[78]; and

(ii) where the owner of an entail dies without having barred it.[78]

In both these cases coparcenary in equity can still arise if two or more females or their issue are entitled. The land will be held on trust for sale,[79] so that the coparcenary, like a tenancy in common, will exist in the proceeds of sale and not in the land itself. Coparcenary can no longer arise under the custom of gavelkind, since gavelkind has been abolished even in the above two exceptional cases.[80]

If coparceners become entitled in possession to settled land, they are apparently in the same position as tenants in common, *i.e.*, the land ceases to be settled land and is thenceforward held on the statutory trusts.[81] This is because they hold in undivided shares.

Part 3

TENANCY BY ENTIRETIES

Sect. 1. At Common Law

1. Creation. Before 1883, when land was limited to a husband and wife in such a way that they would have taken as joint tenants

---

[77] L.P.A., 1925, 1st Sched., Pt. IV, para. 1 (10). For these provisions, see *ante*, p. 418.

[78] Explained *post*, p. 531.

[79] In case (i), under A.E.A., 1925, s. 33; in case (ii), under S.L.A., 1925, s. 36 (1), (2).

[80] *Post*, p. 531.   [81] S.L.A., 1925, s. 36, explained *ante*, p. 424.

if they had not been married, they took as tenants by entireties and not as joint tenants,[82] even if the land was expressly conveyed to them "as joint tenants."[83]   Thus before 1883 a conveyance to

"H and W"

made them tenants by entireties, and a conveyance to

"H and W and X"

made H and W tenants by entireties *inter se* and joint tenants with X.[84]   On a severance, H and W would then normally have taken one moiety between them and X the other moiety, in accordance with the rule already explained.[85]   If at the time of the devise or conveyance the parties were not married, their subsequent marriage did not convert their joint tenancy into a tenancy by entireties[86]; and if tenants by entireties were divorced, they became ordinary joint tenants.[87]

2. Nature.   A tenancy by entireties could exist in any estate, whether in fee, for life, for years or otherwise.[88]   The nature of the tenancy was virtually that of an unseverable joint tenancy[89]; neither husband nor wife could dispose of any interest in the land without the concurrence of the other,[90] nor could one of them cause a forfeiture of the land.[91]   The unity of the husband and wife was regarded as being so complete that they were said to be seised "*per tout et non per my*,"[92] the survivor being entitled to the whole of the land by force of the original limitation discharged of the other's

---

[82] *Green* d. *Crew* v. *King* (1778) 2 Wm.Bl. 1211 at 1213; Challis 376; see generally Preston, *Abstracts*, ii, 39–57.

[83] *Pollok* v. *Kelly* (1856) 6 I.C.L.R. 367.

[84] *Back* v. *Andrew* (1690) 2 Vern. 120.

[85] *Ante*, pp. 421, 422.

[86] *Symond's Case* (1568) Moo.K.B. 92; *Ward* v. *Walthewe* (1607) Yelv. 101; *Hollet* v. *Sanders* (1683) 3 Lev. 107 at 108; *Moody* v. *Moody* (1767) Amb. 649 at 650; *Green* d. *Crew* v. *King* (1778) 2 Wm.Bl. 1211 at 1214; Co.Litt. 187b.

[87] *Anon.* (1540) B.N.C. 63; *Thornley* v. *Thornley* [1893] 2 Ch. 229.

[88] *Bredon's Case* (1597) 1 Co.Rep. 67b at 76b, n. D.1; Preston, *Abstracts*, ii, 39. See, *e.g.*, *Marquis of Winchester's Case* (1583) 3 Co.Rep. 1a (tail); *Doe* d. *Dormer* v. *Wilson* (1821) 4 B. & Ald. 303 (life); as to terms of years see note 90 below, and *Hales* v. *Petit* (1562) 1 Plowd. 253; *Whaley* v. *Anderson* (1665) T.Raym. 120 at 122.

[89] See Challis, 376n.; *Atcheson* v. *Atcheson* (1849) 11 Beav. 485 at 490; *Ward* v. *Ward* (1880) 14 Ch.D. 506 at 508.

[90] *Back* v. *Andrew, supra*; *Green* d. *Crew* v. *King, supra*; *Doe* d. *Freestone* v. *Parratt* (1794) 5 T.R. 652 at 654; *Crofton* v. *Bunbury* (1853) 2 Ir.Ch.R. 465 at 472. This rule did not apply to terms of years held by entireties, which the husband could dispose of freely (as indeed he could dispose of leaseholds owned by his wife alone: *post*, p. 994); see Challis 377, discussing the statements in Preston, *Abstracts*, ii, 39, 43, 57.

[91] Preston, i, 131.

[92] *Green* d. *Crew* v. *King* (1778) 2 Wm.Bl. 1211 at 1214; *Chamier* v. *Tyrell* [1894] 1 I.R. 267 at 271; Bl.Comm. ii, 182; Challis 367; *cf. ante*, pp. 392, 396, n. 48, 430, n. 66.

right to participate, and not, as in the case of joint tenancy, by virtue of survivorship on the death of the other tenant.[93]

Unlike joint tenants, neither tenant was regarded as having any potential share in the land; " there are no moieties between husband and wife." [94] Not even the rents and profits were divided: the husband was entitled to the whole of the income accruing during their joint lives.[95] " The husband and wife have not either a joint estate, a sole or several estate, nor even an estate in common. From the unity of their persons by marriage, they have the estate entirely as one individual " [96]; and, it may be added, that individual was the husband.

Sect. 2. The Married Women's Property Act, 1882

This Act did not affect existing tenancies by entireties, but it prevented the creation of such tenancies after 1882; a limitation to a husband and wife after 1882 without words of severance made them ordinary joint tenants.[97] The rule as to limitations to a husband, wife and one or more other people [98] was not changed by the Act.[99]

Sect. 3. The Law of Property Act, 1925

Few tenancies by entireties still existed at the end of 1925. Those that remained were, without prejudice to any beneficial interest (*e.g.*, the husband's right to the whole of the income during the joint lives), forthwith converted into joint tenancies.[1] But if a recent dictum is sound, in certain cases unseverable joint tenancies may still arise between husband and wife, with much the effect of tenancies by entireties.[2]

Part 4

PARTY WALLS

Sect. 1. Before 1926

Boundary walls dividing one property from another may be in the sole ownership of one owner, free from any rights of the other. But often each of the adjoining owners has certain rights over the walls.

---

[93] Tudor L.C. 287 ; 13 S.J. 946.
[94] *Marquis of Winchester's Case* (1583) 3 Co.Rep. 1a at 5b ; *cf. Green* d. *Crew* v. *King, supra.*
[95] *Chamier* v. *Tyrell* [1894] 1 I.R. 267.
[96] Preston, i, 131.
[97] ss. 1, 5; *Thornley* v. *Thornley* [1893] 2 Ch. 229. For this Act, see *post*, p. 994.
[98] *Ante*, p. 421.
[99] *Re Jupp* (1888) 39 Ch.D. 148.
[1] L.P.A., 1925, 1st Sched., Pt. VI ; and see Wolst. & C. i, 372.
[2] See *Bedson* v. *Bedson* [1965] 2 Q.B. 666 at 690; *ante*, p. 410.

Such walls are known as party walls, and need special treatment; for although party walls used to be subject to the ordinary law as to co-ownership or easements of support, they obviously had to be excepted from the new statutory trust for sale.

1. " Party wall." There is no precise definition of the expression " party wall " [3]; it might mean any one of the following [4]:

  (i) a wall of which the two adjoining owners were tenants in common [5]; or

  (ii) a wall divided longitudinally into two strips, one belonging to each of the neighbouring owners [6]; or

  (iii) a wall divided as in (ii), but each half being subject to an easement of support in favour of the owner of the other half [7]; or

  (iv) a wall belonging entirely to one of the adjoining owners, but subject to an easement or right in the other to have it maintained as a dividing wall. [8]

2. Presumptions. The presumption was in favour of a party wall falling within the first category, at all events if evidence was given that each owner had exercised dominion over the entire wall. [9] The first category had the disadvantage that either owner could insist upon a partition, [10] but it was less unsatisfactory than the second category, where either owner, acting with reasonable care, [11] could remove his half of the wall and leave a structure which was perhaps incapable of standing alone. [12] This could not be done in the case of walls in the third category, owing to the easement of support; but this merely prohibited the positive removal of support, and did not require either owner to repair his half of the wall, although

---

[3] *Kempston* v. *Butler* (1861) 12 Ir.C.L.R. 516 at 526.

[4] *Watson* v. *Gray* (1880) 14 Ch.D. 192 at 194, 195.

[5] *Wiltshire* v. *Sidford* (1827) 1 Man. & Ry. 404; *Cubitt* v. *Porter* (1828) 8 B. & C. 257; *Watson* v. *Gray* (1880) 14 Ch.D. 192.

[6] *Matts* v. *Hawkins* (1813) 5 Taunt. 20.

[7] See *Wiltshire* v. *Sidford, supra,* at p. 408; *Jones* v. *Pritchard* [1908] 1 Ch. 630.

[8] See *Sheffield Improved Industrial and Provident Society* v. *Jarvis* [1871] W.N. 208; [1872] W.N. 47.

[9] *Wiltshire* v. *Sidford, supra,* at pp. 407, 408; *Cubitt* v. *Porter, supra*; *Jones* v. *Read* (1876) 10 I.R.C.L. 315; *Standard Bank of British South America* v. *Stokes* (1878) 9 Ch.D. 68 at 71; *Watson* v. *Gray* (1880) 14 Ch.D. 192 at 194, 195.

[10] *Mayfair Property Co.* v. *Johnston* [1894] 1 Ch. 508. The alternative of a sale (introduced by the Partition Act, 1868) was normally unsuitable.

[11] See *Bradbee* v. *Governors of Christ's Hospital* (1842) 4 Man. & G. 714 at 760, 761; *Kempston* v. *Butler* (1861) 12 Ir.C.L.R. 516. It was desirable (see *Massey* v. *Goyder* (1829) 4 C. & P. 161) but not essential (*Chadwick* v. *Trower* (1839) 6 Bing.N.C. 1) to give warning of the intention to pull down the wall.

[12] *Wigford* v. *Gill* (1592) Cro.Eliz. 269; *Wiltshire* v. *Sidford* (1827) 1 Man. & Ry. 404 at 408; *Cubitt* v. *Porter* (1828) 8 B. & C. 257 at 264.

either if he wished might repair his neighbour's half.[13] Neither owner could pull down a wall of the first kind[14] except for the purpose of rebuilding it with all reasonable despatch,[15] nor could either prevent the other from enjoying any part of the wall, as by covering the top with broken glass or replacing it with part of a shed.[16] There was no presumption in favour of the third or fourth categories because these could be established only on proof that the appropriate easements existed.[17]

3. Ownership of soil. The presumption in favour of the first category applied only where the exact situation of the boundary could not be shown, or where the site of the wall could be shown to have been owned in common.[18] Where the wall was built entirely on A's land, the presumption was that the wall was A's[19]; and where the wall was built on the boundary, so that substantially[20] half the soil on which it stood was A's and half B's, the case usually fell into the second or third category,[21] the wall being regarded as divided into two walls each of half the thickness.[22] The principle in these cases was that " as a matter of law, the property in the wall followed the property in the land upon which it stood." [23] Subject to this, the ownership of the wall was a question of fact for the jury.[24] A wall might even be in sole ownership for part of its height and a party wall for the rest.[25]

In some parts of the country, particularly London, these rules have been modified to some extent by statute.[26]

---

13 *Jones* v. *Pritchard* [1908] 1 Ch. 630 at 637, 638; *Sack* v. *Jones* [1925] Ch. 235; *post*, p. 879.
14 *Jones* v. *Read* (1876) 10 Ir.R.C.L. 315.
15 *Cubitt* v. *Porter* (1828) 8 B. & C. 257; *Standard Bank of British South America* v. *Stokes* (1878) 9 Ch.D. 68 at 71, 72; *Joliffe* .v. *Woodhouse* (1894) 38 S.J. 578.
16 *Stedman* v. *Smith* (1857) 8 E. & B. 1 at 6, 7.
17 See *post*, p. 827.
18 See *Wiltshire* v. *Sidford* (1827) 1 Man. & Ry. 404 at 407, 409.
19 *Hutchinson* v. *Mains* (1832) Alc. & N. 155. Similarly, if A makes an addition to B's wall, the addition prima facie belongs to B: *Waddington* v. *Naylor* (1889) 60 L.T. 480.
20 See *Reading* v. *Barnard* (1827) Moo. & M. 71 at 73, 74.
21 *Matts* v. *Hawkins* (1813) 5 Taunt. 20; *Kempston* v. *Butler* (1861) 12 Ir.C.L.R. 516 at 526; compare *Mason* v. *Fulham Corporation* [1910] 1 K.B. 631 at 637. The presumption to this effect was perhaps not very strong: see *Cubitt* v. *Porter* (1828) 8 B. & C. 257 at 263, 264.
22 *Murly* v. *M'Dermott* (1838) 8 A. & E. 138 at 142.
23 *Jones* v. *Read* (1876) 10 I.R.C.L. 315 at 320, *per* Palles C.B.
24 See *Cubitt* v. *Porter* (1828) 8 B. & C. 257; *Thornhill* v. *Davies* (1859) 32 L.T.(o.s.) 261.
25 *Weston* v. *Arnold* (1873) 8 Ch.App. 1084; *Newton* v. *Huggins & Co. Ltd.* (1906) 50 S.J. 617; and see *Drury* v. *Army & Navy Auxiliary Co-operative Supply Ltd.* [1896] 2 Q.B. 271.
26 See the London Building Acts (Amendment) Act, 1939, Part VI, replacing earlier statutes; and see *Standard Bank of British South America* v. *Stokes* (1878) 9 Ch.D. 68 (London); *Weston* v. *Arnold* (1873) 8 Ch.App. 1084 (Bristol). In the London Act the definitions of " party wall " (see, ss. 4 (1), 44) are wide enough to cover walls in sole ownership: see *Knight* v. *Pursell* (1879) 11 Ch.D. 412.

Sect. 2. After 1925

Unless special provision had been made, all party walls in the first category would have become subject to a trust for sale after 1925. It was consequently provided that after 1925 all party walls in this category, whether created before 1926 [27] or after 1925,[28] should be deemed to be severed vertically, and that the owner of each part should have such rights of support and user over the rest of the wall as were requisite for giving the parties rights similar to those which they would have enjoyed had they been tenants in common of the wall.[29] The practical effect of this provision is to translate all party walls in the first category into the third. Apart from this, the law of party walls remains unchanged.

---

[27] L.P.A., 1925, 1st Sched., Pt. V, para. 1.
[28] *Ibid.*, s. 38 (1).
[29] *Ibid.*, s. 38, 1st Sched., Pt. V. In case of dispute the court may make an order declaratory of the rights of the parties: *ibid.*

CHAPTER 8

TRUSTS AND POWERS

THE nature of trusts and powers has already been briefly discussed in connection with settlements.[1] The principal distinction is that whereas a trust is normally imperative, binding the trustee to carry out a duty, a power is discretionary, enabling the donee of the power to exercise it if he wishes but not binding him to do so. Much of the law of trusts and powers is more appropriate to textbooks on equity than to a book on real property, but some account must be given here of the points which most concern the law of land. They will be dealt with under the heads of—

(1) Trusts.
(2) Trustees.
(3) Powers.

Part 1

TRUSTS

Sect. 1. Classification

A. Conveyancing Classification

1. Classification. From the point of view of a conveyancer, a trust of land may fall under one of three heads:

(1) Settled land.
(2) Trust for sale.
(3) Trust for one beneficiary absolutely.

The first two have already been dealt with,[2] and between them cover all cases where the interests of the beneficiaries are successive or concurrent, or where a beneficiary is an infant.

2. Bare trusts. The only remaining class[3] is therefore the third, where the trust is simply to hold or manage the land for the sole benefit of one beneficiary who is of full age. Such a trust is called a bare, or simple, trust.[4] It arises when the nature of the trust is not

---

[1] *Ante*, Chap. 6.
[2] *Ante*, Chap. 6.
[3] This classification is not necessarily exhaustive: consider, *e.g.*, charitable trusts. But for this purpose they may be treated as settled land: see *post*, p. 1001.
[4] Lewin 6; Underhill, *Trusts* (12th ed., 1970) p. 12.

prescribed by the settlor but is left to the ordinary rules of law, as where T purchases land with money provided by A,[5] or X conveys land

" to T in fee simple on trust for A in fee simple."

In such a case the position of the parties is similar to that under a simple use before 1535 [6]; T is bound to permit A to occupy the land or receive the rents and profits and must obey A's instructions about the disposition of the land.[7] A may therefore call for an outright conveyance to himself from T; for it is pointless to keep the legal and equitable interests separated where only one person is entitled to the whole beneficial interest. This is equally true if the trustees are expressly given duties to perform, *e.g.*, to sell, or to accumulate the income, provided that all such duties are for the benefit of one person only, and that person is of full age; this is the basis of the rule in *Saunders* v. *Vautier*,[8] which has already been encountered.[9]

The transitional vesting provisions of the Law of Property Act, 1925 (which were intended to settle the ownership of outstanding legal estates) had the effect of terminating any trusts of the third class which were in existence at the beginning of 1926; for it is provided that where at the beginning of 1926 a person was entitled to require a legal estate (not vested in trustees for sale) to be vested in him, the legal estate automatically vested in him without further formality.[10] But there is nothing to prevent such trusts from being created after 1925.

B. *Equity's Classification*

In equity, the main classification of trusts is as statutory, express, implied, resulting or constructive trusts; but there are also other classifications. The main classification is to some extent one of convenience: there is no general agreement.[11]

1. Trusts imposed by statute. Various trusts are imposed by statute. Some are expressly entitled " statutory trusts," as with the trust for sale in the case of co-ownership [12] and the trusts for

---

[5] See *Dyer* v. *Dyer* (1788) 2 Cox Eq. 92 at 93; *Finch* v. *Finch* (1808) 15 Ves. 43 at 50.
[6] *Ante*, p. 153. [7] Lewin 6; Williams R.P. 191.
[8] (1841) 4 Beav. 115; Cr. & Ph. 240. [9] *Ante*, p. 278.
[10] L.P.A., 1925, 1st Sched., Pt. II, paras. 3, 6 (*d*); but the L.P.(Am.)A., 1926, Sched., protects purchasers for money or money's worth from the trustee without notice of the trust, provided that the documents of title are produced by the trustee or his successor in title.
[11] See Snell, *Equity*, 99.
[12] *Ante*, p. 408.

certain relations on an intestacy.[13] Others, although not given this name, are nevertheless trusts imposed by statute, *e.g.*, the trust for sale imposed on the property of an intestate,[14] or on property which trustees have obtained by foreclosure,[15] or on land purchased by trustees of a personalty settlement [16]; and by statute a trust is created by an attempt to convey a legal estate in land to an infant.[17]

2. Express trusts. These are trusts declared by a settlor. To create an express trust, the " three certainties " of a trust must be present, *i.e.*, imperative words, certainty of subject-matter, and certainty of objects.[18]

(*a*) *Imperative words.* The settlor must indicate that a trust is intended. The old rule was that words such as " in the full confidence " or " recommending " or " my dying request " would prima facie be construed as creating a trust; these were called precatory words.[19] The present law, however, is that precatory words create no trust unless the instrument as a whole shows an intention that they should.[20]

Where the words are not imperative, the donee holds the property beneficially free from any trust.[21]

(*b*) *Certainty of subject-matter.* Both the property to be vested in the trustee and the beneficial interest to be taken by each beneficiary must be defined with sufficient certainty. If there is no certainty as to what is conveyed to the trustee, the entire transaction is ineffective, *e.g.*, if a testator purports to leave " the bulk of my property " to trustees.[22] Examples of uncertainty of beneficial interest occur where defined property is given to X on trust that he should leave to A and B " the bulk " of it [23] or " such parts of my estate as he shall not have sold or disposed of." [24] In. such cases the donee holds the property beneficially free from any trust,[25]

---

[13] *Post*, p. 527.
[14] *Post*, p. 523.
[15] L.P.A., 1925, s. 31; *ante*, p. 364.
[16] L.P.A., 1925, s. 32. This applies only to settlements coming into operation after 1911, and can be negatived by the settlement.
[17] S.L.A., 1925, s. 27; *ante*, p. 408; *post*, p. 988.
[18] See Snell, *Equity*, 111 *et seq.*; *Knight* v. *Knight* (1840) 3 Beav. 148 at 173; Glanville Williams (1940) 2 M.L.R. 20.
[19] See, *e.g.*, *Harding* v. *Glyn* (1739) 1 Atk. 469; Wh. & T. ii, 285.
[20] See *Re Adams and the Kensington Vestry* (1884) 27 Ch.D. 394 at 410; *Re Williams* [1897] 2 Ch.. 12; *Comiskey* v. *Bowring-Hanbury* [1905] A.C. 84; *Re Johnson* [1939] 2 All E.R. 458.
[21] See, *e.g.*, *McCormick* v. *Grogan* (1869) L.R. 4 H.L. 82.
[22] *Palmer* v. *Simmonds* (1854) 2 Drew. 221; contrast *Bromley* v. *Tryon* [1952] A.C. 265.   [23] See note 22, *supra*.
[24] *Re Jones* [1898] 1 Ch. 438; *cf. Re Sanford* [1901] 1 Ch. 939. But as to executory trusts, see *post*, p. 447; and see Snell, *Equity*, 116.
[25] See, *e.g.*, *Fox* v. *Fox* (1859) 27 Beav. 301.

unless it is clear that the whole of the property was intended to be held on trust and the only uncertainty is which part was intended for each beneficiary; in that case the donee will hold on a resulting trust for the settlor.[26]

(c) *Certainty of objects.* The objects (*i.e.,* the persons or purposes intended to benefit by the trust) must be defined with sufficient certainty. Trusts for " encouraging undertakings of general utility " [27] or " parish work " [28] or " such charitable or benevolent objects in England as the trustees may select " [29] are void for uncertainty of object. But there is an exception in favour of trusts for charities where the settlor has limited the objects to charity in the strict legal sense, since the Crown in some cases and the court in others will direct a suitable mode of application.[30] Thus it happens that a trust for " charitable and benevolent " objects is valid but a trust for " charitable or benevolent " objects is void.[31]

If a trust is void for uncertainty of objects, there is a resulting trust for the settlor.[32]

3. Implied trusts. An implied trust is said to arise where, without any conveyance of the property in question having been made, two people enter into such a relationship with each other that equity implies therefrom that one holds on trust for the other. Thus if one person agrees for value to make a settlement or conveyance of his estate, equity forthwith deems him to be a trustee of that estate for the beneficiaries or the purchaser.[33] In the case of a contract of sale, the trust is of a peculiar nature, for the vendor has certain valuable rights against the purchaser, such as the right of occupation until the date agreed for completion, and an equitable lien for the price.[34] Nevertheless the trust relationship is established, for it will be a breach of trust for the vendor to convey the land to anyone except the purchaser, or negligently to allow the land to be damaged.[34] Another case of an implied trust arises where two people agree to leave their property in the same way (*e.g.,* to the survivor for life, with remainder to X) and make mutual wills in pursuance thereof. In such a case, on the death of one of them, the

---

[26] See, *e.g., Boyce* v. *Boyce* (1849) 16 Sim. 476 ; *cf. Re Clarke* [1923] 2 Ch. 407.
[27] *Kendall* v. *Granger* (1842) 5 Beav. 300.
[28] *Farley* v. *Westminster Bank* [1939] A.C. 430.
[29] *Chichester Diocesan Fund* v. *Simpson* [1944] A.C. 341.
[30] *Morice* v. *Bishop of Durham* (1804) 9 Ves. 399 at 405.
[31] *Chichester Diocesan Fund* v. *Simpson* [1944] A.C. 341.
[32] See, *e.g., Kendall* v. *Granger* (1842) 5 Beav. 300 ; *Re Carville* [1937] 4 All E.R. 464.
[33] *Ante,* p. 132 ; *post,* p. 575.
[34] *Post,* p. 575.

property then owned by the survivor is forthwith impressed with an implied trust for X, so that even if the survivor revokes his will (as he can still do) he cannot frustrate the agreement.[35]

4. Constructive trusts. These are primarily trusts arising by operation of equity from a fiduciary relationship already in existence. Thus if by virtue of his position a trustee obtains any valuable interest in the trust property for himself, the general rule is that he holds it on a constructive trust for the beneficiaries.[36] An example is where a trustee of a lease obtains a renewal for his own benefit.[37] Again, anyone to whom trust property is conveyed usually holds it on a constructive trust if he knew that the conveyance was in breach of trust, or if, without being protected by the plea of purchaser without notice, he afterwards deals with the property in a way he knows to be inconsistent with the trust.[38] There are also other types of case, of a somewhat uncertain ambit, where equity imposes a constructive trust in order to prevent someone profiting from his wrong-doing.[39]

5. Resulting trusts. A resulting trust is said to exist where, on a conveyance of property, a trust arises by operation of equity.[40] Three cases must be considered.

(*a*) *Trusts not exhaustive.* Where a disposition of property is made by the owner, and all or part of the equitable interest is not effectively disposed of, there is a resulting trust for the owner. If the property is conveyed expressly on trust, *e.g.,*

" to X on trust,"

there is no difficulty; a trustee can take no benefit from the fact that the declared trusts do not exhaust the beneficial interest, and so much of the equitable interest as is not disposed of results to the grantor.[41] Thus if G conveys property to X on trust for a beneficiary who is dead, there is a resulting trust of the entire beneficial interest in favour of G.[42] Again, where before 1926 G conveyed land to trustees on trust for herself for life and then on trust for her heir-at-law, without words of limitation, the heir took only a life estate and there was a resulting trust in fee simple in favour of

---

[35] *Dufour* v. *Pereira* (1769) Dick. 419; *Re Hagger* [1930] 2 Ch. 190; Snell, *Equity*, 182–184; *post*, p. 475.
[36] Lewin 141, 142; and see *Re Biss* [1903] 2 Ch. 40.
[37] *Keech* v. *Sandford* (1726) Sel.Ca.t.King 61; *cf. Re Morgan* (1881) 18 Ch.D. 93. See generally Snell, *Equity*, 236–238.
[38] *Soar* v. *Ashwell* [1893] 2 Q.B. 390 at 396; Snell, *Equity*, 185–188.
[39] See Snell, *Equity*, 185; *ante*, p. 407.
[40] For the distinction between automatic and presumed resulting trusts, see *Re Vandervell's Trusts (No. 2)* [1974] Ch. 269 at 289 (not affected on appeal).
[41] See *Merchant Taylors' Co.* v. *Att.-Gen.* (1871) 6 Ch.App. 512 at 518.
[42] *Re Tilt* (1896) 74 L.T. 163.

G.[43] But the rule that there is a resulting trust yields to any contrary intention that the trustee is to take beneficially.[44]

(b) *Voluntary conveyance.* Where before 1926 property was conveyed without any consideration, but not expressly on trust, difficult questions could arise. Resulting uses and resulting trusts must be distinguished, for after the Statute of Uses, 1535, a resulting use would be executed by the statute and so carry the legal estate back to the grantor,[45] whereas a resulting trust was purely equitable, so that the grantee would continue to hold the legal estate as trustee for the grantor.

(1) RESULTING USES. Before 1535 it had been settled that on a voluntary conveyance in fee simple by A to B in which no use was expressed, there was a presumption of a resulting use to the grantor of the whole estate granted.[46] If it appeared that a gift was intended, as where a use was expressed in the conveyance (*e.g.*, in favour of B), that of course prevented a resulting use from being implied. A resulting use was also excluded if the conveyance was made either for valuable consideration (even if nominal [47]) or for good consideration, *e.g.*, the " natural love and affection " that indicated a genuine gift if B was a near relation of A.[48] If B held of A in tenure, that also sufficed, so that no resulting use arose on a grant in tail, for life or for years.[49]

(2) RESULTING TRUSTS. After the Statute of Uses, 1535, a resulting use was executed by the Statute, with the result that such a conveyance was totally ineffective, and A was regarded as holding the same estate as before.[50] When trusts later came into use and a grant " unto and to the use of B " became common form merely for the purpose of vesting the legal estate in B, whether or not upon further trusts,[51] it was arguable that a voluntary grant in such terms raised a resulting trust in equity· for the grantor, by analogy with the old doctrine of resulting uses. But, rather curiously, this question

---

[43] *Re Davison's Settlement* [1913] 2 Ch. 498.
[44] See, *e.g.*, *Smith* v. *Cooke* [1891] A.C. 297.
[45] *Ante*, p. 156.
[46] H.E.L. iv, 424; *Beckwith's Case* (1589) 2 Co.Rep. 56b at 58a; *Armstrong* d. *Neve* v. *Wolsey* (1755) 2 Wils.K.B. 19; Sanders, *Uses*, i, 60, 97, 365; Williams R.P. 185, 186; Norton, *Deeds*, 410; and see *ante*, pp. 156, 157.
[47] *Case of Sutton's Hospital* (1612) 10 Co.Rep. 1a.
[48] See Sanders, *Uses*, ii, 98–100; Snell, *Equity*, 124; *ante*, p. 116.
[49] H.E.L. iv, 429. The statute *Quia Emptores*, 1290, prevented tenure arising between grantor and grantee on grants in fee simple (*ante*, p. 31) but not on grants of lesser estates.
[50] See the authorities cited in n. 46, *supra*, and *Godbold* v. *Freestone* (1694) 3 Lev. 406 at 407; *Harris* v. *Bishop of Lincoln* (1723) 2 P.Wms. 135; Preston, *Conveyancing*, ii, 487. Such a conveyance did not even " break the descent " so as to make A a " purchaser " (see *post*, p. 509): Williams, *Seisin*, 60–63, 84.
[51] *Ante*, p. 171.

was never settled. The old authorities seem to show that a resulting trust would arise if circumstances pointed to the conclusion that the grantee was not intended to take beneficially,[52] but that in the absence of such evidence the grantee would take for his own use.[53] Unlike resulting uses, resulting trusts were not excluded merely by the presence of a nominal consideration.[54] In practice it would nearly always be made clear whether a voluntary conveyance was intended as a gift or not, so that the point was never squarely raised in a modern case.[55]

(3) AFTER 1925. The Law of Property Act, 1925, has disposed of the difficulty in the case of conveyances executed after 1925. Since uses can no longer be executed and so turned into legal estates, the old form of conveyance " unto and to the use of A " is now obsolete: a conveyance simply " to A " now suffices.[56] But upon this formula in a voluntary conveyance a resulting use would still arise in equity, and take effect as a trust, for the repeal of the Statute of Uses does not alter the equitable principle under which the use resulted. This is however prevented by the new rule that " in a voluntary conveyance a resulting trust shall not be implied merely by reason that the property is not expressed to be conveyed for the use or benefit of the grantee." [57] Since in a voluntary grant made after 1925 " to A for his own benefit " the last four words would undoubtedly rebut a resulting trust, it follows that a resulting trust cannot now arise merely from the omission of any such formula in a grant made simply " to A," with no indication whether or not A was intended to take for his own benefit.[58] Where there is evidence that A was to take as trustee for the grantor, there will be a resulting trust to that effect.[59]

---

52 *Duke of Norfolk* v. *Browne* (1697) Prec.Ch. 80; *R.* v. *Williams* (1735) Bunb. 342.
53 *Lloyd* v. *Spillet* (1740) 2 Atk. 148; *Young* v. *Peachey* (1741) 2 Atk. 254. Lord Hardwicke was clearly of opinion that there was no imperative rule demanding a resulting trust.
54 See *Hayes* v. *Kingdome* (1681) 1 Vern. 33 at 34; *Sculthorp* v. *Burgess* (1790) 1 Ves.Jun. 91 at 92.
55 Though see the remarks of Jessel M.R. in *Strong* v. *Bird* (1874) L.R. 18 Eq. 315 at 318; and (in the opposite sense) of James L.J. in *Fowkes* v. *Pascoe* (1875) 10 Ch.App. 343 at 348. The authorities are collected in the editorial note to Maitland, *Equity*, 1936 ed., 330. Text-writers conflict equally freely on the question: see Wh. & T. ii, 762. A resulting trust was favoured by Maitland, *Equity*, 77; Williams R.P. 194; Lewin 131; and opposed by Sanders, *Uses*, i, 365; Ashburner, *Equity*, 107.
56 *Ante*, p. 171.
57 L.P.A., 1925, s. 60 (3), (4).
58 The contrary view in Underhill, *Trusts* (12th ed., 1970) pp. 206, 219 (repeating earlier editions) cannot be relied upon as it appears to ignore L.P.A., 1925, s. 60 (3).
59 *Hodgson* v. *Marks* [1971] Ch. 892, admitting evidence of oral agreement not indicated in the grant.

(4) ADVANCEMENT. One class of cases was always outside the doctrine of resulting trusts: where the grantee was the wife or child of the grantor there was a contrary presumption ("the presumption of advancement") that a beneficial gift was intended.[60] But other relationships (*e.g.*, where the grantee was husband or nephew of the grantor) raised no such presumption. The presumption could always be rebutted by evidence that the wife or child was intended to take as trustee.[61]

(*c*) *Purchase with another's money.* Where land is conveyed to one person, but the purchase-money is provided by another as purchaser,[62] there is a resulting trust in favour of the person providing the purchase-money. If V conveys land to P, A being the real purchaser and as such providing the purchase-money, prima facie P holds on a resulting trust for A.[63] Similarly if A provides part of the purchase-money [64] he acquires a proportionate share in equity.[65] Nevertheless these are only presumptions which can be rebutted either—

  (i) by evidence that P was intended to benefit,[66] or
  (ii) by the presumption of advancement (itself rebuttable) which arises if P is the wife or child of A.[67]

(*d*) *Expenditure on another's land.* Where A spends money on buildings or improvements on B's land, with B's agreement but with no intention of a gift or a loan, there will be a resulting or constructive trust for A proportionate to his expenditure. An example of this was where A was B's mother-in-law and had paid for an extension to accommodate her in B's house, but later had to leave owing to differences.[68] Alternatively, the court may impose an equitable lien for the sum expended.[69]

(*e*) *Spouses and fiancés.* As the result of much litigation over the rights of husband and wife in the matrimonial home (usually after the breakdown of the marriage) it is now established that there is no special law of "family assets," and that the ordinary law

---

[60] See Snell, *Equity*, 176–178.
[61] *Stock* v. *McAvoy* (1872) L.R. 15 Eq. 55.
[62] And not, for example, as mortgagee.
[63] *Dyer* v. *Dyer* (1788) 2 Cox Eq. 92.
[64] *Secus* rent under a tenancy, for this purchases no asset but merely pays for the use of the property: *Savage* v. *Dunningham* [1974] Ch. 181.
[65] *Wray* v. *Steele* (1814) 2 V. & B. 388; *Heseltine* v. *Heseltine* [1971] 1 W.L.R. 342 (money provided by wife).
[66] *e.g.*, *Standing* v. *Bowring* (1885) 31 Ch.D. 282.
[67] See above.
[68] *Hussey* v. *Palmer* [1972] 1 W.L.R. 1286.
[69] *Unity Joint Stock Mutual Banking Association* v. *King* (1858) 25 Beav. 72; *cf. Chalmers* v. *Pardoe* [1963] 1 W.L.R. 677. Such a lien is one manifestation of proprietary estoppel: see Snell, *Equity*, 565–568.

of ownership is modified only where there is some trust, whether implied, resulting or constructive.[70] As between husband and wife, and (by statute) as between engaged couples who break off the engagement,[71] such a trust will be inferred when the result would otherwise be inequitable, and in particular when they have acquired a home in the name of one or both of them with the intention of sharing the ownership between them. A general intention to share without specifying the proportions will produce a resulting trust for them in equal shares. If proportions have been agreed at the time of acquisition, the court will give effect to the agreement, even though oral.[72] If they have both contributed, their shares will be proportionate to their contributions,[73] unless they have agreed otherwise.

In these cases the court is concerned with "the cold legal question"[74] of what were the respective interests originally intended. Where these are determined by contributions, any contributions arranged at the time of the purchase may suffice, even if they are indirect, as where the wife agreed to go out to work so that her earnings would enable her husband to pay the mortgage instalments[75]; but no trust arises merely from contributions arranged subsequently, even if they are direct payments of mortgage instalments.[76] Improvements, however, are an exception: the Matrimonial Proceedings and Property Act 1970[77] has "declared" that substantial contributions in money or money's worth by a husband or wife to the improvement of real or personal property[78] belonging beneficially to either or both of them are to entitle the contributor to such a share as was agreed, or, in default "as may seem in all the circumstances just." The Act does not explain how this rule is to take effect,[79] but presumably there will be a trust for sale analogous to a resulting trust.

---

[70] *Gissing* v. *Gissing* [1971] A.C. 886.
[71] Law Reform (Miscellaneous Provisions) Act 1970, s. 2, applying the general law of matrimonial property to cases where an agreement to marry is terminated.
[72] *Gissing* v. *Gissing, supra*, at pp. 905, 906, *per* Lord Diplock. Analytically it may depend upon an assumed agreement as to the relative financial contributions: see *Cowcher* v. *Cowcher* [1972] 1 W.L.R. 425 at 436, a valuable judgment of Bagnall J.
[73] See *Heseltine* v. *Heseltine* [1971] 1 W.L.R. 342.
[74] *Gissing* v. *Gissing* [1969] 2 Ch. 85 at 93, *per* Lord Denning M.R.
[75] *Hazell* v. *Hazell* [1972] 1 W.L.R. 301.
[76] *Cowcher* v. *Cowcher, supra*; *Kowalczuk* v. *Kowalczuk* [1973] 1 W.L.R. 930 at 934, 935, *per* Buckley L.J.
[77] s. 37, extended to engaged couples as explained above, n. 71. This provision, being declaratory, is retrospective: *Davis* v. *Vale* [1971] 1 W.L.R. 1022. But it does not accord with *Pettitt* v. *Pettitt* [1970] A.C. 777, where the House of Lords held that improvements made by the husband did not entitle him to a share.
[78] See *Harnett* v. *Harnett* [1973] Fam. 156 (contributions must be identifiable with relevant improvements: not discussed on appeal, [1974] 1 W.L.R. 219); *Re Nicholson* [1974] 1 W.L.R. 476.
[79] It is not stated whether the share is a legal or equitable interest or a "mere equity" (*ante*, p. 119). An equitable interest seems most probable.

The logical result in conveyancing would be to make marriage a blot on the title to the matrimonial home. Without making intimate inquiries a purchaser from a husband or wife will have no means of knowing whether resulting or statutory trusts exist in favour of the other spouse and whether he should obey the rules for trusts for sale.[80] But the court has recoiled from extending the doctrine of notice so as to require " embarrassing " and " intolerable " inquiries which would turn purchasers into " snoopers and busybodies " and " create impossible difficulties for those dealing with the property of a married man." [81] Inevitably, therefore, any equitable interest of the other spouse is exceptionally insecure, since it may easily be defeated by a purchase of the legal estate without notice.[82]

6. Other classifications. In addition to the main classification considered above, equity classified trusts in other ways. Two of these must be considered here.

(*a*) *Executed and executory trusts.* Executory trusts are trusts which call for the execution of some further instrument for the purpose of defining the beneficial interests exactly. For example, marriage articles often provided that certain property belonging to one of the parties should be settled upon them and their children. The property is at once subject to a valid trust, but until the settlement is duly executed the trust is executory. The importance of the distinction between executed and executory trusts lies in the more liberal manner in which executory trusts are construed for some purposes.[83]

(*b*) *Completely and incompletely constituted trusts*

(1) CLASSIFICATION. This classification must not be confused with the preceding. A trust is completely constituted as soon as the trust property is vested in the trustee; until this has been done, it is incompletely constituted. All trusts created by will are completely constituted, but they may be either executed or executory; a bequest of £10,000 to A and B on trust to buy land with it, and settle the land on C and his children, is executory but nevertheless completely constituted.

---

[80] *Ante,* p. 378.
[81] *Caunce* v. *Caunce* [1969] 1 W.L.R. 286 at 294, *per* Stamp J. (house mortgaged to bank by husband as sole owner; wife's equitable interest as joint tenant defeated by bank as purchaser without notice); *National Provincial Bank Ltd.* v. *Ainsworth* [1965] A.C. 1175 at 1234, 1248. The phrase last quoted in the text is Lord Wilberforce's (*ibid.* p. 1248).
[82] In the case of registered land it must be protected by registering a minor interest: *post,* p. 1068.
[83] See, *e.g., ante,* pp. 131, 403; and see Snell, *Equity,* 116–118.

(2) COMPLETELY CONSTITUTED TRUSTS. A trust may be completely constituted in either of two ways [84]—

(i) By the trust property being vested in the trustees upon the requisite trusts.

(ii) By " a present irrevocable declaration of trust " being made by the settlor.[85] It is not essential that the settlor should use the words " I declare myself a trustee," but he must do something equivalent to this. Thus where a merchant in Canton wrote to his London agents directing them to set aside £1,000 to be employed for the benefit of his children, and by a later letter declared that he considered himself as having no further control over it, he was held to have declared himself a trustee.[86]

Although words of direct gift have occasionally been construed as declarations of trust,[87] it is now generally regarded as settled that an imperfect attempt to transfer property to a volunteer [88] (a person giving no valuable consideration) or to trustees for a volunteer [89] will not be construed as a declaration of trust. Nor will the court compel the settlor to perfect his attempted transfer at the suit of a volunteer, for " there is no equity in this court to perfect an imperfect gift." [90] Thus if A owns leasehold property and, wishing to give it to E, indorses on the lease " This deed and all thereto belonging I give to E from this time forth," neither this indorsement nor the delivery of the lease to E's mother on his behalf (E being an infant) will give E any beneficial interest in the lease; the legal term of years has not been vested in E or his mother, for a deed is required to do this,[91] and A's words of gift will not be construed as a declaration of trust.[92]

(3) VOLUNTEERS. The importance of the distinction between a completely and incompletely constituted trust lies in the fact that if a trust is completely constituted, it can be enforced by the beneficiaries

84 *Milroy* v. *Lord* (1862) 4 De G.F. & J. 264 at 274; *Richards* v. *Delbridge* (1874) L.R. 18 Eq. 11 at 14.
85 *Re Cozens* [1913] 2 Ch. 478 at 486. There is no power of revocation unless it is expressly reserved: *Re Bowden* [1936] Ch. 71.
86 *Vandenberg* v. *Palmer* (1858) 4 K. & J. 204.
87 See, *e.g.*, *Richardson* v. *Richardson* (1867) L.R. 3 Eq. 686; and see *Bowman* v. *Secular Society Ltd.* [1917] A.C. 406 at 436, 437.
88 *Jones* v. *Lock* (1865) 1 Ch.App. 25; *Re Swinburne* [1926] Ch. 38.
89 *Jefferys* v. *Jefferys* (1841) Cr. & Ph. 138; *cf. Re Wale* [1956] 1 W.L.R. 1346.
90 *Milroy* v. *Lord* (1862) 4 De G.F. & J. 264 at 274, *per* Turner L.J. For statutory exceptions, see S.L.A., 1925, s. 9 (2) (*ante*, p. 305), and s. 27 (*post*, p. 988); Snell, *Equity*, 123. For an equitable exception, see *post*, p. 778.
91 *Post*, p. 621.
92 *Richards* v. *Delbridge* (1874) L.R. 18 Eq. 11.

even if they are volunteers,[93] whereas if the trust is incompletely constituted, it will be enforced at the suit of beneficiaries who gave valuable consideration [94] (including those regarded as "within the marriage consideration" under a marriage settlement [95]) but cannot be enforced by volunteers.[96] The difference may be compared with the familiar distinction between grants and contracts at common law. A grant by deed at once vests the property in the grantee, whether or not he gave consideration for it; a contract to make a grant in the future will be enforceable only if supported by valuable consideration. It is therefore in the case of an incompletely constituted trust that one can apply the maxim "equity will not help a volunteer." But completely constituted trusts are, of course, enforceable at the suit of volunteer beneficiaries.

Sect. 2. Formalities Required for the Creation of a Trust

A. Pure Personalty

An enforceable trust of pure personalty can be validly created by word of mouth, whether the owner is declaring himself a trustee of the property or is transferring it to a third party on trust for the beneficiaries.[97]

B. Land

Before 1677 a trust of land could be created by word of mouth; but thereafter, by the Statute of Frauds, 1677 [98] (now replaced by the Law of Property Act, 1925 [99]), "a declaration of trust respecting any land or any interest therein must be manifested and proved by some writing signed by some person who is able to declare such trust or by his will." [1] The chief points to note on this provision are as follows.

(a) "*Any land.*" This includes leaseholds,[2] and included copyholds before they were abolished.[3]

---

[93] *Paul* v. *Paul* (1882) 20 Ch.D. 742.
[94] *Pullan* v. *Koe* [1913] 1 Ch. 9. If they do so, other beneficiaries who are volunteers may also do so: *Davenport* v. *Bishopp* (1843) 2 Y. & C.C.C. 451; (1846) 1 Ph. 698.
[95] *Ante*, p. 116.
[96] *Re Plumptre's Marriage Settlement* [1910] 1 Ch. 609; *Re Pryce* [1917] 1 Ch. 234.
[97] *e.g., Harris* v. *Truman* (1881) 7 Q.B.D. 340 at 356.
[98] ss. 7, 8.
[99] s. 53 (1) (*b*), (2).
[1] Most wills are required to be in writing, but some may be oral: see *post*, p. 486.
[2] See *Forster* v. *Hale* (1798) 3 Ves. 696; affirmed 5 Ves. 308.
[3] See *Withers* v. *Withers* (1752) Amb. 151 at 152 (but see n. 2 thereto); *ante*, p. 23.

(*b*) *Evidenced*. It is settled that the statutory words " manifested and proved " merely require that the trust should be evidenced by writing. The declaration need not actually be made in writing [4]; it suffices if an oral declaration is supported by some signed acknow-ledgment or declaration [5] in existence when the action is begun,[6] such as a letter,[7] or a recital in a deed,[8] even if this is made some time after the trust is declared.[9] The writing must show not only that there is a trust but also what its terms are.[10]

(*c*) " *Some person who is able to declare such trust*." This means the owner of the beneficial interest, so that if a trust is declared of an equitable interest held under an existing trust, the writing must be signed by the beneficiary; the signature of the trustees is not sufficient.[11]

(*d*) " *Or by his will*." These words allow even an informal oral will (if valid as such [12]) to suffice.

To these requirements there are two important exceptions.

(i) They do not affect the creation or operation of resulting, implied or constructive trusts.[13] Where A conveys land to B who orally agrees to hold on trust for A, the absence of writing will not prevent a resulting trust arising in favour of A.[14] A may therefore be able to enforce this trust both against B (and see (ii) below) and against B's successors in title, subject to the usual rules about equitable interests.

(ii) The court will not permit them to be used as an engine of fraud.[15] " It is a fraud on the part of a person to whom land is conveyed as a trustee, and who knows it was so conveyed, to deny the trust and claim the land himself. Consequently, notwithstanding the statute, it is competent for a person claiming land conveyed to another to prove by parol evidence that it was so conveyed upon trust for the claimant, and that the grantee, knowing the facts, is

---

[4] *Randall* v. *Morgan* (1805) 12 Ves. 67 at 74.
[5] See *Ambrose* v. *Ambrose* (1717) 1 P.Wms. 321.
[6] See *Forster* v. *Hale, supra.*
[7] *Morton* v. *Tewart* (1842) 2 Y. & C.C.C. 67; *Childers* v. *Childers* (1857) 1 De G. & J. 482.
[8] See *Deg* v. *Deg* (1727) 2 P.Wms. 412; and see *Re Holland* [1902] 2 Ch. 360.
[9] *Rochefoucauld* v. *Boustead* [1897] 1 Ch. 196 at 206; and see *Barkworth* v. *Young* (1856) 4 Drew. 1.
[10] *Smith* v. *Matthews* (1861) 3 De G.F. & J. 139.
[11] *Tierney* v. *Wood* (1854) 19 Beav. 330; *Kronheim* v. *Johnson* (1877) 7 Ch.D. 60.
[12] See *post*, p. 486.
[13] L.P.A., 1925, s. 53 (2), replacing Statute of Frauds, 1677, s. 8.
[14] *Hodgson* v. *Marks* [1971] Ch. 892.
[15] *Stickland* v. *Aldridge* (1804) 9 Ves. 516; *Lincoln* v. *Wright* (1859) 4 De G. & J. 16; *Re Duke of Marlborough* [1894] 2 Ch. 133; *cf. Hodgson* v. *Marks, supra*, at p. 933.

denying the trust and relying upon the form of conveyance and the statute, in order to keep the land himself."[16] Thus if P persuades V to sell his cottage in return for an oral promise of a rent-free tenancy of it, the court will hold P a trustee for V to the extent of the promised tenancy; for even if P initially intended no fraud, it would be a fraud for him to plead the statute.[17]

It is on this principle that secret trusts are enforced.[18] If a testator informs X of his intention to leave property to X to be held on trust for Y, and X acquiesces, whether expressly or by silence, this trust will be enforced even though it is not contained in the will or evidenced by writing.[19] This applies whether the will discloses that the property is held upon trust without disclosing the beneficiary (*e.g.*, " to X upon trusts which I have already communicated to him ")[20] or whether the gift is apparently beneficial (*e.g.*, " to X absolutely ").[21] However, in the latter case it suffices if the trusts are communicated at any time before the testator's death,[22] whereas in the former case there is some rather unsatisfactory authority for saying that the trusts must have been declared to and agreed by X before or at the time of making the will,[23] and that the will must show this to be the case.[24]

Sect. 3. Formalities Required for the Transfer of an Interest Under a Trust

By the Law of Property Act, 1925,[25] replacing the Statute of Frauds, 1677,[26] " a disposition of an equitable interest or trust subsisting at the time of the disposition, must be in writing signed by the person disposing of the same, or by his agent thereunto lawfully authorised in writing or by will." The following points should be noted.

(*a*) " *Disposition*." " Disposition " is given a very wide meaning.[1] It includes oral instructions given by a beneficiary to a bare trustee

---

[16] *Rochefoucauld* v. *Boustead* [1897] 1 Ch. 196 at 206, *per* Lindley L.J.; and see *Haigh* v. *Kaye* (1872) 7 Ch.App. 469 at 474.

[17] *Bannister* v. *Bannister* [1948] 2 All E.R. 133; *cf. Hodgson* v. *Marks, supra,* at p. 933.

[18] See Snell, *Equity,* 106 *et seq.*; *Drakeford* v. *Wilks* (1747) 3 Atk. 539.

[19] *Jones* v. *Badley* (1868) 3 Ch.App. 362; *Re Maddock* [1902] 2 Ch. 220; *Re Falkiner* [1924] 1 Ch. 88.

[20] *Blackwell* v. *Blackwell* [1929] A.C. 318; *Re Colin Cooper* [1939] Ch. 811.

[21] *Re Boyes* (1884) 26 Ch.D. 531. As to the position where only one of several beneficiaries is told of the trust, see *Re Stead* [1900] 1 Ch. 237 at 241, on which see (1972) 88 L.Q.R. 225 (B. Perrins).

[22] *Moss* v. *Cooper* (1861) 1 J. & H. 352. The trust is destroyed if the trustee predeceases the testator (*Re Maddock* [1902] 2 Ch. 220 at 231) but not if the beneficiary does so: *Re Gardner (No. 2)* [1923] 2 Ch. 230.

[23] *Johnson* v. *Ball* (1851) 5 De G. & Sm. 85; *Blackwell* v. *Blackwell* [1929] A.C. 318, 339; *Re Colin Cooper* [1939] Ch. 811. But see Holdsworth (1937) 53 L.Q.R. 501.

[24] *Re Keen* [1937] Ch. 236.   [25] s. 53 (1) (*c*).

[26] s. 9. Previously a parol assignment was valid.

[1] By L.P.A., 1925, s. 205 (1) (ii).

for him to hold the property on trust for other persons,[2] but not instructions to the trustee to transfer the legal and equitable interests together to others.[3]

(*b*) " *In writing.*" A parol assignment supported by evidence thereof in writing is not enough. Unlike the rule for the creation of trusts,[4] the rule here requires the assignment itself to be written,[5] and is thus not a mere rule of evidence.

(*c*) " *Signed by the person disposing of the same, or by his agent* [6] *thereunto lawfully authorised in writing.*" This should be contrasted with—

  (i) the rule for the creation of a trust of land, where the signature of an agent is not enough [7]; and

  (ii) the rule for contracts for the disposition of land, where the signature of an agent suffices even if his authority was given only by word of mouth.[8]

(*d*) *The rule applies to pure personalty as well as land.* Although a trust of pure personalty is enforceable even if it is not evidenced in writing,[9] once the trust has been created, a disposition of any interest under it is void unless it is in writing.[10]

Part 2

TRUSTEES

Sect. 1. Appointment of Trustees

A. Original Appointment

1. Appointment. Trustees are usually appointed by the settlor when creating the trust. If he neither makes an appointment nor makes any provision for one, the court may appoint trustees [11]; once the trust has been created, the settlor has no power of making an appointment unless he has reserved such a power. A person appointed trustee need not accept the trust [12] even if he had agreed

---

[2] *Grey* v. *I.R.C.* [1960] A.C. 1; see (1960) 76 L.Q.R. 197 (R.E.M.).
[3] *Vandervell* v. *I.R.C.* [1967] 2 A.C. 291.
[4] *Ante*, p. 449.
[5] See *Re Tyler* [1967] 1 W.L.R. 1269.
[6] The provision for an agent is new.
[7] *Ante*, p. 450.
[8] *Post*, p. 560.
[9] *Ante*, p. 449.
[10] See *Oughtred* v. *I. R. C.* [1960] A.C. 206 ; and see para. (*a*) above.
[11] *e.g.*, *Re Smirthwaite* (1871) L.R. 11 Eq. 251.
[12] *Robinson* v. *Pett* (1734) 3 P.Wms. 249 at 251.

to do so before it was created,[13] provided he disclaims the trust before he has accepted it either expressly or by acting as trustee.[14] A disclaimer is void if it relates only to part of the trusts.[15] It should preferably be express but it may be inferred from conduct [16]; and although the presumption is in favour of acceptance, a person appointed a trustee who maintains a complete inactivity in relation to the trust for a long period (*e.g.*, for more than 25 years) may be held thereby to have disclaimed the trust.[17] Disclaimer operates retrospectively to divest the person appointed both of his office and the trust property.[18]

2. Maximum number. Not more than four trustees of settled land or land held on trust for sale can be appointed if the settlement or trust for sale is created after 1925.[19] If more than four are named as trustees, the first four who are able and willing to act become trustees to the exclusion of the others.[19] Where, at the beginning of 1926, there were more than four trustees of settled land or land held on trust for sale, all the trustees continue to act but no new trustees can be appointed until the number has dropped below four.[20] These provisions apply only to land,[21] and in general there is no limit to the number of trustees of pure personalty.[22]

3. Minimum number. There is no minimum number of trustees even in the case of land.[23] But in the case of settled land or land held on trust for sale, notwithstanding any contrary provision, a sole trustee cannot give a valid receipt for capital money unless that trustee is a trust corporation.[24] This restriction, however, does not affect the right of a sole personal representative acting as such to give valid receipts for purchase-money,[25] *e.g.*, where a sole administrator sells under the trust for sale which is imposed on all the property of an intestate.[26]

---

[13] See *Doyle* v. *Blake* (1804) 2 Sch. & Lef. 231 at 239 (executor).

[14] *Conyngham* v. *Conyngham* (1750) 1 Ves.Sen. 522; *Noble* v. *Meymott* (1851) 14 Beav. 471.

[15] *Re Lord and Fullerton's Contract* [1896] 1 Ch. 228.

[16] *Stacey* v. *Elph* (1833) 1 My. & K. 195. This is so even for freehold land: *Re Gordon* (1877) 6 Ch.D. 531 and *Re Birchall* (1889) 40 Ch.D. 436, ignoring the doubts expressed in *Re Ellison's Trusts* (1856) 2 Jur.(N.S.) 62.

[17] *Jago* v. *Jago* (1893) 68 L.T. 654; *Re Clout and Frewer's Contract* [1924] 2 Ch. 230.

[18] *Peppercorn* v. *Wayman* (1852) 2 De G. & Sm. 230; *Re Martinez' Trusts* (1870) 22 L.T. 403.

[19] T.A., 1925, s. 34 (2); *ante*, pp. 357, 417.

[20] T.A., 1925, s. 34 (1).

[21] *Ibid.*, s. 34 (3).

[22] See Lewin 163.

[23] See *Re Myhill* [1928] Ch. 100; *Re Wight & Best's Brewery Co. Ltd.'s Contract* [1929] W.N. 11; L.P.A., 1925, s. 27 (2).

[24] S.L.A., 1925, s. 18 (1); L.P.A., 1925, s. 27 (2); *ante*, pp. 376, 378.

[25] *Ibid.*

[26] By A.E.A., 1925, s. 33; *post*, p. 523.

B. Replacement

1. Power to appoint. Even if there are properly appointed trustees when the trust is created, it may later become necessary to appoint new trustees, *e.g.*, owing to the death of trustees. The events upon which new trustees can be appointed may be specified in the trust instrument; this is not usual, however, and reliance is normally placed on the statutory provisions, which apply notwithstanding any such express provision [27] unless a contrary intention is shown.[28] By the Trustee Act, 1925,[29] a new trustee or trustees (including Settled Land Act trustees [30]) may be appointed if a trustee—

(i) is dead (and this includes a person nominated trustee by a will who predeceases the testator [31]); or

(ii) remains outside the United Kingdom for a continuous [32] period exceeding twelve months; or

(iii) desires to be discharged from all or any of his trusts or powers; or

(iv) refuses to act (*e.g.*, if he disclaims [33]); or

(v) is unfit to act (*e.g.*, if he is bankrupt [34]); or

(vi) is incapable of acting, as by lunacy,[35] or age and infirmity,[36] or, in the case of a corporation, by dissolution [37]; or

(vii) is an infant [37a]; or

(viii) is removed under a power in the trust instrument.[38]

2. Mode of appointment. The appointment must be made in writing [39] and must be made—

(i) by the person or persons [40] nominated by the trust instrument

---

[27] See *Re Wheeler and De Rochow* [1896] 1 Ch. 315.
[28] T.A., 1925, s. 69 (2).
[29] s. 36 (1), replacing T.A., 1893, s. 10 (1), and C.A., 1881, s. 31 (1).
[30] See *Re Dark* [1954] Ch. 291.
[31] T.A., 1925, s. 36 (8), replacing T.A., 1893, s. 10 (4), and C.A., 1881, s. 31 (6).
[32] See *Re Walker* [1901] 1 Ch. 259 (continuity broken by return for a week).
[33] *Re Birchall* (1889) 40 Ch.D. 436.
[34] *Re Roche* (1842) 2 Dr. & War. 287 at 289; *Re Hopkins* (1881) 19 Ch.D. 61 at 63.
[35] *Re East* (1873) 8 Ch.App. 735; *Re Blake* [1887] W.N. 173.
[36] *Re Lemann's Trusts* (1883) 22 Ch.D. 633.
[37] T.A., 1925, s. 36 (3), operating retrospectively.
[37a] An implied, resulting or constructive trust may make an infant a trustee, though he cannot be *appointed* one: *post*, p. 455.
[38] T.A., 1925, s. 36 (2), a new provision.
[39] But the last surviving trustee cannot appoint by his will: *Re Parker's Trusts* [1894] 1 Ch. 707.
[40] In the absence of a contrary intention, the power does not pass to the survivor of two or more nominees, unless the property is vested in them (see *Re Bacon* [1907] 1 Ch. 475; *Re Harding* [1923] 1 Ch. 182; Farwell, *Powers*, 514, 515) or they are trustees and hold the power as such: T.A., 1925, s. 18 (1), replacing T.A., 1893, s. 22 (1), and C.A., 1881, s. 38; see *Re Smith* [1904] 1 Ch. 139.

for the purpose of appointing new trustees, *i.e.*, nominated generally [41] and not merely in certain stated events [42]; in default of there being any such person able and willing to act (as where the persons nominated cannot be found,[43] or disagree [44]), the appointment may be made

(ii) by the " surviving or continuing trustees or trustee," a term which includes a trustee who is retiring or refuses to act [45] but not a trustee removed against his will [46]; or, if there is no such trustee,

(iii) by the personal representatives of the last remaining (or sole [47]) trustee [48]; or, finally, if there is no such person,[49] or it is doubtful.[50]

(iv) by the court.[51]

3. Who may be appointed. It is expressly provided that the person making the appointment may appoint himself.[52] Even if he appoints a person whom the court would not normally [53] appoint, such as a beneficiary,[54] or the husband of a beneficiary,[55] or the solicitor to the trustees or beneficiaries,[56] the appointment will not thereby be rendered invalid; but an appointment of an infant as trustee, whether of realty or personalty, is void.[57]

4. Number. Where a single trustee was originally appointed, the appointment of a single trustee in his place is valid [58]; but, in the case of settled land or land held on trust for sale, a sole trustee (not being a trust corporation) cannot be appointed under the statutory power if, after his appointment, he would be unable to give receipts

---

[41] *Re Walker & Hughes' Contract* (1883) 24 Ch.D. 698.
[42] *Re Wheeler & De Rochow* [1896] 1 Ch. 315; *Re Sichel's Settlements* [1916] 1 Ch. 358.
[43] *Cradock* v. *Witham* [1895] W.N. 75.
[44] *Re Sheppard's S. T.* [1888] W.N. 234.
[45] T.A., 1925, s. 36 (8), replacing T.A., 1893, s. 10 (4), and C.A., 1881, s. 31 (6).
[46] *Re Stoneham S. T.* [1953] Ch. 59.
[47] *Re Shafto's Trusts* (1885) 29 Ch.D. 247; but see *Nicholson* v. *Field* [1893] 2 Ch. 511.
[48] T.A., 1925, s. 36 (1), replacing T.A., 1893, s. 10 (1), and C.A., 1881, s. 31 (1).
[49] See *Re Higginbottom* [1892] 3 Ch. 132.
[50] See *Re May's W. T.* [1941] Ch. 109 (trustee in enemy territory).
[51] T.A., 1925, s. 41, replacing T.A., 1893, s. 25 (1), T.A., 1852, s. 9, and T.A., 1850, s. 32. For the principles guiding the court, see *Re Tempest* (1866) 1 Ch.App. 485; *Re Northcliffe's Settlements* [1937] 3 All E.R. 804.
[52] T.A., 1925, s. 36 (1); contrast s. 36 (6), *post*, p. 456.
[53] For exceptional cases, see, *e.g.*, *Re Clissold* (1864) 10 L.T. 642; *Re Marquis of Ailesbury and Lord Iveagh* [1893] 2 Ch. 345.
[54] *Forster* v. *Abraham* (1874) L.R. 17 Eq. 351 (tenant for life); *cf. ante*, p. 326.
[55] *Re Coode* (1913) 108 L.T. 94.
[56] *Re Earl of Stamford* [1896] 1 Ch. 288.
[57] L.P.A., 1925, s. 20.
[58] T.A., 1925, s. 37 (1) (*c*), replacing T.A., 1893, s. 10 (2), and C.A., 1881, s. 31 (3).

for capital money,[59] as would be the case if there were no other trustee. There is never any obligation to appoint more than two trustees even if originally more than two were appointed.[60] The appointment may increase the number of trustees, provided that, in the case of settled land or land held on trust for sale, the number is not increased above four.[61] Further, a separate set of trustees may be appointed for any part of the trust property held on distinct trusts.[62]

C. Additional Trustees

Even though no occasion has arisen for the appointment of new trustees, if there are not more than three trustees and none of them is a trust corporation, one or more additional trustees may be appointed, provided the effect of the appointment is not to increase the number above four.[63] The appointment must be made by the same persons and in the same way as an appointment of new trustees,[64] except that there is no provision for an appointment by the personal representatives of the last remaining trustee, or for the appointor to appoint himself.[65]

Sect. 2. Retirement and Removal of Trustees

1. Retirement. A trustee may retire—

(i) If another trustee is appointed in his place; this has already been considered.[66]

(ii) If no new trustee is being appointed in his place, provided that after his discharge there will be left either two or more individuals or a trust corporation to act in the trust.[67] The retirement is effected by a deed declaring the trustee's desire to retire; this is executed by the retiring trustee, the continuing trustees and the person entitled to appoint new trustees, all of whom must concur in the retirement.[67]

(iii) If authorised to do so by an express power in the trust instrument.[68]

---

[59] T.A., 1925, s. 37 (2).
[60] *Ibid.*, s. 37 (1) (c).
[61] *Ibid.*, ss. 37 (1) (a) (replacing T.A., 1893, s. 10 (2) (a), and C.A., 1881, s. 31 (2)), 34 (2).
[62] T.A., 1925, s. 37 (1) (b).
[63] *Ibid.*, s. 36 (6). The limit is not confined to trusts of land.
[64] *Ibid.*
[65] *Re Power's S. T.* [1951] Ch. 1074. This is an accident of drafting: see (1952) 68 L.Q.R. 19 (R.E.M.).
[66] *Ante*, p. 454.
[67] T.A., 1925, s. 39 (1), replacing T.A., 1893, s. 11 (1), and C.A., 1881, s. 32 (1).
[68] *e.g.*, *Lord Camoys* v. *Best* (1854) 19 Beav. 414

(iv) With the consent of all the beneficiaries if they are all *sui juris* and between them absolutely entitled to the trust property.[69]

(v) With the leave of the court [70]; this method should be employed only in cases of difficulty,[71] for if the trustee applies to the court without good cause he may have to pay his own costs.[72]

2. Removal. A trustee may be removed—

(i) Under the power to appoint new trustees considered above.[73]

(ii) Under any express power to do so contained in the trust instrument.[74]

(iii) Under the court's inherent jurisdiction to remove a trustee where it is necessary for the safety of the trust property or the welfare of the beneficiaries, as where the trustee has been inactive for a long while,[75] or his interests conflict with those of the beneficiaries,[76] or there has been friction with the beneficiaries on the mode of administering the trust.[77]

Sect. 3. Vesting of Trust Property

Some trustees have no property vested in them, as is normally the case with trustees of settled land [78]; in such cases, no question of the devolution of trust property arises. But where property is vested in trustees, questions of the transfer of the trust property arise on their death, retirement or removal, or on the appointment of new trustees.

A. On Death

Trustees are always made joint tenants or joint owners of the trust property, whether it is real or personal. The advantage of this is that on the death of one trustee the estate or interest vested in him passes to the surviving trustees by the doctrine of survivorship.[79]

---

[69] Consider *Wilkinson* v. *Parry* (1828) 4 Russ. 272 at 276.

[70] *Forshaw* v. *Higginson* (1855) 20 Beav. 485; *Gardiner* v. *Downes* (1856) 22 Beav. 395.

[71] See *Re Stokes' Trusts* (1872) L.R. 13 Eq. 333; *Re Chetwynd's Settlement* [1902] 1 Ch. 692.

[72] *Howard* v. *Rhodes* (1837) 1 Keen 581; *Porter* v. *Watts* (1852) 21 L.J.Ch. 211.

[73] *Ante*, p. 454.

[74] *e.g., London and County Banking Co.* v. *Goddard* [1897] 1 Ch. 642.

[75] *Reid* v. *Hadley* (1885) 2 T.L.R. 12.

[76] *Passingham* v. *Sherborn* (1846) 9 Beav. 424.

[77] *Letterstedt* v. *Broers* (1884) 9 App.Cas. 371.

[78] *Ante*, p. 296.

[79] *Ante*, p. 391. Powers given to the trustees jointly also pass to the survivors: T.A., 1925, s. 18 (1), replacing T.A., 1893, s. 22 (1), and C.A., 1881, s. 38 (1).

Before 1882, however, if a sole surviving trustee died, any realty which he held on trust passed under his will or intestacy in the same way as the property which he owned beneficially, except that it was still subject to the trust.[80] Thus the devisee or heir would automatically become a trustee.

This inconvenience was removed by the Conveyancing Act, 1881 [81] (now replaced by the Administration of Estates Act, 1925,[82]), which provided that in the case of deaths after 1881, the estate or interest held on trust [83] should vest in the personal representatives of the deceased trustee notwithstanding any provision in his will. Until new trustees are appointed, the personal representatives may exercise any power or trust exercisable by the former trustee,[84] without being obliged to do so.[85]

B. On Appointment of New Trustees

1. Vesting declaration. On an appointment of new trustees, the trust property has to be vested in the new trustees jointly with any continuing trustees. Formerly there had to be a formal conveyance of the trust property by the persons in whom it was vested. Thus if A and B were trustees and C was appointed a new trustee on A's death, B had to convey the trust property to himself and C jointly.[86] But by the Trustee Act, 1925,[87] replacing earlier legislation, if an appointment of new trustees is made by deed, a declaration therein by the appointor that the property shall vest in the trustees (a " vesting declaration ") is sufficient to vest the property in them. This applies to all deeds executed after 1881 [88]; and if the deed is executed after 1925, a vesting declaration is implied in the absence of an express provision to the contrary.[89] It should be noted that

---

[80] Williams R.P. 202. For a minor exception (bare trust of a fee simple), see Vendor and Purchaser Act, 1874, s. 5, replaced by L.T.A., 1875, s. 48.

[81] s. 30.

[82] s. 1, replacing L.T.A., 1897, s. 1.

[83] This included copyholds (*Re Hughes* [1884] W.N. 53; and see *Hall* v. *Bromley* (1887) 35 Ch.D. 642) until the Copyhold Act, 1887, s. 45 (replaced by the Copyhold Act, 1894, s. 88), provided otherwise (on this see *Re Mills' Trusts* (1887) 37 Ch.D. 312; on appeal 40 Ch.D. 14).

[84] T.A., 1925, s. 18 (2), replacing C.A., 1911, s. 8 (1): see *Re Waidanis* [1908] 1 Ch. 123. Two or more personal representatives of a sole trustee may give valid receipts for capital money: see Wolst. & C. iv, 21.

[85] See *Re Ridley* [1904] 2 Ch. 774; *Re Benett* [1906] 1 Ch. 216.

[86] See *ante*, p. 162.

[87] T.A., 1925, s. 40 (1) (*a*), replacing T.A., 1893, s. 12 (1), and C.A., 1881, s. 34 (1).

[88] T.A., 1925, s. 40 (6), replacing T.A., 1893, s. 12 (5), and C.A., 1881, s. 34 (5).

[89] T.A., 1925, s. 40 (1) (*b*). An express declaration subjects the deed to stamp duty of 50p., whereas the implied declaration does not: see *Hadgett* v. *C. I. R.* (1877) 3 Ex.D. 46; Lewin 434. The danger that an express declaration might be defective in form is now met by T.A., 1925, s. 40 (3).

these provisions apply even if the trust property is not vested in the appointor. He has a statutory power to transfer what he has not got.[90] Thus where A and B are the trustees and X has the power to appoint new trustees, if A dies and X appoints C a trustee in his place, the deed of appointment will vest the trust property in B and C jointly.

2. Exceptions. In certain cases, however, the trust property cannot be transferred by a vesting declaration, either express or implied. These cases are when the property consists of—

(a) (before 1926) legal estates in copyholds [91];

(b) land which the trustees hold by way of mortgage for securing trust money [92];

(c) land held under a lease with a provision against assigning or disposing of the land without consent, unless—

    (i) the requisite consent has first been obtained, or

    (ii) the vesting declaration would not be a breach of covenant or give rise to a forfeiture [93];

(d) any share, stock or other property which is transferable only in books kept by a company or other body, or in a way directed by statute.[94]

In these excepted cases the trust property must be transferred by the method appropriate to the subject-matter, *e.g.*, in the case of shares, by a duly registered transfer. The reasons for (a) and (d) are apparent when the normal mode of transfer of such property is considered; (b) is included to avoid bringing the trusts on to the title,[95] for otherwise when the borrower sought to repay the loan, he would have to investigate the trust documents to see that he was paying the right persons; and (c) is included to avoid accidental breaches of the terms of the lease.[96]

The court has a wide jurisdiction to make vesting orders where this is desirable.[97]

C. On Retirement or Removal

Where a trustee retires or is discharged from a trust without a new trustee being appointed, and the transaction is effected by

---

[90] See L.P.A., 1925, s. 9 (1).
[91] T.A., 1893, s. 12 (3), replacing C.A., 1881, s. 34 (3).
[92] T.A., 1925, s. 40 (4) (a), replacing T.A., 1893, s. 12 (3), and C.A., 1881, s. 34 (3). But land conveyed on trust to secure debenture stock is now excepted: T.A., 1925, s. 40 (4) (a).
[93] T.A., 1925, s. 40 (4) (b).
[94] T.A., 1925, s. 40 (4) (c), replacing T.A., 1893, s. 12 (3), and C.A., 1881, s. 34 (3).
[95] Lewin 435.
[96] Wolst. & C. iv, 67.
[97] T.A., 1925, ss. 44–56.

deed, the trust property can be divested from the former trustee and vested solely in the continuing trustees by means of a vesting declaration.[98] This applies only if the deed is executed by the retiring trustee, the continuing trustees and any person with power to appoint new trustees; if the deed is executed after 1925, a vesting declaration is implied.[99] There are the same exceptions as in the case of vesting declarations on the appointment of new trustees.[1]

This special provision is necessary since the right of survivorship operates only on death and not on retirement.

Sect. 4. Procedure in the Case of Settled Land and Trusts for Sale

1. One instrument. Although it is undesirable, a trust for sale may be created by only one instrument. In this case, when a new trustee is appointed, the appointment may be made by a single document. This may be merely in writing, but it should be by deed so that the legal estate may be vested in the new and continuing trustees by virtue of the Trustee Act, 1925,[2] thus avoiding the necessity of a separate conveyance. In addition, a memorandum must be indorsed on or annexed to the instrument creating the trust for sale, stating the names of those who are the trustees after the appointment is made,[3] and not merely the names of the new trustees.

2. Two instruments. Normally, however, a trust for sale is created by two documents.[4] In this case and in the case of settled land, the procedure is more complicated. There must be [5]—

　　(i) An instrument to go with the conveyance on trust for sale or the vesting instrument.

　　(ii) An appointment to go with the trust instrument.

　　(iii) An indorsement on the conveyance on trust for sale or on the vesting instrument stating the names of those who are the trustees after the appointment.

In the case of settled land, the first document must be a deed; but it merely states who are now the trustees. In the case of a trust for sale, it may be merely in writing, but, as before, should be by deed in order to take advantage of section 40 of the Trustee Act, 1925; in either case it effects the actual appointment of the persons

[98] *Ibid.*, s. 40 (2) (*a*), replacing T.A., 1893, s. 12 (3), and C.A., 1881, s. 34 (3).

[99] T.A., 1925, s. 40 (2) (*b*).

[1] See above.

[2] s. 40; *ante*, p. 458.

[3] T.A., 1925, s. 35 (3).

[4] *Ante*, p. 363.

[5] T.A., 1925, s. 35; S.L.A., 1925, s. 35 (1); *cf. ante*, p. 357.

named in it as trustees for sale. A similar procedure applies if a trustee of settled land is discharged without a new trustee being appointed.[6] The second document, both for settled land and trusts for sale, is an appointment which may be made either in writing or by deed.

Part 3

POWERS

The word " power " is normally used in the sense of an authority given to a person to dispose of property which is not his.[7] The person giving the power is called the donor and the person to whom it is given the donee.

Sect. 1. Classification

One classification of powers is the following [8]:

  (i) Powers simply collateral, *i.e.*, those where the donee has no interest in the property subject to the power.

 (ii) Powers in gross, where the donee has some interest in the property but the exercise of the power cannot affect that interest, *e.g.*, where property is given to X for life with power to appoint after his death.

(iii) Powers appendant or appurtenant, where the donee has some interest in the property and the exercise of the power can affect that interest.

This classification was formerly important for determining whether the donee could release the power, and so put an end to it [9]; powers in gross and powers appendant or appurtenant could always be released, but this rule did not apply to powers simply collateral [10] until 1882.[11] Today, this classification is of little value; a more useful classification is the following:

1. Common law powers. Before power to devise legal estates in land was given by the Statute of Wills, 1540, customs existed in some boroughs enabling land to be devised.[12] In such cases it was

---

  [6] S.L.A., 1925, s. 35 (1): there is no corresponding provision for trusts for sale.
  [7] See *Freme* v. *Clement* (1881) 18 Ch.D. 499 at 504; *Re Armstrong* (1886) 17 Q.B.D. 521. The only modern text on Powers is Halsb. xxx, 205–289.
  [8] See *Re D'Angibau* (1880) 15 Ch.D. 228 at 232, 233.
  [9] See *post*, p. 470.
 [10] See *Digge's Case* (1600) 1 Co.Rep. 173a; *Re Mills* [1930] 1 Ch. 654; Sugden, *Powers*, 49.
 [11] C.A., 1881, s. 52; see now L.P.A., 1925, ss. 155, 160.
 [12] *Ante*, p. 22.

possible for a testator to give his executors power to sell the land without devising it to them.[13] Such a power was a common law power, for by virtue of the common law, a legal estate could be conveyed by a person in whom it was not vested. Powers of attorney, under which one person authorises another to do certain acts on his behalf, such as to convey land, are much more important examples of common law powers.[14]

2. Powers operating under the Statute of Uses, 1535. If after 1535 land was given—

" to A and his heirs to such uses as B shall appoint,"
upon B making an appointment in favour of X, the legal estate vested in X forthwith; until this happened, there was a resulting use to the grantor.[15] This remained the law until the repeal of the Statute of Uses in 1925.[16]

3. Statutory powers. A number of statutes have given powers to convey legal estates. For example, the Settled Land Act, 1882, authorised a tenant for life to convey a legal estate not vested in him,[17] and the Law of Property Act, 1925, gives a mortgagee a similar power.[18]

4. Equitable powers. Unlike the powers mentioned above, equitable powers enable the donee to transfer only an equitable interest. For example, a conveyance in 1920—

" unto and to the use of X and his heirs in trust for Y for
life, with remainder on such trusts as Z shall appoint "

gave Z an equitable power.[19]

The 1925 legislation increased the number of equitable powers. The Law of Property Act, 1925,[20] provides that " every power of appointment over, or power to convey or charge land or any interest therein, whether created by a statute or other instrument or implied by law, and whether created before or after the commencement of this Act (not being a power vested in a legal mortgagee or an estate owner in right of his estate and exercisable by him or by another person in his name and on his behalf) operates only in equity." It will be seen that this rule contains some exceptions;

[13] H.E.L. iii, 136, 137, 271; vii, 153. Until the executors sold, the legal estate was in the heir: Litt. 169.
[14] Sugden, *Powers*, 45. They are now regulated by Powers of Attorney Act 1971.
[15] *Ante*, p. 162.
[16] *Ante*, p. 171.
[17] *Ante*, p. 293.
[18] *Post*, p. 913.
[19] *Cf. ante*, pp. 170, 390.
[20] s. 1 (7).

and others appear elsewhere in the legislation of 1925. Thus the
following powers may still operate at law, and not only in equity—

(i) a legal mortgagee's power of sale, by which he can convey
a legal estate vested in the mortgagor [21];

(ii) a power of attorney, enabling one person to convey a legal
estate vested in another [22];

(iii) the power of Settled Land Act trustees, acting in the name
of the tenant for life and on his behalf, to convey the legal
estate vested in him on certain special occasions.[23]

Apart from cases such as these, a legal estate can be conveyed only
by the person in whom it is vested. A conveyance of a legal estate
by a tenant for life is no longer a conveyance under a statutory
power enabling him to sell what was not vested in him, but a conveyance by the estate owner.[24] This, together with the abolition of
legal powers operating under the Statute of Uses, 1535, makes it
possible to say that by the 1925 legislation " the basis of conveyancing
was shifted from powers to estates." [25]

Sect. 2. Powers of Appointment

A. *Introductory*

1. Classification. Statutory powers are more conveniently considered under their appropriate heads, but powers of appointment,
which are powers given under some settlement or trust authorising
the donee to make an appointment of some or all of the trust
property, must be discussed here. Such powers are traditionally
classified as either general or special. A general power imposes no
restrictions upon the donee's choice, allowing him, without obtaining
the concurrence of any other person,[26] to appoint to anyone, including
himself.[27] Thus a gift—

" to X for life, remainder as he shall appoint "

gives X a life interest and a general power of appointment. A
special power fetters the donee's choice by providing that he can
appoint the property only among a limited class of persons, known

---

[21] *Post*, p. 913. See also L.P.A., 1925, s. 22 (1) (lunatics).
[22] See the exception (in brackets) to L.P.A., 1925, s. 1 (7); *cf.* s. 7 (4). For details
see Powers of Attorney Act 1971.
[23] *Ante*, p. 350.
[24] Though much restricted in its effect by S.L.A., 1925, s. 18; *ante*, p. 313.
[25] Prideaux, 24th ed., 1948, i, 5. Yet sales by a mortgagee run contrary to this
principle; before 1926, the mortgagee conveyed an estate vested in him, whereas
after 1925 he conveys under a statutory power: see *post*, p. 913.
[26] *Re Churston S. E.* [1954] Ch. 334; *ante*, p. 253.
[27] Farwell, *Powers*, 8; *Re Penrose* [1933] Ch. 793.

as the " objects " of the power, as where X is given a power to appoint among his issue. A power to appoint to anyone except a named person or group of persons is perhaps best regarded as forming a third category,[28] sometimes called a "hybrid "[29] or "intermediate "[29a] power; but if the dichotomy of general and special powers is adopted, such a power may be classified as special for the purposes of section 27 of the Wills Act, 1837,[30] as it now clearly is for the purposes of the rule against perpetuities.[31]

2. Default of appointment. Provision is usually made for some person or persons to take in default of appointment; if this is not done, the grantor is entitled in default of appointment. The effect of an appointment is to divest the interest of those entitled in default of appointment to the extent of the appointment.[32] Where, however, it appears that the objects of the power are intended to take in any event, the power is not a mere power, but " a power in the nature of a trust " (or, more simply, a trust), under which the objects take vested interests in the property in equal shares,[33] subject to being divested by any appointment.[34] It is often difficult to determine whether a power is intended to be in the nature of a trust [35]; but an express gift in default of appointment is conclusive against it, whereas the absence of such a gift is some indication of a trust, though not conclusive.[36]

B. *Formalities for Exercise of Powers*

1. Formalities. The general rule is that any condition prescribed for the execution of a power must be observed, otherwise the appointment will be void.[37] It is immaterial how absurd or unreasonable the conditions are.[38] But this position has been modified by statute.

---

[28] See *Re Jones* [1945] Ch. 105; *Re Harvey* [1950] 1 All E.R. 491; (1948) 13 Conv.(N.S.) 20 (J. G. Fleming); (1950) 66 L.Q.R. 304 (R.E.M.). See the discussion in *Re Lawrence's W. T.* [1972] Ch. 418. If the excepted person does not and cannot exist when the power comes to be exercised, it is a general power: *Re Harvey, supra.*

[29] See, *e.g., Re Triffitt's Settlement* [1958] Ch. 852.

[29a] See, *e.g., Re Manisty's Settlement* [1974] Ch. 17 at 21.

[30] *Post,* p. 505.

[31] *Ante,* pp. 252, 253.

[32] *Re Brooks' S. T.* [1939] Ch. 993 at 996, 997.

[33] *Wilson* v. *Duguid* (1883) 24 Ch.D. 244.

[34] *Robinson* v. *Smith* (1821) 6 Madd. 194 at 198; *Faulkner* v. *Lord Wynford* (1845) 15 L.J.Ch. 8; *cf. ante,* p. 176.

[35] Contrast *Burrough* v. *Philcox* (1840) 5 My. & Cr. 72 with *Re Weekes' Settlement* [1897] 1 Ch. 289.

[36] *Re Mills* [1930] 1 Ch. 654; *Re Perowne* [1951] Ch. 785.

[37] Farwell, *Powers,* 147 *et seq.*

[38] *Rutland* v. *Doe* d. *Wythe* (1843) 10 Cl. & F. 419 at 425. For an example of stringent requirements, see *Hawkins* v. *Kemp* (1803) 3 East 410.

(*a*) *Wills.* By the Wills Act, 1837,[39] an appointment by will is valid so far as concerns execution and attestation, if it is executed with the formalities required for wills (*i.e.*, signed by the testator in the presence of two witnesses who then sign their names [40]), even if the instrument creating the power requires other formalities, such as ten witnesses.[41]

(*b*) *Deeds.* By the Law of Property Act, 1925,[42] an appointment by deed is valid as regards execution and attestation if it is signed [43] in the presence of, and attested by, two witnesses, even if the instrument creating the power requires other formalities.

2. Substance. Deeds and wills are thus on a similar footing in this respect. But it must be noticed that these provisions apply only to formalities concerning execution and attestation, such as a requirement that the document should be executed in a certain place in the presence of three witnesses.[44] There is nothing in these provisions to make it unnecessary to comply with other requirements (*e.g.*, as to obtaining the consent of specified persons [45]), and an appointment not made in accordance with such requirements is void.[46] Whether the power is general, special or hybrid, an appointment must also (apart from statute [46a]) sufficiently indicate an intention to exercise the power.[47]

3. Relief in equity. In one limited class of such cases equity will intervene and treat the defective appointment as valid. This will be done only if both the following conditions are satisfied:

  (i) The defect is merely formal and not one of substance. Thus if under a power to appoint by deed the donee appoints by will, equity will grant relief.[48] But if there is a power exercisable only by will, equity will not aid an appointment

[39] s. 10.
[40] *Post*, p. 476.
[41] As to the operation of a will in exercising a power, see also *post*, p. 504.
[42] s. 159, replacing L.P.(Am.)A., 1859, s. 12.
[43] L.P.A., 1925, s. 73; before 1926 signature was not essential, and sealing and delivery alone would be effective: *Taunton* v. *Pepler* (1820) 6 Madd. 166; *post*, p. 611.
[44] See *Hawkins* v. *Kemp* (1803) 3 East 410.
[45] See, *e.g.*, *Hulton* v. *Simpson* (1716) 2 Vern. 722.
[46] See, *e.g.*, *Cooper* v. *Martin* (1867) 3 Ch.App. 47 (appointment to be made before a specified child was 25).
[46a] See *post*, p. 504.
[47] *Re Lawrence's W. T.* [1972] Ch. 418.
[48] *Tollet* v. *Tollet* (1728) 2 P.Wms. 489.

by deed, for the power was not intended to be exercised until the donee's death, and the donee was meant to be free to modify the appointment until then.[49]

(ii) The relief is sought by a purchaser, creditor or charity, or the wife or legitimate child of the donee of the power.[50]

It should be noted that although equity gives relief against the defective exercise of the power in these cases, it never gives relief against failure to exercise the power at all.[50a]

C. *Excessive Execution*

An appointment which exceeds the limits set to the power either expressly or by law is said to be an excessive execution of the power. This may be illustrated by an appointment which infringes the rule against perpetuities[51] or appoints £8,000 under a power that authorises the appointment of only £7,000[52] or attaches an unauthorised condition to the interest appointed,[53] or an appointment to an illegitimate child which is made under a power to appoint to legitimate children.[54] In such cases the rule is that the appointment is valid so far as it is proper and void as to the excess only; but if it is impossible to draw a clear boundary between what is proper and what is excessive, the whole appointment is bad.[55] Thus if under a power to appoint to children, an appointment is made to a child for life with remainder to a grandchild, the appointment is valid as to the life interest of the child only.[56] Again, a lease for 26 years granted under a power to lease for 21 years is valid for 21 years.[57] But if under a special power there is an appointment to a class of persons composed partly of persons who are not objects of the power, and the shares in which they are to take are not specified, the whole appointment fails, for it is impossible to sever the good from the bad.[58]

---

[49] *Reid* v. *Shergold* (1805) 10 Ves. 370; *Coffin* v. *Cooper* (1865) 13 W.R. 571 at 572; *secus*, it seems, if the deed was not to take effect until death, and was to be revocable until then.

[50] See Farwell, *Powers*, 385 *et seq.*

[50a] *Holmes* v. *Coghill* (1806) 12 Ves. 206.

[51] *Re Brown and Sibly's Contract* (1876) 3 Ch.D. 156; *ante*, p. 256.

[52] *Parker* v. *Parker* (1714) Gilb.Eq. 168.

[53] *e.g.*, *Re Neave* [1938] Ch. 793; *Re Morris's S. T.* [1951] 2 All E.R. 528 (appointment on protective and discretionary trusts held invalid on the ground that appointor's discretion could not be delegated); and see *Re Hunter's W. T.* [1963] Ch. 372.

[54] *Re Kerr's Trusts* (1877) 4 Ch.D. 600.

[55] See *Re Witty* [1913] 2 Ch. 666; Farwell, *Powers*, 343 *et seq.*

[56] *Doe* d. *Nicholson* v. *Welford* (1840) 12 A. & E. 61.

[57] *Campbell* v. *Leach* (1775) Amb. 740; but see Cru.Dig. iv, 202.

[58] *Harvey* v. *Stracey* (1852) 1 Drew. 73 at 117; *Re Brown's Trust* (1865) L.R. 1 Eq. 74.

No appointment is bad merely because little or nothing is appointed to one or more of the objects, unless the power provides that each object shall receive some minimum amount at least and the donee does not comply with this requirement.[59] The law was once otherwise,[60] hence the phrase " Cut off with a shilling."

D. *Fraud on a Power*

I. INVALIDITY OF APPOINTMENT

1. Bona fide. A special power of appointment must be exercised " bona fide for the end designed, otherwise it is corrupt and void." [61] The donee must, in making the appointment, act in relation to the power as a trustee would act [62]; he must " act with good faith and sincerity and with an entire and single view to the real purpose and object of the power, and not for the purpose of accomplishing or carrying into effect any bye or sinister object (I mean sinister in the sense of it being beyond the purpose and intent of the power) which he may desire to effect in the exercise of the power," [63] even if there is no " fraud " in the ordinary sense.[64] If an appointment does not satisfy these requirements, it is void as a fraud on the power; but the doctrine does not apply to a power to revoke an appointment.[65]

2. Fraud. An appointment may be deemed fraudulent and void on any of three grounds.

(a) *Corrupt purpose*: the appointment was made with a corrupt purpose, as by the donee appointing to one of his children who is seriously ill, expecting that the child would die and that he would

[59] L.P.A., 1925, s. 158, replacing the Illusory Appointments Act, 1830, and the Powers of Appointment Act, 1874.

[60] Originally something more than a nominal sum had to be appointed to every object, unless the contrary was intended: *Thomas* v. *Thomas* (1705) 2 Vern. 513. Thus an appointment would be set aside if nothing, or only a nominal sum such as five shillings, was appointed to one of the objects: *Gibson* v. *Kinven* (1682) 1 Vern. 66. The Illusory Appointments Act, 1830, provided that appointment of a nominal sum should not invalidate the exercise of the power, unless it directed otherwise. But until the Powers of Appointment Act, 1874, the total exclusion of any object still prima facie invalidated the appointment: *Gainsford* v. *Dunn* (1874) L.R. 17 Eq. 405 at 407. "The Act of 1830 enabled an appointor to cut off any object of the power with a shilling: the Act of 1874 enables him to cut off the shilling also": Farwell, *Powers*, 427.

[61] *Aleyn* v. *Belchier* (1758) 1 Eden 132 at 138, *per* Henley L.K.

[62] See *Scroggs* v. *Scroggs* (1755) Amb. 272 at 273.

[63] *Duke of Portland* v. *Lady Topham* (1864) 11 H.L.C. 32 at 54, *per* Lord Westbury L.C.; and see *Henty* v. *Wrey* (1882) 21 Ch.D. 332 at 354.

[64] *Vatcher* v. *Paull* [1915] A.C. 372 at 378.

[65] *Re Greaves* [1954] Ch. 434.

take the property appointed as the child's next-of-kin.[66] " If a father . . . charges a portion for his child, not because the child wants it, but because the child is delicate in health, and likely to die, this court has authority to defeat such an act." [67]

(*b*) *Foreign purpose*: the appointment was made for purposes foreign to the power. Thus where a mother appoints property to a child with the intent that the child should use it for the benefit of the father, who was not an object of the power, the appointment will be set aside even though the child was ignorant of the mother's intention.[68] But pressure on the appointee to settle the property on himself and his issue (who were not objects of the power) does not necessarily indicate a fraud on the power, for it may well be compatible with a genuine intention to benefit the appointee.[69]

(*c*) *Bargain to benefit non-objects*: the appointment was made in pursuance of a previous agreement with the appointee whereby persons who were not objects of the power obtained some benefit, as where the donee bargained for some advantage for himself [70] or a stranger [71] as a condition of making the appointment. In the case of a power to appoint to one person only, an appointment may be fraudulent and void under this head but not under the previous head, for there is no exercise of a power of selection among two or more objects which might be warped by the mere pressure of a foreign purpose, as distinct from a bargain.[72]

3. Effect of fraud. An appointment which is a fraud on the power under the above rules is usually treated as a whole even if the fraud affects only part; the entire appointment is thus bad.[73] But if the fraudulent part is clearly separable from the rest,[74] the court may hold only the fraudulent part void [75] and the rest valid.[76] Further, a fraudulent appointment is merely void, and does not stop

---

[66] *Lord Hinchinbroke* v. *Seymour* (1789) 1 Bro.C.C. 395; *Lord Wellesley* v. *Earl of Mornington* (1855) 2 K. & J. 143; contrast *Henty* v. *Wrey* (1882) 21 Ch.D. 332 (appointment to healthy children not invalid merely because of their youth).
[67] *Keily* v. *Keily* (1843) 4 Dr. & War. 38 at 55, 56, *per* Sugden L.C.
[68] *Re Marsden's Trusts* (1859) 4 Drew. 594; *Re Crawshay* [1948] Ch. 123 (family pressure); *Re Dick* [1953] Ch. 343 (request in memorandum left with will).
[69] *Re Burton's Settlements* [1955] Ch. 82.
[70] *Farmer* v. *Martin* (1828) 2 Sim. 502 (agreement to pay appointor's debts); *Cochrane* v. *Cochrane* [1922] 2 Ch. 230 (agreement to divorce appointor).
[71] *Birley* v. *Birley* (1858) 25 Beav. 299.
[72] *Re Nicholson's Settlement* [1939] Ch. 11 (see at pp. 18, 19).
[73] See, *e.g., Agassiz* v. *Squire* (1854) 18 Beav. 431.
[74] See *Whelan* v. *Palmer* (1888) 39 Ch.D. 648 at 659.
[75] *Ranking* v. *Barnes* (1864) 33 L.J.Ch. 339.
[76] *Harrison* v. *Randall* (1852) 9 Hare 397.

the appointor subsequently making a fresh appointment [77]; but if this appointment is in favour of the same person, he must show that it is not tainted with the same fraud as the original appointment.[78]

II. POSITION OF A PURCHASER

1. Before 1926. Before 1926 the position of a purchaser of an interest which had been fraudulently appointed depended upon the question whether that interest was legal or equitable. If the interest was legal, the appointment was not void but voidable, *i.e.*, it was good until set aside, so that if before the appointment was avoided the interest passed to a purchaser for value without notice of the fraud, he took a good title.[79] But if the interest was equitable, the appointment was void *ab initio*; even a purchaser without notice got no title, for he had not the security of the legal estate and was merely a subsequent equitable claimant.[80]

2. After 1925. Since 1925 all powers of appointment are equit-able,[81] and so the position of a purchaser is now more precarious. But the Law of Property Act, 1925,[82] gives a very limited measure of protection to purchasers and those deriving title under them.[83] The Act applies whenever the appointment was made, provided the purchase was made after 1925.[84] The purchaser must show—

    (i) that he bought for money or money's worth without notice of the fraud or circumstances from which it might have been discovered upon making reasonable inquiries [85]; and

    (ii) that the appointee with whom he dealt was not less than 25 years of age.[85]

Even if he proves this, he is protected only to the extent of the amount to which, at the time of the appointment, the appointee was presumptively entitled in default of appointment.[86] For example, if A has power to appoint £5,000 among his children and in default of appointment the children share equally, a purchaser from one of the children is protected to the extent of only £1,000 if A had five

---

[77] See *Topham* v. *Duke of Portland* (1869) 5 Ch.App. 40.
[78] *Re Chadwick's Trust* [1939] 1 All E.R. 850.
[79] *M'Queen* v. *Farquhar* (1805) 11 Ves 467; *Cloutte* v. *Storey* [1911] 1 Ch. 18 at 24, 31. In other words, the appointment operated at law but the right to have it set aside for fraud was merely equitable.
[80] *Cloutte* v. *Storey* [1911] 1 Ch. 18; *cf. ante,* p. 117.
[81] L.P.A., 1925, s. 1 (7); *ante*, p. 462.
[82] s. 157.
[83] s. 157 (3).
[84] s. 157 (4).
[85] s. 157 (2).
[86] s. 157 (1).

children at the date of the appointment; if A had two children at that time, £2,500 is the limit of the protection. This is so even if the whole £5,000 has been appointed to one child. A purchaser would have no protection if in default of appointment some third party was entitled to the property.

E. Determination of Powers

A power may be extinguished in two ways.

1. Expressly : by release, or by contract not to exercise it.[87] This rule now [88] applies to all powers except a power coupled with a duty or in the nature of a trust, where a release would be a breach of that duty or trust.[89] Such a release or contract may either totally extinguish the power, or be partial. A partial release may exclude part of the property from the operation of the power, leaving the rest subject to it,[90] or prevent the power being exercised in favour of one or more of the objects.[91] The rules relating to frauds on a power do not apply to the release of a power,[92] so that a bargain to release the power may be made by the donee of the power with those entitled to take in default.

The donee of a power may also disclaim it.[93] Disclaimer does not destroy the power but renders the donee who disclaims incapable of exercising it; it can still be exercised by any other donees.[94]

2. Impliedly : by any dealing inconsistent with the further exercise of the power.[95] Thus if a husband appoints one-quarter of the income to his wife for life, and subject thereto he appoints the property to his children, he cannot, after the death of his wife, appoint a life interest in one-fourth to his second wife, for he has exhausted the power.[96] There is also an implied release when all the purposes for which the power was created cease to exist.[97]

---

[87] L.P.A., 1925, s. 155, replacing C.A., 1881, s. 52. A contract not to exercise a power operates as a release : Farwell, *Powers*, 19.
[88] See *ante*, p. 462.
[89] *Re Eyre* (1883) 49 L.T. 259; and see *Re Mills* [1930] 1 Ch. 654; *Re Wills' Trust Deed* [1964] Ch. 219, distinguished in *Muir* v. *I. R. C.* [1966] 1 W.L.R. 1269.
[90] *Re Evered* [1910] 2 Ch. 147 at 157.
[91] *Re Brown's Settlement* [1939] Ch. 944.
[92] *Re Somes* [1896] 1 Ch. 250.
[93] L.P.A., 1925, s. 156, replacing C.A., 1882, s. 6.
[94] L.P.A., 1925, s. 156 (2).
[95] *Smith* v. *Death* (1820) 5 Madd. 371 at 374; *Foakes* v. *Jackson* [1900] 1 Ch. 807.
[96] *Re Hancock* [1896] 2 Ch. 173.
[97] See *Wolley* v. *Jenkins* (1856) 23 Beav. 53.

CHAPTER 9

WILLS AND INTESTACY

THIS chapter falls into three parts. The first two parts deal with wills and intestacy respectively, setting out the rules which determine who is beneficially entitled to property after the death of the owner. The third part deals with personal representatives, who hold the property of the deceased not for their own benefit but for the purpose of administering it (including the payment of debts and the like) and then vesting what is left in the persons beneficially entitled.

Part 1

WILLS

Sect 1. Freedom of Testation

1. Historical development. For some while after the Norman Conquest it was possible for a man to dispose of both his realty and his personalty by will. At first his powers of disposition over personalty were confined to a fixed proportion, his widow and children being entitled to the rest.[1] During the fourteenth century this restriction disappeared in nearly all parts of the country; but in some places it survived until the seventeenth and eighteenth centuries, the last case being that of London, where it was abolished in 1725.[2] Realty, on the other hand, could at first be freely devised, but by the end of the thirteenth century all power of testamentary disposition had disappeared except in the case of local customs, such as gavelkind.[3] But this restriction was soon evaded by means of uses [4]; and the general belief that the Statute of Uses, 1535, had abolished this indirect power of testamentary disposition provoked such an outcry that the Statute of Wills, 1540,[5] authorised the devise of all socage land and two-thirds of land held by knight

---

[1] P. & M. ii, 348; H.E.L. iii, 550. The fraction varied locally; often he was free to dispose of only a third if he left a widow and children, but a half if he left either a widow or children but not both.
[2] 11 Geo. I, c. 18, 1724, ss. 17, 18; and see H.E.L., iii, 552.
[3] *Ante*, pp. 20, 68; H.E.L. iii, 75, 76.
[4] *Ante*, p. 154.
[5] As explained by the Statute of Wills, 1542.

service.[6] When the Tenures Abolition Act, 1660, converted all land held by knight service into land of socage tenure, all land became devisable. But this power extended only to estates in fee simple: land held in tail could not be disposed of by will before the Law of Property Act, 1925 [7]; and land held *pur autre vie* did not become devisable until the Statute of Frauds was enacted in 1677.[8]

Copyhold land was not within the Statute of Wills, 1540, and devises were effected by the testator in his lifetime making a surrender to the uses of his will.[9] If the testator was a joint tenant, this had the incidental effect of severing the joint tenancy.[10] But by Preston's Act, 1815,[11] a devise without a previous surrender was rendered effective, and the Wills Act, 1837, applied to copyholds as well as to lands of other tenures. It is this latter Act which governs wills of all property, real or personal, today.

2. Inheritance (Family Provision) Act, 1938

(a) *Freedom of testation.* From the fourteenth century until 1939 there was in general no restriction upon a testator's power to dispose of property as he thought fit: for good reasons or bad, he might give all his property to a mistress or to charities, and leave his family penniless. The Inheritance (Family Provision) Act, 1938, gives the court a limited power to modify the effect of a will in certain cases, and the Intestates' Estates Act, 1952, gives the court power to modify even the rules of succession on intestacy. These powers have since been extended by the Family Provision Act 1966.[11a] The Act of 1938 applies to any testator (or testatrix) dying domiciled in England after July 13, 1939,[12] and the Act of 1952 applies to any person dying so domiciled after December 31, 1952.[13]

(b) *Power to make an order.* If the deceased leaves a spouse, son under 21, unmarried daughter,[13a] or a son or daughter incapable of supporting himself or herself through some mental or physical defect, for whom reasonable [14] provision is not made by his will, or by the intestacy law, or by both will and intestacy law in combination, the court may order that reasonable provision for

---

[6] *Ante*, p. 160.
[7] *Ante*, p. 95.
[8] *Ante*, p. 101.
[9] Scriven 146.
[10] *Porter* v. *Porter* (1605) Cro.Jac. 100; *Gale* v. *Gale* (1789) 2 Cox Eq. 136; *Edwards* v. *Champion* (1847) 1 De G. & Sm. 75; (1853) 3 De G.M. & G. 202; and see *ante*, pp. 392, 405, 406.
[11] 55 Geo. 3, c. 192.
[11a] Brought into force by S.I. 1966 no. 1453 and 1967 no. 275.
[12] ss. 1 (1), 6 (2).   [13] s. 7.
[13a] Including one whose marriage has been annulled for incapacity: *Re Rodwell* [1970] Ch. 726.
[14] See *Re Styler* [1942] Ch. 387 at 389; *Re Pugh* [1943] Ch. 387 at 395; *Re E.* [1966] 1 W.L.R. 709; *Re Clayton* [1966] 1 W.L.R. 969; *Re Ducksbury* [1966] 1 W.L.R. 1226; *Re Sivyer* [1967] 1 W.L.R. 1482; *Re Clarke* [1968] 1 W.L.R. 415.

maintenance shall be made out of the net estate.[15] After some fluctuations, it now seems clear that the test is not subjective but objective, *i.e.*, not whether the deceased acted reasonably but whether as events have turned out the provision made is in fact reasonable.[15a] Application must be made not later than [16] six months after the grant of probate or letters of administration, but the court has a free discretion to permit later application if it thinks fit.[17] " Son " and " daughter " include an adopted child [18] and a child *en ventre sa mère*,[19] and also, where the deceased died after 1969, an illegitimate child.[20] " Net estate " excludes property bequeathed in satisfaction of a contractual obligation.[21]

(c) *Maintenance*. The maintenance [22] so ordered may take the form of periodical payments or a lump sum or both.[23] Periodical payments may be determined as the court thinks fit, *e.g.*, as fixed annual sums or as allotments of income of part or the whole of the estate.[23a] Pending final determination the court may make an interim order.[24] The maintenance must cease at latest—

(i) in the case of a spouse, on remarriage;

(ii) in the case of a daughter who has not married or is under disability, on marriage or the cesser of. her disability, whichever is the later [25];

(iii) in the case of a son under 21, on his attaining 21;

(iv) in the case of a son under disability, on the cesser of his disability;

and in any case, it ceases at death.[26]

The court may charge any sum awarded on any part of the deceased's estate, so that it may fall to some extent on specific

---

[15] Act of 1938, s. 1 (1), as amended by Act of 1952, s. 7 and 3rd Sched. The whole Act as further amended is conveniently set out in the Act of 1966, 3rd Sched.; but see Family Law Reform Act 1969, s. 5 (1).

[15a] *Re Goodwin* [1969] 1 Ch. 283, approved in *Re Shanahan* [1973] Fam. 1 and *Millward* v. *Shenton* [1972] 1 W.L.R. 711.

[16] *Re Searle* [1949] Ch. 73 (application before probate valid).

[17] Family Provision Act 1966, s. 5. See *Re Ruttie* [1970] 1 W.L.R. 89.

[18] If adopted in the U.K., Isle of Man or Channel Islands: Family Provision Act 1966, s. 8.

[19] Act of 1938, s. 5 (1).

[20] Family Law Reform Act 1969, s. 18; but not previously: *Re Makein* [1955] Ch. 194.

[21] See *Schaefer* v. *Schuhmann* [1972] A.C. 572, decided under the corresponding Act of New South Wales.

[22] See *Re Vrint* [1940] Ch. 920; (1940) 56 L.Q.R. 441 (R.E.M.).

[23] Family Provision Act 1966, s. 4.

[23a] *Ibid.*, s. 3 (2).

[24] *Ibid.*, s. 6 and 1st Sched.

[25] See *Re Pointer* [1941] Ch. 60 at 68; (1941) 57 L.Q.R. 20 (R.E.M.).

[26] s. 1 (2), as amended by Family Law Reform Act 1969, s. 5 (1).

legatees as well as on those entitled to the residue.[27] If there is any possibility of an application being made under the Act, therefore, it is inadvisable for the executors to begin distribution of any part of the estate until the time limit has expired.[27]

(d) *Discretion of court.* The court's power is entirely discretionary, and all the relevant factors must be considered, including the conduct of the dependant in question [28] and the deceased's reasons (if ascertainable) for not providing for the dependant, including those in any statement in writing signed by the deceased and dated.[29] There is a limited power for the court to vary any order.[30]

(e) *Nullity or divorce.* Similar but by no means identical provisions have been made for applications for maintenance by a person whose marriage to the deceased has been ended by a decree of nullity or divorce.[31]

Sect. 2. Nature of a Will

1. A will is ambulatory. Until the death of the testator a will has no effect at all,[32] but operates as a mere declaration of his intention, which may be changed from time to time. For this reason, a will is said to be "ambulatory." This distinguishes a will from a conveyance, settlement or other dealing *inter vivos,* which operates at once or at some fixed time.[33]

A will is also ambulatory in that it "speaks from death," *i.e.,* it is capable of disposing of all property owned by the testator at his death, even if acquired after the date of the will. Before 1838 this was true only of personalty: a will could not dispose of realty acquired between the making of the will and death. But by the Wills Act, 1837,[34] unless a contrary intention appears, a will now speaks from death with regard to both real and personal property.

---

27 *Re Simson* [1950] Ch. 38.

28 See *Re Andrews* [1955] 1 W.L.R. 1105; (1956) 72 L.Q.R. 18 (R.E.M.).

29 s. 1 (5)–(8), as amended (see Act of 1966, 3rd Sched.). For examples of applications made under the Act see the cases cited above and *Re Lidington* [1940] Ch. 927; *Re Inns* [1947] Ch. 576; *Re Bidie* [1949] Ch. 121; *Re Borthwick* [1949] Ch. 395; *Re Smallwood* [1951] Ch. 369; *Re Doring* [1955] 1 W.L.R 1217.

30 s. 4, as amended: see Act of 1966, 3rd Sched.

31 Matrimonial Causes Act 1965, ss. 26–28, as amended by Matrimonial Causes Act 1973, Sched. 2; *Re Eyre* [1968] 1 W.L.R. 530; *Re Harker-Thomas* [1969] P. 28; *Re Shanahan* [1973] Fam. 1.

32 *Re Baroness Llanover* [1903] 2 Ch. 330 at 335; *Re Thompson* [1906] 2 Ch. 199 at 205.

33 See Jarman 26. But a will_may, as soon as made, rank as a "disposition" for certain statutory purposes: see *Re Gilpin* [1954] Ch. 1, and contrast *Berkeley* v. *Berkeley* [1946] A.C. 555 (" provision "), noted (1946) 62 L.Q.R. 340 (R.E.M.).

34 s. 24; *post,* p. 500.

2. A will is revocable. Notwithstanding any declaration in the will itself or any other document, a will can be revoked at any time.[35] A binding contract not to revoke a will does not prevent its revocation,[36] though it gives a right of action for damages against the testator's estate if the will is revoked.[37] Such a contract will usually be construed as confined to acts of revocation performed as such, and not to the revocation that usually results automatically from marriage[38]; and even if the contract is wide enough to extend to marriage, it will be valid only so far as it is not in restraint of marriage.[39] In the case of land,[40] or where an implied trust arises from an agreement to make mutual wills,[41] the effect of a contract not to revoke the will is that the person to whom the assets have passed may be compelled to hold these on trust in accordance with the terms of the contract.[42]

3. Codicils. A codicil is similar to a will and is governed by the same rules. A testamentary document is usually called a codicil if it is supplementary to a will and adds to, varies or revokes provisions in the will: if it is an independent instrument, it is called a will. Although sometimes indorsed on a will, a codicil may be a separate document, and can stand by itself even if the will to which it is supplementary is revoked.[43] Codicils are construed in such a way as to disturb the provisions of a will no more than is absolutely necessary to give effect to the codicil.[44]

4. Infants. Before 1838 a male infant could make a will of personalty (but not realty [45]) if fourteen years old, and a female infant if twelve.[46] Since 1837 no infant can make a valid will,[47] except in the special cases of privilege (soldiers, sailors, marines and airmen)

---

[35] *Vynior's Case* (1610) 8 Co.Rep. 81b.
[36] *In b. Heys* [1914] P. 192.
[37] *Synge* v. *Synge* [1894] 1 Q.B. 466.
[38] *Re Marsland* [1939] Ch. 820; for revocation by marriage, see *post*, p. 484.
[39] *Robinson* v. *Ommanney* (1883) 23 Ch.D. 285; for restraint of marriage, see *ante*, p. 80.
[40] *i.e.*, where the contract creates an equitable interest: *ante*, p. 132; *Goylmer* v. *Paddiston* (1682) 2 Ventr. 353; and see note 42 below.
[41] *Ante*, p. 441.
[42] *Dufour* v. *Pereira* (1769) Dick. 419; *Stone* v. *Hoskins* [1905] P. 194; *Re Oldham* [1925] Ch. 75 (reviewing the authorities); *Re Green* [1951] Ch. 148. But a purchaser of a legal estate without notice, or against whom the contract is void for want of registration, will take free from it: *ante*, p. 134. Yet *quaere* whether a contract to devise is an estate contract within the meaning of the L.C.A. 1972. For the statutory definition, see *post*, p. 1040.
[43] *Black* v. *Jobling* (1869) L.R. 1 P. & D. 685; *In b. Savage* (1870) L.R. 2 P. & D. 78.
[44] *Doe* d. *Hearle* v. *Hicks* (1832) 1 Cl. & F. 20; Jarman 194.
[45] Statute of Wills, 1542, s. 14.
[46] *Hyde* v. *Hyde* (1711) Prec.Ch. 316; and see Co.Litt. 89b, n. 6.
[47] Wills Act, 1837, s. 7, as amended by Family Law Reform Act 1969, s. 3 (1), reducing the age of majority from 21 to 18 with effect from January 1, 1970.

explained later.[48] But infants of sixteen years or more have statutory power to make nominations of certain property (*e.g.*, money in savings banks) to take effect on death.[49]

Sect. 3. The Formalities of a Will

A. History

The Statute of Wills, 1540,[50] required a will of realty to be made in writing, although it was unnecessary for it to be signed by the testator, or witnessed. Wills of personalty could be made by word of mouth. The Statute of Frauds, 1677,[51] required all wills of realty [52] not only to be in writing but also to be signed by the testator (or by some person in his presence and by his direction) and attested in his presence by at least three credible witnesses. The statute also laid down such stringent requirements for nuncupative (*i.e.*, oral) wills of personalty over £30 [53] that thereafter wills of personalty were usually made in writing. Written wills of personalty required no witnesses and did not need to be signed by the testator if written or acknowledged by him.[54]

The Wills Act, 1837, repealed these provisions as regards all wills made after 1837 [55] and substituted a uniform code for both realty and personalty.

Rules as to formality for foreigners' wills and for wills made abroad were formerly laid down by the Wills Act, 1861, and are now to be found in the Wills Act 1963.

B. Formal Wills

I. EXECUTION

" No will shall be valid unless it shall be in writing and . . . signed at the foot or end thereof by the testator, or by some other person in his presence and by his direction, and such signature shall be

---

[48] *Post*, p. 487.

[49] See Jarman 35, 36; Lawton's *Guide to the Law of Trustee Savings Banks* (3rd ed., 1962), pp. 368–388; Administration of Estates (Small Payments) Act 1965 (raising the maximum amount for nominations to £500).

[50] s. 1. This did not affect customary wills: Rob.Gav. 299.

[51] s. 5. This expressly applied to land devisable by custom, *e.g.*, gavelkind.

[52] Leaseholds and copyholds were not within the statute (Cru.Dig. vi, 69); *secus* if the will, instead of assigning an existing lease, created a new one: *ibid.*, 63.

[53] ss. 19, 20 (three witnesses; made during testator's last sickness, and (usually) in his own home; and the witnesses' evidence was inadmissible after six months unless the will was committed to writing within six days).

[54] See H.E.L. iii, 538; Bailey, *Wills*, 21, 22.

[55] ss. 2, 34.

made or acknowledged by the testator in the presence of two or more witnesses present at the same time, and such witnesses shall attest and shall subscribe the will in the presence of the testator, but no form of attestation shall be necessary." [56]

This is the primary provision of the Wills Act, 1837, which today governs the form of a will; and like other such provisions it has given rise to much litigation.

1. Writing : the will must be in writing.[57] Any form of writing, printing, typewriting and the like may be employed,[58] or a combination of these, *e.g.*, a printed form completed in manuscript [59]; but pencil writing on a will made in ink is presumed to be merely deliberative, and will be excluded from probate unless it appears to be intended to be operative.[60] No special form of words need be used: all that is required is an intelligible document [61] which indicates an *animus testandi* (intention to make a will).[62]

2. Signature by testator : the will must be signed by the testator, or by someone else in his presence and by his direction.[63] The testator's signature may be made in any way, provided there is an intention to execute the will. Thus initials,[64] a stamped name,[65] a mark [66] (even if the testator could write [67]), or a signature in a former [68] or assumed [69] name all suffice.[70] But a seal is not enough, for the will must be signed, and sealing is not signing.[71] Similar principles apply to signature by someone on behalf of the testator. Thus signature of his own name instead of that of the testator is

---

[56] Wills Act, 1837, s. 9.

[57] *Ibid.*

[58] See, *e.g.*, *In b. Usborne* (1909) 25 T.L.R. 519.

[59] *In b. Moore* [1892] P. 378.

[60] *In b. Adams* (1872) L.R. 2 P. & D. 367.

[61] *e.g.*, *Thorn* v. *Dickens* [1906] W.N. 54 (entire will consisting of words " all for mother ").

[62] In *Re Meynell* [1949] W.N. 273 probate was granted of written instructions to a solicitor, which had been duly witnessed because of fears that the testator might die suddenly. Where these formalities are observed there is a strong presumption of *animus testandi: ibid.*

[63] Wills Act, 1837, s. 9.

[64] *In b. Savory* (1851) 15 Jur. 1042.

[65] *Jenkins* v. *Gaisford* (1863) 3 Sw. & Tr. 93.

[66] *e.g.*, a thumb-mark: *In b. Finn* (1936) 53 T.L.R. 153.

[67] *Baker* v. *Dening* (1838) 8 A. & E. 94.

[68] *In b. Glover* (1847) 11 Jur. 1022.

[69] *In b. Redding* (1850) 2 Rob.Ecc. 339.

[70] And see *In b. Chalcraft* [1948] P. 222 (testatrix too ill to complete more than part of her surname: held valid); *In b. Cook* [1960] 1 W.L.R. 353 (" your loving Mother ": held valid).

[71] *Wright* v. *Wakeford* (1811) 17 Ves. 454.

sufficient.[72] But it is essential that the signature should be made in the testator's presence and authorised by him, either expressly or by implication.[73]

3. Position of signature: the signature must be at the " foot or end " of the will.[74] At first this requirement was interpreted liberally,[75] but later the courts insisted upon a strict compliance, and probate was refused to a will which left no room for signature at the end of the third side and was signed in the middle of a blank fourth side.[76] Consequently the Wills Act Amendment Act, 1852,[77] made elaborate provisions for most of the positions in which a signature could possibly appear: it might be placed " at or after, or following or under or beside or opposite to the end of the will "; or it might be put in the attestation clause, or below the witnesses' signatures, or on a separate sheet, or after a blank space below the will. The effect of the Act is that if it is apparent from the face of the will that the testator intended by his signature to give effect to the will, probate will be granted; but nothing which was inserted after the will was signed,[78] or which follows the signature in space, will be effective. Probate will therefore be granted to every part of the will except that which comes after the signature either in time or in space.

For example, where a will ended in the middle of the third page of a sheet of paper and was executed at the bottom of the fourth page, the intervening space being left blank, probate was granted.[79] In another case the will was written on one sheet of paper, one side of which contained all the bequests and the other the usual opening words " This is the last Will and Testament," the appointment of an executor and, beneath these, the signature of the testatrix. It was held that the proper way to read the will was to start with the bequests and then to turn over; the will was thus admitted to probate.[80] The court may even ignore the numbered order of the pages in order to reduce the signature to the foot or end of the will,[81] or be satisfied with a signature in the margin [82] or in a space

---

[72] *In b. Clark* (1839) 2 Curt. 329.   [73] *In b. Marshall* (1866) 13 L.T. 643.
[74] Wills Act, 1837, s. 9. Formerly the signature might be anywhere in the will (*Lemoyne* v. *Stanley* (1681) 3 Lev. 1), and a holograph will (*i.e.*, one made in the testator's own handwriting) might be effective even if unsigned: *In b. Cooper* (1848) 1 Rob.Ecc. 633.
[75] See *Smee* v. *Bryer* (1848) 1 Rob.Ecc. 616 at 623.
[76] *Smee* v. *Bryer* (1848) 1 Rob.Ecc. 616.
[77] See Bailey, *Wills*, 53.
[78] *e.g.*, *In b. Arthur* (1871) L.R. 2 P. & D. 273; *In b. Little* [1960] 1 W.L.R. 495.
[79] *Hunt* v. *Hunt* (1866) L.R. 1 P. & D. 209.
[80] *In b. Long* [1936] P. 166.
[81] *In b. Smith* [1931] P. 225 (pages numbered 1, 2, 3 and signed on p. 1, read in the order 2, 3, 1); compare *Royle* v. *Harris* [1895] P. 163.
[82] *In b. Usborne* (1909) 25 T.L.R. 519; *Re Roberts* [1934] P. 102.

ruled off halfway down the only page of the will,[83] or on the envelope containing the will [84]; and words written before the will was signed but following the signature in space will be effective if incorporated by words above the signature, *e.g.,* " see other side for completion," [85] though it is not enough that a sentence begun on the signed page is continued on an unsigned page.[86] Although the court will go to all lengths within the limit of reasonable construction to save a will from defeat by such formal defects [87] it will not resort to physical interference with it, such as folding or bending the paper.[88]

Effect will be given to dispositions contained in a document which has not been executed as a will if the document is incorporated in a will. For this to be the case—

(i) the will must clearly [89] identify the document to be incorporated [90];

(ii) the will must refer to the document as being already in existence [91] and not as one subsequently to be made [92]; and

(iii) the document must in fact be in existence when the will [93] (or a codicil confirming it [94]) is executed.

4. Presence of witnesses: the testator must make the whole [94a] of the signature (or acknowledge it) in the presence of two witnesses present at the same time.[95] Whether the signature to the will is made by the testator or by someone in his presence and by his direction, there is no need for witnesses to be present at the time of the signature if they are present when the testator subsequently makes a proper acknowledgment [95a] of the signature. But either the signature or the acknowledgment must be made in the simultaneous presence of two witnesses. An express acknowledgment is desirable but not

[83] *In b. Hornby* [1946] P. 171; contrast *In b. Harris* [1952] P. 319 (signature in top right-hand corner insufficient).

[84] *In b. Mann* [1942] P. 146 (see (1943) 59 L.Q.R. 20 (R.E.M.)); contrast *In b. Bean* [1944] P. 83. See also *Re Beadle* [1974] 1 W.L.R. 417.

[85] *Palin* v. *Ponting* [1930] P. 185. Contrast *In b. Bercovitz* [1962] 1 W.L.R. 321 (will signed at beginning and end but only first signature attested: probate refused).

[86] *In b. Gee* (1898) 78 L.T. 843; *Practice Direction* [1953] 1 W.L.R. 689.

[87] *In b. Jones* (1865) 34 L.J.P. 41; *Re Roberts* [1934] P. 102.

[88] *Re Stalman* (1931) 145 L.T. 339 (will signed at top cannot be folded in a circle).

[89] But see *In b. Saxton* [1939] 2 All E.R. 418.

[90] *In b. Garnett* [1894] P. 90.

[91] *In b. Sutherland* (1866) L.R. 1 P. & D. 198.

[92] *University College of North Wales* v. *Taylor* [1908] P. 140.

[93] *Singleton* v. *Tomlinson* (1878) 3 App.Cas. 404.

[94] *In b. Hunt* (1853) 2 Rob.Ecc. 622. But the will, speaking from the date of the codicil, must here refer to the document as existing (*In b. Truro* (1866) L.R. 1 P. & D. 201); it is not enough that in fact the document was made before the codicil: *In b. Smart* [1902] P. 238. [94a] *Re Colling* [1972] 1 W.L.R. 1440.

[95] Wills Act, 1837, s. 9.

[95a] See *Re Groffman* [1969] 1 W.L.R. 733 (will in testator's pocket: no sufficient acknowledgment).

essential[96]; a gesture by the testator may suffice,[97] and an acknowledgment by a third party is effective if it can be shown that it should
be taken to be the acknowledgment of the testator.[98]

It is immaterial if the witnesses do not know that the document
is a will[99]; it suffices if they see the testator write something (even
if they do not know that it is his signature[1]), or if he asks them to
sign a document on which they see his signature,[2] or could have seen
it if they had looked.[3]   But there is no signature in the presence of a
witness if, although in the room, he had no knowledge that the
testator was writing; a man cannot be a witness to an act of which
he is unconscious.[4]   Similarly, a blind person cannot witness a will.[5]

It is desirable but not essential[6] that the witnesses should be of
full age and sound intelligence.

5. Signature by witnesses : the witnesses must then sign in the
presence of the testator.[7]   No form of attestation is necessary,[8]
although a proper attestation clause showing that the will has been
executed in accordance with the statutory requirements will facilitate
the grant of probate.   All that is necessary is that after the testator's
signature has been made or acknowledged in the joint presence of
two witnesses, they should sign their names in the testator's presence.
It suffices that the testator knew that they were signing,[9] and either
saw them sign,[10] or could have seen them if he had wished,[11] or if he
had not been blind.[12]

---

[96] Except where the testator is acknowledging a signature made by someone else
on his behalf: see *In b. Summers* (1850) 14 Jur. 791.
[97] *In b. Davies* (1850) 2 Rob.Ecc. 337.
[98] *Inglesant* v. *Inglesant* (1874) L.R. 3 P. & D. 172; but see *Morritt* v. *Douglas*
(1872) L.R. 3 P. & D. 1.
[99] *Daintree* v. *Fasulo* (1888) 13 P.D. 102; *In b. Benjamin* (1934) 150 L.T. 417.
[1] *Smith* v. *Smith* (1866) L.R. 1 P. & D. 143.
[2] *Fischer* v. *Popham* (1875) L.R. 3 P. & D. 246; and see *Brown* v. *Skirrow*
[1902] P. 3 at 5.
[3] *In b. Gunstan* (1882) 7 P.D. 102 (see at p. 108); *secus* if the signature is
covered up: *ibid.*
[4] *Brown* v. *Skirrow* [1902] P. 3.
[5] *In b. Gibson* [1949] P. 434.
[6] Wills Act, 1837, s. 14; Jarman 143, 144; *Smith* v. *Thompson* (1931) 146 L.T.
14 (effective attestation by infant).
[7] Wills Act, 1837, s. 9.   The testator must be mentally as well as physically
present, but latitude is allowed if a proper signature in the presence of witnesses
has already been made: *In b. Chalcraft* [1948] P. 222 (testatrix losing conscious-
ness after signature and during attestation: will held valid).
[8] Wills Act, 1837, s. 9; and see *In b. Colyer* (1889) 60 L.T. 368 (will executed in
form of a deed held valid); *In b. Denning* [1958] 1 W.L.R. 462 (mere presence
of two other signatures).
[9] *Jenner* v. *Finch* (1879) 5 P.D. 106.
[10] *e.g., Casson* v. *Dade* (1781) 1 Bro.C.C. 99 (view from carriage of witnesses
signing in attorney's office).
[11] *In b. Trinnell* (1865) 11 Jur.(N.S.) 248.
[12] *In b. Piercy* (1845) 1 Rob.Ecc. 278.

There is no provision allowing a witness to acknowledge his signature. Thus if the testator signs in the presence of A, who signs his name, and then B is called in and both the testator and A acknowledge their signatures to B, who then signs, probate will be refused.[13] The testator did not sign or acknowledge his signature in the presence of two witnesses until B was called in, and A's subsequent acknowledgment of his signature is no substitute for signing after the testator as required by the Act.[13]

There is no need for the witnesses to sign in each other's presence,[14] although this is both usual and desirable. They may sign by a mark[15] or initials,[16] and the position of their signatures is immaterial, provided they are made with intent to attest the operative[17] signature of the testator.[18]

II. ALTERATIONS

"No obliteration, interlineation, or other alteration made in any will after the execution thereof[19] shall be valid or have any effect, except so far as the words or effect of the will before such alteration shall not be apparent, unless such alteration shall be executed in like manner as hereinbefore is required for the execution of the will[20] . . ." The Act goes on to provide that the signatures of the testator and the witnesses may be written either opposite or near to the alteration (*e.g.*, in the margin) or else at the foot or end of, or opposite to, a memorandum referring to the alteration.[20] Signature by means of initials suffices.[21] A codicil confirming a will gives effect to any alterations of the will existing at the date of the codicil,[22] unless the codicil shows that the testator was treating the will as being unaltered.[23]

An obliteration or erasure of part of a will, even though unattested, has the effect of revoking that part in so far as it makes that part impossible to read (" not apparent "), provided that there

---

13 *In b. Allen* (1839) 2 Curt. 331; *In b. Simmonds* (1842) 2 Curt. 79; *Wyatt* v. *Berry* [1893] P. 5.
14 *In b. Webb* (1855) Dea. & Sw. 1.
15 *In b. Amiss* (1849) 2 Rob.Ecc. 116. But a seal does not suffice: *In b. Byrd* (1842) 3 Curt. 117.
16 *In b. Streatley* [1891] P. 172.
17 *Phipps* v. *Hale* (1874) L.R. 3 P. & D. 166.
18 *In b. Braddock* (1876) 1 P.D. 433 (witnesses to codicil signed on will to which it was pinned: held valid); *In b. Streatley, supra.*
19 See *In b. Campbell* [1954] 1 W.L.R. 516 (interlineation prior to execution).
20 Wills Act, 1837, s. 21.
21 *In b. Blewitt* (1880) 5 P.D. 116.
22 *In b. Hall* (1871) L.R. 2 P. & D. 256 at 257, 258.
23 *Re Hay* [1904] 1 Ch. 317 (unattested deletion of three legacies in will; codicil revoked one legacy: *held*, the other two stood).

was an intention to revoke.[24] The same applies to the pasting of paper over part of a will,[25] provided the words are not decipherable by any natural means, such as by the use of magnifying glasses or by holding the will up to the light.[26] The court will not permit physical interference with the will, as by using chemicals[27] or removing paper pasted over the words[28]; for they must be " apparent " on the will as it stands. Similarly, they are not " apparent " if they can be read only by making some other document, such as an infra-red photograph.[29] But intention to revoke is always necessary, and where paper is pasted over the amounts of legacies, but not the names of the recipients, the intention is evidently to revoke only by substituting new amounts. The doctrine of conditional revocation (explained below[30]) may then come to the rescue, so that the original amounts are unrevoked and can be proved by any means, including infra-red photography.[31]

III.   REVOCATION

A will or codicil may be revoked by another will or codicil, by destruction, or by marriage; and revocation may be conditional.

1. By another will or codicil. A revocation clause expressly revoking all former wills is effective,[32] provided it is contained in a document[33] executed with the proper formalities.[34] This is so even if the testator had been misled as to the effect of the clause,[35] but not if the testator did not know of the presence of the clause.[36] A misapprehension may, however, admit the doctrine of conditional revocation, explained below.[37] A will is not revoked merely through a later will being entitled (as is usual) " This is the last will and testament of me " or some similar phrase.[38]

---

[24] *Townley* v. *Watson* (1844) 3 Curt. 761. For revocation by destruction, see *post*, p. 483.   [25] *In b. Horsford* (1874) L.R. 3 P. & D. 211.
[26] *Ffinch* v. *Combe* [1894] P. 191; *In b. Brasier* [1899] P. 36.
[27] *Ffinch* v. *Combe, supra*, at p. 193.
[28] *In b. Horsford* (1874) L.R. 3 P. & D. 211. Where words illegible in 1874 had gradually become legible, they were admitted to probate in 1894: *Ffinch* v. *Combe* [1894] P. 191; and see *In b. Gilbert* [1893] P 183 for removal of paper in order to ascertain whether an earlier will had been revoked, for the obliteration of the revoking words would not revive it: *post*, p. 486.
[29] *In b. Itter* [1950] P. 130.   [30] *Post*, p. 485.
[31] *In b. Itter, supra.*
[32] Including, in the absence of special circumstances (*Smith* v. *Thompson* (1931) 146 L.T. 14), the exercise of any power of appointment made thereby: *Re Kingdon* (1886) 32 Ch.D. 604; *Lowthorpe-Lutwidge* v. *Lowthorpe-Lutwidge* [1935] P. 151.
[33] See *Re Spracklan's Estate* [1938] 2 All E.R. 345 (duly executed letter directing destruction of will in recipient's custody held effective).
[34] Wills Act, 1837, s. 20.
[35] *Collins* v. *Elstone* [1893] P. 1; *Re Horrocks* [1939] P. 198 at 216; but see *Re Phelan* [1972] Fam. 33.
[36] *In b. Oswald* (1874) L.R. 3 P. & D. 162; *In b. Moore* [1892] P. 378.
[37] *Post*, p. 485.   [38] *Simpson* v. *Foxon* [1907] P. 54.

A will is revoked by implication if a later will is executed which merely repeats the former will [39] or is inconsistent with it [40]; but if the repetition or inconsistency is merely partial, those parts of the former will which are not repeated in the later will or inconsistent with it remain effective.[41] Any number of testamentary documents may be read together, each being effective except so far as subsequently varied or revoked; the sum total constitutes the testator's will.[42]

2. By destruction. A will is revoked "by the burning, tearing, or otherwise destroying the same by the testator, or by some person in his presence and by his direction, with the intention of revoking the same." [43] There are thus two elements: an act of destruction, and an *animus revocandi* (intention to revoke).

(*a*) *Destruction.* It is not necessary that the will should be completely destroyed; there must, however, be some burning, tearing or other destruction of the whole will or some essential part of it, as by cutting off [44] or obliterating [45] the signature of the testator [46] or the witnesses.[47] It is not enough for the testator to draw a line through part of the will, indorse it "all these are revoked" and kick it into the corner.[48] Destruction of part of a will normally revokes that part alone,[49] unless the part destroyed is so important as to lead to the conclusion that the rest cannot be intended to stand alone.[50] Destruction by someone other than the testator is ineffective unless carried out both in his presence [51] and by his direction [52]; the testator cannot ratify an unauthorised destruction.[53]

---

[39] *Re Hawksley's Settlement* [1934] Ch. 384: see at pp. 397, 398. But consider *In b. Musgrave* (1932) [1934] Ch. 402 at 405.

[40] *In b. Bryan* [1907] P. 125.

[41] *Lemage* v. *Goodban* (1865) L.R. 1 P. & D. 57.

[42] *In b. Fenwick* (1867) L.R. 1 P. & D. 319; *cf. Townsend* v. *Moore* [1905] P. 66 (two inconsistent wills of uncertain priority: probate refused to each); *Re Robinson* [1930] 2 Ch. 332 (no revocation by ineffective disposition).

[43] Wills Act, 1837, s. 20.

[44] *In b. Gullan* (1858) 1 Sw. & Tr. 23.

[45] *In b. Morton* (1887) 12 P.D. 141; contrast *In b. Godfrey* (1893) 69 L.T. 22 (signature remaining legible).

[46] *In b. Gullan, supra.*

[47] *Williams* v. *Tyley* (1858) John. 530.

[48] *Cheese* v. *Lovejoy* (1877) 2 P.D. 251.

[49] See *In b. Woodward* (1871) L.R. 2 P. & D. 206 (seven or eight lines out of a will written on seven sheets); *In b. Nunn* (1936) 105 L.J.P. 57 (part of will cut out and remaining parts stitched together; partial revocation only).

[50] *Leonard* v. *Leonard* [1902] P. 243 (two out of five sheets destroyed).

[51] *In b. Dadds* (1857) Dea. & Sw. 290; *In b. De Kremer* (1965) 110 S.J. 18 (solicitor burns will on client's telephone instructions).

[52] *Gill* v. *Gill* [1909] P. 157.

[53] *Ibid.*

If a will has been destroyed without being revoked (*e.g.*, because an *animus revocandi* was lacking), it is proved by means of a draft or copy, or even by oral evidence.[54] A will kept in the testator's possession but which cannot be found at the testator's death is presumed to have been destroyed by him *animo revocandi* and cannot be proved[55] unless the presumption is rebutted by evidence of non-revocation.[56]

(*b*) *Intent to revoke.* The testator must have an *animus revocandi* at the time of the destruction. If a will is intentionally torn up by a testator who is drunk[57] or believes the will to be ineffective,[58] it is not revoked, for an intent to destroy the document is no substitute for the requisite intent to revoke the will.[59] " All the destroying in the world without intention will not revoke a will, nor all the intention in the world without destroying: there must be the two." [60]

3. By marriage. Marriage automatically revokes all wills made by the parties to the marriage.[61] There are two exceptions.

(*a*) *Certain appointments.* An appointment by will under a power of appointment is not revoked by the marriage of the testator unless, in default of appointment, the property would pass as on his intestacy.[62] The general intention of this provision is that if the testator's new " family " will get the property even if the will is revoked, there is no harm in allowing marriage to revoke it. But if in default of appointment the property would pass out of the " family," as defined by the rules of intestacy, or only partly to that family,[63] the will is allowed to stand so far as it exercises the power of appointment, though the rest of the will is revoked.[64]

(*b*) *Contemplation of marriage.* A will made after 1925 and expressed to be made in contemplation of a marriage is not revoked

---

54 *In b. Dadds* (1857) Dea. & Sw. 290 (copy); *Sugden* v. *Lord St. Leonards* (1876) 1 P.D. 154 (oral evidence of a beneficiary: the leading case on this subject); *Mills* v. *Millward* (1889) 15 P.D. 20 (affidavit by executor); *Re Webb* [1964] 1 W.L.R. 509.
55 *Eckersley* v. *Platt* (1866) L.R. 1 P. & D. 281; *Allan* v. *Morrison* [1900] A.C. 604.
56 *Sugden* v. *Lord St. Leonards, supra.*
57 *In b. Brassington* [1902] P. 1.
58 *In b. Thornton* (1889) 14 P.D. 82; *cf. In b. Southerden* [1925] P. 177 at 185.
59 See *Giles* v. *Warren* (1872) L.R. 2 P. & D. 401.
60 *Cheese* v. *Lovejoy* (1877) 2 P.D. 251 at 253, *per* James L.J.
61 Wills Act, 1837, s. 18. There is no corresponding provision for divorce.
62 *Ibid.*, as explained in *In b. Gilligan* [1950] P. 32 at 38, discussed at (1951) 67 L.Q.R. 351 (J. D. B. Mitchell); see A.E.A., 1925, s. 50 (1), and *post*, p. 523, for the intestacy rules.
63 See *In b. McVicar* (1869) L.R. 1 P. & D. 671; *Re Paul* [1921] 2 Ch. 1.
64 *In b. Russell* (1890) 15 P.D. 111; see also *In b. Gilligan* [1950] P. 32 at 38, which contains a helpful explanation of the enactment.

by the solemnisation of the marriage contemplated.[65] This exception applies only if the will refers to the particular marriage in fact celebrated; it is not enough for the testator to declare in the will that it is " made in contemplation of marriage," [66] though it suffices if the will gives everything [67] to an identified beneficiary described as " my fiancée " [67a] or possibly " my wife." [68]

4. Conditional revocation. Revocation of a will may be conditional, in which case the will remains unrevoked until the condition has been fulfilled.[69] One particular kind of conditional revocation is known as dependent relative revocation.[70] If revocation is relative to another will and intended to be dependent upon the validity of that will, the revocation is ineffective unless that other will takes effect. Thus if a will is destroyed by a testator who is about to make a new will, and the evidence shows that he intended to revoke the old will only in order to make way for the new one, the old will remains valid if the new will is never executed.[71] No special declaration of intention is necessary, since the court will readily infer it from the fact that a new will was contemplated.[72]

Another example arises in the case of revival: if Will No. 1 is revoked by Will No. 2, the revocation of Will No. 2 is not sufficient to revive Will No. 1,[73] so that if the testator revokes Will No. 2 in the mistaken belief that he is thereby reviving Will No. 1, the doctrine of dependent relative revocation applies and the revocation of Will No. 2 is ineffective.[74] Similarly with obliterations [75]: if a testator obliterates a legacy and by unattested writing substitutes a new

---

[65] L.P.A., 1925, s. 177.   [66] *Sallis* v. *Jones* [1936] P. 43.
[67] *Re Coleman* [1975] 2 W.L.R. 213 (gift of part not enough).
[67a] *In b. Langston* [1953] P. 100, preferred on this point in *Re Coleman, supra,* to *Burton* v. *McGregor* [1953] N.Z.L.R. 487.
[68] *Pilot* v. *Gainfort* [1931] P. 103, doubted in *Re Coleman, supra.*
[69] *e.g., In b. Southerden* [1925] P. 177 (will destroyed in mistaken belief that testator's widow would take all his property on his intestacy: *held,* not revoked); *cf. Campbell* v. *French* (1797) 3 Ves. 321 (mistaken belief that legatee was dead); *In b. Greenstreet* (1930) 74 S.J. 188.
[70] A title " somewhat overloaded with unnecessary polysyllables. The resounding adjectives add very little, as it seems to me, to any clear idea of what is meant. The whole matter can be quite simply expressed by the word ' conditional ' ": *In b. Hope Brown* [1942] P. 136 at 138, per Langton J.
[71] *Onions* v. *Tyrer* (1716) 2 Vern. 742; *Dixon* v. *Solicitor to the Treasury* [1905] P. 42 (testator gave instructions for new will, tore off his signature from old will, and died before new will completed: old will admitted to probate); *In b. Hope Brown* [1942] P. 136 (new will incomplete by reason of omission of names of beneficiaries: both old and new wills admitted to probate); *In b. Davies* [1951] 1 All E.R. 920 (new will invalid owing to defective attestation: old will admitted to probate); *In b. Bromham* [1952] 1 All E.R. 110 (will mutilated with intention (never completed) of making a new will: old will admitted to probate); *In b. Cocke* [1960] 1 W.L.R. 491; [1960] 2 All E.R. 289; contrast *Re Feis* [1964] Ch. 106.
[72] See cases cited in previous note.   [73] *Post,* p. 486.
[74] *Powell* v. *Powell* (1866) L.R. 1 P. & D. 209; *In b. Bridgewater* [1965] 1 W.L.R. 416 (letter by testator admissible evidence both of destruction and of his intent).
[75] For obliterations, see *ante,* p. 481.

legacy,[76] or pastes over the amount of a legacy an unattested slip of paper bearing a new amount,[77] the old legacy remains effective if the court is satisfied that it was revoked only on the erroneous supposition that the new legacy would be effective.

IV. REVIVAL

A will revoked by destruction *animo revocandi* can never be revived.[78] Any other will can be revived, but only by re-execution with the proper formalities or by a codicil showing an intention to revive it.[79] If a will has been revoked by a subsequent will, the first will is thus not revived merely by the revocation of the later will.[80] If a will is first partially revoked, then wholly revoked, and then revived, the revival does not extend to the part partially revoked unless an intention to this effect is shown.[81]

C. *Informal Wills*

A long-standing dispensation from the rules of formality is confirmed by the Wills Act, 1837, in the following words: " Provided always, that any soldier being in actual military service, or any mariner or seaman being at sea, may dispose of his personal estate as he might have done before the making of this Act." [82] Under this privilege completely informal dispositions are permitted, even by infants, and it has since been extended to realty as well as personalty.[83] The underlying doctrine, borrowed from Roman law,[84] is that a soldier or sailor may at times be *inops consilii*, cut off from skilled advice and help; but the privilege is not lost merely because such advice and help is available, nor are the rules of Roman law incorporated.[85]

---

76 *In b. Horsford* (1874) L.R. 3 P. & D. 211; *In b. McCabe* (1873) L.R. 3 P. & D. 94 (substitution of different legatee); *Sturton* v. *Whellock* (1883) 52 L.J.P. 29 (gifts to grandchildren at twenty-one: " one " obliterated and unattested " five " substituted); *cf. In b. Hope Brown* [1942] P. 136, *supra*.

77 *In b. Itter* [1950] P. 130 (new amounts signed but not attested).

78 *Rogers* v. *Goodenough* (1862) 2 Sw. & Tr. 342; *In b. Reade* [1902] P. 75.

79 Wills Act, 1837, s. 22; see *Goldie* v. *Adam* [1938] P. 85; *In b. Davis* [1952] P. 279 (revival by duly attested inscription on envelope containing will; intention to revive inferred from facts); *Re Pearson* [1963] 1 W.L.R. 1358 (revival of will containing revocation clause revokes later will).

80 *In b. Hodgkinson* [1893] P. 339. The law was otherwise before 1838: *Usticke* v. *Bawden* (1824) 2 Add. 116.

81 Wills Act, 1837, s. 22.

82 s. 11, replacing Statute of Frauds, 1677, s. 22, which was in similar terms. Before 1677 anyone might make an informal will of personalty: *ante*, p. 476.

83 *Post*, pp. 488, 489.

84 *Drummond* v. *Parish* (1843) 3 Curt. 522 at 531.

85 *Re Booth* [1926] P. 118; *Re Wingham* [1949] P. 187.

I. PRIVILEGED TESTATORS

1. A soldier in actual military service. It is not enough that the testator was in an army; he must have been " in actual military service " when he made the will. This phrase means active service in the armed forces in connection with hostilities, whether past, present or believed to be imminent in the future; and it is interpreted liberally.[86] A soldier is deemed to be on actual military service from the moment he received mobilisation orders [87] until the full conclusion of the operations,[88] which may last for many years beyond the end of hostilities.[89] Thus the privilege extends to an escort for those delimiting a frontier after fighting is over,[90] and to a member of an army of occupation, even though fighting ended nine years earlier,[91] but not to a wounded soldier in a London hospital.[92]

" Soldier " includes both officers and other ranks, a female army nurse,[93] and a member of the Air Force [94]; and in the Second World War it included members of the Women's Auxiliary Air Force,[95] Auxiliary Transport Service, and Home Guard.[96]

2. A mariner or seaman at sea.[97] This includes both members of the Royal Navy [98] and merchant seamen; it has been held to extend to a female typist employed on a liner.[99] It includes an admiral directing naval operations on a river,[1] and a master mariner in his ship lying in the Thames before starting on her voyage.[2] A seaman on shore leave is deemed to be at sea, if he is a member of a ship's crew [3] or has received orders to join a ship.[4] It makes no difference that his ship is in dock for refitting [5] or is permanently stationed in harbour,[6] provided that he has not been paid off.

---

[86] The leading case is *Re Wingham* [1949] P. 187, where an airman undergoing training in Canada was held to be privileged. It resolves some of the difficulties in the earlier cases: see (1941) 57 L.Q.R. 481 (R.E.M.), criticising *In b. Gibson* [1941] 2 All E.R. 91, disapproved in *Re Wingham, supra*.
[87] *Gattward* v. *Knee* [1920] P. 99; *Re Booth* [1926] P. 118.
[88] *Re Limond* [1915] 2 Ch. 240.
[89] *Re Colman* [1958] 1 W.L.R. 457.
[90] *Re Limond, supra*.
[91] *Re Colman, supra* (British army in Germany).
[92] *In b. Grey* [1922] P. 140.
[93] *In b. Stanley* [1916] P. 192.
[94] Wills (Soldiers and Sailors) Act, 1918, s. 5.
[95] *In b. Rowson* [1944] 2 All E.R. 36.
[96] See *Re Wingham* [1949] P. 187 at 196.
[97] Wills Act, 1837, s. 11, repeating Statute of Frauds, 1677, s. 23.
[98] The restrictions on informal dispositions of wages, prize money, etc., by seamen in the Navy and Marines imposed by the Navy and Marines (Wills) Acts, 1865, 1930 and 1939, have been repealed: Navy and Marines (Wills) Act, 1953.
[99] *In b. Hale* [1915] 2 I.R. 362.
[1] *In b. Austen* (1853) 2 Rob.Ecc. 611.
[2] *In b. Patterson* (1898) 79 L.T. 123.
[3] *In b. Newland* [1952] P. 71; but see *In b. Thomas* (1918) 34 T.L.R. 626, which seems not to have been cited.
[4] *In b. Wilson* [1952] P. 92.
[5] *In b. Newland, supra*.
[6] *In b. M'Murdo* (1867) L.R. 1 P. & D. 540; *In b. Anderson* [1916] P. 49 at 52.

3. A member of Her Majesty's Naval or Marine Forces so circumstanced that, had he been a soldier, he would have been in actual military service.[7] This enables a member of the navy or marines who has been called up to make an informal will even though he has not joined his ship.[8]

II. EXTENT OF THE PRIVILEGE

A testator within one of the above categories has the following privileges:

1. He can make or revoke a will even if he is an infant.[9]

2. He can make or revoke a will informally. The will may be in writing, with or without witnesses or signature, or it may be nuncupative, *i.e.*, oral. Thus farewell words spoken at a railway station may constitute a valid will.[10] The testator need not know that he is making a will, provided he gives deliberate expression to his wishes as to the destination of his property on his death.[11] Those entitled to make informal wills are also entitled to revoke a will, even if it has been made formally, in an informal manner, as by an unattested letter to a relative asking that the will should be burned, " for I have already cancelled it "[12]; and marriage also effects revocation.[13]

A will properly made under the above conditions remains valid indefinitely unless revoked. This is so even after the military or other service is over[14]; but thereafter any revocation must be formal. It formerly seemed that an infant was unable to revoke the will save by marriage, but a general power of revocation has now been conferred.[15]

3. The will can dispose of all kinds of property. The statutory privileges at first applied only to wills of personalty.[16] They were

[7] Wills (Soldiers and Sailors) Act, 1918, s. 2.
[8] See *In b. Anderson* [1916] P. 49 at 52; *In b. Yates* [1919] P. 93.
[9] Wills (Soldiers and Sailors) Act, 1918, s. 1 (declaratory, removing doubts raised by *Re Wernher* [1918] 1 Ch. 339), as amended by Family Law Reform Act 1969, s. 3 (1) (reduction of age of majority from 21 to 18). This is contrary to the usual rule: *ante*, p. 476.
[10] *In b. Yates* [1919] P. 93.
[11] *Re Stable* [1919] P. 7 (" If I stop a bullet, everything of mine will be yours "); *In b. Spicer* [1949] P. 441. Contrast *In b. Donner* (1917) 34 T.L.R. 138 (soldier told, incorrectly, that on intestacy his mother would get all his property: " That is just what I want. I want my mother to have everything ": *held* no will but rather a reason for making no will); similarly *In b. Knibbs* [1962] 1 W.L.R. 852.
[12] *In b. Gossage* [1921] P. 194.
[13] *In b. Wardrop* [1917] P. 54.
[14] *Re Booth* [1926] P. 118 (over 40 years); and see *In b. Coleman* [1920] 2 I.R. 352.
[15] Family Law Reform Act 1969, s. 3 (3).
[16] Wills Act, 1837, s. 11.

extended to realty by the Wills (Soldiers and Sailors) Act, 1918 [17]; but as regards infant testators there seems to be ground for supposing that the latter enactment has been unintentionally frustrated by the Administration of Estates Act, 1925,[18] except in the case of married infants or devises of interests *pur autre vie*. The Act of 1918 also allows a guardian for the testator's infant children to be appointed by a privileged will.[19]

Sect. 4. Operation of Wills

A. Lapse

I. GENERAL RULE

A legacy or bequest (*i.e.*, a testamentary gift of personalty) or a devise (*i.e.*, a testamentary gift of realty) is said to lapse if the beneficiary dies before the testator.[20] In such a case, unless a contrary intention is shown, the gift fails and the property comprised in it falls into residue,[21] which means that it passes under any general or residuary gift in the will, such as " all the rest of my property I leave to X." If there is no residuary gift, or if the gift which lapses is itself a gift of all or part of the residue, there is a partial intestacy and the property passes to the persons entitled on intestacy.[22]

II. EXCLUSION OF THE GENERAL RULE

1. Moral obligation. A legacy which is not mere bounty but is intended to satisfy some moral obligation recognised by the testator, whether legally enforceable or not, is outside the doctrine of lapse, so that even if the legatee predeceases the testator the legacy can be claimed by the legatee's personal representatives.[23] A legacy bequeathed in order to pay a debt barred by lapse of time [24] or by the bankruptcy law,[25] or intended to pay the debts of someone for whom the testator felt morally responsible,[26] may thus be saved from lapse.

---

[17] s. 3, giving power to dispose of real estate in England and Ireland if the testator died after February 5, 1918.
[18] s. 51 (3); see *post*, p. 991.
[19] s. 4, reversing *In b. Tollemache* [1917] P. 246.
[20] The term " lapse " is also sometimes applied to the failure of gifts through events which occur after the testator's death, such as failure to satisfy a contingency: see, *e.g.*, *Smell* v. *Dee* (1707) 2 Salk. 415; *Re Parker* [1901] 1 Ch. 408; *Re Fox's Estate* [1937] 4 All E.R. 664.
[21] Wills Act, 1837, s. 25. Previously the same rule applied to personalty, but realty passed to the heir: *Wright* v. *Hall* (1724) Fort. 182.
[22] *Ackroyd* v. *Smithson* (1780) 1 Bro.C.C. 503; *Re Forrest* [1931] 1 Ch. 162; *Re Midgley* [1955] Ch. 576.
[23] *Stevens* v. *King* [1904] 2 Ch. 30; but see Theobald, *Wills* (13th ed., 1971), p. 719.
[24] *Williamson* v. *Naylor* (1838) 3 Y. & C.Ex. 208.
[25] *Re Sowerby's Trusts* (1856) 2 K. & J. 630.
[26] *Re Leach* [1948] Ch. 232 (bequest to pay son's debts).

2. Wills Act, 1837. The general rule is also modified in two important cases by the Wills Act, 1837:

(a) *Entails*: by section 32, subject to any contrary intention, there is no lapse if property is given to a person in tail and he predeceases the testator, leaving issue living at the testator's death capable of inheriting under the entail.

(b) *Gifts to issue*: by section 33, subject to any contrary intention, there is no lapse if property is given to a child or other issue of the testator who leaves issue living (and not merely *en ventre sa mère* [27]) at the testator's death. " Issue " includes legitimated issue [27a] and, for testators dying after 1969, illegitimate issue as well.[28]

3. Fictional survival. In neither case does the Act give anything to the issue whose survival prevented the lapse; it merely provides that the gift shall take effect as if the legatee or devisee had died immediately after the testator. Thus if T leaves £2,000 by his will to his daughter D, who dies some years before him, the legacy lapses unless she left issue who survived both herself and T, in which case the £2,000 forms part of D's estate, even if when the will was made the testator knew that she was dead.[29] If D died a bankrupt, it passes to her trustee in bankruptcy[30]; if she was solvent but bequeathed all her property to charities or strangers, it passes to them under her will,[30a] even if it is worded as giving "everything I die possessed of "[31]; and if the property concerned was realty, D's husband was formerly entitled to curtesy out of it[32] if the necessary conditions were fulfilled.[33] Only if D's issue are entitled under her will or intestacy will they benefit.

4. Limits of fiction. The fiction, however, is applied only so far as is necessary to prevent a lapse.[34] Thus where it saves from lapse a gift by a father who died in 1940 to a son who died intestate in 1920, the property carried to the son's estate passes under the rules of intestacy in force at the date of the son's real, and not his notional,

---

[27] *Elliott* v. *Joicey* [1935] A.C. 209, disapproving *Re Griffiths' Settlement* [1911] 1 Ch. 246.
[27a] *Re Brodie* [1967] Ch. 818; Family Law Reform Act 1969, s. 16 (2).
[28] Family Law Reform Act 1969, s. 16.
[29] *Barkworth* v. *Young* (1856) 4 Drew. 1.
[30] *Re Pearson* [1920] 1 Ch. 247. Any surplus would pass under her will or intestacy.
[30a] *Johnson* v. *Johnson* (1843) 3 Hare 157.
[31] *Re Hayter* [1937] 2 All E.R. 110.
[32] *Eager* v. *Furnivall* (1881) 17 Ch.D. 115.
[33] For these, see *post*, p. 516.
[34] *Re Basioli* [1953] Ch. 367, resolving the doubts arising from two conflicting lines of cases and the curious case of *Re Hensler* (1881) 19 Ch.D. 612, discussed at 91 L.J.News. 252 (R.E.M.).

death,[35] and the persons entitled are ascertained as at the same date.[36] Further, section 33 no longer results in estate duty being payable a second time (even at reduced rates [37]) by reason of the notional survivorship of the testator's child or other issue.[38]

5. Exceptions. In certain cases section 33 does not apply to prevent a lapse.

(a) *Appointments under special powers*: section 33 does not apply to an appointment by will under a special power,[39] for it is confined to cases where property is "devised or bequeathed." It does, however, apply to appointments under general powers,[40] for the property is then in effect devisable by the appointor.[41]

(b) *Class gifts*: section 33 does not apply to class gifts,[42] such as a gift to "all my children," [43] even if in fact there is only one member of the class.[44] The reason for this is that membership of a class is normally ascertained at a testator's death and those dying before the testator fail to become members of the class. Strictly, there is no question of lapse; it is merely that nothing has ever been given to those who predecease the testator. But a gift of property "to be equally divided between the five daughters of X" is not a class gift, for there is a gift to each individual alive at the date of the will [45]; there is accordingly nothing to prevent section 33 from applying if one of the children predeceases the testator.

(c) *Interests terminable on donee's death*: section 33 does not preserve gifts which would in any case terminate with the donee's death, *e.g.*, gifts of a life interest or joint tenancy.[46]

(d) *Certain contingent gifts*: section 33 does not preserve a contingent gift such as a bequest "to X as and when he is twenty-five" if X dies aged twenty-four, even if he would have attained the requisite age had he in fact outlived the testator.[47]

---

[35] *Re Hurd* [1941] Ch. 196.
[36] *Re Basioli, supra.*
[37] Finance Act, 1958, s. 30.
[38] *Ibid.*, s. 29 (2), in effect reversing *Re Scott* [1901] 1 K.B. 228, for deaths after April 15, 1958; and see *post*, p. 492.
[39] *Holyland* v. *Lewin* (1883) 26 Ch.D. 266. For powers of appointment, see *ante*, p. 463.
[40] *Eccles* v. *Cheyne* (1856) 2 K. & J. 676.
[41] Wills Act, 1837, s. 27; *post*, p. 504.
[42] For class gifts, see *ante*, p. 228.
[43] *Olney* v. *Bates* (1855) 3 Drew. 319.
[44] *Re Harvey's Estate* [1893] 1 Ch. 567.
[45] *Re Smith's Trusts* (1878) 9 Ch.D. 117.
[46] *Re Butler* [1918] 1 I.R. 394.
[47] *Re Wolson* [1939] Ch. 80.

III. COMMORIENTES

1. Before 1926. Where a devisee or legatee dies at nearly the same time as the testator, it is necessary to determine which of them survived the other in order to know whether the gift lapsed. Similar questions between *commorientes* (those dying together) arise on intestacy and in respect of joint tenancies. Before 1926 there was no means of settling the question if there was no evidence of the order of deaths. Thus if two people perished in a shipwreck, in the absence of evidence of survivorship the estate of one could not benefit under the will or intestacy of the other, for it was impossible for the personal representatives of either to establish the survivorship essential to their case.[48]

2. After 1925. The Law of Property Act, 1925, resolves this problem for deaths occurring after 1925 by providing that where it is uncertain which survived the other, for all purposes affecting the title to property the younger shall be deemed to have survived the elder, subject to any order of the court.[49] The section applies equally to cases of simple uncertainty, as where one of the parties is on a ship which founders with all hands on an uncertain date and the other dies at home during that period, and to common disasters, such as practically simultaneous deaths in an air-raid,[50] or deaths in an unknown sequence in a common shipwreck [50a]; but it does not apply where one person is merely presumed to have died because he disappeared over seven years before the other died.[51]

3. Modifications. This rule has now been modified as between husband and wife if one of them dies intestate.[52] Further, for the purposes of estate duty the old rule has been restored, and each of the deceased is deemed to have died simultaneously with the other.[53] This obviates a second liability (even though at the much reduced rates for a " quick succession " [54]) on the death of the notional survivor. Even so, it is still prudent to insert a survivorship clause in a will, making gifts by a husband to his wife conditional upon her surviving him for (say) a month. Then, if both are killed in an

---

48 *Wing* v. *Angrave* (1860) 8 H.L.C. 183; and see *Re Phené's Trusts* (1870) 5 Ch.App. 139; *Ross's Judicial Factor* v. *Martin*, 1955 S.C.(H.L.) 56.

49 s. 184. The last two words probably do not confer any general discretion on the court, *e.g.*, to avoid hardship: see *Re Lindop* [1942] Ch. 377 at 382 (reserved in *Hickman* v. *Peacey* [1945] A.C. 304 (see at p. 337)).

50 *Hickman* v. *Peacey* [1945] A.C. 304, the majority of the House of Lords rejecting the argument that the section is inapplicable where the deaths may have been simultaneous.

50a *Re Rowland* [1963] Ch. 1.

51 *Re Albert* [1967] V.R. 875. 	52 See *post*, p. 527.

53 Finance Act, 1958, s. 29 (1), applying to deaths after April 15, 1958; and see *ante*, p. 491.

54 Finance Act, 1958, s. 30.

accident with all their issue and the wife actually or notionally survives the husband for a short while, the husband's property will pass to (for example) his own parents rather than to his wife's parents.

B. Gifts to Witnesses

1. Former law. In the case of wills of realty, the Statute of Frauds, 1677,[54a] required that all wills should be attested by at least three *credible* witnesses. If a witness to such a will was given either a devise or a legacy by the will, he was deemed not to be credible, and if his disqualification left less than three credible witnesses, the will was void as to the realty comprised in it.[55] The same applied to legacies or devises to the spouse of a witness.[56] The Wills Act, 1751,[57] provided that a legacy or devise to a witness should be void but that his attestation should no longer be invalidated. The Act somewhat curiously made no provision for legacies or devises to the spouse of a witness, and these still invalidated the attestation of the witness.[58]

2. No benefit for witness. The Wills Act, 1837,[59] put matters on a more rational basis by providing that the attestation of a beneficiary or his or her spouse should be valid, but that the beneficiary could claim no benefit under the will, as to either realty or personalty. Formerly this applied even if there were two other witnesses to the will, so that the beneficiary's signature was superfluous.[60] But where the testator dies after May 29, 1968, the attestations of any beneficiaries (or their spouses) are for this purpose to be disregarded if without them the will is duly executed.[60a] Thus if one of the three witnesses is a legatee, the legacy is good; if two of them are legatees, both legacies fail.

3. Limits. The limits of the rule should be noticed :

    (i) It does not apply if no witnesses at all were necessary for the validity of the will, such as the will of a soldier in actual military service.[61]

[54a] s. 5.
[55] Cru.Dig. vi, 60.
[56] Williams R.P. 259.
[57] s. 1.
[58] *Hatfield* v. *Thorp* (1822) 5 B. & Ald. 589.
[59] s. 15.
[60] *Randfield* v. *Randfield* (1863) 32 L.J.Ch. 668.
[60a] Wills Act 1968, s. 1.
[61] *Re Limond* [1915] 2 Ch. 240.

(ii) It does not apply to a person who signs the will not as a witness but merely, for example, to show that he agrees with the testator's leaving him less than his brothers and sisters.[62]

(iii) A beneficiary who marries a witness after the date of the will is not disabled from claiming under it.[63]

(iv) The rule applies only to beneficial gifts and not to gifts to a person as trustee.[64] But the trustee cannot himself benefit; thus a solicitor trustee who attested the will cannot charge professional fees, although expressly so empowered by the will,[65] unless he is not appointed trustee until after the will has been made.[66]

(v) The rule does not apply if the gift is made or confirmed by any will or codicil not attested by the beneficiary.[67] Thus if there is a gift by will confirmed by codicil, a beneficiary who witnesses only one document is entitled to the gift since he can claim under the other document; this is so even where the residuary legatee under a will attests a codicil which, by revoking certain legacies, will swell the residue.[68]

4. Limited interests. The effect of the rule in the case of a limited interest is to accelerate the subsequent interests. Thus if property is given to A for life, with remainder to B, the effect of A attesting the will is that B is entitled to the property as soon as the testator dies.[69] Similarly if property is given to X, Y and Z as joint tenants, and X attests the will, Y and Z are entitled to the whole of the property[70]; had they been tenants in common, X's third would have fallen into residue or passed on intestacy.[71]

C. Murder or Manslaughter of Testator

A person guilty of murder or manslaughter can take no benefit under the will or intestacy of his victim.[72] Thus a murderer's prospective share under his victim's intestacy devolves as if he did not

---

[62] *Kitcat* v. *King* [1930] P. 266; *In b. Bravda* [1967] 1 W.L.R. 1080.

[63] *Thorpe* v. *Bestwick* (1881) 6 Q.B.D. 311.

[64] *Cresswell* v. *Cresswell* (1868) L.R. 6 Eq. 69; *Re Ray's W. T.* [1936] Ch. 520 (prior to testatrix's death witness becomes Abbess to whom property is given on trust: gift effective).

[65] *Re Pooley* (1888) 40 Ch.D. 1.

[66] *Re Royce's W. T.* [1959] Ch. 626.

[67] *Re Marcus* (1887) 56 L.J.Ch. 830; *Re Trotter* [1899] 1 Ch. 764.

[68] *Gurney* v. *Gurney* (1855) 3 Drew. 208.

[69] *Jull* v. *Jacobs* (1876) 3 Ch.D. 703. Contrast *Re Doland's W. T.* [1970] Ch. 267 (substitutional or dependent gift falls with offending gift).

[70] *Young* v. *Davies* (1863) 2 Dr. & Sm. 167.

[71] *Hoare* v. *Osborne* (1864) 33 L.J.Ch. 586.

[72] *In b. Hall* [1914] P. 1 (will: manslaughter); *Re Sigsworth* [1935] Ch. 89 (intestacy: murder); but *quaere* whether this applies to manslaughter by negligence: *Beresford* v. *Royal Insurance Co. Ltd.* [1938] A.C. 586 at 598. See also *ante*, p. 407.

exist, *e.g.*, on his brothers and sisters, and not on the Crown.[73] This rule applies equally in cases of diminished responsibility,[73a] but not where the slayer was insane.[74]

Sect. 5. Construction of Wills

The construction of wills is a vast and difficult subject [75] of which only a few of the more important rules can be mentioned here.

A. General Rule

1. Ascertaining intention. The cardinal rule of construction is that effect must be given to the intention of the testator as expressed in the will, the words being given their natural meaning. The will alone must be looked at, and, in general,[76] no evidence can be received to contradict the meaning of the words used in the will. " The will must be in writing, and the only question is, what is the meaning of the words used in that writing." [77]

The words of the will must normally be given their natural meaning, or the most appropriate of their several natural meanings, except so far as that leads to absurdities or inconsistencies. But there is nothing to prevent words from being construed in some special sense if the will clearly shows that they are used in that sense; and in recent years the courts have been rather more ready to accept that the testator may have used words otherwise than in accordance with their " strict " meaning. Thus " money," in its strict legal meaning, comprises only cash and debts due, but a bequest in a home-made will of " all moneys of which I die possessed " may be construed as including stocks and shares and personal property generally.[78] The court may invoke what is sometimes known as the " dictionary principle ": the testator, by showing in the will that he has used a word in a particular sense, has made his own dictionary for the purposes of the will.[79]

2. Illegitimate children. It was a settled rule that " children " bore the natural meaning of " legitimate children," [80] so that an illegiti-

---

[73] *Re Callaway* [1956] Ch. 559.   [73a] *Re Giles* [1972] Ch. 544.
[74] *Re Pitts* [1931] 1 Ch. 546 (intestacy).
[75] " Wills and the construction of them do more perplex a man, than any other learning, and to make a certain construction of them, this *excedit juris prudentum artem* ": *Roberts* v. *Roberts* (1613) 2 Bulstr. 123 at 130, *per* Coke C.J. Lord Eldon L.C. began one judgment: " Having had doubts upon this Will for 20 years . . .": *Earl of Radnor* v. *Shafto* (1805) 11 Ves. 448 at 453 ; but see Megarry, *Miscellany-at-Law* (1955) p. 244.
[76] Contrast *Re Jones' W. T.*, *infra*, and *Re Jebb*, *infra* (cases on " contrary intention ").
[77] *Grey* v. *Pearson* (1857) 6 H.L.C. 61 at 106, *per* Lord Wensleydale.
[78] *Perrin* v. *Morgan* [1943] A.C. 399.
[79] See *Hill* v. *Crook* (1873) L.R. 6 H.L. 265 at 285.
[80] *Wilkinson* v. *Adam* (1812) 1 V. & B. 422 at 462.

mate child was excluded even if he passed as legitimate.[81] But if the testator included some provision showing that by "children" he meant to include illegitimate children, the word would bear the wider meaning. Thus a gift "to all J's children except X," where X was illegitimate, operated to include all J's children, legitimate or illegitimate, except X.[82] Further, in a will or codicil made after 1969 statute now requires a provision for the benefit of a child, children or relations of any kind to be construed as including those illegitimately related, unless the contrary intention appears.[83] The Act has also abolished the rule of public policy which invalidated gifts to illegitimate children not yet born.[83a]

3. Adopted children. In the case of adopted children, if the adoption preceded the testator's death and the will was made after 1949 [84] or confirmed after April 1, 1959,[85] the adopted children are treated as "children" of the adopter for purposes of dispositions of property, unless a contrary intention appears from the will or the surrounding circumstances.[86] In the case of wills made before 1950 the rule is the contrary, subject of course to any contrary intention [87]; and such an intention may be deduced from the circumstances, *e.g.*, if when the will is made the only child is an adopted child and the birth of legitimate children is most improbable.[88]

4. Mistakes and inept language. Where a will fails to provide for some obvious contingency the court will not in general insert the missing provision, for that would be to rewrite the will.[89] Yet in some cases, where the testator's precise intention is sufficiently manifest, the court will omit or supply words which have clearly been inserted or omitted by mere mischance.[90] Similarly, senseless and incongruous words may be disregarded.[91] Vague expressions such

---

81 *Re Pearce* [1914] 1 Ch. 254.
82 *Re Lowe* (1895) 61 L.J.Ch. 415; see also *Re Helliwell* [1916] 2 Ch. 580.
83 Family Law Reform Act 1969, s. 15, extending to all dispositions but not affecting the meaning of "heir," or entailed interests, or property intended to accompany titles of honour, or pre-1970 wills or codicils confirmed by post-1969 codicils. As to legitimated children, see s. 15 (4).
83a s. 15 (7).
84 Adoption Act, 1958, ss. 16 (2), 17 (2), 59 and 5th Sched., para. 4, not affected by Family Law Reform Act 1969, s. 15.
85 Adoption Act, 1958, 5th Sched., para. 4 (3).
86 *Re Jones' W. T.* [1965] Ch. 1124 (statement by testator admitted in evidence); *Re Brinkley's W. T.* [1968] Ch. 407.
87 Adoption of Children Act, 1926, s. 5 (2).
88 *Re Jebb* [1966] Ch. 666; but see (1966) 82 L.Q.R. 196 (J. H. C. Morris).
89 *Re Hammersley* [1965] Ch. 481.
90 *Re Smith* [1948] Ch. 49; *Re Follett* [1955] 1 W.L.R. 429; *Re Whitrick* [1957] 1 W.L.R. 884; *Re Riley's W. T.* [1962] 1 W.L.R. 344; *Re Morris* [1971] P. 62; *Re Phelan* [1972] Fam. 33 (revocation clause omitted).
91 *Re Macandrew's W. T.* [1964] Ch. 704.

as "X's relations" or "X's successors" may be construed as references to the persons who would be entitled on X's intestacy, so as to save the gift from being void for uncertainty.[92]

B. Extrinsic Evidence

Since only the words of the will may be considered, extrinsic evidence (*i.e.*, evidence not gathered from the will itself) is normally inadmissible.[92a] But this is subject to certain qualifications.

1. Surrounding circumstances. Evidence of facts and circumstances existing when the will was made is always admissible. " You may place yourself, so to speak, in [the testator's] armchair." [93] Thus extrinsic evidence is admissible to show that certain words had a peculiar meaning to the testator by the custom of the district or the usage of the class of persons to which he belonged,[94] or that a description was mistaken, in which case the testator's true intention is carried out: *falsa demonstratio non nocet* (a mistake in description does no harm).[95] Nicknames,[96] or symbols used by the testator in his trade,[97] may be explained by evidence; thus it may be shown that a gift for " mother " was intended for the testator's wife, whom he always described thus.[98]

2. Equivocations

(a) *Ambiguity.* Evidence of the testator's intention is admissible to explain an equivocation. There is said to be an equivocation or ambiguity in a will when there is a description of a person or thing which can apply equally well to two or more persons or things. Thus if a testator devises his close (enclosed land) " in the occupation of W " and he has two such closes, there is an equivocation.[99]

(b) *Latent or patent.* An ambiguity is said to be latent when the will is apparently perfect on the face of it, but on attempting to apply

[92] *Rowland* v. *Gorsuch* (1789) 2 Cox Eq. 187; *Re Gansloser's W. T.* [1952] Ch. 30; *Re Kilvert* [1957] Ch. 388. As to the share taken, see *ante*, p. 400.
[92a] See the general survey in the Nineteenth Report of the Law Reform Committee (1973) Cmnd. 5301, proposing the admission of all extrinsic evidence except (by a majority) that of the testator's dispositive intention.
[93] *Boyes* v. *Cook* (1880) 14 Ch.D. 53 at 56, *per* James L.J.; but the testator is not to be assumed to have a well-stocked law library: *Re Follett* [1955] 1 W.L.R. 429; (1955) 71 L.Q.R. 17, 326 (R.E.M.).
[94] *Shore* v. *Wilson* (1839) 9 Cl. & F. 355 at 498 *et seq*.
[95] See, *e.g.*, *Re Ray* [1916] 1 Ch. 461; *Re Price* [1932] 2 Ch. 54; *Re Posner* [1953] P. 277 (bequest to " my wife R," upheld although R was not the testator's wife); but see *Re Tetsall* [1961] 1 W.L.R. 938.
[96] *Re Ofner* [1909] 1 Ch. 60.
[97] *Kell* v. *Charmer* (1856) 23 Beav. 195 (jeweller's bequest of " the sum of i.x.x." which was the trade symbol for £100).
[98] Consider *Thorn* v. *Dickens* [1906] W.N. 54 (the entire will was " all for mother ").
[99] *Richardson* v. *Watson* (1833) 4 B. & Ad. 787.

it an ambiguity appears.[1] Extrinsic evidence of the testator's intention is always admissible to explain such an ambiguity. Thus if a testator makes a devise " to my son John " and leaves two sons of that name, extrinsic evidence is admissible to show that the testator believed the elder son to be dead and intended the land for the younger son.[2] An ambiguity is said to be patent when the will itself discloses that the description fits more than one person or thing.

Extrinsic evidence of the testator's intention is often said to be inadmissible in the case of patent ambiguities,[3] but this is not universally true, and the position is far from clear.[4] Thus evidence of the testator's intention was admitted in one case where there was a gift to " George Gord the son of Gord," and other parts of the will showed that there were two men called Gord with sons named George.[5]

(c) *Effect of extrinsic evidence.* Once extrinsic evidence of the testator's intention is admitted, it will be given effect to even if it shows that someone apparently outside the scope of the gift was intended. Thus in one case [6] a testatrix gave part of her property " to my nephew Arthur Murphy." She had two legitimate nephews of that name and extrinsic evidence was admitted to explain this ambiguity. The evidence admitted showed that the testatrix intended to benefit an illegitimate nephew called Arthur Murphy, and it was held that he took to the exclusion of the two legitimate nephews. Had there been only one legitimate and one illegitimate nephew, there would have been no ambiguity, for " nephew " prima facie means " legitimate nephew "; consequently no extrinsic evidence would have been admitted and the legitimate nephew would have taken.[7]

(d) *Uncertainty.* If extrinsic evidence fails to resolve an ambiguity, the gift is void for uncertainty.[8] The same applies where the description is on the face of it indefinite, *e.g.*, a gift by a testator " to one of the sons of X," X having at the time several sons.[9]

C. Contradictions

1. Inconsistency. Extrinsic evidence is not admissible to explain a contradiction in a will, *e.g.*, a gift of " one hundred pounds (£500)

1 *Doe d. Hiscocks* v. *Hiscocks* (1839) 5 M. & W. 363 at 368, 369.
2 *Lord Cheyney's Case* (1591) 5 Co.Rep. 68a at 68b; *In b. Hubback* [1905] P. 129; and see *Goldie* v. *Adam* [1938] P. 85.
3 Bacon, *Maxims*, Reg. 23.
4 See Phipson, *Evidence* (11th ed., 1970), p. 840.
5 *Doe d. Gord* v. *Needs* (1836) 2 M. & W. 129 (the sidenote misses the point).
6 *Re Jackson* [1933] Ch. 237.   7 *Re Fish* [1894] 2 Ch. 83.
8 *Richardson* v. *Watson, supra*, where the evidence showed that in fact the testator intended both closes to pass.
9 *Strode* v. *Russel* (1708) 2 Vern. 621 at 624, 625; *cf. Dowset* v. *Sweet* (1753) Amb. 175.

to X." In such a case, the rule is that the second expression prevails over the first [10] since it is the latest in the testator's mind. This contrasts with a deed, where the former of two inconsistent expressions prevails, for what has once been done cannot be undone.[11] Before resorting to such a rule of thumb, however, the court tries to reconcile the two provisions in some way.[12]

2. Lassence v. Tierney. An important example of such a reconciliation is the rule in *Lassence* v. *Tierney*,[13] which applies to deeds as well as to wills,[14] and to realty as well as to personalty.[15] This rule has been stated as follows: " If you find an absolute gift to a legatee in the first instance, and trusts are engrafted or imposed on that absolute interest which fail, either from lapse or invalidity or any other reason, then the absolute gift takes effect so far as the trusts have failed, to the exclusion of the residuary legatee or next of kin, as the case may be." [16]

Thus if there is a gift to X of a fee simple or an absolute interest in personalty, and later in the will [17] or in a codicil [18] there is a direction that the property given to X shall be held for X for life with remainder to his children, if the gift to the children fails, whether partly [19] or wholly (*e.g.*, through there being no children [20] or through the perpetuity rule being infringed [21]), the gift of the fee simple or absolute interest to X takes effect instead of the property passing under a residuary gift or as on intestacy.[22] For the rule to apply, there must be an initial absolute gift which is subsequently cut down [23]; one continuous limitation containing both gift and restrictions will normally not bring the doctrine into play,[24] nor will a gift in which the names of the beneficiaries are immediately followed by the words " subject to the provisions hereinafter contained." [25]

---

[10] *Perkins* v. *Baynton* (1781) 1 Bro.C.C. 118; *Re Hammond* [1938] 3 All E.R. 308 (refusing to apply the rule for commercial documents that the words control the figures).

[11] *Doe* d. *Leicester* v. *Biggs* (1809) 2 Taunt. 109 at 113; *Forbes* v. *Git* [1922] 1 A.C. 256 at 259; *cf. ante*, pp. 159, 400. The rule was laid down as early as 1309: see *Blaunket* v. *Simonson* (1309) Y.B. 2 Edw. 2 (S.S.) 126 at 127.

[12] See *Wallop* v. *Darby* (1611) Yelv. 209 (gift to X in tail, followed by a separate gift of the same property to Y in fee simple: *held*, Y took a remainder after X's entail); *Fyfe* v. *Irwin* [1939] 2 All E.R. 271 at 281.

[13] (1849) 1 Mac. & G. 551.

[14] *Re Gatti's Voluntary S. T.* [1936] 2 All E.R. 1489; *Att.-Gen.* v. *Lloyds Bank Ltd.* [1935] A.C. 382.   [15] *Moryoseph* v. *Moryoseph* [1920] 2 Ch. 33.

[16] *Hancock* v. *Watson* [1902] A.C. 14 at 22, *per* Lord Davey.

[17] *Hulme* v. *Hulme* (1839) 9 Sim. 644.

[18] *Norman* v. *Kynaston* (1861) 3 De G.F. & J. 29.

[19] *Re Coleman* [1936] Ch. 528. See also *Re Litt* [1946] Ch. 154; *Re Atkinson's W. T.* [1957] Ch. 117.   [20] *Watkins* v. *Weston* (1863) 3 De G.J. & S. 434.

[21] *Ring* v. *Hardwick* (1840) 2 Beav. 352.

[22] *Whittell* v. *Dudin* (1820) 2 Jac. & W. 279.

[23] See, *e.g.*, *Re Burton's S. T.* [1955] Ch. 348, on the distinction between a true gift and mere administrative direction.   [24] *Re Payne* [1927] 2 Ch. 1.

[25] *Re Cohen's W. T.* [1936] 1 All E.R. 103.

D. A Will Speaks from Death

I. AS TO PROPERTY

By the Wills Act, 1837,[26] a will speaks from death as regards all property comprised in it, unless it shows a contrary intention. This means that a will is capable of disposing of all property owned by the testator at his death even if he acquired it after making his will. Thus a gift of " my shares in the Great Western Railway Company " includes not only those owned when the will was made but those acquired subsequently [27]; and a devise of " all the lands of which I am seised " carries with it land acquired after the will was made,[28] together with all fixtures attached to the land, even if they were affixed after the will was made.[29]

This rule applies to all generic descriptions (*i.e.*, descriptions of a class of objects which may increase or decrease [30]) and is not confined to general or residual gifts [31]; but it has no application to a gift of a specific object existing at the date of the will.[32] Thus if a testator makes a will giving " my piano " to X and subsequently sells that piano and buys another, X has no claim to it,[33] unless the will is confirmed by a codicil made after the sale.[34] The bequest is said to have been adeemed, meaning that the gift has failed because the specified property ceased to exist, or ceased to belong to the testator, between the date of his will and his death.[35] A gift will also be adeemed if before his death the testator contracts to sell the property,[36] or if an option to purchase it granted by him before his death is exercised even after his death [37]; for in each case the specific asset has become a mere right to receive the purchase price.

II. AS TO PERSONS

1. Class gifts

(a) *The problem of distribution.* Class gifts [38] are construed on

---

[26] s. 24; see *Re Bancroft* [1928] Ch. 577. Previously the law was otherwise as to realty (*Att.-Gen.* v. *Vigor* (1803) 8 Ves. 256 at 283) but not personalty: see *Re Chapman* [1904] 1 Ch. 431 at 436.
[27] *Trinder* v. *Trinder* (1866) L.R. 1 Eq. 695.
[28] *Doe* d. *York* v. *Walker* (1844) 12 M. & W. 591.
[29] For fixtures, see *post*, p. 711.
[30] *Re Slater* [1906] 2 Ch. 480 at 485. See *All Souls College* v. *Coddrington* (1719) 1 P.Wms. 597 (bequest of library " now in the custody " of X includes after-added books). [31] *Re Ord* (1879) 12 Ch.D. 22 at 25.
[32] *Emuss* v. *Smith* (1848) 2 De G. & Sm. 722 at 733, 736.
[33] *Re Sikes* [1927] 1 Ch. 364.
[34] *Re Reeves* [1928] Ch. 351.
[35] See Bailey, *Wills*, 109, 113; *cf. Re Heilbronner* [1953] 1 W.L.R. 1254, and see *ante*, p. 474. [36] *Re Edwards* [1958] Ch. 168.
[37] *Lawes* v. *Bennett* (1785) 1 Cox Eq. 167; *Re Isaacs* [1894] 3 Ch. 506; *Re Carrington* [1932] 1 Ch. 1; *Re Rose* [1948] Ch. 78.
[38] For definition, see *ante*, p. 228.

the ordinary principle that the testator's intention shall govern the persons who are to take.[38a] But a special problem arises where one member of the class becomes qualified to take before the maximum number of members can be fixed. Suppose, for example, that the testator leaves property " to all my grandchildren who attain 21 in equal shares." So soon as a grandchild attains 21 he becomes entitled to a share. But to how much? If all future grandchildren are to be included, nothing can safely be paid out to him until all the parents, uncles and aunts are dead, so that the maximum number of shares is known. The essence of the problem, therefore, is an inconsistency in the testator's directions: *all* are to take, yet each is to *take* rather than have to await the completion of the class.

(*b*) *Andrews* v. *Partington.* In order to expedite the distribution of the property, the courts have adopted the rule, already discussed in relation to the rule against perpetuities,[39] known as the rule in *Andrews* v. *Partington.*[40] This rule cuts down the class by confining it to persons in existence when the first capital[41] share becomes payable.[42] The interests of after-born members of the class are sacrificed for the purpose of fixing the maximum number of shares. Because this is unfair to them, the rule " has been repeatedly attacked over the two hundred years or so that it has survived," [43] and it has artificial limits. It may be generally stated as follows [44]:

A class closes when the first member becomes entitled in possession; but where the shares of its members are to vest at birth, it will remain open indefinitely unless a member was born before the testator's death or before the end of some intermediate limitation. All persons born after the closing of the class are excluded from it.

[38a] Thus a gift, after a life interest to X (a spinster), to X's issue who attain 21 may be confined to issue born before X's death, without the aid of the rule in *Andrews* v. *Partington* (below): *Re Cockle's W. T.* [1967] Ch. 690.

[39] *Ante*, p. 231.

[40] (1791) 3 Bro.C.C. 401. It applies to both realty and personalty (see *Re Canney's Trust* (1910) 101 L.T. 905) and to settlements as well as wills: see *Re Knapp's Settlement* [1895] 1 Ch. 91; *Re Wernher's S. T.* [1961] 1 W.L.R. 136.

[41] The rule will not therefore apply to gifts of income only, *e.g.*, for joint lives: *Re Stephens* [1904] 1 Ch. 322 (also holding that the closing of the class may be postponed by a period of accumulation of income); *Re Ward* [1965] Ch. 856 (discretionary trusts). But it is not excluded because land is held upon trust for sale and sale is postponed: *Re Edmondson's W. T.* [1972] 1 W.L.R. 183.

[42] *Re Emmet's Estate* (1880) 13 Ch.D. 484.

[43] *Re Harker's W. T.* [1969] 1 W.L.R. 1124 at 1127, *per* Goff J.

[44] The best general account of the rule and its various refinements is that given by J. H. C. Morris (1954) 70 L.Q.R. 61 *et seq.*, where he also deals with its effect on the operation of the perpetuity rule (already considered, *ante*, p. 231); and see Jarman, 1660 *et seq.* Helpful statements of the rule will be found in *Re Chartres, infra*, at pp. 471, 472, and in [1958] C.L.J. 39 (S. J. Bailey).

The artificial element is the exception in the case of shares which vest at birth and not on some later contingency such as attainment of full age or marriage.

This is a rule of convenience for resolving the testator's contradictory directions.[45] He can therefore exclude it by expressing a contrary intention,[45a] so that the contradiction disappears. He may exclude it by implication, as by giving trustees a power of advancement under which they can pay out presumptive shares.[46] But it will not normally be excluded by expressions such as " all," " each and every," or " all or any " [47]; and if the class gift is in remainder even expressions like " born or to be born " may be taken as referring to persons born between the testator's death and the falling into possession of the remainder.[48] But the words " whenever born " have been held to exclude the rule, being emphatic and expressly unlimited as to time.[49]

(c) *Examples.* The operation of the rule is best explained by examples.

(i) Devise " to all my sisters." Sisters alive at the testator's death take, and any sisters born afterwards are excluded. But if no sister was alive at the testator's death, the exception applies and any sister born subsequently can take.[50] Similarly a devise " to all A's children " or " to all my grandchildren " will benefit only those born before the testator's death, unless no member of the class has by then been born.[51] If only one member of the class was born before the testator's death, he or she takes the whole.

(ii) Devise " to all my grandchildren who attain 21." The class closes when the first grandchild attains 21,[52] whether or not he was born before the testator's death. When the class closes, all grandchildren then alive are included in it: those under 21 will obtain their shares on attaining 21; if any of them dies under 21, his potential share is divided among

---

[45] *Re Emmet's Estate, supra,* at p. 490; *Re Stephens* [1904] 1 Ch. 322 at 328; *Re Chartres* [1927] 1 Ch. 466 at 474; [1958] C.L.J. 39 at 42 (S. J. Bailey).
[45a] *Scott* v. *Earl of Scarborough* (1838) 1 Beav. 154 (" now born or who shall hereafter be born "); *Hodson* v. *Micklethwaite* (1854) 2 Drew. 294; *Re Ransome* [1957] Ch. 348.
[46] *Re Henderson* [1969] 1 W.L.R. 651.
[47] See *Re Emmet's Estate* (1880) 13 Ch.D. 484.
[48] *Scott* v. *Earl of Scarborough, supra,* at p. 168.
[49] *Re Edmondson's W. T.* [1972] 1 W.L.R. 183.
[50] *Weld* v. *Bradbury* (1715) 2 Vern. 705.
[51] See *Re Chartres, supra.* Provided that the gift vests at once, it makes no difference that there are special trusts during minority: *Re Manners* [1955] 1 W.L.R. 1096.
[52] *Andrews* v. *Partington* (1791) 3 Bro.C.C. 401; *Re Deloitte* [1919] 1 Ch. 209; *Re Chartres, supra.* If a grandchild has attained 21 before the testator's death, the class closes at once: *Picken* v. *Matthews* (1878) 10 Ch.D. 264.

those who reach 21. Even if there is no grandchild alive
at the testator's death, the class will nevertheless close when
the first grandchild attains 21 (since the shares were not
to vest at birth).[53] There is however some doubt on this
last point.[54]

(iii) Devise " to A for life, remainder to all his grandchildren
who attain 21." Here the class closes at A's death, if by
then any grandchild who survived the testator, or was born
after his death, has attained 21.[55] As any such grandchild's
interest will have vested, it will make no difference if he has
predeceased A, for someone will be entitled to take his share
under his will or intestacy,[56] and so the class must close. If
at A's death there are no grandchildren,[57] or only infant
grandchildren,[58] the class closes when the first of them
attains 21.[59]

Where the remainders are accelerated by the premature
determination of the prior life interest (*e.g.*, by disclaimer
or release [59a]) and a remainderman is already qualified to take,
the rule will not apply unless, it seems, the limitation is one
to which the rule would in any case apply. Thus if the gift
is to A for life with remainder to his children who attain 21,
no remainderman could be born after A's death, and so the
premature determination of A's life interest will not bring
within the rule a limitation which otherwise would stand outside it.[60] But had the remainder been to A's *grandchildren*
who attain 21, the rule would apply to the limitation so as
to exclude some remaindermen, as explained above, and so
it has been held also to apply if A's life interest is prematurely determined.[61] Yet it seems contrary to principle
for the class to be closed as a result of a disposition not
made by the testator, and for the rule to be open to mani-
pulation at the expense of the unborn.[62]

(*d*) *Individual gifts.* An even more drastic rule of convenience is
applied where there is not one gift divisible among a class, but a

---

[53] *Pearse* v. *Catton* (1839) 1 Beav. 352; and see *Re Bleckly* [1951] Ch. 740 at 749.
[54] See Morris (1954) 70 L.Q.R. 61 at 68, 69.
[55] *Re Emmet's Estate* (1880) 13 Ch.D. 484; *Re Knapp's Settlement* [1895] 1 Ch. 91 at 96.   [56] *Greenwood* v. *Greenwood* [1939] 2 All E.R. 150.
[57] *Re Bleckly* [1951] Ch. 740.   [58] See authorities cited in n. 55, *supra*.
[59] Similarly on a gift of a reversionary interest the class remains open until the reversion falls into possession: *Walker* v. *Shore* (1808) 15 Ves. 122.
[59a] See [1958] C.L.J. 39 (S. J. Bailey); [1973] C.L.J. 246 (A. M. Prichard).
[60] *Re Kebty-Fletcher's W. T.* [1969] 1 Ch. 339; *Re Harker's W. T.* [1969] 1 W.L.R. 1124.
[61] *Re Davies* [1957] 1 W.L.R. 922, as explained in *Re Harker's W. T.*, *supra*.
[62] See generally *Re Harker's W. T.*, *supra*.

series of gifts to each member of a class, for example, a gift of £100 to each of the children of X who attains 21. Here the class closes at the testator's death, and if X has then no living child the gift fails altogether.[63] The object of this rule is to enable the personal representatives to deal with the residue by fixing the maximum number of legacies at once. But the testator may exclude the rule by a sufficiently clear direction, and it will not be applied unless the circumstances require it.[64]

2. Gifts to individuals. In the case of gifts to existing individuals, the date of the will, and not the date of the testator's death, is normally the relevant time. Thus a gift " to the eldest son of my sister," there being such a son living at the date of the will, is a gift to him personally; if he dies before the testator, the gift lapses and the eldest son at the testator's death has no claim.[64a] Similarly, a bequest " to Lord Sherborne " is a gift to the holder of the title at the date of the will.[65] But like all rules of construction, this yields to a contrary intention, and a legacy " to the Lord Mayor of London for the time being " operates as a gift to the person holding that office at the testator's death,[66] while a gift " to the Mayor of Lowestoft for the benefit of poor and needy fishermen of Lowestoft " takes effect as a gift to the Mayor of Lowestoft for the time being, on the stated trusts, and not as a gift to a particular person who is Mayor at a particular time.[67]

E. *Exercise of Powers of Appointment*

A general devise or bequest (*e.g.*, " I give all my property to X ") operates to exercise a general power of appointment unless a contrary intention (and not merely an absence of intention [67a]) is shown by the will,[68] or unless the general power is expressed to be exercisable only in some special way, *e.g.*, by referring to the power [69] or the property.[70] On the other hand, a special power

---

[63] *Rogers* v. *Mutch* (1878) 10 Ch.D. 25 ; *Re Belville* [1941] Ch. 414.
[64] *Re Belville, supra.* Presumably, therefore, if the residue is not distributable until some future date, *e.g.*, after a life interest, all persons living at that date will be admitted.
[64a] *Amyot* v. *Dwarris* [1904] A.C. 268.
[65] *Re Whorwood* (1878) 34 Ch.D. 446.
[66] *Re Daniels* (1918) 87 L.J.Ch. 661.
[67] *Re Pipe* (1937) 106 L.J.Ch. 252.
[67a] *Re Thirlwell* [1958] Ch. 146; (1958) 74 L.Q.R. 21 (R.E.M.).
[68] Wills Act, 1837, s. 27; see, *e.g.*, *Re Lawry* [1938] Ch. 318. For the rule apart from the section, see *ante*, p. 464.
[69] *Phillips* v. *Cayley* (1889) 43 Ch.D. 222; contrast *Re Lane* [1908] 2 Ch. 581 (reference to " any power " which the testator might have held sufficient).
[70] *Re Phillips* (1889) 41 Ch.D. 417.

(which for this purpose includes a power to appoint to "anyone except X "[71]) is not exercised by a general bequest or devise unless the will shows a contrary intention, as by referring expressly to the power or to the property.[72]

F. *" To A, but if He Die Without Issue, to B "*

1. Before 1838. The construction put on a gift " to A, but if he die without issue, to B " before the Wills Act, 1837, was that in the case of realty A took an entail with remainder to B, while in the case of personalty A took an absolute interest. This odd result was achieved by construing " if he die without issue " as meaning " if he dies and his issue die out," so that B was only to take when the last of A's descendants was dead. Unless a contrary intention appeared in the gift,[73] this was treated as displaying an intention to create an entail which was given effect to in the case of realty [74]; and this was so whether the gift that was subject to the gift over to B was " to A," " to A for life " or " to A in fee simple." [75] The gift to B not only followed an entail but was also vested and so did not infringe the perpetuity rule [76]; but A might bar the entail even if he had no issue and so B's chance of taking the land was remote. In the case of personalty, A took an absolute interest,[77] for personalty could not be entailed [78]; and even if A had no issue the gift over could not be effective because it infringed the perpetuity rule.[79]

2. The Wills Act, 1837. The Wills Act, 1837,[80] in effect provided that the natural meaning should be given to such gifts and that A should take the fee simple in realty and the absolute interest in personalty, subject in each case to a gift over to B if at A's death no issue of A was living. The inconvenience of this was that A could never know during his lifetime whether or not the gift over to B would take effect. Even if A had many children and grandchildren alive, they might all perish in some calamity before his death and so leave him to " die without issue."

---

[71] *Re Byron's Settlement* [1891] 3 Ch. 474.
[72] See *Re Ackerley* [1913] 1 Ch. 510; compare *Re Beresford's W. T.* [1938] 3 All E.R. 566 (mere use of " I appoint . . ." not enough).
[73] *Roe* d. *Sheers* v. *Jeffery* (1798) 7 T.R. 589 at 595, 596.
[74] *Counden* v. *Clerke* (1614) Hob. 29.
[75] *Machell* v. *Weeding* (1836) 8 Sim. 4 at 7.
[76] *Ante,* p. 208.
[77] *Chandless* v. *Price* (1796) 3 Ves. 99.
[78] *Doe* d. *Ellis* v. *Ellis* (1808) 9 East 381; *ante,* p. 94.
[79] *Candy* v. *Campbell* (1834) 2 Cl. & F. 421.
[80] s. 29.

3. After 1882. Where any such gift was made after 1882 in the case of land, or after 1925 in the case of any property, it has accordingly been provided that the gift over to B becomes void as soon as any issue of A attains his majority.[81] This does not apply where an entail is given to A, though it is not excluded merely because A's " children " are specified instead of his " issue." [82] Where it applies, A's interest thus becomes absolute either if any issue attains full age (even if none survives A) or if A dies leaving any issue (even if none attains full age). Further, even before A's interest has become absolute, land subject to such a gift over is alienable, for the gift over makes the land settled land and A is in the position of a tenant for life, although if he sells under his statutory powers the purchase-money will be subject to a corresponding gift over.

G. " To A and his children " : The Rule in Wild's Case

1. Before 1926. Under the Rule in *Wild's Case*,[83] the effect of a devise " to A and his children " depended upon the facts existing when the will was made. Its peculiarity is that it has continued to obey the old principle that the time of making the will is the significant time, even after the modern rule that the will speaks from death was adopted for other forms of gift.[84]

(i) If A had no children when the will was made, he took an estate tail, even if children had been born before the testator's death. " Children " was construed as a word of limitation, for the only way in which the testator could have intended to benefit A's children under an immediate gift was by their being entitled to succeed under A's entail.[85] Yet by barring the entail, A could of course prevent his children from taking anything.

(ii) If A had children living (and not merely *en ventre sa mère* [86]) when the will was made, the word " children " was treated as a word of purchase and A took jointly with all his children living at the testator's death, in accordance with the usual rules for class gifts.

2. After 1925

(i) If no children were living at the date of the will, A cannot now take an entail, for an entail can no longer be created by informal words.[87] In such cases a fee simple interest passes; and

---

[81] L.P.A., 1925, s. 134, extending C.A., 1882, s. 10, amended by Family Law Reform Act 1969, s. 1 (3) and 1st Sched.

[82] *Re Booth* [1900] 1 Ch. 768.

[83] (1599) 6 Co.Rep. 16b at 17a, 17b.

[84] See S. J. Bailey (1936) 6 C.L.J. 78.

[85] *Wild's Case, supra*, at 17a.

[86] *Roper* v. *Roper* (1867) L.R. 3 C.P. 32.

[87] *Ante*, p. 60.

A, it seems, is solely entitled to it, even if children are born after the will is made but before the testator dies [88]; but it may be that A takes a life interest, with remainder to his children in fee simple.[89]

(ii) The second branch of the rule has not been affected. As before, A takes jointly with all his children living at the testator's death.[90]

3. Intention. The Rule in *Wild's Case* yielded to any contrary intention. It was laid down in terms which included a devise " to A and his issues " as well as a devise " to A and his children " [91]; but in modern times it seems never to have been applied to the former expression, since " issue " was prima facie a word of limitation [92] which in a will (as already explained [93]) created an entail until 1926. Nor did the rule apply to a bequest; prima facie A would take the personalty jointly with all issue living at the testator's death.[94]

H. Life Estate by Implication

1. Basis. Normally a will confers no interest on a person unless it shows a clear intent to do so. But in certain circumstances, a life estate may arise by implication. If upon an intestacy property would pass to X, and the testator devises or bequeaths it " to X after A's death," then unless the income during A's life is caught by a residuary gift, A takes a life estate by implication, whether the property given is realty [95] or personalty.[96]

The reason for this is that there is no other destination for the income until A's death. Undisposed of property passes primarily under any residuary gift, and in default to the person entitled under an intestacy. Here, the income until A's death is caught by no residuary gift, and the testator has clearly shown that the person entitled upon the intestacy is not to have it during A's lifetime. " A must have the thing devis'd or none else can have it." [97]

2. Conditions. For the rule to apply the following conditions had to be satisfied.

[88] L.P.A., 1925, s. 130 (2); *ante*, p. 60; see (1945) 5 C.L.J. 46 (R.E.M.).
[89] See S. J. Bailey (1936) 6 C.L.J. 80; (1946) 9 C.L.J. 185.
[90] *Ibid.*
[91] *Wild's Case, supra,* at 17a.
[92] *Slater* v. *Dangerfield* (1846) 15 M. & W. 263 at 272; *Re Coulden* [1908] 1 Ch. 320 at 324.
[93] *Ante*, p. 59.
[94] *Re Hammond* [1924] 2 Ch. 276.
[95] *Horton* v. *Horton* (1606) Cro.Jac. 74.
[96] *Ralph* v. *Carrick* (1879) 11 Ch.D. 873 at 876.
[97] *Gardner* v. *Sheldon* (1671) Vaugh. 259 at 262, *per* Vaughan C.J.

(i) X must be the person presumptively entitled on intestacy when the will was made.[98]

(ii) X must be the sole person so entitled, and not one of several persons together entitled.[99]

(iii) The intermediate income must not be caught by any residuary gift,[1] *i.e.*, there must either be no residuary gift, or the property in question must itself be comprised in a residuary gift.

3. After 1925. It seems that no life estate by implication can arise where the testator dies after 1925 in the case of specific devises and bequests, for these will carry the intermediate income to the devisee or legatee unless it is *expressly* disposed of.[2] But it can still apply to pecuniary legacies, or general or residuary devises or bequests.[3]

I. *The Meaning of " Land "*

A gift of " land " has always included freeholds,[4] though before the Wills Act, 1837, it did not include leaseholds unless the testator had no freeholds[5] or showed an intention to include leaseholds[6]; and similarly as to copyholds.[7] Since the Act, " land " has included leaseholds and (before their abolition in 1926) copyholds unless a contrary intention appears in the will.[8] But a gift of " real estate " does not[9] include leaseholds, unless the testator had no freeholds.[10] A gift of " land " or " real property " does not pass an interest in land held upon trust for sale.[11]

Part 2

INTESTACY

The rules relating to intestacy must now be explained. If the deceased dies wholly intestate, leaving no effective will, these rules govern the devolution of all his property, while if he dies partly

---

[98] *Aspinall* v. *Petvin* (1824) 1 Sim. & St. 544; *Stevens* v. *Hale* (1862) 2 Dr. & Sm. 22 at 28.

[99] *Ralph* v. *Carrick* (1879) 11 Ch.D. 873; *Re Springfield* [1894] 3 Ch. 603; and see *Re Willatts* [1905] 1 Ch. 378, reversed on other grounds [1905] 2 Ch. 135.

[1] *Stevens* v. *Hale* (1862) 2 Dr. & Sm. 22 at 28.

[2] L.P.A., 1925, s. 175 (1). On this provision, see *Re McGeorge* [1963] Ch. 544; (1963) 79 L.Q.R. 184 (P.V.B.).

[3] Bailey, *Wills*, 268.

[4] *Thompson* v. *Lady Lawley* (1800) 2 B. & P. 303.

[5] *Rose* v. *Bartlett* (1631) Cro.Car. 292.

[6] *Hobson* v. *Blackburn* (1833) 1 My. & K. 571.

[7] See *Roe* d. *Pye* v. *Bird* (1779) 2 Wm.Bl. 1301 at 1306.

[8] Wills Act, 1837, s. 26.

[9] *Butler* v. *Butler* (1884) 28 Ch.D. 66.

[10] *Re Holt* [1921] 2 Ch. 17.

[11] *Ante*, p. 288.

testate and partly intestate, they apply to all the property which does not pass under his will.

Before 1926 realty and personalty descended differently. All the realty vested in the heir; the personalty devolved through the personal representatives upon the next-of-kin. If a widower died intestate leaving three sons and four daughters, the eldest son was the heir and took all the realty, but all seven children shared the personalty equally. In the case of deaths occurring after 1925, both realty and personalty devolve in the same way under the new code of intestacy; and for those dying after 1952, the Intestates' Estates Act, 1952, as amended, has made some important modifications to the new code. Three separate sets of rules must therefore be considered:

1. Realty before 1926.
2. Personalty before 1926.
3. All property after 1925, subject to modifications after 1952.

Sect. 1. Realty Before 1926

The general rule was that all realty which was vested in the intestate passed to his heir, subject to the rights of the surviving spouse. The heir was ascertained at the moment of the death of the intestate and not before, for *nemo est haeres viventis*.[12] The rules for ascertaining the heir were partly common law and partly statutory; the Inheritance Act, 1833, made a number of important changes in the old law. The rules for ascertaining the heir will be explained first, then the rights of the surviving spouse.

A. Ascertainment of the Heir

The ten rules for ascertaining the heir fall under the four heads of the purchaser, the issue, ancestors and collaterals, and relatives of the half blood.

I. THE PURCHASER

1. Descent was traced from the last purchaser.[13]

The purchaser was defined [14] as the person who last acquired the land otherwise than by descent on intestacy, escheat,[15] partition [16]

---

[12] *Ante*, p. 52.

[13] Inheritance Act, 1833, s. 2. Previously descent was traced from the person last seised (except in the case of an entail: see *infra*, note 20). But this required proof of his seisin as distinct from his title: Williams R.P. 241. The alteration of the law had the effect of improving the position of persons who were only half brothers or sisters of the person last seised but direct descendants of the purchaser: *ibid.*, 250; and it altered the order of tracing descent through ancestors among collateral heirs (*post*, p. 512) where the property had been inherited through a woman standing between the purchaser and the intestate.

[14] *Ibid.*, s. 1.

[15] *Ante*, p. 18.

[16] *Ante*, p. 427.

or inclosure,[17] *i.e.*, otherwise than by operation of law. A person who acquired the land by buying it or having it given or devised to him was a purchaser for this purpose, and the descent was traced from the last purchaser. Until the contrary was shown, the person last entitled was deemed to be the last purchaser.[18]

For example, if F bought land and died intestate, his eldest son S inherited it as heir to F. If S then died intestate, descent was traced from F; the land descended to the heir of F and not to the heir of S. But if F had devised the land to S, on the death of S intestate, descent had to be traced from S, for he was the last purchaser.[19]

A similar example is the descent of an entail: provided the entail had not been barred, descent was traced from the original tenant to whom the estate tail was first granted, for he was the last purchaser.[20] Thus if the entail had remained unbarred for several generations, it was capable of descending to collateral relations of the tenant in tail for the time being, and not only to the heirs of his body.

There was one modification of this rule. By the Law of Property Amendment Act, 1859,[21] if there was no heir of the purchaser, descent could be traced from the person last entitled to the land. For example, if B, a bastard, bought land and died intestate leaving a widow and one child, that child inherited the land. If the child then died intestate and without issue, descent had to be traced afresh from B. Since B's issue had died out and in the eyes of the law he had no ancestors (for in law a bastard is *filius nullius*, the child of no one), there was a failure of the heirs of B; B's widow was not entitled, for she was no blood relation of B. In these circumstances the Act of 1859 allowed descent to be traced from the person last entitled, namely, B's child, in which case B's widow could inherit the land; although no blood relation of B, she was a blood relation of her child.

II.   THE ISSUE

2. The issue were preferred to the other relatives, the male issue being preferred to the female issue.[22]

---

[17] *Post*, p. 868.

[18] Inheritance Act, 1833, s. 2.

[19] *Ibid.*, s. 3. Before the Act, on a devise to the heir he was considered to have taken the land by descent and not under the devise: Williams R.P. 276; *cf. ante*, p. 61.

[20] The law was similar before the Act: Williams R.P. 245.

[21] s. 19.

[22] Bl.Comm. ii, 212; Cru.Dig. iii, 331, 332.

3. The elder male was preferred to the younger male, but females of the same degree all took equally as coparceners.[23]

4. Issue of a deceased person represented him, being preferred among themselves according to rules 2 and 3.[24]

These three rules were common law rules. They are perhaps best illustrated by diagrams. (In the following examples, "P" stands for the purchaser, and the other letters indicate the relationship to him of the others concerned. Thus "S" and "D" stand for "son" and "daughter" respectively, "GS" and "GD" for "grandson" and "granddaughter," "U" and "A" for "uncle" and "aunt," and the like. The numerals are used to distinguish two or more of the same relationship, and, where relevant, show the order of birth.)

(*a*)

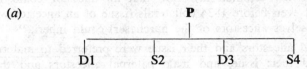

   (i) S2 is the heir.

   (ii) If S2 predeceased P leaving no issue, S4 is the heir.

   (iii) If both S2 and S4 predeceased P leaving no issue, D1 and D3 took as coparceners, together constituting the heir. The nature of coparcenary has already been explained.[25]

(*b*)

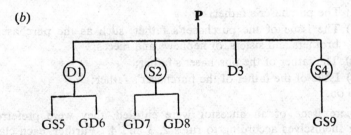

Here, D1, S2 and S4 have all predeceased P, leaving children.

   (i) GD7 and GD8 inherit as coparceners.

   (ii) If they predeceased P leaving no issue, GS9 is the heir.

   (iii) If GS9 also predeceased P leaving no issue, GS5 and D3 inherit as coparceners,[26] and if GS5 had also predeceased P, leaving a son, that son inherited the share of D1.[27]

23 Bl.Comm. ii, 214; Cru.Dig. iii, 332. For coparcenary, see *ante*, p. 429.
24 Bl.Comm. ii, 216; Cru.Dig. iii, 333.
25 *Ante*, p. 430.
26 *Cooper* v. *Frame* (1850) 19 L.J.Ch. 313.
27 *Re Matson* [1897] 2 Ch. 509.

If a man died without issue leaving his widow *enceinte,* the person who would be heir if not displaced by birth of issue was entitled as "qualified heir" to possession of the land and to the rents and profits until issue was born.[28] The qualified heir could obtain a writ *de ventre inspiciendo* for a jury to determine whether the widow was in fact pregnant.[29]

III. ANCESTORS AND COLLATERALS

5. If the purchaser left no issue, his nearest lineal ancestor was entitled, issue of a deceased ancestor representing the ancestor according to rule 4.[30]

This reversed the common law rule that an ancestor could not inherit[31]; but even before 1834 collaterals (issue of an ancestor who are not themselves ancestors of the purchaser) could inherit.[32]

6. Paternal ancestors and their issue were preferred to maternal ancestors and their issue, and male paternal ancestors and their issue were preferred to female paternal ancestors and their issue.[33]

Rules 5 and 6 meant that the purchaser's mother and her relations could not inherit the land unless every single relation on the father's side was dead, ancestors as well as collaterals. A second cousin twice removed on the paternal side was preferred to the purchaser's mother herself. Thus the order of succession was—

(i) The purchaser's father;

(ii) The issue of the purchaser's father, such as the purchaser's brothers and sisters, or nephews and nieces;

(iii) The father of the purchaser's father;

(iv) Issue of the father of the purchaser's father;

and so on.

Where issue of an ancestor were entitled, they were preferred among themselves according to rules 2, 3 and 4. Further, each class had to be entirely exhausted before moving on to the next; a single member of class (ii) excluded the paternal grandfather. Before 1834 the position was similar to the extent that collaterals on the father's side were preferred to those on the mother's side; but ancestors could not inherit.[34]

---

[28] *Richards* v. *Richards* (1860) John. 754.
[29] See, *e.g., Ex p. Aiscough* (1730) 2 P.Wms. 591; Co.Litt. 8b.
[30] Inheritance Act, 1833, s. 6.
[31] See, *e.g., Ratcliff's Case* (1592) 3 Co.Rep. 37a at 40a, 40b. The reasons are obscure: see *ibid.* and notes thereto; [1959] C.L.J. 203 (S. E. Thorne).
[32] Bl.Comm. ii, 220; Williams R.P. 247.
[33] Inheritance Act, 1833, s. 7.
[34] Cru.Dig. iii, 351.

7. The mother of the more remote male paternal ancestor and her heirs were preferred to the mother of the less remote male paternal ancestor and her heirs.[35]

When it became impossible to trace any further male paternal ancestors and their issue, the female paternal ancestors and their issue came next. Among these, the mother of the more remote male paternal ancestor came first: " up the male and down the female line." This may be illustrated thus:

```
                        ┌──────────GGM
                 GF─────┤
                        └──GM
            F───────┬───────M
                    │
                    P
```

If neither F nor GF nor their issue exist, and the father of GF cannot be traced, then GGM and her heirs are preferred to GM and her heirs, and M comes last.

8. On failure of paternal ancestors and their issue, similar rules applied to the maternal ancestors and their issue.[36]

IV. RELATIVES OF THE HALF BLOOD

Two persons are said to be related by the half blood when they trace descent from different marriages of a common ancestor. Before 1834 no person could take as heir if he was related only by the half blood.[37] The Inheritance Act, 1833, altered the general rule, as follows:

9. If the common ancestor was a male, relatives of the half blood took next after relatives of the whole blood of the same degree.[38]

---

[35] Inheritance Act, 1833, ss. 7, 8, confirming the opinions of Blackstone (Comm. ii, 238) and Watkins (*Descents*, 146): see Williams R.P. 249.
[36] Inheritance Act, 1833, ss. 7, 8.
[37] Bl.Comm. ii, 228; P. & M. ii, 300; Cru.Dig. iii, 342.
[38] Inheritance Act, 1833, s. 9. For examples of the operation of this and the next head, see 3rd edition of this book, p. 521

10. If the common ancestor was a female, relatives of the half blood took next after her.[39]

Variations by local custom. So far as the rules set out above were statutory, they overrode any local custom. The rules which were not statutory, however, applied only if there was no local custom to the contrary. Thus rule 3 was varied by the customs of gavelkind and borough English[40]; and frequently the heir to copyhold land was ascertained according to some local custom, so that the customary heir and the heir at common law were different persons.

Escheat. If no heir could be traced, the land escheated *propter defectum sanguinis*[41] to the feudal lord. If no mesne lord could prove that the land was held of him, it escheated to the Crown.[42] Equitable interests did not escheat until the Intestates Estates Act, 1884[43]; previously the trustees took the property beneficially.[44]

B. Rights of a Surviving Spouse

Occasionally there would be a marriage between two persons so related by blood that on the death of one, the other was the heir. This was a rare occurrence, and the law of succession made special provision for widowers and widows which gave them rights prior to the rights of the heir. The interests so given were called curtesy and dower.

I. A WIDOWER

A widower was entitled to a life estate in the whole of the real property of his deceased wife. This right was known as curtesy, or, more fully, an estate by the Curtesy of England.[45] Equity followed the law, and allowed curtesy out of equitable interests,[46] even in the case of property held to the separate use of the wife,[47] unless there was an express direction to the contrary.[48]

Curtesy could be claimed only if the following requirements were satisfied.

[39] Inheritance Act, 1833, s. 9.
[40] *Ante*, pp. 20, 22.
[41] *Ante*, p. 18.
[42] Cru.Dig. iii, 416. See, *e.g.*, *Re Lowe's W. T.* [1973] 1 W.L.R. 882.
[43] ss. 4, 7.
[44] *Burgess* v. *Wheate* (1759) 1 Wm.Bl. 123; *ante*, p. 130.
[45] Litt. 35.
[46] *Watts* v. *Ball* (1708) 1 P.Wms. 108; *ante*, p. 130.
[47] *Cooper* v. *Macdonald* (1877) 7 Ch.D. 288; *post*, p. 994.
[48] *Bennet* v. *Davis* (1725) 2 P.Wms. 316; *Morgan* v. *Morgan* (1820) 5 Madd. 408 at 411.

1. Estate of inheritance: the wife must have been entitled to a freehold estate of inheritance otherwise than as a joint tenant.[49] There was no curtesy out of estates less than freehold such as leaseholds, nor out of life estates[50] or estates *pur autre vie*[51] which were not estates of inheritance. Nor could there be curtesy out of a joint tenancy, for the right of survivorship of the other tenants excluded any such claim.[52] But if the wife was entitled either solely or as tenant in common or coparcener to a fee simple or fee tail, the husband might claim his curtesy.[53]

2. Seisin or possession: the wife must have been either seised "in deed" or else entitled in possession to an equitable interest. There was no curtesy out of estates either in remainder or reversion,[54] apart from the reversion upon a term of years, where seisin was in the reversioner.[55] The common law rule was that even an estate in possession gave rise to no curtesy unless the wife (or the husband in her name) had taken possession of the land.[56] In the case of equitable interests there had to be some equivalent act, such as receipt of the income of the land from the trustees, which showed that the wife had the present enjoyment of the equitable interest.[57]

3. Actual birth of heritable issue: the husband had no claim to curtesy unless issue of the marriage capable of inheriting the land had been born alive. Thus if the wife was seised in tail male and only female issue had been born, the husband took no curtesy[58]; but if a son was born alive, the husband at once became prospectively entitled to curtesy even if the son died a few minutes later[59] leaving nobody to inherit the entail after the wife's death.[60]

4. No disposition of land: the land must not have been disposed of either *inter vivos* or by will. At common law a wife could not alienate realty *inter vivos* without her husband's concurrence and

---

[49] Litt. 35.
[50] *Boothby* v. *Vernon* (1725) 9 Mod. 147.
[51] *Stead* v. *Platt* (1853) 18 Beav. 50.
[52] *Palmer* v. *Rich* [1897] 1 Ch. 134 at 141 ; Cru.Dig. ii, 375.
[53] Cru.Dig. ii, 394, 408.
[54] Williams R.P. 334.
[55] *De Grey* v. *Richardson* (1747) 3 Atk. 469 ; *ante*, p. 48.
[56] Co.Litt. 29a ; but seisin in law sometimes suffered: *ibid*.
[57] *Casborne* v. *Scarfe* (1737) 1 Atk. 603 at 606.
[58] Co.Litt. 29b.
[59] See, *e.g.*, *Jones* v. *Ricketts* (1862) 10 W.R. 576.
[60] Co.Litt. 30b.

could not devise land even with his consent.[61] The husband could thus prevent her from disposing of her land; but if it was alienated, his claim to curtesy was defeated.[62]

Both equity and statute modified this rule. If realty was conveyed to the " separate use " of the wife, equity allowed her to dispose of it by herself either *inter vivos* or by will; and by the Married Women's Property Act, 1882, if a married woman had married or acquired property after 1882, she was able to dispose of it by herself as if she were unmarried.[63] In each case the husband could claim curtesy only if his wife had not disposed of the property either *inter vivos* or by will.[64]

Variations of curtesy. The existence of curtesy and the conditions under which it could be claimed were modified in the case of land subject to customs such as gavelkind.[65] Further, there was no curtesy out of copyholds unless the custom of the particular manor allowed it.[66]

II. A WIDOW

A widow's rights fell under two heads: dower, and the Intestates Estates Act, 1890.

Dower

Provided the necessary conditions were satisfied, a widow was entitled to dower, which was a life interest in one-third of the realty of her deceased husband. Her interest was not terminated by remarriage, nor by adultery,[67] unless she left her husband for her paramour and was not reconciled to her husband,[68] in which case it was immaterial that she left under a separation agreement [69] or was driven away by her husband's cruelty and misconduct.[70] The requirements for dower were as follows.

1. Estate of inheritance: the husband must have been entitled, at some time during the marriage, to a freehold estate of inheritance otherwise than as a joint tenant. The same rules applied here as in the case of curtesy.[71]

---

[61] *Post*, p. 993.
[62] Challis 344.
[63] *Post*, p. 994.
[64] *Cooper* v. *Macdonald* (1877) 7 Ch.D. 288 (separate use); *Hope* v. *Hope* [1892] 2 Ch. 336 (separate property under the Act).
[65] *Ante*, p. 20.
[66] Scriven 74.
[67] *Hethrington* v. *Graham* (1829) 6 Bing. 135 at 138.
[68] Statute of Westminster II, 1285, c. 34.
[69] *Hethrington* v. *Graham* (1829) 6 Bing. 135.
[70] *Woodward* v. *Dowse* (1861) 10 C.B.(N.S.) 722; *Bostock* v. *Smith* (1864) 34 Beav. 57.
[71] Litt. 36; *ante*, p. 514.

2. Seisin or possession: the husband must have been either seised in law or else (after 1833) entitled in possession to an equitable interest. Seisin in deed was not required,[72] for the wife had no means of compelling the husband to make an actual entry. But the estate had to be in possession; there was no dower out of remainders or reversions.[73]

Equity refused to follow the law, and gave no dower out of equitable interests.[74] The reason was that a potential claim to dower was a serious fetter on alienability, since no disposition by the husband could defeat it. But the Dower Act, 1833,[75] made equitable interests in possession subject to dower provided that the parties married after 1833. At the same time the Act made dower defeasible by alienation, as explained below.

3. Birth of heritable issue possible: it must have been possible for heritable issue of the marriage to be born[76]; the actual birth of such issue was immaterial. Thus if land was given " to A and the heirs male of his body," his widow could claim dower even if no issue, or only female issue, had been born. But if land was given " to A and the heirs of his body begotten on Mary," and A married Jane, Jane could not claim dower.

4. Dower not barred: dower could be claimed only if it had not been effectively barred. Before 1834 it was common to employ the somewhat complicated " uses to bar dower " invented by Fearne in the eighteenth century.[77] An intending husband would before marriage convey his land to certain uses which gave him a mere life interest but also an unlimited power of appointment, and a remainder to his heirs in case he died intestate.[78] Thus he had absolute powers of disposition, but no estate which would attract dower. Any land to be acquired after marriage would, at the husband's instance, be conveyed to similar uses, giving the husband a mere life interest coupled with a power of appointment.

---

[72] Litt. 448. A mere right of entry or action sufficed if the parties married after the Dower Act, 1833: see ss. 3, 14.

[73] Except reversions upon leases: Cru.Dig. i, 162.

[74] *Chaplin* v. *Chaplin* (1733) 3 P.Wms. 229 (trust estate); *Dixon* v. *Saville* (1783) 1 Bro. C.C. 326 (equity of redemption).

[75] ss. 2, 14.

[76] Litt. 53.

[77] Fearne 347; Williams R.P. 424, 425 and Appendix A. For an earlier device, see *ibid.*, 352.

[78] Merger of the life interest with the remainder to the heirs, under the rule in *Shelley's Case (ante,* p. 60), was prevented by interposing a vested interest which was unlikely to take effect: see *Duncomb* v. *Duncomb* (1695) 3 Lev. 437: *Parkhurst* v. *Smith d. Dormer* (1740) 6 Bro.P.C. 351.

Such devices were rendered unnecessary [79] by the Dower Act, 1833,[80] which provided that if the parties married after 1833, dower could not be claimed out of any land disposed of by the husband either in his lifetime or by his will,[1] nor out of land in respect of which he had made a declaration by deed or will in bar of dower. The Act also made dower subject to the husband's debts [2]; formerly it took precedence over them.

Variations of dower. The rules applying to dower in gavelkind land have already been noticed.[3] The extent of dower varied in different parts of the country, so that dower might extend to the whole of the land, or to half or one-quarter of it.[4] There was no dower in copyholds, but in many manors there was a custom for widows to have freebench, which corresponded to dower, and was normally a life estate in one-third of the land.[5] The Dower Act, 1833, did not apply to copyholds.[6]

Mode of enjoyment of dower. A widow was entitled to have one-third of the land assigned to her for her life. This assignment was to be effected within the quarantine, namely, the period of forty days after the husband's death during which *Magna Carta*, 1215,[7] allowed the widow to remain in his house.[8] The assignment was made by the person entitled to the land [9] and the widow was usually entitled to have it made " by metes and bounds," *i.e.,* by having the boundaries of her portion marked out. She might, however, accept dower in some other form, as by receiving one-third of the rents and profits of the land.[10] In default of agreement she could apply to the court, which would order the sheriff to assign one-third of the land by metes and bounds.[11] Where this was impossible, dower was assigned in the most convenient manner; thus

---

[79] The Dower Act, 1833, s. 2, in fact made this ineffective if the parties married after 1833: *Re Mitchell* [1892] 2 Ch. 87 at 99.

[80] ss. 4, 6, 7.

[1] See *Lacey* v. *Hill* (1875) L.R. 19 Eq. 346.

[2] s. 5.

[3] *Ante,* p. 20.

[4] Litt. 37; Co.Litt. 33b.

[5] See Scriven 69. In some manors freebench was *dum casta et sola* (*cf. ante,* p. 21), but if lost by unchastity could be retrieved by a remarkable ceremony: Megarry, *Miscellany-at-Law,* 156.

[6] *Smith* v. *Adams* (1854) 3 De G.M. & G. 712.

[7] c. 7.

[8] Co.Litt. 32b.

[9] Tudor L.C. 124.

[10] See *Williams* v. *Thomas* [1909] 1 Ch. 713 at 731, 732; Cru.Dig. i, 170.

[11] Cru.Dig. i, 171, mentioning a case where a sheriff who had chalked out a third part of each room in a house was committed to prison for making an " idle and malicious assignment."

dower out of an advowson entitled the widow to each third presentation.[12]

Intestates Estates Act, 1890

A widow, in addition to any right of dower, was sometimes entitled to £500. This right arose under the Intestates Estates Act, 1890,[13] if her husband—

(i) died after September 1, 1890,
(ii) leaving no issue surviving him, and
(iii) leaving no will of any effect.

The Act made no provision for surviving husbands.

Sect. 2. Personalty Before 1926

As has been seen, all realty descended on intestacy to the heir, thus preserving the estate intact. Leaseholds and other personalty, on the other hand, passed to the next-of-kin as ascertained according to the rules laid down by the Statute of Distribution, 1670,[14] as explained and amended by the Statute of Frauds, 1677, and the Statute of Distribution, 1685.

Subject to certain special rules the property devolved upon all next-of-kin of the same degree in equal shares. The degrees of relationship were ascertained by counting the number of steps between the deceased and the relative in question, counting directly in the case of those related lineally and through the common ancestor in the case of collaterals. Thus suppose X to die intestate leaving the following relatives:

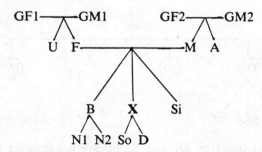

F, M, So and D are relatives of the first degree, GF1, GF2, GM1, GM2, B and Si are relatives of the second degree, and U, A, N1 and N2, relatives of the third degree.

---

[12] Co.Litt. 32a, where it is also said that dower might be taken out of a villein (*ante*, p. 24) in the form of every third day's work.

[13] s. 1.

[14] This appears to have been modelled on rules of Roman law: see *Re Ross's Trusts* (1871) L.R. 13 Eq. 286 at 293.

The special rules were as follows:

I. SURVIVING SPOUSE

1. Widower: if the deceased left a husband, he took the whole of the personalty absolutely, to the exclusion of the other relatives.[15]

2. Widow and issue: if the deceased left a widow and issue, the widow took one-third absolutely [16]; this contrasts with dower, where the widow's third was hers for life only.

3. Widow and no issue: if the deceased left a widow and no issue, the widow took—

    (*a*) her £500 under the Intestates Estates Act, 1890, if the necessary conditions had been fulfilled [17];

    (*b*) one-half of the residue absolutely.[18]

II. OTHER RELATIVES

Subject to the above claims of the surviving spouse, if any, personalty devolved as follows:

4. Issue: the issue of the deceased (including any issue *en ventre sa mère* [19]) took *per stirpes*, males taking equally with females and the younger equally with the elder [20]; "*per stirpes*" means "through the stocks of descent." An example will make this clear.

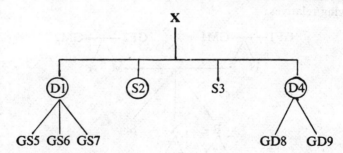

X died intestate, D1 and S2 having predeceased him. Each of X's children who is either alive or represented by issue forms a stock of descent. There are thus three stocks of

---

15 Statute of Frauds, 1677, s. 25.
16 Statute of Distribution, 1670, s. 5.
17 *Ante,* p. 519.
18 Statute of Distribution, 1670, s. 6.
19 *Wallis* v. *Hodson* (1740) 2 Atk. 114.
20 Statute of Distribution, 1670, s. 5.

descent, namely, those of D1, S3 and D4. X's personalty would therefore be divided into thirds. One-third would be divided among the children of D1, who take her share and so get one-ninth each. One-third would pass to S3, and the remaining third to D4; GD8 and GD9 would take nothing, for their mother, D4, was still alive. This rule of descent *per stirpes* applied even if all the children were dead.[21] Thus if all X's children had predeceased him, the grandchildren would not take *per capita* (one share for each head) but still *per stirpes*; in other words, instead of taking one-fifth each, each of the children of D1 would take one-sixth and each of the children of D4 one-quarter.

Where the intestate was a father, any advances made in his lifetime to his child had to be brought into hotchpot (*i.e.*, into account) when distributing the estate [22]; but this rule did not apply if the intestate was the mother,[23] or in cases of partial intestacy.[24]

5. Father : in default of surviving issue, the intestate's father was entitled absolutely.[25]

6. Mother, brothers and sisters : if the father also predeceased the intestate, the mother, brothers and sisters shared equally.[26] Children, but not remoter descendants, of a deceased brother or sister took their parents' share.[27] Thus the mother (first degree), a brother (second degree) and the child of a deceased sister, *i.e.*, a nephew or niece (third degree) might share the personalty equally. But if the mother, brothers and sisters had all predeceased the intestate, the children of the brothers and sisters did not take *per stirpes* under this rule but *per capita* under the general rule.[28]

In default of mother, brothers and sisters, the general rule applied, and the next-of-kin of the same degree took *per capita*.[29] Any relative of one degree would exclude all relatives of remoter degrees.[30]

It will be noted that there was no preference for the whole blood; relatives of the half blood took equally with those of the whole blood.[31] Nor were males preferred to females, or the elder

---

[21] *Re Natt* (1888) 37 Ch.D. 517.
[22] Statute of Distribution, 1670, s. 5; see *post*, p. 528.
[23] *Holt* v. *Frederick* (1726) 2 P.Wms. 356.
[24] *Re Roby* [1908] 1 Ch. 71.
[25] *Blackborough* v. *Davis* (1701) 1 P.Wms. 41 at 51.
[26] Statute of Distribution, 1685, s. 7.
[27] Statute of Distribution, 1670, s. 7.
[28] *Re Ross's Trusts* (1871) L.R. 13 Eq. 286.   [29] Statute of Distribution, 1670, s. 6.
[30] *Bowers* v. *Littlewood* (1719) 1 P.Wms. 594.
[31] *Watts* v. *Crooke* (1690) Show.P.C. 108.

to the younger. In these respects the rules were perhaps more reasonable than those applying to realty; but there seems little to justify some of the complexities.

Bona vacantia. If no next-of-kin could be found according to the above rules, the Crown [32] was entitled to the personalty of the intestate in this country as *bona vacantia* (goods without an owner).[33] But if the deceased had appointed an executor (*e.g.*, if he had made a will which, apart from appointing an executor, was totally or partially ineffective through the premature death of the beneficiaries or some other cause), the executor might be entitled for his own benefit.[34] Before the Executors Act, 1830, the appointment of an executor entitled him to undisposed-of personalty even in preference to the next-of-kin unless they could show from the will that they were intended to benefit [35]; and the words " to be disposed of as my executors shall think fit " did not suffice to do this.[36] The Act,[37] however, obliged the executor to hold the property on trust for the next-of-kin unless a contrary intention could be shown. The Act did not alter the position as between the executor and the Crown, and on deaths before 1926 the executor was entitled unless a contrary intention was shown.[38]

Heirlooms. Heirlooms were chattels which descended to the heir [39]; they were therefore exceptions from the foregoing rules since they obeyed the law of realty rather than the law of personalty. This they did either by ancient custom or because they were so directly connected with land as to " savour of the inheritance." [40] Examples of the latter class were title deeds,[41] letters patent creating dignities,[42] the Crown jewels,[43] the Pusey horn,[44] deer in a deer-park, fishes in a pond, doves in a dovecote [45]; of the former class were household utensils or furniture, such as the best bed,[46] in localities

---

[32] Or Duchy of Lancaster or Duke of Cornwall.
[33] Bl.Comm. i, 298. This applied even to a foreigner domiciled abroad: *Re Barnett's Trusts* [1902] 1 Ch. 847. See generally N. D. Ing, *Bona Vacantia* (1971).
[34] See *Androvin* v. *Poilblanc* (1745) 3 Atk. 299: and see at p. 300 (legacy to executor shows intention that he should not take the residue beneficially).
[35] *Bishop of Cloyne* v. *Young* (1750) 2 Ves.Sen. 91.
[36] *Re Carville* [1937] 4 All E.R. 464; and compare *Re Howell* [1915] 1 Ch. 241 with *Re Chapman* [1922] 2 Ch. 479.
[37] Repealed by A.E.A., 1925, 2nd Sched. For the new law, see *post*, p. 531.
[38] *Att-Gen.* v. *Jefferys* [1908] A.C. 411; *Re Jones* [1925] Ch. 340.
[39] Co.Litt. 18b; Bl.Comm. ii, 427. For " heirlooms " in the wider sense, *i.e.*, settled chattels, see *ante*, p. 342.
[40] *Hill (Viscount)* v. *Hill (Dowager Viscountess)* [1897] 1 Q.B. 483 at 494, 495.
[41] *Atkinson* v. *Baker* (1791) 4 T.R. 229. See *post*, p. 599.
[42] *Hill (Viscount)* v. *Hill (Dowager Viscountess)*, *supra*.
[43] Co.Litt. 18b.
[44] *Pusey* v. *Pusey* (1684) 1 Vern. 273. By this token the Pusey lands were held in cornage (*ante*, p. 16): Litt. 156; Co.Litt. 107a; Blount, Frag., 71.
[45] Co.Litt. 8a; Bl.Comm. ii, 427, 428.
[46] Co.Litt. 18b; *Hill (Viscount)* v. *Hill (Dowager Viscountess)*, *supra*.

where a valid custom could be proved.[47] Heirlooms could not be created otherwise: man " cannot turn a chattel into freehold land." [48] But chattels could be settled upon trust to devolve with land, as has been explained elsewhere.[49]

Heirlooms could not be devised away from the land with which they devolved [50]; but they would presumably pass under a devise of it. It is settled that title deeds pass with the land, and belong to the freeholder in possession.[51]

The subject of heirlooms is of less importance since 1925 owing to the unification of the rules of descent for realty and personalty, next to be considered. But questions may still arise where a testator owning heirlooms devises, for example, his land to A and his other property to B.

Sect. 3. All Property After 1925

A. *The New Rules of Intestacy*

Where a person dies intestate after 1925, no distinction is made between realty and personalty. The heir and all the law associated with him is therefore obsolete. Under the Administration of Estates Act, 1925,[52] all property, whether real or personal, which does not already consist of money is held on trust for sale. The personal representatives of the deceased have power to postpone sale for such period as they think proper. But unless required for the purpose of administration for want of other assets, " personal chattels " [53] are not to be sold without special reason, and reversionary interests (such as an interest in a trust fund which will not fall into the intestate's estate until the life interest of some third person has ceased) are similarly not to be sold without special reason.

Out of the fund thus produced, the personal representatives must pay all funeral, testamentary and administration expenses, debts and other liabilities, and set aside a fund to meet the pecuniary legacies (if any) bequeathed by the will of the deceased.[54] The residue must then be distributed to the persons beneficially entitled. The rules for ascertaining these persons are stated as amended by the Intestates' Estates Act, 1952, and they apply in the case of persons who die

[47] Proof of a custom was not easy: *post*, p. 821.
[48] *Hill (Viscount)* v. *Hill (Dowager Viscountess)*, *supra*, at p. 495, *per* Chitty L.J.; see also *Re Johnston* (1884) 26 Ch.D. 538, and contrast *Re Penton's S. T.* [1924] 2 Ch. 192. But it can be done by making a chattel a fixture: *post*, p. 711.
[49] *Ante*, p. 342.
[50] Co.Litt. 185b. See generally, Williams & Mortimer, *Executors, Administrators and Probate*, 480 *et seq.*
[51] *Atkinson* v. *Baker*, *supra*.
[52] s. 33 (1). [53] See *post*, p. 524.
[54] A.E.A., 1925, s. 33 (2). See *Re Midgley* [1955] Ch. 576; [1956] C.L.J. 22, 80.

intestate after 1952. The Act of 1925 is still the primary Act, but the Act of 1952 has made important amendments to it, particularly by increasing the rights of a widower or widow. The rules which applied to intestates dying between 1925 and 1953 are summarised in a footnote.[55] Certain fixed sums were increased by the Family Provision Act 1966 and the Family Provision (Intestate Succession) Order 1972,[55a] and these are stated as they apply where the intestate died after June 30, 1972.

1. The surviving spouse. Widowers and widows have equal rights. But these rights vary greatly according to the state of the intestate's family. In the following summary[56] " specified relatives " means parent, brother or sister of the whole blood, or issue of a brother or sister of the whole blood. " Issue " is used in its normal meaning, as including children, grandchildren, or remoter descendants, but references to " leaving issue " and " leaving no issue " refer only to issue who attain an absolutely vested interest.[57]

(a) *No issue and no specified relative.* If the intestate leaves no issue and no specified relative, the surviving spouse takes the whole residuary estate *absolutely*.

(b) *Issue.* If the intestate leaves issue (whether or not there are any specified relatives), the surviving spouse takes the following interests.

(1) THE " PERSONAL CHATTELS " ABSOLUTELY. These are elaborately defined.[58] They include furniture, horses, cars, plate, books, jewellery, wines and " articles of household or personal use or

---

55 The 1926–52 rules are as stated in the original version of the A.E.A., 1925, ss. 46–49. The following brief summary may be compared with the new rules stated in the text. A surviving spouse took (i) the personal chattels absolutely, (ii) £1,000 free of death duties and costs with interest at 5 per cent., (iii) if there were no surviving issue, a life interest in the whole of the residue; if there were surviving issue, a life interest in half the residue. Subject to these rights the residue was held on the statutory trusts (*post*, p. 527) for the surviving issue, and in default of issue for other relatives in the same manner as since 1952 (*post*, p. 529); except that if no one in classes 3–8 took, a surviving spouse would take absolutely, so as to exclude the Crown. A surviving spouse's life interest might be purchased by the personal representatives (s. 48), but the spouse had no right to compel them to do so. They might, and often did, appropriate the matrimonial home in satisfaction of the surviving spouse's share (see s. 41), but again they could not be compelled to do so. Until 1953 a surviving spouse's £1,000 was not subject to deduction of any benefit received by will (s. 49); and in case of doubt as to the order of two deaths the younger person was deemed to survive the elder under L.P.A., 1925, s. 184, for intestacy purposes as well as others.
55a S.I. 1972 No. 916.
56 For full details see Intestates' Estates Act, 1952, s. 1 (2), and the table therein contained. The effect of the amendments on A.E.A., 1925, ss. 46–49, may conveniently be seen from the 1st Sched. to the I.E.A., 1952.
57 A.E.A., 1925, s. 47 (2) (*b*), (*c*); see *post*, p. 527.
58 A.E.A., 1925, s. 55 (1) (x).

ornament," but exclude chattels used at the death of the intestate for business purposes, money and securities for money. Roughly speaking, the phrase includes everything that goes to make a home (though not the house itself), and more besides, such as a small yacht used for family purposes,[59] and a stamp collection kept as a hobby.[60] The phrase thus has a meaning quite distinct from " personalty " or " personal property."

(2) £15,000 ABSOLUTELY, free of death duties and costs, with interest thereon at the rate of 4 per cent. per annum from the date of death until payment. Both the £15,000 and the interest thereon are charged on the residuary estate and are therefore payable out of capital,[61] but the interest is *primarily* payable out of income.[62]

(3) A LIFE INTEREST in half of the residuary estate. Provision is made whereby the surviving spouse may call upon the personal representatives to purchase the life interest for a lump sum [63] (ascertained in accordance with the Act [64]), thus enabling the estate to be distributed forthwith. This right may only be exercised within twelve months from the first grant of representation, unless the court extends the time limit for special reasons,[65] and it is exercisable only in so far as the property is in possession.[66] A written notice must be served on the personal representatives [67]; but if the surviving spouse is the sole personal representative, the right is effective only if written notice is given to the principal probate registrar.[68]

(c) *No issue but specified relatives.* If the intestate leaves no issue, but one or more of the specified relatives, the surviving spouse takes—

(i) THE " PERSONAL CHATTELS " ABSOLUTELY (as above);

(ii) £40,000 ABSOLUTELY (as above);

(iii) HALF OF THE RESIDUARY ESTATE ABSOLUTELY.[69]

These provisions are subject to a number of rules.

(1) INCREASE OF FIXED SUMS. The Lord Chancellor may by order increase the above-mentioned sums of £15,000 and £40,000.[69a] Formerly they were respectively £5,000 and £20,000 under the Intestates Estates Act, 1952 and £8,750 and £30,000 under the Family Provision Act 1966.

---

[59] *Re Chaplin* [1950] Ch. 507.
[60] *Re Reynolds' W. T.* [1966] 1 W.L.R. 19; see (1966) 82 L.Q.R. 18 (R.E.M.). See also *Re Crispin's W. T.* [1974] 3 W.L.R. 657 (collection of clocks and watches worth £50,000 included). [61] *Re Saunders* [1929] 1 Ch. 674.
[62] I.E.A., 1952, s. 1 (4).
[63] *Ibid.*, s. 2.
[64] *Ibid.* (now A.E.A., 1925, s. 47A (2)). [65] *Ibid.* (now A.E.A., 1925, s. 47A (5)).
[66] *Ibid.* (now A.E.A., 1925, s. 47A (3)). [67] *Ibid.* (now A.E.A., 1925, s. 47A (6)).
[68] *Ibid.* (now A.E.A., 1925, s. 47A (7)). [69] I.E.A., 1952, s. 1 (2), Table.
[69a] Family Provision Act 1966, s. 1.

526 *Wills and Intestacy*

(2) MATRIMONIAL HOME. The surviving spouse has a special right to have appropriated to him or her any dwelling-house forming part of the residuary estate in which he or she was resident at the intestate's death [70]; this will usually be the matrimonial home. The spouse may require the personal representatives (even if he or she is one of them [71]) to appropriate the house, at a proper valuation, as part of the property to which he or she is entitled absolutely [72]; and it must be exercised within twelve months of the first grant of representation.[73] It applies to whatever interest the intestate had in the house, even if only a leasehold; but it does not apply in the case of a leasehold which would expire or be determinable within two years of the intestate's death.[74] The mere right to call for an appropriation of the house does not, however, give the surviving spouse even an equitable interest in it, or any right to retain possession of it.[75] The Act contains a number of other provisions about the details of this right.[76]

(3) PARTIAL INTESTACY. These rules apply equally to partial intestacies. But the Act of 1952 requires the sums of £15,000 and £40,000 (see above) to be diminished by the value of any beneficial interest which the surviving spouse may take under the deceased's will.[77] It sometimes happens, for example, that the surviving spouse is given a life interest by the will, and the rest of the property passes as on intestacy; in that case the surviving spouse may at once claim the statutory legacy of £15,000 or £40,000, but it must be diminished by the actuarial value of the life interest.[78] Alternatively the surviving spouse may disclaim the benefit of the will and take under the intestacy rules alone.[79]

(4) SEPARATION. If the spouses are separated by a judicial separation and the separation is continuing, the property of either of them who dies intestate will devolve as if the other were already dead.[80]

[70] I.E.A., 1952, s. 5 and 2nd Sched.
[71] *Ibid.*, 2nd Sched., para. 5 (1).
[72] *Ibid.*, para. 1 (1).
[73] *Ibid.*, para. 3 (1).
[74] *Ibid.*, para. 1 (2).
[75] *Lall* v. *Lall* [1965] 1 W.L.R. 1249.
[76] I.E.A., 1952, 2nd Sched., para. 1 (2). If the house is worth more than the surviving spouse's absolute interest (which will be only £15,000 where there are issue and no personal chattels), the spouse may pay the balance in cash: para. 5 (2).
[77] I.E.A., 1952, s. 3 (now A.E.A., 1925, s. 49 (*aa*)).
[78] *Re Bowen-Buscarlet's W. T.* [1972] Ch. 463, not following the assumption in *Re McKee* [1931] 2 Ch. 145.
[79] See *Re Sullivan* [1930] 1 Ch. 84; *Re Thornber* [1937] Ch. 29.
[80] Matrimonial Causes Act 1973, s. 18 (2), replacing Matrimonial Proceedings and Property Act 1970, s. 40 (applying to deaths after July 31, 1970). For the previous law, see Matrimonial Causes Act 1965, s. 20 (3).

(5) COMMORIENTES. If spouses die in circumstances which make it uncertain which survived the other (a phrase which is held to cover simultaneous deaths [81]) the statutory presumption that the younger survived the elder [82] is modified for the purposes of applying the rules of intestate succession. It is now always to be presumed that the spouse predeceased the intestate,[83] and so takes no benefit as a *surviving* spouse. Thus if H (husband, aged 60) and W (wife, aged 50) are simultaneously killed in an accident and both die intestate, in distributing H's property W will be presumed to have predeceased H and so will have no rights in his intestacy, although she will be deemed to have survived him for other purposes. In distributing W's property, however, H will be presumed to have predeceased W,[84] and the same presumption will hold good for other purposes. It is only in the case of spouses that the normal presumption of the younger person's survival is modified: if H and his son are simultaneously killed, both intestate, the son can take under H's intestacy; but H cannot take under his son's, for H is presumed to have died first.

2. The issue. Subject to the rights of the surviving spouse, if any, the property is held on special statutory trusts for the surviving issue.[85] Under these trusts the property is held upon trust for all the children of the deceased living at his death in equal shares, but qualified as follows—

(a) *Subject to representation, i.e.,* subject to the rule that surviving issue of a deceased child stand in his shoes and take his share [86]; descent is thus *per stirpes.*

(b) *Subject to the rule that no issue attains a vested interest until he is eighteen* [86a] *years old or married.*[87] This in effect means that if an infant dies without having married, the property must be dealt with from that moment as if the infant had never existed.[88] Thus if X dies leaving a widow and infant son, the widow takes a life interest in half the residue. If the son dies before either marrying or attaining his majority, the widow forthwith takes either all or half the residue absolutely, just as if there had been no issue.

---

[81] *Hickman* v. *Peacey* [1945] A.C. 304; *ante*, p. 492.
[82] L.P.A., 1925, s. 184; *ante*, p. 492.
[83] I.E.A., 1952, s. 1 (4) (now A.E.A., 1925, s. 46 (3)).
[84] This is by the operation of L.P.A., 1925, s. 184; I.E.A., 1952, s. 1 (4), does not apply, since it is confined to cases where the L.P.A., 1925, would otherwise require the spouse to have survived the intestate.
[85] A.E.A., 1925, ss. 46 (1) (i), (ii), 47.
[86] *Ibid.*, s. 47.
[86a] Family Law Reform Act 1969, s. 3 (2). For deaths prior to 1970 the prescribed age is 21.
[87] A.E.A., 1925, s. 47.
[88] *Ibid.*, s. 47 (2).

(c) *Subject to hotchpot.* There are two rules governing this.

(1) INTER VIVOS. Children (but not remoter issue) must bring into account any money or property which by way of advancement or upon their marriage the intestate has paid to them or settled for their benefit, if they wish to share in the distribution of the estate.[89] For example, if the estate is worth £16,000 and there are three children, one of whom has received an advancement of £2,000 in the intestate's lifetime, that child can claim only £4,000 out of the £16,000; the other two children each receive £6,000. Had the first child received an advancement of £10,000, he could not be compelled to refund any part of it for distribution between the others. The obligation to bring property into hotchpot is subject to any contrary intention appearing from the circumstances of the case, but applies even if the deceased was the mother of the children.[90]

In determining what advances must be brought into hotchpot, a distinction must be drawn between payments made to start a child in life or make permanent provision for him, on the one hand, and, on the other hand, casual or periodical payments made in the ordinary course of events (*e.g.*, for education or maintenance,[91] or annual allowances,[92] or small gifts [93]), or in order to relieve the child from temporary difficulties [94] : the former alone need be brought into hotchpot, and then only if the amounts are sufficiently substantial, judged absolutely and not merely in relation to the size of the estate.[95] Further, property appointed to the child by the deceased under a special power of appointment need not be brought into account.[96]

(2) PARTIAL INTESTACY. In the case of partial intestacy, issue of the deceased, whether children or remoter descendants, must, subject to any contrary intention shown by the deceased, bring into hotchpot any benefit received under his will.[97] Thus if a grandchild of the deceased has received £1,000, he need not bring it into hotchpot if it was an advancement made *inter vivos* (for he is not a child of the deceased), but he must bring it into account if it is given him by will. Property bequeathed in effect to a child of the deceased for life

---

[89] *Ibid.*, s. 47 (1) (iii). See generally (1961) 25 Conv.(N.S.) 469 (J. T. Farrand).
[90] Contrast *ante*, p. 521.
[91] *Edwards* v. *Freeman* (1727) 2 P.Wms. 435.
[92] *Hatfeild* v. *Minet* (1878) 8 Ch.D. 136 at 144.
[93] *Schofield* v. *Heap* (1858) 27 Beav. 93.
[94] See *Taylor* v. *Taylor* (1875) L.R. 20 Eq. 155 at 157; *Re Scott* [1903] 1 Ch. 1 at 3.
[95] *Re Hayward* [1957] Ch. 528 (£507 held, on the facts, not sufficiently substantial, although estate totalled under £2,300); see (1957) 73 L.Q.R. 21, 302 (R.E.M.).
[96] *Re Reeve* [1935] Ch. 110.
[97] A.E.A., 1925, s. 49 (*a*).

and then to his children absolutely must therefore be brought in by them at its full capital value, for their interests amount to the whole,[98] whereas a mere life interest is brought in only at its actuarial value.[99]

If no issue attains a vested interest, then, subject to the claim of the surviving spouse (if any), the relatives of the deceased are entitled in the following order; any member of one class who takes a vested interest excludes all members of subsequent classes.

3. The parents of the deceased are entitled in equal shares absolutely [1]; if one is dead, the survivor is entitled absolutely.[2]

4. The brothers and sisters of the whole blood, on the statutory trusts.

A division may be made here, for at this point the " specified relatives " end. Those included in the foregoing classes may take an interest even though the intestate left a surviving spouse; those in the subsequent classes cannot.

5. The brothers and sisters of the half blood, on the statutory trusts.

6. The grandparents, if more than one in equal shares.

7. The uncles and aunts of the whole blood, on the statutory trusts.

8. The uncles and aunts of the half blood, on the statutory trusts.

9. The Crown (or the Duchy of Lancaster or Duke of Cornwall) as *bona vacantia* in lieu of any right to escheat.[3]

A number of points arise on the foregoing list.

(1) STATUTORY TRUSTS. The statutory trusts for the brothers, sisters, uncles and aunts are the same as those for the issue, save that the provisions relating to hotchpot do not apply.[4] Thus deceased brothers, sisters, uncles and aunts are represented by their surviving descendants (*e.g.,* nephews, nieces and cousins of the

---

[98] *Re Young* [1951] Ch. 185; *Re Grover's W. T.* [1971] Ch. 168.
[99] *Re Morton* [1956] Ch. 644; (1956) 72 L.Q.R. 483 (R.E.M.).
[1] A.E.A., 1925, s. 46 (1) (iii).
[2] *Ibid.,* s. 46 (1) (iv).
[3] *Ibid.,* s. 46 (1) (vi).
[4] *Ibid.,* s. 47 (3).

intestate),[5] and their interests in every case are contingent upon their attaining full age or marrying. " Uncles " and " aunts " include only blood relations; an aunt's husband, although bearing the courtesy title of uncle, has no claim.

(2) ILLEGITIMATE CHILDREN. Where the intestate dies after 1969, an illegitimate child (or his issue if he is dead) can take on the intestacy of either of his parents as if he had been born legitimate; and similarly on his intestacy each of his parents can take.[6] But in other relationships illegitimacy bars all rights under an intestacy. Even in the case of parent and child it bars any claim to an entailed interest.[6] Where the death occurred before 1970, an illegitimate child or his issue could take on his mother's intestacy, if there were no legitimate children; and the mother of an illegitimate child could take on the child's intestacy as if she were the only surviving parent.[7] No disabilities attach to persons legitimated by the subsequent marriage of their parents.[7a]

(3) ADOPTED CHILDREN. Adopted children are now treated as children of their adopting (not their natural) parents, provided that the death occurred after the adoption and after 1949; and members of the adopting family may take under the intestacy of an adopted child.[8] In the case of deaths prior to 1950 the rule was the opposite.[9] An adopted child whose natural parent died intestate before 1950 and whose adopting parent died intestate after 1949 could therefore benefit under both intestacies.

(4) CROWN DISCRETION. The Crown usually modifies its strict rights under head No. 9 by making provision for dependants of the deceased, whether related to him or not, and for others for whom he might reasonably have been expected to make provision. This purely discretionary power, which the Act confirms,[10] is made all the more necessary by the increased prospects of the Crown of succeeding to property of an intestate. Before 1926 any relative, however remote, could claim as heir or next-of-kin, and mesne lords

---

[5] *Ibid.*, s. 47 (5), added by I.E.A., 1952. This contains a slip in drafting which appears to exclude the descendants unless one of the brothers, uncles, etc., also survives; but this is to be ignored: *Re Lockwood* [1958] Ch. 231 ; see (1958) 74 L.Q.R. 25 (R.E.M.).

[6] Family Law Reform Act 1969, s. 14.

[7] Legitimacy Act 1926, s. 9.

[7a] Legitimacy Acts 1926 and 1959 (save in relation to the descent of titles of honour: Act of 1926, s. 10).

[8] Adoption Act, 1958, ss. 16 (1), 17 (1), 59 and 5th Sched. Property entailed before the adoption order was made is excepted.

[9] Adoption of Children Act, 1926, s. 5 (2).

[10] A.E.A., 1925, s. 46 (1) (vi). For the practice, see N. D. Ing, *Bona Vacantia* (1971) Chap. 10.

could claim land by escheat. After 1925 no relation more remote than a grandparent or the descendant of a grandparent can claim,[11] and there can be no escheat to a mesne lord on intestacy.[12]

(5) EXECUTOR'S CLAIM. On a partial intestacy the executor cannot take undisposed of property beneficially unless an intention to this effect is shown by the will [13]; this rule now applies to an executor as against the Crown and also as against the statutory next-of-kin.[14]

B. Survivals of the Old Rules

I. THE HEIR

In the case of all persons dying after 1925 the foregoing rules supersede the old rules relating to intestacy. But in the case of realty the old general law of descent still has to be applied in three cases.

1. Lunatic : if the deceased was a lunatic of full age at the end of 1925 and dies without having recovered testamentary capacity, any realty as to which he died intestate descends according to the general law in force before 1926.[15] Since the *general* law in force before 1926 applies, customs such as gavelkind are ignored [16]; and a child legitimated under the Legitimacy Act, 1926, has no claim.[17] An interest under a trust for sale is included if the land was owned by the lunatic before 1926 and was not previously subject to a trust for sale (as where the lunatic was a tenant in common),[18] but not otherwise, *e.g.*, if the lunatic took under a trust for sale arising under an intestacy after 1925.[19]

2. Entail : an entail not disposed of by the will of the deceased [20] descends in accordance with the general law in force before 1926.[21] Since entails were to be preserved, this could only be done by preserving their peculiar rules of devolution.

3. Limitation to heir : if property is limited after 1925, whether *inter vivos* or by will, to the heir of a deceased person, the " heir "

---

11 See *Re Bridgen* [1938] Ch. 205 at 209.
12 A.E.A., 1925, s. 45 (1) (*d*).
13 s. 49 (*b*). See *Re Skeats* [1936] Ch. 683.
14 Contrast the position before 1926: *ante*, p. 522.
15 A.E.A., 1925, s. 51 (2).
16 *Re Higham* [1937] 2 All E.R. 17.
17 *Re Berrey* [1936] Ch. 274.
18 *Re Bradshaw* [1950] Ch. 582 ; *Re Sirett* [1969] 1 W.L.R. 60.
19 *Re Donkin* [1948] Ch. 74.
20 *Ante*, p. 95.
21 L.P.A., 1925, s. 130 (4); A.E.A., 1925, ss. 45 (2), 51 (4); *ante*, p. 509.

is ascertained according to the general law in force before 1926.[22]
This is not a case of descent on intestacy, for the heir takes as
purchaser. Prima facie, " heir " is taken in its strict sense,[23] though
the context may show that the heir apparent or heir presumptive is
intended,[24] or even that the new law of intestacy is to apply[25]; and
the court is more ready today than formerly to find such a context.[26]
A devise to the testator's own right heirs except X is void if X is
the heir.[27]

II.   CURTESY

Curtesy has been abolished in the case of all persons dying after
1925.[28]   There are two exceptional cases where curtesy according to
the general law in force before 1926 may still arise:

1. Lunatic : in the case of realty as to which a wife dies intestate,
if she was a lunatic of full age at the end of 1925 and dies without
having recovered testamentary capacity.[29]

2. Entail : in the case of an unbarred entail.[30]

III.   DOWER

Dower has been abolished in the case of all persons dying after
1925.[31]   The only exception is in the case of a lunatic: dower
according to the general law in force before 1926 can still arise out
of realty as to which a husband dies intestate, if he was of full age
and insane at the end of 1925 and dies without recovering
his testamentary capacity.[32]

Dower cannot now arise out of an entail.   There is no provision
for it in the enactment governing the descent of entails,[33] and since
the Dower Act, 1833, which gave dower. out of equitable interests,[34]
has been repealed,[35] there seems to be no means of attaching dower
to an interest which is now always equitable.

---

[22] L.P.A., 1925, s. 132; A.E.A., 1925, s. 51 (1).   By the former section the heir
appears to take only an equitable interest, even in the (highly unlikely) event
of an immediate conveyance by deed.
[23] See *Doe* d. *Winter* v. *Perratt* (1826) 5 B. & C. 48; affd. 9 Cl. & F. 606.
[24] *Darbison* d. *Long* v. *Beaumont* (1713) 1 P.Wms. 229.
[25] See *Re Kilvert* [1957] Ch. 388 (" heirs and successors " held to refer to general
law of intestacy).
[26] See *Lightfoot* v. *Maybery* [1914] A.C. 782 at 794.
[27] *Re Smith* [1933] Ch. 847; contrast *Re Hooper* [1936] Ch. 442.
[28] A.E.A., 1925, s. 45 (1).
[29] *Ibid.*, s. 51 (2).
[30] L.P.A., 1925, s. 130 (4).
[31] A.E.A., 1925, s. 45 (1).
[32] *Ibid.*, s. 51 (2); *ante*, p. 531.
[33] L.P.A., 1925, s. 130 (4).
[34] *Ante*, p. 516.
[35] A.E.A., 1925, 2nd Sched., Pt. I; Wolst. & C. iii, 30.   From the wording of
L.P.A., 1925, s. 130 (4), it seems that the result is not accidental.

IV. PERSONALTY

In the case of personalty, the old rules never apply to deaths occurring after 1925.[36] These rules still retain some of their importance, however, particularly in showing title to leaseholds, and in the practice of reversion conveyancing. Thus if in 1920 personalty was settled upon A for life with remainder to B absolutely, and B died intestate in 1924, B's reversion (which is called by this name, although technically a remainder [37]) passed to his next-of-kin. If the person at present entitled to B's reversion (A still being alive) wishes to sell or mortgage it, he will have to prove that he is duly entitled to it, thus invoking the old rules of intestacy.

Part 3

DEVOLUTION OF LEGAL ESTATES

Sect. 1. Introductory

1. Vesting of property. Hitherto we have examined only the beneficial devolution of property on death. We must now turn to machinery by which the property becomes vested in those beneficially entitled. The general rule today is that all property first vests in the personal representatives of the deceased, who in due course transfer to the beneficiaries any of the property not required in the due administration of the estate, *e.g.,* for payment of debts. In this context, " estate " is used not in the technical sense of an estate in land, but as a collective expression for the sum total of the assets and liabilities of the deceased.

2. Executors. " Personal representatives " is a phrase which includes both executors and administrators. If a person makes a will, he may (but need not) appoint one or more persons to be his executor or executors, with the duty of paying debts, death duties and funeral expenses, and ultimately of distributing the estate to those entitled. The executor derives his powers from the will, although he must obtain confirmation of his position by " proving the will," *i.e.,* obtaining a grant of probate from the court.[38] If a sole or only surviving executor who has obtained probate dies having himself appointed an executor, the latter, on proving the original executor's will, becomes executor of the original testator also. This " chain

---

[36] A.E.A., 1925, s. 45 (1).
[37] *Ante,* p. 178.
[38] See, *e.g., Chetty* v. *Chetty* [1916] 1 A.C. 603; *Bainbridge* v. *I. R. C.* [1955] 1 W.L.R. 1329 at 1335; *Biles* v. *Caesar* [1957] 1 W.L.R. 156; *Re Crowhurst Park* [1974] 1 W.L.R. 583.

of representation " may be continued indefinitely until broken by failure to appoint an executor, or failure of an executor to obtain a grant of probate.[39]

3. Administrators. If a person dies without having appointed an executor, or if none of the executors he has appointed is able and willing to act, application must be made to the court by some person or persons interested in the estate for " letters of administration " appointing an administrator or administrators. The duties of an administrator are substantially the same as those of an executor. If the deceased left no will, simple administration is granted; if he left a will, administration *cum testamento annexo* (" with the will annexed ") is granted.[40] Provision is also made for certain limited grants of administration, such as grants confined to settled land,[41] grants " save and except " settled land,[42] and grants *durante minore aetate* (" during the minority " of the sole executor).[43] There is no " chain of representation " for administrators. If a sole or last surviving administrator dies without completing the administration of the estate, application must be made for a grant of administration *de bonis non administratis* (more shortly, *de bonis non*), which is a grant " in respect of the goods left unadministered."

Sect. 2. Devolution of Property on Personal Representatives

The devolution of the property of the deceased upon his personal representatives can be divided into three stages :

1. Before 1898;
2. Between 1897 and 1926; and
3. After 1925.

A. *Before* 1898

I. REALTY

The common law rule was that the realty of the deceased did not vest in his personal representatives but passed immediately to the heir or devisee as the case may be. If any dispute arose as to who was entitled under the will or intestacy, it was settled by the common law courts. There was never any need for the grant of probate or letters of administration. Even if executors had been appointed,

---

[39] A.E.A., 1925, s. 7, replacing 25 Edw. 3, St. 5, c. 5, 1351.
[40] J.A., 1925, s. 166.
[41] *Ibid.*, s. 162; *ante*, p. 309.
[42] See A.E.A., 1925, s. 23; *ante*, p. 309.
[43] J.A., 1925, s. 165.

they had no power over the realty of the deceased and were thus unable to sell it to pay debts. Instead, the creditors had to sue the heir or devisee, and their right to do this did not extend to all debts until the Administration of Estates Act, 1833; even then, the claim did not arise against an assignee who took in good faith before action brought.[44] The position was the same if, there being no executor, someone had obtained a grant of administration. The only case in which the personal representatives could exercise control over the realty was if the deceased gave them some express or implied power to deal with it, as by devising it to them for the purposes of administration or by charging it with the payment of debts.[45]

II. PERSONALTY

In the case of personalty the position was very different. All personalty (including, as usual, leaseholds) vested in the personal representatives. If an executor was appointed, the property vested in him from the moment of death, although it was necessary for him to confirm his position by obtaining probate of the will. If no executor was appointed, a grant of administration had to be obtained by some person interested in the estate, and until then the property vested in the Ordinary (*i.e.*, the Bishop [46]) or (after the Court of Probate Act, 1858 [47]) in the Probate judge, now the President of the Family Division.[48] When the grant is made, the administrator's title for most purposes [49] relates back to the moment of death.[50] In either case the personal representatives had full control over the property and could use it for the payment of debts and other liabilities, handing over the surplus to those entitled under the will or intestacy. Probate and letters of administration were originally granted by the ecclesiastical courts, but the Court of Probate Act, 1857, substituted a Court of Probate which was subsequently replaced by the High Court under the Judicature Acts, 1873 and 1875.

B. *Between* 1897 *and* 1926

1. Vesting in personal representatives. The Land Transfer Act, 1897, was passed to establish a " Real Representative." Under the Act,[51] in the case of deaths after 1897, all property, whether real or

---

[44] *Re Atkinson* [1908] 2 Ch. 307.
[45] L.P.(Am.)A., 1859, ss. 14–18.
[46] Statute of Westminster II, 1285, c. 19.
[47] s. 19.
[48] A.E.A., 1925, ss. 9, 55 (1) (xv), as amended by Administration of Justice Act 1970, s. 1, Sched. 2 (5); see, *e.g.*, *Smith* v. *Mather* [1948] 2 K.B. 212 (notice to quit served on President).
[49] See *Hilton* v. *Sutton Steam Laundry* [1946] K.B. 63 (invalid writ not retrospectively validated).
[50] *Foster* v. *Bates* (1843) 12 M. & W. 226 at 233.
[51] s. 1 (1). Part I of the Act has been called " one of the worst-drawn enactments of modern times "; Jarman, 6th ed., 64; and see *post*, p. 537, n. 76.

personal, vested in the personal representatives in the same way as leaseholds had vested before 1898, save that on an intestacy the legal estate in realty vested in the heir (instead of the Probate judge) until an administrator was appointed.[52] The personal representatives thus became " real " as well as " personal " representatives, although their old name is still used. They had full powers of administration[53] and could thus sell realty to raise money for the payment of debts. There were a few exceptions to the rule that all property vested in them,[54] including legal (but not equitable[55]) interests in copyholds; and in one case property not owned by the deceased vested in them, namely, property over which he had a general power of appointment which he exercised by his will.[56]

2. Vesting in beneficiaries. During the administration of the estate, the ownership of all assets not specifically devised or bequeathed was in the personal representatives; the beneficiaries had no equitable interest in them,[57] but merely a right to compel the personal representatives to administer the estate properly.[58] But subject to due administration, the personal representatives held the property on trust for those beneficially entitled, who could call for a transfer of it to themselves.[59] If the heir was entitled, the realty had to be transferred by a conveyance; but if a devisee was entitled, the personal representatives might either assent to the devise or convey the land to the devisee.[60] An assent did not even need to be in writing; any conduct by the personal representatives showing that they assented to the gift would suffice, as, for example, allowing the beneficiary to take possession of the property.[61] This was unsatisfactory, since the title to a legal estate might depend upon facts which were difficult to prove, instead of appearing plainly from title deeds.

To make a valid transfer of realty, all the personal representatives who had taken out a grant had to concur[62]; but over personalty

---

[52] *Re Griggs* [1914] 2 Ch. 547.
[53] L.T.A., 1897, s. 2.
[54] *Ibid.*, s. 1 (4); see *post*, p. 537.
[55] *Re Somerville and Turner's Contract* [1903] 2 Ch. 583.
[56] L.T.A., 1897, s. 1 (2).
[57] See *post*, p. 539.
[58] See *Williams* v. *Holland* [1965] 1 W.L.R. 739 (executor entitled to possession as against beneficiary).
[59] L.T.A., 1897, s. 2 (1).
[60] *Ibid.*, s. 3 (1).
[61] *Wise* v. *Whitburn* [1924] 1 Ch. 460.
[62] L.T.A., 1897, s. 2 (2), as amended by C.A., 1911, s. 12. Before 1912 all persons named as executors had to concur: *Re Pawley and London & Provincial Bank's Contract* [1900] 1 Ch. 58. There was an exception where the deceased was a sole surviving mortgagee or trustee: C.A., 1881, s. 30, for the main provisions of which see *ante*, p. 458, and *post*, p. 953.

(including leaseholds) they had a joint and several power, so that one of several personal representatives could make a good title by himself.[63]

C. After 1925

1. Vesting of property. The Administration of Estates Act, 1925, substantially repeats the provisions of the Land Transfer Act, 1897. In the case of deaths after 1925, all land owned by the deceased, including leaseholds [64] and Crown land,[65] vests in the personal representatives [66] with the following exceptions:

(i) Entails, unless disposed of by the deceased's will.[67] Probably entails did not vest in the personal representatives before 1926, but the position was somewhat uncertain.[68]

(ii) Property to which the deceased was entitled as a joint tenant [69]; this was so before 1926.[70]

(iii) Property to which the deceased was entitled as a corporation sole.[71] This repeats the former rule.[72]

(iv) Interests which ceased on the death of the deceased, such as an interest for his life.[73] This was probably so before 1926 also.[74]

As before 1926, property subject to a general power of appointment exercised by the will of the deceased passes to his personal representatives.[75]

2. Assents

(a) *Writing required.* Before 1926 an assent was a mere recognition by the executor that the land was not needed for purposes of administration, and the devisee's title was founded on the will, not the assent.[76] After 1925 an assent operates as a conveyance whereby an

---

[63] *Anon.* (1536) 1 Dy. 23 (b); *Simpson* v. *Gutteridge* (1816) 1 Madd. 609; *Warner* v. *Sampson* [1958] 1 Q.B. 404, reversed on other grounds [1959] 1 Q.B. 297.
[64] A.E.A., 1925, s. 3 (1).
[65] *Ibid.,* s. 57; *e.g.,* land passing as *bona vacantia.* The L.T.A., 1897, did not bind the Crown, so that land escheating to the Crown did not vest in the personal representatives: *In b. Hartley* [1899] P. 40.
[66] A.E.A., 1925, s. 1 (1).
[67] *Ibid.,* s. 3 (3).
[68] See Williams R.P. 116, 239.
[69] A.E.A., 1925, s. 3 (4).
[70] L.T.A., 1897, s. 1 (1).
[71] A.E.A., 1925, s. 3 (5).
[72] Litt. 647; Challis 101; *ante,* p. 54. This was the exceptional case of an abeyance of seisin until a new holder of the office was appointed.
[73] A.E.A., 1925, s. 1 (1).
[74] See Williams R.P. 239, 240 on the " careless wording of the Land Transfer Act, 1897," as regards life interests and entails.
[75] A.E.A., 1925, s. 3 (2).
[76] See *Attenborough* v. *Solomon* [1913] A.C. 76 at 83; Williams, *Assents,* 22 *et seq.*

estate or interest vested in the deceased which has devolved [77] upon his personal representatives is vested in the person named.[78] No assent made after 1925 (even if the deceased died before 1926 [79]) will pass a legal estate in land [80] unless it is in writing and signed by the personal representative.[81] Thus the law now provides for a proper paper title to the legal estate. If A dies leaving land to B and B wishes to sell the land to C, B establishes his title by proving (i) the grant of representation to certain persons as A's personal representatives (ii) an assent or conveyance by those persons as personal representatives in favour of B. Before 1926 he also had to prove A's will, showing that he was beneficially entitled.[81a]

(b) *Documents of title.* The effect of the new machinery is that both the grant of probate [82] and the written assent [83] have a new character: they are essential documents of title, and if the land is subsequently sold the assent has the effect of overreaching the equitable interests declared by the will.[84] In other words, a bona fide purchaser for value [85] from a post-1925 devisee is not now concerned with the terms of the will: he is concerned only to see that the legal estate has devolved upon the personal representatives, and that they have in turn vested it by assent or conveyance in the vendor.[86] Unless the purchaser has evidence to the contrary,[87] he cannot require the will to be disclosed [88]; and even if the assent is in favour of the wrong person the purchaser is protected, for the assent passes the legal estate,[89] and the purchaser will have no notice of the bene-ficiary's claim.[90] Interests arising under wills are therefore now kept off the title to the legal estate, just as are beneficial interests arising under trusts for sale and settlements.

---

[77] If the property was conveyed to the personal representatives by a third party, it has not " devolved " within A.E.A., 1925, s. 36 (1), and cannot be transferred by assent: *Re Stirrup's Contract* [1961] 1 W.L.R. 449. Contrast (1961) 25 Conv. (N.S.) 490 (Sir L. Elphinstone).

[78] A.E.A., 1925, s. 36 (2), (4).

[79] *Ibid.*, s. 36 (12).

[80] Including leaseholds: A.E.A., 1925, s. 55 (1) (xix).

[81] *Ibid.*, s. 36 (4). [81a] See n. 76, *supra.*

[82] *Re Miller and Pickersgill's Contract* [1931] 1 Ch. 511 at 514. The same applies to letters of administration: *ibid.* Grants of representation, being orders of the court, cannot be invalidated against purchasers on account of lack of jurisdiction, or the absence of any consent, even though there was notice of the defect: L.P.A., 1925, s. 204 (replacing C.A., 1881, s. 70); *Hewson* v. *Shelley* [1914] 2 Ch. 13; *Re Bridgett and Hayes' Contract* [1928] Ch. 163.

[83] A.E.A., 1925, s. 36 (2), (4); Williams V. & P. 281, n. (g); Emmet 191.

[84] A.E.A., 1925, s. 39 (1) (ii), giving personal representatives the overreaching powers of trustees for sale (for which see *ante*, p. 377); but a sole personal representative can receive purchase-money: L.P.A., 1925, s. 27 (2), as amended by L.P.(Am.)A., 1926, Sched.

[85] A.E.A., 1925, s. 55 (1) (xviii).

[86] *Ibid.*, s. 36 (7).

[87] *Re Duce and Boots Cash Chemists (Southern) Ltd.'s Contract* [1937] Ch. 642.

[88] A.E.A., 1925, s. 36 (7).

[89] *Ibid.*, s. 36 (4). [90] See also *post*, p. 580.

(*c*) *Precautions.* Two supplemental provisions further illustrate the functions of the grant of representation and of the personal representatives in the new machinery of devolution. (i) The person in whose favour an assent or conveyance of a legal estate is made may require notice of it to be indorsed on the grant of probate or letters of administration [91]; thus the grant of representation may be made a kind of register of dispositions,[92] indicating that some specific assent or conveyance is the right one. (ii) A written statement by a personal representative that he has not disposed of a legal estate is sufficient evidence to a purchaser that no previous assent or conveyance has been made, unless notice is indorsed on the grant of representation as provided above [93]; thus a purchaser can obtain from the personal representative a document which acts as a curtain over all the personal representative's acts. Both these provisions are permissive, not mandatory; but it is always advisable to employ them.

(*d*) *Changes of capacity.* A personal representative is often given power to act in some other capacity, as where the will appoints X and Y both personal representatives and trustees for sale. In such a case the legal estate will not vest in them as trustees for sale unless as personal representatives they make a written assent in favour of themselves as trustees for sale.[94] An assent thus remains an essential link in the title to the legal estate, showing that the property is no longer subject to the personal representatives' powers of administration, even where it is to remain vested in the same persons.

3. Ownership of assets. Although the personal representatives are in a fiduciary position, it is not right to regard them as holding only the legal estate in the assets, with the equitable interests in the beneficiaries. Not until there has been an assent can it be said whether any particular asset will be needed for the payment of debts or discharge of other liabilities, and so no beneficiary can assert that he has any interest in it, legal or equitable. Apart from any property specifically devised or bequeathed,[94a] the personal representatives thus have the whole ownership of the assets vested in them, and the rights of the beneficiaries, whether under a will [95] or an intestacy,[96] are protected, not by vesting in them any equitable interest in any of the assets, but by the rule that the court will control the personal representatives and ensure that the assets are duly administered in the

---

[91] A.E.A., 1925, s. 36 (4).
[92] See n. 82, *supra.*
[93] A.E.A., 1925, s. 36 (5).
[94] *Re King's W. T.* [1964] Ch. 542, criticised in (1964) 80 L.Q.R. 328 (R. R. A. Walker) and (1964) 28 Conv.(N.S.) 298 (J. F. Garner); *cf. Re Yerburgh* [1928] W.N. 208.
[94a] *Kavanagh* v. *Best* [1971] N.I. 89.
[95] *Commissioner of Stamp Duties (Queensland)* v. *Livingston* [1965] A.C. 694.
[96] *Eastbourne Mutual Benefit B. S.* v. *Hastings Corporation* [1965] 1 W.L.R. 861.

interests of the beneficiaries and all other persons concerned.[97] A beneficiary prospectively entitled to any such asset can thus at most be said to have a species of " floating equity " in it, which may or may not crystallise. Accordingly, even a beneficiary who is solely entitled under an intestacy cannot, for the purposes of a statutory right to compensation, claim to be " entitled to an interest " in a house which forms part of an unadministered estate[98]; and a surviving spouse with the right to call for the matrimonial home to be appropriated to her[99] has no *locus standi* to defend an action for possession of it.[1]

4. Powers of personal representatives. Personal representatives no longer have a several power of disposition over leaseholds if the deceased died after 1925,[2] though an act of forfeiture of a lease by one will affect all.[3] They still have joint and several powers over pure personalty or, if the deceased died before 1926, over leaseholds; but over realty[4] and, if the deceased died after 1925, over leaseholds, they have only joint authority.[4a]

Personal representatives now have all the powers of trustees for sale,[5] and thus all the powers of a tenant for life and trustees under the Settled Land Act, 1925.[6] Although they should sell the property only if this is necessary for the purposes of administration, *e.g.*, to pay the deceased's debts, a conveyance to a purchaser for value in good faith is not invalidated merely because he knows that all the debts and other liabilities have been met.[7] Nor is a conveyance to a purchaser for value in good faith invalidated merely because the probate or letters of administration under which the personal representatives acted are subsequently revoked.[8]

---

[97] See *Commissioner of Stamp Duties (Queensland)* v. *Livingston, supra*, at pp. 712, 713, a passage of fundamental importance (not cited in *Williams* v. *Holland* [1965] 1 W.L.R. 739).

[98] *Eastbourne Mutual Benefit B. S.* v. *Hastings Corporation, supra*.

[99] See *ante*, p. 526.

[1] *Lall* v. *Lall* [1965] 1 W.L.R. 1249; and see Snell, *Equity*, 326, 327.

[2] A.E.A., 1925, s. 2 (2) (unless the conveyance is made under an order of the court: *ibid.*).

[3] *Warner* v. *Sampson* [1958] 1 Q.B. 404; reversed on other grounds [1959] 1 Q.B. 297.

[4] See, however, C.A., 1881, s. 30; L.P.A., 1925, 7th Sched. (deaths before 1926).

[4a] But see *Fountain Forestry Ltd.* v. *Edwards* [1975] Ch. 133 as to contracts.

[5] A.E.A., 1925, s. 39.

[6] L.P.A., 1925, s. 28 (1); *ante*, p. 365. Probably they have the " *ad hoc* " powers (*ante*, p. 379) as being " approved or appointed by the court."

[7] A.E.A., 1925, ss. 36 (8), 55 (1) (xviii). Before 1926 a purchaser would not be compelled to accept a title in such circumstances: *Re Verrall's Contract* [1903] 1 Ch. 65. *Quaere* what time had to elapse after the testator's death to raise a presumption that all debts had been paid: see *Re Venn & Furze's Contract* [1894] 2 Ch. 101; *Re Tanqueray-Willaume & Landau* (1882) 20 Ch.D. 465 (20 years sufficient).

[8] A.E.A., 1925, ss. 37, 55 (1) (xviii), retrospectively confirming *Hewson* v. *Shelley* [1914] 2 Ch. 13.

Sect. 3. Number of Personal Representatives

A. Maximum

No grant of probate or letters of administration can be made to more than four personal representatives in respect of the same property.[9] If more than four executors are appointed by a testator, they must decide among themselves who shall apply for probate.

B. Minimum

A sole personal representative, whether original or by survivorship, has full power to give valid receipts for capital money or any other payments.[10] Therefore personal representatives have the powers of trustees for sale[11] without their disability as to receiving capital money severally.[12] But if any person interested in the estate is an infant or has a life interest in it, a sole administrator (other than a trust corporation) must not be appointed by the court after 1925.[13] A sole executor can act under such circumstances, but the court has power to appoint additional personal representatives.[14]

---

[9] J.A., 1925, s. 160 (1). This is strictly construed: see *In b. Holland* (1936) 105 L.J.P. 113.
[10] L.P.A., 1925, s. 27 (2), as amended by L.P.(Am.)A., 1926, Sched.
[11] *Ante*, p. 365.
[12] *Ante*, p. 378.
[13] J.A., 1925, s. 160 (1).
[14] *Ibid*., s. 160 (2).

CHAPTER 10

CONTRACTS AND CONVEYANCING

Part 1

CONTRACTS

A CONTRACT to sell or make any other disposition of land is made in the same way as any other contract. As soon as there is an agreement for valuable consideration between the parties on definite terms, there is a contract; and this is so whether the agreement was made orally or in writing.

But although a valid contract relating to land may be made orally, it will be unenforceable by the most important method of enforcing contracts, namely, by action, unless either the statutory requirements as to written evidence of the contract, or the requirements of equity as to part performance, have been satisfied. These requirements put contracts for dispositions of land into a special category by themselves. Another distinguishing rule, peculiar to such contracts, is the rule that a purchaser, even before conveyance, acquires an immediate equitable interest in the property.[1]

Moreover, contracts for the sale of land are so much part and parcel of the whole system of conveyancing that they have many peculiarities drawn from the land law. In default of any express terms there will be many implied terms as to proof of title and other matters. Between the contract and the conveyance, which are respectively the first and last formal steps in a sale of land, many questions arise which have to be decided according to the settled practice of conveyancers. The performance of the contract is thus affected in numerous ways, and there is a body of rights and duties which are special to such contracts.

The questions which must first be considered are:

(1) whether there is a contract at all;

(2) if so, whether that contract is enforceable by action.

A short account will also be given of—

(3) the rights and duties created by contracts relating to land.
This last topic will serve as an introduction to some of the general principles of conveyancing.

[1] *Ante,* p. 132.

Sect. 1. The Existence of a Contract

1. Terms. There must be a final and complete agreement between the parties on the terms,[2] which must include—

(i) the parties;

(ii) the property;

(iii) the consideration; and

(iv) the interest to be granted.

There is no necessity for a contract to be made by any formal document or phrases. Provided the parties intend to enter into a legally enforceable contract,[3] and there is an agreement upon the essential terms made for valuable consideration, a contract is made. The agreement may be reached by an offer by one party followed by an unqualified acceptance by the other, or an offer may be met by a counter-offer (or by a qualified acceptance, which operates as a rejection of the offer and a counter-offer[4]) followed by another counter-offer and so on, until at last a counter-offer is accepted without qualification.[4]

2. " Subject to contract." If an offer is accepted not finally but conditionally, for example with the common formula " subject to contract "[5] or " subject to the preparation and approval of formal contract "[6] or " subject to suitable arrangements being arranged between your solicitors and mine,"[7] the effect is that until the necessary contract or arrangements have been made, there is no contract and either party can withdraw.[8] This follows the ordinary rule that a contract to make a further contract (on terms unspecified) is no binding contract at all.[9] If such a reservation is made, therefore, both parties have complete freedom of action; and if one of

---

[2] See *Harvey* v. *Pratt* [1965] 1 W.L.R. 1025 at 1027.
[3] *Rose & Frank Co.* v. *Crompton & Brothers Ltd.* [1925] A.C. 445; *Appleson* v. *H. Littlewood Ltd.* [1939] 1 All E.R. 464.
[4] *Hyde* v. *Wrench* (1840) 3 Beav. 334.
[5] *Tiverton Estates Ltd.* v. *Wearwell Ltd.* [1974] 2 W.L.R. 176; *post*, p. 551.
[6] *Winn* v. *Bull* (1877) 7 Ch.D. 29.
[7] *Lockett* v. *Norman-Wright* [1925] Ch. 56.
[8] Under the usual kind of agency contract an estate agent's commission is commonly payable as soon as an unqualified offer to purchase at the agreed price is made by a person introduced by the agent, even if no actual contract ensues: see *Fowler* v. *Bratt* [1950] 2 K.B. 96; *Graham and Scott (Southgate) Ltd.* v. *Oxlade* [1950] 2 K.B. 257; *Dennis Reed Ltd.* v. *Goody* [1950] 2 K.B. 277; *Christie, Owen & Davies Ltd.* v. *Stockton* [1953] 1 W.L.R. 1353; *Dellafiora* v. *Lester* [1962] 1 W.L.R. 1208; contrast *E. P. Nelson & Co.* v. *Rolfe* [1950] 1 K.B. 139; *Boots* v. *E. Christopher & Co.* [1952] 1 K.B. 89; *Scheggia* v. *Gradwell* [1963] 1 W.L.R. 1049; but see *Wilkinson Ltd.* v. *Brown* [1966] 1 W.L.R. 194. See the analysis at (1963) 79 L.Q.R. 497 (P.V.B.).
[9] *Cf. King's Motors Ltd.* v. *Lax* [1970] 1 W.L.R. 426 (contract to let at rent to be agreed: void).

them has paid a deposit, he can demand its return at any time.[10]
" Subject to contract " is therefore commonly inserted in letters from
solicitors and agents conducting negotiations for purchasers as a protection against legal liability in the preliminary stages. Meanwhile
the vendor remains at liberty to withdraw or to raise the price (the
abuse known as gazumping), but this is the inevitable counterpart
of the protection which the purchaser needs.[11] There can
be an unconditional acceptance (so that the parties are bound at
once) even though they intend to make a more formal contract later,[12]
as for example where they say " this is a provisional agreement until
a fully legalised agreement, drawn up by a solicitor and embodying
all the conditions herewith stated, is signed." [13] The difference lies
between (a) mere negotiation preliminary to, or subject to, a contract which has not yet been made, and (b) an immediate binding
contract, which can nevertheless be superseded by some later contract if the parties so wish. It is also possible for an agreement
" subject to contract " to become legally binding if the parties later
agree to waive that condition; for then, in effect, they are making a
firm contract by reference to the terms of the earlier agreement.[14]

3. Conditional contract. There may, of course, be a binding
contract in conditional terms. If a contract which is otherwise final
contains such a term as " subject to the right of either party to withdraw on payment of £100," or " subject to the purchaser's solicitor
approving the title," [15] the parties are bound at once but the obligation may never be enforceable since the condition may defeat it.
This kind of conditional term is quite different from a reservation
like " subject to contract " which prevents the formation of a contract
at all.

---

[10] If the deposit is paid to the vendor's agent as such and the agent goes bankrupt,
the vendor is liable to return it: *Goding* v. *Frazer* [1967] 1 W.L.R. 286; *Burt* v.
Claude Cousins & Co. Ltd. [1971] 2 Q.B. 426. This is so even where the agent
is stakeholder for both parties, unless judgment has already been recovered
against him: *Barrington* v. *Lee* [1972] 1 Q.B. 326. But see the strong dissents
by Lord Denning M.R. in the last two cases, and the opinion of Russell L.J.
in *Maloney* v. *Hardy* [1971] 2 Q.B. at 442 (note); also (1972) 88 L.Q.R. 184
(F. M. B. Reynolds). For stakeholders see *post,* p. 590.
[11] See Law Commission Working Paper No. 51, para. 80.
[12] Even though no formal contract is ever prepared: *Chinnock* v. *The Marchioness
of Ely* (1865) 4 De G.J. & S. 638 at 645; *Rossiter* v. *Miller* (1878) 3 App.Cas.
1124 at 1139, 1151; *Bonnewell* v. *Jenkins* (1876) 8 Ch.D. 70 (agent's letter:—
" We are instructed to accept your offer of £800 for these premises and have
asked [our principal's] solicitor to prepare a contract." *Held,* this completed
the contract).
[13] *Branca* v. *Cobarro* [1947] K.B. 854.
[14] *Griffiths* v. *Young* [1970] Ch. 675; *post,* p. 552.
[15] Conditions of this kind are common, but the courts tend to interpret them as
permitting objection on fair grounds only and not as conferring an arbitrary
right of withdrawal: see *Curtis-Moffat Ltd.* v. *Wheeler* [1929] 2 Ch. 224;
Caney v. *Leith* [1937] 2 All E.R. 532; *cf. Chipperfield* v. *Carter* (1895) 72 L.T.
487; *Hussey* v. *Horne-Payne* (1879) 4 App.Cas. 311.

Where a formal agreement is drawn up, usually each party signs one copy, and there is no binding contract until these copies have been exchanged in accordance with ordinary conveyancing practice.[16] But the circumstances may preclude any idea of a formal exchange of contracts, as where a solicitor acts for both parties.[17]

Sect. 2. The Enforceability of the Contract

The contract will be unenforceable by action unless there is either a sufficient memorandum in writing or a sufficient act of part performance. This branch of the law dates from the Statute of Frauds, 1677, the object of which was to prevent fraud and perjury by false allegations of contracts. The statute required contracts of certain kinds to be evidenced in writing signed by or on behalf of the party sued.

Much law has accumulated around the statute because of the reluctance of judges to allow unmeritorious parties to take advantage of it and escape from their bargains. Times have changed since the era when Titus Oates and his contemporaries made a lucrative profession of perjury. Equity also checked abuse of the statute by inventing the doctrine of part performance, which in effect created an important exception, recently widely extended.

A. *Memorandum in Writing*

By the Law of Property Act, 1925, s. 40 (1), replacing part of section 4 of the Statute of Frauds, 1677, it is provided that " no action may be brought upon any contract for the sale or other disposition of land or any interest in land, unless the agreement upon which such action is brought, or some memorandum or note thereof, is in writing, and signed by the party to be charged or by some other person thereunto by him lawfully authorised." [18]

---

[16] *Eccles* v. *Bryant & Pollock* [1948] Ch. 93. Where the exchange is intended to be carried out through the post, the moment of completion is at any rate not earlier than the putting of the later copy in the post; but *quaere* whether the effective time is that of posting or of receipt by the other party (*ibid*).

[17] *Smith* v. *Mansi* [1963] 1 W.L.R. 26; and see *Storer* v. *Manchester City Council* [1974] 1 W.L.R. 1043.

[18] Lord Nottingham, prime author of the Statute of Frauds, declared that " every line was worth a subsidy." After a century and a half of litigation upon it Lord St. Leonards retorted that every line had cost one. Litigation about the necessary formalities for contracts for the disposition of land shows no sign of abating. It has been said that " little is left of the statute. The courts are bound by decisions which they may well think to be out of harmony both with the spirit and the letter of the enactment ": *Hanau* v. *Ehrlich* [1911] 2 K.B. 1056 at 1066, *per* Fletcher Moulton L.J. See (1967) 31 Conv.(N.S.) 182, 254 (H. W. Wilkinson), advocating repeal. The statute was repealed as regards sale of goods and certain other contracts by Law Reform (Enforcement of Contracts) Act, 1954.

1. "No action may be brought." It is settled that the effect of non-compliance with the statute is not to make the contract void [19] but merely to make it unenforceable by action.[20] "The Statute of Frauds does not avoid parol contracts, but only bars the legal remedies by which they might otherwise have been enforced." [21] It is the entire contract that is unenforceable, including those parts of it which do not relate to land but, *e.g.*, to the goodwill and stock-in-trade of a business sold with the land.[22]

It is true that to deprive a party to a contract of his right to bring an action upon it is to deprive him of what is usually his most important right; but it does not always render that contract useless, for the Act is no bar to the contract being enforced in any way except by action. Thus if a purchaser pays a cash deposit to the vendor under an oral contract, the vendor may keep that deposit if the purchaser defaults.[23] This fulfils an implied term in the contract, for a deposit is ordinarily paid as a guarantee against breach of contract by the purchaser and it is forfeited to the vendor in that event.[24] If there were no contract at all, the deposit would have to be returned [25]: for then it is "impossible to say that the purchasers pay the deposit as a guarantee to carry out the bargain, when . . . they have not bound themselves to carry out any bargain." [26] If there is no contract, the deposit is recoverable as money paid for a consideration which wholly fails [27]; if there is a contract, even though it is unenforceable by action, the money is properly paid under it and the vendor is entitled to retain it if the purchaser repudiates.[28] But if it is the vendor who repudiates, the purchaser

---

[19] As has been held in cases such as *Carrington* v. *Roots* (1837) 2 M. & W. 248 at 255, *per* Lord Abinger C.B.: "It means that the contract shall be altogether void." Contrast *Crosby* v. *Wadsworth* (1805) 6 East 602 at 611, *per* Lord Ellenborough C.J.: "It only precludes the bringing of actions to enforce [contracts]."

[20] *Leroux* v. *Brown* (1852) 12 C.B. 801; *Britain* v. *Rossiter* (1879) 11 Q.B.D. 123. "Action" includes "prosecution": *Banks* v. *Crossland* (1874) L.R. 10 Q.B. 97.

[21] *Madison* v. *Alderson* (1883) 8 App.Cas. 467 at 474, *per* Lord Selborne L.C. (and see at p. 488); *Bristol, Cardiff & Swansea Aërated Bread Co.* v. *Maggs* (1890) 44 Ch.D. 616 at 622.

[22] *Hawksworth* v. *Turner* (1930) 46 T.L.R. 389.

[23] *Thomas* v. *Brown* (1876) 1 Q.B.D. 714; *Monnickendam* v. *Leanse* (1923) 39 T.L.R. 445.

[24] *Howe* v. *Smith* (1884) 27 Ch.D. 89; *cf. Soper* v. *Arnold* (1889) 14 App.Cas. 429 at 435; *Smith* v. *Butler* [1900] 1 Q.B. 694. As to "deposit and part payment" see *post*, p. 589.

[25] As to the court's power to order the return of a deposit under L.P.A., 1925, s. 49 (2), see *post*, p. 590.

[26] *Chillingworth* v. *Esche* [1924] 1 Ch. 97 at 112, *per* Warrington J.; and see *post*, p. 589.

[27] The basis of this claim is quasi-contract: Leake, *Contracts*, 8th ed., 72–74; Goff & Jones, *The Law of Restitution*, 357.

[28] See above. Similarly if the deposit is paid by cheque he may sue on the cheque, for a cheque given for value may be sued upon under the Bills of Exchange Act, 1882, quite apart from contract: *Low* v. *Fry* (1935) 152 L.T. 585. For an action on a promissory note, see *Jones* v. *Jones* (1840) 6 M. & W. 84.

can recover his money, for he can bring his action not upon the contract but upon the ground of failure of consideration.[29]

Although an oral contract is merely made unenforceable by action, it does not follow that it is enforceable by self-help. In one case [30] the vendor repudiated an oral agreement but the purchaser, nothing daunted, made a clandestine entry into the property; then, on being forcibly ejected by the vendor, the purchaser claimed that he had been lawfully in possession under the contract and so could not be disturbed. But this argument failed; for the vendor was still the legal owner of the property and the purchaser's title could be proved against him only if the action was founded on the contract, which was precisely what the statute forbade.[31] It is only where the property has been effectively transferred (as in a payment of money) that the contract will be of any avail. It may, in short, be a shield,[32] but it cannot be a sword.

2. " The sale or other disposition of land or any interest in land "

(a) " *Any interest*." The section applies to a contract for any disposition of any interest in land, whether by sale, mortgage, lease or otherwise. Thus it will apply to the letting of a part of a house furnished,[33] though not to a mere contract of lodging which creates no interest in land.[34] The section applies as much to a contract for the creation of a new interest in land as to a contract for the disposition of an existing interest. Nor does it apply any the less because the contract is part of a wider transaction concerning other things.[35]

(b) *Crops as " land."* " Land " is very widely defined,[36] but it never includes annual crops such as wheat,[37] corn [38] or potatoes,[39] which require the periodical application of labour for their produc-

---

[29] *Pulbrook* v. *Lawes* (1876) 1 Q.B.D. 284.
[30] *Delaney* v. *T. P. Smith Ltd.* [1946] K.B. 393 (agreement for a lease).
[31] But if the purchaser had entered with the vendor's agreement, and then the vendor had repudiated, the purchaser might have succeeded on the ground of part performance: *post*, p. 568.
[32] See, *e.g.*, *Dawson* v. *Ellis* (1820) 1 Jac. & W. 524.
[33] *Inman* v. *Stamp* (1815) 1 Stark. 12 ; *Edge* v. *Strafford* (1831) 1 Cr. & J. 391.
[34] *Wright* v. *Stavert* (1860) 2 E. & E. 721; for this distinction, see *post*, p. 618.
[35] See *Steadman* v. *Steadman* [1974] Q.B. 161 (affirmed [1974] 3 W.L.R. 56; *post*, p. 566), discussing possible exceptions in cases of partnerships involving land.
[36] L.P.A., 1925, s. 205 (1) (ix).
[37] See *Mayfield* v. *Wadsley* (1824) 3 B. & C. 357.
[38] *Jones* v. *Flint* (1839) 10 A. & E. 753.
[39] Whether mature (*Parker* v. *Staniland* (1809) 11 East 362 ; *Warwick* v. *Bruce* (1813) 2 M. & S. 205) or still growing (*Evans* v. *Roberts* (1826) 5 B. & C. 829 ; *Sainsbury* v. *Matthews* (1838) 4 M. & W. 343). For the anomalous character of growing crops, see *Brantom* v. *Griffits* (1876) 1 C.P.D. 349 at 353, 354 (affirmed 2 C.P.D. 212).

tion [40]; these are known as *fructus industriales*.[41] *Fructus naturales*, on the other hand, are sometimes included. This term applies to the natural products of the soil, such as grass and timber, and also the products of those plants and trees which, although needing attention when first planted, do not require it each year to produce a crop,[42] such as fruit from fruit trees.[43] *Fructus naturales* are treated as land within the statute [44] unless either they are to be severed by the vendor and not by the purchaser [45] or else the contract binds the purchaser to sever them at once, so that they will not remain part of the land for any long time after purchase.[46]

The principle behind these rules is not easy to discern; the statute was perhaps never intended to apply even to *fructus naturales*, though it is now too late to establish the law in this sense.[47] One possible test is whether the produce will derive benefit from the land between sale and severance [48]; yet the effect of such a rule, strictly applied, would vary with the season of the year.[49] Another possible test is whether any property in the products passes to the purchaser while they are still in the soil.[50] In truth, however, " taking the cases altogether, . . . no general rule is laid down in any one of them that is not contradicted by some other." [51]

(c) *Other property as " land."* In addition to the rules governing crops, the cases have established that the following are " interests in land," namely—

[40] *Duppa* v. *Mayo* (1669) 1 Wms.Saund. 275 at 276, n. (*f*); and see Dart, *Vendor and Purchaser*, 8th ed., I, 207 and cases cited *supra* in nn. 37–39; see also *Poulter* v. *Killingbeck* (1789) 1 B. & P. 397. *Waddington* v. *Bristow* (1801) 2 B. & P. 452 (hops) and *Emmerson* v. *Heelis* (1809) 2 Taunt. 38 (turnips) are authorities to the contrary, but the former was questioned in *Rodwell* v. *Phillips* (1842) 9 M. & W. 501 at 503, *per* Parke B. (" That case would now probably be decided differently "), and the latter in *Evans* v. *Roberts* (1826) 5 B. & C. 829 and *Jones* v. *Flint* (1839) 10 A. & E. 753; and in *Marshall* v. *Green* (1875) 1 C.P.D. 35, it was accepted that *fructus industriales* had become an established exception from the statute.

[41] See *Duppa* v. *Mayo* (1669) 1 Wms.Saund. 275 at 276, n. (*f*); *Dunne* v. *Ferguson* (1832) Hayes 540.

[42] *Rodwell* v. *Phillips* (1842) 9 M. & W. 501 at 503; *Marshall* v. *Green* (1875) 1 C.P.D. 35 at 40; see generally *Benjamin's Sale of Goods* (1st ed. 1974), pp. 55–64.   [43] *Rodwell* v. *Phillips* (1842) 9 M. & W. 501.

[44] *Crosby* v. *Wadsworth* (1805) 6 East 602 (grass); *Scorell* v. *Boxall* (1827) 1 Y. & J. 396 (underwood); *Carrington* v. *Roots* (1837) 2 M. & W. 248 (grass); and see *Teal* v. *Auty* (1820) 2 Brod. & B. 99 (trees).

[45] *Smith* v. *Surman* (1829) 9 B. & C. 561; *Washbourn* v. *Burrows* (1847) 1 Exch. 107 at 115.

[46] *Marshall* v. *Green* (1875) 1 C.P.D. 35, reviewing the decisions; and see Blackburn, *Contract of Sale*, 3rd ed., 7–16.

[47] *Marshall* v. *Green* (1875) 1 C.P.D. 35 at 38.

[48] See *Parker* v. *Staniland* (1809) 11 East 362; *Evans* v. *Roberts* (1826) 5 B. & C. 829 (both cases on *fructus industriales*).

[49] *Marshall* v. *Green*, *supra*, at p. 39.

[50] See *Smith* v. *Surman* (1829) 9 B. & C. 561 at 573, 576; Blackburn, *Contract of Sale* (3rd ed.), 5 *et seq.*; Amos & Ferard, *Fixtures* (3rd ed.), 330; Adkin & Bowen, *Fixtures* (3rd ed.), 149.

[51] *Rodwell* v. *Phillips* (1842) 9 M. & W. 501 at 505, *per* Lord Abinger C.B.

the building materials contained in a house, where the buyer was to demolish the house and remove the materials within a fixed time [52];

slag and cinders which had become part of the land [53];

an interest under a trust for sale of land [54];

an easement or profit [55];

fixtures (*i.e.*, objects attached to land [56]), even when sold separately from the land.[57] But a tenant who has the right to sever and remove his fixtures [58] can sell them without formality: although the fixtures, while attached, are still land,[59] he is not selling either land or goods, but merely assigning his right to sever and remove what is legally part of his landlord's premises.[60] The same applies to an agreement by the landlord to extend the tenant's time for removing the fixtures.[61]

(*d*) *Sale of Goods Act,* 1893. A further complication is that the Sale of Goods Act, 1893,[62] defines " goods " as including not only " industrial growing crops " but also " things attached to or forming part of the land which are agreed to be severed before sale or under the contract of sale." This last phrase would cover " *fructus naturales* " and such things as building materials or fixtures if sold separately, for then there must be a severance under the contract. Can the same thing be land for the purpose of one statute and goods for the purpose of another? Inconvenient as this result may be, there is no necessary impossibility about it.[63]

3. " Some memorandum or note thereof, is in writing "

(*a*) *Subsequent memorandum.* The contract itself may be made orally; all that is required is that a written memorandum of the contract should have come into existence.[64] This must have occurred

---

52 *Lavery* v. *Pursell* (1888) 39 Ch.D. 508.
53 *Morgan* v. *Russell and Sons* [1909] 1 K.B. 357.
54 *Cooper* v. *Critchley* [1955] Ch. 431; and see (1955) 71 L.Q.R. 177; [1955] C.L.J. 155.
55 *Webber* v. *Lee* (1882) 9 Q.B.D. 315 (a case on a profit in gross). For these rights, see *post*, pp. 805 *et seq*. The definition of " land " in L.P.A., 1925, s. 205 (1) (ix), expressly includes " an easement, right, privilege, or benefit in, over, or derived from land." 56 See *post*, p. 711.
57 *Jarvis* v. *Jarvis* (1893) 63 L.J.Ch. 10 at 13.
58 See *post*, p. 715.
59 See *Lee* v. *Risdon* (1816) 7 Taunt. 188 at 191.
60 *Hallen* v. *Runder* (1834) 1 Cr.M. & R. 266; *Lee* v. *Gaskell* (1876) 1 Q.B.D. 700.
61 *Thomas* v. *Jennings* (1896) 66 L.J.Q.B. 5 at 8.
62 s. 62 (1).
63 Compare *Sims* v. *Thomas* (1840) 12 A. & E. 536 with *Ex p. Foss* (1858) 2 De G. & J. 230; for a discussion, see Blackburn, cited above, n. 46.
64 *Shippey* v. *Derrison* (1805) 5 Esp. 190 at 193; *Re Holland* [1902] 2 Ch. 360.

before the action is commenced,[65] so that an affidavit sworn in that action, which did not exist when the writ was issued, will not suffice.[66] But such a memorandum may be relied upon by a person who later becomes a party to the action,[67] or by a party to a subsequent action,[68] even if he was a party to the original action, as where the original action is discontinued and a new action is started.[69] A memorandum made over 14 years after the contract may suffice[70]; and if the memorandum has been lost or destroyed, it may, like any other missing document, be proved by oral or other secondary evidence.[71]

(b) *Prior memorandum.* Normally the contract will have been made before or at the same time as the memorandum. But there is one exceptional case in which it is possible for the memorandum to precede the contract: this is where a written offer is made by the party to be charged and the other party unconditionally accepts it, whether orally[72] or in writing[73]; and similarly if one of two alternatives in a written offer is accepted.[74] The acceptance of a mere offer as a memorandum has been said to have " pushed the literal construction of the Statute of Frauds to a limit beyond which it would perhaps be not easy to go," [75] and " the onus of proving an unconditional verbal acceptance of an offer in writing to sell real estate ought to be regarded as a heavy one." [76] But the doctrine is well established[77]; and it is within the policy of the Statute, for there is no danger of the vendor being held by perjured evidence to an offer which he never made.

(c) *Memorandum " thereof."* Apart from the exceptional case last mentioned, there must always be a written record of a concluded contract, *i.e.* of a binding legal commitment by the defendant.[78] The

---

[65] *Jackson* v. *Oglander* (1865) 2 H. & M. 465.
[66] *Lucas* v. *Dixon* (1889) 22 Q.B.D. 357.
[67] *Farr, Smith & Co. Ltd.* v. *Messers Ltd.* [1928] 1 K.B. 397 (a pleading).
[68] *Barkworth* v. *Young* (1856) 4 Drew. 1.
[69] *Lucas* v. *Dixon, supra,* at p. 368; and see the discussion in *Hardy* v. *Elphick* [1974] Ch. 65. See also R.S.C., Ord. 21.
[70] *Barkworth* v. *Young, supra.*
[71] *Barber* v. *Rowe* [1948] 2 All E.R. 1050. But the court will proceed with care, recognising the danger of this course. *Cf. post,* p. 553, n. 16.
[72] *Powers* v. *Fowler* (1855) 4 E. & B. 511; *Benecke* v. *Chadwicke* (1856) 4 W.R. 687; *Warner* v. *Willington* (1856) 3 Drew. 523 at 532; *Smith* v. *Neale* (1857) 2 C.B.(N.S.) 67; *The Liverpool Borough Bank* v. *Eccles* (1859) 4 H. & N. 139; *Reuss* v. *Picksley* (1866) L.R. 1 Ex. 342.
[73] *Parker* v. *Clark* [1960] 1 W.L.R. 286.
[74] See *Lever* v. *Koffler* [1901] 1 Ch. 543.
[75] *Re New Eberhardt Co.* (1889) 43 Ch.D. 118 at 129, *per* Bowen L.J.
[76] *Watson* v. *Davies* [1931] 1 Ch. 455 at 468, *per* Maugham J.
[77] See cases in n. 72, *supra.*
[78] *Munday* v. *Asprey* (1880) 13 Ch.D. 855 (letter referring to draft conveyance reciting agreement insufficient).

law requires " a signed admission that there was a contract and a signed admission of what that contract was." [79] If the written record is " subject to contract " it is therefore of no avail.[1] In its anxiety to prevent parties escaping from their bargains the Court of Appeal recently twice held the contrary, saying that " subject to contract " was a suspensive condition which could be waived orally in a later conversation.[2] These decisions embodied the fallacy that a transaction subject to contract is a potential contract, whereas in reality it is not a contract at all. They also gravely weakened the protection which " subject to contract " is designed to give. But the Court of Appeal has now reversed itself and has restored the rule that the written record must indicate a firm contract.[3]

(*d*) *Form.* The memorandum need be in no special form.[4] It need not even have been intended to act as a memorandum [5] : " the question is not one of intention of the party who signs the document, but simply one of evidence against him." [6] Examples [7] of documents which have served as effective memoranda are a letter, even if written to the writer's own solicitor or agent,[8] or to a third party,[9] an entry in a diary,[10] company's minute book,[11] auctioneer's book,[12] or order book,[13] a note in a rent book,[14] a receipt,[15] a telegram [16] (or the written instructions therefor [17]), a recital in a

79 *Thirkell* v. *Cambi* [1919] 2 K.B. 590 at 597, *per* Scrutton L.J.

1 See *ante*, p. 543.

2 *Griffiths* v. *Young* [1970] Ch. 675; *Law* v. *Jones* [1974] Ch. 112. Both decisions could have rested on orthodox grounds since the oral agreements were adequately confirmed by later letters.

3 *Tiverton Estates Ltd.* v. *Wearwell Ltd.* [1974] 2 W.L.R. 176.

4 *Barkworth* v. *Young* (1856) 4 Drew. 1 at 13. As early as 1682 a mere letter sufficed: *Moore* v. *Hart* (1682) 1 Vern. 110, 201.

5 *Welford* v. *Beezely* (1747) 1 Ves.Sen. 6; *Daniels* v. *Trefusis* [1914] 1 Ch. 788 at 799 (" nothing could have been further from his thoughts ": *per* Sargant J.).

6 *Re Hoyle* [1893] 1 Ch. 84 at 99, *per* Bowen L.J.

7 Some of the decisions are on s. 17 of the statute, replaced by Sale of Goods Act, 1893, s. 4, now repealed by Law Reform (Enforcement of Contracts) Act, 1954; but the same principles applied: Williams, *Statute of Frauds, Section IV*, 75.

8 *Gibson* v. *Holland* (1865) L.R. 1 C.P. 1; *Smith-Bird* v. *Blower* [1939] 2 All E.R. 406 (disapproved on another point in *Davies* v. *Sweet* [1962] 2 Q.B. 300).

9 *Moore* v. *Hart*, *supra*; *Longfellow* v. *Williams* (1804) Peake Add.Cas. 225.

10 *Re Hoyle*, *supra*, at p. 100.

11 *Jones* v. *Victoria Graving Dock Co.* (1877) 2 Q.B.D. 314. This point was not considered in *Eley* v. *Positive Government Security Life Assurance Co. Ltd.* (1875) 1 Ex.D. 20 (on appeal, *ibid.*, 88).

12 *Cohen* v. *Roche* [1927] 1 K.B. 169.

13 *Sarl* v. *Bourdillon* (1856) 1 C.B.(N.S.) 188.

14 *Hill* v. *Hill* [1947] Ch. 231.

15 *Evans* v. *Prothero* (1852) 1 De G.M. & G. 572; *Boun* v. *Stroud* (1870) 21 L.T. 695; *Auerbach* v. *Nelson* [1919] 2 Ch. 383.

16 *McBlain* v. *Cross* (1871) 25 L.T. 804.

17 *Godwin* v. *Francis* (1870) L.R. 5 C.P. 295.

will [18] or settlement,[18a] a pleading in an action,[19] a rough draft of an agreement,[20] a statement of evidence,[21] an escrow.[22]

A party who writes a letter solely for the purpose of repudiating the contract may provide the evidence needed for an action against him. This happened where a purchaser wrote a letter beginning " I beg to repeat that I have made no purchase or contract whatever " but admitting that he had made a bid at the auction and referring to the particulars of sale in which all the terms were specified.[23] Repudiation of an admitted contract must, however, be distinguished from denial of a contract. A letter disputing the terms of a contract, or denying (without further admissions) that any contract was ever made, cannot be evidence of any contract at all.[24]

(e) *Two or more documents*

(1) CONNECTION. A memorandum may be made up of more than one document. Two physically separable documents may be regarded as one if they are treated as such, *e.g.*, a paper book slipped into a leather cover.[25] But often the record of the transaction will be contained in separate papers, as for example in correspondence, so that the memorandum must be pieced together.[26] In that case it is normally necessary that the paper bearing the defendant's signature should refer to the others [1]; in building up a memorandum out of several documents the starting point must always be the document signed by the party to be charged.[2] The principle is that the defendant must be protected against fraud, and that his signed paper must itself indicate the other document or documents.[3]

---

[18] *Re Hoyle* [1893] 1 Ch. 84.   [18a] *Re Holland* [1902] 2 Ch. 360.

[19] *Grindell* v. *Bass* [1920] 2 Ch. 487; *Farr, Smith & Co. Ltd.* v. *Messers Ltd.* [1928] 1 K.B. 397; see *ante*, p. 549.

[20] *Wanchford* v. *Fotherley* (1694) 2 Free.Ch. 201 at 202; *Gray* v. *Smith* (1889) 43 Ch.D. 208.

[21] *Daniels* v. *Trefusis* [1914] 1 Ch. 788.

[22] *Moritze* v. *Knowles* [1899] W.N. 40 (reversed on other grounds, *ibid.*, 83). For escrows, see *post*, p. 601.

[23] *Dewar* v. *Mintoft* [1912] 2 K.B. 373; and see *Bailey* v. *Sweeting* (1861) 9 C.B. (N.S.) 843; *Wilkinson* v. *Evans* (1866) L.R. 1 C.P. 407; *cf. Thirkell* v. *Cambi* [1919] 2 K.B. 590.

[24] *Smith* v. *Surman* (1829) 9 B. & C. 561; *Archer* v. *Baines* (1850) 5 Exch. 625; *Goodman* v. *Griffiths* (1857) 1 H. & N. 574; *Thirkell* v. *Cambi, supra.*

[25] See *Jones Brothers* v. *Joyner* (1900) 82 L.T. 768, where the cover supplied the plaintiff's name; compare *Kenworthy* v. *Schofield* (1824) 2 B. & C. 945 at 948.

[26] The doctrine, which first appeared in *Tawney* v. *Crowther* (1791) 3 Bro.C.C. 318, was developed cautiously at first: see cases in n. 4, *infra*.

[1] *Long* v. *Millar* (1879) 4 C.P.D. 450.

[2] See *Timmins* v. *Moreland Street Property Co. Ltd.* [1958] Ch. 110 at 130.

[3] See, *e.g., Jackson* v. *Lowe* (1822) 1 Bing. 9; *Hodges* v. *Horsfall* (1829) 1 Russ. & M. 116 (plan); *Morris* v. *Wilson* (1859) 5 Jur.(N.S.) 168 (letter); *Pickles* v. *Sutcliffe* [1902] W.N. 200 (conditions of sale).

(2) ORAL EVIDENCE. At first it was required that the signed document should refer to some other document as such; a reference to a transaction which might be oral or written was not enough, even if in fact it was written.[4] But in 1857 evidence was admitted to show that the "instructions" referred to were in fact written,[5] and since 1879 it has been accepted that even an implied reference suffices.[6] Thus today oral evidence may be given to identify a reference in a signed document even if it merely refers to "instructions," without indicating whether they were given on paper or not.[7] Similarly a telegram accepting "your offer" may be proved by oral evidence to refer to a written offer received by the sender[8]; and the words "as agreed on,"[9] "the purchase,"[10] the "terms agreed on,"[11] or "our arrangement"[12] may refer to documents containing the agreed terms.[13]

(3) IMPLIED REFERENCE. An implied reference may be as effective as an express one,[14] so that a signed receipt for £50 may refer to a cheque for £62 which included the £50[15]; and the reference may rest on nothing more than the nature of the document. A letter, for example, has been held to refer to the envelope in which it arrived, thereby connecting "Dear Sir" with the name of the addressee[16]; and a carbon copy of a memorandum signed by the defendant has been held to refer to the original signed by the plaintiff, thereby providing evidence of the plaintiff's name.[17] But a signed document cannot be taken to refer to a paper of which the writer did not know,[18] or to a paper which was not in existence at the time of the signature,[19] unless they were virtually contemporaneous[20]; thus where

[4] See *Boydell* v. *Drummond* (1809) 11 East 142; *Dobell* v. *Hutchinson* (1835) 3 A. & E. 355; *Smith* v. *Dixon* (1839) 3 Jur. 770.
[5] *Ridgway* v. *Wharton* (1857) 6 H.L.C. 238.
[6] *Long* v. *Millar* (1879) 4 C.P.D. 450.
[7] *Ridgway* v. *Wharton* (1857) 6 H.L.C. 238; *Oliver* v. *Hunting* (1890) 44 Ch.D. 205 at 208, 209; see, *e.g.*, *Franco-British Ship Store Co. Ltd.* v. *Compagnie des Chargeurs Française* (1926) 42 T.L.R. 735 (reference to "the agreement").
[8] *Godwin* v. *Francis* (1870) L.R. 5 C.P. 295.
[9] *Wylson* v. *Dunn* (1887) 34 Ch.D. 569.
[10] *Long* v. *Millar, supra*; *cf. Nene Valley Drainage Commissioners* v. *Dunkley* (1876) 4 Ch.D. 1.
[11] *Baumann* v. *James* (1868) 3 Ch.App. 508.
[12] *Cave* v. *Hastings* (1881) 7 Q.B.D. 125.
[13] See also *Fowler* v. *Bratt* [1950] 2 K.B. 96 at 101, 102.
[14] *Long* v. *Millar, supra*; and see *Fitzmaurice* v. *Bayley* (1860) 9 H.L.C. 78 at 99; *Caton* v. *Caton* (1867) L.R. 2 H.L. 127 at 139.
[15] *Stokes* v. *Whicher* [1920] 1 Ch. 411; contrast *Chaproniere* v. *Lambert* (1917) 86 L.J.Ch. 726, and see *Coombs* v. *Quiney* (1917) 142 L.T.News. 258 (letter and counterfoil of cheque).
[16] *Pearce* v. *Gardner* [1897] 1 Q.B. 688; *cf. Freeman* v. *Freeman* (1891) 7 T.L.R. 431. Loss of the envelope will not be fatal, if the court accepts evidence that it existed: *Last* v. *Hucklesby* (1914) 58 S.J. 431; *cf. ante*, p. 549.
[17] *Stokes* v. *Whicher* [1920] 1 Ch. 411.   [18] *Peirce* v. *Corf* (1874) L.R. 9 Q.B. 210.
[19] *Turnley* v. *Hartley* (1848) 3 New Pr.Cas. 96.
[20] *Timmins* v. *Moreland Street Property Co. Ltd.* [1958] Ch. 110.

a cheque and a receipt for it are signed on the same occasion, the precise order of the signatures will not be material.[21] Nor is evidence admissible to connect one document with another when, on being placed side by side,[22] the signed document still does not appear to refer to the unsigned document.[23]

(4) APPARENT CONNECTION. Where two documents are signed, and when placed side by side, they obviously refer to the same subject-matter, there is no need for evidence to connect them [24]; they proclaim their connection themselves.[25] They may therefore be read together even in the absence of any reference by one to the other. This doctrine may even extend to cases where only one document is signed,[26] for it is not so much the signature as the common subject-matter which establishes the connection. But in any such case the signed document must itself make some reference (express or implied) to the transaction to which both documents evidently relate, for otherwise the principle [27] would be infringed. Thus a cheque, which is merely an order for payment of money and by itself gives no clue as to the transaction, cannot be linked with a receipt containing the terms of the sale so as to render the signer of the cheque liable.[28]

(f) *Terms.* It is essential that the memorandum should contain all the terms of the contract which have been expressly agreed.[29] " If the memorandum is not in accordance with the true contract, it is a bad memorandum." [30] The omission of a single term, even though a subsidiary one, is fatal; for then the contract evidenced

21 *Timmins* v. *Moreland Street Property Co. Ltd., supra.*
22 See *Long* v. *Millar* (1879) 4 C.P.D. 450 at 454.
23 See *Boydell* v. *Drummond* (1809) 11 East 142; *North Staffordshire Ry.* v. *Peek* (1860) E.B. & E. 986 at 1000 (10 H.L.C. 473); *Kronheim* v. *Johnson* (1877) 7 Ch.D. 60; *Oliver* v. *Hunting* (1890) 44 Ch.D. 205 at 208, 209; *Taylor* v. *Smith* [1893] 2 Q.B. 65; *L. D. Turner Ltd.* v. *R. S. Hatton (Bradford) Ltd.* [1952] 1 All E.R. 1286.
24 *Allen* v. *Bennet* (1810) 3 Taunt. 169; *Verlander* v. *Codd* (1823) T. & R. 352; *Studds* v. *Watson* (1884) 28 Ch.D. 305. *Smith* v. *Dixon* (1839) 3 Jur. 770 and *Potter* v. *Peters* (1895) 64 L.J.Ch. 357 to the contrary seem unsound.
25 See *Sheers* v. *Thimbleby & Son* (1897) 76 L.T. 709 at 711, 712.
26 *Burgess* v. *Cox* [1951] Ch. 383, treating *Sheers* v. *Thimbleby & Son, supra,* as applying to such a case.
27 *Ante,* p. 552.
28 *Timmins* v. *Moreland Street Property Co. Ltd.* [1958] Ch. 110. The headnote states that reference to some document is essential, but this is wrong: see at p. 130 (" document or transaction "). The question here is whether there is reference to a transaction. For reference to a document, see *ante,* pp. 551, 552. A cheque with a perforated edge presumably refers to its counterfoil, and if the terms were there noted there could be a complete memorandum. See (1958) 74 L.Q.R. (R.E.M.); [1958] C.L.J. 36 (H.W.R.W.).
29 See *Peirce* v. *Corf* (1874) L.R. 9 Q.B. 210 at 214; *Beckett* v. *Nurse* [1948] 1 K.B. 535; and see *Caddick* v. *Skidmore* (1857) 2 De G. & J. 52 at 55, 56.
30 *Crane* v. *Naughten* [1912] 2 I.R. 318 at 324, *per* Gibson J.; and see *Allsopp* v. *Orchard* [1923] 1 Ch. 323; *Smith* v. *MacGowan* [1938] 3 All E.R. 447 (three distinct contracts recorded as single contract). But as to rectification, see *post,* p. 595.

by the writing is different from the contract actually made. Similarly a subsidiary memorandum that supplies a missing term is ineffective if it also introduces new terms not agreed between the parties.[31] It is wrong to suppose that a memorandum is sufficient merely because it specifies the parties, the property and the price: only if no other terms were expressly agreed to will it be an adequate memorandum. Thus actions have failed where the memorandum did not mention the conditions of sale which had been agreed on,[32] or a stipulation about the date for vacant possession,[33] or a promise to transfer deposits on advance bookings along with the property.[34]

There are two exceptions to the rigour of this rule.

(1) VARIATION. If the term not recorded in writing was not part of the original contract, but was introduced by way of variation after a complete memorandum of the original contract had been made, the original contract remains enforceable and the parol variation is disregarded.[35] Strictly speaking, this is illogical, for after the variation the true contract between the parties is the contract as varied, and this is not wholly evidenced in writing.[36] But the rule is now well settled. Variation has to be distinguished from complete rescission or abandonment of the original contract, which unlike variation can be done by a simple oral agreement without evidence in writing.[37]

(2) WAIVER. If the memorandum merely omits a stipulation which is for the benefit of one party alone, that party can enforce the contract if he waives the stipulation.[38] But this exception is a narrow one, for the term must benefit the plaintiff exclusively. If for example the contract contained an oral term that vacant possession should be given at a particular date, the term may well be to the advantage of both parties since each may be glad to have a definite date fixed.[39]

---

[31] *Nesham* v. *Selby* (1872) 7 Ch.App. 406.
[32] *Rishton* v. *Whatmore* (1878) 8 Ch.D. 467; compare *M'Meekin* v. *Stevenson* [1917] 1 I.R. 348.
[33] *Johnson* v. *Humphrey* (1946) 174 L.T. 324: *Hawkins* v. *Price* [1947] Ch. 645.
[34] *Burgess* v. *Cox* [1951] Ch. 383.
[35] See *Morris* v. *Baron & Co.* [1918] A.C. 1 at 16 (Lord Haldane), and cases there cited.
[36] *Ibid.* at 31 (Lord Atkinson); *cf. British and Beningtons Ltd.* v. *North Western Cachar Tea Co. Ltd.* [1923] A.C. 48 at 68, 69 (Lord Sumner). The paradox is probably caused by confusion with the easily misunderstood rule that oral evidence may not be given to contradict a written contract, even though that rule does not prevent the subsequent oral variation of a written contract: *Goss* v. *Lord Nugent* (1833) 5 B. & Ad. 58 at 65. Oral evidence may always be given to show that the memorandum does not represent the true contract: *Beckett* v. *Nurse, supra*; n. 30, *supra*.
[37] *Morris* v. *Baron & Co.* [1918] A.C. 1.
[38] *Morrell* v. *Studd and Millington* [1913] 2 Ch. 648 at 660; *North* v. *Loomes* [1919] 1 Ch. 378 at 385, 386 (purchaser to pay vendor's costs); *cf. Van Hatzfeldt-Wildenburg* v. *Alexander* [1912] 1 Ch. 284.
[39] *Hawkins* v. *Price* [1947] Ch. 645 at 657, 658.

There is also some authority for saying that the exception operates only when the term omitted is " of no great importance," [40] though it is difficult to see how this phrase could be given any precise meaning. There is a corresponding rule that a party may cure the omission of a term to his detriment by offering to perform it.[41]

(g) *Certainty.* The memorandum must state the terms of the contract with certainty. But help may be had from the maxim *id certum est quod certum reddi potest* (that is certain which can be made certain).[42]

(1) PARTIES. It is essential, of course, that the parties (or their agents [43]) should be. stated [44]; but it is not essential to give their names, provided that they are identifiable from a description.[45] Thus references to the " proprietor," [46] " mortgagees " [47] or " trustees " [48] of the property, or to " the legal personal representatives of X " [49] will suffice; such descriptions, although not excluding all uncertainty, may be more precise than the names of those concerned, for there may be many a man of the same name.[50]

Even " personal representatives " (without saying of whom) has been held to be adequate [51]; and the words " you having this day paid me the sum of £50 " have been held to identify the person who paid.[52] But references to " the vendor," [53] " landlord," [54] " proposing lender," [55] " my friend " [56] or " my clients " [57] will not do by themselves,[58] for such descriptions are indefinite: land may be sold or

---

[40] See *Hawkins* v. *Price* [1947] Ch. 645; *Burgess* v. *Cox* [1951] Ch. 383; Fry S.P. 243n.; but see *Martin* v. *Pycroft* (1852) 2 De G.M. & G. 785.

[41] *Martin* v. *Pycroft, supra* (tenant to pay premium of £200); *Scott* v. *Bradley* [1971] Ch. 850 (purchaser to pay half vendor's costs), not following *Burgess* v. *Cox, supra,* as being contrary to *Martin* v. *Pycroft, supra.* See (1951) 67 L.Q.R. 299 (R.E.M.). A party may similarly waive an express term in writing which is solely for his benefit: see, *e.g., Heron Garage Properties Ltd.* v. *Moss* [1974] 1 W.L.R. 148.

[42] *Shardlow* v. *Cotterell* (1881) 20 Ch.D. 90 at 98.   [43] See *infra,* p. 557.

[44] *Williams* v. *Lake* (1859) 2 E. & E. 349; *Williams* v. *Byrnes* (1863) 1 Moo.P.C.(N.S.) 154 at 196; *Stokell* v. *Niven* (1889) 61 L.T. 18.

[45] *Potter* v. *Duffield* (1874) L.R. 18 Eq. 4 at 7; *Carr* v. *Lynch* [1900] 1 Ch. 613 at 615; and see *Rossiter* v. *Miller* (1878) 3 App.Cas. 1124 at 1153; *Goldsmith Ltd.* v. *Baxter* [1970] Ch. 85.

[46] *Sale* v. *Lambert* (1874) L.R. 18 Eq. 1; *Rossiter* v. *Miller* (1878) 3 App.Cas. 1124.   [47] *Allen & Co. Ltd.* v. *Whiteman* (1920) 89 L.J.Ch. 534 at 538.

[48] *Catling* v. *King* (1877) 5 Ch.D. 660, esp. at p. 664.

[49] *Towle* v. *Topham* (1877) 37 L.T. 308; and see *Hood* v. *Lord Barrington* (1868) L.R. 6 Eq. 218.   [50] See *Catling* v. *King* (1877) 5 Ch.D. 660 at 664.

[51] *Fay* v. *Miller Wilkins & Co.* [1941] Ch. 360. *Sed quaere*: see (1941) 57 L.Q.R. 452 (R.E.M.).

[52] *Carr* v. *Lynch* [1900] 1 Ch. 613; *cf. Stokes* v. *Whicher* [1920] 1 Ch. 411 at 419–422.   [53] *Potter* v. *Duffield* (1874) L.R. 18 Eq. 4.

[54] *Coombs* v. *Wilkes* [1891] 3 Ch. 77.   [55] *Pattle* v. *Anstruther* (1893) 69 L.T. 175.

[56] *Rossiter* v. *Miller* (1878) 3 App.Cas. 1124 at 1141.

[57] *Lovesy* v. *Palmer* [1916] 2 Ch. 233.

[58] The circumstances may, however, narrow down the descriptions so that they suffice: see, *e.g., Commins* v. *Scott* (1875) L.R. 20 Eq. 11; *Sidle* v. *Bond-Cabbell* (1885) 2 T.L.R. 44.

let by many persons besides the fee simple owner, *e.g.*, by tenants, mortgagees or even complete strangers [59]; and to decide who is one of the parties is " exactly what the Act says shall not be decided by parol evidence." [60]   Conversely, it is not enough to give the names of the parties if the memorandum does not indicate their capacities, [61] *e.g.*, which is vendor and which is purchaser. [62]   But where there is an agent for an undisclosed principal, a memorandum in the name of the agent is good and binds both him and his principal, even if the other party knows that he is merely an agent. [63]

(2) OTHER TERMS.   Similar principles apply to the other terms: " Mr. O's house," [64] " the house in Newport," [65] " my house " [66] and even " this place " [67] have all been upheld, with the aid of oral evidence, as descriptions of the property. [68]   The Court of Appeal has gone so far as to hold that " twenty-four acres of land, freehold, at Totmonslow " could be identified by oral evidence, [69] although destitute of " my " or " the " or any other defining particular.   This straining of language must be attributed to the court's reluctance to allow the contract to be broken with impunity.   An example of a defective description is the case of a sub-lease for the residue of the head lease " less a few days " [70]; both the beginning [71] and the length [72] of the term of a lease must be indicated in some way which can be made precise.   It will not be assumed that a term is to commence on the date of the agreement, [73] or when the tenant is to take possession, [74] or begin paying rent. [75]   Likewise the consideration must be stated with reasonable precision. [76]   But a right of first

[59] See *Donnison* v. *People's Cafe Co.* (1881) 45 L.T. 187.

[60] *Potter* v. *Duffield, supra*, at p. 8, *per* Jessel M.R.

[61] *Stokell* v. *Niven* (1889) 61 L.T. 18.

[62] *Vandebergh* v. *Spooner* (1866) L.R. 1 Ex. 316 (vendor); *Dewar* v. *Mintoft* [1912] 2 K.B. 373 (purchaser).

[63] *Basma* v. *Weekes* [1950] A.C. 441 (purchaser's agent); *Davies* v. *Sweet* [1962] 2 Q.B. 300 (vendor's agent).   Yet does such a memorandum really record the *true* contract?   [64] *Ogilvie* v. *Foljambe* (1817) 3 Mer. 53.

[65] *Owen* v. *Thomas* (1834) 3 My. & K. 353; and see *Bleakley* v. *Smith* (1840) 11 Sim. 150 (" the property in Cable Street "); *Wood* v. *Scarth* (1855) 2 K. & J. 33 (" the intended new public-house at Putney ").

[66] *Cowley* v. *Watts* (1853) 17 Jur. 172.

[67] *Waldron* v. *Jacob* (1870) 5 I.R.Eq. 131.

[68] See *Sheers* v. *Thimbleby & Son* (1897) 76 L.T. 709 at 712.

[69] *Plant* v. *Bourne* [1897] 2 Ch. 281; *cf. Wesley* v. *Walker* (1878) 38 L.T. 284; Williams V. & P. 6.   [70] *Dolling* v. *Evans* (1867) 36 L.J.Ch. 474.

[71] *Blore* v. *Sutton* (1817) 3 Mer. 237; *Cartwright* v. *Miller* (1877) 36 L.T. 398.

[72] *Fitzmaurice* v. *Bayley* (1860) 9 H.L.C. 78; *Clarke* v. *Fuller* (1864) 16 C.B.(N.S.) 24.   [73] *Marshall* v. *Berridge* (1881) 19 Ch.D. 233.

[74] *Edwards* v. *Jones* (1921) 124 L.T. 740; and see *Rock Portland Cement Co. Ltd.* v. *Wilson* (1882) 52 L.J.Ch. 214.   Prima facie, however, a renewed lease will run from the expiration of the existing lease: see *Verlander* v. *Codd* (1823) T. & R. 352; *Wood* v. *Aylward* (1888) 58 L.T. 667.

[75] *Humphrey* v. *Conybeare* (1899) 80 L.T. 40.

[76] *Blagden* v. *Bradbear* (1806) 12 Ves. 466; *cf. Baumann* v. *James* (1868) 3 Ch.App. 508 (agreement to do repairs costing " from about £150 to £200 " held sufficiently precise).

refusal " at a price to be agreed upon " has been upheld as meaning the lowest price at which the vendor was willing to sell.[76a]

(*h*) *Implied terms.* There is, of course, no need for the memorandum to specify the many implied terms which a contract for the disposition of land often contains. For example, if nothing is expressly agreed about the date for completion (conveyance and payment) it will be subject to an implied time limit which need not be mentioned.[77] If nothing is said of the date for giving vacant possession, it will be implied that it shall be given at the time of completion.[78] Similarly if the sale is expressly made subject to some incumbrance, such as a lease, but the memorandum makes no mention of it, the omission will not matter if the purchaser has waived his right to object,[79] for the missing provision is then present by implication.[80]

4. " Signed by the party to be charged or by some other person thereunto by him lawfully authorised "

(*a*) " *Party to be charged.*" The Statute requires signature by or on behalf of the party to be charged, namely, the party against whom as defendant the action is brought. No other signature is needed.[81] Thus where there is a contract between A and B, and A alone has signed a memorandum, the contract is enforceable by action by B against A but not by A against B.[82]

(*b*) " *Signed.*" The word " signed " has been given an extended meaning by the courts. Provided the name of the party to be charged appears in some part of the document in some form, whether in writing, typewriting, print or otherwise,[83] there will be a sufficient signature if that party has shown in some way that he recognises the document as an expression of the contract.[84] The difference is between inserting the name in the document merely to make it intelligible,[85] and inserting it in such a way as to " have the effect of authenticating the instrument," [86] or " to govern what follows." [87]

[76a] *Smith* v. *Morgan* [1971] 1 W.L.R. 803.   [77] *Post*, p. 573.
[78] *Post*, p. 585.   [79] For this doctrine, see *post*, p. 584.
[80] *Timmins* v. *Moreland Street Property Co. Ltd.* [1958] Ch. 110.
[81] *Backhouse* v. *Mohun* (1736) 3 Swans. 434; *Laythoarp* v. *Bryant* (1836) 2 Bing.N.C. 735.
[82] See *Child* v. *Comber* (1723) 3 Swans. 423; *Boys* v. *Ayerst* (1822) 6 Madd. 316.
[83] *Tourret* v. *Cripps* (1879) 48 L.J.Ch. 567; *Halley* v. *O'Brien* [1920] 1 I.R. 330 at 339.
[84] *Evans* v. *Hoare* [1892] 1 Q.B. 593; *Leeman* v. *Stocks* [1951] Ch. 941; *Bilsland* v. *Terry* [1972] N.Z.L.R. 43.
[85] See *Hubert* v. *Treherne* (1842) 3 Man. & G. 743 at 753.
[86] *Ogilvie* v. *Foljambe* (1817) 3 Mer. 53 at 62, *per* Grant M.R. See Williams, *Statute of Frauds, Section IV*, 82 *et seq.*
[87] *Lobb* v. *Stanley* (1844) 5 Q.B. 574 at 582, *per* Coleridge J.; compare *Halley* v. *O'Brien* [1920] 1 I.R. 330.

Thus memoranda in the handwriting of A, the defendant, which began " I, A, agree " [88] or " A agrees " [89] or " Mr. A presents his compliments " [90] or " sold A " [91] without any other signature, have all been held sufficiently signed on the ground that A has shown by his writing that he recognises the existence of the contract mentioned in the document. But the form of the document may imply that the name is not to be regarded as a signature [92] : thus if A writes out a document beginning " Articles of agreement made between A and B " and ending " As witness our hands " without any signatures, the Statute is not satisfied. [93] Yet even this implication may be rebutted by oral evidence. [94]

It may be said generally that if the defendant has prepared the document, and it contains his name in full [95] or is headed by his name, [96] the name is likely to suffice as a signature. If the memorandum is altered after signature, in principle a further signature is necessary; but the Court of Appeal has held that oral approval of the alterations by the defendant will extend the effect of his signature to them. [97] This was perhaps no great extension of the law, since the courts had long before reached the point of allowing oral evidence to be given to show what words were governed by the signature. [98] Initials may be a signature. [99] Even signature as a witness may be operative, provided the witness can be shown to be attesting the document itself and not merely someone else's signature to it. [1]

---

[88] *Knight* v. *Crockford* (1794) 1 Esp. 190; *cf. Sims* v. *Landray* [1894] 2 Ch. 318.
[89] *Bleakley* v. *Smith* (1840) 11 Sim. 150; or " Mr. A has agreed ": *Propert* v. *Parker* (1830) 1 Russ. & M. 625.
[90] *Ogilvie* v. *Foljambe* (1817) 3 Mer. 53.
[91] *Johnson* v. *Dodgson* (1837) 2 M. & W. 653.
[92] See *Stokes* v. *Moore* (1786) 1 Cox Eq. 219; *Caton* v. *Caton* (1867) L.R. 2 H.L. 127 at 143.
[93] *Hubert* v. *Treherne* (1842) 3 Man. & G. 743; and see *Selby* v. *Selby* (1817) 3 Mer. 2 (letter to son concluding " believe me to be the most affectionate of mothers " held insufficient).
[94] *Leeman* v. *Stocks* [1951] Ch. 941 (evidence admitted to show that the words " as witness the hands of the parties " applied to the plaintiff's signature only, since it was intended that he alone should sign beneath them).
[95] *Evans* v. *Hoare* [1892] 1 Q.B. 593 at 596.
[96] *Ibid.*; *Schneider* v. *Norris* (1814) 2 M. & S. 286; *Tourret* v. *Cripps* (1879) 48 L.J.Ch. 567 (letter headed in print " from A "); contrast *Hucklesby* v. *Hook* (1900) 82 L.T. 117.
[97] *Koenigsblatt* v. *Sweet* [1923] 2 Ch. 314.
[98] See *Evans* v. *Hoare, supra,* and *cf. Hawkins* v. *Holmes* (1721) 1 P.Wms. 770. It is *a fortiori* if the defendant wrote the words himself, even if only the plaintiff signed the addition: *Bluck* v. *Gompertz* (1852) 7 Exch. 862.
[99] *Hill* v. *Hill* [1947] Ch. 231. So also a rubber stamp: consider *Bennett* v. *Brumfit* (1867) 37 L.J.C.P. 25; *Goodman* v. *J. Eban Ltd.* [1954] 1 Q.B. 550.
[1] *Coles* v. *Trecothick* (1804) 9 Ves. 234; *Jones* v. *Victoria Graving Dock Co.* (1877) 2 Q.B.D. 314 at 324 (as to which, see *John Griffiths Cycle Corpn. Ltd.* v. *Humber & Co. Ltd.* [1899] 2 Q.B. 414 at 418, reversed on other grounds [1901] W.N. 110); *Wallace* v. *Roe* [1903] 1 I.R. 32.

(c) *Agent's authority.* The Statute says nothing about the mode in which an agent must be " lawfully authorised " to sign, and this is consequently governed by the rules of common law. Thus written authority is not required,[2] and a signature made without authority may be ratified.[3] But the courts guard against the possibility of fraud by holding that one party cannot sign as agent for the other.[4] It must also be shown that the agent was " thereunto " authorised, and had authority to sign a memorandum of a contract of the nature relied on by the plaintiff.[5] His authority need not have extended to the making of a contract, for example if he was employed to write a letter purely for the other party's information[6]; and authority to " carry out " a contract,[7] or to sell at a defined price (as opposed to merely finding a purchaser),[8] is sufficient. But the mere fact that he is the defendant's solicitor will not necessarily give him such authority,[9] nor will instructions to deny that there is a contract,[10] or to inquire into title,[11] or to make a draft of a formal contract,[12] or to prepare a contract for signature.[13]

(d) *Agent for both parties.* The same agent may act for both parties[14] (provided that he is not himself one of them[15]), as often happens in the case of sales by auction. An auctioneer is primarily agent for the vendor, with authority to sign a memorandum as such.[16] But by a special rule the purchaser (the highest bidder at the fall of the hammer) is deemed to have given the auctioneer authority to sign a memorandum on his behalf also[17]; and the auctioneer commonly signs a note of the sale of each lot which makes the contract enforceable against either party. An agent's authority is revocable without formality up to the moment when a contract is made, and accordingly

[2] *Heard* v. *Pilley* (1869) 4 Ch.App. 548; *Gavaghan* v. *Edwards* [1961] 2 Q.B. 220 (note made by solicitor to both parties of purchaser's oral agreement to date for completion held binding); and see *Smith* v. *Mansi* [1963] 1 W.L.R. 26.
[3] *Maclean* v. *Dunn* (1828) 4 Bing. 722.
[4] *Sharman* v. *Brandt* (1871) L.R. 6 Q.B. 720; but consider *Bird* v. *Boulter* (1833) 4 B. & Ad. 433; Blackburn, *Contract of Sale*, 3rd ed., 76, 77.
[5] *Thirkell* v. *Cambi* [1919] 2 K.B. 590 at 598.
[6] *Daniels* v. *Trefusis* [1914] 1 Ch. 788.
[7] *North* v. *Loomes* [1919] 1 Ch. 378.
[8] *Keen* v. *Mear* [1920] 2 Ch. 574 at 579; see the cases there cited, and *Saunders* v. *Dence* (1885) 52 L.T. 644 and *Lewcock* v. *Bromley* (1922) 127 L.T. 116.
[9] *Bowen* v. *Duc d'Orleans* (1900) 16 T.L.R. 226.
[10] *Thirkell* v. *Cambi* [1919] 2 K.B. 590.
[11] *Matthews* v. *Baxter* (1873) 28 L.T. 669.
[12] *Smith* v. *Webster* (1876) 3 Ch.D. 49.
[13] *Bowen* v. *Duc d'Orleans, supra.*
[14] *Durrell* v. *Evans* (1862) 1 H. & C. 174; *Thompson* v. *Gardiner* (1876) 1 C.P.D. 177; *Gavaghan* v. *Edwards* [1961] 2 Q.B. 220 (*supra*, n. 2).
[15] See previous paragraph.
[16] Blackburn, *Contract of Sale*, 3rd ed., 78.
[17] *Warlow* v. *Harrison* (1858) 1 E. & E. 295 at 307; *Sims* v. *Landray* [1894] 2 Ch. 318 at 320; *Chaney* v. *Maclow* [1929] 1 Ch. 461; *Richards* v. *Phillips* [1969] 1 Ch. 39.

in the case of auctions it seems that neither vendor [18] nor purchaser [19] can revoke it after the fall of the hammer. The auctioneer's authority to sign for the purchaser is confined to the time of the sale,[20] but his authority to sign for the vendor lasts throughout the period for which he was expressly made the vendor's agent.[21] Signature by an auctioneer's clerk normally [22] binds neither party,[23] for an agent cannot delegate his authority.[24]

B. A Sufficient Act of Part Performance

1. Fraud. The Statute of Frauds, 1677, was intended to prevent the fraud and perjury which were possible when contracts for the transfer of land could be alleged upon merely oral testimony. This it did, but it opened new and different possibilities of deception: a person who had made a genuine contract might repudiate it on the ground that there was no proper memorandum as required by the Statute. In some cases of this kind equity would invoke its wide jurisdiction to grant relief against fraud, even though this meant "decorously disregarding an Act of Parliament." [25] "In cases of fraud, equity should relieve, even against the words of the statute." [26] The commonest and most important example of this principle is found in the doctrine of part performance. Certain other examples will be mentioned elsewhere.[27]

2. Part performance. The doctrine of part performance appeared in the reports in 1686 [28] and was firmly established by a decision of

---

[18] See *Day* v. *Wells* (1861) 30 Beav. 220 at 224; *Bell* v. *Balls* [1897] 1 Ch. 663 at 672; contrast *Farmer* v. *Robinson* (1805) 2 Camp. 337.

[19] *Van Praagh* v. *Everidge* [1902] 2 Ch. 266 at 270, not questioned on appeal [1903] 1 Ch. 434; *Chaney* v: *Maclow, supra,* at pp. 467, 481; Williams V. & P. 23, n. (s).

[20] *Mews* v. *Carr* (1856) 1 H. & N. 484 at 488. And see *Chaney* v. *Maclow* [1929] 1 Ch. 461 (auctioneer's signature made an hour and a half after end of sale but as part of transaction of sale: held binding on purchaser); contrast *Bell* v. *Balls, supra* (signature a week after auction: purchaser not bound).

[21] *Mews* v. *Carr, supra*; *M'Meekin* v. *Stevenson* [1917] 1 I.R. 348 at 354 (the party to be charged was the vendor, not the purchaser as stated in Williams, *Statute of Frauds, Section IV,* 112).

[22] For examples of implied authority, see *Bird* v. *Boulter* (1833) 4 B. & Ad. 443 at 488 (nodding head as clerk writes); *Sims* v. *Landray* [1894] 2 Ch. 318 (standing by while clerk makes memorandum); but compare *Murphy* v. *Boese* (1875) L.R. 10 Ex. 126.

[23] *Peirce* v. *Corf* (1874) L.R. 9 Q.B. 210 at 214, 215; *Bell* v. *Balls* [1897] 1 Ch. 663.

[24] *Dyas* v. *Stafford* (1881) 7 L.R.Ir. 590 at 600, not questioned on appeal (1882) 9 L.R.Ir. 520.

[25] *Spencer* v. *Hemmerde* [1922] 2 A.C. 507 at 519, *per* Lord Sumner, in relation to another statute.

[26] *Viscountess Montacute* v. *Maxwell* (1720) 1 P.Wms. 618 at 620, *per* Lord Parker L.C. Cf. *Le Neve* v. *Le Neve* (1747) Amb. 436.

[27] *Post*, pp. 910, 1054.

[28] *Butcher* v. *Stapley* (1686) 1 Vern. 363 (a decision of Lord Jeffreys L.C., not of Lord Guilford L.K. as stated in (1883) 8 App.Cas. at 477). See S.S. Vol. 73 at p. ciii (D. E. C. Yale).

the House of Lords in 1701.[29]   From then on it could be said that,
even if it was invented in error, it was a case of *communis error
facit jus* (universal error amounts to law).[30]   Its fundamental proposition is that if the plaintiff has partly carried out the contract on
his side, in reliance on the promise of the defendant, it is inequitable
to allow the defendant to plead the statute.[31] Equity will not allow
the statute to be made an instrument of fraud.[32] The principle has
been expressed in another way by saying that " the defendant is
really ' charged ' upon the equities resulting from the acts done in
execution of the contract, and not (within the meaning of the statute)
upon the contract itself. . . . The matter has advanced beyond the
stage of contract; and the equities which arise out of the stage which
it has reached cannot be administered unless the contract is
regarded." [33]   Specific performance of the contract will therefore be
decreed, and all its terms may be proved by oral evidence.[34]

3. Connection with land. As the doctrine developed, it was confined to acts of part performance which in some way indicated the
land concerned.[35] The object was " to prevent a recurrence of the
mischief which the statute was passed to suppress," [36] since otherwise there could be nothing but oral evidence to support a claim to
the land.   In the case of a contract for sale, it was thus a sufficient act
of part performance if the purchaser was let into possession by the
vendor, for then it was clear that there must be some transaction
between them concerning that land: the contract could not be
fabricated by perjured evidence. But if the purchaser merely paid
the vendor without taking possession, this was not a sufficient act of
part performance because it did not by itself indicate a transaction
about any land: it was a mere payment of money, which in any case
could be recovered.[37]   Thus there emerged the rule, discussed
below, that the performance must be referable to the contract.
Originally based broadly on fraud, the doctrine acquired an evidentiary character: an essential safeguard was " some *evidentia rei* to

[29] *Lester* v. *Foxcroft* (1701) Colles P.C. 108.
[30] See *Maddison* v. *Alderson* (1883) 8 App.Cas. 467 at 489.
[31] *Mundy* v. *Joliffe* (1839) 5 My. & Cr. 167 at 177; and see *Buckmaster* v. *Harrop*
(1802) 7 Ves. 341, (1807) 13 Ves. 456.
[32] *Whitbread* v. *Brockhurst* (1784) 1 Bro.C.C. 404 at 413; *Mestaer* v. *Gillespie*
(1805) 11 Ves. 621 at 628.
[33] *Maddison* v. *Alderson, supra,* at pp. 475, 476, *per* Lord Selborne L.C.
[34] *Post,* p. 570.
[35] See *Maddison* v. *Alderson, supra,* at pp. 478–481, *per* Lord Selborne L.C.; at
p. 485, *per* Lord O'Hagan; at p. 489, *per* Lord Blackburn; and at p. 491, *per*
Lord FitzGerald. And see *post,* p. 565, n. 67.
[36] *Ibid.,* at p. 478, *per* Lord Selborne L.C.
[37] See *Clinan* v. *Cooke* (1802) 1 Sch. & Lef. 22 at 41, 42; *Chaproniere* v. *Lambert*
[1917] 2 Ch. 356. Yet the defendant may become insolvent: see *Buckmaster* v.
Harrop (1807) 13 Ves. 456 at 460n.

connect the alleged part performance with the alleged agreement." [38]
This was at least a partial substitute for the statutory safeguard of
signed writing.

The House of Lords confirmed this limitation decisively in the
leading case of *Maddison* v. *Alderson*.[39] A housekeeper had agreed
to continue in her employer's service without wages in consideration
of his oral promise to leave her by his will a life interest in a farm,
which he omitted to do. Her claim based on part performance
failed, since her service " was not such an act as to be in itself
evidence of a new contract, much less of a contract concerning her
master's land." [40] But now the House of Lords has no less decisively
rejected this restriction, as explained below.[40a]

4. Statute. Statutory recognition has been given to the doctrine
of part performance, for section 40 (2) of the Law of Property Act,
1925, provides that subsection (1), which requires writing,[41] " does
not affect the law relating to part performance."

I. ELEMENTS OF PART PERFORMANCE

The essentials of the doctrine of part performance may be classified
as follows.

1. Evidence of the contract. The court requires clear evidence,
whether parol or otherwise, that there was a contract " certain and
definite in its terms " [42] between the parties.[43] The court will not
assist the plaintiff if there was no final contract, matters being still
in the stage of negotiations.[44] No amount of what would otherwise
be part performance will render certain a contract which is void for
uncertainty [45] or make into an agreement that which is not an
agreement at all, such as an agreement " subject to contract." [46]

---

[38] *Maddison* v. *Alderson, supra*, at p. 478, *per* Lord Selborne L.C. See likewise
Britain v. *Rossiter* (1879) 11 Q.B.D. 123 at 130; *Rawlinson* v. *Ames* [1925] Ch.
109.

[39] (1883) 8 App.Cas. 467 (will made as promised but not witnessed).

[40] *Ibid.*, at p. 481, *per* Lord Selborne L.C.

[40a] *Post*, p. 566.

[41] Cited *ante*, p. 545.

[42] *Cooth* v. *Jackson* (1801) 6 Ves. 12 at 38, *per* Lord Eldon L.C.

[43] *Reynolds* v. *Waring* (1831) You. 346; *Mortal* v. *Lyons* (1858) 8 I.Ch.R. 112
at 118; *Price* v. *Salusbury* (1863) 32 L.J.Ch. 441; (1866) 14 L.T. 110.

[44] *Thynne* v. *Earl of Glengall* (1848) 2 H.L.C. 131 at 158; *Bertel* v. *Neveux* (1878)
39 L.T. 257; *Ex p. Foster* (1883) 22 Ch.D. 797 at 811; *Lockett* v. *Norman-Wright*
[1925] Ch. 56.

[45] See *Waring & Gillow Ltd.* v. *Thompson* (1912) 29 T.L.R. 154.

[46] See *Ex p. Foster, supra*, at p. 808; *Lockett* v. *Norman-Wright* [1925] Ch. 56.
But equity will sometimes, independently of any contract, protect a person who
has spent money on the land of another: see *post*, p. 778.

2. Contract specifically enforceable. Even if the terms of the contract are clear, it is essential that the plaintiff should establish a case for specific performance of the contract.[47] In equity, part performance raises a right to full performance, but not to any other remedy: "the choice is between undoing what has been done (which is not always possible, or, if possible, just) and completing what has been left undone."[48] It is only by statute that the plaintiff can claim damages in addition to, or in lieu of, specific performance.[49] It was of course necessary for equity to set strict bounds to its exception to the Statute of Frauds. Specific performance, being itself an equitable and therefore discretionary remedy,[50] might be refused on a number of grounds, such as misrepresentation, hardship or unreasonable delay.[51] It might also be refused if the interest was to last only for a very short period, *e.g.*, a tenancy for a month or two; no specific performance could be granted if the term had expired before the action was heard, and so part performance would not avail.[52] It has been said that a contract for a lease for a year or less is not specifically enforceable[53]; but probably there is no rigid rule,[54] and in any case a contract for a yearly tenancy is specifically enforceable.[55]

As against a plaintiff who has partly performed the contract, the court is loth to exercise its discretion merely because the contract itself is of a kind which the court might otherwise hesitate to enforce specifically.[56] If, for example, the terms of the contract appear somewhat vague, "the court is bound to struggle against the difficulty arising from the vagueness."[57]

3. Act by the plaintiff. The act of part performance must have been done by the plaintiff, or on his behalf or at his request.[58] It will be noticed that whereas in the case of a memorandum in writing it is the signature of the defendant that is necessary, what is required in the case of part performance is an act by the plaintiff, who is

---

47 *Elliott* v. *Roberts* (1912) 28 T.L.R. 436 at 437, 438; and see *McManus* v. *Cooke* (1887) 35 Ch.D. 681 at 697; *Lavery* v. *Pursell* (1888) 39 Ch.D. 508 at 518.
48 *Maddison* v. *Alderson* (1883) 8 App.Cas. 467 at 476, *per* Lord Selborne L.C.
49 See *ante*, p. 126.   50 *Ante*, p. 126, *post*, p. 593.
51 See Fry S.P., Part III; Snell, *Equity*, 588 *et seq.*
52 *Lavery* v. *Pursell* (1888) 39 Ch.D. 508.
53 *Ibid.*, at p. 519; *Glasse* v. *Woolgar* (1897) 41 S.J. 573.
54 See *De Brassac* v. *Martyn* (1863) 11 W.R. 1020; *Lever* v. *Koffler* [1901] 1 Ch. 543 at 547; *cf. Gilbey* v. *Cossey* (1912) 106 L.T. 607 at 608, 609; and see Fry S.P., 31, 32.
55 *Lever* v. *Koffler, supra.*   56 *Hart* v. *Hart* (1881) 18 Ch.D. 670.
57 *Ibid.*, at p. 685, *per* Kay J.
58 *Williams* v. *Evans* (1875) L.R. 19 Eq. 547 (repairs and alterations executed by plaintiff's lessee). See also *Re Cooke's Trustee's Estate* (1880) 5 L.R.Ir. 99 (surrender of lease by existing tenant held part performance of agreement to grant a lease to a new tenant in place of old lease: *sed quaere*); and see *Parker* v. *Smith* (1845) 1 Coll.C.C. 608; Fry S.P. 297.

seeking to enforce the contract [59]; for if the party refusing to perform the contract has done the only act of part performance, there is no fraud but merely a loss to himself. [60]

Since the element of fraud is essential, the act of part performance must have been known by the defendant to have been done on the faith of the contract. [61] The defendant's acquiescence in the act ensures that he is not himself the victim of a falsely alleged contract. [62]

For this last-mentioned reason it has been held that an oral contract by a tenant for life for a lease which would bind the remaindermen is not made enforceable against either of them by part performance unless they both knew that the act was being done in reliance on the contract [63]; but it is difficult to understand these decisions, since there was no need for the remaindermen to consent to any such lease, and whether they knew of the contract or not should have been irrelevant. A tenant for life with power to lease can certainly bind the remaindermen by a *written* contract. [64]

4. Act referable to the contract. According to the classic rule, observed consistently in many cases, acts of part performance must be " unequivocally, and in their own nature, referable to some such agreement as that alleged." [65] Yet, as was truly said, " in the nature of things no act of part performance could be so eloquent as to point unequivocally to one particular contract and no other." [66] What the rule really meant, as its judicial context showed, [67] was that the act of part performance must satisfy the court that the land in question was the subject of some agreement between the parties.

---

[59] *Caton* v. *Caton* (1865) 1 Ch.App. 137 (on appeal, L.R. 2 H.L. 127); *Rawlinson* v. *Ames* [1925] Ch. 96 at 108. For argument to the contrary see Williams, *Statute of Frauds, Section IV*, 260, 261.

[60] *Buckmaster* v. *Harrop* (1802) 7 Ves. 341 at 346.

[61] *Dann* v. *Spurrier* (1802) 7 Ves. 231; Fry S.P. 281; *cf. Broughton* v. *Snook* [1938] Ch. 505.

[62] See examples, *infra*, pp. 568, 569. But see also *Steadman* v. *Steadman, infra*.

[63] *Blore* v. *Sutton* (1817) 3 Mer. 237 (remainderman held not liable); *Trotman* v. *Flesher* (1861) 3 Giff. 1 (tenant for life held not liable because of remainderman's ignorance); Fry S.P. 281.

[64] *Shannon* v. *Bradstreet* (1803) 1 Sch. & Lef. 52.

[65] *Maddison* v. *Alderson* (1883) 8 App.Cas. 467 at 479, *per* Lord Selborne L.C. This rule first emerged in *Gunter* v. *Halsey* (1739) Amb. 586.

[66] Williams, *Statute of Frauds, Section IV*, 253, note; and see *Broughton* v. *Snook, supra*, at p. 515.

[67] The most authoritative context is Lord Selborne's speech in *Maddison* v. *Alderson, supra*. The Court of Appeal had similarly held that " unequivocally referable " meant that " there must be a necessary connection between the acts of part performance and the interest in the land which is the alleged subject-matter of the agreement ": *Alderson* v. *Maddison* (1881) 7 Q.B.D. 174 at 178.

This was the indispensable evidence which protected the defendant against fraud, as already explained.[69]

Accordingly, if A took possession of B's land with B's consent,[70] or B altered his own house at A's request,[71] the explanation could only be that there was some agreement that A should obtain an interest in the land. These were therefore sufficient acts of part performance, even though they did not indicate whether the agreement was that A should have a weekly tenancy, a life tenancy [72] or the fee simple. This and the other terms could then be proved by oral evidence. But if A merely paid money to B,[73] or continued to occupy B's land after the expiry of a lease by B to A,[74] or acted as B's housekeeper without wages,[75] or married B,[76] none of these acts would lead anyone to suppose that there must be some contract between them for the sale or lease of any land. Such acts were therefore held to be equivocal and inadequate. The mere payment or part-payment of purchase money, in particular, could not be part performance.[77]

5. Relaxation of the rule. The courts are now so much more concerned with preventing breach of contract than with upholding the policy of the statute that they have abandoned the principle explained above, long settled though it was. It was first held that a house-keeper, who gave up her home and moved into her employer's house and worked without wages, could enforce an oral contract that he would leave her the house and contents by his will.[78] This was a clear departure from *Maddison* v. *Alderson* in a closely analogous case.[79] The House of Lords then went still further in *Steadman* v. *Steadman*,[80] where a wife had orally agreed with her husband to sell her interest in their house to him for £1,500 and he had at the same time agreed to pay £100 towards arrears of maintenance due to her.

---

[69] *Ante*, p. 562.
[70] *Post*, p. 568.
[71] *Post*, p. 569.
[72] *Kingswood Estate Co. Ltd.* v. *Anderson* [1963] 2 Q.B. 169 at 189.
[73] *Chaproniere* v. *Lambert* [1917] 2 Ch. 356; Fry S.P. 290–292. Contrast *Steadman* v. *Steadman* [1974] 3 W.L.R. 56, *infra*.
[74] *Post*, p. 568.
[75] *Maddison* v. *Alderson, supra*. Contrast *Wakeham* v. *Mackenzie* [1968] 1 W.L.R. 1175, *infra*.
[76] Fry S.P. 293.
[77] *Maddison* v. *Alderson, supra*, at p. 479; *Broughton* v. *Snook* [1938] Ch. 505 at 514, *per* Farwell J.
[78] *Wakeham* v. *Mackenzie* [1968] 1 W.L.R. 1175. The judgment was based on these acts alone and not on the housekeeper having taken exclusive possession of a room in the house into which she moved her furniture, though this might well be equivocal.
[79] See also *National Provincial Bank Ltd.* v. *Moore* (1967) 111 S.J. 357, criticised in (1968) 32 Conv.(N.S.) 384 (P. H. Pettit).
[80] [1974] 3 W.L.R. 56, Lord Morris of Borth-y-Gest (in H.L.) and Edmund Davies L.J. (in C.A.) dissenting with much force. See (1974) 90 L.Q.R. 433 (H.W.R.W.).

The House held that payment of the £100, and also the sending of a deed of transfer for signature by the wife, were good acts of part performance by the husband. Yet no rule was better established than that mere payment of money was insufficient; and the sending of the transfer was a unilateral act, not in itself conclusive as to any agreement by the husband.

It now seems that " you take the whole circumstances, leaving aside evidence about the oral contract, to see whether it is proved that the acts relied on were done in reliance on a contract: that will be proved if it is shown to be more probable than not."[81] The acts themselves need no longer show that the contract must concern land.[82] The court is concerned with " equities resulting from *res gestae* subsequent to and arising out of the contract," [1] and evidence of any acts, including spoken words, may be admitted.[2] It seems that no more is required than " that the acts in question be such as must be referred to some contract, and may be referred to the alleged one; that they prove the existence of some contract, and are consistent with the contract alleged." [3] These are the words of a venerated textbook which were, in truth, an inaccurate and misleading statement of the principle, but which have now been judicially sanctified.

It is difficult to see what can be the limits of so loose a doctrine as that now laid down. It seems possible that any purchaser who pays a deposit under an oral contract may be able to enforce it, and that the mere sending of a draft conveyance may by itself suffice. It is clear that the doctrine is now stripped of the evidentiary character, explained earlier,[4] which the courts impressed upon it in the nineteenth century and which kept it within logical limits. It appears to have reverted to its primeval eighteenth-century state, when the courts would accept any acts, however equivocal.[5]

---

[81] *Steadman* v. *Steadman, supra,* at p. 61, *per* Lord Reid.
[82] The payment of money already due under a court order, accepted as part performance in *Steadman* v. *Steadman, supra,* was the most equivocal type of act imaginable.
[1] *Maddison* v. *Alderson, supra,* at p. 476, *per* Lord Selborne L.C., approved in *Steadman* v. *Steadman, supra.*
[2] *Steadman* v. *Steadman, supra,* at pp. 71, 72, 82, 90.
[3] Fry S.P. 278, approved in *Steadman* v. *Steadman, supra,* and also, though unnecessarily, in *Kingswood Estate Co. Ltd.* v. *Anderson* [1963] 2 Q.B. 169 at 189. Fry's later editions paid little attention to *Maddison* v. *Alderson* and the principle there confirmed. His inaccuracy was pointed out by Lord Salmon in *Steadman* v. *Steadman, supra,* at p. 87 and by Edmund Davies L.J., [1974] Q.B. 161 at 171.
[4] *Ante,* p. 562.
[5] Thus Lord Hardwicke L.C. held in *Lacon* v. *Mertins* (1743) 3 Atk. 1 that " paying of money has been always held in this court as à part-performance." But these decisions were overruled: see *Maddison* v. *Alderson, supra,* at p. 478. Other exceptional decisions were *Parker* v. *Smith* (1845) 1 Coll.C.C. 608 (dissolution of partnership and release from liability under lease); *Hammersley* v. *De Biel* (1845) 12 Cl. & F. 45 at 64n. (settlement of annuity; but the decision was on other grounds).

6. Examples of part performance. Certain situations where part performance is often pleaded require further illustration.

(*a*) *Taking possession.* Taking possession of land with the vendor's consent is " the act of part performance *par excellence*." [6] It is, furthermore, a part performance by both parties: the vendor gives up the land,[7] and the purchaser takes it.[8] Accordingly it is the general rule that once the purchaser has been let into possession (for however short a time [9]) it is too late for either party to repudiate an oral contract. This does not, of course, hold good where the purchaser takes possession by force after the vendor has repudiated the contract.[10] It is essential that the vendor should authorise the purchaser to take possession [11]; but it suffices if a purchaser who was let into possession by the vendor before the contract was made continues in possession thereafter.[12]

(*b*) *Continuing in possession.* Where the plaintiff already has possession under some other title before the contract is made, his continuance in possession is not by itself part performance. A leasehold tenant who holds over after the end of his term cannot enforce an oral contract for a new lease [13] or for the purchase of the reversion [14] on the strength of his continuing possession alone, for tenants very commonly hold over as tenants at will or at sufferance merely: " his remaining in possession is a mere continuance of the character, which he all along filled." [15] But holding over may be one of several acts which, though insufficient by themselves, amount to part performance when taken together. An example of this is the holding over by a tenant who also pays an increased rent; for this combination of circumstances points strongly to an agreement to grant a new lease on different terms.[16] Acceptance of such a rent will equally imply the making of the agreement by the landlord.[17]

---

6 Williams, *Statute of Frauds, Section IV*, 256.
7 See the cases cited in Fry S.P. 286, 287, and *Bowers* v. *Cator* (1798) 4 Ves. 91 (lease); *Smallwood* v. *Sheppards* [1895] 2 Q.B. 627 (lease); *Hohler* v. *Aston* [1920] 2 Ch. 420 (assignment).
8 See the cases cited in Fry S.P. 286, 287; *Sharman* v. *Sharman* (1893) 67 L.T. 834; *Kingswood Estate Co. Ltd.* v. *Anderson* [1963] 2 Q.B. 169.
9 *Ungley* v. *Ungley* (1876) 4 Ch.D. 73 at 76.
10 *Delaney* v. *T. P. Smith Ltd.* [1946] K.B. 393; *ante*, p. 547.
11 But an unauthorised entry will not invalidate other good acts of part performance, such as doing repairs or improvements: see *Gregory* v. *Mighell* (1811) 18 Ves. 328 at 333 (acquiescence in purchaser's unauthorised entry and expenditure), and cases cited in n. 18, *infra*.
12 *Hodson* v. *Heuland* [1896] 2 Ch. 428 at 433–435.
13 *Wills* v. *Stradling* (1797) 3 Ves. 378 at 381, 382; *Morphett* v. *Jones* (1818) 1 Swans. 172 at 181; *Re National Savings Bank Association* (1867) 15 W.R. 753.
14 *Savage* v. *Carroll* (1810) 1 Ball & B. 265 at 282; *Lincoln* v. *Wright* (1859) 4 De G. & J. 16 at 20.
15 *Brennan* v. *Bolton* (1842) 2 Dr. & War. 349 at 384, *per* Sugden L.C.
16 *Wills* v. *Stradling* (1797) 3 Ves. 378 at 382; *Miller & Aldworth Ltd.* v. *Sharp* [1899] 1 Ch. 622.
17 *Conner* v. *Fitzgerald* (1883) 11 L.R.Ir. 106 at 113.

(c) *Alterations.* The making of expensive alterations or improve-ments to the property will often be part performance, *e.g.*, when carried out by someone who has no apparent right to possession,[18] or who is a tenant holding over,[19] or who is a tenant under a lease which is so near to expiry as to indicate that the tenant must be relying on an extension of his tenure in order to make the expenditure worth while.[20] Thus where with the vendor's consent the purchaser of an inn gave up his business and by arrangement with the tenant of the inn (whose tenancy had only some two months to run) moved into the inn and made substantial improvements to it, this was held sufficient part performance of the contract of sale. The argument that this was equally consistent with a purchase merely of the tenant's interest was rebutted by the fact that the tenant's interest was then too short to explain the purchaser's expenditure of nearly £200 on improvements. The inference was, therefore, that the purchaser had gone into possession under a con-tract with the vendor. An important fact was that the vendor expressly approved of what was done,[1] so that it could not be said that he was committed to liability on the contract merely by what had taken place between the purchaser and a third party.

No contract can be inferred (or so at least was the law formerly [2]) merely because a party does work on his own land. But if he can prove from the surrounding facts that he did it at some other person's request or instructions, or for some other person's benefit,[3] he then rebuts the explanation that he was acting simply on his own account. One such case [4] concerned the lease of a flat under an oral contract in which one of the terms was that the owner should carry out alterations before the tenant took possession. While this was being done the intending tenant frequently visited the flat, and at her suggestion further alterations were made by the owner. When the intended tenant later repudiated the transaction the owner brought a successful action for specific performance.[5]

---

[18] *Lester* v. *Foxcroft* (1701) Coll.P.C. 108; *Shillibeer* v. *Jarvis* (1856) 8 De G.M. & G. 79; *Reddin* v. *Jarman* (1867) 16 L.T. 449; *Broughton* v. *Snook* [1938] Ch. 505.

[19] *Dowell* v. *Dew* (1842) 1 Y. & C.C.C. 345.

[20] *Broughton* v. *Snook, supra.*

[1] *Ibid.* at pp. 508, 509, 516.

[2] See *Dickinson* v. *Barrow* [1904] 2 Ch. 339 at 343; *Rawlinson* v. *Ames* [1925] Ch. 96 at 114; *Hawkesworth* v. *Turner* (1930) 46 T.L.R. 389 (keeping business together). But *Steadman* v. *Steadman, supra,* may have changed the law.

[3] *McManus* v. *Cooke* (1887) 35 Ch.D. 681 (lowering of party wall so as to allow neighbour more light).

[4] *Rawlinson* v. *Ames* [1925] Ch. 96.

[5] *Dickinson* v. *Barrow* [1904] 2 Ch. 339 shows that such acts would also have been sufficient to support a contract for sale.

7. " Performance." The so-called " performance " need not in fact be performance of an obligation imposed by the contract.[6] Many valid acts of part performance, such as the taking of possession by a purchaser [6a] or the making of alterations by him for his own purposes,[7] are cases where he is exercising his rights under the agreement rather than performing his duties. Likewise it is part performance where a vendor makes alterations at the purchaser's request, even though the contract imposes no obligation to make them and the cost is charged to the purchaser [8]; and also where at the purchaser's request the vendor gives notice to quit to his tenants.[9] Acts of this kind suffice because the primary requirement is for evidence that a contract exists rather than for performance of it as such.[10]

Acts which are merely preparatory will not suffice,[11] *e.g.* if the plaintiff has merely viewed the land,[12] or measured it,[13] or has had the land [14] or the timber on it [15] valued, or has given instructions for a conveyance to be prepared.[16] For then there is no assurance that any binding commitment has been made. Part performance requires " the parties on both sides acting as if the agreement had been carried into execution." [17]

II. EFFECT OF PART PERFORMANCE

1. Evidence of all terms admissible. The effect of a sufficient act of part performance is to enable evidence to be given of all the terms of the contract, including terms to which the acts of part performance have no relation.[18] " The effect of the removal of the barrier set up by the statute . . . is to open the door to parol evidence of the whole agreement." [19] Thus if a landlord agrees to grant a tenant a lease

---

[6] Lord Brougham is incorrect in *Thynne* v. *Earl of Glengall* (1848) 2 H.L.C. 131 at 158.

[6a] *Ante,* p. 568.

[7] *Broughton* v. *Snook* [1938] Ch. 505. Contrast *Nunn* v. *Fabian* (1865) 1 Ch.App. 35 at 40.

[8] *Rawlinson* v. *Ames* [1925] Ch. 96 (see facts stated at p. 102); similarly in *Dowell* v. *Dew* (1842) 1 Y. & C.C.C. 345 (*ante,* p. 569), the works executed were not obligatory. On this point, see Williams, *Statute of Frauds, Section IV,* 260, 261.   [9] *Daniels* v. *Trefusis* [1914] 1 Ch. 788.

[10] *Ante,* p. 563.

[11] Fry S.P. 295; and see *Whitbread* v. *Brockhurst* (1784) 1 Bro.C.C. 404 at 412.

[12] *Clerk* v. *Wright* (1737) 1 Atk. 12 at 13.

[13] *Pembroke* v. *Thorpe* (1740) 3 Swans. 437 at 441–443.

[14] *Cooth* v. *Jackson* (1801) 6 Ves. 12 at 17, 18.

[15] See *Whitbread* v. *Brockhurst* (1784) 1 Bro.C.C. 404.

[16] *Whitchurch* v. *Bevis* (1789) 2 Bro.C.C. 559; *Cooke* v. *Tombs* (1794) 2 Anst. 420. Similarly as to instructions for a lease: `Cole` v. *White* (1767) 1 Bro.C.C. 559.

[17] *Phillips* v. *Edwards* (1864) 33 Beav. 440 at 444, *per* Romilly M.R. (lease executed but not delivered: no part performance).

[18] *Sutherland* v. *Briggs* (1841) 1 Hare 26 at 32: *Brough* v. *Nettleton* [1921] 2 Ch. 25.

[19] *Brough* v. *Nettleton, supra,* at p. 28, *per* P. O. Lawrence J.

with an option to purchase the freehold, part performance by the tenant which is unequivocally referable to the agreement to grant a lease entitles him to demand not merely the term of years but also the option.[20] Similarly if there is a contract to grant a lease of a plot of land and the tenant does an act of part performance which affects only part of the land, he can nevertheless insist on a lease of the whole of the land.[21] But part performance of one contract will not enable a party to enforce another, independent, contract even if it was entered into between the same parties at the same auction.[22]

2. Enforceable only in equity. Nevertheless, a party seeking to enforce a contract merely supported by part performance is not in as good a position as if the contract were evidenced in writing [23]; for part performance makes the contract enforceable only in equity and not at law,[24] and then only if the plaintiff can establish a case for specific performance.[25] A contract properly evidenced in writing is enforceable at law and the plaintiff, on proving his case, is entitled as of right to an award of damages; equity may in addition grant him the discretionary remedy of specific performance.[26] A contract merely supported by part performance, on the other hand, may be enforced by specific performance if the case is a proper one, but that lies in the discretion of the court; and no damages can be awarded if the case is one where the court could not, or would not, grant specific performance.[27]

C. Cases in which neither Writing nor Part Performance is Required

Neither writing nor part performance is required in the following cases.

1. Sale by court: where the sale is by the court [28]; for here, when a purchaser has been found, there is in effect an order by the court that the sale shall be carried through, and this is enforceable as such without further proof of the contract.

2. Statute not pleaded: where the defendant does not plead the absence of writing as a defence.[29] The defendant is not bound to take advantage of the statute, and if he fails to plead it he renounces

[20] *Brough* v. *Nettleton, supra.*   [21] *Sutherland* v. *Briggs, supra.*
[22] *Buckmaster* v. *Harrop* (1807) 13 Ves. 456 at 474.
[23] *Obiter dicta* to the contrary in *O'Herlihy* v. *Hedges, infra,* at p. 130 and *Brough* v. *Nettleton, supra,* at p. 29, should not be relied on.
[24] *O'Herlihy* v. *Hedges* (1803) 1 Sch. & Lef. 123 at 130.
[25] *Ante,* p. 564.
[26] See *ante,* p. 564, *post,* p. 593.   [27] See *ante,* p. 126.
[28] Fry S.P. 269; Dart V. & P. 988; L.P.A., 1925, s. 40 (2).
[29] *Broughton* v. *Snook* [1938] Ch. 505 at 511.

the benefit of it. This now depends upon rules of court,[30] which in substance follow earlier decisions to the effect that a contract admitted by both parties was outside the mischief which the statute was designed to remedy, and that even where the contract was denied, the statute must be specially pleaded if it was to be made a defence.[31]

3. Fraud: where it was due to the fraud of the defendant that the contract was not put into writing.[32] This exception is founded on the same principle as the doctrine of part performance: the court will not allow the section to be used as an engine of fraud.[33] It is no fraud that the defendant merely refused to sign a memorandum after having agreed to do so.[34] It has been said that it would be fraud " if one agreement in writing should be proposed and drawn, and another fraudulently and secretly brought in and executed in lieu of the former." [35] But there is little authority on the scope of this exception.

Sect. 3. Contracts in Practice

A. *Cases where it is Usual to Have a Contract*

Whenever a transaction involves payment of a lump sum it is usual for a contract to be made first and a conveyance some time later. This is because the purchaser wishes to be sure of his bargain and yet to have time to investigate the title fully before paying his money and taking over the liabilities of ownership. Thus where land is being sold by a fee simple owner, or by a tenant who holds under a lease at a ground rent (a rent representing the value of the land without the buildings on it), a formal contract is normally made. If, on the other hand, no capital payment is to be made, there is often no contract, *e.g.*, on the grant or assignment of a lease at a rack rent (a rent representing the full value of the land and buildings). A mortgage, although involving a capital payment, is rarely preceded by a contract; for it is in essence an investment of money rather than a purchase of land, and it will probably be no loss to the mortgagee if the deal falls through before completion. In practice there are many exceptions to these generalisations. In particular, agreements for the grant of leases are often made.

---

30 R.S.C., Ord. 18, rr. 8, 13.
31 Fry S.P. 270; Williams, *Statute of Frauds, Section IV*, 275; *Gunter* v. *Halsey* (1739) Amb. 586; *James* v. *Smith* [1891] 1 Ch. 384.
32 *Viscountess Montacute* v. *Maxwell* (1720) 1 P.Wms. 618 at 620; Fry S.P. 271–276.
33 See *Bannister* v. *Bannister* [1948] 2 All E.R. 133 (*ante*, p. 451) for an analogous case.
34 *Wood* v. *Midgley* (1854) 1 De G.M. & G. 41 at 45, not following earlier cases.
35 *Viscountess Montacute* v. *Maxwell, supra*, at p. 620, *per* Lord Parker L.C.

B. Types of Contract

There are three main types of contract.

1. Open contracts. An open contract means a contract where only certain terms have been expressly agreed, leaving others to be implied by the general law. The simplest possible contract is where only the parties, property and price are specified, *e.g.*, where A agrees to buy Blackacre from B for £1,000.[36] This is the most "open" contract of all and though it is unbusinesslike it is perfectly effective in law. It is implied that the vendor must show a good title within a reasonable time and then execute a proper conveyance to the purchaser against payment of the purchase-money. It is for the purchaser to · prepare the draft conveyance for the vendor to execute, and to pay his own solicitor's costs, but most other expenses fall on the vendor. The effect of such a contract is more fully considered below.[37]

2. Contracts made by correspondence. In the case of "contracts by correspondence,"[38] the Law of Property Act, 1925,[39] provides that the Statutory Form of Conditions of Sale, 1925,[40] made by the Lord Chancellor, shall govern the contract, subject to any modification or contrary intention expressed in the correspondence. The statutory conditions are contained in nine clauses, which provide a time-table for the various steps in the proof of title, fix the date and place for completion, and provide for various other incidental matters. By clause 7 the vendor is given a power to rescind the contract in certain conditions.[41]

3. Formal contracts. There are so many matters to be dealt with between the contract and the conveyance, and conveyancing is so specialised an art, that it is generally inadvisable to sell land by open contract. In the first place it is convenient to fix dates for the various stages of the investigation of title and for completion. Furthermore, it may be necessary to sell the land subject to incumbrances, *e.g.*, leases or rights of way, and the vendor must protect himself either by making specific reservations, or by reserving a general right to rescind the contract if an incumbrance is discovered which he cannot dispose of. In practice various standard forms of

---

[36] See *ante*, p. 543. [37] *Post*, p. 574.

[38] There appears to be no definition of the meaning of " by correspondence." The contract in *Bigg* v. *Boyd Gibbins Ltd.* [1971] 1 W.L.R. 913 seems to have been a contract by correspondence, but without mention of L.P.A., 1925, s. 46, it was said to be an open contract: see at p. 916. See generally (1974) 90 L.Q.R. 55 (A. M. Prichard).

[39] s. 46.

[40] For these, see Wolst. & C, i, 405. [41] See *post*, p. 592.

conditions [42] have been settled and may be purchased from law stationers. These conditions, with such emendations as are desirable to fit the particular case, are very commonly employed, since they avoid the labour of preparing a special set of conditions for every transaction.

These types of contract are not mutually exclusive; the parties may agree upon a few special conditions and leave the rest to the ordinary rules of law, thus creating a contract which is partly formal and partly open.

C. Terms of a Contract

The following are examples of the matters usually dealt with in a formal contract for the sale of land. Most of them are explained in more detail below.

(i) Provision for the payment of a deposit (usually 10 per cent. of the purchase-money) [43] and for the payment of interest on the purchase-money if completion is delayed.

(ii) The length and nature of the title to be shown by the vendor [44] and any special provisions, *e.g.*, as to making no objection to some specified defect in title or flaw in the evidence of title. [45]

(iii) The time within which the abstract of title, [46] requisitions on title and other matters must be dealt with.

(iv) The date and place for completion of the sale.

(v) Power for the vendor to rescind the contract or resell the property in certain circumstances, such as the purchaser's insistence on objections to the title or failure to perform the contract. [47]

D. Effect of a Contract

There is a great deal of law peculiar to contracts for the sale of land, but it cannot be fully expounded without opening the wider subject of conveyancing. The boundary between real property and conveyancing is, however, uncertain [48]; and although conveyancing lies outside the scope of this book, some of its borderland must be explored in order to understand the special rights and liabilities which contracts for the sale of land create. Contracts for sale include contracts for leases, except where a distinction is expressly made.

---

[42] *e.g.*, The Law Society's Conditions of Sale, and the National Conditions of Sale. See H. W. Wilkinson, *The Standard Conditions of Sale* (1972), commenting on both sets of conditions. The minor amendments to the 1970 edition of The Law Society's Conditions of Sale made in the 1973 revision are summarised at (1973) 70 *The Law Society's Gazette* 150†.

[43] As to deposits, see *post*, p. 589.   [44] *Post*, p. 578.

[45] *Post*, p. 582.   [46] *Post*, p. 597.

[47] *Post*, p. 592.   [48] *Ante*, p. 2.

1. The purchaser at once becomes owner in equity

(a) *The purchaser as owner.* If the purchaser is potentially entitled to the equitable remedy of specific performance,[49] he obtains an immediate equitable interest in the property contracted to be sold[50]: for he is, or soon will be, in a position to call for it specifically. It does not matter that the date for completion, when the purchaser may pay his money and take possession, has not yet arrived: equity looks upon that as done which ought to be done, and from the date of contract the purchaser becomes owner in the eyes of equity[51] (he cannot, of course, become owner at law until the land is conveyed to him by deed). This equitable ownership is, as has been seen, a proprietary interest, enforceable against third parties, though it must be registered to protect it against purchasers.[50]

(b) *The vendor as trustee.* As between the parties to it, the contract creates a relationship of trustee and beneficiary: the vendor is said to be trustee for the purchaser, and the purchaser to be beneficial owner.[52] The vendor must therefore manage[53] and preserve the property with the same care as is required of any other trustee, until it is finally handed over to the purchaser. For example, a vendor was held liable when between contract and conveyance a trespasser removed a large quantity of surface soil from the land, for with reasonable vigilance he should have observed and prevented the damage.[54] But, provided that the vendor has acted with due care since the date of the contract, the purchaser cannot complain of the condition of the property which he has agreed to buy, even if (for example) a house turns out to be unfit for habitation.[55]

(c) *Nature of trusteeship.* The vendor's trusteeship is of a peculiar kind,[56] for he himself has a beneficial interest which is valuable though temporary. He may occupy the land and take the rents and profits for himself up to the day fixed for handing over possession; and until the purchase-money is paid he may stay in possession under his common law lien as vendor,[57] which arises at

[49] *Ante,* p. 126; *post,* p. 593.   [50] *Ante,* pp. 132, 147; *post,* p. 1040.
[51] See *Lysaght* v. *Edwards* (1876) 2 Ch.D. 499 at 506–510; Williams V. & P. 59, 545.
[52] *Lysaght* v. *Edwards, supra; Clarke* v. *Ramuz* [1891] 2 Q.B. 456; *Lake* v. *Baylis* [1974] 1 W.L.R. 1073.
[53] See *Earl of Egmont* v. *Smith* (1877) 6 Ch.D. 469; *Abdulla* v. *Shah* [1959] A.C. 124.
[54] *Clarke* v. *Ramuz, supra;* and see *Phillips* v. *Lamdin* [1949] 2 K.B. 33 (removal of door by vendor: order for specific restitution). If the vendor conveys the property to another, he is accountable to the purchaser for the purchase money: *Lake* v. *Baylis, supra.*
[55] *Hoskins* v. *Woodham* [1938] 1 All E.R. 692; *Scott-Polson* v. *Hope* (1958) 14 D.L.R. (2d) 333; *cf. Miller* v. *Cannon Hill Estates Ltd.* [1931] 2 K.B. 113.
[56] See *Rayner* v. *Preston* (1881) 18 Ch.D. 1.
[57] *Phillips* v. *Silvester* (1872) 8 Ch.App 173 at 176; *post,* p. 885.

the date of contract.[58] Ordinarily both these rights will expire on the date of completion, when the conveyance is delivered, the purchase-money is paid, and the purchaser is let into possession. But if the vendor parts with possession of the land before he receives payment, he has an equitable lien on the land which entitles him, if he cannot obtain payment, to ask the court for an order for sale.[59]

The vendor must pay all expenses properly attributable to his period of beneficial enjoyment, *e.g.*, rates and taxes apportioned up to the date of completion, for in respect of these he has not the ordinary trustee's right of indemnity against the beneficiary.[60] Conversely he may take the benefit of statutory compensation falling due to the " owner " before completion.[61] But broadly speaking " as between vendor and purchaser generally the powers of the vendor to act as owner of the property, and (*inter alia*) to change tenants and holdings, are suspended pending completion of the purchase." [62]

(*d*) *The risk passes.* Since in equity the property at once belongs to the purchaser, the risk also passes to him at once. Thus if a house has been sold and is, without fault of the vendor, destroyed by fire before completion, the purchaser must nevertheless pay the full purchase-money and take the land as it is.[63] It is important for a purchaser of buildings to insure at once in his own name, since he undertakes the risk of accidents before he takes the property itself. He cannot take the benefit of any insurance maintained by the vendor in the vendor's name alone [64]; for insurance is normally only a personal indemnity against loss, and since the vendor is entitled to the whole purchase-money and so loses nothing he can recover nothing under his policy.[65] If the vendor does in fact obtain payment of the insurance money, the insurers can recover it.[66] Even

---

[58] *Re Birmingham* [1959] Ch. 523.
[59] *Mackreth* v. *Symmons* (1808) 15 Ves. 329; Wh. & T. ii, 848; Snell, *Equity*, 445; *post*, p. 886. This is an equitable interest in land (*ante*, p. 119), registrable as a general equitable charge (*post*, p. 1040).
[60] *Re Watford Corporation and Ware's Contract* [1943] Ch. 82; Williams V. & P. 560.
[61] *Re . Hamilton-Snowball's Conveyance* [1959] Ch. 308 (compensation on derequisition).
[62] *Raffety* v. *Schofield* [1897] 1 Ch. 937 at 945, *per* Romer J.
[63] *Paine* v. *Meller* (1801) 6 Ves. 349; *Rayner* v. *Preston* (1881) 18 Ch.D. 1. The same principle applies if between contract and completion the land is made the subject of a compulsory purchase order and notice to treat: there is no frustration, and the purchaser must take the land subject to the compulsory purchase: *Hillingdon Estates Co.* v. *Stonefield Estates* [1952] Ch. 627; *post*, p. 585.
[64] *Rayner* v. *Preston, supra.* 　　　　　　　[65] See next following note.
[66] *Castellain* v. *Preston* (1883) 11 Q.B.D. 380. Yet if the contract of insurance is framed not as an indemnity against loss but as a guarantee against fire, the vendor will be entitled to the insurance money: *Collingridge* v. *Royal Exchange Assurance Corpn.* (1877) 3 Q.B.D. 173. But the purchaser may then require it to be laid out in reinstating the property under the Fires Prevention (Metropolis) Act, 1774, s. 83; or he may claim the money itself under L.P.A., 1925, s. 47, discussed below.

if they do not, equity does not require the vendor to pay the money to the purchaser, for his qualified trusteeship extends only to the land, and not to the proceeds of a personal contract of insurance.[67]

(e) *Insurance by purchaser.* It is therefore essential for the purchaser, if he wishes to insure buildings, to take out insurance on his own account. A common practice is to arrange, with the consent of the insurers, for the vendor's existing insurance to be extended to cover the purchaser. Before 1926 it was usual to stipulate that this should be done and that the purchaser should pay the premium as from the date of the contract.[68] It is now provided by section 47 of the Law of Property Act, 1925, that any insurance money which becomes payable under the vendor's policy in respect of damage to the property after the date of the contract shall be paid by the vendor to the purchaser at completion, subject to (a) the terms of the contract, (b) any requisite consents of the insurers, and (c) the payment by the purchaser of his share of the premium. Where, therefore, the insurers consent to include the purchaser in the insurance, it is now unnecessary to make further terms about the insurance money or premium. Where the insurance is left in the vendor's name only, section 47 will not normally apply at all; for if the vendor can prove no personal loss no insurance money will ever become payable under the policy.

(f) *Conversion.* Another consequence of the change in beneficial ownership brought about by the contract is that the equitable doctrine of conversion applies.[69] If, for example, A contracts to sell land to B and then dies leaving all his land to X and all his other property to Y, Y will be entitled to the purchase-money when the contract is duly completed by the executors; for A's beneficial interest consisted of money due from B rather than of land.

(g) *Specific enforceability.* All these consequences—the passing of the beneficial interest and risk, and conversion—flow from the fact that the contract is specifically enforceable. If it is not,[70] they are all excluded. For example, there might be a flaw in the vendor's title, so that the purchaser refuses to complete. In that case the vendor would not be liable for negligent damage to the property, he could recover any insurance money payable for accidental damage, and the land would pass under a devise of real property.[71]

[67] *Rayner* v. *Preston* (1881) 18 Ch.D. 1.
[68] Williams V. & P. 88, 89.
[69] See ante, p. 286; Snell, *Equity*, 473; cf. *Lysaght* v. *Edwards* (1876) 2 Ch.D. 499.
[70] See post, p. 593.
[71] Cf. *Broome* v. *Monck* (1805) 10 Ves. 597; *Re Thomas* (1886) 34 Ch.D. 166.

It is only when the title has been proved or accepted that it becomes clear that the parties have from the beginning been in the position of trustee and beneficiary, and can enforce their rights on that footing.[72]

(h) *Options.* An option to purchase seems to operate as an offer, open to acceptance in accordance with the terms of the option, rather than as a conditional contract of sale.[73] Nevertheless, it creates an immediate interest in the land, for by granting it the grantor has empowered the grantee to bring into being a binding contract of sale.[74] A mere right of pre-emption (*i.e.*, a right of " first refusal ") differs in requiring the owner's decision to sell as well as the purchaser's decision to purchase.[75] The effect of such a right is uncertain. There are decisions that it does not create an interest in land,[76] and a decision that it can do so,[77] supported by assumptions in statutes that it can.[78] It may also be capable of binding the land as a restrictive covenant, if it fulfils the necessary conditions.[79]

2. The vendor must show a good title

(a) *Proof of title.* Under the traditional system (*i.e.*, if the title is not registered [79a]) proof of title is made by exhibiting to the purchaser the records of past transactions in the land, *e.g.*, sales, mortgages and grants of probate, and by proving other relevant events such as deaths. This procedure has two main purposes: to persuade the purchaser that the vendor owns the land; and to give the purchaser his opportunity to inquire about the existence of equitable interests by which, if he made no inquiries, he would be bound. For the first purpose the vendor's title deeds are merely evidence; it is possible that owing to fraud, forgery or mistake he is not really the true owner, so that the purchaser will not obtain a

---

[72] See *Rayner* v. *Preston* (1881) 18 Ch.D. 1 at 13; *Ridout* v. *Fowler* [1904] 1 Ch. 658. *Lysaght* v. *Edwards* (1876) 2 Ch.D. 499 at 507 should be read in this sense.
[73] *Stromdale & Ball Ltd.* v. *Burden* [1952] Ch. 223 at 235; (1958) 74 L.Q.R. 242 (W. J. Mowbray).
[74] See *L. & S. W. Ry.* v. *Gomm* (1882) 20 Ch.D. 562 at 581; *Griffith* v. *Pelton* [1958] Ch. 205 at 225; *Webb* v. *Pollmount Ltd.* [1966] Ch. 584 at 597; *McCarthy & Stone Ltd.* v. *Julian S. Hodge & Co. Ltd.* [1971] 1 W.L.R. 1547; *Mountford* v. *Scott* [1975] 2 W.L.R. 114 (consideration nominal: specific performance granted); and see *post*, pp. 1040, 1041, for options as estate contracts requiring registration.
[75] See *Brown* v. *Gould* [1972] Ch. 53 at 58.
[76] *Manchester Ship Canal Co.* v. *Manchester Racecourse Co.* [1901] 2 Ch. 37 (Court of Appeal, reversing Farwell J. on this point, but giving no reasons); *Murray* v. *Two Strokes Ltd.* [1973] 1 W.L.R. 823.
[77] *Birmingham Canal Co.* v. *Cartwright* (1879) 11 Ch.D. 421, not disapproved on this point in *L. & S. W. Ry.* v. *Gomm, supra.* See (1973) 89 L.Q.R. 462 (M. J. Albery). See generally (1974) 38 Conv.(N.S.) 8 (A. M. Prichard).
[78] L.C.A. 1972, s. 2 (4), Class C (iv), includes it in the definition of " estate contract." See also L.P.A., 1925, s. 186; Perpetuities and Accumulations Act 1964 s. 9 (2).
[79] It may involve an implied negative contract not to part with the land so as to defeat the right of pre-emption: *Gardner* v. *Coutts & Co.* [1968] 1 W.L.R. 173.
[79a] For registered titles, see *post*, p. 1054.

good title.[80] For the second purpose the proof of title is conclusive: if the purchaser has made all reasonable inquiries and found nothing, he is safe from all equitable interests except such as are registered.[81]

For the purpose of proving title the parties may agree on as much, or as little, disclosure of documents as they wish. For the purpose of searching for equities the purchaser is required to search back for a certain period. If he fails to do so, he has constructive notice of anything he would have discovered by doing so.[82] Until 1970, when the length of title was reduced (as mentioned below), it was not uncommon for purchasers to agree to accept a short title and take the risk of equities.

(b) *Fifteen years' title*. If there is no agreement to the contrary, and the contract was made after 1969, the period is now at least fifteen years under the Law of Property Act 1969.[83] Previously it was at least thirty years under the Law of Property Act, 1925.[84] Before that it was at least forty years under the Vendor and Purchaser Act, 1874,[85] and before that it was at least sixty years under the general practice of conveyancers which the law adopted.[1] There are special rules in the case of leases, which are explained elsewhere.[2]

The period is " at least " fifteen years because the title must start from a document known as a good root of title, and it will only be by chance that such a document among the title deeds will be exactly fifteen years old; normally the title will have to start from a date more than fifteen years ago, since only a document at least fifteen years old can be used for the purpose.[3]

The progressive shortening of the period has proved possible because complications are in practice rare and the work saved is great. But the latest and most drastic reduction to fifteen years has been accompanied by a scheme, explained later, for compensating

---

[80] For relative titles and " true owners," see *post*, pp. 1006, 1009.
[81] See *ante*, pp. 123, 144, 145.
[82] *Ante*, p. 121.
[83] s. 23.
[84] s. 44 (1). But see *Bolton* v. *London School Board* (1878) 7 Ch.D. 766 and *Re Wallis and Grout's Contract* [1906] 2 Ch. 210. These cases concerned the provision of the Vendor and Purchaser Act, 1874, s. 2 (now replaced by L.P.A., 1925, s. 45 (6)), that recitals, descriptions and statements of fact contained in instruments twenty years old should be deemed to be correct in default of proof to the contrary. In the former case it was held that a deed reciting seisin in fee simple was therefore a good root of title, if at least twenty years old. But the later decision disapproved the conclusion that the full statutory period for title was thus cut down, and in practice the earlier decision is usually regarded as wrong.
[85] s. 2.
[1] Williams V. & P. 114. The minimum period of 60 years may have been adopted since that was the longest of the periods of limitation which applied to the real actions: *post*, p. 1010. But in the opinion of Mr. Brodie (one of the Real Property Commissioners) the analogy was rather with the length of human life: see Hayes, i, 566.
[2] *Post*, p. 704.
[3] *Cf. ante*, p. 123.

purchasers affected by registered land charges which they could not discover from the title shown.[4] It has proved worth while to take considerable risks for the sake of economy in conveyancing.[5]

(c) *Good root of title.* A good root of title is a document which describes the land sufficiently to identify it, which shows a disposition of the whole legal and equitable interest contracted to be sold, and which contains nothing to throw any doubt on the title.[6] Examples of documents which commonly serve as roots of title are—

> a conveyance on sale;
> a legal mortgage[7];
> a specific devise (*i.e.*, a will mentioning the property specifically) which took effect before 1926[8];
> an assent by a personal representative made after 1925 (after 1925 devises of land take effect not by force of the will but by force of the personal representatives' assent or conveyance,[9] which should describe the property[10]); and
> a voluntary conveyance.[11]

Examples of documents which will not serve as roots of title on a sale of the fee simple are—

> a will taking effect after 1925[12];
> a lease;
> an equitable mortgage;
> a disentailing assurance executed after 1925.[13]

A squatter's title, *i.e.*, a title obtained by adverse possession for twelve years or more,[14] must be proved from a good root of title, by showing the full title of the person from whom the squatter took

---

[4] L.P.A., 1969, s. 25; *post*, p. 1046.
[5] Reduction to 20 years was recommended as long ago as 1911 by the Royal Commission on Land Transfer, Cd. 5483, para. 59.
[6] Williams V. & P. 124.
[7] Since 1925 a mortgage may no longer be made by a conveyance in fee simple (*post*, p. 892) and it is therefore questionable whether a mortgage made after 1925 is a good root of title. It is suggested that it may be so if it recites the mortgagor's ownership in fee simple: Williams V. & P. 124; but a mere recital will not ordinarily serve in place of a disposition: see n. 84, *supra*.
[8] Strictly speaking since 1897 a will has been only an equitable disposition (*ante*, pp. 536, 538); but the will and the assent of the personal representatives together founded a legal title. Dart V. & P. 295 denies that a specific devise was a good root of title before 1926, but no reason is given.
[9] *Ante*, p. 538. An assent under seal by a person with no power to make an assent takes effect as a conveyance: *Re Stirrup's Contract* [1961] 1 W.L.R. 449.
[10] See examples given in Prideaux, Vol. iii, 874 *et seq*.
[11] As to this, see Williams V. & P. 127.
[12] The assent is now the effective disposition of the legal estate: *ante*, p. 538.
[13] Since 1925 a disentailing assurance is only an equitable disposition. Previously the rule was that the purchaser was entitled to see the instrument creating the entail; but if that was lost, he could be compelled to take the disentailing assurance as the root of title: Preston, *Abstracts*, i, 6, 7; Sugden V. & P. 366.
[14] See *post*, p. 1003.

the land and then proving the adverse possession.[15] This will often be difficult, and the vendor will generally try to stipulate that the purchaser shall accept a title beginning with the adverse possession.

(*d*) *Deduction of title.* Having established a good root of title of the necessary age, the vendor must then prove all the later steps in the title which lead it down to himself. If he personally has held the land for more than fifteen years there may be nothing more to prove. But more probably there will have been intervening transfers on sale, death or otherwise, which are necessary links in deducing the title to be proved. If the proof is defective at any point, or if the title shown appears to be bad or doubtful,[16] the purchaser is entitled to rescind the contract on the ground that the vendor is unable to perform it.

(*e*) *Defects anterior to the root of title.* The purchaser may not make any inquiry or objection about matters anterior to the root of title.[17] There are certain exceptions to this rule,[18] one being any contrary provision in the contract.[19] But in general the purchaser must be content with a title starting with a good root in accordance with the contract. If he discovers (for example, from an accidental disclosure of older documents) that the earlier title is technically defective, so that it is questionable whether the vendor is really owner at all, he must nevertheless take the property with the title as it stands.[1] But if he can prove that the title is patently indefensible, so that if he took the property he would at once be liable to ejection by the true owner, then he may rescind [2]; for he has the right not only to have evidence of a good title shown to him over a certain period but to be satisfied that the property is effectively conveyed to him by the vendor at completion.[3] Similarly he may object to an incumbrance which, although created before the date of the root of title, still affects the existing title.[4]

---

[15] *Re Atkinson and Horsell's Contract* [1912] 2 Ch. 1 ; Williams V. & P. 122.

[16] *e.g.*, *Re Handman and Wilcox's Contract* [1902] 1 Ch. 599 (title dependent upon purchase without notice, insufficiently proved).

[17] L.P.A., 1925, s. 45 (1), replacing C.A., 1881, s. 3 (3), which confirmed earlier practice.

[18] *Ibid.*, proviso. This entitles the purchaser to see (i) any power of attorney under which an abstracted document is executed, (ii) any document creating a subsisting incumbrance, (iii) any document creating any limitation or trust by reference to which a disposition is made by a document appearing in the abstract. [19] L.P.A., 1925, s. 45 (10), proviso.

[1] See *Re Scott and Alvarez' Contract (No. 1)* [1895] 1 Ch. 596, awarding specific performance to vendor and removing (it is thought) the doubt expressed in *Re National Provincial Bank and Marsh* [1895] 1 Ch. 190 at 192. Since specific performance will be awarded, L.P.A., 1925, s. 45 (11) does not apply.

[2] *Re Scott and Alvarez' Contract (No. 2)* [1895] 2 Ch. 603, refusing specific performance when fresh evidence turned doubt into certainty. L.P.A., 1925, s. 45 (11) therefore applies and frees the purchaser from s. 45 (1).

[3] Williams V. & P. 233.   [4] See *post*, p. 583.

Merely raising a doubt upon the earlier title does not disprove the vendor's prima facie ability to convey, for it is more than likely that so old a blot upon the title will have been cured by the law of limitation of actions [5] or otherwise. A mere conveyancer's objection (*e.g.*, that the wrong person appears to have taken under a will), although it may be insisted upon in the title agreed to be shown, cannot be made good against the title prior to the root. " There are bad titles and bad titles; bad titles which are good holding titles, although they may be open to objections which are not serious, are bad titles in a conveyancer's point of view, but good in a business man's point of view." [6]

(*f*) *Agreement not to investigate.* If the purchaser expressly agrees not to question the earlier title, or some intermediate step in the title to be shown under the contract, his position is less favourable than that just described: for he is liable at law on the contract even though it turns out that the vendor cannot give him any title at all owing to the part of the title which he has agreed not to question. [7] In that case the purchaser's only consolation is that specific performance will not be ordered so as to compel him to take the property if he would then be liable to instant ejection. [8] Equity, it is said, will compel no one to buy a law-suit. [9]

The purchaser, however, is the party who is in breach of the contract at law, [10] for the express condition, at least if sufficiently stringently framed, [11] amounts to an agreement that he will take the whole risk of the title turning out to be bad on account of the matters mentioned. [12] The vendor may therefore keep any deposit paid to him by the purchaser. [13] Indeed there appears to be no reason why the vendor should not bring an action for damages for loss of the sale. The worse his title, the greater the damages will be, since the greater will be the difference between the agreed price and the price which the vendor could get on resale after discovery of the defect in his title [14]; the purchaser, by imprudently agreeing to accept the title unproved, has in effect become the vendor's insurer.

[5] *Post*, p. 1003.
[6] *Re Scott and Alvarez' Contract (No. 2)* [1895] 2 Ch. 603 at 613, *per* Lindley L.J.
[7] The difference between express and implied terms arises because an express term normally contains no provision corresponding to L.P.A., 1925, s. 45 (11).
[8] *Re Scott and Alvarez' Contract (No. 2)* [1895] 2 Ch. 603.
[9] Fry S.P. 416 and cases there cited; *Re Nichols' & Von Joel's Contract* [1910] 1 Ch. 43 at 46; *Hope* v. *Walter* [1900] 1 Ch. 257 (liability to prosecution).
[10] See *Re Scott and Alvarez' Contract (No. 2)* [1895] 2 Ch. 603 at 612.
[11] *Jones* v. *Clifford* (1876) 3 Ch.D 779. The condition must prohibit the purchaser from raising objections, and not merely exempt the vendor from answering them.
[12] *Cf. Corrall* v. *Cattell* (1839) 4 M. & W. 734.
[13] *Re Scott and Alvarez' Contract (No. 2)* [1895] 2 Ch. 603. As to deposits, see *post*, p. 589.
[14] See Williams V. & P. 1015 for measure of damages.

(g) *Freedom from incumbrances.* A good title means a title free from incumbrances. The term " incumbrances " covers all subsisting third party rights such as leases,[15] rentcharges, mortgages, easements and restrictive covenants. It also includes statutory liabilities, if they are not merely potential [16] or imposed on all property generally.[17] But a statutory liability which first attaches to the property after the date of the contract must be borne by the purchaser [18] (for the risk is on him), except to the extent that it is an outgoing which the vendor must meet as attributable to the period of his own occupation,[19] and except where it prevents the vendor from giving vacant possession on completion.[20]

The purchaser may refuse to complete if any other incumbrance comes to light which he has not agreed to accept, and which will bind him if he takes the land.[21] It makes no difference that the incumbrance was created by a document older than the root of title, for although the purchaser may not object to the earlier title as such he may object to the incumbrance itself as a defect which continues throughout the later title as well.[22]

(h) *Waiver.* A purchaser under an open contract is held to have waived his right to object to an incumbrance if (i) he knew that it was irremovable, and (ii) despite this, he contracted to purchase the property or took some other step inconsistent with his right to rescind the contract, such as entering into possession.[23] An incumbrance is irremovable if the vendor cannot compel the incumbrancer to give it up, *e.g.,* a restrictive covenant or an easement; examples of removable incumbrances are mortgages or death duty charges, which may be paid off at any time.

15 Though see *District Bank Ltd.* v. *Webb* [1958] 1 W.L.R. 148. The meaning of " incumbrance " can vary with the circumstances.
16 *Re Allen and Driscoll's Contract* [1904] 2 Ch. 226 (street paving); *Re Forsey and Hollebone's Contract* [1927] 2 Ch. 379 (resolution by local authority to prepare a town planning scheme, held no incumbrance); *Re Winslow Hall Estates Co. and United Glass Bottle Manufacturers Ltd.'s Contract* [1941] Ch. 503 (preliminary notice of future requisition held no incumbrance); and see *Manning* v. *Turner* [1957] 1 W.L.R. 91 (potential liability to estate duty: rescission held valid).
17 For example, local rates: Williams V. & P. 214.
18 *Re Farrer and Gilbert's Contract* [1914] 1 Ch. 125; *Hillingdon Estates Co.* v. *Stonefield Estates Ltd.* [1952] Ch. 627.
19 *Ante*, p. 575.   20 *Post*, p. 585.
21 Incumbrances created (otherwise than by statute) between contract and completion may be objected to even though the purchaser could have protected himself against them by registering his estate contract, for he has no duty to register: *post*, p. 1049.
22 *Nottingham Patent Brick and Tile Co.* v. *Butler* (1885) 15 Q.B.D. 261; (1886) 16 Q.B.D. 778; *Re Cox and Neve's Contract* [1891] 2 Ch. 109; *Re Nisbet and Potts' Contract* [1906] 1 Ch. 386.
23 *Re Gloag and Miller's Contract* (1883) 23 Ch.D. 320 at 327 (where a distinction is drawn); *Ellis* v. *Rogers* (1888) 29 Ch.D. 661; *McGrory* v. *Alderdale Estates Co.* [1918] A.C. 503. As to the question, there left unresolved, whether the right to a good title is founded on contract or on the general law, see Williams V. & P. 35, n. (e).

(i) *Land charges.* A serious stumbling-block was created in 1927 by a decision that an irremovable land charge (*e.g.,* a restrictive covenant created since 1925), unknown to the purchaser but already registered at the time of the contract, had to be accepted under the above doctrine, since registration is " deemed to constitute actual notice to all persons for all purposes." [24] This violated conveyancing principles, since the proper time for searching the register is between contract and completion [25]; and in any case the purchaser could not usually make a full search before contract since he would not then know the names of previous owners on the title. Nor did the decision appear to be right in law, since willingness to waive objection to the incumbrance could hardly be imputed to a purchaser who in fact had no knowledge of it at all. The Law of Property Act 1969 [26] has now removed the difficulty for contracts made after 1969. Any question of the purchaser's knowledge of a registered land charge is to be determined by reference to his actual knowledge [27] and without regard to the statutory " deemed " notice; and furthermore any stipulation to the contrary, or which restricts the purchaser's remedies in respect of such a charge, is void.

(j) *Express terms.* It is only where the contract is open as to the title that waiver can be implied from the making of the contract. If the vendor expressly contracts to show, for example, " a valid title " [28] or " a good marketable title," [29] he must carry out his promise and show a title entirely free from incumbrances. Even if the purchaser knows that there are incumbrances of an irremovable kind, nevertheless he is entitled to assume that the vendor will find some means of removing them, *e.g.,* by obtaining releases from the incumbrancers. But if, having discovered irremovable incumbrances, he takes some step indicating a desire to proceed (such as going into possession of the property) without reserving his rights as to the title, this may amount to a waiver even of an express promise of a clear title.[30] The essence of the matter is that no waiver can be implied merely from the purchaser's entering into the contract if that is inconsistent with the express terms of the contract.[31]

[24] *Re Forsey and Hollebone's Contract* [1927] 2 Ch. 379 (Eve J.). For notice by registration see *post*, p. 1044.
[25] See *Re White and Smith's Contract* [1896] 1 Ch. 637.
[26] s. 24, not applying to local land charges (*post*, p. 1053) or to land with registered title (*post*, pp. 1057, 1058). This reform was recommended by the Committee on Land Charges (1956) Cmd. 9825, paras. 30–33. For a fuller discussion, see [1954] C.L.J. 89 (H.W.R.W.); and contrast *Coles* v. *White City (Manchester) Greyhound Association Ltd.* (1928) 45 T.L.R. 125, 230, noted *post*, p. 1044, n. 4.
[27] Or that of his counsel, solicitor or other agent : s. 24 (4).
[28] *Re Gloag and Miller's Contract* (1883) 23 Ch.D. 320.
[29] *Cato* v. *Thompson* (1882) 9 Q.B.D. 616.
[30] *Re Gloag and Miller's Contract, supra.*
[31] *Re Gloag and Miller's Contract, supra,* at p. 327.

Here again, it was held that the rule was different where the incumbrance was registered, and that even a sale "free from incumbrances" was made subject to incumbrances deemed to be known to the purchaser because of registration prior to the contract.[32] By the Law of Property Act 1969 [33] this further pitfall for purchasers was only removed as regards contracts made after 1969, as explained above.

In practice, the traps which existed before 1970 caused little inconvenience. Purchasers usually make such searches as they can before contract, *e.g.*, as to local land charges [34]; and the parties may contract on terms which allow the purchaser to rescind if he did not have written notice of certain matters such as land charges and the service of notices adversely affecting the land.[35]

3. The vendor must give vacant possession on completion. This rule is, of course, subject to any agreement to the contrary. Its importance is that it requires the vendor to make the property available at the due date of completion; to evict any tenants or other occupiers; to remove his own chattels from it [36]; and to bear the risk of any event, even after the contract, which makes it impossible for him to give vacant possession at the proper time. Thus if between contract and conveyance the property is requisitioned and the vendor put out of possession, the purchaser may rescind and recover his deposit.[37] But a compulsory purchase order, if possession has not yet been taken under it, does not prevent the vendor from giving vacant possession, and the purchaser must therefore complete.[38] This clear-cut obligation of the vendor avoids the problem of frustration in various unexpected situations arising between contract and conveyance.[39]

4. Stipulations as to time. At common law, time was " of the essence of the contract." If either party was late in performance,

---

[32] *Re Forsey and Hollebone's Contract* [1927] 2 Ch. 379 at 387. See [1954] C.L.J. 89, 102, 103 (H.W.R.W.); and see Emmet, 7.

[33] s. 24; *ante*, p. 584.

[34] See *post*, p. 1053.

[35] See The Law Society's Conditions of Sale : the wide provisions of the 1953 edition, cll. 20, 21, appear in cl. 2 of the 1970 and 1973 editions in a greatly curtailed form, especially in omitting land charges.

[36] *Cumberland Consolidated Holdings Ltd.* v. *Ireland* [1946] K.B. 264 (large quantities of rubbish left on the premises).

[37] See *Cook* v. *Taylor* [1942] Ch. 349 : *James Macara Ltd.* v. *Barclay* [1945] K.B. 148. Contrast *Re Winslow Hall Estate Co. and United Glass Bottle Manufacturers Ltd.'s Contract* [1941] Ch. 503 (*ante*, p. 583), where the requisition had not yet taken effect.

[38] *Hillingdon Estates Co.* v. *Stonefield Estates Ltd.* [1952] Ch. 627.

[39] Contrast leases, *post*, p. 673. There is some discussion of frustration in the *Hillingdon* case, *supra*.

he was in breach of the contract and could not enforce it. But equity regarded time less strictly, and would grant specific performance to a party who was out of time, provided that was not inequitable.[40] Now, by the Law of Property Act, 1925,[41] the equitable doctrine applies equally to common law remedies: " stipulations in a contract, as to time or otherwise, which according to the rules of equity are not deemed to be or to have become of the essence of the contract, are also construed and have effect at law in accordance with the same rules." But time is of the essence, even in equity—

(i) where the contract expressly says so;

(ii) where the nature of the contract requires it, *e.g.,* on the sale of a wasting asset such as a short leasehold,[42] or of a business such as a public-house sold as a going concern,[43] or of a house required for immediate occupation[44]: but often in such cases the terms of the standard conditions of sale will negative the inference that time is of the essence[45];

(iii) where, after one party has delayed unreasonably, the other gives him notice requiring performance at a reasonable future date[46]; and

(iv) where a contract is made conditional upon some act being done by a fixed date, or within a reasonable time.[47]

In any case, whether time is of the essence or not, a party who is actually injured by breach of a time stipulation can recover damages. Thus where the purchaser needed the property for professional purposes, and her practice was injured by the vendor's delay in completion, she recovered damages for this and other expenses.[48]

5. Discharge of the contract. The principal obligations of both parties are discharged at completion, *i.e.,* when the title has been accepted, the conveyance executed, and delivered, and the purchase-

---

[40] See, generally, Fry S.P. 500 *et seq.*; Wh. & T. ii, 455 *et seq.*
[41] s. 41; *cf.* J.A., 1873, s. 25 (7).
[42] See *Hudson* v. *Temple* (1860) 29 Beav. 536.
[43] *Lock* v. *Bell* [1931] 1 Ch. 35. In *Coslake* v. *Till* (1826) 1 Russ. 376 a delay of one day was held a breach.
[44] *Tilley* v. *Thomas* (1867) 3 Ch.App. 61 at 67. Contrast *Smith* v. *Hamilton* [1951] Ch. 174 at 179, not citing this or other authorities to the same effect.
[45] See (1967) 86 L.N. at 192, 193.
[46] *Stickney* v. *Keeble* [1915] A.C. 386; *Finkielkraut* v. *Monahan* [1949] 2 All E.R. 234; *Smith* v. *Hamilton* [1951] Ch. 174; *Re Barr's Contract* [1956] 1 W.L.R. 918. Such a notice binds both parties: *Quadrangle Development and Construction Co. Ltd.* v. *Jenner* [1974] 1 W.L.R. 68. But where it is plain that the party in default is not intending to proceed, no notice need be given: *Re Stone and Saville's Contract* [1963] 1 W.L.R. 163.
[47] *Aberfoyle Plantations Ltd.* v. *Cheng* [1960] A.C. 115.
[48] *Phillips* v. *Lamdin* [1949] 2 K.B. 33.

money paid. From then onwards, as regards any defect of title which may appear, the purchaser must rely on the limited covenants for title which are given by the conveyance. These are explained below,[49] and it need only be noted here that the purchaser is entitled to the usual covenants for title except in so far as the vendor's obligation is qualified by special terms in the contract.

But completion does not bring about an automatic discharge of the whole contract if there are terms which are not intended to be so discharged. For example, if the contract gives a warranty of quality, or promises compensation for errors of description, or if the purchaser gives undertakings as to the use of the land, or indemnities against future liabilities,[50] all these can be enforced after completion,[51] though in the last case there would more usually be a covenant by the purchaser in the conveyance, which would discharge the initial contractual obligation. There are in fact many situations in which the contract remains of importance, as where it creates specific equitable rights which are only vaguely described in the conveyance.[52]

6. Certain terms are void. By the Law of Property Act, 1925,[53] certain terms are made void. This is partly to protect purchasers from having bad titles foisted upon them, and partly to compel the use of the new conveyancing machinery. Examples of void terms of the former class are stipulations that the purchaser shall not employ his own solicitor,[54] or that he shall accept a title which does not give him the legal estate.[55] Examples of terms which are void for purely technical reasons are terms requiring title to be made with the concurrence of the owner of an interest which could be overreached,[56] or requiring the purchaser to pay the costs of obtaining a vesting order or appointment of trustees.[57]

7. Remedies. One or more of the following remedies will be available to a vendor or purchaser in case of dispute about the effect of the contract.

(a) *Action for damages.* This is the primary remedy under the law of contract, but perhaps the remedy least often sought as

---

[49] *Post*, p. 603.
[50] See, *e.g.*, *Eagon* v. *Dent* [1965] 3 All E R. 334.
[51] Williams V. & P. 981, 982; *Hancock* v. *B. W. Brazier (Anerley) Ltd.* [1966] 1 W.L.R. 1317; and see *Hissett* v. *Reading Roofing Co. Ltd.* [1969] 1 W.L.R. 1757.
[52] *White* v. *Taylor (No. 2)* [1969] 1 Ch. 150.
[53] L.P.A., 1925, ss. 42, 48.
[54] s. 48 (1).
[55] s. 42 (3).
[56] s. 42 (1). For examples, see *ante*, pp. 319, 379; and for overreaching see *ante*, p. 371.
[57] s. 42 (2).

between vendor and purchaser of land. The measure of damages is the loss to the plaintiff from the non-performance of the contract. A vendor, for example, can recover the difference between the price agreed to be paid and the net value of the property left on his hands.[58] A purchaser can claim for the loss of a bargain, *i.e.*, the amount by which the net value of the property when conveyed to him at the due date would have exceeded the purchase price [59]; but where the property has risen in value damages awarded in substitution for specific performance will, in order to be a true substitute, be calculated as at the date of the hearing.[60] If there is no such loss, he can recover his costs, *e.g.*, for investigation of title.

There is one exceptional rule: a vendor who fails to show a good title because of some irremovable defect, which is not due to his own fault, is not liable to pay damages for the purchaser's loss of his bargain.[61] This rule is said to be founded on " the peculiar difficulty of making a title to land in England." [62] The exception is a wide one, and applies even where a good title was expressly promised but the vendor knew he had not got one, provided that he was not actually fraudulent. Thus if leasehold property is agreed to be sold, but the lease is not assignable without the lessor's consent and that consent is refused, the purchaser cannot recover more than his costs.[63] Where, on the other hand, the sale is frustrated because, after contract, the vendor's wife registers her statutory rights of occupation,[64] it is held that the exception does not apply, so that the purchaser can recover full damages.[65]

The vendor may be liable in damages for misrepresentation, whether fraudulent or innocent, unless he can show that he had reasonable grounds to believe and did believe up to the time of the contract, that the facts represented were true.[66]

(b) Rescission

(1) RIGHT TO RESCIND. If either party breaks a term of the

---

[58] *Noble* v. *Edwards* (1877) 5 Ch.D. 378.

[59] Together with damages in respect of any special circumstances known to the vendor: *Cottrill* v. *Steyning and Littlehampton B.S.* [1966] 1 W.L.R. 753.

[60] *Wroth* v. *Tyler* [1974] Ch. 30; and see *Grant* v. *Dawkins* [1973] 1 W.L.R. 1406. Both decisions were made under the jurisdiction conferred by the Chancery Amendment Act, 1858 (*ante*, p. 126), which is wider than the jurisdiction at common law.

[61] *Flureau* v. *Thornhill* (1776) 2 W.Bl. 1078; *Bain* v. *Fothergill* (1874) L.R. 7 H.L. 158.

[62] *Elliott* v. *Pierson* [1948] 1 All E.R. 939 at 942, *per* Harman J.

[63] *Bain* v. *Fothergill* (1874) L.R. 7 H.L. 158; *aliter* if the vendor dissuades the lessor from consenting (*Day* v. *Singleton* [1899] 2 Ch. 320) or if the defect is removable, *e.g.*, a mortgage: *Re Daniel* [1917] 2 Ch. 405; *cf. Thomas* v. *Kensington* [1942] 2 K.B. 181; *J. W. Cafés Ltd.* v. *Brownlow Trust Ltd.* [1950] 1 All E.R. 894 (the exception applies as between landlord and tenant).

[64] For these rights, see *post*, p. 785.

[65] *Wroth* v. *Tyler, supra.*

[66] Misrepresentation Act 1967, s. 2 (1).

contract which is a condition precedent to the liability of the other (for example, if the vendor does not prove a good title or if the purchaser refuses to pay the purchase-money), the other party may, as an alternative to suing for damages,[67] rescind the contract.[68] Rescission means cancelling the contract and restoring the parties to their original position, whereas an action for damages means giving effect to the contract so far as is possible by a money payment. At common law rescission effected a discharge of the contract, and any money paid under it (*e.g.*, a part payment) could be recovered by an action in quasi-contract.[69] But an action to enforce rescission by a judgment could be brought only in equity; for judgments merely declaratory of the parties' rights were not available until 1850,[70] and the only relief which could be asked for in earlier times was an injunction to prevent the defendant enforcing the contract or an order that it should be delivered up to be cancelled.[71] Rescission is therefore substantially an equitable remedy.

(2) RETURN OF DEPOSIT. The court will allow rescission only on condition of *restitutio in integrum*, that is to say the restoration of each party to his original position. A purchaser lawfully rescinding may therefore recover not only any deposit or part payment but also his costs of investigating title and the like, and for this money he has an equitable lien on the land agreed to be sold.[72] Similarly a vendor lawfully rescinding on account of default by the purchaser must return any part payment already received, for he cannot both cancel the contract and keep the payment.[73]

A deposit in the vendor's hands [74] may sometimes be retained by a vendor who rescinds, for unlike a mere part payment a deposit is intended to be security for performance by the purchaser and to be forfeited if he makes default. " Everybody knows what a deposit is . . . it is a guarantee that the purchaser means business." [75] " In the event of the contract being performed it shall be brought into account, but if the contract is not performed by the payer it shall remain the property of the payee." [76] It makes no difference that the deposit is paid to some third party (often in practice the vendor's

---

[67] *Barber* v. *Wolfe* [1945] Ch. 187; *Horsler* v. *Zorro* [1975] 2 W.L.R. 183.
[68] Williams V. & P. 991–994; *Myton Ltd.* v. *Schwab-Morris* [1974] 1 W.L.R. 331 (deposit).
[69] *Flight* v. *Booth* (1834) 1 Bing.N.C. 370; *cf. Pulbrook* v. *Lawes* (1876) 1 Q.B.D. 284.
[70] Court of Chancery Act, 1850, ss. 1, 14.
[71] *Mackreth* v. *Marlar* (1786) 1 Cox Eq. 259; *King* v. *King* (1883) 1 My. & K. 442.
[72] Williams V. & P. 1006; Snell, *Equity*, 448; *Lee-Parker* v. *Izzet* [1971] 1 W.L.R. 1688. For equitable liens, see *post*, p. 886.
[73] *Mayson* v. *Clouet* [1924] A.C. 980.
[74] As distinct from an unpaid balance of a deposit: *Lowe* v. *Hope* [1970] Ch. 94.
[75] *Soper* v. *Arnold* (1889) 14 App.Cas. 429 at 435, *per* Lord Macnaghten.
[76] *Howe* v. *Smith* (1884) 27 Ch.D. 89 at 101, *per* Fry L.J.; this is a leading case on deposits.

estate agent or solicitor) " as stakeholder." [77] A stakeholder is a person who holds the deposit as agent of both parties, with authority to pay it to the person who becomes entitled to it under the contract.[78] If the sale goes off by the vendor's fault, the purchaser may recover the deposit from the stakeholder direct. On the other hand, if the deposit is paid to a person who is merely the vendor's agent, any action to recover it must be brought against the vendor,[79] and the vendor can at any time require his agent to pay over the deposit to him.[80] A stakeholder resembles a banker in that he is not accountable for any interest earned by the deposit, whereas an agent must account for it to the vendor.[81]

(3) DISCRETION OF COURT. It is important, however, to notice that under the Law of Property Act, 1925,[82] the court now has discretion to order the return of a deposit in any case where specific performance is refused or return of the deposit is claimed in an action. This provision does not seem to have made much difference in practice. A deposit is forfeited only when the purchaser is in breach of the contract, and whether the court will exercise its discretion so as to relieve such a person from his liability for the breach is at least doubtful. Hitherto the discretion has been exercised only in cases where the purchaser could have rescinded,[83] and it seems to be proving useful as a means for restoring deposits without going into the technicalities of rescission. It will naturally not be used to deprive a purchaser of a deposit which he is legally entitled to have returned to him.[84]

(4) MISREPRESENTATION. In one class of cases rescission is allowed even where there has been no breach of contract: this is where one party has been induced to enter into the contract because the other has misled him by some misrepresentation as to a material fact, even though the contract itself contains no reference to that fact. Common law allowed either rescission or an action for damages if the misrepresentation was fraudulent. Equity went further, and allowed rescission (but not, of course, damages) even for innocent

---

[77] *Hall* v. *Burnell* [1911] 2 Ch. 551.
[78] *Collins* v. *Stimson* (1883) 11 Q.B.D. 142 at 144; and see *Barrington* v. *Lee* [1972] 1 Q.B. 326; Williams, *Contract of Sale of Land*, 104.
[79] *Ellis* v. *Goulton* [1893] 1 Q.B. 350.
[80] *Edgell* v. *Day* (1865) L.R. 1 C.P. 80.
[81] *Harington* v. *Hoggart* (1830) 1 B. & Ad. 577 at 586, 587.
[82] s. 49 (2).
[83] *Charles Hunt Ltd.* v. *Palmer* [1931] 2 Ch. 287 (misrepresentation by vendor); *Finkielkraut* v. *Monohan* [1949] 2 All E.R. 234 (breach by vendor).
[84] *James Macara Ltd.* v. *Barclay* [1945] K.B. 148.

misrepresentation if it both misled the other party and induced him to enter into the contract.[85]

This is a particularly important remedy for a purchaser,[1] since if thus misled by the vendor he may escape from a contract which would otherwise bind him to complete or pay damages.[2] But formerly there was a severe limitation: for an innocent (as opposed to a fraudulent) misrepresentation the equitable right to rescind ceased at completion. The purchaser had his opportunity for inspection and objection between the contract and the conveyance; and after the conveyance the transaction was final. Thus where the intending tenant of a house was honestly but wrongly assured that the drains were good, he was held to have no remedy after executing the lease and staying in possession for six months.[3] The hardship of this rule was that the purchaser might well not be able to discover that he had been misled until he had taken possession.[4] Its justification was that the vendor would otherwise not be safe in spending the purchase-money.[5]

The rule was abolished by the Misrepresentation Act 1967, which provides generally that a person may rescind a contract, notwithstanding that it has been performed, if he would otherwise be entitled to rescind without alleging fraud [6]; and contracting out of the Act is ineffective except so far as the court considers it fair and reasonable.[7] But the court is given a wide discretion to declare the contract subsisting and to award damages in lieu of rescission if this would be equitable, having regard (*inter alia*) to any loss that would be caused by upholding the contract or rescinding it.[8] The court can accordingly relieve the vendor from the hardship of having to refund the whole of the purchase-money, *e.g.*, where he has spent it on buying another house. Nevertheless, the Act substantially weakens the maxim *caveat emptor*, and calls for great caution on the part of vendors.

---

[85] See works on contract; Williams V. & P. 800, n. (*e*); *cf. Gilchester Properties Ltd.* v. *Gomm* [1948] 1 All E.R. 493 (innocent misrepresentation as to rents of the property: purchaser's remedy held to be rescission, not specific performance with abatement of price, as to which see *post*, p. 595).

[1] It is not available to a sub-purchaser or successor in title: *Gross* v. *Lewis Hillman Ltd.* [1970] Ch. 445.

[2] He has no other remedy. He cannot, for example, claim specific performance with abatement of price: see n. 85, *supra*.

[3] *Angel* v. *Jay* [1911] 1 K.B. 666; followed in *Edler* v. *Auerbach* [1950] 1 K.B. 359.

[4] See *Lever Brothers Ltd.* v. *Bell* [1931] 1 K.B. 557 at 588 (reversed [1932] A.C. 161); *Solle* v. *Butcher* [1950] 1 K.B. 671 at 695, 696; *Leaf* v. *International Galleries* [1950] 2 K.B. 86 at 90.

[5] *Allen* v. *Richardson* (1879) 13 Ch.D. 524 at 541. The Law Reform Committee (10th Report, 1962, Cmnd. 1782) recommended that the rule should be maintained except in the case of leases not exceeding three years at a full rent.

[6] s. 1, effective for misrepresentations made after April 21, 1967.

[7] s. 3.

[8] s. 2 (2).

The Act merely entitles the misled party " to rescind the contract," without saying what is to happen to any executed conveyance, which may be a grant but not a contract. If the right to rescind after performance is to be effective, the grant must necessarily be set aside [9]; though the court may prefer to award damages in lieu of rescission.

(5) NON-DISCLOSURE.   Mere non-disclosure of some defect in the property known to the vendor is not misrepresentation; for the purchaser has his opportunity to inspect it, and buys at his own risk.[10] But if there is a condition in the contract which requires the purchaser to assume some fact, there is an implied representation that the vendor knows nothing to make that fact untrue.[11] Therefore if the vendor fails to disclose the true facts, the purchaser may rescind as for misrepresentation.   In one case the condition required the purchaser to assume that a predecessor in title was the fee simple owner by a title which could not be explained, whereas in fact he had an incomplete squatter's title and the facts were known to the vendor; and the purchaser was held entitled to rescind unless a title was shown according to the contract, disregarding the condition.[11] It may be said generally that mere non-disclosure may contribute to misrepresentation if it renders the vendor's own statements misleading.[12]

(6) CONTRACTUAL RIGHT TO RESCIND.   Quite apart from breach of the contract or misrepresentation, a right to rescind for some specified cause may be one of the terms of the bargain.   Vendors very commonly make it a condition that they shall have the right to rescind in case they fail to make a good title,[13] so that they can escape from

---

[9] For the court's power to do so, see *post*, pp. 596, 611. It is clear from the legislative history that the Act is intended to authorise the cancellation of conveyances and leases where *restitutio in integrum* is possible: see 277 H.L.Deb. cols. 48–53 (October 18, 1966).

[10] Williams V. & P. 763, 810, lays down a rule that non-disclosure of a defect in title, as opposed to a defect in quality, amounts to a misrepresentation. But the authorities do not appear to justify this. The cases are of three kinds: (i) where the defect entitles the purchaser to rescind in any case, *e.g.*, a restrictive covenant; (ii) where the purchaser may not rescind, but the vendor is not awarded specific performance: see *post*, p. 593; and (iii) where the rule next stated in the text applies. The language used by Joyce J. in *Carlish* v. *Salt* [1906] 1 Ch. 335 perhaps supports Williams' rule, but that case seems clearly to fall within class (i): see *Re Flynn and Newman's Contract* [1948] I.R. 104.

[11] *Re Banister* (1879) 12 Ch.D. 131 at 146, 147. It is difficult to reconcile with this the decision of Russell J. in *Beyfus* v. *Lodge* [1925] Ch. 350, where he held that a condition required the purchaser to assume facts known to the vendor to be untrue but that the purchaser had no right to rescind.

[12] *McKeown* v. *Boudard Peveril Gear Co. Ltd.* (1896) 74 L.T. 712; *Re Englefield Holdings Ltd. and Sinclair's Contract* [1962] 1 W.L.R. 1119; and see *Becker* v. *Partridge* [1966] 2 Q.B. 155.

[13] For the common form, see Williams V. & P. 73; *cf.* the Lord Chancellor's Conditions of Sale, clause 7.

any unforeseen expense in perfecting the title as the purchaser could otherwise demand. But the courts construe these conditions strictly, and do not allow vendors to take advantage of them arbitrarily or unreasonably, *e.g.*, if the vendor has recklessly assumed that mortgagees would agree to the sale,[14] if the expense is one which any vendor should be prepared to incur, or if the vendor has misled the purchaser.[15] The provision against contracting out of the Misrepresentation Act 1967 [16] may also restrict the operation of these conditions.

(*c*) *Equitable relief.* The court's jurisdiction (rarely exercised) to grant relief against the consequences of a mistake is considered below in connection with rectification.[16a] Relief against a forfeiture clause may also be granted, *e.g.*, where instalments of purchase money are in arrear.[16b]

(*d*) *Specific performance*

(1) RIGHT TO SPECIFIC PERFORMANCE. An order of the court compelling specific performance of the contract is the remedy most commonly sought by vendors and purchasers of land. The performance which can be compelled is the due completion of the transaction in proper form according to the contract. This remedy is purely equitable, and in principle is confined to cases where the common law remedy of damages is inadequate.[17] But land is always treated as being of unique value, so that the remedy of specific performance is available to the purchaser as a matter of course; and even though the vendor is merely concerned to obtain the purchase-money, so that he could be adequately compensated in damages for the purchaser's refusal to complete, the remedy of specific performance is equally available to him. A vendor can in fact " thrust the property down the purchaser's throat " [18]; and claims by vendors for specific performance are very common, since it is usually more convenient to them to get rid of the property than to resell and claim damages.

(2) REMEDY DISCRETIONARY. Like other equitable remedies, specific performance is discretionary; but the court's discretion is governed by settled principles. The remedy may be refused, for example, in proper cases where there is mistake or great hardship,[19] even though these do not invalidate the contract at law; or where

[14] *Baines* v. *Tweddle* [1959] Ch. 679.
[15] See *Re Des Reaux and Setchfield's Contract* [1926] Ch. 178 and authorities there cited; contrast *Selkirk* v. *Romar Investments Ltd.* [1963] 1 W.L.R. 1415.
[16] *Ante*, p. 591.   [16a] *Post*, p. 595.
[16b] *Starside Properties Ltd.* v. *Mustapha* [1974] 1 W.L.R. 816.
[17] As to specific performance of agreements for short leases, see *ante*, p. 564.
[18] *Hope* v. *Walter* [1900] 1 Ch. 257 at 258, *per* Lindley L.J.
[19] Snell, *Equity*, 589, 597.

the vendor would be required to take hostile proceedings against his wife, in order to put an end to her statutory rights of occupation [20]; or where the property is being used for illegal purposes, which would make the purchaser liable to prosecution,[1] even though on this ground he has no right to rescind the contract; or where the vendor has not made a full and fair disclosure of known defects in title, even though the purchaser has agreed to accept any defects there may be.[2] In these cases the contract will remain binding at law, so that the party in default will be liable in damages, but equity will not assist with an order for specific performance. On the other hand, specific performance may be decreed before the legal time for performance has arrived if there has been an anticipatory breach, *e.g.*, by repudiation.[3]

(3) NO REMEDY AT LAW. Normally, of course, there can be no claim to specific performance where there could be no possible remedy at law, *e.g.*, where a contract is void because of fundamental mistake,[4] or where the defendant has a right to rescind, *e.g.*, for misrepresentation or fraud.[5] But occasionally specific performance is available where there is no remedy at law at all. One example of this is in cases where the contract is not evidenced in writing but there has been part performance.[6] Another is in cases of misdescription in the contract. A vendor who cannot convey precisely what he agreed to sell cannot claim damages at law; but he may claim specific performance if the misdescription is not a substantial one, provided he makes allowance for it in money.[7] Thus where a large estate was sold but the title proved bad as to six acres not material to the enjoyment of it, the vendor was awarded specific performance with abatement of the purchase price by £500.[8] If the misdescription is substantial the purchaser may rescind [9]; but

[20] *Wroth* v. *Tyler* [1974] Ch. 30.
[1] *Hope* v. *Walter* [1900] 1 Ch. 257.
[2] *Heywood* v. *Mallalieu* (1883) 25 Ch.D. 357; *Beyfus* v. *Lodge* [1925] Ch. 350 (but as to this case see *ante*, p. 592, n. 11). But if the purchaser has agreed to take the risk of the title being bad, specific performance will be refused only if it is plainly indefensible: *Re Scott and Alvarez' Contract (No. 2)* [1895] 2 Ch. 603, *ante*, p. 581.
[3] *Hasham* v. *Zenab* [1960] A.C. 316. See (1960) 76 L.Q.R. 200 (R.E.M.).
[4] See *Hartog* v. *Colin* [1939] 3 All E.R. 566.
[5] For a case based on fraud where the court, although it refused specific performance to the party defrauded owing to the vague terms of the agreement, ordered a sale of the property and an inquiry as to the proper basis of division of the proceeds, see *Pallant* v. *Morgan* [1953] Ch. 43 ; and see Snell, *Equity*, 568.
[6] *Ante*, p. 563.
[7] Fry S.P. 567 *et seq.*
[8] *McQueen* v. *Farquhar* (1805) 11 Ves. 467.
[9] *Re Russ and Brown's Contract* [1934] Ch. 34 (underlease described as lease); contrast *Cunningham* v. *Shackleton* [1935] L.J.N.C.C.A. 177; *Becker* v. *Partridge* [1966] 2 Q.B. 155 (sub-underlease described as underlease). See also *Re Brine and Davies' Contract* [1935] Ch. 388.

he may, if he prefers, claim specific performance with abatement. But he has this choice only where the misdescription amounts to a breach of contract. If there is merely misrepresentation as to some matter outside the terms of the contract the purchaser may be able to rescind but he cannot claim specific performance with abatement of price.[10]

It is often stipulated that errors of description shall not annul the sale or entitle the purchaser to compensation, and where this is agreed there will be no abatement. But such a clause will not deprive the purchaser of his right to rescind for substantial misdescription.[11]

(e) *Injunction.* This equitable remedy, the negative counterpart of specific performance, is rarely appropriate in cases of vendor and purchaser, but it may be useful to prevent a breach of contract, *e.g.*, if the vendor threatens to demolish a building while he is still in possession of the property.[12]

(f) *Rectification and setting aside.* These are equitable remedies based on mistake.

Rectification may be sought where the parties intended to put their contract into writing, but by a common mistake failed to record it correctly. The court may then correct the mistake so that the writing accurately represents the contract; and the court may order specific performance of the contract as so rectified, even in the same action.[13] This might be done, for example, where there was an agreement to build and let four houses but the written contract wrongly gave the number as six,[14] or where the rent agreed upon was wrongly stated.[15] The requirement that the contract must be evidenced in writing is no bar to rectification, for when the writing has been rectified it can then form the evidence.[16] But the burden of proof in actions for rectification is heavy[17]; the court requires " strong irrefragable evidence "[18] (or, in modern terms, " convincing proof "[19]) that the written words were contrary to the concurrent intention of all parties.

Rectification is also useful for correcting mistakes in a convey-

[10] *Gilchester Properties Ltd.* v. *Gomm* [1948] 1 All E.R. 493.
[11] *Flight* v. *Booth* (1834) 1 Bing.N.C. 370; *Jacobs* v. *Revell* [1900] 2 Ch. 858; *Lee* v. *Rayson* [1917] 1 Ch. 613; *cf. Watson* v. *Barton* [1957] 1 W.L.R. 19.
[12] Williams V. & P. 558.
[13] *Craddock Brothers* v. *Hunt* [1923] 2 Ch. 136; *U.S.A.* v. *Motor Trucks Ltd.* [1924] A.C. 196. For details of the remedy, see generally Snell, *Equity*, 610–619; *Riverlate Properties Ltd.* v. *Paul* [1974] 3 W.L.R. 564.
[14] *Olley* v. *Fisher* (1886) 34 Ch.D. 367.
[15] *Garrard* v. *Frankel* (1862) 30 Beav. 445; but see *Riverlate Properties* v. *Paul, supra,* at p. 571.
[16] *Thomas* v. *Davis* (1757) 1 Dick. 301; *Johnson* v. *Bragge* [1901] 1 Ch. 28 at 36; *Craddock Brothers* v. *Hunt* [1923] 2 Ch. 136; Williams V. & P. 775, 776.
[17] Fry S.P. 373; Williams V. & P. 776, 777.
[18] *Countess of Shelburne* v. *Earl of Inchiquin* (1784) 1 Bro.C.C. 338 at 341, *per* Lord Thurlow L.C.   [19] *Joscelyne* v. *Nissen* [1970] 2 Q.B. 86 at 98.

ance, *e.g.*, if it gives the purchaser more land,[20] or wider rights,[21] than he was entitled to under the contract, or if it creates a joint tenancy when a tenancy in common was intended.[22] But, being an equitable remedy, it will not be available where there has been long delay, or where the land affected has passed into the hands of a bona fide purchaser who had no notice of the mistake in the conveyance.[23] Since the right to rectification is a " mere equity," such a purchaser need not necessarily acquire the legal estate.[24]

There is also a wide equitable jurisdiction to set aside or adjust transactions vitiated by mistake, even after execution of a conveyance. In one case A took a lease of a fishery from B, both supposing it to be B's property when in fact it was A's property. The House of Lords set aside the lease in equity, subject to terms under which (*inter alia*) A was to reimburse B for his expenditure in obtaining a private Act of Parliament and in improving the fishery.[25] In another case A took a lease of a flat from B at a rent of £250, both believing that the former restricted rent of £140 did not apply, when in fact it did apply. The Court of Appeal set aside the lease on elaborate terms designed to protect the tenant but to allow the landlord to claim a statutory increase of rent.[26] In such cases there must either be mutual mistake or inequitable conduct by one party.[26a]

(g) *Declaration by the court* (*Vendor and Purchaser Summons*). The most suitable way of deciding disputes which may arise in the investigation of title (*e.g.*, whether a good title has been shown according to the contract, or whether some incumbrance must be accepted by the purchaser) is to ask the court to make a declaration, and this remedy is always available.[27] A convenient form of procedure is the Vendor and Purchaser Summons, introduced by the Vendor and Purchaser Act, 1874,[28] and now authorised by the Law of Property Act, 1925.[29] This is a summary procedure designed for the decision of particular points arising between contract and conveyance. It may not be used to question the existence or validity of the contract, but only for matters arising under it. The court may make such order as it thinks just. This will normally be a declaration, but it may sometimes include an order for rescission and

---

[20] *Beale* v. *Kyte* [1907] 1 Ch. 564.
[21] *Clarke* v. *Barnes* [1929] 2 Ch. 368; *cf. post*, p. 840.
[22] *Re Colebrook's Conveyances* [1972] 1 W.L.R. 1397.
[23] Williams V. & P. 791; *Smith* v. *Jones* [1954] 1 W.L.R. 1089; *cf. Garrard* v. *Frankel* (1862) 30 Beav. 445.　　　　　[24] *Ante*, pp. 121, 122.
[25] *Cooper* v. *Phibbs* (1867) L.R. 2 H.L. 149.
[26] *Solle* v. *Butcher* [1950] 1 K.B. 671 (Jenkins L.J. dissenting on the ground that the mistake was one of law against which the court could not grant relief).
[26a] *Riverlate Properties Ltd.* v. *Paul* [1974] 3 W.L.R. 564.
[27] R.S.C. Ord. 15, r. 16.　　　　　　　　　　　　　　[28] s. 9.
[29] s. 49 (1). The use of a vendor and purchaser summons is indicated by the title " *Re A's and B's Contract.*"

repayment of deposit and expenses. If a party wishes for a declaration as to the validity of the contract, or any other matter outside the scope of a Vendor and Purchaser Summons, he must claim it in an ordinary action.

Part 2

CONVEYANCING

There is no hard and fast line to be drawn between contracts and conveyancing, and conveyancing in its wide sense includes most of the subjects which have already been treated under contracts. The title " conveyancing " is here used to cover some brief notes on the procedure for investigation of title and completion, and the form and effect of an ordinary conveyance.

Sect. 1. From Contract to Completion

The usual sequence of events on the sale of a freehold by V to P is as follows; most of the steps are normally taken by the solicitors for the parties rather than by the parties in person.

1. Signature of the contract. This has been dealt with above. The modern practice is for a purchaser to make certain searches before signing the contract [30]; to make inquiries of local authorities about such things as roads, drainage and planning matters [31]; and also, if it is possible (which is usually not the case in sales by auction), to make a series of written " Inquiries on Draft Contract," addressed to the vendor and designed to clear up any uncertainties as to the state of the property.[32] The contract may also contain a provision permitting rescission if certain specified classes of defects are not disclosed, and so make searches and inquiries to some extent unnecessary.[33]

2. Delivery of abstract. Within the time mentioned in the contract, V must deliver to P the abstract of title. This document consists in part of an epitome of the various documents, and in part of a recital of the relevant events, such as births, deaths and marriages, which affect the title.[34] The abstract starts with a good

[30] See *ante*, p. 585.
[31] These are made in approved form and answered for a fixed fee.
[32] See Emmett, Chap. 1, for pre-contract searches and inquiries.
[33] *Ante*, p. 585.
[34] Williams V. & P. 123.

root of title [35] and traces the devolution of the property down to V.
Thus a very simple abstract might consist of—

   (i) an epitome of a conveyance by A to B;

   (ii) a recital of B's death;

   (iii) a recital of probate of B's will being granted to X and Y [36];

   (iv) an epitome of the assent by X and Y in favour of V.[36]

3. Consideration of abstract. P then peruses the abstract of title,
considers the validity of the title shown, and checks the abstract
against V's title deeds, grants of probate, and other papers which
prove the statements made in the abstract.

4. Requisitions on title. P's examination of the abstract usually
discloses a number of points upon which he requires further
information. This further explanation is obtained by means of
" requisitions on title," a series of written questions which P delivers
to V. Requisitions usually consist of a mixture of requests for
information genuinely needed (*e.g.*, as to the date of a death not
revealed by the abstract, or as to some incumbrance which the
abstract mentions but does not explain), statements of the obvious
(*e.g.*, that V, having agreed to sell free from incumbrances, must
discharge a mortgage or obtain the concurrence of his mortgagee
to the sale of the property free from the mortgage), and general
inquiries designed to make V commit himself to a definite statement
(*e.g.*, whether there are any incumbrances other than those specifically
mentioned). In addition to dealing with matters disclosed in the
abstract of title, requisitions cover most or all of the points taken
in the Enquiries on Draft Contract.

5. Replies to requisitions. V then answers the requisitions within
the agreed time; if his answers are unsatisfactory on any point, P
may make further requisitions.

6. Draft conveyance. P next prepares a draft conveyance in the
form which he thinks it should take. He sends this draft to V for
his approval; V makes in red ink any emendations he considers
necessary, returns it to P, who makes any further amendments in
green ink, and so on until the conveyance is agreed. P then prepares
an engrossment (fair copy) of the conveyance and sends it to V for
signature and sealing.

---

[35] *Ante*, p. 580.
[36] The will itself is no longer abstracted if the testator died after 1925: see *ante*,
p. 538, and see the examples given in L.P.A., 1925, 6th Sched.

7. Searches. A few days before the day fixed for completion, P makes his searches. Normally this will be limited to searching the Land Charges Register and the Registers of Local Land Charges.[37]

8. Completion. Completion then takes place, usually at the office of V's solicitor. V delivers [38] to P the conveyance duly executed; only if P is entering into some obligation towards V, as by binding himself to observe restrictive covenants, will P have to execute the conveyance as well, though even if he does not do so he will still be bound by the covenants if he takes possession under the deed.[39] In addition to receiving the conveyance, P is entitled to receive the title deeds. This is more than a contractual right, for the owner of land has a right to the title deeds under a general rule.[49] However, V may retain any deed which—

(i) relates to other land retained by him; or

(ii) creates a trust which is still subsisting; or

(iii) relates to the appointment or discharge of trustees of a subsisting trust.[41]

If V retains any deeds, he must give P an acknowledgment of P's right to production of the deeds and, unless V is a mortgagee or trustee of the land, an undertaking for their safe custody.[42] In return P pays V the purchase-money either in cash or by banker's draft. The exact amount due is settled by the " completion statement " which apportions the rates and other outgoings up to the day of completion. It is for the purchaser to have the conveyance duly stamped, which is usually done after completion.

Sect. 2. The Conveyance

A. *Precedent of a Conveyance*

Commencement and date.　　THIS CONVEYANCE is made the 1st day of June, 1965,

---

[37] See *post*, pp. 1051, 1053.
[38] Deeds take effect by delivery, not by signature: *post*, p. 601. Sealing without signature is no longer sufficient: L.P.A., 1925, s. 73.
[39] Litt. 374; Dart V. & P. 507; and see *post*, pp. 749, 750.
[40] Co.Litt. 6a (" the purchaser shall have all the charters, deeds and evidences, as incident to the lands . . . for the evidences are, as it were, the sinews of the land."); *Harrington* v. *Price* (1832) 3 B. & Ad. 170; *Loosemore* v. *Radford* (1842) 9 M. & W. 657; *cf. Re Knight's Question* [1958] Ch. 381. And see Halsb. xxxii, 256, 257, where special rules as to tenants for life, mortgagees, etc., are stated.
[41] L.P.A., 1925, s. 45 (9), replacing Vendor and Purchaser Act, 1874, s. 2, r. 5.
[42] As to the effect of such acknowledgments and undertakings see L.P.A., 1925, s. 64, and notes thereto in Wolst. & C. The benefit of these covenants runs with the land at common law (*post*, p. 736), the burden runs with the deeds by L.P.A., 1925, s. 64 (2), (9).

Parties.

BETWEEN Victor Vendor of No. 1 Smith Street Dorking in the County of Surrey Clerk (hereinafter called " the vendor ") of the one part and Percy Purchaser of No. 2 Brown Street Lewes in the County of Sussex Auctioneer (hereinafter called " the purchaser ") of the other part

WHEREAS—

Recitals.

(1) The vendor is the estate owner in respect of the fee simple of the property hereby assured for his own use and benefit absolutely free from incumbrances (2) The vendor has agreed with the purchaser to sell to him the said property free from incumbrances for the price of £5,000

Testatum.
Consideration.
Receipt clause.

NOW THIS CONVEYANCE WITNESSETH that in consideration of the sum of £5,000 now paid by the purchaser to the vendor (the receipt whereof the vendor hereby acknowledges) the vendor As Beneficial

Operative words.

Owner hereby conveys to the purchaser

Parcels.

ALL THAT messuage or dwelling house with the yard gardens offices and outbuildings thereto belonging known as No. 703 Robinson Street Ashford in the County of Kent which premises are more particularly delineated and coloured pink on the plan annexed to these presents

Habendum.

TO HOLD the same unto the purchaser in fee simple

Testimonium.

IN WITNESS WHEREOF the parties to these presents have hereunto set their hands and seals the day and year first above written

Attestation clause.

Signed sealed and delivered by the vendor in the presence of Charles Brown clerk to Benham and Gambling solicitors } VICTOR VENDOR

B. Details of the Conveyance

In the very simple form of conveyance set out above, the following matters should be considered. The titles refer to the side-notes to its various parts.

1. Commencement. The old practice was for the initial words to be " This Indenture." An indenture was a deed made in two counterparts, each having an indented or irregular edge. The deed was written out twice on a single sheet of parchment, which was then severed by cutting it with an irregular edge; the two halves of the parchment thus formed two separate deeds which could be fitted together to show their genuineness. This contrasted with a " deed poll," a deed to which there was only one party, which at the top had been polled, or shaved even.[43] The modern practice is for the commencement to describe the general nature of the document, *e.g.,* " This Conveyance," " This Mortgage " and the like.[44]

2. Date. Whatever date is in fact inserted in the conveyance, the document takes effect from the date upon which it was signed, sealed and delivered by the parties to it.[44a] A deed which has been signed and sealed but not delivered is ineffective [45]; delivery is effected formally by uttering words such as " I deliver this as my act and deed," or informally by doing some act showing that the deed is intended to be operative. A deed may be delivered in escrow, *i.e.,* delivered on the condition that it is not to become operative until some stated event occurs,[46] in which case it takes effect as soon as the event occurs; it is not revocable in the meantime.[47] Usually a vendor of land will execute the conveyance some days before completion and deliver it to his solicitor in escrow, the condition being the completion of the purchase by the purchaser. The deed then takes effect when the solicitor delivers it to the purchaser (or his solicitor) on completion.

3. Parties. If any other person is an essential party to the transaction, such as a mortgagee who is releasing the property from his mortgage, he will be included as a party.

4. Recitals. These are of two types:

    (a) *Narrative recitals,* which deal with such matters as how the vendor became entitled to the land; and

    (b) *Introductory recitals,* which explain how and why the existing state of affairs is to be altered, *e.g.,* that the parties have agreed for the sale of the property.

---

[43] Norton, *Deeds,* 27.
[44] See L.P.A., 1925, s. 57.
[44a] Norton, *Deeds,* 189.
[45] Co.Litt. 35b, 171b; Norton, *Deeds,* 10. But the deed of a corporation aggregate sealed in accordance with L.P.A., 1925, s. 74, apparently takes effect without delivery: *D'Silva* v. *Lister House Development Ltd.* [1971] Ch. 17, criticised in (1973) 89 L.Q.R. 14 (M. J. Albery).
[46] Norton, *Deeds,* 18 *et seq.*
[47] *Beesly* v. *Hallwood Estates Ltd.* [1961] Ch. 105.

These recitals can create estoppels. For example, the common form of recital of ownership set out above will estop the vendor from denying that he owns the legal estate. If at the time of the conveyance he does not own the legal estate but later acquires it, it will in effect pass to the purchaser under the doctrine of " feeding the estoppel " (explained elsewhere [48]) as against the vendor and persons claiming through him.[49]

5. Testatum. This is the beginning of the operative part of the conveyance.

6. Consideration. The consideration is stated to show (*inter alia*) that the transaction is not a voluntary one.[50]

7. Receipt clause. This is inserted to save a separate receipt being given. A solicitor who produces a conveyance containing such a clause which has been executed by the vendor thereby shows the purchaser that he has authority from the vendor to receive the purchase-money.[51]

8. Operative words. These effect the actual conveyance of the property. A most important part of them is the phrase " As Beneficial Owner." These words have great technical significance, as has already been seen in the case of a conveyance by the survivor of joint tenants.[52] Their principal function is to imply covenants for title, which are the nearest thing to a guarantee that the purchaser receives from the vendor.

(*a*) *Warranty of title.* Although it is the general rule that the purchaser, after making all his investigations, takes the land at his own risk (*caveat emptor*), he has always had some kind of remedy against the vendor for certain defects of title. In medieval times he had the benefit of the law of warranty, which took its origin from the feudal lord's duty to protect his tenant in exchange for his services.[53] When tenure between vendor and purchaser of a fee simple was abolished by the Statute *Quia Emptores,* 1290,[54] it became customary for vendors to give an express warranty of title.[55] If the purchaser was then disturbed by anyone having a superior

---

48 *Post,* p. 646.
49 *Cumberland Court (Brighton) Ltd.* v. *Taylor* [1964] Ch. 29.
50 See *ante,* p. 442.
51 L.P.A., 1925, s. 69.
52 *Ante,* p. 413.
53 P. & M. i, 306; H.E.L. iii, 159–161.
54 *Ante,* p. 30.
55 H.E.L. iii, 161 ; Challis 307, 308.

title, the vendor could be made liable in damages or, in case of eviction, be compelled to give lands of equal value in compensation. The old law of warranty was bound up with the real actions and the feudal land law, and it fell out of use with them.[56]

(*b*) *Covenants for title.* The old system of warranties was replaced by the practice of giving express covenants for title, and in the course of the sixteenth and seventeenth centuries the ordinary form for these became settled.[57] These modern covenants sounded in damages only, and the idea of specific compensation was forgotten. The question is, therefore, how far a purchaser may now claim damages from the vendor for breach of a covenant for title.

Since 1881 it has been unnecessary to set out the covenants in the conveyance, for by the Law of Property Act, 1925, s. 76 and Second Schedule,[58] they are implied if the following conditions are satisfied:

(i) the conveyance is for valuable consideration; and

(ii) the vendor " conveys and is expressed to convey as beneficial owner." The conveyance must therefore state in terms that he conveys " as beneficial owner." It has been held that the inept statutory formula [59] requires in addition that the vendor should in fact be a beneficial owner.[60] This would deprive the purchaser of the protection of the covenants in exactly the case where he ought to have it, namely, where the vendor's title is not as represented, *e.g.*, where the vendor is not a beneficial owner but a trustee. The object of the Act is to allow short forms of words to take the place of the lengthy covenants which used to be set out in full [61]; and the Act becomes a trap unless the covenants are uniformly implied whenever the statutory forms of words are used. If they are not, it is safer to incorporate the covenants by express reference to the Second Schedule.

---

[56] H.E.L. vii, 257; and see *post*, p. 1167.

[57] H.E.L. iii, 103; vii 374, 557–559. The invention of the modern form of covenants is attributed to Sir O. Bridgeman (1606–1674): see Platt on *Covenants* 304.

[58] Replacing (with amendments) C.A., 1881, s. 7.

[59] Contrast L.P.A., 1925, s. 77, which substitutes " or " for " and." The drafting seems quite indiscriminate. To substitute " or " would remove the whole difficulty.

[60] *Fay* v. *Miller, Wilkins & Co.* [1941] Ch. 360; and see *Pilkington* v. *Wood* [1953] Ch. 770 at 777. This interpretation conflicts with the policy of the Act, with conveyancing practice, and with previous decisions which imply that the nature of the vendor's actual interest is irrelevant, as it ought to be: *David* v. *Sabin* [1893] 1 Ch. 523 (*post*, p. 609); *Re Ray* [1896] 1 Ch. 468; *Parker* v. *Judkin* [1931] 1 Ch. 475. See Farrand, *Contract and Conveyance*, 341; (1968) 32 Conv.(N.S.) 123 (M. J. Russell).

[61] See *Re Ray* [1896] 1 Ch. 468 at 475, where Kay L.J. made this a reason for giving the Act a wide construction, holding that a tenant for life who conveyed " as beneficial owner " gave the full covenant.

(*c*) *The covenants.* The implied covenants are set out in the lengthy and long-settled but " extremely difficult " [62] form of words which conveyancers inserted in full before 1882.[63] They may be summarised as follows:

(i) Full power to convey: the vendor has a good right to convey the whole property and interest agreed to be sold.

(ii) Quiet enjoyment: the purchaser shall have quiet enjoyment of the land.[64]

(iii) Freedom from incumbrances: the land shall be enjoyed free from any incumbrances other than those subject to which the conveyance is expressly made. This covenant applies even to incumbrances known to the purchaser, unless the conveyance is expressed to be subject to them.[65]

(iv) Further assurance: the vendor will execute such assurances and do such things as are necessary to cure any defect in the conveyance.

(*d*) *Leaseholds.* In the case of a sale of leaseholds, the following additional covenants are implied on such a conveyance [66]:

(v) That the lease is valid and in full force.

(vi) That the rent has been paid and the covenants in the lease duly performed.

It should be noted that this set of covenants applies to leases only when an existing lease is sold, *i.e.*, assigned. Where a new lease or sub-lease is granted, *i.e.*, where a new estate is created as between landlord and tenant, the landlord's liability for the title is different; this is explained elsewhere.[67] We are here concerned with vendor and purchaser, not with landlord and tenant.

(*e*) *Limited covenants.* Where a person conveys and is expressed to convey " as settlor " the only covenant implied is one for further assurance, binding that person and those claiming under him [68]; and this applies whether the settlement is voluntary or for value. On the other hand, where a person conveys (whether or not for value) " as trustee," " as mortgagee," " as personal representative," [68a] or " under

---

[62] *Pilkington* v. *Wood* [1953] Ch. 770 at 777, *per* Harman J.
[63] The practice of shortening conveyances by using special words to imply covenants is not a modern invention: see Statute *De Bigamis*, 1276, cited in H.E.L. vii, 251, 255.   [64] *Cf., post,* p. 676.
[65] *Page* v. *Midland Ry.* [1894] 1 Ch. 11; *Great Western Ry.* v. *Fisher* [1905] 1 Ch. 316. Contrast the rule for contracts, *ante,* p. 583.
[66] L.P.A., 1925, s. 76 (1) (B) and 2nd Sched., Pt. II.   [67] *Post,* p. 676.
[68] s. 76 (1) (E) and 2nd Sched., Pt. V.
[68a] The covenant may be implied in an assent as well as in a deed: L.P.A., 1925, s. 76 (1).

an order of the court " the only covenant implied is that the grantor has not himself incumbered the land.[69] Where the vendor sells in any such capacity the purchaser is entitled only to covenants limited accordingly. For example, a tenant for life who sells under the Settled Land Act, 1925, or co-owners who hold on trust for sale for themselves, will convey merely as trustees, for that is the capacity in which they hold the legal estate. And in any case where the vendor's liability for the state of the title is limited by the contract, the vendor may insert corresponding limitations in the conveyance.[70] But if the purchaser has agreed to buy subject to a mortgage or a right of way, the effect of conveying expressly subject to them will be the automatic exclusion of liability for them.

(f) *Enforceability of the covenants.* The rules for enforcing covenants for title are as follows.

(1) BENEFIT. The benefit of the covenants runs with the land, so that each person in whom the land is for the time being vested is entitled to enforce the covenant. This was so at common law,[71] but there is now a statutory provision to the same effect.[72] Thus if V enters into the covenants with P, and later P sells the land to Q, Q is entitled to enforce the covenants for title against V, even though Q was not a party to the conveyance from V to P which created the obligations.

(2) BURDEN. As regards the burden of the covenant, the person liable is the individual who gives the covenant; the obligation is a purely personal one, which does not run with the land. The vendor who conveys " as beneficial owner " personally guarantees the title; but, as will be seen from the full form of the covenants, his liability is limited to the consequences of the conduct of certain persons. This is a very important restriction of the scope of the covenants: they are not a warranty of title, but qualified covenants only. The general rule is that they extend only to the lawful acts and omissions of—

    (i) the covenantor himself, and

    (ii) anyone claiming through, under, or in trust for him, and

    (iii) anyone through whom he claims otherwise than by purchase for money or money's worth, and

---

[69] s. 76 (1) (F) and 2nd Sched., Pt. VI, as amended by Mental Health Act, 1959, 8th Sched., Pt. I (eliminating " as committee " and " as receiver ").
[70] Williams V. & P. 662–665. If they are omitted by mistake, the conveyance may be rectified: *Stait v. Fenner* [1912] 2 Ch. 504.
[71] Smith's L.C. i, 72, 73; *post*, p. 746.
[72] L.P.A., 1925, s. 76 (6). As to the position of mortgagees, see (1964) 28 Conv.(N.S.) 205 (A. M. Prichard).

(iv) anyone claiming through or under those in class (iii).[73]

Thus if V conveys land to P for value " as beneficial owner " and P subsequently discovers undisclosed incumbrances, he can sue V on the covenants for title if those incumbrances were created by V, or by V's tenant, mortgagee, or trustee (all examples of class (ii)); or by a person who left the land to V by will, or gave it to him by deed of gift or marriage settlement (class (iii)). Class (iv) extends class (iii) in the same way as class (ii) extends class (i).

(3) EXAMPLE. A simple example will show how these qualified covenants operate. Suppose that V allows his neighbour X to acquire a right of way over V's land by prescription; then V sells and conveys to P " as beneficial owner "; then P sells similarly to Q; and finally X asserts his rights against Q. For this defect in title and disturbance of quiet enjoyment Q may sue V, for Q obtains the benefit of V's covenants with P, which run with the land. Q cannot sue P, for P is not responsible for incumbrances created by V, who sold to him for value. But if the land had passed from V to P under V's will, Q could then sue P, for P's covenants would extend to V's acts. Yet Q could not sue V, for V would have given no covenant at all.

(4) MORTGAGES. Where a person creates a mortgage " as beneficial owner," the covenants for title implied are absolute [74]; the mortgagor thus makes himself responsible for the acts of everyone, and gives a complete warranty that his title is good. This is because it has long been the practice for mortgagees to insist on these unqualified covenants, and this situation is now recognised by statute.[74] As stated under (e) above, the liability on the covenants implied by using phrases other than " as beneficial owner " is limited to the grantor's own acts.

(5) GIFTS. Even where the phrase " as beneficial owner " is used, it implies covenants only where the conveyance is made for valuable consideration, e.g., by way of sale or marriage settlement.[75] In a deed of gift, therefore, it has no effect; but the phrase " as settlor " may be used so as to give the limited covenant already mentioned in (e) above. If for any special reason more extensive covenants for title are desired in a voluntary conveyance, they must be set out expressly.

---

[73] See, e.g., *David* v. *Sabin* [1893] 1 Ch. 523 at 532, 542.
[74] s. 76 (1) (D) and 2nd Sched., Pt. IV. See (1964) 28 Conv.(N.S.) 205 (A. M. Prichard).
[75] s. 76 (1) (A). For a case where executors conveyed " as beneficial owners," see *Parker* v. *Judkin* [1931] 1 Ch. 475.

(g) *Limitation.* The covenants are subject to the usual period of limitation (twelve years).[76] The covenant for full power to convey stands broken, if at all, at the moment when the conveyance is made,[77] so that the right to sue upon it expires twelve years after the conveyance.[78] The same rule has been held to apply to the covenant for freedom from incumbrances [79]; but more probably this is merely part of the covenant for quiet enjoyment,[80] operating not as a separate warranty that the land is free from incumbrances when conveyed, but as a covenant that the purchaser shall not be disturbed by incumbrancers.[81] The covenant for quiet enjoyment is not broken until the purchaser is actually disturbed by someone with a valid prior right, *e.g.* the owner of an easement, so that this covenant can be sued on at any time within twelve years of the disturbance.[82] Although this covenant covers much of the same ground as the other two, it is of particular value for this reason. Similarly the covenant for further assurance is not broken until execution of some necessary document is demanded and refused.[83]

(h) *Effect of the system of vendors' covenants*

(1) CHAIN OF COVENANTS. Since the benefit of the covenants runs with the land, but the burden is purely personal, the purchaser normally gets the benefit of a chain of covenants given by all previous vendors of the land. Each vendor's covenants extend back to the acts of the last previous purchaser, so that the chain is continuous even though between purchases the land passes by will or intestacy, or by deed of gift. "The covenant by a vendor in fee is not understood as extending to acts done previously to the last preceding sale. On each sale the title is investigated, and conveyancers are content with a series of covenants of title each of which covers the time which has elapsed since the last conveyance from a vendor in fee." [84] Therefore, although no one vendor gives a full warranty of title, the various covenants added together amount to a comprehensive

---

[76] Limitation Act, 1939, s. 2 (3); *post*, p. 1011.
[77] *Spoor* v. *Green* (1874) L.R. 9 Ex. 99 at 110, adopted in *Turner* v. *Moon* [1901] 2 Ch. 825; and see *Pilkington* v. *Wood* [1953] Ch. 770 at 777.
[78] See *post*, p. 1011.
[79] *Turner* v. *Moon*, *supra*.
[80] *Nottidge* v. *Dering* [1909] 2 Ch. 647, affd. [1910] 1 Ch. 297; and see *Vane* v. *Lord Barnard* (1708) Gilb. Eq. 6 at 8; Williams V. & P. 1080, 1081; Platt, *Covenants*, 331. The language of the covenant (L.P.A., 1925, 2nd Sched., Pt. I) is clumsy and obscure, but the words relating to freedom from incumbrances (which as a separate covenant would lack a main verb) appear to be part of the covenant for quiet enjoyment. *Turner* v. *Moon*, *supra*, at p. 828 appears incorrectly to promote the subsidiary verbs "freed and discharged."
[81] A further argument for this construction is that the general purpose of the covenant is to give an indemnity.
[82] See *Spoor* v. *Green*, *supra*, at p. 111.
[83] *King* v. *Jones* (1815) 4 M. & S. 188.
[84] *David* v. *Sabin* [1893] 1 Ch. 523 at 534, *per* Lindley L.J.

guarantee to the purchaser, provided that he sues the proper defendant in each case. But this is assuming that the full covenants are given on each sale. The chain may be broken if a vendor sells as trustee or executor,[85] or if a previous vendor sold with limited covenants; and the right to sue a previous vendor who is dead may be valueless if his estate has been fully distributed.

(2) ACTS AND OMISSIONS. The covenants extend both to acts and omissions. Thus they cover adverse claims caused not only by the grant of rights (*e.g.*, easements) or bankruptcy,[86] but also by the failure to contest a squatter's rights while the period of limitation is running.[87] But only rightful acts are covered: if the purchaser is disturbed by a trespasser or a claimant with no title he has his own remedies and needs no recourse against his vendor.

(3) POWER TO CONVEY. The first covenant (full power to convey) is qualified even more strictly than the others, despite its somewhat ambiguous language.[88] It makes the vendor liable only in respect of the acts or omissions of himself and persons through whom he claims otherwise than by purchase for money or money's worth. It does not therefore extend to eviction by title paramount. If the vendor is merely a squatter and the purchaser is evicted by the true owner, or if the vendor purports to sell land to which neither he nor his predecessors (other than previous vendors) has ever had title at all, then the purchaser has no remedy under the ordinary covenants.

For example, owing to a mistake about his boundary the vendor of a farm may sell and purport to convey a field which is in fact his neighbour's property; but the purchaser will have no remedy if he fails to detect the flaw in the title before completion.[89] On the other hand the vendor will be liable if the defect in title is one which he had power to remove, for then it subsists because of his omission to remove it. Thus where a tenant in tail purported to dispose of the fee simple, and the purchaser was evicted by the remainderman, the tenant in tail was held liable because he could have barred the

---

[85] *Ante*, p. 604.
[86] *Jenkins* v. *Jones* (1882) 9 Q.B.D. 128.
[87] *Eastwood* v. *Ashton* [1915] A.C. 900.
[88] See L.P.A., 1925, 2nd Sched., Pt. I. " Notwithstanding " (the second word of the covenant) is used in the sense of " to the extent of " ; but see (1961) 105 S.J. 743.
[89] See *Browning* v. *Wright* (1799) 2 B. & P. 13, and the remarks of Lord Eldon C.J. at pp. 22, 23. Where a tenant for life purported to sell the fee, the purchaser would have no remedy on the covenants unless the vendor (or his ancestor, etc.) himself once had the fee and then disposed of it ; in other cases the purchaser bears the risk of the title.

entail and so perfected his title.[90] Similarly, as already mentioned, the covenant covers loss of title under the Limitation Acts, for that is caused by omission to eject the squatter while there is yet time. And it covers ejection by anyone claiming through a person who left the land by will to the vendor, as where after the fee simple had been sold and (as it was thought) conveyed, it was discovered that the will gave the vendor only a life interest: for then the remainderman's claim was caused by the act (*i.e.*, the will) of a person in class (iii) for whom the vendor was answerable under the covenant.[91] But the burden of proof is on the purchaser, so that if the origin of the adverse claimant's title is uncertain, the vendor is not liable.[92]

(4) PREDECESSORS AND SUCCESSORS IN TITLE. The meaning of "through" in the phrases "claiming through" and "through whom he claims"[93] is apparently not the same throughout all the covenants; for in class (iii) it extends to the vendor's predecessors in title in fee simple if he acquired the land from them without giving money or money's worth for it, whereas in classes (ii) and (iv) the corresponding expression does not extend to successors in title to the fee simple, or whatever else the vendor's whole interest may be. This is best explained by examples. If A grants an easement to X and then devises the fee simple to V, and then V sells and conveys to P with the usual covenants for title, V is liable to P for the easement because V claims through A and is responsible for his act, *viz.*, the granting of the easement. Here "claiming through" is used in its widest sense, including all successors in title. But on the other hand if V sells first to L, then L grants a lease to T, then L resells the fee simple to V and conceals the lease, and then V sells and conveys to P, V's covenant with P does not make V liable for the lease, even though L derives title through V in the first place.[94] Here, therefore, "claiming through" means claiming a derivative interest (*e.g.*,

---

[90] *Cavan* v. *Pulteney* (1795) 2 Ves.Jun. 544 (a case of landlord and tenant, with an express covenant); *cf. Howes* v. *Bushfield* (1803) 3 East 491, discussed in Sugden V. & P. 602, 603, where the question is raised whether this principle extends to a mortgage created by an earlier vendor which the latter vendor might have paid off even though he was not responsible for its creation; and see *Stock* v. *Meakin* [1900] 1 Ch. 683, where a statutory charge for sewers (which the vendor had no power to prevent) was held within the covenant, apparently because the vendor "omitted" to pay it off (see argument at pp. 688, 689). See also *Chivers & Sons Ltd.* v. *Air Ministry* [1955] Ch. 585.

[91] *Page* v. *Midland Ry.* [1894] 1 Ch. 11.

[92] *Howard* v. *Maitland* (1883) 11 Q.B.D. 695; *Stoney* v. *Eastbourne R.D.C.* [1927] 1 Ch. 367.

[93] As regards predecessors in title the precise words are "through whom he derives title"; as regards successors they are "claiming through, under or in trust for."

[94] Based on an example given by Romer J. in *David* v. *Sabin* [1893] 1 Ch. 523 at 530, and approved by A. L. Smith L.J., at p. 544; *cf. Steping* v. *Gladding* (1671) 1 Free.K.B. 18 at 20; *Butler* v. *Swinerton* (1623) Palm. 339; Cru.Dig. iv. 386.

under a lease) and not merely being a successor in title to the fee simple.

A contrasting case, on the other hand, in which V was held liable, was where V, being fee simple owner, first granted a *lease* to T, then T sub-leased to S, then T surrendered his lease back to V for payment and concealed the sub-lease, and then V sold and conveyed to P.[95] Here T claimed through V in the sense of having a derivative interest carved out of V's fee simple, and the fact that V also claimed through T for value (by the surrender) did not prevent him being liable in his original capacity as a person through whom T claimed, who was therefore answerable for T's sub-lease under the ordinary covenants against incumbrances. In this case it was also held that V was liable under the covenant for full power to convey, because of his own act in granting the lease to T; for " it is a mere convey- ancing illusion to suppose that the defendant ever by the so-called surrender . . . got back the term which he had granted so as to extinguish it. He only recovered it mangled by the sub-leases and shorn of all right to possession." [96]

(*i*) *Purchaser's covenants.* Where the land sold is leasehold, or is subject to a rentcharge, a conveyance for value implies covenants by the purchaser that he and his successors in title will perform all covenants connected with the lease or rentcharge and will indemnify the vendor against liability.[97] No special words need be used to imply these covenants. They are designed as a safeguard to vendors who may remain personally liable by privity of contract even after they have parted with the land affected.[98]

9. Parcels. This is the description of the property. Description by reference to an annexed plan is a common alternative, but is not essential if an accurate verbal description can be given.[99] Very often a conveyance both describes the property verbally and also includes a plan. In that case it is advisable to provide that one or the other shall prevail in case of inconsistency. For example, if the plan is expressed to be included " by way of identification and not of limita- tion," the verbal description will prevail [1]; but if the property is said to be " more particularly described in the plan," then the plan will prevail.[2]

---

[95] *David* v. *Sabin* [1893] 1 Ch. 523 (the leading case on covenants for title).
[96] *Ibid.*, at p. 538, *per* Bowen L.J.
[97] L.P.A., 1925, s. 77 and 2nd Sched., Pts. VII–X. These provisions are new, but follow previous practice. [98] See *post*, p. 723.
[99] *Re Sharman's Contract* [1936] Ch. 755. [1] K. & E. i, 586, n. (*a*).
[2] *Eastwood* v. *Ashton* [1915] A.C. 900; for other examples, see Lord Sumner's speech at p. 914, and Norton on *Deeds*, 237, 238, 243. See, however, *Truckell* v. *Stock* [1957] 1 W.L.R. 161, and contrast *Grigsby* v. *Melville* [1974] 1 W.L.R. 80. If both phrases are used, they are " mutually stultifying ": *Neilson* v. *Poole* (1968) 20 P. & C.R. 909 at 916.

The conveyance will pass all fixtures without special mention, for they are part of the land and pass with it.[3] But it will not pass removable chattels such as movable greenhouses.[4] The purchaser is entitled on completion to all fixtures attached to the land at the date of the contract.[5]

10. Habendum. This shows that the purchaser is to hold the land for his own benefit and not upon trust for a third party. It also contains the usual words of limitation.[6] It is followed by the acknowledgment and undertaking [7] where these are to be included.

11. Testimonium, and

12. Attestation clause. Since 1925 deeds executed by individuals must be signed as well as sealed.[8] Witnessing is not legally necessary for the validity of a deed, but is an invariable practice.[9]

C. Setting Aside and Modification of Conveyances

An executed conveyance may be avoided, set aside or modified by the court [10] in various cases of fraud, undue influence, or mistake; and where this occurs the court may order the document to be delivered up for cancellation.[11] The jurisdiction is either equitable or statutory. In either case the conveyance is not void but voidable, and unless and until it is avoided it can pass a good title to an innocent purchaser who has no notice of the vitiating facts.[12]

The court may always set aside a conveyance induced by fraudulent misrepresentation.[13] Conveyances induced by innocent misrepresentation may also, it seems, be set aside under the Misrepresentation Act 1967, as already mentioned.[14]

Conveyances made with intent to defraud creditors (including any intent to prejudice them [15]) are by statute voidable at the instance of any person thereby prejudiced.[16] Disentailing assurances

---

[3] L.P.A., 1925, s. 62, expressly includes " buildings, erections, fixtures."
[4] *H. E. Dibble Ltd.* v. *Moore* [1970] 2 Q.B. 181 ; *post*, p. 718.
[5] As to fixtures, see *post*, p. 711.
[6] *Ante*, p. 50.
[7] *Ante*, p. 599.
[8] L.P.A., 1925, s. 73 ; as to corporations, see s. 74.
[9] Norton on *Deeds*, 24.
[10] For infants' dispositions, see *post*, p. 991.
[11] See Snell, *Equity*, 608.
[12] He need not acquire a legal estate: *ante*, p. 119.
[13] *Ante*, pp. 591–592.
[14] *Ante*, p. 591.
[15] *Lloyds Bank Ltd.* v. *Marcan* [1973] 1 W.L.R. 1387 (lease by mortgagor intended to prejudice mortgagee's remedies).
[16] L.P.A., 1925, s. 172, replacing 13 Eliz. 1, c. 5, 1571. See generally Snell, *Equity*, 127–130; and see *Re Eichholz* [1959] Ch. 708 at 728; *cf.* Bankruptcy Act, 1914, s. 42 (Snell, *Equity*, 131–133).

are not affected.[17] A purchaser of any estate or interest for valuable
or good consideration is protected if at the time of the conveyance
he had no notice of the intent to defraud.[18]

Every voluntary disposition of land made with intent to defraud
a subsequent purchaser is by statute voidable at the instance of that
purchaser.[19] A subsequent conveyance for value is not *per se* evidence of fraudulent intent.[20]

Conveyances made under undue influence, *e.g.,* by a child to a
parent or by a client to a solicitor, may be set aside under equitable
jurisdiction.[21] The same may be done where a relationship of confidence is abused. The Court of Appeal has set aside a guarantee and
legal charge, made in favour of a bank by its customer, when the
bank knew that the customer relied on its advice but did not warn him
of the dangers of the transaction.[22]

In some cases conveyances may be rectified, set aside or modified for mutual mistake. This has already been explained.[23]

---

[17] s. 172 (2).
[18] s. 172 (3); *Lloyds Bank Ltd.* v. *Marcan, supra* (imputed notice).
[19] L.P.A., 1925, s. 173 (1), replacing 27 Eliz. 1, c. 4, 1584. See generally Snell,
  Equity, 130, 131.
[20] s. 173 (2), replacing Voluntary Conveyances Act, 1893. Formerly the law was
  otherwise.
[21] See Snell, *Equity,* 546.
[22] *Lloyds Bank Ltd.* v. *Bundy* [1974] 3 W.L.R. 501.
[23] *Ante,* p. 596.

CHAPTER 11

LEASES AND TENANCIES

Part 1

INTRODUCTORY

Sect. 1. History

A LEASE, as generally understood today, is a document creating an interest in land for a fixed period of certain duration, usually in consideration of the payment of rent. The interest so created is called a term of years, but it is also often referred to as a lease or a leasehold interest. There are also certain tenancies which are not created by documents, or which are not for fixed periods, which are nevertheless part of the subject of leases. The most comprehensive title for the law governing these various interests is " the law of landlord and tenant."

1. Leases as interests in land. Something has already been said of leases in relation to other estates in land [1]; and elsewhere will be found an account of the manner in which leases developed from mere personal contracts (rights *in personam*) into rights of property (rights *in rem*) after the invention of the action of ejectment in the fifteenth century.[2] Just as this development brought the term of years into the category of estates, so also, as has been seen, it brought it within the principle of tenure [3]; for the theory of tenure requires that all land which is held for any estate shall be held of a lord. Thus it was that the relationship of landlord and tenant (for years), which had no place in the old feudal land law, came to be based upon tenure; and, indeed, it is now the only form of tenure which retains any practical importance after 1925. It is owing to the existence of tenure, for example, that the tenant's rent is properly called rent-service (as opposed to rentcharge) and that the landlord has the remedy of distraint for rent owed to him [4]; and in theory, at least, every tenant probably still owes fealty to his landlord.[5]

---

[1] *Ante*, p. 43.
[3] *Ante*, p. 45.
[2] *Post*, p. 1168.
[4] *Post*, p. 691.
[5] Litt. 213; Co.Litt. 142a. For fealty, see *ante*, p. 16. It may be for this reason that a man cannot grant a lease to himself (*Rye* v. *Rye* [1962] A.C. 496), though the House of Lords stressed the absurdity of a man contracting with himself rather than that of his holding in tenure of himself. See (1962) 78 L.Q.R. 175 (P. V. Baker).

2. Duration of leases. Leases came into common use long before they obtained full protection as interests in land [6]; they appear frequently from the early thirteenth century onwards.[7] There is a tradition that in ancient times leases might not exceed forty years,[8] but there is no clear evidence that such a rule ever existed. A lease cannot be granted to endure in perpetuity,[9] but subject to this the law allows the creation of leases of any length. For example an ordinary mortgage now takes the form of a lease for 3,000 years [10]; and even a tenant for life, who at common law could not grant a lease which would continue after his death, may now grant a building or forestry lease of 999 years under the Settled Land Act, 1925.[11]

The system of farming under agricultural leases became widespread in the seventeenth century. Farming leases were generally granted for terms up to 21 years.[12] Much longer terms (*e.g.*, 60 or 99 years) were used for building or mining leases, which were useful means for the development or exploitation of land. Under a building lease, for example, the land is let for a long term at a ground rent, the tenant puts up a building at his own expense, and at the end of the term this becomes the landlord's property [13]; such a lease is therefore a valuable long-term investment for the landlord. Leases of anything up to 999 years, or even more, are sometimes granted for similar purposes; here the reversion is too remote to have any value, but the advantage to the landlord is that he can control the use of the land by means of covenants in the lease, and a greater variety of covenants are enforceable under a lease than under an outright conveyance of the fee simple.[14] Such very long leases may therefore be useful when a landlord is developing an estate and wishes to keep control over its appearance and character.

3. Leases as conveyancing devices. Leases are also much used as a mere conveyancing device, usually in order to provide security for the payment of money. For this purpose a long lease is granted, free of rent or other obligations, so that the lessee simply takes a valuable interest in the land which is a good security for money advanced by him. The two most important examples are:

---

[6] For the history of leaseholders' remedies and the growth of leasehold interests in land, see *post*, p. 1169.

[7] P. & M. ii, 110–112.

[8] Co.Litt. 45b, 46a.

[9] *Sevenoaks, Maidstone & Tunbridge Ry.* v. *London, Chatham & Dover Ry.* (1879) 11 Ch.D. 625 at 635.

[10] *Post*, p. 892.

[11] *Ante*, p. 334.

[12] See *Att.-Gen.* v. *Owen* (1805) 10 Ves. 555 at 560.

[13] But legislation has now in many cases expropriated the landlord's interest in the building in favour of the tenant and enabled the tenant to acquire the land compulsorily; alternatively the tenant is given security of tenure: see *post*, p. 1149.

[14] *Post*, p. 724.

(i) the lease granted by a mortgagor to the mortgagee as security for the money lent; and

(ii) the lease granted under a settlement to trustees to secure payment of portions for younger children.

In both cases it is unusual for the lessee to take possession of the land. These leases are dealt with under mortgages [15] and settlements [16] respectively. The leases dealt with in this chapter are leases where the lessee has the right to occupy the land or to receive the rent from a sub-tenant.

4. Leases for lives. Formerly leases were often granted not for a term of years but for a life or lives. A lease for life or lives [17] had the advantage of giving the lessee a freehold estate, instead of a mere term of years, so that even before the action of ejectment was invented he could recover the land itself.[18] Further, a lease for 21 years or three lives was formerly the longest term which could be granted by a tenant in tail or by an ecclesiastical or charitable corporation (*e.g.,* a college).[19] By the middle of the nineteenth century wider leasing powers had been given to tenants in tail,[20] ecclesiastical corporations,[21] and certain universities and colleges,[22] and so the practice of granting leases for life had declined. A lease for life, like a lease for years, created tenure between the parties, so that rent or other services could be reserved. Such leases were usually commercial transactions which were quite distinct from tenancies for life under family settlements, where a beneficial interest was granted free of any rent or services. The scheme of the 1925 legislation required life interests to be merely equitable, and this, though suitable for settlements, was unsuitable for leaseholds. Accordingly, most leases for life have now been converted into terms of years, as will be seen later.[23]

5. Law and equity. Unlike life tenancies, leases are commonly legal estates, and any number of leases and sub-leases can exist as legal estates concurrently. A term of years can, of course, subsist

[15] *Post,* p. 896.
[16] *Ante,* p. 387.
[17] For this phrase, see Challis 65.
[18] *Ante,* p. 613.
[19] See *ante,* p. 93 ; Platt on *Leases,* i, 66, 67, 247.
[20] See Fines and Recoveries Act, 1833 ; *ante,* p. 90.
[21] Ecclesiastical Leases Act, 1842.
[22] Universities and College Estates Act, 1858. The Universities and College Estates Acts, 1925 and 1964, continue the policy of the Universities and College Estates Act, 1898, of giving these universities and colleges powers resembling those given to tenants for life under S.L.A., 1882, which are narrower than those given by S.L.A., 1925.
[23] *Post,* p. 642.

as an equitable interest under a trust, or as a result of a failure to employ the formalities required for the grant of a legal term; but legal leases are much more common. In order to be capable of existing as a legal estate the leasehold interest must be a "term of years absolute" within the meaning of the Law of Property Act, 1925, s. 1 (1). The wide meaning of this expression has already been explained,[24] and should be borne in mind in reading this chapter.

Sect. 2. Terminology

It is important to be familiar with the terms used in the law of leases. The grantor of a lease is known as the lessor, the person to whom it is granted as the lessee. On the grant of a lease, the lessor retains a reversion, which he may assign; similarly, the lessee may assign the lease. Instead of assigning the lease (*i.e.*, transferring the property for the whole of the period for which it is held), the owner of the lease may grant a sub-lease (or underlease) for a period at least one day shorter than the lease, the parties to this sub-lease being known as the sub-lessor and the sub-lessee respectively. Where the original lessor and original lessee have both assigned their interests, the new owners of the reversion and the lease are sometimes referred to as the lessor and lessee, although it is better to reserve these expressions for the original parties to the lease, and refer to the owners for the time being of the reversion and the lease, whether original or by assignment, as the landlord and the tenant.

These expressions may be illustrated as follows:

$$X \longrightarrow Y$$
$$\downarrow 99$$
$$A \longrightarrow B$$
$$\downarrow 21$$
$$C \longrightarrow D$$

This diagram is the usual way of representing the following events. X grants a 99-years lease to A and then assigns the reversion to Y. B takes an assignment of A's lease and grants a sub-lease

---

[24] *Ante*, p. 140.

to C for 21 years, and C assigns his sub-lease to D. As to the 99-years lease, X is the " lessor," Y is the " assignee of the reversion " or " landlord," and A the " lessee." B is in a dual position: as to the 99-years lease, he is the " assignee " or " tenant "; as to the 21-years lease, he is " sub-lessor " or " landlord." The 99-years lease is then called the " head lease," so as to distinguish it from the sub-lease. C is the " sub-lessee," and D the " assignee " of the sub-lease, or the " sub-tenant." By annexing the dates of each transaction to each link in the diagram the sequence of events may be shown.

" Demise " is the technical term for " let " or " lease "; thus a lease may be referred to as a " demise " and the premises in question as the " demised premises." " Lease " and " term of years " are nearly synonymous terms today [24a]; before 1926 a term of years could only be regarded as one kind of lease,[25] since leases for lives were by no means unknown. Today leases for lives have nearly all disappeared.[26] " Lease " is often used interchangeably, either for the document or for the " term of years " or " leasehold interest " created by it, although primarily it means the document.[27]

Part 2

CREATION OF LEASES

Sect. 1. Essentials of a Lease

A lease in its simplest possible form is the grant of a leasehold interest in land. But in practice leases are almost invariably bilateral contracts, in which the tenant is not only given an estate in the land but also himself gives covenants, *e.g.*, to pay rent and execute repairs. Leases must now be distinguished from other contracts concerning the use of land, for there is an infinite variety of such contracts which are not leases. Parties may make any bargain they like between themselves, and enforce it between themselves as a contract. But if one wishes to give the other an estate, that is to say a proprietary interest which will bind not only the grantor but also the rest of the world, then that interest must conform to the requirements by which the law limits the kinds of estates which can be created. For example,

---

[24a] But see *Re Land and Premises at Liss, Hants.* [1971] Ch. 986.
[25] See *ante*, p. 615.
[26] See *post*, p. 642.
[27] In the L.P.A., 1925, " lease " includes any tenancy: ss. 154, 205 (1) (xxiii): and see *post*, p. 735. Further, the L.P.A., 1925, s. 54 (2), speaks of parol " leases " (and see s. 52 (2) (*d*)), and " oral lease " and its less correct relative " verbal lease " are common expressions.

if A gives B a mere licence [28] to use A's land, even though for payment, and then A sells the land to X, B can sue A for damages for breach of contract but he has no rights over the land as against X.[29] But if A grants B a lease, then B has a legal estate subject to which X takes, so that B can enforce his rights against X as well as against A. It is therefore of great importance to know what transactions come within the definition of a lease.

A. The Right to Exclusive Possession must be Given

1. Exclusive possession. It is of the essence of a lease that the tenant should be given the right to exclusive possession, that is, the right to exclude all other persons from the premises. A right to occupy certain premises for a fixed period cannot be a tenancy if the person granting the right remains in general control of the property. This is normally the case with rooms in an inn or boarding-house, so that a lodger is commonly a mere licensee and not a tenant.[30] It makes no difference that the parties make a formal agreement purporting to be a lease and call themselves landlord and tenant [31]; for the test is one of fact, not one of form. Conversely, a person described as a lodger or other licensee may be a tenant if he is, in fact, given exclusive possession of some definite part of the premises together with the right to exclude all other people including the landlord,[32] even if the landlord lives on the premises,[33] and notwithstanding a clause expressly negativing any tenancy.[34] Yet although exclusive possession is essential, it does not necessarily establish a tenancy; other facts may show that there is only a licence.[34a] In case of a tenancy the landlord commits a trespass if he enters without the tenant's permission and without authority under the lease, whereas if only a licence is granted, the licensor by entering may commit a breach of contract, but not a trespass.

---

28 See *post*, p. 776.
29 But X may possibly be bound if he purchases with notice: *post*, p. 782.
30 *Smith* v. *St. Michael's, Cambridge, Overseers* (1860) 3 E. & E. 383 (a rating case); *cf. Helman* v. *Horsham & Worthing Assessment Committee* [1949] 2 K.B. 335; *R.* v. *Battersea, etc., Rent Tribunal, ex p. Parikh* [1957] 1 W.L.R. 410; *Appah* v. *Parncliffe Investments Ltd.* [1964] 1 W.L.R. 1064.
31 *Daly* v. *Edwardes* (1900) 83 L.T. 548; *Frank Warr & Co. Ltd.* v. *L.C.C.* [1904] 1 K.B. 713; *Clore* v. *Theatrical Properties Ltd.* [1936] 3 All E.R. 483.
32 *Newman* v. *Anderton* (1806) 2 B. & P.N.R. 224; *Addiscombe Garden Estates Ltd.* v. *Crabbe* [1958] 1 Q.B. 513. *Cf. The Three D's Co. Ltd.* v. *Barrow* (1949) 99 L.J.News. 564.
33 *Kent* v. *Fittall* [1906] 1 K.B. 6.
34 See *Facchini* v. *Bryson* [1952] 1 T.L.R. 1386.
34a *Abbeyfield (Harpenden) Society Ltd.* v. *Woods* [1968] 1 W.L.R. 374 (exclusive possession of one room in old people's home); *Barnes* v. *Barratt* [1970] 2 Q.B. 657 (house-sharing arrangement without rent or fixed term); *Shell-Mex and B.P. Ltd.* v. *Manchester Garages Ltd.* [1971] 1 W.L.R. 612 (petrol filling station); and see n. 35, *infra*.

2. Intention. The distinction is thus governed by the situation created by the parties rather than by their expressed intentions. But the court will, it seems, now sometimes be swayed by the purpose of the transaction, and even a right of exclusive occupation may be held no more than a licence.[35] In one case a landlord refused to grant a lease to a daughter of the deceased tenant but accepted the weekly rent which she paid; it was held that there was only a licence, and that the licensee (unlike a tenant) was not protected by the Rent Restriction Acts.[36] A desire to prevent these Acts from operating too widely has thus weakened the former rule that exclusive occupation necessarily resulted in a tenancy.[37] But, as will appear later, there are other cases also in which the established rule has not been followed.[38]

3. Illustrations. Since the line dividing leases from licences is a fine one, a few more examples may be given. In one well-known case [39] a graving dock was let by a corporation subject to certain rights of control, *e.g.*, as to opening and shutting the dock gates and seeing that the dock was cleaned out each day; it was held that no lease had been created. Similarly it has been held that nothing more than a licence is given by an agreement to let the " front of the house rights " of a theatre, *i.e.*, the right to sell refreshments in the theatre and use the refreshment rooms for that purpose [40]; or for the hire of a stall between certain hours daily at an exhibition [41]; or for the grant of the exclusive right to put up advertisements on a building.[42] Nor can there be any lease if no defined premises are let, as where there is a contractual obligation to store goods but the rooms in which they are stored may be changed from time to time at the convenience of the owner of the premises.[43] But if the premises are clearly defined, and exclusive occupation of them is

---

[35] *Marcroft Wagons Ltd.* v. *Smith* [1951] 2 K.B. 496; *Errington* v. *Errington* [1952] 1 K.B. 290; *Cobb* v. *Lane* [1952] 1 All E.R. 1199; *Gorham (Contractors) Ltd.* v. *Field* [1952] C.P.L. 266; *Murray Bull & Co. Ltd.* v. *Murray* [1953] 1 Q.B. 211; *Isaac* v. *Hotel de Paris Ltd.* [1960] 1 W.L.R. 239; *Finbow* v. *Air Ministry* [1963] 1 W.L.R. 697. For criticism of this new trend, see " Licensed Possessors " (1953) 69 L.Q.R. 466 (A. D. Hargreaves); and for the criteria for determining whether a transaction creates a lease or a licence, see Megarry's *Rent Acts*, 10th ed., pp. 54–60; and *cf. post*, p. 776. See also n. 34a, *supra*.

[36] *Marcroft Wagons Ltd.* v. *Smith, supra*; and see *Murray Bull & Co. Ltd.* v. *Murray, supra.*

[37] *Marcroft Wagons Ltd.* v. *Smith, supra.* at p. 501; *Cobb* v. *Lane* [1952] 1 All E.R. 1199 at 1202; *Heslop* v. *Burns* [1974] 1 W.L.R. 1241.

[38] *Errington* v. *Errington* [1952] 1 K.B. 290; *post*, p. 782; *Cobb* v. *Lane, supra*; *post*, p. 1018. See also *Brooker* v. *Palmer* [1942] 2 All E.R. 674; *Isaac* v. *Hotel de Paris Ltd.* [1960] 1 W.L.R. 239.

[39] *Wells* v. *Kingston-upon-Hull Corporation* (1875) L.R. 10 C.P. 402.

[40] See cases cited, *supra*, n. 31.

[41] *Rendell* v. *Roman* (1893) 9 T.L.R. 192.

[42] *King* v. *David Allen & Sons, Billposting, Ltd.* [1916] 2 A.C. 54; *Walton Harvey Ltd.* v. *Walker & Homfrays Ltd.* [1931] 1 Ch. 274.

[43] *Interoven Stove Co. Ltd.* v. *Hibbard* [1936] 1 All E.R. 263.

given, the mere imposition of severe restrictions on the use which can be made of them will not prevent a lease from being created.[44] A document calling itself a " licence," but modelled upon the common form of a lease, and containing undertakings for " delivery up " of the premises, for the " licensor " to enter and view the state of repair, and for re-entry for breach of the " licensee's " undertakings, may for these reasons be construed as granting an exclusive right of occupation, and so creating a lease.[45]

4. Service occupation. There is also no tenancy where a servant occupies his master's premises because that is required by the nature of his duties. This may apply, for example, to a gamekeeper's or stockman's cottage.[46] In such cases there is no tenancy but merely a " service occupancy," and the occupant is a licensee. Here again fine distinctions may have to be drawn between occupation which is required for the better performance of the servant's duties, and occupation which is for the convenience of the servant. In any case the parties may show by their language that they created a lease and not a licence.[47]

B. *The Requirements as to Duration must be Satisfied*

A lease may fail because the estate is not clearly marked out, *e.g.*, if it purports to be a lease for an indefinite period instead of for a fixed term. The various periods for which leases can validly be granted are treated separately below.[48]

C. *The Lease must be Created in the Proper Way*

I. FORMAL LEASES

In order to create a legal estate which can rank as a term of years absolute within section 1 (1) of the Law of Property Act, 1925,[49] a lease must be made with the proper formalities. The present position has been reached in four stages.

1. At common law a lease of corporeal land could be granted in any way, even orally. This illustrates the ancient conception of a lease as a simple contract. But incorporeal rights which are within

---

[44] *Joel* v. *International Circus and Christmas Fair* (1920) 124 L.T. 459.
[45] *Addiscombe Garden Estates Ltd.* v. *Crabbe* [1958] 1 Q.B. 513.
[46] See *Dover* v. *Prosser* [1904] 1 K.B. 84; *Ramsbottom* v. *Snelson* [1948] 1 K.B. 473; *Glasgow Corporation* v. *Johnstone* [1965] A.C. 609.
[47] *The Three D's Co. Ltd.* v. *Barrow* (1949) 99 L.J.News. 564. This may still be true where there is an express clause stating that no tenancy shall arise: *Facchini* v. *Bryson* [1952] 1 T.L.R. 1386.
[48] *Post*, p. 630.
[49] *Ante*, p. 140.

the definition of real property,[50] such as easements and profits, could be created at common law only by deed: they lay in grant, not in livery.[51] This rule was applied to leases, when they came to be considered estates in land, so that a lease of (for example) shooting or fishing rights had to be made by deed. But if land was leased to which such incorporeal rights were appurtenant, they could pass with the land without a deed.

2. 1677–1845. The common law rule that a lease could be established on oral evidence alone was a fertile source of fraud and perjury. The Court of Chancery manifested an unwillingness to enforce parol leases, " considering the plenty of witnesses now-a-days, which were *testes diabolices, qui magis fame quam fama moventur.*" [52] To remedy this, the Statute of Frauds, 1677,[53] required (*inter alia*) that every lease should be in writing (though not necessarily by deed) signed by the party creating it or his agent authorised in writing; in default of this, only a tenancy at will was created. An exception was made for a lease for a period not exceeding three years from its creation at a rent of at least two-thirds of the full improved value (*i.e.*, the value taking into consideration any improvements to the property[54]); such a lease could still be made orally. The rule that leases of incorporeal rights must be made by deed was not altered by the statute.[55]

3. 1845–1926. The Real Property Act, 1845,[56] required a deed in all cases in which the existing law required writing. The exception as to leases for three years or less therefore remained as before, but all other leases had to be made by deed. The Act said " a lease required by law to be in writing . . . shall be void at law unless also made by deed."

4. Since 1925

(*a*) *The statute.* The provisions of the two previous Acts were repeated by the Law of Property Act, 1925, but with certain alterations. No attempt has been made to state the combined effect of the earlier Acts: section 54 follows the Statute of Frauds, 1677, and

---

[50] *Ante*, p. 136, *post*, p. 787.
[51] *Post*, p. 810.
[52] *Anon.* (1603) Cary 27 at 28, *per* Egerton L.K.; and see *Anon.* (1598) Cary 7.
[53] s. 1.
[54] s. 2.
[55] *Duke of Somerset* v. *Fogwell* (1826) 5 B. & C. 875; *Bird* v. *Higginson* (1835) 6 A. & E. 824.
[56] s. 3, replacing the Transfer of Property Act, 1844, s. 4.

section 52 follows the Real Property Act, 1845, so that their differing provisions still stand side by side. This is presumably because
they had become so familiar that it was thought best to preserve
them.

(*b*) *The rule.* The present law may be stated as follows. A lease
cannot create a legal estate unless it is made by deed; for all grants
are " void for the purpose of conveying or creating a legal estate
unless made by deed." [57] But no formality is required for a lease
which—

    (i) takes effect in possession,

    (ii) for a term not exceeding three years, whether or not the
        lessee is given power to extend the term,

    (iii) at the best rent reasonably obtainable without taking a fine.[58]

It will be seen that (i) is new, and (iii) is a modification of the
previous law.

(*c*) " *Possession.*" A lease taking effect in possession is to be
contrasted with one taking effect in reversion, *e.g.*, a lease granted
today to take effect in 19 days' time [59]; reversionary leases are considered below.[60] " Possession " is not confined to physical possession,
but includes receipt of rents and profits, *e.g.*, from sub-tenants in
physical possession.[61]

(*d*) " *Three years.*" The phrase " a term not exceeding three
years " includes a monthly or other periodic tenancy,[62] even though
it will continue indefinitely unless determined by notice,[63] for it is
wholly uncertain that it will endure for more than three years. The
phrase also includes a fixed term for three years or less which contains an option for the tenant to extend it beyond three years,[64] but
not a fixed term for more than three years, even though it is determinable within that period.[65] The three years must be computed
from the date of the grant.[66]

---

[57] s. 52 (1); and see ss. 54 (1), 205 (1) (ii).
[58] s. 54 (2). A " fine " in this sense is a lump sum payment made in consideration
of a reduced rent; it is often called a " premium." Thus premises worth £100
per annum may be let for three years at £100 per annum (*i.e.*, at a full, or
" rack " rent) or at £10 per annum with a premium of £270.
[59] See *Foster* v. *Reeves* [1892] 2 Q.B. at 257.
[60] *Post*, p. 631.
[61] L.P.A., 1925, s. 205 (1) (xix), *ante*, p. 140.
[62] *Ex p. Voisey* (1882) 21 Ch.D. 442; *Hammond* v. *Farrow* [1904] 2 K.B. 332
at 335.
[63] See *post*, p. 633.
[64] See *Hand* v. *Hall* (1877) 2 Ex.D. 355.
[65] *Kushner* v. *Law Society* [1952] 1 K.B. 264.
[66] See *Rawlins* v. *Turner* (1699) 1 Ld.Raym. 736.

(e) *Application.* If all three conditions are complied with, a legal lease can be created either orally or in writing. But the legislation seems to preserve the exception as to incorporeal rights, such as shooting or fishing, which therefore can be leased only by deed.[67] Further, an oral lease is not a " conveyance " within the Law of Property Act, 1925,[68] and so it may be less effective than a lease by deed, *e.g.*, for creating easements.[69] In any case, the concession in favour of informal leases applies only to the *grant* of a lease; a *contract* for a lease, *i.e.*, a promise to grant a lease at a future date, for however short a period, will be unenforceable by action unless evidenced by sufficient writing or part performance. Contracts for leases must be evidenced in exactly the same way as contracts for sale,[70] and there is no exception in favour of contracts for short terms; but, as has been explained elsewhere, the doctrine of part performance will often protect a tenant who has taken possession under an informal agreement for a lease.[71]

(f) *Assignment.* Once a legal lease has been validly granted, a deed is required to effect a legal assignment of it,[72] no matter how short the term; thus a legal assignment of a yearly tenancy can be effected only by deed, even if the tenancy was created orally.[73]

II. INFORMAL LEASES

1. Informal lease void at law. A lease which did not satisfy the above requirements was void at law and passed no legal estate. But a tenancy might arise independently of the lease; for if the tenant took possession with the landlord's consent, a tenancy at will arose, and as soon as rent was paid and accepted, the tenancy at will was converted into a yearly or other periodic tenancy, depending on the way in which the rent was paid.[74] Such a yearly tenancy was a legal estate, for the law implied an oral grant from one acceptance of rent by the landlord. Furthermore, it was held subject to any terms which the parties had agreed upon, so far as they were consistent with a yearly tenancy.[75]

---

[67] *Wood* v. *Leadbitter* (1845) 13 M. & W. 838 at 843; *Swayne* v. *Howells* [1927] 1 K.B. 385; *Mason* v. *Clarke* [1954] 1 Q.B. 460; [1955] A.C. 778; [1954] C.L.J. 189; Woodfall L. & T. 22; *post*, p. 827.
[68] *Rye* v. *Rye* [1962] A.C. 496.
[69] *Post*, p. 838.
[70] *Ante*, p. 545.
[71] *Ante*, p. 561.
[72] L.P.A., 1925, s. 52 (1), replacing R.P.A., 1845, s. 3.
[73] *Botting* v. *Martin* (1808) 1 Camp. 317. As to the effect of an informal assignment, see *post*, p. 650.
[74] *Martin* v. *Smith* (1874) L.R. 9 Ex. 50; *post*, p. 634.
[75] *Doe* d. *Rigge* v. *Bell* (1793) 5 T.R. 471; *Doe* d. *Thomson* v. *Amey* (1840) 12 A. & E. 476.

An informal lease which was "void at law" under the Real Property Act, 1845, was thus not entirely ineffective if a yearly tenancy later arose. If, for example, the tenant had covenanted to do repairs, this became one of the terms of the yearly tenancy. Other examples of such terms which are transferable to a yearly tenancy are given later.[76] Before 1875, therefore, the position *in a common law court* of a tenant who had entered and paid rent under a void lease was generally that of a yearly tenant subject to certain of the terms of the lease. The landlord was in a corresponding position. But both parties might have had other rights *in equity*, as will shortly be explained.

2. Effect as contract. Although such a lease failed to create any legal estate, it might be treated as a contract to grant the lease agreed upon. A lease is clearly distinct from a contract to grant a lease: the difference is between " I hereby grant you a lease " and " I hereby agree that I will grant you a lease." [77] Nevertheless both law and equity concurred in treating an imperfect lease as a contract to grant a lease,[78] provided it was made for value and was sufficiently evidenced in writing or, in the case of equity, supported by a sufficient act of part performance. The attitude of equity was particularly important, for under the doctrine of *Parker* v. *Taswell* [79] equity would first treat an imperfect lease of this kind as a contract to grant the lease, and then order specific performance of that contract.[80] Once a proper lease had been granted in pursuance of the decree of specific performance, the position of the parties was the same for the future as if the lease had been granted by deed in the first place. Specific performance is, of course, an equitable remedy, and it was not available in any except the courts of equity until 1875.[81]

---

[76] *Post*, p. 634.

[77] The difference is often not so clear in practice, where the " agreement " made by the parties may be either a contract or a grant, depending on its language. In doubtful cases the court leans towards the interpretation which will give the greater validity to the transaction: *Browne* v. *Warner* (1807) 14 Ves. 156; *Rollason* v. *Leon* (1861) 7 H. & N. 73 (" A agrees to let and B agrees to take "); *cf. Wright* v. *Macadam* [1949] 2 K.B. 744 at 747 (" Agreement " held to be a lease).

[78] *Bond* v. *Rosling* (1861) 1 B. & S. 371; *Tidey* v. *Mollett* (1864) 16 C.B. (N.S.) 298. An imperfect lease is not treated as an agreement for every purpose: see, *e.g.*, *Harte* v. *Williams* [1934] 1 K.B. 201 (unsealed lease prepared by unqualified person).

[79] (1858) 2 De G. & J. 559; and see *Zimbler* v. *Abrahams* [1903] 1 K.B. 577, following *Mardell* v. *Curtis* [1899] W.N. 93: this, and not *Cheshire Lines Committee* v. *Lewis* (1880) 50 L.J.Q.B. 121, represents the present law on this point. As to incorporeal rights, see *Frogley* v. *Earl of Lovelace* (1859) John. 333.

[80] If the lease was void because it exceeded the lessor's power to grant it, it might similarly be treated as a contract for a properly limited lease; *cf.* L.P.A., 1925, s. 152, *ante*, p. 337.

[81] J.A., 1873, 1875; *ante*, p. 128.

3. Walsh v. Lonsdale [82]

(*a*) *Effect of right to specific performance.* The rights of the parties under an imperfect lease sufficiently evidenced by writing or part performance were thus clear whenever specific performance had been decreed. What was not so clear was the position if, as was far more often the case, no decree of specific performance had been granted but the parties were entitled to obtain one. In equity the principle is " equity looks on that as done which ought to be done," so that the parties were treated as if the lease had been granted with proper formalities. But there was no such principle at law; for at law the transaction was void as a lease, and as a contract for a lease it was remediable only by an action for damages.

The difference in the position in equity is founded on the difference between damages and specific performance. A person entitled merely to damages has no rights in the land; but a person entitled to specific performance has the right to demand the land itself, and so in the eyes of equity such a person is the rightful occupant. Just as a purchaser becomes equitable owner under a contract for sale,[83] so an intended lessee becomes equitable tenant under a contract for a lease. If a proper lease ought already to have been executed, he is in the same position as if it had been executed, with one important reservation, namely, that until he has obtained a proper lease his rights are equitable, not legal.

(*b*) *Fusion of courts.* A tenant holding under a mere contract for a lease, *i.e.*, merely in equity, could, before 1875, always enforce his rights against the other party by recourse to the Court of Chancery. Here he could obtain a decree of specific performance, and he could meanwhile ask for an injunction to prevent the landlord interfering with the exercise of his equitable rights. After 1875 the tenant no longer needed to rely on the protection of one special court, for the result of the Judicature Acts, 1873–1875,[84] was that " there is only one court, and the equity rules prevail in it." [85] This is shown in the leading case of *Walsh* v. *Lonsdale*,[1] which laid down that where there is a yearly tenancy at common law but a tenancy for years in equity, both parties can insist on their equitable rights against one another and that these prevail over their legal rights.

(*c*) *The decision.* The facts and decision in *Walsh* v. *Lonsdale* [2] were as follows. L agreed in writing to grant a seven years' lease of a mill to T at a rent which was to vary with the number of looms

[82] (1882) 21 Ch.D. 9.
[84] See J.A., 1873, s. 25 (11).
[85] *Walsh* v. *Lonsdale* (1882) 21 Ch.D. 9 at 14, *per* Jessel M.R.
[1] (1882) 21 Ch.D. 9.
[83] *Ante*, p. 575.
[2] *Ibid.*

run. One of the agreed terms was that on demand T would pay a year's rent in advance. No lease was executed, but T was let into possession and paid rent in arrear for a year and a half, thereby becoming a yearly tenant at law. L then demanded a year's rent in advance, and on T's refusal to pay, distrained for it. T then brought an action for damages for wrongful distress (in effect, for trespass), for an injunction and for specific performance of the agreement, and he applied for an interim injunction restraining the landlord's acts meanwhile. It was upon this last application that the case was decided.

T's argument was that distress was a legal, and not an equitable, remedy, and that since at law he was only a yearly tenant and no obligation to pay rent in advance could be implied, especially in view of the variable nature of the rent, L could not distrain for the rent.[3] It was held, however, that since the distress would have been legal had the lease agreed upon been granted by deed, and since equity treated the parties as if this had been done, the distress was lawful in equity. In equity's eyes T was already tenant for seven years subject to all the terms of the agreement, not a yearly tenant subject to some terms only. Since 1875 the equitable rule prevailed over the rule at law in all courts and so T could not complain of the distress.

4. Differences between legal and equitable leases. The effect of *Walsh* v. *Lonsdale* was often summed up in the words " a contract for a lease is as good as a lease."[4] For many purposes this is true, but as a generalisation it is misleading,[5] for it ignores the vital difference between legal and equitable interests. The difference between a contract and a lease is in reality substantial: a contract falls short of a lease in the following respects.

(*a*) *Dependence upon specific performance.* The effect of *Walsh* v. *Lonsdale* in equity depends upon the willingness of the court to grant the discretionary remedy of specific performance.[6] If for any reason an agreement for a lease is one of which the court cannot or will not grant specific performance the position under it is very different from that under a legal lease: the parties can have nothing more than a right to sue for damages under the agreement, though a yearly or other periodic tenancy may arise in the usual way. For

---

[3] See *Manchester Brewery Co.* v. *Coombs* [1901] 2 Ch. 608 at 617, 618, *per* Farwell J.

[4] See *Re Maughan* (1885) 14 Q.B.D. 956 at 958; *Furness* v. *Bond* (1888) 4 T.L.R. 457; *Allhusen* v. *Brooking* (1884) 26 Ch.D. 551 at 565; *Lowther* v. *Heaver* (1889) 41 Ch.D. 248 at 264.

[5] See *Manchester Brewery Co.* v. *Coombs* [1901] 2 Ch. 608 at 617.

[6] *Ibid.*; *ante*, p. 593; and see *ante*, p. 561 (specific performance of agreements for short leases).

example, there can normally be no specific performance in favour of a tenant whose tenancy agreement is subject to a condition precedent (*e.g.*, to repair) which he has not performed,[7] or who is already in breach of one of the terms of the agreement,[8] or whose claim is to an underlease which can be granted to him only in breach of a covenant against sub-letting in the head-lease.[9] He who comes into equity must come with clean hands, and he who seeks equity must do equity.[10] In such cases the tenant must stand or fall by his rights (if any) at law. Further, limits to a court's jurisdiction may create difficulties. Thus a plaintiff's right to specific performance in a county court is strictly limited,[11] whereas a defendant's is not.[12]

(*b*) *Third parties.* There are basic differences as to third parties. A lease creates a legal estate, good against all the world. A contract for a lease creates only an equitable interest, *viz.*, the right to the equitable remedy of specific performance; and this must share the usual frailty of equitable interests, that it will not be good against a bona fide purchaser for value of a legal estate without notice.[13] Thus if before 1926 L made a specifically enforceable contract for a lease with T, but then conveyed a legal estate to X by a lease, mortgage or conveyance on sale in proper form, X's rights would prevail over T's provided that X acted in good faith and had no notice of T's rights when he took the conveyance. But if T had taken possession he was normally secure, for a later purchaser would have actual or constructive notice of his rights.[14]

This rule still applies to tenants holding under pre-1926 contracts for leases, provided that they have not acquired their rights by assignment made since 1925. But a contract for a lease made after 1925 is registrable as an estate contract, and if unregistered is void against a purchaser for money or money's worth of a legal estate in the land; and there are somewhat similar provisions where the contract was made before 1926 and the tenant has assigned his rights after 1925.[15] Therefore if the tenant fails to register the contract against the landlord, he may be defeated by a later purchaser (including a lessee) from the landlord, even though that purchaser has notice of the contract.[16]

---

[7] *Cornish* v. *Brook Green Laundry Ltd.* [1959] 1 Q.B. 394.
[8] *Coatsworth* v. *Johnson* (1886) 55 L.J.Q.B. 220.
[9] *Warmington* v. *Miller* [1973] Q.B. 877.   [10] See Snell, *Equity*, 30–33.
[11] *Foster* v. *Reeves* [1892] 2 Q.B. 255.
[12] *Kingswood Estate Co. Ltd.* v. *Anderson* [1963] 2 Q.B. 169; and see *Cornish* v. *Brook Green Laundry Ltd.*, *supra*; (1959) 75 L.Q.R. 168 (R.E.M.).
[13] *Ante*, p. 114.
[14] See *Daniels* v. *Davison* (1809) 16 Ves. 249; *Mumford* v. *Stohwasser* (1874) L.R. 18 Eq. 556; *Hunt* v. *Luck* [1902] 1 Ch. 428 at 432, 433; *ante*, p. 123.
[15] As to this, see *post*, p. 1050.
[16] L.P.A., 1925, s. 14, is not in point: see *post*, p. 1049, n. 3.

In one respect, therefore, the disadvantages of holding under a mere contract have been aggravated by the 1925 legislation: the tenant can no longer rely on his possession as protection against third parties claiming for value under his landlord. On the other hand if he registers the contract he is fully protected even though he does not take possession, for registration is deemed to be actual notice to all persons for all purposes.[1] In practice, agreements (especially for short terms) are often not registered, even though this may leave the tenant with no remedy but an action for damages if the lessor later grants another lease of the land, or sells or mortgages it; and it is in such cases that the lessor is often not worth suing. It is to the interest of the landlord as well as of the tenant to see that the agreement is registered, since the tenant is under no duty to register, and failure to register will usually greatly increase the damages.[2]

(c) *Assignment.* A further difference affecting third parties lies in the rules about assignment. These rules must be considered later,[3] but here we may notice the differing effects of a lease and a contract. A proper lease gives the lessee a legal estate, and an assignment of it passes to the assignee not only the lessee's rights but also his obligations as to the observance of all ordinary covenants, such as covenants to pay rent and to repair.[4] A contract for a lease, on the other hand, creates no legal estate with which the burden of such a covenant can run, *i.e.,* there is no " privity of estate "[5]; and it is governed by the ordinary rule that the benefit but not the burden of a contract is assignable.[6] The lessee can therefore assign his right to specific performance and all his other rights under the agreement, so that the assignee can sue the landlord to enforce them[7]; but for breach of any of the tenant's obligations the landlord can sue only the lessee and not the assignee,[8] even

---

1 L.P.A., 1925, s. 198; *post,* p. 1044.
2 See *post,* p. 1049.
3 *Post,* p. 650.
4 As to covenants which run with the land and with the reversion, see *post,* p. 721.
5 As to the importance of privity of estate to the running of positive (not restrictive) covenants, see *post,* p. 721.
6 The assignment takes effect in equity or under L.P.A., 1925, s. 136. As to statutory assignment of equitable rights, see *Re Pain* [1919] 1 Ch. 38; Snell, *Equity,* 72.
7 " It is well settled that the assign of one of the parties to a contract can obtain specific performance of that contract against the other contracting party ": *Manchester Brewery Co.* v. *Coombs* [1901] 2 Ch. 608 at 616, *per* Farwell J. The assignor must usually be made a party: *ibid.*
8 *Camden* v. *Batterbury* (1859) 7 C.B.(N.S.) 864; *Purchase* v. *Lichfield Brewery Co.* [1915] 1 K.B. 184 (mortgagee by assignment held not liable for rent). But see *Boyer* v. *Warbey* [1953] 1 Q.B. 234, *post,* p. 728. The assignee may be liable to forfeiture, or for non-observance of restrictive covenants.

though the assignee has taken possession.[9] It is possible that disregard of covenants might affect the assignee's right to specific performance (on which his whole interest in the land depends [10]), even though the covenants were not binding upon him; but it is also possible that the assignee, not being himself bound by the covenants, will not be penalised in equity for not observing them.

So much for the position where the lessee assigns his interest. Where the lessor assigns his reversion the position has, it seems, been simplified by statute, with the result that the rules are the same whether the lessee holds under a proper lease or under a mere contract. The statutory provisions must be explained in a later place.[11]

(*d*) *Miscellaneous.* Various other differences flow from the fundamental distinction between a grant and a contract, or from the wording of statutes. For example, (i) it is only under a lease, and not under a contract, that the tenant can plead purchase without notice against the owner of an unregistrable equitable interest (*e.g.*, a pre-1926 restrictive covenant) as opposed to a " mere equity " (*e.g.*, a right to rescission); for it is essential to this plea that the purchaser should obtain the legal estate before notice reaches him.[12] Similarly, some important registrable interests are void against a purchaser unless registered " before the completion of the purchase " [13]: a person who has contracted to take a legal lease but has not had it granted to him has not " completed the purchase," and is therefore presumably bound by such interests even though they are not registered. (ii) A contract for a lease entitles the landlord to " the usual covenants," which oblige the tenant to repair, and make the lease forfeitable for non-payment of rent; but an executed lease in proper form implies no such covenants.[14] (iii) A mere contract for a lease is not a " conveyance " within section 62 of the Law of Property Act, 1925, so as to pass all the appurtenant rights therein mentioned.[15]

D. Sub-leases

The same rules apply to sub-leases as apply to leases.

---

[9] *Cox* v. *Bishop* (1857) 8 De G.M. & G. 815 at 824. But if rent is paid and accepted a common law tenancy may arise.
[10] *Ante,* p. 577.
[11] *Post,* pp. 734, 735.
[12] *Ante,* pp. 117, 118 ; *L. & S. W. Ry.* v. *Gomm* (1882) 20 Ch.D. 562 at 583.
[13] L.C.A., 1925, ss. 10, 13 ; *post,* p. 1047.
[14] *Post,* p. 687.
[15] *Post,* p. 838. This does not exhaust the catalogue of possible differences. For example, a lease is not, but a contract sometimes is, affected by the rule against perpetuities : *ante,* p. 259.

Sect. 2.   Types of Leases and Tenancies

A. Classification

Leases and tenancies may be classified under the five following heads.

1. Leases for a fixed period

(a) *Length of term.* A lease may be granted for any certain period of certain duration, no matter how long or short. Leases for a week or for three thousand years are equally valid. A lease may be for discontinuous periods, *e.g.*, for three successive bank holidays.[17]

(b) *Certainty of term.* Both the commencement and the maximum duration of the term must be either certain or capable of being rendered certain before the lease takes effect.[18] If no time for commencement is stated, a grant of a tenancy usually takes effect at once [19]; but a contract for a future lease will be void, unless some definite time for the commencement of the lease can be inferred from it.[20] As regards duration, a lease for 99 years from January 1 next, or a lease for 7 years from the determination of an existing tenancy, are examples of terms which are valid under the above rule. A lease to take effect from January 1 next " for so many years as X shall name " will be valid if X names the term before January 1, but not otherwise.[21]

The court sometimes succeeds in construing vague transactions as being sufficiently certain. Thus a lease " for years " may be held to mean a lease for two years [22]; an " option of a lease " (naming no period) may entitle the tenant to a lease for life [23]; and where the lessor has only a limited power of disposition, *e.g.*, because his own interest is leasehold, an agreement to grant an indefinite tenancy may entitle the tenant to the longest term which the lessor has power to grant.[23a]

---

[17] *Smallwood* v. *Sheppards* [1895] 2 Q.B. 627.
[18] *Lace* v. *Chantler* [1944] K.B. 368 at 370, 371; *cf.* Co.Litt. 45b.
[19] *Doe* d. *Phillip* v. *Benjamin* (1839) 9 A. & E. 644 (" agrees to let " construed as grant rather than contract); *Furness* v. *Bond* (1888) 4 T.L.R. 457.
[20] *Harvey* v. *Pratt* [1965] 1 W.L.R. 1025, applying to contracts the rule established by *Marshall* v. *Berridge* (1881) 19 Ch.D. 233 for the sufficiency of a memorandum: *ante*, p. 557. Contrast *Re Lander and Bagley's Contract* [1892] 3 Ch. 41.
[21] *Lace* v. *Chantler, supra*, at pp. 370, 371; *cf.* Co.Litt. 45b.
[22] *Bishop of Bath's Case* (1605) 6 Co.Rep. 34b.
[23] *Austin* v. *Newham* [1906] 2 K.B. 167; contrast *Buck* v. *Howarth* (1947) 63 T.L.R. 195 (tenancy at will); and see *ante*, p. 66.
[23a] *Re King's Leasehold Estates* (1873) L.R. 16 Eq. 521; *Kusel* v. *Watson* (1879) 11 Ch.D. 129; *Siew Soon Wah* v. *Yong Tong Hong* [1973] A.C. 836.

After some hesitation [24] it was finally settled in 1944 that a lease granted during wartime " for the duration of the war " is void for uncertainty at common law.[25] But this would have led to so much inconvenience during the Second World War that such leases, and contracts therefor, were converted by statute into terms, or contracts for terms, of ten years, determinable after the end of the war by (usually) one month's notice.[26] But the Act was made applicable only to the Second World War [27]; nor did it rescue tenancies for other uncertain periods, such as the duration of a partnership,[28] from the common law rule declaring them void. Leases for life, however, stood outside the rule, for they conferred a recognised freehold estate.[29]

It is important to note that the rule invalidating uncertain terms applies only where the maximum duration is uncertain: if the maximum extent of the term is fixed, it may be made determinable on any uncertain event happening within the term.[30] Thus valid leases may be made " for 90 years if X shall so long live " [31] or " for 21 years determinable if the tenant ceases to live on the premises." It is therefore perfectly possible to make a lease determinable upon some future uncertain event, provided that the device of a determinable fixed term is employed. Similarly the landlord may (and most commonly does) reserve a right of re-entry [32] to arise if some event happens during the term, *e.g.*, if the tenant commits a breach of covenant. In that case the lease is subject to a condition subsequent and may be determined upon some quite uncertain event in the future.

(*c*) *Reversionary leases.* Before 1926 there was no restriction upon the length of time that might elapse before the term began; a lease could thus be granted in 1917 to commence in 1946.[33] Such a lease was known as a reversionary lease.[34] For leases were not subject to the common law rule for freehold estates, based upon the need for livery of seisin in old times, that grants could not be made so as to take effect in the future.[35] The perpetuity rule was

---

[24] *G. N. Ry.* v. *Arnold* (1916) 33 T.L.R. 114; *Swift* v. *Macbean* [1942] 1 K.B. 375.

[25] *Lace* v. *Chantler* [1944] K.B. 368.

[26] Validation of War-Time Leases Act, 1944.

[27] s. 7 (2).

[28] The present point was not considered in *Pocock* v. *Carter* [1912] 1 Ch. 663.

[29] See *Platt on Leases* (1847), Vol. 1, p. 678; *Lace* v. *Chantler, supra*, at pp. 371, 372. Most of such leases are now converted into terms of years: see *post*, p. 642.

[30] Co.Litt. 45b, 46a. But see (1963) 27 Conv.(N.S.) 111 (F. R. Crane).

[31] See *post*, p. 642.

[32] *Post*, p. 654.

[33] *Mann, Crossman & Paulin Ltd.* v. *Registrar of the Land Registry* [1918] 1 Ch. 202.

[34] Contrast a lease of the reversion: *post*, p. 648; and see Preston, *Conveyancing*, ii, 145, 146; *Hyde* v. *Warden* (1877) 3 Ex.D. 72, at 83, 84.

[35] *Ante*, p. 183.

not infringed since the lessee took a vested interest forthwith; only the vesting in possession was postponed.[36] But now the grant of a term at a rent or in consideration of a fine, limited to take effect more than 21 years from the date of the instrument creating it, is void; and the same applies to any contract to create such a term.[37]

This does not affect grants or contracts made before 1926 or leases taking effect in equity under a settlement, *e.g.*, portions terms.[38] Nor does it affect contracts for leases which, when eventually granted, will take effect in possession within 21 years of the grant; for these, subject to the perpetuity rule in certain cases after assignment,[39] are valid even after longer periods, as for example a contract to renew a 50-years lease at the tenant's option. The prohibition applies only to immediate grants the operation of which is suspended for more than 21 years, and to contracts for such grants.[40]

(*d*) *Interesse termini.* Before 1926 there was a common law rule that a lessee acquired no actual estate in the land until he had taken possession in accordance with the lease. Until he had exercised his right to take possession he had a legal proprietary right in the land which carried with it a right of entry and was called an *interesse termini*, an interest of a term.[41] This was no mere equitable interest, nor a mere licence or right of action, but was an interest in land which could be freely assigned, and enabled the lessee to sue any person interfering with his entry on the land.[42] But since it was not an estate, no reversion could exist upon it; therefore there could be no release of the grantor's interest to the holder of an *interesse termini*.[43] A reversionary lease could create no more than an *interesse termini* until the time came for the tenant to take possession; and even then the tenant would have no estate until he did in fact enter.

The doctrine of *interesse termini* sometimes led to unfortunate results. Thus in one case[44] T held land under a lease from L which had two years to run. L then granted T a new lease for 73 years,

[36] *Ante*, p. 209.
[37] L.P.A., 1925, s. 149 (3), excepting certain equitable terms. The reason for requiring a rent or fine is explained below: *post*, p. 642.
[38] L.P.A., 1925, s. 149 (3); and see *ante*, p. 387.
[39] *Ante*, p. 260.
[40] *Re Strand and Savoy Properties Ltd.* [1960] Ch. 582; *Weg Motors Ltd.* v. *Hales* [1962] Ch. 49, not following *Northchurch Estates Ltd.* v. *Daniels* [1947] Ch. 117; see (1960) 76 L.Q.R. 352 (R.E.M.).
[41] Co.Litt. 270a.
[42] *Gillard* v. *Cheshire Lines Committee* (1884) 32 W.R. 943.
[43] Co.Litt. 270a. This was important in conveyancing by " lease and release "; but the difficulty was met by employing the Statute of Uses: *ante*, p. 162.
[44] *Lewis* v. *Baker* [1905] 1 Ch. 46.

to run from the end of the two years. During the two years, T sub-leased the land to S for 21 years and S became in arrear with his rent. It was held that T had no reversion on the 21-years sub-lease,[44a] for he had not entered upon the land under the 73-years lease and so had only an *interesse termini*; consequently, he could not distrain for rent due under S's sub-lease, for distress is a remedy available only to reversioners or those authorised by statute. This trouble-some doctrine was usually avoided by means of a grant to uses: if a grant was made to X and his heirs to the use that Y should have a lease for 21 years, the Statute of Uses, 1535, conferred legal posses-sion and thus a legal lease on the tenant without entry.[45] The doctrine has now been abolished in respect of all leases, whether made before or after 1925.[46]

(*e*) *Determination.* A lease for a fixed period automatically determines when that period expires. There are certain statutory exceptions to this rule.[47]

2. Yearly tenancies

(*a*) *Nature.* A yearly tenancy is one which continues from year to year indefinitely until determined by proper notice, not-withstanding the death of either party or the assignment of his interest. It is not affected by the rule against leases of uncertain maximum duration, for originally it is treated as a grant for one year which, if not determined at the end of that year, will auto-matically and without any fresh letting run for another year, and so on from year to year[48]; similar rules apply to all periodic tenancies.[49] Thus the law treats each successive yearly term, when it takes effect, as part and parcel of the original term, which there-fore grows as the years pass; after 50 years, for example, the tenant's interest is regarded in retrospect as a 50-year term, but as to the future as a yearly tenancy.[50] The characteristics of yearly tenancies were laid down by the courts mainly in cases where such tenancies were held to arise by implication.[51] But they may equally well be created by express grant, *e.g.*, to A " from year to year " or " as a yearly tenant." A grant " to X for one year and thereafter

---

[44a] The so-called sub-lease was therefore an assignment: *post*, p. 650.
[45] *Ante*, p. 164.
[46] L.P.A., 1925, s. 149 (1) (2).
[47] See *post*, p. 653.
[48] *Gandy* v. *Jubber* (1865) 9 B. & S. 15 at 18 (an undelivered judgment); and see *Centaploy Ltd.* v. *Matlodge Ltd.* [1974] Ch. 1 (weekly tenancy).
[49] *Bowen* v. *Anderson* [1894] 1 Q.B. 164; *Wilchick* v. *Marks* [1934] 2 K.B. 56 at 65; *Re Midland Railway Co.'s Agreement* [1971] Ch. 725.
[50] Preston, *Conveyancing* iii, 76, 77; *Legg* v. *Strudwick* (1708) 2 Salk. 414; *Oxley* v. *James* (1844) 13 M. & W. 209 at 214; *Cattley* v. *Arnold* (1859) 1 J. & H. 651.
[51] For their origin, see Smith's L.C. ii, 122, 123.

from year to year " will give X a tenancy for at least two years; for he has been given a definite term of one year followed by a yearly tenancy which cannot be determined before the end of the first year thereof.[52]

(*b*) *Creation.* A yearly tenancy arises by implication whenever a person occupies land with the owner's consent and rent measured with reference to a year is paid and accepted.[53] This is so unless there is sufficient evidence to show that some other kind of tenancy was intended, as where there is an express agreement for a tenancy at will,[54] or for a tenancy determinable by three months' notice expiring on any quarter day, whether or not at the end of a year of the tenancy.[55] Thus where a tenant under a lease for a fixed term holds over (*i.e.,* remains in possession at the end of his term) and rent is paid and accepted on a yearly basis, a yearly tenancy will be implied in the absence of any other explanation. But if, for example, the tenant had a right to remain in possession as a " statutory tenant " under the Rent Acts, a yearly tenancy will not be implied from his continuing in possession and paying rent.[56] Nor will it be implied where the landlord does not know the relevant facts; thus if the tenant has died, acceptance of rent from the tenant's widow will not make her a tenant herself, unless the landlord knows that she is paying it in that capacity.[57]

(*c*) *Terms.* Where a tenant holds over and a yearly tenancy is implied, the tenancy will be subject to such of the terms of the expired or informal lease or agreement as are not inconsistent with a yearly holding.[58] The same applies to a tenant who enters and pays yearly rent under a mere agreement or an informal lease: he is tenant from year to year at law, although he may have other rights in equity.[59] Covenants to repair,[60] to pay rent in advance,[61] to carry on some specified trade on the premises,[62] and provisos for re-entry by the landlord on non-payment of rent or breach of covenant,[63] may all be

---

[52] *Re Searle* [1912] 1 Ch. 610.
[53] Woodfall L. & T. 270, 271.
[54] *Doe* d. *Bastow* v. *Cox* (1847) 11 Q.B. 122; *Morgan* v. *William Harrison Ltd.* [1907] 2 Ch. 137.
[55] *Kemp* v. *Derrett* (1814) 3 Camp. 510.
[56] *Morrison* v. *Jacobs* [1945] K.B. 577; *Bowden* v. *Rallison* [1948] 1 All E.R. 841 at 843; *Marcroft Wagons Ltd.* v. *Smith* [1951] 2 K.B. 496. For the Acts, see *post,* pp. 1124 *et seq.*
[57] *Tickner* v. *Buzzacott* [1965] Ch. 426.
[58] *Hyatt* v. *Griffiths* (1851) 17 Q.B. 505 (holding over after a term of four years); *Dougal* v. *McCarthy* [1893] 1 Q.B. 736 (holding over after term of one year).
[59] *Ante,* p. 624.
[60] *Wyatt* v. *Cole* (1877) 36 L.T. 613.
[61] *Lee* v. *Smith* (1854) 9 Exch. 662.
[62] *Sanders* v. *Karnell* (1858) 1 F. & F. 356.
[63] *Thomas* v. *Packer* (1857) 1 H. & N. 669.

implied in a yearly tenancy. But a covenant to paint every three years [64] or a provision for two years' notice to quit [65] are inconsistent with a yearly tenancy and cannot be implied in this way.[66]

(*d*) *Frequency of rent days.* The payment of rent at more frequent intervals than a year will not prevent a yearly tenancy from arising by implication.[67] The test is the period by reference to which the parties calculated the rent. Thus an agreement for "£104 per annum payable weekly" prima facie creates a yearly tenancy; had the agreement been for "£2 per week," a weekly tenancy would be presumed, despite the fact that in each case the tenant would in fact have made precisely the same payments, namely, £2 every week.[68] The same principle applies in the case of other periods, *e.g.*, months or quarters.[69] But every case may be affected by its own special facts, if any contrary intention can be inferred from them. The question is sometimes difficult where a tenant holds over after the expiry of a lease for a fixed term of years at a weekly rent, and continues to pay rent weekly as before.[70] In such a case the court will infer a weekly tenancy unless there is evidence that the weekly payments were instalments of an annual rent.[71]

(*e*) *Determination.* A yearly tenancy is determinable by notice. The parties may agree on any period of notice,[72] and the landlord's period may be different from the tenant's.[73] A term that the landlord shall not give notice either at all [74] or so long as the tenant observes his undertakings [75] is void at law as being repugnant to the nature of

---

[64] *Pinero* v. *Judson* (1829) 6 Bing. 206; contrast *Martin* v. *Smith* (1874) L.R. 9 Ex. 50 (tenant under unsealed lease held liable on covenant to paint in seventh year, since he had stayed for seven years).

[65] *Tooker* v. *Smith* (1857) 1 H. & N. 732.

[66] *Cf. Re Leeds & Batley Breweries Ltd. and Bradbury's Lease* [1920] 2 Ch. 548 (option to purchase reversion not implied).

[67] *Shirley* v. *Newman* (1795) 1 Esp. 266.

[68] *Ladies Hosiery and Underwear Ltd.* v. *Parker* [1930] 1 Ch. 304 at 328, 329, where, however, it is pointed out that the days in a year are not precisely divisible into 52 weeks.

[69] The statement of Chambre J. in *Richardson* v. *Langridge* (1811) 4 Taunt. 128 at 132 that payment of rent measured by any aliquot part of a year is evidence of a yearly tenancy must not be read as extending Mansfield C.J.'s phrase (at p. 131) "a yearly rent, though payable half-yearly or quarterly."

[70] See *Ladies Hosiery and Underwear Ltd.* v. *Parker, supra; cf. Richardson* v. *Langridge* (1811) 4 Taunt. 128 at 132.

[71] *Adler* v. *Blackman* [1953] 1 Q.B. 146, overruling *Covered Markets Ltd.* v. *Green* [1947] 2 All E.R. 140. For the implication of express terms in yearly tenancies, see *Godfrey Thornfield Ltd.* v. *Bingham* [1946] 2 All E.R. 485, and n. 64 above.

[72] *Re Threlfall* (1880) 16 Ch.D. 274 at 281, 282; *Allison* v. *Scargall* [1920] 3 K.B. 443.

[73] *Breams Property Investment Co. Ltd.* v. *Stroulger* [1948] 2 K.B. 1; *Wallis* v. *Semark* [1951] 2 T.L.R. 222.

[74] *Centaploy Ltd.* v. *Matlodge Ltd.* [1974] Ch. 1.

[75] *Warner* v. *Browne* (1807) 8 East 165; and see *Cheshire Lines Committee* v. *Lewis & Co.* (1880) 50 L.J.Q.B. 121 at 124, 128 (landlord not to give notice until premises required for demolition).

the tenancy, though the tenant may be entitled to protection in equity.[76] Yet a term that unless the landlord requires the premises for some specified purpose (*e.g.*, his own occupation) he is not to give notice to the tenant either during a fixed period [77] or even at all,[78] has been held valid, provided it is not in substance an attempt to prevent the landlord from ever determining the tenancy.

In default of agreement, a yearly tenancy can be determined by at least half a year's notice expiring at the end of a completed year of the tenancy.[79] It is desirable but not essential that the notice should be in writing.[80] It cannot, it seems, be given before the tenancy begins.[81] But once a valid notice is given, it automatically terminates the tenancy on the date stated, and cannot be withdrawn; even a purported agreement to withdraw it cannot prevent it operating, though the agreement will create a new tenancy in place of the old.[82]

Either the last day of a year of the tenancy (*i.e.*, the day *before* the anniversary of the commencement of the year), or the next following day, may be specified in the notice as the day on which the tenant shall quit.[83] If the tenancy began on one of the usual quarter days (Lady Day (March 25), Midsummer Day (June 24), Michaelmas (September 29) or Christmas (December 25)), " half a year " means " two quarters "; otherwise " half a year " means 182 days.[84] Thus the period of the notice is not necessarily six months,[85] although of course the parties may agree that such shall be the notice required.[1]

Periods of notice must be strictly observed, and the court will not grant equitable relief against the consequences of forgetfulness or mistake.[2]

---

[76] *Doe* d. *Browne* v. *Warner* (1807) 14 Ves. 156; (1808) 14 Ves. 409; *Re King's Leasehold Estates* (1873) L.R. 16 Eq. 521 (tenant protected for duration of landlord's leasehold interest; suggestion of protection for life against a freeholder).

[77] *Breams Property Investment Co. Ltd.* v. *Stroulger, supra.*

[78] *Re Midland Railway Co.'s Agreement* [1971] Ch. 725, not following *Cheshire Lines Committee* v. *Lewis & Co., supra.*

[79] *Sidebotham* v. *Holland* [1895] 1 Q.B. 378.

[80] *Doe* d. *Lord Macartney* v. *Crick* (1805) 5 Esp. 196.

[81] *Lower* v. *Sorrell* [1963] 1 Q.B. 959; but the decision on this point may be confined to agricultural holdings. See generally (1963) 79 L.Q.R. 178 (R.E.M.).

[82] *Dagger* v. *Shepherd* [1946] K.B. 215 at 221; *Lower* v. *Sorrell, supra.*

[83] *Sidebotham* v. *Holland, supra*; for a year that begins on, say June 1, ends on May 31.

[84] *Anon.* (1575) 3 Dy. 345a. The odd half-day is ignored.

[85] The phrase " six months " should be avoided, since " half a year " is the proper expression (*Doe* d. *Williams* v. *Smith* (1836) 5 A. & E. 350 at 351) although " six months " is sometimes used in judgments where the point is not material. Six months may be more than two quarters or 182 days, or less, depending on the quarters or months.

[1] " Month " formerly meant " lunar month " unless otherwise defined: *Rogers* v. *Kingston-upon-Hull Dock Co.* (1864) 13 W.R. 217. But in documents made since 1925 it means " calendar month ": L.P.A., 1925, s. 61. The same rule is applied by the Interpretation Act, 1889, s. 3, to Acts of Parliament passed after 1850.

[2] See *Samuel Properties (Developments) Ltd.* v. *Hayek* [1972] 1 W.L.R. 1296 (notice of rent increase served too late).

(f) *Commencement.* Where a yearly tenancy is created by a tenant under a lease for a fixed period holding over and paying rent, the yearly tenancy is calculated from the end of the original tenancy, so that where a tenant held over after a tenancy from November 11, 1915, to December 25, 1916, his yearly tenancy was terminable on Christmas Day, 1917, or any subsequent Christmas Day.[3]

(g) *Agricultural holdings.* There are special statutory rules for the determination of yearly agricultural tenancies. These can generally be determined only by a year's notice expiring at the end of the current year of the tenancy, even if the parties have otherwise agreed[4] and even if it is the tenant who gives the notice.[5] Even if such a notice is given, it may not take effect if the tenant takes advantage of his statutory power to serve a counter-notice.[6]

3. Weekly, monthly and other periodic tenancies

(a) *Creation.* A tenancy from week to week, month to month, quarter to quarter, and the like,[7] can be created in a similar way to a yearly tenancy, namely, either by express agreement, or by inference, such as that arising from the payment and acceptance of rent measured with reference to a week, month or quarter, as the case may be,[8] or from an express provision that the tenancy is to be determinable by some specified period of notice, *e.g.,* a quarter's notice.[9]

(b) *Termination.* In general the position of the parties under any such tenancy is similar to that under a yearly tenancy. save that notice of termination is not half a period but a full period, expiring at the end of a completed period.[10] The period is computed in the usual way, so that for a weekly tenancy, unless otherwise agreed,[11] the notice need not be seven *clear* days (reckoned by excluding both the day on which it is given and the day on which it expires, *e.g.,* notice given on Sunday to quit on the following Monday week). Thus a weekly tenancy commencing on a Monday can be determined by

---

[3] *Croft* v. *William F. Blay Ltd.* [1919] 2 Ch. 343.
[4] Agricultural Holdings Act, 1948, s. 23 (1). The section contains a number of exceptions.
[5] *Flather* v. *Hood* (1928) 44 T.L.R. 69.
[6] *Post,* p. 1120.
[7] *e.g.,* for successive periods of 364 days: *Land Settlement Association Ltd.* v. *Carr* [1944] K.B. 657.
[8] *Cole* v. *Kelly* [1920] 2 K.B. 106 at 132. See, *e.g., Huffell* v. *Armitstead* (1835) 7 C. & P. 56.
[9] *Kemp* v. *Derrett* (1814) 3 Camp. 510. This is subject to any contrary indication, as in a yearly tenancy with a special period of notice.
[10] *Lemon* v. *Lardeur* [1946] K.B. 613.
[11] *Weston* v. *Fidler* (1903) 88 L.T. 769.

notice given on or before one Monday [12] to expire at midnight on
the following Sunday; yet the notice may be given simply either
for "Sunday" or for "Monday," for if possible this will be
benevolently construed as referring to the midnight that divides the
two days.[13] A notice to quit "on or before," or "by," the proper date
is valid if given by the landlord [14] but void if given by the tenant [15];
for in the former case the tenant knows when he must go, though he
can go earlier, whereas in the latter case the landlord is left uncertain
when the tenant will go.

Both the length of notice and the date of expiration are subject
to any contrary agreement,[16] and in the case of premises genuinely [17]
let as a dwelling, at least four weeks' [18] notice is now required.[19]
Similarly, and subject also to any contrary agreement, a monthly
tenancy requires a month's notice expiring at the end of a month
of the tenancy,[1] and a quarterly tenancy requires a quarter's notice
expiring at the end of one of the quarters of the tenancy.[2] A quarterly
tenancy commencing on October 29 could thus be determined only
on the 29th of January, April, July or October, in default of any
contrary agreement.[2]

4. Tenancies at will

(a) *Creation.* A tenancy at will arises whenever a tenant, with
the consent of the owner, occupies land as tenant (and not merely
as a servant or agent [3]) on the terms that either party may determine
the tenancy at any time. This kind of tenancy may be created either
expressly [4] or by implication. Common examples are where a tenant
whose lease has expired holds over with the landlord's permission,
without having yet paid rent on a periodic basis [5]; where a tenant
takes possession under a void lease, or under a mere agreement for
a lease, and has not yet paid rent; where a person is allowed to
occupy a house rent free and for an indefinite period; and (usually)

---

12 *Crate* v. *Miller* [1947] K.B. 946; *Newman* v. *Slade* [1926] 2 K.B. 328.
13 *Crate* v. *Miller, supra*; *Bathavon R.D.C.* v. *Carlile* [1958] 1 Q.B. 461.
14 *Dagger* v. *Shepherd* [1946] K.B. 215; *Eastaugh* v. *Macpherson* [1954] 1 W.L.R. 1307.
15 *Perduzzi* v. *Cohen* [1942] L.J.N.C.C.R. 136; *Dagger* v. *Shepherd, supra*, at p. 224.
16 *Re Threlfall* (1880) 16 Ch.D. 274; *H. & G. Simonds Ltd.* v. *Haywood* [1948] 1 All E.R. 260.
17 Thus excluding a mere formal tenancy under an attornment clause (see *post*, p. 917): *Alliance B. S.* v. *Pinwill* [1958] Ch. 788.
18 See *Schnabel* v. *Allard* [1967] 1 Q.B. 627 (notice given on Friday to expire on Friday valid).
19 Rent Act, 1957, s. 16. The notice must also contain prescribed information: Housing Act 1974, s. 123.   1 *Precious* v. *Reedie* [1924] 2 K.B. 149.
2 *Kemp* v. *Derrett* (1814) 3 Camp. 510.
3 *Mayhew* v. *Suttle* (1854) 4 E. & B. 347.
4 *e.g., Manfield & Sons Ltd.* v. *Botchin* [1970] 2 Q.B. 612.
5 See, *e.g., Meye* v. *Electric Transmission Ltd.* [1942] Ch. 290.

where a purchaser has been let into possession pending completion.[6] Unless the parties agree that the tenancy shall be rent free, or the tenant has some other right to rent free occupation,[7] the landlord is entitled to compensation for the " use and occupation " of the land.[8] But if rent is agreed upon, it may be distrained for as such in the usual way.[9]

(b) *Determination.* The essence of the tenancy is that either party can determine it at will, even if it is made determinable at the will of the landlord only, for the law will imply that it is to be determinable at the will of the tenant also.[10] A tenancy at will also comes to an end when either party does any act incompatible with the continuance of the tenancy, as where the tenant commits voluntary waste,[11] or the landlord enters the land and cuts trees or carries away stone,[12] or serves a writ claiming possession of the land,[13] or either party gives notice to the other determining the tenancy.[14] The tenancy is likewise determined if either party dies [15] or assigns his interest in the land.[16] But the tenant may not be ejected until he has knowledge of the act or event which has determined the tenancy.[17]

(c) *Conversion.* If a tenancy at will is created without any agreement as to payment of rent, and rent is subsequently paid and accepted upon some regular periodical basis, a yearly, monthly or other periodical tenancy will be created in accordance with the rules set out under Heads 2 and 3 above.[18]

(d) *Legal or equitable.* It is sometimes suggested that a tenancy at will must now be an equitable interest,[19] since it is not a " term of years absolute " within the statutory definition.[20] But its exclusion from this very wide definition is not quite certain. Another possibility

---

[6] *Howard* v. *Shaw* (1841) 8 M. & W. 118; *Wheeler* v. *Mercer* [1957] A.C. 416 at 425; Tudor L.C. 16–18.
[7] *e.g.,* as in preceding note.
[8] *Howard* v. *Shaw* (1841) 8 M. & W. 118; *post,* p. 689.
[9] Litt. 72; *Anderson* v. *Midland Ry.* (1861) 3 E. & E. 614.
[10] Co.Litt. 55a.
[11] *Countess of Shrewsbury's Case* (1600) 5 Co.Rep. 13b.
[12] *Turner* v. *Doe* d. *Bennett* (1842) 9 M. & W. 643.
[13] *Martinali* v. *Ramuz* [1953] 1 W.L.R. 1196 (a writ is not a notice to quit).
[14] See *Crane* v. *Morris* [1965] 1 W.L.R. 1104 at 1108 (such a notice not within Rent Act, 1957, s. 16 (*ante,* p. 638).
[15] *Turner* v. *Barnes* (1862) 2 B. & S. 435; *James* v. *Dean* (1805) 11 Ves. 383 at 391.
[16] *Doe* d. *Davies* v. *Thomas* (1851) 6 Exch. 854 at 857; *Pinhorn* v. *Souster* (1853) 8 Exch. 763 at 772.
[17] *Doe* d. *Davies* v. *Thomas, supra.* As to the tenant's rights to emblements, see *post,* p. 686.
[18] *Ladies Hosiery and Underwear Ltd.* v. *Parker* [1930] 1 Ch. 304.
[19] For the authorities for and against. see Foa L. & T. 2, n. (*i*).
[20] *Ante,* p. 140; possibly L.P.A., 1925, s. 14, may affect the position, but that is at least highly doubtful.

is that a tenancy at will is not a species of estate but a mere relationship of tenure unaccompanied by any estate.[21] An estate cannot exist without tenure, as already explained [22]; but there would seem to be no reason why tenure should not exist without any estate. A may hold land of B, but for no fixed period and merely for so long as B may allow. This, indeed, was probably the original type of tenure on to which the doctrines of estates were superimposed. It is true that the expression " estate at will " has been used by some writers,[23] but it would seem to have no special significance. A tenant at will " hath no certain nor sure estate " [24]; there is merely " privity " [25] *i.e.*, tenure, between him and his landlord. If it is remembered that tenure by itself is a purely personal relationship when unconnected with any estate or interest which can exist as a right *in rem*, this may explain why a tenancy at will cannot survive death or alienation; and it may also explain why tenancy at will is possible despite the rule which requires every leasehold estate to be for a term certain.

5. Tenancies at sufferance

(*a*) *Creation.* A tenancy at sufferance arises where a tenant, having entered under a valid tenancy, holds over without the landlord's assent or dissent.[26] Such a tenant differs from a trespasser in that his original entry was lawful, and from a tenant at will in that his tenancy exists without the landlord's consent. A tenancy at sufferance can arise only by operation of law,[27] and not by express grant, for it assumes an absence of agreement between landlord and tenant. Indeed, it is strictly incorrect to call it " tenancy " at all, for there is no " privity," *i.e.*, tenure, between the parties.[28] But since it normally arises between parties who have been landlord and tenant it has acquired the title of tenancy; and the tenant is liable to a claim for " use and occupation," which properly lies against a tenant,[29] rather than to an action for damages for trespass. There can, of course, be no claim for rent as such, for rent is a *service* which depends upon a proper tenure by consent.[30] The landlord

---

[21] See *ante*, p. 45. Crown land is, of course, an exception.
[22] *Ante*, p. 13.
[23] *Ante*, p. 45, n. 30.
[24] Litt. 68.
[25] Litt. 460; Co.Litt. 270b and note by Butler. In Co.Litt. 271a Coke distinguishes between privity of estate and privity of tenure.
[26] Co.Litt. 57b; *Remon* v. *City of London Real Property Co. Ltd.* [1921] 1 K.B. 49 at 58.
[27] Tudor L.C. 8; *Meye* v. *Electric Transmission Ltd.* [1942] Ch. 290.
[28] Co.Litt. 270b, note by Butler, and 271a.
[29] *Bayley* v. *Bradley* (1848) 5 C.B. 396 at 406; *Leigh* v. *Dickeson* (1884) 15 Q.B.D. 60; *post*, p. 689. And see Woodfall L. & T. 437 *et seq.*
[30] *Post*, p. 689.

may eject the tenant, or sue for possession, at any time, and the tenant will have no right to emblements.[31]

(b) *Legal or equitable interest.* As in the case of tenancy at will, so in the case of tenancy at sufferance it has been said that it must be an equitable interest since 1925.[32] But it can hardly be true that the landlord holds on trust for his tenant at sufferance. In reality it would seem that a tenant at sufferance is simply in the position of a squatter, *i.e.,* an adverse claimant[33]; and a squatter's interest may still be a legal estate, as will later be explained.[34]

(c) *Conversion.* A tenancy at sufferance may be converted into a yearly or other periodic tenancy in the usual way, *e.g.,* if rent is paid and accepted with reference to a year.

(d) *Holding over.* There are statutory penalties for tenants who wrongfully hold over after giving or receiving notice to quit.

(1) DOUBLE VALUE. If the landlord gives the tenant *written* notice to quit and the tenant is a tenant *for life or for years,* the tenant is liable to pay the landlord a sum calculated at double the annual value of the land in respect of the period for which he wilfully[35] holds over after the notice expires; this can be enforced by action but not otherwise, *e.g.,* not by distress.[35a] This provision applies to tenancies from year to year[36] as well as to tenancies for fixed terms of years or for a year certain,[37] but not to weekly[38] or, it seems, other similar periodic tenancies.[39]

(2) DOUBLE RENT. If the tenant gives the landlord *written or oral*[40] notice to quit, then whatever the type of tenancy (provided it is determinable by notice[41]), the tenant is liable to pay double rent in respect of the period for which he holds over after the notice expires; payment can be enforced by action or distress.[42]

The differing terms of these aged provisions will be noticed. The rent and the annual value may be the same, but they often

---

[31] *Doe* d. *Bennett* v. *Turner* (1840) 7 M. & W. 226 at 235.
[32] See *ante,* pp. 140, 141, where this question is discussed.
[33] This was not so for the purposes of acquiring title by limitation before 1833; but the doctrine of adverse possession upon which the distinction was founded was abolished by the Real Property Limitation Act, 1833; Tudor L.C. 9; *post,* p. 1013.
[34] *Post,* p. 1007.
[35] *French* v. *Elliott* [1960] 1 W.L.R. 40 (reasonable claim of right is a defence).
[35a] Landlord and Tenant Act, 1730, s. 1.
[36] See *Ryal* v. *Rich* (1808) 10 East 48.
[37] *Cobb* v. *Stokes* (1807) 8 East 358.
[38] *Lloyd* v. *Rosbee* (1810) 2 Camp. 453.
[39] See *Williamson* v. *Hall* (1837) 3 Bing.N.C. 508.
[40] *Timmins* v. *Rowlison* (1764) 1 Wm.Bl. 533.
[41] *Johnstone* v. *Hudlestone* (1825) 4 B. & C. 922.
[42] Distress for Rent Act, 1737, s. 18.

differ, as where premises have been let at a reduced rent in consideration of a fine.

B. Statutory Modifications

Although leases can in general be created for such periods as the parties think fit, there are special statutory rules for some cases, which sometimes produce surprising results.

1. Leases for lives or until marriage

(a) *Conversion to 90-year terms.* By the Law of Property Act, 1925,[43] a lease at a rent or a fine " for life or lives or for any term of years determinable with life or lives or on the marriage of the lessee," is converted into a term of 90 years, whether it was granted before or after 1925. A contract for such a lease is treated in a similar way; but a term " taking effect in equity under a settlement or created out of an equitable interest under a settlement for mortgage, indemnity, or other like purposes " is excluded, even if a rent is reserved. When a lease falls within the statute, neither death nor marriage determines the lease, but " on the death or marriage (as the case may be) of the original lessee " either party may determine it by serving on the other at least one month's written notice to expire on one of the quarter days applicable to the tenancy, or, if no special quarter days are applicable, on one of the usual quarter days. If the lease is determinable with " the lives of persons other than or besides the lessees," the notice is " capable of being served " on the dropping of their lives, " instead of after the death of the original lessee."

(b) *Operation of the statute.* For example, leases at a rent or fine granted—

" to A for life,"
" to B for 10 years if he so long lives," and
" to C for 99 years if he so long remains a bachelor,"

are all converted into terms which will continue for 90 years unless by the proper notice they are determined on any quarter-day (not necessarily the first) after the event has occurred. In most cases this position will cause little change in the effective rights of the parties. But it may drastically cut down the lessor's reversion if, in a case like the second of the above examples, he wishes to grant only a short term, conditional upon the lessee remaining alive or unmarried.[44] And the drafting of the statute seems ill-adapted for

---

[43] s. 149 (6).
[44] *Cf.* Wolst. & C. i, 278.

leases such as " to A during B's life," [45] or " to C for 50 years if D so long remains unmarried," or " to E until he remarries."

(c) *Contrast with life interests.* The general object of these provisions is to bring leases for life within the general scheme of the 1925 legislation, and to distinguish between leases for life which involve the relationship of landlord and tenant [46] and beneficial life tenancies under a settlement. Normally the former are commercial transactions, whereas the latter are family transactions. This distinction is usually marked by whether or not a premium or rent is payable; and this is the test adopted by the statute. Life interests of a family character thus remain subject to the law of settled land, and exist only in equity; life tenancies of a commercial character are converted into true terms of years, free from the complications of the law of settled land.

The distinction is, however, not always clear cut. Thus where a testator gives one of his relations the right to be granted a tenancy for life at a nominal rent,[47] or at less than the market rent,[48] the transaction, though at a rent, is also partly of a beneficial or family nature. On the other hand, a commercial transaction in which there is no beneficial or family element may create a tenancy for life which makes the land settled land.[49] Further, the statute itself provides for the exclusion of certain leases even though granted at a rent, *e.g.*, those taking effect in equity under a settlement.[50] Nevertheless, in most cases the distinction is valid.[51]

2. Perpetually renewable leases

(a) *Renewability.* A perpetually renewable lease is a lease which gives the tenant the right to renew it for another period as often as it expires. Such leases are seldom deliberately created today.[52] But they may be created inadvertently by unrestricted renewal clauses, as by an option giving the tenant a right of renewal " on the same terms and conditions, including this clause," [53] or " on identical terms and conditions." [54] The lease is then held to be perpetually renewable even

---

[45] For it seems that a notice could be served after the death of A even if B is still living.
[46] For these, see *ante*, p. 615.
[47] *Re Catling* [1931] 2 Ch. 359 (£1 a year).
[48] *Blamires* v. *Bradford Corporation* [1964] Ch. 585 (30s. a week).
[49] See, *e.g.*, *Bannister* v. *Bannister* [1948] 2 All E.R. 133.
[50] *Re Catling, supra,* seems to be an example of this.
[51] See, *e.g.*, *Kingswood Estate Co. Ltd.* v. *Anderson* [1963] 2 Q.B. 169 (clearly commercial).
[52] They used to be common in Ireland : see *Swinburne* v. *Milburn* (1884) 9 App.Cas. 844 at 855.
[53] *Hare* v. *Burges* (1857) 4 K. & J. 45 ; *Parkus* v. *Greenwood* [1950] Ch. 644 ; *Caerphilly Concrete Products Ltd.* v. *Owen* [1972] 1 W.L.R. 372.
[54] *Northchurch Estates Ltd.* v. *Daniels* [1947] Ch. 117 (tenancy for a year becomes a term of 2,000 years).

though the parties may have had no such intention: " the courts have manoeuvred themselves into an unhappy position " [55] in these decisions.

(*b*) *Conversion.* Formerly there was always the danger that the tenant might lose his perpetual right by omitting to give notice of renewal. This danger has been obviated by statute. By the Law of Property Act, 1922,[56] all such leases existing at the end of 1925 were converted into terms of two thousand years, calculated from the beginning of the existing terms; and perpetually renewable leases granted after 1925 take effect as terms of two thousand years from the date fixed for the commencement of the term. Any perpetually renewable sub-lease created out of a perpetually renewable lease is converted into a term of two thousand years less one day.[57]

(*c*) *Terms.* The two thousand years lease is subject to the same terms as the original lease, with the following modifications.

(i) The tenant (but not the landlord) may terminate the lease on any date upon which, but for the conversion by the Act, the lease would have expired if it had not been renewed, provided he gives at least ten days' written notice to the landlord.[58]

(ii) Every assignment or devolution of the lease must be registered with the landlord or his solicitor or agent within six months, and a fee of one guinea paid.[59]

(iii) A tenant who assigns the lease is not liable for breaches of covenant committed after the assignment.[60] The general rule is that the original lessee remains liable for all breaches occurring during the term, even if he parts with the lease.[61] Perpetually renewable leases have been made a statutory exception to this rule, because otherwise the original lessee's liability might last for ever.

(iv) Any fine or other payment for renewal for which the lease provides is converted into additional rent and spread over the period between the renewal dates, except where the lease is granted after 1925, when the obligation for payment is void.[62]

---

[55] *Caerphilly Concrete Products Ltd.* v. *Owen, supra*, at p. 376, *per* Sachs L.J.
[56] s. 145 and 15th Sched.
[57] L.P.A., 1922, 15th Sched., paras. 2, 5.
[58] *Ibid.*, para. 10 (1) (i).
[59] *Ibid.*, para. 10 (1) (ii). This operates by way of covenant and is subject to any proviso for forfeiture for breach of the covenants of the lease: *ibid.* As to forfeiture, see *post*, p. 654.
[60] L.P.A., 1922, 15th Sched., para. 11.
[61] See *post*, p. 723.
[62] L.P.A., 1922, 15th Sched., para. 12.

(*d*) *Right to determine.* It should be noted that the landlord has no right to determine the lease at the renewal dates. Before 1926, if L granted T a lease for 21 years with a perpetual right of renewal, it was T alone who had the right to decide each 21 years whether or not to renew the lease. This position is preserved, save that now the lease continues unless determined, instead of requiring renewal: the tenant may contract out, but he need no longer contract in.

3. Over-lengthy renewals. A contract made after 1925 to renew a lease for over 60 years from its termination is void.[63] This is aimed at single renewals, not perpetual renewals, and does not affect contracts made before 1926.

4. Reversionary leases. A lease at a rent or a fine cannot be granted after 1925 to commence at too distant a future date. This has already been dealt with.[64]

C. *Tenancy by Estoppel*

1. Estoppel between landlord and tenant. There is a general rule that a tenant is estopped from denying his landlord's title, and a landlord from denying his tenant's.[65] Estoppel is a principle of the law of evidence which, in this case, precludes parties who have created a tenancy from denying their respective capacities as against one another. Thus the landlord cannot question the validity of his own grant, nor can the tenant question it while he is enjoying possession of the land.[66] The estoppel operates from the time when the landlord puts the tenant into possession [67] until the time when the tenant goes out of possession. Once the tenant has gone, he can dispute the landlord's title and, apparently, deny liability on any covenants broken during the term.[68] Even while still in possession

---

[63] L.P.A., 1922, 15th Sched., para. 7.

[64] *Ante*, p. 631.

[65] *Cooke* v. *Loxley* (1792) 5 T.R. 4; *Achorne* v. *Gomme* (1824) 2 Bing. 54; *Cuthbertson* v. *Irving* (1860) 6 H. & N. 135; Halsb. xv, 247, 248, approved in *Mackley* v. *Nutting* [1949] 2 K.B. 55 at 62. This is connected with the rule that if A has permitted B to take possession of A's land, B may not dispute A's title and so plead *jus tertii* (see *post*, p. 1009) against him: *Tadman* v. *Henman* [1893] 2 Q.B. 168 at 171. This rule is important in actions for the recovery of land; but it is now settled that there is no rule confining pleas of tenancy by estoppel to such actions: Spencer Bower, *Estoppel by Representation*, 1st ed., pp. 251, 252.

[66] *Webb* v. *Austin* (1844) 7 Man. & G. 701; *Cuthbertson* v. *Irving*, *supra*; and for the limits of the estoppel, see Spencer Bower and Turner, *Estoppel by Representation*, 2nd ed., p. 176; *Rhyl U.D.C.* v. *Rhyl Amusements Ltd.* [1959] 1 W.L.R. 465 (*ultra vires*).

[67] See *Hall* v. *Butler* (1839) 10 A. & E. 204; *Doe* d. *Marlow* v. *Wiggins* (1843) 4 Q.B. 367; and see n. 65, *supra*.

[68] *Harrison* v. *Wells* [1967] 1 Q.B. 263. This inequitable result is questionable.

the tenant may show that the landlord's title has expired (*e.g.*, if it was a life interest), provided that he does not question the landlord's right to have granted him any tenancy.[69]

This estoppel applies to all types of tenancy, including periodic tenancies, tenancies at will and at sufferance,[70] and statutory tenancies under the Rent Acts [71]; it applies similarly to licences [72]; and it operates whether the tenancy was created by deed or writing or orally.[73] Those claiming through the parties concerned are also estopped, so that the estoppel binds the successors in title to both landlord and tenant.[74]

2. Tenancy by estoppel. In addition to the general estoppel just described, there are certain cases in which there is said to be a tenancy by estoppel.[75] If a person with no estate in land purports to grant a tenancy of the land, the grant can pass no actual estate. Yet, even though the lessor's want of title is apparent to the parties,[76] both the parties and their successors in title will be estopped from denying that the grant was effective to create the tenancy that it purported to create.[77] There is thus brought into being a tenancy by estoppel under which the parties and their successors in title have (as against one another) most of the rights and liabilities of an estate in land, although no estate is actually granted. Such a tenancy will, for example, devolve and may be alienated in the same way as any other tenancy,[78] and the landlord may distrain for rent in the ordinary way.[79] But since estoppels do not bind strangers, he cannot exercise his normal right [80] to distrain goods not owned by the tenant.[81]

3. Feeding the estoppel. If after creating a tenancy by estoppel the landlord later acquires a legal estate out of which the tenancy

---

[69] *Mountnoy* v. *Collier* (1853) 1 E. & B. 630; Foa L. & T. 474. See (1968) 32 Conv.(N.S.) 249 (C. J. W. Allen) for a general survey.

[70] *Doe* d. *Bailey* v. *Foster* (1846) 3 C.B. 215 at 229, apparently meaning that all such tenancies come within the rule mentioned in note 65, *supra*. As to concurrent leases, see *post*, p. 648.

[71] See *Stratford* v. *Syrett* [1958] 1 Q.B. 107; and for statutory tenancies, see *post*, p. 1134.

[72] *Doe* d. *Johnson* v. *Baytup* (1835) 3 A. & E. 188; *Terunnanse* v. *Terunnanse* [1968] A.C. 1086; compare *Tadman* v. *Henman* [1893] 2 Q.B. 168 at 171.

[73] *E. H. Lewis & Son Ltd.* v. *Morelli* [1948] 2 All E.R. 1021. The limits stated in Co.Litt. 47b no longer apply: see, *e.g.*, *Mackley* v. *Nutting* [1949] 2 K.B. 55.

[74] *Webb* v. *Austin* (1844) 7 Man. & G. 701; *Cuthbertson* v. *Irving* (1859) 4 H. & N. 742 at 758 (affirmed (1860) 6 H. & N. 135).

[75] The doctrine is discussed in (1964) 80 L.Q.R. 370 (A. M. Prichard).

[76] *Morton* v. *Woods* (1869) L.R. 4 Q.B. 293.

[77] See *Cuthbertson* v. *Irving, supra*, at pp. 757, 758.

[78] *Gouldsworth* v. *Knights* (1843) 11 M. & W. 337; *Webb* v. *Austin* (1844) 7 Man. & G. 701; *Cuthbertson* v. *Irving, supra*, at p. 758; *Mackley* v. *Nutting* [1949] 2 K.B. 55; *cf. Church of England B. S.* v. *Piskor* [1954] Ch. 553, *post*, p. 648.

[79] *Gouldsworth* v. *Knights, supra*.

[80] See *post*, p. 691.   [81] *Tadman* v. *Henman* [1893] 2 Q.B. 168.

could be created (as where he purchases the fee simple), this is said to "feed the estoppel": the tenant then at once acquires a legal tenancy in place of his tenancy by estoppel.[82] Similarly, if a tenant dies or leaves the premises and another tenant occupies them and pays rent to the landlord, the second tenant has an implied lease by estoppel while the first tenancy remains in existence, and a true tenancy as from its determination [83]; for upon its determination the landlord recovers his immediate legal title, and that feeds the estoppel. But no tenancy by estoppel can arise if the lessor had any present legal estate (as distinct from a mere equitable interest [84]) in the land when he granted the lease.[85] If the lessor's interest was a freehold, or a leasehold which would outlast the lease which he granted, the lease takes effect in the ordinary way; if it was a leasehold equal to [1] or smaller than [2] the subsequent lease, the grant of that lease operates as an assignment of the lessor's interest.[3] Thus if L grants T a lease for 99 years and subsequently acquires the fee simple (*e.g.*, under his father's will), T will take a lease for 99 years by estoppel if L had no interest in the land when the lease was granted. But if L had a lease for ten years at that time, the lease for 99 years will operate only as an assignment to T of L's lease for ten years,[4] and L will not be estopped from recovering the land when the ten-year term expires.

4. Purchaser in possession before completion. Sometimes a purchaser of land is allowed to go into possession before completion. If he then grants a tenancy of the land, and subsequently, on completion, mortgages the land in order to raise the purchase-money, the question arises whether the lease (which, until it was "fed" by completion of the purchase, was a mere lease by estoppel) is binding upon the mortgagee. After some uncertainty it is now settled that

---

[82] *Rawlin's Case* (1587) Jenk. 254; 4 Co.Rep. 52a; *Webb* v. *Austin* (1844) 7 Man. & G. 701 at 724; *Sturgeon* v. *Wingfield* (1846) 15 M. & W. 224; *Rajapakse* v. *Fernando* [1920] A.C. 892 at 897; *cf.* L.P.A., 1925, s. 152 (2), *ante*, p. 337.

[83] *Edward H. Lewis & Son Ltd.* v. *Morelli* (1948) 65 T.L.R. 56; *Mackley* v. *Nutting* [1949] 2 K.B. 55; *Moses* v. *Warsop* (1949) 100 L.J.News. 51.

[84] *Universal Permanent B. S.* v. *Cooke* [1952] Ch. 95 at 102 (tenancy by estoppel where the lessor had contracted to buy the property let but had not completed the purchase). A lease by a mortgagor may also take effect by estoppel despite the equity of redemption still vested in him: *post*, p. 932.

[85] Co.Litt. 47b; *Doe d. Strode* v. *Seaton* (1835) 2 C.M. & R. 728 (lease granted by tenant for life not binding on successors in title); *Cuthbertson* v. *Irving* (1859) 4 H. & N. 742, affd. (1860) 6 H. & N. 135.

[1] *Beardman* v. *Wilson* (1868) L.R. 4 C.P. 57; *Hallen* v. *Spaeth* [1923] A.C. 684 at 687.

[2] *Wollaston* v. *Hakewill* (1841) 3 Man. & G. 297 at 323 (not a case of estoppel).

[3] For this rule, see *post*, p. 650.

[4] See *post*, p. 651.

the purchase and the mortgage are two distinct transactions,[5] although the practice is for the conveyance (by the vendor to the purchaser) and the mortgage (by the purchaser to the mortgagee) to be executed simultaneously, the mortgagee paying the mortgage money direct to the vendor. The legal estate must therefore be vested in the purchaser before the mortgage can become effective, and at the moment when it becomes so vested the lease becomes a legal incumbrance by the feeding of the estoppel. The lease therefore takes priority to the mortgage,[5a] which is in effect only a mortgage of the reversion.

The tenant may, however, lose his priority if he is party to a fraudulent representation to the mortgagee that the property is not let.[6] If the transaction between the purchaser and the tenant was not a lease but an agreement for a lease, it would only be binding upon the mortgagee if registered as an estate contract under the Land Charges Act, 1925.[7] Further problems may arise if the purchaser has entered into a contract for the mortgage before the date of completion, but these have not yet been explored by the courts.[8]

D. *Concurrent Leases*

1. Grant. If a landlord who has granted a lease subsequently grants another lease of the same land for some or all of the period of the existing lease, so that there are concurrent leases, he is said to have granted a lease of the reversion.[9] The second grant is *pro tanto* a disposition of the reversion,[10] and so creates a relationship of landlord and tenant between the second and the first lessee respectively,[11] with all rights and liabilities as to rent and other

---

[5] *Church of England B. S.* v. *Piskor* [1954] Ch. 553, following *Woolwich Equitable B. S.* v. *Marshall* [1952] Ch. 1 and *Universal Permanent B. S.* v. *Cooke* [1952] Ch. 95, and overruling on this point *Coventry Permanent Economic B. S.* v. *Jones* [1951] 1 All E.R. 901.

[5a] *Church of England B. S.* v. *Piskor, supra.*

[6] It is on this ground that the decision in *Coventry Permanent Economic B. S.* v. *Jones, supra,* may be supported: see *Church of England B. S.* v. *Piskor, supra,* at p. 561.

[7] *Coventry Permanent Economic B. S.* v. *Jones, supra.* Registration is no less necessary because the tenant has taken possession (*ibid.; ante,* p. 628; *post,* p. 1049) or because the agreement was not made in writing: *Universal Permanent B. S.* v. *Cooke, supra,* at p. 104.

[8] *Church of England B. S.* v. *Piskor, supra,* at p. 566. If the lease by estoppel precedes the mortgage, the lease should in principle have priority since the estoppel binds persons claiming through the lessor. If the contract for the mortgage precedes the lease, the mortgage should have priority if an estate contract was registered before the estoppel was fed (no title deeds will be available for deposit with the mortgage until the purchase is completed).

[9] Contrast a reversionary lease: *ante,* p. 631.

[10] Shep.Touch. 275, 276; *Neale* v. *Mackenzie* (1836) 1 M. & W. 747; *Harmer* v. *Bean* (1853) 3 C. & K. 307; *Wordsley Brewery Co.* v. *Halford* (1903) 90 L.T. 89; *Cole* v. *Kelly* [1920] 2 K.B. 106.

[11] *Birch* v. *Wright* (1786) 1 T.R. 378 at 384, *per* Buller J. (there is "immediate privity between the grantee and the tenant"; the grantee is "perfect landlord to the tenant"). The apparent dictum to the contrary by Lush J. at first instance in *Cole* v. *Kelly, supra.* at p. 120 seems wrong.

matters which are capable of running with the tenancy [12]; and this supplants the relationship of landlord and tenant between the landlord and the first lessee.[13] Thus if L grants a lease of Blackacre to T for 21 years, and soon afterwards grants a lease of Blackacre to X for 30 years, X becomes the immediate reversioner upon T's lease so long as it continues, and is thus T's landlord. When T's lease determines, X becomes entitled to possession of Blackacre. The result would be the same if X's lease was for a term shorter than T's,[14] except, of course, that X's lease would normally expire before he had become entitled to take possession. X could collect rent and enforce covenants against T,[15] and if T's lease prematurely determined before X's term expired, X would be entitled to possession of the land.[16] Statute has expressly preserved this rule that a legal term (whether or not a mortgage term) may be created to take effect in reversion expectant upon a longer term.[17]

2. Effect. A lease of the reversion, being *pro tanto* an assignment of it, must obey the rules governing assignments of reversions, explained below.[18] Such a lease can therefore have no effect at law unless made by deed. If, in the above example, X's lease was created merely by parol, it was wholly void at common law during the full term of T's lease, even if T's lease determined prematurely.[19] And this was equally true if the term of X's lease did not exceed three years.[20] But once T's term had expired, X's lease (if still in being) could take effect as a lease of the land, not as a disposition of the reversion, and so be valid as a reversionary lease if it conformed to the rules for the creation of such leases.[1] It is not clear, however, whether the relationship between L and X during T's term is that of landlord and tenant or that of assignor and assignee,[2] or whether there is a lease by estoppel between them.[3] Nor is it clear whether

---

[12] *Burton* v. *Barclay* (1831) 7 Bing. 745; *Horn* v. *Beard* [1912] 3 K.B. 181; *Cole* v. *Kelly, supra*; Preston, *Conveyancing*, ii, 145, 146.
[13] See *Wordsley Brewery Co.* v. *Halford, supra* (notice to quit by landlord to first lessee bad).
[14] *Neale* v. *Mackenzie* (1836) 1 M. & W. 747; *Re Moore & Hulm's Contract* [1912] 2 Ch. 105.
[15] *Burton* v. *Barclay* (1831) 7 Bing. 745.
[16] *Stephens* v. *Bridges* (1821) 6 Madd. 66 at 67; *Re Moore & Hulm's Contract, supra.*
[17] L.P.A., 1925, s. 149 (5). The statement in Wolst. & C. i, 277, that this and s. 149 (2) overrule *Neale* v. *Mackenzie* is puzzling.
[18] *Post*, p. 652.
[19] *Neale* v. *Mackenzie, supra* (where the lease was held void only as to the part of the land already leased).
[20] *Brawley* v. *Wade* (1824) M'Clel. 664 (tenancy from year to year).
[1] *Doe* d. *Thomas* v. *Jenkins* (1832) 1 L.J.K.B. 190.
[2] The authorities appear to be silent on this point.
[3] Bacon's *Abridgement*, 7th ed. (1832), iv, 848; *Platt on Leases*, ii, 59. For tenancy by estoppel, see *ante*, p. 645.

the Law of Property Act, 1925, has now made it possible for X's lease to be created by parol if its term does not exceed three years.[4]

Part 3

ASSIGNMENT OF LEASES AND REVERSIONS

Sect. 1. Assignment of Leases

1. Need for deed. A legal lease, once created, can be transferred *inter vivos* only by deed, in accordance with the general rule.[5] This applies to all legal leases, even those created orally, *e.g.*, a yearly tenancy. However, on principles similar to those applicable to the creation of leases, an oral or written assignment will be effective in equity as between the assignor and the assignee as a contract to assign, if sufficiently evidenced by writing or part performance.[6] But such an assignment does not make the assignee liable to the landlord on the covenants of the lease,[7] even if he enters and pays rent, though in special cases he may be estopped from denying liability.[8]

2. Contrast with sub-lease. The difference between an assignment of a lease and a sub-lease has already been mentioned. As will appear later,[9] this is of fundamental importance to the question of liability for breaches of covenant, if the original tenant has made some disposition of the land. If he assigns his lease, he grants his whole estate to the assignee, thus putting the assignee in his shoes as immediate tenant of the head landlord. If he grants a sub-lease, he does not cease to be tenant, for he retains his estate: he has merely carved out of it a lesser estate, in respect of which he owns the immediate reversion. The assignment of a lease transfers an estate but creates no new tenure; the grant of a sub-lease creates a new tenure between sub-lessor and sub-lessee.

3. Sub-lease as assignment. Since the distinction between an assignment and a sub-lease is one of substance, not one of form, it

---

4 s. 54 (2) (*ante*, p. 621) requires the lease to take effect in possession, but X's lease can take effect only in reversion upon T's lease. By s. 205 (1) (xix) " possession " includes the right to receive rents and profits. But presumably this right can pass only under a grant by deed, *i.e.*, as incident to the reversion. See Woodfall L. & T. 265.
5 L.P.A., 1925, s. 52, *ante*, p. 623.
6 *Ante*, p. 624.
7 There is no privity of estate: see *ante*, p. 628; *post*, p. 729.
8 *Rodenhurst Estates Ltd.* v. *W. H. Barnes Ltd.* [1936] 2 All E.R. 3, where the landlord had granted a licence for a legal assignment which had been acted upon in all respects save the execution of a formal assignment; for estoppel, see *supra*. Compare *Official Trustee of Charity Lands* v. *Ferriman Trust Ltd.* [1937] 3 All E.R. 85; and see *Richmond* v. *McGann* [1954] 1 W.L.R. 1282.
9 *Post*, p. 721.

follows that if the tenant disposes of the whole residue of his estate, the transaction must operate as an assignment even though the parties intend it to operate as a sub-lease.[10] For example, if three years ago L granted a lease to A for seven years, and A now purports to grant a sub-lease to B for ten years, the sub-lease operates as an assignment despite its terms, and any covenants and conditions contained in it (*e.g.*, as to rent, repair or forfeiture) have such operation as they may have under an assignment.[11] A is then no longer tenant of L; there is direct tenure between L and B. A cannot therefore distrain for rent due to him from B under the so-called sub-lease,[12] although it has the legal quality of being rent, and can be sued for.[13] And if the so-called sub-lease is followed by a yearly or other periodic tenancy (*e.g.*, to B for five years and thereafter from year to year), A cannot give B notice to quit under the periodic tenancy since A is not B's landlord.[14] But if A had granted to B a sub-lease for the residue of A's term less one day, this would have been a valid sub-lease.

This rule applies only where the tenant creates an interest which is certain to last as long as, or longer than, his own. Therefore where a tenant from year to year granted a sub-lease of 34 years, this took effect as a sub-lease, not as an assignment; for the yearly tenancy might have outlasted the sub-lease, and so left a reversion in the sub-lessor.[15] Similarly a tenant from year to year can create a sub-lease from year to year[16]; and it would seem that a tenant for a fixed term may grant a sub-lease of a yearly or other periodic kind, provided that the head lease will outlast at least the initial period of the sub-lease; for there is then always a potential reversion in case the periodic sub-tenancy should be determined by notice.

4. Formalities. Assignments which result from " sub-leases " of the tenant's whole interest are brought about by operation of law, and so seem to be excepted from the rule that they must be made by deed.[17] Thus if a tenant with less than three years of his term unexpired purports to grant an informal sub-lease for three years at

---

[10] *Hicks* v. *Downing* (1696) 1 Ld.Raym. 99; *Palmer* v. *Edwards* (1783) 1 Doug. K.B. 187; *Wollaston* v. *Hakewill* (1841) 3 Man. & G. 297; *Milmo* v. *Carreras* [1946] K.B. 306. See (1967) 31 Conv.(N.S.) 159 (P. Jackson); *post*, p. 896.

[11] As between L and A there is no longer privity of estate (*post*, p. 721); but a forfeiture clause may still operate: *Doe* d. *Freeman* v. *Bateman* (1818) 2 B. & Ald. 168.

[12] For distress, see *post*, p. 691.

[13] *Williams* v. *Hayward* (1859) 1 E. & E. 1040.

[14] *Milmo* v. *Carreras* [1946] K.B. 306.

[15] *Oxley* v. *James* (1844) 13 M. & W. 209.

[16] *Pike* v. *Eyre* (1829) 9 B. & C. 909.

[17] L.P.A., s. 52 (2) (*g*), excepting " conveyances which take effect by operation of law." See *Preece* v. *Corrie* (1828) 5 Bing. 24; *Milmo* v. *Carreras* [1946] K.B. 306. But this point has not yet been finally settled.

a rack-rent, this operates as an assignment of the residue of the term. If this doctrine is sound, as judicial opinion indicates, it produces a paradox in cases like the foregoing: if described correctly as an assignment, an informal disposition of a lease is void at law and can operate only in equity; but if described incorrectly as a sub-lease, it takes effect as a valid assignment by operation of law. Perhaps it is illogical to describe an assignment as being brought about by operation of law when in fact it is brought about by act of the parties, particularly since the question is one of substance rather than form.

Assignments of only part of the demised land are treated later.[18]

5. Covenants and conditions. The assignment may contain covenants by either or both parties, and covenants by the assignee may be reinforced by a forfeiture clause entitling the assignor to resume the lease in case of breach. Such a clause creates an equitable right of entry,[19] and where the clause merely provides security for the attainment of a primary purpose which can still be achieved, the court has jurisdiction to grant relief.[20]

Sect. 2. Assignment of Reversions

1. Need for deed. The landlord's reversion is freely assignable by him, but in order to take effect at law the assignment must be made by deed.[21] This was always the rule at common law, since a reversion was regarded as analogous to an incorporeal hereditament which "lay in grant." [22] The rule is now part of the general rule, enacted by the Law of Property Act, 1925, that legal estates in land can be conveyed or created only by deed.[23]

2. Effect. An absolute assignment of the reversion, if validly made by deed, transfers the assignor's fee simple or leasehold legal estate to the assignee, subject to the subsisting lease, so that the assignee becomes the landlord.[23a] The effect of the assignment on the enforceability of the covenants in the lease is explained in the next chapter, as is also the effect of a partial assignment.[24] Assignment for a term of years, often called a lease of the reversion or a concurrent lease, has been discussed above.[25]

---

18 *Post*, p. 730.   19 *Ante*, p. 143.
20 *Shiloh Spinners Ltd.* v. *Harding* [1973] A.C. 691. For relief against forfeiture, see *post*, p. 660.
21 *Brawley* v. *Wade* (1824) M'Clel. 664; *ante*, p. 164.
22 *Ibid.*; Challis 48 (but see also 53); and see *post*, pp. 788, 790.
23 L.P.A., 1925, s. 52.
23a If the property includes a dwelling, it is an offence if the assignee fails to give the tenant written notice of the assignment and his name and address within (usually) two months: Housing Act 1974, s. 122.
24 *Post*, p. 734.   25 *Ante*, p. 648.

Part 4

DETERMINATION OF TENANCIES

A lease or tenancy may come to an end in the following ways:

    (1) By expiry.
    (2) By notice.
    (3) By forfeiture.
    (4) By surrender.
    (5) By merger.
    (6) By becoming a satisfied term.
    (7) By enlargement.
    (8) By disclaimer.

Perhaps, though doubtfully, there should be added—

    (9) By frustration.

The first three of these modes of determination are subject to statutory restrictions on the landlord's right to recover possession, as mentioned later.[26] All nine must now be explained successively.

Sect. 1. By Expiry

At common law, as has already been mentioned,[27] a lease or tenancy for a fixed period automatically determines when the fixed period expires. There are, however, important statutory exceptions under which the existing tenancy is automatically prolonged, with further provision for the grant of a new tenancy,[28] or the tenant may be entitled to remain in possession indefinitely as a statutory tenant.[29]

It has also been explained [30] how a lease for a fixed period may be made determinable upon the happening of some event within that period, *e.g.*, a death. In that case, at common law, the lease automatically ended when the event happened; but such tenancies, in so far as they belong to the law of landlord and tenant, have now been converted into long terms determinable by notice after the event.[31] But in the case of other events, *e.g.*, if the tenant parts with possession of the property,[32] the lease will still determine automatically if limited so as to last only until the condition is fulfilled.[33] Yet a lease until the tenant commits a breach of covenant

---

[26] *Post*, pp. 660, 683.
[27] *Ante*, p. 633.
[28] *Post*, p. 1111.
[29] *Post*, p. 1134.
[30] *Ante*, p. 631.
[31] *Ante*, p. 642.
[32] *Doe* d. *Lockwood* v. *Clarke* (1807) 8 East 185.
[33] See, however, (1963) 27 Conv.(N.S.) 111 (F. R. Crane).

falls within the provisions of the Law of Property Act, 1925, relating to forfeiture and relief therefrom in the same way as if the lease were determinable under a proviso for re-entry.[34]

Such determinable terms must be distinguished from terms made subject to some proviso or condition subsequent,[35] for in the latter case the lease does not end until the landlord re-enters; this is explained below in connection with forfeiture.[36]

Sect. 2. By Notice

A lease or tenancy for a fixed period cannot be determined by notice unless this is expressly agreed upon. Thus a lease for a substantial term such as 21 years often contains provisions enabling the tenant to determine it, *e.g.*, at the end of the seventh or fourteenth year, in which case the length of the notice required, the time when it is to be given, and other matters of this kind, depend on the terms of the lease. In the absence of any such provision the lease will continue for the full period.

Yearly, weekly, monthly and other periodical tenancies can be determined by notice. These rules, and the determination of tenancies at will and at sufferance, have already been explained.[37] As in the case of tenancies for a fixed term,[38] there are important statutory exceptions to these rules which prevent a landlord from determining the tenancies, or entitle the tenants to remain after the tenancies have been determined.[39]

Sect. 3. By Forfeiture

A. Right to Forfeit

The landlord may become entitled to re-take the premises, and so prematurely put an end to the lease, either under the terms of the lease or by operation of law. The former reason is by far the more common, and must be treated in detail. The latter is to be seen in the rules relating to denial of title, which will be considered first.

1. Denial of title. The rule is that a tenant who denies his landlord's title is automatically made liable to forfeit his lease,[40] a rule derived from the feudal principle that repudiation of the lord

---

[34] L.P.A., 1925, s. 146 (7); for these provisions, see *post*, p. 662.
[35] In principle the distinction is similar to that between determinable and conditional fees: *ante*, p. 75.
[36] *Infra.*
[37] *Ante*, p. 638.
[38] See above.
[39] *Post*, pp. 1109 *et seq.*
[40] See Woodfall L. & T. 961; Foa L. & T. 589. As to relief, see *post*, p. 664.

destroys the tenure.[41] This outmoded doctrine was even held to apply where the tenant inadvertently denied the landlord's title in a pleading in an action.[42] But a mere pleader's general denial which sets up no adverse title has now been held to be innocuous [43]; and the tenant may in any case save himself if given leave to amend his pleading before the landlord claims forfeiture.[44] Nor will a merely oral denial of title produce forfeiture in the case of a tenancy for years.[45] But it will do so in the case of a yearly (or other periodic) tenancy; for the tenant, by denying that he has a tenancy, is taken to waive any notice to quit, and the landlord can claim possession at once.[46]

2. Covenants. In other cases the lease is subject to forfeiture only if there is some provision to that effect in the lease. Nearly every lease contains a list of things which the tenant shall and shall not do, and these may be framed as conditions or as covenants. If, as is normally the case, they are framed as covenants (*e.g.*, " The tenant hereby covenants with the landlord as follows . . ."), the landlord has no right to determine the lease if they are broken unless the lease contains an express provision for forfeiture on breach of a covenant.[47] There is no necessary connection between the tenant failing to perform a covenant made by him and the determination of the lease; even a breach of covenant which the other party accepts as a repudiation will not put an end to the estate in the land created by the lease.[47a] Every well-drawn lease consequently contains a forfeiture clause.

3. Conditions. The tenant's obligations may, however, be worded as conditions, as, for example, if the lease is granted " upon condition that " or " provided always that " certain things are done or not done. In this case the term created by the lease becomes liable to forfeiture if the condition is broken, even if there is no forfeiture

41 *Doe* d. *Ellerbrock* v. *Flynn* (1834) 1 C.M. & R. 137; *Wisbech St. Mary Parish Council* v. *Lilley* [1956] 1 W.L.R. 121. The same applies if a tenant assists another person to deny the landlord's title: *Doe* d. *Ellerbrock* v. *Flynn, supra.*
42 *Kisch* v. *Hawes Bros. Ltd.* [1935] Ch. 102; *cf. Barton* v. *Read* [1932] 1 Ch. 362 at 367. R.S.C., Ord. 21, r. 21, which brought about the forfeiture in these cases, was later amended so as to prevent it applying to tenants as against their landlords, and has now been revoked.
43 *Warner* v. *Sampson* [1959] 1 Q.B. 297.
44 *Ibid.*
45 *Doe* d. *Graves* v. *Wells* (1839) 10 A. & E. 427.
46 *Wisbech St. Mary Parish Council* v. *Lilley* [1956] 1 W.L.R. 121; Woodfall L. & T. 962; such a statement is sometimes called a disclaimer of the lease (see *post,* p. 672) but that is inaccurate: *Warner* v. *Sampson* [1958] 1 Q.B. 404, reversed on other grounds [1959] 1 Q.B. 297.
47 *Doe* d. *Willson* v. *Phillips* (1824) 2 Bing. 13.
47a *Total Oil Great Britain Ltd.* v. *Thompson Garages (Biggin Hill) Ltd.* [1972] 1 Q.B. 318; and see *post,* p. 673.

clause,[48] and even if the lease is made merely in writing and not by deed.[49] In such a case the continuance of the lease has been made conditional upon the tenant performing his obligations, and upon breach of one of them the lease becomes voidable at the landlord's option. It does not become void automatically, even if the proviso expressly declares that it shall: the tenant will not be allowed to set up his breach of condition as determining the lease unless the landlord chooses to determine it by re-entry or by claiming possession.[50] In one case, where it was " stipulated and conditioned that the lessee should not underlet," these words were held to create a condition subsequent, so that the landlord was entitled to re-enter upon breach of the covenant, even though there was no other forfeiture clause.[51]

4. Forfeiture clauses. The more usual practice is to set out the tenant's duties in the form of covenants merely, but to add a forfeiture clause on the following lines: " provided always that if the tenant commits a breach of covenant or becomes bankrupt it shall be lawful for the lessor to re-enter upon the premises and immediately there-upon the term shall absolutely determine." Under this sort of proviso the lessor reserves to himself a right of re-entry,[52] and the lease continues unless and until he exercises it. As in the case of a condition, even if a proviso for re-entry also states that the lease shall determine or become void immediately upon the breach, it is settled that the lease remains valid until the lessor re-enters[53] or, perhaps, otherwise indicates his unequivocal intention to determine the lease[54]; the lease is thus not void but merely voidable[55] by the lessor (not by the lessee[56]).

5. Forfeiture. If a landlord is entitled to re-enter, he can enforce his right either by making peaceable entry on the land[57] or by

[48] *Doe* d. *Lockwood* v. *Clarke* (1807) 8 East 185.
[49] *Doe* d. *Henniker* v. *Watt* (1828) 8 B. & C. 308 at 315.
[50] For the similar rule governing conditional fees, see *ante*, p. 77. Formerly this principle did not apply to leases (Co.Litt. 214b); but the law appears to have changed: *Doe* d. *Bryan* v. *Bankes* (1821) 4 B. & Ald. 401; *Roberts* v. *Davey* (1833) 4 B. & Ad. 664.
[51] *Doe* d. *Henniker* v. *Watt* (1828) 8 B. & C. 308.
[52] A proprietary interest, not merely a contractual right: cf. L.P.A., 1925. s. 1 (2) (e), *ante*, p. 143. For its application against third parties, *e.g.*, underlessees, see *post*, p. 739.
[53] *Arnsby* v. *Woodward* (1827) 6 B. & C. 519; *Davenport* v. *R.* (1877) 3 App.Cas. 115 at 128; *Quesnel Forks Gold Mining Co. Ltd.* v. *Ward* [1920] A.C. 222; Smith's L.C. i, 45, 46.
[54] *Moore* v. *Ullcoats Mining Co. Ltd.* [1908] 1 Ch. 575 at 588; *quaere* how far this view can stand with the authorities in n. 53, *supra*.
[55] *Quesnel Forks Gold Mining Co. Ltd.* v. *Ward, supra*, at p. 227.
[56] *Rede* v. *Farr* (1817) 6 M. & S. 121.
[57] *Aglionby* v. *Cohen* [1955] 1 Q.B. 558. Merely reletting does not suffice: *Parker* v. *Jones* [1910] 2 K.B. 32; but see, *contra, Edward H. Lewis & Son Ltd.* v. *Morelli* [1948] 1 All E.R. 433, reversed on other grounds, [1948] 2 All E.R. 1021.

commencing an action for possession. It is usually inadvisable for a landlord to adopt the first method, for if any force is used, he may be criminally (but not civilly [58]) liable under the Forcible Entry Acts, 1381, 1391, 1429 and 1623.[59] And now, if the premises are let as a dwelling, it is unlawful to enforce a forfeiture otherwise than by proceedings in court while any person is lawfully residing on any part of the premises.[60] Consequently the normal method of enforcing a forfeiture is by issuing a writ for possession.

A writ which unequivocally claims possession (as distinct from one which includes alternative claims for injunctions based on the lease and its covenants continuing to exist) operates as a re-entry in law and so brings about a forfeiture as soon as it is served on the tenant [61]; the mere issue of such a writ is not enough.[62] But the forfeiture does not become final until the landlord has obtained judgment for possession, thereby establishing that the forfeiture is justified and that no relief against it will be granted.[63]

B. Waiver of Breach

1. Waiver. Even if the landlord has shown that he is treating the lease as forfeited, he may subsequently prevent himself from proceeding with the forfeiture if he waives the breach of covenant; and *a fortiori* a waiver of the breach may take place before the landlord has shown that he is treating the lease as forfeited. Waiver may be express or implied. It will be implied if—

(i) the landlord is aware of the acts or omissions of the tenant which make the lease liable to forfeiture, and

(ii) the landlord does some unequivocal act recognising the continued existence of the lease.[64]

Both elements must be present to constitute a waiver: knowledge of the breach accompanied by a merely passive attitude in the

---

[58] *Hemmings* v. *Stoke Poges Golf Club Ltd.* [1920] 1 K.B. 720.
[59] 5 Ric. 2, st. 1, c. 7; 15 Ric. 2, c. 2; 8 Hen. 6, c. 9; 21 Jac. 1, c. 15. Another reason for not making a re-entry in person may be gathered from *R.* v. *Hussey* (1924) 18 Cr.App.R. 160 (*held*, a tenant was not guilty of the crime of unlawful wounding if he shot his landlady while she was trying to evict him forcibly under an invalid notice to quit).
[60] Rent Act 1965, s. 31.
[61] See *Calabar Properties Ltd.* v. *Seagull Autos Ltd.* [1969] 1 Ch. 451.
[62] *Moore* v. *Ullcoats Mining Co. Ltd.* [1908] 1 Ch. 575 at 584; *Elliott* v. *Boynton* [1924] 1 Ch. 236; *Canas Property Co. Ltd.* v. *K. L. Television Services Ltd.* [1970] 2 Q.B. 433.
[63] See *Serjeant* v. *Nash Field & Co.* [1903] 2 K.B. 304 at 311; *Driscoll* v. *Church Commissioners for England* [1957] 1 Q.B. 330; *Borzak* v. *Ahmed* [1965] 2 Q.B. 320; but see (1965) 29 Conv.(N.S.) 267 (D. G. Barnsley).
[64] *Matthews* v. *Smallwood* [1910] 1 Ch. 777 at 786, approved in *Fuller's Theatre & Vaudeville Co. Ltd.* v. *Rofe* [1923] A.C. 435. But a transaction with a third party, not communicated to the tenant, does not imply waiver: *post*, p. 737..

landlord will not be a waiver.[65] But a waiver will be implied where a landlord, with knowledge of the breach, demands [66] or sues for [67] or accepts [68] rent falling due after the breach,[69] or distrains for rent, whether due before or after the breach [70] or agrees to grant a new lease to the tenant to commence from the normal determination of the existing lease.[71] These acts, however, will not amount to a waiver if done after the landlord has shown his final decision to treat the lease as forfeited, as by commencing an action for possession [72]; but a waiver by demand or acceptance of rent is not excluded merely because the lease provided that any waiver must be in writing,[73] or because the rent was accepted " without prejudice," [74] or because the demand and acceptance were due to clerical error.[74a] Although it is a question of fact whether money has been tendered and accepted as rent, its acceptance as such is in law conclusive against the landlord, who cannot then deny the waiver.[75]

2. Extent of waiver. As would be expected, the waiver of a covenant or condition extends only to the particular breach in question and does not operate as a general waiver of all future breaches [76]; but the law was once different.[77] The same applies to a licence to do any act granted to the tenant.[78] Waiver which is implied from the mere recognition of the continuance of the tenancy is waiver of the right to re-enter only, and not of the right to sue for damages for the breach.[79] Nor does it affect the legality of acts done before the waiver.[80]

3. Continuing breaches. Where the breach is of a continuing nature, as, for example, breach of a covenant to repair [81] or to use

---

[65] *Perry* v. *Davis* (1858) 3 C.B.(N.S.) 769.
[66] *Segal Securities Ltd.* v. *Thoseby* [1963] 1 Q.B. 887.
[67] *Dendy* v. *Nicholl* (1858) 4 C.B.(N.S.) 376.
[68] *Doe* d. *Gatehouse* v. *Rees* (1838) 4 Bing.N.C. 384.
[69] *Goodright* d. *Charter* v. *Cordwent* (1795) 6 T.R. 219.
[70] *Doe* d. *David* v. *Williams* (1835) 7 C. & P. 322.
[71] *Ward* v. *Day* (1864) 5 B. & S. 359.
[72] *Grimwood* v. *Moss* (1872) L.R. 7 C.P. 360; *Civil Service Co-operative Society Ltd.* v. *McGrigor's Trustee* [1923] 2 Ch. 347.
[73] *R.* v. *Paulson* [1921] 1 A.C. 271.
[74] *Davenport* v. *R.* (1877) 3 App.Cas. 115; *Segal Securities Ltd.* v. *Thoseby* [1963] 1 Q.B. 887.
[74a] *Central Estates (Belgravia) Ltd.* v. *Woolgar (No. 2)* [1972] 1 W.L.R. 1048.
[75] *Ibid.*; *David Blackstone Ltd.* v. *Burnetts (West End) Ltd.* [1973] 1 W.L.R. 1487.
[76] L.P.A., 1925, s. 148, replacing L.P.(Am.)A., 1860, s. 6.
[77] *Dumpor's Case* (1603) 4 Co.Rep. 119b, holding that a condition against assignment was not severable and that therefore if it was once waived it was destroyed. See Smith's L.C. i, 35.
[78] L.P.A., 1925, s. 143, replacing L.P.(Am.)A., 1859, ss. 1, 2.
[79] *Stephens* v. *Junior Army and Navy Stores Ltd.* [1914] 2 Ch. 516; *Norman* v. *Simpson* [1946] K.B. 158 at 160.
[80] *Muspratt* v. *Johnston* [1963] 2 Q.B. 383.
[81] *Coward* v. *Gregory* (1866) L.R. 2 C.P. 153; *Spoor* v. *Green* (1874) L.R. 9 Ex. 99 at 111, *per* Bramwell B. (" the covenant is broken afresh every day the premises are out of repair ").

the premises in a particular way,[82] a waiver will extend only to the time for which the landlord knew that the breaches would continue [83]; and breaches continuing after the date of the waiver will normally give a fresh right of forfeiture.[84] But waiver of a breach of one covenant will extend to a consequential continuing breach of another covenant which the tenant cannot discontinue, *e.g.*, where an unauthorised sub-letting has been waived and the sub-tenancy also involves a breach of a covenant as to user.[85]

C. Conditions for Forfeiture

The law leans against forfeiture, and a landlord suing for it is put to strict proof of his case. Moreover, both equity and statute have intervened so as to allow tenants to rescue themselves from liability to forfeiture in certain cases. There are different sets of rules for forfeiture for non-payment of rent and forfeiture for other causes. This is because equity would very commonly relieve a tenant against forfeiture for failure to pay rent, but as a general rule refused relief in all other cases.[86] Accordingly, relief in cases of non-payment of rent is given by the equitable jurisdiction, as amended by statute; in other cases there is a purely statutory jurisdiction, which is quite distinct.[1]

I. FORFEITURE FOR NON-PAYMENT OF RENT

A landlord who according to the lease has the right to re-enter for non-payment of rent must sometimes nevertheless make a formal demand for the rent before he may re-enter; and on complying with certain conditions the tenant may be able to have the proceedings for forfeiture terminated, or obtain relief against the forfeiture.

1. Landlord's formal demand. The landlord must either have made a formal demand for the rent, or else be exempted from making such a demand.

(*a*) *Formal demand.* To make a formal demand, the landlord or his authorised agent must demand the exact sum due on the day when it falls due at such convenient hour before sunset as will give

---

[82] *Marsden* v. *Edward Heyes Ltd.* [1927] 2 K.B. 1; *Creery* v. *Summersell* [1949] Ch. 751.

[83] *Segal Securities Ltd.* v. *Thoseby* [1963] 1 Q.B. 887.

[84] *Doe* d. *Ambler* v. *Woodbridge* (1829) 9 B. & C. 376. The fact that the rent is payable in advance is immaterial. [85] *Downie* v. *Turner* [1951] 2 K.B. 112.

[86] See *Shiloh Spinners Ltd.* v. *Harding* [1973] A.C. 691. Equitable relief in cases other than non-payment of rent was consistently refused after 1811: *Hill* v. *Barclay* (1811) 18 Ves. 56 (and see 16 Ves. 402); *Reynolds* v. *Pitt* (1812) 19 Ves. 134 (covenant to insure).

[1] But the statutory jurisdiction does not preclude the grant of equitable relief in proper cases: see *Shiloh Spinners Ltd.* v. *Harding, supra,* at pp. 724, 725.

time to count out the money, the demand being made upon the demised premises and continuing until sunset.[2]

(*b*) *Exemption from formal demand.* In order to avoid the technicalities of a formal demand, every well-drawn lease provides that the lease may be forfeited if the rent is a specified number of days in arrear, " whether formally demanded or not." The words quoted exempt the landlord from making a formal demand. Even if a lease contains no such clause, the Common Law Procedure Act, 1852,[3] dispenses with a formal demand in any action for forfeiture if—

(i) half a year's rent is in arrear, and

(ii) any goods to be found upon the premises available for distress [4] are not sufficient to satisfy all the arrears due.[5]

2. Tenant's right to stay proceedings. If the landlord brings an action for possession, the tenant has a statutory right to have the action discontinued (*i.e.,* terminated) by himself [6] paying all arrears of rent and costs at any time before trial.[7] But the ill-drafted statute has been held [8] to confine this right to cases where at least half a year's rent is in arrear.[9]

3. Tenant's claim to relief. Even where the tenant has no other defence, he may still be able to escape forfeiture by claiming relief. This jurisdiction is much used. It is of great importance to tenants, and it greatly qualifies the landlord's common law right of forfeiture.

(*a*) *The claim.* Equity considered that a right of re-entry was merely security for payment of the rent, so that if—

(i) the tenant paid the rent due; and

(ii) the tenant paid any expenses to which the landlord had been put; and

(iii) it was just and equitable to grant relief,

---

[2] See 1 Wms.Saund. (1871) 434 *et seq.,* being notes to *Duppa* v. *Mayo* (1669).

[3] s. 210, replacing L. & T. Act, 1730, s. 2. See also County Courts Act, 1959, s. 191 (2).

[4] See *post,* p. 692. If the premises are locked, no distress can be " found " and the Act is satisfied: *Hammond* v. *Mather* (1862) 3 F. & F. 151.

[5] " All arrears ": not merely half a year's rent, if more is due: *Cross* v. *Jordan* (1853) 8 Exch. 149.

[6] See *Matthews* v. *Dobbins* [1963] 1 W.L.R. 227 (payment by stranger insufficient under similar provision in County Courts Act, 1959, s. 191 (1)).

[7] Common Law Procedure Act, 1852, s. 212.

[8] *Standard Pattern Co. Ltd.* v. *Ivey* [1962] Ch. 432; but see (1962) 78 L.Q.R. 168 (R.E.M.). Contrast County Courts Act, 1959, s. 191 (1). The county court can now extend the time for payment: Administration of Justice Act, 1965, s. 23.

[9] *Semble,* when the writ is issued.

equity would restore the tenant to his position despite the forfeiture of the lease.[10]

(*b*) *Time limit.* Originally there was no limit to the time within which application for relief had to be made,[11] apart from the general principle that equity would give no assistance to stale claims. But this was inconvenient; and therefore the Common Law Procedure Act, 1852 [12] (replacing earlier legislation [13]), provided that where the landlord had obtained judgment for possession in the circumstances which dispensed him from making a formal demand,[14] an application for relief must be made within six months of execution of the judgment. In other cases the equitable jurisdiction to grant relief is unimpaired [15]; and though the court may possibly adopt a similar time limit,[16] it will not " boggle at a matter of days." [17]

(*c*) *Discretion.* Even if application for relief is made within the six months, relief will not necessarily be granted, *e.g.*, if no application is made until the six months have nearly expired, and the landlord has arranged to let the premises to others,[1] or if no rent has been paid for many years and the tenancy has been treated as at an end [2]; and relief may be granted on terms, *e.g.*, that the tenant should execute outstanding repairs.[3] If relief is granted, the tenant holds under the old lease, and the execution of a new document is not required.[4] It makes no difference whether the tenant applies for relief in an action for forfeiture by the landlord [5] or whether he applies after re-entry.[6]

(*d*) *Underleases.* Where a lease is forfeited, any underleases created out of it automatically come to an end [7]; for " every subordinate interest must perish with the superior interest on which it is dependent." [8] But an underlessee or mortgagee has the same right

---

[10] See *Howard* v. *Fanshawe* [1895] 2 Ch. 581; *Belgravia Insurance Co. Ltd.* v. *Meah* [1964] 1 Q.B. 436.
[11] *Hill* v. *Barclay* (1811) 18 Ves. 56 at 59, 60.
[12] ss. 210–212. See also County Courts Act, 1959, s. 191.
[13] L. & T. Act, 1730, ss. 2, 4.
[14] For these, see *ante*, pp. 659, 660.
[15] *Lovelock* v. *Margo* [1963] 2 Q.B. 786. *Cf.* County Courts Act, 1959, s. 191 (3).
[16] *Howard* v. *Fanshawe* [1895] 2 Ch. 581 at 589.
[17] *Thatcher* v. *C. H. Pearce & Sons (Contractors) Ltd.* [1968] 1 W.L.R. 748 at 756, *per* Simon P. (non-contentious re-entry; relief granted on application made six months and four days later).
[1] *Stanhope* v. *Haworth* (1886) 3 T.L.R. 34.
[2] *Public Trustee* v. *Westbrook* [1965] 1 W.L.R. 1160 (bombed site: no rent paid for 22 years).
[3] *Newbolt* v. *Bingham* (1895) 72 L.T. 852; *Belgravia Insurance Co. Ltd.* v. *Meah* [1964] 1 Q.B. 436.
[4] *Howard* v. *Fanshawe, supra.*
[5] Common Law Procedure Act, 1852, s. 212. See *Gill* v. *Lewis* [1956] 2 Q.B. 1.
[6] Common Law Procedure Act, 1860, s. 1, now Judicature Act, 1925, s. 46.
[7] *G. W. Ry.* v. *Smith* (1876) 2 Ch.D. 235 at 253.
[8] *Bendall* v. *McWhirter* [1952] 2 Q.B. 466 at 487, *per* Romer L.J

of applying for relief against forfeiture of the head lease as has the tenant under the head lease.[9] Relief cannot be applied for by a person who has no legal interest in the term created by the lease, such as a person in adverse possession (a squatter).[10]

II. FORFEITURE FOR BREACH OF OTHER COVENANTS OR CONDITIONS

The general rule is that the right to re-enter for breach of any covenant or condition other than for payment of rent is subject to the landlord's obligation to serve a notice in the statutory form, and the tenant's right to relief. Relief against forfeiture for non-payment of rent must be sought before re-entry or within six months thereafter; relief in other cases may be sought only before re-entry,[11] but the procedure of serving a preliminary notice gives the tenant his opportunity to apply for relief if he wishes.[12]

The tenant's right to apply for relief prevails over any stipulation to the contrary.[13] It cannot be defeated by framing the lease so that it continues only so long as the lessee abstains from committing a breach of covenant,[14] or by devices such as an undated surrender executed by the tenant as a guarantee against breach: a forfeiture disguised as a surrender is still a forfeiture.[14a] There are some exceptions to the general rule, and there are special provisions for sub-tenants.

1. General rule

(a) *Service of notice*

(1) THE NOTICE. Before proceeding to enforce forfeiture either by action or re-entry, the landlord must serve the statutory notice on the tenant under the Law of Property Act, 1925, s. 146,[15] or else the forfeiture will be void.[16] The notice must—

(i) specify the breach complained of; and

(ii) require it to be remedied, if this is possible; and

(iii) require the tenant to make compensation in money for the breach if the landlord requires such compensation.

---

9 Common Law Procedure Act, 1852, s. 210; *Doe* d. *Wyatt* v. *Byron* (1845) 1 C.B. 623. Relief may also be sought by an underlessee under L.P.A., 1925, s. 146 (4) (replacing C.A., 1892, s. 4), but only before re-entry: *Rogers* v. *Rice* [1892] 2 Ch. 170; *Belgravia Insurance Co. Ltd.* v. *Meah* [1964] 1 Q.B. 436 (mortgagee); and see *post*, p. 666.
10 *Tickner* v. *Buzzacott* [1965] Ch. 426.
11 *Rogers* v. *Rice* [1892] 2 Ch. 170.
12 See *Horsey Estate Ltd.* v. *Steiger* [1899] 2 Q.B. 79 at 91.
13 L.P.A., 1925, s. 146 (12).
14 *Ibid.*, s. 146 (7).
14a *Plymouth Corporation* v. *Harvey* [1971] 1 W.L.R. 549.
15 Replacing C.A., 1881, s. 14; C.A., 1892, ss. 2, 4.
16 *Re Riggs* [1901] 2 K.B. 16.

(2) TERMS OF NOTICE. The subsection says that money compensation shall be required " in any case," but it has been held that the landlord need not ask for it if he does not want it.[17] Thus, if the breach cannot be remedied and no compensation is desired, a notice merely specifying the breach will suffice.[18] Reasonable details of the breach must be given, so that the tenant may know what is required of him [19]; and a notice is not invalidated merely because it includes more than the landlord is entitled to require.[20]

A sub-letting in breach of covenant is a breach once and for all which cannot be remedied, *e.g.*, by obtaining a surrender of the sub-tenancy.[20a] A breach is also irremediable where the premises have been used for gambling [21] or for immoral purposes,[22] so that " the breach was of such a nature that it must cast a stigma on the premises." [23] But in some cases the question may be one of fact; thus use of premises for immoral purposes by a sub-tenant may not represent an irremediable breach on the part of the tenant if he takes prompt steps to stop it and to claim forfeiture of the sub-lease.[24] The safe course for the landlord, therefore, is to require in his notice that the breach be remedied " if it is capable of remedy," so that he can proceed with his action for forfeiture if in fact the breach is not remedied within a reasonable time.[25] The argument that all breaches of negative covenants are irremediable [26] is regarded as unsound.[27]

(3) MODE OF SERVICE. The notice may be served under the general provisions governing all notices under the Act, *i.e.*, by a written notice being left at the tenant's last known abode or business address, or being left for him on the demised premises; and it is sufficient service, to despatch the written notice to his last known abode or business address by registered letter or recorded delivery [28] (but not ordinary post [29]), provided it is not returned as undelivered.[30] But if a repairing covenant is broken, the landlord must prove that

---

[17] *Lock* v. *Pearce* [1893] 2 Ch. 271.
[18] *Rugby School (Governors)* v. *Tannahill* [1935] 1 K.B. 87.
[19] *Fletcher* v. *Nokes* [1897] 1 Ch. 271; and see *Fox* v. *Jolly* [1916] 1 A.C. 1.
[20] *Blewett* v. *Blewett* [1936] 2 All E.R. 188; *Silvester* v. *Ostrowska* [1959] 1 W.L.R. 1060.
[20a] *Scala House & District Property Co. Ltd.* v. *Forbes* [1974] Q.B. 575.
[21] *Hoffman* v. *Fineberg* [1949] Ch. 245, where the subject is generally discussed.
[22] *Rugby School (Governors)* v. *Tannahill* [1935] 1 K.B. 87; *Egerton* v. *Esplanade Hotels London Ltd.* [1947] 2 All E.R. 88.
[23] *Egerton* v. *Esplanade Hotels London Ltd.*, *supra*, at p. 91, *per* Morris J.
[24] *Glass* v. *Kencakes Ltd.* [1966] 1 Q.B. 611.
[25] *Ibid.*
[26] *Rugby School (Governors)* v. *Tannahill* [1934] 1 K.B. 695 at 701, *per* MacKinnon J. (affirmed [1935] 1 K.B. 87).
[27] *Ibid* [1935] 1 K.B. 87 at 90, 92. Yet see *Scala House & District Property Co. Ltd.* v. *Forbes*, *supra*, at p. 588; (1973) 89 L.Q.R. 460 at 462 (P.V.B.).
[28] Recorded Delivery Service Act, 1962, s. 1.
[29] *Holwell Securities Ltd.* v. *Hughes* [1973] 1 W.L.R. 757.
[30] L.P.A., 1925, s. 196, replacing C.A., 1881, s. 67.

the tenant [31] had knowledge of the service of the notice,[32] and service by registered post is only prima facie proof of this [33]; in other cases service by registered post or recorded delivery suffices by itself, and is deemed to have been made when in the ordinary course the letter would have been delivered.[34]

If there are several tenants, the notice must be served on all of them.[35] The definition°of " lessee " for this purpose includes successors in title,[36] but a sub-lessee or mortgagee need not be served,[37] nor need an assignee who takes after proper service on the tenant for the time being.[38]

(b) *Time for compliance.* The landlord must then allow the tenant a reasonable time in which to comply with the notice.[39] The Act does not define what is a reasonable time, but three months is usually considered to be enough in normal circumstances.[40] Even if the breach cannot be remedied (as where the provision is for forfeiture on the bankruptcy of the tenant), reasonable notice must be given so as to enable the tenant to consider his position [41]; in such cases, two days' notice has been held inadequate [42] and fourteen days' has sufficed.[43]

(c) *Relief.* If within a reasonable time the notice has not been complied with, the landlord may proceed to enforce the forfeiture. This he may do in person or by action, and the same considerations apply as before.[44] But while the landlord " is proceeding," by action or otherwise, to enforce the forfeiture (*i.e.*, at any time before he has actually entered,[45] even if judgment for possession has been given [46]), the tenant [47] may apply to the court for relief, either in any action

---

[31] Or an undertenant holding under a sub-lease nearly as long as the lease, or the person who last paid rent.
[32] Landlord and Tenant Act, 1927, s. 18 (2).
[33] *Ibid.*
[34] L.P.A., 1925, s. 196 (4).
[35] *Blewett* v. *Blewett* [1936] 2 All E.R. 188.
[36] L.P.A., 1925, s. 146 (5).
[37] *Egerton* v. *Jones* [1939] 2 K.B. 702; *Church Commissioners for England* v. *Ve-Ri-Best Manufacturing Co. Ltd.* [1957] 1 Q.B. 238.
[38] *Kanda* v. *Church Commissioners for England* [1958] 1 Q.B. 332. See also *post*, p. 703.
[39] L.P.A., 1925, s. 146 (1).
[40] See *Penton* v. *Barnett* [1898] 1 Q.B. 276 (though here the terms of the lease expressly provided for repairs to be done within this time).
[41] *Horsey Estate Ltd.* v. *Steiger* [1899] 2 Q.B. 79 at 90.
[42] *Ibid.*, at p. 92.
[43] *Civil Service Co-operative Society Ltd.* v. *McGrigor's Trustee* [1923] 2 Ch. 347; *Scala House & District Property Co. Ltd.* v. *Forbes* [1974] Q.B. 575 (breach of covenant against assigning or sub-letting held incapable of remedy).
[44] *Ante*, p. 656.
[45] *Rogers* v. *Rice* [1892] 2 Ch. 170.
[46] *West* v. *Rogers* (1888) 4 T.L.R. 299; and see *Egerton* v. *Jones* [1939] 2 K.B. 702.
[47] If the premises are held by joint tenants, the application must be made by all of them: *Fairclough & Sons Ltd.* v. *Berliner* [1931] 1 Ch. 60.

by the landlord enforcing the forfeiture or by a separate action of his own.[48] The court may grant relief on such terms as it thinks fit,[49] and if relief is granted the effect is as if the lease had never been forfeited.[50] If the breach has been remedied, relief is nearly always granted; but it may be refused if, *e.g.*, the tenant's personal qualifications are of importance and he has proved to be an unsatisfactory tenant.[51] There is nothing to enable the court to grant relief after actual entry, even within six months.[52]

2. Exceptional cases. No relief is available against forfeiture at common law for denial of the landlord's title, for section 146 of the Law of Property Act, 1925, applies only to forfeiture " under any proviso or stipulation in a lease." [53] Apart from that, the provisions of section 146 concerning the landlord's notice and the tenant's right to apply for relief govern all covenants and conditions (other than those for payment of rent) with three exceptions. These three exceptions are as follows.

(*a*) *Pre-*1926 *assignment*: when there was a breach before 1926 of a covenant against assigning, underletting or parting with the possession of the property.[54] This exception is now obsolete, for all such breaches will have been dealt with or waived long ago. The general rule applies to breaches of such a covenant committed after 1925.

(*b*) *Mining lease*: when there has been a breach of a covenant in a mining lease providing for inspection of the books, accounts, weighing machines or other things, or of the mine itself.[55] Since the rent reserved on such a lease usually varies with the quantity of minerals got, such a covenant is most important to the landlord; there is consequently no restriction upon the landlord forfeiting the lease without serving a notice, and no provision enabling the tenant to obtain relief.

---

[48] L.P.A., 1925, s. 146 (2).
[49] *Ibid.* For an example of an elaborate order made on different terms for different parties, see *Duke of Westminster* v. *Swinton* [1948] 1 K.B. 524.
[50] *Dendy* v. *Evans* [1910] 1 K.B. 263; *Driscoll* v. *Church Commissioners for England* [1957] 1 Q.B. 330; *ante*, p. 661.
[51] *Bathurst (Earl)* v. *Fine* [1974] 1 W.L.R. 905.
[52] *Rogers* v. *Rice, supra*; *cf. Re Rexdale Investments Ltd. and Gibson* [1967] 1 O.R. 251 to the contrary (" is proceeding " treated as including " has proceeded.").
[53] *Warner* v. *Sampson* [1958] 1 Q.B. 404, reversed on other grounds [1959] 1 Q.B. 297; *ante*, p. 654.
[54] L.P.A., 1925, s. 146 (8) (i). This apparently applies equally whether the prohibition is absolute, or merely against assignment without the landlord's consent: see *Barrow* v. *Isaacs & Son* [1891] 1 Q.B. 417.
[55] L.P.A., 1925, s. 146 (8) (ii).

(c) *Bankruptcy or execution*: when there has been a breach of a condition against the bankruptcy of the tenant (which includes the winding-up of a corporation [56]) or the taking of the lease in execution.[57] This must be divided into two heads:

(1) SECTION 146 EXCLUDED. In five specified cases,[58] on breach of such a condition, section 146 has no application at all; the lease can thus be forfeited at once without service of notice and without possibility of relief. These cases are those where the lease is of—

   (i) agricultural or pastoral land, or

   (ii) mines or minerals, or

   (iii) a public house or beershop, or

   (iv) a furnished house, or

   (v) property with respect to which the personal qualifications of the tenant are of importance for the preservation of the value or character of the property, or on the ground of neighbourhood to the landlord or to any person holding under him.[58]

(2) SECTION 146 APPLIES FOR ONE YEAR. In all other cases, on breach of such a condition, the protection of section 146 applies for one year from the bankruptcy [59] or taking in execution; if during that year the landlord wishes to forfeit the lease, he must serve the notice and the tenant can apply for relief.[60] But once the year has elapsed, the tenant is no longer protected; the landlord can enforce the forfeiture of the lease (provided the breach has not been waived) without serving notice and the court has no power to grant relief.[60]

In one case under this head, however, the provisions as to notice and relief apply without limit of time: if the tenant's lease is sold during the year, the protection of section 146 continues indefinitely.[60] This allows the trustee in bankruptcy or sheriff [61] to dispose of the lease to a purchaser at a reasonable price, for if the lease were liable to be forfeited after the year without the service of notice or the chance of relief, it would be hard to find a purchaser.

3. Sub-tenants and mortgagees. Under the Law of Property Act, 1925,[62] as amended by the Law of Property (Amendment) Act,

---

[56] L.P.A., 1925, s. 205 (1) (i).
[57] These provisions were first introduced by C.A., 1892, s. 2, now replaced by L.P.A., 1925, s. 146 (9), (10).
[58] L.P.A., 1925, s. 146 (9). See *Bathurst (Earl)* v. *Fine* [1974] 1 W.L.R. 905 (personal qualifications).
[59] Probably the date of adjudication.
[60] L.P.A., 1925, s. 146 (10).
[61] *i.e.*, under the execution.
[62] s. 146 (4), replacing C.A., 1892, s. 4.

1929,[63] a sub-tenant (including a mortgagee [64]) may apply for relief against the forfeiture of his landlord's lease on whatever ground that forfeiture is being enforced.[65] A sub-tenant has this right whether the head lease is being forfeited for non-payment of rent,[66] for one of the exceptional matters mentioned above or for any other reason, even if the tenant himself cannot claim relief.[67] Thus even if a mining lease is forfeited for breach of a covenant for inspection, a sub-tenant (but not the tenant) can ask for relief.

The court may make an order vesting the whole or any part of the demised premises in the sub-tenant " for the whole term of the lease or any less term " on such conditions as it thinks fit, but the sub-tenant is in no case " entitled to require a lease to be granted to him for any longer term than he had under his original sub-lease." [68] The latter of these conflicting provisions prevails, and the court will not grant the sub-tenant a longer term than his sub-lease.[69] Conditions may be imposed requiring, for example, the sub-tenant to pay a higher rent to the head landlord,[70] to covenant with him to perform the covenants of the forfeited lease,[71] and to make good any subsisting breaches.[72]

An adverse occupier or squatter, having no interest in the term, has no right to apply for relief.[73]

Sect. 4. By Surrender

1. Effect of surrender. If a tenant surrenders his lease to his immediate landlord, who accepts the surrender, the lease merges in the landlord's reversion and is extinguished. The surrender must be to the immediate landlord; the transfer of the lease to a superior landlord does not work a surrender but operates merely as an assign-

---

[63] s. 1, restoring the law as first enacted by C.A. 1892, s. 4, and inadvertently altered by L.P.A., 1925, s. 146 (8)–(10).
[64] If the mortgage is by sub-demise or legal charge: *Re Good's Lease* [1954] 1 W.L.R. 309; *Grand Junction Co. Ltd.* v. *Bates* [1954] 2 Q.B. 160; *Chelsea Estates Investment Trust Co. Ltd.* v. *Marche* [1955] Ch. 328 (vesting order in favour of mortgagee held not to extinguish right of redemption).
[65] Before the C.A., 1892, a sub-tenant could not obtain relief if the tenant's lease was forfeited otherwise than for non-payment of rent: *Burt* v. *Gray* [1891] 2 Q.B. 98.
[66] The jurisdiction is then as described *ante*, p. 661: *Belgravia Insurance Co. Ltd.* v. *Meah* [1964] 1 Q.B. 436.
[67] See *Imray* v. *Oakshette* [1897] 2 Q.B. 218.
[68] L.P.A., 1925, s. 146 (4).
[69] *Ewart* v. *Fryer* [1901] 1 Ch. 499 at 515, *per* Romer L.J., *obiter* (in H.L. [1902] A.C. 187). The point seems to have been expressly decided in *Ellerman* v. *Lillywhite* (1923) unrep.: see *Factors (Sundries) Ltd.* v. *Miller* [1952] 2 All E.R. 630 at 634.
[70] *Chatham Empire Theatre (1955) Ltd.* v. *Ultrans Ltd.* [1961] 1 W.L.R. 817.
[71] *Gray* v. *Bonsall* [1904] 1 K.B. 601 at 608.
[72] See *Ewart* v. *Fryer* [1901] 1 Ch. 499.
[73] *Tickner* v. *Buzzacott* [1965] Ch. 426.

ment of the lease. Thus if A leases land to B for 99 years and B sub-leases it to C for 21 years, C's lease will be extinguished by surrender if he transfers it to B but not if he transfers it to A.

If, however, the tenant who surrenders has granted an under-lease or created some incumbrance, this is binding on the landlord for so long as it would have bound the tenant had the lease not been surrendered. To return to the above example, if B surrendered his lease to A before C's sub-lease expired, A would take subject to C's sub-lease, for during the residue of the 99-year period A's title is derived from B and is subject to such other interests as B validly created before surrendering his lease to A.[73]

2. Express surrender. Surrender may be either express or by operation of law. For an express surrender, a deed is required by the Law of Property Act, 1925,[74] even though the lease was created orally. But probably an oral surrender made for value and supported by sufficient evidence in writing or part performance would be effective in equity as a contract to surrender.

3. Surrender by operation of law. Surrender by operation of law requires some act by the parties showing an intention to terminate the lease, in circumstances such that it would be inequitable for them to rely on the fact that there has been no surrender by deed.[75] The basis of this doctrine is the law of estoppel,[76] which operates at the determination of a tenancy much as at the creation of one.[77] Surrender by operation of law will take place if the tenant accepts a fresh (and valid [78]) lease from his immediate reversioner, even though the new lease is for a shorter term than the old one [79] or starts at a future date [80]; or where it is agreed between landlord and tenant that the term of the lease shall be extended, thereby creating a different estate in the land [81]; or where they agree that the tenancy shall cease but that the tenant shall in future occupy the property rent-free as a licensee.[82] Other variations of the terms of the tenancy may merely

---

[73] Co.Litt. 338a : " having regard to strangers ... the estate surrendered hath in consideration of law a continuance "; *David* v. *Sabin* [1893] 1 Ch. 523, explained *ante*, p. 609; *Phipos* v. *Callegari* (1910) 54 S.J. 635.
[74] s. 52, replacing R.P.A., 1845, s. 3. Previously, writing signed by the surrenderor or his agent sufficed : Statute of Frauds, 1677, s. 3.
[75] *Nicholls* v. *Atherstone* (1847) 10 Q.B. 944; *Glynn* v. *Coghlan* [1918] 1 I.R. 482 at 485; *Foster* v. *Robinson* [1951] 1 K.B. 149; Smith's L.C. ii. 771.
[76] *Lyon* v. *Reed* (1844) 13 M. & W. 285; *Wallis* v. *Hands* [1893] 2 Ch. 75; *Foster* v. *Robinson, supra.* [77] *Ante*, p. 645.
[78] *Corporation of Canterbury* v. *Cooper* (1908) 99 L.T. 612; 100 L.T. 597; *Rhyl U.D.C.* v. *Rhyl Amusements Ltd.* [1959] 1 W.L.R. 465.
[79] *Dodd* v. *Acklom* (1843) 6 Man. & G. 672.
[80] *Ive's Case* (1597) 5 Co.Rep. 11a.
[81] *Baker* v. *Merckel* [1960] 1 Q.B. 657; *Jenkin R. Lewis & Son Ltd.* v. *Kerman* [1971] Ch. 477 at 496. Similarly if the area of the holding is later extended : *ibid.*
[82] *Foster* v. *Robinson, supra.*

vary the existing tenancy or they may be so substantial that they will operate by way of surrender and regrant.[83] In particular, an agreed increase in the rent does not necessarily result in a surrender and regrant.[84]

There will naturally be a surrender if the tenant gives up possession of the premises and the landlord accepts it. But mere abandonment of the premises by the tenant is not by itself a surrender, for the landlord may wish the tenant's liability under the lease to continue. The mere delivery of the key of the premises to the landlord is not enough by itself,[85] and even if he accepts it, it must be shown that he did so with intent to determine the tenancy (as when he proceeds to re-let the premises [1]) and not merely because he could not help himself, *e.g.*, where the tenant leaves the country.[2] Nor will a contract by the tenant to purchase the reversion normally effect a surrender.[3]

Sect. 5. By Merger

1. Effect of merger. Merger is the converse of surrender. A surrender occurs where the landlord acquires the lease; merger occurs where the tenant retains the lease and acquires the reversion, or a third party acquires both lease and reversion. The principle is the same in both surrender and merger: the lease is absorbed by the reversion and destroyed.

2. Requirements. For merger to be effective, the lease and the reversion must be vested in the same person in the same right with no vested estate intervening. If he holds the lease and reversion in different capacities, *e.g.*, if he holds the lease as his own, and the reversion as executor or administrator, there is no merger.[4] Merger could take place at common law even if the immediate reversion consisted of a lease shorter than the lease merged.[5] Thus, if A, a tenant in fee simple, leased land to B for a thousand years and a few years later leased the same land to C for five hundred years, the result was to give C the reversion on B's lease for five hundred

---

[83] See *Re Arkwright's Settlement* [1945] Ch. 195; *Barclays Bank Ltd.* v. *Stasek* [1957] Ch. 28 (*post*, p. 936); *Collins* v. *Claughton* [1959] 1 W.L.R. 145; *Joseph* v. *Joseph* [1967] Ch. 78.
[84] *Jenkin R. Lewis & Sons Ltd.* v. *Kerman*, *supra*, explaining *Donellan* v. *Read* (1832) 3 B. & Ad. 899.
[85] *Cannan* v. *Hartley* (1850) 9 C.B. 634; *Oastler* v. *Henderson* (1877) 2 Q.B.D. 575.
[1] *Oastler* v. *Henderson*, *supra*; and see *Smith* v. *Roberts* (1892) 9 T.L.R. 77 (eviction).
[2] *Ibid.*
[3] *Nightingale* v. *Courtney* [1954] 1 Q.B. 399.
[4] *Chambers* v. *Kingham* (1878) 10 Ch.D. 743.
[5] *Hughes* v. *Robotham* (1593) Cro.Eliz. 302. An earlier rule to the contrary is stated in Co.Litt. 273b: " one chattel cannot drowne another, and years cannot be consumed in yeares."

years.[6] If X then acquired both C's reversion and B's lease, the thousand years' lease merged in the five hundred years' reversion and left X with five hundred years.[7] The same would have applied if A had granted C a life estate instead of a term of five hundred years.

3. Law and equity. But in equity the inconveniences of the doctrine of merger were often mitigated. At common law merger was automatic, by operation of law. In equity merger was a matter of intention, so that it did not occur unless intended by the person who acquired the two estates [8]; and there was a presumption against merger if it was against that person's interest.[9] The common law rules have now been amended by statute so as to follow the equitable doctrine: "there is no merger by operation of law only of any estate the beneficial interest in which would not be deemed to be merged or extinguished in equity." [10] Thus there is no merger either at law or in equity if it is intended that there shall be none.[11]

The position of a sub-tenant where the head lease has been surrendered or has become merged is discussed below.[12]

Sect. 6. By Becoming a Satisfied Term

This has already been dealt with.[13]

Sect. 7. By Enlargement

1. The power. Under certain conditions, not frequently encountered in practice, a lease may be enlarged into a fee simple by the tenant executing a deed of enlargement. Under the Law of Property Act, 1925,[14] this can be done only if—

    (i) there is not less than two hundred years of the lease unexpired; and

---

[6] C is of course not entitled to possession, but he has the right to receive the rent from B for 500 years, after which B pays his rent to A as before. C thus has only part of the reversion, as distinct from the reversion of a part of the land: *cf. post*, p. 735.

[7] *Stephens* v. *Bridges* (1821) 6 Madd. 66. Before 1926 there would have been no merger if C's term had been granted to commence after B's 1,000 years had expired, for C would then have had a mere *interesse termini* with which no term could merge: *Doe* d. *Rawlings* v. *Walker* (1826) 5 B. & C. 111; *Hyde* v. *Warden* (1877) 3 Ex.D. 72; and see *ante*, p. 632. The position in such a case after 1925 is doubtful.

[8] See *Capital and Counties Bank Ltd.* v. *Rhodes* [1903] 1 Ch. 631.

[9] *Ingle* v. *Vaughan Jenkins* [1900] 2 Ch. 368.

[10] L.P.A., 1925, s. 185, replacing J.A., 1873, s. 25 (4).

[11] See *Re Fletcher* [1917] 1 Ch. 339.

[12] *Post*, p. 738.

[13] *Ante*, p. 388.

[14] s. 153, replacing C.A., 1881, s. 65, and C.A., 1882, s. 11.

    (ii) the lease was originally granted for at least three hundred years; and

    (iii) no trust or right of redemption [15] exists in favour of the reversioner; and

    (iv) the lease is not liable to be determined by re-entry for condition broken; and

    (v) no rent of any money value is payable. A rent of " one silver penny if lawfully demanded " is a rent of no money value,[16] but a rent of three shillings is not.[17] A rent in such a lease which does not exceed one pound per annum and which has not been paid for a continuous period of twenty years (five having elapsed since 1925) is deemed to have ceased to be payable [18] and can no longer be recovered.[19]

For a sub-lease to be capable of enlargement under the section, it must, in addition, be derived out of a lease which is itself capable of enlargement.[20]

    2. The resulting fee. A fee simple acquired by enlargement is subject to all the same covenants, provisions and obligations as would have applied to the lease had it not been enlarged.[1] The lessor's reversion, however, presumably disappears, for the existence of a fee simple absolute in possession excludes the possibility of any estate in reversion.[2]

    3. Effect of enlargement. This statutory power has been little used, and its possibilities have not yet been worked out. On its face it seems to provide a means of subinfeudation in fee simple (since there is no indication that the previous tenure from the landlord is to be destroyed),[3] of making positive covenants run with freehold land,[4] and of making a fee simple subject to drastic restraints upon alienation,[5] as where the enlarged lease contains a covenant to repair and a covenant not to assign without licence. If long leases

---

[15] This excludes mortgages: *post*, p. 889.
[16] *Re Chapman and Hobbs* (1885) 29 Ch.D. 1007.
[17] *Re Smith and Stott* (1883) 29 Ch.D. 1009. Similarly, it seems, one shilling a year: see *Blaiberg v. Keeves* [1906] 2 Ch. 175.
[18] L.P.A., 1925, s. 153 (4).
[19] *Ibid.*, subs. (5).
[20] *Ibid.*, subs. (2).
[1] *Ibid.*, subs. (8).
[2] But see Challis 334, 335, who seems inclined to the opinion that the reversion continues and that the enlarged term may become a base fee. This argument is unconvincing, and if correct would make such interests subject to the Settled Land Act, 1925: *ante*, p. 314. See also (1958) 22 Conv.(N.S.) 101 at 106–112 for another opinion that the reversion subsists (T. P. D. Taylor).
[3] For subinfeudation (prohibited in fee simple by the Statute *Quia Emptores*, 1290), see *ante*, pp. 30–32.
[4] See *post*, p. 749.
[5] See *ante*, p. 78.

followed by enlargements can be deliberately used as a conveyancing device for these purposes, the barriers between freehold and leasehold principles will be liable to break down in some important respects.[6]

Sect. 8. By Disclaimer

1. The term. The term *disclaimer* is sometimes used as meaning repudiation of the tenancy in cases where the tenant denies the landlord's title. This type of disclaimer, which can bring about the termination of a lease, has already been explained under the heading of forfeiture, where it properly belongs.[7]

2. Statute. A right to end a lease by disclaimer sometimes arises by statute. Thus tenants whose premises were rendered unfit by war damage were given a statutory power to disclaim their tenancies; the effect of a valid disclaimer was the same as if there had been a surrender.[8] Similar rights were given to certain tenants of premises which had been requisitioned.[9]

3. Bankruptcy. There is a rather different form of disclaimer under the Bankruptcy Act, 1914.[10] This Act authorises a trustee in bankruptcy to disclaim onerous property belonging to the bankrupt which has become vested in the trustee under the bankruptcy law. Leaseholds are often onerous if near to expiry and subject to liabilities, *e.g.*, to repair; but they may not be disclaimed without leave of the court except in certain cases.[11] Disclaimer, if properly made, puts an end to the bankrupt's rights and liabilities in the lease, but except so far as is necessary to release him and his trustee from liability, it does not affect third parties [12]; and the court may make a vesting order in favour of any person interested in the property,[13] *e.g.*, a mortgagee.[14] Thus the disclaimer of a head lease leaves any sublease still in being,[15] and does not prevent the head landlord from distraining on the sub-tenant for rent due under the head lease.[16] But if the only person interested in the tenancy is the original lessee and he is bankrupt, disclaimer seems to determine the lease, at least for all practical purposes.

---

6 For these and other possibilities, see (1958) 22 Conv.(N.S.) 101 (T. P. D. Taylor); and see George & George, *The Sale of Flats* (3rd ed. 1970) p. 16 (the attractions of this method are " wholly spurious ").
7 *Ante*, p. 654.   8 Landlord and Tenant (War Damage) Acts, 1939 and 1941.
9 Landlord and Tenant (Requisitioned Land) Acts, 1942 and 1944.
10 s. 54; and similarly under the Companies Act, 1948, s. 323, for companies in liquidation.
11 Bankruptcy Act, 1914, s. 54 (3); Bankruptcy Rules, 1952, r. 278.
12 s. 54 (2).
13 s. 54 (6); *Re Holmes* [1908] 2 K.B. 812; *Re Carter and Ellis* [1905] 1 K.B. 735.
14 *Re Finley* (1888) 21 Q.B.D. 475.
15 *Re Thompson & Cottrell's Contract* [1943] Ch. 97.
16 *Ex p. Walton* (1881) 17 Ch.D. 746.

Sect. 9. Frustration

1. Leases. The doctrine of frustration is part of the law of contract, and may sometimes be invoked to discharge a party from contractual liability when some unforeseen event has made performance impossible. In general, the doctrine does not apply to executed leases; for a lease creates an estate which vests in the lessee, and cannot be divested except in one or other of the ways enumerated above. In other words, the lessor's principal obligation is executed when he grants the lease and puts the tenant into possession. The doctrine of frustration can apply only to obligations which are executory and which can therefore be rendered impossible of performance by later events.

2. Covenants. A covenant in a lease may accordingly be suspended or discharged by impossibility of performance if it creates a continuing or future obligation. If the impossibility ceases before the time for performance is past, the covenant is merely suspended until performance is possible; if the impossibility continues throughout the time for performance, the covenant is discharged. For example, under a building lease the landlord may let the site to the tenant for 99 years at a fixed rent, the tenant undertaking to erect a building which at the end of the term will pass to the landlord. If, after the grant of the lease, the building is prevented by some unforeseen cause such as wartime regulations or requisitioning, the lease continues and the rent remains payable.[17] But the landlord will perhaps have no remedy in damages against the tenant for the failure to build [18]; and even if he has reserved a power of re-entry for breach of the building covenant, he will probably not be able to exercise it,[19] for the supervening impossibility destroys the tenant's obligation and there is therefore no breach.[20] There is no hard-and-fast rule, since every covenant must be interpreted according to the intention of the parties to it, and it is quite possible to frame it so that the landlord may re-enter for non-fulfilment of some condition even if its performance is impossible.[21]

---

[17] *Cricklewood Property and Investment Trust Ltd.* v. *Leighton's Investment Trust Ltd.* [1945] A.C. 221.

[18] Cf. *Baily* v. *De Crespigny* (1869) L.R. 4 Q.B. 180 (covenant by tenant that neither he nor his assigns would build on certain land; land acquired by railway company, under compulsory powers, for building railway station; tenant held not liable in damages); contrast n. 25, *infra*. *Baily's* case may turn merely on the construction of " assigns " and so not apply to the case in the text.

[19] *Doe* d. *Marquis of Anglesea* v. *Churchwardens of Rugeley* (1844) 6 Q.B. 107.

[20] *Brewster* v. *Kitchell* (1698) 1 Salk. 198.

[21] Cf. *Moorgate Estates Ltd.* v. *Trower* [1940] Ch. 206 (a case of mortgagor and mortgagee); *Edward H. Lewis & Son Ltd.* v. *Morelli* [1948] 1 All E.R. 433, reversed on other grounds [1948] 2 All E.R. 1021.

3. Mere difficulty. An obligation to pay money (*e.g.*, rent) is never regarded as impossible of performance, unless prohibited by statute. Nor does the doctrine apply merely because performance is made much more onerous or expensive by some accident, or because the tenant loses the use of the land. In a well-known case a tenant who was evicted by the King's forces during the Civil War was held still liable to pay rent to his landlord.[22] Similarly tenants who have covenanted to repair are not relieved of liability if a building is accidentally destroyed by fire [23] or by enemy action,[24] for it is still possible to repair it; and even legislation which prohibits the effecting of repairs without a licence does not relieve a tenant who is sued for damages for not repairing, for even if he is refused a licence the legislation does not prevent him paying damages.[25]

4. Exceptional cases. Although the principle of frustration will not normally apply to a lease itself, as distinct from the covenants contained in it, there is high authority for the view that in a sufficiently strong case a term might be implied to the effect that the lease should be terminable in case of unforeseen disaster—" if, for example, some vast convulsion of nature swallowed up the property altogether, or buried it in the depths of the sea." [26] But there is equally high authority to the contrary: it is a principle of land law that the risk of accidents passes to the purchaser,[27] and this should apply just as much where he takes a lease as where he buys the fee simple outright. This rule may of course be displaced by an express agreement to the contrary; but the view that it can be displaced by mere implication would seem to go counter to the ordinary rule as to the incidence of risks. Furthermore the termination of an estate, unlike the discharge of a contract, may affect the rights of third parties, and it could hardly be right to destroy the interests of sub-lessees or mortgagees, whose titles depend upon the lease.[28]

---

22 *Paradine* v. *Jane* (1647) Aleyn 26; and see *Cyprus Cinema & Theatre Co. Ltd.* v. *Karmiotis* [1967] 1 Cy.L.R. 42.
23 *Matthey* v. *Curling* [1922] 2 A.C. 180; and see n. 30, *infra*.
24 *Redmond* v. *Dainton* [1920] 2 K.B. 256. But for the possibility of disclaimer under statute, see *ante*, p. 672.
25 *Maud* v. *Sandars* [1943] 2 All E.R. 783; *Eyre* v. *Johnson* [1946] K.B. 481. These cases appear to interpret the covenant as a covenant to repair or else to pay compensation.
26 *Cricklewood* case, *supra*, at p. 229, *per* Lord Simon L.C.; and see at pp. 239–241, *per* Lord Wright.
27 *Ante*, p. 575.
28 *Cricklewood* case, *supra*, at pp. 244, 245, *per* Lord Goddard; similarly Lord Russell of Killowen at pp. 233, 234. In this conflicting state of the authorities the Court of Appeal is bound by its own decision that the doctrine of frustration is inapplicable to leases: *Denman* v. *Brise* [1949] 1 K.B. 22 at 28: *Cusack-Smith* v. *London Corporation* [1956] 1 W.L.R. 1368; and see *Total Oil Great Britain Ltd.* v. *Thompson Garages (Biggin Hill) Ltd.* [1972] 1 Q.B. 318.

5. Destruction of buildings. If there is a lease of land and buildings, the destruction of the buildings does not affect the continuance of the lease, so that the lessee remains entitled to possession of the land and any buildings that may subsequently be erected on it.[29] But the complete destruction of the whole of the demised premises, as where an upper-floor flat is destroyed by fire, produces problems that yet have to be solved.[30] One view is that the tenancy would come to an end, and with it liability on the covenants,[31] for there would no longer be any physical entity which the tenant could hold of his landlord for any term,[32] and there can hardly be tenure without a tenement.[33] Another view is that the tenancy (and with it liability on the covenants) would endure in the air space formerly occupied by the flat,[34] and would thus attach to the corresponding flat in any building erected to replace the building destroyed. The former view has theoretical attractions, and the latter view practical merits,[35] not free from possible complications, *e.g.*, if there were substantial differences between the segments of air space occupied by the old flats and the new.

Part 5

RIGHTS AND DUTIES OF THE PARTIES UNDER A LEASE OR TENANCY

The rights and duties of the landlord and tenant under a lease or tenancy fall under four heads. First, the lease may be silent as to everything except the essential terms as to parties, premises, rent and duration. This is not infrequently the case with weekly and other periodic tenancies. Secondly, the parties may have agreed to be bound by the " usual covenants." Thirdly, the lease may provide in the orthodox way not only for the matters dealt with by the " usual covenants " but also for a number of other matters. Fourthly,

---

[29] *Simper* v. *Coombs* [1948] 1 All E.R. 306; *Denman* v. *Brise* [1949] 1 K.B. 22.
[30] Suggestions in Rolle's and Bacon's *Abridgements* that rent abates in case of partial loss or destruction seem to be based on no authority: see Foa L. & T. 111, n. (*g*).
[31] Thus the reddendum usually runs "yielding and paying therefor *during the said term* a rent of £x."
[32] Contrast *Izon* v. *Gorton* (1839) 5 Bing.N.C. 501; but that was a case of partial, not total, destruction.
[33] For the dependence of leases upon tenure, see *ante*, p. 614.
[34] See *Izon* v. *Gorton, supra*, at p. 507; and see 14 Vin.Abr. 320.
[35] *e.g.*, if the tenant has paid a premium for his tenancy, and the landlord is under covenant to rebuild.

there are a number of statutory provisions relating to the rights and duties of the parties to a lease, which at this stage can only be mentioned briefly.

The question how far covenants in a lease can be enforced between persons other than the original lessor and original lessee is considered separately.[36]

Sect. 1. Position of the Parties in the Absence of Express Provision

Except so far as the lease or tenancy agreement otherwise provides, the position of the parties is as set out below.

A. *Position of the Landlord*

1. Implied covenant for quiet enjoyment

(*a*) *Implication.* The relationship of landlord and tenant automatically implies a covenant for quiet enjoyment by the lessor.[37] This position has been established only after much conflict of judicial opinion, for it was long thought that the covenant was implied only if the word " demise " was used in the grant.[38]

(*b*) *Effect.* The covenant gives the tenant the right to be put into possession of the whole of the premises demised,[39] and to recover damages from the landlord if the landlord, or any other person to whom the covenant extends, physically interferes with the tenant's enjoyment of the land.[40] The covenant is not one for " quiet " enjoyment in the acoustic sense [41]; the lessor undertakes not that the tenant will be free from the nuisance of noise, for which the tenant has the ordinary remedy in tort, but that he will be free from disturbance by the exercise of adverse rights over the property or over other neighbouring land occupied by the lessor or some person for whom he is responsible.[42] For example, the covenant will be broken if a lessor who has reserved the right to work the minerals under the

---

[36] *Post*, p. 721.

[37] *Budd-Scott* v. *Daniel* [1902] 2 K.B. 351; *Markham* v. *Paget* [1908] 1 Ch. 697.

[38] *Baynes & Co.* v. *Lloyd & Sons* [1895] 2 Q.B. 610; *cf. Jones* v. *Lavington* [1903] 1 K.B. 253; *Hart* v. *Windsor* (1843) 12 M. & W. 68 at 85. See Woodfall L. & T. 562; and consider the covenants implied by the use of certain words in freehold conveyances: *ante*, p. 602.

[39] *Ludwell* v. *Newman* (1795) 6 T.R. 458; *Miller* v. *Emcer Products Ltd.* [1956] Ch. 304.

[40] See *Jaeger* v. *Mansions Consolidated Ltd.* (1903) 87 L.T. 690.

[41] *Jenkins* v. *Jackson* (1888) 40 Ch.D. 71; *Matania* v. *National Provincial Bank Ltd.* [1936] 2 All E.R. 633.

[42] *Hudson* v. *Cripps* [1896] 1 Ch. 265 at 268.

land demised causes a subsidence of the land by his mining activities [43]; and similarly if the landlord tries to drive out the tenant by
persistent threats,[44] or inflicts physical discomfort on him by cutting
off his gas and electricity.[45]

(c) *Reduction of enjoyment.* Usually there is no breach of the
covenant unless the tenant suffers some physical interference with his
enjoyment of the property. Thus where a landlord erected an
external staircase which passed the tenant's bedroom windows and
so destroyed his privacy, the tenant's action for damages failed.[46]
Nor can punitive damages be given if the landlord's conduct, though a
breach of contract, does not amount to a tort; in such cases the
effective remedy is an injunction.[47]

Independently of this covenant, it is a criminal offence for any
person to interfere with the peace or comfort of a residential occupier
or his household or to withdraw services reasonably required for
residential occupation if the intention is to drive him out of the
premises or to prevent him from exercising his rights.[48] It is similarly
an offence for any person unlawfully to deprive the residential
occupier of his occupation of any of the premises unless he proves
that, with reasonable cause, he believed that the residential occupier
had ceased to reside in the premises.[49]

(d) *Acts of others.* The scope of the landlord's covenant for
quiet enjoyment may be contrasted with that of the covenant for
quiet enjoyment ordinarily given by the vendor of a fee simple.[50]
The landlord's covenant extends to his own acts, whether rightful or
wrongful, but to only the rightful acts of persons claiming under him.
For the wrongful acts of persons claiming under the landlord the
tenant has his remedies against them [51]; but for their rightful acts
under any title derived from the landlord the landlord is made
answerable by his covenant, for it is through him that they are
enabled to disturb the tenant. For example, the tenant of a farm
suffered damage from the flooding of drains on two neighbouring
farms; all the farms were held by tenants of one landlord, but the
flooding from one farm was caused by defective drains properly used

---

[43] *Markham* v. *Paget* [1908] 1 Ch. 697.
[44] *Kenny* v. *Preen* [1963] 1 Q.B. 499.
[45] *Perera* v. *Vandiyar* [1953] 1 W.L.R. 672.
[46] *Browne* v. *Flower* [1911] 1 Ch. 219; contrast *Owen* v. *Gadd* [1956] 2 Q.B. 99
    (scaffolding).
[47] *Perera* v. *Vandiyar, supra; Kenny* v. *Preen, supra.*
[48] Rent Act 1965, s. 30 (2); *cf. post*, p. 683.
[49] *Ibid.*, s. 30 (1).
[50] *Ante*, p. 604.
[51] See *Malzy* v. *Eichholz* [1916] 2 K.B. 308 (no breach of the covenant where
    other tenants of the lessor caused a nuisance without his concurrence); *Matania*
    v. *National Provincial Bank Ltd.* [1936] 2 All E.R. 633.

and from the other by sound drains excessively used. The landlord was held liable for the former but not for the latter, since only in the former case was the interference caused by his tenant's lawful act.[52] A landlord, it may be added, does not use the words " as beneficial owner " when granting a lease; and even if he did, these words would not import the covenants for title applicable to a conveyance.[53]

(*e*) *Title paramount*. The covenant does not give the tenant any remedy if he is ejected by title paramount, at all events if the word " demise " is not used,[54] and probably even if it is.[55] There is thus in general no remedy if the landlord's title turns out to be bad. In one case a tenant having 8½ years of his lease unexpired mistakenly granted a sub-lease for 10½ years, but when in due course the sub-lessee was evicted by the freeholder he was held to have no remedy against the sub-lessor.[56] Similarly where the property turned out to be subject to a restrictive covenant the tenant had no remedy against his landlord on the covenant for quiet enjoyment.[57]

(*f*) *Lease not by deed*. Where the lease is not granted by deed, there cannot be any covenant in the technical sense, for the essence of a covenant is that it should be entered into by deed; but there will be corresponding contractual obligations.[58]

2. Obligation not to derogate from his grant

(*a*) *The obligation*. It is a principle of general application that a grantor must not derogate from his grant [59]; he must not seek to take away with one hand what he has given with the other. This obligation binds not only the grantor himself but persons claiming under him [60]; and the right to enforce it passes to those who claim under the grantee. In the case of leases, the covenant for quiet enjoyment will extend to many of the acts which might be construed as a derogation from the lessor's grant; but acts not amounting to a breach of the covenant or to a tort may nevertheless be restrained as being in

---

52 *Sanderson* v. *Berwick-upon-Tweed Corporation* (1884) 13 Q.B.D. 547.
53 L.P.A., 1925, s. 76 (5); *ante*, p. 604.
54 *Jones* v. *Lavington* [1903] 1 K.B. 253; *Markham* v. *Paget* [1908] 1 Ch. 697.
55 See *Baynes & Co.* v. *Lloyd & Sons* [1895] 2 Q.B. 610. But contrast an express covenant for quiet enjoyment: *Williams* v. *Burrell* (1845) 1 C.B. 402.
56 *Baynes & Co.* v. *Lloyd & Sons* [1895] 2 Q.B. 610.
57 *Jones* v. *Lavington* [1903] 1 K.B. 253. The law was previously doubtful: Woodfall L. & T. 562. See also *Commissioners of Crown Lands* v. *Page* [1960] 2 Q.B. 274; *post*, p. 690.
58 *Baynes & Co.* v. *Lloyd & Sons* [1895] 1 Q.B. 820 at 826 (in C.A., [1895] 2 Q.B. 610).
59 *Palmer* v. *Fletcher* (1663) 1 Lev. 122; and see *post*, p. 820; (1964) 80 L.Q.R. 244 (D. W. Elliott).
60 *Aldin* v. *Latimer Clark, Muirhead & Co.* [1894] 2 Ch. 437.

derogation of the grant. Thus if land is leased for the express purpose of storing explosives, the lessor and those claiming under him
will be restrained from using adjoining land so as to endanger the
statutory licence necessary for the storage of explosives.[61] Again, if
land is leased to a timber merchant for use for his business, the
landlord and his assigns will be restrained from building on adjoining
land so as to interrupt the flow of air to sheds used for drying
timber.[62] In neither case would there have been any remedy against
such acts by strangers, for they were not torts.

(*b*) *Extent of the obligation.* To constitute a derogation from
grant there must be some act rendering the premises substantially
less fit for the purposes for which they were let.[62a] No action will
lie if the tenant's business is abnormally sensitive to interference and
its abnormality was unknown to the landlord when the lease was
granted,[63] or if the landlord, having let the premises for some
particular trade, *e.g.*, for use as a wool shop only, lets adjoining
premises for a similar trade which competes with it: for the original
premises are still fit for use as a wool shop even if the profits will be
diminished.[64] Nor, as in the case of the covenant for quiet enjoyment,
will mere invasion of privacy amount to a breach of the obligation,
even though the property is let for residential purposes.[65] But
interference with the stability of the house by vibrations caused by
powerful engines on adjoining land may be restrained on this
ground [66]; and so may excessive noise, such as that caused in altering
another flat in the same building,[67] or a substantial interference with
the light reaching the tenant's windows.[68]

The rule against derogation from grant may therefore give the
tenant a wider protection against his landlord than he has against
strangers under the ordinary law.

3. Implied condition of safety or fitness in certain cases. In general
the landlord gives no implied undertaking that the premises are or
will be fit for habitation, or for any particular use,[69] or that any

---

[61] *Harmer* v. *Jumbil (Nigeria) Tin Areas Ltd.* [1921] 1 Ch. 200. This was an
extension of the principle, for the landlord's acts had no direct physical effect
on the premises: see *Port* v. *Griffith* [1938] 1 All E.R. 295 at 298.
[62] *Aldin* v. *Latimer Clark, Muirhead & Co.* [1894] 2 Ch. 437. [62a] *Ibid.*
[63] *Robinson* v. *Kilvert* (1889) 41 Ch.D. 88.
[64] *Port* v. *Griffith* [1938] 1 All E.R. 295; *cf. O'Cedar Ltd.* v. *Slough Trading Co.*
[1927] 2 K.B. 123 (adjoining premises let for purposes increasing fire insurance
premiums of the original premises: held, no derogation from grant).
[65] *Browne* v. *Flower* [1911] 1 Ch. 219; *Kelly* v. *Battershell* [1949] 2 All E.R. 830.
[66] *Grosvenor Hotel Co.* v. *Hamilton* [1894] 2 Q.B. 836.
[67] *Newman* v. *Real Estate Debenture Corpn. Ltd.* [1940] 1 All E.R. 131.
[68] *Coutts* v. *Gorham* (1829) Moo. & M. 396; *Cable* v. *Bryant* [1908] 1 Ch. 259.
[69] *Hart* v. *Windsor* (1843) 12 M. & W. 68.

particular use is lawful,[70] or that he will do any repairs [71] or rebuild the premises (*e.g.*, if destroyed by fire), even if he has covenanted for quiet enjoyment.[72] This rule is subject to four qualifications.

(*a*) *Furnished lettings.* Where a house is let furnished, the landlord impliedly undertakes, and there is an implied condition, that it is fit for human habitation when let.[73] If this is not the case, the tenant may repudiate the tenancy [74] and recover damages for any loss he has suffered.[75] But if the premises are fit for human habitation when let, the landlord need do no more; he is under no obligation to keep them in this condition.[76] Nor does the implied undertaking extend to unfurnished premises.[77] Nor is there any implied undertaking by the tenant that he is a suitable tenant, *e.g.*, by freedom from contagious diseases.[78]

(*b*) *Houses let at a low rent*

(1) HUMAN HABITATION. Under the Housing Act, 1957,[79] if a house is let at a comparatively low rent there is an implied condition that the house is fit for human habitation at the beginning of the tenancy, and an implied undertaking by the landlord that he will keep it in this condition throughout the tenancy. This provision, which cannot be excluded by any stipulation to the contrary,[80] applies to houses let at a rent [81] not exceeding £80 a year in inner London and £52 elsewhere, or half these amounts if the contract of letting was made before July 6, 1957.[81] " Rent " here means the gross rent payable to the landlord, without deduction for any rates or other outgoings for which the landlord is liable.[82]

---

[70] *Edler* v. *Auerbach* [1950] 1 K.B. 359 (covenant to carry on profession forbidden by Defence Regulations); *Hill* v. *Harris* [1965] 2 Q.B. 601 (user by sub-tenant in accordance with sub-lease but prohibited by covenant in head lease).
[71] *Gott* v. *Gandy* (1853) 2 E. & B. 845; *Sleafer* v. *Lambeth B. C.* [1960] 1 Q.B. 43 (landlord not liable for failure to repair dangerous door, where landlord in practice did repairs and knew of the defect).
[72] *Brown* v. *Quilter* (1764) Amb. 619.
[73] *Smith* v. *Marrable* (1843) 11 M. & W. 5 (bugs); *Wilson* v. *Finch-Hatton* (1877) 2 Ex.D. 336 (drains); *Collins* v. *Hopkins* [1923] 2 K.B. 617 (tuberculosis).
[74] *Wilson* v. *Finch-Hatton* (1877) 2 Ex.D. 336; this is because the implied covenant is also a condition: see *ante*, p. 655.
[75] *Charsley* v. *Jones* (1889) 53 J.P. 280.
[76] *Sarson* v. *Roberts* [1895] 2 Q.B. 395.
[77] *Hart* v. *Windsor* (1843) 12 M. & W. 68, correcting *Smith* v. *Marrable*, *supra*; *Cruse* v. *Mount* [1933] Ch. 278.
[78] *Humphreys* v. *Miller* [1917] 2 K.B. 122.
[79] s. 6 (1), (2), replacing provisions of the earlier Housing Acts, dating from 1885 onwards. See (1962) 26 Conv.(N.S.) 132 (W. A. West).
[80] Housing Act, 1957, s. 6 (2).
[81] Housing Act, 1957, s. 6 (1), as amended by London Government Act, 1963, Sched. 8, Pt. I, para. 2. See s. 6 (1) (*a*) (iii) of the Act of 1957 for a case where the limit is £16 a year.
[82] *Rousou* v. *Photi* [1940] 2 K.B. 379.

(2) NOTICE. The undertaking is confined to defects of which the landlord has notice.[83]

(3) EXTENT OF DEFECTS. A small defect such as a broken sashcord may constitute a breach of the statute, for the test is not how difficult it is to repair the defect but whether the state of repair of the house " is such that by ordinary user damage may naturally be caused to the occupier, either in respect of personal injury to life or limb or injury to health." [84] There is now a statutory list of the matters to be considered (including repair, freedom from damp, natural lighting and drainage) in determining whether a house is unfit for human habitation.[85] But the obligation is limited to cases when the house is capable of being made fit for human habitation at reasonable expense.[1]

(4) CONTRACT. Since this statutory duty operates by way of implying a term into the contract,[2] it makes the landlord contractually liable only to the tenant personally.[3] But in certain cases he may be liable to visitors and others for breach of a statutory duty of care.[4]

(5) EXCEPTIONS. This provision does not apply to tenancies of houses for not less than three years, which are not determinable by option within three years, and which provide that the lessee is to put the house into a condition reasonably fit for human habitation.[5] But it is curious that there is no exception for building leases or other cases where the house is already habitable and a repairing lease is granted at a low rent. Under an ordinary building lease the tenant, having built the house, is then given a long lease of it at a low ground rent, and the tenant is made liable for repair and insurance. Obviously the Act should not apply to such cases, for example if the house is damaged by fire; but there seems to be no way of escape from its terms.[6]

(c) *Houses let for a short term.* The Housing Act, 1961,[7] provides that in any lease of a dwelling-house granted after October 24, 1961, for a term of less than seven years there shall be an implied covenant by the landlord—

---

[83] *McCarrick* v. *Liverpool Corporation* [1947] A.C. 219; *Morgan* v. *Liverpool Corporation* [1927] 2 K.B. 131. For this doctrine, see *post*, p. 700.

[84] *Summers* v. *Salford Corporation* [1943] A.C. 283 at 289, *per* Lord Atkin.

[85] Housing Act, 1957, ss. 4, 5, 189 (1).

[1] *Buswell* v. *Goodwin* [1971] 1 W.L.R. 92.

[2] See *McCarrick* v. *Liverpool Corporation, supra,* discussed in *O'Brien* v. *Robinson* [1973] A.C. 912.

[3] *Ryall* v. *Kidwell* [1914] 3 K.B. 135.

[4] See *post*, p. 682.

[5] Housing Act, 1957, s. 6 (2). For other exceptions, see ss. 29 (4), 46 (5), 48 (4).

[6] See (1944) 8 Conv.(N.S.) 219 (E. O. Walford).

[7] ss. 32, 33. See (1962) 26 Conv.(N.S.) 187 (W. A. West).

(1) to keep in repair the structure and exterior [7a] (including drains, gutters and external pipes) and

(2) to keep in repair and proper working order the installations in the house—
    (i) for the supply of water, gas and electricity and for sanitation (including basins, sinks, baths and sanitary conveniences but not other fixtures, fittings and appliances for making use of water, gas and electricity) and
    (ii) for space heating or heating water.

Any covenant by the tenant to repair or pay money in lieu of repair is modified accordingly, and contracting out is forbidden except to the extent that the county court may authorise as reasonable. But the tenant remains liable to use the premises in a tenant-like manner,[8] and the landlord is not required to rebuild or reinstate after fire or other inevitable accident or to repair tenant's fixtures. The tenant must also allow the landlord to enter and view the premises at reasonable times after twenty-four hours' notice in writing to the occupier. There are other supplementary provisions. The landlord is liable only for defects of which he has notice.[9]

" Lease " for this purpose includes an agreement for a lease and any other tenancy. If the landlord can [9a] determine the lease within seven years it is treated as a lease for less than seven years, but it is not so treated if the tenant can extend it to seven years or more. The rent and rateable value are irrelevant.

(*d*) *Duty of care for safety.* In certain cases a landlord owes to all persons who might reasonably be expected to be affected by defects in the premises a statutory duty to take reasonable care to see that they and their property are reasonably safe from injury or damage.[10] This duty arises when under the tenancy the landlord is either under an obligation to the tenant (whether it is statutory or otherwise) for the maintenance or repair of the premises,[11] or else is or can become entitled to enter the premises to maintain or repair them [12]; but the duty is owed only if the defect falls within the landlord's obligation or right to maintain or repair, and he knows or ought to have known of the defect.[13] This rule applies to all types of tenancy, including

---

[7a] See *Brown* v. *Liverpool Corporation* [1969] 3 All E.R. 1345 (outside steps and paved access path included).   [8] See *post*, p. 685.

[9] *O'Brien* v. *Robinson* [1973] A.C. 912, applying the same approach as for the statutory obligation for habitability: *ante*, p. 681. Similarly for the liability on covenant: *post*, p. 700.

[9a] A right to do so only in certain events is not enough: *Parker* v. *O'Connor* [1974] 1 W.L.R. 1160.

[10] Defective Premises Act 1972, s. 4, replacing Occupiers' Liability Act, 1957, s. 4.

[11] Defective Premises Act 1972, s. 4 (1).

[12] *Ibid.*, s. 4 (4), not benefiting a tenant who has failed in his own express obligations.

[13] *Ibid.*, s. 4 (2), (3).

statutory tenancies and tenancies at will or sufferance, but not to mortgage terms or tenancies under attornment clauses in mortgages [14]; and it also applies to mere rights of occupation given by contract or statute, which for this purpose are treated as if they were tenancies.[15] No contracting out of this duty is possible.[16]

4. Statutory restrictions on the recovery of possession. When a lease or tenancy comes to an end, whether by effluxion of time or by notice to quit, the landlord's right at common law to recover possession is subject to certain statutory restrictions.

(*a*) *Protected tenancies.* Many tenancies are protected by statutory systems of control which either prolong the tenancy or else restrict the landlord's right to recover possession. These systems include the Rent Acts, 1968–1974, for most dwellings and the Landlord and Tenant Act, 1954, Part II, for most business tenancies. They are discussed later.[17]

(*b*) *Forcible entry.* The Forcible Entry Acts, 1381–1623, have already been mentioned.[18] They may make a landlord who takes forcible possession of the premises liable criminally, though not civilly.[19] They have engendered many differences of judicial opinion [20]; but the better view seems to be that they do not apply to tenants at will or at sufferance,[21] so that a landlord who forcibly evicted a tenant who was holding over would commit no offence under the Acts. Nevertheless it is possible that the landlord must first obtain an order of the court.[22]

(*c*) *Dwellings.* The Rent Act 1965 (replacing the Prevention from Eviction Act 1964) now restricts the recovery of possession of premises which have been let as a dwelling and are not protected by the Rent Acts, the Landlord and Tenant Act, 1954, or the Agricultural Holdings Act, 1948.[23] When such a tenancy comes to an end but any person lawfully residing in the premises continues to reside in any part of them, it is unlawful for the person entitled to possession to enforce his right of possession otherwise than by proceedings in the county court or, if it has no jurisdiction, the High Court.[24] A

---

[14] *Ibid.*, s. 6 (1); see *post*, p. 917. [15] *Ibid.*, s. 4 (6).
[16] *Ibid.*, s. 6 (3). [17] See *post*, pp. 1109 *et seq.*
[18] *Ante*, p. 657.
[19] *Hemmings* v. *Stoke Poges Golf Club Ltd.* [1920] 1 K.B. 720.
[20] *Ibid.*, at p. 731.
[21] *Ibid.*, at p. 744.
[22] See *McPhail* v. *Persons Unknown* [1973] Ch. 447 at 459, *per* Lord Denning M.R. But perhaps these *obiter dicta* apply only to dwellings under the Act next mentioned.
[23] Rent Act 1965, ss. 32 (1), 34.
[24] *Ibid.*, ss. 32, 35. The Act lays down no penalty, but breach of it is a tort: *Warder* v. *Cooper* [1970] Ch. 495. S. 32 is slightly amended by the Rent Act 1968, 1st Sched.

service occupancy is treated as a tenancy for this purpose. The court has some discretion in fixing the date for the surrender of possession.[25] The Act does not, however, affect the jurisdiction of the High Court in proceedings for forfeiture of a lease, or to enforce a mortgagee's right to possession where there is a tenancy not binding on him.[26] The Act also makes special provisions for the court to suspend the execution of any order for possession of an agricultural " tied dwelling," *i.e.,* a dwelling occupied by an agricultural worker under the terms of his employment.[1]

B. Position of the Tenant

1. Obligation to pay rent. This is discussed below.[2]

2. Obligation to pay rates and taxes. The tenant is under an obligation to pay all rates and taxes except those for which the landlord is liable. The landlord is liable for any tithe redemption annuity unless the tenant agrees to bear it[3] or the lease in question is for over fourteen years and the rent less than two-thirds of the annual value.[4] Formerly the landlord was also liable for income tax under Schedule A[5] (commonly called landlord's property tax) and land tax,[6] but both those taxes have been abolished. In place of Schedule A tax, the landlord became liable to income tax on the rent, at first under Schedule D but latterly under a new Schedule A.[6a] If he does not pay the tax, any tenant of the land may be required to pay it instead, up to the amount of any rent due from him, and he may deduct any such payment from any subsequent rent due from him.[7]

3. Obligation not to commit waste

(a) *Tenants for years.* The law of voluntary and permissive waste has already been explained in connection with freehold estates.[8] Under the ancient common law it had no application to leaseholds.[9]

---

[25] *McPhail* v. *Persons Unknown, supra,* at pp. 459, 460.
[26] Rent Act 1965, s. 35 (3); and see *Borzak* v. *Ahmed* [1965] 2 Q.B. 320 (forfeiture); *Bolton B. S.* v. *Cobb* [1966] 1 W.L.R. 1 (tenancy not binding on mortgagee; for such tenancies, see *post,* p. 935).
[1] Rent Act 1965, s. 33. See *e.g., Crane* v. *Morris* [1965] 1 W.L.R. 1104.
[2] *Post,* p. 689.
[3] Such agreement used not to be permitted in the case of tithe rentcharge, which tithe redemption annuity replaces: see Tithe Act, 1891, s. 1.
[4] Tithe Act, 1936, s. 17; for tithe, see *post,* p. 801.
[5] Abolished by Finance Act 1963, Pt. II.
[6] Abolished by Finance Act 1963, Pt. V, 14th Sched. Formerly it was open to the tenant to agree to bear this tax.
[6a] Income and Corporation Taxes Act 1970, Pt. III.
[7] *Ibid.,* s. 70.   [8] *Ante,* p. 103.
[9] At common law only tenants whose estates arose by operation of law, such as by curtesy or dower, were liable for waste. Tenants whose estates arose by act of parties were not liable unless the grantor had imposed this liability upon them.

But since 1267 it has been laid down by statute that a tenant for a fixed term of years is liable for both voluntary and permissive waste, unless there is a contrary agreement.[10] This means that if the terms of the tenancy make no provision about repairs, the tenant is liable for them and must maintain the property in the condition in which he took it.[11]

(b) *Yearly tenancies.* Under yearly and other periodic tenancies, the tenant must use the premises in a tenant-like manner.[12] Thus he will be liable for voluntary waste,[13] and he must not alter the character of the property, as by converting premises let as a shop and dwelling into one large shop.[14] As regards permissive waste, a yearly tenant is merely liable to keep the premises wind- and water-tight,[15] fair wear and tear excepted.[16]

(c) *Weekly tenancies.* A weekly tenant is, it seems, normally absolved from any liability for permissive waste by the implied understanding that " the house will be kept in reasonable and habitable condition . . . by the landlord and not by the tenant." [17] This does not make the landlord liable to repair [18]; it merely absolves the tenant. But the tenant is under a duty to use the premises in a tenant-like manner [19] : he must " take proper care of the place. He must, if he is going away for the winter, turn off the water and empty the boiler. He must clean the chimneys, when necessary, and also the windows. He must mend the electric light when it fuses. He must unstop the sink when it is blocked by his waste. . . . But apart from such things, if the house falls into disrepair through fair wear and tear or lapse of time, or for any reason not caused by him, then the tenant is not liable to repair it." [20] The position of a monthly or quarterly tenant, though uncertain, is probably similar.

---

[10] Statute of Marlbridge, 1267, making lessees for life or years liable for waste; *Yellowly* v. *Gower* (1855) 11 Exch. 274; *Davies* v. *Davies* (1888) 38 Ch.D. 499 at 504. The severe penalties imposed by the Statute of Gloucester, 1278, were repealed by the Civil Procedure Acts Repeal Act, 1879.

[11] Contrast the statement by Denning L.J. in *Warren* v. *Keen* [1954] 1 Q.B. 15 at 20 that a tenant is prima facie not liable for repair. This branch of the law is strangely uncertain: see (1954) 70 L.Q.R. 9 (R.E.M.); [1954] C.L.J. 71 (H.W.R.W.).

[12] *Marsden* v. *Edward Heyes Ltd.* [1927] 2 K.B. 1; *Warren* v. *Keen* [1954] 1 Q.B. 15.

[13] See *Warren* v. *Keen, supra,* at p. 21.

[14] *Marsden* v. *Edward Heyes Ltd., supra.*

[15] *Wedd* v. *Porter* [1916] 2 K.B. 91; but the test is doubtful: see *Warren* v. *Keen, supra.*

[16] See *Warren* v. *Keen, supra;* for fair wear and tear, see *post,* p. 700.

[17] *Mint* v. *Good* [1951] 1 K.B. 517 at 522, *per* Somervell L.J.

[18] *Mint* v. *Good, supra,* at p. 522; *Sleafer* v. *Lambeth B. C.* [1960] 1 Q.B. 43 (weekly tenancy).

[19] *Warren* v. *Keen, supra.*

[20] *Ibid.,* at p. 20, *per* Denning L.J.

(*d*) *Tenancies at will and at sufferance.* A tenant at will is not liable for permissive waste [21]; but if he commits voluntary waste his tenancy is thereby terminated and he is liable to an action for damages.[22] A tenant at sufferance is liable for voluntary waste [23] but probably not for permissive waste.

4. Landlord's right to view. The tenant is under an obligation to permit the landlord to enter and view the state of repair of the premises in cases where the landlord is liable to repair them.[24] The landlord may also have a statutory right to enter and view the premises in certain other cases.[25] But apart from these, unless he has reserved a right of entry, he has no right to enter the premises during the term, however good his reason,[26] for he has given the tenant the right of exclusive occupation as long as the tenancy endures.

5. Right to take emblements. The nature of emblements has already been considered.[27] A tenant at sufferance has no right to emblements,[28] but at common law a tenant at will,[29] a yearly tenant [30] or a tenant for years determinable with lives [31] was entitled to them provided the determination of the tenancy was not caused by his own act. A tenant for a fixed term of years could also claim emblements if his lease came to a premature end without his fault, *e.g.*, if the landlord had only a life estate and his death brought the lease to an end.[32]

The importance of these rules has been greatly diminished by statute. By the Landlord and Tenant Act, 1851,[33] a tenant at a rack-rent [34] whose tenancy determined by the death of the landlord or cesser of his interest was given the right to continue his tenancy on the existing terms until the expiration of the current year of the

---

21 *Harnett* v. *Maitland* (1847) 16 M. & W. 257.
22 *Countess of Shrewsbury's Case* (1600) 5 Co.Rep. 13b.
23 *Burchell* v. *Hornsby* (1808) 1 Camp. 360.
24 See *Saner* v. *Bilton* (1878) 7 Ch.D. 815 (express covenant); *Mint* v. *Good* [1951] 1 K.B. 517 (implied obligation).
25 See, *e.g.*, Agricultural Holdings Act, 1948, s. 17; Landlord and Tenant Act, 1927, s. 10; Housing Act, 1957, s. 6 (3); *ante*, p. 680.
26 *Stocker* v. *Planet B. S.* (1879) 27 W.R. 877.
27 *Ante*, p. 109.
28 *Doe* d. *Bennett* v. *Turner* (1840) 7 M. & W. 226 at 235.
29 Litt. 68.
30 *Kingsbury* v. *Collins* (1827) 4 Bing. 202; *Haines* v. *Welch* (1868) L.R. 4 C.P. 91.
31 *Graves* v. *Weld* (1833) 5 B. & Ad. 105.
32 *Knevett* v. *Pool* (1596) Cro.Eliz. 463; but the Settled Land Acts, 1882 and 1925, have given life tenants power to grant leases not determining on their death: see *ante*, p. 334. Yet the old law might apply if the lease was not granted under the statutory powers (see, *e.g.*, *Kisch* v. *Hawes Brothers Ltd.* [1935] Ch. 102), so that it did not bind the successors of the tenant for life.
33 s. 1.
34 *i.e.*, full rent; *see ante*, p. 622.

tenancy, in lieu of any right to emblements. In the case of agricultural holdings, the Agricultural Holdings Act, 1948,[35] provides that in such a case the tenancy continues until determined at the end of a year of the tenancy by twelve months' notice to quit. These provisions, coupled with the conversion of most leases for lives into terms of ninety years,[36] have made this subject of little consequence.

6. Right to estovers. A tenant for years has the same right to estovers and botes as a tenant for life.[37]

Sect. 2. Position of the Parties under a Lease Containing the Usual Covenants

1. Contracts for leases. The rights and duties set out above are those which arise when a lease is granted and there is no agreement to the contrary. But where, as occasionally happens, the lease is preceded by a contract that such a lease shall be granted,[38] the position of the parties is usually rather different, even where the contract is silent as to the covenants to be included. For the rule is that it is an implied term in a contract for a lease that the lease shall contain " the usual covenants." [39] If nevertheless the lease does not contain them, owing to the mistake of both parties when drawing it up, the lease may be rectified so as to accord with the contract.[40]

Where the "usual covenants" are to be included, they do not weaken the ordinary implied obligations of both parties, which have already been explained. In some instances they merely make express provision for what would otherwise be implied; in others they impose rather more extensive liabilities.

2. The usual covenants. The following covenants and conditions are always " usual." [41]

(a) On the part of the landlord—
a covenant for quiet enjoyment in the usual qualified form,[42] *i.e.*, extending only to the acts of the lessor or the rightful acts of anyone claiming from or under him.

(b) On the part of the tenant—
(i) a covenant to pay rent;

---

[35] s. 4, replacing Agricultural Holdings Act, 1923, s. 24; see *post*, p. 1117. .
[36] *Ante*, p. 642.
[37] Co.Litt. 41b: *ante*, p. 113.
[38] For the distinction between lease and contract, see *ante*, p. 624.
[39] *Propert* v. *Parker* (1832) 3 My. & K. 280.
[40] For rectification, see *ante*, p. 595.
[41] See *Hampshire* v. *Wickens* (1878) 7 Ch.D. 555.
[42] *Hampshire* v. *Wickens, supra.*

(ii) a covenant to pay tenant's rates and taxes, *i.e.*, all rates and taxes except those which statute requires the landlord to bear[43];

(iii) a covenant to keep the premises in repair and deliver them up in repair at the end of the term;

(iv) (if the landlord has undertaken any obligation to repair) a covenant to permit the landlord to enter and view the state of repair;

(v) a condition of re-entry for non-payment of rent, but not for breach of any other covenant.[44]

3. Other usual covenants. In addition to the above provisions, which are always " usual," other covenants may be " usual " in the circumstances of the case, by virtue, for example, of the custom of the neighbourhood or trade usage[45]; in each case this is a question of fact for the court. " It may very well be that what is usual in Mayfair or Bayswater is not usual at all in other parts of London, such, for instance, as Whitechapel." [46]

4. Covenants commonly inserted. In the absence of such special circumstances, however, many covenants which in practice are usually inserted in leases and are therefore literally " usual " are nevertheless not deemed to be " usual " in the technical sense of the word. Examples are covenants against assignment,[47] covenants against carrying on specified trades,[48] and provisos for forfeiture for breaches of any covenant, whether for payment of rent or otherwise.[49] Such provisions are frequently inserted when no contract to take a lease has been made and the terms of the lease are a matter for negotiation between the parties. But if a contract for a lease has been made, no covenant can be inserted in the lease without the concurrence of both parties unless either the contract provides for it or the covenant is technically a " usual " covenant.

[43] See *ante*, p. 684.

[44] *Hodgkinson* v. *Crowe* (1875) 10 Ch.App. 662; *Re Anderton & Milner's Contract* (1890) 45 Ch.D. 476. This is so even in the case of a lease of a public-house: *Re Lander and Bagley's Contract* [1892] 3 Ch. 41.

[45] See *Flexman* v. *Corbett* [1930] 1 Ch. 672 at 678, *per* Maugham J.: " if it is established that (to put a strong case) in nine cases out of ten the covenant would be found in a lease of premises of that nature for that purpose and in that district, I think the court is bound to hold that the covenant is usual."

[46] *Ibid.*, at p. 678, *per* Maugham J.

[47] *Lady De Soysa* v. *De Pless Pol* [1912] A.C. 194.

[48] *Propert* v. *Parker* (1832) 3 My. & K. 280.

[49] *Re Anderton & Milner's Contract* (1890) 45 Ch.D. 476. See Woodfall L. & T. 182 for other examples.

Sect. 3. Position under Certain Covenants Commonly Found in Leases

In addition to the covenants already considered there are a number of others which are very often agreed upon and need brief explanation.

1. Covenant to pay rent

(*a*) *Liability*. A landowner has the right at common law, founded on implied contract and reinforced by a statute,[50] to recover from any person occupying his land as tenant a reasonable sum for use and occupation of the land, unless the circumstances otherwise indicate.[51] Usually, however, a landlord need not rely upon this right because he will be able to enforce an express agreement for the payment of rent. Rent reserved by a lease is properly called rent-*service*, because there is a tenure and privity of estate[52]: it is said to be "incident to the reversion" of the landlord.[53] By this it is distinguished from a rent-*charge*,[54] which is a rent reserved out of land but not attached to any reversion. But today rent is for the most part regarded as a contractual payment.[54a]

A rent may be made to vary with circumstances (as was done in *Walsh* v. *Lonsdale*[55]), and there is nothing to prevent rent being reserved in kind,[56] *e.g.*, bottles of wine,[57] or in services, *e.g.*, the doing of team work[58] or cleaning the parish church.[59] Yet a "gold clause" reserving an annual rent equivalent to £1,900 in gold sterling has been held to entitle the lessor only to £1,900 in bank notes.[60] A contract for a tenancy is void for uncertainty if the rent is "to be agreed,"[61] but not if the rent is to be fixed "having regard to the market value," even if the contract provides no machinery for fixing

---

[50] Distress for Rent Act, 1737, s. 4.
[51] *Gibson* v. *Kirk* (1841) 1 Q.B. 850; Foa L. & T. 403–414.
[52] Litt. 213, 214, 215; see *ante*, p. 46.
[53] Co.Litt. 143a. For the question whether a later increase in the rent originally reserved is rent-service or a rent-charge, see *Jenkin R. Lewis & Son Ltd.* v. *Kerman* [1971] Ch. 477 at 484, 497.
[54] See *post*, p. 792.
[54a] *C. H. Bailey Ltd.* v. *Memorial Enterprises Ltd.* [1974] 1 W.L.R. 728.
[55] *Ante*, p. 625. See also *Selby* v. *Greaves* (1868) L.R. 2 C.P. 594 at 602; *Smith* v. *Cardiff Corporation (No.* 2) [1955] Ch. 159 at 173; (1957) 21 Conv.(N.S.) 265 (B. Hargrove); *ante*, p. 20, n. 53.
[56] Co.Litt. 142a.
[57] *Pitcher* v. *Tovey* (1692) 4 Mod. 71.
[58] *Duke of Marlborough* v. *Osborn* (1864) 5 B. & S. 67.
[59] *Doe* d. *Edney* v. *Benham* (1845) 7 Q.B. 976. Contrast *Barnes* v. *Barratt* [1970] 2 Q.B. 657 (services not "rent" for purposes of Rent Acts).
[60] *Treseder-Griffin* v. *Co-operative Insurance Society Ltd.* [1956] 2 Q.B. 127: see (1957) 73 L.Q.R. 181 (F. A. Mann); (1957) 21 Conv.(N.S.) 265 (B. Hargrove).
[61] *King's Motors (Oxford) Ltd.* v. *Lax* [1970] 1 W.L.R. 426: contrast *Smith* v. *Morgan* [1971] 1 W.L.R. 803 (mere right of pre-emption).

the rent [62]; nor is a provision entitling the landlord to vary the rent by giving notice void for uncertainty.[63]

Unless the lease provides for payment in advance, rent is normally payable in arrear.[64] It continues to be payable even if the premises cannot be used, *e.g.,* owing to destruction by fire [65] or other calamity, or seizure by military authorities for the occupation of troops,[66] or legislation prohibiting the tenant from occupying them.[67] But this stern common law rule has now been mitigated in the case of war damage and requisitioning (but not other events) by giving the tenant a statutory right to disclaim his tenancy.[68]

The tenant remains liable for the rent, and to forfeiture for non-payment of it, even though the amount owing has been paid by a third party under a contract of guarantee.[69] But a husband or wife with statutory rights of occupation may pay rent on behalf of the other spouse.[70] If the tenant is wrongfully evicted from any part of the premises by the landlord [71] or by any person claiming under the landlord,[72] the whole of the rent (but not liability under the other covenants) is suspended while the eviction lasts. But if the eviction is by some person lawfully claiming by title paramount, only an apportioned part of the rent is suspended [73]; and if the landlord is the Crown, the requisitioning of the land under statutory powers is not an unlawful eviction, and the rent is not suspended.[74]

No rent is recoverable if the tenancy was granted for an immoral purpose,[75] or for some illegal purpose, such as deceiving the rating authorities.[76]

Where a weekly rent is payable for a residence the landlord is required to provide a rent book containing the landlord's name and address and certain other information.[77] Failure to provide a proper

---

[62] *Brown* v. *Gould* [1972] Ch. 53.
[63] *Greater London Council* v. *Connolly* [1970] 2 Q.B. 100.
[64] *Coomber* v. *Howard* (1845) 1 C.B. 440.
[65] *Belfour* v. *Weston* (1786) 1 T.R. 310. There was no relief in equity: *Holtzapffel* v. *Baker* (1811) 18 Ves. 115.
[66] *Whitehall Court Ltd.* v. *Ettlinger* [1920] 1 K.B. 680.
[67] *London & Northern Estates Co.* v. *Schlesinger* [1916] 1 K.B. 20.
[68] *Ante,* p. 672.
[69] *London and County (A. & D.) Ltd.* v. *Wilfred Sportsman Ltd.* [1971] Ch. 764. *Sed quaere.* Perhaps receipt of the money will imply waiver of the forfeiture: *ibid.* Contrast *Re Hawkins* [1972] Ch. 714 at 727, 728 (where the *London and County* case was not cited): the precise terms of the guarantee may be of importance, too (*ibid.*).
[70] Matrimonial Homes Act 1967, s. 1 (5), applying also to mortgage payments and other outgoings. For this Act, see *post,* p. 785.
[71] *Morrison* v. *Chadwick* (1849) 7 C.B. 266.
[72] *Neale* v. *Mackenzie* (1836) 1 M. & W. 747. See *ante,* p. 648.
[73] *Neale* v. *Mackenzie, supra,* at pp. 758, 759.
[74] *Commissioners of Crown Lands* v. *Page* [1960] 2 Q.B. 274.
[75] *Upfill* v. *Wright* [1911] 1 K.B. 506.
[76] *Alexander* v. *Rayson* [1936] 1 K.B. 169.   [77] Landlord and Tenant Act, 1962.

rent book is a criminal offence, but it does not prevent the landlord from recovering rent due.[78]

In general, a rent cannot be increased or decreased while the tenancy subsists unless the tenancy so provides or the parties so agree. But formerly under the Housing Act 1964 a landlord who carried out improvements to a dwelling as a result of an improvement notice under the Act could obtain an order of the county court increasing the rent even if the dwelling was not subject to rent control.[79]

(*b*) *Enforcement.* The landlord may enforce payment of the rent—

    (*a*) directly, by—
        (i) an action for the money, or
        (ii) distress, *i.e.*, seizing the tenant's goods [80];
    (*b*) indirectly, by the threat of forfeiture if the lease contains a forfeiture clause.

Forfeiture has already been dealt with [81] and there is no need to discuss an action for the money. But distress must be considered in outline.

(*c*) *Distress*

(1) FEUDAL REMEDY. The subject of distress is extremely intricate.[82] It is " an archaic remedy which has largely fallen into disuse." [83] In essence distress is the ancient feudal remedy by which a lord could coerce his tenant into rendering his services. It is only where there is a relationship of landlord and tenant (legal or equitable) that a right to distrain for rent automatically arises.[84] Distress may therefore be levied against a tenant at will,[85] but not against a tenant at sufferance.[1]

The right of distress at common law was the right of the land-lord, as soon as any rent was due and unpaid,[2] to enter the premises and impound any chattels found thereon.[3] No formal demand for

---

[78] *Shaw* v. *Groom* [1970] 2 Q.B. 504.
[79] Housing Act 1964, s. 34, now repealed by Housing Act 1974, 15th Sched. For rent control, see *post*, pp. 1124 *et seq.*
[80] Suing or distraining will normally waive any right of forfeiture (*ante*, p. 658), so that they are alternative and not additional remedies to forfeiture. But in actions for forfeiture arrears of rent may be claimed (see, *e.g.*, *Evans* v. *Enever* [1920] 2 K.B. 315).
[81] *Ante*, p. 654.   [82] See Woodfall L. & T. 336; Foa L. & T. 467.
[83] *Abingdon R.D.C.* v. *O'Gorman* [1968] 2 Q.B. 811 at 819, *per* Lord Denning M.R.
[84] See *ante*, pp. 613, 626.
[85] Co.Litt. 142b; *Turner* v. *Barnes* (1862) 2 B. & S. 435.
[1] *Williams* v. *Stiven* (1846) 9 Q.B. 14; Woodfall L. & T. 338.
[2] Compare the statutory remedy of distress in the case of a rentcharge, exercisable only when the rent is 21 days in arrear; see *post*, p. 796.
[3] Statute of Marlbridge, 1267, c. 15.

the rent was first necessary. The landlord might enter himself, or by his bailiff acting on his behalf. He might take only enough property to provide reasonable security for the outstanding rent and expenses.[4] He had no right to sell the chattels: distress originally was merely coercive, not compensatory. But the Distress for Rent Act, 1689,[5] gave a right of sale after five days, provided notice was given to the tenant.

(2) THIRD PARTIES. Under a distress the landlord could take chattels found on the land,[6] even if they belonged to third parties,[7] *e.g.*, lodgers. This caused little hardship so long as there was no power of sale, for the landlord had no benefit from seizing property not belonging to his tenant. But the Act of 1689 was, as regards third parties, " a very harsh and unjust law "[8]; and relief is now available under the Law of Distress Amendment Act, 1908,[9] which enables most third parties[10] to protect their goods by making a written declaration in a prescribed form to the landlord.[11] There are also statutory provisions as to stock and machinery on agricultural holdings.[12]

(3) PRIVILEGED GOODS. Many classes of goods, even if they belong to the tenant, are privileged against distress.[13] For example, things in actual use[14] and perishables[15] may not be taken at all; and tools and implements of trade[16] and certain farm animals may be taken only if there is no other sufficient distress on the premises.[17]

---

[4] Statute of Marlbridge, 1267, c. 4.

[5] s. 1.

[6] Or elsewhere, if fraudulently removed: Distress for Rent Act, 1737, s. 1. In such a case the landlord may, with a number of qualifications, seize the goods wherever they are found and sell them as if they had actually been distrained on the premises, provided he seizes them within thirty days after the removal (*ibid.*). If goods are fraudulently removed to avoid distress, an action for double the value of the goods removed lies against the tenant or anyone knowingly assisting him (*ibid.*, s. 3).

[7] *Lyons* v. *Elliott* (1876) 1 Q.B.D. 210.

[8] *Ibid.*, at p. 213, *per* Blackburn J.

[9] Replacing and extending the Lodgers' Goods Protection Act, 1871.

[10] Including lodgers, certain undertenants and persons having no interest in the property, but excluding (*inter alia*) goods belonging to the tenant's spouse and goods comprised in a hire-purchase agreement with the tenant: Law of Distress Amendment Act, 1908, ss. 1, 4 (1).

[11] *Ibid.*, s. 1.

[12] Agricultural Holdings Act, 1948, ss. 19, 20.

[13] A synoptic table is given in Foa L. & T. 485; and see Agricultural Holdings Act, 1948, ss. 18–22.

[14] Otherwise a breach of the peace would be probable: see *Storey* v. *Robinson* (1795) 6 T.R. 138.

[15] *e.g.*, the carcases of pigs (*Morley* v. *Pincombe* (1848) 2 Exch. 101), for they could not be returned in the same condition if the tenant subsequently paid his rent.

[16] *e.g.*, a cab-driver's cab: *Lavell* v. *Richings* [1906] 1 K.B. 480, where the cab also fell within a statutory provision giving absolute privilege.

[17] *Lyons* v. *Elliott* (1876) 1 Q B.D. 210 at 215; Agricultural Holdings Act 1948, s. 19.

Fixtures may not be taken, even though they may be removable as tenant's fixtures, since in law they are land, not chattels.[18] Similarly growing crops could not be distrained at common law,[19] nor could sheaves of corn, which could not be returned in the same state [20]; but both these privileges were taken away by statute.[21] In the case of agricultural holdings distress must be made within a year of the default.[22] And there are general rules, some of ancient origin, as to time: distress may not be levied between dusk and dawn, or on a Sunday.

(4) POUND-BREACH, RESCUE AND REPLEVIN. The landlord may impound the goods (*i.e.*, secure them for safe custody) either on the premises [23] or elsewhere. If the tenant interferes with them he commits " pound-breach " and becomes liable to an action for treble damages.[1] But if the distress is illegal [2] or irregular [3] or excessive [4] the landlord is liable as for a trespass. In the case of illegal (but not irregular or excessive) distress the tenant has two other remedies: he may " rescue," *i.e.*, re-take his goods, provided they are not yet impounded [5]; or he may " replevy," *i.e.*, obtain in the county court an order for the return of the goods on his giving security for the rent and costs due, and undertaking to bring an action against the landlord.

(5) LEVY. A landlord who does not distrain in person is now required to employ a certificated bailiff, and it is by such that distress is ordinarily levied.[6] It may be done by taking " walking possession," *i.e.*, by leaving the goods impounded *in situ* on the premises under

---

[18] *Provincial Bill Posting Co.* v. *Low Moor Iron Co.* [1909] 2 K.B. 344.
[19] Co.Litt. 47a.
[20] *Ibid.*
[21] Distress for Rent Acts, 1689 and 1737.
[22] Agricultural Holdings Act, 1948, s. 18.
[23] This is the more usual. It was authorised by the Distress for Rent Act, 1737, s. 10; before that, the tenant's consent was required before the goods could be impounded on the premises.
[1] Distress for Rent Act, 1689, s. 3. Once the goods have been distrained, it is a " rescue " to take them out of the custody of the distrainer, and treble damages can be recovered (*ibid.*). Pound-breach is also an indictable offence: Woodfall L. & T. 404. No action will lie against someone who innocently assists in the removal of the goods after the pound has been broken: *Lavell & Co. Ltd.* v. *O'Leary* [1933] 2 K.B. 200.
[2] *i.e.*, wrongful from the start, as where no rent is due.
[3] *i.e.*, where the distress was lawful initially, but the procedure required by law has not been complied with, as where the goods are sold before the five days have expired.
[4] *i.e.* where more goods are seized than are reasonably necessary to satisfy the rent and costs.
[5] Once impounded they are " in the custody of the law."
[6] Law of Distress Amendment Act, 1888, s. 7. Certificates are granted by the county court.

an agreement with the tenant.[7] But a third party who removes his goods without knowing that they are thus impounded does not commit pound-breach.[8]

The remedy of distress is not available for breach of any covenant except a covenant to pay rent.

2. Covenant against assignment, underletting or parting with possession

(a) *Rights of tenants.* If the lease is silent on the matter, the tenant may assign or underlet without the landlord's consent.[9] Accordingly, a covenant against assignment, underletting or parting with possession of all or any part of the property is often inserted in leases. This cannot by itself invalidate an assignment or sub-lease as against the grantee, for the tenant has an estate which is always alienable property [10]; but there will be a breach of covenant which, if reinforced by a forfeiture clause, may result in determination of the lease, and the landlord may in any case sue the assignor for damages. If, however, the landlord accepts rent from an assignee or sub-lessee, that amounts to an implied consent to the transaction.[11]

(b) *Withholding consent.* If the covenant is absolute, *i.e.*, stating simply that the tenant shall not assign or underlet, the landlord is entitled to waive it in any particular instance, although he cannot be compelled to do so even if his attitude is entirely unreasonable.[12] But if the covenant is one against assigning, sub-letting or parting with possession " without licence or consent," the Landlord and Tenant Act, 1927,[13] requires that notwithstanding any contrary provision the covenant shall be deemed to be subject to a proviso that the licence or consent is not to be unreasonably withheld. In view of the landlord's power to waive even an absolute covenant, the distinction between an absolute and a qualified covenant of this kind is purely one of form; yet in its result it is important.

---

[7] This practice became less popular when it was held that the tenant could not be made to pay the bailiff even under an express agreement: *Day* v. *Davies* [1938] 2 K.B. 74. But there is now a right to charge for taking " walking possession " and inspecting the goods thereunder: Distress for Rent Rules, 1953, (S.I. 1953 No. 1702), r. 7, App. I (as replaced by Distress for Rent (Amendment) Rules 1971, (S.I. 1971 No. 1333), Sched.); S.I. 1973 No. 474.

[8] *Abingdon R.D.C.* v. *O'Gorman* [1968] 2 Q.B. 811.

[9] See *Doe* d. *Mitchinson* v. *Carter (No.* 1) (1798) 8 T.R. 57 at 60.

[10] *Parker* v. *Jones* [1910] 2 K.B. 32 at 38; *Property & Bloodstock Ltd.* v. *Emerton* [1968] Ch. 94 at 119. Contrast *Elliott* v. *Johnson* (1866) L.R. 2 Q.B. 120 at 126, 127.

[11] *Hyde* v. *Pimley* [1952] 2 Q.B. 506. For waiver implied from acceptance of rent, see *ante*, p. 657.

[12] See *Lilley and Skinner* v. *Crump* (1929) 73 S.J. 366: *F. W. Woolworth & Co. Ltd.* v. *Lambert* [1937] Ch. 37 at 58, 59; but note *Property & Bloodstock Ltd.* v. *Emerton, supra*, at p. 119.

[13] s. 19. This section does not apply to agricultural holdings: s. 19 (4). But it applies to leases whether granted before or after the Act.

(c) *Operation of rule.* The section has been held not to affect the somewhat unusual covenant [13a] that the tenant shall offer a free surrender of his tenancy to the landlord before assigning or under-letting.[14] Even where it does apply, it does not permit the tenant to assign or sub-let without seeking the landlord's consent; if he does so, he has committed a breach of covenant even if the landlord could not properly refuse his consent.[15] But if he seeks consent and it is unreasonably withheld, he may forthwith assign or sub-let without the consent,[16] or seek a declaration from the court [17] of his right to do so [18]; yet the landlord is not liable for damages, as he would be had he expressly convenanted not to refuse consent unreasonably.[19]

(d) *Reasonableness.* It is for the tenant to show that the with-holding of consent was unreasonable.[20] This is a question of fact; there are no fixed rules, but many decided cases.[21] Examples of reasonable refusal are—

where the proposed assignee's references were unsatisfactory [22];

where the tenant had altered and failed to repair the property and proposed to assign before putting matters right [23];

where the property would be used by the proposed assignee for trade competition detrimental to other property belonging to the landlord [24];

where a proposed sub-letting was to be at a high premium and a low rent, which would depreciate the landlord's interest in the property [25];

where the proposed assignee was a development company interested only in development to take place after the end of the lease and conflicting with the landlord's plans [26];

13a See *Cardshops Ltd.* v. *Davies* [1971] 1 W.L.R. 591.
14 *Adler* v. *Upper Grosvenor Street Investment Ltd.* [1957] 1 W.L.R. 227, discussed in (1957) 73 L.Q.R. 157 (R.E.M.), followed in *Creer* v. *P. & O. Lines of Australia Pty. Ltd.* (1971) 125 C.L.R. 84, but doubted in *Greene* v. *Church Commissioners for England* [1974] Ch. 467, where the *Creer* case was not mentioned.
15 *Eastern Telegraph Co. Ltd.* v. *Dent* [1899] 1 Q.B. 835; *cf. Moat* v. *Martin* [1950] 1 K.B. 175, a slightly different case leading to a different result.
16 *Treloar* v. *Bigge* (1874) L.R. 9 Ex. 151.
17 The county court now has jurisdiction to make such a declaration: Landlord and Tenant Act, 1954, s. 53 (1).
18 *Young* v. *Ashley Gardens Properties Ltd.* [1903] 2 Ch. 112.
19 *Ideal Film Renting Co. Ltd.* v. *Nielsen* [1921] 1 Ch. 575.
20 *Shanly* v. *Ward* (1913) 29 T.L.R. 714; *Mills* v. *Cannon Brewery Co. Ltd.* [1920] 2 Ch. 38 at 46.
21 See *Houlder Brothers & Co. Ltd.* v. *Gibbs* [1925] Ch. 575; *Viscount Tredegar* v. *Harwood* [1929] A.C. 72; *Governors of Bridewell Hospital* v. *Fawkner and Rogers* (1892) 8 T.L.R. 637; *Swanson* v. *Forton* [1949] Ch. 143.
22 *Shanly* v. *Ward, supra.*   23 *Goldstein* v. *Sanders* [1915] 1 Ch. 549.
24 *Premier Confectionery (London) Co. Ltd.* v. *London Commercial Sale Rooms Ltd.* [1933] Ch. 904.
25 *Re Town Investments Ltd. Underlease* [1954] Ch. 301.
26 *Pimms Ltd.* v. *Tallow Chandlers Company* [1964] 2 Q.B. 547.

where consent to the transaction would necessarily preclude the landlord from preventing the premises from being used for purposes prohibited by the lease [26a]; and

where the assignee would acquire a statutory protection (*e.g.*, under the Rent Restriction Acts [27]) that the assignor could not claim or did not want.[28]

Examples of unreasonable refusal are—

where the landlord's motive was that he wished to recover the premises for himself [29];

where the proposed assignee was also his tenant, and would vacate another house which would be difficult to re-let [30];

where the proposed assignee was a diplomat with diplomatic immunity against legal proceedings [31]; and

where permission was refused unless the proposed sub-tenant covenanted with the head landlord to pay him the rent.[32]

If the tenant is granted a licence to sub-let on condition that the sub-lessee covenants not to assign without the consent of both the tenant and the head landlord, the tenant impliedly covenants not to consent to an assignment without the head landlord's consent.[33]

(e) *Reasons.* The Court of Appeal has held that objections not connected with the person of the assignee or with the nature of his proposed use or occupation of the premises are not reasonable.[34] But the House of Lords has cast doubt upon this principle,[35] for in the management of large estates there may be considerations connected with other properties which may reasonably influence a landlord. It is not clear whether the landlord is bound to state any reasons for withholding his consent, or whether, if he does so, he can

---

26a *Killick* v. *Second Covent Garden Property Co. Ltd.* [1973] 1 W.L.R. 658, distinguishing *Packaging Centre Ltd.* v. *Poland Street Estate Ltd.* [1961] E.G.D. 377.

27 For these, see *post*, pp. 1124, 1125.

28 *Lee* v. *K. Carter Ltd.* [1949] 1 K.B. 85; *Swanson* v. *Forton* [1949] Ch. 143 (distinguishing *Re Swanson's Agreement* [1946] 2 All E.R. 628, *contra*); *Dollar* v. *Winston* [1950] Ch. 236; *Thomas Bookman Ltd.* v. *Nathan* [1955] 1 W.L.R. 815.

29 *Bates* v. *Donaldson* [1896] 2 Q.B. 241.

30 *Houlder Brothers & Co. Ltd.* v. *Gibbs* [1925] Ch. 575.

31 *Parker* v. *Boggon* [1947] K.B. 346.

32 *Balfour* v. *Kensington Gardens Mansions Ltd.* (1932) 49 T.L.R. 29.

33 *Drive Yourself Hire Co. (London) Ltd.* v. *Strutt* [1954] 1 Q.B. 250; or the landlord may be made a covenantee under the L.P.A., 1925, s. 56: see *post*, p. 745.

34 *Houlder Bros. & Co. Ltd.* v. *Gibbs*, *supra*. Despite the case next cited, the Court of Appeal will still follow its own decision: *Lee* v. *K. Carter Ltd.* [1949] 1 K.B. 85.

35 *Viscount Tredegar* v. *Harwood* [1929] A.C. 72, a case on insurance: see *post*, p. 703, and see *Pimms Ltd.* v. *Tallow Chandlers Company* [1964] 2 Q.B. 547.

also rely on any other reasons which in fact he has.[36] The test, however, is not subjective but objective, and so depends on what a reasonable landlord would think.[36a]

(*f*) *Racial objections.* By statute, the consent of a landlord or any other person to an assignment, sub-letting or parting with possession of any premises comprised in a tenancy is unreasonably withheld " if and so far as it is withheld on the ground of colour, race or ethnic or national origins "; but where the tenancy is of part of a dwelling-house this does not apply if the person whose consent is required occupies the remainder as his residence and the tenant is entitled to the use of any accommodation (other than that required for access) in common with him.[37] Any provision which purports to prohibit any such disposition of the demised premises by reference to any such ground is construed as prohibiting the disposition without the landlord's consent, such consent not to be unreasonably withheld.[38] There is also a wider and overlapping provision against racial discrimination by any person concerned with the disposal of land, subject to a similar exception where residential accommodation in small premises is shared with a resident landlord.[39]

(*g*) *Fines.* Covenants to which the Act of 1927 applies are subject to a further restriction under the Law of Property Act, 1925,[40] namely, a proviso that no " fine " or similar sum shall be payable in respect of any licence or consent unless the lease expressly provides for it. " Fine " is defined in wide terms [41] which include any valuable consideration given in circumstances such that, if it were money, it would be what is commonly known as a fine [42]; and it thus includes a stipulation in a lease of a public-house which makes it a house " tied " to the landlord, a brewer.[43] But reasonable sums for legal and other expenses relating to the licence are expressly excepted.[44] If a fine which a tenant need not pay is in fact paid without protest, the tenant cannot recover it, for the payment is not unlawful but merely unnecessary.[45]

[36] See *Parker* v. *Boggon* [1947] K.B. 346 and *Lovelock* v. *Margo* [1963] 2 Q.B. 786, as discussed at (1963) 79 L.Q.R. 479 (R.E.M.).
[36a] *Searle* v. *Burroughs* (1966) 110 S.J. 248; contrast *Lovelock* v. *Margo, supra,* at p. 789.
[37] Race Relations Act 1965, s. 5 (1).
[38] *Ibid.,* s. 5 (2).
[39] Race Relations Act 1968, ss. 5, 7.
[40] s. 144, replacing C.A., 1892, s. 3.
[41] L.P.A., 1925, s. 205 (1) (xxiii).
[42] *Waite* v. *Jennings* [1906] 2 K.B. 11 at 18.
[43] *Gardner & Co. Ltd.* v. *Cone* [1928] Ch. 955. See also *Comber* v. *Fleet Electrics Ltd.* [1955] 1 W.L.R. 566.
[44] L.P.A., 1925, s. 144.
[45] *Andrew* v. *Bridgman* [1908] 1 K.B. 596.

(*h*) *Building leases.* In one case no consent is required. If a building lease (*i.e.*, a lease granted in consideration wholly or partially of the erection, or the substantial improvement, addition or alteration of buildings) is granted for more than forty years, and contains a covenant against assigning, underletting or parting with possession without the landlord's consent, there is implied a proviso (notwithstanding any contrary provision) that no consent is required to an assignment, underlease or parting with possession made more than seven years before the end of the term, provided that written notice is given to the landlord within six months.[46] But this does not apply where the lessor is one of certain public and statutory authorities,[47] or in the case of mining or agricultural leases.[48]

(*i*) *Breaches.* To amount to a breach of a covenant against assignment, underletting, or parting with possession there must in general be some voluntary dealing with the property *inter vivos.* Thus a bequest of the lease is no breach,[49] nor is the involuntary vesting of the lease in the trustee in bankruptcy upon the tenant's bankruptcy[50] (as distinct from a voluntary sale by the trustee in bankruptcy[51]), or the compulsory sale of the lease under statutory provisions.[52] Loss of the lease by the execution of a judgment is not regarded as a breach, even where the covenant extends to parting with possession,[53] unless the action and judgment were collusive and designed solely to evade the covenant.[54] A mortgage made by the grant of a sub-lease is a breach,[55] but one made by a mere deposit of the title deeds is not,[56] nor is a declaration of trust made by the tenant for the benefit of his creditors.[57] It is neither an assignment[58] nor a parting with possession[59] if the tenant merely allows other persons to share in the use of the premises, or grants a licence for the limited use of part of the premises.

---

[46] L. & T.A., 1927, s. 19 (1).   [47] *Ibid.*
[48] *Ibid.*, s. 19 (4).
[49] *Fox* v. *Swann* (1655) Sty. 482; *Doe* d. *Goodbehere* v. *Bevan* (1815) 3 M. & S. 353; Woodfall L. & T. 526 (but see *Berry* v. *Taunton* (1594) Cro.Eliz. 331). *Quaere* as to an assent giving effect to a bequest: see Williams on *Assents* 130. *Re Wright* [1949] Ch. 729 suggests that consent is needed; and see (1963) 27 Conv.(N.S.) 159 (D. G. Barnsley).
[50] *Re Riggs* [1901] 2 K.B. 16.   [51] *Re Wright* [1949] Ch. 729.
[52] *Slipper* v. *Tottenham & Hampstead Junction Ry.* (1867) L.R. 4 Eq. 112.
[53] *Doe* d. *Mitchinson* v. *Carter* (*No.* 1) (1798) 8 T.R. 57.
[54] *Doe* d. *Mitchinson* v. *Carter* (*No.* 2) (1799) 8 T.R. 300.
[55] *Serjeant* v. *Nash, Field & Co.* [1903] 2 K.B. 304; *cf.* a legal charge (*post*, p. 897).
[56] *Doe* d. *Pitt* v. *Hogg* (1824) 4 Dow. & Ry. 226.
[57] *Gentle* v. *Faulkner* [1900] 2 Q.B. 267.
[58] *Gian Singh & Co.* v. *Devraj Nahar* [1965] 1 W.L.R. 412 (premises shared with partners); *Edwardes* v. *Barrington* (1901) 85 L.T. 650 (licence to use refreshment bar, etc., in theatre).
[59] *Chaplin* v. *Smith* [1926] 1 K.B. 198 (company permitted to run demised garage); *Stening* v. *Abrahams* [1931] 1 Ch. 470 (advertisement hoarding); *Lam Kee Ying Sdn. Bhd.* v. *Lam Shes Tong* [1974] 3 W.L.R. 784.

A covenant merely against underletting is perhaps not broken by an assignment [60] or by letting lodgings.[61] A covenant against parting with possession would presumably be broken by allowing a squatter to obtain a title under the Limitation Act, 1939. Underletting or parting with possession of a part of the property is no breach of a general covenant not to underlet or part with possession [62]; but it is of course otherwise if the covenant is worded (as it usually is) so as to extend to the property " or any part thereof."

3. Covenant to use the premises as a private dwelling-house only.

This covenant is broken if the house is divided into two, or if part of the house is sub-let, even though for private use, since it is implicit in the covenant that the premises shall be used as one single dwelling-house.[63] But taking a paying guest will normally be no breach [64]; and there is statutory jurisdiction for the county court to authorise the division of a house in certain circumstances.[65]

4. Covenant to repair

(a) *The covenant.* In long leases the tenant often covenants to do all repairs; in short leases the landlord often assumes liability for external and structural repairs. In every case the matter is one for negotiation. If no provision is made for repairs, the tenant is sometimes liable for them because of the general law relating to waste.[66]

(1) " REPAIR." The extent of the liability of any party under a repairing covenant depends of course upon the wording of the covenant, but expressions such as " tenantable repair," " sufficient repair," or " good and substantial repair " seem to add little to the meaning of the word " repair." [67] In general, the obligation to repair requires the replacement of subsidiary parts of the premises (*e.g.,* a wall) that can no longer be repaired,[68] or, if the premises have been

---

[60] *Re Doyle & O'Hara's Contract* [1899] I.R. 113 (no breach); *Greenaway* v. *Adams* (1806) 12 Ves. 395 (breach).
[61] *Doe d. Pitt* v. *Laming* (1814) 4 Camp. 73, doubted in *Greenslade* v. *Tapscott* (1834) 1 Cr.M. & R. 55.
[62] *Wilson* v. *Rosenthal* (1906) 22 T.L.R. 233; *Cottell* v. *Baker* (1920) 36 T.L.R. 208; *Cook* v. *Shoesmith* [1951] 1 K.B. 752; *Esdaile* v. *Lewis* [1956] 1 W.L.R. 709 (see (1956) 72 L.Q.R. 325: R.E.M.).
[63] *Barton* v. *Keeble* [1928] Ch. 517; *Dobbs* v. *Linford* [1953] 1 Q.B. 48, distinguishing *Downie* v. *Turner* [1951] 2 K.B. 112; and see *Re Endericks' Conveyance* [1973] 1 All E.R. 843.
[64] *Segal Securities Ltd.* v. *Thoseby* [1963] 1 Q.B. 887.
[65] *Post,* p. 774.
[66] *Ante,* pp. 684–686, where the exceptions are also stated.
[67] See *Anstruther-Gough-Calthorpe* v. *McOscar* [1924] 1 K.B. 716 at 722, 723, *per* Bankes L.J., and at 729, *per* Scrutton L.J.: but see *per* Atkin L.J. at 731, 732.
[68] *Lurcott* v. *Wakely* [1911] 1 K.B. 905.

destroyed by a calamity such as a fire, the whole of the premises.[69]
But it does not extend to requiring the rebuilding of premises
which through inherent defects have passed beyond repair,
or to doing work which cannot fairly be called repairing the premises
as they stood when demised.[70] The insertion of words such as " fair
wear and tear excepted " relieve the tenant from liability for any
disrepair which he can show has resulted from the reasonable use of
the premises and the ordinary operation of natural forces; but he
remains liable for any consequential damage, such as damage to the
interior resulting from the tenant's failure to prevent rain entering
where tiles have slipped from the roof or a skylight has become
defective.[71]

(2) NOTICE OF DISREPAIR. In general, a landlord is not liable on
his covenant to repair until he has notice of the need for repair.[72]
Usually the tenant will give him notice; but the tenant may not know
of the defect,[73] and probably express notice from any source will
suffice.[74] The mere means of knowing, as where the exterior is
visibly out of repair,[75] or the landlord has reserved the right to enter
and view the state of repair,[76] is not enough. But prior notice is
required only where the tenant can be said to have the better means
of knowledge. Thus where the landlord covenants to repair a roof
retained in his own control,[77] or a sea-wall,[78] road or bridge [79] which
is not itself in the tenant's occupation, his liability on the covenant
does not depend upon notice.

(3) LIABILITY TO OTHERS. As already explained, a landlord who
is liable to repair the premises, or who has a right of entry for that
purpose, now has a wide duty of care under the Defective Premises
Act 1972 towards all persons likely to be affected by his failure to
repair.[80] Parliament has abolished the former rule that the landlord's

---

[69] *Bullock* v. *Dommitt* (1796) 2 Chit. 608 (fire); *Redmond* v. *Dainton* [1920] 2
K.B. 256 (bomb).
[70] *Lister* v. *Lane* [1893] 2 Q.B. 212 (tenant's covenant); *Torrens* v. *Walker* [1906]
2 Ch. 166 (landlord's covenant); *Brew Brothers Ltd.* v. *Snax (Ross) Ltd.* [1970]
1 Q.B. 612 (tenant's covenant).
[71] *Regis Property Co. Ltd.* v. *Dudley* [1959] A.C. 370, overruling *Taylor* v. *Webb*
[1937] 2 K.B. 283, and restoring *Haskell* v. *Marlow* [1928] 2 K.B. 45 at 58, 59.
[72] *Makin* v. *Watkinson* (1870) L.R. 6 Ex. 25; *Torrens* v. *Walker* [1906] 2 Ch. 166;
McCarrick v. *Liverpool Corporation* [1947] A.C. 219.
[73] See *O'Brien* v. *Robinson* [1973] A.C. 912.
[74] *Griffin* v. *Pillet* [1926] 1 K.B. 17; and see *McCarrick* v. *Liverpool Corporation*,
supra, at p. 232; *Uniproducts (Manchester) Ltd.* v. *Ross Furnishers Ltd.* [1956]
1 W.L.R. 45; *O'Brien* v. *Robinson*, [1973] A.C. 912 at 926. Contrast *Torrens*
v. *Walker*, *supra*, at p. 172.
[75] *Torrens* v. *Walker*, *supra*; and see *Makin* v. *Watkinson*, *supra*, at p. 28.
[76] *Hugall* v. *M'Lean*, *supra*; *Torrens* v. *Walker*, *supra*; *McCarrick* v. *Liverpool
Corporation*, *supra*.
[77] *Melles & Co.* v. *Holme* [1918] 2 K.B. 100; *Bishop* v. *Consolidated London
Properties Ltd.* (1933) 148 L.T. 407.   [78] *Murphy* v. *Hurly* [1922] 1 A.C. 369.
[79] See *Murphy* v. *Hurly*, *supra*.   [80] *Ante*, p. 682.

liability, being contractual, did not cover injury to the tenant's family or visitors.[81]

(b) *Damages.* Apart from forfeiture, the remedy for breach of a repairing covenant is damages. No injunction or decree of specific performance can normally be obtained to enforce a tenant's covenant to repair,[82] since damages are an adequate remedy for the landlord.[83] But where it is the landlord who breaks a repairing covenant, damages may not be an adequate remedy for the tenant, particularly if the breach concerns property not comprised in the lease and so not accessible to the tenant. Specific performance may therefore sometimes be decreed against a landlord.[83a]

The measure of damages recoverable for the breach of a repairing covenant formerly varied according to the time of the breach. If the breach occurred during the term, the damages were calculated on the decrease in the value of the reversion caused by the breach [84]; the longer the lease had to run, the less would be the damages. But if the breach occurred at the end of the term, the cost of repairing the premises was recoverable by the landlord [85]; and (by way of exception to the ordinary rule that the measure of damages is the damage actually suffered) it was held to make no difference that the landlord did not propose to carry out the repairs but intended to demolish the premises instead.[86]

Now, however, by the Landlord and Tenant Act, 1927,[87] damages for breach of a repairing covenant are not to exceed the diminution in the value of the reversion,[88] *i.e.,* the difference between the value of the reversion with the repairs done and its value without.[89] In normal cases when the repairs are likely to be done the cost of doing them represents the diminution in the value of the reversion [90]; and the landlord's claim is not reduced merely because he has let the premises to a new tenant who has covenanted to repair them,[91] or

---

[81] *Cavalier* v. *Pope* [1906] A.C. 428; *Ryall* v. *Kidwell* [1914] 3 K.B. 135.
[82] *Hill* v. *Barclay* (1810) 16 Ves. 402.
[83] See Fry S.P. 45–50; Snell, *Equity*, 581.
[83a] *Jeune* v. *Queens Cross Properties Ltd.* [1974] Ch. 97 (balcony not part of demised premises). This power now always exists in the case of dwellings: see Housing Act 1974, ss. 125, 129 (1).
[84] *Doe* d. *Worcester Trustees* v. *Rowlands* (1841) 9 C. & P. 734; *Ebbetts* v. *Conquest* [1895] 2 Ch. 377, affirmed, *Conquest* v. *Ebbetts* [1896] A.C. 490.
[85] *Joyner* v. *Weeks* [1891] 2 Q.B. 31.
[86] *Ibid.,* at pp. 44, 45. But this exception does not apply to a covenant to reinstate after alterations: *James* v. *Hutton* [1950] 1 K.B. 9. As to the effect of the Landlord and Tenant Act, 1927, s. 19 (2), in such a case, *quaere*: *ibid.*
[87] s. 18.
[88] See, *e.g.,* *Smiley* v. *Townshend* [1950] 2 K.B. 311.
[89] *Hanson* v. *Newman* [1934] Ch. 298.
[90] *Jones* v. *Herxheimer* [1950] 2 K.B. 106.
[91] *Haviland* v. *Long* [1952] 2 Q.B. 80.

because his reversion is of very short duration.[92] But no damages at all are recoverable if the premises are to be demolished, or structurally altered in such a way as to make the repairs valueless, at or soon after the end of the term.[93] This is so even if in the event no demolition is carried out[94]; but it is otherwise if the reason for demolition is merely the tenant's breach of his repairing obligations.[94a] These rules relate only to repairing covenants; damages for breach of other covenants (*e.g.*, against making alterations) are recoverable in the usual way.[95]

(c) *Internal decorative repairs.* The Law of Property Act, 1925,[96] enables the court in certain cases to relieve the tenant from liability for internal decorative repairs if the landlord acts unreasonably. But there are a number of exceptions, *e.g.*, when the tenant has never performed a contract to put the property into decorative repair. This power of the court is not confined to proceedings for forfeiture but extends to actions for damages.

(d) *The Leasehold Property (Repairs) Act*, 1938

(1) OBJECT OF ACT. The Act was passed in order to protect tenants of small houses under long leases from having to pay heavy bills for dilapidations under the threat of forfeiture for breach of covenant. The mischief which the Act was designed to remedy was that speculators could buy the reversion of dilapidated house property for a small price, enforce forfeiture of the lease on account of non-repair, and so get the residue of the term for nothing.[97] As now extended,[98] the Act applies to all types of property (except agricultural holdings) where the tenancy was granted for a term certain of not less than seven years, and has at least three years unexpired.[99]

(2) LEAVE OF COURT. Where the Act applies, the landlord may neither sue for damages nor enforce forfeiture for failure to repair[1] unless he first serves on the tenant a notice under section 146 of the

[92] *Jaquin* v. *Holland* [1960] 1 W.L.R. 258; *Lloyds Bank Ltd.* v. *Lake* [1961] 1 W.L.R. 884.
[93] See, *e.g.*, *Cunliffe* v. *Goodman* [1950] 2 K.B. 237.
[94] *Keats* v. *Graham* [1960] 1 W.L.R. 30.
[94a] *Hibernian Property Co. Ltd.* v. *Liverpool Corporation* [1973] 1 W.L.R. 751, also holding that the intention to demolish must be that of the landlord: *sed quaere.*
[95] *Eyre* v. *Rea* [1947] K.B. 567.
[96] s. 147.
[97] See *National Real Estate and Finance Co. Ltd.* v. *Hassan* [1939] 2 K.B. 61 at 78.
[98] By the Landlord and Tenant Act, 1954, s. 51, removing (*inter alia*) the former limits as to rateable value.
[99] Leasehold Property (Repairs) Act, 1938, ss. 1, 7. The Act applies to leases created before or after the Act (s. 5).
[1] *Ibid.*, s. 3.

Law of Property Act, 1925,[2] which informs the tenant of his right to serve a counter-notice, and one month elapses thereafter.[3] Within 28 days after service of the notice the tenant may serve a counter-notice claiming the benefit of the Act. The result of this is that the landlord can take no further proceedings without leave of the court, and this may be given only on establishing at least a prima facie or arguable case [4] that certain specified grounds exist, *e.g.*, that immediate repair is necessary to comply with a by-law relating to the safety or repair of houses, or that the cost of immediate repair would be small compared with the cost of future repair.[5] One important feature of the Act is that it shifts the onus of applying to the court from the tenant to the landlord in cases to which it extends.

(3) SERVICE OF NOTICE. There is no need to serve a notice under the Act on a mortgagee of the lease [6]; and if a notice was properly served on the tenant for the time being, no notice need be served on a subsequent assignee, though if the tenant served a counter-notice, leave to proceed against the assignee must be obtained.[7] Further, the Act does not protect the original lessee after he has assigned, even though by privity of contract he remains liable on the repairing covenant.[8]

5. Covenant to insure. A covenant to insure against fire is broken if the premises are uninsured for any period, however short, even if no fire occurs.[9] If the covenant is to insure with a named company, or with some other responsible company with the landlord's approval, the landlord, who may wish to have all his properties insured with one company, can withhold his approval of an alternative company without giving any reasons.[10] A covenant to insure with a named company binds the tenant to take out such policy of the company as is usual at the time, so that if such a policy excepts some specified risks, the tenant is not liable under this covenant if the house is destroyed in one of the excepted ways.[11]

---

[2] For this, see *ante*, p. 662.
[3] Leasehold Property (Repairs) Act, 1938, ss. 1 (2), (4), 3.
[4] *Sidnell* v. *Wilson* [1966] 2 Q.B. 67.
[5] s. 1 (5). See *Phillips* v. *Price* [1959] Ch. 181; *Re Metropolitan Film Studio Ltd.'s Application* [1962] 1 W.L.R. 1315.
[6] *Church Commissioners for England* v. *Ve-Ri-Best Manufacturing Co. Ltd.* [1957] 1 Q.B. 238.
[7] *Kanda* v. *Church Commissioners for England* [1958] 1 Q.B. 332.
[8] See *Cusack-Smith* v. *Gold* [1958] 1 W.L.R. 611; but see *Baker* v. *Sims* [1959] 1 Q.B. 114 at 129. For this liability, see *post*, p. 723.
[9] *Penniall* v. *Harborne* (1848) 11 Q.B. 368.
[10] *Viscount Tredegar* v. *Harwood* [1929] A.C. 72.
[11] *Upjohn* v. *Hitchens* [1918] 2 K.B. 48. It is otherwise if no company is named: see *Enlayde Ltd.* v. *Roberts* [1917] 1 Ch. 109.

In one case a tenant covenanted to insure against fire in the joint names of himself and the landlord, to pay the premiums and to lay out the policy moneys in restoring the premises in case of fire. The premises were destroyed by fire, but statutory restrictions and later a compulsory purchase order made reinstatement impossible, and so the policy moneys were held to be the tenant's alone; for they were intended merely to give security for the tenant's obligation to reinstate, and not to be the landlord's.[12] But where a landlord covenanted to insure at the tenant's expense, and reinstatement was possible, the landlord was held liable to apply the policy moneys in reinstatement despite the absence of any covenant to do so; for the covenant was intended to benefit both landlord and tenant.[13]

Sect. 4. Special Statutory Restrictions

The modern tendency is to make special statutory provisions to protect tenants from landlords, irrespective of any agreement between the parties; the movement is from contract to status. Some examples of this have already been noticed; another example is that anyone who demands or receives rent or acts as agent for a landlord of a dwelling must now comply with a written request by the tenant of the dwelling for his landlord's name and address.[13a] Other examples, much more far-reaching, go beyond the scope of this book. In particular, agricultural tenancies, under the Agricultural Holdings Act, 1948, most tenancies of dwelling-houses, under the Rent Acts, 1968–1974, and business premises, under the Landlord and Tenant Acts, 1927 and 1954, are now governed by extensive codes, one primary purpose of which is to restrict the landlord's right to determine a tenancy. This legislation would need another book to expound it, and it cannot well be studied before the general law of real property has been mastered. It is therefore best regarded as a separate subject, and is summarised in a later chapter.[14]

Part 6

LEASEHOLD CONVEYANCING

Contracts and conveyancing have been treated in a former chapter,[15] but primarily with reference to the sale of a fee simple. The same principles apply generally to the creation and assignment of leases; for example, we have already seen that a contract to grant or assign a lease must be evidenced by writing or part performance in the

---

12 *Re King* [1963] Ch. 459.
13 *Mumford Hotels Ltd.* v. *Wheler* [1964] Ch. 117.
13a Housing Act 1974, s. 121; failure to comply without reasonable excuse is an offence.
14 See *post*, pp. 1109 *et seq.*   15 *Ante*, p. 542.

same way as a contract for sale, and that its operation in equity is similar.[16] On the other hand, the rules as to formality in granting (but not assigning) legal leases are in some ways different from the rules for freehold conveyances. The following paragraphs show in outline the principal points of similarity and divergence in the rules for freehold and leasehold dispositions.

1. Contracts

(a) *Formality.* A contract to grant or assign a lease requires the same formalities as any other contract for the disposition of an interest in land,[16] and there is the same exception for contracts supported by part performance.[17]

(b) *Effect in equity.* A contract to grant or assign a lease creates an equitable interest, analogous to that created by a contract to sell a freehold, which is registrable as an estate contract. This has been explained in connection with *Walsh* v. *Lonsdale*.[18]

(c) *Implied terms*

(1) TITLE. The only important difference is in the title which may be called for by an intending lessee or assignee of a lease. At common law a contract to grant or assign a lease conferred on the purchaser the right to call for a full disclosure of the title, which the purchaser would usually insist upon since otherwise he might have constructive notice of incumbrances.[19] This was a necessary right in the case of a long and valuable term, particularly where a fine or other capital sum was paid. But in the case of short terms at rack rents it was inconvenient to have a full disclosure of title at every letting, and landlords or assignors would often stipulate against it in the contract. The assignor of a lease or the grantor of a sub-lease was in a particular difficulty, for he had no means of compelling the landlord to disclose the title deeds relating to the freehold.

The law was changed by the Vendor and Purchaser Act, 1874,[20] now replaced by the Law of Property Act, 1925,[21] which provides that in default of any express provision to the contrary—

    (i) Under a contract for the grant or assignment of a lease or sub-lease, there is no right to call for the title to the freehold[22];

---

[16] *Ante*, pp. 547, 563, 624.
[17] *Ante*, p. 563.
[18] *Ante*, p. 625.
[19] *Ante*, p. 121.
[20] s. 2; further changes were introduced by C.A., 1881, ss. 3, 13, also now replaced by L.P.A., 1925, s. 44.
[21] s. 44 (2)–(4).
[22] s. 44 (2).

(ii) Under a contract for the assignment of a sub-lease, there is no right to call for the title to the superior lease [23]; and

(iii) Under a contract to grant a sub-sub-lease there is no right to call for the title to the head lease.[24]

These provisions are obscurely worded. It is assumed in practice that the " title to " a lease or sub-lease includes the lease or sub-lease itself.[25] The effect of these rules may then conveniently be summed up by saying that an intending tenant or assignee may always inspect any lease under which the other contracting party holds,[25] but that is all; and there is never a right to inspect the title to the freehold.

Since these rules yield to contrary provision in the contract, it is for the intending tenant to stipulate for a fuller disclosure if he wishes it. It is most desirable that he should do so in the case of a long lease, especially if he pays a premium or fine, or purchase-money, or undertakes an obligation to build, for he bears the risk of the title turning out to be bad.

(2) THE PROBLEM OF NOTICE. Statutory limitation of the purchaser's ordinary right to inspect the title has naturally led to difficulties over equitable incumbrances which bind a purchaser with notice. In *Patman* v. *Harland* [26] it was held that the lessee had constructive notice of all matters which he would have discovered had he stipulated for and made a full investigation of title, even though under an open contract he was deprived by statute of the right to investigate: for he might, had he wished, have contracted out of the statute, and by not doing so he was in the same position as if he had agreed to accept a short title.[27] This was a reasonable interpretation of the Act [28]; but it revealed a statutory trap for tenants, and the law was amended by the Law of Property Act, 1925.[29] This provides that where, by reason of the statutory restrictions, an intending lessee or assignee is unable to make a full

---

[23] s. 44 (3).

[24] s. 44 (4).

[25] The dictum to the contrary in *Gosling* v. *Woolf* [1893] 1 Q.B. 39 is thought to be wrong, and is not supported by the report in (1892) 68 L.T. 89, indicating that the case concerned the grant (not the assignment) of a sub-lease. See Wolst. & C. i, 111; Farrand, *Contract and Conveyance*, 151.

[26] (1881) 17 Ch.D. 353 (restrictive covenant on freehold title prohibiting buildings other than private dwelling-houses; the owner, being ignorant of the covenant, let to the tenant for use as an art school; the tenant was unable to inspect the freehold title, but at the suit of the covenantee was restrained by injunction from carrying on the school); and see *Mogridge* v. *Clapp* [1892] 3 Ch. 382 at 397; *Imray* v. *Oakshette* [1897] 2 Q.B. 218.

[27] See *ante*, p. 123.

[28] The previous practice was for lessors to stipulate against disclosure of title (Wolst. & C., 12th ed., i, 298) and it was reasonable to regard the Act as making such clauses unnecessary, but as otherwise not changing the law.

[29] s. 44 (5).

investigation of title, " he shall not be deemed to be affected with notice of any matter or thing of which, if he had contracted that such title should be furnished, he might have had notice." The amendment applies only to contracts made after 1925.

Taken by itself, this provision merely shifts the hardship from the shoulders of the lessee on to those of the owner of the equitable incumbrance; for the lessee, when his lease is granted, becomes a purchaser of a legal estate for value without notice, and the equitable interest is void against him. For example, he could build in violation of a restrictive covenant, so that the person entitled to the benefit of it would lose it. And similarly, extraordinary as it may seem, he could take free from an equitable mortgage made by deposit of title deeds.[30] The Law of Property Act, 1925, has provided a remedy which is worse than the disease, for it creates insecurity of property.

The Act protects a purchaser only from the consequences of being unable to investigate title fully. It does not, it appears, protect him if he has notice *aliunde, e.g.,* actual notice.[31] This is particularly important where the equitable incumbrance is registered as a land charge, as often it will be, since registration is deemed to be actual notice.[31a] Registered incumbrances will therefore in any case bind a lessee or sub-lessee or the assignee of a sub-lease.[32]

(3) DEFECTS OF MACHINERY. The defects of the registration machinery, discussed later,[33] may make it impossible for a purchaser to discover a registered incumbrance which is binding on him as explained above. Unless he has access to all the title deeds he cannot discover the names of the owners against which he must search, excepting only those of his immediate vendor and of persons named in such documents as he is allowed to see. Suppose that a restrictive covenant has been entered into since 1925 by some previous owner of the freehold: under an open contract an intending tenant will have no means of discovering the name of the covenantor, but the covenant will nonetheless bind him if registered.[34] When this obstacle arises the tenant is in much the same position as under

---

[30] Such a mortgage is not registrable (see *post*, p. 970), nor does it seem likely that it is protected by L.P.A., 1925, s. 13, as to possession of deeds: see (1944) 8 Conv.(N.S.) at 146 (M. J. Albery). Under s. 44 (5) it would seem that any unregistrable equity can be barred by granting a long lease (enlargeable into a fee simple: *ante*, p. 670) to a tenant who has no notice from any other quarter.

[31] The burden of proving notice is on the person seeking to enforce the adverse interest: *Shears* v. *Wells* [1936] 1 All E.R. 832.

[31a] *Post*, p. 1044. For the equivalent rule for registered land, *see post*, p. 1069.

[32] *White* v. *Bijou Mansions Ltd., infra.*

[33] See *post*, p. 1045.

[34] *White* v. *Bijou Mansions Ltd.* [1937] Ch. 610 (in C.A., [1938] Ch. 351). This was a similar point concerning registered land. " It may perhaps be a blot that the lessee, unless he makes some bargain to that effect, is not permitted to inspect the register ": *ibid.*, at p. 621, *per* Simonds J.

the rule in *Patman* v. *Harland* : he is bound by an incumbrance which he has no means of discovering. On the other hand, in the case of a restrictive covenant created before 1926, and therefore not registrable, the tenant is rendered immune but the owner of the benefit loses it.[35] Two opposite injustices are therefore inflicted. It is only where the covenant is entered into after 1925 by a person whose name the tenant is entitled to discover that the law appears to operate fairly to all parties.[36] In certain cases, however, the tenant may now be entitled to compensation.[36a]

The rule in *Patman* v. *Harland* has been abolished only as regards contracts made since 1925. Leases granted under earlier contracts and still on foot may at any time turn out to be subject to some unregistrable incumbrance made before the lease was granted, so that the tenant may be bound by an undiscoverable liability.

(*d*) *Remedies.* These are in general the same as under contracts for the sale of a freehold.[37] It used to be thought that equity would not grant specific performance of agreements for short leases, *e.g.*, leases of a year or less, but the modern authorities indicate that there is no such rule.[38]

2. Conveyances. The grant or assignment of a lease by deed is a " conveyance " within the meaning of the Law of Property Act, 1925,[39] except where provision is made to the contrary.[40]

(*a*) *Form.* A specimen of a simple lease is given in the next section. The rules governing the creation and assignment of leases have already been explained. The notable difference from freehold conveyancing is, of course, that certain leases for three years or less may be granted [41] (but not assigned [42]) orally or in writing.

(*b*) *Covenants for title and indemnity.* The *grant* of a lease is outside the provisions of the Law of Property Act, 1925, which imply certain covenants from the use of certain words.[43] As already explained, the tenant has the benefit of the landlord's qualified covenant for quiet enjoyment only, and this is implied not from the use of any particular words or by statute but from the relationship of landlord and tenant.[44]

---

[35] See *Shears* v. *Wells* [1936] 1 All E.R. 832.
[36] For further discussion, see [1956] C.L.J. 230 (H.W.R.W.) and the Report of the Committee on Land Charges, Cmd. 9825 (1956) 13–16.
[36a] Under L.P.A. 1969, s. 25. For this, see *post*, p. 1046.
[37] *Ante*, p. 587.
[38] *Ante*, p. 564.
[39] s. 205 (1) (ii).
[40] As in ss. 76 (5), 77 (3).
[41] *Ante*, p. 621.
[42] *Ante*, p. 650.
[43] L.P.A., 1925, s. 76 (5).
[44] *Ante*, p. 676.

The *assignment* of a lease, on the other hand, is within the provisions for statutory covenants, and the assignor must normally convey " as beneficial owner." These words import not only the usual statutory covenants for title,[45] but also a covenant that the lease is valid and in full force at the time of assignment, and that all rent has been paid and all covenants observed.[46] On the other side the assignee, who may be required to execute the deed of assignment, thereby (and without the need for any special words) covenants that he will pay the rent and observe all the covenants in the lease, and will indemnify the assignor against the consequences of any breach.[47] The covenant by the assignee is dealt with below.[48]

3. Precedent of a lease

Commencement and date. Parties.

THIS LEASE made the 1st day of January, 1974, between Leslie Landlord of No. 15 South Street Seaford in the County of Sussex solicitor (hereinafter called " the landlord ") of the one part and Timothy Tenant of No. 525 West Road Newnham in the County of Gloucester bookseller (hereinafter called " the tenant ") of the other part

Testatum.

WITNESSETH as follows:—

Demise.

1. The landlord hereby demises unto the tenant ALL THAT messuage or dwelling-house with the yard gardens offices and outbuildings thereto belonging known as " The Pines " Highfield in the County of Surrey which premises for purposes of identification and not of limitation are coloured pink on the plan annexed to these presents TO HOLD the same unto the tenant from the 25th day of December, 1973, for the term of five years PAYING therefor the net yearly rent of £200 clear of all deductions (except only such as the tenant may by law be entitled to make notwithstanding any agreement to the contrary [48a]) by equal quarterly instalments commencing on the 25th day of March next and thereafter on the usual quarter days.

Habendum.

Reddendum.

Tenant's covenants.

2. The tenant hereby covenants with the landlord as follows:—

[45] *Ante*, p. 602.
[46] L.P.A., 1925, s. 76 (1) (B) and 2nd Sched., Pt. II.
[47] *Ibid.*, s. 77 (1) (C) and (D), and 2nd Sched., Pts. IX and X. These provisions do not apply to mortgages.
[48] *Post*, p. 733.
[48a] See *ante*, p. 685.

(i) To pay the rent hereby reserved on the days hereinbefore mentioned.

(ii) To pay all rates taxes assessments charges and outgoings now or hereafter legally payable in respect of the property hereby demised (save only as aforesaid) whether payable by the owner or occupier thereof.

[*Then follow other covenants by the tenant, e.g., to repair, to insure, not to assign, underlet or part with possession of the premises.*]

Landlord's covenants.

3. The landlord hereby covenants with the tenant as follows: —

(i) That the tenant paying the rent hereby reserved and observing and performing the covenants on his part herein contained shall peaceably hold and enjoy the premises hereby demised during the said term without any interruption or disturbance [49] by the landlord or any person rightfully claiming under or in trust for him.

[*Then follow any other covenants by the landlord, e.g., to execute certain classes of repairs or improvements, or to renew the lease at the tenant's request.*]

Provisos.

4. PROVIDED ALWAYS and it is hereby expressly agreed and declared as follows: —

Forfeiture clause.

(i) that if the rent hereby reserved or any part thereof shall remain unpaid for twenty-one days after becoming payable (whether formally demanded or not) or if any covenant on the part of the tenant herein contained shall not be performed or observed or if the tenant shall become bankrupt or enter into any composition with his creditors or suffer any distress or execution upon his goods then and in any of the said cases it shall be lawful for the landlord at any time thereafter to re-enter upon the demised premises or

---

[49] The word "lawful" is often (but inaccurately) inserted before "interruption or disturbance." It does not absolve the landlord from unlawful disturbance of the tenant (*Crosse* v. *Young* (1685) 1 Show.K.B. 425; *Lloyd* v. *Tomkies* (1787) 1 T.R. 671), and it merely duplicates "rightfully claiming" in the case of third parties.

any part thereof in the name of the whole and thereupon this demise shall absolutely determine.
[*Then follow any other provisos, e.g., that the tenant may determine the lease by giving notice.*]

IN WITNESS etc.

(signatures, seals and witnesses)

The PLAN above referred to.

This short form of lease may be compared with the brief precedent of a conveyance in fee simple given in Chapter 10.[50]

Subject to any written agreement to the contrary, no party to a lease or tenancy agreement is now liable to pay any of the legal costs of any other party.[51] Formerly the tenant was usually liable for the costs of both parties, save that the landlord bore the cost of his counterpart (*i.e.*, duplicate) if he had one.[52] The normal practice is for the landlord to take a counterpart executed by the tenant, in order to facilitate the enforcement of the tenant's covenants.

Part 7

FIXTURES

The question whether an object affixed to the land by a tenant can be removed by him or his representatives at the end of the term is one on which there has been much litigation. Similar problems arise, though less frequently, in the case of mortgages, sales, devises and settlements, and these also will be considered here.

The meaning of "real property" in law extends, as has been seen, to a great deal more than "land" in everyday speech.[53] It comprises, for instance, incorporeal hereditaments; and it also includes fixtures. The general rule as to fixtures is "*quicquid plantatur solo, solo cedit*"[54] (whatever is attached to the soil becomes part of it). Thus if a building is erected on land and objects are permanently attached to the building, then the soil, the building and the objects affixed to it are all in law "land," *i.e.*, they are real property, not chattels. They will all become the property of the owner of the land, unless otherwise granted or conveyed.

[50] *Ante*, p. 599.
[51] Costs of Leases Act, 1958.
[52] Foa, L. & T. 339.
[53] *Ante*, p. 136; *post*, p. 788.
[54] *Minshall* v. *Lloyd* (1837) 2 M. & W. 450 at 459.

But if there is an intention to the contrary, merger of ownership may not take place.[54a]

In general, the word " fixture " means anything which has become so attached to land as to form in law part of the land.[55] But the context may restrict this meaning: thus if part of a house is leased, a covenant to repair the interior " including all landlord's fixtures " does not extend to the windows which, *quoad* what was demised, are not fixtures but part of the original structure.[56]

A.   *Distinction between Fixtures and Chattels*

A physical object will usually be either land or a chattel, but its nature may change according to the use made of it. The materials used for building a house are thereby converted from chattels into land, and so automatically pass out of the ownership of the person who owned them as chattels and become the property of the owner of the land to which they are attached; and it makes no difference whether the person who attached them had a right to do so or not.[57] Conversely, when a house is pulled down, the person who severs the materials from the building converts them from land into chattels. The question whether an object has become a fixture, and so is part of the land to which it has been fixed, will therefore often determine the question of ownership as between competing claimants. A tenant, for example, who attaches fixtures to the demised premises may thereby make them the property of his landlord; and a purchaser of land may claim as part of his purchase all objects which were fixtures at the date of the contract, for they form part of the land sold to him. The first need, therefore, is to be able to decide what is a fixture and what is not. In borderline cases this is often difficult; but in principle it depends upon two tests, namely—

　　　　(1) the degree of annexation, and

　　　　(2) the purpose of annexation.

1. Degree of annexation. This is the primary test. An article is prima facie a fixture if it has some substantial connection with the land or a building on it. An article which merely rests on the ground by its own weight, such as a cistern [58] or a " Dutch barn "

[54a] *Simmons* v. *Midford* [1969] 2 Ch. 415 (right to lay and maintain drains in another's land; drains held to remain property of the person laying them); *Montague* v. *Long* (1972) 24 P. & C.R. 240.

[55] See *Hulme* v. *Brigham* [1943] K.B. 152 at 154; and see *Reynolds* v. *Ashby & Son* [1904] A.C. 466.

[56] *Boswell* v. *Crucible Steel Co.* [1925] 1 K.B. 119, discussed in *Holiday Fellowship Ltd.* v. *Hereford* [1959] 1 W.L.R. 211; and see *Pole-Carew* v. *Western Counties and General Manure Co. Ltd.* [1920] 2 Ch. 97.

[57] See *post,* p. 719.　　　　[58] *Mather* v. *Fraser* (1856) 2 K. & J. 536.

standing in sockets let into the ground,[59] is prima facie not a fixture. On the other hand a chattel attached to the land or a building on it in some substantial manner, *e.g.*, by nails or screws, will prima facie be a fixture even if it would not be difficult to remove it; examples in this category are fireplaces, panelling, wainscot, and a conservatory on a brick foundation.[60]

2. Purpose of annexation. Originally, the common law looked only to the degree of annexation, and held everything substantially attached to the land to be the property of the owner of the land. But this rule was unduly severe, and two classes of exceptions arose. In the first class, certain kinds of chattels were held to remain chattels even after annexation, if the purpose of annexation was not to effect a permanent improvement in the land as such but merely to enable the owner of the chattel to enjoy it as a chattel. The second class of exceptions went further: even though an object was clearly a fixture, and so part of the land, a tenant for years or for life was allowed to sever and remove it if he had annexed it to the land for certain purposes.

In principle the distinction is plain: objects of the first class are removable because they never cease to be the property of the person who affixed them; objects of the second class are fixtures properly so called, and become the property of the owner of the land, but the law confers a special power of removal on the person who was owner of the object while it was a chattel. But in practice the two classes of exceptions tend to merge into each other.

This may be illustrated by a leading case concerning tapestry: a tenant for life put up valuable tapestries on the walls of the mansion house, fixed them by tacks to a framework of wood and canvas nailed on to the walls, and then surrounded each piece of tapestry with a moulding which was also fastened firmly to the wall. When the tenant for life died the question arose whether the tapestries passed with the settled land or were part of the tenant for life's personal estate. It was held that they were personal estate: by the Court of Appeal, apparently on the ground that, even though fixtures, the tenant for life (and her executor or legatee) had the power to remove them [61]; by the House of Lords (affirming the Court of Appeal) on the ground that the tapestries never ceased to

---

[59] *Culling* v. *Tufnal* (1694) Bull.N.P. 34; and see *Elwes* v. *Maw* (1802) 3 East 38; Smith's L.C. ii, 193; *Wiltshear* v. *Cottrell* (1853) 1 E. & B. 674; *Webb* v. *Frank Bevis Ltd.* [1940] 1 All E.R. 247; *H. E. Dibble Ltd.* v. *Moore* [1970] 2 Q.B. 181 (free-standing greenhouses held removable chattels).
[60] *Buckland* v. *Butterfield* (1820) 2 Brod. & B. 54.
[61] *Re De Falbe* [1901] 1 Ch. 523; contrast *Re Whaley* [1908] 1 Ch. 615, *post*, p. 718, n. 4.

be chattels, since fixing them to the walls was no more than was necessary for their enjoyment as objects of personal property.[62]

As was stated in an earlier case, " Perhaps the true rule is, that articles not otherwise attached to the land than by their own weight are not to be considered as part of the land, unless the circumstances are such as to show that they were intended to be part of the land, the onus of showing that they were so intended lying on those who assert that they have ceased to be chattels, and that, on the contrary, an article which is affixed to the land even slightly is to be considered as part of the land, unless the circumstances are such as to show that it was intended all along to continue a chattel, the onus lying on those who contend that it is a chattel." [63] " Thus blocks of stone placed one on top of another without any mortar or cement for the purpose of forming a dry stone wall would become part of the land, though the same stones, if deposited in a builder's yard and for convenience' sake stacked on top of each other in the form of a wall, would remain chattels." [64] Again, " the anchor of a large ship must be very firmly fixed in the ground . . . yet no one could suppose that it became part of the land." [65] Yet material such as piles of abandoned spoil from a slate quarry may become a permanent accretion to the land.[65a]

These examples are clear, but others are less so. Looms in a worsted mill, fixed by nails to wooden beams and plugs in the floor, have been held to be part of the land,[66] although they were easily removable without damage to the building, and by the test " is there any more fixing than was necessary for the enjoyment of the chattel as such? " [67] they might have been thought to be chattels. But machinery standing merely by its own weight remains personalty,[68] unless (perhaps) it can be shown to be installed for the permanent improvement of the premises. Statues, figures, vases and stone garden seats have been held to become part of the land because they

---

[62] *Leigh* v. *Taylor* [1902] A.C. 157; the speeches of Lord Halsbury and Lord Macnaghten may be contrasted with that of Lord Shand; and it is remarkable that none of the numerous authorities were discussed. *Cf. Viscount Hill* v. *Bullock* [1897] 2 Ch. 482 (collection of stuffed birds in cases fixed to walls held chattels, as between tenant for life and remainderman).

[63] *Holland* v. *Hodgson* (1872) L.R. 7 C.P. 328 at 335, *per* Blackburn J. In *Bradshaw* v. *Davey* [1952] 1 All E.R. 350 this dictum was applied to a yacht's mooring (a movable arrangement of anchors and chains) which was held to be a chattel and not a hereditament for rating purposes.

[64] *Holland* v. *Hodgson, supra,* at p. 335, *per* Blackburn J.

[65] *Ibid.*

[65a] *Mills* v. *Stokman* (1967) 116 C.L.R. 61.

[66] *Holland* v. *Hodgson, supra* (as between mortgagor and mortgagee); *cf. Reynolds* v. *Ashby & Son* [1904] A.C. 466 (machinery fixed by bolts passed to mortgagee with land); *Jordan* v. *May* [1947] K.B. 427 (electric light generating engine fixed by bolts held a fixture, but batteries held to be chattels).

[67] *Re De Falbe* [1901] 1 Ch. 523 at 536, *per* Vaughan Williams L.J.

[68] *Hulme* v. *Brigham* [1943] K.B. 152 (mortgagor and mortgagee).

were essentially part of the design of a house and grounds, even though standing merely by their own weight.[69] Similarly, movable dog grates, substituted for fixed grates, have been held to be fixtures,[70] and so have some temporary structures, such as a corrugated iron shed bolted to metal straps fixed in concrete foundations.[71]

Similar articles may remain chattels or become fixtures depending on the circumstances of their annexation, *e.g.*, tip-up seats fastened to the floor of a cinema or theatre.[72]

B. Right to remove Fixtures

If according to the above rules an article is not a fixture, it can be removed by the person bringing it on to the land or by his successors in title, though not by a subsequent tenant who takes a fresh tenancy from the landlord.[73] But if the article is a fixture, prima facie it cannot be removed from the land and must be left for the fee simple owner. Nevertheless, as already mentioned, there are some exceptional cases where something which is undeniably part of the land may be removed by the person who affixed it: the object is a fixture, but the person who affixed it has a power to sever and remove it. This power arises in certain cases if the object has been affixed for certain purposes. The test of " purpose of annexation " therefore applies again here, although in a different way. It is best to consider separately the classes of cases in which the power of removal can and cannot arise.

1. Landlord and tenant. Prima facie, all fixtures attached by the tenant are " landlord's fixtures," *i.e.*, must be left for the landlord. But important exceptions to this rule have arisen, and fixtures which can be removed under these exceptions are known as " tenant's fixtures." This expression must not be allowed to obscure the fact that the legal title to the fixture is in the landlord until the tenant chooses to exercise his power and sever it.[74] The

---

[69] *D'Eyncourt* v. *Gregory* (1866) L.R. 3 Eq. 382; but the authority of this decision is not great: see *Re De Falbe* [1901] 1 Ch. 523 at 531, 532.

[70] *Monti* v. *Barnes* [1901] 1 Q.B. 205.

[71] *Webb* v. *Frank Bevis Ltd.* [1940] 1 All E.R. 247 (tenant's fixture), not cited in *Billing* v. *Pill* [1954] 1 Q.B. 70 (army hut similarly attached held a mere chattel and so the subject of larceny). *Cf. L.C.C.* v. *Wilkins* [1957] A.C. 362.

[72] Contrast *Lyon & Co.* v. *London City & Midland Bank* [1903] 2 K.B. 135 (seats hired for temporary use: held, not fixtures) with *Vaudeville Electric Cinema Ltd.* v. *Muriset* [1923] 2 Ch. 74 (seats owned by cinema owner: held, fixtures).

[73] *Re Thomas* (1881) 44 L.T. 781; and see *Leschallas* v. *Woolf* [1908] 1 Ch. 641; *Smith* v. *City Petroleum Co. Ltd.* [1940] 1 All E.R. 260.

[74] A neat illustration of the position is *Crossley* v. *Lee* [1908] 1 K.B. 86 at 90 (tenant's fixtures may not be taken on a distress (*ante*, p. 691), since they are not chattels but part of the demised premises).

tenant may do so only during the tenancy or (except in cases of forfeiture or surrender [75]) within such reasonable time thereafter as may properly be attributed to his possession *qua* tenant.[76]

Where the tenancy is determinable by a week's notice, for example, and the fixtures cannot reasonably be removed within a week,[77] the tenant will be allowed a reasonable time after the notice has expired. Once that time has elapsed, the tenant loses his right of removal and the landlord's title to the fixture is absolute [78]; any extension of time that he grants to the tenant binds only him and not, *e.g.*, a mortgagee who has taken possession.[79] If a tenant surrenders his tenancy, *e.g.*, in order to take a new and longer term, he thus will normally lose his right to remove fixtures unless the contrary is provided.[80] But in general a tenant is under no obligation to remove anything that he has lawfully affixed to the land.[81]

The following are tenant's fixtures.

(a) *Trade fixtures.* Fixtures attached by the tenant for the purpose of his trade or business have long been removable by the tenant at any time during the term, but not after it has come to an end.[82] Vats, fixed steam engines and boilers,[83] a shed for making varnish,[84] shrubs planted by a market gardener,[85] the fittings of a public-house [86] and petrol pumps affixed to tanks embedded in the ground [87] have all been held to come within this category.

(b) *Ornamental and domestic fixtures.* This exception appears to be rather more limited than the previous one, and seems to extend only to chattels perfect in themselves which can be removed without substantial injury to the building.[88] An article which can be moved entire is more likely to fall within this exception than one which cannot.[89] Thus a conservatory on brick foundations has

---

[75] *Pugh* v. *Arton* (1869) L.R. 8 Eq. 626; *Ex p. Brook* (1878) 10 Ch.D. 100.
[76] See *Ex p. Stephens* (1877) 7 Ch.D. 127 at 130. The exact limits of the rule are rather obscure: see *Ex p. Brook* (1878) 10 Ch.D. 100 at 109.
[77] *Smith* v. *City Petroleum Co. Ltd., supra.*
[78] *Lyde* v. *Russell* (1830) 1 B. & Ad. 394; *Smith* v. *City Petroleum Co. Ltd., supra.* [79] *Thomas* v. *Jennings* (1896) 66 L.J.Q.B. 5.
[80] *Leschallas* v. *Woolf* [1908] 1 Ch. 641; *Slough Picture Hall Co. Ltd.* v. *Wade* (1916) 32 T.L.R. 542.
[81] See *Never-Stop Railway (Wembley) Ltd.* v. *British Empire Exhibition (1924) Incorporated* [1926] Ch. 877 (licensee).
[82] *Poole's Case* (1703) 1 Salk. 368.
[83] *Climie* v. *Wood* (1869) L.R. 4 Ex. 328.
[84] *Penton* v. *Robart* (1801) 2 East 88.
[85] *Wardell* v. *Usher* (1841) 3 Scott N.R. 508.
[86] *Elliott* v. *Bishop* (1854) 10 Exch. 496.
[87] *Smith* v. *City Petroleum Co. Ltd.* [1940] 1 All E.R. 260.
[88] See *Martin* v. *Roe* (1857) 7 E. & B. 237 at 244; *Spyer* v. *Phillipson* [1931] 2 Ch. 183.
[89] *Grymes* v. *Boweren* (1830) 6 Bing. 437.

been held not to be removable [90]; but looking glasses, [91] ornamental chimney pieces, [92] panelling, [93] window blinds, [94] stoves, grates and kitchen ranges, [95] pumps and coppers, [96] and bells, [97] have all been held to be removable during the tenancy.

(*c*) *Agricultural fixtures.* At common law agricultural fixtures were not regarded as falling within the exception of trade fixtures. [98] Market gardeners were regarded as being engaged primarily in trade, not agriculture, and so could remove their fixtures [99]; but farmers were liable in damages if they removed sheds, sties and the like erected by them, even if they removed them before the end of the term and did no damage. [1] But by the Agricultural Holdings Act, 1948, [1a] replacing earlier legislation, [2] a tenant of an agricultural holding who has attached fixtures to the land may remove them before, or within two months after, the determination of the term, provided the following conditions are observed:

(i) one month's written notice must be given to the landlord;
(ii) all rent due must be paid and all the tenant's obligations under the tenancy satisfied by him;
(iii) no avoidable damage may be done in the removal and any damage done must be made good; and
(iv) the landlord may retain the fixtures if he serves a counter-notice in writing and pays the tenant their fair value to an incoming tenant.

Contrary to the general rule already stated, the Act provides that such fixtures remain the tenant's property so long as he has the right to remove them.

2. Tenant for life and remainderman. If land is settled on A for life with remainder to B, on the death of A the question arises whether fixtures which A has attached to the land can be removed and treated as part of A's estate or whether they must be left for B. The position here is similar to that between landlord and tenant.

---

[90] *Buckland* v. *Butterfield* (1820) 2 Brod. & B. 54.
[91] *Beck* v. *Rebow* (1706) 1 P.Wms. 94.
[92] *Leach* v. *Thomas* (1835) 7 C. & P. 327.
[93] *Spyer* v. *Phillipson* [1931] 2 Ch. 183.
[94] *Colegrave* v. *Dias Santos* (1823) 2 B. & C. 76 at 77.
[95] *Darby* v. *Harris* (1841) 1 Q.B. 895.
[96] *Grymes* v. *Boweren* (1830) 6 Bing. 437 at 439.
[97] *Lyde* v. *Russell* (1830) 1 B. & Ad. 394.
[98] *Elwes* v. *Maw* (1802) 3 East 38.
[99] *Wardell* v. *Usher* (1841) 3 Scott N.R. 508 (shrubs and young trees); *Mears* v. *Callender* [1901] 2 Ch. 388 (glass-houses).
[1] *Elwes* v. *Maw, supra.*
[1a] s. 13.
[2] Landlord and Tenant Act, 1851, s. 3, Agricultural Holdings Act, 1923, s. 22, and various intervening statutes.

Prima facie all the fixtures must be left for B, with the common law exception of trade, ornamental and domestic fixtures, which applies to a tenant for life in the same way as to a tenant for years [3]; but the statutory exception of agricultural fixtures does not apply.

3. Devisee and personal representative. If land is given by will, the rule is that all fixtures pass under the devise; the testator's personal representatives are not entitled to remove them for the benefit of the testator's estate, whether they are ornamental, trade or any other kind of fixture.[4] For the devise naturally carries with it everything which can fairly be said to be part of the land [5]; and there is no question of hardship upon a limited owner, as in the case of a lessee or life tenant. The same rule applied to descent to the heir on intestacy.[6]

4. Vendor and purchaser. Without exception, all fixtures attached to the land at the time of a contract of sale must be left for the purchaser unless otherwise agreed.[7] The conveyance will be effective to pass the fixtures to the purchaser without express mention.[8] The statutory "general words" also operate to convey all buildings, erections and fixtures along with the land, in default of contrary intention [9]; but they will not convey structures which are not fixtures, such as greenhouses merely resting on the land and not attached to it.[10]

5. Mortgagor and mortgagee. If land is mortgaged, all fixtures on it are included in the mortgage without special mention [11]; the exceptions as between landlord and tenant do not apply.[12] The mortgagor is not even entitled to remove fixtures which he has attached after the date of the mortgage.[13]

---

3 *Lawton* v. *Lawton* (1743) 3 Atk. 13; *Re Hulse* [1905] 1 Ch. 406 at 410; but it has been said that a tenant for life is less favoured than a tenant for years: see *Norton* v. *Dashwood* [1896] 2 Ch. 497 at 500.

4 *Bain* v. *Brand* (1876) 1 App.Cas. 762 (machinery); *Re Whaley* [1908] 1 Ch. 615 (tapestry so fixed as to improve the premises as such held not to be removable even though ornamental); *Re Lord Chesterfield's S. E.* [1911] 1 Ch. 237 (wood carvings).   5 See *Re Hulse* [1905] 1 Ch. 406 at 410.

6 See *Norton* v. *Dashwood* [1896] 2 Ch. 497 at 500.

7 *Colegrave* v. *Dias Santos* (1823) 2 B. & C. 76; *Phillips* v. *Lamdin* [1949] 2 K.B. 33. For the effect of hire-purchase agreements, see (1963) 27 Conv.(N.S.) 30 (A. G. Guest and J. Lever).

8 *Colegrave* v. *Dias Santos, supra.*

9 L.P.A., 1925, s. 62, replacing C.A. 1881, s. 6; *ante,* p. 611.

10 *H. E. Dibble Ltd.* v. *Moore* [1970] 2 Q.B. 181.

11 L.P.A., 1925, ss. 62 (1), 205 (1) (ii). As to hire-purchase, see note 7, *supra.*

12 *Monti* v. *Barnes* [1901] 1 Q.B. 205; *Climie* v. *Wood* (1869) L.R. 4 Ex. 328 at 330 (trade fixtures); cf. *Lyon & Co.* v. *London City & Midland Bank* [1903] 2 K.B. 135.

13 *Reynolds* v. *Ashby & Son* [1904] A.C. 466.

C. *Rights of Third Parties*

It has already been seen that the primary rule governing fixtures, namely, that they become the property of the owner of the land, applies irrespective of the title of the person who affixed them: " the title to chattels may clearly be lost by being affixed to real property by a person who is not the owner of the chattels." [14] If, for example, X steals Y's bricks and builds them into a house on Z's land, the owner of the bricks is not Y but Z; there is no room for the principle that a man cannot give a better title than he has (*nemo dat quod non habet*), since the title to the object as a chattel is extinguished entirely when it is turned into land.[15]

Again, if A hires machinery from B and fixes it to the floor of A's factory, and the factory is mortgaged (whether prior to the fixing or not), the machinery becomes subject to the mortgage as against B.[16] But if the machinery is hired under a hire-purchase agreement which entitles B to enter and retake it if A fails to pay the instalments, this creates an equitable interest in land (apparently a right of entry [17]) which will bind all later takers except a bona fide purchaser of a legal estate for value without notice. In such a case, therefore, B can enforce his rights against a subsequent equitable mortgagee of the land,[18] or a purchaser who has not yet taken his conveyance. Such an equitable interest does not appear to be registrable.[19] A person who lets out goods on hire may thus be able to protect himself to some extent against the consequences of the law of fixtures if he reserves a right of entry against the owners of the land on which the goods are used.

---

[14] *Reynolds* v. *Ashby & Son, supra*, at p. 475, *per* Lord Lindley; see also *Gough* v. *Wood* [1894] 1 Q.B. 713 at 718, 719; *Crossley* v. *Lee* [1908] 1 K.B. 86.
[15] But, of course, Y may have a personal remedy against X in tort (conversion).
[16] *Hobson* v. *Gorringe* [1897] 1 Ch. 182 (before); *Reynolds* v. *Ashby & Son* [1904] A.C. 466 (after).
[17] *Re Morrison, Jones & Taylor Ltd.* [1914] 1 Ch. 50 at 58; *ante*, p. 143.
[18] *Re Samuel Allen & Sons Ltd.* [1907] 1 Ch. 575; *Re Morrison, Jones & Taylor Ltd.* [1914] 1 Ch. 50.
[19] *Poster* v. *Slough Estates Ltd.* [1968] 1 W.L.R. 1515; *Shiloh Spinners Ltd.* v. *Harding* [1973] A.C. 691, *post*, p. 1043. See also (1963) 27 Conv.(N.S.) 30 (A. G. Guest and J. Lever).

CHAPTER 12

COVENANTS AND LICENCES AFFECTING LAND

THIS chapter comprises three related branches of the law:

(1) The running of covenants in leases. Here the rules are mostly of long standing, and the basis of the subject is common law, extended by statute.

(2) The running of covenants with freehold land. Much of this topic consists of the law of restrictive covenants, a nineteenth-century development which was the creature of equity.

(3) Licences for the use of land. This subject has become prominent in the present century, a number of important rules being new, but uncertain. Claims have been made for a new doctrine of equity, and Parliament has intervened on the subject of matrimonial homes.

Part 1

COVENANTS : GENERAL PRINCIPLES

A covenant is a promise under seal, *i.e.*, contained in a deed. Such a promise is enforceable, according to the ordinary law of contract, between the persons who are parties to it or their personal representatives. But certain kinds of covenants are so much part of the system of transactions in land that they are enforceable in cases which the law of contract does not cover: they partake, so to speak, of the nature of the estates in connection with which they are made, so that like those estates they may benefit and bind third parties. Therefore they belong to the category of interests in land as well as to the law of contract, and two sets of rules have to be considered together. Common examples of these kinds of covenants are covenants in a lease, *e.g.*, to repair, and restrictive covenants taken on a sale, *e.g.*, binding the purchaser and future occupiers not to carry on a business on the property sold. The rules which govern such covenants also apply, in general, to contractual promises not made under seal, such as " covenants " contained in a mere agreement for a lease.[1]

---

[1] See, *e.g.*, *post*, p. 727.

The primary question is, how far are covenants made in connection with transactions in land enforceable outside the law of contract. The fundamental principles are as follows.[2]

1. If there is privity of contract, all covenants are enforceable. There is said to be privity of contract when the parties are in direct contractual relations, *i.e.*, bound to one another by the ordinary law of contract. Clearly, if two people have agreed to do or not to do certain things, their obligations bind them whether their contract has anything to do with land or not. Contractual liability is enforceable by or against the estate of a party who is dead; and in general the benefit, but not the burden, of the contract is assignable, so that assignees of the benefit can sue the original promisor or his personal representatives without the aid of the law of property.

The covenant can be enforced both at law, by an action for damages, and in equity, by an injunction or specific performance.

2. If there is privity of estate, but not privity of contract, only covenants which touch and concern the land are enforceable. Privity of estate means that there is tenure between the parties, *i.e.*, that the relationship of landlord and tenant exists between them[3]; cases in this category are thus confined to leases and tenancies.[4] If L grants a lease to T and then T assigns it to A, there is no privity of contract between L and A since there has been no direct transaction between them; but there is privity of estate, for A has become L's tenant by acquiring the estate which L created and which is held of L as the immediate landlord. Similarly if L assigns his reversion to X, there is privity of estate between X and A. In such cases any covenants in the lease which " touch and concern " the land, *e.g.*, repairing covenants, are enforceable both at law and in equity.

Covenants which do not relate to the land are not enforceable under this head, for they have nothing to do with the relationship of landlord and tenant on which this right to enforce covenants against third parties is founded. Nor do all covenants in leases " touch and concern " the land for this purpose, even though they concern the land in a general sense. For we are here outside the

---

[2] See *Manchester Brewery Co.* v. *Coombs* [1901] 2 Ch. 608 at 614.

[3] *Milmo* v. *Carreras* [1946] K.B. 306; *ante*, p. 613. Privity of estate is a legal relationship, not equitable: *Cox* v. *Bishop* (1857) 8 De G.M. & G. 815 at 824. For its meaning in this context, see *Manchester Brewery Co.* v. *Coombs, supra,* at pp. 613, 614; *Purchase* v. *Lichfield Brewery Co.* [1915] 1 K.B. 184.

[4] " Privity of estate " was, however, also used to describe the relationship of grantor and grantee of the fee simple, where the grantee claimed the *benefit* of a covenant (running with land) as a successor in title to the grantor: see *David* v. *Sabin* [1893] 1 Ch. 523 at 537, 545; *Campbell* v. *Lewis* (1820) 3 B. & Ald. 392; Co.Litt. 271a.

bounds of the law of contract, and the law of property as usual sets limits to the kinds of interests which can be made to bind all comers. For example, as will be seen shortly, an option to purchase the freehold is not a covenant which " touches and concerns " the land, though it may bind an assignee as an estate contract.[5]

3. If there is privity neither of contract nor of estate, then with two exceptions, no covenants are enforceable. There is privity neither of contract nor of estate between a lessor and a sub-lessee, or between the vendor of freehold land and a person who buys it from the purchaser. In such cases the general rule is that covenants concerning the land are not enforceable between the parties mentioned. To this rule there are two important exceptions.

First, even the common law allowed the *benefit* of a covenant (*i.e.*, the right to sue on it) to be assigned with land for the benefit of which it was made, provided that the covenant was one which " touched and concerned " that land. One example already mentioned [6] is that of a grantor's covenants for title in a conveyance: the benefit of these runs with the land conveyed so that whoever is entitled to the land is entitled to the benefit of the covenants. Equity went further, and enforced assignments of the *benefit* of contracts generally, whether or not connected with land; and there is now a statutory procedure for assignment which takes effect at law.[7] Thus it has become the general rule that the benefit of a contract is assignable. But the burden of a contract (*i.e.*, the liability to be sued on it) has never been assignable by itself: assignment applies only to rights, not to duties. Nevertheless the burden of certain covenants concerning land can pass with the land affected under the rules of the law of property: either at law, because there is privity of estate, as already mentioned; or in equity, under the next following exception.

Secondly, equity allows the transmission of both the benefit and the burden of restrictive covenants. A restrictive covenant is a covenant imposing a negative obligation (*e.g.*, not to build) as opposed to a positive covenant (*e.g.*, to build); and the benefit and burden of a restrictive covenant can run in equity only if there is both land which is benefited and land which is burdened. As usual, however, a purchaser of a legal estate without notice [8] takes free from the burden.

These three principles should always be borne in mind in considering the enforceability of covenants. They should be applied

---

in the given order: if there is privity of contract, there is no need to look further; and if there is privity of estate, there is no need to consider whether the covenant is restrictive. Privity of contract need not be discussed at length, for it operates according to the ordinary law of contract. The other two principles, on the other hand, are peculiar to the law of property and demand detailed explanation.

Part 2

PRIVITY: COVENANTS IN LEASES

Sect. 1. Privity of Contract : Position of the Original Parties

If a lease is granted by L to T, there is privity of contract between them. The effect of this is not only that L may enforce all the covenants in the lease against T while he retains it, but also that T remains liable on the covenants for the whole term, notwithstanding any assignment of the lease.[9] For covenants in leases (like other covenants affecting land [10]) are ordinarily framed as promises that neither the covenantor nor any of his successors in title will infringe the covenant; that is to say, the covenantor gives a personal warranty against future breaches by himself or anyone else. This does not, of course, make the successor in title personally liable [11]: it merely makes the covenantor personally liable for what his successor does. It is a long-established practice, which helps to induce the tenant to choose an assignee who is financially responsible.

Formerly, in drafting such covenants, it was necessary to provide expressly for this extensive liability by stating that the covenantor covenanted on behalf of his successors in title as well as of himself. But by the Law of Property Act, 1925, s. 79,[12] covenants made after 1925 which relate to the land of a covenantor are now deemed to be made on behalf of himself and his successors in title and those deriving title under him or them, unless a contrary intention is expressed,[13] *i.e.*, is to be found in the instrument, whether expressed or implied.[14] Section 79 is essentially a " word-saving " provision,

---

[9] *Thursby* v. *Plant* (1670) 1 Wms.Saund. 230; *Auriol* v. *Mills* (1790) 4 T.R. 94 at 98; *Staines* v. *Morris* (1812) 1 V. & B. 8 at 11; *Bickford* v. *Parson* (1848) 5 C.B. 920 at 929; *John Betts & Sons Ltd.* v. *Price* (1924) 40 T.L.R. 589.

[10] *Cf. post*, p. 747.

[11] See *Tophams Ltd.* v. *Earl of Sefton* [1967] 1 A.C. 50; *cf. post*, p. 754.

[12] For the corresponding s. 78 as to covenantees, see *post*, p. 748.

[13] As, for example, in the case of perpetually renewable leases (*ante*, p. 644) or by the terms of the covenant: *Bryant* v. *Hancock & Co. Ltd.* [1898] 1 Q.B. 716; [1899] A.C. 442; *Wilson* v. *Twamley* [1904] 2 K.B. 99; and see *post*, p. 731. [14] *Re Royal Victoria Pavilion, Ramsgate* [1961] Ch. 581.

which makes it unnecessary to set out the stereotyped formula about successors, but does not otherwise change the law.[15]

The benefit of the tenant's covenants will run with the reversion,[16] so that after an assignment of the reversion it is the assignee and not the lessor who can enforce the tenant's continuing contractual liability.[17] Likewise, if the lease is assigned, it is the assignee and not the tenant who can sue the lessor.

An example will illustrate the position. If T takes a lease for 99 years, he makes himself liable for 99 years, even if he assigns the lease after only one year has run; T cannot divest himself of his personal contractual liability by parting with the land, and the fact that the assignee may also be liable to L by reason of privity of estate is no defence to T if L prefers to sue T on the contract. L may accordingly sue T for unpaid rent, or for damages if a covenant to repair is not observed by the assignee. Two different persons may therefore be liable for one breach of covenant, one by privity of contract and the other by privity of estate. But if the landlord obtains satisfaction from one, he cannot then sue the other[18]; the liabilities are alternative, not cumulative. Similarly, L remains liable on his covenants for the whole term, notwithstanding any assignment of the reversion by him.[19]

Where a lease contains an option for renewal which is exercised by an assignee, the new lease will normally be a new contract which will not involve the original tenant in liability. But his liability will continue where the old lease is merely extended under its own terms, *e.g.*, where the lease is for 7 years but if the tenant shall give due notice then for 11 years.[20]

Sect. 2. Privity of Estate : Position of Assignees

A. *Covenants Touching and Concerning Land*

The rights and liabilities of assignees, either of the lease or of the reversion, depend upon two things : whether there is privity of

---

15 *Tophams Ltd.* v. *Earl of Sefton* [1967] 1 A.C. 50 at 73. *Re Royal Victoria Pavilion, Ramsgate* [1961] Ch. 581 suggests that s. 79 may be held to affect the liability of successors in title, but the point may be merely that their inclusion helps to show that the covenant was intended to run with the land (see *post*, p. 753, n. 46).

16 See *post*, p. 734.

17 *Arlesford Trading Co. Ltd.* v. *Servansingh* [1971] 1 W.L.R. 1080; *post*, pp. 737, 738.

18 *Brett* v. *Cumberland* (1619) Cro.Jac. 521; *cf. B. O. Morris Ltd.* v. *Perrott and Bolton* [1945] 1 All E.R. 567; *Kohnke* v. *Karger* [1951] 2 K.B. 670.

19 *Stuart* v. *Joy* [1904] 1 K.B. 368; *cf.* L.P.A., 1925, s. 142 (2). This decision is unsound on the question who may sue for breaches committed after the assignment; on this see *post*, p. 737.

20 *Baker* v. *Merckel* [1960] 1 Q.B. 657.

estate [21] between the plaintiff and the defendant, and whether the covenant in question " touches and concerns the land " [22] or, to use more modern phraseology, " has reference to the subject-matter of the lease." [23] These are technical expressions which bear the same meaning,[24] and refer to the limited class of covenants which can be made to bind third parties so that the right to enforce them is a proprietary interest as well as a merely contractual right. A covenant which does not " touch and concern " the land cannot run with the land by reason of privity of estate.

Any covenant which affects the landlord *qua* landlord or the tenant *qua* tenant will probably be within the class of covenants which touch and concern the land.[25] But no general definition will solve all cases: difficulties can still arise over covenants which are out of the ordinary run of covenants found in leases, and the rule is best explained by examples. The covenants in the left-hand column below have been held to touch and concern the land, while those in the right-hand column have been held not to do so. It will be seen that some of the examples are not easy to reconcile by any general test.

1. Covenants by a lessee

Touching and concerning	*Not touching and concerning*
To pay rent.[26]	To pay an annual sum to a third person.[31]
To repair the property or fixtures on it.[27]	To pay rates in respect of other land.[32]
To pay £40 towards redecoration on quitting.[28]	Not to employ persons living in other parishes to work in the demised mill (the landlord's motive being to benefit his other property in the parish).[33]
To insure against fire.[29]	
To use as a private dwelling-house only.[30]	

[21] *Ante,* p. 721.
[22] *Spencer's Case* (1583) 5 Co.Rep. 16a.
[23] L.P.A., 1925, ss. 141, 142.
[24] *Davis* v. *Town Properties Investment Corporation Ltd.* [1903] 1 Ch. 797.
[25] *Breams Property Investment Co. Ltd.* v. *Stroulger* [1948] 2 K.B. 1 at 7, approving the test suggested by Cheshire, *Modern Real Property,* 5th ed., 214, 215.
[26] *Parker* v. *Webb* (1693) 3 Salk. 5.
[27] *Matures* v. *Westwood* (1598) Cro.Eliz. 599; *Williams* v. *Earle* (1868) L.R. 3 Q.B. 739.
[28] *Boyer* v. *Warbey* [1953] 1 Q.B. 234; and see *Moss' Empires Ltd.* v. *Olympia (Liverpool) Ltd.* [1939] A.C. 544 (covenant to spend specified sum on repairs or pay the sum to the landlord).
[29] *Vernon* v. *Smith* (1821) 5 B. & Ald. 1.
[30] *Wilkinson* v. *Rogers* (1864) 2 De G.J. & S. 62.
[31] *Mayho* v. *Buckhurst* (1617) Cro.Jac. 438.
[32] *Gower* v. *Postmaster-General* (1887) 57 L.T. 527.
[33] *Congleton Corporation* v. *Pattison* (1808) 10 East 130.

Not to assign the lease without the landlord's consent.[34]

Not to let X be concerned in the conduct of the business carried on upon the premises.[35]

To buy beer for a public-house[36] or petrol for a filling station[37] only from the lessor.

To repair and renew the tools of a smithy standing on the land (the tools were movable chattels, not fixtures).[38]

2. Covenants by a lessor

Touching and concerning

To renew the lease[39] (the inclusion of this is somewhat anomalous[40]).

To supply the demised premises with water.[41]

Not to build on a certain part of the adjoining land.[42]

Not to determine a periodic (quarterly) tenancy during its first three years.[43]

Not touching and concerning

To sell the reversion at a stated price, at the tenant's option.[44]

To pay at the end of the lease for chattels not amounting to fixtures.[45]

To pay the tenant £500 at the end of the lease unless a new lease is granted.[46]

Not to open another public-house within half a mile (in a lease of a public-house).[47]

To keep in repair a large number of houses in the district.[48]

To allow the tenant to display advertising signs on other premises.[49]

---

[34] *Goldstein* v. *Sanders* [1915] 1 Ch. 549; *Cohen* v. *Popular Restaurants Ltd.* [1917] 1 K.B. 480; *cf. Re Robert Stephenson & Co. Ltd.* [1915] 1 Ch. 802.

[35] *Lewin* v. *American & Colonial Distributors Ltd.* [1945] Ch. 225, where there is a useful review of the authorities.

[36] *Clegg* v. *Hands* (1890) 44 Ch.D. 503; *Manchester Brewery Co.* v. *Coombs* [1901] 2 Ch. 608.

[37] *Regent Oil Co. Ltd.* v. *J. A. Gregory (Hatch End) Ltd.* [1966] Ch. 402.

[38] *Williams* v. *Earle* (1868) L.R. 3 Q.B. 739.

[39] *Richardson* v. *Sydenham* (1703) 2 Vern. 447; *Muller* v. *Trafford* [1901] 1 Ch. 54 at 60; *Weg Motors Ltd.* v. *Hales* [1962] Ch. 49.

[40] *Woodall* v. *Clifton* [1905] 2 Ch. 257 at 279.

[41] *Jourdain* v. *Wilson* (1821) 4 B. & Ald. 266.

[42] *Ricketts* v. *Enfield Churchwardens* [1909] 1 Ch. 544.

[43] *Breams Property Investment Co. Ltd.* v. *Stroulger* [1948] 2 K.B. 1.

[44] *Woodall* v. *Clifton, supra*; see *post*, p. 742, n. 3. Similarly a right of pre-emption over adjoining land: *Collison* v. *Lettson* (1815) 6 Taunt. 224.

[45] *Gorton* v. *Gregory* (1862) 3 B. & S. 90.

[46] *Re Hunter's Lease* [1942] Ch. 124.

[47] *Thomas* v. *Hayward* (1869) L.R. 4 Ex. 311.

[48] *Dewar* v. *Goodman* [1909] A.C. 72.

[49] *Re No. 1, Albemarle Street* [1959] Ch. 531.

In particular, a covenant does not touch and concern the land merely because its non-performance may cause a lease of the land to be forfeited. Thus where several properties are leased, and then one of these is sub-leased, and the sub-lessor covenants that he will perform all the covenants in the head lease in respect of the properties not included in the sub-lease, this covenant will not bind an assignee of the head lease, even though his breach of a covenant causes a forfeiture of the head lease, and so of the sub-lease also.[50]

B. *Principles of Transmission*

Having seen which covenants touch and concern the land, we must now examine the rights and liabilities of assignees. As in every other case of enforcing rights of property, two separate points must be considered:

(i) Is the defendant liable? and

(ii) Is the plaintiff entitled to sue?

In the case of the rights and liabilities of assignees under covenants concerning land, it is more usual to put these questions as follows:

(i) Has the burden of the covenant passed? and

(ii) Has the benefit of the covenant passed?

In discussing these questions it will be convenient to deal first with assignments of leases, then with assignments of reversions, then with incorporeal hereditaments, and finally with forfeiture clauses. The reader should be warned that a distinguished judge once said of this branch of the law that " the established rules . . . are purely arbitrary, and the distinctions, for the most part, quite illogical." [51]

I. WHERE THE LESSEE ASSIGNS HIS LEASE

If L leases land to T, and T assigns the lease to A, the common law rule laid down in *Spencer's Case* [52] is that A is entitled to the benefit, and subject to the burden, of all covenants and conditions touching and concerning the land, because there is privity of estate between L and A. Where there is privity of estate, both the benefit and the burden of the covenants run with the land demised.

The details of this fundamental rule must now be studied.

1. The lease must be in due form. It used to be held that only a lease made by deed would carry the benefit or burden of special

---

[50] *Doughty* v. *Bowman* (1848) 11 Q.B. 444; *Dewar* v. *Goodman* [1909] A.C. 72; but a sub-lessee may apply for relief: *ante*, p. 666.
[51] *Grant* v. *Edmondson* [1931] 1 Ch. 1 at 28, *per* Romer L.J.
[52] (1583) 5 Co.Rep. 16a.

stipulations to an assignee, since they could not otherwise be annexed to the estate.[53] But if the assignee of an informal lease went into possession and paid rent the court would readily infer a new agreement on the same terms as the old, so that the assignee would become bound by privity of contract [54]; and under equitable doctrines, if there was a specifically enforceable agreement for a lease the benefit, but not the burden, of its terms could be assigned.[55] The Court of Appeal has now, however, held that the burden (and presumably also the benefit) of a stipulation can run with a lease for three years or less made by unsealed writing [56]; and dicta in the same case would apparently extend the concession to mere agreements for a lease,[57] thus conflicting with the rule that the burden of a mere agreement is not assignable. The very reasonable decision to hold the assignee bound by the terms of a legal lease made by unsealed writing is rather strangely attributed to " the fusion of law and equity " made by the Judicature Act, 1873, which is said to have largely obliterated the distinction between agreements under hand and covenants under seal.[58] Whether the new doctrine extends to tenancies for three years or less which are made merely orally (i.e., without writing) is uncertain.[59]

2. There must be a legal assignment of the whole term

(a) Legal assignment. The benefit and burden of covenants run with the lease only in the case of a legal assignment of the whole of the remainder of the term.[60] Where instead of an assignment there has been a sub-lease, the sub-lessee takes neither the benefit nor the burden of the covenants in the lease,[61] even if his sub-lease is only one day shorter than the head lease. Thus if L leases land to T for

---

53 Elliott v. Johnson (1866) L.R. 2 Q.B. 120 at 127.
54 Buckworth v. Johnson (1835) 1 Cr.M. & R. 833; Cornish v. Stubbs (1870) L.R. 5 C.P. 334 at 338, 339.
55 Ante, p. 628.
56 Boyer v. Warbey [1953] 1 Q.B. 234 (lease of a flat for three years made by unsealed writing, with a term that the tenant on quitting would pay £40 towards cost of redecoration: held, this term was binding on an assignee of the lease); cf. Weg Motors Ltd. v. Hales [1962] Ch. 49 (burden of covenant written but unsealed running with reversion)
57 Boyer v. Warbey, supra, at p. 246 (Denning L.J.).
58 Ibid.
59 Boyer v. Warbey, supra, appears to overrule Elliott v. Johnson, supra, where there was a mere oral agreement implied in the case of a tenant who had held over after the expiration of a lease for fourteen years. There are obvious difficulties for an assignee in ascertaining the terms of an oral tenancy unless, as in that case, they are contained in an earlier lease.
60 West v. Dobb (1869) L.R. 4 Q.B. 634.
61 South of England Dairies Ltd. v. Baker [1906] 2 Ch. 631; but it is possible that the sub-lessee can now take the benefit under the principle of Smith v. River Douglas Catchment Board [1949] 2 K.B. 500, post, p. 748. A sub-lessee may be bound by restrictive covenants: post, p. 756. For the difference between an assignment and a sub-lease, see ante, p. 616.

99 years, T assigns the lease to A, and A sub-leases the land to S for the residue of the term of 99 years less one day, S is not an assignee and there is privity neither of contract nor of estate between L and S. A is still the tenant under the lease for 99 years and remains liable upon it. Consequently if S does some act which is contrary to a covenant in the 99 years' lease, L cannot sue S but can sue A. If the lease contains a forfeiture clause, L can also take proceedings for forfeiture and so put an end to both head lease and sub-lease together. In practice the covenants inserted in a sub-lease are made at least as stringent as those in the head lease, so that the sub-lessor may have a remedy against the sub-lessee in case the sub-lessee's acts render the sub-lessor liable to the head landlord.

(b) *Other assignments.* Since the covenants run only where there is privity of estate, a mere equitable assignment (*e.g.*, under a contract to assign) cannot pass the burden of covenants.[62] But the benefit may itself be assigned as such; and if the covenant creates an interest in land (*e.g.*, a restrictive covenant, or an option), the burden will affect subsequent occupiers in accordance with the ordinary rules governing legal and equitable interests. These cases are explained more fully below.[63]

(c) *Squatters.* A squatter, *i.e.*, a person who bars the lessee's interest by adverse possession for twelve years under the Limitation Act, 1939, is not an assignee of the lessee, and cannot therefore sue or be sued on covenants in the lease which run only where there is privity of estate.[64] But if he claims some advantage under the lease, *e.g.*, a reduction of rent which is conditional on observance of the covenants, he may estop himself from denying that he is bound by the lease.[65]

(d) *Personal representatives.* A personal representative of the tenant is an assignee by operation of law, for when the tenant dies the lease devolves automatically upon his executor or administrator.[66] But the extent of a personal representative's liability varies. If he takes possession of the land, he is personally liable to the same extent as an ordinary assignee,[67] though by proper pleading he may

---

[62] *Cox* v. *Bishop* (1857) 8 De G.M. & G. 815; *Friary, Holroyd & Healey's Breweries Ltd.* v. *Singleton* [1899] 1 Ch. 86, reversed on other grounds [1899] 2 Ch. 261. But there may be facts cogent enough to estop the assignee from denying liability: see *ante*, p. 650.

[63] See *post*, pp. 741, 742.

[64] *Tichborne* v. *Weir* (1892) 67 L.T. 735; *post*, p. 1030.

[65] *Ashe* v. *Hogan* [1920] 1 I.R. 159; *post*, p. 1031.

[66] *Ante*, p. 537.

[67] *Tilny* v. *Norris* (1700) 1 Ld.Raym. 553; *Stratford-upon-Avon Corpn.* v. *Parker* [1914] 2 K.B. 562 at 567.

limit his liability to the annual value of the land.[68] If he does not take possession, he is liable only[69] in his representative capacity, *i.e.*, to the extent of the deceased tenant's assets.[70] The representative liability of an original lessee's estate endures for the whole term of the lease, despite any assignment by him[71] or by his personal representatives.[72]

This representative liability formerly made it unsafe for a personal representative to distribute the assets to the persons beneficially entitled so long as any liability might arise under the covenants in the lease[73] without setting aside a fund to meet possible liabilities, although the landlord could not require this to be done.[74] The difficulty was removed by legislation of 1859[75] now re-enacted by the Trustee Act, 1925.[76] This provision protects a personal representative or trustee against his representative liability if he has first satisfied any existing claims, set aside any *fixed* sum agreed to be laid out on the land, and assigned the lease to a beneficiary[77] or purchaser. But this provides no protection if the personal representative or trustee has taken possession and so is liable as an assignee; in such cases he may set aside a fund for his protection,[78] though this will be distributable when all possible claims have been paid or barred by lapse of time.[79]

(e) *Several assignees.* If the tenancy is vested in two or more assignees, each is liable for the full amount of any damages for breach of covenant and not merely a proportionate share, even if in equity they are not joint tenants but tenants in common.[80]

3. Partial assignment. It is possible for part only of the demised land to be assigned separately from the rest. In that case covenants capable of running with the land will bind the assignee in so far

---

68 *Rendall* v. *Andreae* (1892) 61 L.J.Q.B. 630.
69 *Wollaston* v. *Hakewill* (1841) 3 Man. & G. 297 at 320.
70 *Helier* v. *Casebert* (1665) 1 Lev. 127; *Youngmin* v. *Heath* [1974] 1 W.L.R. 135 (weekly tenancy).
71 *Brett* v. *Cumberland* (1619) Cro.Jac. 521; and see *Matthews* v. *Ruggles-Brise* [1911] 1 Ch. 194.
72 *Pitcher* v. *Tovey* (1692) 4 Mod. 71 at 76.
73 See *Davis* v. *Blackwell* (1832) 9 Bing. 6; *Collins* v. *Crouch* (1849) 13 Q.B. 542.
74 *King* v. *Malcott* (1852) 9 Hare 692.
75 L.P.Am.A., 1859, s. 27.
76 s. 26.
77 Before 1926 assignment to a purchaser was essential: see *Re Lawley* [1911] 2 Ch. 530.
78 *Re Owers* [1941] Ch. 389; compare *Re Bennett* [1943] 1 All E.R. 467, a curious case.
79 *Re Lewis* [1939] Ch. 232.
80 See *United Dairies Ltd.* v. *Public Trustee* [1923] 1 K.B. 469 (repair: legal tenancy in common before 1926); *cf. ante*, p. 408.

as they relate to the part assigned to him.[81] In an action for rent the assignee is liable only for the proportion attributable to his part,[82] which in default of agreement,[83] may be determined by the court,[84] or by the appropriate Secretary of State if application is made to him.[85] But although the landlord can sue only for this proportion, the ancient right of distress is available against every part of the demised land for the whole of the rent.[1] If the assignee of part is thus compelled to pay the whole rent, he can claim contribution from the tenant of the other part, on the principle which gives a right of indemnity to persons compelled to pay a debt for which some other person is primarily liable.[2]

4. Covenants relating to things in posse. If a covenant made before 1926 imposed an obligation upon the tenant to do some entirely new thing, such as to erect a building, the burden of the covenant ran with the land only if the lessee expressly covenanted for himself *and for his assigns* that the covenant would be performed.[3] This rule did not apply to covenants relating to things *in esse* (in existence) nor even to covenants relating only conditionally to something *in posse* (not in existence), such as a covenant to repair a new building if it is erected [4]; in such cases it was immaterial whether or not the covenant mentioned assigns. This unreasonable distinction between covenants relating to things *in posse* and those relating to things *in esse* is still in force as regards all leases granted before 1926; but by the Law of Property Act, 1925,[5] it does not apply to leases made after 1925.

5. Duration of liability. The original lessee is liable for all breaches of covenant throughout the term of the lease, even after assignment, because there is still privity of contract.[6] But an assignee is liable only for breaches committed while the lease is

---

[81] *Congham* v. *King* (1631) Cro.Car. 221 (repair), approved in *Stevenson* v. *Lambard* (1802) 2 East 575.
[82] *Curtis* v. *Spitty* (1835) 1 Bing.N.C. 756. But see *Whitham* v. *Bullock* [1939] 2 K.B. 81 at 86. On the doubt there raised as to privity of estate, see *Gamon* v. *Vernon* (1678) 2 Lev. 231.
[83] Such an agreement will not bind persons not parties to it : *Bliss* v. *Collins* (1882) 5 B. & Ald. 876 (severance of reversion).
[84] See *Whitham* v. *Bullock*, *supra*, at p. 86, citing *Bliss* v. *Collins*, *supra*.
[85] Landlord and Tenant Act, 1927, s. 20.
[1] *Whitham* v. *Bullock*, *supra*, at p. 86.
[2] *Whitham* v. *Bullock*, *supra* (payment under threat of distress). For another example of this principle, see *post*, p. 733.
[3] *Spencer's Case* (1583) 5 Co.Rep. 16a, second resolution ; though see *Minshull* v. *Oakes* (1858) 2 H. & N. 793 ; *Re Robert Stephenson & Co. Ltd.* [1915] 1 Ch. 802 at 807.
[4] *Minshull* v. *Oakes*, *supra*.
[5] s. 79.
[6] *Ante*, p. 723.

vested in him,[7] for privity of estate exists only while the estate is held. An assignee is under no liability for breaches committed before the lease was assigned to him [8] unless they are continuing breaches (as of a covenant to repair),[9] nor is he liable for breaches committed after he has assigned the lease.[10] But if a covenant is broken while the lease is vested in him, his liability for this breach continues despite any assignment.[11] Thus while the original lessee of an onerous lease cannot divest himself of liability for future breaches, an assignee can do so by assigning the lease, even if the assignee is a pauper.[12]

6. Indemnities by assignee. If a covenant which runs with the land has been broken, the lessee and the assignee entitled to the lease at the time of the breach are each liable to be sued by the lessor.[13] But although the lessor may obtain judgment against either or both, he can only have one satisfaction [14]; he has no right to recover twice. The same rule applies to all the other cases in the examples given below where one person may sue more than one defendant in respect of one liability: both may be sued, but the money may be recovered only once. The value of alternative rights of enforcement is that if one defendant is inaccessible or insolvent, satisfaction may be had from the other.

(a) *Implied indemnity.* The primary liability is that of the assignee, since he has the exclusive benefit of the lease.[15] If the lessee is sued, he may claim indemnity from the assignee in whom the lease was vested at the time of the breach, whether that assignee obtained the lease from the lessee directly or from some intermediate assignee.[16] The principle here is a branch of quasi-contract, by which the law implies an obligation between joint debtors to repay money paid by one of them for the exclusive benefit of the other, when both were legally liable to a common creditor. Since the assignee is solely entitled to enjoy the lease, the satisfaction of the lessor's claim enures to the assignee's benefit alone. The lessee has, in fact, paid the assignee's debt for him, and has the same right of indemnity as has a surety.[17]

---

[7] *Chancellor* v. *Poole* (1781) 2 Doug.K.B. 764.
[8] *Grescot* v. *Green* (1700) 1 Salk. 199.
[9] *Granada Theatres Ltd.* v. *Freehold Investment (Leytonstone) Ltd.* [1959] Ch. 592.
[10] *Paul* v. *Nurse* (1828) 8 B. & C. 486.
[11] *Harley* v. *King* (1835) 2 Cr.M. & R. 18.
[12] *Valliant* v. *Dodemede* (1742) 2 Atk. 546.
[13] Unless liability for other persons' acts is expressly restricted: *ante,* p. 723. *Wilson* v. *Twamley* [1904] 2 K.B. 99.
[14] *Ante,* p. 724.
[15] *Moule* v. *Garrett* (1872) L.R. 7 Ex. 101.
[16] *Ibid.*; *Wolveridge* v. *Steward* (1833) 1 Cr. & M. 644.
[17] *Moule* v. *Garrett, supra,* at p. 104; *cf. ante,* p. 730.

(b) *Express indemnity.* It is also the usual practice for an assignor to require a covenant of indemnity by the assignee against liability for future breaches of covenant, by whomsoever committed. The Law of Property Act, 1925,[18] sets out the common form of covenant, which is now implied in any assignment for value made after 1925.[1] This covenant is purely personal and cannot, of course, run with the land, since it is not made between landlord and tenant.

(c) *Effect.* The effect of these rights of indemnity may be illustrated thus:

$$A$$
$$| \ 99 \ \text{years}$$
$$B\text{---}C\text{---}D\text{---}E$$
$$| \ 21 \ \text{years.}$$
$$F$$

A has leased land to B for 99 years; by successive assignments E has become entitled to the lease and has granted a sub-lease to F for 21 years. If F does some act which is contrary to a covenant in the head lease, A can sue either B (privity of contract) or E (privity of estate).[2] A cannot sue C, D or F, for with them he has no privity of any kind. If A sues B, B has an implied right of indemnity (quasi-contractual) against E, but not against F.[3] Alternatively, if on the assignment to C a covenant of indemnity was given to B (either expressly or by the statutory implication), B may claim indemnity (contractual) from C. C in turn may claim a similar indemnity from D, and D from E, provided in each case that the covenant for indemnity was given on the assignment.

If such a covenant was given but not taken by C or D, or in any case if C prefers to sue E rather than D, C and D may presumably claim quasi-contractual indemnity from E for anything which they have been compelled to pay; for E is liable quasi-contractually to B, and therefore also to C if C is compelled to discharge this liability for E's sole benefit; and by parity of reasoning E, being liable to idemnify C, must indemnify D if D is compelled to pay C under a covenant for indemnity. Apart from the rules relating to restrictive covenants,[4] F incurs no liability to anyone except so far

---

[18] 2nd Sched., Pt. IX.

[1] L.P.A., 1925, s. 77 (1). This covenant includes liability for continuing breaches (e.g., of a repairing covenant) existing when the lease was assigned: *Middlegate Properties Ltd.* v. *Bilbao* (1972) 24 P. and C.R. 329.

[2] But see n. 13, *supra.*

[3] *Bonner* v. *Tottenham & Edmonton Permanent Investment B. S.* [1899] 1 Q.B. 161; this is because F is not jointly liable with B to A, and payment by B to A does not relieve F of any liability. The principle of *Moule* v. *Garrett, supra,* does not therefore apply. [4] *Post,* p. 750.

as his act was a breach of a covenant in the sub-lease and so makes him liable to E; for it is only with E that F has any privity of any kind.

II.   WHERE THE LESSOR ASSIGNS HIS REVERSION

The common law rule was that covenants touching and concerning the land could run with the lease, but not with the reversion.[5] If L, a tenant in fee simple, leased his land to T, and then L sold his fee simple, subject to the lease, to R, R was neither able to sue nor liable to be sued on the covenants in the lease. But R could sue and be sued on the obligations (often called implied covenants [6]) inherent in the relationship of landlord and tenant, since these arose automatically from the privity of estate (*i.e.*, tenure) between R and T.[7] Thus R could sue T for the rent, for rent was due not merely under a personal covenant but as a service incident to the tenant's estate.[8] The same applied to any services analogous to rent, *e.g.*, grinding corn at the lessor's mill.[9]

But before *Spencer's Case* laid down the principles upon which covenants could run with leases, statute enabled them to run with reversions. When the monastic lands were seized and distributed it was necessary to enable grantees to enforce the terms of leases, and the Grantees of Reversions Act, 1540,[10] altered the law generally.

The effect of the Act was that the benefit and burden of all covenants, provisions and conditions contained in a lease which touched and concerned the land [11] (or, in the modern phrase, had reference to the subject-matter of the lease [12]) passed with the reversion. The meaning of " touching and concerning the land " was here the same as in *Spencer's Case,* discussed above.[13] These provisions have twice been re-enacted in more modern form, first by the Conveyancing Acts, 1881–1911,[14] and now by the Law of Property Act, 1925, ss. 141 (benefit) and 142 (burden).

---

[5] (1871) 1 Wms.Saund., pp. 299, n. (b), 300, n. (10).   Distinguish the cases where the benefit of a covenant could run with other land belonging to the reversioner (not with the reversion itself): *post,* p. 747.

[6] *Ante,* p. 676.

[7] *Wedd* v. *Porter* [1916] 2 K.B. 91 at 100, 101; and see Platt on *Covenants,* 532.

[8] *Cf.* Co.Litt. 215a (rent payable to lord who took reversion by escheat).

[9] *Vyvyan* v. *Arthur* (1823) 1 B. & C. 410.

[10] 32 Hen. 8, c. 34.

[11] This qualification was added by judicial legislation, by analogy to the principle of *Spencer's Case* (*ante,* p. 725): see Smith's L.C. i, 59.

[12] See L.P.A., 1925, ss. 141, 142; *Davis* v. *Town Properties Investment Corporation* [1903] 1 Ch. 797.

[13] *Ante,* p. 725.

[14] 1881, ss. 10, 11; 1911, s. 2.

The following points must be observed.

1. The lease must be in due form. The Act of 1540 applied only to leases under seal,[15] but that of 1881 applied also to leases evidenced in writing,[16] though not to mere oral tenancies.[17] Since 1925 it appears that even a mere oral tenancy is sufficient, for by section 154 of the Law of Property Act, 1925, sections 141 and 142 extend to an underlease " or other tenancy " [18]; and " covenant " is not confined to promises made under seal.[19]

By a liberal construction it has been held that even a contract for a lease, if properly proved and specifically enforceable, is " a lease," and the intending lessor's interest a " reversionary estate," within the Acts of 1881 and 1925.[20] This implies an extension of the doctrine of *Walsh* v. *Lonsdale* [21] so as to affect third parties: not only the benefit but also the burden of the stipulations becomes assignable by the proposed lessor, although as has been seen only the benefit is assignable by the proposed lessee.[22] The decisions so far given concern only the benefit of the lessor's covenants, but their reasoning applies equally to the burden. This difference between the lessor's and lessee's positions under a mere contract may perhaps rest in principle on the fact that the burden of an estate contract can run with the land of the lessor as an equitable burden of a proprietary kind, carrying with it the burden of covenants [23]; but the lessee's obligations are purely contractual until a lease is executed, and therefore they cannot be assigned.

2. The reversion may have been assigned in whole or in part. The assignee of the entire reversion takes the benefit and burden of the provisions in the lease; and if the reversion is held on trust, it is the trustee, as legal reversioner, and not the beneficiaries who can enforce the covenants.[24] Where the reversion is not assigned in its entirety, the position is not so simple. Two separate cases must be considered.

---

[15] *Smith* v. *Eggington* (1874) L.R. 9 C.P. 145 (burden); *Standen* v. *Chrismas* (1847) 10 Q.B. 135 (benefit).

[16] *Cole* v. *Kelly* [1920] 2 K.B. 106; *Rye* v. *Purcell* [1926] 1 K.B. 446.

[17] *Blane* v. *Francis* [1917] 1 K.B. 252.

[18] See also the dictum of Denning L.J. in *Boyer* v. *Warbey, ante,* p. 728. That case concerned the assignment of a lease, but the dictum extends to assignment of the reversion.

[19] *Weg Motors Ltd.* v. *Hales* [1962] Ch. 49.

[20] Doubted in *Manchester Brewery Co.* v. *Coombs* [1901] 2 Ch. 608 at 619, but so held in *Rickett* v. *Green* [1910] 1 K.B. 253 and *Rye* v. *Purcell* [1926] 1 K.B. 446.

[21] *Ante,* p. 625.

[22] *Ante,* p. 628.

[23] *Ante,* p. 132.

[24] See *Schalit* v. *Joseph Nadler Ltd.* [1933] 2 K.B. 79.

(*a*) *Severance as regards the estate.* Where the assignee has part of the reversion, *e.g.*, where a fee simple reversioner grants a lease of his reversion to X (whether for a shorter or longer period than the existing lease), the reversion is severed as regards the estate.[25] An assignee of part of the reversion falls within the Acts of 1540–1925, so that the benefit and burden of all covenants and conditions pass to him.[26] That is to say, the covenants run with the *immediate* reversion, for it is the person entitled to the next immediate reversion upon the lease who has privity of estate with the tenant.[27] This explains why the benefit and burden of the covenants passes to a mere lessee of the reversion, but does not pass to a sub-lessee of the lease.

(*b*) *Severance as regards the land.* Where the assignee has the reversion of part, *e.g.*, where a fee simple reversioner grants the fee simple of half the land to X, the reversion is severed as regards the land. It has been held that this does not sever the tenancy, so that although there is a severed reversion, there is still a single tenancy.[27a] In such a case rent was apportionable at common law between the two reversioners in proportion to the value of their respective parts.[28] Other covenants ran with the reversion under the Act of 1540 in so far as they related to the part assigned.[29] But conditions (*e.g.*, a condition for forfeiture on non-payment of rent) did not,[30] because the Act did not alter the curious common law rule that conditions were not severable.[31] But now, by the Law of Property Act, 1925,[32] replacing earlier legislation,[33] all conditions and rights of re-entry are apportioned on the severance of the reversion. The old law continues to apply if the lease was made before 1882 and the reversion was severed before 1926.

There is a new statutory rule about a notice to quit which is served after a severance of the reversion and so applies to part of

25 For this, see *ante*, p. 649.
26 Co.Litt. 215a, 215b, and notes by Butler; *Wright* v. *Burroughes* (1846) 3 C.B. 685.
27 Preston, *Conveyancing*, ii, 145, 146; *ante*, p. 649.
27a *Jelley* v. *Buckman* [1974] Q.B. 488.
28 Co.Litt. 148a; *Bliss* v. *Collins* (1822) 5 B. & Ald. 876; *Mayor of Swansea* v. *Thomas* (1882) 10 Q.B.D. 48; Hood and Challis, 254.
29 *Twynam* v. *Pickard* (1818) 2 B. & Ald. 105.
30 Co.Litt. 215a, rule 5.
31 *Dumpor's Case* (1603) 4 Co.Rep. 119b; Smith's L.C. i, 35, *ante*, p. 659. There were two exceptions: where the King was assignee; and where an assignee took by operation of law, *e.g.*, where part of the demised land was subject to the custom of Borough English (*ante*, p. 22) and descended differently from the rest (Co.Litt. 215a), or where the reversion was severed by compulsory acquisition: *Piggott* v. *Middlesex County Council* [1909] 1 Ch. 134.
32 s. 140 (1).
33 L.P.(Am.)A., 1859, s. 3 (non-payment of rent); C.A., 1881, s. 12 (other conditions).

the demised land only. The tenant may elect to quit the whole, provided that within one month he serves on the other reversioner a counter-notice expiring at the same time as the original notice.[34]

3. Assignee's right to sue for previous breaches. An assignee of the reversion acquires the right to sue for breaches of covenant committed before the assignment, and the assignor loses this right.[35] This is held to be the result of the Law of Property Act, 1925, s. 141, replacing earlier legislation,[36] which provides in effect that rent and the benefit of leasehold covenants (if they touch and concern the land) and conditions shall pass with the reversion.[37] The legislation has changed the previous law, which was that the assignor and not the assignee could sue for rent due and other breaches of covenant committed before the assignment, not being breaches of a continuing character.[38] Thus in a case where, at the time of the assignment of the reversion, there were outstanding breaches of covenants to repair and reinstate the property, the assignee and not the assignor is the person entitled to sue.[39] But this rule will, it seems, yield to any contrary intention in the assignment.[40]

A right of re-entry for breach of covenant could not be assigned at common law, so that if a reversion was assigned after a covenant had been broken, the new reversioner could not take advantage of a forfeiture clause.[41] By the Law of Property Act, 1925,[42] replacing earlier legislation,[43] such rights of re-entry are enforceable by the new reversioner provided they have not been waived.[43a] Although the court will often imply waiver,[44] it will not do so merely because the reversion is conveyed to a third party " subject to the lease," since this is *res inter alios acta* and the reference to the lease is a conveyancing formality.[45]

---

[34] L.P.A., 1925, s. 140 (2), altering the law as laid down in *Re Bebington's Tenancy* [1921] 1 Ch. 559: *Smith* v. *Kinsey* [1936] 3 All E.R. 73.

[35] *Re King* [1963] Ch. 459; *London and County (A. & D.) Ltd.* v. *Wilfred Sportsman Ltd.* [1971] Ch. 764.

[36] C.A., 1881, s. 10. This in turn replaced the Grantees of Reversions Act, 1540, but in different terms.

[37] subs. (1); and see sub-ss. (2), (3).

[38] *Flight* v. *Bentley* (1835) 7 Sim. 149 (rent); *Re King, supra* (where Lord Denning M.R., dissenting, was of opinion that the previous law remained unaltered).

[39] *Re King, supra.*

[40] *Re King, supra,* at p. 488.

[41] *Hunt* v. *Bishop* (1853) 8 Exch. 675; *Hunt* v. *Remnant* (1854) 9 Exch. 635. The Real Property Act, 1845, s. 6 (*ante,* p. 81), did not apply: *ibid.*

[42] s. 141 (3).

[43] C.A., 1911, s. 2.

[43a] *Rickett* v. *Green* [1910] 1 K.B. 253; *London and County (A. & D.) Ltd.* v. *Wilfred Sportsman Ltd.* [1971] Ch. 764.

[44] For waiver generally, see *ante,* p. 657.

[45] *London and County (A. & D.) Ltd.* v. *Wilfred Sportsman Ltd., supra,* overruling *Davenport* v. *Smith* [1921] 2 Ch. 270, which had treated the phrase as recognising that the lease still existed.

4. Privity of estate not required. Covenants run with the reversion by force of the statute, and not because of the doctrine of privity of estate. Thus if the original lessee assigns the lease and later the landlord assigns the reversion, the new landlord can sue the original lessee for rent previously due from him, even though there has never been privity of estate between them.[46]

5. Merger or surrender of the reversion. If the reversion disappeared,[47] no covenants could run with it, for the privity of estate was destroyed. Before this rule was amended by statute a sub-tenant might find himself released from all his covenants by merger or surrender of the head lease, provided that he was not also liable by privity of contract. For example, if L leased land to T for 99 years and T sub-leased to S for 21 years, and then P purchased both L's and T's interests, T's lease would then cease to exist by merger or surrender (depending on the order of P's two purchases) and no covenants could be enforced by or against S by reason of privity of estate.[48] But since the Real Property Act, 1845,[49] now repealed and re-enacted by the Law of Property Act, 1925,[50] the benefit and burden of covenants have been preserved from destruction in this way.[51]

III. INCORPOREAL HEREDITAMENTS

Where the subject-matter of the lease is not land itself but some right over land in the nature of an incorporeal hereditament,[52] the benefit and burden of covenants will sometimes run with the lease and with the reversion under the general principles explained above.[53] Thus in a lease of tithes[54] a covenant not to let certain farmers have any part of the tithes was held to bind an assignee of the lessee[55]; and similarly an assignee of the lease was held liable on a covenant to pay rent under a lease of market-tolls.[56] Covenants can, likewise, run with the reversions in such cases, for the Act of 1540[57] applied to reversions in " rents, . . . tithes,

---

[46] *Arlesford Trading Co. Ltd.* v. *Servansingh* [1971] 1 W.L.R. 1080.
[47] For merger and surrender, see *ante*, p. 667.
[48] *Webb* v. *Russell* (1789) 3 T.R. 393.
[49] s. 9. The Landlord and Tenant Act, 1730, s. 6, had previously given a small measure of relief in the case of rent.
[50] s. 139.
[51] For examples, see *Phipos* v. *Callegari* (1910) 54 S.J. 635; *Plummer* v. *David* [1920] 1 K.B. 326.
[52] For incorporeal hereditaments, see *post*, p. 787.
[53] *Norval* v. *Pascoe* (1864) 34 L.J.Ch. 82. See Smith's L.C. i, 98.
[54] For tithes, see *post*, p. 801.
[55] *Bally* v. *Wells* (1769) Wilm. 341.
[56] *Earl of Egremont* v. *Keene* (1837) 2 Jo.Ex.Ir. 307; and see *Norval* v. *Pascoe*, *supra* (mining lease).
[57] *Ante*, p. 734.

portions, or any other hereditaments," and the statutory provisions [58] which have now replaced it may be presumed to have a similar scope. A purchaser of land was thus able to sue a person to whom the right to excavate china clay from it had been let for a term of years, and who failed to observe a covenant to yield up the works in repair.[59]

It seems, however, that covenants are incapable of running with rentcharges,[60] except possibly under the above-mentioned statutes. This is a region where judges have despaired of finding logical distinctions.[61]

IV. OPERATION OF FORFEITURE CLAUSES

1. Lack of privity. An occupier of leasehold land (*e.g.,* a sub-tenant) may be in neither privity of contract nor privity of estate with the head landlord, and so not be bound by the covenants of the head lease; yet he may have to observe them under penalty of forfeiture. This question can arise only where there is an express forfeiture clause.[62] Normally this will be found in the head lease, but it may also be one of the terms of an assignment of a lease,[63] or of a grant in fee simple.[64] It creates a conditional right of entry which can be exercised against anyone when it arises; for such a right of entry is a proprietary interest,[65] and not merely the benefit of a covenant, and, being usually a legal interest,[66] it binds all later occupiers. The fact that the latter may not be bound by the covenants themselves is immaterial.[67] It may indeed be just for this reason that a forfeiture clause is employed.

For example, L demises property to T, T covenanting to repair and L reserving a right of re-entry for breach of this covenant. If T sub-demises to S, and S fails to repair, L can then re-enter and determine both T's and S's estates, subject to the statutory restrictions on enforcing forfeiture and the provisions for relief against forfeiture.[68] T could give S no better rights against L than

---

[58] *Ibid.*
[59] *Martyn* v. *Williams* (1857) 1 H. & N. 817; and see *Lord Hastings* v. *N. E. Ry.* [1898] 2 Ch. 674; aff'd. [1899] 1 Ch. 656; [1900] A.C. 260.
[60] *Milnes* v. *Branch* (1816) 5 M. & S. 411; *Grant* v. *Edmondson* [1931] 1 Ch 1. These cases, however, concerned freehold, not leasehold, rentcharges.
[61] See *Grant* v. *Edmondson, supra,* at pp. 26, 28.
[62] *Ante,* p. 654.
[63] As in *Shiloh Spinners Ltd.* v. *Harding* [1973] A.C. 691 (right of re-entry reserved by assignor of lease to enforce covenants given by assignee).
[64] *i.e.,* a conditional fee: *ante,* p. 77.
[65] L.P.A., 1925, s. 1 (2) (*e*); *ante,* p. 143.
[66] But in *Shiloh Spinners Ltd.* v. *Harding, supra,* the House of Lords held the right of entry to be equitable: *ante,* p. 143.
[67] *Ibid.*
[68] See *ante,* p. 659.

T had himself, and T's rights were subject to forfeiture. The person who has committed the breach of covenant is not S but T, since T's covenant to repair amounted to a warranty (assuming no stipulation to the contrary) [69] that neither T nor any of his successors in title would fail to repair.

2. Covenants not touching and concerning the land. The law is less clear where the covenant which precipitates the forfeiture is a covenant of the kind which does not " touch and concern the land." In the first place, section 79 of the Law of Property Act, 1925, does not apply to such covenants, so that they only apply to the covenantor personally: he is not liable for the acts of his successors in title unless the covenant expressly so provides. Secondly, in the case of an assignment of the reversion, the right of re-entry was not assignable at common law, but was made to run with the reversion by the Act of 1540.[70] That Act dealt with covenants and conditions in similar terms, so that when the courts engrafted on to it the qualification that it applied only to covenants which touched and concerned the land,[71] this restriction was applied equally to conditional rights of re-entry. Accordingly, an assignee of the reversion could enforce a forfeiture clause only in respect of a breach of a covenant which touched and concerned the land.[72]

But the statutory provision which has superseded the Act of 1540 (now section 141 of the Law of Property Act, 1925) gives to the assignee of a reversion the benefit of " every covenant or provision therein contained, having reference to the subject-matter thereof . . . and every condition of re-entry and other condition therein contained." This wording, it will be noticed, qualifies covenants but not conditions, and appears to intend that the assignee shall be entitled to re-enter even where the condition is something unrelated to the land. This seems reasonable, for now that rights of re-entry are freely assignable [73] there would seem to be no reason why the assignee should not take all the assignable rights of the assignor, and take advantage of a condition that (for example) the lease should be determinable " when X returns from Rome." The House of Lords appears to favour this view.[74]

---

[69] *Ante*, p. 723.

[70] *Ante*, p. 734.

[71] *Ante*, p. 734.

[72] *Stevens* v. *Copp* (1868) L.R. 4 Ex. 20 (proviso for re-entry in case of offence against game laws; breach by sub-tenant of an assignee of the lease; action for possession brought by an assignee of reversion failed).

[73] L.P.A., 1925, s. 4 (2), replacing R.P.A., 1845, s. 6; *ante*, p. 81.

[74] See *Shiloh Spinners Ltd.* v. *Harding* [1973] A.C. 691 at 717, disparaging *Stevens* v. *Copp, supra.*

3. Assignment or sub-lease. There remain the cases where the lease is assigned, or a sub-lease is granted. The latter case presents no difficulty: the sub-lease depends upon the head lease, and shares its fate if it is determined by forfeiture, unless the sub-tenant succeeds in obtaining relief.[75] The more difficult question is whether an assignee of a lease is subject to forfeiture for non-observance of a covenant which does not touch and concern the land. On principle, a right of re-entry for breach of covenant should be exercisable against any assignee of the lease, as well as against any other third party, whether or not the covenant touches and concerns the land; for a right of re-entry is a proprietary interest in its own right,[76] and may be made exercisable on any event, *e.g.,* " when X returns from Rome." The House of Lords again seems to favour this view.[77] But the only direct decision holds that the burden of a condition of re-entry will run with the lease at law only if the condition touches and concerns the land.[78] If this is right, the condition will be exercisable against an assignee only if the covenant itself runs with the land.

C. *Transmission by Other Means*

In certain cases benefits and burdens which will not be transmitted under the foregoing rules will nevertheless pass to assignees. This is of a special importance in relation to options in a lease to purchase the freehold,[79] which do not touch and concern the land.[80]

1. Benefit. The general principle is that the benefit of any contract is assignable.[81] Accordingly, the benefit of a covenant in a lease is assignable as such, even though it does not touch and concern the land and so run with the land automatically under the foregoing rules. For example, a lease may contain an option to purchase the freehold, which will not run automatically [82]; but the benefit of the option will pass to an assignee of the lease if the assignment is construed as extending to the benefit of the option as such. The benefit does not cease to be separately assignable merely because the option

---

[75] *Ante,* p. 667. See *e.g., Cresswell* v. *Davidson* (1887) 56 L.T. 811; *Westminster (Duke)* v. *Swinton* [1948] 1 K.B. 524. [76] See n. 65, *supra.*
[77] *Shiloh Spinners Ltd.* v. *Harding, supra* (assignee not bound by covenants but right of entry effective).
[78] *Horsey Estate Ltd.* v. *Steiger* [1899] 2 Q.B. 79 at 88, 89, where, however, the difference between conditions and covenants was not observed, and the condition (against the tenant company's liquidation) in any case touched and concerned the land. The only authority relied on related to assignments of reversions, which are governed by the special construction of the Act of 1540; *ante,* p. 740. See also the hostile reference to this case in *Shiloh Spinners Ltd.* v. *Harding, supra,* at p. 717.
[79] On the nature of options, see (1958) 74 L.Q.R. 242 (W. J. Mowbray).
[80] *Ante,* p. 726. [81] *Ante,* p. 628.
[82] *Ante,* p. 726.

is contained in a lease, or because it is assigned along with the lease.[83] Even the conventional definition in the lease of " lessee " as including successors in title has been treated as evidence that an ordinary assignment of the lease was intended to carry also the benefit of the option.[84]

2. Burden. Leases may contain covenants of the kind which, under principles explained elsewhere, create interests in land, so that the burden will run with the land. Thus restrictive (as opposed to positive) covenants are equitable interests which are capable of binding assignees and others,[85] and their effect is not reduced merely because they occur in a lease.[1] Similarly an equitable interest will normally arise if the owner of land binds himself to sell it or let it, or grants an option for sale or lease.[2] Subject to the rules as to purchase without notice and registration as land charges, such covenants will accordingly bind any assignee or other person interested in the land.[3] Even legal interests can sometimes be created by what in form are mere covenants, for example by covenants creating rentcharges[4] and covenants creating easements, such as rights of way.[5]

Part 3

NO PRIVITY: COVENANTS RUNNING WITH FREEHOLD LAND

1. Classification. Where there is no privity either of contract or of estate between the parties, the liability to observe a covenant is less

---

[83] *Griffith* v. *Pelton* [1958] Ch. 205; *Re Button's Lease* [1964] Ch. 263.

[84] *Ibid.* Yet provided the lease does not indicate that the option is purely personal, it should be the terms of the assignment rather than of the lease that are decisive: see [1957] C.L.J. 148 (H.W.R.W.). See also *Re Adams and the Kensington Vestry* (1883) 24 Ch.D. 199 at 206 (on appeal, (1884) 27 Ch.D. 394); *Batchelor* v. *Murphy* [1926] A.C. 63; (1957) 73 L.Q.R. 452 (R.E.M.); (1958) 74 L.Q.R. 242 (W. J. Mowbray). *County Hotel and Wine Co. Ltd.* v. *L. N. W. Ry.* [1918] 2 K.B. 251 at 256, 257 (on appeal [1919] 2 K.B. 29; [1921] 1 A.C. 85) seems to show the right approach.

[85] *Post,* p. 750.

[1] But for a difference as to registration, see *post,* p. 1042.

[2] *Ante,* pp. 132, 575; *post,* p. 1040.

[3] Consider *Woodall* v. *Clifton* [1905] 2 Ch. 257, where the option, had it not been void for perpetuity, would have bound the reversion in equity, even though it did not touch and concern the land and so run at law. The reason why the court decided that it did not run at law was because it had been argued that all covenants capable of running at law were exempt from the perpetuity rule. See the fuller explanation at (1955) 19 Conv.(N.S.) 255 (H.W.R.W.).

[4] *Post,* p. 794.

[5] *Post,* p. 828.

like a condition of tenure and more like an incumbrance; a right over the land has been created in favour of someone who is a stranger to it, and the occupier is bound by it just as by any other third party right like an easement or a mortgage. At this point, therefore, we leave the subject of landlord and tenant and enter that of incumbrances, which is continued in Chapters 13 and 14. Nevertheless it is best to deal with all types of covenant together in this chapter, since they have so much in common. There is, furthermore, some overlapping, for a landlord may be able to sue a sub-tenant on a covenant in the head lease if it qualifies as a restrictive covenant and is binding on the sub-tenant under the rules about to be given.

2. Divergence of law and equity. At common law the rule is that under certain conditions the benefit but not the burden of a covenant can run with land. Thus if P, on buying a plot of land from V, enters into a covenant with V for the benefit of V's other land (*e.g.*, if P covenants to clean annually the ditches on V's side of the boundary), the benefit of this covenant may pass at law to V's successors in title, so enabling them to enforce the covenant against P.[6] But this does not apply to the burden of the covenant; P's successors in title will not be bound by it,[7] for the covenant binds only P himself and (after his death) his estate.[8]

In equity the rules are of more modern invention, and much wider. In the first place, equity allowed the benefit of a contract or covenant to be assigned, whether or not it concerned land, as a chose in action[9]; and express assignments may now have legal as well as equitable effect if they comply with the Law of Property Act, 1925.[10] Next, equity followed the law in allowing the benefit of certain covenants to be annexed to the land, so as to run with the land without express assignment. But the revolutionary contribution of equity was the rule that subject to certain conditions the *burden* of restrictive (*i.e.*, negative or prohibitory) covenants could run with land which was subject to them.

This transformed the law of covenants in cases where there was privity neither of contract nor of estate. The effectiveness of a covenant concerning the covenantor's land was no longer confined

---

[6] *Post*, p. 744.
[7] *Austerberry* v. *Corporation of Oldham* (1885) 29 Ch.D. 750 at 781–785; *Smith* v. *Colbourne* [1914] 2 Ch. 533 at 542; *E. & G. C. Ltd.* v. *Bate* (1935) 79 L.J.News. 203 (covenant to build road; assignee of benefit failed in action against devisee of covenantor); *Cator* v. *Newton* [1940] 1 K.B. 415; *Jones* v. *Price* [1965] 2 Q.B. 618.
[8] See, *e.g.*, *Hall* v. *National Provincial Bank Ltd.* [1939] L.J.N.C.C.R. 185.
[9] Thus a right to specific performance is assignable: *ante*, p. 628.
[10] s. 136, replacing J.A., 1873, s. 25 (6); see Snell, *Equity*, 70 *et seq.*

to the period for which the original covenantor retained his land, but might continue indefinitely. Once it could be shown that the necessary conditions had been satisfied, a restrictive covenant might continue to burden one plot of land for the benefit of another irrespective of the number of times each plot changed hands. The position must now be examined in some detail; for the sake of completeness, the position of the original parties to the covenant will be considered as well, although that is simply a matter of privity of contract.

Sect. 1.   At Law

A.   *The Benefit of the Covenant*

I.   THE ORIGINAL COVENANTEE

1. Enforcement.   The original covenantee can always enforce any express [11] covenant against the original covenantor, provided that the covenantee has not expressly assigned the benefit to some other person.[12] But if the covenant was made for the benefit of land belonging to the covenantee, and the covenantee has parted with the land before the breach occurred, he may only recover nominal damages, for the loss is likely to fall not on him but on the assignee of the land. The assignee himself may or may not be able to sue, as is explained below.

2. Parties to the deed.   Normally the original covenantee will be a party to the deed containing the covenant. At common law it was a strict rule that no one could sue on a deed made *inter partes* who was not a party to it.[13] This rule was never applied to a deed poll, *i.e.*, a .deed executed by one party alone as a unilateral act, so that any person with whom he purported to contract could enforce the contract.[14]

3. Non-parties.   The rule for deeds *inter partes* has been qualified by the Law of Property Act, 1925, s. 56,[15] under which a person may take an interest in " land or other property " or the benefit of any

---

[11] Implied covenants may be sued upon only where there is a present relationship of landlord and tenant, *i.e.*, they depend upon privity of estate, not privity of contract: *ante*, p. 676.

[12] *Ante*, p. 724, n. 17.

[13] *Lord Southampton* v. *Brown* (1827) 6 B. & C. 718.

[14] *Chelsea & Walham Green B. S.* v. *Armstrong* [1951] Ch. 853 (registered transfer (see *post*, p. 1073) held equivalent to deed poll, so that a covenant therein could be enforced by the covenantee, even though not a party to the transfer).

[15] Replacing with amendments R.P.A., 1845, s. 5, which replaced the Transfer of Property Act, 1844, s. 11, in a narrower form.

condition, covenant or agreement respecting land or other property, " although he may not be named as a party to the conveyance or other instrument." " Land or other property " may mean " land or other real property " or it may extend to personal property as well [16]; but on any footing the section appears to apply only to agreements which relate to some pre-existing property and not, *e.g.*, to contracts for personal services.[17] To this extent this provision has abolished the common law rule requiring anyone claiming any benefit under a deed to be named as a party to it, and so it extends in an important way the class of persons who can be brought within the benefit of a covenant. For example, if V sells land to P, and P enters into a covenant with V " and also with the owners for the time being " of certain adjacent plots of land, the persons who are the adjoining owners at the time of the covenant can sue, for although they are not named as parties to the conveyance, they are covenantees just as much as is V [18]; and if the benefit of the covenant is capable of running with land (as explained below), it can benefit the successors in title of the adjoining owners.

4. Ambit of section 56. The true aim of section 56 seems to be not to allow a third party to sue on a contract merely because it is made for his benefit; the contract must purport to be made *with* him.[19] Just as, under the first part of the section, a person cannot benefit by a conveyance unless it purports to be made *to* him (as grantee), so he cannot benefit by a covenant which does not purport to be made *with* him (as covenantee).[20] On this view, if A covenants

---

[16] See the differing views in *Beswick* v. *Beswick* [1968] A.C. 58, where the majority took the former view and the minority took the latter (and preferable) view: see at pp. 76, 81, 87, 94, 105.

[17] But see *Beswick* v. *Beswick, supra*, at p. 76.

[18] *Westhoughton U. D. C.* v. *Wigan Coal & Iron Co. Ltd.* [1919] 1 Ch. 159; *Re Ecclesiastical Commissioners for England's Conveyance* [1936] Ch. 430. The suggestion that the section is confined to covenants running with the land is denied at p. 438; but there is the authority of the Court of Appeal for it in *Forster* v. *Elvet Colliery Co. Ltd.* [1908] 1 K.B. 629 (affd. *sub nom. Dyson* v. *Forster* [1909] A.C. 98) and *Grant* v. *Edmondson* [1931] 1 Ch. 1. Since s. 56 may now extend to property other than land the suggestion seems difficult to justify.

[19] *Beswick* v. *Beswick, supra*, at p. 106 *per* Lord Upjohn, Lord Pearce concurring. Though said (at p. 105) to be " obiter and tentative," this judgment confirms what has long been the better opinion: see *White* v. *Bijou Mansions Ltd.* [1937] Ch. 610 at 624 (in C.A. [1938] Ch. 351); *Re Sinclair's Life Policy* [1938] Ch. 799; *Re Foster* [1938] 3 All E.R. 357 at 365; *Re Miller's Agreement* [1947] Ch. 615. For Lord Denning's opinions to the contrary see *Drive Yourself Hire Co. (London) Ltd.* v. *Strutt* [1954] 1 Q.B. 250 (*cf. Smith* v. *River Douglas Catchment Board* [1949] 2 K.B. 500); *Beswick* v. *Beswick* [1966] Ch. 538. For criticism, see [1954] C.L.J. 66 (H.W.R.W.); and *cf.* (1954) 70 L.Q.R. 467 (E.J.P.).

[20] s. 56 of the L.P.A., 1925, " can be called in aid only by a person who, although not a party to the conveyance or other instrument in question, is yet a person to whom that conveyance or other instrument purports to grant something or with whom some agreement or covenant is thereby purported to be made ": *Re Foster, supra*, at p. 365, *per* Crossman J., summarising earlier cases; and similarly *White* v. *Bijou Mansions Ltd., supra*, at p. 625, *per* Simonds J.

with B that A will convey land to C, B can enforce the covenant but C cannot; for B is a covenantee, but C is merely a third party. But if A's covenant is expressed to be made with B and C, C can enforce it as well as B, even though B was a party to the deed and C was not.[21] This interpretation follows the sound principle that a promisor should be liable only to those to whom he chooses to engage himself.

The Court of Appeal, however, has asserted that section 56 enables a mere third party, not being a promisee, to enforce a contract made for his benefit.[22] Although the House of Lords rejected this argument, the opinion of the majority was that section 56 was inapplicable because it was confined to real property,[23] not because it could not benefit a mere third party. On this footing the Court of Appeal's revolutionary doctrine may still be operative as regards real property.[24] But two opinions were given to the contrary,[25] after a review of the history and true purpose of the section, and these are altogether more convincing.

5. Non-existent persons. It seems to be clear that a person cannot be a covenantee within the scope of section 56 unless he is in existence and identifiable at the time when the covenant is made.[26] Thus in the example given,[1] the covenant cannot be made to benefit future purchasers of plots directly; but they may obtain the benefit of it through V or one of the previous plot-owners under the rules relating to assignees. In the same way, if a covenant is expressed to be made with an owner of land and his successors in title, only the present owner is an original covenantee; successors in title can claim the benefit only as assignees.

II. ASSIGNEES

The benefit of a covenant can run with land at common law if three conditions are fulfilled. Before setting them out it is well to observe that two other matters are immaterial at law although very important

---

[21] *Stromdale & Ball Ltd.* v. *Burden* [1952] Ch. 223 is a borderline case.
[22] *Beswick* v. *Beswick* [1966] Ch. 538 (C.A.); [1968] A.C. 58 (H.L.). A coal merchant transferred his business to his nephew, the nephew promising to pay an annuity of £5 a week to the merchant's widow; held (by the Court of Appeal), the widow could enforce the promise under s. 56. The House of Lords upheld her claim, but only *qua* the merchant's administratrix, representing the promisee personally. The House surmounted the difficulty that the merchant's estate suffered no loss by granting specific performance.
[23] See note 16, *supra.*
[24] Lords Hodson and Guest seem to support this: see at pp. 80, 85, 87.
[25] *Per* Lords Upjohn and Pearce. See note 19, *supra.*
[26] See cases cited in n. 18, *supra.*
[1] *Ante*, p. 745.

in equity, as will appear later. (i) It is immaterial whether the covenant is negative (not to do something) or positive (to do something). Thus the common law doctrine applies equally to a covenant not to build on the land purchased by P or a covenant to supply pure water to the land retained by V.[2] (ii) It makes no difference that the covenant has nothing to do with any land of the covenantor.[3] In an old case a prior covenanted with the lord of a manor that he and his convent would always sing divine service in the chapel of the manor; and it was held that the lord's successors in title could sue the prior for non-performance.[4] Similarly the benefit of the covenants for title in a conveyance ran with the land conveyed at common law.[5]

For the benefit of a covenant to run at common law, the following conditions must be satisfied.

1. The covenant must touch and concern land of the covenantee.[6] Since it is the benefit, not the burden, of the covenant which can run with land, there must be land to be benefited even though there is not land to be burdened. The covenant must therefore be made for the benefit of land owned by the covenantee (*i.e.*, V in the above examples) at the time of the covenant, and not merely for V's personal advantage.[7] Where the covenant is made between landlord and tenant the lessor's reversion alone will not rank as " land " for this purpose, for it will be recalled that the benefit of covenants could not run with the reversion at common law, before the statute of 1540.[8] But some incorporeal hereditaments rank as " land." Thus the benefit of a covenant to repair a footpath may run with an easement of way over the path,[9] although the benefit of a covenant to pay a rentcharge will not run with the rentcharge.[10]

In general the test for determining whether a covenant touches and concerns the land is the same as for covenants in a lease.[11] The

---

[2] *Sharp* v. *Waterhouse* (1857) 7 E. & B. 816; *Shayler* v. *Woolf* [1946] 1 All E.R. 464 at 467 (affd. [1946] 2 All E.R. 54; [1946] Ch. 320).

[3] *Smith* v. *River Douglas Catchment Board* [1949] 2 K.B. 500 (covenant by Board to maintain river banks held enforceable both by assignee of covenantee and by assignee's tenant).

[4] *The Prior's Case* (also known as *Pakenham's Case*) Y.B. 42 Edw. 3, Hil., pl. 14 (1368); Co.Litt. 385a; Smith's L.C. i, 55.

[5] Smith's L.C. i, 73; *ante*, p. 605. These covenants now run by force of L.P.A., 1925, s. 76 (6).

[6] Co.Litt. 385a; *Rogers* v. *Hosegood* [1900] 2 Ch. 388; *Formby* v. *Barker* [1903] 2 Ch. 539 at 554; *Dyson* v. *Forster* [1909] A.C. 98; *Smith* v. *River Douglas Catchment Board* [1949] 2 K.B. 500 at 506.

[7] *Rogers* v. *Hosegood, supra*.

[8] *Ante*, p. 734.

[9] *Gaw* v. *Coras Iompair Eireann* [1953] I.R. 232; but *Grant* v. *Edmondson, infra*, was not cited.

[10] *Grant* v. *Edmondson* [1931] 1 Ch. 1; *ante*, p. 739, *post*, p. 796.

[11] *Ante*, p. 724.

connection between the covenant and the land concerned need not appear from the terms of the covenant, but may be proved by extrinsic evidence.[12]

2. The covenantee must have a legal estate in the land benefited.

A common law court could take no cognisance of an equitable interest before 1875,[13] and if the covenantee was merely an equitable owner (*e.g.*, a mortgagor, prior to 1926) the benefit of a covenant could not run with his interest at law.[14]

The old rule was that the assignee seeking to enforce the covenant must have the same legal estate as the covenantee, the benefit being annexed to that estate alone.[15] Thus if the covenant was made with the fee simple owner, a purchaser of the fee simple could enforce it but a lessee could not.[16] But covenants made after 1925 can be enforced by any tenant or other successor in title of the covenantee. Accordingly, in a case [17] where a catchment board covenanted to maintain the banks of a river, and the land was later sold to a purchaser who let it to a tenant, both the purchaser and his tenant were able to recover damages for injury to their respective interests (the reversion and the tenancy) after the land had been inundated due to breach of the covenant.

This beneficial change is held to have been effected by the Law of Property Act, 1925, s. 78,[18] which provides that " a covenant relating to any land of the covenantee shall be deemed to be made with the covenantee and his successors in title and the persons deriving title under him or them, and shall have effect as if such successors and other persons were expressed." This provision seems, like its partner section 79,[19] to be merely a " word-saving " section, intended to save trouble to draftsmen but not to alter general rules of law. But the court has now interpreted it as making a substantial amendment, apparently because of the wide reference to derivative titles, specially inserted in 1925.[20] Even if this reasoning provokes doubt, the result is welcome.

---

12 *Smith* v. *River Douglas Catchment Board, supra*, at p. 508.
13 *Ante*, p. 128.
14 *Webb* v. *Russell* (1789) 3 T.R. 393; *Rogers* v. *Hosegood* [1900] 2 Ch. 388 at 404.
15 See H.E.L. iii, 158; Holmes, *The Common Law*, 394 *et seq*. But in *The Prior's Case, supra*, the covenantee was owner in fee simple and the successful plaintiff was tenant in tail.
16 *Westhoughton U. D. C.* v. *Wigan Coal & Iron Co. Ltd.* [1919] 1 Ch. 159; but this point was not clearly decided.
17 *Smith* v. *River Douglas Catchment Board* [1949] 2 K.B. 500; *ante*, p. 747, n. 3.
18 Replacing a more restricted provision of C.A., 1881, s. 58: see *post*, p. 764.
19 See *ante*, p. 723.
20 *Smith* v. *River Douglas Catchment Board, supra*. For this argument see Smith's L.C. i, 76. For criticism, see (1956) 20 Conv.(N.S.) 43 at 53 (D. W. Elliott). Before 1882 the usual words to insert were " heirs and assigns," and this was the

B. The Burden of the Covenant

The rule at law is that the burden of a covenant will not pass with freehold land.[21] Yet what cannot be done directly may to some extent be done indirectly. There are the following possibilities.[22]

1. Chain of covenants. If V sells land to P, and P covenants, for example, to erect and maintain a fence, P will remain liable to V on the covenant by virtue of privity of contract even if P sells the land to Q. P will accordingly protect himself by extracting from Q a covenant of indemnity against future breaches of the covenant to fence. If Q then fails to maintain the fence, V cannot sue Q, but he can sue P, and P can then sue Q on the covenant for indemnity.[23] Similarly if P dies without having parted with the land, P's personal representatives remain liable in damages, and may require an indemnity from anyone to whom P may have left the land by his will.[24] But a chain of purely personal covenants is unsatisfactory for many reasons. The longer it grows, the more liable it is to be broken by the insolvency or disappearance of one of the parties, or by the neglect of one of them to take a covenant of indemnity from his successor; and the remedy can only be in damages, whereas an injunction is the remedy usually desired.

2. Enlarged long lease. A more direct method, though an artificial device of untested validity, and subject to difficulties, is to insert the covenant in a long lease which can be enlarged into a fee simple under the statutory power.[25] If the lease is enlarged, the resultant fee simple is by statute made subject to all the same covenants, provisions and obligations as the lease would have been subject to had it not been enlarged.[26] It seems that a fee simple may by these means be made subject to any covenant which touches and concerns the land, *e.g.*, a covenant to repair.[27]

phrase used in C.A., 1881, s. 58. Those words were not necessary in order that the benefit should run (*Lougher* v. *Williams* (1673) 2 Lev. 92), but they helped to show that it was not intended to be personal to the covenantee and so incapable of running. "Heirs" is now an obsolete term, and further explanation of the change of language in 1925 hardly seems necessary.

21 *Ante*, p. 722.
22 See Report of the Committee on Positive Covenants Affecting Land, 1965, Cmnd. 2719, para. 8. Difficulties and additional possibilities are canvassed in Farrand, *Contract and Conveyance* (2nd ed. 1973), p. 423 *et seq.*; (1973) 37 Conv. (N.S.) 194 (A. Prichard). *Shiloh Spinners Ltd.* v. *Harding* [1973] A.C. 691 at 717 suggests the further possibility of supporting the covenant by a right of entry for breach.
23 All the actions may be heard together by bringing in indemnifiers as third parties: R.S.C. 1965, Ord. 16. This makes no difference to the substantive law.
24 A.E.A., 1925, s. 36 (10).
25 L.P.A., 1925, s. 153, for which see *ante*, p. 670; and see *Re M'Naul's Estate* [1902] 1 I.R. 114. See generally (1958) 22 Conv.(N.S.) 101 (T. P. D. Taylor).
26 L.P.A., 1925, s. 153 (8).
27 Challis 334, 335; Hood & Challis, *Property Acts*, 282.

3. Condition of taking benefits. When adjacent owners make reciprocal covenants containing some positive obligation, it may seem anomalous that the benefit will run with their lands but the burden will not. A problem of this kind has, however, been solved by an extension of an old rule relating to deeds: it is said that a person who claims the benefit of a deed must also submit to its obligations.[27a] Thus where purchasers of plots on a building estate execute deeds of covenant which give them the right to use the roads on the estate but require them and their successors to pay periodical contributions towards the cost of upkeep, their successors in title cannot take the benefit of the right to use the roads without submitting to liability for the contributions.[28] The result is that positive burdens may in this way be made to run with the land not absolutely but conditionally: the burden will bind successors in title only so long as they choose to take the benefit,[28a] though often they will have little real choice in the matter.

This result hardly seems to be supported by the old rule as to deeds, which is narrow and technical. In its ordinary form it is no more than a rule that he who is named as a party to a deed and knowingly takes the benefit of it is bound by it, even if he does not execute it[29]; in another form it is that a person to whom an estate is granted subject to conditions can take the estate only if he becomes bound by the conditions, even if he is not a party to the grant.[30] But in its new form the rule does not operate unreasonably, provided that the benefit claimed is one to which the claimant would not otherwise be entitled.[31] The same result could be reached by the alternative method of treating use of the roads by each successor as acceptance of an implied offer of the right to use them on payment of the contributions.

Sect. 2. In Equity : Restrictive Covenants

1. Law and equity. The relationship between the divergent rules of common law and of equity is best understood by imagining the two separate jurisdictions which existed before 1875.[32] Equity's

---

27a For this principle as affecting licences, see *post* p. 779.
28 *Halsall* v. *Brizell* [1957] Ch. 169; see (1957) 73 L.Q.R. 154 (R.E.M.); [1957] C.L.J. 35 (H.W.R.W.). See also *Westhoughton U. D. C.* v. *Wigan Coal & Iron Co. Ltd.* [1919] 1 Ch. 159 at 174. *Cf. ante,* p. 599, *post,* pp. 1030, 1031.
28a *Parkinson* v. *Reid* (1966) 56 D.L.R. (2d) 315.
29 *R.* v. *Houghton-le-Spring* (1819) 2 B. & Ald. 375; *Webb* v. *Spicer* (1849) 13 Q.B. 886 at 893; *Lady Naas* v. *Westminster Bank Ltd.* [1940] A.C. 366 at 373; Norton, *Deeds,* 26, 27.   30 Co.Litt. 230b.
31 Otherwise an owner could be said to be subject to any positive covenants contained in his title deeds merely because he derives title through those deeds. That would contradict the rules as to the running of covenants.
32 *Ante,* p. 127.

jurisdiction had, furthermore, two distinct aspects of its own. First, equity followed the law and provided better remedies than damages. Secondly, equity broke away from the rule that the burden of a covenant affecting land can only run with a lease, and allowed *restrictive* covenants to be enforced even against later owners of a freehold.

2. Equitable remedies. The special equitable remedies may be disposed of shortly. The value of a covenant affecting land is generally of a " real " character; that is to say, it lies in continued observance rather than in monetary compensation for a breach. Therefore an injunction, an equitable remedy, is usually more valuable than damages, at any rate where the obligation is merely negative. An injunction would normally be awarded [33] in a court of equity (and since 1875 in any Division of the High Court [34]) in any case where a covenant was enforceable at law.

3. Restrictive covenants. In inventing special rules about restrictive covenants equity added a new chapter to the law of property. The essentials of a restrictive covenant are that it is negative, and made for the benefit of land belonging to the covenantee. An example is where V, having two adjacent houses, sells one of them to P, and P covenants not to carry on any trade or business in the house he has bought, in order to preserve the residential value of V's other house.[34a] The real starting point, after some doubts [35] and precursors,[36] was the decision in *Tulk* v. *Moxhay* [37] in 1848, a time when the full effect of the vast expansion in industrial and building activities was being felt. It was held that a restrictive covenant could be enforced against a later purchaser unless (as always, in equity) he bought without notice of the covenant. Many rules developed round this new doctrine, first as regards the burden and then as regards the benefit of such covenants. In practice today it is the rules about the benefit which most often present difficulties. The heart of the subject, however, lies in the rules about the burden.

[33] *Doherty* v. *Allman* (1878) 3 App.Cas. 709 at 719.
[34] *Ante*, p. 128.
[34a] Such covenants are not in unlawful restraint of trade when given on the acquisition of new property. It may be otherwise when the property already belonged to the covenantor: *Esso Petroleum Co. Ltd.* v. *Harper's Garage (Stourport) Ltd.* [1968] A.C. 269 ; *Cleveland Petroleum Co. Ltd.* v. *Dartstone Ltd.* [1969] 1 W.L.R. 116. The remarkable operation of this distinction, suggested for the first time during the argument in the *Esso* case in the House of Lords, is illustrated by the example put in argument at p. 289 of that case.
[35] The doctrine was denied in *Keppell* v. *Bailey* (1834) 2 My. & K. 517 at 546, 547 (on which see Challis 185) and treated as still unsettled in *Bristow* v. *Wood* (1844) 1 Coll.C.C. 480.
[36] *Whatman* v. *Gibson* (1838) 9 Sim. 196; *Mann* v. *Stephens* (1846) 15 Sim. 377.
[37] 2 Ph. 774.

A. The Burden of the Covenant

1. The decision. *Tulk* v. *Moxhay*,[38] decided in 1848, laid the
first foundations of the modern doctrine of restrictive covenants.
Previously the burden of a covenant (not made in a lease) would no
more run in equity than it would at law. But in that case it was
held by Lord Cottenham L.C., affirming Lord Langdale M.R.,[38a] that a
covenant to maintain the garden at Leicester Square uncovered with
any buildings would be enforced by injunction against a purchaser
of the land who bought with notice of the covenant. Thus was
invented a new interest in land,[39] purely equitable in nature. No
longer was a negative covenant enforceable only against the covenantor or his personal representatives as a mere contract: it was now
enforceable against his successors in title as an incumbrance, a right
over some other person's land.

2. Original basis. For some while the question was thought to
depend on two things only: the character of the covenant, and the
fact of notice. A person who took land with notice that it was bound
by some restriction could not, it was thought, disregard that restriction. On this footing it was immaterial whether the restriction had
been imposed to benefit other land or merely the covenantee personally.[40] In fact, the suit in *Tulk* v. *Moxhay* had been brought by
the original covenantee, who had other property in Leicester Square,
and Lord Cottenham had relied on the argument that if the covenant
did not run " it would be impossible for an owner of land to sell part
of it without incurring the risk of rendering what he retains
worthless." [41]

3. Dominant tenement. This indeed is the foundation of the
doctrine; and since 1903 it has been settled that equity will enforce a
restrictive covenant against a purchaser only if it was made for the
protection of other land.[42] Restrictive covenants came to resemble
easements as being rights over one plot of land (" the servient tenement ") existing for the benefit of another plot of land (" the dominant
tenement "). It was said that the new principle was " either an
extension in equity of the doctrine of *Spencer's Case* to another line
of cases, or else an extension in equity of the doctrine of negative
easements; such, for instance, as a right to the access of light, which

---

38 (1848) 2 Ph. 774. For a sequel, see *Tulk* v. *Metropolitan Board of Works* (1868)
   16 W.R. 212.
38a (1848) 11 Beav. 571. The appeal was decided a mere 16 days after the decision
   below.
39 *Cf. ante*, p. 132. See the survey at (1971) 87 L.Q.R. 539 (D. J. Hayton).
40 *Catt* v. *Tourle* (1869) 4 Ch.App. 654 and *Luker* v. *Dennis* (1877) 7 Ch.D. 227
   are two examples which are no longer good law.
41 *Tulk* v. *Moxhay, supra*, 2 Ph. at p. 777.
42 *Formby* v. *Barker* [1903] 2 Ch. 539; *L.C.C.* v. *Allen* [1914] 3 K.B. 642 at 659,
   660. There are certain exceptions to this rule; *post*, p. 756.

prevents the owner of the servient tenement from building so as to obstruct the light."[43] But in reality the rule was a new departure, and eventually it was recognised that a new type of equitable interest had been created.[44]

4. Essentials. It was accordingly established that this new liability could run with land only where (i) the covenant was restrictive, *i.e.*, negative, in nature; (ii) two plots of land were concerned, one bearing the burden and the other receiving the benefit; and (iii) the defendant could not set up the overriding defence in equity of purchase of the legal estate for value without notice. After noticing the special position of the person who originally entered into the covenant, we will deal with these conditions *seriatim*.

I. THE ORIGINAL COVENANTOR

The original covenantor normally remains liable on the covenant, even if there is no dominant tenement, and even if he has parted with the servient tenement. This is because his liability is purely contractual and exists quite apart from the law of property, just as in the case of an original tenant who has assigned his lease.[45] Before 1926 the covenantor would usually covenant " for himself, his heirs and assigns, and other persons claiming under him," so giving in effect a personal warranty that neither he nor any of his successors in title would infringe the terms.[46] If the covenant is made after 1925 the effect is the same even though these words are omitted,[47] and the covenantor can escape liability only if there is an express exemption in the covenant.

II. ASSIGNEES

An assignee of the original covenantor's land is bound by the covenant only if four conditions are fulfilled.

---

[43] *London and South Western Ry.* v. *Gomm* (1882) 20 Ch.D. 562 at 583, *per* Jessel M.R. The three criticisms of this in Behan's *Covenants* (pp. 45, 46) are based on inserting into the quotation words which Jessel M.R. did not use (" common law "), and ignoring words that he did use (" extension " and " in equity ").

[44] *Re Nisbet and Potts' Contract* [1905] 1 Ch. 391 at 396 (on appeal, [1906] 1 Ch. 386).

[45] *Ante,* p. 723.

[46] *L.C.C.* v. *Allen* [1914] 3 K.B. 642 at 660, 673 ; *cf. Baily* v. *De Crespigny* (1869) L.R. 4 Q.B. 180 at 186. But a covenant mentioning assigns might sometimes be construed as doing so only in order to make the covenant run with the land, and not in order to make the covenantor personally liable for their acts : *Powell* v. *Hemsley* [1909] 1 Ch. 680 ; 2 Ch. 252 ; but *quaere* whether this interpretation was correct.

[47] L.P.A., 1925, s. 79, explained *ante,* p. 723.

1. The covenant must be negative in nature

(a) *Negativity.* After a few cases in which the court was prepared to enforce a positive covenant,[48] the rule was settled in 1881 that only a negative covenant would be enforced by equity.[49] The equitable interest created by the covenant is one primarily enforceable by injunction, and whereas a negative injunction restraining the commission or continuance of specified acts normally presents no difficulties of enforcement, equity has long been chary of making orders to perform a series of acts requiring supervision,[50] even though it has the necessary jurisdiction to decree specific performance or grant a mandatory injunction,[51] ordering specified acts to be done. The doctrine is confined to negative covenants because effect can be given to these " by means of the land itself." [52]

(b) *Substance.* The question is whether the covenant is negative in nature: it is immaterial whether the wording is positive or negative. Thus the covenant in *Tulk* v. *Moxhay*[53] was positive in wording (to maintain the Leicester Square garden " in an open state, uncovered with any buildings ") but negative in nature, for it merely bound the covenantor to refrain from building, without requiring him to do any positive act. A test which is often applied is whether the covenant requires expenditure of money for its performance; if the covenant requires the covenantor " to put his hand into his pocket," it is not negative in nature.[54] But the converse does not necessarily follow; a covenant that can be performed without expense may still require some positive act and so not be restrictive. A covenant to use the premises as a private dwelling-house only is negative in nature, for really it is a prohibition against use for other purposes[55]; and the same applies to a covenant to give the first refusal of a plot of land,[56] for in effect it is a covenant not to sell to anyone else until the covenantee has had an opportunity of buying. But a covenant " not to let the premises fall into disrepair," despite its apparently negative form, is in substance positive, for it can be performed only by the expenditure of money on repairs.

(c) *Severance.* If a covenant has both positive and negative elements in it, the negative element may bind the land even though

---

48 *Morland* v. *Cook* (1868) L.R. 6 Eq. 252 ; *Cooke* v. *Chilcott* (1876) 3 Ch.D. 694. For the enforcement of positive covenants today, see *ante*, p. 749.
49 *Haywood* v. *Brunswick Permanent Benefit B. S.* (1881) 8 Q.B.D. 403.
50 See *ante*, p. 701.
51 See *Jackson* v. *Normanby Brick Co.* [1899] 1 Ch. 438 (order to demolish buildings erected in breach of covenant).
52 *Re Nisbet & Potts' Contract* [1905] 1 Ch. 391 at 397, *per* Farwell J.
53 *Ante*, p. 757.
54 *Haywood* v. *Brunswick Permanent Benefit B. S.*, *supra*, at pp. 409, 410.
55 *e.g.*, *German* v. *Chapman* (1877) 7 Ch.D. 271.
56 See *Manchester Ship Canal Co.* v. *Manchester Racecourse Co.* [1901] 2 Ch. 37 ; *Lange* v. *Lange* [1966] N.Z.L.R. 1057.

the positive cannot.[57] Even a positive obligation may be binding if it is no more than a condition of a negative one; thus a covenant to submit plans before building may be enforceable against a purchaser as a covenant not to build without first submitting plans.[58]

(d) *Common covenants.* The restrictive covenants most frequently met with in practice are covenants against building on land, and against carrying on any trade or business (or certain specified trades or businesses) on the premises.[58a] It is common to find such covenants inserted in conveyances or leases of urban property.

(e) *Positive covenants.* It has been recommended that the law should provide for the running of positive as well as negative covenants. Apart from limited statutory exceptions, there is at present no satisfactory way of imposing positive obligations (*e.g.*, to repair walls and fences) so as to bind successors in title where the property is freehold. There is no such difficulty with leasehold property, but the declining popularity of leasehold tenure makes the leasehold system less useful. This handicap on freehold property is illogical. It is particularly troublesome in the case of divided buildings, blocks of flats and building estates, where there is a need for permanent obligations to maintain the property and to contribute to the maintenance of common facilities and services, and where in the absence of binding covenants owners may be unable to obtain mortgages. Schemes for allowing such obligations to run with land have therefore been proposed.[59] Other countries have made statutory provision for this, including elaborate schemes of management which can be adopted for blocks of flats and similar developments. This is known in North America as the law of condominium, and in Australasia as that of strata titles.

2. The covenant must be made for the protection of land retained by the covenantee.[60] It is axiomatic that the justification for con-

---

[57] *Shepherd Homes Ltd.* v. *Sandham (No. 2)* [1971] 1 W.L.R. 1062. Thus in *Tulk* v. *Moxhay* (*ante*, p. 751) the covenant was to maintain the garden as well as not to build upon it.

[58] *Powell* v. *Hemsley* [1909] 1 Ch. 680; 2 Ch. 252; and see *Westhoughton U. D. C.* v. *Wigan Coal & Iron Co. Ltd.* [1919] 1 Ch. 159 (not to let down surface without paying compensation).

[58a] See, however, *Petrofina (Gt. Britain) Ltd.* v. *Martin* [1966] Ch. 146. *Quaere* whether a covenant restraining alienation is within the doctrine: see *Caldy Manor Estate Ltd.* v. *Farrell* [1974] 1 W.L.R. 1303 at 1307; *ante*, p. 78.

[59] Report of the Committee on Positive Covenants Affecting Land, 1965, Cmnd. 2719; Law Commission, Working Paper No. 36 (Appurtenant Rights). The Committee recommended a model management scheme like that of the New South Wales Conveyancing Strata Titles Act 1961. The Commission put forward a new system of "land obligations" comprising and assimilating both easements and covenants, positive and negative. See [1972B] C.L.J. 157 (H.W.R.W.). For the statutory exceptions, see p. 6 of the Report, and *post*, p. 757; see also the Pastoral Measure 1968, cited in (1970) 34 Conv.(N.S.) 1. For flats, see George & George, *The Sale of Flats* (3rd ed. 1970).

[60] *Millbourn* v. *Lyons* [1914] 2 Ch. 231 (the relevant date is that of the covenant, not the contract therefor); *L.C.C.* v. *Allen* [1914] 3 K.B. 642.

verting a personal covenant into an equitable incumbrance is to enable the covenantee to preserve the value of other land of his in the neighbourhood.[61] As with easements,[62] therefore, there must be two plots of land in the case: the doctrine depends on a relation of "dominancy" and "serviency" of lands.[63] Whether this relationship exists is a question of fact in each case, and proof of the facts may make the relationship plain.[64] Proximity is essential: covenants binding land in Hampstead will be too remote to benefit land in Clapham.[65] A covenantee similarly ceases to be able to enforce a covenant (except as against the original covenantor) if he parts with all the land for the benefit of which the covenant was taken,[66] or if it ceases to be reasonably possible to regard the covenant as being for the benefit of the land.[66a] And a covenant made for the protection of a leasehold interest ceases to be enforceable when the lease determines, *e.g.*, by merger in the freehold.[67]

To this rule requiring the covenantee to hold adjacent land there are the following exceptions and qualifications.

(a) *Leases and Mortgages.* The doctrine of *Tulk* v. *Moxhay* applies equally to covenants contained in leases. Moreover, the landlord enjoys an important dispensation: his reversion is apparently a sufficient interest to enable him to sue a sub-lessee in equity on a restrictive covenant contained in the lease. There is therefore no need for any other land which could be called a dominant tenement.[68] This is an important extension of the reversioner's rights, for where the covenant is negative he may have a remedy against someone, such as a sub-tenant, with whom he has neither privity of contract nor privity of estate.[69] A similar dispensation appears to apply to mortgages, so that the mortgagee's interest in the mortgaged land likewise suffices.[70] The authority for these exceptions is not, however, beyond question.

---

61 *Ante*, p. 752.   62 *Post*, p. 806.
63 *Formby* v. *Barker* [1903] 2 Ch. 539 at 552 (Vaughan Williams L.J.). For a detailed account of the evolution of this rule, see *L.C.C.* v. *Allen, supra*, at pp. 664 *et seq.* For dominant and servient tenements, see *post*, p. 806.
64 In other words, it need not appear from the covenant itself: *Tulk* v. *Moxhay* (1848) 2 Ph. 774; *Marten* v. *Flight Refuelling Ltd.* [1962] Ch. 115.
65 *Kelly* v. *Barrett* [1924] 2 Ch. 379 at 404.
66 *Chambers* v. *Randall* [1923] 1 Ch. 149 at 157, 158.
66a *Wrotham Park Estate Co. Ltd.* v. *Parkside Homes Ltd.* [1974] 1 W.L.R. 798.
67 *Golden Lion Hotel (Hunstanton) Ltd.* v. *Carter* [1965] 1 W.L.R. 1189. L.P.A., 1925, s. 139 (*ante*, p 738) does not cover this situation.
68 *Hall* v. *Ewin* (1887) 37 Ch.D. 74, decided before the requirement of benefited land was firmly settled, but approved by Harman L.J. in *Regent Oil Co. Ltd.* v. *J. A. Gregory (Hatch End) Ltd.* [1966] Ch. 402 at 433; and see *Teape* v. *Douse* (1905) 92 L.T. 319.
69 *Cf. ante*, p. 722.
70 *John Brothers Abergarw Brewery Co.* v. *Holmes* [1900] 1 Ch. 188; *Regent Oil Co. Ltd.* v. *J. A. Gregory (Hatch End) Ltd., supra*, per Harman L.J.

(b) *Scheme of development.* The meaning of " scheme of development " will shortly be explained.[71] When, under such a scheme, the common vendor disposes of the last of the plots laid out for development, he may retain no adjacent land. But even though the owners of the other plots are not expressly made covenantees,[72] the last purchaser's covenants are enforceable by them against both the last purchaser himself and his successors in title, so that the rule in *Tulk* v. *Moxhay* applies.

(c) *Statutory exceptions.* The rules applied to private landowners have been modified by numerous statutes for the benefit of public bodies. For example, under the Housing Act, 1957,[73] a local housing authority which is itself the covenantee may enforce a covenant against the covenantor's successors in title to the same extent as if it had been made for the benefit of land belonging to the authority; and so similarly may the National Trust.[74]

(d) *Remedies in contract and tort.* It has recently been held [75] that where there is a covenant not to " cause or permit " land to be used otherwise than for specified purposes, it will be no breach of the covenant for the covenantor to agree to sell the land to a purchaser whom he knows to intend to use it for other purposes, and to assist him in obtaining planning permission for that use. For the vendor, on selling, loses control of the property, and " one cannot permit that which one does not control." [1] But if the covenant had been framed so as to prohibit parting with control in such circumstances, it appears that both the vendor and the purchaser could have been restrained by injunction from completing the sale, and that the covenantee, if he suffered damage, could also have sued the purchaser in tort for wrongfully inducing a breach of contract.[2] A purchaser must therefore remember that even when a covenant will not bind him as a successor in title,[3] he may yet become implicated in a breach of contract by the vendor.

3. The burden of the covenant must have been intended to run with the covenantor's land. A covenant may be so worded as to bind the covenantor alone, and of course in such a case assignees of

---

[71] *Post*, p. 768.   [72] *Ante*, p. 745.
[73] s. 151, replacing Housing Act, 1936, s. 148; and see Town and Country Planning Act 1971, s. 52 (2).
[74] National Trust Act, 1937, s. 8. See, *e.g., Gee* v. *The National Trust* [1966] 1 W.L.R. 170.
[75] *Tophams Ltd.* v. *Earl of Sefton* [1967] 1 A.C. 50 (proposal to build houses on Aintree Racecourse).
[1] *Ibid.*, at p. 65, *per* Lord Hodson.
[2] *Sefton* v. *Tophams Ltd.* [1965] Ch. 1140 (C.A.); reversed, *supra*, n. 75. But there was no appeal against this part of the decision.
[3] In the *Sefton* case, *supra*, the vendor retained no land benefited by the covenant.

the covenantor's land will not be bound by the covenant.[4] But if the covenant is made by the covenantor for himself, his heirs and assigns, the burden will normally run with his land. Covenants relating to the covenantor's land which are made after 1925 are deemed to have been made by the covenantor on behalf of himself, his successors in title, and the persons deriving title under him or them, unless a contrary intention appears.[5] The burden of a covenant restricting the use of land and made since 1925 will therefore prima facie run with the land.[6]

4. The burden of the covenant runs only in equity. There are two principal consequences of the rule that the burden of the covenant runs only in equity.

(a) Only equitable remedies are available. This means in practice that the case must be remediable by injunction, which is the only equitable remedy appropriate to a negative covenant. This is in keeping with the nature of a restrictive covenant as an equitable interest: it is not intended as a subject for monetary compensation, but as a means of preserving the value of land specifically. But it must be remembered that since the Chancery Amendment Act, 1858,[7] the court has been empowered to award damages in any case where an injunction or specific performance could have been awarded. Even now, however, the plaintiff is not, as in an action at law, entitled to insist upon some damages being awarded if he makes out his case,[8] nor can he be awarded damages if he could not have been awarded an injunction.[9]

Like other equitable remedies, an injunction lies in the discretion of the court. This does not mean that it will not be granted as a matter of course in an ordinary case. But it will be refused if it would be inequitable to grant it, as it may be where, for example, the plaintiff has known of the breach for five years, and taken no action[10]; and although failure to enforce a covenant against one person does not necessarily waive it as against others,[11] an injunction may be refused if the plaintiff has exhibited such inactivity in the

---

4 *Re Fawcett and Holmes' Contract* (1889) 42 Ch.D. 150; *Re Royal Victoria Pavilion, Ramsgate* [1961] Ch. 581.
5 L.P.A., 1925, s. 79, explained *ante*, p. 723.
6 The burden of positive covenants cannot run with the land, irrespective of the intention of the parties, and s. 79 does not appear intended to alter this rule: see *ante*, pp. 723, 742, 749. The suggestion in (1955) 19 Conv.(N.S.) 261 seems unsound.
7 s. 2. Though the Act is repealed, the jurisdiction still exists: *Leeds Industrial Co-operative Society Ltd.* v. *Slack* [1924] A.C. 851.
8 See *Kelly* v. *Barrett* [1924] 2 Ch. 379; *cf. ante*, p. 126.
9 *Ante*, p. 126.
10 *Gaskin* v. *Balls* (1879) 13 Ch.D. 324.
11 *German* v. *Chapman* (1877) 7 Ch.D. 271.

face of open breaches of covenant as to justify a reasonable belief that he no longer intends to enforce the covenant.[12] It is also possible for an injunction to be refused because the character of the neighbourhood has been so completely changed that the covenant has become valueless.[13] But otherwise a restrictive covenant remains enforceable indefinitely, even after the perpetuity period has run.[14]

(*b*) *A purchaser without notice is not bound.* A restrictive covenant suffers from the infirmity of all equitable interests, namely, that it will not be enforced against a bona fide purchaser for value of a legal estate [15] without notice of the covenant,[16] or someone claiming through such a person.[17] A restrictive covenant is therefore enforceable against a squatter (a wrongful occupier), for he is not a purchaser.[18]

Since any restrictive covenants are usually part of the terms of a sale or other disposition, they are normally set out or referred to in the conveyance. Thus they are "brought on to the title," so that any later purchaser will have notice of them, and there is little danger of a purchase without notice destroying the benefit. Even if the covenant was given in a document lying behind the root of title, any later conveyance will probably allude to the covenant's existence, so that notice will be transmitted to future purchasers. This used to be the position in the case of freehold conveyances. In the case of leases the situation is much less satisfactory, owing to the set of problems created by the rule in *Patman* v. *Harland* and its reversal by the Law of Property Act, 1925, s. 44 (5). As has already been explained,[19] the dangers which the Act has created apply particularly to such restrictive covenants as are not registrable.

The doctrine of notice was radically altered by the Land Charges Act, 1925.[20] A restrictive covenant made after 1925 otherwise than between lessor and lessee is registrable as a land charge [21]; and if it is not registered it is void against a subsequent purchaser for money or money's worth of a legal estate in the land, even

---

12 See *Chatsworth Estates Co.* v. *Fewell* [1931] 1 Ch. 224.
13 *Chatsworth Estates Co.* v. *Fewell, supra*; and see *Westripp* v. *Baldock* [1939] 1 All E.R. 279. In the former case (at pp. 227, 228), it was doubted whether it was legitimate to consider (as was done in *Sober* v. *Sainsbury* [1913] 2 Ch. 513) changes in property outside the district. For the discharge of obsolete covenants, see *post*, p. 773.
14 *Mackenzie* v. *Childers* (1889) 43 Ch.D. 265 at 279.
15 Not a mere equitable interest: *London & South Western Ry.* v. *Gomm* (1882) 20 Ch.D. 562 at 583 ; *Osborne* v. *Bradley* [1903] 2 Ch. 446 at 451.
16 *Ibid.*; *ante*, p. 121.
17 *Wilkes* v. *Spooner* [1911] 2 K.B. 473; *ante*, p. 125.
18 *Re Nisbet and Potts' Contract* [1906] 1 Ch. 386.
19 See *ante*, p. 706.
20 Replaced by L.C.A. 1972. See *ante*, p. 144; *post*, p. 1048.
21 *Post*, p. 1042.

though he purchases with notice of it. The importance of this change has been stressed elsewhere, [21a] and the Land Charges Acts will be dealt with later.[21b] Restrictive covenants are among the commonest of registrable interests, and the covenantee must now protect himself by registration, otherwise the covenant will become unenforceable by injunction upon a sale of the burdened land. But two large classes of restrictive covenants are unaffected by the Act: those made before 1926, and those made between landlord and tenant.[22] Registration after 1925 was clearly impracticable for the first class, and was probably thought unduly troublesome for the second. Covenants of these two classes are therefore still governed by the old doctrine of notice (with the variations already mentioned in the case of leases). Therefore whenever it is sought to enforce a restrictive covenant against a purchaser, the first questions to ask are what was the date of the covenant and what was the relationship of the parties to it.

B. The Benefit of the Covenant

In order to enforce a covenant, the plaintiff must show that he is entitled to the benefit of it. The original covenantee can of course sue the original covenantor, and he can also sue successors in title of the original covenantor, if the burden has passed to them. But he cannot sue the successors in title if he has parted with all the land for the benefit of which the covenant was taken,[23] for equity would not enforce the doctrine of *Tulk* v. *Moxhay* where the covenant was divorced from the land that it was intended to protect.[24]

As for successors in title of the original covenantee, it should be remembered that the benefit of a restrictive covenant could, and still can, run with the covenantee's land at common law, without the help of equity, under the rules already stated.[25] In order to succeed at law the plaintiff must be legal owner of the land to which the covenant relates. But in equity he can succeed if he has some lesser estate,[26] or is merely an equitable owner, such as a successor under the covenantee's will or intestacy who has not yet obtained a legal title,[27] or a person for whom the benefit of the covenant is

---

[21a] *Ante*, p. 145; *post*, p. 1049. [21b] *Post*, p. 1042.

[22] See *Newman* v. *Real Estate Debenture Corpn. Ltd.* [1940] 1 All E.R. 141 at 149, 150.

[23] *Chambers* v. *Randall* [1923] 1 Ch. 149.

[24] See *ibid.*, at pp. 157, 158; *post*, p. 763.

[25] *Ante*, p. 746.

[26] *Taite* v. *Gosling* (1879) 11 Ch.D. 273 (tenant of purchaser from covenantee).

[27] *Lord Northbourne* v. *Johnston* [1922] 2 Ch. 309; *Newton Abbot Co-operative Society Ltd.* v. *Williamson & Treadgold Ltd.* [1952] Ch. 286; *Earl of Leicester* v. *Wells-next-the-Sea U.D.C.* [1973] Ch. 110. Another such case is that of a mortgagor before 1926: *Fairclough* v. *Marshall* (1878) 4 Ex.D. 37; *Rogers* v. *Hosegood* [1900] 2 Ch. 388 at 404.

otherwise held upon trust.[28] The benefit is regarded as an interest in property which devolves on death in the ordinary way.[29] In addition there is the possibility, discussed later,[30] that any occupier of the benefited land may be able to sue under section 78 of the Law of Property Act, 1925.

Since 1875 it ought to make no practical difference whether the benefit passes under the rules of law or of equity, since the same court can enforce both. In one leading case the court was prepared to allow the benefit to run with the benefited land at law even where the defendant, being a successor of the covenantor, was liable only in equity.[31] Equity here merely followed the law. But more complicated rules have developed which are now assumed to apply in all actions against such defendants, so making the law follow equity.[32] Some of these rules have been formulated too stringently,[33] and there is now a tendency to relax them. It is also questionable whether they entirely displace the rules of law, which are altogether simpler. This part of the subject has therefore become difficult. The rules may be stated as follows.[34]

1. The covenant must touch and concern land of the covenantee.
This is the same as the rule at common law.[35] The benefit of a covenant can run only with land to which the covenant in fact relates; and in the case of a restrictive covenant the essential object, on which the doctrine of *Tulk* v. *Moxhay* depends,[36] is to preserve the value of the covenantee's other land. Whether that land is in fact benefited must be established by extrinsic evidence.[37]

2. The benefit of the covenant must have passed to the plaintiff in one of three ways: by annexation; by assignment; or under a scheme of development.

Originally this rule was perhaps another way of stating the preceding one. But in the case of negative covenants it has grown to great importance. Where there is a positive covenant requiring the covenantor to do some act on or for the benefit of the land of

---

[28] *Lord Northbourne* v. *Johnston, supra*; *Marten* v. *Flight Refuelling Ltd.* [1962] Ch. 115.
[29] *Ives* v. *Brown* [1919] 2 Ch. 314.　　　　　　　　[30] *Post*, p. 764.
[31] *Rogers* v. *Hosegood* [1900] 2 Ch. 388 at 394, 404.
[32] See *Re Union of London and Smith's Bank Ltd.'s Conveyance* [1933] Ch. 611 at 630, saying that equity prescribed special rules.
[33] *e.g.*, as to identifying the benefited land in the covenant (*post*, p. 762, note 40); as to annexation to each part as well as to the whole (*post*, p. 763); as to schemes of development (*post*, p. 768); and perhaps as to annexation implied from circumstances (*post*, pp. 763, 764).
[34] For a valuable discussion of the earlier cases, see (1938) 6 C.L.J. 343 (S. J. Bailey).
[35] *Rogers* v. *Hosegood* [1900] 2 Ch. 388; *Re Union of London & Smith's Bank Ltd.'s Conveyance* [1933] Ch. 611; *Re Ballard's Conveyance* [1937] Ch. 473; see *ante*, p. 747.　　　　　　　　　　[36] *Ante*, p. 752.
[37] See, *e.g.*, *Re Ballard's Conveyance, supra*.

the covenantee (*e.g.*, to maintain a boundary wall, or to repair river banks), it is usually obvious that the covenant benefits a definable area of land. But a restrictive covenant which merely prohibits the covenantor from some kind of activity on his own land does not on the face of it indicate whether it is intended to benefit any land, still less any particular land, of the covenantee. If the benefit of a restrictive covenant is to run with the covenantee's land, therefore, something further must be done to indicate the land; and that can be done *either* by showing that the benefit is annexed to that land, *or* by expressly assigning the benefit of the covenant along with that land at the time of a later disposition, *or* by showing that that land lies within a scheme of development. The details of these three alternatives are as follows.

I. ANNEXATION

(a) Express annexation

(1) LANGUAGE. The benefit will be effectively annexed to the land so as to run with it if in the instrument the land is sufficiently indicated and the covenant is either stated to be made for the benefit of the land, or stated to be made with the covenantee in his capacity of owner of the land [38]; for then in either case it is obvious that future owners of that land are intended to benefit. A classic formula is " with intent that the covenant may enure to the benefit of the vendors their successors and assigns and others claiming under them to all or any of their lands adjoining." [39] It will be noted that this formula indicates the benefited land only in general terms,[40] so that precise definition is not required.[41] On the other hand, to covenant merely with " the vendors their heirs executors administrators and assigns " is insufficient, for no reference is made to any land, and the reference to executors and others is so wide that it indicates no particular purpose.[42]

---

[38] See *Osborne* v. *Bradley* [1903] 2 Ch. 446 at 450; *Drake* v. *Gray* [1936] Ch. 451 at 466.

[39] *Rogers* v. *Hosegood* [1900] 2 Ch. 388.

[40] Reliance should not be placed on unduly strict statements in *Renals* v. *Cowlishaw* (1879) 11 Ch.D. 866 at 868; *Re Union of London and Smith's Bank Ltd.'s Conveyance* [1933] Ch. 611 at 625; *Newton Abbot Co-operative Society Ltd.* v. *Williamson & Treadgold Ltd.* [1952] Ch. 286 at 289. See [1972B] C.L.J. 157 at 166 (H.W.R.W.).

[41] It is recommended by the Committee on Positive Covenants Affecting Land (Cmnd. 2719 (1965), para. 15) and suggested by the Law Commission (Working Paper No. 36, p. 84) that in future the dominant and servient land should have to be plainly identified by plan or description. This seems unduly formalistic: see [1972B] C.L.J. 157 at 163, 171 (H.W.R.W.).

[42] *Renals* v. *Cowlishaw* (1878) 9 Ch.D. 125; affd. (1879) 11 Ch.D. 866. " Assigns " has been said to be ambiguous, for it may mean assigns of the benefit of the covenant as well as assigns of the land benefited: see *Rogers* v. *Hosegood* [1900] 2 Ch. 388 at 396. " Heirs and assigns " sufficed in *Mann* v. *Stephens* (1846) 15 Sim. 377, though this was before it had been settled that there must be dominant land (*ante*, p. 752).

(2) AREA. There will be no effective annexation if the area is greater than can reasonably be benefited. Thus, where restrictive covenants were stated to be made for the benefit of the " owners for the time being of the Childwickbury estate " (which was about 1,700 acres in extent), it was held that the benefit of a covenant could not run with the estate even in favour of someone acquiring the whole of the estate: the covenant could not benefit the whole of the estate, and the court could not sever the covenant.[43] Had the covenant been expressed to be for the benefit of the whole *or any part* of the estate, it could have been enforced by the successor in title to any part of the land which the covenant in fact benefited.[44] In drafting restrictive covenants it is therefore desirable to annex them to the covenantee's land " or any part or parts thereof."

An additional reason for using this form of words is that, if there is no indication to the contrary, the benefit may be held to be annexed only to the whole of the covenantee's land, so that it will not pass with portions of it disposed of separately.[45] But even without such words the court may find that the covenant is intended to benefit any part of the retained land [46]; and small indications may suffice,[47] since the rule that presumes annexation to the whole only is arbitrary and inconvenient.[48] In principle it conflicts with the rule for assignments, which allows a benefit annexed to the whole to be assigned with part,[49] and it also conflicts with the corresponding rule for easements.[50]

(3) TRANSMISSION. Once the benefit of the covenant is annexed to land, it passes with the land to each successive owner, tenant or occupier,[51] even if he knew nothing of it when he acquired the land.[52]

(b) Other possibilities

(1) IMPLIED ANNEXATION. Although it has sometimes been stated

---

[43] *Re Ballard's Conveyance* [1937] Ch. 473 (a case of liability at law), criticised at (1941) 57 L.Q.R. 210 (G. R. Y. Radcliffe), and in Elphinstone, *Covenants,* 60.

[44] *Marquess of Zetland* v. *Driver* [1939] Ch. 1 (liability in equity).

[45] *Re Union of London & Smith's Bank Ltd.'s Conveyance* [1933] Ch. 611 at 628, per Romer L.J.; *Re Freeman-Thomas Indenture* [1957] 1 W.L.R. 560; *Russell* v. *Archdale* [1964] Ch. 38 (on appeal [1963] E.G.D. 366); *Re Jeff's Transfer (No. 2)* [1966] 1 W.L.R. 841; *Ellison* v. *O'Neill* [1968] 2 N.S.W.R. 246.

[46] *Re Selwyn's Conveyance* [1967] Ch. 674 ("land part of or lately part of the Selwyn estate ").

[47] See *Drake* v. *Gray* [1936] Ch. 451 at 465 (" lands retained by the vendor "). But contrast *Russell* v. *Archdale, supra*; *Re Selwyn's Conveyance, supra.*

[48] See (1968) 84 L.Q.R. 22 at 28 (P. V. Baker); (1971) 87 L.Q.R. 539 at 552, 562 (D. J. Hayton). In Victoria the presumption was reversed by the Transfer of Land (Restrictive Covenants) Act 1964, s. 3; see *Re Miscamble's Application* [1966] V.R. 596.

[49] *Post,* p. 766.

[50] See (1962) 78 L.Q.R. 334, 482 (R.E.M.).

[51] L.P.A., 1925, s. 78, discussed below; *Taite* v. *Gosling* (1879) 11 Ch.D. 273.

[52] *Rogers* v. *Hosegood* [1900] 2 Ch. 388.

that annexation must appear from the covenant itself,[53] this may
not be an invariable rule where the facts make the connection with
the benefited land so obvious that to ignore it would be " not only
an injustice but a departure from common sense." [54] No formal
annexation is required in order that the benefit of a covenant may
run at law, even when negative: it need only touch and concern
the benefited land [55]; and it is out of character for equity to be more
formalistic than common law. The leading case on annexation is
apparently merely a case of equity following the law,[56] requiring
some " indication in the original conveyance, *or in the circumstances
attending it,* that the burden of the restrictive covenant is imposed
for the benefit of the land reserved." [57] Nor is express annexation
of benefit required in order that the burden may run [58]; nor for
purposes of assignment [59]; nor by the doctrine of *Spencer's Case*
nor by the rules for easements, the two closest analogies at common
law.[60] Consequently there is little force in the argument that an
express formula is required in order to protect purchasers of the
burdened land. Schemes of development, discussed below, are a
special instance of annexation implied merely from circumstances.

   (2) SECTION 78. Another question is whether annexation is
assisted by section 78 of the Law of Property Act, 1925.[61] This

---

[53] *Re Union of London and Smith's Bank Ltd.'s Conveyance* [1933] Ch. 611 at
   628 (but the decisive factor in this case was the complete absence of evidence as
   to benefited land: see at pp. 636–637); *Marquess of Zetland* v. *Driver* [1939]
   Ch. 1 at 8; *Newton Abbot Co-operative Society Ltd.* v. *Williamson & Treadgold
   Ltd.* [1952] Ch. 286 at 289.
[54] *Marten* v. *Flight Refuelling Ltd.* [1962] Ch. 115 at 133. See [1972B] C.L.J. 157 at
   168 (H.W.R.W.). This decision does not support the doctrine of implied
   annexation suggested in the previous edition of this book: see (1968) 84 L.Q.R.
   at p. 30 (P. V. Baker); (1972) 36 Conv.(N.S.) at p. 32 (E. C. Ryder). As the
   latter critic explains, the decision is in terms of the rules for assignment: its
   place is therefore at p. 767, *infra.* An example of self-evident annexation is a
   covenant not to let down the surface of overlying land (see next note), where the
   benefited land is obvious.
[55] *Westhoughton U. D. C.* v. *Wigan Coal & Iron Co. Ltd.* [1919] 1 Ch. 159 at 170
   (covenant not to let down surface of land " deemed to be annexed to the
   land "). See *ante,* p. 747.
[56] *Rogers* v. *Hosegood* [1900] 2 Ch. 388 at 404. This passage clearly indicates that
   the Court of Appeal did not intend to impose more stringent requirements than
   those of common law. See likewise *Torbay Hotel Ltd.* v. *Jenkins* [1927] 2 Ch.
   225 at 239. In the early case of *Mann* v. *Stephens* (1846) 15 Sim. 377 a restrictive
   covenant made merely with the covenantee, his heirs and assigns, was enforceable
   by and against successors in title: but see *ante,* p. 762, n. 42.
[57] *Rogers* v. *Hosegood, supra,* at p. 408 (italics supplied). Similarly in *Renals* v.
   Cowlishaw (1878) 9 Ch.D. 125 at 129, Hall V.-C. referred to " the expressed *or
   otherwise apparent* purpose or object of the covenant, in reference to its being
   intended to be annexed to other property " (italics supplied).
[58] See *ante,* p. 756.
[59] See *post,* p. 767.
[60] See *ante* p. 752; *post,* p. 807.
[61] See [1972B] C.L.J. 157 at 171 (H.W.R.W.); Farrand, *Contract and Conveyance,*
   (2nd ed. 1973) p. 413.

provides that a covenant relating to any land of the covenantee shall be deemed to be made with him and his successors in title, and shall have effect as if they were expressed; and that in the case of restrictive covenants, " successors in title " includes owners and occupiers for the time being of the land intended to be benefited.[62] If the covenant in fact touches and concerns land of the covenantee, therefore, successors in title to that land are within the intended benefit. Inserting these prescribed words, including the reference to the land, produces what is tantamount to a formula of annexation, closely similar to the classic formula " the vendors their heirs and assigns and others claiming under them to all or any of their lands adjoining." [63] The latter is, indeed, just such a clause of common form as section 78 is designed to render unnecessary. The earlier version of 1881 makes this seem even more probable.[1] Yet section 78 is never invoked in the cases, and is said not to alter the need for express annexation.[2]

(3) SECTION 62. Yet a further possibility is that the benefit should pass on any conveyance of the benefited land by virtue of section 62 of the Law of Property Act, 1925, a provision which the courts have interpreted generously.[3] This has been argued but not decided.[4]

II. ASSIGNMENT

Even if the benefit of the covenant has not been annexed to the land to be benefited, an assignee of the land may nevertheless succeed in enforcing the covenant if the benefit of the covenant has also been assigned to him.

(a) *Form of assignment.* The assignment must ordinarily be made expressly. But even if it is not, the assignee of the land may succeed if it was agreed between him and the vendor that he should have the benefit of the covenant.[5] What is necessary is a distinct

---

[62] These words appear to recognise the wider operation of restrictive covenants as interests in property.
[63] *Rogers* v. *Hosegood* [1900] 2 Ch. 388; *ante,* p. 762.
[1] C.A. 1881, s. 58 was enacted shortly after *Renals* v. *Cowlishaw (ante,* p. 762) had shown that the benefit would not run where successors to property of all kinds were mentioned. S. 58, which differentiated the classes of successors for realty and personalty, may well have been intended to remedy this difficulty where the covenant in fact related to land of the covenantee, thus removing a technical obstacle to the running of the benefit.
[2] Preston and Newsom, *Restrictive Covenants,* 5th ed., 52, 53. This view, formerly supported also in this book, assumes that s. 78 merely explains the class of successors without importing any reference to the land.
[3] See *post,* p. 837.
[4] *Rogers* v. *Hosegood, supra,* at pp. 394, 398 (on narrower " general words "). See (1971) 87 L.Q.R. 539 at 570 (D. J. Hayton).
[5] *Renals* v. *Cowlishaw* (1878) 9 Ch.D. 125 at 129–131 ; affd. (1879) 11 Ch.D. 866; *Re Union of London & Smith's Bank Ltd.'s Conveyance, supra,* at p. 628; *Drake* v. *Gray* [1936] Ch. 451 at 455.

agreement that the benefit of the covenant shall run to the assignee, as opposed to a mere sale of the land without reference to the covenant. In the latter case the benefit will not run unless previously annexed to the land.[6]

(b) *Assignment with land.* If the assignee is suing the original covenantor or his personal representative (who are liable at law), he has only to prove that the benefit of the covenant has been properly assigned to him as a chose in action and ask for damages or an injunction.[7] But if he is suing some successor in title to the covenantor's land (who can be liable only in equity under the rule in *Tulk* v. *Moxhay*), he must also prove that the benefit was assigned to him together with the land benefited, *i.e.*, as part of the same transaction. It is possible that a covenantee, so long as he retains some part of the land benefited by the covenant, may assign the benefit separately to someone who has previously bought a plot without the benefit.[8] But the better view is probably that the covenant must be assigned together with the land or some parcel of it. For the primary purpose of the covenant is to preserve the value of the vendor's retained land, and " if he has been able to sell any particular part of his property without assigning to the purchaser the benefit of the covenant, there seems no reason why he should at a later date and as an independent transaction be at liberty to confer upon the purchaser such benefit." [9] This is a special rule of equity, for the purposes of an action against a successor in title to the covenantor's land. There is naturally no objection to a later assignment which merely gives effect to an existing equitable right to the benefit of the covenant, *e.g.*, where the benefited land is conveyed by trustees to a beneficiary and they later assign the benefit of the covenant to him.[10] For then the value of the benefited land has not been realised.

(c) *Assignment with part.* Assignment is therefore normally a transaction whereby the benefit of a covenant, though not originally annexed to the land benefited, becomes annexed to it on its sale.[11] " Express assignment is delayed annexation." [12] But assignment

---

6 *Renals* v. *Cowlishaw, supra.*

7 Elphinstone, *Covenants,* 96.

8 At least, a vendor who has parted with the whole of the benefited land can no longer assign the benefit of the covenant in equity: *Chambers* v. *Randall* [1923] 1 Ch. 149; *Re Union of London & Smith's Bank Ltd.'s Conveyance* [1933] Ch. 611.

9 *Ibid.*, at p. 632, *per* Romer L.J.; this is the leading case on express assignment of benefit. See also *Re Rutherford's Conveyance* [1938] Ch. 396.

10 *Lord Northbourne* v. *Johnston* [1922] 2 Ch. 309 (assignment to devisee of beneficiary). This decision appears to assume that the benefit ran in equity without either annexation or assignment.

11 *Rogers* v. *Hosegood* [1900] 2 Ch. 388 at 408.

12 (1968) 84 L.Q.R. at 29 (P. V. Baker).

may have a part to play even where there was an effective initial annexation, if that annexation was only to the benefited land as a whole: for equity allows the benefit to be assigned with any part or parts of the benefited land,[13] with which (irrationally) it will not run by virtue of the annexation alone.[14] In such a case, also, an express assignee can sue even though he has parted with part of the benefited land.[15] This shows how one anomaly may be tempered by another.

(*d*) *Intention to benefit.* A purchaser of the benefited land who seeks to sue the covenantor's successor in title in equity on the strength of an express assignment of the benefit of the covenant (as above described) must of course be able to show that the covenant was intended to benefit the land which he has purchased. Since *ex hypothesi* the benefit of the covenant was not expressly annexed to the land, there will probably be insufficient evidence in the deed containing the covenant. But the surrounding circumstances may be proved, and they may establish the connection clearly.[16] Thus, where the vendor was an ironmonger and took a covenant against any competing trade from the purchaser of other premises opposite to her shop, it was held that the facts plainly proved that the covenant was intended to benefit the shop, and so a later purchaser of the shop, to whom the benefit of the covenant had been expressly assigned by a person who succeeded to it under the will of the covenantee, could maintain an action against an assignee of the covenantor.[17] The principle of this decision was approved in a later case where the purchaser of a farm covenanted with the vendors to use the land for agricultural purposes only, and the facts showed clearly that the object was to benefit the remainder of a large agricultural estate which the vendors retained as a unit.[18] From the standpoint of conveyancing it is inconvenient that the enforceability of the covenant should depend on whatever dominant tenement is indicated by the circumstances when the deeds were executed,

---

[13] *Re Union of London & Smith's Bank Ltd.'s Conveyance, supra,* at p. 630; *Russell* v. *Archdale* [1964] Ch. 38 (on appeal [1963] E.G.D. 366); *cf. Stilwell* v. *Blackman* [1968] Ch. 508.

[14] *Ante,* p. 763. [15] *Stilwell* v. *Blackman, supra.*

[16] *Newton Abbot Co-operative Society Ltd.* v. *Williamson & Treadgold Ltd.* [1952] Ch. 286, not following the statement by Bennett J. in *Re Union of London & Smith's Bank Ltd.'s Conveyance, supra,* at p. 625, that the deed containing the covenant must define the benefited land; see also *Marten* v. *Flight Refuelling Ltd.* [1962] Ch. 115; *ante,* p. 764.

[17] *Newton Abbot Co-operative Society Ltd.* v. *Williamson & Treadgold Ltd., supra.*

[18] *Marten* v. *Flight Refuelling Ltd.* [1962] Ch. 115 (*ante,* p. 764), where Wilberforce J. advocated " a broad and reasonable view." In fact the plaintiffs were original covenantees, not assignees, and the reasoning appears to be that since assignees would have succeeded, so *a fortiori* should the plaintiffs. Why this circuitous argument was employed is not clear. But at least it is clear that the decision is adverse to technical restrictions. See (1972) 36 Conv.(N.S.) 20 (E. C. Ryder).

perhaps many years earlier [19]; but this inconvenience is inherent in many kinds of property rights,[20] and must be accepted if they are not to be defeasible on merely formal grounds.

(e) *Assignment as annexation.* It is not clear whether the effect of expressly assigning the benefit of a restrictive covenant on the sale of the benefited land is to annex it to the land so that it will thereafter pass to future owners without express assignment. On principle, supported by the older authorities,[21] it seems that such an assignment should annex the benefit of the covenant to the land, for it demonstrates that the benefit of the covenant is intended to pass with the land and not remain a separate right; and there appears to be no rule that the benefit of a covenant can be annexed only at the moment of its creation and not subsequently. But it has since been held that the covenant can be enforced in such a case only if there is a complete chain of assignments of the benefit.[22]

(f) *Assignor.* It is not always necessary that the assignment should be made by the original covenantee: it may be made by anyone in whom the land and the benefit of the covenant are both vested. If, for example, the original covenantee dies, and under his will or intestacy his son becomes entitled both to the benefited land and to the benefit of the covenant (two separate assets of the deceased), the son can effectively assign the benefit of the covenant if he subsequently sells the land.[23] The benefit of the covenant will pass to him automatically with the benefited land if it is clear from the facts that the covenant was intended to protect the land.[24]

III. SCHEMES OF DEVELOPMENT

(a) *An independent equity.* Building and other development schemes have special rules of their own, which derive from the wider principle that the benefit of covenants runs in equity according to

---

[19] See (1952) 68 L.Q.R. 353 (Sir L. Elphinstone); Preston & Newsom, *Restrictive Covenants* (2nd ed., 1955), pp. 41–48; contrast 5th ed. 1971, pp. 30–31.

[20] *Cf. ante*, p. 764.

[21] *Renals* v. *Cowlishaw* (1878) 9 Ch.D. 125 at 130, 131 (affd. (1879) 11 Ch.D. 866); *Rogers* v. *Hosegood* [1900] 2 Ch. 388 at 408; *Reid* v. *Bickerstaff* [1909] 2 Ch. 305 at 320, 326, 328.

[22] *Re Pinewood Estate, Farnborough* [1958] Ch. 280, where the authorities to the contrary were not cited: see [1957] C.L.J. 146 (H.W.R.W.); (1968) 84 L.Q.R. 22 at 31 (P. V. Baker).

[23] *Newton Abbot Co-operative Society Ltd.* v. *Williamson & Treadgold Ltd., supra.*

[24] *Earl of Leicester* v. *Wells-next the-Sea U.D.C.* [1973] Ch. 110. The personal representatives hold the benefit of the covenant upon trust for him, so that he can sue in equity: *ibid.* Alternatively they themselves can sue: *Ives* v. *Brown* [1919] 2 Ch. 314.

the common intention and common interest of the original parties.[25]
Where land is to be sold or let in lots according to a plan, restrictions
are often imposed on the purchasers of each lot for the benefit of
the estate generally, such as covenants restraining trading on the
estate, or prohibiting the erection of cheap buildings. Much of the
purpose of the covenants given by a purchaser of one lot would be
lost if they could not be enforced—

    (i) by those who have previously bought lots, and

    (ii) by those who subsequently buy the unsold lots.

Both these results could be achieved without any special rules for
schemes of development. The first could be achieved if the purchaser's covenants were expressed to be made with the owners of
the lots previously sold as well as with the vendor.[26] The second
could be achieved by framing the covenants expressly for the benefit
of the whole or any part of the land retained by the vendor, and
so annexing the benefit of them to each lot to be sold in the future,
or by express assignment to the later purchasers, as already described.

The special character of schemes of development makes it
possible to dispense with these formalities. If such a scheme exists,
the covenants given on the sale of each plot are enforceable by the
owner for the time being of any plot on the estate. " Community
of interest necessarily . . . requires and imports reciprocity of
obligation." [27] The covenants in effect form a sort of local law for
the estate.[28] They give rise to " an equity which is created by
circumstances and is independent of contractual obligation," [29] thus
transcending ordinary restrictions. In particular, (i) the annexation
of the benefit of the covenants to every plot still unsold proves
itself from the surrounding facts much as in the case of a positive
covenant,[30] so that no special formula for annexation need be used;
(ii) the owners of plots sold previously are shown by the facts to be
within the benefit of the covenants, even though not expressly
mentioned as covenantees [31]; (iii) no unsold plot may later be dis-

---

25 *Re Dolphin's Conveyance* [1970] Ch. 654. The doctrine can be traced back to
Whatman v. *Gibson* (1838) 9 Sim. 196, thus antedating *Tulk* v. *Moxhay* (1848)
2 Ph. 774. It was approved by the House of Lords in *Spicer* v. *Martin*
(1888) 14 App.Cas. 12; see *Lawrence* v. *South County Freeholds Ltd.* [1939]
Ch. 656 at 675. And see S. J. Bailey (1938) 6 C.L.J. 363, 364.

26 L.P.A. 1925, s. 56, replacing R.P.A. 1845, s. 5, discussed *ante*, p. 744. But
the possibility of this was not fully understood until *Forster* v. *Elvet Colliery
Co. Ltd.* [1908] 1 K.B. 629 (affd. *sub nom. Dyson* v. *Forster* [1909] A.C. 98),
and the rules relating to schemes had by then been settled.

27 *Spicer* v. *Martin* (1888) 14 App.Cas. 12 at 25, *per* Lord Macnaghten.

28 *Reid* v. *Bickerstaff* [1909] 2 Ch. 305 at 319; *Brunner* v. *Greenslade* [1971] Ch.
993 at 1004.

29 *Lawrence* v. *South County Freeholds Ltd.* [1939] Ch. 656 at 682 (Simonds J.);
Brunner v. *Greenslade* [1971] Ch. 993.

30 *Ante*, p. 764.

31 *Spicer* v. *Martin* (1888) 14 App.Cas. 12.

posed of by the vendor without his requiring the purchaser to enter into the covenants of the scheme; and (iv) the vendor is himself bound by the covenants of the scheme, even if he has not himself entered into them. As soon as the first disposition under the scheme has been made, the scheme crystallises, and all the land within the scheme is bound.[32] The vendor himself is in the position of a trustee, and is not at liberty to authorise breaches of the covenants.[33]

Whether or not a scheme of development exists is a question of fact which may depend upon extraneous circumstances as well as upon the terms of the conveyances.[34]

(b) Elements of a scheme

(1) INTENTION. The classic statement of the facts to be proved required that there should have been a common vendor who first laid out the property for sale in lots subject to restrictions consistent only with a scheme of development; that the common vendor should have intended the restrictions to benefit all the lots to be sold; and that the purchasers from the common vendor should have purchased on the footing that the restrictions were for the benefit of the other lots.[35] But later decisions have shown that what matters above all is that there should have been an intention to impose a scheme of mutually enforceable restrictions in the interest of all the purchasers and their successors. If this appears from the facts, and if the area affected by it is likewise clearly defined,[36] neither a common vendor nor laying out in lots is indispensable.[37] The present tendency is to relax formal requirements and to give effect to the manifest intention of the transaction.

(2) EVIDENCE. It is not necessary to prove an express undertaking by each purchaser that the covenants given by him are to be enforceable by the owners of all the other lots, provided the circumstances show that he must have realised it. This will be so if before his purchase he saw some plan of the estate with the restrictions indorsed on it. But the absence of a proper plan may prove fatal,[38] if the intention to impose a scheme of mutually enforceable restrictions

---

[32] *Brunner* v. *Greenslade, supra,* at p. 1003, summarising the first principles of schemes; and see *post,* p. 771.
[33] *Brunner* v. *Greenslade, supra,* at p. 1003.
[34] *Texaco Antilles Ltd.* v. *Kernochan* [1973] A.C. 609.
[35] *Elliston* v. *Reacher* [1908] 2 Ch. 374 at 384 (Parker J.); affirmed [1908] 2 Ch. 655.
[36] *Reid* v. *Bickerstaff* [1909] 2 Ch. 305; and see *Kelly* v. *Barrett* [1924] 2 Ch. 379 at 401.
[37] *Baxter* v. *Four Oaks Properties Ltd.* [1965] Ch. 816 (no lotting: size of plots variable); *Re Dolphin's Conveyance* [1970] Ch. 654 (two successive vendors; no lotting; no plan).
[38] *e.g., Osborne* v. *Bradley* [1903] 2 Ch. 446; *Kelly* v. *Barrett* [1924] 2 Ch. 379; *Re Wembley Park Estate Co. Ltd.'s Transfer* [1968] Ch. 491; *cf. Hodges* v. *Jones* [1935] Ch. 657 (plan with no restrictions on it not enough).

does not otherwise appear.[39] The evidence must, of course, show that the vendor intended to do more than merely benefit himself.[40] The reservation of a power for the vendor to release all or part of the land from the restrictions does not negative a scheme,[41] nor does an express formula of annexation in the conveyances [42]; nor is it essential that the restrictions imposed on each plot should be identical.[43] But if the agreement provides for the covenants to be enforced by the vendor on behalf of all parties, that is inconsistent with mutual enforceability.[44]

(3) SUB-SCHEMES. If one of the plots is later subdivided, the covenants of the scheme will be mutually enforceable between the sub-purchasers *inter se*, so far as they are applicable, as well as between them and the occupiers of the other plots, even though none of the sub-purchasers themselves gave covenants.[45] If the sub-purchasers themselves entered into " scheme of development " covenants differing from those of the main scheme, they can enforce only their own sub-scheme *inter se*, but can still enforce the head scheme against others.[46] The covenants of the head scheme thus remain operative unless some contrary intention appears.[47] This illustrates the special operation of such covenants as " a local law for the area of the scheme." [48] Another illustration is that if two plots come into common ownership but are later separated, the covenants are not discharged (*e.g.*, by unity of seisin), but will continue to operate.[49]

(*c*) *Extent of principle.* The law for schemes of development originated with building schemes, but the principle applies to numerous other types of schemes of development involving uniform covenants; the term " schemes of development " is the genus and " building scheme " is merely a species.[50] If an estate already fully built upon is disposed of in sections, whether freehold or leasehold, and the appropriate conditions for schemes of development are satis-

---

[39] As in *Re Dolphin's Conveyance, supra.*
[40] *Tucker* v. *Vowles* [1893] 1 Ch. 195; *Willé* v. *St. John* [1910] 1 Ch. 325.
[41] *Elliston* v. *Reacher* [1908] 2 Ch. 665 at 672; *Pearce* v. *Maryon-Wilson* [1935] Ch. 188 (leaseholds); *Newman* v. *Real Estate Debenture Corpn. Ltd.* [1940] 1 All E.R. 131; *Re Wembley Park Estate Co. Ltd.'s Transfer, supra.*
[42] *Texaco Antilles Ltd.* v. *Kernochan, supra.*
[43] *Collins* v. *Castle* (1887) 36 Ch.D. 243 at 253, 254; *Reid* v. *Bickerstaff* [1909] 2 Ch. 305 at 319.
[44] *White* v. *Bijou Mansions Ltd.* [1938] Ch. 351 at 363.
[45] *Brunner* v. *Greenslade* [1971] Ch. 993.
[46] On sub-schemes see *Knight* v. *Simmonds* [1896] 1 Ch. 653; *Lawrence* v. *South County Freeholds Ltd.* [1939] Ch. 656; *Brunner* v. *Greenslade, supra.*
[47] *Brunner* v. *Greenslade, supra*, at p. 1006.
[48] *Ibid.*, at p. 1004.
[49] *Brunner* v. *Greenslade, supra*; *Texaco Antilles Ltd.* v. *Kernochan, supra.*
[50] *Brunner* v. *Greenslade, supra*, at p. 999.

fied, the covenants will be enforceable as in building schemes.[51] The principle of such schemes can apply to a block of residential flats let on similar leases,[52] so that the landlord will be restrained from letting[53] or using[54] any of them otherwise than for residential purposes, even though it was only the tenants, and not the landlord, who entered into any express covenant as to user.

If the parties to a scheme modify it by releasing the covenants and substituting new covenants, it seems that the new covenants will not have the benefit of the rules as to schemes.[55]

Covenants under a scheme of development enjoy no dispensation from the requirement of registration, so that the " local law " principle depends upon due registration against all the purchasers if the land is freehold and developed after 1925.[56] Registration governs the running of the burden of the covenant, whereas the development scheme rules govern the running of the benefit.

Sect. 3. Declaration as to Restrictive Covenants

In the case of freehold land (or certain long leaseholds[57]) it is now possible to apply to the court for a declaration stating whether the land is or would be affected by any restriction, and if so, the nature, extent and enforceability of it.[58] This provision is a convenience to intending purchasers or lessees who wish to find out whether some long-standing restriction is really operative or not. It is often used to test the many nineteenth-century covenants which may today be unenforceable through non-compliance with the rules governing the transfer of the benefit of the covenants.

Sect. 4. Discharge of Restrictive Covenants

1. The power. In some cases a covenant may be still enforceable, but it may be undesirable for this state of affairs to continue. Con-

---

51 *Nottingham Patent Brick & Tile Co.* v. *Butler* (1886) 16 Q.B.D. 778; *Spicer* v. *Martin* (1888) 14 App.Cas. 12 (leasehold); *Torbay Hotel Ltd.* v. *Jenkins* [1927] 2 Ch. 225.
52 *Hudson* v. *Cripps* [1896] 1 Ch. 265; *Alexander* v. *Mansions Proprietary* (1900) 16 T.L.R. 431; *Gedge* v. *Bartlett* (1900) 17 T.L.R. 43; *Jaegar* v. *Mansions Consolidated Ltd.* (1903) 87 L.T. 690; *cf. Kelly* v. *Battershell* [1949] 2 All E.R. 830 (no scheme found).
53 *Gedge* v. *Bartlett* (1900) 17 T.L.R. 32.
54 *Newman* v. *Real Estate Debenture Corpn. Ltd.* [1940] 1 All E.R. 131 (" the high water-mark of cases where a scheme can be inferred ": *Kelly* v. *Battershell, supra,* at p. 841, *per* Cohen L.J.).
55 *Re Pinewood Estate, Farnborough* [1958] Ch. 280. This seems questionable: see [1957] C.L.J. 146 (H.W.R.W.).
56 *Ante,* p. 759.
57 See *post,* p. 774.
58 L.P.A., 1925, s. 84 (2), as amended by L.P.A. 1969, s. 28 (4). See, *e.g., Re Freeman-Thomas Indenture* [1957] 1 W.L.R. 560; *Re Gadd's Land Transfer* [1966] Ch. 56.

sequently a discretionary [59] power has been given to the Lands Tribunal (subject to appeal on a point of law to the Court of Appeal [60]) to modify or discharge the restrictive covenant with or without the payment of compensation.[61] The applicant must satisfy the Lands Tribunal that one of the following four grounds exists.

(*a*) *Obsolete.* That by reason of changes in the character of the property or neighbourhood or other material circumstances the restriction ought to be deemed obsolete. This requirement is not satisfied if the covenant still provides real protection to persons entitled to enforce it.[62]

(*b*) *Obstructive.* That its continued existence would impede some reasonable use of the land for public or private purposes, in a case where either it confers no practical benefit of substantial value or is contrary to the public interest and (in either case) any loss can be adequately compensated in money.

(*c*) *Agreement.* That the persons of full age and capacity entitled to the benefit of the restrictions have agreed, either expressly or by implication by their acts and omissions, to the discharge or modification sought.

(*d*) *No injury.* That the discharge or modification will not injure the persons entitled to the benefit of the covenant.[63]

The Lands Tribunal must take account of the development plan and of any ascertainable planning policy for the area and of any other material circumstances, *e.g.*, permissions granted by those entitled to enforce the covenant.[64] As a condition of modification or discharge the Tribunal may require the applicant to compensate those persons in money either for any loss on their part or for any reduction in the price of the land due to the imposition of the covenant. They may also require him to accept reasonable alternative restrictions.

2. Covenants within the power. These provisions as to discharge, and the provisions mentioned above as to declarations, apply to

---

[59] *Driscoll* v. *Church Commissioners for England* [1957] 1 Q.B. 330.
[60] Lands Tribunal Act, 1949, s. 3.
[61] L.P.A., 1925, s. 84 (1) as extended by L.P.A. 1969, s. 28. For the amended text, see *ibid.*, 3rd Sched. See Preston & Newsom, *Restrictive Covenants*, 5th ed., Chap. 7.
[62] *Re Truman, Hanbury, Buxton & Co. Ltd.'s Application* [1956] 1 Q.B. 261; *Re Miscamble's Application* [1966] V.R. 596.
[63] See *Re Freeman-Thomas Indenture* [1957] 1 W.L.R. 560 (estate broken up and no one entitled to benefit); *Ridley* v. *Taylor* [1965] 1 W.L.R. 611 at 622 (discouragement of frivolous objections); contrast *Gee* v. *The National Trust* [1966] 1 W.L.R. 170.
[64] See *Re Ghey and Galton's Application* [1957] 2 Q.B. 650.

restrictions whenever made and of whatever kind, even if they are not capable of running with land [65]; but they do not apply to restrictions imposed on a disposition made either gratuitously or for a nominal consideration for public purposes.[66] They apply as between the original contracting parties as well as between successors in title,[67] though discretion may be exercised against an original covenantor who himself accepted the restriction not long previously.[68] They apply to restrictions on freehold land, and to restrictions on leasehold land if the lease was made for more than forty years and at least twenty-five have expired; but they do not apply to mining leases.[69] The court may be less willing to modify or discharge covenants affecting leaseholds than covenants affecting freeholds, because of the landlord's interest in the future of the property.[70]

3. Stay of proceedings. A defendant in an action to enforce a restrictive covenant may apply for a stay of proceedings in order that he may apply to the Lands Tribunal for an order of discharge or modification [71]; but there is no similar power to stay proceedings for forfeiture of a lease for breach of a restrictive covenant.[72]

4. Conversion of houses. There is also provision for the county court, on such terms as the court thinks fit, to authorise the conversion of a house into two or more tenements in contravention of a restrictive covenant or a provision in a lease if owing to changes in the neighbourhood the house cannot readily be let as a whole, or if planning permission for the conversion has been granted.[73]

Sect. 5. Restrictive Covenants and Planning

The extension of planning control has somewhat reduced the importance of restrictive covenants. The effect of this control [74] is to restrict any change in the use of any land in the whole country, subject to various exceptions; landowners thus have less need to impose restrictive covenants for more limited purposes. Nevertheless, restrictive covenants have by no means been superseded by planning control. A landowner must see that what he proposes to do will contravene neither the private system of restrictive covenants nor

---

[65] *Shepherd Homes Ltd.* v. *Sandham* (*No. 2*) [1971] 1 W.L.R. 1062.
[66] L.P.A., 1925, s. 84 (7).
[67] *Ridley* v. *Taylor* [1965] 1 W.L.R. 611.
[68] *Cresswell* v. *Proctor* [1968] 1 W.L.R. 906 (two years).
[69] L.P.A., 1925, s. 84 (12) as amended by Landlord and Tenant Act, 1954, s. 52.
[70] *Ridley* v. *Taylor, supra.*
[71] See L.P.A., 1925, s. 84 (9); *Fielden* v. *Byrne* [1926] Ch. 620; *Richardson* v. *Jackson* [1954] 1 W.L.R. 447; *Shepherd Homes Ltd.* v. *Sandham* (*No. 2*), *supra.*
[72] *Iveagh* v. *Harris* [1929] 2 Ch. 281.
[73] Housing Act, 1957, s. 165. For the limits of this, see *Josephine Trust Ltd.* v. *Champagne* [1963] 2 Q.B. 160.
[74] *Ante*, p. 70; and *post*, p. 1086.

the public system of planning control; restrictive covenants sometimes extend to matters not covered by the planning legislation, as for example a change of the business carried on on the premises; and it may be better to be able to enforce a restrictive covenant as of right than to be dependent on a local planning authority enforcing planning control.[75]

The grant of planning permission does not by itself authorise the breach of restrictive covenants. But there are special provisions where a local authority has acquired land, or appropriated its own land, for planning purposes: the erection, construction or carrying out, or maintenance, of any building or work on land in accordance with planning permission is then authorised by statute even though this involves a breach of restrictive covenants or interference with easements and similar rights of third parties. This provision extends both to the local authority and to their successors in title; but there is an exception to protect statutory undertakers.[76] For this expropriation the owners of such rights may claim compensation as mentioned below.[77]

Sect. 6. Restrictive Covenants and Compulsory Acquisition

Where land which is subject to a restrictive covenant is acquired compulsorily[78] by a public authority under statutory powers, no action lies for breach of the covenant if what is done on the land is validly done in the exercise of statutory powers.[79] The authority of Parliament then overrides the contractual restriction, and the covenantee's only remedy is to claim compensation for the injurious affection of his own land which was previously benefited by the covenant.[80] But this does not extinguish the covenant, which continues to bind the acquired land as regards any use not authorised by statute. Thus where the Air Ministry compulsorily purchased agricultural land for use as an aerodrome and later let it to a firm for use for commercial flying, an injunction was granted to prevent the firm from so using the land in breach of a covenant restricting it to agricultural use; but an injunction to prevent them from using it for Air Ministry work was refused.[81]

---

[75] For further discussion, see (1964) 28 Conv.(N.S.) 190 (A. R. Mellows).
[76] Town and Country Planning Act 1971, s. 127.
[77] *Ibid.*, s. 81 (3).
[78] As to purchase by agreement under statutory powers, see *Kirby* v. *Harrogate School Board* [1896] 1 Ch. 437; *Cripps on Compulsory Purchase*, 11th ed., p. 322.
[79] *Kirby* v. *Harrogate School Board*, *supra*; *Marten* v. *Flight Refuelling Ltd.* [1962] Ch. 115.
[80] *Long Eaton Recreation Grounds Co. Ltd.* v. *Midland Ry.* [1902] 2 K.B. 574. *Cf. Hawley* v. *Steele* (1877) 6 Ch.D. 521.
[81] *Marten* v. *Flight Refuelling Ltd.*, *supra*.

Part 4

LICENCES

Sect. 1. Nature of Licences

1. Licences. A licence is a permission given by the occupier of land which allows the licensee to do some act which would otherwise be a trespass,[82] *e.g.*, to lodge in his house,[83] or to go on to his land to play cricket.[84] The law about licences, like the law about covenants, concerns transactions which are primarily personal, but which have developed in the direction of interests in property, thus raising difficult questions. Until recently it could be said that a licence was merely a personal arrangement between two parties and did not create any proprietary interest which could bind a third party, *i.e.*, a successor in title to the licensor's land. Thus if A owned a lodging-house and sold it to B, B could turn out the lodgers, whose only remedy would be to sue A for damages. If A had granted leases to tenants, the tenants would of course have interests in land (legal estates) which would be binding on B. But even this fundamental distinction has been shaken by a number of recent decisions; and it may be that the law relating to licences is at the beginning of a period of development like that by which restrictive covenants were transformed from mere contracts into equitable interests in land after the decision in *Tulk* v. *Moxhay* in 1848. Thus a new chapter in the subject of real property may possibly be opening. At present the two most important questions are:

(i) whether contractual licences are inherently revocable; and

(ii) how far licences can create interests in land capable of binding third parties.

At present the law on both these questions is unsettled. For the purposes of the law of property the vital question is the second one.

2. No right to exclusive possession. The general rule for distinguishing a lease from a licence is, as mentioned elsewhere,[85] that a lease gives the right to exclusive possession of the land, whereas a licence usually does not.[86] Examples of licences are—

---

[82] See *Thomas* v. *Sorrell* (1673) Vaugh. 330 at 351.
[83] *Ante*, p. 618.
[84] *Frank Warr & Co. Ltd.* v. *L. C. C.* [1904] 1 K.B. 713 at 723.
[85] *Ante*, p. 618.
[86] *Wilson* v. *Tavener* [1901] 1 Ch. 578 at 591. For examples of licences giving exclusive possession, see *ante*, p. 618.

the hire of a concert hall for several days without the hirer being entitled to exclusive possession [87];

permission to erect and use an advertisement hoarding [88] or electric sign [89];

the letting of bookstalls on a station platform [90];

permission to use pleasure boats on a canal [91];

the grant of the "front of the house rights" in a theatre, *i.e.*, the exclusive right to supply refreshments coupled with other rights such as the use of refreshment rooms [92];

permission to view a race [93] or cinema performance [94]; and

permission to use the front part of a shop at night for the sale of tickets for a night-club carried on in the basement.[95]

Sect. 2. Types of Licences

There is no limit to the possible variety of licences, since they are mostly purely personal transactions. The simplest type is a bare licence, *i.e.*, a licence granted otherwise than for valuable consideration, such as a gratuitous permission to enter a house or a field. It can be revoked at any time [96] on reasonable notice without rendering the licensor liable in damages,[97] but the licensee will not be a trespasser until he has had reasonable time to withdraw.[98] Even a licence granted by deed may be revocable,[99] provided that there is no covenant not to revoke it. A revocable licence is automatically determined by the death of the licensor or the assignment of the land.[1] While it continues [2] the licensee is estopped from

[87] *Taylor* v. *Caldwell* (1863) 3 B. & S. 826.
[88] *Wilson* v. *Tavener* [1901] 1 Ch. 578.
[89] *Walton Harvey Ltd.* v. *Walker and Homfrays Ltd.* [1931] 1 Ch. 274.
[90] *Smith & Son* v. *Lambeth Parish Assessment Committee* (1882) 10 Q.B.D. 327.
[91] *Hill* v. *Tupper* (1863) 2 H. & C. 121.
[92] *Frank Warr & Co. Ltd.* v. *L. C. C.* [1904] 1 K.B. 713; *Clore* v. *Theatrical Properties Ltd.* [1936] 3 All E.R. 483.
[93] *Wood* v. *Leadbitter* (1845) 13 M. & W. 838.
[94] *Hurst* v. *Picture Theatres Ltd.* [1915] 1 K.B. 1.
[95] *Jackson* v. *Simons* [1923] 1 Ch. 373; *cf. Isaac* v. *Hotel de Paris Ltd.* [1960] 1 W.L.R. 239 (use of one floor of hotel as a night bar at a monthly rent: held a licence).
[96] But there are traces of a doctrine that a licence is irrevocable after being acted upon: *Webb* v. *Paternoster* (1619) 2 Roll. 152, Palm. 71 at 74; *Feltham* v. *Cartwright* (1839) 5 Bing.N.C. 569: see *Hounslow L.B.C.* v. *Twickenham Garden Developments Ltd.* [1971] Ch. 233 at 255.
[97] *Aldin* v. *Latimer Clark, Muirhead & Co.* [1894] 2 Ch. 437 (where the licensor gave no reasonable notice and so was liable in damages); *Armstrong* v. *Sheppard and Short Ltd.* [1959] 2 Q.B. 384.
[98] *Post*, p. 782.
[99] *Wood* v. *Leadbitter* (1845) 13 M. & W. 838 at 845.
[1] *Terunnanse* v. *Terunnanse* [1968] A.C. 1086.
[2] *Government of Penang* v. *Beng Hong Oon* [1972] A.C. 425 (licensee no longer estopped after giving up possession).

denying the licensor's title, so that he cannot resist making any agreed payment by pleading that the licensor is not the true owner.[3]

The licences which are important in the law of property are those which are, or may be, capable of affecting third parties. Three different types may be distinguished.

1. Licence protected by estoppel or in equity. The principle of estoppel may operate to prevent revocation of a right which one party has led the other to suppose was permanent. If neighbours agree that one of them may build up to a certain boundary line, the other cannot later require the building to be removed as an encroachment, even though it stands partly on his land, since his own conduct estops him.[4] An estoppel of this kind both binds and benefits successors in title at common law, so that in effect it creates a legal interest in land.[5]

The revocation of a licence may also be restrained by injunction on equitable grounds. One example is the case of certain contractual licences, discussed below. Another is the "equity arising out of acquiescence,"[6] where a landowner allows a licensee to spend substantial sums of money on improvements in circumstances which raise a reasonable expectation that the licence will not be revoked. In this latter case revocation will be restrained not only against the licensor but against his successors in title, so that the licence becomes an equitable interest in the land, similar in some ways to an interest by estoppel[7]; indeed, the process has been called "proprietary estoppel."[8] Thus where a father encouraged his son to build a house on the father's land, in the expectation that he would be allowed to remain there indefinitely, the court refused to allow the trustees of the father's will to dispossess the son, whose licence therefore gave him a protected equitable title.[9] Similarly, where A built a garage on his own land which was accessible only over B's land, and B acquiesced in the building and allowed access as of right, purchasers from B with notice of A's right of access were not entitled to revoke it.[10] Licences may, additionally, be protected by the

---

3 *Terunnanse* v. *Terunnanse, supra.* For this type of estoppel see *ante,* p. 645.
4 *Hopgood* v. *Brown* [1955] 1 W.L.R. 213.
5 *Ibid.*; *Taylor* v. *Needham* (1810) 2 Taunt. 278.
6 *E. R. Ives Investment Ltd.* v. *High* [1967] 2 Q.B. 379 at 394.
7 *Inwards* v. *Baker* [1965] 2 Q.B. 29. And see *Att.-Gen. of Southern Nigeria* v. *John Holt & Co. (Liverpool) Ltd.* [1915] A.C. 599 (building erected on foreshore belonging to Crown).   8 See Snell, *Equity,* 565.
9 *Inwards* v. *Baker, supra,* criticised in *Dodsworth* v. *Dodsworth* (1973) 228 E.G. 1115. See similarly *Dillwyn* v. *Llewellyn* (1862) 4 De G.F. & J. 517; *Plimmer* v. *Mayor etc. of Wellington* (1884) 9 App.Cas. 699 (wharf and warehouse erected at licensor's request and with his consent); *Siew Soon Wah* v. *Yong Tong Hong* [1973] A.C. 836; *cf. Cullen* v. *Cullen* [1962] I.R. 268. See generally Snell, *Equity,* 565 *et seq.*
10 *E.R. Ives Investment Ltd.* v. *High, supra.* This right was held not to be registrable: *post,* p. 1043.

doctrine that " he who takes the benefit must accept the burden." [11]
In the last-mentioned case A's right of access had been given in
exchange for a right for foundations of B's building to encroach on
A's land, and B's successors were therefore bound to honour A's
right while the encroachment persisted. This doctrine is here said
to operate " in equity."

One factor which may induce the court to restrain revocation
may be the owner's knowledge that the licensee mistakenly supposed
that he had himself some title to the land.[12] As an alternative remedy
the court may instead give the licensee a lien on the land for his
outlay,[13] or even declare him to be entitled to the fee simple.[14] But
if the licensor was unaware of his own title to the land and merely
indicated no objection to the licensee's occupation, equity will not
restrain the licensor from asserting his title when he discovers it.[15]

The court may also resort to the device of a constructive trust.
Where a purchaser took a conveyance expressly subject to a licence
allowing the widow of an employee of the vendor to occupy a
cottage for her life, and on that account paid a reduced price, the
Court of Appeal held that the purchaser was a constructive trustee,
so that the widow's licence could be enforced in equity against him.[16]

These decisions show that the court is well furnished with means
of enforcing licences against successors in title when special circumstances so require.

2. Licence coupled with an interest. A licence may be coupled
with some proprietary interest in other property. Thus the right to
enter another man's land to hunt and take away the deer killed, or
to enter and cut down a tree and take it away, involves two
things, namely, a licence to enter the land and the grant of an interest
(a profit *à prendre* [17]) in the deer or tree.[18] At common law such a
licence is both irrevocable [19] and assignable,[20] as an adjunct of the
interest with which it is coupled. This is probably an example of
the principle that a man may not derogate from his grant,[21] which is

---

[11] For this see *ante*, p. 750; *Hopgood* v. *Brown* [1955] 1 W.L.R. 213 (licensor
unable to revoke licence for use of drains while enjoying reciprocal licence).
[12] *Ramsden* v. *Dyson* (1865) L.R. 1 H.L. 129.
[13] *Unity Joint Stock Mutual Banking Association* v. *King* (1858) 25 Beav. 72.
[14] *Dillwyn* v. *Llewellyn, supra.*
[15] *Armstrong* v. *Sheppard and Short Ltd., supra.*
[16] *Binions* v. *Evans* [1972] Ch. 359; *ante*, p. 314. Formidable conveyancing problems
are raised by interests arising thus: see (1974) 38 Conv.(N.S.) 226.
[17] For such interests, see *post*, pp. 822, 881.
[18] See *Thomas* v. *Sorrell* (1673) Vaugh. 330 at 351; *Wood* v. *Leadbitter* (1845)
13 M. & W. 838 at 845.
[19] *James Jones & Sons Ltd.* v. *Earl of Tankerville* [1909] 2 Ch. 440 at 442 (sale
of timber); *Doe* d. *Hanley* v. *Wood* (1819) 2 B. & Ald. 724 at 738 (sale of hay);
Wood v. *Manley* (1839) 11 A. & E. 34; *Wood* v. *Leadbitter* (1845) 13 M. & W.
838 at 845.   [20] *Muskett* v. *Hill* (1839) 5 Bing.N.C. 694 at 707, 708.
[21] *Cf. Wood* v. *Manley* (1839) 11 A. & E. 34 at 37, 38.

mentioned again below.[22] In other words, if a man has granted an interest in property accompanied by certain privileges, he may not later repudiate them in a way which diminishes the value of his grant. On this principle the licence is not only irrevocable but is enforceable by and against successors in title of the grantee and grantor respectively, as will later be explained.[22]

The interest in question must, of course, have been validly created. If the licence was to go upon land to take game or dig for minerals, these rights, being profits *à prendre*, must have been duly granted by deed[23] or acquired by prescription.[24] An interest in chattels, however, can be created with less formality, as where there is a sale of hay or timber already cut, coupled with a licence to the purchaser to cart them away.[25] An interest in standing timber or growing crops can be created, it seems, only by the formalities appropriate for land.[26] In equity, as usual, effect will be given to a specifically enforceable agreement to grant an interest; and thus a licence coupled with a profit *à prendre* granted for value but merely in writing[27] can be enforced by injunction.[28]

Licences have occasionally been held to be coupled with an interest, and so irrevocable, even though no recognisable interest was involved.[29] But the better view must be that some kind of proprietary interest is necessary.[30]

Licences of this class may be compared with rights of entry, which are recognised interests in land.[31]

3. Contractual licence. Midway between a bare licence and a licence coupled with an interest is a licence which is supported merely by the licensor's contract not to revoke it. Such are the rights of lodgers in a lodging house, or of ticket-holders at a cricket match or on the railway. There are two particular problems concerning contractual licences: are they inherently revocable; and do they bind third parties, *i.e.*, successors in title?

---

[22] *Post*, p. 820; and see *ante*, p. 678.
[23] *Duke of Somerset* v. *Fogwell* (1826) 5 B. & C. 875 at 886 (fishing lease).
[24] *Post*, p. 841.   [25] See n. 19 above.
[26] Although a sale of timber to be cut forthwith is not a contract for the sale of an interest in land (see *ante*, p. 547), the property in the timber cannot pass until it is cut, *i.e.*, no proprietary interest can be created informally so long as the timber is in fact part of the land: *Morison* v. *Lockhart*, 1912 S.C. 1017, followed in *Kursell* v. *Timber Operators and Contractors Ltd.* [1927] 1 K.B. 298. " Timber trees cannot be felled with a goose quill ": *Liford's Case* (1614) 11 Co.Rep. 46b at 50a.
[27] A contract to grant such an interest is unenforceable unless supported by sufficient writing or part performance: see *ante*, pp. 545, 561.
[28] *Frogley* v. *Earl of Lovelace* (1859) John. 333; *cf. Duke of Devonshire* v. *Eglin* (1851) 14 Beav. 530; *McManus* v. *Cooke* (1887) 35 Ch.D. 681; *cf. ante*, p. 624.
[29] As in *Vaughan* v. *Hampson* (1875) 33 L.T. 15 (successful action for assault by licensee ejected from meeting); *Hurst* v. *Picture Theatres Ltd.*, *infra*.
[30] *Hounslow L.B.C.* v. *Twickenham Garden Developments Ltd.* [1971] Ch. 233.
[31] *Ante*, pp. 143, 656, 719.

A. *Revocability*

At common law contractual licences suffered from a peculiarity rooted in the law of property: it was held that they were always revocable, since the licensee was not possessed of any estate or interest in the land. Thus in *Wood* v. *Leadbitter* [32] a ticket-holder was wrongfully turned off the Doncaster racecourse, but failed in an action for assault even though he would have succeeded in an action for breach of contract. The defect of the common law remedy in contract is that the plaintiff can merely recover the price of the ticket; he cannot insist on his right to remain on the land. But if the contract is specifically enforceable in equity, *e.g.*, by an injunction against wrongful interference with the licensee, the licensee has then a specific equitable right to remain on the land: an injunction will be granted to restrain a threatened revocation of the licence and also to restrain a wrongful revocation from being enforced. [33] Equity may thus protect the licensee effectively, at least during the period of the licence. Even if he cannot seek an equitable remedy until afterwards, the fact that it was due to him at the time of the wrongful revocation may entitle him to sue for assault if ejected. [34]

But what if equity will not assist, so that the question is one of common law? In one case two schools agreed to share premises owned by one of them, and after revocation of the licence the licensee re-entered forcibly. The Court of Appeal held that he was a trespasser, even if the revocation was a breach of contract. [35] Equity would not assist him, since " the court cannot specifically enforce an agreement for two people to live peaceably under the same roof." [36] This affirmed the old doctrine that at common law a licensor has a *power* to eject his licensee even though he has no *right* to do so. Shortly afterwards this doctrine was repudiated in the House of Lords, but in a case where the question did not really arise, for it was held that the contract impliedly permitted revocation of the licence, which was for the use of a theatre for the production

---

[32] (1845) 13 M. & W. 838. Contrast *Feltham* v. *Cartwright* (1829) 5 Bing.N.C. 569, where a contractual licence was held irrevocable after being acted upon (*ante*, p. 777, n. 96), and *Butler* v. *Manchester, Sheffield & Lincolnshire Ry.* (1888) 21 Q.B.D. 207, where the Court of Appeal allowed an action for assault to a ticket-holder who was wrongfully turned off a railway train.

[33] *Winter Garden Theatre (London) Ltd.* v. *Millennium Productions Ltd.* [1946] 1 All E.R. 678 at 684 (reversed on other grounds, *infra*), *per* Lord Greene M.R.; and see *Hounslow L.B.C.* v. *Twickenham Garden Developments Ltd.* [1971] Ch. 233.

[34] This appears to be the explanation of *Hurst* v. *Picture Theatres Ltd.* [1915] 1 K.B. 1 (successful action for assault by ticket-holder ejected from cinema).

[35] *Thompson* v. *Park* [1944] K.B. 408.

[36] *Ibid.*, at p. 409, *per* Goddard L.J.

of plays.[37] The position of a licensee protected only by a contract which is not enforceable by an equitable remedy is therefore still speculative. Normally the court will at least not grant equitable remedies, such as injunctions, to assist a licensor who is in breach of his contract.[38] But it remains obscure whether such a licensor is liable for assault if he forcibly removes a licensee who is not entitled to protection in equity. The question is whether the *ratio decidendi* of the Court of Appeal is outweighed by *obiter dicta* in the House of Lords.[39]

 Unless the agreement otherwise provides,[40] no period of notice need be given before revoking a revocable licence, but the licensee must be given a reasonable time in which to leave the premises.[41]

B. Position of Third Parties

It is not clear how far contractual licences are interests in land which can affect third parties, *e.g.*, purchasers or devisees of the licensor's land. Until quite recently the authorities indicated that, except in the special cases already discussed,[42] licences were personal transactions which created no proprietary interests in land, so that a purchaser of the licensor's land had no concern with any mere licence, even when he bought with express notice of it.[43] Thus, where a licence had been granted to sellers of refreshments giving them the exclusive use of the refreshment rooms of a theatre, a purchaser of the theatre was able to prevent an assignee of the licensee from enforcing his rights, and the Court of Appeal held that the proper remedy was in damages against the licensor.[44]

---

[37] *Winter Garden Theatre (London) Ltd.* v. *Millennium Productions Ltd.* [1948] A.C. 173, *per* Lord Simon, holding that the mere contract gives the licensee a right to remain. His explanation of *Wood* v. *Leadbitter, supra,* was not accepted by Lord Porter. Lord Porter and Lord Uthwatt, however, speak only of cases where equity will assist.

[38] *Hounslow L.B.C.* v. *Twickenham Garden Developments Ltd., supra* (injunction against contractor remaining on building site refused). Contrast *Thompson* v. *Park, supra* (injunction granted to expel violent intruder). In each case the decision preserved the *status quo*: see the *Hounslow* case at p. 250.

[39] The subject is discussed in (1948) 64 L.Q.R. 57 *et seq.* (H.W.R.W.).

[40] *Winter Garden Theatre (London) Ltd.* v. *Millennium Productions Ltd.* [1948] A.C. 173.

[41] *Cornish* v. *Stubbs* (1870) L.R. 5 C.P. 334; *Mellor* v. *Watkins* (1874) L.R. 9 Q.B. 400; *Aldin* v. *Latimer Clark, Muirhead & Co.* [1894] 2 Ch. 437 (damages awarded but injunction refused); *Canadian Pacific Ry.* v. *The King* [1931] A.C. 414; *Minister of Health* v. *Bellotti* [1944] K.B. 298; *Australian Blue Metal Ltd.* v. *Hughes* [1963] A.C. 74.

[42] *Ante*, p. 778.

[43] *King* v. *David Allen & Sons, Billposting Ltd.* [1916] 2 A.C. 54 (agreement for licence to display advertisements on a building held not binding on tenant to whom licensor later demised the land); *Clore* v. *Theatrical Properties Ltd., infra; cf. Plimmer* v. *Mayor, etc., of Wellington* (1884) 9 App.Cas. 699 at 714; contrast *Webb* v. *Paternoster* (1619) Poph. 151, *per* Montague C.J.

[44] *Clore* v. *Theatrical Properties Ltd.* [1936] 3 All E.R. 483.

Errington v. *Errington,*[45] however, laid down new and wider propositions. The Court of Appeal held that a contractual licence for the occupation of a dwelling-house will bind a person to whom the licensor leaves the house by will; and it was said that a contractual licence created an equitable interest in land which would bind all comers except a purchaser without notice. In that case a father bought a house, raising part of the money on mortgage, and allowed his son and daughter-in-law to live in it, saying that if they paid off the mortgage instalments the house would become theirs. Before the instalments had all been paid the father died, having by his will left the house to his widow. The widow failed in an action to recover the house, on the ground that it was occupied under a licence [46] which was binding upon her. For reasons which are hard to understand the court rejected the argument that the transaction was a contract to convey the house on completion of the payments, which would have created an equitable interest (an estate contract) of a familiar type.[47]

In a later case the House of Lords left this whole question open, but their comments are damaging to *Errington* v. *Errington* as an authority for any new principle that contractual licences, merely as such, may be interests in land.[48] It has also been distinguished as being a case of a licence coupled with an interest, namely, the right to a conveyance (as suggested above).[49] It seems likely that, if directly challenged, the doctrine of *Errington* v. *Errington* would be overruled as being inconsistent with long-settled principles of property law, and that it would share the fate of the analogous decisions about the rights of deserted wives, to be mentioned next.

Sect. 3. Matrimonial Homes

1. The short-lived " deserted wife's equity." At about the same time as *Errington* v. *Errington*, and equally without precedent,

---

[45] [1952] 1 K.B. 290; amplified in *Bendall* v. *McWhirter* [1952] 2 Q.B. 466 at 474 *et seq.* and repeated by Lord Denning M.R. in *Binions* v. *Evans* [1972] Ch. 359; criticised in (1952) 68 L.Q.R. 337 (H.W.R.W.) and (1953) 69 L.Q.R. 466 (A. D. Hargreaves); approved in (1953) 16 Mod.L.R. 1 (G. C. Cheshire). See also (1956) 20 Conv. (N.S.) 281 (R. H. Maudsley); (1972) 88 L.Q.R. 336 (P.V.B.). *Cf. Kelaghan* v. *Daly* [1913] 2 I.R. 328, and contrast *Wallace* v. *Simmers*, 1960 S.C. 225.

[46] See *ante*, p. 618.

[47] *Ante*, p. 575. A written contract would not have been necessary, since the taking of possession would have amounted to part performance: *ante*, p. 568. Nor would non-registration have mattered, for the plaintiff was not a purchaser. The court rejected this interpretation on the ground that there is no equitable interest where there is no obligation to complete the transaction. But this is contrary to well-recognised authority, *e.g.*, in the case of options: see *ante*, p. 578. See similar criticism in *National Provincial Bank Ltd.* v. *Ainsworth* [1965] A.C. 1175 at 1239, *per* Lord Upjohn; *Re Solomon* [1967] Ch. 573 at 585, *per* Goff J.

[48] *National Provincial Bank Ltd.* v. *Ainsworth, supra*, especially at pp. 1239 (Lord Upjohn), 1251 (Lord Wilberforce).

[49] *Re Solomon, supra.*

there appeared the " deserted wife's equity." This was based on the notion of a matrimonial rather than a contractual licence.[50] Despite authority to the contrary,[51] it was held that a wife who had been deserted by her husband had an irrevocable licence enforceable in equity against third parties, such as her husband's trustee in bankruptcy[52] or a purchaser with notice of her situation.[53] This right was held to be at most a " mere equity," [54] and not an equitable interest,[55] and to be determinable at the discretion of the court.[56] Unless otherwise agreed it became revocable on divorce[57] or, apparently, on commission of a matrimonial offence by the wife.[58]

All this new law, which was the subject of much criticism,[59] was summarily swept away by the House of Lords in 1965. The case was one where the husband had deserted his wife and then conveyed the matrimonial home to a company, whereupon the company charged it to a bank as security for money owed. The House of Lords held that the bank could enforce its security and take possession of the property, and that the wife must vacate it.[60] The decisions to the contrary were overruled, including the original decision enforcing the wife's right to possession against the husband's trustee in bankruptcy: for there is no reason why the fact of desertion should give the wife priority over the husband's creditors. It was made clear that a wife was not a licensee in her husband's house, and that if it was his sole property she had no sort of proprietary interest in it, even if deserted.[60] She had rights against her husband personally which flowed from her status as wife, and she might be able to obtain an injunction restraining him from dealing with the matrimonial home in a way which infringed these rights.[61] But she could enforce them against her husband alone, and not against his successors in title or other third parties.

[50] See *Re Solomon, supra* (husband's undertaking to court not contractual).
[51] See *Thompson* v. *Earthy* [1951] 2 K.B. 596; *Bradley-Hole* v. *Cusen* [1953] 1 Q.B. 300 at 306.
[52] *Bendall* v. *McWhirter* [1952] 2 Q.B. 466, *per* Denning L.J.
[53] *Ferris* v. *Weaven* [1952] 2 All E.R. 233; *Street* v. *Denham* [1954] 1 W.L.R. 624.
[54] See *ante*, p. 119.
[55] *Westminster Bank Ltd.* v. *Lee* [1956] Ch. 7; see (1955) 71 L.Q.R. 481 (R.E.M.); [1955] C.L.J. 158 (H.W.R.W.).
[56] *Jess B. Woodcock and Sons Ltd.* v. *Hobbs* [1955] 1 W.L.R. 152; *Churcher* v. *Street* [1959] Ch. 251.
[57] *Vaughan* v. *Vaughan* [1953] 1 Q.B. 762.
[58] *Wabe* v. *Taylor* [1952] 2 Q.B. 735; but contrast *Short* v. *Short* [1960] 1 W.L.R. 833.
[59] See (1952) 68 L.Q.R. 379 (R.E.M.). See generally (1953) 16 Mod.L.R. 215 (O. Kahn-Freund); (1952) 16 Conv.(N.S.) 323 (F. R. Crane); (1953) 17 Conv.(N.S.) 440 (L. A. Sheridan); see also *Brennan* v. *Thomas* [1953] V.L.R. 111; *Dickson* v. *McWhinnie* [1958] S.R.(N.S.W.) 179 (a full survey); (1956) 72 L.Q.R. 477 (R.E.M.).
[60] *National Provincial Bank Ltd.* v. *Ainsworth* [1965] A.C. 1175, approving *Thompson* v. *Earthy, supra*, and overruling *Bendall* v. *McWhirter, supra*, *Street* v. *Denham, supra*, and *Jess B. Woodcock & Sons Ltd.* v. *Hobbs, supra*.
[61] *Lee* v. *Lee* [1952] 2 Q.B. 489. *Cf. Short* v. *Short* [1960] 1 W.L.R. 833.

2. Matrimonial Homes Act 1967. The collapse of the "deserted wife's equity" admittedly left an unsatisfactory situation. The solution was to give statutory "rights of occupation" of the matrimonial home to husbands and wives alike. These rights are more properly described as matrimonial rights than as licences, but they may be explained here. They are not conditional on desertion, but arise automatically [52] from the fact of marriage in cases where one spouse is entitled [53] to the home and the other is not.[54] This far-reaching change was effected by the Matrimonial Homes Act 1967, a statute which bristles with difficulties.[55]

(a) *Rights of occupation.* The new "rights of occupation" are the right not to be excluded from occupation, and, with leave of the court, to enter and occupy.[56] They continue so long as the marriage exists, unless previously terminated by an order of the court. The court has wide discretion to act as it thinks is just and reasonable for enforcing, restricting or terminating these rights, having regard to all the circumstances of the case, including the conduct and resources of the spouses and the needs of children.[57] While the rights exist, the court may also "regulate" the occupational rights of *either* spouse; but this power does not extend to ordering the spouse who owns the home to vacate it.[58] As amended in 1970 the Act protects a spouse who has not a legal (fee simple or leasehold) estate in the home, whether solely or jointly.[59] If therefore the husband is sole legal owner upon trust for himself and his wife jointly or in common, the wife but not the husband can claim the benefit of the Act; yet neither can benefit if the legal estate is vested in them both jointly.[60] The Act may apply to several houses simultaneously: the non-owning spouse can claim to occupy any dwelling which the owning spouse is entitled to occupy, if it has at some time been their matrimonial home.[61]

(b) *Successors in title.* Successors in title may be bound by these rights of occupation, but only where the owning spouse's rights are

---

[52] But they can be released: s. 6.
[53] *i.e.* is entitled to occupy by virtue of an estate or interest, contract or statute, *e.g.* the Rent Acts (see *Penn* v. *Dunn* [1970] 2 Q.B. 686 at 692).
[54] For cases where the spouse is co-owner see *ante*, p. 447.
[55] See the discussion in *Wroth* v. *Tyler* [1974] Ch. 30. For details of the Act, see Snell, *Equity*, 528–530.
[56] s. 1 (1).
[57] s. 1 (2), (3).
[58] s. 1 (2); *Tarr* v. *Tarr* [1973] A.C. 254.
[59] s. 1 (9), added by Matrimonial Proceedings and Property Act 1970, s. 38. Previously the Act protected only what Lord Denning M.R. called a "bare" wife, having no proprietary, contractual or statutory right in the home: *Gurasz* v. *Gurasz* [1970] P. 11 at 17.
[60] It is not clear why the Act is now based on legal ownership, for this may be merely as trustee, as in the case of a joint legal owner.
[61] s. 1 (8).

founded on an estate or interest, as opposed to a contract or statute.[62] In the former case the non-owning spouse's rights are a charge on the estate or interest with "priority as if it were an equitable interest" created on January 1, 1968, on marriage, or on the acquisition of the estate or interest, whichever is the latest[63]; and the charge is registrable.[64] So long as the owning spouse is alive and the marriage lasts, therefore, the non-owning spouse can enforce the charge against third parties,[65] provided that, in the case of a purchaser, it has been duly registered.[66] But, as under the previous law, the charge is in any case void against persons representing creditors in the owning spouse's bankruptcy or insolvency.[67] Successors in title may apply to the court to have it restricted or terminated as above.[68] Where it extends to two or more dwelling houses, it is registrable against only one of them at any one time, and only the later registration may stand.[69] The power to register a charge naturally makes it possible for the non-owning spouse to impede transactions with the property by the owning spouse, even if the non-owner is in no danger of being left homeless and merely objects to moving; the non-owner can, indeed, register a charge without the knowledge of the owner, so rendering the owner liable in damages by frustrating a prior contract of sale.[70] This is therefore another case where marriage has been made into a blot on the title to the matrimonial home.[71] But probably most charges are in practice left unregistered, so that conveyancing proceeds on the curious basis of the mass invalidation of the charges for want of registration.[72]

---

[62] Rights under a contract for sale or lease, which creates an equitable interest, ought in principle to count as an interest rather than as a contract, but the position is not clear.

[63] s. 2. "The charge seems to be neither legal nor equitable, but a pure creature of statute, with a priority (though not a nature) defined by reference to equity ": Wroth v. Tyler [1974] Ch. 30 at 43.

[64] See post, p. 1044.

[65] s. 2 (4) also protects it against merger, e.g., where the owning spouse acquires the freehold of a leasehold home.

[66] A spouse not in occupation may register effectively: Watts v. Waller [1973] Q.B. 153.

[67] s. 2 (5).

[68] s. 2 (3).

[69] s. 3.

[70] Watts v. Waller, supra; Wroth v. Tyler [1974] Ch. 30.

[71] Cf. ante, p. 447.

[72] See Wroth v. Tyler, supra, at p. 46. For the conveyancing implications of the decision, see (1974) 38 Conv.(N.S.) 110 (D. J. Hayton).

CHAPTER 13

INCORPOREAL HEREDITAMENTS

1. Meaning of term. Incorporeal hereditaments are rights of property of certain special classes. Their distinguishing feature is that the law of real property applies to them, just as it applies to corporeal land.[1] But since the property owned is a mere right, and not a physical object, it is called incorporeal. The list of incorporeal hereditaments is a varied one, and it includes several curiosities; for it was for historical rather than logical reasons that certain rights were treated as real property instead of personal property. Most of them are, indeed, closely connected with land. But there is no logic in treating a rentcharge (the right to an income charged upon land) as real property and a lease as personal property; yet so it is.

2. Rules governing realty. The effect of denominating some particular right as an *hereditament* is most naturally illustrated, as the name indicates, by the old law of devolution on intestacy. If the owner of a rentcharge in fee simple died intestate before 1926, the rentcharge would devolve upon his heir as realty rather than upon his next-of-kin as personalty. In a similar way the system of estates and interests, both present and future, applied to incorporeal hereditaments.[2] For example, a rentcharge owned in fee simple by A could be settled by deed upon B for life with remainder to C in fee simple, whereas a lease, however long, could not at common law be granted by deed to B for life with remainder to C; any such grant would be an outright assignment to B, for no future interest could exist in personalty.[3]

---

[1] *Ante*, p. 11; *cf.* L.P.A., 1925, s. 205 (1) (ix).

[2] But complications arose in the case of entails, since the Statute *De Donis*, 1285 (*ante*, p. 94), applied only to "tenements." A tenement is something held in tenure, and strictly can include only corporeal land (*cf.* Challis 38; Williams R.P. 479) and, it seems, an advowson: Co.Litt. 85a; P. & M. ii, 148. But for the purposes of the statute "tenements" was held to mean all hereditaments which "savoured of the realty," *i.e.*, were connected with corporeal land: Co.Litt. 20a; Challis 43, 47, 61. Thus rentcharges were entailable (*ibid.*); but "tenements" could not include any kind of personalty, so that until 1926 leaseholds were not entailable even when it had become recognised that they involved tenure (*ante*, p. 613): Co.Litt. 20a, Hargrave's note; Fearne 463. For other purposes incorporeal hereditaments other than advowsons were not tenements, so that, for example, there was no escheat of a rentcharge or right of common: Challis 38; but *contra* Y.B. 10 Hen. 6, Mich., fo. 12, pl. 40 (1431), speaking of tenure of rent; and see Pike (1889) 5 L.Q.R. 32. The truth perhaps is that medieval concepts here led into deep waters which were never plumbed.

[3] Fearne 401, 402; *ante*, p. 46.

This old common law rule was not in practice a great handicap, for with the aid of a trust (equity here not following the law) or under a will (by reason of the indulgence shown towards a man's last will and testament) a life estate in a lease could be created.[4] Other examples of the " real " character of incorporeal hereditaments are that they can be conveyed only by deed, for they " lie in grant " [5]; and a will leaving " all my real property to X and all my personal property to Y " will pass a rentcharge to X but a lease to Y. It is therefore necessary to notice what rights rank as incorporeal hereditaments. Moreover, several of them are important interests in land which must be treated at length: these are rentcharges, easements and profits.

3. Contrast with corporeal hereditaments. Corporeal and incorporeal hereditaments together make up what is " real property " in the wide sense.[6] Corporeal hereditaments are physical objects, not rights, and they are of only one type: land, including buildings and other fixtures.[7] Incorporeal hereditaments are rights, not physical objects, and are of many types. This classification of *rights* and *things* as if they were similar has been ridiculed on theoretical grounds in Austin's *Jurisprudence*,[8] but in reality it is the inevitable outcome of having two separate systems of property law. A line has to be drawn between real and personal property in terms of the *things* which are governed by each set of rules. But there are many species of property which are not physical things but yet must be governed by property law. Personal property must include, for example, choses in action, *e.g.*, debts, money in a bank, stocks and shares; real property must equally necessarily include certain special interests of an intangible kind. The illogical part of the subject is not the inclusion of mere rights, but the kinds of rights which have been allotted to realty and personalty respectively. The early tendency to treat all rights as proprietary if that was at all possible made our law " rich with incorporeal things ": this is " the most medieval part of medieval law." [9]

---

[4] Fearne 401, 402, explaining that even pure personalty (*e.g.*, chattels) could be settled on a person for life under a trust, but not by will unless a trust was employed. But even by a trust it was impossible to create an entailed interest in leaseholds or any other personalty, for on this point equity followed the law: see n. 2 above.   [5] *Post*, p. 810.

[6] *Ante*, p. 11. But " real property " and " hereditaments " were not exactly coterminous. An annuity of inheritance (see next paragraph of text) was an hereditament but not real property, since real property was property recoverable by a real action: *cf*. Wolst. & C. i, 337.

[7] For fixtures, see *ante*, p. 711. Heritable chattels (" heirlooms ") should perhaps be classed separately, for they were chattels which descended like hereditaments: *ante*, p. 522.

[8] i, 372; *cf*. Cheshire, *Modern Real Property*, 11th ed., 111.

[9] P. & M. ii, 124, 149.

4. Principal incorporeal hereditaments. The following may be listed as incorporeal hereditaments.

(i) Rentcharges. A rentcharge is an annuity secured on some specified land.[10]

(ii) Annuities and corodies. These differ from rentcharges in not being secured upon or connected with land. An annuity, *e.g.*, £100 a year, could be granted or devised to a person and his heirs and would then devolve as an hereditament, like land.[11] A corody was paid in kind, and was a grant, usually by a religious house, to some person of board and lodging, and sometimes of clothing, of a certain kind for a certain period.[12] In early times corodies were popular as a form of salary or pension, but they have long been obsolete.

(iii) Advowsons. An advowson is the right of presentation to an ecclesiastical living.[13]

(iv) Tithes.[14] A rather similar right was " multure " of a mill, being the right of the owner to take a certain proportion of the corn ground.[15]

(v) Easements.[16] An example of an easement is a private right of way. It is only in modern times that easements have been recognised as incorporeal hereditaments.[16]

(vi) Profits *à prendre*,[17] for example, rights of common or of shooting or fishing.

(vii) Titles of honour, *e.g.*, peerages.[18] A baronetcy has been held to be " land," and also a " tenement " capable of being entailed.[19]

(viii) Offices. Offices, like titles of honour, were in early times governed by land law, since an office holder was commonly remunerated by a grant of land. When this feudal practice died out offices were still thought of as property; they could be granted in fee simple, or for life, or in tail, and an aspirant to an office might

---

[10] Litt. 218; *post*, p. 792.
[11] H.E.L. iii, 152; Wolst. & C. v, 79; Challis 46; such a " personal hereditament " could not be entailed: *ibid.*; it was enforceable only against the grantor or his estate.
[12] P. & M. ii, 133; H.E.L. iii, 152, 153.
[13] Co.Litt. 17b.
[14] *Post*, p. 801.
[15] Co.Litt. 47a.
[16] *Post*, p. 805.
[17] *Post*, p. 805.
[18] Cru.Dig. iii, 167; Cruise, *Dignities*, 2nd ed., 468.
[19] *Re Rivett-Carnac's Will* (1885) 30 Ch.D. 136. The decision has been criticised on the ground that only territorial dignities " savoured of the realty " so as to be entailable (n. 2, *supra*): Hood & Challis, *Property Acts*, 485; Challis 45n. A reasoned attack on the proprietary character of titles of honour is made by Sweet in his edition of Challis, pp. 468–472.

obtain a grant of the reversion to it.[20] Thus the office of Marshal of England could be entailed, as could also those of Chamberlain of the Exchequer, steward of a manor, or forester. Other offices of inheritance mentioned by Coke [21] are those of constable, bedell, parker (*i.e.*, keeper of a park), falconer and master of hounds. Indeed, any office properly granted can probably be made inheritable [22]; but the only inherited offices now to be found are probably ancient. Even in early times the grant of an office for a term longer than life was a rarity. But grants for life or for a term of years were common.

(ix) Franchises. These were royal rights or privileges granted by the Crown to a subject.[23] In the early Middle Ages they were of many kinds. Examples are fairs, markets, the right to wrecks and treasure trove,[24] and free fisheries.[25] Lords of manors, also, were often given special rights of jurisdiction, such as the right to hang thieves, or the right to the chattels of condemned felons which normally belonged to the Crown.[26]

5. Future interests. Reversions and remainders have been called incorporeal hereditaments by most modern authorities [27]; but this is thought to be wrong.[28] The relationship between hereditament and estate is expressed by saying that *land* is always held (if corporeal, in *tenure* [29]) for some *estate*; and estates are either in possession, in remainder or in reversion.[30] If this is accepted, reversions and remainders cannot themselves be hereditaments; they describe merely the nature of the estate for which some hereditament is held. If corporeal land is settled upon A for life, with remainder to B in fee simple, B's property is not a mere incorporeal right but the actual land, subject to A's life interest. Again, a right

---

20 For conditions of tenure, see Litt. 378 and Coke's commentary. The sale of judicial offices was prohibited by statute in 1552: 5 & 6 Edw. 6, c. 16.
21 Co.Litt. 20a; 233a, b. Not all of these were entailable.
22 *Contra*, Challis 45n., but there seems to be no clear authority for his opinion. For dispositions of public offices (civil service) see D. W. Logan (1945) 61 L.Q.R. 249–253.
23 P. & M. i, 571, 642; H.E.L. i, 87; iii, 169; Bl.Comm. i, 302.
24 See *ante*, p. 71.
25 See *post*, p. 824.
26 P. & M. i, 576, ii, 6.
27 Preston i, 14; Challis 48; Williams R.P. 30. The reason for this doctrine is probably an inversion of the rule that incorporeal hereditaments lay in grant (*post*, p. 810); but it does not follow that everything which lay in grant was an incorporeal hereditament. Williams (*ibid.*) also calls a seignory (*ante*, p. 14) an incorporeal hereditament; and *cf.* P. & M. ii, 125. A seignory, at any rate in one possible view, was simply a special kind of interest in corporeal land, much like a reversion but in the realm of tenure, not estate.
28 See Sweet's critical note in Challis 52, 53.
29 *Ante*, p. 787, n. 2.
30 *Ante*, p. 47.

of entry and a possibility of reverter [31] are probably simply attenuated forms of ownership of corporeal land, not incorporeal hereditaments in themselves.[32] If Y wrongfully occupies X's land, X's property is not changed from a corporeal to an incorporeal thing (a mere right to recover his land) [33]: X remains owner of the land itself, though his title may be barred if he does not assert it within twelve years.[34]

6. Variations of law. All incorporeal hereditaments were, and are, subject to the law of real property, but their nature has demanded concessions of various kinds. We have already noticed the mode of taking dower out of an advowson, by allowing the widow to make each third presentation.[35] Neither dower nor curtesy could be taken out of a title of honour, which was impartible. Nor, for the same reason, could it be held in co-parcenary; a title which descended upon co-parceners went into abeyance,[36] subject to the king's prerogative to revive it in any of them or their issue.[37] But the Crown, the highest inheritance in the kingdom, descends to an elder heiress to the exclusion of a younger, by a special and necessary rule.[38] An office could, it seems, be held in co-parcenary.[39]

7. 1925 legislation. The legislation of 1925, like other legislation affecting land, generally applies to incorporeal hereditaments, since they are within the meaning of the term " land." The Law of Property Act, 1925 applies to them, " subject only to the qualifications necessarily arising by reason of the inherent nature of the hereditament affected." [40] The provisions of the Administration of Estates Act, 1925, which abolish the old law of inheritance and lay down the new order of succession,[41] appear to be intended to apply only to property which is disposable by will,[42] thus excluding titles of honour, which are inalienable.[43]

---

[31] For these interests, see *ante*, p. 74.
[32] *Contra*, Challis 46n.
[33] *Contra*, Williams R.P. 30, 31; Challis 46n. curiously speaks of a right to bring a writ of error as a hereditament, which Coke, whom he cites, does not.
[34] *Post*, p. 1003.   [35] *Ante*, p. 518.
[36] Cruise, *Dignities*, 2nd ed., 181.   [37] *Ibid.*, 183, 184.
[38] Co.Litt. 15b, 165a; Bl.Comm. ii, 194.
[39] See the case of the Great Chamberlain, Hargrave's note to Co.Litt. 165a; Challis 115.
[40] s. 201, which also precludes any power to dispose of an advowson except as permitted by the Benefices Act, 1898, or of an inalienable title or dignity of honour.
[41] *Ante*, p. 523.
[42] A.E.A., 1925, s. 52; but the section is faultily drafted: Wolst. & C. v, 99. It is said (*ibid.*, 10) that titles of honour are not within s. 1, but that appears to be doubtful. Most titles are entailed and so excepted from s. 1 by s. 3 (3) (*cf.* s. 45 (2)). Others are presumably outside it because the modern scheme of devolution cannot apply to property incapable of being conveyed.
[43] Cruise, *Dignities*, 2nd ed., 111; they cannot even be surrendered to the Crown: *Norfolk Peerage Claim* [1907] A.C. 10. But see now Peerage Act 1963.

The principal incorporeal hereditaments of any importance today are rentcharges, easements and profits; and in addition, something must be said of advowsons and tithes. These will now be examined.

Part 1

RENTCHARGES

Sect. 1.   Nature of Rentcharges

1. Rentcharges and rent services. Periodical payments in respect of land fall under the two main heads of rentcharges and rent services. Where the relationship of lord and tenant exists between the parties, any rent payable by virtue of that relationship by the tenant to the lord is a rent service.[44] If there is no relationship of lord and tenant, the rent is a rentcharge. Thus if L grants a lease to T at £100 per annum and X charges his fee simple estate with the payment of £200 per annum to Y, L has a rent service and Y a rentcharge. Since the Statute *Quia Emptores*, 1290, it has been impossible for a grantor to reserve any services on a conveyance of freehold land in fee simple, for the grantee holds of the grantor's lord, and not of the grantor.[45] Consequently no rent reserved on a conveyance of freehold land in fee simple after 1290 can be a rent service. Although at law services could be reserved on the grant by a fee simple owner of a life estate or a fee tail,[46] it was most unusual to do so.

The only rent service met with in practice is thus the rent reserved upon the grant of a lease for a term of years. A rent reserved by a lease is annexed to a reversion in land, while a rentcharge stands on its own as an incorporeal hereditament. The majority of rent services reserved on the grant of a fee simple in freehold land before *Quia Emptores*, 1290, have remained uncollected for so long (the fall in the value of money having made them not worth collecting) that they have been both forgotten and barred by lapse of time.[47] Such rents were usually known as chief rents or

[44] *Ante*, p. 689.
[45] *Ante*, p. 30.
[46] It should be remembered that if any rent service is reserved on the grant of an estate for life, the estate is now automatically converted into a term of 90 years: *ante*, p. 642.
[47] *Owen* v. *de Beauvoir* (1847) 16 M. & W. 547. Uncollected freehold rent services were barred after twenty years under the Real Property Limitation Act, 1833, s. 2; but *quaere* whether they are within the Limitation Act, 1939; *post*, p. 1018.

quit rents in the case of freehold land. Any still existing at the end of 1925 were likely to be manorial (for only then was the preservation of an ancient title probable) and these were classed with those manorial incidents in copyhold land which were extinguished at the end of 1935 at the latest.[48]

2. Rents seck. At common law the relationship of lord and tenant carried with it an automatic right of distress for any rent.[49] If no such relationship existed, there was no common law right of distress, and consequently an express clause of distress was frequently inserted when reserving the rent. A rent supported by no right of distress was known as a rent seck,[50] and the name rentcharge was reserved for a rent supported by a power of distress given by the instrument creating the rent or by statute. Rents seck ceased to exist many years ago, for by the Landlord and Tenant Act, 1730,[51] the owners of rents seck were given the same rights of distress as a landlord has against his tenant under a lease; that is to say, the landlord might impound such chattels as were to be found on the land charged with the rent.[52] Since even this was a far from perfect remedy, a right of entry might also be inserted in the original grant, which would enable the payee to take possession of the land to enforce payment of arrears.[53] This in turn was rendered unnecessary by the Conveyancing Act, 1881, the provisions of which (as now re-enacted) are explained below.[54]

3. Legal and equitable rentcharges. A rentcharge is real property, so that both at law and in equity it could be held for any of the usual estates or interests, such as an estate tail[55] or a term of years.[56] But now, since 1925, an interest in a rentcharge can be legal only if it is—

(a) in possession,[57] and

(b) either perpetual or for a term of years absolute.[58]

Further, a legal rentcharge cannot be created at law without certain

[48] *Ante*, p. 36.
[49] *Ante*, p. 691.
[50] Litt. 218 (Latin *siccus*=dry, barren).
[51] s. 5; *cf. Re Lord Gerard and Beecham's Contract* [1894] 3 Ch. 295.
[52] For distress, see *ante*, p. 691.
[53] For an example, see *ante*, p. 138. Such a right of entry was incident to the rentcharge and transferable with the right to receive it.
[54] *Post*, p. 797.
[55] *Ante*, p. 787, n. 2; *Chaplin* v. *Chaplin* (1733) 3 P.Wms. 229.
[56] *Re Fraser* [1904] 1 Ch. 726.
[57] As to when a rentcharge is deemed to be in possession, see *ante*, pp. 141, 142.
[58] L.P.A., 1925, s. 1 (2) (*b*); *ante*, p. 141.

formalities.[59] A mere contract for a rentcharge may however create an equitable interest in the usual way.[60]

4. Rentcharge on a rentcharge. At common law a rentcharge could be charged only upon a corporeal hereditament. There could be no rentcharge charged upon another rentcharge [61] or other incorporeal hereditament,[62] since obviously there could then be no right of distress. But this technical obstacle was removed both for the past and for the future by the Law of Property Act, 1925,[63] which validates rentcharges charged on other rentcharges and provides special machinery for enforcing payment.

Sect. 2. Creation and Transfer of Rentcharges

1. Creation. A rentcharge may be created by statute, by an instrument *inter vivos*, or by will.

(a) *By statute.* A rentcharge may be created by statute, or by virtue of powers conferred thereby.[64]

(b) *By instrument inter vivos.* Apart from statute, a legal rentcharge can be created *inter vivos* only by a deed,[65] although it has always been possible for a person disposing of land to reserve a rentcharge to himself, without the grantee of the land executing the deed.[66]

An equitable rentcharge may be created merely by contract [67] or by signed writing.[68]

(c) *By will.* A will now operates only in equity [69]; therefore, if a rentcharge is created or devised by will, the beneficiary gets no legal interest until the personal representatives have assented to the gift. The assent must be in writing, but need not be by deed.[70]

---

[59] See *infra*.
[60] *Jackson* v. *Lever* (1792) 3 Bro.C.C. 605; *cf. ante*, p. 624.
[61] Co.Litt. 47a ; *Earl of Stafford* v. *Buckley* (1750) 2 Ves.Sen. 170 at 178.
[62] *Re The Alms Corn Charity* [1901] 2 Ch. 750 at 759.
[63] s. 122; *post*, p. 798.
[64] See, *e.g.*, Improvement of Land Acts, 1864 and 1899, which empowered a landowner (*e.g.*, a tenant for life) to obtain an order from the Ministry of Agriculture, Fisheries and Food charging the land with repayment of money borrowed to finance improvements. These Acts were in general superseded by the Settled Land Acts, 1882 and 1925 (*ante*, p. 282), but the Act of 1864 is still occasionally resorted to because (by s. 59) it may give the rentcharge priority over other incumbrances.
[65] *Hewlins* v. *Shippam* (1826) 5 B. & C. 221 at 229. The usual exceptions apply : see L.P.A., 1925, s. 52.
[66] Co.Litt. 143a.
[67] Above, n. 60.
[68] L.P.A., 1925, s. 53, replacing Statute of Frauds, 1677, ss. 3, 7.
[69] L.P.(Am.)A., 1924, Sched. IX; *ante*, p. 535.
[70] A.E.A., 1925, s. 36; *ante*, p. 537.

2. Words of limitation

(a) *Transfer.* The words of limitation required for the transfer of an existing rentcharge are governed by the ordinary rules for dispositions of land,[71] so that a will made after 1837 or a deed executed since 1925 will pass the whole interest in the rentcharge unless a contrary intention is shown.[72]

(b) *Creation.* On the creation of a new rentcharge the Wills Act, 1837, s. 28, has been held not to apply; it is confined to the transfer of an existing interest.[73] Accordingly the devisee of a rentcharge created by the will can take it only for life unless a contrary intention appears.[74]

It is not so clear whether the Law of Property Act, 1925, s. 60,[75] applies to the creation of rentcharges by deed. Its general form is very like that of the Wills Act, 1837, s. 28; but it applies to every " conveyance of freehold land " executed since 1925, and " conveyance " includes a " mortgage, charge, lease " (all of which create interests *de novo*, although these are not new hereditaments) and " every other assurance of property or of an interest therein by any instrument except a will." [76] It would be a narrow construction of this definition to hold that a deed creating a rentcharge was not an " assurance of property or of an interest therein," and it is perhaps the more likely prospect that a perpetual rentcharge will now be held to need no special words of limitation when created by deed. If this is wrong, the pre-1926 rules will apply and only a life interest will result unless proper words of limitation are used.[77]

Sect. 3. Means of Enforcing Payment of Rentcharges

A. *Rentcharge Charged on Land*

There are four remedies available to the owner of a rentcharge if it is not paid. The first remedy, namely, an action for the money, is given by the common law; the other three are given by statute,[78] thus making unnecessary the express powers of corresponding effect

---

[71] *Ante*, pp. 50 *et seq.*
[72] Wills Act, 1837, s. 28; L.P.A., 1925, s. 60 (1).
[73] *Nichols* v. *Hawkes* (1853) 10 Hare 342.
[74] *Ante*, p. 56.
[75] *Ante*, p. 56; *cf. post*, p. 828, n. 66.
[76] L.P.A., 1925, s. 205 (1) (ii).
[77] The decision in *Grant* v. *Edmondson* [1930] 2 Ch. 245; [1931] 1 Ch. 1 seems to be founded not on any rule peculiar to rentcharges but on the rule that words of limitation might be incorporated by reference to another instrument: *ante*, p. 53; *cf.* (1931) 47 L.Q.R. 380 (W. Strachan).
[78] L.P.A., 1925, s. 121, replacing C.A., 1881, s. 44, and C.A., 1911, s. 6.

which were often inserted in deeds creating rentcharges. These statutory remedies avail only in so far as they might have been conferred by express stipulation,[79] so that they do not extend the law. They also yield to any contrary intention expressed in the instrument creating the rentcharge.[80]

1. Action for the money. A personal action for the rent (as for a debt) will lie against the "terre tenant" (the freehold tenant for the time being of the land upon which the rent is charged), even if the rent was not created by him [81] and even if it exceeds the value of the land.[82] If the land charged has been divided, the terre tenant of any part is liable for the full amount.[83] A mere lessee for a term of years is not liable,[84] for the action is the modern successor of one of the ancient real actions,[85] which lay only against the person seised of the land, *i.e.*, the freeholder in possession. Its "real" nature is attested by the fact that though nominally a personal action it lies against assignees of the land. In truth, "the land is the debtor," [86] and the action asserts title to an incorporeal hereditament.

Although the right to sue and the liability to be sued run with the rentcharge and the land, respectively, the benefit of an express covenant for payment does not run with the rentcharge without express assignment.[87] Thus if a rentcharge created by A in favour of X is conveyed to Y and the land to B, Y cannot sue A on his covenant for payment if B fails to pay: A is liable to Y only while A is entitled in possession, unless Y is an express assignee of X's rights under the covenant to pay. This is another illustration of the medieval view of a rent as a thing rather than a promise.

2. Distress. If an express power of distress is given by the instrument creating the rentcharge, the extent of the right is a question of construction. If there is no such express power, and the rentcharge was created before 1882, the rentcharge owner can distrain upon the land as soon as the rent or any part of it is in

---

[79] L.P.A., 1925, s. 121 (1).
[80] *Ibid.*, s. 121 (5), (7).
[81] *Thomas* v. *Sylvester* (1873) L.R. 8 Q.B. 368.
[82] *Pertwee* v. *Townsend* [1896] 2 Q.B. 129.
[83] *Christie* v. *Barker* (1884) 53 L.J.Q.B. 537.
[84] *Re Herbage Rents* [1896] 2 Ch. 811. A mortgagee is therefore not liable since 1925, for he holds a mere term of years: previously he was liable if he took a freehold estate: *Cundiff* v. *Fitzsimmons* [1911] 1 K.B. 513.
[85] *Post*, p. 1167.
[86] *Thomas* v. *Sylvester, supra*, at p. 372, *per* Quain J.
[87] *Grant* v. *Edmondson* [1931] 1 Ch. 1, where the rentcharge was created before 1926; for rentcharges created after 1925, see Halsbury, 2nd. ed., Vol. 28, p. 242. For criticism of *Grant* v. *Edmondson*, see (1931) 47 L.Q.R. 380 (W. Strachan). *Cf.* Law Commission Working Paper No. 49, para. 109.

arrear.[88] If the rentcharge was created after 1881,[89] then, subject to any contrary intention,[90] the rentcharge owner can distrain as soon as the rent or any part of it is twenty-one days in arrear.[91]

3. Entry into possession. If a rentcharge was created after 1881[92] and shows no contrary intention,[93] the rentcharge owner may, when the rent or any part of it is forty days in arrear, enter and take possession of the land without impeachment of waste and take the income until he has paid himself all rent due with costs.[94]

4. Demise to a trustee. If the rentcharge was created after 1881[95] and shows no contrary intention,[96] the rentcharge owner may, if the rent or any part of it is forty days in arrear, demise the land to a trustee for a term of years, with or without impeachment of waste, on trust to raise the money due, with all costs and expenses, by creating a mortgage, receiving the income or any other reasonable means.[97] If a rentcharge owner has only an equitable interest, he can grant only an equitable lease to the trustees,[98] but the estate owner can be compelled to clothe the equitable lease with the legal estate.[99]

These last three remedies are expressly excepted from the law relating to perpetuities, together with like powers conferred by any instrument for enforcing payment of a rentcharge.[1] This provision is perhaps not wide enough to cover a clause which is sometimes inserted entitling the rentcharge owner to effect a permanent forfeiture of the land if the rent is unpaid for a specified period, properly called a right of re-entry as opposed to a right of entry.[2] The general rule that such a power is void unless confined to the perpetuity period[3] probably applies in such a case.[4] However, if the rentcharge was created after July 15, 1964, the rule against perpetuities does not apply to any powers or remedies for recovery or enforcing payment, whether statutory or otherwise.[5]

---

[88] L. & T.A., 1730, s. 5.
[89] L.P.A., 1925, s. 121 (7).
[90] *Ibid.*, s. 121 (5).
[92] *Ibid.*, s. 121 (7).
[94] *Ibid.*, s. 121 (3).
[96] *Ibid.*, s. 121 (5).
[98] *Ibid.*
[91] *Ibid.*, s. 121 (2).
[93] *Ibid.*, s. 121 (5).
[95] *Ibid.*, s. 121 (7).
[97] *Ibid.*, s. 121 (4).
[99] L.P.A., 1925, ss. 3 (1), 8 (2); S.L.A., 1925, s. 16.
[1] L.P.A., 1925, s. 121 (6) (amended by Perpetuities and Accumulations Act 1964, s. 11 (2)), replacing C.A., 1911, s. 6 (1).
[2] *Ante*, p. 138.
[3] *Ante*, p. 247, discussing *Re Hollis' Hospital Trustees & Hague's Contract* [1899] 2 Ch. 540.
[4] The combined effect of L.P.A., 1925, ss. 4 (3), 121 (6), 162, 190 (8), is not at all plain: see Law Reform Committee's Fourth Report, 1956, Cmnd. 18, paras. 42, 43.
[5] Perpetuities and Accumulations Act 1964, ss. 11 (1), 15 (5).

B. *Rentcharge Charged on Another Rentcharge*

Instead of the statutory remedies of distress, entry into possession, and demise to a trustee, the owner of a rentcharge charged upon another rentcharge may appoint a receiver if the rent or any part of it is twenty-one days in arrear.[6] The receiver has all the powers of a receiver appointed by a mortgagee.[7] Thus if Blackacre is charged with a rent of £100 per annum and that rentcharge is charged with a rent of £25 per annum in favour of X, a receiver of the £100 can be appointed by X if the £25 is unpaid for twenty-one days.

There is no provision for any personal action against an assignee of the rentcharge upon which the second rentcharge is charged; but since the latter can be created " in like manner as the same could have been made to issue out of land "[8] it may be that the right to such a rentcharge is implicitly accompanied by the usual common law remedy.[9]

Sect. 4. Extinguishment of Rentcharges

A rentcharge may be extinguished by release, merger, lapse of time or statutory discharge.[9a]

1. Release. The owner of a rentcharge may by deed release the land from the rent, either wholly or in part. A partial release may take the form of releasing all of the land from part of the rent,[10] or releasing part of the land from the whole of the rent.[11] An informal release may be valid in equity.

A limited owner, *e.g.*, a life tenant, of a rentcharge cannot release more than his own interest, except under the powers conferred by the Settled Land Act, 1925.[12] Nor can the owner of a rentcharge charged upon several different properties increase the liability on one of them by releasing another, unless the owner of the property to be burdened concurs in the release.[13] Thus if a rent of £100 is charged on five plots of land owned by five different persons, and one plot is released, the rentcharge owner can recover £100 in respect of the four remaining plots if the owners concurred in the release,[14] but only £80 if they did not concur.[15]

---

[6] L.P.A., 1925, s. 122.
[7] *Ibid.*; and see *post*, p. 920, for such a receiver's powers.
[8] L.P.A., 1925, s. 122 (1).   [9] *Ante*, p. 795.
[9a] Proposals for extinguishment after a fixed period are made in Law Commission Working Paper No. 49, paras. 60, 67.   [10] Co.Litt. 148a.
[11] L.P.A., 1925, s. 70, replacing L.P.(Am.)A., 1859, s. 10. Under the old law the result was to release the whole of the land : Co.Litt. 147b.
[12] *Ante*, p. 313.
[13] L.P.A., 1925, s. 70, replacing L.P.(Am.)A., 1859, s. 10.
[14] *Price* v. *John* [1905] 1 Ch. 774.   [15] *Booth* v. *Smith* (1884) 14 Q.B.D. 318.

2. Merger. At common law, if a rentcharge became vested in the same person as the land upon which it was charged, the rentcharge became extinguished by merger, even if this was not the intention.[16] For this to occur, both the rent and the land must have been vested in the same person at the same time and in the same right.[17] This automatic rule of the common law no longer applies, for by the Law of Property Act, 1925,[18] there is to be no merger at law except in cases where there would have been a merger in equity, and the equitable rule is that merger depends upon the intention of the parties.[19] Even if an intention that there should be no merger cannot be shown, there will be a presumption against merger if it is to the interest of the person concerned to prevent it.[20]

3. Lapse of time. If a rentcharge is not paid for twelve years and no sufficient acknowledgment of the owner's title is made, it is extinguished.[21]

4. Statutory discharge. By the Law of Property Act, 1925,[22] provision is made for landowners to obtain the discharge of their land from rentcharges on paying to the rentcharge owner a sum representing the capital value as certified by the appropriate Secretary of State.

Sect. 5. Note on the Types of Rent

A summary of the various kinds of rent may be useful.[22a]

1. Rent service: this is rent due from a tenant to his lord by reason of tenure. It is now met with only in the case of rent due under a lease or tenancy.

2. Rentcharge: this is a periodical sum charged on land independently of any relationship of lord and tenant, supported by a power of distress.

3. Rent seck: this was a rentcharge with no power of distress. It is now obsolete.

---

[16] *Capital and Counties Bank Ltd.* v. *Rhodes* [1903] 1 Ch. 631 at 652, 653.
[17] *Re Radcliffe* [1892] 1 Ch. 227 at 231.
[18] s. 185, replacing J.A., 1873, s. 25 (4).
[19] *Ingle* v. *Vaughan Jenkins* [1900] 2 Ch. 368.
[20] *Re Fletcher* [1917] 1 Ch. 339; but see *Re Attkins* [1913] 2 Ch. 619.
[21] Limitation Act, 1939, s. 18 (1); *Shaw* v. *Crompton* [1910] 2 K.B. 370; *post*, p. 1018.
[22] s. 191, extending C.A., 1881, s. 45. Provision is made for payment into court in case of difficulty, *e.g.*, if the owner of the rentcharge cannot be found, or cannot prove his title to it.
[22a] For a summary of these and many other types of rent, related to economics and the like, see (1974) 232 E.G. 349.

4. Chief rent: this was a rent service reserved on the subinfeudation of freehold land in fee simple. The Statute *Quia Emptores,* 1290, for the most part prevented such rents being created.[23] Those previously created mostly fell into abeyance long ago, but some survived in manors where there were freehold tenants. Any manorial chief rents existing in 1925 were extinguished by the end of 1935.[24] In some parts of the country, *e.g.*, Manchester, rentcharges are sometimes called chief rents.

5. Fee farm rent: this was the name originally used for chief rents; latterly it has been applied to rentcharges reserved on a conveyance in fee simple.[25]

6. Quit rent: this was a rent service payable by a copyholder to his lord, whereby he went quit of his obligation to perform agricultural services; and chief rents were sometimes called quit rents. Quit rents existing in 1925 were extinguished by the end of 1935.[26]

7. Rents of assize: this term is rarely encountered today; it was applied both to chief rents and quit rents.

Part 2

ADVOWSONS

An advowson (from the Latin *advocatio*) is the perpetual right of presentation to an ecclesiastical living.[27] The owner of an advowson is known as the patron. When a living becomes vacant, as when a rector or vicar dies or retires, the patron of the living has a right to nominate the clergyman who shall next hold the living. Subject to a right of veto on certain specified grounds, the bishop is bound to institute (formally appoint) any duly qualified person presented. This is a relic of the days when it was common for the lord of a manor to build and endow a church and in return have the right of patronage.

---

23 *Ante*, p. 792.
24 *Ante*, p. 793.
25 *Ante*, p. 138; *cf.* Cru.Dig. iii, 274; Co.Litt. 143b, n. 5 by Hargrave, disapproving a note to *Bradbury* v. *Wright* (1781) 2 Doug.K.B. 624 at 627n. which suggests that the rent must be at least one-quarter of the value of the land, and contending that only rent service can be a fee farm rent. *Sed quaere.*
26 *Ante*, p. 793.
27 Co.Litt. 17b.

It is one of the curiosities of English law that an advowson is real property. There is no physical land of which the patron is owner, but the advowson is an incorporeal hereditament and the patron has an estate in what in law is real property. His estate in an advowson will accordingly pass under a devise of " all my real property."

Under the old law of inheritance advowsons could be subject to dower or curtesy on an intestacy.[28] What happens to them under the new law of intestate succession [29] is far from clear.[30]

Legal estates and equitable interests may exist in an advowson as in other real property; thus a life interest in an advowson is necessarily equitable, while a fee simple absolute in possession may exist as a legal estate.[31]

Advowsons may be either appendant, *i.e.*, annexed to a manor, so that the right of presentation will pass to the owner for the time being of the manor; or in gross, *i.e.*, held independently of land. They are subject to a number of important restrictions (in particular, upon their sale) both at common law and by statute,[32] which prevents serious abuses of this incursion of property into religion. These are more appropriate to books on ecclesiastical law [33] than to a textbook on real property.

Part 3

TITHES

A tithe was the right of a rector to a tenth part of the produce of all the land in his parish. In some cases a rector was an individual while in others the rectory was vested ("appropriated") in a monastery, who appointed a vicar to perform the necessary

---

[28] *Ante*, p. 518.
[29] *Ante*, p. 523.
[30] They are disposable by will, and so within Pt. IV of A.E.A., 1925: see s. 52. That makes them subject to a trust for sale on an intestacy (*ante*, p. 523) but their sale is restricted by the Benefices Act, 1898, and the Benefices Act, 1898 (Amendment) Measure, 1923, which in most cases prohibit sale after two vacancies subsequent to July 14, 1924, or after a declaration made under seal by the owners. Vaisey J. described this conflict as " an insoluble problem ": *The Times*, November 10, 1944; but see 1945 Conv.Y.B. 296. A similar problem arises if an advowson is devised to joint tenants or tenants in common. But the Measure does not prevent the sale of land to which an advowson is appendant.
[31] *Ante*, p. 134; L.P.A., 1925, ss. 1, 205 (1) (ix).
[32] See n. 30 above.
[33] *e.g.*, Cripps on *Church and Clergy*, 8th ed., 253–263.

ecclesiastical duties "vicariously" for the monastery.[34] On the dissolution of the monasteries in the reign of Henry VIII many rectories passed into the royal hands and were granted to laymen; the result was that the right to tithes in many cases passed into lay hands, and was said to be "impropriated" by the lay rector. This carried with it the rector's common law liability to repair the chancel of the church,[35] and any other customary duties which could be performed by a layman.[36] Like rentcharges and advowsons, tithes were deemed to be land in which the various estates could exist. The history of tithes falls into four periods.

1. Before the Tithe Act, 1836. Originally tithe was payable in kind, a tenth of the corn, wood, milk, eggs and so on being handed to the tithe owner, as witness the many tithe barns still standing. To avoid the inconvenience of each landowner paying his tithe in a variety of products, in many cases an agreement was made for the satisfaction of tithe by, say, the delivery of one quarter of the hay instead of one tenth of all the produce of the land, or the payment of a sum of money. This was often known as a "modus" (or *modus decimandi, i.e.,* method of taking one tenth).[37]

In the numerous local Inclosure Acts of the seventeenth, eighteenth and early nineteenth centuries, under which communal agriculture gave way to individual holdings, tithes were commuted either by allotments of land to the rector, or by the creation of rentcharges, or by both. Liability for the repair of the chancel then fell upon the owner for the time being of the rectorial property. Although technically it was a personal liability rather than a charge on land,[37a] it was in effect an incumbrance affecting future owners.[38] If the land was subdivided each owner remained fully liable, though he could claim contribution from the others.[39]

Rentcharges resulting from Inclosure Acts in this way were known as corn rents, and were made variable with agricultural prices, generally with the price of wheat. Corn rents must be

---

[34] The rector might grant some or all of the tithes to the vicar. Vicars often took the "small tithes," *i.e.,* all except corn, hay and wood; but such practices were very varied: see Millard, *Tithes,* 8, 9.

[35] See *Wickhambrook Parochial Church Council* v. *Croxford* [1935] 2 K.B. 417; *Chivers & Sons Ltd.* v. *Air Ministry* [1955] Ch. 585; Millard, *Tithes,* 143–145; Chancel Repairs Act, 1932.

[36] *e.g.,* to keep a bull and a boar for the common use of parishioners: *Lanchbury* v. *Bode* [1898] 2 Ch. 120.

[37] Strictly speaking, a "modus" was a composition existing since time immemorial, *i.e.,* made before 1189; a later composition was called a "composition real." *Cf.* Millard, *Tithes,* 7; *Roberts* v. *Williams* (1810) 12 East 33 (where a modus of 1d. for every turkey laying eggs was disputed on the ground that turkeys were not known in England until about 1555).

[37a] *Wickhambrook Parochial Church Council* v. *Croxford, supra.*

[38] It is an overriding interest (*post,* p. 1065) under L.R.A., 1925, s. 70 (1) (c).

[39] *Wickhambrook Parochial Church Council* v. *Croxford, supra.*

distinguished from tithes, since they have received different treatment from the legislature.

2. Between the Tithe Act, 1836, and the Tithe Act, 1925. The Tithe Act, 1836, abolished the payment of tithe in kind and substituted therefor a tithe rentcharge on the land. Commissioners fixed a yearly amount which each plot of land was to bear, and this was known as the " commuted value." The actual sum payable each year, however, varied according to the average prices of wheat, barley and oats for the previous seven years, and thus varied directly according to the prosperity of agriculture. Tithe rentcharge was not recoverable in the same way as an ordinary rentcharge, but only under an order of the county court; the landowner was not, as in the case of ordinary rentcharges, personally liable for the money payable.

Corn rents continued as before, but provision was made for converting them into tithe rentcharge by obtaining a ministerial order under the Tithe Act, 1860. If this was done they came within the Tithe Acts of 1925 and 1936. Schemes for their apportionment and redemption may now be made under the Corn Rents Act 1963.

3. Between the Tithe Act, 1925, and the Tithe Act, 1936. The Tithe Act, 1925, stabilised the amount payable for tithes. For each £100 commuted value of tithe rentcharge, £105 became payable, irrespective of fluctuations in the price of corn. In the case of ecclesiastical tithe rentcharge (*i.e.*, rentcharge still payable to some church authority) a further £4 10s. was payable, making £109 10s. 0d. per £100 commuted value; this additional sum went to a sinking fund which by the end of a fixed period [40] would have produced approximately enough income to replace the rentcharge and so allow its extinguishment. There was no similar provision for lay tithe rentcharge or for corn rents, but the landowner could insist on discharging his land from them by paying a lump sum ascertained by a prescribed method.[41]

4. After the Tithe Act, 1936. The Tithe Act, 1936,[42] extinguished all tithe rentcharge, whether ecclesiastical or lay, as from October 2, 1936. The Act put an end to the collection of the money by the tithe owner direct from the landowner, for this had too often been made only with the assistance of the county court aided by the police and had given rise to much friction in agricultural districts,

[40] 85 years if the charge was annexed to a benefice; 81½ years if payable to an ecclesiastical corporation.

[41] Redemption at the landowner's option had already been introduced, but subject to restrictions, by the Tithe Act, 1918.

[42] s. 1. The Act was amended by the Tithe Act, 1951 and the Corn Rents Act 1963.

especially where farmers who were not supporters of the Church
of England were compelled to provide that Church with substantial
financial assistance in years when their profits from farming were
small.

The main provisions of the Act are as follows.

(*a*) *Tithe redemption annuities.* Land formerly charged with
a tithe rentcharge payable to the tithe owner now stands charged
with a " tithe redemption annuity " payable to the Crown, for which
the landowner is personally liable.[42a] These annuities are collected
by the Commissioners of Inland Revenue.[43]

(*b*) *Amount of annuities.* The amount of the annuity is—

  (i) £91 11s. 2d. per £100 commuted value of rentcharge if
    any of the land was agricultural land on April 1, 1936;

  (ii) £105 per £100 commuted value of rentcharge in other
    cases.

Thus for agricultural land the Act has reduced the annual sum
payable per £100 commuted value from £109 10s. to £91 11s. 2d.
in the case of ecclesiastical tithe rentcharge, and from £105 to
£91 11s. 2d. in the case of lay tithe rentcharge. In the case of
non-agricultural land, ecclesiastical tithe rentcharge has been reduced
by £4 10s. 0d.; otherwise it is unchanged.

(*c*) *Period of annuities.* The annuities are payable for sixty
years and then cease. From the money paid during this period a
fund is being built up out of which the tithe redemption stock (see
(*e*) below) will be redeemed. From the tithe payer's point of view
the period of sixty years compares favourably with the former
provision for redemption of ecclesiastical tithe rentcharge. However,
on any disposition or creation of an estate or interest in the land
after October 1, 1962, which brings about a change in the person
who is the owner of the land, any tithe redemption annuity charged
on the land must be redeemed.[44] For this purpose, the owner of
the land is the owner of the fee simple, or, if the land is subject to
a lease for more than fourteen years at a rent less than two-thirds
of the annual value, the owner of that lease.[45]

(*d*) *Status of annuities.* The annuities are legal interests within
section 1 (2) of the Law of Property Act, 1925 [46]; they are not
registrable under the Land Charges Act 1972.

[42a] Tithe Act, 1936, s. 16 (1). Where the land is settled, the burden falls on the
  tenant for life: *Re Leicester's Settled Estates* [1939] Ch. 77.
[43] S.I. 1959 No. 1971.   [44] Finance Act, 1962, s. 32 (1).
[45] Finance Act, 1962 s. 32 (2), applying Tithe Act, 1936, s. 17.
[46] See *ante*, p. 144.

(e) Tithe redemption stock. Tithe owners were compensated by the issue to them of "tithe redemption stock" upon which interest of 3 per cent. per annum is paid. The payment, being charged on the Consolidated Fund, is guaranteed by the government and is redeemable within sixty years. The stock can be bought and sold in the same way as other stock and is not, of course, an interest in real property. The interest produced by the stock is rather less than the amount of tithe formerly payable, but the tithe owner now has the certainty of receiving his income in full and without trouble, independently of the financial position of any landowner. At the same time the liability of most [47] lay tithe owners to repair chancels was extinguished, a proportionate part of the redemption stock being allotted to the diocesan authorities instead of to the tithe owner.

The Act did not apply to corn rents, unless they had previously been converted into tithe rentcharge. Corn rents are therefore still payable under the various Inclosure Acts, but there is statutory machinery for their redemption. [47a]

Part 4

EASEMENTS AND PROFITS

The common law recognised a limited number of rights which one landowner could acquire over the land of another; and these rights were called easements and profits. Examples of easements are rights of way, rights of light and rights of water. Examples of profits are rights to dig gravel, or cut turf, or to take game or fish.

Nowadays both these classes of rights are incorporeal hereditaments. [48] But before the eighteenth century easements were not properly so described, because an easement could exist only if it was "appurtenant" (*i.e.*, annexed) to some piece of land (the dominant tenement) so as to benefit it. It was therefore said that easements were not incorporeal hereditaments, but rights appurtenant to corporeal hereditaments [49]; or, in other words, that an easement

---

[47] For the exceptions (*e.g.*, Queen Anne's Bounty and the Ecclesiastical Commissioners (now both replaced by the Church Commissioners), Universities and Colleges), see Tithe Act, 1936, s. 31 (2)–(4).

[47a] *Ante*, p. 803, n. 41.

[48] *Hewlins* v. *Shippam* (1826) 5 B. & C. 221 at 229; *Hill* v. *Midland Ry.* (1882) 21 Ch.D. 143; *Great Western Ry.* v. *Swindon Ry.* (1882) 22 Ch.D. 677; 9 App.Cas. 787; *Jones* v. *Watts* (1890) 43 Ch.D. 574 at 585; contrast *Re Brotherton's and Markham's S. E.* (1907) 97 L.T. 880 at 882; on appeal 98 L.T. 547; Sweet's note to Challis 55, 56.

[49] Challis 51, 52, 55.

was not an object of property in itself, but was a privilege which could be obtained for the benefit of corporeal land. The same could be said of a profit (or even of an advowson) when it was attached to and passed with some particular parcel of land. But profits, like advowsons but unlike easements, could also exist " in gross," that is to say without any dominant tenement. For example, rights of mining or of shooting are often held by persons who are not adjacent landowners; but rights of way or rights of light are not. Rights held in gross were clearly incorporeal hereditaments.

In modern times the attempt to distinguish rights which are merely appurtenances has been abandoned, and easements and profits are classed together indiscriminately as incorporeal hereditaments.[50] This is convenient, for they have many common points and both should fall within the definition of land. Logically, no doubt, restrictive covenants [51] should also be included. But they, being a recent innovation and purely equitable, have a quite separate history and many different characteristics, and therefore stand apart from the older interests which are hereditaments in themselves.

Sect. 1. Nature of Easements

In order to explain, first of all, what rights can and cannot exist as easements we must examine—

(a) the essentials of an easement, and

(b) the distinction between easements and certain analogous rights.

A. Essentials of an Easement

1. There must be a dominant and a servient tenement. If X owns Blackacre and grants a right to use a path across Blackacre to the owner for the time being of the neighbouring plot White-acre, Blackacre is the servient tenement and Whiteacre the dominant tenement. Had X granted the right to A who owned no land at all, A would have acquired a licence to walk over Blackacre, but his right could not exist as an easement, for a dominant tenement was lacking. Put technically, according to the distinction already explained, an easement cannot exist in gross [52] but only as

---

[50] Note 48, *supra*.

[51] *Ante*, p. 750. And perhaps some licences may now have to be classed with restrictive covenants as equitable interests in land; *ante*, p. 783.

[52] *Rangeley* v. *Midland Ry.* (1868) 3 Ch.App. 306 at 310; *Hawkins* v. *Rutter* [1892] 1 Q.B. 668. See, however, Challis 54, 55; Gale 7, 42.

appurtenant to a dominant tenement. On any transfer of the dominant tenement, the easement will pass with the land, so that the occupier for the time being can enjoy it,[53] even if he is a mere lessee.[54] A dominant tenement may be wholly incorporeal,[55] or partly corporeal and partly incorporeal, as where it consists of the whole undertaking of a waterworks company and thus comprises both physical land and rights over the land of others, such as the right to lay pipes.[56]

Where an easement is created by an express grant there is no legal necessity for it to specify or refer to the dominant tenement. The court will consider all the relevant facts to see whether there was in fact a dominant tenement for the benefit of which the easement was granted,[57] and what its extent and identity were.[58] Documentary evidence to identify the dominant tenement is certainly desirable in practice, but as in the parallel case of restrictive covenants [59] it is not required by law.

2. The easement must accommodate the dominant tenement

(a) *Benefit to land.* A right cannot exist as an easement unless it confers a benefit on the dominant tenement as such.[60] It is not sufficient that the right should give the owner for the time being some personal advantage; the test is whether the right makes the dominant tenement a better and more convenient property. This may be done not only by improving its general utility, as by giving means of access or light, but also by benefiting some trade which is carried on on the dominant tenement, at least if the trade is one long established. For example, a public house may have an easement to fix a signboard to the house next door,[61] and a shop may have an easement to put out a stall in the street on market day.[62]

(b) *Propinquity.* The servient tenement must be close enough to the dominant tenement to confer a practical benefit on it. Thus if X owns land in Northumberland, he cannot burden it with an

---

[53] *Leech* v. *Schweder* (1874) 9 App.Cas. 463 at 474, 475; L.P.A., 1925, s. 187 (1).
[54] *Thorpe* v. *Brumfitt* (1873) 8 Ch.App. 650.
[55] *Hanbury* v. *Jenkins* [1901] 2 Ch. 401 at 422 (several profit of piscary).
[56] *Re Salvin's Indenture* [1938] 2 All E.R. 498.
[57] *Thorpe* v. *Brumfitt* (1873) 8 Ch.App. 650; *Johnstone* v. *Holdway* [1963] 1 Q.B. 601. Cf. *Callard* v. *Beeney* [1930] 1 K.B. 353.
[58] *The Shannon Ltd.* v. *Venner Ltd.* [1965] Ch. 682 (easement held appurtenant not only to land acquired when it was granted but also to land acquired previously).
[59] *Ante,* pp. 763, 764.
[60] See *Mason* v. *Shrewsbury and Hereford Ry.* (1871) L.R. 6 Q.B. 578 at 587.
[61] *Moody* v. *Steggles* (1879) 12 Ch.D. 261; and see the examples at p. 266.
[62] *Ellis* v. *Mayor, etc., of Bridgnorth* (1863) 15 C.B.(N.S.) 52.

easement of way in favour of land in Kent, for although it may be very convenient for the owner of the Kentish land to walk across X's Northumberland estate when he goes north, the right of way does not improve the Kentish land.[63] This does not mean that a right cannot exist as an easement unless the dominant and servient tenements are contiguous; even if they are separated by other land, an easement can still exist, provided that they are near enough for the dominant tenement to receive some benefit as such.[64] For example, a right to use a cart track may be appurtenant to a farm even though the track crosses properties lying at some little distance from the farm and does not lead directly to it. And the use of a pew in a church may belong to the owners of a house in the parish.[65] Nor will a right be any less an easement merely because it benefits other land as well as the dominant tenement.[66]

(c) *Disconnected user.* In *Ackroyd* v. *Smith* [67] it was held that a right of way granted " for all purposes " to the tenant of Blackacre and his successors in title was not an easement, for the grant permitted the way to be used for purposes not connected with Blackacre. Had the grant been worded " for all purposes connected with Blackacre " it could have created an easement; and probably the words used in *Ackroyd* v. *Smith* would today be construed in this sense, as they were in the later case of *Thorpe* v. *Brumfitt.*[68]

(d) *Personal advantage.* In *Hill* v. *Tupper* [69] the owner of a canal leased land on the bank of the canal to Hill and granted him the sole and exclusive right of putting pleasure boats on the canal. Tupper, without any authority, put rival pleasure boats on the canal. The question was whether Hill could successfully sue Tupper. If Hill's right amounted to an easement, he could sue anyone who interfered with it, for it was a right of property enforceable against all the world. If it was not an easement, then it could only be a licence,[70] *i.e.,* a mere personal permission given to Hill

---

[63] See *Bailey* v. *Stephens* (1862) 12 C.B.(N.S.) 91 at 115.
[64] *Todrick* v. *Western National Omnibus Co. Ltd.* [1934] Ch. 561 ; *Pugh* v. *Savage* [1970] 2 Q.B. 373.
[65] *Philipps* v. *Halliday* [1891] A.C. 228. This easement is of an exceptional kind.
[66] *Simpson* v. *Mayor, etc., of Godmanchester* [1897] A.C. 696 (right to open sluice gates to protect dominant tenement from flooding: held, this could be an easement even though it protected other land as well).
[67] (1850) 10 C.B. 164.
[68] (1873) 8 Ch.App. 650 at 655–657; and see *Todrick* v. *Western National Omnibus Co. Ltd.* [1934] Ch. 561 at 583 ; *Gaw* v. *Coras Iompair Eireann* [1953] I.R. 232 at 243 ; contrast *Clapman* v. *Edwards* [1938] 2 All E.R. 507 (" for advertising purposes " held not restricted to user for the benefit of the business carried on upon the dominant tenement, and therefore not an easement).
[69] (1863) 2 H. & C. 121.
[70] For licences, see *ante,* p. 776.

by the canal owner, and not a proprietary interest which Hill could defend against third parties in his own right. It was held that the right to put out pleasure boats was not an interest in property which the law could recognise as being appurtenant to land. The monopoly which Hill had obtained was therefore a merely personal or commercial advantage, not connected with the use of his land as such.[71] The result would have been different if the right granted had been to cross and recross the canal to get to and from Hill's land, and Tupper's boats had been so numerous as to interfere with it. If Hill had taken a lease of the canal itself he could, of course, have sued Tupper for trespassing on it.[72] Similarly Tupper could have been sued, on the facts as they were, by the owner of the canal.

3. The dominant and servient tenements must not be both owned and occupied by the same person. An easement is essentially a right *in alieno solo* (in the soil of another). A man cannot have an easement over his own land.[73] " When the owner of Whiteacre and Blackacre passes over the former to Blackacre, he is not exercising a right of way in respect of Blackacre; he is merely making use of his own land to get from one part of it to another." [74] As this observation implies, the same person must not only own both tenements but also occupy both of them before the existence of an easement is rendered impossible. Thus there is no difficulty about the existence of an easement in favour of a tenant against his own landlord, or another tenant of his landlord, although the landlord owns the freehold of both dominant and servient tenements.[75]

The rule is therefore really no more than the self-evident proposition that a man cannot have rights against himself. When an easement has once come into existence as between two different landowners, and both their properties later come into the hands of a single person, *e.g.*, under a lease,[76] the question arises whether the easement is extinguished or merely suspended while the two properties are in one hand. This question is dealt with later in connection with the extinguishment of easements.[77]

---

[71] For another aspect of this case, see *post*, p. 811.

[72] *Lord Chesterfield* v. *Harris* [1908] 2 Ch. 397 at 412 (a river or canal is treated as land covered with water, and the trespass is to the land underlying the water).

[73] *Metropolitan Ry.* v. *Fowler* [1892] 1 Q.B. 165 at 171.

[74] *Roe* v. *Siddons* (1888) 22 Q.B.D. 224 at 236, *per* Fry L.J.

[75] See, *e.g.*, *Borman* v. *Griffith* [1930] 1 Ch. 493, *post*, p. 839. See also *Richardson* v. *Graham* [1908] 1 K.B. 39; *Buckby* v. *Coles* (1814) 5 Taunt. 311 at 315. There are difficulties about acquiring such easements by prescription: *post*, p. 845.

[76] See, *e.g.*, *Thomas* v. *Thomas* (1835) 2 Cr.M. & R. 34.

[77] *Post*, p. 871.

Rights habitually exercised by a man over part of his own land which, if the part in question were owned and occupied by another would be easements, are often called quasi-easements.[78] The term is sometimes also used to include other rights similar to easements, such as customary rights of way[79]; but in this book it is used only in the stricter sense. Quasi-easements are of some importance, for they may sometimes become true easements if the land is subsequently sold in separate parcels.[80]

4. The easement must be capable of forming the subject-matter of a grant. All easements "lie in grant"; that is to say, no right can exist as an easement unless it could have been granted by deed. The principles underlying this rule are that only certain kinds of rights are capable of being rights of property which one man can convey to another,[81] and that every easement in theory owes its existence to a grant by deed; although in practice many easements are established by long user, the presumption always is that a grant was once made.[82]

This assumption that an easement must have been created by deed leads to the following rules.

(a) *The right must be within the general nature of rights capable of being created as easements*

(1) THE LIST NOT CLOSED. Although most easements fall under one of the well-known heads of easements, such as way, light, support or water, the list of easements is not closed.[83] "The category of servitudes and easements must alter and expand with the changes that take place in the circumstances of mankind." [84] An example of this might be a right for a house to have telephone lines running across a neighbour's land. There has as yet been no decision that this can be an easement. But a right to use a clothes line is probably capable of being one,[85] and the analogy may be close enough for the purpose.

(2) LIMITS. But there are limits. "It must not therefore be supposed that incidents of a novel kind can be devised and attached

---

[78] See, *e.g.*, *Wheeldon* v. *Burrows* (1879) 12 Ch.D. 31 at 49.
[79] *Brocklebank* v. *Thompson* [1903] 2 Ch. 344 at 348.
[80] See *post*, p. 833.
[81] *Cf. ante*, p. 721.
[82] For prescription, see *post*, p. 841. Exceptions to the presumption of a lost grant occur under the Prescription Act, 1832: *post*, p. 864.
[83] See the 35 varieties of easement listed by Gale, 35.
[84] *Dyce* v. *Lady James Hay* (1852) 1 Macq. 305 at 312, 313, *per* Lord St. Leonards.
[85] *Drewell* v. *Towler* (1832) 3 B. & Ad. 735; *cf.* the right to run a timber "traveller" (aerial tramway) over other land: *Harris* v. *De Pinna* (1886) 33 Ch.D. 238 at 251, 260, 261.

to property, at the fancy or caprice of any owner." [86] This expresses the overriding principle that the various kinds of proprietary interests are fixed by the law, and finite in number.[87] Even though the list of easements is not closed, it is not open to interests which do not conform to the rules about the general nature of easements. For example, a right to an unspoilt view [88] cannot exist as an easement. Nor can a right to have the wall of a house protected from weather by an adjoining house,[89] as contrasted with a right of support which is a well-recognised easement and which often exists in favour of semi-detached houses.

It used to be said that a right to use a path or a garden merely for taking walks, being a mere *jus spatiandi*, is incapable of being an easement [90]; but this right, which is of value to many houses adjacent to parks and gardens, has now been admitted into the company of easements,[91] and the same may apply to a right to boat on a neighbouring lake.[92] The law of easements may protect projecting buildings, or even the projecting bowsprits of ships using a dock [93]; but it will not extend to overhanging trees.[94] More examples of the various species of easements are given below.[95]

(3) EXPENDITURE. It is most unlikely that a right would be accepted as an easement if it involved the servient tenant in the expenditure of money [96]; for none of the recognised easements does so,[97] except the obligation to fence land in order to keep out cattle, which has been described as " in the nature of a spurious easement." [98] An easement of support for a semi-detached house, for example, does not require the servient owner to keep the supporting premises in repair.[99] The general principle is that the dominant owner may enter and execute repairs upon the servient land, *e.g.*, to a building from which he is entitled to support or to a pipe or pump which he is entitled to use; all this is implicit in the concept of grant.[1] The servient owner need do nothing.[2]

---

[86] *Keppell* v. *Bailey* (1834) 2 My. & K. 517 at 535, *per* Lord Brougham L.C.
[87] *Ante*, p. 810.
[88] *Post*, p. 812.
[89] *Phipps* v. *Pears* [1965] 1 Q.B. 76; see (1964) 80 L.Q.R. 318 (R.E.M.).
[90] *International Tea Stores Co.* v. *Hobbs* [1903] 2 Ch. 165 at 172.
[91] *Re Ellenborough Park* [1956] Ch. 131.
[92] *Ibid.*: see at p. 175. Contrast a mere commercial right to hire or boats on the water: *ante*, p. 808.
[93] *Suffield* v. *Brown* (1864) 4 De G.J. & S. 185.
[94] *Lemmon* v. *Webb* [1895] A.C. 1.
[95] *Post*, p. 872.
[96] *Regis Property Co. Ltd.* v. *Redman* [1956] 2 Q.B. 612 (covenant to supply hot water creates no easement, being a right to services).
[97] See *Pomfret* v. *Ricroft* (1669) 1 Wms.Saund. 321.
[98] *Lawrence* v. *Jenkins* (1873) L.R. 8 Q.B. 274 at 279, *per* Archibald J.; *post*, p. 879.
[99] See *post*, p. 879.
[1] Gale 44 *et seq.*; *Jones* v. *Pritchard* [1908] 1 Ch. 630 at 637, 638.
[2] *Ibid.*; *cf. Bond* v. *Nottingham Corporation* [1940] Ch. 429 at 438, 439.

(4) NEW EASEMENTS. New rights not involving the servient owner in expenditure have from time to time been recognised as easements. Thus in 1896 the courts recognised as an easement the right to go upon the land of another to open sluice gates,[3] in 1915 the right to store casks and trade produce on land,[4] in 1955 the right to use a neighbour's lavatory,[5] and in 1973 the right to use an airfield.[5a] But such rights must always conform to the general nature of easements. For example, a wheelwright failed to make good a claim to stand an unlimited number of vehicles on a strip of his neighbour's land, since this really amounted to a claim to joint possession of the land and went beyond the ordinary bounds of an easement.[6] It is not, however, an objection that the easement merely benefits a business carried on on the dominant land.[7]

(b) *The right must be sufficiently definite.* The extent of the right claimed must be capable of reasonably exact definition, for otherwise it could not be granted at all. This rule is really a corollary of the preceding one, but it helps to explain the exclusion of certain kinds of rights. Thus although there can be an easement of light where a defined window receives a defined amount of light,[8] there can be no easement of indefinite privacy[9] or prospect (*i.e.*, the right to a view).[10] Again, an easement may exist for the passage of air through a defined channel[11]; but there can be no easement for the general flow of air over land to a windmill,[12] chimney,[13] drying shed for timber,[14] or otherwise.[15] A catalogue of

---

[3] *Simpson* v. *Mayor, etc., of Godmanchester* [1896] 1 Ch. 214; [1897] A.C. 696.
[4] *Att.-Gen. of Southern Nigeria* v. *John Holt & Co. (Liverpool) Ltd.* [1915] A.C. 599 at 617 (*ante*, p. 778, and *post*, p. 820). See also *Smith* v. *Gates* [1952] C.P.L. 814, where the Court of Appeal upheld a claim to keep chicken coops on a common, but rejected a claim to keep fish boxes there since until 1938 the boxes had been greengrocers' boxes and the claimant had changed his business in that year.
[5] *Miller* v. *Emcer Products Ltd.* [1956] Ch. 304; see (1956) 72 L.Q.R. 172 (R.E.M.).
[5a] *Dowty Boulton Paul Ltd.* v. *Wolverhampton Corporation (No. 2)* [1973] 2 W.L.R. 618.
[6] *Copeland* v. *Greenhalf* [1952] Ch. 488, not citing *Wright* v. *Macadam* [1949] 2 K.B. 744, where a right to store coal in a shed was held to be an easement, and distinguished in *Ward* v. *Kirkland* [1967] Ch. 194; and see *Grigsby* v. *Melville* [1972] 1 W.L.R. 1355 (claim to exclusive use of cellar probably too extensive to be an easement). [7] *Copeland* v. *Greenhalf, supra.*
[8] *Post*, pp. 875, 876. [9] *Browne* v. *Flower* [1911] 1 Ch. 219 at 225.
[10] *William Aldred's Case* (1610) 9 Co.Rep. 57b at 58b, *per* Wray C.J.: "for prospect, which is a matter only of delight, and not of necessity, no action lies for stopping thereof . . . the law does not give an action for such things of delight."
[11] *Bass* v. *Gregory* (1890) 25 Q.B.D. 481 (ventilation shaft for cellar); *Cable* v. *Bryant* [1908] 1 Ch. 259 (aperture in stable).
[12] *Webb* v. *Bird* (1862) 13 C.B.(N.S.) 841. [13] *Bryant* v. *Lefever* (1879) 4 C.P.D. 172.
[14] *Harris* v. *De Pinna* (1886) 33 Ch.D. 238.
[15] *Chastey* v. *Ackland* [1895] 2 Ch. 389. In earlier times the law was different (Gale 256), and in some other jurisdictions, it is different today: see, *e.g.*, *Commonwealth* v. *Registrar of Titles of Victoria* (1918) 24 C.L.R. 348 (express grant of general access of light and air to proposed building held an easement), where, however, the cases in notes 12–14, *supra*, were not cited.

recognised species of easements and profits will be found at the end of this chapter.[16]

Of course, it is often possible to secure by way of contract rights which are too indefinite to be easements; and a restrictive covenant properly framed may be used to confer a right of amenity, *e.g.*, an unspoilt view, upon one piece of land as against another,[17] so as in substance to create a right of property to that effect. Another doctrine which may sometimes circumvent the limits of easements is the rule against "derogation from grant," explained below.[18]

(*c*) *There must be a capable grantor.* There can be no claim to an easement if at the relevant time the servient tenement was owned by someone incapable of granting an easement, *e.g.*, a statutory corporation with no power to grant easements,[19] or a tenant under a lease who has no power to bind the reversion.[20] Where the claim is based on an express grant, the grantor must, of course, have been capable of granting the easement: thus an easement over a common cannot be granted by some only of the commoners.[21]

(*d*) *There must be a capable grantee.* An easement can be claimed only by a legal person capable of receiving a grant.[22] Thus a claim by a company with no power to acquire easements must fail.[23] A fluctuating body of persons, such as "the inhabitants for the time being of the village of X," cannot claim an easement, for no grant can be made to them. But they may have similar rights if there is a valid custom to that effect,[24] such as a customary right of way across land to reach the parish church,[25] or a customary right to take water from a spout,[26] or to water cattle at a pond,[27] or to play games [27a] or dry nets [28] on certain land.

B. *Distinctions between Easements and Certain Analogous Rights*

It will have been gathered that the attempt to define an easement leads to a list of miscellanous examples rather than to a precise definition. Some further help may be had from contrasting easements with certain other rights which are distinct from them.

---

[16] *Post*, p. 872.   [17] *Ante*, p. 751; *post*, p. 819.
[18] *Post*, p. 820.   [19] *Mulliner* v. *Midland Ry.* (1879) 11 Ch.D. 611.
[20] *Derry* v. *Sanders* [1919] 1 K.B. 223 at 231. The position of a tenant for life was formerly the same (*ibid.*), but he can now grant easements: S.L.A., 1925, s. 38 (i), replacing S.L.A., 1882, s. 3 (i).
[21] *Paine & Co. Ltd.* v. *St. Neots Gas & Coke Co.* [1939] 3 All E.R. 812.
[22] See *Re Salvin's Indenture* [1938] 2 All E.R. 498.
[23] *National Guaranteed Manure Co. Ltd.* v. *Donald* (1859) 4 H. & N. 8.
[24] For custom, see *post*, p. 821.   [25] *Brocklebank* v. *Thompson* [1903] 2 Ch. 344.
[26] *Harrop* v. *Hirst* (1868) L.R. 4 Ex. 43.
[27] *Manning* v. *Wasdale* (1836) 5 A. & E. 758.
[27a] *New Windsor Corporation* v. *Mellor* [1974] 1 W.L.R. 1504.
[28] *Mercer* v. *Denne* [1905] 2 Ch. 538.

I. NATURAL RIGHTS

1. Support for land. The most obvious difference between an easement and a natural right is that a natural right exists automatically but an easement must be acquired. A "natural right" is, in fact, simply a right protected by the law of tort, *i.e.*, the right to damages or an injunction for nuisance. In addition to his rights over his own land [29] every landowner has a natural right [30] of support. This is often described as a man's right to have his land supported by his neighbour's land, but it is more accurately described as a right not to have that support removed by his neighbour; for no action lies when the support is removed by natural causes, such as the action of water lying in a gravel pit.[31] There is a similar right where the surface of the land and the soil underneath are owned by different persons; the owner of the surface has a natural right to have it supported by the subjacent soil, and even if he has let or sold minerals lying below the surface he can sue if the mining causes subsidence,[32] provided of course that he has not agreed to the surface being let down.[33]

2. No support for buildings. This natural right, however, extends only to land in its natural state [34]; there is no natural right to support for buildings or for the additional burden on land which they cause.[35] "The owner of the adjacent soil may with perfect legality dig that soil away, and allow his neighbour's house, if supported by it, to fall in ruins to the ground." [36] But if withdrawing support would have caused actionable damage even if nothing had been built, the damages recoverable include any damage to the buildings.[37] Similarly there is no natural right to have buildings supported by neighbouring buildings.[38] If no more damage is done than is necessary, a man may pull down his house without having to provide support for his neighbour's house.[39] The right to have

[29] *e.g.*, to walk over his land to reach his house. Such rights are for certain purposes called " quasi-easements "; see *ante*, p. 810.
[30] *Backhouse* v. *Bonomi* (1861) 9 H.L.C. 503; *Dalton* v. *Angus & Co.* (1881) 6 App.Cas. 740 at 791.
[31] *Rouse* v. *Gravelworks Ltd.* [1940] 1 K.B. 489; contrast *Redland Bricks Ltd.* v. *Morris* [1970] A.C. 652 (support removed by excavation of clay; damages awarded but mandatory injunction refused).
[32] *L. & N. W. Ry.* v. *Evans* [1893] 1 Ch. 16 at 30.
[33] See, *e.g.*, *Butterknowle Colliery Co. Ltd.* v. *Bishop Auckland Industrial Co-operative Co. Ltd.* [1906] A.C. 305 at 309.
[34] *Hunt* v. *Peake* (1860) Johns. 705.
[35] *Wyatt* v. *Harrison* (1832) 3 B. & Ad. 871.
[36] *Dalton* v. *Angus & Co.* (1881) 6 App.Cas. 740 at 804, *per* Lord Penzance.
[37] *Stroyan* v. *Knowles* (1861) 6 H. & N. 454; *Lotus Ltd.* v. *British Soda Co. Ltd.* [1972] Ch. 123 (where, however, the real injury was abstraction of the plaintiff's own subsoil); *Ray* v. *Fairway Motors (Barnstaple) Ltd.* (1968) 20 P. & C.R. 261.
[38] *Peyton* v. *The Mayor & Commonalty of London* (1829) 9 B. & C. 725.
[39] *Southwark & Vauxhall Water Co.* v. *Wandsworth District Board of Works* [1898] 2 Ch. 603 at 612, 613.

buildings supported by land or by other buildings can, however, be acquired as an easement [40]; and the provision of statutory rights of this kind, subject to safeguards, has been suggested.[41]

3. Light and water. " No natural right exists to a single ray of light." [42] This is, no doubt, because land in its natural state must always receive light through the air-space above it, which is protected by the law of trespass.[43] There are no natural rights in respect of buildings. But there is a natural right to water, where it flows naturally in a definite channel. Therefore if the stream is dammed or diverted the riparian owners can sue.[44] The right to dam or divert it, on the other hand, may be acquired as an easement.[45] There is no natural right to water percolating underground, for there is then no definite channel.[46]

II. PUBLIC RIGHTS

An easement must always be appurtenant to land; it is a right exercisable by the owner for the time being by virtue of his estate in the land.[47] A public right, on the other hand, is a right exercisable by anyone, whether he owns land or not, merely by virtue of the general law. Thus there is a public right to fish and navigate over the foreshore (the area between the ordinary high and low water marks) when it is covered with water, but no right of bathing, walking or beachcombing on it.[48]

The public rights which most closely resemble easements are public rights of way. The land over which a public right of way exists is known as a highway; and although most highways have been made up into roads, and most easements of way exist over footpaths, the presence or absence of a made road has nothing to do with the distinction. There may be a highway over a footpath, while a well-made road may be subject only to an easement of way, or may exist only for the landowner's benefit and be subject to no easement at all. A highway may exist as such even if it does not lead to another highway or any public place.[49] If it is maintainable

---

[40] *Post*, p. 879.
[41] Law Reform Committee, 14th Report, Cmnd. 3100 (1966), paras. 89, 90; Law Commission Working Paper No. 36, para. 82.
[42] Gale, 12th ed., 6. An easement of light can be acquired for a building, however: *post*, p. 875.
[43] *Ante*, p. 70.
[44] *Swindon Waterworks Co. Ltd.* v. *Wilts and Berks Canal Navigation Co.* (1875) L.R. 7 H.L. 697; and see *ante*, p. 72.
[45] Gale, 36, 218.
[46] *Acton* v. *Blundell* (1843) 12 M. & W. 324; *Chasemore* v. *Richards* (1859) 7 H.L.C. 376; *Bradford Corporation* v. *Pickles* [1895] A.C. 587.
[47] *Ante*, p. 806.
[48] *Brinckman* v. *Matley* [1904] 2 Ch. 313; *Alfred F. Beckett Ltd.* v. *Lyons* [1967] Ch. 449. Such activities are enjoyed not as of right but by tolerance.
[49] *Williams-Ellis* v. *Cobb* [1935] 1 K.B. 310.

at public expense under the Highways Act, 1959, it vests in the statutory highway authority,[50] which then holds the surface of the land affected, together with so much of the land below and the air-space above as is required by their statutory duties, for " a determinable statutory fee simple interest." [51]

1. Creation. A public right of way may be created in the following ways:

(a) *By statute.* This needs no explanation.

(b) *By dedication and acceptance.*

(1) AT COMMON LAW. To establish a highway at common law by dedication and acceptance it must be shown—

  (i) that the owner of the land dedicated the way to the public, and

  (ii) that the public accepted that dedication, the acceptance normally being shown by user by the public.[52]

Dedication may be formal, although this is comparatively infrequent.[53] It is usually inferred from long user by the public, so that user is thus effective to prove both dedication and acceptance.[54] But in order to raise a presumption of dedication there must have been open user as of right [55] for so long a time and in such a way that the landowner must have known that the public were claiming a right.[56] User with the landowner's permission or tolerance is not user as of right,[57] and the court is slow to find a claim of right where the user is attributable to the landowner's indulgence.[58] The user must also have been without interruption by the owner. A practice frequently adopted to disprove any intention to dedicate is to close the way for one day in each year, for this asserts the landowner's right to exclude the public at will.[59]

The length of the enjoyment to be shown depends on the circumstances of the case. Where the circumstances have pointed to an intention to dedicate, eighteen months has been held to be enough [60]; where the circumstances are against dedication, a substantially greater period may be insufficient,[61] especially if in recent years

---

50 s. 226.
51 *Foley's Charity Trustees* v. *Dudley Corporation* [1910] 1 K.B. 317 at 322; and see *Tithe Redemption Commission* v. *Runcorn U. D. C.* [1954] Ch. 383.
52 See *Cubitt* v. *Lady Caroline Maxse* (1873) L.R. 8 C.P. 704 at 715.
53 *Simpson* v. *Att.-Gen.* [1904] A.C. 476 at 494.
54 *Cubitt* v. *Lady Caroline Maxse, supra.*
55 See *Hue* v. *Whiteley* [1929] 1 Ch. 440 at 445; and see *post*, p. 842.
56 *Greenwich District Board of Works* v. *Maudslay* (1870) L.R. 5 Q.B. 397 at 404.
57 *R.* v. *Broke* (1859) 1 F. & F. 514; *cf. post*, p. 843.
58 *Att.-Gen.* v. *Antrobus* [1905] 2 Ch. 188 (no public right of access to Stonehenge).
59 *British Museum Trustees* v. *Finnis* (1833) 5 C. & P. 460.
60 *North London Ry.* v. *Vestry of St. Mary's, Islington* (1872) 27 L.T. 672.
61 *R.* v. *Hudson* (1732) 2 Stra. 909 (four years).

there has been no occupier capable of dedicating a highway in perpetuity.[62]

At common law it is possible for an occupier of adjoining land to be liable for repair of the highway under the conditions of tenure of the land, *ratione tenurae*.[63] This liability is in effect a burden running with land,[64] since it falls on successive owners and occupiers, though it seems that they bear only personal liability. In theory, the tenure must have been created before 1290,[65] but in practice liability is proved by showing that the occupier and his predecessors have repaired the highway over a long period of time.

(2) UNDER THE HIGHWAYS ACT, 1959. The Highways Act, 1959, has replaced the Rights of Way Act, 1932. The object of this legislation is to simplify proof of dedication by laying down a definite period of use which will suffice to show that a right of way exists. The public can still claim a right of way based on use for a shorter period than that laid down by the Act if an intent to dedicate can be inferred.[66] As will appear later, the Act of 1932 was to a certain extent modelled upon its predecessor by a century, the Prescription Act, 1832.[67]

The principal provision [68] is that a right of way can be established by twenty years' enjoyment of a way over land [69] by the public as of right [70] and without interruption, unless the landowner can show that during that period there was no intention to dedicate a way. " Without interruption " means " without physical obstruction," and not merely " not contentious " [71]; and even a physical obstruction at times when nobody was likely to use the way is no interruption.[72] The absence of any intention to dedicate can be shown either in one of the usual ways, as by closing the way for one day in each year,[73] or in one of the special statutory ways, namely, by exhibiting a notice visible to those using the way,[74] or by depositing a map with the local authorities with a statement of what ways the landowner admits to be highways, and lodging statutory declarations at intervals of not more than six years stating whether any other ways have been dedicated.[75]

---

[62] See *Williams-Ellis* v. *Cobb* [1935] 1 K.B. 310.
[63] See Pratt & Mackenzie on *Highways*, 21st ed., 76.
[64] It is an overriding interest under L.R.A., 1925, s. 70: *post*, p. 1065.
[65] *Ante*, pp. 30, 31.   [66] Highways Act, 1959, s. 34 (9).
[67] *Post*, p. 850.   [68] Highways Act, 1959, s. 34 (1).
[69] Including land covered with water: *ibid.*, s. 34 (11).
[70] This has the same meaning as in the case of easements, explained *post*, p. 842; *Jones* v. *Bates* [1938] 2 All E.R. 237.
[71] See *Merstham Manor Ltd.* v. *Coulsdon and Purley U. D. C.* [1937] 2 K.B. 77.
[72] *Lewis* v. *Thomas* [1950] 1 K.B. 438.
[73] *Merstham Manor Ltd.* v. *Coulsdon and Purley U. D. C.*, *supra*, at p. 85.
[74] Highways Act, 1959, s. 34 (3). If this is torn down or defaced, a written notice to the local council will be effective: s. 34 (4). If the land is leased, the landlord is entitled to enter and erect a notice: s. 34 (5).   [75] *Ibid.*, s. 34 (6).

The twenty years' period is to be calculated as that next before the time when the right to use the way was brought into question by a notice exhibited to the public negativing the dedication or otherwise.[76] Enjoyment prior to the date of the Act suffices.[77]

The Act of 1932 originally provided a further defence, *viz.*, that there was no one who could have dedicated a way at any time during the period.[78] This prevented acquisition by twenty years' user against tenants for life or years, for normally only a fee simple owner could dedicate a highway.[79] But if forty years' user could be shown, this defence was not available. These provisions were repealed in 1949,[80] so that the forty-year period is no longer of any special use and the defence can no longer be raised. But reversioners and remaindermen can protect themselves in other ways. If the land is let on lease, the reversioner may exhibit a notice rebutting dedication[81]; if it is held by a tenant for life, the reversioner or remainderman may take proceedings for trespass as if he were already in possession.[82]

Local authorities are required to maintain definitive maps and statements, subject to the hearing and determination of objections, of public footpaths and bridleways in their areas.[83] These maps and statements are conclusive even though manifestly wrong, *e.g.*, where shown as crossing impassable country.[84]

2. Extinguishment. Once a highway has been established, it can be extinguished only if it is closed or diverted by an order made under certain statutory provisions,[85] or if closing orders have extinguished all ways leading to it.[1] The mere obstruction of the highway or the failure of the public to use it will not destroy the rights of the public, for " once a highway always a highway." [2] A mere closing order for a highway leaves unaffected any easement over the route of the highway,[3] while the statutory extinguishment of an easement may not affect a highway over the route.[3a]

76 *Ibid.*, s. 34 (2); *cf. post*, pp. 850, 851.
77 *Att.-Gen. and Newton Abbot R. D. C.* v. *Dyer* [1947] Ch. 67; *Fairey* v. *Southampton C. C.* [1956] 2 Q.B. 439. See [1956] C.L.J. 172 (R. N. Gooderson).
78 See *Williams-Ellis* v. *Cobb* [1935] 1 K.B. 310. As to a corporation's power to dedicate, see *British Transport Commission* v. *Westmorland C. C.* [1958] A.C. 126.   79 But see S.L.A., 1925, s. 56, *ante*, p. 349.
80 National Parks and Access to the Countryside Act, 1949, s. 58.
81 Highways Act, 1959, s. 34 (5).   82 *Ibid.*, s. 36.
83 National Parks and Access to the Countryside Act, 1949, Pt. IV; and see Countryside Act, 1968, ss. 27–29.
84 National Parks and Access to the Countryside Act, 1949, s. 32; *Morgan* v. *Hertfordshire C. C.* (1965) 63 L.G.R. 456; contrast *Att.-Gen.* v. *Honeywill* [1972] 1 W.L.R. 1506 (a vehicular way may exist even if the map shows only a footpath).
85 *e.g.*, Highways Act, 1959, s. 108; Town and Country Planning Act 1971, s. 210.
1 See *Bailey* v. *Jamieson* (1876) 1 C.P.D. 329.
2 *Dawes* v. *Hawkins* (1860) 8 C.B.(N.S.) 848 at 858, *per* Byles J.
3 *Walsh* v. *Oates* [1953] 1 Q.B. 578.
3a *Att.-Gen.* v. *Shonleigh Nominees Ltd.* [1974] 1 W.L.R. 305.

III. RESTRICTIVE COVENANTS

Easements and restrictive covenants [4] are similar in that an easement, like a restrictive covenant, may entitle a landowner to restrict the use that his neighbour makes of his land; thus the owner of an easement of light may prevent the servient owner from obstructing his light by erecting a building on the adjoining land. There are other similarities, such as the need for dominant and servient tenements. In general it is possible to say that the law of restrictive covenants is an equitable extension of the law of easements.[5] But, historically, this was not a case of equity following the law. The enforcement of restrictive covenants against purchasers with notice was really a new departure, founded on equitable principles. It will be seen from the section on restrictive covenants [4] that although they have some elements in common with easements they are a fundamentally different kind of interest. Unlike restrictive covenants, easements may exist at law as well as in equity, and they may be acquired by prescription (*i.e.*, long enjoyment).

There is some overlap, nevertheless. Certain rights of a negative kind, as rights to light, air, support, or water, may be either acquired as easements or secured by restrictive covenants. But more often restrictive covenants are used for some purpose outside the scope of easements, such as preserving the amenity of a neighbourhood. On the other hand a restrictive covenant cannot confer a positive right like a right of way.

IV. LICENCES

Here again there is some overlap. If A permits B to use a path across A's land, this may simply be a licence [6] given by A to B. But if the requirements for an easement are satisfied, the same right may be an easement (an easement of way). Yet not all licences have their counterparts in the law of easements. In general the categories of easements are old and restricted, whereas the categories of licences are new and flexible. In particular, there are the following differences:

(i) An easement requires a dominant tenement, a licence does not.

(ii) An easement is either a legal or equitable interest in land, usually the former; a licence is a mere equity, at the most.[7]

---

[4] For restrictive covenants generally, see *ante*, p. 750.
[5] See *ante*, p. 753.
[6] For licences, see *ante*, p. 776.
[7] *Ante*, p. 784.

(iii) There are rules of formality for the creation of easements,[8] but not of licences.

(iv) An easement cannot give a general right to occupy land.[9] A licence may do so.[10] For example, the right to occupy lodgings in a lodging-house is a licence, but cannot be an easement.

V. RIGHTS RESULTING FROM THE RULE AGAINST DEROGATION FROM GRANT

1. Derogation. A person who sells or lets land, knowing that the purchaser intends to use it for a particular purpose, may not do anything which hampers the use of the purchaser's land for the purpose which both parties contemplated at the time of the transaction. A grantor may not derogate from his grant.[11] This is " a principle which merely embodies in a legal maxim a rule of common honesty." [12] " A grantor having given a thing with one hand is not to take away the means of enjoying it with the other." [13] " If A lets a plot to B, he may not act so as to frustrate the purpose for which in the contemplation of both parties the land was hired." [14]

2. A right of property. In so far as this doctrine restricts the grantor's freedom to use any of his neighbouring land which he may have retained, it is really part of the law of property, since the rights which it creates bind not only the grantor but also all who claim title through him; so that, in effect, the grantee and his successors in title have a proprietary interest of a special kind against the grantor's land, into whosesoever hands it may pass. For example, where a lease was granted to a timber merchant who required a free flow of air to his stacks of drying timber, it was held that a purchaser of the lessor's adjoining land could not build upon it so as to obstruct the ventilation required by the lessee.[15] The right claimed, be it noted, was one which could not exist as an easement since the air did not flow through any definable channel or aperture.[16] " The

---

8 *Post*, p. 828.
9 *Ante*, p. 812.
10 *Ante*, p. 618. In *Att.-Gen. of Southern Nigeria* v. *John Holt & Co.* (*Liverpool*) *Ltd.* [1915] A.C. 599, *ante*, p. 812, a claim to occupy foreshore failed as an easement but succeeded as a licence.
11 *Cf. ante*, p. 678, where examples are given. See generally (1964) 80 L.Q.R. 244 (D. W. Elliott).
12 *Harmer* v. *Jumbil* (*Nigeria*) *Tin Areas Ltd.* [1921] 1 Ch. 200 at 225, *per* Younger L.J.
13 *Birmingham, Dudley & District Banking Co.* v. *Ross* (1888) 38 Ch.D. 295 at 313, *per* Bowen L.J.
14 *Lyttelton Times Co. Ltd.* v. *Warners Ltd.* [1907] A.C. 476 at 481, *per* Lord Loreburn L.C.
15 *Aldin* v. *Latimer Clark, Muirhead & Co.* [1894] 2 Ch. 437; *cf. Thomas* v. *Owen* (1887) 20 Q.B.D. 225.
16 *Ante*, p. 812.

implications usually explained by the maxim . . . do not stop short with easements." [17] It is in this that the importance of the doctrine lies. Paradoxically, the law will allow a grant made for a particular purpose to create rights which are really proprietary and which yet, according to the rules for easements, do not lie in grant.

3. Application. The doctrine is not confined to cases of landlord and tenant: it may apply as well to a sale as to a lease.[18] It is sometimes said to rest upon an implied promise [19]; but it is in truth an independent rule of law, and has nothing to do with restrictive covenants or the equitable doctrine of notice.[20]

VI. CUSTOMARY RIGHTS OF FLUCTUATING BODIES

We have already seen examples of customary rights, *e.g.*, for parishioners to use a path to the church, or to water cattle at a pond.[21] Such rights differ from easements in that they are exercisable by all who are included within the custom, independently of ownership of a dominant tenement. They differ from public rights in that they are exercisable only by members of some local community,[22] not by members of the public generally.

A custom really amounts to a special local law, a local variation of the common law. The common law recognises such variations only if they are ancient, certain, reasonable and continuous.[23] To be "ancient" a custom must date back to the year 1189, the beginning of legal memory; but ancient origin may be presumed if there has been long enjoyment and there is no proof of a later origin.[24] Nor is it a fatal objection that the nature of the custom has changed with the times; for example, an ancient custom to play games has been held to cover cricket, "although it is reasonably certain that cricket was unknown until long after the time of Richard I." [25] Customs have been proved for the holding of a fair or wake [1]; for the fishermen of a parish to dry their nets on private

---

[17] *Browne* v. *Flower* [1911] 1 Ch. 219 at 225, *per* Parker J.
[18] *Cable* v. *Bryant* [1908] 1 Ch. 259, where the maxim was resorted to because the adjoining land was in lease at the time of the sale, and it was said that a reversionary easement could not be granted; *Woodhouse & Co. Ltd.* v. *Kirkland (Derby) Ltd.* [1970] 1 W.L.R. 1185.
[19] *North Eastern Ry.* v. *Elliot* (1860) 1 J. & H. 145 at 153.
[20] *Cable* v. *Bryant, supra,* at p. 264.   [21] *Ante*, p. 813.
[22] *Manning* v. *Wasdale* (1836) 5 A. & E. 758 (parish); *Race* v. *Ward* (1855) 4 E. & B. 702 (town).
[23] *Lockwood* v. *Wood* (1844) 6 Q.B. 50 at 64; and see the discussion of such rights in *Mercer* v. *Denne* [1904] 2 Ch. 534 at 552–554; [1905] 2 Ch. 538.
[24] See *Simpson* v. *Wells* (1872) L.R. 7 Q.B. 214 (custom to have stalls in statutory hiring fair held bad because origin of fair was statute of Edward III or later); *Mercer* v. *Denne* [1904] 2 Ch. 534; [1905] 2 Ch. 538.
[25] *Mercer* v. *Denne* [1904] 2 Ch. 534 at 553, *per* Farwell J. (affd. [1905] 2 Ch. 538).
[1] *Wyld* v. *Silver* [1963] Ch. 243 (discussing the mode of enforcement of such rights).

land [2]; and for inhabitants of a parish " to enter upon certain land in the parish, erect a maypole thereon, and dance round and about it, and otherwise enjoy on the land any lawful and innocent recreation at any times in the year." [3] Such rights are not lost by disuse or waiver.[4] Special customs of many kinds were also to be found in manors.

Sect. 2. Nature of a Profit à Prendre

A profit *à prendre* has been described as " a right to take something off another person's land." [5] This it is, but not all such rights are profits. If the right is to be a profit, the thing taken must be either part of the land,[6] *e.g.*, minerals or crops, or the wild animals existing on it [7]; and the thing taken must at the time of taking be susceptible of ownership.[8] A right to " hawk, hunt, fish and fowl " may thus exist as a profit,[9] for this gives the right to take creatures living on the soil which, when killed, are capable of being owned.[10] But a right to take water from a spring or a pump,[11] or the right to water cattle at a pond,[12] may be an easement but cannot be a profit; for the water, when taken, was not owned by anyone [13] nor was it part of the soil.[14]

Rights exercised by a man over part of his own land which, if that part were owned and occupied by another, would be profits, are sometimes called quasi-profits; and similar principles apply to them as apply to quasi-easements.[15]

A. Classification of Profits à Prendre

I. AS TO OWNERSHIP

A profit *à prendre* may be enjoyed—

[2] *Mercer* v. *Denne* [1905] 2 Ch. 538.
[3] *Hall* v. *Nottingham* (1875) 1 Ex.D. 1, headnote.
[4] *Wyld* v. *Silver, supra*; *New Windsor Corporation* v. *Mellor* [1974] 1 W.L.R. 1504.
[5] *Duke of Sutherland* v. *Heathcote* [1892] 1 Ch. 475 at 484, *per* Lindley L.J.
[6] *Manning* v. *Wasdale* (1836) 5 A. & E. 758 at 764.
[7] Halsb. xii, 522.
[8] *Race* v. *Ward* (1855) 4 E. & B. 702 at 709; *Lowe* v. *J. W. Ashmore Ltd.* [1971] Ch. 545 at 557.
[9] *Wickham* v. *Hawker* (1840) 7 M. & W. 63.
[10] *Case of Swans* (1592) 7 Co.Rep. 15b at 17b; *Blades* v. *Higgs* (1865) 11 H.L.C. 621; *Lord Fitzhardinge* v. *Purcell* [1908] 2 Ch. 139 at 168.
[11] See *Polden* v. *Bastard* (1865) L.R. 1 Q.B. 156.
[12] *Manning* v. *Wasdale, supra*. As to water stored in a tank, see (1938) 2 Conv. (N.S.) 203 (J. S. Fiennes); but the authorities seem unsatisfactory.
[13] *Embrey* v. *Owen* (1851) 6 Exch. 353 at 369. Game becomes the subject of ownership as soon as killed (see n. 10, *supra*), *i.e.*, sometimes before being taken; water is reduced into ownership only at the time of taking. Yet the difference between taking fish in a net and taking water in a bucket seems slight.
[14] *Manning* v. *Wasdale, supra*, at p. 764; *Race* v. *Ward, supra*, at p. 709.
[15] See *ante*, p. 810.

(i) by one person to the exclusion of all others: this is known as a several profit; or

(ii) by one person in common with others: this is known as a profit in common, or a common.

II. IN RELATION TO LAND

Unlike an easement, a profit is not necessarily appurtenant to land. It may exist in the following forms.

1. A profit appurtenant. This is a profit, whether several or in common, which by act of parties, actual or presumed,[16] is annexed to some nearby dominant tenement and runs with it. In general there must be compliance with the four conditions necessary for the existence of an easement, which is always appurtenant.[17] Thus a profit of piscary appurtenant cannot be exploited for commercial purposes; the number of fish taken must be limited to the needs of the dominant tenement.[18]

2. A profit appendant. This is a profit annexed to land by operation of law; probably it exists only in the form of a common of pasture.[19] If before the Statute *Quia Emptores*, 1290,[20] the lord of a manor subinfeudated arable land to a freeholder, the freeholder obtained as appendant to the arable land, the right to pasture, on the waste land of the manor, animals to plough and manure the land granted to him [21]; for " he must have some place to keep such cattle in whilst the corn is growing on his own arable land." [22] This right was known as a common of pasture appendant and was limited both as to the kind and number of animals which could be depastured. It extended only to horses and oxen (to plough the land) and cows and sheep (to manure it),[23] and only to the number of these " levant and couchant " on the land to which the right was appendant, *i.e.*, the number which the dominant tenement was capable of maintaining during the winter.[24] It was immaterial that the land was at any particular time used for purposes temporarily rendering the maintenance of cattle impossible, for the test was

---

16 *i.e.*, by prescription. See *White* v. *Taylor* [1969] 1 Ch. 150 at 158.
17 *Ante*, p. 806.
18 *Harris* v. *Earl of Chesterfield* [1911] A.C. 623.
19 See Halsb., 4th ed., vi, 212. Tudor L.C.R.P. states that other profits appendant exist, *e.g.*, piscary (p. 713), estovers (p. 714) and turbary (p. 716), but authority for this seems to be lacking.
20 *Ante*, p. 31.
21 *Earl of Dunraven* v. *Llewellyn* (1850) 15 Q.B. 791 at 810.
22 *Bennett* v. *Reeve* (1740) Willes 227 at 231, *per* Willes C.J.
23 *Tyrringham's Case* (1584) 4 Co.Rep. 36b at 37a.
24 *Robertson* v. *Hartopp* (1889) 43 Ch.D. 484 at 516.

not the number actually supported but the number which the land could be made to support.[25]

No common appendant could be created after 1290, for a conveyance of freehold land in a manor after that date resulted in the feoffee holding of the feoffor's lord, and the land passed out of the manor altogether.[26]

3. A profit pur cause de vicinage. This also exists only in the form of a common of pasture. If two adjoining commons are open to each other, there is a common *pur cause de vicinage* if the cattle put on one common by the commoners have always been allowed to stray to the other common and *vice versa*.[27] The claim fails if in the past the cattle have been driven off one common by the commoners thereof,[28] or if the commons have been fenced off,[29] or if the two commons are not contiguous to each other, even if they are separated only by a third common.[30]

4. A profit in gross. This is a profit, whether several or in common, exercisable by the owner independently of his ownership of land; there is no dominant tenement.[31] Thus a right to take fish from a canal without stint (*i.e.*, without limit) can exist as a profit in gross,[32] but not, as already seen,[33] as a profit appurtenant. A profit in gross is an interest in land which will pass under a will or intestacy or can be sold or dealt with in any of the usual ways,[34] being an incorporeal hereditament.[35]

B. Distinctions between Profits à Prendre and Certain Analogous Rights

I. PUBLIC RIGHTS

The public right which most closely resembles a profit is the right of the public to fish in the sea and all tidal waters. In theory the right is the Crown's, and it was formerly possible for the Crown to grant to an individual the exclusive right to fish in a specified part of the sea or tidal waters. Such a franchise[36] was known as a free fishery.[37] The public may therefore fish in all tidal waters except

---

[25] *Ibid.*, at pp. 516, 517.
[26] *Baring* v. *Abingdon* [1892] 2 Ch. 374 at 378; *ante*, p. 31.
[27] *Pritchard* v. *Powell* (1845) 10 Q.B. 589 at 603.
[28] *Heath* v. *Elliott* (1838) 4 Bing.N.C. 388.
[29] *Tyrringham's Case* (1584) 4 Co.Rep. 36b.
[30] *Commissioners of Sewers* v. *Glasse* (1874) L.R. 19 Eq. 134.
[31] *Lord Chesterfield* v. *Harris* [1908] 2 Ch. 397 at 421 (in H.L. [1911] A.C. 623).
[32] *Staffordshire and Worcestershire Canal Navigation* v. *Bradley* [1912] 1 Ch. 91.
[33] *Ante*, p. 823.
[34] *e.g.*, leased (*Staffordshire and Worcestershire Canal Navigation* v. *Bradley*, *supra*). [35] *Webber* v. *Lee* (1882) 9 Q.B.D. 315.
[36] A franchise is an incorporeal hereditament: *ante*, p. 790.
[37] Cru.Dig. iii, 261; see, *e.g.*, *Stephens* v. *Snell* [1939] 3 All E.R. 622.

a free fishery. But it has been held that the effect of *Magna Carta*, 1215, was to prevent the Crown from creating any new free fisheries,[38] although any already existing remain valid and transferable to this day.[39]

The right of fishery in non-tidal waters is dealt with below.[40]

II. RIGHTS OF FLUCTUATING BODIES

There can be no custom for a fluctuating body of persons to take a profit.[41] The reason is said to be that otherwise the subject-matter would be destroyed, " and such a claim, which might leave nothing for the owner of the soil, is wholly inconsistent with the right of property in the soil." [42] Neither can such rights exist as profits, for a profit lies in grant just like an easement[43] and a fluctuating body is not a capable grantee.

Yet if such a right has in fact been enjoyed for a long time, as of right[43a] and not merely by toleration,[44] the courts will strive to find a legal origin for it. " The first thing the court looks at as the criterion of property is usage and enjoyment. . . . Very high judges have said they would presume any thing in favour of a long enjoyment and uninterrupted possession." [45] Upon this principle two methods have been evolved for circumventing the rule against these customs, which in modern times finds little favour with the courts.

1. Presumed incorporation by Crown grant. The Crown is able to incorporate any body of persons and so endow them, as a corporation, with a single legal personality. Thus the Crown could grant a charter to a village making it a city or borough. Consequently there is nothing to prevent the Crown from making a grant of a profit to the inhabitants of a district and providing therein that for the purposes of the grant they should be treated as a corporation, though for other purposes they remain unincorporated. The obstacle that there is no definite person or persons in whose favour a grant could be presumed[46] is thus surmounted by

---

[38] *Malcolmson* v. *O'Dea* (1863) 10 H.L.C. 593 at 618, criticised in Theobald, *Law of Land*, 2nd ed., pp. 58 *et seq.*
[39] *Neill* v. *Duke of Devonshire* (1882) 8 App.Cas. 135 at 180.
[40] *Post*, p. 826.
[41] *Gateward's Case* (1607) 6 Co.Rep. 59b; *Commissioners of Sewers of the City of London* v. *Glasse* (1872) 7 Ch.App. 456 at 465; *Alfred F. Beckett Ltd.* v. *Lyons* [1967] Ch. 449.
[42] *Race* v. *Ward* (1855) 4 E. & B. 702 at 709, *per* Lord Campbell C.J.; and see *Chesterfield* v. *Fountaine* (1895) [1908] 1 Ch. 243n.   [43] *Ante*, p. 810.
[43a] See *post*, p. 842.
[44] *Alfred F. Beckett Ltd.* v. *Lyons, supra.*
[45] *Att.-Gen.* v. *Lord Hotham* (1823) T. & R. 209 at 217, 218, *per* Plumer M.R.
[46] *Fowler* v. *Dale* (1594) Cro.Eliz. 362.

presuming the existence of a corporation created *ad hoc* in a grant from the Crown. In fact such grants have been made but rarely.[47] Their chief importance is that the court will presume such a grant to have been made [47a] provided that—

(i) long enjoyment is proved; and

(ii) the right claimed derives from the Crown; and

(iii) those claiming the grant and their predecessors have always regarded themselves as a corporation and acted as such as regards the right, as by holding meetings or appointing some officer to supervise the right.[48]

2. Presumed charitable trust. Even when the claimants are destitute of any sign of corporate capacity,[49] the difficulty may not be insuperable. If long enjoyment [50] is shown the court may succeed in finding a legal origin for the right by presuming a grant of the profit to some existing corporation, subject to a trust or condition that the corporation should allow the claimants to exercise the right claimed. Thus in *Goodman* v. *Mayor of Saltash* [51] the free inhabitants of certain ancient tenements had for two hundred years enjoyed an oyster fishery from Candlemas (February 2) to Easter Eve each year. This right had been shared by the local corporation, which had enjoyed the right all the year round from time immemorial. The House of Lords refused to presume a grant incorporating the inhabitants for the purpose of the grant, but by " a splendid effort of equitable imagination " [51a] held that the corporation was entitled to a profit subject to a trust or condition in favour of the free inhabitants. Such a trust is charitable, since it exists to benefit the inhabitants of a particular place, as a section of the public, and so it is not subject to the rule against trusts of perpetual duration.[52] But enjoyment as of right is essential. Local inhabitants claiming to be entitled to collect coal on the foreshore therefore failed when they could show only a practice sufficiently explained by mere toleration.[52a] Nor will a trust be presumed against

---

[47] See, *e.g.*, *Willingale* v. *Maitland* (1866) L.R. 3 Eq. 103, explained in *Chilton* v. *Corporation of London* (*No.* 2) (1878) 7 Ch.D. 735.

[47a] *Re Free Fishermen of Faversham* (1887) 36 Ch.D. 329.

[48] See *Lord Rivers* v. *Adams* (1878) 3 Ex.D. 361 at 366, 367 (where the claim failed for want of corporate acts).

[49] See, *e.g.*, *Harris* v. *Earl of Chesterfield* [1911] A.C. 623 at 639.

[50] *e.g.*, *Haigh* v. *West* [1893] 2 Q.B. 19 (claim to pasturage by roadside succeeded on proof of 115 years' user). Examples of unsuccessful claims under this doctrine are *Lord Fitzhardinge* v. *Purcell* [1908] 2 Ch. 139; *Harris* v. *Earl of Chesterfield* [1911] A.C. 623.

[51] (1882) 7 App.Cas. 633.

[51a] *Harris* v. *Earl of Chesterfield* [1911] A.C. 623 at 633, *per* Lord Ashbourne, dissenting.   [52] *Ante*, p. 271.

[52a] *Alfred F. Beckett Ltd.* v. *Lyons* [1967] Ch. 449. See similarly *Mahoney* v. *Neenan* [1966] I.R. 559 (seaweed).

a landowner who can show a documentary title bearing no trace of it.[53]

Sect. 3. Acquisition of Easements and Profits

An easement or profit can exist as a legal interest in land only if it is—

    (i) held for an interest equivalent to a fee simple absolute in possession or term of years absolute [54]; and

    (ii) created either by statute, deed or prescription.

A document not under seal cannot create a legal [55] easement or profit, not even (it seems) for a term of three years or less.[56] But if made for value it may create a valid equitable easement [57] or profit.[57a] Similarly, an oral agreement for value may create an equitable easement [58] or profit if supported by a sufficient act of part performance.[59]

The various methods of acquisition must now be considered.

A. By Statute

Easements and profits created by statute are most frequently found in the case of local Acts of Parliament, *e.g.*, an Act giving a right of support to a canal constructed under statutory powers,[60] or an Inclosure Act giving the lord of the manor shooting rights over land allotted to the commoners.[61] But statutory rights analogous to easements are also often created by general Acts, *e.g.*, Acts

---

[53] *Goodman* v. *Mayor of Saltash, supra*, at p. 647; *Att.-Gen.* v. *Antrobus* [1905] 2 Ch. 188.

[54] L.P.A., 1925, s. 1 (2); *ante*, p. 141. Although the subsection does not mention profits expressly, it is almost beyond argument that they are covered by the words " easement, right, or privilege." In any case, a profit would fall within the definition of " land " in s. 205 (1) (ix), and would thus come within s. 1 (1). S. 62, which is manifestly intended to include profits, also does not mention them expressly, but is content to use words similar to those in s. 1 (2).

[55] L.P.A., 1925, s. 52, replacing Real Property Act, 1845, s. 3; *Hewlins* v. *Shippam* (1826) 5 B. & C. 221 (easement); *Duke of Somerset* v. *Fogwell* (1826) 5 B. & C. 875 (profit); *Armstrong* v. *Sheppard and Short Ltd.* [1959] 2 Q.B. 384.

[56] *Hewlins* v. *Shippam, supra*, at p. 229; *Wood* v. *Leadbitter* (1845) 13 M. & W. 838 at 843; *Mason* v. *Clarke* [1954] 1 Q.B. 460 at 468, 471, reversed on other grounds, [1955] A.C. 778. L.P.A. 1925, s. 54 (2), will not assist interests which could not validly be created by parol at common law: *Rye* v. *Rye* [1962] A.C. 496, *ante*, p. 623.

[57] *May* v. *Belleville* [1905] 2 Ch. 605.

[57a] *Frogley* v. *Earl of Lovelace* (1859) John 333. But if for any reason the court would refuse specific performance of the contract (*e.g.*, because it is tainted with fraud) there is no such equitable right: see *Mason* v. *Clarke, supra*. For this principle, see *ante*, p. 577.

[58] *McManus* v. *Cooke* (1887) 35 Ch.D. 681.

[59] *Duke of Devonshire* v. *Eglin* (1851) 14 Beav. 530, where under oral permission, given for value, the plaintiff had constructed a watercourse under the defendant's land; an injunction was granted to restrain the defendant from obstructing the watercourse.

[60] See, *e.g.*, *London & North Western Ry.* v. *Evans* [1893] 1 Ch. 16.

[61] Halsb. xii, 626.

giving rights to public utility undertakings in respect of electric cables, gas pipes, water pipes, sewers and similar things.[62]

B. By Express Grant or Reservation

1. Grant. The simplest way to create an easement or profit is by an express grant by deed. No special words are needed for a grant, so that a covenant or agreement, if contained in a deed, will have the same effect.[62a] The provisions of section 62 of the Law of Property Act, 1925, discussed below,[63] often cause a conveyance to operate as an express grant of easements and profits which are not expressly mentioned in the conveyance.

Before 1926 it was uncertain whether a grant of an easement without words of limitation created more than an easement for the life of the grantee[64]; but such a grant made after 1925 seems to give the grantee an easement in fee simple under the ordinary rule,[65] provided that the grantor is able to create such an interest, and that no contrary intention appears.[66]

It has been argued, but not decided, that an easement cannot be granted in reversion, *i.e.*, to take effect at some future time.[66a] Since a grant requires a grantee, a developer selling off plots of land cannot create easements in advance of each sale.[67]

2. Reservation. Reservation is the converse of grant. When a landowner disposes of part of his land and retains the rest, he may wish to reserve easements or profits over the part sold. Today this can be achieved quite simply,[67a] but until recent times there were difficulties. Before 1926 a legal easement or profit could not be created by a simple reservation in favour of the grantor. Any part of the land, or any pre-existing right over it, could be *excepted* from the grant, as, for example, minerals[68]; and some new right could be *reserved* if it was to issue out of the land granted, as did a rentcharge.[69] But an easement or profit created on a sale of the

---

[62] See " Statutory ' Easements ' " (1956) 20 Conv.(N.S.) 208 (J. F. Garner).

[62a] *Russell* v. *Watts* (1885) 10 App.Cas. 590 at 611; *Dowty Boulton Paul Ltd.* v. *Wolverhampton Corporation (No. 2)* [1973] 2 W.L.R. 618.

[63] See *post*, p. 835.

[64] See *Hewlins* v. *Shippam* (1826) 5 B. & C. 221 at 228, 229, for some indication that words of limitation were necessary; and see the controversy between Underhill, Sweet and Williams (1908) 24 L.Q.R. 199, 259, 264.   [65] *Ante*, p. 56.

[66] L.P.A., 1925, s. 60 (1), as read with s. 205 (1) (ii), (ix), defining " conveyance " and " land." The wording of s. 60 (1) is not wholly appropriate to the creation of new interests as distinct from the transfer of existing interests (see *ante*, p. 56), but it would be inconvenient to hold it inapplicable to grants *de novo*.

[66a] *Cable* v. *Bryant* [1908] 1 Ch. 259; *ante*, p. 821.

[67] Law Commission Working Paper No. 36, para. 112.

[67a] A conveyance expressed to be subject to all rights of way may suffice: *Pitt* v. *Buxton* (1970) 21 P. & C.R. 127.

[68] See Co.Litt. 47a; *Durham & Sunderland Ry.* v. *Walker* (1842) 2 Q.B. 940 at 967.

[69] Co.Litt. 143a.

servient tenement fell outside both these rules: it was not a pre-existing right, and it lay only in grant; and before 1926 a man could not grant to himself.[70] This obstacle could be overcome by two different devices.

(a) *Execution by grantee*: the conveyance reserved the right to the grantor and the grantee executed the conveyance.[71] Such a conveyance operated as a conveyance of the land to the grantee followed by the regrant of the easement or profit by the grantee to the grantor.[72]

If the transaction was a sale, but the purchaser did not execute the conveyance, the vendor had an equitable right to compel him to do so in accordance with the contract. Therefore, by analogy with the doctrine of *Walsh* v. *Lonsdale*,[72a] the vendor had an equitable right to the intended easement or profit, even though not a legal one. And since the attempted reservation in the conveyance put later purchasers on notice that such were the terms, the vendor was hardly worse off for failing to obtain execution by the purchaser.[73]

(b) *Executed use*: the grantor conveyed the land to X and his heirs to the use that the grantor should have a legal easement or profit, and subject thereto, to the use of the grantee and his heirs. This method was effective if the conveyance was executed after 1881, for by the Conveyancing Act, 1881,[74] the use relating to the easement or profit[75] was duly executed. Previously it was not, for the grantee was not seised of the easement in the sense required by the Statute of Uses, 1535,[76] and the use could therefore operate only in equity.

After 1925 the first method is unnecessary and the second is impossible. Both the Statute of Uses, 1535, and the Conveyancing Act, 1881, have been repealed[77]; and the Law of Property Act, 1925,[78] has now provided that the reservation of a legal estate or interest shall "operate at law without any execution of the conveyance by the grantee . . . or any regrant by him."

3. Effect of grant or reservation. The effect of a grant or reservation is a question of construction, which must be approached in the light of the rules that a grant is in general construed against

---

[70] *Durham & Sunderland Ry.* v. *Walker, supra,* at p. 967.
[71] Where a simple conveyance is made, it is unusual for the grantee to execute it.
[72] *Durham & Sunderland Ry.* v. *Walker, supra,* at p. 967.
[72a] (1882) 21 Ch.D. 9; *ante,* p. 625.
[73] *May* v. *Belleville* [1905] 2 Ch. 605.   [74] s. 62.
[75] This section applied to " any easement, right, liberty, or privilege."
[76] Sanders, *Uses,* i, 105; *ante,* p. 157.
[77] L.P.A., 1925, 7th Sched.
[78] s. 65.

the grantor [79] and that a man may not derogate from his grant.[80] Examples of the latter rule have already been given,[81] and examples of the former are given below.[82]

These rules governing grants ought also equally to govern reservations. The principle is that in case of doubt a man's legal acts should be construed against him, since the person who dictates the terms of the transaction cannot complain of not being given the benefit of any doubt.[83] But it has several times been said that the creation of easements by reservation under the Law of Property Act, 1925 (explained above) represents a mere change of machinery, and that a reservation is to be construed as if it were a regrant.[84] Yet these dicta conflict not only with the principle but also with express words in the Act which were not cited ("shall operate at law without . . . any regrant . . ."). In the latest decisions the dicta have not been followed, and the reservation has been construed against the party making it, in the same way that other reservations and exceptions have long been construed.[85]

The judicial addiction to the anomaly of the pre-1926 law has even been carried beyond questions of construction. Where land held upon trust was sold and conveyed by a deed which both the legal and the equitable owners executed, and in which the equitable owner reserved a right of way, it was held that this took effect in law as a regrant by the purchaser (to the equitable owner) of a legal easement, so that it did not create a mere equitable easement requiring registration as a land charge.[86]

C. By Implied Reservation or Grant

1. Implied reservation. The general rule, as explained above, is that a grant is construed in favour of the grantee. Therefore normally no easements will be implied in favour of a grantor; if he wishes

---

[79] *Williams* v. *James* (1867) L.R. 2 C.P. 577 at 581; *Neill* v. *Duke of Devonshire* (1882) 8 App.Cas. 135 at 149.   [80] *Ante,* p. 820.

[81] *Ibid.*   [82] *Post,* p. 873.

[83] Thus at common law reservations (*e.g.,* of rent or other services) and exceptions are construed against the person making them: *Lofield's Case* (1612) 10 Co.Rep. 106a; *Savill Bros. Ltd.* v. *Bethell* [1902] 2 Ch. 523; Shep.Touch. 100.

[84] *Bulstrode* v. *Lambert* [1953] 1 W.L.R. 1064; *Mason* v. *Clarke* [1954] 1 Q.B. 460, reversed on other grounds, [1955] A.C. 778; and see *Johnstone* v. *Holdway* [1963] 1 Q.B. 601. See [1954] C.L.J. 191 (H.W.R.W.).

[85] *Cordell* v. *Second Clanfield Properties Ltd.* [1969] 2 Ch. 9; *St. Edmundsbury and Ipswich Diocesan Board of Finance* v. *Clark (No. 2)* [1973] 1 W.L.R. 1572 where at pp. 1587–1591 there is a full discussion; yet although affirmed on appeal (Dec. 18, 1974), the decision is understood to have been disapproved on this point, on the ground that it was concluded by *Johnstone* v. *Holdway, supra.*

[86] *Johnstone* v. *Holdway, supra.* But see the discussion of the basis for such a decision in the *St. Edmundsbury* case, *supra,* at p. 1590.

to reserve any easements he must do so expressly.[87] To this rule there are two exceptions.

(a) Easements of necessity

(1) NECESSITY. If a grantor grants a plot of land in such circumstances as to cut himself off completely from some other part of his own land (*e.g.*, if a plot retained in the middle is completely surrounded by the part granted) there is implied in favour of the part retained a way of necessity over the part granted, for otherwise there would be no means of access to the land retained.[88] Whether the former owner of both plots of land retains or parts with the landlocked close, he may select the particular way to be enjoyed,[89] provided it is a convenient way[90]; and once selected, the route cannot subsequently be changed.[91] A way of necessity will be implied even if some of the surrounding land belongs to third parties[92]; but it is essential that the necessity should exist at the time of the grant and not merely arise subsequently.[93]

(2) ALTERNATIVE WAY. If some other way exists, no way of necessity will be implied unless that other way is merely precarious and not as of right,[94] or unless, perhaps, it would be a breach of the law to use that other way for the purpose in question.[95] Nor will there be a way of necessity if the other way is merely inconvenient,[96] as where the land abuts on a highway in a cutting twenty feet below[97]; for the principle is that an easement of necessity is one " without which the property retained cannot be used at all, and not one merely necessary to the reasonable enjoyment of that property." [98] Thus if a man grants land and retains an adjoining house, no easement of light is implied in his favour, for the house is not unusable

---

[87] *Wheeldon* v. *Burrows* (1879) 12 Ch.D. 31 at 49 (a leading case on reservation of easements, reviewing the authorities); *Liddiard* v. *Waldron* [1934] 1 K.B. 435. For a neat illustration of the different positions of grantor and grantee, see Williams V. & P. 661, 662.

[88] *Pinnington* v. *Galland* (1853) 9 Exch. 1. *Quaere* how far this doctrine depends on public policy: see (1973) 89 L.Q.R. 87 (E. H. Bodkin).

[89] *Bolton* v. *Bolton* (1879) 11 Ch.D. 968 at 972. On a simultaneous grant of both plots (*e.g.*, by devise) it seems that in the absence of any indication from the terms of the grant, any existing way which is used at the time will constitute the way of necessity: *Pearson* v. *Spencer* (1861) 1 B. & S. 571 at 585; affd. (1863) 3 B. & S. 761.   [90] *Pearson* v. *Spencer, supra.*

[91] *Deacon* v. *South Eastern Ry.* (1889) 61 L.T. 377.

[92] *Serff* v. *Acton Local Board* (1886) 31 Ch.D. 679.

[93] *Midland Ry.* v. *Miles* (1886) 33 Ch.D. 632.

[94] *Barry* v. *Hasseldine* [1952] Ch. 835.

[95] See *Hansford* v. *Jago* [1921] 1 Ch. 322 at 342, 343, where it was suggested but not decided that a way of necessity might arise when the only alternative way of emptying earth closets was by carrying the contents through cottages in breach of a by-law.

[96] *Dodd* v. *Burchell* (1862) 1 H. & C. 113.

[97] *Titchmarsh* v. *Royston Water Co. Ltd.* (1899) 81 L.T. 673.

[98] *Union Lighterage Co.* v. *London Graving Dock Co.* [1902] 2 Ch. 557 at 573, *per* Stirling L.J.

without the easement.[99]　Yet where a landowner grants away the subsoil of his land (*e.g.*, for mining), but retains the surface, an easement of support is implied in his favour.[1]

(3) CESSATION OF NECESSITY.　Where under an easement of necessity the necessity subsequently ceases, as where the owner of a way of necessity acquires another way to his land, it has been held that the easement of necessity thereupon ceases,[2] though this view has been criticised in later cases.[3]

(b) *Intended easements.*　Easements required to carry out the common intention of the parties will be implied in favour of the grantor even though not expressed in the conveyance.　Thus on the grant of one of two houses supported by each other, the mutual grant and reservation of easements of support will be implied if (as is usual) such an intention can be inferred.[4]　It is, however, essential in such cases that the parties should intend that the servient tenement should be used in the particular way claimed as an easement: an intent that there should be user which might or might not involve the user claimed as an easement is not enough.[5] A grantor alleging an intended reservation of an easement bears a heavy burden of proof.[6]

2. Implied grant.　In favour of a grantee easements are implied much more readily, on the principle that a grant must be construed in the amplest rather than in the narrowest way.　An express grant of the land is therefore often accompanied by the implied grant of easements.[7]　Rights which will arise by implied grant are as follows:

(a) *Easements of necessity,*[8] and

(b) *Intended easements.*　The rules which apply in these two cases are similar to those in the case of implied reservation, except

---

[99] *Ray* v. *Hazeldine* [1904] 2 Ch. 17.
[1] *Richards* v. *Jenkins* (1868) 18 L.T. 437.
[2] *Holmes* v. *Goring* (1824) 2 Bing. 76.
[3] See, *e.g.*, *Procter* v. *Hodgson* (1855) 10 Exch. 824; *Barkshire* v. *Grubb* (1881) 18 Ch.D. 616 at 620; but see (1939) 3 Conv.(N.S.) 425 at 430 (R. Grundy).
[4] *Richards* v. *Rose* (1853) 9 Exch. 218 at 221; *cf. Shubrook* v. *Tufnell* (1882) 46 L.T. 886, which treats such rights as easements of necessity. For other examples, see *Jones* v. *Pritchard* [1908] 1 Ch. 630 (common flue); *Cory* v. *Davies* [1923] 2 Ch. 95 (use of drive); *Simpson* v. *Weber* (1925) 133 L.T. 46 (right to let creeper climb neighbour's wall, and support for gate); contrast *Pwllbach Colliery Co. Ltd.* v. *Woodman* [1915] A.C. 634 at 647; *Re Webb's Lease* [1951] Ch. 808. There are special provisions in London under the London Building Acts (Amendment) Act, 1939, Part VI, replacing earlier Acts (*ante,* p. 436): see, *e.g.*, *Selby* v. *Whitbread* [1917] 1 K.B. 736.
[5] *Pwllbach Colliery Co. Ltd.* v. *Woodman, supra,* at p. 647.
[6] *Cf. Re Webb's Lease, supra.*
[7] *Phillips* v. *Low* [1892] 1 Ch. 47 at 50.
[8] *Pinnington* v. *Galland* (1853) 9 Exch. 1 at 12.

that the court is readier to imply easements in favour of the grantee than in favour of the grantor.[9] In one case a landlord let cellars to a tenant who covenanted to use them as a restaurant, to eliminate smells and to comply with health regulations. In fact, unknown to the parties, this could not lawfully be done without installing a proper ventilation system, and so it was held that the tenant had an easement of necessity to construct such a system (partly on the landlord's part of the premises) and use it.[10] Similarly, easements necessary for the enjoyment of some right expressly granted will be implied, *e.g.*, a right of way to a spring, on the grant of an easement to draw water from it.[11]

(c) Easements within the rule in Wheeldon v. Burrows

(1) SCOPE OF THE RULE. *Wheeldon* v. *Burrows* [12] determines what easements are implied in favour of the grantee of one part of a holding against the owner of the remainder. It is really a branch of the general rule against derogation from grant.[13] It relates not to the transmission of existing easements over the land of third parties (these, being already appurtenant to the land granted, naturally pass with it) but to the translation into easements of rights over the grantor's retained land which are necessary to the proper enjoyment of the land granted. It is natural for this purpose to look at the grantor's previous use of the land, and to allow the grantee to take easements corresponding to the facilities which the grantor himself found necessary. Before the grant they cannot have been easements because of the common ownership. They are therefore called "quasi-easements," *i.e.*, rights which are potential easements in case of a division of the land.[13a]

(2) THE RULE. *Wheeldon* v. *Burrows* [14] was a case where a long line of earlier authorities was summed up in a general rule.[15] It laid down that upon the grant of part of a tenement, there would pass to the grantee as easements all quasi-easements over the land retained which—

(i) were continuous and apparent, or

---

[9] *Richards* v. *Rose* (1853) 9 Exch. 218; *Pwllbach Colliery Co. Ltd.* v. *Woodman supra*, at p. 646; and see *Wheeldon* v. *Burrows, infra; Barry* v. *Hasseldine, supra.*
[10] *Wong* v. *Beaumont Property Trust Ltd.* [1965] 1 Q.B. 173.
[11] *Pwllbach Colliery Co. Ltd.* v. *Woodman, supra*, at p. 646.
[12] (1879) 12 Ch.D. 31.
[13] *Ibid.*, at p. 49; for the general rule, see *ante*, p. 820.
[13a] See *ante*, p. 810.
[14] *Supra.*
[15] The decision itself, however, was concerned rather with implied reservation than with implied grant. The rules for implied grant were set out by way of contrast.

(ii) were necessary to the reasonable enjoyment of the land granted,[16] and (in either case)

(iii) had been, and were at the time of the grant, used by the grantor for the benefit of the part granted.

It is by no means clear how far requirements (i) and (ii) are distinct. In *Wheeldon* v. *Burrows* they are treated in one place as synonymous[17] and in another as alternative.[18] The distinction between "continuous and apparent" easements and others was unknown to English law until 1839, when it seems to have been imported by a text-writer from the French law of prescription.[19] It then became a source of confusion, since it did not fit easily into the older and wider English rule against derogation from grant[20]; nor was it always insisted upon, or correctly understood. Requirements (i) and (ii) are therefore probably to be regarded as alternatives.

(3) "CONTINUOUS AND APPARENT." A "continuous" easement is one which is enjoyed passively, such as a right to use drains or a right to light, as opposed to one requiring personal activity for its enjoyment, such as a right of way.[21] An "apparent" easement is one which is evidenced by some sign on the dominant tenement[22] (or perhaps the servient tenement[23]) discoverable on "a careful inspection by a person ordinarily conversant with the subject."[24]

---

[16] This does not mean that it must be an easement of necessity, *i.e.*, an easement without which the property cannot be enjoyed *at all*, but merely that *reasonable* enjoyment of the property cannot be had without the easement.

[17] (1879) 12 Ch.D. 31 at 49.

[18] *Ibid.*, at p. 58. See (1967) 83 L.Q.R. 240 at 245 (A. W. B. Simpson).

[19] *Gale on Easements* (1st ed., 1839) 53: see *Dalton* v. *Angus & Co.* (1881) 6 App. Cas. 740 at 821, where Lord Blackburn explains the origins of this expression. In *Suffield* v. *Brown* (1864) 4 De G.J. & S. 185 at 195 Lord Westbury criticises it as "a mere fanciful analogy, from which rules of law ought not to be derived"; and see at p. 199 (though at p. 194 he appears to accept the doctrine for grants as distinct from reservations). In *Wheeldon* v. *Burrows, supra*, the Court of Appeal applied his distinction between grants and reservations, thus rejecting the principle of the French law which applied to both equally. Why the French terminology was nevertheless preserved is a mystery.

[20] The English rule goes back at least to 1663: *Palmer* v. *Fletcher* (1663) 1 Lev. 122.

[21] Code Civil, Art. 688. See (1967) 83 L.Q.R. 240 (A. W. B. Simpson). *Suffield* v. *Brown* (1864) 4 De G.J. & S. 185 at 199, holding that "continuous" requires incessant use, is evidently erroneous. Gale in his 1st ed., 1839, at p. 53, confined his doctrine to "those easements only which are attended by some alteration which is in its nature obvious and permanent; or, in technical language, to those easements only which are apparent and continuous." He thus apparently equated "continuous" with "permanent."

[22] Code Civil, Art. 689; *Schwann* v *Cotton* [1916] 2 Ch. 120 at 141 (affd. at 459); *Ward* v. *Kirkland* [1967] Ch. 194 at 225 (right to go on neighbour's land to maintain wall on edge of dominant land held not continuous and apparent).

[23] See *Ward* v. *Kirkland, supra*, at p. 225.

[24] *Pyer* v. *Carter* (1857) 1 H. & N. 916 at 922, *per* Watson B. In so far as this case applied the same rule to implied reservation it cannot now be good law: *Wheeldon* v. *Burrows* (1879) 12 Ch.D. 31.

Thus an underground drain into which water from the eaves of a house runs may be both continuous and apparent. Other examples are a watercourse running through visible pipes,[25] windows enjoying light [26] and a building enjoying support. On the other hand, a right to take water from a neighbour's pump from time to time [27] or a right to project the bowsprits of ships when in dock over the land of another [28] have been held to be outside the meaning of " continuous and apparent " easements.

Despite their adoption of these unsuitable terms, the courts have not applied them rigidly. Thus a right of way over a made road,[29] or one which betrays its presence by some indication such as a worn track [30] or its obvious use in connection with the land granted,[31] will pass under the Rule in *Wheeldon* v. *Burrows*; and the court will, it seems, turn a blind eye to the obstacle that a right of way is not " continuous." [32] The rule against derogation from grant is a flexible doctrine, capable, indeed, of creating rights which cannot be easements at all.[33]

(4) SIMULTANEOUS GRANTS. The rules relating to implied grant apply also to cases where the grantor, instead of retaining any land himself, makes simultaneous grants to two or more grantees. Each grantee obtains the same easements over the land of the other as he would have obtained if the grantor had retained it.[34]

(5) WILLS. Gifts by will are treated no differently from grants by deed for purposes of implied easements.[35] Thus on a devise of adjoining houses to different devisees, mutual rights of way over a connecting passage running behind the houses have been implied.[36] The rules are rules of common law and do not depend upon the grantee giving valuable consideration.

IMPLIED GRANT AND SECTION 62 OF THE LAW OF PROPERTY ACT, 1925

1. Section 62. The operation of the rules relating to implied grant has been considerably modified by the Law of Property Act, 1925, s. 62. This provision, which dates from 1881 [37] and so applies

---

[25] *Watts* v. *Kelson* (1870) 6 Ch.App. 166.
[26] *Phillips* v. *Low* [1892] 1 Ch. 47 at 53.
[27] *Polden* v. *Bastard* (1865) L.R. 1 Q.B. 156; and see *Ward* v. *Kirkland* [1967] Ch. 194.   [28] *Suffield* v. *Brown* (1864) 4 De G.J. & S. 185.
[29] *Brown* v. *Alabaster* (1887) 37 Ch.D. 490.
[30] *Hansford* v. *Jago* [1921] 1 Ch. 322; *Borman* v. *Griffith* [1930] 1 Ch. 493.
[31] *Borman* v. *Griffith, supra.*
[32] *Ibid.*, at p. 499.   [33] *Ante*, p. 820.
[34] *Swansborough* v. *Coventry* (1832) 2 Moo. & Sc. 362 (a better report than that in 9 Bing. 305: see *Broomfield* v. *Williams* [1897] 1 Ch. 602 at 616); *Hansford* v. *Jago, supra.*
[35] *Phillips* v. *Low* [1892] 1 Ch. 47.
[36] *Milner's Safe Co. Ltd.* v. *Great Northern & City Ry.* [1907] 1 Ch. 208.
[37] It replaces C.A., 1881, s. 6.

to all conveyances executed since then,[38] is designed to make it unnecessary to set out the full effect of every conveyance by " general words " extending it to all kinds of particulars. Now, if no contrary intention is expressed, every conveyance of land passes with it (*inter alia*) " all . . . liberties, privileges, easements, rights, and advantages whatsoever, appertaining or reputed to appertain to the land, or any part thereof, or, at the time of conveyance, . . . enjoyed with . . . the land or any part thereof." [39] " Conveyance " includes, *inter alia*, mortgages, leases, and assents,[40] but not a mere contract, *e.g.*, for a lease for over three years [41] or for the sale of the fee simple.[42] But a contract for sale may be relevant in providing some evidence of what rights exist which can fall within the statutory language when the conveyance is made.[43]

2. Creation of easements and profits. This very comprehensive formula has no effect on existing easements or profits appurtenant to the land conveyed, which automatically pass with it,[44] save that they preclude any argument that they were not intended to pass. But it has the important effect of creating new easements and profits, by way of express grant,[45] out of all kinds of quasi-easements and quasi-profits.[46] It therefore goes beyond the rule in *Wheeldon* v. *Burrows,* which applies only to certain classes of quasi-easements and perhaps not at all to quasi-profits. Under section 62 the difficulty of determining whether a quasi-easement is " continuous " or " apparent " does not arise,[47] provided only that it has been enjoyed with the land conveyed. Even a quasi-easement not reasonably necessary to the enjoyment of the property granted (*e.g.*, an alternative way of access through another person's house) can become an easement under section 62,[48] although it cannot under *Wheeldon* v. *Burrows.*

---

[38] L.P.A., 1925, s. 62 (6).
[39] L.P.A., 1925, s. 62 (1) ; and see subs. (2) for conveyances of land with buildings on it.
[40] L.P.A., 1925, s. 205 (1) (ii).
[41] *Borman* v. *Griffith* [1930] 1 Ch. 493.
[42] *Re Peck and the School Board for London's Contract* [1892] 2 Ch. 315.
[43] See *White* v. *Taylor (No. 2)* [1969] 1 Ch. 160.
[44] *Godwin* v. *Schweppes Ltd.* [1902] 1 Ch. 926 at 932.
[45] *Gregg* v. *Richards* [1926] Ch. 521 at 534, 535.
[46] *White* v. *Williams* [1922] 1 K.B. 727 (quasi-profit of sheepwalk); *Crow* v. *Wood* [1971] 1 Q.B. 77 (quasi-easement of fencing).
[47] See *Ward* v. *Kirkland* [1967] Ch. 194 at 229. Some signs of a judicial disposition to limit the operation of the statutory formula to continuous and apparent quasi-easements appear in *Titchmarsh* v. *Royston Water Co. Ltd.* (1899) 81 L.T. 673 and *Long* v. *Gowlett* [1923] 2 Ch. 177 at 202–204. But the true ground of decision in both cases appears to have been that the quasi-easement was not in fact enjoyed " with " the part of the land conveyed. To limit the words of the Act to any particular class of easements does not seem justifiable.
[48] *Goldberg* v. *Edwards* [1950] Ch. 247.

3. Operation of the section. Illustrations of the wide operation of section 62 are to be found in cases where the grantee has previously been tenant of the quasi-dominant tenement and has enjoyed certain additional rights by permission of the landlord. In one case, for example, the tenant had been allowed to use a roadway leading into a yard belonging to his landlord; the tenant eventually purchased the reversion, and it was held that he acquired an easement to use the roadway, even though his previous user was purely precarious.[49] A mere renewal of the tenant's lease would have had the same result, for a lease is equally a " conveyance " within the meaning of section 62, and nonetheless so because it was made informally,[50] provided that it was made in writing and not merely by word of mouth.[51] A landlord about to renew a lease should therefore take care first to revoke any licences which he has given to the tenant and prevent any further enjoyment of them, or else insert some provision in the new lease to exclude the application of section 62; otherwise section 62 may turn them into easements and give the tenant a right to enjoy them indefinitely.[52] Again, if a landlord lets a tenant into possession before granting a lease, and permits him to pass through a passage in the landlord's other property, the subsequent grant of the lease will turn this revocable licence into an irrevocable easement; for section 62 operates at the date of conveyance, and not at the date appointed by the conveyance for the beginning of the lessee's term.[53] Not surprisingly, the justice of this doctrine has been doubted.[53a]

4. Limits of the section. Section 62 cannot create as an easement or profit a right which is incapable of being an easement or profit.[54] The object of the section is to shorten conveyances, not to extend the categories of interests known to the law. Thus the section cannot confer an easement for the protection of one house by another against weather,[55] or for a precarious right such as a right to take

---

[49] *International Tea Stores Co.* v. *Hobbs* [1903] 2 Ch. 165, not cited in *White* v. *Taylor (No. 2)* [1969] 1 Ch. 160 at 185, which appears to assume the contrary.
[50] *Wright* v. *Macadam* [1949] 2 K.B. 744.
[51] *Rye* v. *Rye* [1962] A.C. 496. For informal leases, see *ante,* p. 622.
[52] The automatic continuance of a weekly or other periodic tenancy for each new period would not be a " conveyance," but merely a continuance of the original grant: see *ante,* p. 633; *Cattley* v. *Arnold* (1859) 1 J. & H. 651. See also (1962) 106 S.J. 483.
[53] *Goldberg* v. *Edwards* [1950] Ch. 247.
[53a] *Wright* v. *Macadam, supra,* at p. 755; *Green* v. *Ashco Horticulturist Ltd.* [1966] 1 W.L.R. 889 at 897; Law Commission Working Paper No. 36, para. 92, suggesting reform.
[54] *International Tea Stores Co.* v. *Hobbs* [1903] 2 Ch. 165 at 172; *Bartlett* v. *Tottenham* [1932] 1 Ch. 114; *Regis Property Co. Ltd.* v. *Redman* [1956] 2 Q.B. 612; *ante,* p. 811, n. 96.
[55] *Phipps* v. *Pears* [1965] 1 Q.B. 76.

water from an artificial watercourse and pond if and when the landowner chooses to let water into them [56]; for such rights cannot exist as easements. Since section 62 operates by way of express grant, it will not create a right which the grantor had no power to grant.[57]

Section 62 has also been held not to apply where the quasi-dominant and quasi-servient tenements are both owned and occupied by the same person.[58] If this is correct, it is an important restriction. The contrary was held in a case of a claim to light [59]; but this easement is an exception to many rules. Even if section 62 is inapplicable, there may of course be an implied grant under the rule in *Wheeldon* v. *Burrows*.[60]

5. Contrary intention. Section 62 applies " only if and as far as a contrary intention is not expressed in the conveyance." [61] An express grant of a more limited right of way than section 62 would carry does not by itself amount to a contrary intention for this purpose.[62] But the section is also subject to any contrary intention which may be implied from circumstances existing at the time of the grant. If, for example, the plot sold and the plot retained are both subject to a building scheme, the purchaser of a house standing on the plot sold will not be able to prevent the plot retained from being built upon so as to diminish his light; for the light was enjoyed " under such circumstances as to show that there could be no expectation of its continuance." [63]

DIFFERENCE BETWEEN EFFECTS OF CONTRACT AND OF GRANT

1. Contract and grant. In the great majority of cases, conveyances of a freehold are intended to give effect to some previous contract for a sale. It is important to realise that the rules which determine the operation of a conveyance do not in any way affect the interpretation of a contract.[64] The rule in *Wheeldon* v. *Burrows* [65] presupposes a grant and proceeds on the principle that a man who

---

[56] *Burrows* v. *Lang* [1901] 2 Ch. 502 ; and see *Green* v. *Ashco Horticulturist Ltd.,* *supra* (right of way exercisable only when convenient to landlord).
[57] *Quicke* v. *Chapman* [1903] 1 Ch. 659.
[58] *Long* v. *Gowlett* [1923] 2 Ch. 177 (unsuccessful claim by purchaser to go on land retained by vendor in order to clear millstream and repair banks). *Cf. Ward* v. *Kirkland* [1967] Ch. 194.
[59] *Broomfield* v. *Williams* [1897] 1 Ch. 602.
[60] *Long* v. *Gowlett, supra.*
[61] L.P.A., 1925, s. 62 (4).
[62] *Gregg* v. *Richards* [1926] Ch. 521.
[63] *Birmingham, Dudley & District Banking Co.* v. *Ross* (1888) 38 Ch.D. 295 at 307, *per* Cotton L.J.
[64] *Re Peck and the School Board for London's Contract* [1893] 2 Ch. 315 at 318.
[65] *Ante,* p. 823.

has made a grant may not derogate from it. Section 62 of the Law
of Property Act, 1925, applies only to a "conveyance," which,
although widely defined,[66] does not include a contract.[67] The rules
which govern the operation of conveyances merely say what the
result will be if the conveyance is made without reservations. But a
vendor of land, even under an open contract, is not necessarily
under any obligation to make such a conveyance: his obligation is
to convey what he has contracted to sell; and while he may not
convey less, he need not convey more.

2. Scope of contract. A purchaser of land is ordinarily entitled
by the contract to existing easements or profits which are appendant
or appurtenant to the land sold.[68] As regards quasi-easements, he
is entitled to such rights as may fairly be implied into the contract.
"When a property with a particular mode of access apparently and
actually constructed as a means of access to it is contracted to be
sold the strong presumption is that the means of access is included
in the sale."[69] Thus in *Borman* v. *Griffith*[70] there was an agreement
to let a house in a large park which stood close to a driveway
leading to a larger house, and it was held that the agreement
included the right to use the driveway for general purposes. This
was plainly within the scope of the contract, since the lease stated
that the house was let to the tenant for his trade of poultry and
rabbit farming, and he proved that the only other way of access
existing at the time of the contract was quite impracticable for
many purposes of this trade. In another case, where there was
a contract to sell house property in London which was approached
by made-up private roads both from the east and the west, the
purchaser was held entitled to the use of one of them only, as a
way of necessity, and not to the use of the other.[71] In such a case,
subject to allowing for the reasonable convenience of the purchaser,
the vendor is entitled to select the way.[72]

3. Scope of grant. It therefore seems that there is no general
rule that a contract entitles the purchaser to all the rights which an
unrestricted conveyance would pass to him. He is rather entitled
only to existing easements, and such quasi-easements as are necessary

---

[66] L.P.A., 1925, s. 205 (1) (ii); see *ante*, p. 836.
[67] *Borman* v. *Griffith* [1930] 1 Ch. 493.
[68] *Re Walmsley & Shaw's Contract* [1917] 1 Ch. 93.
[69] *Ibid.*, at p. 98, *per* Eve J.
[70] [1930] 1 Ch. 493.
[71] *Bolton* v. *Bolton* (1879) 11 Ch.D. 968.
[72] See *Re Peck and the School Board for London's Contract, supra*; *Re Walmsley and Shaw's Contract, supra*. The words "and the appurtenances" do not narrow the scope of a contract but may enlarge the scope of a conveyance: *Hansford* v. *Jago* [1921] 1 Ch. 322.

or intended [73]; and by an action for specific performance he cannot compel the vendor to convey more. The vendor may therefore insert limitations into the conveyance so as to make it accord with the contract.[74] In *Borman* v. *Griffith* [75] it was held that the tenant was entitled by the contract to such rights as would have passed to him under a conveyance executed before 1882, *i.e.*, including quasi-easements within the rule in *Wheeldon* v. *Burrows* [76]; for he was held to be entitled to the same rights as if specific performance had been decreed in his favour before 1882 and the conveyance had made no mention of rights of way.

The reasoning (though not the result) of this case is somewhat difficult. As explained above, a contract to grant land will prima facie comprise only such quasi-easements as are necessary or intended; and it should make no difference to assume specific performance, for a vendor need never convey more than he has contracted to sell. But since the rule governing contracts is so similar in its scope to the rule which governed grants without special words made before 1882, it is not always perceived that they are really two distinct rules. The first rule, for contracts, is still unaltered. The second rule, for grants, has been widened by statute, so that a conveyance may easily transfer more extensive rights than the purchaser is entitled to demand, unless the vendor takes care to make the proper reservations. A way of convenience over the vendor's other land is an example of a quasi-easement which may fall outside a contract for sale but within the wide general words of section 62.[77]

4. Rectification. Even if the vendor mistakenly makes an unrestricted conveyance, and so conveys more rights than he has agreed to sell, there is the possibility of rectification.[78] The court has an equitable jurisdiction to rectify the conveyance, and so make it accord with the contract, if by the common mistake of both parties it has been wrongly worded. The common intention of the parties appears from the contract, so that a mistake in the conveyance is a common mistake. For example, where a conveyance of a plot of land operated by reason of section 62 to create (unintentionally,

---

[73] See Williams V. & P. 658.

[74] *Re Peck and the School Board for London's Contract, supra* (the object and limitations of the statutory formula are well explained by Chitty J. at p. 318); *Re Hughes and Ashley's Contract* [1900] 2 Ch. 595; *Re Walmsley and Shaw's Contract, supra.* [75] [1930] 1 Ch. 493; see the text, *ante*, p. 836.

[76] *Ante*, p. 833.

[77] *Bolton* v. *Bolton, supra*; *Re Peck and the School Board for London's Contract, supra*; *Re Walmsley and Shaw's Contract, supra*; *Clark* v. *Barnes* [1929] 2 Ch. 368 at 380 (purchaser under open contract (but subject to an express oral agreement excluding the right of way in question: see at p. 382) held not entitled to a reputed way which fell within s. 62). [78] *Ante*, p. 595.

as regards the vendor) a right of way over a track across the vendor's other land, because the track had in fact been used in connection with the land sold, the court rectified the conveyance by expressly excluding this right of way, even though the purchaser alleged that he agreed to buy the land on the assumption that he would get the right of way.[79] But there are limits to the use of rectification, and it by no means nullifies the operation of section 62. Since it is an equitable remedy, it will not be awarded to a vendor who has misled the purchaser, or who has unduly delayed claiming it; nor will it be awarded against a bona fide purchaser for value who had no notice of the discrepancy between the contract and the conveyance.[80]

D. By Presumed Grant, or Prescription

The basis of prescription is that if long enjoyment of a right is shown, the court will strive to uphold the right by presuming that it had a lawful origin.[81] Thus the court may presume, on proof of the fact of long enjoyment, that there once was an actual grant of the right, even though it is impossible to produce any direct evidence of such a grant.[82] It is then " the habit, and in my view the duty, of the court, so far as it lawfully can, to clothe the fact with right." [82a] " The court is endowed with a great power of imagination for the purpose of supporting ancient user." [83] This policy extinguishes stale claims, quiets titles, and preserves established property, while at the same time paying lip service to the doctrine that every easement must owe its origin to a grant.

Today it is questionable whether this policy should be preserved; undoubtedly it has produced far too complex a body of law. The Law Reform Committee reported " that the law of prescription is unsatisfactory, uncertain and out of date, and that it needs extensive reform." A majority of the committee recommended its total abolition; but a strong minority recommended that in lieu of all existing forms of prescription there should be an improved Prescription Act for easements, though not for profits, based on a 12-year period of user.[84]

For a claim by prescription it is not enough to show long user by itself; there must have been continuous user " as of right " before the court will go so far as to presume a grant, and even then the court

---

[79] *Clark* v. *Barnes* [1929] 2 Ch. 368; *cf. Barkshire* v. *Grubb* (1881) 18 Ch.D. 616 (rectification in favour of purchaser).

[80] For this purpose the right to rectification is a " mere equity ": *ante*, p. 119.

[81] *Clippens Oil Co. Ltd.* v. *Edinburgh and District Water Trustees* [1904] A.C. 64 at 69, 70.

[82] *Gardner* v. *Hodgson's Kingston Brewery Co. Ltd.* [1903] A.C. 228 at 239.

[82a] *Moody* v. *Steggles* (1879) 12 Ch.D. 261 at 265, *per* Fry J.

[83] *Neaverson* v. *Peterborough R. D. C.* [1902] 1 Ch. 557 at 573, *per* Collins M.R.

[84] 14th Report, Cmnd. 3100 (1966).

will not presume a grant except in fee simple. These fundamental conditions must first be discussed before considering the three methods of prescription, namely, at common law, by lost modern grant, and under the Prescription Act, 1832.

1. User as of right. The claimant must show that he has used the right as if he were entitled to it, for otherwise there is no ground for presuming that he enjoys it under a grant. From early times English authorities have followed the definition of Roman law [85]: the user which will support a prescriptive claim must be user *nec vi, nec clam, nec precario* (without force, without secrecy, without permission).[86] The essence of this rule is that the claimant must prove not only his own user but also circumstances which show that the servient owner acquiesced in it as in an established right.[87] Since the necessary conditions are negative, it is usually the servient owner who alleges that the user was either forcible, secret or permissive; but the burden of proof on these matters nevertheless rests on the claimant.[88]

(*a*) *Vi.* Forcible user (*vi*) extends not only to user by violence, as where a claimant to a right of way breaks open a locked gate, but also to user which is contentious or allowed only under protest.[89] If there is a state of " perpetual warfare " between the parties there can obviously be no user as of right; and if the servient owner chooses to resist not by physical but by legal force, as by making unmistakable protests or taking legal proceedings,[89] the claimant's user will not help a claim by prescription.

(*b*) *Clam.* Secret user (*clam*) is illustrated by cases where the right claimed is exercised underground, *e.g.*, by discharging waste fluid from a factory intermittently and secretly (though without active concealment) into a local authority's sewers,[90] or by fixing the sides of a dock to the adjacent land by underground rods.[91] The same objection may be made to a claim for support of one building by another if the degree of support required for the dominant building is abnormally great because of some peculiarity not apparent to

---

[85] Dig. 8.5.10; 43.17.1; Bracton lib. 2 fo. 51b, 52a, 222b; Co.Litt. 114a. For modern authorities, see Gale 171, and the paragraphs below.

[86] *Solomon* v. *Mystery of Vintners* (1859) 4 H. & N. 585 at 602 (common law prescription); *Sturges* v. *Bridgman* (1879) 11 Ch.D. 852 at 863 (lost modern grant); *Tickle* v. *Brown* (1836) 4 A. & E. 369 at 382 (prescription under the Prescription Act, 1832; and see ss. 1, 2).

[87] *Sturges* v. *Bridgman, supra*, at p. 863.

[88] *Gardner* v. *Hodgson's Kingston Brewery Co. Ltd.* [1903] A.C. 229.

[89] *Eaton* v. *Swansea Waterworks Co.* (1851) 17 Q.B. 267; *Dalton* v. *Angus & Co.* (1881) 6 App.Cas. 740 at 786.

[90] *Liverpool Corporation* v. *H. Coghill & Son Ltd.* [1918] 1 Ch. 307.

[91] *Union Lighterage Co.* v. *London Graving Dock Co.* [1902] 2 Ch. 557.

the servient owner.[92]   But the servient owner cannot make the user secret by shutting his own eyes: it must be " of such a character that an ordinary owner of the land, diligent in the protection of his interests, would have, or must be taken to have, a reasonable opportunity of becoming aware of that enjoyment." [93] Thus a plea of *clam* failed where an outbuilding in a yard had for many years been supported by the wall of a dye-works, even though the outbuilding could not be seen from the servient tenement, for the servient owner should have had sufficient opportunity to discover its existence.[94]

(c) *Precario.*   Permissive user (*precario*) is the most common kind of enjoyment which will vitiate a claim by prescription.   User under licence is of course permissive, whether or not there is a contract or annual payment.[95]   The advantage of a periodic payment is that it shows that permission is regularly sought and renewed; otherwise user which was at first permissive may in time become user as of right if the circumstances indicate that the original permission is no longer relied upon.[96]   The right to receive an artificial flow of water is often permissive by its very nature, since it frequently depends upon the servient owner being willing to continue it.   Thus where waste water pumped from mines had flowed to the claimant's land for over sixty years he had no right to its continuance, since he enjoyed it at all times only because the servient owner chose to supply it.[97]

(d) *User qua easement or profit.*   User during unity of possession, *i.e.*, while the claimant was in possession of both dominant and servient tenements, cannot be user as of right [98]; nor can user enjoyed in the mistaken belief that the claimant was entitled to the

---

[92] *Dalton* v. *Angus & Co.* (1881) 6 App.Cas. 740.
[93] *Union Lighterage Co.* v. *London Graving Dock Co., supra,* at p. 571, *per* Romer L.J.
[94] *Lloyds Bank Ltd.* v. *Dalton* [1942] Ch. 466; contrast *Davies* v. *Du Paver* [1953] 1 Q.B. 184, where the plaintiff claimed a profit of sheepwalk over part of a hill farm in Wales in country where there had been little fencing; the owner lived some distance away and had only recently bought the farm: held, despite some evidence that the enjoyment was " common knowledge " in the district, the plaintiff had failed to show user with the owner's knowledge and his claim failed.   This decision creates difficulties: see *post,* p. 860, n. 20.
[95] *Monmouth Canal Co.* v. *Harford* (1834) 1 Cr.M. & R. 614; *Gardner* v. *Hodgson's Kingston Brewery Co. Ltd.* [1903] A.C. 229. As to an agent's knowledge, see *Diment* v. *N. H. Foot Ltd.* [1974] 1 W.L.R. 1427.
[96] This is a question of fact: *Gaved* v. *Martyn* (1865) 19 C.B.(N.S.) 732.
[97] *Arkwright* v. *Gell* (1839) 5 M. & W. 203; *cf. Wood* v. *Waud* (1849) 3 Ex. 748; *Bartlett* v. *Tottenham* [1932] 1 Ch. 114; and see *ante,* p. 838.
[98] *Bright* v. *Walker* (1834) 1 Cr.M. & R. 211 at 219; *Outram* v. *Maude* (1881) 17 Ch.D. 391 (dominant owner holding servient land under lease); and see *Clayton* v. *Corby* (1842) 2 Q.B. 813 (profit), and *Battishill* v. *Reed* (1856) 18 C.B. 696 and *Damper* v. *Bassett* [1901] 2 Ch. 350 (easements), decided under the Prescription Act, 1832.

servient tenement [99] or that he had the temporary permission of the landlord.[1] But proof that the claimant exercised his right in the mistaken belief that a valid easement or profit had already been granted to him will not prevent the user from being as of right.[2] The principle is that the right must have been exercised *qua* easement or profit and not, for example, under any actual or supposed right of an occupant of both tenements. "The whole law of prescription . . . [rests] upon acquiescence . . . I cannot imagine any case of acquiescence in which there is not shown to be in the servient owner: 1, a knowledge of the acts done; 2, a power in him to stop the acts or to sue in respect of them; and 3, an abstinence on his part from the exercise of such power." [3]

2. User in fee simple

(a) *User by and against the fee.* The user must be by or on behalf of a fee simple owner against a fee simple owner.[4] "The whole theory of prescription at common law is against presuming any grant or covenant not to interrupt, by or with anyone except an owner in fee." [5] An easement or profit for life or for years, for example, may be expressly granted but cannot be acquired by prescription,[6] for the theory of prescription presumes that a permanent right has been duly created at some unspecified time in the past. A claim by prescription must therefore fail if user can be proved only during a time when the servient land was occupied by a tenant for life [7] or for years,[8] for then the fee simple owner may never have been in a position to contest the user.[8a] But if it can be

---

[99] *Lyell* v. *Lord Hothfield* [1914] 3 K.B. 911 (profit); *Att.-Gen. of Southern Nigeria* v. *John Holt & Co. (Liverpool) Ltd.* [1915] A.C. 599 at 617, 618 (easement).

[1] *Chamber Colliery Co.* v. *Hopwood* (1886) 32 Ch.D. 549 (easement).

[2] *Earl de la Warr* v. *Miles* (1881) 17 Ch.D. 535 (profit).

[3] *Dalton* v. *Angus & Co.* (1881) 6 App.Cas. 740 at 773, 774, *per* Fry J.; and see at p. 803, *per* Lord Penzance.

[4] *Bright* v. *Walker* (1834) 1 Cr.M. & R. 211 at 221 (prescription at common law); *Wheaton* v. *Maple & Co.* [1893] 3 Ch. 48 at 63 (lost modern grant); *Kilgour* v. *Gaddes* [1904] 1 K.B. 457 at 460 (Prescription Act, 1832). But see *post*, p. 850, as to lost modern grant.

[5] *Wheaton* v. *Maple & Co.* [1893] 3 Ch. 48 at 63, *per* Lindley L.J. (lost modern grant).

[6] *Wheaton* v. *Maple & Co.*, *supra*, at p. 63; *Kilgour* v. *Gaddes*, *supra*, at p. 460 (Prescription Act, 1832). These decisions of the Court of Appeal appear to be decisive. For contrary opinions, see *Bright* v. *Walker* (1834) 1 Cr.M. & R. 211 at 221 (suggestion that before the Prescription Act, 1832, a grant by a termor could be presumed from long user); *East Stonehouse U. D. C.* v. *Willoughby Bros. Ltd.* [1902] 2 K.B. 318 at 332. In Ireland the law is otherwise: *Flynn* v. *Harte* [1913] 2 I.R. 326; *Tallon* v. *Ennis* [1937] I.R. 549.

[7] *Roberts* v. *James* (1903) 89 L.T. 282; *Barker* v. *Richardson* (1821) 4 B. & Ald. 579. For the question whether any change has been brought about by the Settled Land Acts, 1882-1925, which empower a tenant for life to grant easements in fee simple, see *post*, p. 850, n. 57.

[8] *Daniel* v. *North* (1809) 11 East 372.

[8a] *Pugh* v. *Savage*, *infra*.

shown that user as of right began against the fee simple owner, it will not be less effective because the land was later settled or let [9]; and user against the fee simple will be presumed, unless the servient owner can show the contrary.[9a]

It will be seen, accordingly, that the theory of prescription does not deal properly with cases where the servient land is in the hands of a limited owner. It seems irrational to allow prescription against land if occupied by an owner in fee simple but not if occupied under a 999-year lease, for example. The law in Ireland, where prescription against limited owners is allowed, seems more satisfactory.[10]

(b) *User by lessee.* Where it is the dominant tenement that is let, a tenant cannot make a claim by prescription to an easement as annexed to his limited estate; if he claims an easement on the strength of his own user, he must necessarily claim it for his landlord as well as for himself.[11] It follows that a tenant cannot prescribe for an easement over his landlord's adjacent land, for the landlord can have no right against himself.[12] For the same reason, if A leases two plots of his land to two tenants, one tenant cannot prescribe for an easement against the other, for otherwise the result would be that A would acquire an easement over his own land.[13]

(c) *Exceptions.* There are certain modifications of this rule. First, profits in gross may be acquired by prescription at common law [14] (though not under the Prescription Act, 1832 [15]), which is then known as " prescription in gross." In this case the right is not claimed in respect of any dominant tenement but on behalf of the claimant personally. The claimant must show enjoyment by himself and his predecessors in title to the profit,[16] instead of by himself and his predecessors in title to the dominant tenement. In

---

[9] *Palk* v. *Shinner* (1852) 18 Q.B. 215; *Pugh* v. *Savage* [1970] 2 Q.B. 373, in effect approving this passage, and suggesting that it remains correct even if the tenancy, though granted after the user commenced, began before the 20 years' period next before action under the Prescription Act, 1832, began to run.

[9a] *Davis* v. *Whitby* [1973] 1 W.L.R. 629, affirmed [1974] Ch. 186; contrast *Diment* v. *N. H. Foot Ltd.* [1974] 1 W.L.R. 1427 (onus discharged).

[10] See (1958) 74 L.Q.R. 82 (V. T. H. Delany).

[11] This was important as a rule of pleading before the Common Law Procedure Act, 1852; but the need to plead the landlord's title was removed by the Prescription Act, 1832, s. 5, as regards claims made under that Act (for which see *ante*, p. 844). For the earlier rule, see *Gateward's Case* (1607) 6 Co.Rep. 59b; *Dawney* v. *Cashford* (1697) Carth. 432; 17 Vin.Abr. 288; Cru.Dig. iii, 422; for the later law, see the arguments and judgment in *Ivimey* v. *Stocker* (1866) 1 Ch.App. 396; cf. *Att.-Gen.* v. *Gauntlett* (1829) 3 Y. & J. 93. Similarly a copyholder had to prescribe in the name of his lord: 1 Wms.Saund. 349, n. (11).

[12] *Gayford* v. *Moffat* (1868) 4 Ch.App. 133.

[13] *Kilgour* v. *Gaddes* [1904] 1 K.B. 457. Here again the law is different in Ireland: *Flynn* v. *Harte* [1913] 2 I.R. 326; *Tallon* v. *Ennis* [1937] I.R. 549.

[14] *Johnson* v. *Barnes* (1873) L.R. 8 C.P. 527.

[15] *Shuttleworth* v. *Le Fleming* (1865) 19 C.B.(N.S.) 687.

[16] *Welcome* v. *Upton* (1840) 6 M. & W. 536.

technical terms, prescription in gross is contrasted with prescription " in the *que* estate " [17] where the claimant used to plead user by himself and " *ceux que estate il ad* " [18] (*i.e.,* those whose estate he has). There can be no prescription in gross for easements, which cannot exist in gross.[19] Secondly, certain exceptions arise under the Prescription Act, 1832, as is explained below.[20]

3. Continuous user. The claimant must show continuity of enjoyment.[21] This is interpreted reasonably; in the case of easements of way it is clearly not necessary to show ceaseless user by day and night.[22] User whenever circumstances require it is normally sufficient,[23] provided the intervals are not excessive. A claim which clearly fell on the wrong side of the line was where a right of way had been exercised only on three occasions at intervals of twelve years.[24] But continuity is not broken merely by some agreed variation in the user, as by the parties altering the line of a right of way for convenience.[24a]

The requirement of continuity of user must be distinguished both from the special rule under the Prescription Act, 1832, as to user " without interruption," and from the degree of disuse that may extinguish an easement or profit after it has been acquired.[25]

The three methods of prescription must now be described.

I. PRESCRIPTION AT COMMON LAW

1. Presumption of grant. Prescription and limitation are in many ways similar principles, but as the law has developed they have become quite distinct subjects.[26] By *limitation* one person may acquire the land of another by adverse possession for a period which is now generally twelve years. By *prescription* one person may

---

[17] *Austin* v. *Amhurst* (1877) 7 Ch.D. 689 at 692.
[18] Litt. 183 ; and see Y.B. 1 & 2 Edw. 2 (17 S.S.), p. xlviii.
[19] *Ante,* p. 806.
[20] *Post,* pp. 862, 863.
[21] *Dare* v. *Heathcote* (1856) 25 L.J.Ex. 245 (common law); *Att.-Gen.* v. *Simpson* [1901] 2 Ch. 671 at 698 (lost modern grant); *Hollins* v. *Verney* (1884) 13 Q.B.D. 304 at 314, 315 (Prescription Act, 1832).
[22] *Hollins* v. *Verney, supra,* at p. 308.
[23] *Dare* v. *Heathcote, supra* (easement); see *Earl de la Warr* v. *Miles* (1881) 17 Ch.D. 535 at 600 (profit). But see *Parker* v. *Mitchell* (1840) 11 A. & E. 788 (easement: user shown from fifty years before action down to four years before action, but no user shown during the last four years: claim failed). Compare *Carr* v. *Foster* (1842) 3 Q.B. 581 (profit: thirty years' user shown, except for two years near the middle of the thirty, when the claimant had no commonable cattle: claim succeeded).
[24] *Hollins* v. *Verney* (1884) 13 Q.B.D. 304.
[24a] *Davis* v. *Whitby* [1974] Ch. 186.
[25] *Smith* v. *Baxter* [1900] 2 Ch. 138 at 143, 146; *post,* pp. 852, 870.
[26] For limitation, see *post,* Chap. 16, p. 1003.

acquire rights such as easements and profits over the land of another. One important difference is that limitation is extinctive but prescription is acquisitive: that is to say, adverse possession of land for twelve years extinguishes the previous owner's title, leaving the adverse possessor with a title based on his own actual possession [27]; but prescription creates a new right, an incorporeal hereditament, which no one possessed previously. Prescription therefore must have positive operation, so as to create a new title. This is brought about by presuming a grant. "Every prescription presupposes a grant to have existed." [28]

2. Time immemorial. At common law a grant would be presumed only where user as of right had continued from time immemorial, "from time whereof the memory of men runneth not to the contrary." [29] For this purpose the year 1189 was fixed as the limit of legal memory, so that any right enjoyed at that date was unchallengeable. This date was first fixed by statute in 1275,[30] and applied primarily to limitation; but it was also adopted for prescription. Yet although the law of limitation was changed by later statutes,[31] they were held not to alter the limit of legal memory for purposes of prescription. A claimant by prescription at common law must therefore have the boldness to claim that he and his predecessors have enjoyed the right since 1189.[32]

3. Twenty years' user. It is clearly impossible in most cases to show continuous user since 1189, and so the courts have adopted the rule that if user as of right for twenty years or more is shown, the court will presume that that user has continued since 1189.[33] The period of twenty years was probably adopted by analogy with the limitation period laid down by the Limitation Act, 1623.[34] Such user for less than twenty years requires supporting circumstances to raise the presumption [35]; and if there is evidence of user as far back as the period of living memory, it is immaterial that no continuous period of twenty years is covered.[36] This rule reduced to reasonable proportions a burden of proof which in theory was absurdly onerous.

---

[27] *Post*, p. 1003. For the application of the Statutes of Limitation to incorporeal hereditaments, see Co.Litt. 115a and notes by Hargrave.
[28] Bl.Comm. ii, 265.   [29] Litt. 170.
[30] Statute of Westminster I, 1275, c. 39; *post*, p. 1010.
[31] *Post*, p. 1010.
[32] See the account of this rule given by Cockburn C.J. in *Bryant* v. *Foot* (1867) L.R. 2 Q.B. 161 at 180, 181.
[33] *Darling* v. *Clue* (1864) 4 F. & F. 329 at 334.
[34] *Bright* v. *Walker* (1834) 1 Cr.M. & R. 211 at 217; *post*, p. 1010.
[35] *Bealey* v. *Shaw* (1805) 6 East 208 at 215.
[36] *R. P. C. Holdings Ltd.* v. *Rogers* [1953] 1 All E.R. 1029.

4. Defects. Serious obstacles remained, however. The worst was that the presumption of user from time immemorial could be rebutted by showing that at some time since 1189 the right could not or did not exist.[37] Thus an easement of light cannot be claimed by prescription at common law for a building which is shown to have been erected since 1189.[38] Consequently it was very difficult to establish a claim to light at common law, and many claims based on enjoyment lasting for centuries were liable to be defeated by evidence that there could have been no enjoyment of the light in 1189. Again, if it could be shown that at any time since 1189 the dominant and servient tenements had been in the same ownership and occupation, any easement or profit would have been extinguished [39] and so any claim at common law would fail. Yet again, a man could not prescribe for a right contrary to custom.[40] To remedy these failings the courts invented the " revolting fiction " [41] of the lost modern grant.

II.   LOST MODERN GRANT

1. Nature of doctrine. The weakness of common law prescription was the liability to failure if it was shown that user had begun after 1189. The doctrine of lost modern grant avoided this by presuming from long user that an easement or profit had been actually granted after 1189 but prior to the user supporting the claim,[42] and that the deed of grant had been lost. The doctrine was wholly judge-made, and therefore really a variety of prescription at common law; but it was a fairly late and distinct development,[43] and so may be classified separately.

2. Presumption of grant. " Juries were first told that from user, during living memory, or even during twenty years, they might presume a lost grant or deed; next they were recommended to make such presumption; and lastly, as the final consummation of judicial legislation, it was held that a jury should be told, not only that they might, but also that they were bound to presume the existence of such a lost grant, although neither judge nor jury, nor anyone else, had the shadow of belief that any such instrument had ever really existed." [44]   In their anxiety to find a legal origin for a

---

[37] *Hulbert* v. *Dale* [1909] 2 Ch. 570 at 577.
[38] *Bury* v. *Pope* (1588) Cro.Eliz. 118; *Duke of Norfolk* v. *Arbuthnot* (1880) 5 C.P.D. 390.   [39] See *post,* p. 871; *Keymer* v. *Summers* (1769) Bull.N.P. 74.
[40] *Perry* v. *Eames* [1891] 1 Ch. 658 at 667.
[41] *Angus & Co.* v. *Dalton* (1877) 3 Q.B.D. 85 at 94, *per* Lush J.
[42] See, *e.g., Dalton* v. *Angus & Co.* (1881) 6 App.Cas. 740 at 813.
[43] The earliest case in the reports is said to be *Lewis* v. *Price* (1761), noted in 2 Wms.Saund., 6th ed., 175, 85 E.R. 926: see *Dalton* v. *Angus & Co., supra,* at p. 812.
[44] *Bryant* v. *Foot* (1867) L.R. 2 Q.B. 161 at 181, *per* Cockburn C.J.

right of which there had been open and uninterrupted enjoyment for a long period, unexplained in any other way,[45] the courts presumed that a grant had been made, and so made it immaterial that enjoyment had not continued since 1189. " Grant " is not confined to dispositions by deed: the court may be willing to presume a lost faculty from an ecclesiastical authority,[46] a lost Crown charter, a lost ministerial consent,[46a] and even a lost port authority's regulation,[47] though it is very difficult to presume a lost statute.[48] Twenty years' user will normally raise such presumptions.[49]

3. Improbability of grant. Presuming the existence of grants which had probably never been made was frequently felt to be objectionable, particularly when it fell to juries who were required to find it as a fact upon oath. But the doctrine was elaborately considered and endorsed by the House of Lords in *Dalton* v. *Angus & Co.*,[50] and is now unquestionable. Certain rules survive as relics of judicial reluctance to strain the consciences of juries more than necessary. In the first place, rather stronger evidence of user is required to induce the court to presume a lost modern grant than is required for prescription at common law.[51] Again, the doctrine can be invoked only if something excludes common law prescription.[52] Since the doctrine is admittedly a fiction, the claimant will not be ordered to furnish particulars of the fictitious grant, *e.g.*, as to the parties,[53] though he must plead whether the grant is alleged to have been made before or after a particular date.[54]

4. Impossibility of grant. Probably the presumption cannot be rebutted by evidence that no grant was in fact made.[55] But it is a

---

[45] *Att.-Gen.* v. *Simpson* [1901] 2 Ch. 671 at 698.
[46] *Philipps* v. *Halliday* [1891] A.C. 228.
[46a] *Re Edis's Declaration of Trust* [1972] 1 W.L.R. 1135.
[47] *Att.-Gen.* v. *Wright* [1897] 2 Q.B. 318.
[48] *Harper* v. *Hedges* [1924] 1 K.B. 151.
[49] *Penwarden* v. *Ching* (1829) Moo. & M. 400; *Dalton* v. *Angus & Co.* (1881) 6 App.Cas. 740, *e.g.*, at p. 812.
[50] *Supra.*   [51] *Tilbury* v. *Silva* (1890) 45 Ch.D. 98 at 123.
[52] *Bryant* v. *Lefever* (1879) 4 C.P.D. 172 at 177.
[53] *Palmer* v. *Guadagni* [1906] 2 Ch. 494.
[54] *Tremayne* v. *English Clays Lovering Pochin & Co. Ltd.* [1972] 1 W.L.R. 657; contrast *Gabriel Wade & English Ltd.* v. *Dixon & Cardus Ltd.* [1937] 3 All E.R. 900.
[55] This is supported by Thesiger and Cotton L.JJ., *Angus & Co.* v. *Dalton* (1878) 4 Q.B.D. 162 at 172, 187; Lindley and Lopes JJ. and Lord Blackburn, *Dalton* v. *Angus & Co.* (1881) 6 App.Cas. 740 at 765, 767, 813, 814; and see Gale 121–124, treating the House of Lords as having in effect affirmed the view of Thesiger and Cotton L.JJ. *Tehidy Minerals Ltd.* v. *Norman* [1971] 2 Q.B. 528 probably settles the point. For the contrary view, see Cockburn C.J. and Mellor J., *Angus* v. *Dalton* (1877) 3 Q.B.D. 85 at 113, 118, 130; Brett L.J., S.C. (1878) 4 Q.B.D. 162 at 201; *Duke of Norfolk* v. *Arbuthnot* (1880) 5 C.P.D. 390 at 394 (and see *per* Bramwell L.J. at p. 393); Bowen J., *Dalton* v. *Angus & Co.*, *supra*, at p. 783; and Farwell J., *Att.-Gen.* v. *Simpson* [1901] 2 Ch. 671 at 698.

good defence that during the entire period when the grant could have been made there was nobody who could lawfully have made it.[56] Thus the court has refused to presume a lost grant of a way where the land had been in strict settlement (under which there was no power to make a grant in fee simple) from the time when the user began down to the time of action.[57] Similarly the courts have refused to presume lost grants which would be contrary to statute [58] or custom.[59] But although the English authorities are to the contrary, there seems nothing in principle that necessarily excludes a lost modern grant by or to a person owning less than a fee simple.[60]

III. UNDER THE PRESCRIPTION ACT, 1832

The Prescription Act, 1832, was designed to reduce the difficulties and uncertainties of prescription, and in particular the difficulty of persuading juries to presume grants to have been made when they knew this was not true.[61] In many cases it has substituted certainty for uncertainty and thus simplified a claimant's position. It makes special provisions for easements of light; and these have now been supplemented by the Rights of Light Act, 1959. Accordingly, other easements will be treated first, together with profits, and then easements of light.

The Act of 1832 is notorious as " one of the worst drafted Acts on the Statute Book." [61a] It is perhaps best explained by giving a summary of the effect of the principal sections and annotating the sections in groups. The elements of the Act are as follows.

---

[56] *Neaverson* v. *Peterborough R. D. C.* [1902] 1 Ch. 557.

[57] *Roberts* v. *James* (1903) 89 L.T. 282, where it was also held that an intervening resettlement made no difference; this leaves little, if anything, of *Williams* v. *Ducat* (1901) 65 J.P. 40. The question whether the court could presume a grant under the Settled Land Act (*ante,* p. 333) was not raised and may still be open. Similar cases where lost grants were not presumed are *Barker* v. *Richardson* (1821) 4 B. & Ald. 579 (user against glebe land over which the rector could not grant an easement); *Rochdale Canal Co.* v. *Radcliffe* (1852) 18 Q.B. 287 (corporation with limited power of grant); *Daniel* v. *North* (1809) 11 East 372 (user against leaseholder).

[58] *Neaverson* v. *Peterborough R. D. C.* [1902] 1 Ch. 557; *Hulley* v. *Silversprings Bleaching and Dyeing Co. Ltd.* [1922] 2 Ch. 268.

[59] *Wynstanley* v. *Lee* (1818) 2 Swans. 33; *Perry* v. *Eames* [1891] 1 Ch. 658 at 667 (City of London custom against prescription for light, except under s. 3 of the Prescription Act, 1832: *post,* p. 862).

[60] See (1958) 74 L.Q.R. 82 (V. T. H. Delany), discussing English and Irish authorities; *cf. ante,* p. 844.

[61] *Mounsey* v. *Ismay* (1865) 3 H. & C. 486 at 496.

[61a] Law Reform Committee, 14th Report, Cmnd. 3100 (1966), para. 40.

1. Easements (other than light) and profits

(a) *The statutory periods*

SECTIONS 1 AND 2: (i) An easement enjoyed for twenty years as of right and without interruption cannot be defeated by proof that user began after 1189.[62]

(ii) An easement enjoyed for forty years as of right and without interruption is deemed " absolute and indefeasible " unless enjoyed by written consent.[62]

(iii) The same rules apply to profits, except that the periods are thirty and sixty years respectively.[63]

SECTION 3: This section, which lays down special rules for the easement of light, is dealt with below.[64]

SECTION 4: (i) All periods of enjoyment under the Act are those periods next before some suit or action in which the claim is brought into question.

(ii) No act is to be deemed an interruption until it has been submitted to or acquiesced in for one year after the party interrupted had notice both of the interruption and of the person making it.

(b) *Shorter and longer periods.* The shorter periods (twenty and thirty years for easements and profits respectively) operate negatively, *i.e.*, they assist prescription at common law by prohibiting one kind of defence. The longer periods operate positively, for then the Act declares the right to be " absolute and indefeasible." This important distinction is further discussed below, in the light of other provisions of the Act.[65]

(c) *" Next before some suit or action."* The Act does not say that an easement or profit comes into existence after twenty, thirty, forty or sixty years' user in the abstract; all periods under the Act are those next before some action in which the right is questioned. Thus until some action is brought, there is no right to any easement or profit under the Act, however long the user.[66] It is sometimes said that the right remains merely inchoate until action is brought. The important point is that the fruits of the Act can be reaped only by a litigant. Any person who wishes to consolidate an inchoate right under the Act can issue a writ against the servient

---

[62] s. 2.
[63] s. 1.
[64] *Post*, p. 861.
[65] *Post*, p. 859.
[66] *Colls* v. *Home and Colonial Stores Ltd.* [1904] A.C. 179 at 189, 190; *Hyman* v. *Van den Bergh* [1908] 1 Ch. 167.

owner claiming a declaration that he is entitled to an easement or profit.[67] He need not wait for some interference with it by the servient owner.

Even if there has been user for longer than the statutory periods, the vital period remains the period next before action. Thus if user commenced fifty years ago but ceased five years ago, a claim to an easement will fail if the action is commenced today, for during the twenty or forty years next before the action there has not been continuous user.[68] Similarly a claim under the Act will fail if there has been unity of possession for a substantial time during the period immediately before the action, for then there has not been user as an *easement* during the whole of the vital period.[69]

(d) " Without interruption "

(1) ONE YEAR'S ACQUIESCENCE. The user must be "without interruption"; but a special meaning is given to "interruption." If D has used a way over S's land for over twenty years, and then a gate is locked or a barrier erected barring his way, D can still succeed in establishing an easement providing that, at the time an action is brought, he has not acquiesced in the obstruction for one year after he has known both of the obstruction and of the person responsible for it.[70] While the best way of proving non-acquiescence in the interruption is by commencing an action, protests will do as well if they can be proved[71]; and protests may continue to have effect for some while after they are made, so that protests prior to the year may negative acquiescence during the year.[72]

(2) "INTERRUPTION." "Interruption" means some hostile obstruction[73] (even though by a stranger[73]) and not mere non-user,[74] or natural · occurrences, such as the drying up of a stream.[75] Prolonged non-user, however, may mean that there has been

---

[67] If the case is plain the servient owner will not defend and the plaintiff will obtain judgment on satisfying the court of his claim. There may be procedural difficulties (see, *e.g.*, *Re Clay* [1919] 1 Ch. 66) but these do not seem to be insurmountable: consider Zamir, *The Declaratory Judgment* (1962), Chap. 4, and pp. 125–129.

[68] *Parker* v. *Mitchell* (1840) 11 Ad. & El. 788.

[69] *Damper* v. *Bassett* [1901] 2 Ch. 350, discussing earlier authorities.

[70] Both elements are essential: *Seddon* v. *Bank of Bolton* (1882) 19 Ch.D. 462.

[71] *Bennison* v. *Cartwright* (1864) 5 B. & S. 1; *Glover* v. *Coleman* (1874) L.R. 10 C.P. 108.

[72] The question is one of fact: *Davies* v. *Du Paver* [1953] 1 Q.B. 184 (claim to a profit of sheepwalk).

[73] *Davies* v. *Williams* (1851) 16 Q.B. 546. In certain cases there are special rules for commons: see *post*, p. 859.

[74] *Smith* v. *Baxter* [1900] 2 Ch. 138 at 143; *Carr* v. *Foster* (1842) 3 Q.B. 581 (non-user of right of pasture for two years owing to lack of cattle: claim upheld).

[75] *Hall* v. *Swift* (1838) 4 Bing.N.C. 381.

insufficient enjoyment to support a claim[76]; and, conversely, an interruption may be too intermittent to be effective.[77] It is important to realise that "interruption" does not mean user by permission, which is to be contrasted with user "as of right" rather than with user "without interruption."[78] Interruption means some interference with enjoyment or cessation of enjoyment[78]; enjoyment by permission, or subject to protest,[79] is not interrupted, but rather continuing.

(3) NINETEEN YEARS AND A DAY. The special meaning of "interruption" is illustrated by the case of a claimant who has used an easement for nineteen years and a day, and is then interrupted. For the remainder of the twentieth year he has no right to contest the interruption, for he cannot show twenty years' enjoyment.[80] But there will come one day (the first day of the twenty-first year) when, if he issues his writ on that day, he will succeed; for he can then show twenty years' enjoyment before action brought, the interruption being disregarded since it is one day less than a year. A writ issued on the following day will be too late, for the interruption will then have lasted a full year.[81] But if instead the servient owner starts proceedings disputing the right, he can effectively defeat the claim to the easement; for his action is not an "interruption,"[82] as defined, and the dominant owner cannot complete twenty years' enjoyment as of right.

(e) User " as of right "

(1) MEANING. Sections 1 and 2 provide that the enjoyment must be by a "person claiming the right thereto," and section 5 provides that it is sufficient to plead enjoyment "as of right." Claims under the Act must be based on user of the same character as is required

---

[76] For examples of this, see *Parker* v. *Mitchell* (1840) 11 A. & E. 788 (non-user for four or five years next before action); *Hollins* v. *Verney* (1884) 13 Q.B.D. 304 (intervals of twelve years between each act of user).

[77] *Presland* v. *Bingham* (1889) 41 Ch.D. 268 (piles of packing cases obstructing light to varying extents from time to time).

[78] *Plasterers' Co.* v. *Parish Clerks' Co.* (1851) 6 Exch. 630.

[79] *Reilly* v. *Orange* [1955] 1 W.L.R. 616; see the text, *infra*.

[80] *Lord Battersea* v. *Commissioners of Sewers for the City of London* [1895] 2 Ch. 708; *Barff* v. *Mann, Crossman & Paulin Ltd.* (1905) 49 S.J. 794 (writ issued after 19 years and 352 days held premature).

[81] See *Flight* v. *Thomas* (1840) 11 Ad. & E. 688 at 771; 8 Cl. & F. 231. Perhaps the claimant could save himself by proving that he had contested the interruption, and so had not "submitted to or acquiesced in" it for a full year; see n. 70, *supra*. But non-acquiescence is presumably effective only in the period after the twenty years have expired. Before the expiration of the twenty years the claimant has no right to contest the interruption: therefore he can be compelled to submit to it, and whether he protests or not can hardly matter. As soon as he acquires an enforceable right to contest the interruption, his acquiescence or non-acquiescence becomes important, as in *Glover* v. *Coleman*, *supra*.   [82] *Reilly* v. *Orange, supra*.

at common law.[83]   Under the Act, the requisite user "as of right" means not only user *nec vi, nec clam, nec precario,* but also user by or on behalf of one fee simple owner against another.[84]

(2) PRECARIO.   At common law any consent or agreement by the servient owner, whether oral or written, rendered the user *precario*; it made no difference how long ago the permission was given provided that user was in fact enjoyed under it and not under a claim to use as of right.   Under the Act this rule applies to the shorter periods (twenty years for easements, thirty years for profits). But a dilemma arises in the case of the longer periods (forty years for easements, sixty years for profits) because of the provision that the right shall be absolute unless enjoyed by written consent or agreement.[85]   This clearly implies that enjoyment by oral consent shall be effective; but what then becomes of the rule that enjoyment must be as of right?

(3) ORAL PERMISSION.   The House of Lords has partially solved this puzzle by deciding that a right enjoyed by oral permission renewed every year cannot be acquired as an easement by user, however long, for it is not enjoyed "as of right" in any sense.[86] Even a single oral consent given during the period will vitiate the user, since there is no difference in principle between permission given once or more often.[87]   But if the only oral permission given was given before the period began to run and not later renewed, it is probable that the Act will prevail; that is to say, the claim will succeed because the original licence was not made in writing.[88]   If it were otherwise the provision about written permission would be meaningless.   The position can be summarised as follows:

(i) Any consents, whether oral or written, which have been given from time to time during the period make the user *precario* and defeat a claim based on either the shorter or longer periods.

---

[83] *Tickle* v. *Brown* (1836) 4 Ad. & E. 369 at 382; *Gardner* v. *Hodgson's Kingston Brewery Co. Ltd.* [1903] A.C. 229 at 238, 239.

[84] *Kilgour* v. *Gaddes* [1904] 1 K.B. 457; and see *ante,* p. 844.   [85] ss. 1 and 2.

[86] *Gardner* v. *Hodgson's Kingston Brewery Co. Ltd.* [1903] A.C. 229 (user of a way for at least seventy years, fifteen shillings being paid each year for the user; held, no easement. The result would have been the same if no money had been paid, but annual consents had been given by word of mouth; the payment is merely evidence of the consent); and see *Monmouth Canal Co.* v. *Harford* (1834) 1 Cr.M. & R. 614 at 630, 631 (20 years' period).

[87] *Tickle* v. *Brown* (1836) 4 Ad. & E. 369; and see *Ward* v. *Kirkland* [1967] Ch. 194 (period of permissive user).

[88] *Tickle* v. *Brown, supra,* at p. 383; *cf. Gardner* v. *Hodgson's Kingston Brewery Co. Ltd., supra,* [1901] 2 Ch. 198 at 215; [1903] A.C. 229 at 236.

(ii) A written consent given at the beginning of the user (and extending throughout) defeats a claim based on either the shorter or longer periods.

(iii) An oral consent given at the beginning of the user (and extending throughout) defeats a claim based on the shorter periods but not a claim based on the longer periods.[89]

If user commences by consent, the question whether it continues by consent is one of fact.[90]

(4) POWER TO CONSENT. The person competent to give consent is the occupier of the servient tenement, for it is by his sufferance that the claimant's enjoyment continues.[91] Similarly the occupier of the dominant tenement, who in fact enjoys the right, also may make enjoyment precarious by acknowledging that he has no indefeasible right.[92] It is a question of fact who is occupier: he may be the fee simple owner, or a tenant for life or years, or even a squatter; but a mere lodger or servant is not an occupier.[93] A tenant may thus frustrate his landlord's claim to an easement under the Act by acknowledging that his user is permissive; for then the period immediately before action brought is not a period of continuous user as of right.[93] But if the landlord can make out a case by prescription at common law or lost modern grant, his rights so acquired cannot be given away by a tenant or other occupier of the dominant land, for they are vested rights in fee simple which a tenant has no power to dispose of.[93]

(*f*) *Statutory provisions as to the periods.* The remaining sections of the Act may now be summarised.

SECTION 5 deals with pleadings.

---

[89] *Healey* v. *Hawkins* [1968] 1 W.L.R. 1967 (approving this sentence). As to the shorter period, see *Tickle* v. *Brown, supra,* at p. 383. But Alderson B. gave a contrary opinion in *Kinloch* v. *Nevile* (1840) 6 M. & W. 795 at 806; and see *Gardner* v. *Hodgson's Kingston Breweries Co.* [1900] 1 Ch. 592 at 599 (reversed [1901] 2 Ch. 198; [1903] A.C. 229). Perhaps the question is one of fact in which it is hard to draw the inference that user in such a case is user as of right: see *Gaved* v. *Martyn* (1865) 19 C.B.(N.S.) 732 at 744, 745; (1968) 32 Conv.(N.S.) 40 (P. S. Langan).

[90] *Gaved* v. *Martyn* (1865) 19 C.B.(N.S.) 732; *Healey* v. *Hawkins, supra.*

[91] See, *e.g., Lowry* v. *Crothers* (1871) I.R. 5 C.L. 98 (tenant for life).

[92] *Bewley* v. *Atkinson* (1879) 13 Ch.D. 283; *Hyman* v. *Van den Bergh* [1908] 1 Ch. 167.

[93] See the discussion of these points in *Hyman* v. *Van den Bergh* [1907] 2 Ch. at p. 531 (Parker J.) and [1908] 1 Ch. at p. 179 (Farwell L.J.). This decision concerned the easement of light, but its principle seems applicable to all claims made under the Act. Lost modern grant was not pleaded in the alternative, and conflicting opinions were expressed as to the possibility of pleading it successfully in a case where a defence provided by the Act had been made out. As to pleading claims in the alternative, see *post,* p. 860.

SECTION 6 provides that enjoyment for less than the statutory periods shall give rise to no claim. This does not prevent a lost grant being presumed from user for less than a statutory period if there is some evidence to support it in addition to the enjoyment.[94]

SECTION 7 provides that any period during which the servient tenant has been an infant, lunatic or tenant for life shall automatically be deducted from the shorter periods; and despite the changes made by the 1925 legislation it seems that the periods of infancies and life tenancies will still be deducted.[95] Further, the period during which an action is pending and actively prosecuted is also to be deducted.[96] Married women were formerly included in the section, but coverture is no longer a disability.[97]

SECTION 8 provides that if the servient tenement has been held under a " term of life, or any term of years exceeding three years from the granting thereof," the term shall be excluded in computing the forty years' period in the case of a " way or other convenient [*sic*] watercourse or use of water," provided the claim is resisted by a reversioner upon the term within three years of its determination.

No more need be said about sections 5 and 6. Sections 7 and 8 are complicated and can conveniently be dealt with together.

(g) *Effect of deductions.* Where either section 7 or 8 applies, the period deducted is excluded altogether when calculating the period next before action. Thus if there has been enjoyment of a profit for forty-five years in all, consisting of twenty-five years' user against the fee simple owner, then nineteen years against a life tenant, and then a further year against the fee simple owner, the claim fails, for by section 7 the period of the life tenancy is deducted when calculating the period next before action brought, and thus less than thirty years' user is left. But if the user continues for another four years, the claim will then succeed, for there is thirty years' user consisting of twenty-five years before and five years after the life tenancy; since the period of the life tenancy is disregarded, the thirty years' period is, for the purposes of the Act, next before action

---

[94] *Hanmer* v. *Chance* (1865) 4 De G.J. & S. 626 at 631.

[95] See L.P.A., 1925, s. 12.

[96] The same deduction would probably be allowed in the case of the longer periods ; but the Act makes no provision for it.

[97] Except as to non-separate property, now extinct: see *post*, p. 993; *Hulley* v. *Silversprings Bleaching & Dyeing Co. Ltd.* [1922] 2 Ch. 268.

within section 4.[98] The sections in effect connect the periods immediately before and after the period deducted, but they will not connect two periods separated in any other way, *e.g.*, by a period of unity of possession.[99] Nor will events that have occurred during the life tenancy, such as an interruption, be disregarded; the provision is for the benefit not of the claimant but of those resisting the claim,[1] and it appears to operate not as a cloak of oblivion but merely mathematically.

(*h*) *Rights within the sections.* Section 7 applies to the shorter periods both for easements and profits; but section 8 does not apply to profits at all, and applies to the longer period only in the case of easements of way " or other convenient watercourse or use of water." The word " convenient " is " not unreasonably supposed to be a misprint for ' easement '," [2] so that the phrase should read " or other easement, watercourse or use of water," thus corresponding with the phrase used in section 2. If so, section 8 may apply to all easements; but the point is unsettled.[3]

(*i*) *Disabilities within the sections*

(1) THE DISABILITIES. Section 7 applies if the servient owner is an infant, lunatic or tenant for life; section 8 applies where the servient tenement has been held under a term for over three years, or for life.[4] Thus a life tenancy is the only disability which applies to both the longer and the shorter periods. Infancy and lunacy affect only the shorter periods, and leases affect only the longer periods for the claims mentioned in section 8. Thus if D enjoys a way against S's land for twenty-five years, but S has been insane for the last fifteen of those years, section 7 defeats D's claim. If D continues his user for another fifteen years, however, his claim succeeds, even though S continues insane throughout.

(2) LEASES FOR YEARS. It is curious that leases for years, unlike life tenancies, may be deducted only under section 8 and not under section 7. Thus, where there had been user of a way for twenty years, the servient land being under lease for fifteen of the twenty years, but free from any lease at the beginning of the period, an

[98] *Clayton* v. *Corby* (1842) 2 Q.B. 813.
[99] *Onley* v. *Gardiner* (1838) 4 M. & W. 496.
[1] *Clayton* v. *Corby, supra,* at p. 825.
[2] *Laird* v. *Briggs* (1880) 50 L.J.Ch. 260 at 261, *per* Fry J. (omitted from the report in 16 Ch.D. 440 at 447); and see *Wright* v. *Williams* (1836) Tyr. & G. 375 at 390, by counsel in argument.
[3] In *Laird* v. *Briggs, supra,* the point was reserved on appeal: see S.C. (1881) 19 Ch.D. 22 at 33, 36, 37.
[4] The settled land legislation (*ante,* p. 288) appears to make no difference: *Laird* v. *Briggs* (1881) 19 Ch.D. 22; *Symons* v. *Leaker* (1885) 15 Q.B.D. 629.

easement was established [5]: for section 7 makes no mention of leaseholds, and section 8 does not apply to the twenty years' period. Such user began against a fee simple owner who, by leasing the land, voluntarily put it out of his power to resist the user. Had the lease been granted before the user began and continued throughout, the position would have been different, for there (unlike the case when the servient owner had granted a number of successive tenancies [6]) no user as against a fee simple owner able to resist it could have been shown.[7] It will also be seen that even if there had been user for forty years, the claim would have succeeded only on the last twenty years' user; a claim based on forty years' user would make the lease deductible, leaving a period of twenty-five years' user only. In such a case, therefore, a claim based on the short period may succeed where one based on the long period will fail.

(3) EFFECT OF LEASE. A lease may therefore affect a claim in two ways:

- (i) by showing that there has been no user against a fee simple owner who knows of it and can resist it; and
- (ii) by falling within the provisions of section 8 allowing deduction.

The first of these is a common law rule not affected by the Act [8]; the second is a creature of the statute and can apply only to claims under the Act.

(j) *Right to deduct.* In section 7 the provision for deduction is absolute; in section 8 it is subject to the condition that the reversioner resists the claim within three years of the determination of the term of years or life.[9] Thus if the reversioner fails to resist the claim within the three years, he has no right of deduction at all. Another peculiarity of section 8 is that it extends only to a reversioner and not to a remainderman,[10] so that it will rarely apply to land held by a tenant for life under the usual kind of settlement.

It will be seen that section 7 is wide in its scope, giving an absolute right of deduction from the shorter periods for both easements and profits; section 8, on the other hand, is very narrow,

---

[5] *Palk* v. *Shinner* (1852) 18 Q.B. 568.

[6] See *Bishop* v. *Springett* (1831) 1 L.J.K.B. 13.

[7] *Daniel* v. *North* (1809) 11 East 372; *Bright* v. *Walker* (1834) 1 Cr.M. & R. 211.

[8] Unless it is unnecessary to presume a grant in the case of the longer period: see *post*, p. 860.

[9] *Wright* v. *Williams* (1836) 1 M. & W. 77 at 100.

[10] *Symons* v. *Leaker* (1885) 15 Q.B.D. 629 (remainderman held unable to deduct life tenancy of 55 years). But see *Holman* v. *Exton* (1692) Carth. 246 (remainderman held to be " within the equity " of a statute applicable to reversioners).

giving only a reversioner a conditional right of deduction from the forty years' period in the case of (possibly) only two classes of easements.

(*k*) *Rights of common.* Under the Commons Registration Act 1965, special rules apply to rights of common where during any period the right was not exercised but for the whole or part of that period the servient tenement was requisitioned (*i.e.*, in the possession of a government department under emergency powers), or for reasons of animal health (*e.g.*, restrictions to prevent the spread of animal diseases) the right, being a right to graze animals, could not be or was not exercised.[11] In such cases, that period or part of a period is to be left out of account—

(i) in determining whether there has been an "interruption" within the Act of 1832, and

(ii) in computing the thirty or sixty years' period under that Act.[12]

Further, any objection to the registration of a right of common under the Act of 1965[13] is to be treated as a suit or action within section 4 of the Act of 1832.[14]

(*l*) *Difference between longer and shorter periods*

(1) SHORTER PERIODS. In the case of the shorter periods, the only benefits which the Act of 1832 confers upon a claimant are that the period for which he must show user is clearly laid down, and that he cannot be defeated by proof that his enjoyment began after 1189. The nature of the user required is still substantially the same, so that the claimant must show continuous uninterrupted user as of right by or on behalf of a fee simple owner against a fee simple owner who both knew of the user and could resist it, at least at the time when user began.[15] The effect of the Act is merely to facilitate prescription at common law, by eliminating the objection to user which is not of immemorial antiquity. Apart from that, the Act provides that a claim based on the shorter period "may be defeated in any other way by which the same is now liable to be defeated."[16] "The Act was an Act 'for shortening the time of prescription in certain cases'. And really it did nothing more."[17]

---

[11] Commons Registration Act 1965, s. 16 (1), (3), (4).
[12] *Ibid.*, s. 16 (1).
[13] See *post*, p. 868.   [14] Commons Registration Act 1965, s. 16 (2).
[15] *Ante*, p. 844.
[16] ss. 1, 2.
[17] *Gardner* v. *Hodgson's Kingston Brewery Co. Ltd.* [1903] A.C. 229 at 236, *per* Lord Macnaghten.

(2) LONGER PERIODS. User as of right is equally necessary in the case of the longer periods. But here the language of the Act is positive: the right becomes "absolute and indefeasible." This is held not to alter the fundamental rule that prescription must operate for and against a fee simple estate. "An easement for a term of years may, of course, be created by grant; but such an easement cannot be gained by prescription [*sc.* at common law], and, not being capable of being so acquired, it does not fall within the scope of the statute." [18] A tenant cannot therefore prescribe against his own landlord, or against another tenant of his own landlord. [19]

One difference, however, arises from the positive words of the Act: it is no defence that user began against a mere tenant or other occupier. Thus by forty years' user against a tenant for years or for life the claimant can acquire an easement against the fee simple, even though the fee simple owner was in no position to contest the user, provided that a defence is not available under section 8. [20] In principle also it should be possible under the longer periods to prescribe against corporations which have no power of grant; for the positive right conferred by the Act should require no presumption of a grant by the servient owner. But on this last point the authorities are conflicting. [21]

(*m*) *Limitations.* The Prescription Act, 1832, does not create easements or profits which could not exist as such at common law. [22] Thus a claim by the freemen and citizens of a town to enter land and hold races thereon on Ascension Day cannot be established under the Act. [23] Nor, it is held, does it apply to the acquisition of profits in gross, which can therefore be prescribed for only at common law or by lost modern grant. [24]

(*n*) *Alternative claims.* One of the many uncertainties raised by the Act was whether it had abolished the other methods of prescrip-

18 *Wheaton* v. *Maple* [1893] 3 Ch. 48 at 64, *per* Lindley L.J.; that was a case about light, but its principle was applied to other easements in *Kilgour* v. *Gaddes, infra.*
19 *Kilgour* v. *Gaddes* [1904] 1 K.B. 457 (unsuccessful claim to use of a pump, habitually used for over 40 years, by one tenant against another tenant of the same landlord).
20 *Wright* v. *Williams* (1836) 1 M. & W. 77, not cited in *Davies* v. *Du Paver* [1953] 1 Q.B. 184, where the contrary was held: see (1956) 72 L.Q.R. 32 (R.E.M.).
21 Against the claim: *The Proprietors of the Staffordshire and Worcestershire Canal Navigation* v. *The Proprietors of the Birmingham Canal Navigations* (1866) L.R. 1 H.L. 254 at 268, 278. For the claim: *Lemaitre* v. *Davis* (1881) 19 Ch.D. 281 at 291. In the special case of the easement of light there is clearly no presumption of grant: *post,* p. 864.
22 *Wheaton* v. *Maple & Co.* [1893] 3 Ch. 48 at 65.
23 *Mounsey* v. *Ismay* (1865) 3 H. & C. 486.
24 See *ante,* p. 824.

tion. It is now clearly settled that it did not.[25] The doctrine of lost modern grant is therefore still available, except, perhaps, in the case of light.[26] Consequently all three methods of prescription may be relied upon in the alternative,[27] without (at least in the county court) pleading them individually.[27a] It has been said that lost modern grant should be pleaded last,[28] but in fact the order of pleading seems immaterial.

Claims at common law or by lost modern grant therefore remain of great importance, since in many cases a claim under the Act may be defeated by some technicality, *e.g.*, an interruption, or a consent by a tenant of the dominant land, or unity of possession.[29] Thus in one case[30] a claim by lost modern grant succeeded where a right of way of modern origin had been subject to unity of possession for sixteen out of the last twenty years, so that neither common law nor the Act were of any help. In a comparable case the court presumed a lost modern grant of a right of grazing although the servient land had been under requisition, thus preventing user, for nineteen of the thirty years next before action.[31] In the case of profits, lost modern grant has the substantial advantage that twenty years' user suffices, whereas the Act requires at least thirty.[31]

The Court of Appeal has commented on the unnecessary complication and confusion caused by the co-existence of three separate methods of prescription,[31a] but a much better Act will be required before the judge-made methods can be eliminated.

2. The easement of light. There are special provisions for facilitating claims to light, both under the Prescription Act, 1832, and the Rights of Light Act, 1959.

---

[25] *Aynsley* v. *Glover* (1875) 10 Ch.App. 283; *Healey* v. *Hawkins* [1968] 1 W.L.R. 1967. See also (1958) 74 L.Q.R. at 86, 87 (V. T. H. Delany) and cases cited below.

[26] *Tapling* v. *Jones* (1865) 11 H.L.C. 290. But on that case see *Tisdall* v. *McArthur & Co. (Steel and Metal) Ltd.* [1951] I.R. 228 at 235–238 (holding that lost modern grant may still avail in a claim to light).

[27] See *Bass* v. *Gregory* (1890) 25 Q.B.D. 481; *Aynsley* v. *Glover, supra*, at p. 284.

[27a] *Pugh* v. *Savage* [1970] 2 Q.B. 373 (claim to right of way " by prescription ": lost modern grant presumed).

[28] *Gardner* v. *Hodgson's Kingston Brewery Co. Ltd.* [1903] A.C. 229 at 240.

[29] See *Healey* v. *Hawkins, supra* (lost modern grant where user not continuous to time of action brought). In *Hyman* v. *Van den Bergh* [1908] 1 Ch. 167 at 176–178 Farwell L.J. expressed the opinion that a plea of lost modern grant would not succeed in a case where one of the defences provided by the Prescription Act had been made out; but later decisions impose no such restriction.

[30] *Hulbert* v. *Dale* [1909] 2 Ch. 570.

[31] *Tehidy Minerals Ltd.* v. *Norman* [1971] 2 Q.B. 528 (user as of right, 1920–1941; requisition, 1941–1960; user by consent, 1960–1966).

[31a] *Ibid.*, at p. 543. See the recommendations of the Law Reform Committee, *ante*, p. 841.

(a) Under the Prescription Act, 1832

(1) THE STATUTE. The easement of light, having been perhaps the most difficult easement to acquire by prescription before the Act of 1832,[32] has now become the easiest. Section 3 provides that the actual enjoyment of the access of light to a " dwelling-house, workshop, or other building " for twenty years [33] without interruption shall make the right absolute and indefeasible unless enjoyed by written consent or agreement. " Building " here includes a church,[34] a greenhouse,[35] and a cowshed,[36] but not a structure for storing timber.[36a]

(2) EFFECT. The general effect of section 3, therefore, is that twenty years' enjoyment of light is equivalent to forty years' enjoyment of any other easement.[37] But there are three important differences:

    (i) Section 3 says nothing of user as of right. Enjoyment by itself suffices, even though precarious,[38] unless the consent is in writing.

    (ii) Sections 7 and 8 are inapplicable, so that there are no disabilities which can be pleaded against a claim to light.

    (iii) No easement of light can be acquired over Crown land, for unlike sections 1 and 2, section 3 is not expressed to bind the Crown.[39]

In other respects light is governed by the same rules as other easements: the twenty years' period is that next before action,[40] and subject to the Rights of Light Act, 1959,[41] " interruption " has the same special meaning as in other cases.[42]

(3) USER AS OF RIGHT UNNECESSARY. The fact that user as of right is unnecessary in claims to light under the Act has far-reaching implications, for the whole basis of prescription is thus changed.

---

32 *Ante*, p. 848.
33 Sometimes twenty-seven years: *post*, p. 864.
34 *Ecclesiastical Commissioners for England* v. *Kino* (1880) 14 Ch.D. 213.
35 *Clifford* v. *Holt* [1899] 1 Ch. 698.
36 *Hyman* v. *Van den Bergh* [1908] 1 Ch. 167.
36a *Harris* v. *De Pinna* (1886) 33 Ch.D. 238.
37 *Dalton* v. *Angus & Co.* (1881) 6 App.Cas. 740 at 800.
38 *Colls* v. *Home and Colonial Stores Ltd.* [1904] A.C. 179 at 205.
39 *Wheaton* v. *Maple & Co.* [1893] 3 Ch. 48. This includes land held under Crown leases: *ibid.* The wording also makes s. 3 prevail against any custom to the contrary, *e.g.*, against prescriptive rights of light in the City of London: *Perry* v. *Eames* [1891] 1 Ch. 658 at 667; *ante*, p. 850.
40 *Hyman* v. *Van den Bergh* [1908] 1 Ch. 167.
41 See *post*, pp. 864, 865.
42 *Smith* v. *Baxter* [1900] 2 Ch. 138.

For instance, the provision that written consent defeats the claim is the only fragment of *nec vi, nec clam, nec precario* which is left in claims to light under the Act; oral consent is no bar,[43] even though evidenced by annual payments.[44] From this there arises a crop of peculiarities connected with tenants. A tenant can acquire a right to light against his own landlord,[45] or against another tenant of his own landlord,[46] though in each case the landlord's reservation in the lease of a right to rebuild the adjoining property may amount to a consent in writing that will defeat the claim.[47] Where the easement is acquired against another tenant, and the lease of the servient land expires first, the easement binds the landlord and all subsequent occupiers.[48]

(4) EASEMENTS ONLY IN FEE. Nevertheless, an easement for a term of years cannot be acquired even in the case of light. Thus where there was twenty years' enjoyment against a tenant of the Crown it was held that since the Crown could not be bound, so neither could the tenant.[49] It therefore seems that light must be acquired, if at all, in fee simple, even though user is against a tenant. Thus a common landlord will not only be bound if the lease of the servient land expires first: he will also benefit if the lease of the dominant land expires first. It is of course paradoxical that easements can arise both for and against the same fee simple reversion, but that is attributable to the strength of the words "absolute and indefeasible" when freed from the requirement of user as of right.

(5) UNITY OF POSSESSION. Another divergence appears, though somewhat darkly, in cases where there is unity of possession during the statutory period. In the case of easements other than light we have seen that this vitiates any claim under the Act.[50] In the case of light it has been said that unity of possession merely suspends the running of the period, so that enjoyment for twenty-five years can be successfully pleaded even though during that time there was five years' unity of possession.[51] The principle on which this

[43] *London Corporation v. Pewterers' Co.* (1842) 2 Moo. & R. 409.
[44] *Plasterers' Co. v. Parish Clerks' Co.* (1851) 6 Exch. 630.
[45] *Foster v. Lyons & Co. Ltd.* [1927] 1 Ch. 219 at 227.
[46] *Morgan v. Fear* [1907] A.C. 425. The older authorities were discussed in the Court of Appeal: *Fear v. Morgan* [1906] 2 Ch. 406.
[47] *Willoughby v. Eckstein* [1937] Ch. 167 (landlord and tenant); *Blake & Lyons Ltd. v. Lewis Berger & Sons Ltd.* [1951] 2 T.L.R. 605 (tenant and tenant).
[48] *Morgan v. Fear, supra.*
[49] *Wheaton v. Maple & Co.* [1893] 3 Ch. 48.
[50] *Ante,* p. 852.
[51] *Ladyman v. Grave* (1871) 6 Ch.App. 763.

distinction rests is obscure [52]; and it is difficult to see how it can be reconciled with section 4, requiring all periods to be those next before action.

(6) NO GRANT. It is clear that there is no presumption of a grant in the case of light.[53] Thus it may be acquired under the Act against a corporation having no power of grant.[54] Whether the Act has by implication abolished claims to light under the doctrine of lost modern grant is a difficult question, as mentioned above.[55]

(b) *Under the Rights of Light Act*, 1959. This Act has amended the law by making both temporary and permanent changes.[56] It extends to Crown land, though it preserves the Crown's immunity against claims to light under the Prescription Act, 1832.[57]

(1) TEMPORARY PROVISIONS. The rebuilding of much war-damaged property would be severely hampered if neighbouring owners had acquired rights of light over it. The Act accordingly provides that if an action claiming a right of light was begun after July 13, 1958, but before January 1, 1963, or if an action brought thereafter concerns an infringement begun before January 1, 1963, the statutory period of twenty years [58] is to be extended to twenty-seven years.[59] This allows time to take advantage of the permanent provisions.

(2) PERMANENT PROVISIONS. The interruption of light by screens and hoardings has always been cumbrous; during the last war it was often impossible, and it is now subject to planning control.[60] Instead, a servient owner may now register a notice as a local land charge, provided the Lands Tribunal has certified either that due notice has been given to those likely to be affected or that a temporary notice should be registered on grounds of exceptional urgency.[61] The notice must identify the servient land and the dominant building, and specify the position and size of an obstruction on the servient land to which the notice is intended to be equivalent. It then takes effect, both under the Act of 1832 and

52 According to *Ladyman* v. *Grave, supra,* the same rule applies to all easements; but according to *Damper* v. *Bassett* [1901] 2 Ch. 350 it is confined to light.
53 *Tapling* v. *Jones* (1865) 11 H.L.C. 290 at 304, 318.
54 *Jordeson* v. *Sutton, Southcoates & Drypool Gas Co.* [1898] 2 Ch. 614 at 626 (affd. [1899] 2 Ch. 217).
55 *Ante,* p. 861.
56 Following the Report of the Committee on Rights of Light, 1958, Cmnd. 473.
57 Rights of Light Act, 1959, s. 4; and see *ante,* p. 862.
58 See *ante,* p. 862.
59 Rights of Light Act, 1959, s. 1.
60 See *post,* p. 1086.
61 Rights of Light Act, 1959, s. 2. See also Lands Tribunal Rules 1963 (S.I. No. 483), Part VI; Local Land Charges Rules, 1966 (S.I. No. 579), as amended: see *post,* p. 1053.

otherwise, as if the access of light had in fact been so obstructed, and as if the obstruction had been both known to and acquiesced in by all concerned.[62]

The notice remains effective for one year unless before then it is cancelled or, being temporary, expires.[63] While it is in force the dominant owner may sue for a declaration as if his light had actually been obstructed, and may claim cancellation or variation of the registration; and for this purpose the dominant owner may treat his enjoyment as having begun one year earlier than it did, thus avoiding the problem of interruption during the final year of the period.[64]

Sect. 4. Remedies for Infringement of Easements and Profits

1. Easements. The remedy is either by abatement or by action.[65]

(*a*) *Abatement.* Provided that no more force is used than is reasonably necessary,[66] that there is no injury to innocent third parties or the public,[67] and that the circumstances are not likely to lead to a breach of the peace,[68] the owner of the easement may abate any obstruction to its exercise without notice to the servient owner,[69] *e.g.*, by breaking open a locked gate or removing boards interfering with his light. But the law does not favour abatement.[70]

(*b*) *Action.* The plaintiff may seek damages, an injunction, a declaration,[71] or a combination of these.[72] Trivial or temporary infringements will not justify an injunction.[73] But in other cases an injunction is a valuable remedy, for otherwise the servient owner could in effect make a compulsory purchase of the easement.[74] If damages are sought, some substantial interference with the enjoyment

---

[62] Rights of Light Act, 1959, s. 3; and see *ante*, p. 852.
[63] *Ibid.*, s. 3.
[64] *Ibid.*; and see *ante*, p. 853.
[65] *Lane* v. *Capsey* [1891] 3 Ch. 411.
[66] *Hill* v. *Cock* (1872) 26 L.T. 185 at 186.
[67] *Roberts* v. *Rose* (1865) L.R. 1 Ex. 82 at 89.
[68] *Davies* v. *Williams* (1851) 16 Q.B. 546 (*e.g.*, demolition of an occupied dwelling-house).
[69] See *Perry* v. *Fitzhowe* (1846) 8 Q.B. 757. This and the previous case were cases on profits, but in this respect the same law applies to easements: see *Lane* v. *Capsey, supra.* In practice it will always be prudent to give notice first.
[70] *Lagan Navigation Co.* v. *Lambeg Bleaching, Dyeing and Finishing Co. Ltd.* [1927] A.C. 226 at 244.
[71] *Litchfield-Speer* v. *Queen Anne's Gate Syndicate (No. 2) Ltd.* [1919] 1 Ch. 407.
[72] *Leeds Industrial Co-operative Society Ltd.* v. *Slack* [1924] A.C. 851 at 857.
[73] *Cowper* v. *Laidler* [1903] 2 Ch. 341; *Pettey* v. *Parsons* [1914] 1 Ch. 704 (reversed on another point [1914] 2 Ch. 653), where an injunction was refused, but £5 damages awarded for a " petty " infringement.
[74] *Dent* v. *Auction Mart Co.* (1866) L.R. 2 Eq. 238 at 246.

of the easement must be shown, and not merely injury to the servient land [75]; but proof of actual damage is not essential.[76]

Since the owner of an easement does not occupy the servient tenement in any sense, he has not the occupier's right of protection against third parties without proof of title. In other words, in an action for infringement he must be prepared to prove his title even against a third party. If, for example, an artificial watercourse is polluted by someone other than the servient owner, it is a defence that there was no capable grantor of the right.[77] This is a case where title rests upon the concept of absolute ownership, not possessory rights, and where therefore the defendant may plead *jus tertii*.[78] This applies to the title to the easement, not to the title to the dominant tenement. Any occupier of the land to which an easement (already duly acquired) is appurtenant (*e.g.*, a tenant for life [79] or years [80]) may sue for disturbance of his right without having to prove his title to the land,[81] unless the defendant himself claims title to that land. A reversioner may also sue if the interference is such as to injure the reversion, *e.g.*, by withdrawal of support to a building, or obstruction of light.[82]

2. Profits. Here also the remedy is either by abatement or by action.

(*a*) *Abatement.* This remedy (*e.g.*, pulling down a fence or house which has been erected to the detriment of a profit of pasture) is governed by the same principles as in the case of easements.[83]

(*b*) *Action.* The rules are the same as in the case of easements,[84] with one notable exception. This is that a profit, by conferring a right to take something from the servient land, is held to give a sufficient degree of possession to enable the possessor to sue a third party for infringement without proving his title to the profit.

---

[75] *Weston* v. *Lawrence Weaver Ltd.* [1961] 1 Q.B. 402; *Saint* v. *Jenner* [1973] Ch. 275.

[76] *Nicholls* v. *Ely Beet Sugar Factory Ltd.* (*No.* 2) [1936] Ch. 343 at 349.

[77] *Paine & Co. Ltd.* v. *St. Neots Gas & Coke Co.* [1939] 3 All E.R. 812. But see cases noted *post*, p. 1007, n. 20, which were not cited.

[78] For the rule against this defence in other cases, see *post*, p. 1004; and contrast the rule as to profits given below.

[79] *Simper* v. *Foley* (1862) 2 J. & H. 555.

[80] *Fishenden* v. *Higgs & Hill Ltd.* (1935) 153 L.T. 128.

[81] Gale 361; *cf. William Aldred's Case* (1610) 9 Co.Rep. 57b, n. A.

[82] Gale 365. Similarly where the death of a witness might make a future claim more difficult to prove: see *Shadwell* v. *Hutchinson* (1829) 3 C. & P. 615 at 617; (1831) 2 B. & Ad. 97 at 98, 99.

[83] *Arlett* v. *Ellis* (1827) 7 B. & C. 346, (1829) 9 B. & C. 671; *Davies* v. *Williams* (1851) 16 Q.B. 546.

[84] See, *e.g.*, *Fitzgerald* v. *Firbank* [1897] 2 Ch. 96 at 102 (damages); *Peech* v. *Best* [1931] 1 K.B. 1 (declaration).

Thus where a " several fishery " was injured by the discharge from a factory some miles upstream, it was held that the defendant could not dispute the plaintiff's title and so plead *jus tertii*.[85] This exception is connected with the doctrine that a profit, unlike an easement, may exist in gross.[86] Had the action been against the servient owner, it would have been open to him to contest the title; but a mere stranger cannot contest the title of a person in possession.[87]

Sect. 5. Extinguishment of Easements and Profits

A. By Statute

There is no statutory procedure for the discharge or modification of obsolete or obstructive easements, as there is in the case of restrictive covenants,[88] though it might be equally desirable.[88a] The only statutes of general application relate to commons, which may be extinguished by approvement, by inclosure, and under the Commons Registration Act 1965.

1. Approvement. The lord of a manor had a common law right to " approve " the manorial waste over which the tenants exercised rights of pasture. Approvement was effected by the lord taking part of the waste for his separate enjoyment. The Statutes of Merton, 1235,[89] and Westminster II, 1285,[90] confirmed this practice, but obliged the lord to leave sufficient land for the commoners. The onus of proving sufficiency was on the lord, and there had to be enough pasture for all the animals which the commoners were entitled to turn out, and not merely for those in fact turned out in recent years.[91] Since the Commons Act, 1876,[92] a person seeking to approve a common otherwise than under the Act must advertise his intention in the local press on three successive occasions; and the Law of Commons Amendment Act, 1893,[93] makes the consent of the appropriate Secretary of State, given after holding a local inquiry, essential to approvement.

---

[85] *Nicholls* v. *Ely Beet Sugar Factory Ltd.* (*No. 1*) [1931] 2 Ch. 84. For *jus tertii*, see *post*, p. 1004.
[86] See *Paine & Co. Ltd.* v. *St. Neots Gas & Coke Co.* [1939] 3 All E.R. 812 at 823, *per* Luxmoore L.J. In *Mason* v. *Clarke* [1954] 1 Q.B. 460 at 470 Denning L.J. appears to deny that a claim to a profit may be based on a possessory title, but the decision was reversed by the House of Lords: S.C. [1955] A.C. 778, esp. at p. 794, *per* Viscount Simonds.
[87] See *post*, p. 1006, for discussion of this principle.
[88] *Ante*, p. 772.
[88a] Law Commission Working Paper No. 36, para. 121.
[89] c. 4.
[90] c. 46.
[91] *Robertson* v. *Hartopp* (1889) 43 Ch.D. 484.
[92] s. 31.
[93] ss. 2, 3.

2. Inclosure. Inclosure involves the discharge of the whole manorial waste from all rights of common, whereas approvement applies only to commons of pasture appendant or appurtenant, and discharges only part of the land. From the middle of the eighteenth century onwards a large number of private inclosure Acts were passed. The policy of Parliament was to encourage the efficient production of food, which was hardly possible under the medieval system of communal agriculture. The Inclosure (Consolidation) Act, 1801, and the Inclosure Act, 1845, further facilitated inclosures; but public opinion was aroused by the disappearance of open spaces, and the Inclosure Act, 1852,[94] prevented inclosures being made without the consent of Parliament. The procedure is now governed by the Commons Act, 1876. An application must first be made to the appropriate Secretary of State, and if a prima facie case is made out, regard being had to the benefit of the neighbourhood, a local inquiry is held.[1] A provisional order is then submitted to Parliament for confirmation.[2]

3. The Commons Registration Act 1965

(a) *Object.* With the passage of time and changed social and economic conditions, there are many uncertainties today about what lands are subject to rights of common, and what rights of common exist over these lands.[3] In order to lay a foundation for further legislation to govern the management and improvement of common land (which amounts to over four per cent. of the total area of England and Wales), the Commons Registration Act 1965 enacted provisions for ascertaining what rights are claimed to be still in existence, and for extinguishing the others.

(b) *Registration.* The Act and the regulations made under it required the registration with county and county borough councils of common land,[4] of persons claiming or found to be its owners, and of claims to rights of common over it before August 1970,[5] though all applications for registration had to be made before January 3, 1970.[6] Rights of common held merely for a term of years or from year to year were excluded.[7] Any person might apply for registration of any land as common land.[8] Registration is merely provisional,[9]

---

[94] s. 1; *cf.* Inclosure Act, 1845, s. 12, which had made the consent of Parliament essential in some, but not in all, cases.
[1] Commons Act, 1876, ss. 10, 11.
[2] *Ibid.*, s. 12.
[3] See Report of Royal Commission on Common Land, 1955–58 (Cmnd. 462).
[4] *i.e.* land subject to rights of common: s. 22 (1). The Act also applies to town and village greens (ss. 1 (1), 22 (1)).
[5] ss. 1–4; S.I. 1970 No. 383.
[6] s. 4 (6); S.I. 1966 No. 1470; but see *post,* p. 869.
[7] s. 22 (1).
[8] s. 4 (2).
[9] s. 4 (5). See *Cooke* v. *Amey Gravel Co. Ltd.* [1972] 1 W.L.R. 1310.

pending the determination of any objection, which had to be lodged before August 1972 [10]; and provisional registration is of itself no evidence of the existence of the right registered.[11] Objections are adjudicated under the Act by Commons Commissioners, with a right of appeal to the High Court on a point of law [12]; and now that commissioners have been appointed, their jurisdiction excludes that of the courts in all save cases of bad faith.[13]

Registration becomes final if no objection is duly lodged, or if after determining the objection the Commissioner or the court orders confirmation.[1] There are provisions for rectification or amendment of the register in case of fraud or change of circumstances,[2] such as where land ceases to be common land, or becomes common land, or where registered rights are extinguished, varied or transferred. Otherwise final registration is conclusive evidence as to the land being common land and as to the registered rights of common over it as at the date of registration.[3]

After July 1970 no land capable of being registered is to be deemed to be common land unless it is so registered; and no rights of common " shall be exercisable " over any such land unless they are either registered under the Act or have been registered previously [4] under the Land Registration Acts, 1925 and 1936.[5] These provisions accordingly operate to extinguish all existing unregistered rights. By themselves, they would have prevented any new rights from arising; but elaborate provisions have been made for the registration of any land becoming common land (or a town or village green) after January 2, 1970, and also for the registration of rights of common over such land, and rights of ownership.[5a] The general procedure is similar to that for existing rights.

(c) *Exemptions.* Certain land is outside these provisions, such as the New Forest and Epping Forest, and any other land exempted by ministerial order [6]; and provision is also made for the vesting and protection of land which has been registered as common land but which has no registered owner.[7]

---

[10] S.I. 1968 No. 989; 1970 No. 384.
[11] *Cooke* v. *Amey Gravel Co. Ltd., supra.*
[12] ss. 6, 17, 18. For the procedure before the commissioners, see S.I. 1971 No. 1727; 1973 No. 815.
[13] *Thorne R.D.C.* v. *Bunting* [1972] Ch. 470 (court's jurisdiction before any commissioners were appointed); *Wilkes* v. *Gee* [1973] 1 W.L.R. 742.
[1] ss. 6, 7, 10. For the registers and procedure, see S.I. 1966 No. 1471; 1968 No. 658; 1970 No. 1371; 1972 No. 437.
[2] ss. 13, 14.
[3] s. 10.
[4] See s. 1 (1).
[5] s. 1 (2); S.I. 1970 No. 383. For the latter Acts, see *post*, p. 1056.
[5a] S.I. 1969 No. 1843.
[6] s. 11. See S.I. 1965 Nos. 2000, 2001.
[7] ss. 8, 9.

B. By Release

1. Express release. At law a deed is required for an express release of an easement or profit.[8] In equity, however, an informal release will be effective provided it would be inequitable for the dominant tenant to claim that the right still exists,[9] as where he has orally consented to his light being obstructed and the servient tenant has spent money on erecting the obstruction.[10] A release of a portion of a common appurtenant extinguishes the whole common,[11] but this does not apply to a several profit appurtenant.[12]

2. Implied release

(a) Abandonment. If the dominant owner shows an intention to release an easement or profit, it will be extinguished by implied release. Mere non-user is never enough by itself[13]: an intention to abandon the right must be shown.[14] Nevertheless non-user for a long period may raise a presumption of abandonment.[15] For this purpose twenty years' non-user will usually suffice[16]; but even then the presumption is rebuttable if there is some other explanation.[17]

(b) Intention. It is a question of fact whether an act was intended as an abandonment.[18] Grazing rights have been held not to be abandoned merely by the commoners making temporary arrangements for regulating their rights, even if this is accompanied by payments to the servient owner[18a]; and the bricking-up of a door for over thirty years was held no abandonment of a right of way.[19] On the other hand, replacing a wall containing windows by a blank wall was held to be an abandonment of light after seventeen years[20]; but the servient owner had meanwhile erected buildings which would have obstructed the former lights, and the presumption of abandonment is naturally stronger where the dominant owner has allowed the servient owner to incur expense without any protest.[21]

---

8 Co.Litt. 264b; *Lovell* v. *Smith* (1857) 3 C.B.(N.S.) 120 at 127; but see *Norbury* v. *Meade* (1821) 3 Bli. 211 at 241, 242 (easement).
9 *Davies* v. *Marshall* (1816) 10 C.B.(N.S.) 697 at 710.
10 *Waterlow* v. *Bacon* (1866) L.R. 2 Eq. 514.
11 *Miles* v. *Etteridge* (1692) 1 Show.K.B. 349.
12 *Johnson* v. *Barnes* (1873) L.R. 8 C.P. 527.
13 *Ward* v. *Ward* (1852) 7 Exch. 838 at 839; *Gotobed* v. *Pridmore* (1970) 115 S.J. 78.
14 *Swan* v. *Sinclair* [1924] 1 Ch. 254, affd. [1925] A.C. 227; but see *post,* p. 871, n. 27.   15 *Crossley & Sons Ltd.* v. *Lightowler* (1867) 2 Ch.App. 478 at 482.
16 *Moore* v. *Rawson* (1824) 3 B. & C. 332 at 339; *cf. Lawrence* v. *Obee* (1814) 3 Camp. 514 (window bricked up for 20 years: abandonment of light presumed).
17 *Ward* v. *Ward* (1852) 7 Exch. 838 (acquisition of more convenient way); *James* v. *Stevenson* [1893] A.C. 162 (no occasion for use); and see *Treweeke* v. *36 Wolseley Road Pty. Ltd.* (1973) 128 C.L.R. 274 (way survives despite vertical rock faces, impenetrable bamboo plantation, swimming pool and fence).
18 *Cook* v. *Mayor and Corporation of Bath* (1868) L.R. 6 Eq. 177 at 179.
18a *Tehidy Minerals Ltd.* v. *Norman* [1971] 2 Q.B. 528.
19 *Cook* v. *Mayor and Corporation of Bath* (1868) L.R. 6 Eq. 177.
20 *Moore* v. *Rawson* (1824) 3 B. & C. 332.
21 *Cook* v. *Mayor and Corporation of Bath, supra,* at p. 179; *cf. Waterlow* v. *Bacon* (1866) L.R. 2 Eq. 514.

(c) *Altering dominant tenement.* Alterations to the dominant tenement which make the enjoyment of an easement or profit impossible or unnecessary may show an intent to abandon the right. Thus if a mill to which an easement of water is appurtenant is demolished without any intent to replace it, the easement is released [22]; and a profit of pasture appurtenant will be extinguished if the dominant land becomes part of a town, or a reservoir, but not if the land could easily be turned to the purpose of feeding cattle.[23] Again, the demolition of a house to which an easement of light is appurtenant may amount to an implied release, but not if it is intended to replace the house by another building.[24] It is not essential that the new windows should occupy exactly the same positions as the old, provided they receive substantially the same light [25]; the test is identity of light, not identity of aperture.[26] If the dominant tenement is so altered that the burden of the easement is substantially increased, the right may be extinguished altogether.[27]

(d) *Altering servient tenement.* An alteration of the servient tenement may effect an extinguishment if it is acquiesced in by the dominant owner.[28]

C. By Unity of Ownership and Possession

If the dominant and servient tenements come into the ownership and possession of the same person, any easement or profit is extinguished.[29] Unity of possession without unity of ownership is not enough [30]; and unity of ownership means acquisition of both tenements for a fee simple absolute.[31] If there is only unity of possession, the right is merely suspended until the unity of possession ceases.[32] If there is only unity of ownership the right continues

---

[22] *Liggins* v. *Inge* (1831) 7 Bing. 682 at 693; and see *National Guaranteed Manure Co. Ltd.* v. *Donald* (1859) 4 H. & N. 8 (canal converted into railway: right to water for canal extinguished). [23] *Carr* v. *Lambert* (1866) L.R. 1 Ex. 168.
[24] *Ecclesiastical Commissioners for England* v. *Kino* (1880) 14 Ch.D. 213.
[25] *Scott* v. *Pape* (1886) 31 Ch.D. 554.
[26] *Andrews* v. *Waite* [1907] 2 Ch. 500 at 510. These rules apply equally to alterations made while the light is being acquired: *ibid.* at p. 509.
[27] *e.g.*, *Ankerson* v. *Connelly* [1906] 2 Ch. 544; affd. [1907] 1 Ch. 678 (easement of light for aperture in partly open shed extinguished by enclosing shed and shutting out all other light); *Ray* v. *Fairway Motors (Barnstaple) Ltd.* (1968) 20 P. & C.R. 261 (easement of support extinguishable, irrespective of intention, by greatly increasing weight on dominant land).
[28] *Scrutton* v. *Stone* (1893) 9 T.L.R. 478 (pasture claimed over land which had become covered with buildings).
[29] *Tyrringham's Case* (1584) 4 Co.Rep. 36b at 38a (profit); *Buckby* v. *Coles* (1814) 5 Taunt. 311 (easement).
[30] *Canham* v. *Fisk* (1831) 2 Cr. & J. 126; and see *Thomas* v. *Thomas* (1835) 2 Cr.M. & R. 34 at 40.
[31] Gale 309; *R.* v. *Inhabitants of Hermitage* (1692) Carth. 239 at 241 (union of base fee with fee simple absolute works no extinguishment).
[32] *Canham* v. *Fisk*, supra.

until there is also unity of possession.[33] Thus if both dominant and servient tenements are under lease, the easement or profit will not be extinguished merely because both leases are assigned to X,[34] or both reversions to Y[35]; but if both leases and both reversions become vested in Z, the right is gone. Similarly, if the fee simple owner of one tenement takes a lease of the other, the right is merely suspended during the lease.[36]

A common appurtenant has been held to be wholly extinguished if the dominant owner acquires any part of the servient tenement, since otherwise the remainder of the servient tenement would be unduly burdened.[37] But in the case of a common appendant the burden was apportioned,[38] and much may be said for extending this more liberal rule to commons appurtenant.[39]

Sect. 6. Species of Easements

A. Rights of Way

1. Extent of easements of way

(a) *General or limited.* An easement of way may be either general or limited. A general right of way is one which may be used by the owner of the dominant tenement at any time and in any way. A limited right of way is one which is restricted in some way. The restriction may be as to time, *e.g.,* a way which can be used only in the daytime,[40] or it may be as to the mode in which the way can be used, *e.g.,* a way limited to foot passengers,[41] or to cattle and other animals in charge of a drover,[42] or to wheeled traffic,[43] and the like.

(b) *Other land.* A right of way can normally be used only as a means of access to the dominant tenement. A right to pass over

---

[33] *Richardson* v. *Graham* [1908] 1 K.B. 39. For this reason "unity of seisin" is not a satisfactory term for the unity of both ownership and possession which is required.

[34] *Thomas* v. *Thomas, supra.*

[35] *Richardson* v. *Graham, supra.* This was a case on light, and it is not clear whether the decision was founded on the peculiar nature of the easement of light, or the doctrine of non-derogation from grant (*ante,* p. 820). In principle the rule should be the same for all easements. *Cf. Buckby* v. *Coles* (1814) 5 Taunt. 311 at 315, 316.

[36] *Simper* v. *Foley* (1862) 2 J. & H. 555 at 563, 564.

[37] *White* v. *Taylor* [1969] 1 Ch. 150.

[38] *Wyat Wyld's Case* (1609) 8 Co.Rep. 78b.

[39] Consider *Benson* v. *Chester* (1799) 8 T.R. 396 at 401.

[40] *Collins* v. *Slade* (1874) 23 W.R. 199; *cf. Hollins* v. *Verney* (1884) 13 Q.B.D. 304 (right of way to remove timber cut every 12 years).

[41] *Cousens* v. *Rose* (1871) L.R. 12 Eq. 366.

[42] *Brunton* v. *Hall* (1841) 1 Q.B. 792.

[43] *Ballard* v. *Dyson* (1808) 1 Taunt. 279.

Plot A to reach Plot B cannot be used as a means of access to Plot C lying beyond Plot B.[44]

(c) *Construction and repair.* In the absence of a contrary agreement,[45] or special circumstances,[46] it is for the grantee of a way, not the grantor, to construct the way [47] and to repair it when constructed; the grantee may enter the servient tenement for these purposes.[48] The benefit of a covenant by the grantor to repair the way may run with the easement [49]; but as such a covenant is positive, the burden cannot of course run with the servient land.[50] If the way becomes impassable, there is no right to deviate from it [51] unless the servient owner has obstructed it.[52]

2. Effect of mode of acquisition. The extent of an easement of way depends upon the manner of its acquisition.

(a) *Express grant or reservation.* Here the question is primarily one of construction.[53] The rules of construction, as already explained,[54] are that in case of doubt a grant of an easement and (probably) a reservation is construed against the person making it in accordance with the general rule.[55]

Rights of way are often granted in very wide terms, *e.g.*, " at all times and for all purposes." But even without such words the right, if granted in general terms, is not confined to the purpose for which the land is used at the time of the grant.[56] A right of way for general purposes granted as appurtenant to a house can be used (though not enlarged [57]) for the business of an hotel if that house is subsequently converted into an hotel.[58] A right of way over a strip

---

[44] *Skull* v. *Glenister* (1864) 16 C.B.(N.S.) 81; *Colchester* v. *Roberts* (1839) 4 M. & W. 769 at 774; *Harris* v. *Flower* (1904) 74 L.J.Ch. 127 (building standing partly on B and partly on C).

[45] *Taylor* v. *Whitehead* (1781) 2 Doug.K.B. 745 at 749.

[46] *Miller* v. *Hancock* [1893] 2 Q.B. 177, not affected on this point by *Fairman* v. *Perpetual Investment B. S.* [1923] A.C. 74.

[47] *Ingram* v. *Morecraft* (1863) 33 Beav. 49 at 51.

[48] *Newcomen* v. *Coulson* (1877) 5 Ch.D. 133. Lord Upjohn's denial of this right in *Redland Bricks Ltd.* v. *Morris* [1970] A.C. 652 at 665 seems to have been *per incuriam.*

[49] *Gaw* v. *Coras Iompair Eireann* [1953] I.R. 232; contrast *Grant* v. *Edmondson* [1931] 1 Ch. 1 (rentcharge: *ante*, p. 796).

[50] *Ante*, p. 754.

[51] *Bullard* v. *Harrison* (1815) 4 M. & S. 387.

[52] *Selby* v. *Nettlefold* (1873) 9 Ch.App. 111.

[53] *Robinson* v. *Bailey* [1948] 2 All E.R. 791.

[54] *Ante*, p. 830.

[55] *Williams* v. *James* (1867) L.R. 2 C.P. 577 at 581.

[56] *South Eastern Ry.* v. *Cooper* [1924] 1 Ch. 211.

[57] *White* v. *Grand Hotel, Eastbourne, Ltd.*, *infra*, at p. 116.

[58] *White* v. *Grand Hotel, Eastbourne, Ltd.* [1913] 1 Ch. 113 (affd. 84 L.J.Ch. 938). See also *Robinson* v. *Bailey* [1948] 2 All E.R. 791 (way to building plot held to cover business user).

of land twenty feet wide approached by a narrow gap may be exercisable over the whole width when later the gap is widened [59]; and a right " to pass and repass " along a way may include a right to halt and load or unload vehicles,[60] with a right to adequate space overhead and perhaps a little latitude alongside.[61] A right to cross a railway line " with all manner of cattle " may be a right of way for all purposes and not confined to agricultural purposes.[62] But a way granted as appurtenant to an open space *as such* cannot be used as a means of access to a cottage subsequently built thereon.[63] Nor, of course, can a way be used so as to infringe the rights of others entitled to use it.[64]

If a way is granted " as at present enjoyed," prima facie these words refer to the quality of the user (*e.g.*, on foot or with vehicles) and do not limit the quantity of the user to that existing at the time of the grant.[65] In case of difficulty, as where there is a simple grant or reservation of " a right of way," the surrounding circumstances must be considered [66]: thus both the condition of the way (*e.g.*, whether it is a footpath or a metalled road) and the nature of the dominant tenement (*e.g.*, whether it is a dwelling-house or a factory) may be of assistance in determining whether any vehicles, and if so, which, may use the way.[67]

(b) *Implied grant or reservation.* A way of necessity is limited to the necessity existing at the time the right arose; thus if an encircled plot is used for agricultural purposes at the time of the grant, the way of necessity over the surrounding land is limited to agricultural purposes and cannot be used for the carting of building materials.[68]

In other cases of implied grant the circumstances of the case must be considered. Thus where a testator devised adjoining

---

[59] *Keefe* v. *Amor* [1965] 1 Q.B. 334, a special case depending on special factors: see *St. Edmundsbury & Ipswich Diocesan Board of Finance* v. *Clark* (*No. 2*) [1973] 1 W.L.R. 1572 at 1595.

[60] *Bulstrode* v. *Lambert* [1953] 1 W.L.R. 1064; *McIlraith* v. *Grady* [1968] 1 Q.B. 468; but see *Todrick* v. *Western National Omnibus Co. Ltd.* [1934] Ch. 561 (user by omnibuses excessive).

[61] *V. T. Engineering Ltd.* v. *Richard Barland & Co. Ltd.* (1968) 19 P. & C. R. 890 (" swing space " for loading and unloading vehicles).

[62] *British Railways Board* v. *Glass* [1965] Ch. 538.

[63] *Allan* v. *Gomme* (1840) 11 A. & E. 759.

[64] *Jelbert* v. *Davis* [1968] 1 W.L.R. 589 (user of way for 200-caravan site).

[65] *Hurt* v. *Bowmer* [1937] 1 All E.R. 797.

[66] *St. Edmundsbury & Ipswich Diocesan Board of Finance* v. *Clark* (*No. 2*) [1973] 1 W.L.R. 1572 (the " Iken " case); affirmed Dec. 18, 1974.

[67] *Cannon* v. *Villars* (1878) 8 Ch.D. 415 at 420. See also *Att.-Gen.* v. *Hodgson* [1922] 1 Ch. 429 (carriageway granted in 1861 held to extend to motor-cars); *Kain* v. *Norfolk* [1949] Ch. 163 (grant for use by " carts " held to cover use by motor-lorries). There is a general discussion in *St. Edmundsbury & Ipswich Diocesan Board of Finance* v. *Clark* (*No. 2*), supra, at pp. 1591–1596.

[68] *Corpn. of London* v. *Riggs* (1880) 13 Ch.D. 798.

plots of land to different persons, and one plot was bought by a railway company for conversion into a railway station, it was held that a way which had been used in the testator's lifetime for domestic purposes and for the purposes of warehouses on the land could not be used as a public approach to the station.[69]

(c) *Prescription.* Where an easement of way is acquired by long user, " the right acquired must be measured by the extent of the enjoyment which is proved." [70] Thus a way acquired by long user for farming purposes cannot be used for mineral purposes,[71] or for a camping ground,[72] or for the cartage of building materials.[73] It has been held that user during the prescriptive period as a carriageway does not authorise user for cattle [74]; but it covers user as a footway [75] (since prima facie the greater includes the less [76]) and it extends to user for motor traffic even if the user proved was for horse-drawn vehicles alone, for the right is essentially a right for vehicles, and the mode of propulsion is immaterial.[77] Apart from any radical change in the dominant tenement, the user of the way is not limited by reference to numbers or frequency during the prescriptive period, so that a way acquired for a sparsely occupied caravan site may still be used when the site holds more caravans,[78] and use of a way acquired for business purposes may expand with the expansion of the business.[79]

B. Rights of Light

1. No natural right. There is no natural right to light [80]; a landowner may so build on his land as to prevent any light from reaching his neighbour's windows,[81] unless his neighbour has an easement of light or some other right such as a restrictive covenant against building. The access of light to windows is sometimes

---

[69] *Milner's Safe Co. Ltd.* v. *Great Northern & City Ry.* [1907] 1 Ch. 208.
[70] *Williams* v. *James* (1867) L.R. 2 C.P. 577 at 580, *per* Bovill C.J.; and see *United Land Co.* v. *Great Eastern Ry.* (1875) 10 Ch.App. 586 at 590.
[71] *Bradburn* v. *Morris* (1876) 3 Ch.D. 812.
[72] *R. P. C. Holdings Ltd.* v. *Rogers* [1953] 1 All E.R. 1029.
[73] *Wimbledon & Putney Commons Conservators* v. *Dixon* (1875) 1 Ch.D. 362. The fact that there has been occasional user for the cartage of materials to enlarge the farm house and rebuild a cottage on the farm does not enable the dominant owner to cart materials to build new houses: *ibid.*
[74] *Ballard* v. *Dyson* (1808) 1 Taunt. 279. This seems to have turned to some extent on the danger offered by horned cattle (see at p. 286). And see *British Railways Board* v. *Glass* [1965] Ch. 538.
[75] *Davies* v. *Stephens* (1836) 7 C. & P. 570.
[76] See Gale 265.
[77] *Lock* v. *Abercester Ltd.* [1939] Ch. 861.
[78] *British Railways Board* v. *Glass* [1965] Ch. 538.
[79] *Woodhouse & Co. Ltd.* v. *Kirkland (Derby) Ltd.* [1970] 1 W.L.R. 1185.
[80] *Ante,* p. 815.
[81] *Tapling* v. *Jones* (1865) 11 H.L.C. 290.

deliberately obstructed to prevent an easement of light being
acquired by prescription.[82] Long established rights to light are
sometimes called " ancient lights."

2. Quantum of light. An easement of light can exist only in
respect of a window or other aperture in a building,[83] such as a
skylight.[84] The amount of light to which the, dominant owner is
entitled was finally settled in *Colls* v. *Home and Colonial Stores Ltd.*[85];
this amount is enough light according to the ordinary notions of mankind for the comfortable use of the premises as a dwelling, or, in the
case of business premises, for the beneficial use of the premises as a
warehouse, shop or other place of business. The same test applies,
mutatis mutandis, to any other building, *e.g.*, a church.[1] The measure
is thus " ordinary user ": the dominant owner is not entitled to object
even to a substantial diminution in his light, provided enough is
left for ordinary purposes. The test is not " How much light has
been taken away? ", but " How much light is left? "[2] An easement
of a greater amount of light than that required for ordinary purposes
cannot be acquired even if for twenty years the dominant owner
has enjoyed that quantity of light and has used the premises for
purposes requiring an extraordinary amount of light.[3] Conversely,
the quantum of light to which the dominant owner is entitled is
not affected by the fact that he has used the room in question for
purposes requiring but little light,[4] for a right of light is a right
to have the access of light for all ordinary purposes to which the
room may be put.[5]

3. Infringement. If the dominant owner alters the user of his
premises,[6] or the size or position of the windows,[7] the burden on
the servient tenement is not increased. An obstruction which would
not have been actionable before the alteration will therefore not be
actionable even if it deprives the altered window of most of its
light[8]; the test is identity of light, not identity of aperture.[9] If

---

[82] See, *e.g.*, *Mayor, etc., of Paddington* v. *Att.-Gen.* [1906] A.C. 1.
[83] *Levet* v. *Gas Light & Coke Co.* [1919] 1 Ch. 24.
[84] *Easton* v. *Isted* [1903] 1 Ch. 405.
[85] [1904] A.C. 179.
[1] *Newham* v. *Lawson* (1971) 22 P. & C.R. 852.
[2] See *Higgins* v. *Betts* [1905] 2 Ch. 210 at 215, *per* Farwell J. The Prescription
Act, 1832, has made no change in this rule: *Kelk* v. *Pearson* (1871) 6 Ch.App. 809.
[3] *Ambler* v. *Gordon* [1905] 1 K.B. 417 (architect's office). See Gale 253 for
earlier authorities giving rise to some doubt.
[4] *Price* v. *Hilditch* [1930] 1 Ch. 500 (scullery).
[5] *Yates* v. *Jack* (1866) 1 Ch.App. 295.
[6] *Colls* v. *Home and Colonial Stores Ltd.*, *supra*, at p. 204.
[7] *Smith* v. *Evangelization Society (Incorporated) Trust* [1933] Ch. 515.
[8] *Ankerson* v. *Connelly* [1907] 1 Ch. 678.
[9] *Andrews* v. *Waite* [1907] 2 Ch. 500 at 510; *ante*, p. 871.

the alterations to the dominant tenement render it impossible for the court to determine the extent to which the light received by the old windows is received by the new, the easement is lost.[10] Yet if an easement of light for one set of windows is infringed, and another set of windows (for which no easement exists) is deprived of light by the same obstruction, the dominant owner can recover damages in respect of both sets of windows, for the obstruction is illegal and the damage to both sets of windows is the direct and foreseeable consequence of it.[11]

4. Standard of light. The standard of light varies to some extent from neighbourhood to neighbourhood,[12] the test in each case being that laid down in *Colls'* case. There is no "45 degrees" rule, *i.e.*, no rule that an interference with light is actionable only if the obstruction arises above a line drawn upwards and outwards from the centre of the window at an angle of 45 degrees[13]; at the most, this test provides a very slight presumption.[14] Scientific methods today permit accurate measurement of light, and tests which have been propounded are whether the whole room, or half of it,[15] receives light not below a factor called the "grumble point."[16] But these are not reliable guides, since the court may take account not only of the locality but of the higher standard which may reasonably be required in present times.[17]

5. Other sources of light. In considering whether an easement of light has been obstructed, other sources of light of which the dominant owner cannot be deprived must be taken into account, such as vertical light through a skylight[17a]; and if this has been blocked up by the dominant owner during the prescriptive period, his rights will be assessed on the footing of it being unobstructed.[18] In one case[19] a room was lit through two sets of windows, one set facing A's land and the other facing B's land. It was held that

[10] *Ankerson* v. *Connelly* [1906] 2 Ch. 544 at 548, 549 (affd. [1907] 1 Ch. 678); *News of the World Ltd.* v. *Allan Fairhead & Sons Ltd.* [1931] 2 Ch. 402 at 407.
[11] *Re London, Tilbury & Southend Ry. and the Trustees of the Gower's Walk Schools* (1889) 24 Q.B.D. 326.
[12] *Fishenden* v. *Higgs & Hill Ltd.* (1935) 153 L.T. 128; *Ough* v. *King* [1967] 1 W.L.R. 1547. But see *Horton's Estate Ltd.* v. *James Beattie Ltd.* [1927] 1 Ch. 75.
[13] *Colls* v. *Home and Colonial Stores Ltd.* [1904] A.C. 179 at 210; *Fishenden* v. *Higgs & Hill Ltd., supra.*
[14] *Ecclesiastical Commissioners for England* v. *Kino* (1880) 14 Ch.D. 213 at 220.
[15] *Fishenden* v. *Higgs & Hill Ltd., supra.*
[16] See *Charles Semon & Co. Ltd.* v. *Bradford Corpn.* [1922] 2 Ch. 737 at 747, 748.
[17] *Ough* v. *King, supra*; and see the criticisms in *McGrath* v. *Munster & Leinster Bank Ltd.* [1959] I.R. 313.
[17a] *Smith* v. *Evangelization Society (Incorporated) Trust* [1933] Ch. 515.
[18] *Ibid.*
[19] *Sheffield Masonic Hall Co. Ltd.* v. *Sheffield Corpn.* [1932] 2 Ch. 17.

the light received by both sets of windows had to be considered, but that A could not obscure the greater part of the light passing over his land in reliance upon B supplying a large quantity of light. Neither servient owner could build to a greater extent than, assuming a building of like height on the other servient tenement, would still leave the dominant tenement with sufficient light according to the test in *Colls'* case.

6. Precarious light. Light which the dominant tenement receives from other sources but of which it may be deprived at any time must be ignored.[20] Nor is it a sufficient answer for the servient owner to offer to provide glazed tiles or mirrors to reflect the light,[21] for no provision can be made which will effectively bind future owners of the servient tenement to keep the tiles or mirrors clean.[1] An easement to receive reflected light apparently cannot exist[2]; but in considering whether an easement of light has been infringed, reflected or diffused light entering from ordinary sources cannot be disregarded.[3]

C. Rights of Water

A variety of easements may exist in connection with water,[4] such as rights—

> to take water from a spring[5] or a pump[6];
> to water cattle at a pond[7];
> to take water from a stream running through the dominant tenement for purposes which the natural rights of ownership[8] do not permit[9];
> to pollute the waters of a stream or river[10];
> to discharge water on to the land of another[11];
> to receive the discharge of water from the land of another[12];

[20] *Colls* v. *Home and Colonial Stores, Ltd.*, supra, at p. 211.
[21] *Black* v. *Scottish Temperance Life Assurance Co.* [1908] 1 I.R. 541 (H.L.).
[1] *Dent* v. *Auction Mart Co.* (1866) L.R. 2 Eq. 238 at 251, 252.
[2] *Goldberg* v. *Waite* [1930] E.G.D. 154.
[3] *Sheffield Masonic Hall Co. Ltd.* v. *Sheffield Corpn.*, supra, at pp. 24, 25.
[4] See Gale 199 et seq.   [5] *Race* v. *Ward* (1855) 4 E. & B. 702.
[6] *Polden* v. *Bastard* (1865) L.R. 1 Q.B. 156.
[7] *Manning* v. *Wasdale* (1836) 5 A. & E. 758.
[8] For these, see ante, p. 814.
[9] *McCartney* v. *Londonderry & Lough Swilly Ry.* [1904] A.C. 301 at 313.
[10] *Baxendale* v. *McMurray* (1867) 2 Ch.App. 790.
[11] *Mason* v. *Shrewsbury & Hereford Ry.* (1871) L.R. 6 Q.B. 578 at 587.
[12] *Ivimey* v. *Stocker* (1866) 1 Ch.App. 396. It is harder to obtain this by prescription than the previous right, which is complementary to it; for it is difficult to contend that because a man's pump had dripped on to the land of another for twenty years, the latter had a right to say that the pump must go on leaking: *Chamber Colliery Co.* v. *Hopwood* (1886) 32 Ch.D. 549 at 558. See also *Arkwright* v. *Gell* (1839) 5 M. & W. 203 and *Burrows* v. *Lang* [1901] 2 Ch. 502 for the difficulties which may lie in the way of a claim to continue to receive water temporarily flowing from another person's land.

to enter the land of another to open sluice gates [13];

to permit rain water to drop from a roof on to a neighbour's land ("easement of eavesdrop ").[14]

These rights must be distinguished from the natural rights which a landowner may have in respect of water,[15] which have already been mentioned.[16]

D. Rights of Support

As already mentioned,[17] a landowner's natural right of support for his land extends only to his land in its natural state; it does not include buildings. But a right of support for buildings may be acquired as an easement. Thus where one of two adjoining houses was converted into a coach factory which threw more pressure upon the other house, and was so used for over twenty years, the House of Lords held that an action lay for demolishing the other house and so causing part of the factory to collapse.[18] Where adjoining buildings support one another it is therefore difficult for their owners to preserve their liberty to demolish them for more than twenty years. Probably their only course is to issue a writ claiming a declaration that no easement as yet subsists,[19] so preventing user as of right.

Where an easement of support exists, it entitles the dominant owner to enter and execute repairs to the servient tenement; but it does not put the servient owner under any obligation to keep the supporting building in repair.[20]

E. Rights of Air

These have already been mentioned.[21]

F. Right of Fencing

The right to require a neighbouring landowner to repair his fences has been called a "spurious easement," [22] and even a "quasi-

---

[13] *Simpson* v. *Mayor, etc., of Godmanchester* [1897] A.C. 696.
[14] *Harvey* v. *Walters* (1873) L.R. 8 C.P. 162.
[15] See Gale 199 *et seq.*
[16] *Ante*, p. 815.   [17] *Ante*, p. 814.
[18] *Dalton* v. *Angus & Co.* (1881) 6 App.Cas. 740. This is the leading case on easements of support, and contains a great many important observations about easements generally.
[19] There may be procedural difficulties: but see *ante*, pp. 851, 852.
[20] *Jones* v. *Pritchard* [1908] 1 Ch. 630 at 637, 638; *Bond* v. *Nottingham Corpn.* [1940] Ch. 429 at 438, 439; *ante*, p. 811.
[21] *Ante*, p. 812.
[22] *Coaker* v. *Willcocks* [1911] 2 K.B. 124 at 131, *per* Farwell L.J.; and see *ante*, p. 811. The obligation binds the landowner "to put up such a fence that a pig not of a peculiarly wandering disposition, nor under any excessive temptation, will not get through it" (*Child* v. *Hearn* (1874) L.R. 9 Ex. 176 at 182, *per*

easement." [23]   In fact it appears to be an easement,[24] though exceptional in requiring positive action by the servient owner. It lies in grant [25]; it will pass under section 62 of the Law of Property Act, 1925 [26]; and it can be acquired by prescription.[27] In order to establish the right it must be shown that the servient owner repaired his fence not merely to keep his cattle in or the dominant owner's out, but as a matter of obligation to the dominant owner, *e.g.*, by habitually repairing the fence on his demand.[28] The servient owner cannot be required to repair fences on the dominant owner's land.[29] A corresponding right may also be acquired by custom.[30]

G. Miscellaneous Easements

There are many miscellaneous easements, such as rights—

> to create a nuisance by the discharge of gases, fluids or smoke,[31] or perhaps even by making noises [32] or vibrations [33];
>
> to hang clothes on a line passing over another's land [34];
>
> to fix a signboard on a neighbouring house [35];
>
> to mix manure on the servient tenement for the benefit of the adjoining farm [36];
>
> to place stones on the servient tenement to prevent sand or earth from being washed away by the sea [37];

Bramwell B.); but the fence need not be sufficient to exclude sheep of a " peculiarly wandering and saltative disposition " (*Coaker* v. *Willcocks* [1911] 1 K.B. 649 at 654, *per* Darling J.), nor need it be " so close and strong that no pig could push through it, or so high that no horse or bullock could leap it " (*Child* v. *Hearn*, *supra*, at p. 181, *per* Bramwell B.). For a discussion of this obligation, see Hunt, *Boundaries and Fences*, 6th ed., pp. 100–109; G. L. Williams, *Liability for Animals*, 208.

23 *Jones* v. *Price* [1965] 2 Q.B. 618; for the normal meaning of this term, see *ante*, pp. 810, 833.
24 *Crow* v. *Wood* [1971] 1 Q.B. 77.
25 *Ibid.*
26 *Ante*, p. 837.
27 *Lawrence* v. *Jenkins* (1873) L.R. 8 Q.B. 274; *Jones* v. *Price, supra.*
28 *Hilton* v. *Ankesson* (1872) 27 L.T. 519.
29 *Jones* v. *Price, supra*; *Egerton* v. *Harding* [1974] 3 W.L.R. 437.
30 *Egerton* v. *Harding, supra*, not following *Crow* v. *Wood, supra.*
31 *Crump* v. *Lambert* (1867) L.R. 3 Eq. 409 at 413 (dictum by Romilly M.R.); but see n. 33, below.
32 *Elliotson* v. *Feetham* (1835) 2 Bing.N.C. 134; *Ball* v. *Ray* (1873) 8 Ch.App. 467 at 471, 472; but see n. 33, below.
33 *Sturges* v. *Bridgman* (1879) 11 Ch.D. 852.   This and the three last cited cases are unsatisfactory authorities, for in none did the plaintiff succeed.   If twenty years' user as of right could have been shown, the question would have arisen whether such rights can lie in grant.   This seems highly questionable: there is no direct authority; *contra, Lemmon* v. *Webb* [1895] A.C. 1, *ante*, p. 811.
34 *Drewell* v. *Towler* (1832) 3 B. & Ad. 735.
35 *Moody* v. *Steggles* (1879) 12 Ch.D. 261.
36 *Pye* v. *Mumford* (1848) 11 Q.B. 666 (the right was claimed as a profit *à prendre*).
37 *Philpot* v. *Bath* (1905) 21 T.L.R. 634.

to use a wall for nailing trees thereto [38] or for supporting a creeper [39];

to extend the bowsprits of ships over a wharf [40];

to store casks and trade produce on the servient tenement [41];

to use a coal shed on the servient tenement [42];

to use an airfield [43];

to let down the surface of land by mining operations under it [44];

to use a kitchen [45] or a lavatory [46];

to use a letter-box [47];

to use a pew in a church.[48]

Sect. 7. Species of Profits à Prendre

The following are the main types of profits *à prendre*. They are more often met with as commons than as several profits.

A. Profit of Pasture

A profit of pasture is a true profit; the taking and carrying away is effected by means of the mouths and stomachs of the cattle in question.[49]

1. Forms of profit. A profit of pasture may exist in the following forms.

(a) Appendant. A profit of pasture appendant is limited to horses, oxen, cows and sheep. The numerical test is that of levancy and couchancy.[50]

---

[38] *Hawkins* v. *Wallis* (1763) 2 Wils.K.B. 173.
[39] *Simpson* v. *Weber* (1925) 133 L.T. 46.
[40] *Suffield* v. *Brown* (1864) 4 De G.J. & S. 185.
[41] *Att.-Gen. of Southern Nigeria* v. *John Holt & Co. (Liverpool) Ltd.* [1915] A.C. 599; *ante,* p. 812.
[42] *Wright* v. *Macadam* [1949] 2 K.B. 744.
[43] *Dowty Boulton Paul Ltd.* v. *Wolverhampton Corporation (No. 2)* [1973] 2 W.L.R. 618.
[44] *Rowbotham* v. *Wilson* (1860) 8 H.L.C. 348 at 362. But see *Newcastle-under-Lyme Borough Council* v. *Wolstanton Ltd.* [1939] 3 All E.R. 597 (affd. [1940] A.C. 860) as to the acquisition of such a right by prescription; and see (1940) 56 L.Q.R. 438 (R.E.M.).
[45] See *Heywood* v. *Mallalieu* (1883) 25 Ch.D. 357.
[46] *Miller* v. *Emcer Products Ltd.* [1956] Ch. 304; and see *Simmons* v. *Midford* [1969] 2 Ch. 415 (exclusive right to use a drain).
[47] *Goldberg* v. *Edwards* [1950] Ch. 247.
[48] *Philipps* v. *Halliday* [1891] A.C. 228. But see *Brumfitt* v. *Roberts* (1870) L.R. 5 C.P. 224 at 233.
[49] See Preston, *Estates,* i, 15.
[50] *Ante,* p. 823.

(b) *Appurtenant.* A profit of pasture appurtenant is not confined to any particular animals, but depends on the terms of the grant or, in the case of prescription, the animals habitually turned out to pasture.[51] Thus it may extend to sheep, when it is known as a " foldcourse "[52] or " sheepwalk."[53] The number of animals may either be limited by levancy and couchancy, or be fixed; it cannot be unlimited.[54]

(c) *Pur cause de vicinage.* Under a common of pasture *pur cause de vicinage,*[55] the commoners of one common may not put more cattle upon it than it will maintain; thus if Common A is fifty acres in extent and Common B one hundred acres, the commoners of A must not put more cattle on A than fifty acres will support in reliance upon their cattle straying to B.[56]

(d) *In gross.* A profit of pasture in gross[57] may exist for a fixed number of animals or *sans nombre.* The last phrase means literally " without number " (an alternative form is " without stint "), but such a right is limited to not more cattle than the servient tenement will maintain in addition to any existing burdens.[58]

2. Quantification of commons. For the purpose of registration under the Commons Registration Act 1965[59] rights of common which consist of or include a right, not limited by number, to graze animals must be registered for a definite number of animals. When such registration has become final, the right is exercisable only in relation to the number so registered.[60] Where these provisions apply, they will replace levancy and couchancy as a test, as well as the test for profit *sans nombre*; and commoners may license others to graze their beasts up to the registered number.[60a]

B. *Profit of Turbary*

A profit of turbary is the right to dig and take from the servient tenement peat or turf for use as fuel in a house on the dominant tenement. It may exist as appurtenant, or, where it is limited to

---

[51] Hall, *Profits à Prendre,* 263.
[52] *Robinson* v. *Duleep Singh* (1878) 11 Ch.D. 798. For the distinction between this and a grant of the herbage, see *ibid.,* at p. 820.
[53] *White* v. *Williams* [1922] 1 K.B. 727.
[54] *Benson* v. *Chester* (1799) 8 T.R. 396 at 401. A profit of pasture " without stint " or " *sans nombre* " means a profit for animals *levant et couchant*: Halsb. 4th ed., vi, 204; 1 Wms.Saund., 6th ed., 28, n. (4).
[55] *Ante,* p. 824.
[56] *Sir Miles Corbet's Case* (1585) 7 Co.Rep. 5a.
[57] *Ante,* p. 824.   [58] Halsb. 4th ed., vi, 206.
[59] For registration, see *ante,* p. 868.
[60] Commons Registration Act 1965, s. 15.
[60a] *Davies* v. *Davies* [1974] 3 W.L.R. 607.

some specified quantity, in gross.[61] Where it is appurtenant, the turves can be used only for the benefit of the dominant tenement and not, *e.g.*, for sale,[62] even if the dominant owner is entitled to a fixed quantity.[63]

C. Profit of Estovers

A profit of estovers is the right to take wood from the land of another as hay-bote, house-bote or plough-bote.[64] It may exist as appurtenant, or, if limited to a specified quantity, in gross.[65] If it is appurtenant to a house, the right will not be increased if the house is enlarged.[66] It sometimes includes the right to cut timber,[67] but may be limited to trees of small value.[68] It may extend to furze, gorse, heather, fern or long grass for fuel, manure or litter.[69] In every case the profit must be limited in some way as to quantity, either by reference to some defined quantity or by reference to the needs of the dominant tenement.[70]

Similar rights to profits of estovers are rights of lopwood, *i.e.*, to lop wood for fuel at certain periods of the year,[71] and pannage, *i.e.*, to send pigs on to the servient tenement in order to eat acorns or beech-mast which have fallen to the ground.[72]

D. Profit of Piscary and Other Sporting Rights

A profit of piscary is a right to catch and take away fish. It can exist in gross (when it may be unlimited) [73] or as appurtenant (when it must be limited to the needs of the dominant tenement).[74] Other sporting rights, such as a right of hunting (venery), shooting, fowling (auceptary), and the like, may also exist as profits *à prendre*.[75] It is no infringement of such a right for the servient owner merely

---

[61] *Mellor* v. *Spateman* (1669) 1 Wms.Saund. 339 at 346.
[62] *Valentine* v. *Penny* (1605) Noy 145.
[63] *Hayward* v. *Cunnington* (1668) 1 Lev. 231.
[64] *Ante*, p. 113. This must be distinguished from the similar rights a tenant for life has over the land of which he is tenant, for a profit of estovers is exercised over the land of another.
[65] Halsb. 4th ed., vi, 214, 240.
[66] *Brown & Tucker's Case* (1610) 4 Leon. 241.
[67] *Russel & Broker's Case* (1587) 2 Leon. 209.
[68] *Anon* (1572) 3 Leon. 16.
[69] *Warrick* v. *Queen's College, Oxford* (1871) 6 Ch.App. 716; *Earl de la Warr* v. *Miles* (1881) 17 Ch.D. 535.
[70] *Clayton* v. *Corby* (1843) 5 Q.B. 415 at 419, 420.
[71] *Chilton* v. *Corporation of London (No. 2)* (1878) 7 Ch.D. 735.
[72] *Chilton* v. *Corporation of London (No. 1)* (1878) 7 Ch.D. 562. The servient owner may nevertheless lop the trees in the ordinary course of management, and fell the trees when ripe: *ibid.*
[73] *Staffordshire and Worcestershire Canal Navigation* v. *Bradley* [1912] 1 Ch. 91: *ante*, p. 824.
[74] *Harris* v. *Earl of Chesterfield* [1911] A.C. 623; *ante*, p. 823.
[75] *Ewart* v. *Graham* (1859) 7 H.L.C. 331 at 345. See the extensive rights claimed in *Thorne R.D.C.* v. *Bunting* [1972] Ch. 470.

to cut timber in the ordinary way, even if he thereby drives away game [76]; but it is otherwise if fundamental changes in the land are made, as where the whole or a substantial part of the land is built upon or converted into racing stables.[77] Such a right imposes no obligation to keep down the numbers of birds or animals.[78]

E. *Profit in the Soil*

A profit in the soil is the right to enter the servient tenement and take sand,[79] stone,[80] gravel,[81] brick-earth,[82] coal,[83] minerals [84] and the like.[85] It may exist as appurtenant or in gross.

[76] *Gearns* v. *Baker* (1875) 10 Ch.App. 355.
[77] *Peech* v. *Best* [1931] 1 K.B. 1.
[78] *Seligman* v. *Docker* [1949] Ch. 53.
[79] *Blewett* v. *Tregonning* (1835) 3 A. & E. 544 at 575.
[80] *Heath* v. *Deane* [1905] 2 Ch. 86.
[81] *Constable* v. *Nicholson* (1863) 14 C.B.(N.S.) 230 at 239.
[82] *Church* v. *The Inclosure Commissioners* (1862) 11 C.B.(N.S.) 664.
[83] See *Duke of Portland* v. *Hill* (1866) L.R. 2 Eq. 765.
[84] *Duke of Sutherland* v. *Heathcote* [1892] 1 Ch. 475 at 483.
[85] Co.Litt. 122a. As to a right to take ice from a canal, see *Newby* v. *Harrison* (1861) 1 J. & H. 393; (1938) 2 Conv.(N.S.) 203 at 204 (J. S. Fiennes).

Chapter 14

MORTGAGES

Part 1

NATURE OF A MORTGAGE

When one person lends money to another, he may be content to make the loan without security, or he may demand some security for the payment of the money. In the former case, the lender has a right to sue for the money if it is not duly paid, but that is all; if the borrower becomes insolvent, the lender may lose part or all of his money. But if some security of adequate value is given for the loan, the lender is protected even if the borrower becomes insolvent, for the lender has a claim to the security which takes precedence over other creditors.

The most important kind of security is the mortgage. The essential nature of a mortgage is that it is a conveyance of a legal or equitable interest in property, with a provision for redemption, *i.e.*, that upon repayment of a loan or the performance of some other obligation the conveyance shall become void or the interest shall be reconveyed.[1] The borrower is known as the " mortgagor," the lender as the " mortgagee."

A mortgage must be distinguished from a lien, a pledge and a charge.[2]

1. Lien. A lien may arise at common law, in equity or under certain statutes. A common law lien is the right to retain possession of the property of another until a debt is paid; thus a garage proprietor has a common law lien upon a motor-car repaired by him.[3] This lien is a mere passive right of retention, giving no right to sell[4] or otherwise deal with the property, and is extinguished if the creditor parts with possession to the debtor or his agent.[5] It

---

[1] *Santley* v. *Wilde* [1899] 2 Ch. 474, *per* Lindley M.R., approved in *Noakes & Co. Ltd.* v. *Rice* [1902] A.C. 24 at 28; *London County & Westminster Bank Ltd.* v. *Tompkins* [1918] 1 K.B. 515.
[2] See *Haliday* v. *Holgate* (1868) L.R. 3 Ex. 299 at 302.
[3] *Green* v. *All Motors Ltd.* [1917] 1 K.B. 625.
[4] *Mulliner* v. *Florence* (1878) 3 Q.B.D. 484.
[5] *Pennington* v. *Reliance Motor Works Ltd.* [1923] 1 K.B. 127.

is therefore merely a means of coercing the debtor into payment, rather than a security against payment not being made.

An equitable lien is not dependent upon continued possession of the property [6] and in this respect resembles a mortgage. It is also within the definition of " mortgage " in the Law of Property Act, 1925.[6a] But it differs from a mortgage (*inter alia*) in that a mortgage is intentionally created by contract whereas an equitable lien arises automatically under some doctrine of equity.[7] Thus a vendor of land has an equitable lien on it until the full purchase price is paid, even if he has conveyed the land to the purchaser and put him into possession.[8] This lien gives him no right to possession of the land, but enables him to apply to the court for a declaration of charge and for an order for sale of the land, under which he will be paid the money due.[9] If he is paid off by a third party, the third party can claim the benefit of the lien by subrogation.[9a] An equitable lien is therefore a species of equitable charge arising by implication of law.[10]

A statutory lien is the creature of the statute under which it arises, and the rights which it confers depend on the terms of that statute. Railways, shipowners and solicitors have been given such rights.[11]

2. Pledge. A pledge or pawn is a loan of money secured by the possession of chattels delivered to the lender. Although the lender has certain powers of sale, the general property in the goods remains in the borrower and the lender has possession [12]; in a mortgage, on the other hand, the lender acquires ownership and the borrower usually retains possession. The great advantage of a mortgage, as opposed to a pledge, is that the borrower can thus keep possession of his property for the time being. Land, being immovable, is naturally mortgaged, not pledged; chattels may be either pledged or mortgaged.[13]

3. Charge. For most practical purposes a charge should be regarded as a species of mortgage, and it is so dealt with in this chapter. Nevertheless there is an essential difference between a

---

[6] *Wrout* v. *Dawes* (1858) 25 Beav. 369.
[6a] s. 205 (1) (xvi).
[7] See *Mackreth* v. *Symmons* (1808) 15 Ves. 329 at 340; *Re Beirnstein* [1925] Ch. 12 at 17.
[8] *Ante*, p. 576. There is also a purchaser's lien: *ante*, p. 589.
[9] Williams V. & P. 988.
[9a] *Congresbury Motors Ltd.* v. *Anglo-Belge Finance Co. Ltd.* [1971] Ch. 81; *Coptic Ltd.* v. *Bailey* [1972] Ch. 446.
[10] *Re Birmingham* [1959] Ch. 523.
[11] See Snell, *Equity*, 438 *et seq.*
[12] See *Re Morritt* (1886) 18 Q.B.D. 222.
[13] Mortgages of chattels are effected by bills of sale, which are outside the scope of this book.

mortgage and a charge. A mortgage is a conveyance of property subject to a right of redemption, whereas a charge conveys nothing and merely gives the chargee certain rights over the property as security for the loan.[14]

Part 2

CREATION OF MORTGAGES

Sect. 1. Methods of Creating Legal Mortgages and Charges
The methods of creating a legal mortgage differ for freeholds and leaseholds. In each case it is necessary to understand the history of the subject before considering the effect of the legislation of 1925.

A. *Freeholds*

I. HISTORY BEFORE 1926

1. Twelfth and thirteenth centuries. In the twelfth and thirteenth centuries the forms of mortgage were influenced by the laws against usury, which was both a crime and a sin.[14a] Since lending money at a fixed rate of interest was prohibited, other transactions were resorted to which escaped the usury laws but which were sufficiently profitable to the lender, the mortgagee. Most commonly the mortgagor leased the land to the mortgagee, who went into possession.[15] This therefore resembled a pledge rather than a mortgage. If the income from the land was used to discharge the mortgage debt, the transaction was known as *vivum vadium* (a live pledge), since it was self-redeeming. If the mortgagee kept the income, it was known as *mortuum vadium* (a dead pledge).[16] This latter form was not unlawful, but the Church regarded it as sinful, for the income was taken by way of interest. In either case, if the money was not repaid by the time the lease expired, the mortgagee's lease was enlarged into a fee simple by a condition subsequent expressed in the mortgage.

2. Fifteenth century. By the middle of the fifteenth century the usual form of mortgage had changed. Even in the thirteenth century a form of mortgage by conveyance of the fee simple had

---

[14] See *post*, p. 897.
[14a] H.E.L. viii, 102; Glanvil, Bk. 7, 16.
[15] H.E.L. iii, 130.
[16] H.E.L. iii, 128; Glanvil, Bk. 10, pp. 6, 8. Hence the name "mortgage": mort (dead) gage (pledge).

been known and this form gradually ousted the others, for it gave seisin, and therefore impregnable security, to the mortgagee.[17]   The mortgagor conveyed the land to the mortgagee in fee simple, subject to a condition that the mortgagor might re-enter and determine the mortgagee's estate if the money lent was repaid on a named date.[18] The mortgagee still took possession forthwith.   The condition was construed strictly; if the mortgagor was a single day late in offering to repay the money, he lost his land for ever and yet remained liable for the debt.[19]

3. Seventeenth century onwards

(a) *Form of mortgage.*   By the beginning of the seventeenth century two changes had taken place.   First, the form of a mortgage was usually a conveyance in fee simple with a covenant to reconvey the property if the money was paid on the fixed date.   This was the modern form before 1926, and it simplified proof of title; whether the fee simple was vested in the mortgagor or not no longer depended merely upon whether the money had been paid within the fixed time, but depended upon whether a reconveyance had been executed by the mortgagee.[20]   Mortgages made by granting leases of the property were, however, equally possible,[21] and were employed where there were special reasons for preferring them.[22]

(b) *Intervention of equity.*   Secondly, a far more important change had been made by the intervention of equity.   By this time loans at interest were no longer illegal, but a maximum rate of interest was from time to time fixed by statute.[23]   This greatly altered the function of a mortgage; for instead of providing both security for capital and a source of profit in lieu of interest, the mortgagee ought henceforth to be a security only, and should not yield profit

---

[17] H.E.L. iii, 129, 130; (1967) 83 L.Q.R. 229 (J. L. Barton).   Doubts had also arisen as to the validity of the idea that a term of years could swell into a fee simple: *ibid.*

[18] H.E.L. iii, 129, 130.   A variant of this form was a conveyance of the fee simple subject to a condition that the conveyance should be void if the money was paid on the named date.

[19] *Kreglinger* v. *New Patagonia Meat and Cold Storage Co. Ltd.* [1914] A.C. 25 at 35.

[20] See *Durham Brothers* v. *Robertson* [1898] 1 Q.B. 765 at 772.

[21] See, *e.g., Horne* v. *Darbyshire* (1619) Ritchie's Bac.Cas. 188; *Aldridge* v. *Duke* (1679) Rep.t.Finch 439.

[22] *e.g.,* for raising portions in family settlements (*ante,* p. 387) where a leasehold interest left the other limitations of the settlement undisturbed.

[23] The Usury Acts of 1545 (37 Hen. 8, c. 9) and 1571 (13 Eliz. 1, c. 8) allowed 10 per cent.; this was reduced to 8 per cent. in 1623 (21 Jac. 1, c. 17) and to 5 per cent. in 1714 (13 Ann. c. 15; Ruff., 12 Ann., St. 2, c. 16).   The usury laws were finally repealed by the Usury Laws Repeal Act, 1854.   The court now has wide powers to modify or set aside harsh or unconscionable transactions under the Money-lenders Act, 1900, as modified by the Moneylenders Act, 1927.   See H.E.L. viii, 100–113.

to the mortgagee over and above the interest permitted by law. The Court of Chancery, at this time expanding its jurisdiction and concerned as always to prevent unconscionable dealing, now undertook to enforce this policy. No longer might the mortgagee reap any benefit from his fee simple. If he took possession, equity held him liable to account for a full rent to the mortgagor.[24] Thus it was no longer an advantage to the mortgagee to occupy the land; and there emerged the modern type of mortgage where the mortgagor remains in possession and conveys the fee simple to the mortgagee merely by way of security.[25]

(*c*) *Mortgages as securities*. Equally important, it was repugnant to every idea of equity that the mortgagor should lose his property merely because he was late in repaying the loan. At first equity intervened in cases of accident, mistake, special hardship and the like, but soon relief was given in all cases.[26] Even if the date fixed for repayment had long passed, equity compelled the mortgagee to reconvey the property to the mortgagor on payment of the principal with interest and costs. The mortgagor was thus given an equitable right to redeem at a time when the agreement between the parties provided that the mortgagee was to be the absolute owner.[27] No longer, therefore, did the mortgagee stand to gain by obtaining a property which might be worth much more than the debt. Equity compelled him to treat the property as no more than a security for the money actually owed to him. This equity of redemption became a valuable interest vested in the mortgagor: the measure of its value was the difference between the amount of the debt and the value of the mortgaged property. Since it was an equitable interest in the land,[28] the mortgagor could enforce it not only against the mortgagee personally but against anyone to whom the mortgagee transmitted his fee simple, saving only a bona fide purchaser without notice of the mortgage.[29]

(*d*) *Foreclosure*. There had, of course, to be some limit to the equitable right to redeem, for otherwise the security would not have fulfilled its purpose of enabling the mortgagee to recover his capital when required. Equity therefore devised the decree of foreclosure, which was an order of the court, made on the mortgagee's application,

---

[24] *Holman* v. *Vaux* (c. 1616) Tot. 133; *Pell* v. *Blewet* (1630) Tot. 133; H.E.L. v, 331.

[25] But as to " Welsh mortgages," see Coote, *Mortgages*, Chap. III.

[26] H.E.L. v, 330–332. This may have been due to " the piety " or else to the " love of fees of those who administered equity ": *Salt* v. *Marquess of Northampton* [1892] A.C. 1 at 19, *per* Lord Bramwell.

[27] See *Salt* v. *Marquess of Northampton* [1892] A.C. 1 at 18.

[28] See, *e.g.*, *Casborne* v. *Scarfe* (1738) 1 Atk. 603 at 605.   [29] *Ante*, p. 114.

declaring that the equitable right to redeem was at an end, and thus leaving the mortgagee with an unhampered fee simple.[30] But if the property was much more valuable than the debt the court would order a sale of the property, out of which the mortgagee would receive only the balance due to him, and the mortgagor would take the rest. Foreclosure could not therefore be used oppressively, and in any case a mortgagee who sought it had to come before the court.

(e) *Date for redemption.* These revolutionary changes made mortgages into fair and convenient commercial transactions instead of instruments of extortion. The day fixed for repayment by the mortgage deed (the *legal* date for redemption) became unimportant, for the *equitable* right of redemption extended far beyond it. It therefore became customary to fix the initial legal redemption date very early, commonly at six months' distance, so that the mortgagee might have the right to call in his loan, and if necessary start foreclosure proceedings, at any time thereafter. This was no hardship to the mortgagor, who had his equity of redemption, and was convenient to the mortgagee, for his investment was then in a liquid form.

(f) *The two rights to redeem.* The result was to make the legal effect of a mortgage much less intimidating than its appearance. An ordinary mortgage deed would recite the loan, and then convey the fee simple to the mortgagee subject only to a proviso for redemption in six months' time (a date when neither party, probably, would have the least wish for redemption). This legal redemption date would soon pass by, and then according to the terms of the deed the property would belong absolutely to the mortgagee. But the mortgagor would be fully protected by equity, which would enforce his rights in defiance of the terms of the deed. Mortgages are still frequently made in a similar and no less cryptic form. "No one . . . by the light of nature ever understood an English mortgage of real estate." [31]

It will be seen that the two rights to redeem are quite distinct.

(1) LEGAL RIGHT TO REDEEM: this is a contractual right at law to redeem on the precise day fixed by the mortgage, neither before nor after. This is exercisable as of right, irrespective of any equitable considerations.

---

[30] *How* v. *Vigures* (1628) 1 Ch.Rep. 32; H.E.L. v, 331, 332.
[31] *Samuel* v. *Jarrah Timber and Wood Paving Corporation Ltd.* [1904] A.C. 323 at 326, *per* Lord Macnaghten. And Maitland called a mortgage "one long *suppressio veri* and *suggestio falsi*": *Equity*, 2nd ed., 182. For an example, see *post*, p. 902.

(2) EQUITABLE RIGHT TO REDEEM: this is a right conferred by equity to redeem at any time after [31a] this day; but this is exercisable only on terms considered proper by equity, for "he who seeks equity must do equity." [32]

(g) *The equity of redemption.* The equitable right to redeem must be distinguished from the "equity of redemption," [33] in its wider sense, although sometimes the terms are used interchangeably. First, the equitable right to redeem does not arise until the contractual date for redemption has passed,[34] whereas the equity of redemption arises as soon as the mortgage is made.[35] Secondly, and more important, the equitable right to redeem is a particular right,[36] whereas the equity of redemption is an equitable interest in the land consisting of the sum total of the mortgagor's rights in the property. Although at law he has parted with his land and has only a limited right to recover it, in equity he is the owner of the land, though subject to the mortgage [37]; the mortgagee, on the other hand, is at law the owner but in equity a mere incumbrancer.

The mortgagor's equity of redemption, in the wider sense of the term, is thus an interest in the land [38] which includes his right to redeem it, but is much more than a mere right of redemption. It is an interest in the land which the mortgagor can convey, devise, settle, lease or mortgage, just like any other interests in land.[39] If, for example, a property worth £10,000 is mortgaged to secure a debt of £2,000, the value of the equity of redemption is obvious; and the mortgagor must clearly be at liberty to deal with it like any other property which is subject to incumbrances. He may wish to sell the property (which subject to the mortgage would be worth about £8,000) or to raise a further loan on it by a second mortgage. But since before 1926 the mortgagee usually held the legal fee simple,[40] any such dealings must necessarily have been equitable.

[31a] Or before, if the mortgagee has demanded payment, *e.g.*, by taking possession: *post*, p. 945.

[32] The doctrine of consolidation is an example: see *post*, p. 926.

[33] See *Kreglinger* v. *New Patagonia Meat & Cold Storage Co. Ltd.* [1914] A.C. 25 at 48.

[34] *Brown* v. *Cole* (1845) 14 Sim. 427.

[35] *Kreglinger* v. *New Patagonia Meat & Cold Storage Co. Ltd.*, *supra*, at p. 48.

[36] Perhaps a " mere equity " (for which see *ante*, p. 119).

[37] *Re Wells* [1933] Ch. 29 at 52.

[38] He has "an equitable right inherent in the land": *Pawlett* v. *Att.-Gen.* (1667) Hardres 465 at 469, *per* Hale C.B.

[39] *Casborne* v. *Scarfe* (1738) 1 Atk. 603 at 605; and see *Fawcet* v. *Lowther* (1751) 2 Ves.Sen. 300 at 303 (descent of equity of redemption according to custom of gavelkind).

[40] Before the Dower Act, 1833 (*ante*, p. 518), the conveyance of the fee simple to the mortgagee entitled the mortgagee's widow to dower out of the property, and this complicated the title. It was also inconvenient that the fee simple (realty) and the right to the mortgage money (personalty) devolved differently

Before 1926 a second mortgage was therefore usually an equitable mortgage, *i.e.*, a mortgage of the equity of redemption.

II. AFTER 1925

By the Law of Property Act, 1925,[41] freeholds can no longer be mortgaged by conveyance of the fee simple. This change is probably an example of the policy of requiring the legal fee simple to be vested in the true beneficial owner so far as possible.[42] Two methods only are permitted by the Act[41] for effecting legal mortgages of freeholds:

(i) A demise for a term of years absolute, subject to a provision for cesser on redemption; or

(ii) A charge by deed expressed to be by way of legal mortgage.

A legal mortgage can therefore be created only by deed.

1. Demise for a term of years absolute

(a) Mortgages made after 1925

(1) FORM OF MORTGAGE. The term of years granted to the mortgagee is usually a long term, *e.g.*, three thousand years. The provision for cesser on redemption is a clause providing that the term of years shall cease when the loan is repaid; it is really unnecessary, for on repayment the term becomes a satisfied term and automatically ceases.[43] In other respects the position is much as it was before 1926. A fixed redemption date is still named, and it is still usually six months after the date of the mortgage; thereafter the mortgagor has an equitable right to redeem in lieu of his legal right. The difficulty that a mortgagee by demise has no right to the title deeds[44] is obviated by an express provision giving a first mortgagee the same right to the deeds as if he had the fee simple.[45]

(2) RETENTION OF FEE. The principal change brought about by the new legislation is that the mortgagor now retains the legal fee simple. This brings the legal position rather more into accord with

on the mortgagee's death (*post*, p. 952). For these reasons mortgages were sometimes created by lease, particularly before 1833. But such mortgages had serious inconveniences of their own : the mortgagee could not dispose of the fee simple if he wished to realise the security; nor was he entitled to the title deeds (*Wiseman* v. *Westland* (1826) 1 Y. & J. 117 at 122).

[41] s. 85 (1).
[42] Compare the similar policy of the S.L.A., 1925: *ante*, p. 295 *et seq.*
[43] See *Knightsbridge Estates Trust Ltd.* v. *Byrne* [1939] Ch. 441 at 461 (in H.L. [1940] A.C. 613); and *post*, p. 957.
[44] See n. 40, *supra*.
[45] See *post*, p. 898.

reality, for now the mortgagor remains owner at law as well as in equity, and the mortgagee has an incumbrance only. The change is one of form rather than of substance, for it does not alter the rights of mortgagor and mortgagee; it merely makes the conveyancing machinery more logical.[46]

(3) EQUITY OF REDEMPTION. In particular, the equity of redemption has in no way lost its importance. A fee simple giving the right to possession of land only when a lease for three thousand years has expired is of little value compared with the right to insist that the fee simple shall forthwith be freed from the term of three thousand years on payment of the money due. Indeed, the term " equity of redemption " is sometimes used as including the mortgagor's legal estate, for it is the equity of redemption which is the substantial interest, and the legal estate which is the shadow.

(4) SUCCESSIVE LEGAL MORTGAGES. As the mortgagor now retains the legal fee simple, he can grant further legal terms of years. Consequently second, third and subsequent mortgages may all be legal after 1925. Thus A, the fee simple owner of Blackacre, may create successive legal mortgages in favour of X, Y and Z. The term he grants to each mortgagee is usually [47] at least one day longer than the previous mortgage. Thus X may be given two thousand years, Y two thousand years and a day, and Z two thousand years and two days, so that each mortgagee has a reversion upon the prior mortgage term. Here again the change is purely formal.[48] The rights of Y and Z *at law* are quite nebulous: no one would lend money on the security of one day's reversion at two thousand years' distance. What is valuable security to Y and Z is their interest in the equity of redemption; subject to X's mortgage, they have the next prior claims to the property in equity.[49]

(5) PURPORTED CONVEYANCE. A purported conveyance of a fee simple which in fact [50] is made by way of mortgage now operates as the grant of a term of three thousand years without impeachment of waste but subject to cesser on redemption.[51] An attempt to

---

[46] Save that on a sale by the mortgagee the estate that he conveys is no longer one that is vested in him but one vested in the mortgagor that the mortgagee conveys by virtue of a statutory power: see *post*, p. 913.

[47] This is not essential: *post*, p. 897.

[48] Perhaps there is this substantial difference, that the mortgagor's covenants which touch and concern the land (*e.g.*, his covenants to repair, insure, etc., but not his covenant to repay the loan) will now run with the reversion if the mortgagor assigns his interest: see *ante*, p. 725; *post*, p. 919.

[49] See *post*, p. 943.

[50] See *Grangeside Properties Ltd.* v. *Collingwoods Securities Ltd.* [1964] 1 W.L.R. 139 (on the similar wording of L.P.A., 1925, s. 86 (2): *post*, p. 897).

[51] L.P.A., 1925, s. 85 (2).

create a second or subsequent mortgage in the same way takes effect as the grant of a term one day longer than the preceding term.[51a] The new system is thus foolproof.

A precedent of a legal mortgage in the modern form is given below.[52]

(b) *Transitional provisions.* Mortgages made before 1926 are automatically brought into line with the new scheme.[53] A first or only mortgage made by a conveyance of the legal or equitable fee simple was automatically converted at the end of 1925 into a term of three thousand years without impeachment of waste but subject to cesser on redemption.[54] The fee simple thus taken away from the mortgagee was automatically vested in the mortgagor or whoever else would have been entitled to have the fee simple conveyed to him if all the mortgages were paid off.[55] Second and subsequent mortgages created by a conveyance of the legal or equitable fee simple were similarly converted into terms at least one day longer than the previous term.[56] Thus if before 1926 A had mortgaged his fee simple first to X and then to Y, on January 1, 1926, the legal fee simple vested in A, while X took a term of three thousand years and Y a term of three thousand years and one day. The position would have been the same if A had mortgaged only an equitable fee simple, the legal fee simple being held by T on a bare trust for him absolutely; under the transitional provisions the legal fee simple would have vested in A, and T would have lost all interest in the property.[57]

2. Charge by deed expressed to be by way of legal mortgage. This is a new invention of the Law of Property Act, 1925,[58] which is sometimes for brevity called a " legal charge." The importance of this innovation also is mainly formal. The " legal charge " is a statutory form of legal mortgage which is shorter and simpler than the accustomed form. It states merely that the property has been charged with the debt by way of legal mortgage. There is no conveyance of any estate to the mortgagee. The " legal charge " is intended to provide an optional alternative to the ordinary form of mortgage which, although equally uninformative, is at least not positively misleading to a lay reader.

[51a] L.P.A., 1925, s. 85 (1).
[52] *Post,* p. 902.
[53] L.P.A., 1925, 1st Sched., Pt. VII.
[54] *Ibid.,* para. (1).
[55] *Ibid.,* para. (3).
[56] *Ibid.,* para. (2).
[57] For these provisions, see *ante,* p. 439.
[58] L.P.A., 1925, s. 87 (1).

This statutory legal charge must be—

(i) made by deed [58a]; a charge merely in writing will have no effect at law [59]; and

(ii) expressed to be by way of legal mortgage [60]; the deed must contain a statement that the charge is made by way of legal mortgage.

The effect of such a charge of freeholds is that the chargee (whether first or subsequent) gets "the same protection, powers and remedies" as if he had a term of three thousand years without impeachment of waste.[61] Although he gets no actual legal term of years, he is as fully protected as if he had one,[62] so that he is as able to create tenancies and enforce covenants relating to the land (whether or not they are connected with the charge) as if he had an actual term vested in him.[63] The name "charge" is thus a little misleading, because although a legal charge is by nature a charge and not a mortgage,[64] for all practical purposes it takes effect as a mortgage.

The advantages of a legal charge are considered below.[65]

B. *Leaseholds*

I. BEFORE 1926

The intervention of equity in the case of mortgages of leaseholds produced the same results in matters of substance as in the case of freeholds.[66] As to form, a legal mortgage of leaseholds could be made before 1926 in either of two ways:

(i) By assignment of the lease to the mortgagee with a covenant for reassignment on redemption; or

(ii) By the grant to he mortgagee of a sub-lease at least one day shorter than the lease, with a proviso for cesser on redemption.

[58a] L.P.A., 1925, s. 87 (1).
[59] But it may take effect in equity: see *post*, p. 899.
[60] L.P.A., 1925, s. 87 (1).
[61] *Ibid.*
[62] See *Grand Junction Co. Ltd.* v. *Bates* [1954] 2 Q.B. 160; *Weg Motors Ltd.* v *Hales* [1962] Ch. 49 at 74; *Cumberland Court (Brighton) Ltd.* v. *Taylor* [1964] Ch. 29.
[63] *Regent Oil Co. Ltd.* v. *J. A. Gregory (Hatch End) Ltd.* [1966] Ch. 402.
[64] *Ante*, p. 886.
[65] *Post*, p. 898. For the forms of charge, see *post*, p. 903.
[66] *Ante*, p. 888.

1. Liability under the lease. The first method was rarely employed, for it brought the mortgagee into privity of estate with the landlord, and so made the mortgagee liable for the rent and for the performance of such other covenants in the lease as ran with the land.[67] This was not so under the second method, for then the mortgagee was only an under-lessee and there was privity neither of contract nor of estate between him and the lessor.[68] In either case the mortgage normally contained the usual provision for redemption on a fixed date six months ahead, and thereafter the mortgagor had an equitable right to redeem.

2. Subsequent mortgages. Where a mortgage had been made by assignment, second and subsequent mortgages were made by a mortgage of the mortgagor's equity of redemption. Where the prior mortgage had been made by a sub-lease, subsequent mortgages were made by the grant of other sub-leases, each normally being longer than the previous one. By the second, and usual, method it was therefore possible to create several legal mortgages of a leasehold property. It was desirable to leave a space of, say, ten days between the end of the first sub-lease and the end of the lease, so as to leave room for further mortgage terms, each longer by one day than the preceding sub-lease.[69]

II.   AFTER 1925

By the Law of Property Act, 1925,[70] leaseholds can no longer be mortgaged by assignment. Two methods only are possible at law:

(i) By a subdemise for a term of years absolute, subject to a provision for cesser on redemption, the term being at least one day shorter than the term vested in the mortgagor; or

(ii) By a charge by deed expressed to be by way of legal mortgage.

1. Subdemise for a term of years absolute

(a) *Mortgages made after* 1925. The term of the sub-lease must be at least one day shorter than the term of the lease which is being mortgaged, otherwise it would operate as an assignment.[71]

---

[67] *Ante*, p. 721.
[68] *Ante*, p. 722.
[69] The extra day was not essential to the creation of a legal estate (*ante*, p. 649), but it made it clear beyond doubt that the second or later mortgagee was the immediate reversioner.
[70] s. 86 (1).
[71] *Beardman* v. *Wilson* (1868) L.R. 4 C.P. 57; *ante*, p. 651.

If the lease requires the tenant to obtain the landlord's licence before a subdemise by way of mortgage is made, the licence cannot be unreasonably refused.[72] It is usual to make the sub-term ten days shorter than the lease, so as to allow room for second and subsequent mortgages. Thus if T's fifty years' lease is mortgaged, a first mortgage will be secured by a lease for fifty years less ten days, a second by fifty years less nine days and so on. But this is not essential, for the old rule that a lease may take effect in reversion upon another lease of the same or greater length[73] has been confirmed by the Law of Property Act, 1925.[74] Thus, if the first mortgage was made by a sub-term of fifty years less one day, the second mortgage could be secured by a sub-term of the same length and so on; each mortgage would then take effect in its proper order.

A purported assignment of a lease which in fact[75] is made by way of mortgage after 1925 operates as a subdemise for a term of years absolute subject to cesser on redemption.[76] A first or only mortgagee takes a term ten days shorter than the lease mortgaged. Second and subsequent mortgagees take terms one day longer than the previous mortgagee if this is possible; in every case, however, the sub-term must be at least one day shorter than the term mortgaged.[77]

If the mortgaged lease is subject to forfeiture, a mortgagee by subdemise (or by legal charge) has the same right to relief as any other sub-tenant.[78]

(b) *Transitional provisions.* On January 1, 1926, mortgages made by assignment before 1926 were automatically converted into mortgages by subdemise, subject to cesser on redemption.[79] The terms so created correspond to the terms arising on an attempted mortgage by assignment after 1925.[80]

2. Charge by way of legal mortgage. A charge by deed expressed to be by way of legal mortgage gives the mortgagee (whether first or subsequent) the same rights and remedies as if he

---

[72] L.P.A., 1925, s. 86 (1); *cf. ante*, p. 695.
[73] *Re Moore & Hulm's Contract* [1912] 2 Ch. 105; *ante*, p. 649.
[74] L.P.A., 1925, s. 149 (5).
[75] *Grangeside Properties Ltd.* v. *Collingwoods Securities Ltd.* [1964] 1 W.L.R. 139, holding that the assignment need not be *expressed* to be by way of mortgage.
[76] L.P.A., 1925, s. 86 (2).
[77] *Ibid.* Thus if more mortgages are made than spare days are available, the last mortgagees each take a term of one day less than the term mortgaged.
[78] *Ante*, p. 667, n. 64.
[79] L.P.A., 1925, 1st Sched., Pt. VIII, paras. (1), (2).
[80] *Ibid.* See above.

had a sub-term one day shorter than the term vested in the mortgagor.[81] As in the case of freeholds, he gets no actual term of years but is as fully protected as if he had one.

C. Advantages of a Legal Charge

There is nothing in the Law of Property Act, 1925, which suggests any reason why a statutory legal charge, either of freeholds or leaseholds, should be preferred to an ordinary mortgage.[82] But there seem to be three practical advantages in using a legal charge.

(i) It is a convenient way of mortgaging freeholds and leaseholds together; the deed is shortened by stating that all the properties specified in the Schedule are charged by way of legal mortgage, instead of setting out the length of the various mortgage terms in each case.

(ii) Probably the granting of a legal charge on a lease does not amount to a breach of any covenant in that lease against sub-letting, for the charge creates no actual sub-lease in favour of the mortgagee but merely gives him the same rights as if he had a sub-lease.[83]

(iii) The form of a legal charge is short and simple. This may account in part for its growing popularity, especially in London.

D. Custody of Title Deeds

It has always been to the mortgagee's advantage to take into his custody the title deeds of the property, for then any person to whom the mortgagor might try to convey or re-mortgage it would soon discover from the absence of the deeds that there was a prior mortgage. This precaution was of particular importance in the case

---

[81] L.P.A., 1925, s. 87 (1).

[82] L.P.A., 1925, s. 87 (2), provides that where the estate created by a mortgage made before 1926 has been converted into a term of years by the transitional provisions of the Act, the mortgagee may convert his mortgage into a charge by way of legal mortgage by a written declaration. This seems to contemplate some advantage in legal charges, but does not indicate what that advantage is.

[83] See Wolst. & C. i, 178; *Gentle* v. *Faulkner* [1900] 2 Q.B. 267; *Matthews* v. *Smallwood* [1910] 1 Ch. 777; *Grand Junction Co. Ltd.* v. *Bates* [1954] 2 Q.B. 160 at 168. However, where the covenant in question also prohibits the tenant from parting with possession of the property (as it usually will), there will be a breach if the mortgagee enforces his right to possession. If, as has been suggested ((1950) 100 L.J.News. 473), a house subject to the Rent Restriction Acts cannot be mortgaged owing to the prohibition of premiums by the Landlord and Tenant (Rent Control) Act, 1949, s. 2, the solution would be to use a legal charge. But it seems unlikely that a loan is a " premium " within s. 18, or that s. 2 applies at all (see now the corresponding provisions in the Rent Act 1968, Part VII: *post*, p. 1143).

of equitable mortgages (discussed below), in order to prevent a purchase of the legal estate without notice of the mortgagee's rights. But a legal mortgagee will also wish to have the deeds deposited with him. When mortgages were made by a grant of the fee simple, this automatically entitled the mortgagee to take the deeds. Now that legal mortgages are made by long lease, or by legal charge, the first mortgagee has been given a statutory right to possession of the documents of title,[84] for he would not otherwise be entitled to demand them.[85]

In the rare case of a legal mortgage of a leasehold by *assignment* before 1926, the mortgagee was automatically entitled to possession of the lease. In the more common case of mortgage by *subdemise* he was not so entitled, but he would usually stipulate expressly for it to be handed over. This stipulation is no longer necessary, for a first mortgagee of leaseholds has now, by statute,[86] the same right to possession of documents as if he were mortgagee by assignment.

The expression " title deeds "[87] is used in a wide sense, so as to include all documents necessary to prove the mortgagor's title. It includes, for example, assents by personal representatives made by unsealed writing.[88]

Sect. 2. Methods of Creating Equitable Mortgages and Charges

The fundamental difference between a mortgage and a charge is that a mortgage is a conveyance of property, legal or equitable, subject to a right of redemption, whereas a charge conveys nothing but merely gives the chargee certain rights over the property charged.[89] Only mortgages could be created at common law; but in equity both mortgages and charges were possible. Equitable charges are still occasionally created, but the remedies of an equitable chargee are inferior to those of a mortgagee.[90]

A. Equitable Mortgages

1. Mortgage of an equitable interest. If the mortgagor has no legal estate but only an equitable interest, any mortgage he effects must necessarily be equitable. Thus, before 1926, when once a

---

[84] L.P.A., 1925, s. 85 (1).
[85] *Ante*, p. 892.
[86] L.P.A., 1925, s. 86 (1).
[87] As to what are " title deeds," see *Clayton* v. *Clayton* [1930] 2 Ch. 12 at 21.
[88] *Ante*, p. 538.
[89] *Jones* v. *Woodward* (1917) 116 L.T. 378 at 379; *London County and Westminster Bank Ltd.* v. *Tompkins* [1918] 1 K.B. 515 (esp. at p. 528). Yet a charge by way of legal mortgage is in substance a mortgage, not merely a charge, since the chargee has all the rights of a mortgagee.
[90] See *post*, p. 925.

legal mortgage by conveyance of the fee simple had been created, the mortgagor retained only an equity of redemption and all subsequent mortgages were equitable. Again, the beneficiaries under a trust for sale have mere equitable interests and can create only equitable mortgages.

The 1925 legislation has not affected the form of equitable mortgages of equitable interests.[91] Such mortgages are still made by a conveyance of the whole equitable interest with a proviso for reconveyance. The actual form of words employed is immaterial, provided the meaning is plain.[92] Nor need the mortgage be made by deed, as is essential for a legal mortgage; but it must either be made in writing (not merely evidenced by writing[93]) signed by the mortgagor or his agent authorised in writing, or else be made by will.[94] It is wise, though not essential, for the mortgagee to give notice of his mortgage to the trustees in whom the legal estate is vested, both to prevent the trustees from paying the mortgagor, and to preserve priority.[95]

2. Informal mortgage

(*a*) *Contractual basis.* An informal mortgage is a simple and effective type of security which has long been in common use. Fundamentally it is a contract to create a legal mortgage, which, like other contracts to create legal estates, gives an equitable interest to any party entitled to specific performance.[96] But an equitable mortgage of this type is more than a mere preliminary to a legal mortgage: equity treats it as actual mortgage,[97] for in the great majority of cases the execution of a legal mortgage is never intended and never carried out. In theory the mortgagee may call for a legal mortgage, but in practice he is content to rest upon his equitable rights. Since the basis of the transaction is a contract to convey an estate,[98] the contract is (as explained elsewhere[99]) unenforceable unless supported by written evidence[1] or by part performance. As

---

[91] True, L.P.A., 1925, ss. 85 (2), 86 (2), unlike ss. 85 (1), 86 (1), are not in terms confined to mortgages effected " at law "; yet such a restriction would probably be implied.
[92] *William Brandt's Sons & Co.* v. *Dunlop Rubber Co. Ltd.* [1905] A.C. 454 at 462.
[93] See *ante*, p. 452.
[94] L.P.A., 1925, s. 53 (1) (*c*).
[95] See *post*, pp. 965, 976.
[96] See *ante*, p. 132.
[97] See *Ex p. Wright* (1812) 19 Ves. 255 at 258.
[98] See *Re Earl of Lucan* (1890) 45 Ch.D. 470 (voluntary charge of reversionary interest held ineffective).
[99] *Ante*, p. 545.
[1] *Ex p. Hall* (1879) 10 Ch.D. 615; *Mounsey* v. *Rankin* (1885) Cab. & El. 496.

in the case of imperfect leases,[2] an imperfect legal mortgage may take effect as an agreement for a mortgage, and so as an equitable mortgage,[3] if it contains the necessary particulars. But the money must have been advanced, for normally equity will not specifically enforce an unperformed agreement to lend money.[4]

(b) *Deposit of deeds.* The equitable mortgage was established primarily by extending the doctrine of part performance.[5] Since 1783 [6] a deposit of the title deeds by way of security has been taken both as showing a contract to create a mortgage and also as being part performance of that contract,[7] even if not a word about such a mortgage has been said.[8] A mere deposit of deeds thus creates an equitable mortgage, without any writing. In order to make possible this informal transaction, which proved very useful in commerce, the doctrine of part performance was stretched beyond its normal limits: the deposit of documents was taken as part performance by both parties, despite the rule that only the person who performs may take advantage of the performance.[9] There is therefore no risk of an equitable mortgage by deposit being enforceable on one side only, as may happen in other cases.[9]

The deposit must be made for the purpose of giving a security; delivery of the deeds by mistake,[10] or to enable a mortgage to be drawn up,[11] will not create a mortgage. But it is not essential that all the title deeds should be deposited,[12] provided those which are delivered are material evidence of title [13]; and even one deed out of several may suffice [14] if the intent is to create a mortgage.[15] Prima facie the deposit will secure not only the original loan but also any further advances.[16] But the mortgagee has no lien on the deeds, apart from his right to retain them under the mortgage.[16a]

---

[2] *Ante*, p. 623.

[3] *Parker* v. *Housefield* (1834) 2 My. & K. 419 at 420.

[4] *Rogers* v. *Challis* (1859) 27 Beav. 175; *Sichel* v. *Mosenthal* (1862) 30 Beav. 371; *Fry S.P.* 24, 25; but see now *Beswick* v. *Beswick* [1968] A.C. 58.

[5] The doctrine is explained *ante*, p. 561.

[6] *Russel* v. *Russel* (1783) 1 Bro.C.C. 269.

[7] *Edge* v. *Worthington* (1786) 1 Cox Eq. 211; *Pryce* v. *Bury* (1853) 2 Drew. 41 (affd. L.R. 16 Eq. 153n.); *Carter* v. *Wake* (1877) 4 Ch.D. 605 at 606.

[8] *Ex p. Kensington* (1813) 2 V. & B. 79 at 84; *Bozon* v. *Williams* (1829) 3 Y. & J. 150 at 161; *Bank of New South Wales* v. *O'Connor* (1889) 14 App.Cas. 273 at 282; and see *Re Wallis & Simmonds (Builders) Ltd.* [1974] 1 W.L.R. 391 (deposit of deeds by A for loan to B).

[9] *Ante*, p. 564.　　　　　　　　　　[10] *Wardle* v. *Oakley* (1864) 36 Beav. 27.

[11] *Norris* v. *Wilkinson* (1806) 12 Ves. 192: there was no intent to create a present security.

[12] *Roberts* v. *Croft* (1857) 24 Beav. 223 (conveyance to mortgagor omitted).

[13] *Lacon* v. *Allen* (1856) 3 Drew. 579.　　　[14] *Ex p. Chippendale* (1835) 1 Deac. 67.

[15] See *Ex p. Pearse and Prothero* (1820) Buck 525.

[16] *Ex p. Langston* (1810) 17 Ves. 227; *Ex p. Kensington* (1813) 2 V. & B. 79. For further advances, see *post*, p. 981.

[16a] *Re Molton Finance Ltd.* [1968] Ch. 325 (no lien on the deeds if the mortgage is void).

(c) *Accompanying memorandum.* In practice, equitable mortgages are rarely made without written evidence, since otherwise disputes between the parties will be probable. But, owing to the effect of the deposit of documents, the written evidence may be informal and is therefore free from the pitfalls of the Statute of Frauds.[17] An equitable mortgage is now, moreover, commonly accompanied by a memorandum under seal, which gives the mortgagee additional powers.[18] In this form it is hardly less formal than a legal mortgage or charge, but it is still much used, especially for temporary loans, *e.g.,* to secure an overdraft at a bank. In such cases it is a question of construction whether the mortgage was created by the deposit of deeds or by the execution of the deed accompanying the deposit,[19] *i.e.,* whether the deed is ancillary to the deposit or the deposit to the deed.

B. Equitable Charges

An equitable charge is created by appropriating specific property to the discharge of some debt or other obligation without there being any change in ownership either at law or in equity.[20] No special form of words is required: it is sufficient if an intent that the property should constitute a security can be gathered.[21] Thus if a man signs a written contract agreeing that he thereby charges his real estate with the payment of £500 to A, an equitable charge is created[22]; the same applies where a will or voluntary settlement charges land with the payment of a sum of money.[23]

Sect. 3. Forms of Legal Mortgage and Charge

A. Legal Mortgage

THIS MORTGAGE is made the first day of January 1966 between A of etc. (hereinafter called the borrower) of the one part and B of etc. (hereinafter called the lender) of the other part

WHEREAS—

(1) The borrower is seised in fee simple in possession free from incumbrances of the property hereby mortgaged

---

[17] Now replaced by L.P.A., 1925, s. 40: *ante,* p. 545.
[18] *viz.,* the powers of sale and appointing a receiver: *post,* pp. 908, 919.
[19] See *Paul* v. *Nath Saha* [1939] 2 All E.R. 737.
[20] See *ante,* p. 886.
[21] *Cradock* v. *Scottish Provident Institution* (1893) 69 L.T. 380, affd. 70 L.T. 718; *National Provincial and Union Bank of England* v. *Charnley* [1924] 1 K.B. 431 at 440, 445, 459.
[22] *Matthews* v. *Goodday* (1861) 31 L.J.Ch. 282 at 282, 283.
[23] *Re Owen* [1894] 3 Ch. 220; *Matthews* v. *Goodday, supra.*

(2) The lender has agreed with the borrower to lend him the sum of £5000 upon having the repayment thereof with interest thereon secured in the manner hereinafter appearing

NOW THIS DEED made in pursuance of the said agreement and in consideration of the sum of £5000 now paid to the borrower by the lender (the receipt whereof the borrower hereby acknowledges)

WITNESSETH as follows:—

1. The borrower hereby covenants with the lender to pay to the lender on the first day of July next the said sum of £5000 with interest thereon from the date of this deed at the rate of £7 per cent. per annum and further if the said moneys shall not be so paid to pay to the lender interest at the rate aforesaid by equal half-yearly payments on the first day of January and first day of July in every year on the moneys for the time being remaining due on this security.

2. The borrower as beneficial owner hereby demises unto the lender ALL THAT the property more particularly described in the Schedule hereto TO HOLD unto the lender for a term of 3000 years from the date hereof without impeachment of waste subject to the proviso for cesser on redemption hereinafter contained PROVIDED ALWAYS that if the borrower shall on the first day of July next pay to the lender the sum of £5000 with interest thereon in the meantime at the rate of £7 per cent. per annum, then and in such case the said term hereby granted shall absolutely cease and determine.

3. The borrower hereby covenants with the lender and it is hereby agreed and declared as follows:

[Here follow covenants by the mortgagor to repair, insure, etc., and any other terms agreed upon]

IN WITNESS etc.

Schedule

B. Charge by Way of Legal Mortgage

See the forms set out in the Fifth Schedule to the Law of Property Act, 1925. A charge by way of legal mortgage will be in the same form as the legal mortgage above, except that clause 2 will read as follows:

2. The borrower as beneficial owner hereby charges by way of legal mortgage ALL THAT the property more particularly described

in the Schedule hereto with the payment to the lender of the principal money, interest, and other money hereby covenanted to be paid by the borrower under this deed.

Part 3

RIGHTS OF THE PARTIES UNDER A MORTGAGE OR CHARGE

The rights of the parties under a mortgage or charge will be considered under three heads:

(i) The rights of the mortgagee or chargee;
(ii) Rights common to both parties; and
(iii) The rights of the mortgagor or chargor.

Sect. 1. Rights of the Mortgagee or Chargee

A. *Remedies for Enforcing His Security*

Unless the parties have otherwise agreed, a mortgagee or chargee has certain standard remedies. First of all, he may of course sue for the money due, so soon as the date fixed for repayment has arrived, though not before.[24] But the remedies peculiar to mortgages and charges are the remedies for enforcing the security. These may be classified as follows—

(*a*) *Remedies primarily for recovery of capital*

(i) Foreclosure
(ii) Sale

(*b*) *Remedies primarily for recovery of interest*

(i) Taking possession
(ii) Appointment of receiver.

The first two remedies are necessarily final remedies, since they put an end to the whole transaction; the other two remedies are useful if the mortgagee wishes to keep the mortgage alive, as where there is a favourable rate of interest, and to enforce punctual payment of the interest. The rights to foreclose and to take possession arise from the very nature of the security. The powers to sell and to appoint a receiver are improvements designed by conveyancers and now incorporated by statute in the great majority of mortgages. They may usually be exercised out of court, whereas in most cases

---

[24] See, *e.g.*, *Bolton* v. *Buckenham* [1891] 1 Q.B. 278.

the mortgagee can enforce payment of the money due, foreclose or obtain possession only by proceedings in court. Such proceedings must be brought in the Chancery Division, and no judgment in default of appearance or defence can be entered without leave of the court [25]; but this does not apply if the mortgaged property has already been sold by a prior mortgagee, so that the money is no longer secured on any property. [26]

All the above remedies are available to a legal mortgagee or chargee, and his position will be considered first. An equitable mortgagee or chargee has more restricted remedies, which are considered later.

I. LEGAL MORTGAGE OR LEGAL CHARGE

A legal mortgagee or legal chargee has the following remedies for enforcing his security.

1. To foreclose

(a) *The right of foreclosure*

(1) EQUITY'S INTERVENTION. By giving the mortgagor an equitable right to redeem after he had lost his legal right of redemption, equity interfered with the bargain made between the parties. But equity prescribed limits to the equitable right to redeem which it created. Thus, before 1926, a legal first mortgagee of freeholds had the fee simple vested in him, and once the legal date for redemption had passed, the mortgagor's right to redeem was merely equitable. " Foreclosure " was the name given to the process whereby the mortgagor's equitable right to redeem was declared by the court to be extinguished and the mortgagee was left owner of the property, both at law and in equity. Equity had interfered to prevent the conveyance by way of mortgage from having its full effect; but there had to be some final point at which the mortgagee could enforce his security, and therefore by foreclosure " the court simply removes the stop it has itself put on." [27] The mortgagee was from the first entitled to the property at law; and when he obtained the necessary order of the court, foreclosure made him an absolute owner in equity as well. [28]

---

[25] See J.A., 1925, s. 56; R.S.C. Ord. 88, rr. 2, 7. But for dwelling-houses outside Greater London with a rateable value of £1,000 or less the county court has exclusive jurisdiction in claims for possession unless the mortgagee also genuinely seeks foreclosure or sale: Administration of Justice Act 1970, ss. 36–38, as amended by Administration of Justice Act 1973, s. 6, 2nd. Sched.; *Trustees of Manchester Unity Life Insurance Collecting Society* v. *Sadler* [1974] 1 W.L.R. 770.
[26] *Newnham* v. *Brown* [1966] 1 W.L.R. 875.
[27] *Carter* v. *Wake* (1877) 4 Ch.D. 605 at 606, *per* Jessel M.R.
[28] *Heath* v. *Pugh* (1881) 6 Q.B.D. 345 at 360.

(2) ORDER OF COURT. An order of the court is essential for foreclosure. " Foreclosure is done by the order of the court, not by any person." [29] Since 1925, a mortgagee does not have the whole legal estate of the mortgagor vested in him,[30] but only a long term of years in the case of freeholds and an underlease in the case of leaseholds. Consequently it is no longer sufficient for a decree of foreclosure merely to destroy the mortgagor's equity of redemption; and the Law of Property Act, 1925, provides that a foreclosure decree absolute shall vest the mortgagor's fee simple [31] or term of years [32] in the mortgagee.

(3) RIGHT TO FORECLOSE. The right to foreclose does not arise until repayment has become due at law,[33] for until the equitable right to redeem has arisen, it cannot be extinguished by foreclosure. Repayment is due at law when the legal date for redemption has passed, or, if the mortgage makes the money fall due on breach of any term of the mortgage, on the occurrence of any such breach, such as failure to make due payment of interest [34] or of an instalment of principal.[35] Once this has occurred, the mortgagee may begin foreclosure proceedings unless he has agreed not to do so [36]; and the mere acceptance of a late payment will not by itself waive the right to foreclose for a breach.[37] In practice the mortgagee sometimes contracts not to enforce the security by foreclosure or other means until he has given some specified notice or until the mortgagor has broken one of his covenants in the mortgage.[38] If no redemption date is fixed [39] or if the loan is repayable on demand,[40] the right to foreclose arises when a demand for repayment has been made and a reasonable time thereafter has elapsed.[41]

(b) *Parties to a foreclosure action.* An action for foreclosure can be brought by any mortgagee of property, whether he is the original mortgagee or an assignee,[42] and whether he is a first or subsequent mortgagee.[43] The effect of a foreclosure order absolute

---

[29] *Re Farnol Eades Irvine & Co. Ltd.* [1915] 1 Ch. 22 at 24, *per* Warrington J.
[30] But see *ante*, p. 899, as to equitable mortgages of equitable interests.
[31] s. 88 (2).   [32] s. 89 (2).
[33] *Williams* v. *Morgan* [1906] 1 Ch. 804.
[34] *Keene* v. *Biscoe* (1878) 8 Ch.D. 201; contrast *Burrowes* v. *Molloy* (1845) 2 Jo. & Lat. 521.
[35] *Kidderminster Mutual Benefit B. S.* v. *Haddock* [1936] W.N. 158.
[36] *Ramsbottom* v. *Wallis* (1835) 5 L.J.Ch. 92.
[37] See *Keene* v. *Biscoe, supra*, and contrast *Re Taaffe's Estate* (1864) 14 Ir.Ch.R. 347.   [38] See *Seaton* v. *Twyford* (1870) L.R. 11 Eq. 591.
[39] *Fitzgerald's Trustee* v. *Mellersh* [1892] 1 Ch. 385.
[40] *Balfe* v. *Lord* (1842) 2 Dr. & War. 480.
[41] *Brighty* v. *Norton* (1862) 3 B. & S. 305; *Toms* v. *Wilson* (1862) 4 B. & S. 442. But see Coote, *Mortgages*, Chap. III, for " Welsh mortgages."
[42] *Platt* v. *Mendel* (1884) 27 Ch.D. 246 at 247.
[43] *Rose* v. *Page* (1829) 2 Sim. 471.

in an action brought by the first mortgagee is to make him the sole owner both at law and in equity, free from any subsequent mortgages; if the action is brought by a second or subsequent mortgagee, he will hold the property subject to prior incumbrances [44] but free from all subsequent incumbrances. These are the natural results of extinguishing the equity of redemption.

As will be seen shortly,[45] a foreclosure action gives the mortgagor and all others interested in the equity of redemption an opportunity of redeeming the mortgage or of applying for a sale in lieu of foreclosure. Consequently all persons interested in the equity of redemption must be made parties to the action.[46] Thus if X has made successive mortgages of his property to A, B and C, and B starts foreclosure proceedings,[47] A will not be affected by them and so need not be made a party to the action.[48] But if the action is successful, C will lose his mortgage and X his equity of redemption, and so both must be made parties to the action.[49]

(c) *Procedure*. Where, as is usual, foreclosure proceedings take place in the High Court, the action is started by writ or (in most cases) originating summons. The court then makes a foreclosure order nisi.[50] This directs the taking of the necessary accounts and provides that if the mortgagor pays the money due by a fixed day (usually six months from the accounts being settled by the master), the mortgage shall be discharged; but that if this is not done the mortgage shall be foreclosed. If there are several mortgagees and the first mortgagee is foreclosing, each mortgagee is given the alternative of either losing his security or else redeeming the first mortgage, *i.e.*, buying it up. Sometimes the court will give the mortgagees successive periods (*e.g.*, of six months) to effect this redemption,[51] but usually there will be only one period between them.[52]

In the special case of instalment mortgages of dwelling-houses the court has wide discretionary power to adjourn the proceedings or to suspend its order, as explained below.[52a]

(d) *Sale*. At the request of the mortgagee or of any person interested (*e.g.*, a later mortgagee or the mortgagor) the court may order a sale of the property instead of foreclosure. This jurisdiction

---

[44] See *Slade* v. *Rigg* (1843) 3 Hare 35 at 38.
[45] See (*d*), *infra*.
[46] *Brisco* v. *Kenrick* (1832) 1 Coop.t.Cott. 371; *Westminster Bank Ltd.* v. *Residential Properties Improvement Co. Ltd.* [1938] Ch. 639 (need to join debenture holders of company).   [47] As in *Rose* v. *Page* (1829) 2 Sim. 471.
[48] *Richards* v. *Cooper* (1842) 5 Beav. 304.
[49] *Tylee* v. *Webb* (1843) 6 Beav. 552 at 557.
[50] *i.e.*, the mortgage will be foreclosed unless (nisi) the mortgagor redeems.
[51] *Smithett* v. *Hesketh* (1890) 44 Ch.D. 161.
[52] *Platt* v. *Mendel* (1884) 27 Ch.D. 246.   [52a] *Post*, p. 917.

has always existed, but it is now statutory.[53] It is an important safeguard where the property mortgaged is (as is usual) worth substantially more than the mortgage debt. If, for example, X borrows £2,000 from A on a first mortgage of a property worth £5,000, and then borrows £1,000 from B on a second mortgage, foreclosure by A will be manifestly unjust. For A will obtain far more than is due to him, X will lose far more than he owes, and B will lose his security altogether. Therefore X or B will apply for a sale by order of the court (a " judicial sale "), 'and though the court has a free discretion, an order for sale will almost certainly be made in such a case.[54] When the sale has taken place, each incumbrancer is paid what is due to him according to his priority, and the balance belongs to the mortgagor.[55]

(e) *Opening the foreclosure.* If no order for sale is made and the property is not duly redeemed, a foreclosure order absolute is made. This destroys the mortgagor's equity of redemption and transfers his fee simple [56] or term of years [57] to the mortgagee, who thus becomes sole owner at law and in equity, subject only to prior incumbrances. But even the order of foreclosure absolute is not necessarily final, for the court will sometimes " open [58] the foreclosure." [59] Circumstances which may influence the court to do this are an accident at the last moment preventing the mortgagor from raising the money, any special value which the property had to the mortgagor (e.g., if it was an old family estate), a marked disparity between the value of the property and the amount lent, and the promptness of the application.[60] Even if the mortgagee has sold the property after foreclosure absolute, the court may still open the foreclosure; this is unlikely, however, if the purchaser bought the property some time after foreclosure and without notice of circumstances which might induce the court to interfere.[61] It is the lack of finality in foreclosure proceedings which sometimes leads mortgagees, as well as mortgagors, to apply for judicial sale instead.

2. To sell

(a) *History.* There is no right, either at common law or in equity, for a mortgagee to sell the mortgaged property free from the equity of redemption. He can freely transfer the estate which

---

[53] L.P.A., 1925, s. 91 (2), replacing C.A., 1881, s. 25 (2).
[54] In *Silsby* v. *Holliman* [1955] Ch. 552 special circumstances made a sale inequitable.
[55] Waldock, *Mortgages*, 366, 367.   [56] L.P.A., 1925, s. 88 (2).
[57] *Ibid.*, s. 89 (2).
[58] Or " reopen."
[59] See *Campbell* v. *Holyland* (1877) 7 Ch.D. 166 at 172–175.
[60] *Ibid.*. *per* Jessel M.R.; and see *Lancashire & Yorkshire Reversionary Interest Co. Ltd.* v. *Crowe* (1970) 114 S.J. 435.   [61] See n. 59, *supra.*

is vested in him subject to the equity of redemption, that is to say, he can transfer or assign the mortgage. But he cannot rely upon being able to realise his security in this way, for it may be difficult to find a willing transferee. Yet he desires a better remedy than foreclosure, for foreclosure requires elaborate proceedings before the court and is in many ways an unsatisfactory remedy.

The solution was found by inserting an express power in mortgage deeds enabling the mortgagee to sell the property out of court and free from the equity of redemption.[62] This power was carefully drafted so as to allow the mortgagee to take only what was due to him out of the proceeds of sale, and only to exercise the power in proper circumstances, for otherwise equity would have intervened. The power has long enjoyed statutory approval, and need no longer be inserted expressly. Lord Cranworth's Act, 1860,[63] first gave a limited power of sale in the case of mortgages made after 1860, but this was usually thought too narrow to be relied upon. The Conveyancing Act, 1881,[64] however, gave a satisfactory power of sale and this, as extended by the Conveyancing Act, 1911, is now contained in the Law of Property Act, 1925.[65]

(b) The power

(1) POWER ARISING. Every mortgagee whose mortgage was made after 1881 [66] and shows no contrary intention [67] has a power of sale, provided that—

(i) the mortgage was made by deed [68] (and all legal mortgages must be made thus); and

(ii) the mortgage money is due,[68] *i.e.*, the legal date for redemption has passed; if the mortgage money is payable by instalments, the power of sale arises as soon as any instalment is in arrear.[69]

(2) POWER EXERCISABLE. When the foregoing conditions have been fulfilled, the statutory power of sale *arises*; nevertheless, the power does not become *exercisable* unless one of the three following conditions has been satisfied—

---

[62] This did not become the usual practice until about 1820 or 1830: see *Stevens* v. *Theatres Ltd*. [1903] 1 Ch. 857 at 860; *Clarke* v. *Royal Panopticon* (1857) 4 Drew. 26 at 30.

[63] 23 & 24 Vict. c. 145, ss. 11–16. See Sugden, *Powers*, 877–883.

[64] s. 19.

[65] L.P.A., 1925, ss. 101–107.

[66] *Ibid.*, s. 101 (5). If the mortgage was made before 1882 but after August 28, 1860, Lord Cranworth's Act, 1860, applied; if on or before the latter date, there was no power of sale unless the mortgage gave one.

[67] L.P.A., 1925, s. 101 (4).

[68] *Ibid.*, s. 101 (1).   [69] *Payne* v. *Cardiff R. D. C.* [1932] 1 K.B. 241.

(i) notice requiring payment of the mortgage money has been
served on the mortgagor and default has been made in
payment of part or all of it for three months thereafter [70]; or

(ii) some interest under the mortgage is two months or more
in arrear [71]; or

(iii) there has been a breach of some provision contained in
the Act [72] or in the mortgage deed [73] (other than the covenant
for payment of the mortgage money or interest) which
should have been observed or performed by the mortgagor
or by someone who concurred in making the mortgage.[74]

(c) *Protection of purchaser.* The difference between the power
of sale arising and becoming exercisable is that if the power has not
arisen, the mortgagee has no statutory power of sale at all; he can
only transfer his mortgage. But if the power of sale has arisen,
he can make a good title to a purchaser free from the equity of
redemption even if the power has not become exercisable; the
purchaser's title is not impeachable merely because none of the
three specified events has occurred or the power of sale has in some
way been irregularly or improperly exercised.[75] Any person injured
by an unauthorised, improper or irregular exercise of the power
has a remedy in damages against the person exercising it.[76] Thus
while a purchaser from a mortgagee must satisfy himself that the
power of sale has arisen, he need not inquire whether it has become
exercisable.[77] Proof of title is thereby simplified, for the existence
of the power of sale is proved by the form of the mortgage and
the redemption date specified in it; the purchaser's title does not
depend on the fact of some later default by the mortgagor.

If, however, the purchaser in fact " becomes aware . . . of any
facts showing that the power of sale is not exercisable,[78] or that
there is some impropriety in the sale " (as there would be if the
mortgagee is selling even though the mortgagor has tendered principal
and interest [79]), then notwithstanding the statutory provision that the

---

[70] L.P.A., 1925, s. 103 (i). Alternatively the notice may demand payment in three
months' time, and the mortgagee, if unpaid, may then sell at once: *Barker* v.
Illingworth [1908] 2 Ch. 20.
[71] L.P.A., 1925, s. 103 (ii).
[72] See *Public Trustee* v. *Lawrence* [1912] 1 Ch. 789 (failure to deliver counterpart
of lease as required by s. 99 (11); see *post,* p. 934).
[73] *e.g.,* breach of covenant to repair or insure.
[74] L.P.A., 1925, s. 103 (iii).
[75] *Ibid.,* s. 104 (2). It is no longer necessary (as it was before 1926) to state that
the sale is made in exercise of the statutory power, for that is now presumed:
s. 104 (3).
[76] L.P.A., 1925, s. 104 (2).
[77] *Bailey* v. *Barnes* [1894] 1 Ch. 25 at 35.
[78] See *Selwyn* v. *Garfit* (1888) 38 Ch.D. 273 (decided on an express power of sale).
[79] *Jenkins* v. *Jones* (1860) 2 Giff. 99 (decided on an express power of sale).

purchaser's title is not to be impeachable " he gets no good title on taking the conveyance." [80] To hold otherwise, it has been said, would be to convert the provisions of the statute into an instrument of fraud.[81] Yet the purchaser need not make the inquiries which a suspicious man would make, though he should not shut his eyes to suspicious circumstances.[82]

(d) Mode of sale

(1) THE MORTGAGEE'S RIGHTS. In general, the statutory power of sale is exercisable without any order of the court.[83] This is its principal advantage over foreclosure. The mortgagee may sell by public auction or private contract and has a wide discretion as to the terms and conditions upon which the sale is made [84]; and if the mortgage was made after 1911, his discretion is even wider, *e.g.*, as to making the sale subject to restrictions.[85] The power is exercised as soon as a contract for sale is made, even if it is merely conditional; thereafter the mortgagor's equity of redemption is suspended while the contract subsists, and he cannot stop the sale by tendering the money due.[86] A disposition or contract to sell made by the mortgagor has no effect on the mortgagee's power of sale.[87]

(2) NO TRUSTEESHIP. The mortgagee is not a trustee for the mortgagor of his power of sale,[88] for the power is given to the mortgagee for his own benefit to enable him the better to realise his security.[89] But the mortgagor is the person interested in the proceeds of sale in so far as they exceed the debt, and his interests must not be sacrificed. The mortgagee is accordingly required to act not only in good faith [90] but also with reasonable care.[91] If he

---

[80] *Lord Waring* v. *London and Manchester Assurance Co. Ltd.* [1935] Ch. 310 at 318, *per* Crossman J.
[81] *Bailey* v. *Barnes* [1894] 1 Ch. 25 at 30, *per* Stirling J., impliedly confirmed by the Court of Appeal. For an analogous construction of a different statute, see *Le Neve* v. *Le Neve* (1747) Amb. 436.
[82] See *Bailey* v. *Barnes* [1894] 1 Ch. 25 at 30, 34. This seems to lay down a somewhat different standard from that usually applied under the doctrine of notice: see *ante*, p. 121.
[83] An exceptional case arises under L.P.A., 1925, s. 110, in cases where a post-1925 mortgage provides that a power of sale shall be exercisable in case of bankruptcy. Leave of the court is there required, but a purchaser is not concerned: L.P.A., 1925, s. 104 (2).
[84] L.P.A., 1925, s. 101 (1) (i).
[85] *Ibid.*, s. 101 (2); the date is derived from C.A., 1911, s. 4.
[86] *Lord Waring* v. *London & Manchester Assurance Co. Ltd.* [1935] Ch. 310; *Property & Bloodstock Ltd.* v. *Emerton* [1968] Ch. 94.
[87] *Duke* v. *Robson* [1973] 1 W.L.R. 267.
[88] *Colson* v. *Williams* (1889) 58 L.J.Ch. 539 at 540; *Kennedy* v. *De Trafford* [1897] A.C. 180.
[89] *Warner* v. *Jacob* (1882) 20 Ch.D 220 at 224.
[90] *Kennedy* v. *De Trafford, supra.*
[91] *Tomlin* v. *Luce* (1889) 43 Ch.D. 191 (mortgagee held liable on account of misdescription by auctioneer); *Cuckmere Brick Co. Ltd.* v. *Mutual Finance Ltd.* [1971] Ch. 949.

advertises the property without mentioning that the land has valuable planning permission he will be accountable to the mortgagor for the difference between a proper price and the price obtained.[92] It has been held that he need not advertise the property, or attempt to sell by auction before selling by private contract,[93] or delay a sale so as to obtain a better price,[94] since he is entitled to proceed to a forced sale.[95] His motive for selling, too, such as spite against the mortgagor, has been held immaterial.[96] The House of Lords has even upheld a sale for the exact amount of money due under the mortgage, with costs[97]; but in that case there was no evidence of negligence or undervalue, and the mortgagor delayed for four years before acting. Now that the Court of Appeal has firmly put the law upon the footing that the mortgagee's duty is to take reasonable care to obtain a full price,[1] some of the earlier decisions may need reappraisal, particularly those which suggest that the only duty is to act in good faith and avoid recklessness. The law as now clarified accords with that laid down by statute for building societies, which when selling as mortgagees must take reasonable care to ensure that the price is the best reasonably obtainable.[2]

In any case the sale must be a true sale; a " sale " by the mortgagee to himself, either directly[3] or through an agent,[4] is no true sale and may be set aside[5] or ignored.[6] Thus if the mortgagee sells to himself and later purports to sell as absolute owner, the first sale will be disregarded and so the second will operate as a sale by a mortgagee as such.[7] But there is nothing to prevent a sale to one of two mortgagors being a true sale, and not a mere redemption of the mortgage, even if the price is the exact sum due under the mortgage.[8]

---

[92] *Cuckmere Brick Co. Ltd.* v. *Mutual Finance Ltd., supra* (Salmon L.J. holding that the proper price is the same as the true market value).

[93] *Davey* v. *Durrant* (1857) 1 De G. & J. 535 at 560.

[94] *Ibid.,* at p. 553.

[95] *Farrar* v. *Farrars Ltd.* (1888) 40 Ch.D. 395 at 398. See also *Adams* v. *Scott* (1859) 7 W.R. 213 (property alleged to be worth £20,000 sold for £12,000: sale upheld); *Wright* v. *New Zealand Farmers Co-operative Association of Canterbury Ltd.* [1939] A.C. 439 (rescission and a subsequent sale at a lower price: sale upheld).   [96] *Nash* v. *Eads* (1880) 25 S.J. 95.

[97] *Kennedy* v. *De Trafford* [1897] A.C. 180.

[1] *Cuckmere Brick Co. Ltd.* v. *Mutual Finance Ltd., supra,* explaining *Kennedy* v. *De Trafford, supra.* See also *Holohan* v. *Friends Provident and Century Life Office* [1966] I.R. 1 (duty to act reasonably in selling).

[2] Building Societies Act, 1962, s. 36, replacing earlier legislation; see *Reliance Permanent B. S.* v. *Harwood-Stamper* [1944] Ch. 362.

[3] *Farrar* v. *Farrars Ltd.* (1888) 40 Ch.D. 395 at 409.

[4] *Downes* v. *Grazebrook* (1817) 3 Mer. 200.

[5] And see *Hodson* v. *Deans* [1903] 2 Ch. 647 (sale by auction by mortgagee Friendly Society to one of its trustees who had been concerned with conduct of sale: sale set aside).

[6] *Henderson* v. *Astwood* [1894] A.C. 150.   [7] *Ibid.*

[8] *Kennedy* v. *De Trafford* [1896] 1 Ch. 762 at 776; [1897] A.C. 180.

(*e*) **Proceeds of sale.** Although the mortgagee is not a trustee of his power of sale,[9] he is a trustee of the proceeds of sale.[10] These must be employed in the following order:[11]

(i) in discharge of any prior incumbrances free from which the property was sold;

(ii) in discharge of the expenses of the sale or any attempted sale;

(iii) in discharge of the money due [11a] to the mortgagee under the mortgage [11b]; and

(iv) by paying the balance to the next subsequent incumbrancer or, if none, to the mortgagor.[12]

If the balance is paid to a subsequent incumbrancer, he in turn will hold it on trust to pay his own claim, and pass on the balance, if any. A mortgagee who has a surplus should therefore search in the Land Charges Register [13] to discover the existence of any subsequent mortgagees, for registration is equivalent to notice,[14] and if he pays the money to the mortgagor he will be liable to any mortgagee who is thereby prejudiced.[15] If the rights of all subsequent incumbrancers and the mortgagor have become barred by lapse of time,[16] the mortgagee may retain the money himself.[17] In case of difficulty the money may be paid into court.[18]

(*f*) **Effect of sale.** A sale by a mortgagee under his statutory powers vests the whole estate of the mortgagor, whether it is a fee simple [19] or a term of years,[20] in the purchaser, subject to any prior mortgages, but free from the mortgage of the vendor and all subsequent mortgages, and free from the mortgagor's equity of redemption, which is extinguished. For example, if X has mortgaged

---

[9] *Ante*, p. 911.
[10] L.P.A., 1925, s. 105. And see *Banner* v. *Berridge* (1881) 18 Ch.D. 254 at 269; *Thorne* v. *Heard* [1895] A.C. 495.
[11] L.P.A., 1925, s. 105. See *Re Thompson's Mortgage Trusts* [1920] 1 Ch. 508.
[11a] Including statute-barred arrears of interest: *post*, p. 1033.
[11b] Despite any cross-claim against him by the mortgagor: *Samuel Keller (Holdings) Ltd.* v. *Martins Bank Ltd.* [1971] 1 W.L.R. 43; *Inglis* v. *Commonwealth Trading Bank of Australia Ltd.* (1972) 126 C.L.R. 161 (no injunction to restrain sale).
[12] s. 105 makes the surplus payable "to the person entitled to the mortgaged property." Literally this means the purchaser, but plainly the phrase must be read as "to the person *who immediately before the sale* was entitled to the mortgaged property," *i.e.*, the next mortgagee or the mortgagor: see *British General Insurance Co. Ltd.* v. *Att.-Gen.* [1945] L.J.N.C.C.R. 113 at 115.
[13] *Post*, p. 969.
[14] L.P.A., 1925, s. 198 (1).
[15] *West London Commercial Bank* v. *Reliance Permanent B. S.* (1885) 29 Ch.D. 954.
[16] See *post*, p. 1019.
[17] *Young* v. *Clarey* [1948] Ch. 191.
[18] T.A., 1925, s. 63.
[19] L.P.A., 1925, ss. 88 (1), 104 (1). But see *post*, p. 922.
[20] L.P.A., 1925, ss. 89 (1), 104 (1). See s. 89 (6) as to a sale where the mortgage includes only part of the land which has been leased.

his freehold property successively to A, B and C, and B sells, the purchaser will take the fee simple subject to A's mortgage but free from the claims of B, C and X, which are overreached,[21] *i.e.,* transferred to the purchase-money.

On a sale before 1926 the first mortgagee conveyed the fee simple that was vested in him; after 1925 the mortgagee conveys a fee simple which is not his, by virtue of his statutory power. In the case of leaseholds, before 1926 a mortgage by sub-demise usually included a declaration of trust by the mortgagor of the whole term, and a power for the mortgagee to appoint new trustees in place of the mortgagor, thus enabling the mortgagee to vest the whole term in the purchaser.[22] Such provisions are now unnecessary; and if a licence to assign is required, it must not be unreasonably refused.[23]

(g) *Order for sale.* Quite apart from the mortgagee's power of sale, the court has jurisdiction to order a sale of the mortgaged property on the application of anyone interested either in the mortgage money or in the equity of redemption.[24] The importance of this provision has already been explained.[25] The conduct of the sale is often given to the mortgagor, for this is likely to produce the best price.[26]

3. To take possession

(a) *The right.* Since a legal mortgage gives the mortgagee a legal estate in possession, he is entitled to take possession of the mortgaged property as soon as the mortgage is made, even if the mortgagor is guilty of no default[27]; a legal chargee has a corresponding statutory right.[28] If the property was already let to a tenant before the mortgage was made, or if a subsequent lease is binding on the mortgagee,[29] the mortgagee cannot take physical possession; but he may take possession by directing the tenants to pay their rents to him instead of to the mortgagor.[30] After entry by a

---

21 L.P.A., 1925, s. 2 (1) (iii).
22 See *London & County Banking Co.* v. *Goddard* [1897] 1 Ch. 642, and *cf. post,* p. 923, for a similar device.
23 L.P.A., 1925, s. 89 (1).
24 *Ibid.,* s. 91.
25 *Ante,* p. 907.
26 *Davies* v. *Wright* (1886) 32 Ch.D. 220.
27 *Birch* v. *Wright* (1786) 1 T.R. 378 at 383. The mortgagor thereupon becomes entitled to redeem forthwith without notice: *post,* p. 946.
28 L.P.A., 1925, s. 87 (1).
29 See *post,* p. 933.
30 *Horlock* v. *Smith* (1842) 6 Jur. 478; and see *Heales* v. *M'Murray* (1856) 23 Beav. 401; *cf. Kitchen's Trustee* v. *Madders* [1949] Ch. 588, affd. [1950] Ch. 134.

mortgagee his right to possession dates back to the time at which his legal right to enter accrued. He can therefore bring an action for trespass committed before the entry.[31]

(b) *Mortgagee's liability to account strictly.* A mortgagee's usual object in taking possession is either to sell or to intercept the net rents and profits and so secure punctual payment of interest. The mortgagee may, if he wishes, apply any surplus to paying off the principal debt; but he may, if he prefers, hand it over to the mortgagor, for he cannot be compelled to accept repayment in driblets.[32] What he may not do is to reap any personal advantage beyond what is due to him under the mortgage; for he is liable to account in equity for any such advantage.[33] He is liable to account strictly, " on the footing of wilful default." This means that he must account not only for all that he receives but also for all that he ought to have received, had he managed the property with due diligence.[34] This does not mean that he is bound or allowed to enter into speculation and adventure,[35] but merely that he will be liable for negligence amounting to wilful default.[36]

For example, where the mortgagee was a brewer and the mortgaged property a " free " house, a mortgagee who took possession and let the property as a " tied " house was held liable for the additional rent he would have obtained if he had let the property as a " free " house.[37] If the mortgagee occupies the property himself instead of letting it, he is liable for a fair occupation rent.[38] More usually he will wish to let it; his power to grant binding leases is explained below.[39] The most covenient situation for the mortgagee is where the property is already let, so that he has no responsibility for the amount of the existing rents.

(c) *Powers of mortgagee in possession.* While in possession, a mortgagee whose mortgage was made by deed has a statutory power to cut and sell timber and other trees ripe for cutting which were not planted or left standing for shelter or ornament, or

---

[31] *Ocean Accident and Guarantee Corporation Ltd.* v. *Ilford Gas Co.* [1905] 2 K.B. 493.
[32] *Nelson* v. *Booth* (1858) 3 De G. & J. 119; *Wrigley* v. *Gill* [1905] 1 Ch. 241.
[33] *Ante,* p. 889.
[34] *Chaplin* v. *Young (No. 1)* (1863) 33 Beav. 330 at 337, 338.
[35] *Hughes* v. *Williams* (1806) 12 Ves. 493.
[36] *Ibid.,* at p. 495.
[37] *White* v. *City of London Brewery Co.* (1889) 42 Ch.D. 237. The " tie " was to the mortgagee, but he was held not accountable for the profit on beer sold to the tenant.
[38] *Marriott* v. *Anchor Reversionary Co.* (1861) 3 De G.F. & J. 177 at 193; thus he need pay no rent if the property is too ruinous to be capable of beneficial occupation: *Marshall* v. *Cave* (1824) 3 L.J.(o.s.)Ch. 57.
[39] *Post,* p. 933.

contract for this to be done within twelve months of the contract.[40] Although he is not liable for waste,[41] he will be liable if he improperly cuts timber [42]; and despite his right to work mines already opened,[43] he may not open new mines.[44] But if the property becomes insufficient security for the money due, the court will not interfere if he cuts timber and opens mines, provided he is not guilty of wanton destruction.[45] He must effect reasonable repairs [46] and may without the mortgagor's consent effect reasonable improvements,[47] though not excessive improvements which might cripple the mortgagor's power to redeem [48]; for the cost of the repairs and improvements will be charged to the mortgagor in the accounts.

(*d*) *Relief of mortgagor.* Formerly a mortgagee could obtain summarily an order for possession in the Queen's Bench Division without the matter coming before any judicial officer.[49] But since 1936, when the jurisdiction to hear mortgagees' claims for possession was transferred from the King's Bench to the Chancery Division,[50] the court has assumed a discretionary jurisdiction [51] to refuse an immediate order for possession, whether the proceedings were commenced by writ [52] or originating summons.[53] Under this jurisdiction, a short adjournment may be granted in order to give the mortgagor a chance of paying off the mortgagee in full, or otherwise satisfying him; but if there is no reasonable prospect of this, an adjournment will be refused.[54] It has been suggested that such adjournments will be granted only in cases where (as is common in building society

---

40 L.P.A., 1925, s. 101 (1), replacing C.A., 1881, s. 19 (1). Previously this was allowed in equity only where the security was insufficient.

41 Before 1926 he held the legal fee simple and so was not liable for waste; after 1925 he holds a term of years, normally without impeachment of waste: see L.P.A., 1925, ss. 85 (2), 86 (2), 87 (1), 1st Sched., Pt. VII, paras. 1, 2.

42 *Withrington* v. *Banks* (1725) Ca.t.King 30.

43 *Elias* v. *Snowden Slate Quarries Co.* (1879) 4 App.Cas. 454.

44 *Millett* v. *Davey* (1863) 31 Beav. 470 at 475.

45 *Ibid.*, at p. 476.

46 *Richards* v. *Morgan* (1753) 4 Y. & C. Ex. 570.

47 *Shepard* v. *Jones* (1882) 21 Ch.D. 469 at 479.

48 *Sandon* v. *Hooper* (1843) 6 Beav. 246, affirmed 14 L.J.Ch. 120.

49 *Redditch Benefit B. S.* v. *Roberts* [1940] Ch. 415 at 420.

50 See R.S.C., Ord. 88, rr. 1, 2, replacing R.S.C. 1883, Ord. 55, rr. 5a, 5c; *Norwich Union Life Insurance Society* v. *Preston* [1957] 1 W.L.R. 813.

51 See R.S.C., Ord. 88, r. 7.

52 *Ibid.*

53 *Redditch Benefit B. S.* v. *Roberts, supra,* at p. 421. The benefits of the procedure by originating summons are thus described at p. 420, *per* Clauson L.J.: " the facts and the circumstances of the case were brought before the court, and in proper cases the wind was tempered to the shorn lamb, time being given for payment and so forth."

54 *Hinckley and South Leicestershire Permanent Benefit B. S.* v. *Freeman* [1941] Ch. 32; *Robertson* v. *Cilia* [1956] 1 W.L.R. 1502; *Braithwaite* v. *Winwood* [1960] 1 W.L.R. 1257; *Birmingham Citizens Permanent B. S.* v. *Caunt* [1962] Ch. 883 (reviewing the cases). See (1962) 78 L.Q.R. 171 (R.E.M.).

mortgages) the capital is repayable by instalments currently with the interest, and the mortgagee undertakes not to go into possession so long as the payments are punctually made [55]; but later decisions have thrown doubt on this notion.[56] The precise limits of the court's inherent discretion are at present obscure.

A wide statutory discretion has, however, been given to the court in cases where the property consists of or includes a dwelling-house. The court may then adjourn the proceedings, or suspend execution of its order, or postpone the date for delivery of possession as it thinks fit.[57] But it may do so only where it appears that " the mortgagor is likely to be able within a reasonable period to pay any sums due under the mortgage " or to remedy any default. In the case of an instalment mortgage the " sums due " are merely any instalments in arrear and not the whole capital sum, even if (as is usual) the mortgage makes this payable on any default by the mortgagor [58]; but the court's powers are exercisable only if there is a likelihood of the mortgagor being able by the end of the " reasonable period " also to pay any further instalments then due.[59] Where the mortgage is of this type the court's discretionary powers extend also to foreclosure actions, whether or not possession is sought in the same proceedings.[60]

A summons for possession need be served only on the mortgagor and any other person in possession who claims a right to possession as against the mortgagee.[60a]

(e) *Attornment clause.* Many mortgages contain an attornment clause, whereby the mortgagor attorns, or acknowledges himself to be, a tenant at will or from year to year of the mortgagee, usually at a nominal rent such as a peppercorn or fivepence.[61] Formerly this was inserted because a speedy procedure was available to enable landlords to recover possession of the demised property from their tenants, and no such procedure was available for mere mortgagees; the attornment clause enabled mortgagees to sue for

---

[55] *Four-Maids Ltd.* v. *Dudley Marshall (Properties) Ltd.* [1957] Ch. 317; 73 L.Q.R. 300 (R.E.M.).

[56] *Braithwaite* v. *Winwood, supra*; *Birmingham Citizens Permanent B. S.* v. *Caunt, supra*.

[57] Administration of Justice Act 1970, s. 36.

[58] Administration of Justice Act 1973, s. 8 (1). See also *First Middlesbrough Trading and Mortgage Co. Ltd.* v. *Cunningham* (1974) 28 P. & C.R. 69, not following *Halifax B. S.* v. *Clark* [1973] Ch. 307.

[59] Administration of Justice Act 1973, s. 8 (2).

[60] *Ibid.*, s. 8 (3).

[60a] Despite the repeal of R.S.C., 1883, Ord. 55, r. 5B, *Alliance B. S.* v. *Yap* [1962] 1 W.L.R. 857 and *Brighton & Shoreham B. S.* v. *Hollingdale* [1965] 1 W.L.R. 376 (deserted wife) are probably still good law.

[61] See *Woolwich Equitable B. S.* v. *Preston* [1938] Ch. 129.

possession *qua* landlords.[62] But changes in the rules of court in 1933, 1936 and 1937 [63] made a speedy procedure available to mortgagees as such,[64] and there now seems to be no substantial advantage in an attornment clause. It is true that when any rent was less than £20 a year (as it usually was) possession could be recovered quickly and cheaply by the mortgagee *qua* landlord before Petty Sessions under the Small Tenements Recovery Act, 1838 [65]; but that Act is now repealed.[66]

Despite earlier doubts, it has now been established that an attornment clause still effectually creates the relationship of landlord and tenant.[67] Nevertheless, the substance of the transaction is a mortgage to which the attornment clause is merely ancillary; and so the resulting tenancy has been held to be outside statutes such as the Rent Acts [68] and the Agricultural Holdings Act, 1948,[69] which are intended to protect those who in substance are tenants. But in other respects the general law of landlord and tenant applies. Thus if the mortgagee wishes to take possession, he must first determine the tenancy by proper notice,[70] unless (as is often the case) the attornment clause creates a mere tenancy at will, or makes the tenancy determinable without notice, *e.g.*, upon default being made by the mortgagor.[71] Similarly a mere tenancy at will determines automatically as soon as the mortgagor assigns his interest.[72] But in other cases the assignee will be bound by the tenancy and by covenants which run with it under the ordinary rules.[73] There is, in fact, a duality of positions: under the tenancy arising from the mortgage or charge the mortgagor is the landlord and the mortgagee the tenant, whereas under the sub-tenancy created by the attornment clause their positions are reversed. Nevertheless, any covenants by

---

62 *Mumford* v. *Collier* (1888) 21 Q.B.D. 384. For an earlier reason and its Waterloo, see *Re Willis* (1888) 21 Q.B.D. 384.
63 R.S.C., 1933, No. 1; 1936, No. 3; 1937, No. 1.
64 R.S.C., Ord. 85, r. 1.
65 *Dudley and District Benefit B. S.* v. *Gordon* [1929] 2 K.B. 105.
66 Rent Act 1965, s. 52 (1) and 7th Sched., Pt. II; S.I. 1972 No. 1161.
67 *Regent Oil Co. Ltd.* v. *J. A. Gregory (Hatch End) Ltd.* [1966] Ch. 402.
68 *Portman B. S.* v. *Young* [1951] 1 All E.R. 191. See now in particular the Rent Act 1965, s. 32, protecting tenants of dwellings from eviction except as against a mortgagee on whom their tenancy is not binding: *ante*, p. 684. And see s. 31 (*ante*, p. 657).
69 *Steyning and Littlehampton B. S.* v. *Wilson* [1951] Ch. 1018; and see (1952) 68 L.Q.R. 23; (1958) 74 L.Q.R. 348 (R.E.M.); *Ex p. Isherwood* (1882) 22 Ch.D. 384; *Alliance B. S.* v *Pinwill* [1958] Ch. 788.
70 *Hinckley and Country B. S.* v. *Henny* [1953] 1 W.L.R. 352.
71 See, *e.g.*, *Woolwich Equitable B. S.* v. *Preston* [1938] Ch. 129, where it is said that the issue of a summons for possession takes effect as a re-entry and turns the tenancy into a tenancy at will, and the service of the summons terminates the tenancy at will.
72 *Regent Oil Co. Ltd* v. *J. A. Gregory (Hatch End) Ltd.* [1966] Ch. 402 at 429, 438; *ante*, p. 639.
73 *Regent Oil Co. Ltd.* v. *J. A. Gregory (Hatch End) Ltd.* [1966] Ch. 402.

the mortgagor in the mortgage relating to the premises (*e.g.*, to repair them, or not to use them for certain purposes) are enforceable against the assignee from the mortgagor, for they touch and concern the land and so bind him, whether the mortgagee is enforcing them *qua* tenant or *qua* sub-landlord.[74]

(*f*) *Limitation.* If a mortgagee remains in possession of the mortgaged land for twelve years without acknowledging the mortgagor's title or receiving any payment of principal or interest from him, the right to redeem the land is extinguished[75] and the mortgagee acquires a title to the land.

4. To appoint a receiver

(*a*) *History.* In order to avoid the responsibilities of taking possession and yet achieve substantially the same result, well-drawn mortgages used to provide for the appointment of a receiver with extensive powers of management of the mortgaged property. Thus the mortgagee, without taking possession himself, could ensure that the property was efficiently managed and that his claim for interest was made a first charge on the net rents and profits. At first the appointment was made by the mortgagor at the request of the mortgagee; but subsequently mortgagees began to reserve a power for themselves, acting in theory as agents for the mortgagor, to appoint a receiver.[76] In such circumstances the receiver was, by the terms of the power, deemed the agent of the mortgagor,[77] and the mortgagee was not liable to account strictly in the same way as would have been the case if he had taken possession or the receiver had been his agent.[78] Lord Cranworth's Act, 1860,[79] gave a somewhat unsatisfactory statutory power to appoint a receiver, but the Conveyancing Act, 1881,[80] (now replaced by the Law of Property Act, 1925[81]) conferred a power which satisfies most mortgagees.

Compared with taking possession, the appointment of a receiver has one minor disadvantage: lapse of time may confer a title to the land upon a mortgagee in possession,[82] but not upon a mortgagee who has appointed a receiver.

[74] *Ibid.*
[75] Limitation Act, 1939, s. 12 (and see s. 23 (3) as to the date from which time runs); *Young* v. *Clarey* [1948] Ch. 191. For the law of limitation, see *post*, p. 1019.
[76] *Gaskell* v. *Gosling* [1896] 1 Q.B. 669 at 692.
[77] *Jefferys* v. *Dickson* (1866) 1 Ch.App. 183 at 190; and see *Lever Finance Ltd.* v. *Needlemans' Trustee* [1956] Ch. 375 at 382.
[78] *Ante*, p. 914.
[79] 23 & 24 Vict. c. 145, ss. 17–23. This still applies to mortgages made between August 28, 1860, and 1882. In earlier mortgages there is no power to appoint a receiver unless the mortgage contains an express power.
[80] s. 19.
[81] s. 101 (1) (iii).
[82] *Supra.*

(*b*) *The power*. The statutory power to appoint a receiver arises and becomes exercisable in the same circumstances as the power of sale.[83] A mortgagee has power to appoint a receiver provided—

   (i) his mortgage was made by deed; and
   (ii) the mortgage money is due.[84]

But this power is not exercisable until one of the three events set out on page 910 has occurred,[85] although persons paying money to the receiver are not bound to see that his appointment has been thereby justified.[1] A mortgagee who is in possession is not thereby debarred from appointing a receiver.[2]

The statutory power to appoint a receiver usually makes it unnecessary to apply to the court for a receiver, although since the Judicature Act, 1873,[3] the court has had jurisdiction to make the appointment on such terms as it thinks just in all cases in which it appears to be just or convenient so to do.[4] Formerly the court would usually refuse to appoint a receiver at the instance of a mortgagee who could help himself by taking possession.[5]

(*c*) *Procedure*. The mortgagee must make the appointment by writing,[6] and may remove or replace the receiver in the same way.[7] Though appointed by, and for the benefit of, the mortgagee,[8] the receiver is deemed to be the agent of the mortgagor, who is solely responsible for his acts unless the mortgage otherwise provides,[9] or the mortgagee represents him as being his agent.[10] The receiver has power to recover the income of the property by action, distress or otherwise, and to give valid receipts for it.[11] If the mortgagee so directs in writing, the receiver must insure the property against fire to the same extent as the mortgagee might have insured,[12] and the mortgagee may by writing delegate his powers of leasing [13] and accepting surrenders of leases.[14]

(*d*) *Application of receipts*. The money received by the receiver must be applied in the following order [15]:

[83] *Ante*, p. 909.
[85] *Ibid.*, s. 109 (1).
[2] *Refuge Assurance Co. Ltd.* v. *Pearlberg* [1938] Ch. 687.
[3] See *Re Pope* (1886) 17 Q.B.D. 743 at 749.
[4] J.A., 1925, s. 45 (1), (2), replacing J.A., 1873, s. 25 (8).
[5] *Berney* v. *Sewell* (1820) 1 J. & W. 647; *Sollory* v. *Leaver* (1869) L.R. 9 Eq 22 at 25.
[6] L.P.A., 1925, s. 109 (1).
[7] *Ibid.*, s. 109 (5).
[8] See *Re B. Johnson & Co. (Builders) Ltd.* [1955] Ch. 634 at 644.
[9] L.P.A., 1925, s. 109 (2).
[10] *Chatsworth Properties Ltd.* v. *Effiom* [1971] 1 W.L.R. 144.
[11] L.P.A., 1925, s. 109 (3).
[12] *Ibid.*, s. 109 (7).
[14] *Ibid.*, s. 100 (13). For these powers, see *post*, pp. 933, 936.
[15] L.P.A., 1925, s. 109 (8).

[84] L.P.A., 1925, s. 101 (1) (iii).
[1] *Ibid.*, s. 109 (4).
[13] *Ibid.*, s. 99 (19).

(i) In discharge of rents, rates and taxes.

(ii) In keeping down annual sums and the interest on principal sums having priority to the mortgage.

(iii) In payment of his commission and insurance premiums and, if so directed in writing by the mortgagee, the cost of repairs. His commission is five per cent. on the gross sum received unless his appointment specifies less or the court otherwise directs.[16]

(iv) In payment of the interest under the mortgage.

(v) If the mortgagee so directs in writing, towards the discharge of the principal money lent; otherwise it must be paid to the person who would have received it if the receiver had not been appointed, *i.e.*, normally the mortgagor.

The mortgagee's remedies are cumulative. A mortgagee is not bound to select any one of his remedies and pursue that exclusively: subject to his not recovering more than is due to him, he may employ any or all of the remedies to enforce payment.[17] If he sells the property for less than the mortgage debt, he may still sue the mortgagor upon the personal covenant for payment of the balance,[18] and the same applies on a sale by the court, even if the mortgagee, with the leave of the court, has bought the property at the sale and later resold it at an increased price.[1] If he takes possession, he is not thereby prevented from appointing a receiver.[2]

Foreclosure, however, puts an end to other remedies, since if the mortgagee takes the whole security he cannot also claim payment. He may therefore sue on the personal covenant only if he opens the foreclosure, so that the mortgagor, if he can pay, may also redeem.[3] The mortgagor thus has the option of either paying the whole of the mortgage debt and recovering his property, or paying the difference between the mortgage debt and the value of the property and losing the property. If by disposing of the property after foreclosure (*e.g.*, by selling it) the mortgagee has put it out of his power to reopen the foreclosure, he can no longer sue upon the personal covenant,[4] even though the proceeds of sale are less than the amount of the debt.[5] Further, a foreclosure order nisi

---

[16] L.P.A., 1925, s. 109 (6).
[17] *Palmer* v. *Hendrie* (1859) 27 Beav. 349 at 351.
[18] *Rudge* v. *Richens* (1873) L.R. 8 C.P. 358.
[1] *Gordon Grant & Co. Ltd.* v. *Boos* [1926] A.C. 781.
[2] *Refuge Assurance Co. Ltd.* v. *Pearlberg* [1938] Ch. 687.
[3] *Perry* v. *Barker* (1806) 13 Ves. 198.
[4] *Palmer* v. *Hendrie* (1859) 27 Beav. 349.
[5] *Lockhart* v. *Hardy* (1846) 9 Beav. 349.

suspends the power of sale, and the mortgagee must obtain the leave of the court if he wishes to sell.[6] But a bona fide purchaser without notice gets a good title.[7]

II. EQUITABLE MORTGAGEE

The extent to which the foregoing remedies are exercisable by an equitable mortgagee is as follows.

1. To foreclose. Foreclosure is the primary remedy of an equitable mortgagee. Since he has no legal estate the court's order absolute will direct the mortgagor to convey the land to the mortgagee unconditionally, *i.e.*, free from any right to redeem.[8] It is immaterial whether his mortgage is made merely by deposit of title deeds[9] or is accompanied by a written memorandum.[10]

2. To sell. The statutory power of sale[11] applies only where the mortgage was made by deed[12]; other mortgagees have no power of sale. For this reason, as already mentioned, many equitable mortgages are made by deed, and mortgages by deposit of title deeds are accompanied by a memorandum under seal. But even then there may be a difficulty, for the statutory power to sell " the mortgaged property "[13] has been held to empower the mortgagee to sell only the interest which he has, *i.e.*, the equitable interest[14]; in other words, the power is a power over the equity of redemption and not a power over the legal estate if vested in some other person. But this narrow interpretation has been doubted.[15] Since of course the power of sale is of little value unless it extends to the legal estate, it is often so extended by either or both of two conveyancing devices—

  (a) *Power of attorney*: a power of attorney[16] is inserted in the deed empowering the mortgagee or his assigns[17] to convey

---

6 *Stevens* v. *Theatres Ltd.* [1903] 1 Ch. 857.   7 *Ibid.*

8 *James* v. *James* (1873) L.R. 16 Eq. 153.

9 *Backhouse* v. *Charlton* (1878) 8 Ch.D. 444.

10 *York Union Banking Co.* v. *Artley* (1879) 11 Ch.D. 205.

11 *Ante*, p. 909.

12 L.P.A., 1925, s. 101 (1).

13 *Ibid.*, s. 101 (1) (i).

14 *Re Hodson & Howes' Contract* (1887) 35 Ch.D. 668. It was otherwise in the case of mortgages to which Lord Cranworth's Act, 1860, applied: *Re Solomon & Meagher's Contract* (1889) 40 Ch.D. 508; and see *Re Boucherett* [1908] 1 Ch. 180 at 184.

15 *Re White Rose Cottage* [1965] Ch. 940 at 951, *per* Lord Denning M.R., invoking the contrast in wording between C.A., 1881, s. 21 (1), and L.P.A., 1925, s. 104 (1). Yet the phrase relied on (" the subject of the mortgage ") is the same in each subsection.

16 These powers are now regulated by the Powers of Attorney Act 1971.

17 L.P.A., 1925, s. 128.

the legal estate.[18] This power, being given for value, may be made irrevocable in perpetuity in favour of a purchaser, and so will not be affected by any act of the mortgagor, or by his death.[19]

(b) *Declaration of trust*: a clause is inserted in the deed whereby the mortgagor declares that he holds the legal estate on trust for the mortgagee and empowers the mortgagee to appoint himself or his nominee as trustee in place of the mortgagor.[20] The mortgagee can in this way vest the legal estate in himself or a purchaser.[21]

In the case of an equitable mortgage not made by deed (for example, an informal mortgage by deposit of deeds) there is no power of sale out of court. But the court has power to order a sale [22] on the application of either party, and to vest a legal term of years in the mortgagee, so that he can sell as if he were a legal mortgagee.[23]

3. To take possession

(a) *The right*. It is generally said that an equitable mortgagee has no right to take possession.[24] Certainly he has none at law, for he has no legal estate. But in equity he should be entitled to the same rights as if he had a legal mortgage, and there would seem to be no reason why he should not take possession under the doctrine of *Walsh* v. *Lonsdale*,[25] for the basis of an equitable mortgage is the creation of the relationship of mortgagor and mortgagee forthwith, rather than a mere contract for a future mortgage.[26] The court may, in any case, award him possession [27]; and there is some authority which indicates that he may take possession

---

[18] In *Re White Rose Cottage, supra*, the property was in fact sold by the mortgagor, with a release of the mortgage by the mortgagee; the conveyance was validly executed by the mortgagee but as attorney for the mortgagor.

[19] L.P.A., 1925, s. 126.

[20] See *London & County Banking Co.* v. *Goddard* [1897] 1 Ch. 642.

[21] Under T.A., 1925, s. 40; see *ante*, p. 458.

[22] L.P.A., 1925, s. 91 (2); *ante*, p. 908; *Oldham* v. *Stringer* (1884) 51 L.T. 895.

[23] L.P.A., 1925, ss. 90, 91 (7).

[24] Coote, *Mortgages*, 823; Waldock, *Mortgages*, 235; Halsb. xxvii, 277; and see *Barclays Bank Ltd.* v. *Bird* [1954] Ch. 274 at 280. But no satisfactory authority is cited; see (1954) 70 L.Q.R. 161 (R.E.M.). *Garfitt* v. *Allen* (1887) 37 Ch.D. 48 is a case of charge, not mortgage, and a chargee plainly has no right to take possession. Since the Judicature Acts, 1873–1875, an action for the recovery of land will not be defeated merely for want of the legal estate: *General Finance Mortgage and Discount Co.* v. *Liberator Permanent Benefit B. S.* (1878) 10 Ch.D. 15 at 24; *Re O'Neill* [1967] N.I. 129. For fuller discussion see (1955) 71 L.Q.R. 204 (H.W.R.W.).

[25] (1882) 21 Ch.D. 9; *ante*, p. 625.   [26] See *ante*, p. 901.

[27] *Barclays Bank Ltd.* v. *Bird, supra*; *Re O'Neill, supra*.

in his own right,[28] as in principle one would expect. He may certainly do so if the agreement so provides.[29]

(b) *Collection of rents.* What the mortgagee cannot do without an order of the court [30] is to collect the rents if the land is let [31]; but the true reason for this disability is that rent is payable to the legal reversioner, and that an equitable assignment of the reversion does not create the legal relationship of landlord and tenant (*i.e.*, privity of estate, or tenure) upon which the right to receive rent depends.[32] It does not follow that, because an equitable mortgagee is not entitled to demand rent as against a tenant, he is not entitled to possession as against the mortgagor. For the effect of the contract in equity, as between the contracting parties, is something quite different from its effect upon third parties such as tenants.[33]

(c) *Possible implied term.* The only possible basis for the rule, as commonly stated, that an equitable mortgagee has no right to possession would seem to be an implied term in the contract; it might be said that a contract for a mortgage does not contemplate giving possession to the mortgagee, as contrasted with a contract for a lease, which contemplates possession by the tenant. But there seems to be no authority, and no evident necessity, for implying such a term, nor would it accord with the decisions.[34]

4. To appoint a receiver. An equitable mortgagee has always had the right to have a receiver appointed by the court in a proper case,[35] *e.g.*, when interest is in arrear.[36] If his mortgage is by deed he has also the statutory power,[37] which is more convenient since there is no need to apply to the court.

[28] *Ex p. Bignold* (1834) 4 Deac. & Ch. 259, *per* Erskine C.J. (*contra* the opinion of Sir G. Rose); *Re Gordon* (1889) 61 L.T. 299; *Tichborne* v. *Weir* (1892) 67 L.T. 735; *Antrim County Land Building and Investment Co. Ltd.* v. *Stewart* [1904] 2 I.R. 357 (the judgment of Palles C.B. is particularly helpful); *Spencer* v. *Mason* (1931) 75 S.J. 295. See (1955) 71 L.Q.R. 204 (H.W.R.W.).
[29] *Ocean Accident & Guarantee Corporation Ltd.* v. *Ilford Gas Co.* [1905] 2 K.B. 493.
[30] The court's order is for the appointment of a receiver by way of equitable execution: *Vacuum Oil Co. Ltd.* v. *Ellis* [1914] 1 K.B. 693 at 703. For the appointment of a receiver, see below.
[31] *Re Pearson* (1838) 3 Mont. & A. 592; *Finck* v. *Tranter* [1905] 1 K.B. 427; *Vacuum Oil Co. Ltd.* v. *Ellis* [1914] 1 K.B. 693, where the dicta should probably be limited to the points which were before the court, *i.e.*, that there was no right to possession as against a prior tenant in possession, and no legal title to the rents.
[32] *Cox* v. *Bishop* (1857) 8 De G.M. & G. 815; *Friary Holroyd & Healey's Breweries Ltd.* v. *Singleton* [1899] 1 Ch. 86 at 90 (reversed on the facts [1899] 2 Ch. 261); and see *ante*, pp. 689, 721.
[33] *Ante*, p. 627.
[34] See n. 28, *supra.*
[35] J.A., 1925, s. 45, replacing J.A., 1873, s. 25 (8). Previously there was equitable jurisdiction to the same effect: *ante*, p. 920.
[36] *Shakel* v. *Duke of Marlborough* (1819) 4 Madd. 463.
[37] L.P.A., 1925, s. 101 (1) (iii); *ante*, p. 919.

III. EQUITABLE CHARGEE

The primary remedies of an equitable chargee are to apply to the court for an order for sale or for the appointment of a receiver.[38] But since the statutory definition of a mortgage extends to a charge,[39] an equitable chargee *by deed* is in the same position as an equitable mortgagee as regards sale or the appointment of a receiver out of court. An equitable chargee can neither foreclose [40] nor take possession,[41] since he has neither a legal estate nor the benefit of a contract to create one.

B. *Other Rights of a Mortgagee*

Certain other rights of a mortgagee must now be considered. The law is in general the same for both mortgages or charges, whether legal or equitable, and " mortgage " will accordingly be used hereafter to include all such incumbrances unless the contrary is indicated.

1. Right to fixtures. It is a question of construction to decide what property is included in a mortgage. Subject to any contrary intention, a mortgage includes all fixtures attached to the land either at the date of the mortgage or thereafter [42]; the power to remove certain fixtures which is allowed to tenants [43] is not allowed to mortgagors.

2. Right to possession of the title deeds. We have already seen that a first mortgagee has the same right to the title deeds as if he had the fee simple or an assignment of the lease which has been mortgaged, as the case may be [44]; but notwithstanding any contrary agreement, the mortgagor is entitled to inspect and make copies of the deeds at reasonable times and on payment of the mortgagee's costs.[45] If the mortgage is redeemed by the mortgagor, the mortgagee must deliver the deeds to him,[46] unless he has notice of some subsequent incumbrance, in which case the deeds should be delivered to the incumbrancer next in order of priority of whom the mortgagee has notice.[47]

---

[38] *Tennant* v. *Trenchard* (1869) 4 Ch.App. 537; *Re Owen* [1894] 3 Ch. 220.
[39] L.P.A., 1925, s. 205 (1) (xvi).
[40] *Tennant* v. *Trenchard, supra,* at p. 542; *Re Lloyd* [1903] 1 Ch. 385 at 404.
[41] *Garfitt* v. *Allen* (1887) 37 Ch.D. 48 at 50.
[42] *Ante,* p. 718.
[43] *Ante,* p. 715.
[44] *Ante,* p. 898.
[45] L.P.A., 1925, s. 96 (1), replacing C.A., 1881, s. 16.
[46] See *James* v. *Rumsey* (1879) 11 Ch.D. 398.
[47] See *Corbett* v. *National Provident Institution* (1900) 17 T.L.R. 5.

Contrary to the general rule that registration is notice, registration under the Land Charges Act 1972 or in a local register is not deemed to be notice for this purpose.[48] The mortgagee accordingly need not make a search before returning the deeds, although, as has been seen, a mortgagee is bound to search before he distributes any surplus after a sale.[49] If a mortgage becomes statute-barred by lapse of time,[50] the mortgagee must return the deeds even if no part of the mortgage debt has been or will be paid.[51]

3. Right to insure against fire at the mortgagor's expense. This enables the mortgagee to protect the value of his security. It used to be incorporated expressly, but is now imported[52] by the Law of Property Act, 1925,[53] into every mortgage made by deed. The mortgagee is empowered to insure the mortgaged property against fire and charge the premiums on the property in the same way as the money lent.[54] The power is exercisable as soon as the mortgage is made.[55] The amount of the insurance must not exceed the amount specified in the deed, or, if none, two-thirds of the amount required to restore the property in case of total destruction.[56] But the mortgagee cannot exercise his power if—

(i) the mortgage deed declares that no insurance is required; or

(ii) the mortgagor keeps up an insurance in accordance with the mortgage deed (as is very often stipulated); or

(iii) the mortgage deed is silent as to insurance and the mortgagor keeps up an insurance to the amount authorised by the Act with the mortgagee's consent.[57]

If the mortgagor insures on his own account and not under these provisions, the mortgagee has no right to the policy money.[58]

4. Right to consolidate

(a) *The right.* Consolidation may be described as the right of a person in whom two or more mortgages are vested to refuse to

---

[48] L.P.A., 1925, s. 96 (2), added by L.P.(Am.)A., 1926, Sched. For another case where registration does not constitute notice, see *post*, p. 984.
[49] *Ante*, p. 913.
[50] See *post*, p. 1019.
[51] *Lewis* v. *Plunket* [1937] Ch. 306.
[52] Subject to the provisions of the mortgage: L.P.A., 1925, s. 101 (3), (4).
[53] L.P.A., 1925, ss. 101 (1) (ii), 108, replacing C.A., 1881, ss. 19 (1) (ii), 23.
[54] The premiums are only a charge on the property; they cannot be recovered from the mortgagor as a debt: Halsb. xxvii, 208.
[55] L.P.A., 1925, s. 101 (1) (ii).
[56] *Ibid.*, s. 108 (1).
[57] *Ibid.*, s. 108 (2).
[58] *Halifax B. S.* v. *Keighley* [1931] 2 K.B. 248.

allow one mortgage to be redeemed unless the other or others are also redeemed. If A has mortgaged both Blackacre and Whiteacre to X, each property being worth £1,500 and each loan being £1,000, it would be unfair, if the value of Blackacre subsequently sinks to £500 and the value of Whiteacre doubles, to allow A to redeem Whiteacre and leave Blackacre unredeemed. In such a case equity permits X to consolidate, and so oblige A to redeem both mortgages or neither. In seeking redemption after the legal date for redemption has passed, A is asking for the assistance of equity, and equity puts its own price upon its interference [59]: he who seeks equity must do equity.[60] This is a notable case of equity restricting rather than extending the right to redeem. Even more remarkably, the mortgagee is allowed to consolidate even though each property is still sufficient security for its debt. What was originally a principle of equity is now an automatic right. Even a mortgagee who is foreclosing may insist upon it.[61]

(b) *Conditions of exercise.* The principle of consolidation has been elaborated to some extent, particularly with regard to third parties, *e.g.,* where one of the properties is sold subject to its mortgage, or one of the mortgages is transferred. The rules on the subject are now that there can be no consolidation unless each of the following four conditions is satisfied.

(1) RESERVATION OF RIGHT: either both the mortgages must have been made before 1882 or one of the mortgage deeds must show an intent [62] to allow consolidation.[63]   Before 1882 the right to consolidate existed automatically, provided the other conditions were satisfied; but the Conveyancing Act, 1881,[64] made it necessary to reserve the right. The Law of Property Act, 1925,[65] has in substance re-enacted this provision by excluding consolidation unless all the mortgages were made before 1882, or unless a contrary intention is expressed in the " mortgage deeds or one of them " [66]; these last words perhaps confine consolidation to cases where each mortgage (or possibly one of the mortgages) is by deed. It is common practice for a mortgage to contain a clause excluding this restriction on consolidation.

(2) REDEMPTION DATES PASSED: in the case of both mortgages, the legal dates for redemption must have passed.[67] Consolidation

---

[59] *Cummins* v. *Fletcher* (1880) 14 Ch.D. 699 at 708.
[60] *Willic* v. *Lugg* (1761) 2 Eden 78 at 80.
[61] *Cummins* v. *Fletcher* (1880) 14 Ch.D. 699.
[62] See *Hughes* v. *Britannia Permanent Benefit B. S.* [1906] 2 Ch. 607.
[63] C.A., 1881, s. 17 (2), replaced by L.P.A., 1925, s. 93 (1); *Re Salmon* [1903] 1 K.B. 147.
[65] s. 93.   [64] s. 17.
[66] s. 93 (1).
                                              [67] *Cummins* v. *Fletcher, supra.*

is an equitable doctrine and does not override the legal right to redeem on the date agreed.

(3) SAME MORTGAGOR: both mortgages must have been made by the same mortgagor.[68] Mortgages made by different mortgagors can never be consolidated, even if both properties later come into the same hands. This is so even if X makes one mortgage and Y, as trustee for X, makes the other,[69] or if A makes one mortgage and A and B jointly make the other.[70] But it is immaterial whether or not the mortgages were made to the same mortgagees.

(4) SIMULTANEOUS UNIONS OF MORTGAGES AND EQUITIES: there must have been a time when both the mortgages were vested in one person and simultaneously both the equities of redemption were vested in another.[71] If this state of affairs once existed, it is immaterial that the equities of redemption have subsequently become vested in different persons. The one exception is where consolidation is based on an express contractual right to consolidate, and not merely on the equitable doctrine. In such a case, a purchaser of the equity of redemption takes subject to the risk of the consolidation of mortgages subsequently created by the mortgagor,[72] except where the mortgagee had notice of the purchase before making the subsequent loans.[73] As for the mortgagee, both mortgages must be vested in him when he seeks to consolidate, so that there can be no consolidation if one is vested in him solely and the other jointly.[74]

(c) *Examples.* There is no need to illustrate (1) and (2), but the following examples may be given of the operation of (3) and (4).

(i)

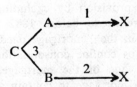

This represents the following steps:

    (a) A mortgages one property to X.
    (b) B mortgages another property to X.
    (c) C purchases the equities of redemption of both properties.

---

[68] *Sharp* v. *Rickards* [1909] 1 Ch. 109.
[69] *Re Raggett* (1880) 16 Ch.D. 117 at 119.
[70] *Thorneycroft* v. *Crockett* (1848) 2 H.L.C. 239; *Cummins* v. *Fletcher* (1880) 14 Ch.D. 699 at 710.   [71] See *Pledge* v. *White* [1896] A.C. 187 at 198.
[72] *Andrew* v. *City Permanent Benefit B. S.* (1881) 44 L.T. 641; *sed quaere.*
[73] *Hughes* v. *Britannia Permanent Benefit B. S.* [1906] 2 Ch. 607, borrowing from the law of tacking (*post*, p. 981).   [74] *Riley* v. *Hall* (1898) 79 L.T. 244.

There can be no consolidation here, even though condition (4) is satisfied, for the mortgages were made by different mortgagors.

(ii)

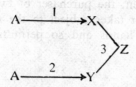

(a) A mortgages one property to X.
(b) A mortgages another property to Y.
(c) Z purchases both mortgages.

Here Z can consolidate, provided conditions (1) and (2) are satisfied. Condition (3) is satisfied, and so is condition (4). Similarly X could consolidate if he acquired Y's mortgage, or Y if he acquired X's.

(iii)

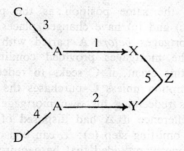

(a) A mortgages one property to X.
(b) A mortgages another property to Y.
(c) C purchases the first property.
(d) D purchases the second property.
(e) Z purchases both mortgages.

There can be no consolidation here, for condition (4) is not satisfied. It is true that at one stage (after step (b)), both equities were in one person's hands, and that at another stage (step (e)) both mortgages were in another person's hands; but at no one moment have both these conditions obtained. The equities of redemption separated before the mortgages came together.[75] The result would be the same if only one of the properties had been

[75] *Harter* v. *Coleman* (1882) 19 Ch.D. 630; *Minter* v. *Carr* [1894] 3 Ch. 498. *Beevor* v. *Luck* (1867) L.R. 4 Eq. 537 is no longer law.

sold (*e.g.*, if step (d) were omitted), since it would be equally true that the equities were separated before the mortgages were united.

If C instead of D had purchased the second property, Z could have consolidated, even though at the time of C's purchase no right to consolidate had arisen; the purchaser of two or more properties from a single mortgagor takes subject to the risk of the mortgages coming into the same hands and so permitting consolidation.[76]

(iv)

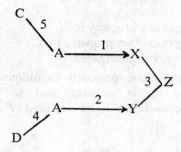

This represents the same position as the previous example, except that steps (c) and (e) have changed places. As Z has now purchased both mortgages *before* A parted with either equity, Z may consolidate the mortgages provided conditions (1) and (2) are satisfied. In this event, if C seeks to redeem his mortgage, Z can refuse redemption unless C purchases the mortgage on D's property as well as redeeming his own mortgage.[77] Here again it would make no difference if A had disposed of only one of the properties, *e.g.*, by omitting step (e): Z can consolidate against the owner of either property provided that he acquired both mortgages while both equities of redemption were still in A's hands.[77]

(*d*) *Three or more mortgages.* These rules of consolidation apply equally when it is sought to consolidate more than two mortgages. Sometimes it will be found that while mortgage I can be consolidated with mortgages II and III, there is no right to consolidate mortgages II and III with each other, *e.g.*, if only mortgage I contains a consolidation clause. Examples containing more than two mortgages are best worked out by taking the mortgages in pairs and applying the rules to each pair in turn.

(*e*) *Application of doctrine.* The nature of the mortgages or of the property mortgaged is immaterial. There can be consolidation

[76] *Vint* v. *Padget* (1858) 2 De G. & J. 611 at 613; *Pledge* v. *White* [1896] A.C. 187.
[77] *Jennings* v. *Jordan* (1880) 6 App.Cas. 698 at 701.

even if one mortgage is legal and one equitable,[78] or if both are equitable,[79] or if one mortgage is of personalty and the other of realty,[80] or if both are mortgages of personalty.[81] The doctrine has even been applied, though probably wrongly, to two mortgages on the same property.[82] It is immaterial whether the equity of redemption has been conveyed outright or whether it has merely been mortgaged,[83] or has devolved under a will or intestacy, or under the bankruptcy law.[84] Thus if a mortgagee has a right of consolidation, it is effective against all the mortgagor's successors in title.

(f) *Danger to purchaser.* It will be seen that the doctrine of consolidation makes it dangerous to buy property subject to a mortgage without careful inquiry, for it may be that the mortgagor may also have mortgaged other property and both mortgages may be held by the same mortgagee. The difficulty is that the purchaser has no means of finding out about this if the two properties are held by different titles; and it is no defence that he bought without notice of the other mortgage,[85] for the right to redeem which he must assert against the mortgagee is an equitable right, and therefore subject to prior equitable interests, irrespective of notice.[86] Even if his own mortgage reserves no right to consolidate, the other mortgage may do so and that will suffice.[87] If he redeems the other mortgage he of course becomes a transferee and takes the benefit of it.[88] But, unreasonable as it seems, he may then have to pay the penalty of the mortgagee's imprudence as a lender, since consolidation is most likely to be enforced where the security for the other mortgage is insufficient.

(g) *Value of doctrine.* In practice, the right to consolidate causes less trouble than might be supposed. But as a source of risk to an innocent purchaser it is a freak of equity; it is " not one of

---

[78] *Cracknall* v. *Janson* (1879) 11 Ch.D. 1 at 18.
[79] *Tweedale* v. *Tweedale* (1857) 23 Beav. 341.
[80] *Tassell* v. *Smith* (1858) 2 De G. & J. 713.
[81] See *Watts* v. *Symes* (1851) 1 De G.M. & G. 240.
[82] *Re Salmon* [1903] 1 K.B. 147. *Pace* Waldock, *Mortgages*, 285, this is not a question of tacking, *i.e.,* of priority, but of the right to redeem. But *Re Salmon* is not a convincing case. A mortgagor who redeems cannot keep the mortgage alive to the prejudice of a mortgagee (*post*, p. 944), and if he redeems the earlier mortgage (*i.e.,* that which is the better secured) he improves the mortgagee's security for the later mortgage. How the principle of consolidation (that redemption of one property alone may impair the security given by the other) can then fit the case is inexplicable.
[83] *Beevor* v. *Luck* (1867) L.R. 4 Eq. 537 at 546.
[84] *Selby* v. *Pomfret* (1861) 3 De G.F. & J. 595.
[85] *Ireson* v. *Denn* (1796) 2 Cox Eq. 425.
[86] The legal estate obtained from the mortgagor is of no avail, since it is subject to the mortgage term and that can only be cleared off by exercising the equitable right to redeem.
[87] *Ante,* p. 927.
[88] *Post,* p. 944.

those doctrines of the Court of Chancery which has met with general approbation." [89] There may well be doubts as to the wisdom of equity in allowing a mortgagee who has made two distinct bargains, one good and one bad, to use the success of one to rescue him from the failure of the other. But the doctrine has existed almost as long as the equity of redemption itself,[90] and is too well settled to be questioned.[91]

5. Right to tack. This is considered below,[92] since it is part of the subject of priorities.

Sect. 2. Rights Common to Both Parties

A. Power of Leasing

1. The mortgagor. The most important right common to both parties is the right of leasing the mortgaged property. Apart from any statutory or contractual provisions, the position of a mortgagor as soon as he has made a mortgage is that he has granted a long term of years to the mortgagee and retains merely the reversion on that lease together with an equity of redemption. But since the mortgagor is usually left in possession of the land he needs an owner's usual powers of management. Any lease which he purports to grant will at least be binding as between him and his tenant, as a lease by estoppel,[93] and so the mortgagor may sue or distrain for the rent.[94] But this is subject to the paramount rights of the mortgagee [95]: the mortgagee is always entitled to take possession or to require the rent (including even arrears [96]) to be paid to himself,[97] though in the latter case he must make an effective demand for payment in order to defeat the claim of the mortgagor.[98] The mortgagor cannot, of course, fetter the mortgagee's right to take possession [99];

---

[89] *Pledge* v. *White* [1896] A.C. 187 at 192, *per* Lord Davey.

[90] It first appeared in *Bovey* v. *Skipwith* (1671) 1 Ch.Cas. 201.

[91] *Pledge* v. *White, supra.*

[92] *Post,* p. 978.

[93] *Webb* v. *Austin* (1844) 7 Man. & G. 701; *Cuthbertson* v. *Irving* (1859) 4 H. & N. 742 at 754 (affd. (1860) 6 H. & N. 135); presumably also it is a good lease in equity. For leases by estoppel, especially as to their effect on mortgages, see *ante,* p. 646.

[94] *Trent* v. *Hunt* (1853) 9 Exch. 14.

[95] L.P.A., 1925, s. 98, replacing J.A., 1873, s. 25 (5). The difficulties arising from the language of this provision, discussed in *Fairclough* v. *Marshall* (1878) 4 Ex.D. 37 and *Matthews* v. *Usher* [1900] 2 Q.B. 535, are perhaps best explained by Farwell L.J. in *Turner* v. *Walsh* [1909] 2 K.B. 484 at 495.

[96] *Moss* v. *Gallimore* (1779) 1 Doug.K.B. 279.

[97] *Pope* v. *Biggs* (1829) 9 B. & C. 245; *Underhay* v. *Read* (1887) 20 Q.B.D. 209.

[98] See *Kitchen's Trustee* v. *Madders* [1950] Ch. 134, *post,* p. 949, n. 57.

[99] See *Thunder* d. *Weaver* v. *Belcher* (1803) 3 East 449.

against the mortgagee therefore the tenant has no defence.[1] Similarly the statutory provisions about protection from eviction after a tenancy has ended do not fetter the mortgagee.[2]

2. The mortgagee. The mortgagee, on the other hand, has the legal right to possession and the power to grant leases; but such leases, like the mortgage itself, will usually be subject to the equity of redemption.[3] Again, therefore, the tenant will have no security against the other party to the mortgage.

3. The statutory power. It will be seen from this that once property had been mortgaged, a satisfactory lease could be made only with the concurrence of both mortgagor and mortgagee. The mortgagee's concurrence might be implied from some later act [4]; but it would not be implied from his mere knowledge of the lease, even though the mortgagor was in default at the time.[5] The only satisfactory solution was for the mortgage to confer upon either or both of the parties a power to grant binding leases.[6] The Law of Property Act, 1925,[7] confers such a power, though subject to contrary agreement. The following provisions apply to all mortgages made after 1881.[8]

(a) *Power to lease.* A power to grant leases and to make agreements for leases [9] which will be binding on both mortgagor and mortgagee is exercisable—

(1) by the mortgagee if he is in possession [10] or has appointed a receiver who is still acting [11] (in which case the mortgagee may by writing delegate his powers of leasing to the receiver [12]); otherwise,

(2) by the mortgagor, being in possession.[13]

---

[1] *Rogers* v. *Humphreys* (1835) 4 A. & E. 299 at 313; *Dudley & District Benefit B. S.* v. *Emerson* [1949] Ch. 707; *Rust* v. *Goodale* [1957] Ch. 33.

[2] *Bolton B. S.* v. *Cobb* [1966] 1 W.L.R. 1. For these provisions, see *ante*, p. 684.

[3] See *Franklinski* v. *Ball* (1864) 33 Beav. 560 at 563; *Chapman* v. *Smith* [1907] 2 Ch. 97 at 102. Before 1926 the mortgagee's tenant would have at least constructive notice of the mortgagor's rights: *cf. Patman* v. *Harland* (1881) 17 Ch.D. 353. But now he may be able to take a legal lease without notice under L.P.A., 1925, s. 44 (5), in which case he will presumably defeat the mortgagor's equity of redemption, unless he had notice of it *aliunde*, *e.g.*, by reason of the mortgagor being in possession. See generally *ante*, pp. 705–708.

[4] See *Parker* v. *Braithwaite* [1952] 2 All E.R. 837; *Stroud B. S.* v. *Delamont* [1960] 1 W.L.R. 431, approved in *Chatsworth Properties Ltd.* v. *Effiom* [1971] 1 W.L.R. 144.

[5] *Taylor* v. *Ellis* [1960] Ch. 368; and see *Barclays Bank Ltd.* v. *Kiley* [1961] 1 W.L.R. 1050.

[6] See, *e.g.*, *Carpenter* v. *Parker* (1857) 3 C.B.(N.S.) 206.

[7] L.P.A., 1925, s. 99, replacing C.A., 1881, s. 18.

[8] L.P.A., 1925, s. 99 (16).

[9] *Ibid.*, s. 99 (17); see *post*, p. 935.

[10] *Ibid.*, s. 99 (2).

[11] *Ibid.*, s. 99 (19).

[12] *Ibid.*; *ante*, p. 920.

[13] *Ibid.*, s. 99 (1).

(b) *Term of lease.* A lease may be granted for the following terms [14]—

(1) if the mortgage was made before 1926, for not more than—
    (i) 21 years for agricultural or occupation purposes;
    (ii) 99 years for building:

(2) if the mortgage was made after 1925, for not more than—
    (i) 50 years for agricultural or occupation purposes;
    (ii) 999 years for building. [15]

(c) *Conditions of lease.* To fall within the statutory powers, any lease granted must comply with the following conditions:

(1) It must be limited to take effect in possession not later than twelve months after its date. [16]

(2) It must reserve the best rent reasonably obtainable, and with certain qualifications, no fine may be taken. [17] But in a building lease the rent may be nominal for not more than the first five years, [18] although the lessee must (whether the rent is nominal or not) agree to erect, improve or repair buildings within five years if he has not done so already. [19]

(3) It must contain a covenant by the lessee for payment of rent and a condition of re-entry on the rent not being paid for a specified period not exceeding thirty days. [20]

(4) A counterpart of the lease must be executed by the lessee and delivered to the lessor. [21] A counterpart of any lease granted by the mortgagor must be delivered within one month to the mortgagee; but the lessee is not concerned to see that this is done, [22] and non-compliance does not invalidate the lease, although it makes the power of sale exercisable. [23]

---

[14] *Ibid.*, s. 99 (3).
[15] Compare leases which may be granted by a tenant for life under the Settled Land Act, 1925, where the date of the settlement makes no difference to the length of the leases which can be granted, and mining and forestry leases can be granted (*ante*, p. 334).
[16] L.P.A., 1925, s. 99 (5).
[17] *Ibid.*, s. 99 (6).
[18] *Ibid.*, s. 99 (10).
[19] *Ibid.*, s. 99 (9).
[20] *Ibid.*, s. 99 (7).
[21] *Ibid.*, s. 99 (8).
[22] *Ibid.*, s. 99 (11).
[23] *Public Trustee* v. *Lawrence* [1912] 1 Ch. 789 (*ante*, p. 910); and see *Rhodes* v. *Dalby* [1971] 1 W.L.R. 1325.

These regulations, however, do not prevent informal transactions, since the definition of " lease " here extends, " as far as circumstances admit . . . to an agreement, whether in writing or not, for leasing or letting." [24] An oral lease or agreement may thus be a valid exercise of the power; but it is not certain whether the above-mentioned conditions as to covenants and conditions of re-entry apply in such a case.[25] A lease by the mortgagor is not invalidated merely because it includes furniture and sporting rights not comprised in the mortgage [25a]; but it will not bind the mortgagee if it includes other land, at an entire rent.[26]

(*d*) *Non-compliance.* By statute,[27] if a lease does not comply with the statutory requirements but is made in good faith, and the tenant has entered under it, it may nevertheless take effect in equity as a contract for a lease, varied so as to comply with the requirements. This provision for assisting defective leases made under powers has already been encountered elsewhere.[28]

(*e*) *Contrary agreement.* The statutory power may be either excluded [29] or extended [30] by agreement of the parties expressed in the mortgage or otherwise in writing. It cannot, however, be excluded in any mortgage of agricultural land made after March 1, 1948 [30a]; nor can its exclusion hamper the power of the court to order the grant of a new lease of business premises under the Landlord and Tenant Act, 1954.[31] In practice, most mortgages expressly exclude the power, and in addition the mortgagor is often required to covenant not to make any letting without the mortgagee's consent.

4. Leases not under the statutory power. If the power is excluded and the mortgagor nevertheless grants an unauthorised lease, the lease is void as against the mortgagee and his successors in title [32] (unless they are estopped from asserting this [33]), but valid as between the parties to it: the statutory powers of leasing do not deprive the

---

[24] L.P.A., 1925, s. 99 (17).
[25] *Pawson* v. *Revell* [1958] 2 Q.B. 360. Wolst. & C. i, 200, retains unchanged the passage doubted in the case at p. 370, and *Rhodes* v. *Dalby* [1971] 1 W.L.R. 1325 now supports the book in saying that the conditions do not apply.
[25a] *Brown* v. *Peto* [1900] 1 Q.B. 346 at 354 (affirmed [1900] 2 Q.B. 653).
[26] *King* v. *Bird* [1909] 1 K.B. 837.
[27] L.P.A., 1925, s. 152, replacing Leases Acts, 1849, 1850. See *Pawson* v. *Revell*, *supra* (omission of condition of re-entry).   [28] *Ante*, p. 337.
[29] L.P.A., 1925, s. 99 (13) (" as far as a contrary intention is not expressed ").
[30] *Ibid.*, s. 99 (14).
[30a] Agricultural Holdings Act, 1948, 7th Sched., para. 2 ; see *Pawson* v. *Revell*, *supra*; *Rhodes* v. *Dalby*, *supra*.
[31] s. 36 (4). For the Act, see *post*, p. 1110.
[32] *Rust* v. *Goodale* [1957] Ch. 33.
[33] *Lever Finance Ltd.* v. *Needlemans' Trustee* [1956] Ch. 375.

parties of their common law rights to create leases not binding upon each other. For example, if a mortgage contains a covenant by the mortgagor not to exercise the statutory power of leasing without the mortgagee's written consent, the mortgagor may nevertheless grant a yearly tenancy which binds the mortgagor under the principle of estoppel but which does not bind the mortgagee.[34]

B. Power of Accepting Surrenders of Leases

In the case of a mortgage made after 1911,[35] if the parties have not expressed a contrary intention, either in the mortgage or otherwise in writing,[36] the Law of Property Act, 1925,[37] enables a surrender of any lease or tenancy to be effected, binding the parties to the mortgage, on the following terms.

1. Power to accept. The surrender may be accepted—

(i) by the mortgagee, if he is in possession [38] or has appointed a receiver who still acts [39] (in which case the mortgagee may by writing delegate his powers of accepting surrenders to the receiver [40]); or

(ii) by the mortgagor, if he is in possession.[41]

2. Conditions of surrender. For the surrender to be valid—

(i) an authorised lease of the property must be granted to take effect in possession within one month of the surrender;

(ii) the term of the new lease must not be shorter than the unexpired residue of the surrendered lease; and

(iii) the rent reserved by the new lease must not be less than the rent reserved by the surrendered lease.[42]

The statutory power of accepting a surrender is thus exercisable only for the purpose of replacing one lease by another; and a surrender which does not comply with these conditions is void.[43] But the power may be extended by an agreement in writing, whether in the mortgage or not.[44]

---

[34] See *Iron Trades Employers Insurance Association Ltd.* v. *Union Land and House Investors Ltd.* [1937] Ch. 313.
[35] L.P.A., 1925, s. 100 (8).   [36] *Ibid.*, s. 100 (7).
[37] s. 100, replacing C.A., 1911, s. 3. Formerly a mortgagor could not accept a surrender of a lease that he had granted under his statutory powers unless the mortgagee concurred: *Robbins* v. *Whyte* [1906] 1 K.B. 125.
[38] L.P.A., 1925, s. 100 (2).   [39] *Ibid.*, s. 100 (13).
[40] *Ibid.*
[41] *Ibid.*, s. 100 (1).
[42] *Ibid.*, s. 100 (5).
[43] See, *e.g.*, *Barclays Bank Ltd.* v. *Stasek* [1957] Ch. 28; (1957) 73 L.Q.R. 14 (R.E.M.).   [44] L.P.A., 1925, s. 100 (10).

Sect. 3. Rights of the Mortgagor

A. *Right of Redemption*

I. PROTECTION OF THE MORTGAGOR

The distinction between the mortgagor's legal right to redeem and his equitable right to redeem has already been considered.[45] The latter right, being the creature of equity, must be protected by equity; for otherwise the mortgagee, who often can bring pressure to bear on a prospective mortgagor by threatening to withhold the loan,[46] might be able to defeat the whole purpose of a mortgage, *i.e.*, that it should provide security and nothing more. The mortgagor's equity of redemption is inviolable; the maxim is " once a mortgage, always a mortgage." [47] The principle is applied in two ways.

1. The test of a mortgage is in substance, not form. If a transaction is in substance a mortgage, equity will treat it as such, even if it is dressed up in some other guise,[48] as by the documents being cast in the form of an absolute conveyance.[49] Thus if a mortgage is expressed in the form of a conveyance with an option for the mortgagor to repurchase the property in a year's time, the mortgagor is entitled to redeem it even after the year has expired.[50] " In all these cases the question is what was the real intention of the parties?",[51] and parol evidence is admissible to show what it was.[52]

2. No clogs on the equity. There must be no clog or fetter on the equity of redemption. This means both that the mortgagor cannot be prevented from eventually redeeming his property on repayment of the sum advanced together with interest due and the mortgagee's proper costs, and also that, after redemption, he is free from all the conditions of the mortgage. This will be considered under the two heads.

---

[45] *Ante*, p. 890.
[46] " For necessitous men are not, truly speaking, free men, but, to answer a present exigency, will submit to any terms that the crafty may impose upon them ": *Vernon* v. *Bethell* (1762) 2 Eden 110 at 113, *per* Lord Henley L.C.
[47] *Seton* v. *Slade* (1802) 7 Ves. 265 at 273, *per* Lord Eldon L.C.
[48] See *Williams* v. *Owen* (1840) 5 My. & Cr. 303 at 306; *Re Watson* (1890) 25 Q.B.D. 27.
[49] *England* v. *Codrington* (1758) 1 Eden 169; *Barnhart* v. *Greenshields* (1853) 9 Moo.P.C. 18.
[50] See *Danby* v. *Read* (1675) Rep.t.Finch 226; *Muttylol Seal* v. *Annundochunder Sandle* (1849) 5 Moo.Ind.App. 72; *Croft* v. *Powel* (1738) 2 Com. 603; *Waters* v. *Mynn* (1850) 15 L.T.(o.s.) 157; *cf. Salt* v. *Marquess of Northampton* [1892] A.C. 1 (Lord Bramwell's attack on the equity of redemption as an interference with freedom of contract is entertaining).
[51] *Manchester, Sheffield and Lincolnshire Ry.* v. *North Central Wagon Co.* (1888) 13 App.Cas. 554 at 568, *per* Lord Macnaghten.
[52] *Lincoln* v. *Wright* (1859) 4 De G. & J. 16; *Barton* v. *Bank of New South Wales* (1890) 15 App.Cas. 379.

(a) No irredeemability [53]

(1) REDEMPTION. " Redemption is of the very nature and essence of a mortgage, as mortgages are regarded in equity." [54] It is inconsistent with the very nature of a mortgage that it shall be totally irredeemable [55] or that the right of redemption shall be confined to certain persons (such as the mortgagor and the heirs male of his body [56]) or to a limited period (such as the joint lives of the mortgagor and mortgagee [57] or the life of the mortgagor alone [58]), or to part only of the mortgaged property. [59] Thus if the property mortgaged is a lease together with an option to renew it, or to purchase the freehold, and the mortgagee exercises the option, the mortgagor is entitled on redemption not only to the lease but also, on paying the cost of acquisition, to the fruits of exercising the option. [60]

(2) EXCLUSION OF REDEMPTION. Any express stipulation which is inconsistent with the right of redemption will be ineffective. No mortgagee can secure, as a condition of the mortgage, that the property shall become his absolutely when some specified event occurs. [61] In all such cases the owner of the equity of redemption may redeem as if there had been no such restriction. If, for example, the mortgage agreement gives the mortgagee an option to purchase the mortgaged property, that term is void, as repugnant to the equity of redemption, even though the transaction is not in itself oppressive to the mortgagor. [62] But a mere right of pre-emption (*i.e.*, of first refusal) is probably unobjectionable if its terms are fair, since the mortgagor cannot be compelled to sell. [62a]

Once the mortgage has been made, equity will not intervene if the mortgagor, by a separate and independent transaction, gives the mortgagee an option of purchasing the property and thus of depriving the mortgagor of his equity of redemption. [63] Equity will protect the mortgagor while he is in the defenceless position of one seeking a loan; once he has obtained his loan, this protection is not needed. But where a mortgagor seeks to escape from his mortgagee by procuring a transfer of the mortgage to a new mortgagee, there

---

[53] *Fairclough* v. *Swan Brewery Co. Ltd.* [1912] A.C. 565 at 570.
[54] *Noakes & Co. Ltd.* v. *Rice* [1902] A.C. 24 at 30, *per* Lord Macnaghten.
[55] *Re Wells* [1933] Ch. 29 at 52.   [56] *Howard* v. *Harris* (1683) 1 Vern. 190.
[57] *Spurgeon* v. *Collier* (1758) 1 Eden 55.
[58] *Newcomb* v. *Bonham* (1681) 1 Vern. 7; *Salt* v. *Marquess of Northampton* [1892] A.C. 1.
[59] See *Re Wells, supra*; *Salt* v. *Marquess of Northampton, supra*.
[60] *Nelson* v. *Hannam* [1943] Ch. 59.
[61] *Toomes* v. *Conset* (1745) 3 Atk. 261.
[62] *Samuel* v. *Jarrah Timber and Wood Paving Corporation Ltd.* [1904] A.C. 323, where the House of Lords expressed a distaste for the rule in the case of a fair commercial bargain, but felt bound to apply it.
[62a] See *Orby* v. *Trigg* (1722) 9 Mod. 2, where the only objection to a right of pre-emption was that the mortgagee exercised it too late and misled the mortgagor.
[63] *Reeve* v. *Lisle* [1902] A.C. 461.

is in effect a new loan, and any option obtained by the new mortgagee will be subject to the rules stated above.[64]

(3) POSTPONEMENT OF REDEMPTION. A provision postponing the date of redemption until some future period longer than the customary six months may be valid, provided the mortgage as a whole is not so oppressive and unconscionable that equity would not enforce it,[65] and provided it does not make the equitable right to redeem illusory.[66] The question here is one of degree. An excessive postponement of the redemption date may in itself be oppressive and thus a clog on the equity of redemption. In one case a lease for twenty years was mortgaged on conditions which prevented its redemption until six weeks before the end of the term. Such a provision rendered the equitable right to redeem illusory; for it prohibited redemption until the lease was nearly valueless and redemption was not worth having. The mortgagor was accordingly allowed to redeem after only three years.[67]

In the case of a wasting security, therefore, any long postponement of the right to redeem is likely to be objectionable. But in other cases it is often not so. In *Knightsbridge Estates Trust Ltd.* v. *Byrne* [68] the Knightsbridge company had mortgaged a large number of properties to an insurance company on terms that repayment should be made by half-yearly instalments over a period of forty years. The mortgagees, for their part, agreed not to call in the money in advance of the due dates. Six years later the Knightsbridge company sought a declaration that the company was entitled to redeem the mortgage, claiming, *inter alia*, that it was oppressive that they should be unable to redeem their properties for forty years. But on this ground their action failed, for it was held that in the circumstances the agreement was a perfectly fair one and the contractual right of redemption was in no way illusory. The court is concerned to see that the essential requirements of a mortgage are observed, and that oppressive or unconscionable terms are not enforced.[69] But it is naturally reluctant to interfere with a contract

---

64 *Lewis* v. *Frank Love Ltd.* [1961] 1 W.L.R. 261. For transfer of mortgages, see *post*, p. 954.
65 *Knightsbridge Estates Trust Ltd.* v. *Byrne* [1939] Ch. 441 at 463 (affd. on other grounds [1940] A.C. 613). 66 *Ibid.*, at p. 456.
67 *Fairclough* v. *Swan Brewery Co. Ltd.* [1912] A.C. 565; *cf. Davis* v. *Symons* [1934] Ch. 442, as explained in the *Knightsbridge* case, *supra*, at pp. 460–462 (same principle applied to mortgage of insurance policies due to mature before redemption date 20 years distant). Contrast *Santley* v. *Wilde* [1899] 2 Ch. 474, where it was held by the Court of Appeal that a ten-year lease of a theatre was irredeemable because part of the mortgagee's security was a covenant by the mortgagor to pay one-third of the profits to the mortgagee during the whole remainder of the lease. The decision proceeded on the ground that without the covenant there would have been insufficient security. It has been criticised in the House of Lords: *Noakes & Co. Ltd.* v. *Rice* [1902] A.C. 24 at 31, 34.
68 [1939] Ch. 441; affd. on other grounds [1940] A.C. 613.
69 *Knightsbridge Estates Trust Ltd.* v. *Byrne* [1939] Ch. 441 at 457.

made as a matter of business by parties well able to look after themselves. "The directors of a trading company in search of financial assistance are certainly in a very different position from that of an impecunious landowner in the toils of a crafty money-lender." [70] A business contract may, however, be in unlawful restraint of trade, and if one element in the transaction is a mortgage which is to be irredeemable during the period of unlawful restraint, the fetter on redemption is inoperative.[70a]

(4) DEBENTURES. The decision of the Court of Appeal in *Knightsbridge Estates Trust Ltd.* v. *Byrne* [71] is now the leading case on postponement of redemption. It was affirmed by the House of Lords,[72] but on the ground that the security was a debenture. A debenture is a written acknowledgment of indebtedness made by a company, and it is usually secured by a mortgage or charge on some property of the company. A factory building may, for example, be mortgaged to trustees for the debenture-holders; and even an ordinary mortgage by a company appears to be a debenture. Mortgages created to secure debentures form a statutory exception to the general rule prohibiting irredeemability,[73] since it is provided by the Companies Act, 1948,[74] that debentures may be made irredeemable, or redeemable only on the happening of a contingency or the expiration of a period of time.

(*b*) *Redemption free from conditions in the mortgage.* The mortgagor cannot be prevented from redeeming the property free from all the conditions of the mortgage. Redemption must be complete redemption, so that the mortgagor is restored to his original position and all the liabilities of the mortgage transaction are ended.

(1) COLLATERAL ADVANTAGES. The essence of a mortgage is a loan of a certain sum of money upon security. Sometimes terms are inserted in a mortgage which give the mortgagee some other advantage in addition to his security and interest. For example, in the case of a mortgage of a public-house to a brewery company the mortgagee will usually stipulate that the mortgagor shall sell only the mortgagee's beer. And in business transactions, which include an investment of

---

[70] *Samuel* v. *Jarrah Timber and Wood Paving Corporation Ltd.* [1904] A.C. 323 at 327, *per* Lord Macnaghten.
[70a] *Esso Petroleum Co. Ltd.* v. *Harper's Garage (Stourport) Ltd.* [1968] A.C. 269 (mortgagor to sell only mortgagee's brand of petrol for 21 years and to redeem only by instalments over 21 years: restraint held excessive and mortgage held redeemable); and see *Texaco Ltd.* v. *Mulberry Filling Station Ltd.* [1972] 1 W.L.R. 814.
[71] [1939] Ch. 441.   [72] [1940] A.C. 613.
[73] Strictly, however, an irredeemable debenture "is not a mortgage at all ": *Samuel* v. *Jarrah Timber and Wood Paving Corporation Ltd.*, *supra*, at p. 330, *per* Lord Lindley.   [74] s. 89, replacing Companies Act, 1929, s. 74.

money secured by mortgage, there may be other provisions giving some commercial advantage to the mortgagee. These " collateral advantages " were at one time held void,[75] for before the repeal of the usury laws in 1854 [76] any such advantage was an evasion of the law limiting the rate of interest. But since 1854 the attitude has changed,[77] and it is clear that collateral advantages are objectionable only if they are unconscionable [78] or clog the equity of redemption.

An example of an unconscionable advantage is an excessive premium. In one case a property company sold a house to one of its tenants, advancing £2,900 under a mortgage which made no provision for interest but which required repayment of £4,553. This premium of £1,653 was held to be an unreasonable collateral advantage, since it was far more than a fair rate of interest and, by making the charge exceed the value of the house, it rendered the equity of redemption worthless. The mortgagor was therefore entitled to redeem by paying £2,900 with reasonable interest fixed by the court.[78a]

(2) INVALIDITY AFTER REDEMPTION. A collateral advantage which is not unconscionable is valid until redemption but not afterwards. The principle is illustrated by a mortgage of a public-house under which the mortgagor covenants to sell only the mortgagee's beer. While the mortgage is still on foot the mortgagor is bound by the covenant.[79] But so soon as he redeems he is free from it,[80] even though it was intended to bind him for a fixed period, for otherwise he could not redeem his property completely; he mortgaged a " free house," and if he could redeem only a " tied house " he would still be fettered by the terms of the mortgage after redemption. The same principle appears in *Bradley* v. *Carritt*,[81] where the mortgagor mortgaged to a tea broker the shares which gave him a controlling interest in a tea company. As a condition of the loan he guaranteed that the mortgagee should always remain broker to the company thereafter. The mortgagor, having paid off the mortgage, was held to be free from this apparently unlimited guarantee. Had it been otherwise he could never have disposed of his shares after redemption, for he would have been compelled to keep control of the company.

---

[75] *Jennings* v. *Ward* (1705) 2 Vern. 520 at 521.   [76] *Ante*, p. 888.
[77] *Biggs* v. *Hoddinott* [1898] 2 Ch. 307 at 316; *Kreglinger* v. *New Patagonia Meat & Cold Storage Co. Ltd.* [1914] A.C. 25 at 54, 55; and see at p. 46, *per* Lord Mersey (" an unruly dog ").
[78] See *Barrett* v. *Hartley* (1866) L.R. 2 Eq. 789 at 795; *James* v. *Kerr* (1889) 40 Ch.D. 449.
[78a] *Cityland and Property (Holdings) Ltd.* v. *Dabrah* [1968] Ch. 166.
[79] *Biggs* v. *Hoddinott* [1898] 2 Ch. 307.
[80] *Noakes & Co. Ltd.* v. *Rice* [1902] A.C. 24 (covenant to buy mortgagee's beer during whole residue of mortgagor's lease: House of Lords unanimous).
[81] [1903] A.C. 253 (House of Lords divided 3–2).

(3) VALIDITY AFTER REDEMPTION. In some cases the courts, in their desire not to unsettle commercial contracts for doctrinal reasons, have allowed collateral stipulations in mortgages to remain binding even after redemption. The leading case is *Kreglinger* v. *New Patagonia Meat and Cold Storage Co. Ltd.*,[82] where the meat company had raised a loan from a firm of woolbrokers on a mortgage by way of a floating charge [83] on the company's undertaking. It was made a condition that for five years the company should not sell any sheepskins to any other person without first offering them to the woolbrokers at the best price obtainable elsewhere, and that the woolbrokers should have a commission on all sheepskins sold by the company to other persons. The company redeemed the property after two years and claimed to be freed from the option [84] and commission clauses. But the House of Lords held that they remained bound, on the ground that these clauses were in truth a separate agreement, part of the consideration for the mortgage but not part of the mortgage itself, and therefore no impediment to complete redemption.

(4) DISTINCTIONS. The reasons given for these decisions are, as a matter of logic, far from easy to reconcile. There is clearly a distinction between a case where the parties negotiate a loan, and the mortgagee then succeeds in getting the mortgagor to agree to a stipulation giving the mortgagee some additional advantage, and a case where from the outset the bargain is for some advantage in return for a loan.[85] Further, it may be important whether, as in *Bradley* v. *Carritt*, specific property is bound, or whether, as in the *Kreglinger* case, there is merely a floating charge.[1]

Perhaps even more important, though less specifically laid down, is the distinction between transactions by private individuals, who may require the protection of the law, and transactions by traders, whether companies or individuals, who do not. When a collateral advantage is bargained for as a condition of a personal loan, it is much less easy to regard it as an independent transaction than when it forms part of an elaborate commercial agreement. In the former case the advantage can generally be terminated on redemption with-

---

[82] [1914] A.C. 25 (House of Lords unanimous); applied in *Re Cuban Land & Development Co. (1911) Ltd.* [1921] 2 Ch. 147; and *cf. De Beers Consolidated Mines Ltd.* v. *British South Africa Co.* [1912] A.C. 52; *post*, p. 943.

[83] *i.e.*, a charge on such assets as the company had from time to time, which would " crystallize " on certain specified events occurring, and attach to the company's then assets.

[84] *Quaere* whether the right was not merely a right of pre-emption; and see *ante*, p. 938, n. 62.

[85] See, *e.g.*, *Biggs* v. *Hoddinott* [1898] 2 Ch. 307 at 316, 317; *Kreglinger* v. *New Patagonia Meat & Cold Storage Co. Ltd.*, *supra*, at pp. 39, 45, 61.

[1] See *Kreglinger's Case*, *supra*, at pp. 41, 42.

out hardship to the mortgagee. In the latter case the court, by interfering with a transaction negotiated as a matter of business, might destroy the fruits of a prudent investment of many thousands of pounds. The test of " severability," which *Kreglinger's* case introduced, provides a convenient but indefinable rule for dealing with such cases on their merits. " The question is one not of form but of substance, and it can be answered in each case only by looking at all the circumstances, and not by mere reliance on some abstract principle, or upon the dicta which have fallen *obiter* from judges in other and different cases." [2]

It is also important to consider what has been included in the mortgage. Thus where a company agreed to grant a perpetual licence for mining on its land, and later mortgaged the land to the licensee, it was held that after redemption the agreement to grant the licence still bound the company. This was so even though the agreement for the licence expressly contemplated the subsequent mortgage, for the two transactions were substantially independent of each other.[3] When the property was mortgaged, it had already been " burdened and encumbered with the prior obligation, superior to the mortgage security, to grant the licence," [4] and so there was no clog on the equity; for on redemption " everything which had been charged was restored to the mortgagor." [5]

II. WHO CAN REDEEM

Redemption is usually sought by the mortgagor; but the right to redeem is not confined to him and may be exercised by any person interested in the equity of redemption,[6] however small his interest.[7] Once the mortgagor has parted with his whole interest in the property he ceases to be able to redeem [8]; but if he is subsequently sued on the covenant for payment he acquires a fresh right of redemption.[9] The right to redeem extends to assignees of the equity of redemption (even if the assignment was voluntary [10]), subsequent mortgagees,[11] unless they are statute-barred,[12] and even a lessee under a lease granted by the mortgagor but not binding on the mortgagee.[13]

2 *Kreglinger's Case, supra,* at p. 39, *per* Lord Haldane: his speech is analysed in *Re Petrol Filling Station, Vauxhall Bridge Road, London* (1968) 20 P. & C.R. 1.
3 *De Beers Consolidated Mines Ltd.* v. *British South Africa Co.* [1912] A.C. 52. Compare the principle explained in connection with options: *ante,* p. 938.
4 *Ibid.,* at p. 66, *per* Lord Atkinson.
5 *Ibid.,* at p. 73, *per* Earl Loreburn L.C.
6 *Pearce* v. *Morris* (1869) 5 Ch.App. 227 at 229.
7 *Hunter* v. *Macklew* (1846) 5 Hare 238.
8 Consider *Moore* v. *Morton* [1886] W.N. 196.
9 *Kinnaird* v. *Trollope* (1888) 39 Ch.D. 636.
10 *Howard* v. *Harris* (1683) 1 Vern. 190.
11 *Fell* v. *Brown* (1787) 2 Bro.C.C. 276.
12 *Cotterell* v. *Price* [1960] 1 W.L.R. 1097.
13 *Tarn* v. *Turner* (1888) 39 Ch.D. 456.

If several persons simultaneously seek to redeem a mortgage the first in order of priority has the first claim.[14]

III. EFFECT OF REDEMPTION

1. Discharge or transfer. Where redemption is effected by the only person interested in the equity of redemption, and the mortgage redeemed is the only incumbrance on the property, the effect of redemption is to discharge the mortgage and leave the property free from incumbrances. But in other cases, as where a second mortgagee redeems the first mortgage, the effect of redemption will normally be that the person paying the money takes a transfer of the mortgage[15]; for, of course, the redemption enures to the benefit of the person redeeming, and the second mortgagee must be able to maintain the first mortgage as against the mortgagor.

2. Redemption by mortgagor. By contrast, if the mortgagor himself redeems a mortgage which has priority over one or more subsequent mortgages, this discharges the mortgage, and the mortgagor cannot claim to have it kept alive to the prejudice of the subsequent mortgagees[16]; he " cannot derogate from his own bargain by setting up the mortgage so purchased against a second mortgagee." [17] This is so even if some third party provided him with the money.[18] Thus if the property proves insufficient to satisfy all the claims the mortgagor cannot claim priority for the amount due on the first mortgage. If the mortgagor redeems a first mortgage he therefore improves the security for any later mortgagees.

3. Subsequent purchaser. The above rule applies only to the mortgagor, and not to later purchasers of the equity of redemption. Thus if Blackacre has been mortgaged first to A and then to B, and is then sold or mortgaged (subject to the mortgages) to X, X may pay off A's mortgage but keep it alive against B.[19] Similarly, if the sale is made not to X but to A, A can keep his mortgage alive against B. It will be presumed in such cases, in the absence of contrary evidence, that there is no intention of a merger of the two interests

---

[14] *Teevan* v. *Smith* (1882) 20 Ch.D. 724 at 730.

[15] *Cf.* L.P.A., 1925, s. 115 (2).

[16] *Otter* v. *Lord Vaux* (1856) 6 De G.M. & G. 638 (purported sale by mortgagee to mortgagor under power of sale, intended to give mortgagor a title free from claims of later mortgagees: held ineffective for this purpose); and see L.P.A., 1925, s. 115 (3), recognising the rule.

[17] *Whiteley* v. *Delaney* [1914] A.C. 132 at 145, *per* Lord Haldane L.C.

[18] *Parkash* v. *Irani Finance Ltd.* [1970] Ch. 101.

[19] *Adams* v. *Angell* (1877) 5 Ch.D. 634; *Thorne* v. *Cann* [1895] A.C. 11; *Whiteley* v. *Delaney* [1914] A.C. 132.

if it is to the advantage of the purchaser that merger should not take place.[20]

4. Right to compel transfer. Instead of redeeming, a person who is entitled to redeem a mortgage may usually insist upon the mortgagee transferring the mortgage to a nominee of the person paying the money.[21] This right exists notwithstanding any stipulation to the contrary, and applies irrespective of the date of the mortgage,[22] though it is exercisable only upon the same terms as the right of redemption.[1] If there are competing claims they take effect in order of priority,[2] as in the case of redemption. The right is excluded, however, if the mortgagee is or has been in possession,[3] for he thereby became liable to account strictly[4] despite any transfer of the mortgage and is liable for any defaults of the transferee[5] unless he transferred under an order of the court[6]; it would thus be unfair if the mortgagor could compel him to make a transfer.[7]

IV. TERMS OF REDEMPTION

1. Method. A mortgage may be redeemed either in court or out of court; the latter is the more usual except in complicated cases. The mortgage remains in being until the money due has actually been paid and accepted[8]; and the mortgagor remains liable for interest under it until either he duly tenders repayment and, if it is not accepted, sets the money aside,[9] or else the mortgagee waives tender, *e.g.*, by unequivocally refusing a proposed repayment.[10] If a mortgagee unreasonably refuses to accept a proper tender of the money due and so makes an action for redemption necessary, he may be penalised in costs.[11]

2. Notice. The mortgagor may redeem on the legal date for redemption (or before, if the mortgagee has sought payment, *e.g.*, by

---

[20] *Ante*, p. 669; L.P.A., 1925, s. 185. The decision in *Toulmin* v. *Steere* (1817) 3 Mer. 210, to the effect that merger will not be presumed if the purchaser has notice of later mortgages at the time he redeems, is of doubtful authority: see *Whiteley* v. *Delaney, supra*, at pp. 144, 145.
[21] L.P.A., 1925, s. 95 (1), (2); and see Hood and Challis, pp. 190, 191.
[22] L.P.A., 1925, s. 95 (5).
[1] *Ibid.*, s. 95 (1). Thus it may be subject to a right of consolidation.
[2] L.P.A., 1925, s. 95 (2); see *Teevan* v. *Smith* (1882) 20 Ch.D. 724.
[3] *Ibid.*, s. 95 (3).
[4] See *ante*, p. 914.
[5] *Hinde* v. *Blake* (1841) 11 L.J.Ch. 26; and see 1 Eq.Ca.Abr. 328, pl. 2.
[6] *Hall* v. *Heward* (1886) 32 Ch.D. 430.
[7] But see Hood and Challis, pp. 190, 191.
[8] *Samuel Keller (Holdings) Ltd.* v. *Martins Bank Ltd.* [1971] 1 W.L.R. 43.
[9] *Barratt* v. *Gough-Thomas (No. 3)* [1951] 2 All E.R. 48.
[10] *Chalikani Venkatarayanim* v. *Zamindar of Tuni* (1922) L.R. 50 Ind.App. 41.
[11] *Graham* v. *Seal* (1918) 88 L.J.Ch. 31.

taking possession [12]) without giving notice of his intention to do so.[13] After that date, when he is forced to rely upon his equitable right to redeem, it is a rule of practice [14] that he must either give the mortgagee reasonable [15] notice (*i.e.*, normally, or perhaps always,[16] six months) of his intention to redeem,[17] or else pay him six months' interest in lieu thereof [18]; it is only fair that the mortgagee should have a reasonable opportunity of finding another investment for his money.[19] But the mortgagee is not entitled to any notices or interest in lieu thereof—

    (i) if the loan is merely of a temporary nature, as is usually the case in an equitable mortgage by deposit of title deeds [20]; or

    (ii) if he had taken steps to enforce his security,[21] as by taking possession,[22] or starting foreclosure proceedings,[23] or giving the mortgagor notice to repay the loan so as to entitle the mortgagee to sell on default being made.[24] " It is said, ' You have demanded payment by your proceedings, and here is payment: you cannot decline what you have demanded '." [25]

If the mortgagor gives six months' notice and fails to pay on the proper day, he must usually give a further six months' notice or pay six months' interest in lieu thereof,[26] unless he can give a reasonable explanation of his failure to pay, in which case it suffices to give reasonable notice, *e.g.*, three months.[27]

    3. Interest and costs. Even if the mortgage makes no provision for interest, the mortgagor, on redeeming, must pay interest on the loan, and the rate will, if necessary, be fixed by the court.[28] If a redemption action is brought the mortgagor must also pay the mortgagee's proper costs, including any expenses incurred for protecting his security.[29]

---

12 *Bovill* v. *Endle* [1896] 1 Ch. 648; 65 L.J.Ch. 542.
13 See *Crickmore* v. *Freeston* (1870) 40 L.J.Ch. 137.
14 *Smith* v. *Smith* [1891] 3 Ch. 550.
15 *Browne* v. *Lockhart* (1840) 10 Sim. 420 at 424.
16 See *Cromwell Property Investment Co. Ltd.* v. *Western & Toovey* [1934] Ch. 322; at p. 332 Maugham J. calls the rule " harsh."
17 *Shrapnell* v. *Blake* (1737) West t.Hard. 166.
18 *Johnson* v. *Evans* (1889) 61 L.T. 18.
19 *Browne* v. *Lockhart, supra*, at p. 424.
20 *Fitzgerald's Trustee* v. *Mellersh* [1892] 1 Ch. 385.
21 *Re Alcock* (1883) 23 Ch.D. 372 at 376.
22 *Bovill* v. *Endle, supra.*
23 *Hill* v. *Rowlands* [1897] 2 Ch. 361 at 363.
24 *Edmonson* v. *Copland* [1911] 2 Ch. 301.
25 *Bovill* v. *Endle, supra*, at p. 651, *per* Kekewich J.
26 *Re Moss* (1885) 31 Ch.D. 90 at 94.
27 *Cromwell Property Investment Co. Ltd.* v. *Western & Toovey* [1934] Ch. 322.
28 See *Cityland and Property (Holdings) Ltd.* v. *Dabrah* [1968] Ch. 166. Even statute-barred interest must be paid: *post*, p. 1033.
29 See *Sinfield* v. *Sweet* [1967] 1 W.L.R. 1489. Though a charge on the property, the mortgagor is not personally liable for these expenses: *ibid.*

V. SALE IN LIEU OF REDEMPTION

Any person entitled to redeem may apply to the court for an order for sale, and is apparently entitled to such an order as of right.[30]

VI. " REDEEM UP, FORECLOSE DOWN "

1. Parties to action. The maxim " Redeem up, foreclose down " applies where there are several incumbrancers and one of them seeks by action to redeem a superior mortgage. The effect is best shown by an example. X has mortgaged his property successively to A, B, C, D and E, the mortgages ranking in that order; X thus ranks last, *e.g.*, in claiming any surplus if the property is sold. Suppose that D wishes to redeem B, and owing to the complexity of the accounts or some other circumstance an action for redemption is begun. Before B can be redeemed, the exact amount due to him must be settled by the court. This amount, however, does not affect only B and D, for C, E and X are all concerned with the amount which has priority to their interests; thus if the property were to be sold, C, E and X would all wish to know whether what B was entitled to was, say, £6,000 or £7,000, for upon that figure might depend their chances of receiving anything from the proceeds of sale. Consequently the court will insist upon their being made parties to D's action for redemption, so that they can be represented in the taking of the accounts between B and D and thus be bound by the final result.[31]

2. Rights of the parties. It would, however, be unfair to give C, E and X the trouble and expense of taking part in the action merely to watch accounts being taken,[32] with the risk of a similar event taking place in the future; and so the court insists that the right of all parties concerned in the action shall be settled once and for all. A is not concerned[33]; it is immaterial to him what is due to B, for A's mortgage has priority to B's. A, therefore, need not be joined in the action,[34] and will be left undisturbed in his position of first mortgagee.[35] But all the other parties are concerned, and the order of the court will be that D shall redeem not only B, but also C, for both their mortgages have priority to D's. E and X must also

---

[30] L.P.A., 1925, s. 91 (1), replacing C.A., 1881, s. 25 (1). See *Clarke* v. *Pannell* (1884) 29 S.J. 147; and see *ante*, pp. 907, 925.

[31] This also protects B against a further taking of his account if a later incumbrancer should offer to redeem both B and D: *Johnson* v. *Holdsworth* (1850) 1 Sim.(N.S.) 106 at 109.

[32] *Ramsbottom* v. *Wallis* (1835) 5 L.J.Ch. 92.

[33] *Slade* v. *Rigg* (1843) 3 Hare 35 at 38.

[34] *Rose* v. *Page* (1829) 2 Sim. 471; *Slade* v. *Rigg, supra.*

[35] *Brisco* v. *Kenrick* (1832) 1 L.J.Ch. 116; 1 Coop.t.Cott. 371.

be disposed of, and that can be done only by foreclosure: that is, each of them will have the opportunity of saving his rights by paying off the prior mortgages concerned in the action, or of asking for a sale; but if he does neither, he will be foreclosed.[36] " The natural decree is, that the second mortgagee shall redeem the first mortgagee, and that the mortgagor shall redeem him or stand foreclosed." [37] Thus if E and X fail to redeem and are foreclosed, the final result will be that D, at the price of redeeming B and C, now holds the equity of redemption subject only to the first mortgage in favour of A.

3. The principle. The principle may be stated thus: a mortgagee who seeks to redeem a prior mortgage by action must not only redeem any mortgages standing between him and that prior mortgage,[38] but must also foreclose all subsequent mortgagees and the mortgagor [39]; in short, " redeem up, foreclose down."

4. Limits to the principle. It is important to notice that this principle has no application to redemptions made out of court.[40] And there is no converse rule " foreclose down, redeem up ": a mortgagee who forecloses is under no obligation to redeem any prior mortgages,[41] although he must foreclose all subsequent mortgagees as well as the mortgagor.[42] In other words, for foreclosure the rule is simply " foreclose down ": a mortgagee cannot foreclose a subsequent mortgagee or the mortgagor unless he forecloses everyone beneath him.[43]

VII. TERMINATION OF EQUITY OF REDEMPTION

An equity of redemption may be extinguished against the mortgagor's will—

    (i) by foreclosure [44];

    (ii) by sale [45]; or

    (iii) by lapse of time.[46]

In addition, the mortgagor may himself extinguish it by releasing it to the mortgagee,[47] or by redeeming.

---

[36] *Fell* v. *Brown* (1787) 2 Bro.C.C. 276 at 278.
[37] *Fell* v. *Brown, supra,* at p. 278, *per* Lord Thurlow L.C.
[38] *Teevan* v. *Smith* (1882) 20 Ch.D. 724 at 729.
[39] *Farmer* v. *Curtis* (1829) 2 Sim. 466.
[40] See *Smith* v. *Green* (1844) 1 Coll.C.C. 555.
[41] *Richards* v. *Cooper* (1842) 5 Beav. 304.
[42] *Bishop of Winchester* v. *Beavor* (1797) 3 Ves. 314; *Anderson* v. *Stather* (1845) 2 Coll.C.C. 209.   [43] *Cockes* v. *Sherman* (1676) Free.Ch. 13.
[44] *Ante*, p. 905.   [45] *Ante*, p. 908.
[46] *Post*, p. 1019.
[47] *e.g.*, *Knight* v. *Marjoribanks* (1849) 2 Mac. & G. 10; *Reeve* v. *Lisle* [1902] A.C. 461; see *ante*, p. 938.

B. Right to Bring Actions

1. Mortgagor's right to sue. A mortgagor's right to bring actions of various kinds needs special consideration, since he is normally left in possession of the property but has no immediate legal title to possession as against the mortgagee. As against third parties, *e.g.*, trespassers or neighbours committing nuisances, the mortgagor, like any other person lawfully in possession of land, could sue at common law to protect that possession,[48] and thus, *e.g.*, recover the land from anyone other than the mortgagee or someone claiming through him. In equity, he was regarded as owner of the land, subject to the mortgage, and so could obtain equitable remedies (such as an injunction [49]) against any person, *e.g.*, to prevent injury to the property,[50] or to enforce a restrictive covenant.[51]

2. Actions as landlord. Difficulties arose, however, when the right of action depended on the legal relationship of landlord and tenant, for example in the case of actions for rent or to enforce covenants against tenants to whom the land had been let before the date of the mortgage.[52] In such cases the mortgage was of course an assignment of the reversion, and thereafter the covenants became enforceable by the mortgagee only.[53] Moreover the court would only allow the mortgagor to sue in the mortgagee's name if the mortgagor offered to redeem,[54] though without doing this he could distrain for rent as agent of the mortgagee.[55]

This difficulty is now remedied by statute.[56] Provided that the mortgagee has not given effective [57] notice of his intention to take possession or enter into receipt of the rents and profits,[57] the mortgagor in possession may sue in his own name for possession or for the rent and profits; he may bring an action to prevent, or recover damages for, any trespass or other wrong [58]; and he may enforce

---

[48] See *post*, p. 1004, where the possessory nature of title to land is explained.

[49] *Van Gelder, Apsimon & Co.* v. *Sowerby Bridge United District Flour Society* (1890) 44 Ch.D. 374.

[50] *Matthews* v. *Usher* [1900] 2 Q.B. 535 at 538; *Turner* v. *Walsh* [1909] 2 K.B. 484 at 487.

[51] *Fairclough* v. *Marshall* (1878) 4 Ex.D. 37.

[52] If the mortgage was made before the lease the mortgagor could of course sue: *Turner* v. *Walsh*, *supra*, at p. 495. As to the nature and effect of such leases, which operate by estoppel, see *ante*, p. 932, also p. 646.

[53] *Turner* v. *Walsh*, *supra*, at p. 495; *Matthews* v. *Usher* [1900] 2 Q.B. 535. For the general law, see *ante*, pp. 650, 734.

[54] *Turner* v. *Walsh*, *supra*, at pp. 495, 496.

[55] *Trent* v. *Hunt* (1853) 9 Exch. 14.

[56] L.P.A., 1925, ss. 98 (replacing J.A., 1873, s. 25 (5)) and 141 (replacing C.A., 1881, s. 10).

[57] Proceedings for possession which by a technical defect are a nullity do not suffice: *Kitchen's Trustee* v. *Madders* [1949] Ch. 588, affd. [1950] Ch. 134.

[58] L.P.A., 1925, s. 98 (1). For the limits of this, see *Turner* v. *Walsh*, *supra*.

all covenants and conditions in leases of the property.[59] It is immaterial whether the mortgage [60] or lease [61] was made before or after the statutory amendment.

C. Other Rights

The mortgagor's rights to have the property sold under an order of the court,[62] to inspect the title deeds,[63] and to compel a transfer of the mortgage,[64] have been explained in earlier sections.

Part 4

TRANSFER OF RIGHTS

Sect. 1. Death of Mortgagor

1. Discharge of mortgage out of assets. A mortgagor's equity of redemption was always considered to be realty,[65] and accordingly passed to the devisee or heir in the same way as other realty.[66] Unless the mortgagor left a will showing a contrary intention,[67] his devisee or heir was entitled to call upon the personal representatives of the deceased to pay off the mortgage out of the deceased's estate in the same way as the other debts of the deceased had to be paid,[68] so that if the personal representatives had sufficient assets to discharge the debt the devisee or heir could compel them to clear off the mortgage free of charge to himself.[69] The rule applied only where the deceased was the original mortgagor and so was personally liable on the covenant to repay the loan [70]; it had no application if the mortgage had been created before the deceased acquired the property (whether by purchase [71] or as heir or devisee [72]), so that he was under no personal liability to repay the loan but merely held subject to the mortgage.

---

[59] L.P.A., 1925, s. 141 (2).
[60] *Ibid.*, s. 98 (3).
[61] *Ibid.*, s. 141 (4).
[62] *Ante*, p. 907.
[63] *Ante*, p. 925.
[64] *Ante*, p. 945.
[65] *Ante*, p. 891.
[66] *e.g.*, subject to curtesy: *Casborne* v. *Scarfe* (1738) 1 Atk. 603; *ante*, p. 514.
[67] *Hancox* v. *Abbey* (1805) 11 Ves. 179.
[68] *Bartholomew* v. *May* (1737) 1 Atk. 487.
[69] *Galton* v. *Hancock* (1743) 2 Atk. 427.
[70] *Lawson* v. *Hudson* (1779) 1 Bro.C.C. 58; *Duke of Ancaster* v. *Mayor* (1785) 1 Bro.C.C. 454.
[71] *Butler* v. *Butler* (1800) 5 Ves. 534.
[72] *Scott* v. *Beecher* (1820) 5 Madd. 96 (devisee); *Earl of Ilchester* v. *Earl of Carnavon* (1839) 1 Beav. 209 (heir).

2. Locke King's Acts. The law was altered by the Real Estate Charges Acts, 1854, 1867 and 1877 (known as Locke King's Acts), now replaced by the Administration of Estates Act, 1925.[73]

The Act of 1854 provided that where a person died after 1854, any of his realty[74] which was subject to a mortgage should be the primary source for satisfaction of the mortgage debt, unless the deceased had shown a contrary intention in any document. The Act did not affect the mortgagee's right to recover any deficiency from the deceased's estate, but it did ensure that, as between the devisee or heir on the one hand, and the deceased's estate on the other, the burden should fall primarily on the devisee or heir.

The Act of 1867 provided that in the case of a testator dying after 1867, a general direction by the testator that his debts should be paid out of his personal estate should not by itself be sufficient contrary intention so as to entitle the devisee or heir to have the mortgage paid off by the personal representatives.[75] It also provided that the Acts should apply to a lien for unpaid purchase-money[76] on lands purchased by the testator.[77]

The Act of 1877 extended these provisions to leaseholds[78] and to all equitable charges, provided the testator died after 1877. But except for leaseholds, the Acts did not apply to personalty,[79] *e.g.*, land held on trust for sale.[80]

3. Modern law. The Administration of Estates Act, 1925, replaces these patchwork provisions in the case of all deaths after 1925, and extends their scope to all property, whether real or personal.[81] It provides accordingly that property mortgaged or charged shall, as between the different persons claiming through a deceased person, be primarily liable to answer the debt, unless the deceased has signified a contrary intention in some document; and that a general direction to pay debts out of personal estate or out of residue is not by itself to be deemed to show contrary intention.[82] Such an intention may be shown in any document (*e.g.*, a letter[83]),

---

[73] s. 35. Maitland described the Act of 1877 as "the last word in the history of a muddle": *Equity*, 267.
[74] Not leaseholds: *Re Wormsley's Estate* (1876) 4 Ch.D. 665.
[75] s. 1.   [76] See *ante*, p. 886.
[77] s. 2, altering the law laid down in *Hood* v. *Hood* (1857) 26 L.J.Ch. 616.
[78] *Re Kershaw* (1888) 37 Ch.D. 674.   [79] *Re Bourne* [1893] 1 Ch. 188 at 191.
[80] *Lewis* v. *Lewis* (1871) L.R. 13 Eq. 218.
[81] A.E.A., 1925, ss. 35, 55 (1) (xvii). See, *e.g.*, *Re Turner* [1938] Ch. 593 (bequest of shares subject to lien of company).
[82] s. 35 (2). This slightly modifies the earlier provisions.
[83] See, *e.g.*, *Re Wakefield* [1943] 2 All E.R. 29 (letter to solicitors directing them to complete a purchase held to show no intention that the devisee should take the property free from the vendor's lien for unpaid purchase-money); and see *Re Birmingham* [1958] Ch. 523.

and it may be partial, *e.g.*, applying to mortgages but not to liens.[84] A direction to pay mortgages out of a special fund suffices,[85] though only to the extent of that fund[86]; but it is not enough merely to make a specific devise of part of the mortgaged land, as distinct from the whole.[87]

These provisions do not affect any rights the mortgagee may have against the estate of the mortgagor; they merely ensure that as between the person taking the mortgaged property and the other beneficiaries, the burden of the mortgage should fall primarily upon the former. They do not apply to a person who is given by a will the right to purchase part of the estate, even at a favourable price; for he is a purchaser and not a devisee or legatee.[88]

Sect. 2. Death of Mortgagee

A. Death of Sole Mortgagee

1. Rights vested in mortgagee. A mortgagee of freeholds who had the whole legal estate conveyed to him before 1926 had two separate rights vested in him:

(i) the legal estate, which was realty; and

(ii) the right to the money lent, which was personalty.[89]

At common law, therefore, on the death of a sole mortgagee the right to the mortgage money passed to his personal representatives,[90] and the legal estate passed to his devisee or heir, who held it on trust for the persons entitled to the money.[91] Thus if the mortgagor wished to redeem he had to pay the money to the persons entitled to it under the will or intestacy, and obtain a reconveyance of the legal estate from the devisee or heir. Apart from requiring two separate transactions, this might well be inconvenient, as where the mortgagee had devised his realty equally between his fifteen children, so making it necessary for all of them to execute the reconveyance.

2. Vesting in personal representatives. This difficulty was sometimes avoided by the testator devising the legal estate to his executors;

---

[84] *Re Beirnstein* [1925] Ch. 12.
[85] *Allie* v. *Katah* [1963] 1 W.L.R. 202.
[86] *Re Fegan* [1928] Ch. 45.
[87] *Re Neeld* [1962] Ch. 643, overruling *Re Biss* [1956] Ch. 243.
[88] *Re Fison's W. T.* [1950] Ch. 394.
[89] *Thornborough* v. *Baker* (1675) 3 Swans. 628.
[90] *Stanley* v. *Mandesley* (1666) 1 Rep.Ch. 254.
[91] *Att.-Gen.* v. *Meyrick* (1750) 2 Ves.Sen. 44 at 46.

and it was in all cases remedied by the Conveyancing Act, 1881,[92] which provided that where a mortgagee died after 1881 the legal estate in such cases should vest in his personal representatives notwithstanding any disposition by the mortgagee's will.

This problem did not arise where the mortgagee's estate was a lease, for that was personalty and followed the same course of devolution as the debt. Since 1897 even the provision made by the Conveyancing Act, 1881, is unnecessary, for realty and personalty alike have since then vested in the personal representatives under the general law.[93]

B. *Death of One of Several Mortgagees*

1. At law. Where two or more persons lent money on mortgage, the legal estate was usually conveyed to them as joint tenants. On the death of one, his interest passed to the others by virtue of the *jus accrescendi*,[94] and the survivors could reconvey the legal estate to the mortgagor when he redeemed.

2. In equity. In equity, however, there is a presumption of a tenancy in common where two or more together lend money on mortgage.[95] Accordingly, in the absence of any provision to the contrary, when one of the mortgagees died his equitable share passed to his personal representatives,[96] and if the mortgagor redeemed they would have to join in the transaction[97]; for otherwise the mortgagor would not obtain a good receipt for the money from the persons entitled to receive it, and the reconveyance would not give him a good title. The same problem arose where the mortgagees were trustees investing trust money, for if it was disclosed that there were beneficiaries who were entitled to the money in equity, the trusts were brought on to the title.[98] The beneficiaries would thus have to join in giving a receipt for the money, for there were no powers of overreaching which dealt with this situation.

3. Joint account clause. In order to meet this difficulty, it became the practice to insert a " joint account clause " in mortgages where two or more persons lent money. This clause recited that the mort-

---

[92] s. 30, now replaced by the more general provisions of A.E.A., 1925, ss. 1 (1), 3 (1).
[93] A.E.A., 1925, ss. 1 (1), 3 (1), replacing provisions of the L.T.A., 1897: *ante*, p. 535.   [94] *Ante*, p. 391.
[95] *Rigden* v. *Vallier* (1751) 2 Ves.Sen. 252 at 258: *ante*, p. 402.
[96] *Petty* v. *Styward* (1632) 1 Ch.Rep. 57.
[97] *Vickers* v. *Cowell* (1839) 1 Beav. 529.
[98] Thus it might be necessary to investigate whether or not the trustees were the duly appointed trustees of the trusts in question: see *Re Blaiberg and Abrahams* [1899] 2 Ch. 340.

gage money belonged to the mortgagees jointly in equity as well as at law. This, as the mortgagor would generally know, was untrue, but he was entitled to rely on it, and could safely pay the surviving mortgagees.[99] In mortgages made since 1881 such a clause is unnecessary (although still often found), for statute [1] has provided that as between the mortgagor and the mortgagees, the mortgagees are deemed to have advanced the money on a joint account unless a contrary intention appears from the mortgage. The result is that the survivor or survivors can give a complete discharge for all moneys due notwithstanding any notice of severance which the mortgagor may have.

This is, of course, mere conveyancing machinery, enabling the surviving mortgagees to overreach the beneficial interests in the mortgaged property. It does not affect the rights of the mortgagees *inter se*; if they are beneficially entitled and not trustees, the survivors must account to the personal representatives of the deceased mortgagee for his share. The joint account clause by itself does not alter the presumption as to a tenancy in common.[2]

Sect. 3. Transfer of Equity of Redemption Inter Vivos

A mortgagor may at any time without the mortgagee's consent make a conveyance of his property subject to the mortgage. Notwithstanding any such conveyance, and even if the transferee undertakes personal liability to the mortgagee,[3] the mortgagor remains personally liable on the covenant to pay the money.[4] He therefore usually takes an express covenant for indemnity from the transferee, but even if he does not [5] a transferee for value [6] will be under an implied obligation to indemnify him.[7]

A mortgagor who wishes to sell free from the mortgage may do so—

    (i) if he redeems; or

    (ii) if the mortgagee consents (as he may well do if the security is adequate or if some other property is substituted for the property in question); or

---

[99] See *Re Harman and Uxbridge and Rickmansworth Ry.* (1883) 24 Ch.D. 720.
[1] C.A., 1881, s. 61, replaced by L.P.A., 1925, s. 111. By s. 112 (replacing C.A., 1911, s. 13) a purchaser is absolved from notice of trusts merely because a transfer of the mortgage is stamped 50p instead of *ad valorem*; and by s. 113 trusts of the mortgage money do not concern a person dealing in good faith with the mortgagee, or with the mortgagor after discharge.
[2] *Re Jackson* (1887) 34 Ch.D. 732.
[3] *West Bromwich B. S.* v. *Bullock* [1936] 1 All E.R. 887.
[4] *Kinnaird* v. *Trollope* (1888) 39 Ch.D. 636.
[5] *Mills* v. *United Counties Bank Ltd.* [1912] 1 Ch. 231 (implied obligation excluded by express but limited obligation).
[6] But not a volunteer: see *Re Best* [1924] 1 Ch. 42.
[7] *Bridgman* v. *Daw* (1891) 40 W.R. 253.

(iii) if the mortgagor takes advantage of the statutory provision enabling the court to declare property free from an incumbrance upon sufficient money being paid into court.[8]

An assignee of the equity of redemption in general steps into the shoes of the mortgagor; but he does not merely by the assignment become personally liable to the mortgagee to pay the mortgage debt to him.[9]

Sect. 4. Transfer of Mortgage Inter Vivos

A. In General

A mortgagee may transfer his mortgage at any time.[10] He may now do so by a simple form of transfer: for since 1925 [11] a deed executed by a mortgagee purporting to transfer his mortgage, or the benefit of it, transfers to the transferee the estate in the land together with the right to the money and the benefit of all covenants, powers and securities therefor, unless a contrary intention appears.[12] The transfer can be made without the concurrence of the mortgagor, but he should always be made a party if possible,[13] for then he admits the state of accounts, *i.e.*, he acknowledges that some specified sum is still due under the mortgage. If he does not join in the transfer, the transferee gets the benefit only of that sum which is actually due,[14] even if the transferor represents that more is owing.[15]

Once the transfer has been made, the transferee should give notice of it to the mortgagor, unless the mortgagor has notice already, *e.g.*, because he was a party to the transfer. If the mortgagor has no actual or constructive notice, the transferee cannot complain if the mortgagor pays to the transferor money due under the mortgage.[16]

---

[8] L.P.A., 1925, s. 50 (1), (2), replacing C.A., 1881, s. 5 (1), (2). This provision is particularly useful if the legal right to redeem has not arisen.

[9] *Re Errington* [1894] 1 Q.B. 11; *cf. ante*, p. 950, n. 72.

[10] See, *e.g.*, *Turner* v. *Smith* [1901] 1 Ch. 213.

[11] The usual practice before 1926 was to transfer both the security and the debt expressly. This was not always essential: the transfer of the estate alone would carry with it the benefit of the debt charged on it (*Jones* v. *Gibbons* (1804) 9 Ves. 407 at 411). But the transfer for value of the debt alone meant that the transferor was still a necessary party to any suit to enforce the security, although any money so recovered would be held on trust for the transferee (*Morley* v. *Morley* (1858) 25 Beav. 253 at 258); and a voluntary transfer of the debt alone was held to be an incomplete gift which equity would not perfect: *Woodford* v. *Charnley* (1860) 28 Beav. 96; but see *Re Patrick* [1891] 1 Ch. 82 at 88.

[12] L.P.A., 1925, s. 114. *Cf.* C.A., 1881, s. 27, and *Re Beachey* [1904] 1 Ch. 67.

[13] 2 K. & E. 266.

[14] *Bickerton* v. *Walker* (1885) 31 Ch.D. 151 at 158. He cannot add the costs of the transfer to the mortgage debt: *Re Radcliffe* (1856) 22 Beav. 201.

[15] *Turner* v. *Smith, supra.*

[16] *Dixon* v. *Winch* [1900] 1 Ch. 736 at 742.

B. Sub-Mortgages

A sub-mortgage is a mortgage of a mortgage.[17] A mortgagee may, instead of transferring his mortgage outright, borrow money upon the security of it. A well-secured debt is in itself a good security for another loan. Thus if X has lent £20,000 upon a mortgage made by B, and X then wishes to raise a temporary loan of £2,000 himself, it would clearly be inadvisable for X to call in the whole of his loan. Consequently, X would raise the money by mortgaging his mortgage, *i.e.*, by making a sub-mortgage.

Before 1926 a sub-mortgage was effected by the mortgagee conveying his estate and assigning the mortgage debt to the sub-mortgagee subject to a proviso for redemption.[18] After 1925 this form is still available if the mortgage is equitable or is a legal charge; but where it has been created by the grant of a term of years, a legal sub-mortgage can be made only by the grant of a sub-term or by a legal charge,[19] though an equitable sub-mortgage can still be made in such a case, *e.g.*, by deposit of title deeds. In general, the sub-mortgagee takes over the mortgagee's rights of enforcing payment under the original mortgage; thus he may sell the property under a power of sale. Alternatively he may exercise his remedies against the mortgage; if the sub-mortgage confers a power of sale, he may sell the mortgage itself.

Sub-mortgages made before 1926 by conveyance of the fee simple or assignment of the lease were converted after 1925 into terms one day shorter than that held by the sub-mortgagor.[20]

Sect. 5. Discharge of Mortgage

A. Before 1926

Upon the redemption of a legal mortgage of a fee simple before 1926, the mortgagee had to execute a reconveyance of the fee simple[21]; meanwhile he held the legal estate upon trust for the mortgagor. In the case of leaseholds there was a reassignment or, if the mortgage had been made by subdemise, a surrender of the sub-lease.[22] In each case the document contained a receipt for the money paid. In the case of a mortgage to a building society, a special form of receipt indorsed on the mortgage deed operated both

---

17 Sub-mortgages are discussed in (1948) 12 Conv.(N.S.) 171 (H. Woodhouse).
18 Fisher & Lightwood, *Mortgages*, 219.
19 L.P.A., 1925, s. 86 (1), (3).
20 L.P.A., 1925, 1st Sched., Pts. VII, para. 4, VIII, para. 4.
21 *Rourke* v. *Robinson* [1911] 1 Ch. 480; Fisher & Lightwood, *Mortgages*, 484.
22 *Re Moore & Hulm's Contract* [1912] 2 Ch. 105, holding the Satisfied Terms Act, 1845 (*ante*, p. 388), inapplicable to terms carved out of leaseholds.

as a discharge of the mortgage and a reconveyance of the estate.[23] An equitable mortgage was sufficiently discharged by an indorsed receipt.[24]

B. *After* 1925

1. Indorsed receipt. In the case of any mortgage discharged after 1925,[25] a receipt indorsed on or annexed to the mortgage deed, signed [26] by the mortgagee and stating the name of the person paying the money, normally operates as a surrender of the mortgage term or a reconveyance, as the case may be, and discharges the mortgage.[27] The mortgagor may, if he prefers, have a reassignment, surrender, release or transfer executed instead [28]; this is necessary if only part of the debt is being paid and part of the property redeemed.[29]

2. Transfer. If the receipt shows that the person paying the money was not entitled to the immediate equity of redemption and makes no provision to the contrary, it operates as a transfer of the mortgage to him.[30] Thus where a third mortgagee pays off the first mortgage, the statutory receipt will transfer the mortgage to him. But this does not enable the mortgagor, on paying off a mortgage, to keep it alive against a subsequent mortgagee.[31]

3. Building societies. A building society may use either a reconveyance or else a special form of statutory receipt. This receipt does not state who paid the money and cannot operate as a transfer of the mortgage; but otherwise it takes effect under these provisions.[32]

4. Satisfied term. Apart from these provisions, once a mortgage by subdemise has been redeemed, the sub-term becomes a satisfied term and ceases forthwith.[33] Under this provision an ordinary receipt (*i.e.*, one not complying with the conditions relating to indorsed receipts and bearing, prior to February 1971,[33a] only a 2d.

---

[23] Building Societies Acts, 1836, s. 5; 1874, s. 42: see *Fourth City Mutual Benefit B. S.* v. *Williams* (1879) 14 Ch.D. 140.
[24] Halsbury, xxvii, 405. But see *Firth & Sons Ltd.* v. *C. I. R.* [1904] 2 K.B. 205.
[25] L.P.A., 1925, s. 115 (8).
[26] *Simpson* v. *Geoghegan* [1934] W.N. 232.
[27] L.P.A., 1925, s. 115 (1).
[28] *Ibid.*, s. 115 (4).
[29] Fisher & Lightwood, *Mortgages*, 485.
[30] L.P.A., 1925, s. 115 (2).
[31] *Otter* v. *Lord Vaux* (1856) 6 De G.M. & G. 638; L.P.A., 1925, s. 115 (3); see *Cumberland Court (Brighton) Ltd.* v. *Taylor* [1964] Ch. 29; and see *ante*, p. 944.
[32] Building Societies Act, 1962, s. 37, 6th Sched., replacing earlier provisions: n. 23, *supra*. See the discussion in Wurtzburg & Mills, *Building Society Law* (13th ed. 1970) pp. 217–221.
[33] L.P.A., 1925, ss. 5, 116; *cf. supra.* This now applies to terms created out of leaseholds as well as as those created out of freeholds.
[33a] See Finance Act 1970, s. 32, Sched. 7, Pt. I, abolishing the stamp duty on a receipt.

stamp [34]) might be thought to operate as a sufficient discharge and save the stamp duty of 1s. per £100 [34a] formerly [35] required on a discharge of a mortgage,[36] whether indorsed or not; but conveyancers do not in practice rely upon such a receipt, for it is only prima facie proof of payment.[37]

Part 5

PRIORITY OF MORTGAGES

Where there is more than one mortgage on the same property, it is sometimes necessary to determine the priority of the mortgages, *e.g.*, if the property is sold by one mortgagee and there is not enough money to satisfy all. There is no question of the various mortgagees sharing the loss. Each mortgagee takes his full claim in order of priority, and it is for a later mortgagee to satisfy himself as to the security before he takes his mortgage. Cases of dispute as to priority are most likely to arise where, perhaps because of the fraud of the mortgagor, a later mortgagee advances his money in ignorance of an earlier mortgage. " It happens with unfortunate frequency that a man having title to land contrives by means of fraudulent conceal-ment to get money from a number of different persons on the security of the land—then disappears—and the lenders are left to dispute among themselves as to the order in which they are to be paid out of the value of the land which is insufficient to pay all of them." [38]

Fundamentally the rules which govern priority are general rules about the relationship of estates, both legal and equitable. Thus the question whether a first equitable mortgage takes priority over a second legal mortgage is essentially the same as the question whether an equitable mortgage binds a later purchaser of the fee simple. The rules are not peculiar to mortgages, but it is in con-nection with mortgages that they most frequently present problems. The question whether a lease takes priority over a mortgage, in a case where a purchaser of land lets it before completion and mortgages it at the time of completion, has been considered in a previous chapter.[39]

The general rules for determining priority will be discussed first, followed by the rules relating to tacking, which is a mode of altering

---

[34] Or none, if indorsed : see *Firth & Sons Ltd.* v. *C. I. R., supra.*
[34a] Under Finance Act 1970, s. 32, Sched. 7, Pt. II, this became 5p per £200.
[35] Until the abolition of this duty on August 1, 1971, by Finance Act 1971, s. 64.
[36] Stamp Act, 1891, 1st Sched. ; Finance Act, 1947, s. 52.
[37] Wolst. & C. i, 225.
[38] Maitland, *Equity*, 125.
[39] *Ante*, p. 647.

the priorities settled by the general rules. In each case the 1925 legislation has made important changes, so that separate consideration must be given to the law before 1926 and after 1925.

Sect. 1. General Rules

A. *Priority Before* 1926

Before 1926 there was one set of rules for determining priorities where the property mortgaged was an interest in land and a separate set of rules for cases where the property mortgaged was an interest in pure personalty, *i.e.*, personalty other than leaseholds.[39a] These will be considered in turn.

I. MORTGAGES OF AN INTEREST IN LAND

Two main rules applied to mortgages of land, including sub-mortgages, *i.e.*, mortgages of a mortgage of land.[40] These rules applied whether the interest was legal or equitable[41] and whether the land was freehold or leasehold.[42]

(i) "*Qui prior est tempore, potior est jure*" (he who is first in time is stronger in law); mortgages primarily ranked in the order of their creation, or "First made, first paid"; but

(ii) "*Where the equities are equal, the law prevails*"; if, apart from the order of their creation, a legal and an equitable mortgage had equal claims to be preferred, the legal mortgage would have priority.[43]

A conflict between two mortgages accordingly fell into one of four classes:

(i) Where both mortgages were legal;
(ii) Where the first was legal and the second equitable;
(iii) Where the first was equitable and the second legal; and
(iv) Where both were equitable.

These will be considered in order.

1. Both mortgages legal. Conflicts where both mortgages were legal rarely came before the courts, since most mortgages of free-

---

[39a] See n. 42, *infra*.
[40] *Taylor* v. *London & County Banking Co.* [1901] 2 Ch. 231.
[41] *Wilmot* v. *Pike* (1845) 5 Hare 14; *Wiltshire* v. *Rabbits* (1844) 14 Sim. 76.
[42] *Rooper* v. *Harrison* (1855) 2 K. & J. 86; *Union Bank of London* v. *Kent* (1888) 39 Ch.D. 238.
[43] *Bailey* v. *Barnes* [1894] 1 Ch. 25 at 36. "Equality means the non-existence of any circumstance which affects the conduct of one of the rival claimants, and makes it less meritorious than that of the other": *ibid., per* Lindley L.J. Formerly these rules might be affected by the Yorkshire and Middlesex Registry Acts in those countries: *post*, p. 1034.

holds were effected by a conveyance of the fee simple, which made the creation of subsequent legal mortgages impossible. Successive legal mortgages could, however, be created by the grant of successive terms of years,[44] and a lease might be mortgaged by the grant of two successive sub-leases.[45] One source of mortgages by demise was the portions term which was commonly inserted in a strict settlement in order that the trustees might mortgage it and raise lump sums for the benefit of the younger children.[46] In any such cases, where two or more legal mortgages were created in succession, priority normally[47] depended on the order of creation, for after the grant of one lease, the second lease must take effect in reversion upon the first, and a legal estate in reversion was postponed to one in possession.[48]

2. Legal mortgage followed by equitable mortgage. Where a legal mortgage was followed by an equitable mortgage, the legal mortgagee had a double claim to priority, both as being prior in point of time and as being a legal mortgagee in competition with a mere equitable mortgagee. But this natural priority might be displaced in a number of ways.

(*a*) *By fraud.* If the legal mortgagee was party to some fraud whereby the equitable mortgagee was deceived into believing that there was no legal mortgage on the property, the legal mortgagee was postponed to the equitable mortgagee.[49]

(*b*) *By estoppel.* If the legal mortgagee either expressly or by implication made some misrepresentation by which the equitable mortgagee was deceived, the legal mortgagee might be estopped from asserting his priority.[50] Thus if the legal mortgagee indorsed a receipt for his money on the mortgage and somebody was thereby induced to lend money on an equitable mortgage of the property, the legal mortgagee could not afterwards claim priority for his loan if in fact it had not been discharged.[51] Again, if the legal mortgagee

---

44 *Aldridge* v. *Duke* (1679) Rep.t.Finch 439.
45 *Jones* v. *Rhind* (1869) 17 W.R. 1091.   46 *Ante*, p. 387.
47 As explained later (see *infra*), a legal mortgagee could lose priority by negligently parting with the title deeds (see *Jones* v. *Rhind*, *supra*), and no doubt also by failure to obtain them, or by fraud.
48 Coote, *Mortgages*, 1240. See *Ex p. Knott* (1806) 11 Ves. 609; *Hurst* v. *Hurst* (1852) 16 Beav. 372. See also *Re Russell Road Purchase-Moneys* (1871) L.R. 12 Eq. 78 (lease mortgaged first by the grant of a legal sub-term and then by legal assignment; the mortgagee by assignment claimed priority over an intervening equitable mortgage of which he had no notice, but the case was compromised before the Court of Appeal could give judgment).
49 *Peter* v. *Russel* (1716) 1 Eq.Ca.Abr. 321.
50 *Dixon* v. *Muckleston* (1872) 8 Ch.App. 155 at 160.
51 *Rimmer* v. *Webster* [1902] 2 Ch. 163; *cf. Rice* v. *Rice* (1853) 2 Drew. 73 (two equitable incumbrances).

returned the deeds to the mortgagor in order to enable him to raise
a further loan, he was postponed to any subsequent mortgagee who
lent money without notice of the first mortgage, even if the mortgagor had agreed to inform the second mortgagee of the first
mortgage,[52] or had agreed to borrow only a limited amount which
in fact he exceeded.[53] Once the mortgagee had clothed the mortgagor
with apparent authority to deal with the property freely, he could
not afterwards claim the protection of any undisclosed limits set
to this authority.[54]

(c) *By gross negligence in relation to the title deeds.* It was
held in one case that an earlier legal mortgagee could never lose his
priority by mere carelessness or want of prudence, falling short of
fraud.[55] But the law appears rather to have been that by gross
negligence in failing to obtain the title deeds,[56] or, perhaps, to retain
them,[57] he could lose priority as against a later equitable mortgagee
who exercised due diligence himself.[58] " Gross negligence " is an
indefinable expression, but it was used to indicate a degree of
negligence which made it unjust to enforce the natural order of
priority.[59] A legal mortgagee who failed to ask for the deeds at
all [60] would certainly be postponed. But a legal mortgagee might
claim the benefit of the doctrine, explained below,[61] which preserves
priority for mortgagees who ask for the deeds and are given a

---

[52] *Briggs* v. *Jones* (1870) L.R. 10 Eq. 92; and see *Martinez* v. *Cooper* (1826) 2 Russ. 198.

[53] *Perry Herrick* v. *Attwood* (1857) 2 De G. & J. 21.

[54] *Brocklesby* v. *Temperance Permanent B. S.* [1895] A.C. 173; *Rimmer* v. *Webster*, *supra*, at p. 173; *Abigail* v. *Lapin* [1934] A.C. 491.

[55] *Northern Counties of England Fire Insurance Co.* v. *Whipp* (1884) 26 Ch.D. 482. See n. 57, *infra*.

[56] *Colyer* v. *Finch* (1856) 5 H.L.C. 905; *Clarke* v. *Palmer* (1882) 21 Ch.D. 124; *Walker* v. *Linom* [1907] 2 Ch. 104. In the last case W conveyed land to trustees, handing over a bundle of title deeds but keeping the last previous deed, a conveyance to himself; later he made, or purported to make, a mortgage with the help of this deed: held, that the mortgagee took priority over the trustees, and that a beneficiary under the trust was in no better position than the trustees. It might have been thought that the mortgagee, who saw only one deed (seven years old) and cannot have investigated the title properly, had little claim in equity against the legal owner. But this point does not appear to have arisen. For this case, see further below, n. 65.

[57] This is less certain. In *Northern Counties of England Fire Insurance Co.* v. *Whipp*, *supra*, the manager of a company mortgaged his property to the company. Later he took back the deeds, which had been placed in a safe to which he had a key, and gave them to X under a mortgage. Held, that the company had priority over X. A distinction between failure to obtain deeds and failure to retain them is difficult to justify, and the Court of Appeal's decision is probably open to question in the light of *Derry* v. *Peek* (1889) 14 App.Cas. 337: see Waldock, *Mortgages*, 397.

[58] *Hunt* v. *Elmes* (1860) 2 De G.F. & J. 578 at 586, 587. See *Walker* v. *Linom* [1907] 2 Ch. 104 at 114.

[59] See *Oliver* v. *Hinton* [1899] 2 Ch. 264 at 274, *post*, p. 964, n. 75.

[60] *Clarke* v. *Palmer* (1882) 21 Ch.D. 124; *Walker* v. *Linom*, *supra*.

[61] *Post*, p. 964.

reasonable excuse for their non-production.[62] Further, where the mortgagee knew that the deeds were in the hands of a prior equitable mortgagee but gave him no notice, so that when the mortgagor paid off the equitable mortgage the mortgagor recovered the deeds and was enabled to create a later equitable mortgage,[63] he was held not guilty of such gross negligence as would postpone him. Nor was the legal mortgagee postponed merely because he failed to obtain all the title deeds: if he obtained some of them reasonably believing them to be all, he was not postponed.[64]

The postponement of an earlier legal to a later equitable incumbrancer for any of the above three reasons is explicable only as an intervention by equity against the ordinary rules governing estates, in particular against the rule that no one can convey what he has not got. The later equitable mortgagee could obtain from the mortgagor only a mortgage of the equity of redemption: the legal estate was outstanding in the first mortgagee, and could be obtained only by redeeming. Nevertheless, if the conduct of the first mortgagee raised a case of fraud, estoppel or gross negligence, the second mortgagee could enforce a prior equitable right to the legal estate, and so ultimately obtain it without redemption. If, for example, his mortgage gave him a power of sale, he could give a good title to a purchaser, free from the earlier mortgage which in law stood first but which in equity stood second.[65] Conversely, it seems probable that if the earlier legal mortgagee transferred his mortgage to a transferee for value who took without notice of the circumstances, *e.g.*, of fraud, the transferee would take free from the equitable liability to postponement.

3. Equitable mortgage followed by legal mortgage

(a) *Purchaser without notice.* Where an equitable mortgage was followed by a legal mortgage, the primary rule that the mortgages

---

[62] *Manners* v. *Mew* (1885) 29 Ch.D. 725. *Quaere* whether the excuse given there would be treated as reasonable today; but the case can perhaps be supported on the relationship between the parties: see, *e.g.*, *Hewitt* v. *Loosemore* (1851) 9 Hare 449; *post*, pp. 963–964.

[63] *Grierson* v. *National Provincial Bank of England Ltd.* [1913] 2 Ch. 18.

[64] *Cottey* v. *The National Provincial Bank of England Ltd.* (1904) 20 T.L.R. 607. *Contra, Walker* v. *Linom, supra,* n. 56.

[65] *Walker* v. *Linom* (*supra*, n. 56). In a note to Maitland, *Equity*, 138, the learned editor (J. W. Brunyate) draws attention to the second incumbrancer's lack of title in that case. The facts were striking, since the prior disposition was an outright conveyance, not a mere mortgage (see *supra*, n. 56). But a mere mortgage would have had the same effect before 1926, as regards the legal estate. In fact the peculiarity seems to apply equally to all the cases in this class. The legal estate remains vested in the person to whom it was first conveyed (*Walker* v. *Linom*, at p. 110), but presumably the person entitled to priority in equity can compel a transfer of it. He is said to have " a subsequent equitable estate " (at p. 114), but this seems to arise from an intervention of the court rather than from any interest which the mortgagor had power to create.

rank in the order of creation might be displaced by the superiority of a legal estate. For this to occur, the legal mortgagee had to show that he was a bona fide purchaser [66] for value of a legal estate without notice [67] of the prior equitable mortgage.[68] In general, a failure to inquire for the deeds at all,[69] or the inability of the mortgagor to produce the title deeds, would amount to constructive notice to the legal mortgagee that some prior mortgage or conveyance had already been made.[70] But there might be good reason for the absence of the deeds (*e.g.*, that they had been destroyed in a fire), and if the later legal mortgagee accepted a " reasonable excuse " for the non-production of the deeds, he was held to have no notice of the prior mortgage.

(*b*) *Excuses for not producing deeds.* The courts have, however, been satisfied by surprisingly frail excuses, imperfectly investigated. The excuse that the deeds also relate to other property has been held insufficient [71]; but prior equitable mortgagees, in possession of the deeds, have lost priority over later legal mortgagees who have been told by the mortgagor that he was busy then, but would produce the deeds later,[72] or that the deeds were in Ireland, where the property was.[73] Such cases appear to deviate from the ordinary principle of notice, which absolves a purchaser of a legal estate only if he has taken all the steps which a prudent man of business, properly advised, would be expected to take [74]; a mere story invented by the mortgagor and not investigated may deprive the first mortgagee of his priority.

This rule probably owes its origin to a doctrine about " gross negligence " which has caused some confusion. It has often been

---

[66] " Purchaser " includes a mortgagee: *Brace* v. *Duchess of Marlborough* (1728) 2 P.Wms. 491; *Pilcher* v. *Rawlins* (1872) 7 Ch.App. 259.

[67] It was only when the equities were equal that the law prevailed, and " he that has Notice has no Equity at all ": *Oxwith* v. *Plummer* (1708) Gilb.Ch. 13 at 15, *per* Lord Cowper L.C.

[68] *Ante*, p. 118. As there mentioned, a better equitable right to an outstanding legal estate would do; see the case put in *Wilmot* v. *Pike* (1845) 5 Hare 14 at 21, 22, which may be paraphrased thus: successive mortgages are made to A (legal), B (equitable) and C (equitable); A joins in the mortgage to C and (neither A nor C then knowing of B's mortgage) declares himself trustee for C subject to A's own mortgage. C then takes priority to B because of his better title to the legal estate; but not if either A or C knew of B's mortgage at the time of the declaration of trust. This shows the importance of B giving notice to A. C could not secure priority merely by giving notice to A before B did so, for the rule in *Dearle* v. *Hall* (1828) 3 Russ. 1 (see *infra*) did not apply to realty; therefore a declaration of trust was essential to C's claim.

[69] *Berwick & Co.* v. *Price* [1905] 1 Ch. 632.

[70] That, indeed, is a primary object in depositing the deeds: see *ante*, p. 898.

[71] *Oliver* v. *Hinton* [1899] 2 Ch. 264.

[72] *Hewitt* v. *Loosemore* (1851) 9 Hare 449, and earlier cases there cited; *cf. Ratcliffe* v. *Barnard* (1871) 6 Ch.App. 652 (receipt by legal mortgagee of some only of the deeds, in reasonable belief that they were all).

[73] *Agra Bank Ltd.* v. *Barry* (1874) L.R. 7 H.L. 135.

[74] *Ante*, p. 121.

said that the later legal mortgagee is entitled to priority if he has not been fraudulent or grossly negligent.[75] But in this class of case, unlike the class previously discussed, the rule contradicts the principle that an equitable interest should bind a purchaser who does not investigate the title. The exception is, however, firmly established.

4. Both mortgages equitable. Where both mortgages were equitable, the primary rule was that priority depended upon the order in which the mortgages were created.[76] This, however, was subject to the equities being in other respects equal,[77] so that although the vested interest of the prior mortgagee would not lightly be displaced,[78] the order might be altered by the inequitable behaviour of the prior mortgagee.[79] Accordingly, a first mortgagee who failed to ask for the title deeds,[80] or who, having obtained them, redelivered them to the mortgagor without pressing for their early return,[81] might be postponed to a second mortgagee who took all proper precautions but who was nevertheless deceived. But a first mortgagee who accepted some only of the title deeds, on the mortgagor's written assurance that they were all, did not lose his priority.[82]

II.   MORTGAGES OF AN EQUITABLE INTEREST IN PURE PERSONALTY

1. The rule in Dearle v. Hall. Legal mortgages of chattels fall under the head of bills of sale and are outside the scope of this book;

---

[75] See *Hewitt* v. *Loosemore, supra*; *Oliver* v. *Hinton* [1899] 2 Ch. 264; *Hudston* v. *Viney* [1921] 1 Ch. 98. In *Oliver* v. *Hinton* there was first an equitable mortgage by deposit, followed by an outright sale of the legal estate to a purchaser who had no actual notice of the mortgage but who accepted an inadequate excuse for non-production of the deeds (*viz.*, that they related also to other property). It was held that the purchaser took subject to the mortgage. On general grounds it should have sufficed to say that the purchaser had constructive notice, and the case was so decided by Romer J. at first instance, at p. 268 (this was also the view of Parker J. in *Walker* v. *Linom* [1907] 2 Ch. 104 at 114). But the Court of Appeal held the purchaser liable not because of notice but because of his " gross negligence ": see Lindley M.R.'s judgment at pp. 273, 274. Why this doctrine was needed, or how, if at all, it differs from the doctrine of notice, is not explained.

[76] *Rice* v. *Rice* (1853) 2 Drew. 73 at 78.

[77] *Ibid.*

[78] *Cory* v. *Eyre* (1863) 1 De G.J. & S. 149 at 167.

[79] Whether priority will be lost only by the same degree of gross negligence as will displace a legal mortgagee is doubtful: see *Taylor* v. *Russell* [1891] 1 Ch. 8 at 14–20 where the authorities are reviewed. See also the decision of the House of Lords in that case ([1892] A.C. 244 at 262) and *National Provincial Bank of England* v. *Jackson* (1886) 33 Ch.D. 1, for the view that a smaller degree of negligence may suffice to displace an equitable mortgagee.

[80] *Farrand* v. *Yorkshire Banking Co.* (1888) 40 Ch.D. 182.

[81] *Waldron* v. *Sloper* (1852) 1 Drew. 193; *Dowle* v. *Saunders* (1864) 2 H. & M. 242.

[82] *Dixon* v. *Muckleston* (1872) 8 Ch.App. 155.

so also are mortgages of choses in action. Equitable interests in pure personalty, on the other hand, include the rights of those interested under a trust for sale [83] (as distinct from land subject to a mere *power* of sale,[84] or money deemed by statute to be land,[85] such as capital money under the Settled Land Act, 1882 [86]) and so must be dealt with here. Mortgages of such interests were governed by the rule in *Dearle* v. *Hall*.[87] This laid down that priority depended upon the order in which notice of the mortgages or other dealings was received by the owner of the legal estate or interest (the trustees, in the case of a trust for sale), but that a mortgagee who, when he lent his money, had actual or constructive notice of a prior mortgage could not gain priority over it by giving notice first.

2. Basis of the rule. The rule in *Dearle* v. *Hall* is a general principle of equity governing dealings with equitable interests in pure personalty. Various explanations of the basis of the rule have been given.[88] The " leading consideration " is that as between two equally innocent incumbrancers, priority should be given to the one who, by giving notice, had prevented the mortgagor from representing himself to be the unincumbered owner of the property and so defrauding third parties.[89] The rule may also be based on an analogy with chattels, where title passes by delivery of possession. An assignee of an equitable interest in personalty must, it was held, take steps to obtain the equivalent to possession by giving notice to the trustee, and so perfecting his title.[90] An imperfect title would not prevail over a later assignee's perfected title; and the earlier assignee's equity was all the weaker for his own negligence in allowing the trustees to suppose that the later assignee was the first.

Although the rule was founded on equitable principles, it soon crystallised into a rigid rule [91] and by the beginning of this century it was settled that it would not be extended.[92]

---

[83] *Lee* v. *Howlett* (1856) 2 K. & J. 531; *ante*, p. 369.
[84] *Rooper* v. *Harrison* (1855) 2 K. & J. 86.
[85] *Re Carew's Estate* (1868) 16 W.R. 1077; but see *Re Sandes' Trusts* [1920] 1 I.R. 216.
[86] s. 26: see *ante*, p. 376.
[87] (1828) 3 Russ. 1, approved by the House of Lords in *Foster* v. *Cockerell* (1835) 3 Cl. & F. 456; and see *Ward* v. *Duncombe* [1893] A.C. 369.
[88] See, *e.g.*, *Ward* v. *Duncombe* [1893] A.C. 369 at 392.
[89] *Ibid.*, at p. 378.
[90] But see Lord Macnaghten's criticisms in *Ward* v. *Duncombe* [1893] A.C. 369 at 392; *cf.* Lord Herschell's speech at p. 378. The House of Lords discussed the rule in *B. S. Lyle Ltd.* v. *Rosher* [1959] 1 W.L.R. 8.
[91] See, *e.g.*, *Re Dallas* [1904] 2 Ch. 385 (X charged a legacy he was expecting under the will of a living testator, who had become insane, first to A and then to B: the testator then died and A and B each gave notice to the administrator as soon as they knew of his appointment, B's notice being received first: held B had priority).
[92] *Ward* v. *Duncombe, supra*, at p. 394; *Hill* v. *Peters* [1918] 2 Ch. 273.

3. Loan without notice. It will be noticed that for a second mortgagee to claim priority over a first mortgagee by giving notice first, he must be able to show that at the time of lending his money he had no notice of the first mortgage.[93] If at that time he had notice, and yet he lent his money, it would be inequitable for him subsequently to claim priority merely because he gave notice first, for the failure of the first mortgagee to give notice had in no way prejudiced him; he lent his money knowing of the first mortgage. But if he lent his money without notice of the first mortgage, it was immaterial that he had notice of the first mortgage at the time when he gave notice to the trustees.[94] Indeed, such knowledge is just what would impel him to give notice.[95]

4. Details of the rule. The details of the rule were worked out in a series of cases, which may be summarised under three main heads.

(*a*) *Priority depended upon notice being received, not given.* Although it was both usual and advisable for a mortgagee to give express notice, the test was not whether the mortgagee had taken active steps to give notice but whether the trustees had received knowledge of the mortgage from any reliable source. For example, where one chargee left written notice with the legal owner, a bank, after closing hours, and other chargees gave notice the next day, as soon as the bank opened, it was held that the bank must be treated as having received all notices simultaneously, and consequently that the charges ranked in the order of creation.[96]

Clear and distinct oral notice sufficed,[97] but a statement made in a casual conversation with a trustee did not.[98] Knowledge received through reading a notice in a paper,[99] and knowledge acquired by a trustee before his appointment which continued to operate on his mind after his appointment,[1] have both been held sufficient to protect a mortgagee against a later mortgagee who gave express notice, although neither would obtain priority for a later mortgagee over a prior mortgagee[2]; stronger measures are needed to upset the natural order of the mortgages than are needed to maintain it.

[93] *Re Holmes* (1885) 29 Ch.D. 786.
[94] *Mutual Life Assurance Society* v. *Langley* (1886) 32 Ch.D. 460.
[95] *Cf. Wortley* v. *Birkhead* (1754) 2 Ves.Sen. 571 at 574. *Cf. post*, p. 979, for a somewhat similar situation in the old law of tacking.
[96] *Calisher* v. *Forbes* (1871) 7 Ch.App. 109; and see *Johnstone* v. *Cox* (1880) 16 Ch.D. 571 (affirmed, 19 Ch.D. 17). *Re Dallas* [1904] 2 Ch. 385 at 405 must, it seems, be taken to refer to simultaneous notices.
[97] *Browne* v. *Savage* (1859) 4 Drew. 635 at 640; *Re Worcester* (1868) 3 Ch.App. 555 (statement at directors' meeting); compare the simultaneous notices in *Calisher* v. *Forbes, supra.*   [98] *Re Tichener* (1865) 35 Beav. 317.
[99] *Lloyd* v. *Banks* (1868) 3 Ch.App. 488.
[1] *Ipswich Permanent Money Club Ltd.* v. *Arthy* [1920] 2 Ch. 257.
[2] *Ibid.*, at p. 271; *Arden* v. *Arden* (1885) 29 Ch.D. 702.

(*b*) *It was advisable to give notice to all the trustees.* This was because :

    (i) Notice given to all the existing trustees remained effective even though they all retired or died without communicating the notice to their successors.[3]

    (ii) Notice given to one of several trustees was effective against all incumbrances created during his trusteeship, and for this purpose remained effective after his death or retirement.[4]

    (iii) But notice given to one of several trustees was not effective against incumbrancers who advanced money after the death or retirement of that trustee, unless he had communicated the notice to one or more of the continuing trustees.[5]

    (iv) If the mortgagor was a trustee, the mere fact that he knew of the transaction would not affect priorities, for such notice afforded no protection to subsequent mortgagees.[6] But if the mortgagee was a trustee, his knowledge of the transaction did affect priorities; for to protect his mortgage he would readily disclose its existence to any prospective incumbrancers.[7]

(*c*) *A mortgagee who lent his money with notice of a prior mortgage could not gain priority over it by giving notice first.* This has been discussed above.[8]

5. Protection on distribution. In addition to securing priority, notice to the trustees, though not essential to the validity of the mortgage,[9] safeguarded the mortgagee by ensuring that his claims would not be disregarded when the funds were distributed. Trustees were bound to give effect to all claims of which they knew,[10] but were not liable if they distributed the trust funds to the prejudice of a mortgagee of whom they did not know.[11] Nor were they bound to answer inquiries either by the beneficiary or a prospective

---

[3] *Re Wasdale* [1899] 1 Ch. 163.
[4] *Ward* v. *Duncombe* [1893] A.C. 369.
[5] *Timson* v. *Ramsbottom* (1836) 2 Keen 35, criticised by Lord Macnaghten in *Ward* v. *Duncombe, supra,* at p. 394, but accepted by Lord Herschell at pp. 381, 382, and followed in *Re Phillips' Trusts* [1903] 1 Ch. 183. For the problems which this rule can present, see *post,* p. 974, n. 39.
[6] *Lloyds Bank* v. *Pearson* [1901] 1 Ch. 865. To hold otherwise would make the rule in *Dearle* v. *Hall* " a mere trap " : *ibid.* at p. 873, *per* Cozens-Hardy J.
[7] *Browne* v. *Savage* (1859) 4 Drew. 635 at 641.
[8] *Ante,* p. 965.
[9] *Burn* v. *Carvalho* (1839) 4 My. & Cr. 690 ; *Gorringe* v. *Irwell India Rubber & Gutta Percha Works* (1886) 34 Ch.D. 128.
[10] *Hodgson* v. *Hodgson* (1837) 2 Keen 704.
[11] *Phipps* v. *Lovegrove* (1873) L.R. 16 Eq. 80.

mortgagee as to the extent to which the beneficiary's share was incumbered: " it is no part of the duty of a trustee to assist his *cestui que trust* in selling or mortgaging his beneficial interest and in squandering or anticipating his fortune." [12]

B. *Priority After* 1925

The general scheme of the 1925 legislation called for some amendment of the rules relating to priority. In particular, the old rule of the superiority of the legal estate was clearly inappropriate to a system which encouraged the creation of more than one legal mortgage of the same property; and since the interests of beneficiaries under strict settlements could no longer be legal, for the purposes of priority they could conveniently be classed with interests arising under a trust for sale.

Before 1926 the line of cleavage was the line between interests in land and interests in pure personalty: if the former, the case was governed by the rules relating to the order of creation and the superiority of the legal estate; if the latter, by the rule in *Dearle* v. *Hall*. After 1925 the question is whether the interest mortgaged is legal or equitable. A mortgage of a legal estate in land now depends for its priority upon possession of the title deeds, or, in default, upon registration; a mortgage of an equitable interest in realty or personalty depends upon the rule in *Dearle* v. *Hall*. Thus if an equitable interest in settled land was mortgaged before 1926, priority depended on the order in which the mortgages were created; if it is mortgaged after 1925, priority is governed by the rule in *Dearle* v. *Hall*.

Priorities acquired before 1926 are not affected by the new rules, which apply only to mortgages created after 1925.[13]

I. MORTGAGES OF A LEGAL ESTATE

This title includes all mortgages of a legal estate, whether the mortgage itself is legal or equitable. The question is " Has a legal estate been mortgaged? ", not " Is the mortgage legal or equitable? " Legal and equitable mortgages need no longer be separated, since the legislation of 1925 treats them both on the same lines.[14]

---

[12] *Low* v. *Bouverie* [1891] 3 Ch. 82 at 99, *per* Lindley L.J.
[13] L.P.A., 1925, ss. 97, 137 (7); L.C.A., 1925, s. 13 (2), replaced by L.C.A. 1972, s. 4 (5). Pre-1926 mortgages belonging to class C become subject to rules about registration if transferred after 1925: *post*, p. 1053; but s. 13 (2) can hardly be intended to affect priority over a pre-1926 purchaser, against whom the mortgagee had no opportunity of registering.
[14] There is a general survey of priorities of such mortgages at (1940) 7 C.L.J. 243 (R.E.M.).

1. Categories of mortgages

(*a*) *The scheme.* The scheme of the legislation is to divide all mortgages of a legal estate into two classes—

(i) mortgages protected by deposit of deeds; and

(ii) mortgages not so protected,

and to make class (ii) registrable as land charges under the Land Charges Act 1972 (replacing the Land Charges Act, 1925). The aim is to make all mortgages readily ascertainable. If a mortgagee has possession of the deeds, their absence will proclaim his mortgage to all other persons seeking to deal with the land. If he has not, he can proclaim his interest to the world by registration. Protection by deposit of deeds is in practice so effective that there is no need to require the registration of mortgages belonging to class (i).[15]

(*b*) *Unregistrable mortgages.* Protected mortgages (class (i) above) are therefore outside the registration machinery and are governed, as regards priority, by the same rules as applied before 1926. They are defined as mortgages " protected " (or " secured ") by a " deposit of documents relating to the legal estate affected." There is no positive enactment about them; they are simply excluded (as will shortly be seen) from the classes of land charges among which unprotected mortgages are intended to be registered. Although it is not clear, probably " protected " (or " secured ") means *originally* protected or secured, rather than *continuously* protected or secured, for otherwise the mortgage would fluctuate between being registrable and unregistrable as often as the mortgagee parted with the deeds and regained them.[16]

(*c*) *Registrable mortgages.* Unprotected mortgages (class (ii) above), if made after 1925, are registrable in the following classes—

(i) if legal, as " puisne mortgages." A puisne mortgage is defined as a legal mortgage not " protected by a deposit of documents relating to the legal estate affected." [17]

(ii) if equitable, as " general equitable charges." A general equitable charge is any equitable charge which, not being " secured by a deposit of documents relating to the legal

---

[15] But see *post*, p. 975, for the risk of " reasonable excuse."

[16] See (1940) 7 C.L.J. 249 (R.E.M.).

[17] L.C.A. 1972, s. 2 (4); the former provision in L.C.A., 1925, s. 10 (1) that a puisne mortgage ranks as such only if not registered in a local deeds registry was repealed by L.P.A. 1969, s. 17 (5): *post*, p. 1039.

estate affected," does not arise under a trust for sale or a settlement, and is not included in any other class of land charge.[18]

(*d*) *Failure to register.* The penalty for failing to register a registrable mortgage is loss of priority over a later purchaser or incumbrancer. The mortgage remains valid as between mortgagor and mortgagee, but as against a later purchaser from the mortgagor (including a later mortgagee) it is void. There are two provisions to be applied—

(i) Section 97 of the Law of Property Act, 1925, which provides that every such mortgage " shall rank according to its date of registration as a land charge pursuant to the Land Charges Act, 1925 or 1972 " [18a]; and

(ii) Section 4 (5) of the Land Charges Act 1972, which provides that a puisne mortgage or general equitable charge created after 1925 shall " be void as against a purchaser of the land charged therewith, or of any interest in such land, unless the land charge is registered in the appropriate register before the completion of the purchase." In the Act, unless the context otherwise requires, " purchaser " means " any person (including a mortgagee or lessee) who, for valuable consideration, takes any interest in land or in a charge on land." [19] Thus a registrable but unregistered mortgage is void against a later mortgagee, even if he had actual knowledge of it; for where an interest is void for non-registration as against a purchaser, he is not prejudicially affected by notice of it.[20]

(*e*) *Equitable mortgages as estate contracts.* Before the operation of these rules is illustrated, one problem must be faced. It is plain that the design of the Land Charges Acts is to exempt all protected mortgages from registration.[21] But it may be argued that a protected *equitable* mortgage is registrable as an " estate contract " (defined as any contract to convey or create a legal estate [22]), since the foundation of an equitable mortgage is a contract to create a legal mortgage,[23] and there is nothing in the definition

---

[18] L.C.A. 1972, s. 2 (4); *post*, p. 1040.
[18a] L.C.A. 1972, s. 18 (6) in effect inserts the last two words.
[19] L.C.A. 1972, s. 17 (1).
[20] L.P.A., 1925, s. 199 (1) (i); *ante*, p. 147; *post*, p. 1040.
[21] The usual view is that they are not registrable: see, *e.g.,* Cheshire, *Modern Law of Real Property*, 11th ed., 684; Waldock, *Mortgages*, 410.
[22] L.C.A. 1972, s. 2 (4) (iv); *post*, p. 1040.
[23] *Ante*, p. 899.

of "estate contract" to exclude equitable mortgages by deposit.[24] This argument is logically strong, but its weakness is that it would upset the scheme of the Act and destroy the security of many equitable mortgages. For these reasons it is probable that the courts would resist it. It could, for example, be argued that an equitable mortgage, although originally a contract to execute a legal mortgage, has now become a distinct and well-recognised transaction which leads not to a legal mortgage but ultimately to foreclosure by order of the court; and this right to enforce the security might be said to fall outside the statutory definition of an estate contract, even though as against a later purchaser the equitable mortgagee may have lost his right to call for a legal mortgage unless the transaction is registered.

(*f*) *Validity as charge.* Even if it could be said that a protected equitable mortgage was wholly deprived of its priority as such for want of registration as an estate contract, it could still be argued that the mortgagee had the benefit of being an equitable chargee[25]; for an equitable mortgage by deposit is a charge as well as a contract to execute a legal mortgage,[26] and a mere charge protected by deposit of deeds is undoubtedly not registrable. While the question remains open, the most prudent course is to advise registration of all equitable mortgages, even though it may be assumed that the courts will not feel compelled to depart from the general intention of the Act merely because the definition of " estate contract " is so widely drawn. The possibility that protected equitable mortgages are registrable will be disregarded in the examples which follow.

2. Operation of the rules. The new rules can operate in four possible combinations of mortgages.

(*a*) *Both mortgages protected by a deposit of deeds.* There is nothing to require the deposit of all the deeds; therefore it may be possible for two or more mortgages of the same property to be exempted from registration provided that the deeds deposited do in fact " protect " or " secure " the mortgage. For example, A may make a mortgage to X and hand over all the existing deeds; A may then sell the property to B, subject to the mortgage; and B may then mortgage it to Y and deposit with Y the conveyance from A to B. In such a case registration is inapplicable and the old law

---

[24] See (1930) 69 L.J.News. 227 (J.M.L.); (1940) 7 C.L.J. 250, 251 (R.E.M.); (1949) 10 C.L.J. 245 (S. J. Bailey); (1962) 26 Conv.(N.S.) 445 (R. F. Rowley).
[25] See (1940) 7 C.L.J. 252 (R.E.M.).
[26] *Pryce* v. *Bury* (1853) 2 Drew. 41.

applies. The 1925 legislation has not altered the basic principle that prima facie mortgages rank in the order of their creation,[27] subject to the rules as to loss of priority, *e.g.*, by fraud, gross negligence, or the plea of purchaser without notice.[28] In this class of case it may therefore still matter whether the mortgages are legal or equitable.

(b) *Neither mortgage protected by a deposit of deeds*

(1) BOTH MORTGAGES REGISTRABLE. In this case both mortgages are registrable. No difficulty arises if the first mortgage is duly registered before the second is made. Even if the first is equitable and the second legal the first prevails, for the provision that registration amounts to notice prevents the legal mortgagee from claiming to be a purchaser without notice.[29] Nor is there any difficulty if neither mortgage is registered. Even if the first mortgage is legal and the second equitable, under section 4 (5) the first is void against the second for want of registration and so the second has priority. Indeed, if there are several successive registrable mortgages, none of which has been registered, the maxim " *qui prior est tempore, potior est jure* " is now reversed, for the last will rank first and so on.

(2) CONFLICT OF STATUTES. The more difficult case is where the first mortgage was registered after the creation of the second mortgage. For example:

January 1	A grants a registrable mortgage to X
February 2	A grants a registrable mortgage to Y
March 3	X registers
March 4	Y registers

Here the provisions of the Law of Property Act, 1925 (s. 97) and the Land Charges Act 1972 (s. 4 (5)) are in apparent conflict. According to section 4 (5) the order of priority is plainly Y, X, for X's mortgage is void against Y. According to a simple reading of section 97 the order should be X, Y, for the section requires every such mortgage to " rank according to its date of registration." [30] How this conflict would be resolved is uncertain, but it might well be that section 4 (5) would be held to prevail, despite the argument

---

[27] See *Roberts* v. *Croft* (1857) 2 De G. & J. 1; *Beddoes* v. *Shaw* [1937] Ch. 81; [1936] 2 All E.R. 1108.

[28] See *Dixon* v. *Muckleston* (1872) 8 Ch.App. 155; *ante*, p. 960.

[29] *Post*, p. 1044.

[30] An argument for this solution, and for the rejection of s. 4 (5), is put forward in (1950) 13 M.L.R. at 534–535 (A. D. Hargreaves). It depends on a distinction between mortgages and other purchases which is not convincing.

(not a strong one [31]) that section 97 would then be meaningless. If X's mortgage is void as against Y, it is difficult to see how the subsequent registration of X's mortgage can give priority to something which, *ex hypothesi*, has no existence as regards Y.[32] Against that, section 4 (5) applies to mortgages only by reason of the statutory definition of " purchaser," which applies only unless the context otherwise requires,[33] whereas section 97 is patently intended to regulate the priority of mortgages; and *generalia specialibus non derogant.*[34]

(3) AVOIDANCE OF CONFLICT. A possible interpretation of section 97 which avoids any conflict is that it merely refers to the machinery of the Land Charges Act and accords with it. The section says that an unprotected mortgage " shall rank according to its date of registration as a land charge pursuant to the Land Charges Act," 1925 or 1972. The operation of section 4 (5) is governed, of course, by the date of registration, but it does not necessarily follow that the mortgage first registered stands first in priority in all cases. Section 97 does not say, to quote the language of another Act of 1925,[35] that registrable charges shall " rank according to the order in which they are entered on the register "; and it might have been more natural to say this had it been intended.[36] On this interpretation section 97 merely provides that registrable mortgages shall rank for priority according to the provisions of the Land Charges Act, *i.e.*, according to section 4 (5).

The argument that the two sections conflict draws its strength from the evident intention of section 97 to deal with the question of priority. Precedents can be found for similar forms of words in Acts requiring registration,[37] and section 97 may have been modelled upon them. If it was intended as a mere reference to the Land Charges Act, it seems both redundant and contradictory. The argument against

---

[31] This could equally well be said of s. 199 (1) (i) for the same reason. Overlapping provisions are by no means rare.

[32] See (1926) 61 L.J.News. 398 (J.M.L.); (1940) 7 C.L.J. 255 (R.E.M.); *Hòllington Bros. Ltd.* v. *Rhodes* [1951] 2 T.L.R. 691 at 696. And technically L.C.A., 1925 (the predecessor of L.C.A. 1972), was a later statute than L.P.A., 1925, and should prevail in the case of irreconcilable conflict. Of two conflicting provisions in the same Act, the later prevails: *Eastbourne Corporation* v. *Fortes Ice Cream Parlour (1955) Ltd.* [1959] 2 Q.B. 92 at 107.   [33] L.C.A. 1972, s. 17 (1).

[34] General provisions do not derogate from special provisions.

[35] L.R.A., 1925, s. 29.

[36] *Cf.* Bills of Sale Act, 1878, s. 10: " shall have priority in the order of the date of their registration."

[37] *Cf.* Yorkshire Registries Act, 1884, s. 14 (" shall have priority according to the date of registration thereof "); Merchant Shipping Act, 1894, s. 33 (mortgages of ships have priority " according to the date at which each mortgage is recorded in the register book "). A lesson in lucid drafting may be taken from the Middlesex Registry Act, 1708, s. 1, which provided that an unregistered assurance is void against a subsequent purchaser unless registered before the registration of the subsequent purchaser's assurance.

conflict, on the other hand, has the merit that this argument should always prevail in case of doubt. The presumption against Parliament simultaneously enacting two contradictory systems is very strong, especially where one of the two supposedly conflicting Acts expressly makes reference to the other.[38]

(4) THREE OR MORE MORTGAGES. Where there are three or more registrable mortgages it is possible to construct insoluble problems. For example:

January 1	A grants a registrable mortgage to X
February 2	A grants a registrable mortgage to Y
March 3	X registers
April 4	A grants a registrable mortgage to Z

Here Y has priority to X and Z has priority to Y; but X has priority to Z, so that the priorities run not in a series but in a circle. There is some authority for solving such problems by recourse to the doctrine of subrogation, by which one creditor is allowed to stand in the shoes of another on equitable grounds.[39] The court's order then might be to pay Z to the extent of Y's claim against X; then to pay X in full; then to pay any balance due to Z on his own claim; and finally to pay any balance to Y. It is easy to find fault with any such solution, for the problem is in fact insoluble. Here Y is sacrificed to X, whereas Y should be paid before X. Subrogation produces an arbitrary result, for there is no logical point at which to break the circle and begin the process; and if begun at a different point it gives a different solution. The cases so far reported seem to show that the court would elect to take the mortgages in order of date of creation and begin by subrogating the latest mortgagee to the earliest, as in the above example.[40]

(5) PRIORITY NOTICES AND OFFICIAL SEARCHES. Since it was physically impossible to register a land charge the instant after it had been created, there was at first a dangerous gap between the creation of a mortgage and its registration. Further, even if a search for prior incumbrances was made, the mortgagee could not

---

[38] "All this property legislation must be construed together; and obviously a result which would make the sections . . . mutually conflict must be avoided, unless there is no escape": *Northchurch Estates Ltd.* v. *Daniels* [1947] Ch. 117 at 123, *per* Evershed J. in another context.

[39] See *Benham* v. *Keane* (1861) 1 J. & H. 685; 3 De G.F. & J. 318; and see *Re Wyatt* [1892] 1 Ch. 188 at 209 (a puzzle suggested by the rule in *Dearle* v. *Hall, ante,* p. 964); *Re Armstrong* [1895] 1 I.R. 87; *Re Weniger's Policy* [1910] 2 Ch. 291. For discussion see (1968) 32 Conv.(N.S.) 325 (W. A. Lee).

[40] See generally (1961) 71 Yale L.J. 53 (G. Gilmore).

be sure that no incumbrance had been registered between the time of his search and the completion of the mortgage. These difficulties have been met by the devices of the priority notice and the official search which are dealt with later in the chapter on registration.[41]

(c) *First but not second mortgage protected by a deposit of deeds.* In this case the first mortgage, by taking its priority from the date of its creation, will normally have priority over the second mortgage, subject to the established rules as to loss of priority, *e.g.*, by fraud or gross negligence.[42]

(d) *Second but not first mortgage protected by a deposit of deeds.* Here section 4 (5) and section 97 must work in harmony, however section 97 is interpreted. If the first mortgage is registered before the second is made, the first ranks for priority " according to its date of registration " (s. 97), *i.e.*, prior to the second mortgage, and section 4 (5) has no application. If the first mortgage is not registered when the second mortgage is made, the first mortgage is void against the second for want of registration; and even if it is subsequently registered, it takes priority from the date of registration and therefore ranks second.

3. Summary

(a) *Deeds.* A mortgage protected by a deposit of deeds ranks according to the date on which it was created. The mortgagee may lose priority—

    (i) by conduct which before 1926 would have had this effect; or

    (ii) if his mortgage is equitable, by a legal mortgage being made to a mortgagee for value without notice, or to a mortgagee who accepts a " reasonable excuse " for non-production of the deeds.[43]

(b) *No deeds.* A mortgage not protected by deposit of deeds should be protected by registration. If the mortgagee fails to do this, he will not be protected against a subsequent mortgagee (s. 4 (5)), even if (as it seems) he registers before him (section 97 notwithstanding). If he does register, he will be protected against all mortgages made thereafter.

Since an equitable mortgagee who has custody of the title deeds may through no fault of his own lose priority to a later legal mortgagee to whom the mortgagor makes some excuse for non-production of the deeds,[43] it seems in theory to be safer for the first mortgagee to refuse to take the title deeds, and to register a

[41] *Post*, p. 1052.   [42] *Ante*, pp. 960, 961.
[43] *Ante*, p. 963.

general equitable charge. But in fact mortgagees prefer the practical security of having the title deeds to the theoretical advantage of refusing them.

II. MORTGAGES OF AN EQUITABLE INTEREST

A mortgage of an equitable interest in any property, whether land or pure personalty, now takes priority according to the rule in *Dearle* v. *Hall*,[44] as amended by the Law of Property Act, 1925.[45] That is to say, the rule in *Dearle* v. *Hall* has now been amended, and extended from the realm of personalty to that of land; but as regards land it applies only to dealings with an equitable interest, *e.g.*, mortgages of the beneficial interest of a tenant for life under a settlement, whether in the land itself or in the capital money representing it. Mortgages of such interests are therefore now governed by the principle that priority depends upon the order in which notice of the mortgages is received by the appropriate trustee or trustees.

The amendments made by the Law of Property Act, 1925, are as follows.

1. Notice in writing. No notice given or received after 1925 can affect priority unless it is in writing.[46] Apart from this, no alteration has been made in the rules relating to notice.[47]

2. Persons to be served. The persons to be served with notice are:

    (i) in the case of settled land,[48] the trustees of the settlement;

    (ii) in the case of a trust for sale, the trustees for sale;

    (iii) in the case of any other land, the estate owner[49] of the land affected.[50]

Thus the person to be served is normally the owner of the legal estate, except in the case of settled land, where notice to the tenant for life might well be no protection, *e.g.*, if it was his life interest which had been mortgaged. In cases other than the three mentioned above, no special provision has been made, so that notice

---

[44] *Ante*, p. 964.
[45] ss. 137, 138. S. 137 does not apply until a trust has been created: subs. (10).
[46] L.P.A., 1925, s. 137 (3). *Quaere* whether the notice in *Lloyd* v. *Banks* (1868) 3 Ch.App. 488 (*ante*, p. 966) would not still be sufficient, for it was " received " by the trustee in printed form. Yet L.P.A., 1925, s. 137 (2), speaks of the persons " to be *served* with notice."   [47] *Ante*, pp. 966, 967.
[48] Including capital money or securities representing capital money.
[49] *i.e.*, the owner of a legal estate: L.P.A., 1925, s. 205 (1) (v); *ante*, p. 135.
[50] L.P.A., 1925, s. 137 (2).

must be given to the legal owner as before 1926. Nor has any alteration been made to the law relating to notice received by one of several trustees.[51]

3. Indorsement of notice. If for any reason a valid notice cannot be served (*e.g.*, where there are no trustees), or can be served only at unreasonable cost or delay, a purchaser [52] may require that a memorandum be indorsed on or permanently annexed to the instrument creating the trust, and this has the same effect as notice to the trustees.[53] He may also require the instrument to be produced in order to prove proper indorsement.[53] In the case of settled land, the trust instrument and, in the case of a trust for sale, the instrument creating the equitable interest, is the document to be used for this purpose.[54] If the trust is created by statute or by operation of law, or there is no instrument creating the trust, the document to be used is that under which the equitable interest is acquired or which evidences its devolution, *e.g.*, in the case of an intestacy, the probate or letters of administration in force when the dealing was effected.[55]

4. Notice to trust corporation. The instrument creating the trust, the trustees, or the court, may nominate a trust corporation to receive notices instead of the trustees.[56] In such cases, only notice to the trust corporation affects priority; notice to the trustees has no effect until they deliver it to the trust corporation, which they are bound to do forthwith.[57] Provision is made for the indorsement of notice of the appointment on the instrument upon which notices may be indorsed,[58] for the keeping of a register of notices,[59] for the inspection of the register,[60] for the answering of inquiries [61] and for the payment of fees therefor.[62] This is in effect machinery for setting up a private register of charges. In practice little use is made of these provisions.

5. Production of notices. On the application of any person interested in the equitable interest, the trustees or estate owner

---

[51] *Ante*, p. 967.
[52] Including, of course, a mortgagee.
[53] L.P.A., 1925, s. 137 (4).
[54] *Ibid.*, s. 137 (5).
[55] *Ibid.*, s. 137 (6).
[56] *Ibid.*, s. 138 (1).
[57] *Ibid.*, s. 138 (3), (4).
[58] *Ibid.*, s. 138 (2).
[59] *Ibid.*, s. 138 (7).
[60] *Ibid.*, s. 138 (9).
[61] *Ibid.*, s. 138 (10).
[62] *Ibid.*, s. 138 (9), (10), (11).

must now produce any notices served on them or their predecessors.[63]
This emasculates *Low* v. *Bouverie* [64]; in that case it had been held
that trustees were under no duty to disclose notices to third parties,
so that a prospective mortgagee might not be able to discover
previous incumbrances.

C. Summary

A summary of the principal divisions of the rules relating to the
priority of mortgages may be useful.

1. Before 1926

(*a*) *Legal or equitable interests in land*: priority was governed by
the order of creation, subject to the doctrine of purchaser without
notice, and special rules as to fraud, estoppel, gross negligence, and
"reasonable excuse" for non-production of title deeds.

(*b*) *Equitable interests in pure personalty*: *Dearle* v. *Hall* applied.

2. After 1925

(*a*) *Legal estates in land*: priority is governed by the same rules
as before 1926, subject to the rules requiring registration of mortgages
not protected by deposit of documents.

(*b*) *Equitable interests in any property*: *Dearle* v. *Hall* applies.

Sect. 2. Tacking

Tacking is a special way of obtaining priority for a secured loan
by amalgamating it with another secured loan of higher priority.
It may apply both to realty and to personalty.[65] Before 1926 there
were two forms of tacking:

    (i) What was called the *tabula in naufragio* ("the plank in the
       shipwreck"); and

    (ii) The tacking of further advances.

The 1925 legislation has abolished the first kind of tacking and
amended the law as to the second. The old law must first be
explained before the amendments can be made intelligible.

---

[63] *Ibid.*, s. 137 (8), (9).
[64] [1891] 3 Ch. 82; *ante*, p. 968.
[65] Coote, *Mortgages*, 1245.

A. *Before* 1926

I. THE TABULA IN NAUFRAGIO

1. The doctrine. In a contest between two equitable mortgagees, the later could sometimes gain priority over the earlier by acquiring a legal mortgage which had priority to both.[66] The insufficiency of the security was the " shipwreck," and the legal estate was the " plank " which any equitable mortgagee might seize without concern for the others.[67] The metaphor implies a disaster where someone must lose, and each party may save himself as best he can. There is no moral equity in the doctrine, which has often been criticised,[68] and " could not happen in any other country but this "[69]; it is a curious example of the deference paid by equity to the legal estate.[70] Where, apart from the order of creation, the equities between the mortgagees were equal, the holder of the legal estate had priority[71]; "where the equities are equal, the law prevails," and so upsets the natural equitable order of priority.

The opportunity for this master-stroke occurred when there was first a legal and then two equitable mortgages, all made to different mortgagees, and the mortgagor managed to conceal the second mortgage at the time when he created the third.[72] Thus if A mortgaged his property to X by a legal mortgage and then to Y and Z by successive equitable mortgages, Z's mortgage could be given priority over Y's if Z bought X's mortgage, provided Z had no notice of Y's mortgage when he advanced his money.[73] X's legal mortgage was the plank in the shipwreck, and if Z could secure it before Y, he could throw on to Y the loss which would otherwise have fallen upon himself. Since Z knew nothing of Y's mortgage when he took his own mortgage, he might naturally have lent more than the security would satisfy. A property worth £10,000 might for example have been mortgaged first to X for £2,000, then to Y for £6,000, and then again to Z for £6,000, Z knowing nothing of Y's mortgage. Thus when the mortgagor defaulted a shipwreck was inevitable.

2. No notice. The mortgagee seeking to tack must have had no notice of the prior equitable mortgage when he advanced his

---

[66] *Marsh* v. *Lee* (1671) 2 Vent. 337; *Peacock* v. *Burt* (1834) 4 L.J.Ch. 33.
[67] The phrase is Hale C.J.'s: see *Brace* v. *Duchess of Marlborough* (1728) 2 P.Wms. 491, *per* Jekyll M.R.   [68] See Waldock, *Mortgages*, 391.
[69] *Wortley* v. *Birkhead* (1754) 2 Ves.Sen. 571 at 574, *per* Lord Hardwicke L.C.
[70] *Bailey* v. *Barnes* [1894] 1 Ch. 25 at 36.
[71] *Wortley* v. *Birkhead* (1754) 2 Ves.Sen. 571 at 574.
[72] See *Phillips* v. *Phillips* (1862) 4 De G.F. & J. 208 at 216.
[73] *Brace* v. *Duchess of Marlborough, supra.*

money [74]; if he had notice, he could not tack, for obviously his equity was then not equal to Y's.[75] But if he had no notice at that time, it was immaterial that he obtained notice later, before he acquired the legal estate [76]; indeed, on a principle similar to the rule in *Dearle* v. *Hall*,[77] notice of the prior equitable mortgage before the later mortgagee acquired the legal estate was " the very occasion, that shews the necessity of it." [78] The natural time for tacking was when the third mortgagee, who when he made his loan imagined that he was taking a second mortgage, discovered later that there was an intervening mortgage, and then took a transfer of the first legal mortgage in order to secure priority. Notice to the first mortgagee (who held the legal estate) was immaterial, so that the second mortgagee could not protect himself against tacking by giving him notice.[79] Such circumstances " look very like a conspiracy between the first and third mortgagees to cheat the second, which cannot be right." [80] But such was the law.

A legal estate which was already held on trust for the intervening mortgagee could not be used against him by a later mortgagee who took it with notice of the trust,[81] for the trust would then bind the later mortgagee [82]; he " must not, to get a plank to save himself, be guilty of a breach of trust." [83] Thus if a third mortgagee took the legal estate from the first mortgagee with notice that the first mortgage had already been paid off (so that the legal estate was held by the first mortgagee merely as trustee for those entitled to it, including the second mortgagee), tacking was impossible.[84] But while the first mortgage was still unredeemed, notice that the second mortgagee wished to redeem did not, it seems, make it a breach of trust for the first mortgagee to give priority to the third mortgagee by transferring the legal estate to him,[85] although he might thus have been able to sell it to the highest bidder.

[74] *Bates* v. *Johnson* (1859) Johns. 304 at 313.
[75] *Lacey* v. *Ingle* (1847) 2 Ph. 413.
[76] *Taylor* v. *Russell* [1892] A.C. 244 at 259.
[77] *Ante*, p. 964.
[78] *Wortley* v. *Birkhead* (1754) 2 Ves.Sen. 571 at 574, *per* Lord Hardwicke L.C.
[79] *Peacock* v. *Burt* (1834) 4 L.J.Ch. 33.
[80] *West London Commercial Bank* v. *Reliance Permanent B. S.* (1885) 29 Ch.D. 954 at 963, *per* Lindley L.J.; and see *Bates* v. *Johnson, supra*, at p. 314.
[81] *Sharples* v. *Adams* (1863) 32 Beav. 213 ; *Mumford* v. *Stohwasser* (1874) L.R. 18 Eq. 556 at 562 ; *cf. Taylor* v. *London & County Banking Co.* [1901] 2 Ch. 231 at 256.
[82] *Saunders* v. *Dehew* (1692) 2 Vern. 271.
[83] *Ibid.*, *per* Lord Nottingham L.C.
[84] See *Bates* v. *Johnson, supra*, at pp. 315–317; *Prosser* v. *Rice* (1859) 28 Beav. 68 at 74; *Harpham* v. *Shacklock* (1881) 19 Ch.D. 207.
[85] *Bates* v. *Johnson, supra*, at pp. 313, 314, criticised in *West London Commercial Bank* v. *Reliance Permanent B. S.* (1885) 29 Ch.D. 954 at 960; the point is reserved at p. 961.

3. Legal estate. It was of the essence of tacking that the mortgagee should secure a legal estate. Any prior [86] legal estate would do, *e.g.*, an outstanding term of years,[87] or even a judgment giving legal rights against the land [88]; but an equitable interest would not suffice.[89] Nevertheless, in accordance with the doctrine that the better right to the legal estate may rank as possession of it,[90] an express declaration of trust by the owner of the legal estate in favour of the mortgagee seeking to tack, or a transfer of the legal estate to a trustee for him, might be sufficient.[91] In all cases the mortgage and the legal estate had to be held in the same right, and not one on trust and the other beneficially.[92] Further, if the mortgagee parted with the legal estate he thereupon lost his right to tack.[93]

Although tacking usually took place when a later mortgagee acquired the legal estate, the principle extended also to a legal incumbrancer who acquired a later mortgage without notice of an intervening incumbrance, *e.g.*, where a first legal mortgagee took a transfer of a third mortgage without notice of the second.[94]

II. TACKING OF FURTHER ADVANCES

1. The doctrine. The tacking of further advances was the more important branch of the doctrine of tacking. It often happened that a mortgagee would wish to lend more money on the same security at some later date. If, then, the borrower had mortgaged the property to another mortgagee between the dates of the first and second loans from the original mortgagee, the question was whether the last loan could be tacked to the first so as to take

---

[86] In *Cooke* v. *Wilton* (1860) 29 Beav. 100 the first (equitable) mortgagee had a right to a legal mortgage, which was in fact executed after the intervening mortgage; this was held to relate back to the date of the original mortgage, and so to be effective for tacking.

[87] *Willoughby* v. *Willoughby* (1756) 1 T.R. 763; and see *Maundrell* v. *Maundrell* (1804) 10 Ves. 246. " Satisfied terms " (see *ante*, p. 387) were formerly valuable for this purpose. The court would not allow such a term to defeat an incumbrance of which the purchaser had notice, save only in the case of dower. But a purchaser without notice, who later obtained notice and then procured an assignment of the term, could protect himself on the principle of tacking: see *ante*, p. 120, esp. n. 84; *Willoughby* v. *Willoughby*, *supra*; Williams R.P. 590, 591. The Satisfied Terms Act, 1845, put an end to this practice: see now L.P.A., 1925, s. 5.

[88] *Morret* v. *Paske* (1740) 2 Atk. 52.

[89] *Brace* v. *Duchess of Marlborough* (1728) 2 P.Wms. 491 at 495, 496.

[90] See *ante*, p. 118.

[91] See *Wilkes* v. *Bodington* (1707) 2 Vern. 599 at 600; *Earl of Pomfret* v. *Lord Windsor* (1752) 2 Ves.Sen. 472 at 486; *Pease* v. *Jackson* (1868) 3 Ch.App. 576; *Crosbie-Hill* v. *Sayer* [1908] 1 Ch. 866 at 875, 876.

[92] *Morret* v. *Paske*, *supra*, at p. 53; *Harnett* v. *Weston* (1806) 12 Ves. 130.

[93] *Rooper* v. *Harrison* (1855) 2 K. & J. 86.

[94] *Morret* v. *Paske*, *supra*, at p. 53.

priority over the second. This question arose very commonly in banking, where a mortgage was made to secure an overdraft which might be increased as further cheques were cashed.

2. Forms of tacking. Before 1926 there were two cases where tacking of this kind was allowed.

(*a*) *Agreement of intervening incumbrancer.* The mortgagee could tack if the intervening incumbrancer agreed; here it was immaterial whether the first mortgage was legal or equitable. Building estates sometimes provided examples of this, when the owner required more money to build on his estate and thus make it a better security. The second mortgagee, not wishing to lend any more money, might agree to the first mortgagee making a further advance to be expended on further building and to rank in priority to the second mortgage. In this case priority was secured simply by contract between the mortgagees.

(*b*) *No notice of intervening incumbrance.* If a further advance was made without notice of the intervening mortgage, it might be tacked if either of the following conditions was satisfied.

(1) LEGAL ESTATE. The further advance was made either by a legal mortgagee,[95] or by an equitable mortgagee with the best right to the legal estate (as where A advanced money and had the legal estate conveyed to the trustee).[96] Priority here resulted from the strength of the legal estate.

(2) CONTRACT. The prior mortgage expressly provided that the security should extend to any further advances, whether or not it was obligatory for the mortgagee to make them. A bank, for example, might take a mortgage to secure an overdraft, with a clause stating that the security should cover any further overdraft which the bank might allow. Such tacking was said to be available to any mortgagee, legal or equitable; for it was tacking not by virtue of a legal estate but by virtue of the contract whereby the equity of redemption was potentially charged with any further advances, so that an intervening mortgagee took it subject to this right.[97]

3. Effect of notice. It was an invariable rule that a further advance could not be tacked if at the time of making it the mortgagee

---

[95] *Wyllie* v. *Pollen* (1863) 3 De G.J. & S. 596.
[96] See *ante*, pp. 118, 981; and see *Wilmot* v. *Pike* (1945) 5 Hare 14, explained *ante*, p. 963, n. 68. See also *Wormald* v. *Maitland* (1866) 35 L.J.Ch. 69, where this point received perfunctory treatment.
[97] See Fisher and Lightwood, *Mortgages*, 397, citing *Calisher* v. *Forbes* (1871) 7 Ch.App. 109 and *Re Weniger's Policy* [1910] 2 Ch. 291 at 295; but see below, n. 1.

had notice of the intervening mortgage.[98] This was a suitable rule for tacking in class (1), for the law should prevail only where the equities are equal. But, after some hesitation, the courts extended it to class (2),[99] whereas it might have been thought that if a paramount right to tack was secured by the terms of the first mortgage, it could not be taken away by a later mortgagee giving notice of his charge. The rule was applied even to the case where the first mortgage obliged the mortgagee to make further advances,[1] though the mortgagee was protected by the rule that he was released from the obligation to make the further advances as soon as the mortgagor, by creating a later incumbrance, prevented any further advance from having the priority of the original mortgage.[2]

The effect of these rules was that a mortgagee with notice of a subsequent incumbrance could never tack further advances against it, and an equitable mortgagee without notice could tack only if his mortgage made provision for further advances, or if he was one of the rare examples of an equitable mortgagee who had some prior claim on the legal estate.[3]

B. After 1925

The law as to tacking is now to be found in section 94 of the Law of Property Act, 1925, which abolishes all tacking except in certain cases of further advances.[4] The position is as follows.

I. THE TABULA IN NAUFRAGIO

Without prejudice to any priority gained before 1926, tacking by means of the *tabula in naufragio* was abolished at the end of 1925.[5]

II. TACKING OF FURTHER ADVANCES

The tacking of further advances has been modified so as to make it immaterial whether any of the mortgages concerned are legal or

---

[98] *Hopkinson* v. *Rolt* (1861) 9 H.L.C. 514, explained in *Bradford Banking Co. Ltd.* v. *Henry Briggs, Son & Co. Ltd.* (1886) 12 App.Cas. 29, and *Union Bank of Scotland* v. *National Bank of Scotland* (1886) 12 App.Cas. 53.

[99] *Hopkinson* v. *Rolt, supra,* where opinions in the House of Lords were divided.

[1] *West* v. *Williams* [1899] 1 Ch. 132. Having reached this point, the authorities had become inconsistent with the notion that an equitable mortgagee could tack at all. The doctrine that an agreement for further advances created a potential charge was denied in *West* v. *Williams* at pp. 143, 146, and this struck at the root of an equitable mortgagee's power to tack.

[2] See *West* v. *Williams, supra,* at pp. 143, 146.

[3] See n. 96 above.

[4] An abortive attempt to abolish tacking was made by the Vendor and Purchaser Act, 1874, s. 7, retrospectively repealed by the Land Transfer Act, 1875, s. 129; see *Robinson* v. *Trevor* (1883) 12 Q.B.D. 423 at 433.

[5] L.P.A., 1925, s. 94 (3). See *ante*, p. 120, n. 84.

equitable,[6] and so as to make the rules more reasonable where the first mortgage expressly contemplates further advances. After 1925 a prior mortgagee may tack further advances so as " to rank in priority to subsequent mortgages "[7] in the three cases set out below. As this exemption from the general abolition of tacking is confined to mortgages, it seems that further advances cannot be tacked so as to take priority over other intervening interests such as estate contracts.[8] The three cases are as follows.

1. Agreement of intervening incumbrancer. The position is unchanged.[9]

2. No notice of intervening incumbrance. A further advance can be tacked if it was made without notice of the intervening mortgage.[10] Where the intervening mortgage is protected by a deposit of deeds and is thus not registrable as a land charge, the normal rules as to notice operate.[11] If the mortgage is not protected in this way and is accordingly registrable (as will usually be the case), the rule that registration amounts to notice [12] will normally apply and so protect it if it is registered. But, by a special exception, if the prior mortgage was made expressly for securing further advances (*e.g.*, in the case of an overdraft at a bank, where the debt is increased or decreased as sums are drawn out or paid in), mere registration of a later mortgage as a land charge [13] is not deemed to be notice, unless that mortgage was registered when the last search was made by the prior mortgagee.[14] The same applies to a spouse's right of occupation under the Matrimonial Homes Act 1967 which is registered after a mortgage has been made; for even if the spouse's charge arose before the mortgage, the charge is deemed for this purpose to be a subsequent mortgage.[14a]

An example may make this clearer. Mortgages have been made to A (who took the deeds) and B, in that order, and A has made further advances. If when A made his further advances he had

---

[6] L.P.A., 1925, s. 94 (1).
[7] *Ibid.*
[8] See Maitland, *Equity*, 214 (J. W. Brunyate); (1958) 22 Conv.(N.S.) 44 at 56 (R. G. Rowley); this is probably a failure in drafting.
[9] L.P.A., 1925, s. 94 (1) (*a*).
[10] *Ibid.*, s. 94 (1) (*b*).
[11] *Ante*, p. 121.
[12] L.P.A., 1925, s. 198 (1).
[13] Before L.P.A. 1969, ss. 16, 17, Sched. 2 took effect, registration in a local deeds register was an alternative.
[14] L.P.A., 1925, s. 94 (2), as amended by L.P.(Am.)A., 1926. The amendment safeguards a mortgage registered (presumably by priority notice; *post*, p. 1052) before the principal mortgage was created.
[14a] Matrimonial Homes Act 1967, s. 2 (8); for the Act, see *ante*, p. 785.

actual, constructive or imputed notice of B's mortgage, he cannot tack under this head even if his mortgage, without obliging him to make further advances, was stated to be security for any further advances he might choose to make.[15] If he had no such notice of B's mortgage when he made his further advances, but B's mortgage was registered at that time, then if A's mortgage is silent as to further advances, the registration amounts to notice and prevents A from tacking. But if A's mortgage was expressed to be security for any further advances he might make, the registration will not prevent him from tacking, and thus he need not search before making each further advance. It would be unreasonable, in particular, to require banks to make a search before cashing each cheque on a secured overdraft.

This points a practical moral. Even if a second mortgage has been duly registered, the mortgagee should still give express notice of his mortgage to the first mortgagee, for this—

(i) prevents tacking under this head; and

(ii) compels the first mortgagee to hand over the deeds to him when the first mortgage is discharged.[16]

In these two respects registration by itself is not notice.

3. Obligation to make further advances. A further advance may be tacked if the prior mortgage imposes an obligation on the mortgagee to make it.[17] In this case, not even express notice will prevent tacking.[18] If in return for a mortgage a bank binds itself to honour a customer's cheques up to an overdraft of £1,000, there is no question of the bank losing priority, for not even express notice will prevent the bank from tacking each further advance.[19] The principle of this is, of course, that the later mortgagee has clear warning that the prior mortgagee has further claims on the security.

<h3 style="text-align:center">Part 6</h3>

<h2 style="text-align:center">MORTGAGES OF COPYHOLDS</h2>

<h3 style="text-align:center">Sect. 1. Before 1926</h3>

<h3 style="text-align:center">A. Legal Mortgages</h3>

A legal mortgage of copyholds could be made in two ways.

---

[15] This confirms *Hopkinson* v. *Rolt, ante*, p. 983.
[16] *Ante*, p. 923.   [17] L.P.A., 1925, s. 94 (1) (c).
[18] This reverses *West* v. *Williams, ante*, p. 983.
[19] *Quaere* whether this affects *Deeley* v. *Lloyds Bank Ltd.* [1912] A.C. 756 (payments into the account prima facie go in reduction of the bank's prior charge, thus improving the later mortgagee's position).

1. By surrender and admittance : the mortgagor covenanted to surrender the property to the use of the mortgagee, with a condition that the surrender should be void if on a fixed day the money lent was repaid with interest. This was followed by the actual surrender and admittance, the latter relating back to the time of the former.[20]

2. By surrender : the procedure was as in 1, except that there was no actual admittance. This was the more usual form, for it saved the fine which was payable on admittance,[21] and if it was likely that the surrender would become void for want of presentment at the manorial court, a fresh surrender could be made.[22] As between lord and tenant, the legal estate remained vested in the tenant until a new tenant was actually admitted; but because the surrender and admittance were merely different parts of the same conveyance [23] (the surrender being the substantial part and the admittance the mere form [24]), as between other parties the title of the mortgagee was perfect from the time of the surrender, which thus constituted a legal mortgage [25]; the mortgagee had " an inchoate legal title." [26]

B. Equitable Mortgages

An equitable mortgage of copyholds could be made :

    (i) By a covenant to surrender [27]; or

    (ii) By a deposit of the title deed, *i.e.*, the copy of the court roll.[28]

C. General Rules

In general, the same rules applied to mortgages of copyholds as to mortgages of freeholds: thus Locke King's Acts applied.[29] One rule relating to priority, however, needs mention. If a mortgage was made to A by surrender without admittance, and later a mortgage was made to B by surrender and admittance, A had priority if he was subsequently admitted even though B had no notice of A's mortgage,[30] for the admittance related back to the date of the sur-

---

[20] *Holdfast* d. *Woollams* v. *Clapham* (1787) 1 T.R. 600.

[21] See, *e.g.*, *Flack* v. *Downing College, Cambridge* (1853) 13 C.B. 945.

[22] *Fawcet* v. *Lowther* (1751) 2 Ves.Sen. 300 at 302.

[23] *Vaughan* v. *Atkins* (1771) 5 Burr. 2764 at 2785.

[24] *Roe* d. *Noden* v. *Griffits* (1766) 4 Burr. 1952 at 1961; *ante*, p. 27.

[25] See *Holdfast* d. *Woollams* v. *Clapham* (1787) 1 T.R. 600 at 601; *Whitbread* v. *Jordan* (1835) 1 Y. & C.Ex. 303.

[26] *Horlock* v. *Priestley* (1827) 2 Sim. 75 at 78, *per* Shadwell V.-C.

[27] See, *e.g.*, *Wainewright* v. *Elwell* (1816) 1 Madd. 627.

[28] *Whitbread* v. *Jordan, supra.*

[29] *Piper* v. *Piper* (1860) 2 L.T. 458; for these Acts, see *ante*, p. 951.

[30] The mere fact that A's conditional surrender was entered on the court rolls did not give B constructive notice of A's mortgage: *Bugden* v. *Bignold* (1843) 2 Y. & C.C.C. 377.

render [31]; and possibly the admittance of A was altogether irrelevant to his priority.[32] The mere fact that A's conditional surrender was entered on the court rolls did not give B constructive notice of A's mortgage.[33] Subject to this, the normal rules relating to priorities applied.

Sect. 2. After 1925

All copyholds were enfranchised at the beginning of 1926,[34] and mortgages of copyholds have been brought into line with the new scheme for mortgages of freeholds. Mortgages of copyholds made by surrender, with or without admittance, or by a covenant to surrender, were automatically converted into legal terms of three thousand years for a first mortgage, and terms one day longer for each successive mortgage, in each case subject to cesser on redemption and without impeachment of waste.[35] The fee simple vested in the mortgagor.[36]

---

[31] *Horlock* v. *Priestley* (1827) 2 Sim. 75; *Doe d. Wheeler* v. *Gibbons* (1835) 7 C. & P. 161.
[32] *Holdfast d. Woollams* v. *Clapham* (1787) 1 T.R. 600 at 601.
[33] *Bugden* v. *Bignold* (1843) 2 Y. & C.C.C. 377.
[34] *Ante*, p. 33.
[35] L.P.A., 1922, 12th Sched., para. (1); L.P.A., 1925, 1st Sched., Pt. VII.
[36] L.P.A., 1922, 12th Sched., para. (8).

CHAPTER 15

DISABILITIES

CERTAIN persons are subject to disabilities as to the interests in land which they can hold, create or alienate.

Sect. 1. Infants

An infant (or " minor " [1]) is a person who has not attained full age. For centuries a person attained full age (or " majority ") at the first moment of the day preceding the twenty-first anniversary of his birth [2]; for a year which begins on, say, July 7, is complete on the following July 6, and the law, which in general ignores fractions of a day, treated any part of a day as a full day. But on January 1, 1970,[3] the age of majority was reduced to eighteen years,[4] and the moment at which a person attained his majority or any other age was altered to the first moment of the relevant anniversary of his birth,[5] so that in law, as in popular belief, ages are now attained on birthdays instead of birthday eves. The following are the main principles governing an infant's rights in land.

1. Ownership of land. Before 1926 an infant was capable of holding both legal estates and equitable interests in land. After 1925 an infant cannot hold a legal estate in land,[6] although he may still hold an equitable interest.

2. Attempted conveyance to an infant. An attempt after 1925 to convey a legal estate to an infant alone or jointly with other infants operates as a contract for value to make a proper settlement by means of a vesting deed and trust instrument, and in the meantime to hold the land in trust for the infant or infants.[7] An attempted conveyance of a legal estate to an infant jointly with a

---

[1] Family Law Reform Act 1969, s. 12.
[2] *Re Shurey* [1918] 1 Ch. 263.
[3] A remarkable day on which nobody attained any age: see Megarry, *A Second Miscellany-at-Law* (1973) pp. 302–304.
[4] Family Law Reform Act 1969, s. 1 ; S.I. 1969 No. 1140.
[5] Family Law Reform Act 1969, s. 9.
[6] L.P.A., 1925, s. 1 (6).
[7] *Ibid.*, s. 19 (1); S.L.A., 1925, s. 27 (1). This is a statutory exception to the rule that an imperfect gift does not create a trust (*ante*, p. 448); and see nn. 11, 17, below. The infant's interest should be registered as an estate contract: *post*, p. 1040. For leases, see *post*, p. 992.

person of full age vests the legal estate in the person of full age on the statutory trusts (*i.e.*, on trust for sale [8]) for himself and the infant.[9] These provisions do not apply to a conveyance to an infant as mortgagee or trustee, for which special provisions are made.[10]

3. Mortgages. An infant cannot be a legal mortgagee or chargee after 1925. An attempt to grant or transfer a legal mortgage or charge to one or more persons who are all infants operates as an agreement for value to execute a proper mortgage or transfer when the infant or infants are of full age, and in the meantime to hold any beneficial interest in the mortgage debt in trust for the persons intended to benefit.[11] But a mortgage to an infant and other persons of full age operates, so far as the legal estate is concerned, as if the infant were not named, although any beneficial interest of his in the mortgage debt is not affected.[12]

4. Personal representatives. An infant can be neither an executor [13] nor an administrator [14]; this was so before 1926. If an infant would but for his infancy be entitled to be an administrator, or is appointed sole executor, he cannot take a grant until he is of full age; in the meantime a grant may be taken by someone on his behalf, *e.g.*, his guardian. In the case of administration, the grant must be made to at least two persons or a trust corporation on the infant's behalf, since an infant is interested in the estate.[15] If an infant is appointed one of several executors, the rest of whom are of full age, he must wait until he attains his majority, when he can join in the grant of probate previously made to the others.

5. Trustees. No infant can be appointed a trustee after 1925.[16] This applies to trusts of any property, real or personal. If there is a purported conveyance of a legal estate in land to an infant as trustee, the effect is as follows:

    (i) If the infant is a sole trustee, the conveyance operates as a declaration of trust by the grantor and no legal estate passes; the effect is the same if the conveyance is to two or more trustees, all of whom are infants.[17]

---

[8] *Ante*, p. 408.
[9] L.P.A., 1925, s. 19 (2); *ante*, p. 411, where it is suggested that this provision extends to a conveyance to an infant and an adult as tenants in common.
[10] L.P.A., 1925, s. 19 (3); see the following paragraphs.
[11] L.P.A., 1925, s. 19 (6); the infant's interest should be registered as an estate contract: *post*, p. 1040.
[12] L.P.A., 1925, s. 19 (6).
[13] J.A., 1925, s. 165, replacing A.E.A., 1798, s. 6, with amendments.
[14] *In b. Manuel* (1849) 13 Jur. 664.
[15] J.A., 1925, s. 160.
[16] L.P.A., 1925, s. 20; for transitional provisions, see below.
[17] L.P.A., 1925, s. 19 (4).

(ii) If the infant is one of two or more trustees, at least one of whom is of full age, the conveyance operates as if the infant were not named, although this does not prejudice any beneficial interest thereby given to him.[18]

These provisions do not prevent an infant from becoming a trustee of property other than a legal estate in land [19] in other ways, *e.g.*, under a constructive trust.[20]

6. Settled land. As was the case before 1926, land to which an infant is entitled in possession is deemed to be settled land.[21] This is so even if the infant is absolutely entitled, for the purpose of applying the Settled Land Act machinery to infants is to make the land freely alienable.[22] Before 1926 the statutory powers were exercisable by the trustees of the settlement, although the legal estate might still be vested in the infant.[23] After 1926 both the legal estate and the statutory powers are vested in the statutory owner.[24]

7. Transitional provisions. Legal estates which were vested in infants before 1926, whether beneficially, as mortgagee, as trustee or otherwise, were automatically vested in persons of full age at the first moment of 1926.[25] In general, if an infant was entitled jointly with other persons of full age, they took the legal estate.[26] If an infant was solely entitled, in the case of settled land the legal estate vested in the trustees of the settlement, or, if none, in the Public Trustee [27]; in other cases it vested in the Public Trustee.[28] However, he will normally not deal with the land, for he is here mainly intended as a temporary home for ownerless legal estates, and unless requested to act by the infant's parents or guardian he has no powers over the land. The parents or guardian may divest the Public Trustee of the legal estate by appointing new trustees in his place, and the legal estate will then vest in them by virtue of the statutory provisions.[29]

---

[18] s. 19 (5).
[19] See *ante*, p. 989.
[20] *Ante*, p. 442.
[21] S.L.A., 1882, s. 59; S.L.A., 1925, s. 1 (1); *ante*, p. 315.
[22] *Ante*, p. 289.
[23] S.L.A., 1882, ss. 59, 60; *ante*, p. 289.
[24] S.L.A., 1925, s. 26; *ante*, p. 297.
[25] L.P.A., 1925, 1st Sched., Pt. III; S.L.A., 1925, 2nd Sched., para. (3).
[26] L.P.A., 1925, 1st Sched, Pt. III, para. (2).
[27] *Ibid.*, para. (1); S.L.A., 1925, 2nd Sched., para. (3).
[28] L.P.A., 1925, 1st Sched., Pt. III, para. (3).
[29] *Ibid.*

8. Dispositions by infants

(a) *Voidable.* Any disposition by an infant of any interest in land is voidable at the option of the infant (but not of the grantee [30]) on the infant attaining his majority,[31] or within a reasonable time thereafter [32]; if the infant dies under age, his personal representatives may avoid the disposition within a reasonable time.[33] This is a long established rule of common law. As the disposition is voidable and not void, it is binding if the infant fails to repudiate it within a reasonable time after attaining his majority.[34]

(b) *Statutory owner.* A binding disposition of an infant's land can now be made under the Settled Land Act, 1925, by the statutory owner, so that in finding a purchaser an infant is no longer handicapped by his privilege of revocation.[35] The Act permits sales, exchanges, leases and mortgages on certain terms; but in general it does not permit gifts or marriage settlements.

(c) *Marriage settlement.* An irrevocable marriage settlement might formerly be made with leave of the court under the Infant Settlements Act, 1855, by a male infant of twenty years or more or a female infant of seventeen years or more.[36] But this Act has now been repealed, since the age of majority is now eighteen.[37]

9. Transfer on death. Normally an infant cannot make a will,[38] and therefore any interest vested in an infant will pass on his death by intestacy. There is one statutory exception.

(a) *Deemed entail.* If an infant who dies after 1925 without having been married would, apart from this provision, have been equitably entitled at his death under a settlement [39] (including a will, or an intestacy [40]) to a vested estate in fee simple,[41] or an absolute interest in property settled to devolve with such land or as freehold land, he is deemed to have had an entailed interest, and the settlement is to be construed accordingly.[42]

---

[30] *Zouch* d. *Abbot* v. *Parsons* (1765) 3 Burr. 1794.
[31] *Ashfeild* v. *Ashfeild* (1628) W.Jo. 157 (lease). See *Chaplin* v. *Leslie Frewin (Publishers) Ltd.* [1966] Ch. 71.
[32] *Carnell* v. *Harrison* [1916] 1 Ch. 328.
[33] Cru.Dig. iv, 69.
[34] *Edwards* v. *Carter* [1893] A.C. 360.
[35] *Ante*, p. 289.
[36] See *Re Sampson and Wall* (1884) 25 Ch.D. 482; *Re Adams* [1943] Ch. 155; *Re Scott* [1891] 1 Ch. 298.
[37] Family Law Reform Act 1969, s. 11; *ante*, p. 988.
[38] Wills Act, 1837, s. 7; the exception is as provided in the Wills (Soldiers and Sailors) Act, 1918; *ante*, p. 488.
[39] As defined by S.L.A., 1925, ss. 1 (1), 117 (1) (xxiv); A.E.A., 1925, s. 55 (1) (xxiv); *ante*, p. 990.
[40] *Re Taylor* [1931] 2 Ch. 242; but see (1932) 76 S.J. 227.
[41] Including perhaps, a fee simple in remainder: see (1932) 76 S.J. 227.
[42] A.E.A., 1925, s. 51 (3).

(b) *Purpose.* The objects of this somewhat strange provision appear to be—

(i) to make it unnecessary always to take out a grant of administration to the infant's estate; and

(ii) to make the land revert to the donor.

For example, if D settled land on A for life with remainder to B (an infant) in fee simple, and B died an infant without having married, he is deemed to have had an entail. Since he can have had no legitimate children, his notional entail comes to an end and D is entitled to the fee simple subject to A's life interest. This is probably closer to D's intentions than that the land should pass under B's intestacy to, perhaps, his father or uncle. If B was solely entitled on D's intestacy, a perpetual oscillation of the land between B's estate and D's estate is avoided by carrying the land from D's estate to the person who, after B, would be entitled on D's intestacy.[43] In any case, no grant of probate or administration to B's estate is needed in respect of the land. But if B had married, then whether or not he had issue, the provision would not apply and the land would pass under his intestacy.

(c) *Consequences.* There seems to be nothing to exclude cases where value has been given for the land, *e.g.,* by the infant or his father. The grotesque result of a purported conveyance for value to the infant seems to be that, if he dies under age, the land reverts to the vendor.[44] If the infant procured a conveyance to trustees, the beneficial ownership of the reversion would be in doubt. It is equally doubtful whether the provision restricts the power of disposition over realty given by the Wills (Soldiers and Sailors) Act, 1918, to infant soldiers and members of the Air Force in actual military service, and mariners at sea [45]; read literally, it deprives them of any testamentary power over realty until they marry, since until then they are deemed to have entails, and an infant cannot dispose of an entail by will.[46]

10. Leases. An attempted grant of a legal term of years to an infant operates merely as a covenant by the lessor to make a settlement on the infant, and in the meantime to hold the term in trust

---

[43] *Re Taylor* [1931] Ch. 242. Yet s. 51 (3) applies only where, independently of the subsection, the infant would *at his death* have been entitled in fee simple and this need not affect a fee simple carried to his estate after his death.

[44] See (1930) 74 S.J. 382, suggesting that reverter would be to the father if he had provided the money : *sed quaere.* Any conveyance to an infant is, of course, a " settlement " for this purpose: see *ante*, p. 990.

[45] *Ante*, p. 488.

[46] *Ante*, p. 95.

for him.[47] The infant can thus take only an equitable interest. He may disclaim this interest within a reasonable time after attaining full age [48]; if he does so, this will discharge him from liability for future rent but not from liability in respect of his past use and occupation of the premises,[49] nor will it enable him to recover rent that he has already paid.[50] If he does not then disclaim, he is bound by the terms of the tenancy even though he was an infant when he entered into it.[51] During his infancy he is, it seems, only liable to pay for the use and occupation of the premises if they can be said to be " necessary." [52] If the lease is set aside by the landlord because the infant obtained it by fraudulently representing himself to be of full age, he cannot also make the infant liable for use and occupation.[53]

Sect. 2. Married Women

In general a married woman is today subject to no disability. She can acquire, hold and dispose of property as if she were a feme sole, *i.e.*, an unmarried woman. This position has been achieved only by legislation. Both common law and equity used to impose special restrictions on married women's property, and it is desirable to have some understanding of these and of the legislation which abolished them. There were two distinct types of disability, namely, as to non-separate property, and under a restraint on anticipation; and after considering these, some mention must be made of the court's special jurisdiction over property in dispute between husband and wife.

1. Non-separate property

(a) *At law.* At common law a married woman was incapable of disposing by herself of any property which she owned; the concurrence of her husband was necessary for an effective disposition to be made.

(1) REAL PROPERTY could be disposed of in fee simple only by a fine levied by the wife in which the husband concurred [54]; this was

---

[47] *Ante*, pp. 988, 989; *Davies* v. *Beynon-Harris* (1931) 47 T.L.R. 424.
[48] *Ketsey's Case* (1613) Cro.Jac. 320; and see *Edwards* v. *Carter* [1893] A.C. 360 (settlement). [49] *Blake* v. *Concannon* (1870) I.R. 4 C.L. 323.
[50] *Valentini* v. *Canali* (1889) 24 Q.B.D. 166.
[51] *Davies* v. *Beynon-Harris, supra.* [52] *Lowe* v. *Griffith* (1835) 4 L.J.C.P. 94.
[53] *Lempriere* v. *Lange* (1879) 12 Ch.D. 675.
[54] *Goodill* v. *Brigham* (1798) 1 B. & P. 192; H.E.L. iii, 525. For fines, see *ante*, p. 87. During the marriage the husband had a freehold estate in the land and was solely entitled to the rents and profits. He could dispose of this limited interest (in effect, with his right to curtesy, a life estate), but of no more. The wife had no power of disposition at all, strictly speaking; but since she could be a co-defendant with her husband, a fine would bind them both and so take effect: see Williams R.P. 333–337; Challis 395, 396.

the same action as was used for barring an entail.[55] The wife had to be separately examined (*e.g.*, by a " Perpetual Commissioner ") so that it could be ascertained in the absence of her husband that she agreed to the transaction. After the Fines and Recoveries Act, 1833, had abolished fines, the form of conveyance was a deed in which the husband concurred, and which the wife acknowledged upon separate examination. This was called a conveyance by " deed acknowledged." [56] Separate examination was not abolished until 1925.[57] The wife had no other power to dispose of her property *inter vivos*; and even with the husband's concurrence she had no power of disposition by will.[58]

(2) LEASEHOLDS remained vested in the wife, but the husband could dispose of them in his lifetime without the concurrence of his wife.[59] They would not, however, pass under his will or intestacy, for on his death the wife's rights revived, free from any charges created by the husband.[60]

(3) PURE PERSONALTY vested in the husband absolutely and passed under any disposition by him whether *inter vivos* or by will, or on his intestacy.[61] He thus could not make a gift to his wife.[62] A wife's will of personalty was effective only if made with her husband's assent.[63]

(*b*) *In equity.* In view of the stringency of the common law rules, equity established a rule, early in the eighteenth century,[64] that any property conveyed either to trustees or to the husband " for the separate use " of the wife could be dealt with by her in equity as if she were unmarried.[65] The Married Women's Property Act,

---

[55] *Ante,* p. 88.
[56] For an historical account, see *Johnson* v. *Clark* [1908] 1 Ch. 303 at 312 *et seq.*; and see Hood and Challis, 106. Separate examination was continued from the old practice required by statute in the case of fines: Challis 396.
[57] L.P.A., 1925, s. 167.
[58] The Statute of Wills, 1542, s. 14, expressly disabled married women from devising land, though they could exercise a testamentary power to appoint land limited to their separate use: see *Peacock* v. *Monk* (1751) 2 Ves.Sen. 190 at 191, 192; *Willock* v. *Noble* (1875) L.R. 7 H.L. 580 at 596.
[59] *Re Bellamy* (1883) 25 Ch.D. 620.
[60] H.E.L. iii, 527.
[61] *Ibid.*, 526.
[62] *Ibid.*; *Ashworth* v. *Outram* (1877) 5 Ch.D. 923 at 941. But she could keep any " paraphernalia " (*i.e.*, clothes and personal ornaments) in her possession when her husband died: see *Masson, Templier & Co.* v. *De Fries* [1909] 2 K.B. 831.
[63] *Willock* v. *Noble, supra*, at pp. 589, 590, 596 597; or if made under a power, or disposing of property held to her separate use: *ibid.* See also H.E.L. iii, 542–544.
[64] *Rollfe* v. *Budder* (1724) Bunb. 187; *Bennet* v. *Davis* (1725) 2 P.Wms. 316.
[65] See Snell, *Equity*, 514; *Ashworth* v. *Outram* (1877) 5 Ch.D. 923 at 941.

1882,[66] extended this principle considerably by providing that all legal estates and equitable interests which either—

(i) were acquired after 1882, or

(ii) belonged to a woman who married after 1882,

should be separate property of the married woman and could be disposed of by her as if she were feme sole.

(c) *Today*. Consequently, property of a married woman could only be non-separate property today, and so subject to the severe restrictions set out above, if it—

(i) was acquired before 1883, and

(ii) the marriage took place before 1883 and still exists, and

(iii) the property was not conveyed to the separate use of the married woman.

There cannot be any such property left today.

The Law Reform (Married Women and Tortfeasors) Act, 1935, rendered obsolete the expression " her separate property," and refers to " her property "; but if any non-separate property still exists, it remains subject to the old law.

2. Property subject to a restraint on anticipation

(a) *Origin*. Although the restraint upon anticipation has now been abolished, it was until recently of considerably greater importance than non-separate property. The invention by equity of " the separate use " made it possible for a married woman to deal by herself with property subject to such a use; but it did not protect her from yielding to the asperities or blandishments of her husband and conveying the property to him, nor did it protect her against her creditors if she were improvident. Consequently, towards the end of the eighteenth century,[67] equity finally[68] made it possible on the grant of property to a married woman for the grantor not only to give it for her separate use but also to subject it to a restraint on anticipation.[69] This was a restraint on alienation which in the

---

[66] ss. 2, 5, as retrospectively extended by the Married Women's Property Act, 1907, s. 1 (replaced by L.P.A., 1925, s. 170 (2), (4)), in certain cases where the land was held upon trust: see *Re Harkness & Allsopp's Contract* [1896] 2 Ch. 358.

[67] There were earlier signs of a willingness to set aside transactions which made excessive anticipations of future income: see *Calverley* v. *Dudley* (1747) 3 Atk. 541.

[68] Lord Thurlow L.C. is mainly to be credited with the invention: see *Pybus* v. *Smith* (1791) 3 Bro.C.C. 340 at 344, n. 1; *Parkes* v. *White* (1805) 11 Ves. 209 at 221, 222; *Jackson* v. *Hobhouse* (1817) 2 Mer. 483 at 487. It was first judicially established for a life interest in *Sockett* v. *Wray* (1794) 4 Bro.C.C. 483, by Arden M.R., and for a fee simple in *Baggett* v. *Meux* (1844) 1 Coll.C.C. 138; (1846) 1 Ph. 627, by Knight Bruce V.-C. and Lord Lyndhurst L.C.

[69] See Snell, *Equity*, 516.

case of a man or a feme sole was invalid, as being repugnant to the nature of property.[70]

(b) *Operation.* The restraint could be declared in a grant to a feme sole, although it became effective only during coverture (marriage); during spinsterhood or widowhood it was inoperative, but attached as soon as the woman became a feme covert (married woman). Thus property given to a spinster subject to a restraint on anticipation would be free from the restraint until she married, when the restraint would attach; on the death or divorce of her husband, it would disattach, and on remarriage would attach again. If a feme sole wished to prevent the restraint from attaching on her marriage, she could execute a deed poll declaring that the trustees of the property should hold it for such purposes as she should appoint, and provided this deed was communicated to the trustees before her marriage, the property would remain free from the restraint.[71]

(c) *Effect.* A restraint on anticipation prevented the married woman from disposing of or charging the capital or future income in any way. Each instalment of income could be disposed of as soon as it was paid, but neither the married woman nor her creditors could attack the capital or future income. However, the court was given power to authorise a disposition of property which was subject to a restraint, provided that the disposition was for the benefit of the married woman, and she consented [72]; the purchase-money was paid to trustees, who held it subject to the restraint.[73] Furthermore, the application of the Settled Land Act, 1925, to property subject to restraint made it possible to dispose of the land under the Act, so that the restraint shifted to the purchase-money.[74]

(d) *Abolition.* By the Law Reform (Married Women and Tortfeasors) Act, 1935,[75] no restraint on anticipation could be imposed by any document (including a settlement or will) executed after 1935, except in pursuance of an obligation imposed before 1936 otherwise than by a special power of appointment; and no will of a testator who died after 1945 could impose a restraint on anticipation, even if the will was made before 1936. The Act did not affect existing restraints but only prevented the imposition of new restraints. Finally the Married Women (Restraint upon Anticipation) Act, 1949, abolished all existing restraints on anticipation and prevented the

---

[70] *Brandon* v. *Robinson* (1811) 18 Ves. 429; *ante*, p. 79.
[71] *Re Chrimes* [1917] 1 Ch. 30.
[72] L.P.A., 1925, s. 169, replacing C.A., 1881, s. 39, and C.A., 1911, s. 7: see Hood and Challis, 294 *et seq.*
[73] See *Re Tippett's and Newbould's Contract* (1888) 37 Ch.D. 444.
[74] *Ante*, p. 317.
[75] s. 2.

creation of any more of such restraints. No restriction on anticipation or alienation is valid if it could not have been attached to the enjoyment of the property by a man. For men and women alike, devices such as discretionary and protective trusts must now be employed in order to protect a beneficiary against his own extravagance.[76]

3. Property disputes between husband and wife. Under the Married Women's Property Act, 1882,[77] " in any question between husband and wife as to the title to or possession of property, either party "[78] may apply in a summary way to the court, and the judge " may make such order with respect to the property in dispute . . . as he thinks fit." [79] After sharp divergences of judicial opinion it is now settled that this is a procedural provision, under which the court is not at liberty to modify the rights of the parties as it thinks just,[80] according to " a kind of palm-tree justice." [81] The court must give effect to the legal and equitable property rights of the parties as they exist, and there is no doctrine of " family assets " which gives the court discretion to depart from the ordinary law of ownership.[81a]

The principles which may entitle a husband or wife to a beneficial interest in the property of the other have been explained earlier,[82] as also have their rights of occupation of the matrimonial home.[83]

Sect. 3. Insane Persons

If a person is insane, there are two necessities: first, some control must be exercised over his person; and secondly, someone must be appointed to manage his property, since he is himself incapacitated. The effect on his property is the only relevant question here.

1. Control over property

(a) *The jurisdiction.* Under statutes dating from the fourteenth-century *De Prerogativa Regis* [84] and later the Lunacy Act, 1890, the

---

[76] See Trustee Act, 1925, s. 33 ; Snell, *Equity*, 134 *et seq.*
[77] s. 17, extended by Matrimonial Causes (Property and Maintenance) Act 1958, s. 7; Matrimonial Proceedings and Property Act 1970, s. 39 ; and Law Reform (Miscellaneous Provisions) Act 1970, s. 2, which extends it to engaged couples who terminate their engagement.
[78] In case of dissolution or annulment of the marriage, application may be made within 3 years thereafter : Matrimonial Proceedings and Property Act 1970, s. 39.
[79] For a modern summary of the jurisdiction, see Snell, *Equity*, 523–526.
[80] *Pettitt* v. *Pettitt* [1970] A.C. 777.
[81] *National Provincial Bank Ltd.* v. *Hastings Car Mart Ltd.* [1965] A.C. 1175 at 1221, *per* Lord Hodson.
[81a] *Pettitt* v. *Pettitt, supra* ; *Gissing* v. *Gissing* [1971] A.C. 886.
[82] *Ante,* pp. 445–447.
[83] *Ante,* p. 785.
[84] Of uncertain date, printed as 17 Ed. II, St. I, cc. 9, 10, 1324 (Ruff.)

Crown had jurisdiction over the property of lunatics; and this was exercised by the Lord Chancellor and certain judges. Today, under the Mental Health Act, 1959, jurisdiction is still exercisable by the Lord Chancellor and nominated judges; but in practice it is usually exercised by the Master, Deputy Master or a nominated officer of the Court of Protection, which is an office of the Supreme Court.[85] The jurisdiction arises when it is established that " a person is incapable, by reason of mental disorder, of managing and administering his property and affairs." [86] The person concerned is now called " the patient," instead of " a person of unsound mind," as formerly, and " lunatic " before that.

(*b*) *Powers*. There are very wide powers of ordering or authorising dispositions and other transactions concerning the patient's property, whether for the benefit of the patient himself or his family or other persons for whom he might have been expected to provide.[87] In cases of emergency these powers may even be exercised before the question of incapacity has been determined.[88] The powers extend, for example, to the making of settlements [89] and wills,[89a] the management of a business, and the conduct of litigation, and include the power, commonly exercised, to appoint a receiver who may exercise any of the powers under the court's directions.[90] Where property of the patient has been disposed of, those who would have taken it under the patient's will or intestacy may claim corresponding interests in the property which represents it.[91]

(*c*) *Former law*. These arrangements have superseded the former law, which distinguished between a " lunatic so found " and a " lunatic not so found." The former, when " so found " by judicial inquisition, was committed to the care of a " committee," who had control both of his person and his property.[92] The latter's property was controlled by a receiver appointed by the court; and in modern times this was the usual procedure.[93]

---

85 Mental Health Act, 1959, s. 100. The Chancery Division may also exercise jurisdiction in certain cases of small trusts: see *Re K.'s S.T.* [1969] 2 Ch. 1.
86 Mental Health Act, 1959, s. 102.
87 *Ibid.*, ss. 102, 103.
88 *Ibid.*, s. 104.
89 See *e.g.*, *Re D. M. L.* [1965] Ch. 1133; *Re L. (W.J.G.)* [1966] Ch. 135. For the previous law, see L.P.A., 1925, s. 171.
89a Administration of Justice Act 1969, ss. 17, 18, not applying to infant patients, and substituting special formalities for those of the Wills Act, 1837, s. 9.
90 Mental Health Act, 1959, s. 105.
91 *Ibid.*, s. 107.
92 Lunacy Act, 1890, Parts III, IV.
93 Lunacy Acts, 1890, s. 116, 1908, s. 1.

2. Patient's incapacity. The former law was that if a committee or receiver had been appointed, the lunatic lost all legal capacity to deal with his property *inter vivos*.[94] Any attempt by him to alienate it was therefore void, and the court would not, while the order remained in force, receive evidence of a lucid interval.[95] But a will made during a lucid interval was valid.[96] If no such order had been made, a disposition made during mental incapacity was voidable at the instance of successors in title, but not at the instance of the person making it unless his incapacity was known to the other party.[97]

The Mental Health Act, 1959, makes no change in these rules. But it is not clear at what point the patient will lose all capacity to deal with his property, *i.e.*, whether this is the result of any intervention by the court, or only the result of the appointment of a receiver. Since the incapacity is based on the inconvenience of having two persons able to deal with the property,[98] and since the appointment of a receiver is now an administrative facility rather than the step by which control is taken, the former suggestion may be correct.

Sect. 4. Traitors and Felons

1. Attainder. At common law, and until 1870, attainder of treason or felony deprived the criminal of his property, both real and personal. In the case of treason the property was forfeit to the Crown; in the case of felony, land escheated to the feudal lord, subject to the Crown's right to enjoy it for a year and a day,[99] and goods were forfeited to the Crown. The escheat or forfeiture of land related back to the commission of the offence, so that dealings between the commission of the crime and conviction were void[1]; in the case of goods, there was no relation back and intermediate dealings were valid.

2. Forfeiture Act, 1870. The Forfeiture Act, 1870, abolished all forfeiture and escheat for attainder of treason or felony.[2] The Act further provided that a convict (as defined in the Act) could not make any disposition of his property during the period of his sentence, either by way of conveyance or contract.[3] There was provision for the appointment by the Home Office of an administrator

---

[94] *Re Walker* [1905] 1 Ch. 160 (lunatic so found); *Re Marshall* [1920] 1 Ch. 284 (receiver appointed).
[95] *Re Walker, supra.*
[96] *In b. Walker* (1912) 28 T.L.R. 466.
[97] See *Imperial Loan Co. Ltd.* v. *Stone* [1892] 1 Q.B. 599. How the purchaser's state of mind can affect the vendor's capacity to convey is somewhat obscure.
[98] See *Re Marshall, supra.* [99] *Ante*, p. 18.
[1] *Ante*, p. 18.
[2] s. 1. [3] s. 8.

in whom vested all property which belonged to the convict beneficially.[4] The administrator had full power to dispose of the property,[5] but he could not bar an entail vested in the convict; if, however, the convict barred the entail, the resulting fee vested in the administrator, who could dispose of it.[6] Pending the appointment of an administrator the justices might appoint an interim curator who could, with the leave of the justices or the court, sell the convict's personal (but not real) property.[7]

3. Criminal Justice Act, 1948. All these provisions for the vesting and administration of a convict's property ceased to have effect on April 18, 1949.[8] Convicts now deal with their property in the normal way, acting through agents where necessary.

Sect. 5. Aliens

An alien is a person who is not a British subject. At common law an alien could not hold land, and any conveyance to an alien made the land liable to forfeiture to the Crown.[9] Both at common law and by statute there were certain minor exceptions to this rule, *e.g.*, permitting friendly aliens to hold certain short leases.[10] By the Status of Aliens Act, 1914,[11] replacing the Naturalisation Act, 1870,[12] an alien can now in general hold and acquire real and personal property in the same way as a British subject.

Sect. 6. Corporations

In general, a corporation which has power to hold land has also the power to dispose of it.[13] But corporations created by statute have only such powers as the statute confers and of course statute may impose restrictions on any corporation.[14] Thus the powers of disposition of the Universities and colleges of Oxford, Cambridge and Durham are restricted by a code of statutory rules somewhat similar to the code which governs tenants for life.[15]

---

[4] ss. 9, 10.   [5] s. 12.
[6] *Re Gaskell and Walters' Contract* [1906] 2 Ch. 1.
[7] ss. 21–26.   [8] Criminal Justice Act, 1948, s. 70 (1); S.I. 1949, No. 139.
[9] Williams R.P. 325–328.
[10] Co.Litt. 2b; Aliens Act, 1844, s. 5. The Crown could by letters patent confer on an alien the status of denizen, which enabled him to hold but not to inherit land; Williams R.P. 326.
[11] s. 17, amended in minor details by the British Nationality Act, 1948, s. 34 and 4th Sched., Pt. II.
[12] s. 2.
[13] *Smith* v. *Barratt* (1663) 1 Sid. 161 at 162; *Mayor & Commonalty of Colchester* v. *Lowten* (1813) 1 V. & B. 226.
[14] See *Davis* v. *Corporation of Leicester* [1894] 2 Ch. 208 at 228.
[15] Universities and College Estates Acts 1925 and 1964. The sanction behind these rules is not clear since the Ecclesiastical Leases Act, 1571, no longer applies: Act of 1964, s. 1. For the curiosities of the Act of 1571, see *Eton College* v. *Minister of Agriculture, Fisheries and Food* [1964] Ch. 274.

Formerly an assurance of land " in mortmain " to a corporation made the land liable to forfeiture to the Crown unless the corporation was authorised to hold land by statute or by licence from the Crown.[16] Most corporations were so authorised, but the ancient law of mortmain remained an anachronism and a trap until it was abolished by the Charities Act, 1960.[17] Its purpose of preventing land from passing into the hands of monasteries had been obsolete for centuries.[18] No title can now be defeated on grounds of mortmain if the possession was in accordance with the title on July 29, 1960, and no step had then been taken to invoke the law of mortmain against it.[19]

Sect. 7. Charities

1. Dispositions to a charity. Formerly dispositions of land to charities were hedged round with restrictions, some obsolete and some illogical.[20] It was for long the policy of the legislature to allow charities to take land by gift from a living person, but not by will.[21] It was considered that a would-be benefactor should be prepared to give at his own expense, not at the expense of his successors, and that it was injurious to families to allow land to pass into mortmain by will. But no such rule applied to personalty; and the rule for land was relaxed by providing that a devise to a charity should be valid, but that the land must be sold by the charity within one year from the testator's death.[22] Gifts to charities made *inter vivos* were also subject to various restrictions, one of which was that the gift must be made at least twelve months before the death of the donor.[23] This restriction on " deathbed gifts " was based on the same policy as the rule against gifts by will, but illogically it was not relaxed at the same time.

All such restrictions have now been abolished by the Charities Act, 1960.[24]

2. Dispositions by a charity. Conveyances by a charity are subject to a number of restrictions. In the first place, persons holding property for charitable purposes are trustees of it, and cannot pass a

---

[16] For the law of mortmain under the Mortmain and Charitable Uses Act, 1888, as amended, see former editions of this book and *Att.-Gen.* v. *Parsons* [1956] A.C. 421.   [17] s. 38.
[18] The statutes began with Magna Carta, 1215: and see *ante*, p. 155.
[19] Charities Act, 1960, s. 38 (2).
[20] For details, see former editions of this book. There were many exceptions.
[21] Mortmain Act, 1736.
[22] Mortmain and Charitable Uses Act, 1891, s. 5. See *Re Hume* [1895] 1 Ch. 422.
[23] Mortmain and Charitable Uses Act, 1888, s. 4; S.L.A. 1925, s. 29 (4).
[24] ss. 38, 48, 7th Sched. But gifts to charities made a year or more before death still have the advantage that they may avoid estate duty.

good title to it unless they have a power of sale. But by the Settled Land Act, 1925,[25] land vested in trustees for charitable, ecclesiastical or public [26] purposes was made settled land, so that the trustees now have all the powers given by the Act to a tenant for life and trustees of a settlement. The land does not become settled land for all purposes. Thus a conveyance to a charity need not be made by a vesting deed and trust instrument, nor is a sole trustee disabled from giving a good receipt for capital money if the scheme governing the charity authorises this.[27] Certain university and college lands are dealt with separately by the Universities and College Estates Acts, 1925 and 1964.

Secondly, the Charities Act, 1960, provides that no land which forms part of the permanent endowment of a charity, or is or has been occupied for the purposes of the charity, may be disposed of in any way without an order of the court, the Charity Commissioners or the Secretary of State for Education and Science.[28] Other land (*e.g.*, land held for investment purposes) is free from this restriction. Nor does it apply to any lease granted without a fine for a term ending not more than 22 years after it is granted, or to any disposition of an advowson.[29] Certain charities are exempt, such as the Universities of Oxford, Cambridge, London and Durham.[30]

---

[25] s. 29.
[26] See *Re Cleveland Literary and Philosophical Society's Land* [1931] 2 Ch. 247.
[27] *Re Booth and Southend-on-Sea Estates Co.'s Contract* [1927] 1 Ch. 579.
[28] Charities Act, 1960, ss. 2, 29; S.I. 1964, No. 490.
[29] Charities Act, 1960, s. 29.
[30] *Ibid.*, and 2nd Sched.

CHAPTER 16

ADVERSE POSSESSION AND LIMITATION

Part 1

GENERAL PRINCIPLES

1. Limitation and prescription. " Limitation " means the extinction of stale claims and obsolete titles; rights of action are limited in point of time, and are lost if not pursued within due time. Some such principle is necessary to every system of law; but in English law it depends wholly on statute, since limitation was unknown to the common law. Different periods of limitation have been laid down for different kinds of actions. In relation to land (for which the period is now in general twelve years) it is in the public interest that a person who has long been in undisputed possession should be able to deal with the land as owner. It is more important that an established and peaceable possession should be protected than that the law should assist the agitation of old claims.[1] A statute which effects this purpose is " an act of peace. Long dormant claims have often more of cruelty than of justice in them." [2]

Limitation has to be distinguished from prescription, for though similar in result they are different in principle. Prescription is primarily a common law doctrine, though extended by statute, by which certain rights (easements and profits) can be acquired over the land of others.[3] Fundamentally it is a rule of evidence, leading to the presumption of a grant from the owner of the land and therefore of a title derived through him. Limitation is wholly statutory, and is concerned with the title to the land itself. It simply extinguishes a former owner's right to recover possession of the land, leaving some other person with a title based on adverse possession. Prescription operates positively, like a conveyance; limitation operates negatively, by eliminating the claim of a person having a superior title.

[1] *Cholmondeley* v. *Lord Clinton* (1820) 2 Jac. & W. at 140; (1821) 4 Bli. 1 at 106; *Manby* v. *Berwicke* (1857) 3 K. & J. 342 at 352.
[2] *A'Court* v. *Cross* (1825) 3 Bing. 329 at 332, *per* Best C.J.
[3] *Ante*, pp. 841 *et seq.*

2. Title. Limitation is thus not *per se* a mode of transferring property from one person to another. But it may operate as such, when combined with the principle that adverse possession gives a title. If S (squatter) wrongfully takes possession of land belonging to O (owner), O immediately acquires a right of action against S for recovery of the land.[4] If O takes no action, in twelve years (normally) his right of action becomes barred and his title extinguished by limitation. S can no longer be disturbed by O, and as against the rest of the world S is protected by the fact of his possession. Possession by itself gives a good title against all the world, except someone having a better legal right to possession.[5]

This last proposition is fundamental to our concept of title to land. If the occupier's possession is disturbed, for example by trespass or nuisance, he can sue on the strength of his possession and does not have to prove his title. It follows that the person disturbing the occupier's possession cannot attack his title, if he admits his possession; in the language of pleading, a defendant sued for trespass in such a case cannot plead *jus tertii* (that the land belongs to some third party, not to the plaintiff [6]). As against a defendant having no title to the land, the occupier's possession is in itself a title. But if the defendant himself lays claim to the land by a title of his own, he may of course plead his own title and so put the plaintiff's title in issue; for then he is alleging a title not in a third party but in himself.[6] Accordingly he may show title in a third party if he himself claims through the third party, *e.g.*, as purchaser, tenant or licensee.[6a]

3. History

(*a*) *Proprietary and possessory actions.* This essentially possessory character of title to land is a product of historical evolution and, in particular, of the old forms of action. For some time after the

---

[4] O may re-enter, but if resisted he will be subject to the Statutes of Forcible Entry, 1381–1623, *ante*, p. 657; O will therefore be put to an action if S refuses to give up possession.

[5] *Asher* v. *Whitlock* (1865) L.R. 1 Q.B. 1. This is the leading decision on the principle in modern times. H enclosed manorial land, and died in 1860 leaving the land by his will to his widow for life or until remarriage, remainder to his daughter in fee simple. The widow remarried, and two years after her death in 1863 the daughter's heir successfully claimed the land from the husband. The reason was that the heir had succeeded to H's possessory rights, and that these were good against the husband since his was a later possession. The lord of the manor was not a party to the proceedings, and it was not shown that his title was barred; and see *Perry* v. *Clissold* [1907] A.C. 73.

[6] " It is well settled that in an action of trespass a defendant may not set up a *jus tertii*. He may set up a title in himself, or show that he acted on the authority of the real owner, but he cannot set up a mere *jus tertii* ": *Nicholls* v. *Ely Beet Sugar Factory (No.* 1) [1931] 2 Ch. 84 at 86, *per* Farwell J. *Cf. Lall* v. *Lall* [1965] 1 W.L.R. 1249.

[6a] " If possession be shown, the defendant is not at liberty to set up the title of a third party unless he justifies what he has done under a licence from such third party ": *Lord Fitzhardinge* v. *Purcell* [1908] 2 Ch. 139 at 145, *per* Parker J.

middle of the twelfth century there were (at least in name) both proprietary and possessory actions, the former asserting title and the latter asserting possessory rights.[7] Thus if S disseised O of a piece of land, O could recover the land by a possessory action. But this did not prejudice the question of title, and if S claimed title he might still recover the land again from O by a proprietary action. Originally the possessory actions were speedy and temporary remedies introduced in the king's courts for the purpose of preserving the peace and preventing forcible dispossessions, whether rightful or wrongful. But they were extended so fast and so far that they soon came to cover almost all claims, and superseded the ancient proprietary actions which lay only in the feudal courts.[8]

(*b*) *Title based on seisin.* Title to land therefore depended on the better right to possession (seisin) rather than *vice versa.* The concept of ownership was never really disentangled from that of possession.[9] As between two rival claimants, the land belonged to him who could lay claim to the earlier and therefore the better seisin, whether that seisin was his own or that of some person to whose rights he had succeeded, *e.g.,* as heir or feoffee. Seisin was thus the root of all titles. When in the seventeenth century the action of ejectment[10] had been perfected as a general action for the recovery of land, it shifted the basis of title from the technical seisin of feudal law to the simple fact of possession.[11] This was because the action of ejectment was a branch of the action of trespass, which lay for a wrongful disturbance of possession, whereas the older possessory actions belonged to the family of the " real actions " which were peculiar to real property and were available only for claims based on seisin.[12]

---

[7] See *post,* p. 1167. Even the proprietary (" droitural ") actions had a strong possessory flavour: Litt. 478; H.E.L. iii, 89, 90; Lightwood, *Possession of Land,* 71–75.　　　　　　　　　　　[8] H.E.L. iii, 8–14; *post,* p. 1168.

[9] H.E.L. ii, 88 *et seq.,* and *ante,* p. 48, for the pre-eminence of seisin in medieval law. An owner disseised had a mere right of entry or action, which at common law was not assignable; he could not convey (being unable to deliver seisin); neither curtesy nor dower could be taken at his death; his death without heirs caused no escheat. Rights of entry did not become assignable at law until the R.P.A., 1845: *ante,* p. 81.　　　　　　　　　　　　　　　[10] *Post,* p. 1170.

[11] In *Doe* d. *Crisp* v. *Barber* (1788) 2 T.R. 749 and *Doe* d. *Carter* v. *Barnard* (1849) 13 Q.B. 945 it was laid down that mere possession (*i.e.,* possession unaccompanied by any other interest) would not support an action of ejectment. But this doctrine was wrong: see *Asher* v. *Whitlock, supra,* n. 5; *Perry* v. *Clissold* [1907] A.C. 73 at 79, 80; *Allen* v. *Roughley* (1955) 94 C.L.R. 98, noted in [1956] C.L.J. 177 (H.W.R.W.); *Oxford Meat Co. Pty. Ltd.* v. *McDonald* [1963] S.R. (N.S.W.) 423; *Nair Service Society Ltd.* v. *K. C. Alexander* A.I.R. 1968 S.C. 1165; *Spark* v. *Whale Three Minute Car Wash (Cremorne Junction) Pty. Ltd.* (1970) 92 W.N. (N.S.W.) 1087; Lightwood, *Time Limit on Actions,* 120–126; and see *Davison* v. *Gent* (1857) 1 H. & N. 744. The shift towards mere possession as the basis of title was further assisted by the Real Property Limitation Act, 1833: see Lightwood, *Possession of Land,* 123, 124.

[12] *Post,* p. 1167.

(c) *Possession as a root of title.* The real actions were abolished in 1833 [13] and the action of ejectment in 1852.[14] But our substantive law is still that developed from the action of ejectment,[15] so that today it is still true that possession is a root of title. Any distinction between seisin and possession as the basis of title [16] is obscured by the well-established rule that possession of land, if exclusive of other claimants [16a] and not otherwise explained, is evidence of seisin in fee simple.[17] Naturally possession by a tenant or an agent is no foundation for a title against the landlord or the principal, for the possession is not adverse. Where the possession is truly adverse, there is little merit today in preserving for this purpose any distinction between seisin and possession; it is possession that forms the recognised root of title.[18] Ownership, as between two rival claimants, is the better right to possession.

4. Titles relative

(a) *Relativity of titles.* "At common law . . . there is no such concept as an 'absolute' title. Where questions of title to land arise in litigation the court is concerned only with the relative strengths of the titles proved by the rival claimants. If party A can prove a better title than party B he is entitled to succeed notwithstanding that C may have a better title than A, if C is neither a party to the action

---

13 Real Property Limitation Act, 1833, s. 36.
14 Common Law Procedure Act, 1852, s. 3.
15 See *Bristow* v. *Cormican* (1878) 3 App.Cas. 641 at 661. An action for the recovery of land, because of its descent through ejectment from trespass, is still regarded as an action in tort, and so was held not to lie between husband and wife before the Law Reform (Husband and Wife) Act 1962: *Bramwell* v. *Bramwell* [1942] 1 K.B. 370 at 373, doubted in *National Provincial Bank Ltd.* v. *Ainsworth* [1965] A.C. 1175 at 1235. Judgment for possession is *in personam* only: *Re Wykeham Terrace, Brighton, Sussex* [1971] Ch. 204; but see R.S.C. Ord. 113; *post*, p. 1174.
16 See (1940) 56 L.Q.R. 376, where in a valuable article A. D. Hargreaves maintains that seisin is still the basis; see esp. the summary at p. 397.
16a Where the alleged trespasser is not a claimant (*i.e.* where he is merely disputing the plaintiff's actual possession), the plaintiff need show only slight evidence of possession: *Wuta-Ofei* v. *Danquah* [1961] 1 W.L.R. 1238; and acts of possession are strengthened by a claim of right: *Fowley Marine (Emsworth) Ltd.* v. *Gafford* [1968] 2 Q.B. 618 (exclusive possession of tidal creek successfully shown); *Ocean Estates Ltd.* v. *Pinder* [1969] 2 A.C. 19 (acts of possession strengthened by documentary title); and see *post*, pp. 1013–1014.
17 *Peaceable d. Uncle* v. *Watson* (1811) 4 Taunt. 16 at 17; *Jayne* v. *Price* (1814) 5 Taunt. 326; *Re Atkinson & Horsell's Contract* [1912] 2 Ch. 1 at 9; Lightwood, *Possession of Land*, 114–121; (1940) 56 L.Q.R. 376 at 381, 382 (A. D. Hargreaves).
18 See Lightwood, *Possession of Land*, 124, 126; Pollock & Wright, *Possession*, 93–96; *Re Atkinson & Horsell's Contract*, *supra*, at p. 9. Holdsworth in H.E.L. vii, 62–68, and in (1940) 56 L.Q.R. 479 maintains that the action of ejectment, instead of making title more possessory, introduced a concept of absolute ownership and enabled the defendant to plead *jus tertii*. This theory is refuted by A. D. Hargreaves, *supra*, conflicts with *Asher* v. *Whitlock* and *Perry* v. *Clissold*, *supra*, note 11, and is treated as wrong in the later cases there cited.

nor a person by whose authority B is in possession or occupation of the land." [18a]

Some examples will illustrate this fundamental doctrine and the right and wrong occasions for the plea of *jus tertii*. If last year S dispossessed O of land which had hitherto belonged to O, and O is taking no action, there are now two incompatible titles to the land: as between O and S, O is the owner, for he can recover the land by bringing an action; but as between S and the rest of the world (except O and persons claiming through him) S is owner, for he is in possession and that is equivalent to ownership as against all persons who have no better right.[19] Thus S can sue strangers for trespass or nuisance, just as O could before.[20] Furthermore, S can convey the land, or make any other disposition which an owner can make.[21] If S dies, the land will pass under his will or intestacy.[22] But all such rights derived through S are subject to O's (or his successor in title's) paramount right to recover the land. S's possession at once [22a] gives him all the rights and powers of ownership: S has, in fact, a legal estate, a fee simple absolute in possession.[23] But so also has O, until such time as his title is extinguished by limitation.

(b) *The better title.* There is thus no absurdity in speaking of two or more adverse estates in the land, for their validity is relative. If O allows his title to become barred by lapse of time, S's title becomes the better, and S then becomes "absolute owner." But if O brings his action within the time allowed, he can successfully assert

---

[18a] *Ocean Estates Ltd.* v. *Pinder, supra,* at pp. 24, 25, *per* Lord Diplock.

[19] *Doe* d. *Hughes* v. *Dyeball* (1829) Moo. & M. 346; 3 C. & P. 610 (one year's possession held a good title as against a stranger); *Doe* d. *Humphrey* v. *Martin* (1841) Car. & M. 32; *Asher* v. *Whitlock* (1865) L.R. 1 Q.B. 1 (*ante*, p. 1004).

[20] *Graham* v. *Peat* (1801) 1 East 244; *Chambers* v. *Donaldson* (1809) 11 East 65; *Nicholls* v. *Ely Beet Sugar Factory (No.* 1) [1931] 2 Ch. 84 at 86 (*ante*, p. 867). Similarly if A supports his house on B's land (having no right), he cannot sue if B removes the support, but he can sue if C does: *Jeffries* v. *Williams* (1850) 5 Exch. 792 at 800; and see *Laing* v. *Whaley* (1858) 3 H. & N. 675. Again, if A uses B's road for access to his house he cannot sue if B obstructs the road, but he can if C does: *Beckett* v. *Midland Ry.* (1867) L.R. 3 C.P. 82 at 103. But contrast *ante*, p. 866.

[21] See Litt. 472, 474, 476, 477.

[22] Litt. 385 (intestacy); *Asher* v. *Whitlock, supra* (will and intestacy: two stages of devolution); *Allen* v. *Roughley, supra,* n. 11 (will).

[22a] The statement in H.E.L. vii, 64 that S has no title until the limitation period has run is erroneous: see cases cited *supra*, note 11.

[23] The old maxim was that a wrongdoer could not qualify his wrong, *i.e.,* he was taken to claim the largest possible interest: Co.Litt. 271a. "For a disseisor, abator, intruder, usurper, etc., have a fee simple, but it is not a lawful fee ": Co.Litt. 2a; and see *ibid.*, 297a; Litt. 519, 520; Williams, *Seisin*, 7, cited with approval by Dixon J. in *Wheeler* v. *Baldwin* (1934) 52 C.L.R. 609 at 632; *Leach* v. *Jay* (1878) 9 Ch.D. 42 at 44, 45; *Spark* v. *Meers* [1971] 2 N.S.W.L.R. 1 at 12. Thus if S is a leasehold tenant, his encroachments are presumed to enure to the benefit of his landlord: *ante*, p. 845; *post*, p. 1016. See also *post*, p. 1029. For the context of modern legislation, see (1964) 80 L.Q.R. 63 (B. Rudden).

his better title based on his prior possession; as against O, S's legal estate is nothing.[24]

(c) *Jus tertii.* We have already seen that other persons who have themselves no title cannot exploit the relative weakness of S's title by pleading *jus tertii.* If X (a stranger) takes possession of the land from S, S or his successors can recover it within the limitation period and X cannot plead that the land is not in fact S's but O's.[24a] This is self-evident, for otherwise anyone could help himself to the land.[25] If X claims the land, he must do so on the strength of some title of his own, not on the weakness of S's.[26]

On the other hand, suppose that, while S is still in undisturbed possession, O dies and by his will leaves all his land to X. If X acts in time he can obtain the land by asserting O's superior title. But here S, who is in possession, can compel X to prove his title, and if X's title (as opposed to O's) is subject to a *jus tertii* then S can plead it.[27] If, for example, S can prove that O revoked the will in favour of X by a later will in favour of Y, S can plead that the land is not X's but Y's; and therefore, since Y's title shows X to be a mere stranger, S's possession is a good title against X. This again is self-evident, for otherwise S would have no protection against anyone purporting to claim through O. *Jus tertii* is therefore a plea which may be used by a person who is in possession in order to attack the documentary part of an adverse title, but not the rights which flow directly from possession.[28] These propositions are really only corollaries of the

---

[24] " When any man is disseised, the disseisor has only the naked possession, because the disseisee may enter and evict him; but against all other persons the disseisor has a right, and in this respect only can be said to have the right of possession, for in respect to the disseisee he has no right at all ": Gilbert, *Tenures*, 21, cited in Butler's note to Co.Litt. 238a.

[24a] *Asher* v. *Whitlock* (1865) L.R. 1 Q.B. 1, *ante*, p. 1004; *Spark* v. *Whale Three Minute Car Wash (Cremorne Junction) Pty. Ltd.* (1970) 92 W.N. (N.S.W.) 1087. It makes no difference that O's title may be registered and " indefeasible ": *ibid.*

[25] " Can it be at the mere will of any stranger to disturb the person in possession?": *Asher* v. *Whitlock, supra,* at p. 6, *per* Cockburn C.J.

[26] *Martin* d. *Tregonwell* v. *Strachan* (1743) 5 T.R. 107n., affd. (1744) Willes 444: *Roe* d. *Haldane* v. *Harvey* (1769) 4 Burr. 2484; *Bristow* v. *Cormican* (1878) 3 App.Cas. 641 at 661.

[27] *Roe* d. *Haldane* v. *Harvey, supra* (the defendant, being in possession, proved that the plaintiff Haldane had conveyed the land to another person, and so had no title); *Doe* d. *Wawn* v. *Horn* (1838) 3 M. & W. 333 (defendant in possession proved that plaintiff had demised the land, so the proper plaintiff was the tenant); *Culley* v. *Doe* d. *Taylerson* (1840) 3 Per. & D. 539 at 552, 557 (defendant in possession proved that plaintiff's claim as heir to A was bad because A had devised the land to B); *cf. Doe* d. *Lloyd* v. *Passingham* (1827) 6 B. & C. 305 (defendant in possession proved that legal estate was outstanding in a trustee). The many cases in which actions of ejectment failed for want of the immediate legal title are in fact cases of *jus tertii* properly pleaded: see n. 30, *infra.* For similar decisions on copyholds, see Scriven 455–457. For modern examples see *ante*, p. 1005, note 11.

[28] " Possession gives the defendant a right against every man who cannot show a good title ": *Roe* d. *Haldane* v. *Harvey, supra,* at p. 2487, *per* Lord Mansfield C.J. See [1956] C.L.J. 177 (H.W.R.W.). For the same principle applied to personalty (a motor-car), see *Wilson* v. *Lombank Ltd.* [1963] 1 W.L.R. 1294.

fundamental rule that possession gives a title against all but a person having a better right.

Where one party has obtained possession by permission of the other, he naturally cannot use that possession to support a plea of *jus tertii* against that other. This explains why a tenant or licensee is estopped from denying the title of his lessor or licensor.[28a]

Sometimes neither party may be able to show possession in fact, and the question then is which of them can show possession in law, *i.e.*, the better right to possession. This is a straight contest of documentary titles, and either can defend an action of trespass by showing that the plaintiff is not the true owner.[29]

5. Equity. Today, an equitable owner who is entitled to possession can bring actions to assert his title and recover land in the same way as a legal owner. Before the Judicature Acts, 1873–1875, an action at law for the recovery of land would fail if only an equitable title could be shown [30]; but since the jurisdictions in law and equity have been amalgamated an equitable title is fully recognised in any court.[31]

6. " Ownership." Although the person with the best ascertained right to possession is often called the " absolute owner," it is clear from the foregoing analysis that English law knows no abstract " ownership " as opposed to the right to recover possession, unless perhaps the Crown's universal seignorial rights [31a] should so be classified. O may be " owner " of Blackacre, but it is always theoretically possible for someone to come forward and prove a better title, as by proving that he owns the reversion on a long term of years which has now expired, or by finding a lost will which alters the devolution of the property.

This " possessory ownership " is well illustrated by the ordinary procedure for proving title to a purchaser.[32] " The standing proof that English law regards, and has always regarded, Possession as a substantive root of title, is the standing usage of English lawyers and landowners. With very few exceptions, there is only one way in which an apparent owner of English land who is minded to deal with

---

[28a] See *ante*, p. 645, n. 65.

[29] *Lord Fitzhardinge* v. *Purcell* [1908] 2 Ch. 139 at 145.

[30] See, *e.g.*, *Doe d. Lloyd* v. *Passingham* (1827) 6 B. & C. 305; *Doe d. Butler* v. *Lord Kensington* (1846) 8 Q.B. 429 at 449; *Cole on Ejectment*, 66, 287.

[31] J.A., 1873, s. 24; *General Finance, Mortgage and Discount Co.* v. *Liberator Permanent Benefit B. S.* (1878) 10 Ch.D. 15 at 24. Exceptions may arise in the county court where jurisdiction is limited by statute: see, *e.g.*, *Foster* v. *Reeves* [1892] 2 Q.B. 255; *ante*, p. 627.

[31a] *Ante*, p. 13.

[32] *Ante*, pp. 578 *et seq.*

it can show his right so to do; and that way is to show that he and those through whom he claims have possessed the land for a time sufficient to exclude any reasonable probability of a superior adverse claim." [33] It is by limitation that any such superior claim will have been excluded. Adverse possession and limitation together are therefore the foundations of a good title; if this is understood, the nature of a title acquired by limitation becomes plain. There is no " parliamentary conveyance " [34] from the one party to the other; one title is extinguished altogether and a new one arises. The new title is, however, subject to the rights of third parties, whether legal or equitable,[35] unless they too have been barred by limitation.[36]

7. The modern system. We must now turn to the details of the statutory system of limitation. At first, periods of limitation were fixed from time to time in relation to particular events or dates of public knowledge, such as the death of Henry I or the last voyage of Henry II into Normandy. Ultimately the Statute of Westminster I, 1275,[37] laid down a prohibition against disputing rights enjoyed in 1189, a date still of significance in relation to prescription.[38] For two centuries and a half this remained the law, so that there gradually ceased to be any effective system of limitation.

The modern type of limitation, which, instead of selecting fixed dates, sets a preclusive period to rights of action as from the time they arise, was introduced by a statute of 1540,[39] which fixed periods of sixty years or less for the various real actions.[40] In 1623 rights of entry were limited to twenty years,[41] and this period therefore

---

[33] Pollock and Wright, *Possession*, 94. Even under the system of registration of title (*post*, p. 1054) titles are still relative, although the mode of proof is different. A person claiming a better title than that of the registered owner can sue for rectification of the register: *post*, p. 1080.

[34] This expression attained some currency (see *Scott* v. *Nixon* (1843) 3 Dr. & War. 388 at 407; *Doe* d. *Jukes* v. *Sumner* (1845) 14 M. & W. 39 at 42; and see *Dawkins* v. *Lord Penrhyn* (1877) 6 Ch.D. 318 at 323), but it is now established that it is erroneous: see *Tichborne* v. *Weir* (1892) 67 L.T. 735; *Re Atkinson & Horsell's Contract* [1912] 2 Ch. 1 at 9. Thus the possessor is not entitled to any right that depends on a grant, *e.g.*, a way of necessity: *Wilkes* v. *Greenway* (1890) 6 T.L.R. 449. For such easements, see *ante*, p. 831.

[35] *Ante*, p. 115; and *post*, p. 1028.

[36] *Post*, pp. 1015 *et seq.*

[37] *Cf. ante*, p. 848; chapter 39 forbade writs of right based on seisin obtained prior to 1189, and fixed 1216 and 1242 as the corresponding dates for other real actions.

[38] See *ante*, p. 848.

[39] 32 Hen. 8, c. 2 (periods of 60, 50 and 30 years).

[40] See the historical sketch in *Bryant* v. *Foot* (1867) L.R. 2 Q.B. 161 at 179–181, *per* Cockburn C.J.; and see P. & M. ii, 81.

[41] Limitation Act, 1623. This Act also provided 6-year limitation periods for actions in contract and tort. Its scope was somewhat extended by the Civil Procedure Act, 1833, which laid down a 20-year period for claims on specialties (statute or covenant) and recognisances, and dealt with certain other types of claim not covered by the Act of 1623.

governed the action of ejectment. A twenty-year limitation period for actions for land generally was fixed by the Real Property Limitation Act, 1833 [42]; but the period was reduced to twelve years by the Real Property Limitation Act, 1874.[43] The earlier statutes have now been repealed and consolidated, in amended form, by the Limitation Act, 1939,[44] which came into force on July 1, 1940.[45]

The provisions of the Limitation Act, 1939, will be treated in three sections:

(1) The length of the limitation period;

(2) When time starts to run; and

(3) The effect of the lapse of time.

Part 2

THE LENGTH OF THE LIMITATION PERIOD

1. Three main periods. The Limitation Act, 1939, lays down three main periods of limitation which are relevant to the law of real property.

(*a*) *Six years*: a period of six years for actions on simple contracts [46] and actions for arrears of rent.[47] The same period applies to actions in tort,[48] except that a three-year period has been imposed for actions for personal injuries.[49]

(*b*) *Specialties*: a period of twelve years for actions on a specialty.[50] A specialty [51] includes a covenant under seal, *e.g.*, a covenant contained in a conveyance or in a lease.

---

[42] s. 2.

[43] s. 1.

[44] The Act has been amended by Law Reform (Limitation of Actions, etc.) Act, 1954, Limitation Act 1963 and Law Reform (Miscellaneous Provisions) Act 1971, but without affecting the law of real property.

[45] Limitation Act, 1939, s. 34 (2).

[46] *Ibid.*, s. 2 (1) (*a*).

[47] s. 17; also arrears of dower: *ibid.*

[48] s. 2 (1) (*a*).

[49] Law Reform (Limitation of Actions, etc.) Act, 1954. This period may sometimes be extended with leave of the court under Limitation Act 1963 as amended by Law Reform (Miscellaneous Provisions) Act 1971.

[50] Limitation Act, 1939, s. 2 (3).

[51] A statute is also a specialty (*Cork & Brandon Ry.* v. *Goode* (1853) 13 C.B. 826), but claims to sums recoverable under statute (other than penalties) are barred in six years: s. 2 (1) (*d*). This was a change made by the Act of 1939. Previously, when the longer period applied to statutory claims, it was often difficult to decide whether claims were statutory or contractual.

(c) *Land*: a period of twelve years for the recovery of land [52] or of money charged on land, *e.g.*, by a mortgage.[53] " Land " for this purpose includes rentcharges and certain tithes, but not other incorporeal hereditaments such as profits *à prendre* or advowsons.[54] Any legal or equitable interest is included; and the definition extends to the proceeds of sale of land held upon trust for sale.[54]

2. **Special cases.** Longer periods are provided in the following special cases.

(a) *Crown lands.* For actions for the recovery of Crown lands the period is now thirty years.[55] Formerly it was sixty years,[56] a period which has been retained in the one case of foreshore owned by the Crown.[57] Claims by subjects to recover lands from the Crown are barred after the ordinary period of twelve years.

(b) *Corporations sole.* The title of a spiritual or eleemosynary (*i.e.*, charitable) corporation sole, such as a bishop, or the master of a hospital, is barred after thirty years.[58] Formerly the period was two successive incumbencies plus six years after the appointment of the third incumbent, or sixty years, whichever was the longer.[59]

(c) *Advowsons.* A claim to an advowson is barred after the period during which three successive incumbencies have been held adversely to the owner of the advowson, or sixty years of adverse possession, whichever is the longer, but subject to a maximum period of one hundred years.[60] This represents no change in the law.

Part 3

THE RUNNING OF TIME

In order to find the moment when a right of action becomes barred, four questions must be considered: first, when time begins to run; second, what will postpone this date; third, what will start time running afresh; and fourth, what will suspend the running of time.

---

[52] Limitation Act, 1939, s. 4 (3).
[53] s. 18 (1).
[54] s. 31 (1).
[55] s. 4 (1).
[56] Crown Suits Acts, 1769, 1861, called the " Nullum Tempus Acts," from the maxim *nullum tempus occurrit regi*. The Limitation Act, 1623, had fixed 1564 as the limitation date for Crown actions.
[57] Limitation Act, 1939, s. 4 (1), proviso.
[58] *Ibid.*, s. 4 (2).
[59] Real Property Limitation Act, 1833, s. 29.
[60] Limitation Act, 1939, s. 14.

Sect. 1. When Time Begins to Run

In the case of actions for the recovery of land or capital sums charged on land, time begins to run in accordance with the following rules.

1. Owner entitled in possession

(a) *Dispossession, discontinuance and adverse possession.* Where the owner of land is entitled in possession, time begins to run as soon as both—

(i) the owner has been dispossessed, or has discontinued his possession,[61] and

(ii) adverse possession has been taken by some other person.[62]

" Dispossessed " merely means that the owner has been driven out of possession by another,[63] whereas " discontinued " means that the owner has abandoned his possession, and some other person has taken possession.[64] It is thus not necessary that the owner should have been driven out of possession; if the owner abandons possession, or if he dies and the person next entitled (*e.g.,* as devisee or remainderman) does not take possession, time will begin to run as soon as adverse possession is taken by another. But it is essential that there should be adverse possession by another, for until there is, there is nobody against whom the owner is failing to assert his rights.

(b) *Adverse possession.* Before 1833, " adverse possession " bore a highly technical meaning.[65] Today it merely means possession inconsistent with the title of the true owner,[66] and not, *e.g.,* possession under a licence from him [67] or by a trustee on his behalf. Possession may continue to be adverse even if the squatter grants a tenancy to the true owner, who takes it in ignorance of his title.[68] In order to amount to adverse possession against the owner, " acts must be done which are inconsistent with his enjoyment of the soil for the purposes for which he intended to use it." [69]

---

[61] *Ibid.,* s. 5 (1).
[62] *Ibid.,* s. 10 (1).
[63] *Rains* v. *Buxton* (1880) 14 Ch.D. 537 at 539.
[64] *Ibid.;* *Cannon* v. *Rimington* (1853) 12 C.B. 18 at 33; *M'Donnell* v. *M'Kinty* (1847) 10 Ir.L.R. 514 at 526; *Smith* v. *Lloyd* (1854) 9 Exch. 562 at 572.
[65] See Lightwood, *Time Limit on Actions,* 6; Lightwood, *Possession,* 180. Thus before the Real Property Limitation Act, 1833, possession by a younger brother was deemed possession by the heir (Co.Litt. 242a); possession by one co-owner was deemed possession by all; possession by a tenant at will or at sufferance was deemed possession by the lessor.
[66] Limitation Act, 1939, s. 10 (1); *Moses* v. *Lovegrove* [1952] 2 Q.B. 533; *Hughes* v. *Griffin* [1969] 1 W.L.R. 23; and see *post,* p. 1018.
[67] *Hughes* v. *Griffin, supra.* Contrast the position of a tenant at will, *post,* p. 1017.
[68] *Bligh* v. *Martin* [1968] 1 W.L.R. 804.
[69] *Leigh* v. *Jack* (1879) 5 Ex.D. 264 at 273, *per* Bramwell L.J.

Possession is a matter of fact, depending on all the circumstances. The type of conduct which indicates possession varies with the type of land: if it is vacant, unenclosed and uncultivated, " there is little which can be done on the land to indicate possession " [70]; and there are obvious difficulties in establishing a squatter's title to part of a swamp.[71] In many cases acts of possession cannot in the nature of things be continuous from day to day.[72] Thus " Enclosure is the strongest possible evidence of adverse possession, but it is not indispensable," [73] nor, it may be added, is it necessarily conclusive.[74]

There may be difficulties when the owner has no present use for the land but only plans for the future. For example, where a strip of land was used as a dump for old boilers, propellers and other foundry refuse by a stranger, this was held not to amount to adverse possession, for it was not inconsistent with the owner's only active intention, which was to dedicate the land as a highway at a future date, and so there was nothing in the nature of an ouster.[75] Nor does the use of land for the breeding of greyhounds (with a consequent erection of sheds and some fencing) and the subsequent cultivation of the land necessarily amount to adverse possession as against owners who merely wish to develop the land when that becomes possible.[76]

2. Successive squatters

(a) *Dispositions by squatter.* As already explained, a squatter has a title based on his own possession, and this title is good against everyone except the true owner.[77] Accordingly, if a squatter who has not barred the true owner sells the land he can give the purchaser a right to the land which is as good as his own. The same applies to devises, gifts or other dispositions by the squatter, and to devolution on his intestacy: in each case the person taking the squatter's interest can add the squatter's period of possession to his own.[78] Thus if X, who has occupied A's land for eight years, sells the land to Y, A will be barred after Y has held the land for a further four years.

(b) *Squatter dispossessed by squatter.* If a squatter is himself dispossessed, the second squatter can add the former period of occupation to his own as against the true owner. This is because

---

[70] *Wuta-Ofei* v. *Danquah* [1961] 1 W.L.R. 1238 at 1243, *per* Lord Guest.
[71] *West Bank Estates Ltd.* v. *Arthur* [1967] 1 A.C. 665; and see *Higgs* v. *Nassauvian Ltd.* [1975] 2 W.L.R. 72 (rotational farming).   [72] *Bligh* v. *Martin, supra.*
[73] *Seddon* v. *Smith* (1877) 36 L.T. 168 at 169, *per* Cockburn C.J.
[74] See *Littledale* v. *Liverpool College* [1900] 1 Ch. 19; *George Wimpey & Co. Ltd.* v. *Sohn* [1967] Ch. 487 (fencing of gardens equivocal as excluding public as well as owner).
[75] *Leigh* v. *Jack* (1879) 5 Ex.D. 264; *Wallis's Cayton Bay Holiday Camp Ltd.* v. *Shell Mex and B.P. Ltd.* [1974] 3 W.L.R. 387 at 392.
[76] *Williams Brothers Direct Supply Ltd.* v. *Raftery* [1958] 1 Q.B. 159.
[77] *Ante,* p. 1004.   [78] *Ante,* p. 1007; *Asher* v. *Whitlock* (1865) L.R. 1 Q.B. 1.

time runs against the true owner from the time when adverse possession began,[79] and so long as adverse possession continues unbroken it makes no difference who continues it.[80] But as against the first squatter, the second squatter must himself occupy for the full period before his title becomes unassailable. This has already been explained,[81] but a simple example may be useful here. If land owned by A has been occupied by X for eight years and Y dispossesses X, A will be barred when twelve years have elapsed from X first taking possession. But although at the end of that time A is barred, X will not be barred until twelve years from Y's first taking possession; for Y cannot claim to be absolutely entitled until he can show that everybody with any claim to the land has been barred by the lapse of the full period.

(c) *Possession abandoned.* There is no right to add together two periods of adverse possession if a squatter abandons possession before the full period has run and some time passes before someone else takes adverse possession of the land. During the gap between the two squatters, the owner has possession in law, and there is no person whom he can sue. The land therefore ceases to be in adverse possession; and when adverse possession is taken by the second squatter a fresh right of action accrues to the true owner, who has the full period within which to enforce it.[82]

3. Future interests. Future interests are governed by two rules.

(a) *Alternative periods.* If adverse possession began before the reversion or remainder fell into possession, the twelve-year period runs against the reversioner or remainderman from the beginning of the adverse possession; but he has an alternative period of six years from the falling into possession of his interest. In other words, he must sue within twelve years of the previous owner's dispossession, or within six years of his own interest vesting in possession, whichever is the longer period.[83] Thus if land is held by A for life with remainder to B in fee simple, and X dispossesses A twenty years before A's death, B still has six years from A's death in which to recover the land. If X had dispossessed A three years before A's death, B would have twelve years from the dispossession of A, *i.e.*, nine years from A's death. But if X had taken no adverse

---

[79] Limitation Act, 1939, s. 10 (1), governing s. 5 (1).
[80] See *Willis* v. *Earl Howe* [1893] 2 Ch. 545.
[81] *Ante,* p. 1007.
[82] *Trustees, Executors and Agency Co. Ltd.* v. *Short* (1888) 13 App.Cas. 793. The rule is now statutory: Limitation Act, 1939, s. 10 (2).
[83] Limitation Act, 1939, s. 6 (2). His trustees may also sue on his behalf: s. 7 (4).

possession until after A's death, the ordinary period of twelve years from the taking of possession would apply, for B's interest would have ceased to be a future interest before time began to run.[84]

(b) *Entails.* A reversioner or remainderman expectant upon an entail in possession is not entitled to the alternative six-year period if his interest could have been barred by the tenant in tail.[85] Thus if B grants land to A in tail, retaining the fee simple reversion, and X dispossesses A or the heirs of his body, B's reversion is barred twelve years after the dispossession, even though B himself had no right to the land during the period. This rule emphasises again the precarious nature of an interest expectant upon an entail: it may be barred by limitation, as well as by disentailment, and the owner is powerless to intervene.

4. Leaseholds

(a) *Reversioner on a lease.* The above provisions do not apply to a reversioner on a lease for a term of years when the tenant has been ousted. No matter when the dispossession occurred, time does not run against the reversioner until the lease expires.[1] Thus if L grants T a lease for ninety-nine years and T is dispossessed by X, the twelve-year period runs against T from the dispossession but against L only from the determination of the lease. X can therefore retain the land as against T during the rest of the term, but L can recover it from X at the end of the term, provided L takes proceedings within twelve years of that date.[2]

(b) *Title acquired by tenant.* A tenant cannot acquire a title against his landlord during the currency of the lease; for occupation by a tenant is never adverse to the landlord's title, which the tenant is estopped from denying.[3] Any encroachments by the tenant on land belonging to third parties will enure for the landlord's benefit,[4] unless a different intention is shown by the conduct of the landlord or tenant.[5] If the tenant occupies other land belonging to the landlord but not included in the demise, that land is presumed to be

---

[84] See ss. 6 (1), 10 (1).
[85] This is the combined effect of ss. 4 (3), 6 (3) and 31 (4), requiring the reversioner or remainderman to be treated as a person claiming through the tenant in tail in such cases, and so to be barred together with him.
[1] s. 6 (2); the words " not being a term of years absolute " confirm *Walter* v. *Yalden* [1902] 2 K.B. 304 on this point.
[2] See further *post*, p. 1029.
[3] *Ante*, pp. 645, 1009.
[4] *Whitmore* v. *Humphries* (1871) L.R. 7 C.P. 1; *Att.-Gen.* v. *Tomline* (1880) 15 Ch.D. 150; *East Stonehouse U. D. C.* v. *Willoughby Bros. Ltd.* [1902] 2 K.B. 318; *King* v. *Smith* [1950] 1 All E.R. 553; *ante*, p. 1007, n. 23.
[5] *Kingsmill* v. *Millard* (1855) 11 Exch. 313; and see cases cited in preceding note.

an addition to the land demised to the tenant (" a mere extension of the *locus* of his tenancy " [6]), so that it becomes subject to the terms of the tenancy [7]; and although the tenant may aquire a title to it against the landlord for the remainder of the term, he must give it up to him when the tenancy ends.[8] But the presumption may be rebutted, *e.g.*, by the tenant conveying the land to a third party and informing the landlord of this while the tenancy is still running.[9]

(c) *Non-payment of rent.* Failure to pay rent merely bars the landlord's claim to recover any particular instalment of rent after six years from its falling due [10]; it has no effect on the landlord's title to the land.

(d) *Right of re-entry.* A right of re-entry under a forfeiture clause (*e.g.*, for non-payment of rent) is a right to recover land,[11] and is therefore barred if not exercised for twelve years. But this does not affect the landlord's title to the reversion, for he will have a fresh right of action when the lease expires.[12] A fresh right of entry arises every time the forfeiture clause is brought into play, *e.g.*, by non-payment of rent falling due subsequently. In the case of continuing breaches of covenant,[13] such as failure to repair or user for a prohibited purpose, time continually begins running afresh, and forfeiture can be claimed at any time.

(e) *Adverse receipt of rent.* A landlord's title may, indeed, be barred if adverse possession is taken not of the land but of the rent from it. The rule is that if a tenant who holds under a written lease pays a rent of at least £1 per annum for twelve years to some person who wrongfully claims the reversion, this bars the landlord's rights altogether.[14] Adverse receipt of rent by a third party is equivalent to adverse possession of the reversion by him,[15] and after twelve years it will extinguish the reversion, even if the true owner of it is also the tenant who paid the rent.[16]

5. Tenants at will and at sufferance. A tenant at will is in a better position than a tenant under a lease for a fixed term of years,

---

[6] *Lord Hastings* v. *Saddler* (1898) 79 L.T. 355 at 356, *per* Lord Russell C.J.
[7] *J. F. Perrott & Co. Ltd.* v. *Cohen* [1951] 1 K.B. 705 (repairing covenant).
[8] *Tabor* v. *Godfrey* (1895) 64 L.J.Q.B. 245.
[9] *Kingsmill* v. *Millard, supra*; *Smirk* v. *Lyndale Developments Ltd.* [1974] 3 W.L.R. 91, not following *Lord Hastings* v. *Saddler, supra*.
[10] See *post*, p. 1033.
[11] Limitation Act, 1939, s. 31 (5).
[12] *Ibid.*, s. 8.
[13] See *ante*, p. 658.
[14] ss. 9 (3), 10 (3). Payment of rent to the true reversioner will stop time running: see s. 9 (3); *Nicholson* v. *England* [1926] 2 K.B. 93. S. 9 (3) does not apply to any tenancy at will or lease granted by the Crown: s. 9 (4).
[15] s. 10 (3).
[16] *Bligh* v. *Martin* [1968] 1 W.L.R. 804.

for time begins to run against the landlord after the expiration of one year after the commencement of the tenancy, or after its determination, whichever is the earlier.[17] Thus if T holds from L as tenant at will, L is barred when thirteen years have elapsed since the tenancy began. But time begins to run afresh if rent is paid or a written acknowledgment is given.[18] And the court may occasionally escape from holding that a rent-free "tenant" has barred the landlord's title by holding that there is only a licence to occupy and not a true tenancy.[19]

In the case of a tenancy at sufferance, time runs from the commencement of the tenancy. This is because a tenancy at sufferance is really not a tenancy at all, but is adverse possession.[20]

6. Yearly or periodic tenants. A tenant under a yearly or other periodic tenancy who does not hold under a lease in writing is in a similar position to a tenant at will.[21] Time runs from the end of the first year or other period of the tenancy, subject to extension by payment of rent or written acknowledgment.[22] An oral tenancy will thus in time ripen into ownership if the rent is not paid.[23] If there is a lease in writing, time runs from the determination of the tenancy.

7. Rentcharges. In the case of a rentcharge [1] in possession, time runs from the last payment of rent to the owner of the rentcharge.[2] Thus the owner's rights are barred—

(i) if no rent is paid for twelve years, in which case the rentcharge is extinguished; or

(ii) if the rent is paid to a stranger for twelve years, in which case the rentcharge remains enforceable against the land but the former owner's claim to it is extinguished in favour of the stranger.

The definition of rentcharge excludes rent service.[3] This is a change from the previous law,[4] and it now appears that any ancient

---

[17] s. 9 (1).

[18] *Post*, p. 1026. A mere oral acknowledgment might suffice to create a new tenancy (see *Jarman* v. *Hale* [1899] 1 Q.B. 994, esp. at 999), and start time running afresh a year later; yet an acknowledgment is unilateral, a tenancy bilateral.

[19] *Cobb* v. *Lane* [1952] 1 All E.R. 1199; *Hughes* v. *Griffin* [1969] 1 W.L.R. 23; *Heslop* v. *Burns* [1974] 1 W.L.R. 1241; see *ante*, p. 1013.   [20] *Ante*, p. 640.

[21] s. 9 (2); *Moses* v. *Lovegrove* [1952] 2 Q.B. 533, holding that the Rent Acts did not prevent time from running, and that a rent book is not a "lease in writing."

[22] And, of course, the grant of a new tenancy would renew the process.

[23] *Hayward* v. *Chaloner* [1968] 1 Q.B. 107, where there was disagreement whether there was adverse possession.   [1] Defined as "land": s. 31 (1).

[2] s. 31 (6).   [3] s. 31 (1).

[4] Real Property Limitation Act, 1833, s. 2; *De Beauvoir* v. *Owen* (1850) 5 Exch. 166.

quit rents payable in respect of freehold land and not extinguished (as most of them were[5]) before 1940 are no longer liable to be barred by non-payment. Copyhold rents have been abolished by other legislation.[6] Rent due under a lease (which is rent service) is dealt with elsewhere.[7]

8. Mortgages

(a) *The mortgagor's right to redeem.* The right to redeem, whether legal or equitable, is barred if the mortgagee remains in possession of the mortgaged land for twelve years without giving any written acknowledgment of the title of the mortgagor or of his equity of redemption and without receiving any payment on account of principal or interest[8] made by or on behalf of the mortgagor; the mere receipt of rents and profits while in possession is not enough,[9] even though he is accountable to the mortgagor for them.[10] The rule that a mortgagee in possession can bar the mortgagor's title is an exception to the general rules that time runs only where there is adverse possession, and that a lessee (here, a mortgagee having a long term of years[11]) may not bar his lessor's title.[12]

When a second mortgagee's rights against the mortgagor are barred, he can no longer exercise his right to redeem the first mortgagee[13]; for his interest in the property is at an end.[14]

(b) *Mortgagee's rights to enforce the mortgage.* The mortgagee's rights to foreclose,[15] to sue for possession,[16] and to sue for the principal[17] all became barred after twelve years from the date when repayment became due under the mortgage[18]; and his title is then extinguished.[19] But time begins to run afresh if during the period the mortgagor makes any written acknowledgment or he or the person in possession of the land makes any payment of interest or of capital which complies with the Act.[20]

---

[5] *Ante,* p. 793.
[6] *Ante,* p. 37.
[7] Mentioned *ante,* p. 1017, and discussed *post,* p. 1032.
[8] ss. 12, 23 (3), 24; *Young* v. *Clarey* [1948] Ch. 191 (mortgagor and second mortgagee barred by mortgagee in possession); and see *post,* p. 1026.
[9] *Harlock* v. *Ashberry* (1882) 19 Ch.D. 539; and see *Re Lord Clifden* [1900] 1 Ch. 774.
[10] *Ante,* p. 915.   [11] See *ante,* p. 896.
[12] *Ante,* p. 1016.   [13] See *ante,* p. 964.
[14] *Cotterell* v. *Price* [1960] 1 W.L.R. 1097.
[15] s. 18 (4), treating this as an action to recover land.
[16] s. 16; *Cotterell* v. *Price, supra.*
[17] s. 18 (1). For interest, see *post,* p. 1033.
[18] See *Lloyds Bank Ltd.* v. *Margolis* [1954] 1 W.L.R. 644 (charge to secure bank overdraft with covenant to pay " on demand ": time runs from demand).
[19] See *Lewis* v. *Plunket* [1937] 1 All E.R. 530 at 534 (omitted from [1937] Ch. 306); *Cotterell* v. *Price, supra.*
[20] s. 23 (1), (4); for the details of acknowledgments, see *post,* p. 1026.

9. Claims through Crown or corporation sole. It has been seen that the Crown is entitled to a period of thirty years instead of the usual twelve.[21] If a person against whom time has started to run conveys his land to the Crown, the only change is that the limitation period becomes thirty years from the dispossession instead of twelve.[22] But in the converse case where time has started to run against the Crown and the Crown then conveys the land to X, the rule is that X is barred at the expiration of thirty years from the original dispossession or twelve years from the conveyance to him, whichever is the shorter.[23] Thus X is entitled to twelve years from the date of the conveyance unless at that time there were less than twelve years of the Crown period unexpired, in which case X merely has the residue of that period.

Similar rules apply to the longer periods for a spiritual or eleemosynary corporation sole.[24]

10. Trusts and equitable remedies

(a) *Adverse possession by a stranger.* In general, the twelve-year period for the recovery of land applies as much to equitable interests in land as to legal estates [25]; and in particular it extends to actions for the proceeds of sale of land, and so to trusts for sale.[26] But adverse possession of trust property by a stranger does not bar the trustee's title to the property until all the beneficiaries have been barred.[27] Thus if land is held on trust for sale for the benefit of A for life with remainder to B, twelve years' adverse possession of the land by X bars A's equitable interest and, but for the provision just mentioned, would bar the trustee's legal estate. But time will not start to run against B's equitable interest until A's death,[28] and the same accordingly applies to the trustee's legal estate. Consequently, after the twelve years have run, the trustee will hold the legal estate on a future trust for B as from A's death.[29] This is so even if A is the trustee, as will normally be the case with settled land.

(b) *Adverse possession by a trustee.* It is a general principle that a trustee can never obtain a title by adverse possession against his beneficiaries. There is, indeed, a limitation period of six years

---

[21] *Ante,* p. 1012.
[22] s. 4 (1).
[23] s. 4 (3), proviso.
[24] s. 4 (2), (3); *ante,* p. 1012.
[25] ss. 7 (1), 18.
[26] s. 7 (1).
[27] s. 7 (2), (3), (4).
[28] *Ante,* p. 1015.
[29] As to X's interest, see *post,* p. 1028.

for actions to recover trust property or in respect of breach of trust, in cases where no other period of limitation is prescribed [30]; but it does not apply to a beneficiary's action against a trustee for any fraud or fraudulent breach of trust to which the trustee was a party or privy, or for recovery of the trust property or its proceeds in the possession of the trustee, or previously received by him and converted to his own use.[31] In these three cases the trustee can never bar the claims of his beneficiaries.

Personal representatives are trustees for this purpose.[32] The limitation period for claims to a deceased person's estate is twelve years,[33] even where the claim is made against a third party, *e.g.*, someone to whom the estate has been wrongly distributed.[34] But personal representatives are often expressly given the duties of trustees, and claims against them in the latter capacity are governed by the rules as to trustees, explained above.[35]

(c) *Adverse possession by a beneficiary.* Formerly a beneficiary in possession of land was treated as a tenant at will to the trustees, though the usual rule that time began to run one year after the commencement of the tenancy [36] was excluded.[37] Thus unless it could be shown that in some way the beneficiary's possession had become adverse (*e.g.*, by actual determination of the tenancy [38]), time would not run against the trustees at all.[39] Under the Limitation Act, 1939, time will not run against a trustee or co-beneficiary in favour of a beneficiary in possession, except where the beneficiary in possession is solely and absolutely entitled.[40] Thus under an uncompleted contract for sale, time runs against the vendor (who is a trustee for the purchaser [41]) if the purchaser is let into possession.[42] It is not, however, clear whether the limitation period is then twelve years,[43] or, on the basis of a tenancy at will,[44] thirteen.[45]

---

[30] s. 19 (2). S. 19 replaces with amendments T.A., 1888, s. 8 (1).
[31] s. 19 (1).
[32] Limitation Act, 1939, s. 31 (1); T.A., 1925, s. 68 (17). And see *ante*, pp. 536, 537.
[33] *Ante*, p. 1012 (land); Limitation Act, 1939, s. 20 (personalty).
[34] *Ministry of Health* v. *Simpson* [1951] A.C. 251.
[35] See *Re Oliver* [1927] 2 Ch. 323.
[36] *Ante*, p. 1018.
[37] Real Property Limitation Act, 1833, s. 7, proviso.
[38] See, *e.g.*, *Doe* d. *Jacobs* v. *Phillips* (1847) 10 Q.B. 130.
[39] See *Garrard* v. *Tuck* (1849) 8 C.B. 231.
[40] Limitation Act, 1939, s. 7 (5).
[41] *Ante*, p. 575.
[42] *Bridges* v. *Mees* [1957] Ch. 475. But for the purchaser's right to specific performance see note 48, *infra*.
[43] See *Re Cussons Ltd.* (1904) 73 L.J.Ch. 296.
[44] See *ante*, pp. 638, 1017, 1018.
[45] The point did not arise in *Bridges* v. *Mees*, *supra*.

(*d*) *Equitable remedies.* Claims for specific performance or for an injunction or for other equitable relief, such as rescission, rectification, or claims to set aside dealings for fraud or mistake,[46] are excepted from the Act,[47] so that they are not subject to any statutory period. The purpose here is not to extend the period (for the court, except in special cases,[48] will not give equitable relief outside the analogous period for an action at law [49]) but to preserve the equitable doctrine of *laches*,[50] *i.e.*, the principle that equitable remedies are available only to those who seek them without unreasonable delay, even though within any analogous limitation period.[51] If a fixed period had been laid down by the Act it would have been more difficult for the court to refuse relief where the plaintiff sought it after undue delay but still within the period.

11. Co-ownership

(*a*) *Ouster.* At common law, the unity of possession between co-owners [52] meant that if one joint tenant or tenant in common occupied the whole of the land, or took the whole of the rents and profits, this by itself was not adverse possession which would start time running; some further act, such as ouster of the other co-owners, was needed.[53] However, a presumption of ouster might arise from long exclusive enjoyment by one co-owner [54]; and after 1833, by statute,[55] time normally began to run as between co-owners as soon as one enjoyed more than his share of the land or of the rents and profits, to the exclusion of the other.[55a]

(*b*) *After 1925.* Since 1925 the law has been changed, perhaps unintentionally, by the imposition of the statutory trust for sale which now operates in all cases of tenancy in common and beneficial joint tenancy.[56] This brings into play the rules relating to trusts, mentioned above,[57] in particular the rules that a trustee cannot bar

---

46 But as to fraud and mistake, see *post*, p. 1024.
47 s. 2 (7).
48 *e.g.*, where possession has been taken by a purchaser but the legal estate has for some reason been left outstanding: *Shepheard* v. *Walker* (1875) L.R. 20 Eq. 659; (1876) 34 L.T. 230 (specific performance awarded after 18 years); *Williams* v. *Greatrex* [1957] 1 W.L.R. 31 (specific performance awarded after 10 years).
49 *Smith* v. *Clay* (1767) 3 Bro.C.C. 639n.
50 See generally Brunyate, *Limitation of Actions in Equity*, 185 *et seq.*
51 Thus insufficiently explained delays of one year (*Watson* v. *Reid* (1830) 1 Russ. & M. 236), or three and a half years (*Eads* v. *Williams* (1854) 4 De G.M. & G. 674) have been held to bar a claim for specific performance. Contrast *Wroth* v. *Tyler* [1974] Ch. 30 at 53. On laches, see generally Snell, *Equity*, 35.
52 See *ante*, p. 393.
53 See Carson's *Real Property Statutes* (2nd ed.), p. 149.
54 See *Doe* d. *Fishar* v. *Taylor* (1774) 1 Cowp. 217; *cf. Doe* d. *Hellings* v. *Bird* (1809) 11 East 49.
55 Real Property Limitation Act, 1833, s. 12.
55a See *Paradise Beach Co. Ltd.* v. *Price-Robinson* [1968] A.C. 1072.
56 *Ante*, p. 408.   57 *Ante*, p. 1020.

his beneficiary, and that one beneficiary cannot bar another beneficiary. Thus in a case [58] where one of two tenants in common took all the rents and profits from 1923 for over twelve years, the other tenant's claim failed in respect of the years 1923–25, when the old law applied; but it succeeded in respect of the later years, for since 1925 the legal estate was vested in the two tenants as trustees for sale on their own behalf, and so neither could plead the Limitation Act against the other. Since 1940, moreover, the position would be the same even if other persons were the trustees,[59] owing to the provision that one beneficiary cannot bar another.[60]

Sect. 2. Postponement of the Period

The date from which time begins to run may be postponed on account of disability, fraud, fraudulent concealment, or (in certain special cases) mistake.

A. Disability

1. Alternative periods. If the owner of an interest in land is under disability when the right of action accrues, he is allowed an alternative period of six years from the time when he ceases to be under a disability or dies, whichever happens first, with a maximum period in the case of land of thirty years from the date when the right of action first accrued.[61] Thus if X takes possession of A's land at a time when A is a lunatic, A will have twelve years from the dispossession or six years from his recovery from lunacy in which to bring his action, whichever period is the longer; but in no case can A sue after thirty years from the dispossession. The following rules should be noted.

2. Disability. A person is under a disability for this purpose if he is an infant or subject to mental treatment.[62] Coverture and absence beyond the seas were once disabilities,[63] but are so no longer[64]; and before April 18, 1949,[65] convicts were under disability if no administrator or curator had been appointed.[66]

---

[58] *Re Landi* [1939] Ch. 828, rejecting the argument that the old law is preserved by L.P.A., 1925, s. 12 (a saving clause for the operation of statutes and the general law of limitation). *Cf. Re Milking Pail Farm Trusts* [1940] Ch. 996; and see (1941) 57 L.Q.R. 26 (R.E.M.); (1971) 35 Conv.(N.S.) 6 (G. Battersby); Preston and Newsom, *Limitation of Actions*, 3rd ed., 149.

[59] For example if the legal estate were vested in personal representatives under L.P.A., 1925, s. 34 (3); *ante*, p. 410.

[60] Limitation Act, 1939, s. 7 (5); *ante*, p. 1021.

[61] s. 22.   [62] s. 31 (2), as amended by Mental Health Act, 1959, 7th Sched.

[63] Civil Procedure Act, 1833, s. 4; Real Property Limitation Acts, 1833, s. 16; 1874, s. 4.

[64] The Limitation Act, 1939, s. 34 (4) and Sched., repeals and does not replace the earlier Acts.   [65] *Ante*, pp. 999–1000.   [66] Limitation Act, 1939, s. 31 (2).

3. Supervening disability. A disability is immaterial unless it existed at the time when the cause of action accrued.[67] Thus if A becomes insane the day before he is dispossessed, the provisions for disability apply, whereas if he becomes insane the day after he has been dispossessed, they do not.[68]

4. Successive disabilities. In the case of successive disabilities, if a person is under one disability and before that ceases another disability begins, the period is extended until both disabilities cease, subject to the thirty years' maximum.[69] But if one disability comes to an end before another disability starts, or if the person under disability is succeeded by another person under disability, time runs from the ceasing of the first disability. For example, A is an infant when the cause of action accrues. If later, during his infancy, he becomes insane, the six-year period does not start to run until he is both sane and of full age.[70] But if he reaches full age before he becomes insane, or if he dies an infant and B, a lunatic, becomes entitled to the land, the six-year period runs from A's majority in the first case and his death in the second. In no case can the right of action survive for more than thirty years after it accrued.

B. Fraud, Fraudulent Concealment and Mistake

1. Fraud or fraudulent concealment. Where—

> (i) an action is based on the fraud of the defendant or his agent (or any person through whom he claims, or his agent), or
> (ii) a right of action is concealed by the fraud of any such person,

time does not begin to run until the plaintiff discovers the fraud or could with reasonable diligence discover it.[71] "Fraud" bears its usual meaning,[72] but "fraudulent concealment"[73] is wide enough to cover not only a deliberately concealed method of doing the act in question (*e.g.*, the surreptitious abstraction of underground minerals[74]), but also the subsequent concealment of the act.[75] Dishonesty is not an indispensable element in fraudulent concealment, for concealment may be unconscionable and so "fraudulent" without

---

[67] *Ibid.*, s. 22; see *e.g.*, *Garner* v. *Wingrove* [1905] 2 Ch. 233.
[68] *Goodhall* v. *Skerratt* (1855) 3 Drew. 216 (where the disability was coverture).
[69] Limitation Act, 1939, s. 22.
[70] See, *e.g.*, *Borrows* v. *Ellison* (1871) L.R. 6 Ex. 128 (infancy and coverture).
[71] Limitation Act, 1939, s. 26.
[72] See *Beaman* v. *A. R. T. S. Ltd.* [1949] 1 K.B. 550 at 558.
[73] See *Willis* v. *Earl Howe* [1893] 2 Ch. 545 at 551.
[74] *Bulli Coal Mining Co.* v. *Osborne* [1899] A.C. 351; compare *Trotter* v. *Maclean* (1879) 13 Ch.D. 574.
[75] *Beaman* v. *A. R. T. S. Ltd.*, *supra*, at p. 559; and see *Eddis* v. *Chichester Constable* [1969] 2 Ch. 345 (mere silence).

any moral turpitude.[76] Thus there may be fraudulent concealment if title deeds are destroyed,[77] or if an eldest son, who knows that he is illegitimate, joins in barring an entail without disclosing the facts to his legitimate brother who was the true tenant in tail,[78] or if a builder covers up what he knows to be defective foundations without saying anything to the purchaser[79]; and where a vendor employs a builder as an independent contractor, the builder may for this purpose be treated as the vendor's " agent." [80] But there is no fraudulent concealment in the open occupation of land, even if it is subterranean and the owner has no knowledge of the occupation.[81]

The plea of fraud will not postpone the beginning of the ordinary period of limitation if the defendant is a purchaser for value who was not a party to the fraud and at the time of his purchase neither knew nor had reason to believe that any fraud had been committed.[82] This rule, now statutory, is a product of the older law under which relief against fraud was given only in equity.[83]

2. Relief from mistake. Similar provisions apply to an action " for relief from the consequences of a mistake." [84] This rule has a narrow scope, and applies only where it is the fact that a mistake has been made that gives a right to apply to the court for relief, as, for example, for the recovery of money paid by mistake.[85] In the case of land, most claims for relief against mistake are based on equitable grounds, *e.g.*, to set aside a conveyance executed under a misapprehension,[1] or by way of rectification[2] or rescission.[3] These are not subject to any period of limitation,[4] and so nothing would be gained by providing that the period shall not begin to run until some later date. There is no general rule that mistake stops time from running,[5] *e.g.*, where a landowner allows his neighbour to take adverse possession of a strip of land owing to a mistake about his boundary; nor does mere ignorance.[6]

[76] *Kitchen* v. *R.A.F. Association* [1958] 1 W.L.R. 563; *Clark* v. *Woor* [1965] 1 W.L.R. 650; *Applegate* v. *Moss* [1971] 1 Q.B. 406.
[77] *Lawrence* v. *Lord Norreys* (1890) 15 App.Cas. 210.
[78] *Vane* v. *Vane* (1872) 8 Ch.App. 383.
[79] *Applegate* v. *Moss, supra*; *King* v. *Victor Parsons & Co.* [1973] 1 W.L.R. 29.
[80] *Applegate* v. *Moss, supra*, perhaps straining the words of the Act in the interests of justice. [81] *Rains* v. *Buxton* (1880) 14 Ch.D. 537.
[82] s. 26, replacing Real Property Limitation Act, 1833, s. 26.
[83] See *Oelkers* v. *Ellis* [1914] 2 K.B. 139. [84] s. 26.
[85] See *Phillips-Higgins* v. *Harper* [1954] 1 Q.B. 411. A person who has mistakenly paid too much has an extension of time, whereas one who has mistakenly received too little has not; for in an action to recover money paid by mistake, the mistake is the gist of the action, whereas the remedy for an underpayment is merely to sue for the balance, and mistake has nothing to do with that.
[1] *Cooper* v. *Phibbs* (1867) L.R. 2 H.L. 149; *cf.* ante, p. 591.
[2] *Ante*, p. 595. [3] *Ante*, p. 588.
[4] *Ante*, p. 1022. [5] See *Phillips-Higgins* v. *Harper, supra.*
[6] See *Cartledge* v. *E. Jopling & Sons Ltd.* [1963] A.C. 758. The Limitation Act, 1963, as amended, allows an extension of time for ignorance in actions for damages for personal injuries, subject to certain conditions.

Sect. 3. Starting Time Running Afresh

1. Acknowledgment or payment. Time may be started running afresh—

(i) by a written and signed acknowledgment of the plaintiff's title [7]; or

(ii) by payment of part of the principal or interest due in respect of a debt.[8]

The acknowledgment or payment must be made by or on behalf of the person in whose favour time is running, and to or for the account of the person whose title is being barred [9]; and it must be signed by the person making it.[10] An acknowledgment signed by a solicitor authorised by a mortgagor to " clear up " his affairs binds the mortgagor [11]; but an acknowledgment to some third party, such as the Inland Revenue, will not satisfy the Act,[12] and interrogatories cannot be used so as to wring an acknowledgment out of a litigant.[13]

2. Sufficiency of acknowledgment or payment. The acknowledgment must be of an existing liability, and not merely of facts which might give rise to liability [14]; but any statement recognising the plaintiff's right to sue is enough.[15] Accordingly, statements in a company's balance-sheets, which relate to past periods, will not suffice [16] unless they are put forward as showing the existing position.[17] No special form is required, nor need there be any intention to make an acknowledgment. Thus a letter by a squatter to the owner offering, subject to contract, to buy the land may be sufficient, by recognising that the owner has the better title [18]; and an acknowledgment of unquantified indebtedness (*e.g.*, the " amount I owe you ") suffices, for extrinsic evidence is admissible to quantify it.[1] But the statement must acknowledge that there is a debt and not merely that there may be a claim, so that it is not enough to state that " the question of outstanding rent can be settled as a separate agreement as soon as you present your account." [2]

3. Expiration of period. When once the full period has run, no payment or acknowledgment can revive any right to recover land,[3] for the lapse of time will have extinguished not only the owner's

---

[7] ss. 23 (1) (*a*), 24.
[9] s. 24 (2).
[11] *Wright* v. *Pepin* [1954] 1 W.L.R. 635.
[12] *Bowring-Hanbury's Trustee* v. *Bowring-Hanbury* [1943] Ch. 104.
[13] *Lovell* v. *Lovell* [1970] 1 W.L.R. 1451.   [14] *Re Flynn* (*No. 2*) [1969] 2 Ch. 403.
[15] *Moodie* v. *Bannister* (1859) 4 Drew. 432.
[16] *Consolidated Agencies Ltd.* v. *Bertram Ltd.* [1965] A.C. 470.
[17] *Jones* v. *Bellgrove Properties Ltd.* [1949] 2 K.B. 700; *Re Gee & Co.* (*Woolwich*) *Ltd.* [1974] 2 W.L.R. 515.
[18] *Edginton* v. *Clark* [1964] 1 Q.B. 367; the question is one of construing the words used: see at p. 377.
[1] *Dungate* v. *Dungate* [1965] 1 W.L.R. 1477; and see *Wright* v. *Pepin, supra.*
[2] *Good* v. *Parry* [1963] 2 Q.B. 418, as construed in *Dungate* v. *Dungate, supra.*
[3] *Nicholson* v. *England* [1926] 2 K.B. 93.

[8] s. 23 (1) (*b*), (3), (4).
[10] s. 24 (1).

remedies for recovering the land but also his right to it.[4] It is otherwise in the case of other actions, *e.g.*, for debts, where lapse of time bars only the remedy and not the right. An acknowledgment or payment by a mortgagor in whose favour time has already run may revive his liability on the personal covenant,[5] but it cannot revive the security.[6]

Sect. 4. Suspension of the Period

In general, once time has begun to run, it runs continuously.[7] Disability or fraud may postpone the date when time begins to run, and an acknowledgment or part payment may start time running afresh, but until recently there was no provision whereby the running of time might be suspended for a time and then resumed. The Limitation (Enemies and War Prisoners) Act, 1945, retroactively provided that as from September 3, 1939, the running of time was suspended while any necessary party to an action was an enemy or was detained in enemy territory; " enemy " and " enemy territory " were widely defined. Two or more periods of suspension were to be treated as a single period beginning with the first period and ending with the last. There was an overriding provision that where the period had been suspended under the Act, it should not expire until a year after the person concerned has ceased to be an enemy or be detained in enemy territory, or a year after March 28, 1945 (when the Act was passed), whichever was the later.

Part 4

THE EFFECT OF THE LAPSE OF TIME

Sect. 1. Title to Land

1. Extinction of title. Before 1833 the effect of the Statutes of Limitation was merely to bar rights of action: they extinguished remedies, not rights.[8] Thus a person whose right to recover land had been barred might, if he could recover it peaceably, reassert

---

[4] See *infra.*
[5] See *Re Lord Clifden* [1900] 1 Ch. 774.
[6] Consider *Lewis* v. *Plunket* [1937] 1 All E.R. 530 at 534 (omitted from [1937] Ch. 306).
[7] *Prideaux* v. *Webber* (1661) 1 Lev. 31; *Rhodes* v. *Smethurst* (1840) 6 M. & W. 351; but see *Bowring-Hanbury's Trustee* v. *Bowring-Hanbury* [1943] Ch. 104, discussed at (1943) 59 L.Q.R. 117 (R.E.M.).
[8] See *Wainford* v. *Barker* (1697) 1 Ld.Raym. 232; *Hunt* v. *Burn* (1703) 2 Salk. 422.

his old title.[9] This principle still applies to pure personalty, other
than chattels [10]; but as regards land it was abolished by the Real
Property Limitation Act, 1833.[11] The rule now is that, at the end
of the limitation period, both the right of action for the land and the
claimant's title are extinguished.[12] This applies equally to
redemption and foreclosure actions.

2. The squatter's title

(a) *Rights of third parties.* The general character of a title
acquired by limitation has already been discussed.[13] The squatter
holds a new estate of his own, founded on his adverse possession
and the absence of any better title, but he holds it subject to any
third party rights which run with the land and have not themselves
been extinguished. Thus a squatter will be bound by easements or
restrictive covenants affecting the land. It makes no difference
whether such incumbrances are legal or equitable or whether (if
registrable) they are registered. If they are legal, they bind all
comers, including squatters; if equitable (and even if registrable but
unregistered [14]) they bind all persons who are not purchasers for
value, and a squatter gives no value.[15]

(b) *Progressive improvement.* A squatter's estate is normally a
fee simple absolute,[16] though it may be cut down by the unextin-
guished rights of other persons. If for example land is settled on A
for life with remainder to B in fee simple, and S occupies it for twelve
years during A's lifetime, A's life interest is extinguished but B will
have at least six years from A's death in which to assert his rights.[17]
Meanwhile S, who has extinguished A's equitable life interest but
not the legal estate which is the subject of the settlement,[18] has an
independent legal estate based upon his own occupation, but subject
to B's future right when it accrues. S's estate is in effect an estate
pur autre vie. But it is probably more correct to call it a fee simple
subject to an adverse title, and so a legal estate [19]; for unless B sues

---

[9] See *Doe* d. *Burrough* v. *Reade* (1807) 8 East 353 (possession taken peaceably
when the land was vacant after a death).
[10] See Limitation Act, 1939, s. 3 (2).
[11] s. 34.
[12] Limitation Act, 1939, s. 16.
[13] *Ante,* pp. 1004 *et seq.*
[14] See *post,* p. 1048.
[15] *Re Nisbet & Potts' Contract* [1906] 1 Ch. 386 (squatter bound by restrictive
covenant: *ante,* p. 115); *Scott* v. *Scott* (1854) 4 H.L.C. 1065 (squatter bound
by trusts of a settlement). Contrast *Bolling* v. *Hobday, ante,* p. 115; and an
equitable title to *possession* may be barred: *ante,* p. 1020.
[16] *Ante,* p. 1007.
[17] *Ante,* p. 1015.
[18] *Ante,* p. 1020.
[19] *Ante,* p. 1007.

within the time allowed his title also will be barred. In other words, S's title is not one which comes to a sudden stop at A's death; it continues indefinitely, until someone having a superior title contests it. The interest gained by S is therefore not necessarily commensurate with the interest lost by A[20]; the principle is that S's title may progressively improve as each successive adverse claimant becomes barred.

(c) Leases

(1) LANDLORD NOT BARRED. Interesting questions can arise where a squatter bars a leasehold tenant. If L leases land to T for ninety-nine years and S occupies the land adversely to T for twelve years, S has extinguished T's title. But this has no effect on L's title: L has disposed of his right to possession for the term of the lease, and nothing done by third parties in the meantime will give it back to him. L cannot therefore eject S, since apart from any right of forfeiture[21] L will have no right of entry until the expiration of the term of T's lease; and S, being in possession, has the best immediate title.[22]

(2) SURRENDER. If, however, T surrenders his lease to L after time has run in S's favour, it is held that L is then entitled to eject S.[23] Thus T, whose title against S is bad, can nevertheless confer upon L a good title against S, and thus accelerate L's right to possession. This is said to follow from the fact that the lease remains valid as between L and T. But it is a notable departure from the principle *nemo dat quod non habet*.[24] It also virtually destroys the squatter's statutory title, by putting it into the power of the person barred (T) to have the squatter ejected by a third party (L). The operation of the Limitation Act, 1939, in respect of leaseholds is thus substantially curtailed.

(3) ACQUISITION OF REVERSION. If T acquires L's reversion after S has taken adverse possession, T has the same rights as L. Thus in one case,[25] where the reversion was purchased by T, a yearly

---

[20] See *Taylor v. Twinberrow* [1930] 2 K.B. 16 at 23; earlier dicta to the contrary are attributable to the " parliamentary conveyance " heresy: see *ante*, p. 1010.

[21] *e.g.*, for breach of covenant against parting with possession (see *infra*), or if T denies L's title: see *ante*, p. 739.

[22] *Ante*, p. 1008. This can perhaps be made clear by comparison with the barring of a fee simple. If A is fee simple owner and sells to B, and B's title is extinguished by S (a squatter), obviously A can assert no title against S. The same is true in the case of a reversioner as regards any time before the reversion is due to fall into possession.

[23] *Fairweather v. St. Marylebone Property Co. Ltd.* [1963] A.C. 510, overruling *Walter v. Yalden* [1902] 2 K.B. 304. For criticism, see (1962) 78 L.Q.R. 541 (H.W.R.W.). [24] *i.e.*, no one can pass a better title than he has.

[25] *Taylor v. Twinberrow* [1930] 2 K.B. 16.

tenant whose title as such had already been barred by another person, it was held that T acquired a fresh right of action at once by stepping into the landlord's shoes; the lease merged [26] in the freehold forthwith, for it was determinable by notice and T could not give notice to himself. The result is held to be the same even if the lease is for a fixed term of years which L could not determine, so that L could not eject S [27]; L's conveyance of the reversion thus gives T a power which L does not possess, despite the principle *nemo dat quod non habet*.

(4) CONTINUING LIABILITY OF TENANT. Where a tenant has lost his title to an interloper by adverse possession, he may still remain liable to the landlord on the covenants in the lease (*e.g.*, for rent) because of the continuing privity of contract. But since the leasehold estate is extinguished, there is no longer any privity of estate, so that if he were an assignee of the lease instead of the original tenant he would cease to be liable on the covenants when his title became barred.[28]

(5) LIABILITY OF SQUATTER. The position of S, the squatter in our example, is that he has a legal estate (probably a fee simple, as explained above) subject to L's right of entry at the end of the period of the original term. Having no privity of estate with L, S is not liable on the covenants in T's lease,[29] except so far as they may be enforceable in equity as restrictive covenants.[30] But if T's lease was determinable by notice, or contained a forfeiture clause, L can enforce these terms against S,[31] and so by threat of notice or forfeiture compel S to perform the covenants; and S has no right to apply for

---

[26] For merger, see *ante*, p. 669.

[27] See dicta in *Fairweather* v. *St. Marylebone Property Co. Ltd.*, *supra*, at pp. 541, 555. The House of Lords treated *Taylor* v. *Twinberrow*, *supra*, as inconsistent with *Walter* v. *Yalden*, *supra*, despite the significance of the landlord's power in the former case to determine the tenancy by notice and so eject the squatter. Without this power the landlord has no present title against the squatter which he can convey to the tenant.

[28] *Re Field* [1918] 1 I.R. 140. *Sed quaere*. It might be more correct to treat T's estate as extinguished *quoad* S but not *quoad* L, as *Taylor* v. *Twinberrow*, *supra*, seems to imply.

[29] *Tichborne* v. *Weir* (1892) 67 L.T. 735 (unsuccessful action for damages on repairing covenant against assignee of a mortgagee of a lease who had taken possession and barred the tenant's equity of redemption; the action was brought after the term had expired). Nor will a squatter be bound by "implied covenants," for they arise from the relationship of landlord and tenant, *i.e.*, from privity of estate; *ante*, p. 675.

[30] *Re Nisbet & Potts' Contract* [1906] 1 Ch. 386; *ante*, p. 1028.

[31] *Humphry* v. *Damion* (1612) Cro.Jac. 300 (forfeiture); and *cf. Taylor* v. *Twinberrow*, *supra*.

relief against forfeiture.[32] The reason why such a clause is enforceable against S, even where the covenant itself is not, is that a covenant creates a purely personal obligation unless it is a restrictive covenant or there is privity of estate; but a clause which reserves to the lessor a conditional right of entry gives him a proprietary interest (a right of entry for condition broken)[33] and therefore binds a squatter just like any other successor in title. Furthermore, although a squatter may not be liable to be sued in covenant for the rent, he may be liable to distress if he does not pay it[34]; for distress is a tenurial remedy enforceable against all occupiers of the land if the rent-service is not paid, with certain statutory exceptions.[35]

(6) THE SQUATTER AS TENANT. It follows that an adverse occupant of leasehold land will almost always have to pay the rent, and so will become a yearly or other periodic tenant of the landlord according to the basis on which rent is paid.[36] If he takes advantage of the previous tenant's lease he may estop himself from denying that he holds under it, and thus (but only thus) he may become bound by the covenants. The principle here is that a person who claims the benefit of a deed is estopped from denying that he has accepted all its terms.[37] Mere payment of the rent reserved by the former lease raises no estoppel against a squatter,[38] for he is not claiming any benefit from the lease but merely performing one of the conditions of tenure. But it was held that an estoppel arose where the squatter took advantage of a clause in the lease that the rent should be halved so long as the covenants were observed; having paid rent at the half rate, he was said to be precluded from denying that he was bound by the covenants.[39]

---

[32] *Tickner* v. *Buzzacott* [1965] Ch. 426. For the question whether T can deliberately bring about a forfeiture, *e.g.*, by not paying rent, and so enable L to eject S, see *Fairweather* v. *St. Marylebone Property Co. Ltd.*, *supra*, at p. 547, and (1962) 78 L.Q.R. 541 at 555 *et seq.*

[33] L.P.A., 1925, ss. 1 (2) (*e*), 4 (2) (*b*); *ante*, p. 143. For the operation of forfeiture clauses against third parties, see *ante*, p. 739.

[34] *Humphry* v. *Damion*, *supra*. But *quaere* whether a squatter's goods are now protected by the Law of Distress Amendment Act, 1908, s. 1, as he might be said to be a person " not being a tenant of the premises . . . and not having any beneficial interest in any tenancy of the premises."

[35] *Ante*, p. 691.

[36] *Ante*, p. 633.

[37] Litt. 374, and authorities cited in Norton on *Deeds*, 26, 27; but this doctrine tends to be stated in wider terms than the authorities justify: see *ante*, p. 750.

[38] *Tichborne* v. *Weir* (1892) 67 L.T. 735, *supra*.

[39] *Ashe* v. *Hogan* [1920] 1 I.R. 159 (999-year lease at rent of £8 reducible to £4 so long as covenants observed); and see *O'Connor* v. *Foley* [1906] 1 I.R. 20. Yet it is not easy to see what other course is open to the squatter than to pay such rent as is legally due, or why by paying the one and only correct amount he makes any representation which estops him.

3. Proof of title

(a) *Long possession not enough.* As between vendor and purchaser, a good title cannot be shown merely by proving adverse possession of land, for however long a period.[40] If A and his predecessors in title have been in possession of land for twenty, fifty, or a hundred years, that does not prove that A is entitled to it, for the true owner—

(i) might have been under disability at the time of dispossession; or

(ii) might have been the Crown; or

(iii) might have been the reversioner or remainderman under a settlement; or

(iv) might be the reversioner on a long lease.

(b) *Proving owner barred.* Consequently, in order to establish a good title by the operation of the Act, the vendor must prove—

(i) the title of the former owner of the interest in land in question; and

(ii) the extinction of that title in the vendor's favour.

This is a heavy burden of proof, particularly since the vendor will often not have access to the title deeds of the land acquired by limitation.[41] But if the vendor can discharge the burden of proof, he can force the purchaser to accept his title.[42] In practice it is comparatively unusual for a title to land to be acquired by limitation except in the case of encroachments upon neighbouring land.

4. Exclusion of limitation. In specified cases statute precludes the acquisition of a title by limitation. Thus no right adverse to the title of the Coal Commission or National Coal Board to any coal or mine of coal can be acquired by limitation.[42a]

Sect. 2. Arrears of Income

1. Rent. The recovery of arrears of income is a matter distinct from the recovery of the land or capital money which produces it.

---

[40] *Moulton* v. *Edmonds* (1859) 1 De G.F. & J. 246 at 250; *Jacobs* v. *Revell* [1900] 2 Ch. 858.

[41] But he may be able to demand them under the rule that the deeds belong to the owner of the land: *ante*, p. 660.

[42] *Scott* v. *Nixon* (1843) 3 Dr. & War. 388; *Games* v. *Bonnor* (1884) 54 L.J.Ch. 517; *Re Atkinson & Horsell's Contract* [1912] 2 Ch. 1. The purchaser may of course agree to accept an imperfect title: see, *e.g.*, the earlier transactions reported in *Re Nisbet and Potts' Contract* [1906] 1 Ch. 386.

[42a] Coal Act, 1938, s. 17 (2); Coal Industry Nationalisation Act, 1946, s. 49 (3).

The arrears of rent which a landlord or the owner of a rentcharge may recover, whether by action or distress, are limited to the arrears accrued due during the preceding six years,[43] whether or not the rent is payable under a deed.[44] Each time a gale of rent falls due, a new cause of action accrues,[45] and so the six years' period begins to run in respect of it. Even if the rent has not been paid for, say, twenty years, a landlord whose title has not become barred[46] may at any time enforce payment of the last six years' arrears of rent, and future rent as it falls due. With the exception of a nominal rent payable under a lease capable of enlargement into a fee simple,[47] mere non-payment of rent never extinguishes the liability for future rent[48]; but it is otherwise with rentcharges.[49] However, in the case of agricultural holdings, the landlord's right of distress is restricted to rent which fell due, or would normally have been paid, in the year preceding the distress[50]; and there are special rules for bankruptcy.[51]

2. Mortgage interest. There is also a six years' period for any action for arrears of mortgage interest.[52] But a mortgagee who exercises his power of sale may retain all arrears of interest, however old, out of the proceeds of sale, for this is not recovery by action[53]; and if the first mortgagee sells, the second mortgagee is similarly entitled to all his arrears of interest out of the surplus proceeds of sale.[54] Further, a mortgagor who seeks to redeem can do so only on the equitable terms of paying all arrears of interest.[55]

3. Part payment. Though payment of part of any arrears of rent or interest may start time running again in respect of the land or the capital,[56] it does not extend the period for claiming the rest of the arrears.[57]

---

[43] Limitation Act, 1939, s. 17.
[44] *Ibid.*, s. 2 (3). Previously a covenant for payment had enlarged the time for arrears of rent service (*Paget* v. *Foley* (1836) 2 Bing.N.C. 679; *Darley* v. *Tennant* (1885) 53 L.T. 257) but not for arrears of rentcharge: *Shaw* v. *Crompton* [1910] 2 K.B. 370.
[45] *Re Jolly* [1900] 2 Ch. 616.   [46] See *ante*, p. 1016.
[47] L.P.A., 1925, s. 153; see *ante*, p. 670. In such cases a rent of £1 a year or less becomes irrecoverable if unpaid for a continuous period of twenty years, of which at least five have elapsed since 1925: *ibid.*
[48] *Ante*, p. 1017.   [49] *Ante*, p. 1018.
[50] Agricultural Holdings Act, 1948, s. 18, replacing Agricultural Holdings Acts, 1923, s. 34 and 1908, s. 28. It does not affect an action for the rent, as distinct from distress.
[51] Bankruptcy Act, 1914, s. 35.
[52] Limitation Act, 1939, s. 18 (5); but see proviso (*a*) for the position where a prior incumbrancer has been in possession; and see proviso (*b*).
[53] *Re Marshfield* (1887) 34 Ch.D. 721; *Re Lloyd* [1903] 1 Ch. 385. *Secus* if the mortgage itself is barred: *Re Hazeldine's Trusts* [1908] 1 Ch. 34.
[54] *Re Thomson's Mortgage Trusts* [1920] 1 Ch. 508; compare *Young* v. *Clarey* [1948] Ch. 191, where the right of redemption was barred.
[55] *Elvy* v. *Norwood* (1852) 5 De G. & Sm. 240; *Dingle* v. *Coppen* [1899] 1 Ch. 726; *Holmes* v. *Cowcher* [1970] 1 W.L.R. 834 (approving this statement); and see Limitation Act, 1939, s. 18 (4).
[56] *Ante*, p. 1026.   [57] Limitation Act, 1939, s. 23 (4).

CHAPTER 17

REGISTRATION

THERE are two types of registration at present in force. These are:

 (i) Registration of incumbrances; and

 (ii) Registration of title.

Registration of incumbrances is designed to strengthen the traditional system of conveyancing by enabling a purchaser to discover incumbrances and transactions affecting the title. Registration of title, as will be seen, is entirely different: it is a new system of conveyancing, designed to supersede the traditional system.

Formerly there was a third type of registration, registration of deeds. This, though much the oldest type of registration,[1] was confined to Middlesex and Yorkshire. It aided the traditional system of conveyancing by providing a register of transactions which gave protection against the loss, destruction or suppression of documents. The Middlesex Deeds Register was closed in 1940 after Middlesex had become subject to compulsory registration of title in 1936[2]; and for a similar reason the Yorkshire Deeds Registries are being closed by stages.[3]

1. Registration of incumbrances. Various registers are provided in which any person claiming to be entitled to certain incumbrances on any land in England should register his claim. There is no investigation or guarantee of the claim by the registrar; all that the applicant need do is to fill in a form containing the necessary particulars and file it in the appropriate registry.

The object of this system is to enable a purchaser of land, when investigating the title, to discover easily whether certain incumbrances exist, and to protect the owners of such incumbrances against defeat by a purchase of the legal estate without notice. Registration of incumbrances is to a large extent a statutory modification of the classical doctrine of notice. It relieves the purchaser of the duty to search further than the register; it insures the owner of an equitable

---

[1] In Yorkshire it dated from 1703 (2 & 3 Ann. c. 4); in Middlesex from the Middlesex Registry Act, 1708.

[2] Middlesex Deeds Act, 1940.

[3] See L.P.A. 1969, s. 16. The Deeds Registries in the North and West Ridings closed in 1972, and that in the East Riding, already closed for new registrations, will finally close on April 1, 1976: see S.I. 1974, No. 221.

incumbrance against the risk of its being defeated; and it eliminates arguments as to whether the purchaser had notice. The incumbrance will, however, be defeated if it is registrable but unregistered, and this principle has been applied to certain legal (as opposed to equitable) incumbrances also.

2. Registration of title. The title to any land in England may be registered [3a]; but only in specified parts of the country, known as the compulsory areas, is registration compulsory. Registration of title differs fundamentally from both the previous types of registration. In particular—

(i) The system deals with registration of the whole title to the land and not merely each individual transaction.

(ii) The registrar not only investigates the title himself but also, when satisfied, guarantees it.

(iii) Registration of title normally puts an end to the usual investigation of title; for instead of having to examine all the deeds for the last fifteen years or more, as is the case with ordinary land, a purchaser of registered land merely inspects the register to see that the vendor is certified to be the owner of the land. This is the principal benefit of the system: it simplifies and cheapens the investigation of title, by requiring full documentary proof once for all to the registrar and not on the occasion of every future disposition as well. The register also discloses many, but not all, of the incumbrances affecting the land.

Registration of title thus creates a new technique of conveyancing, replacing the system which has been traditional for centuries. Its basis remains that of the ordinary law of real property (subject to some important modifications), but the methods of carrying out sales, mortgages and other transactions are revolutionised.

Part 1

REGISTRATION OF INCUMBRANCES

Before 1926 only a few special incumbrances were registrable,[4] and they did not include the most common kinds, such as mortgages and restrictive covenants. The underlying policy was to require registration only of somewhat unusual charges which a purchaser might fail to discover in an ordinary investigation of title.

[3a] But see *post*, p. 1060.

[4] These were, as indicated in the catalogue of registrable interests below, pending actions, annuities, writs and orders affecting land, deeds of arrangement, and land charges of Class A.

The legislation of 1925 extended the system widely (in some respects too widely [5]) by applying it to numerous everyday transactions also. It has thus become an important part of the general system of conveyancing. In particular, the extensions of 1925 have in many important cases superseded the equitable doctrine of notice, which was for so long the foundation of conveyancing practice.[6] The new system is in many ways much more convenient than the old, especially in that it saves time and is certain in its operation. It is designed for mechanical simplicity at the sacrifice, in some cases, of justice and equity. But, as will be seen, it is marred by grave flaws.

Two different classes of registers are in operation: the central Land Charges Register and the various Local Land Charges Registers.

A. *Land Charges Register*

I. REGISTRABLE INTERESTS

The Land Charges Act, 1925, was the primary statute governing the registration of incumbrances. Although to some extent it reproduced earlier statutes, it greatly extended the system by making many interests registrable after 1925 for the first time. This was an important part of the policy of the 1925 legislation.[7] The Act has now been consolidated, with later amendments, in the Land Charges Act 1972,[8] and references in this chapter are to the latter Act. The Land Charges Rules 1974 [9] regulate the procedure, and prescribe the contents of the registers and the forms.

The five registers [10] under the Act are kept in the Land Charges Department of the Land Registry at Plymouth, and searches are now carried out with the aid of a computer.[11] Since the last of these registers contains the extensions made in and since 1925 and is much the most important for discussion in relation to the registration machinery, the order of the registers in the Act of 1925, which is the historical order, has here been retained, although the Act of 1972 has altered it.[12]

Registration must be " in the name of the estate owner or other person whose estate or interest is intended to be affected," save that for land charges only the estate owner suffices.[12a]

---

[5] See *post*, pp. 1046, 1166.   [6] *Ante*, p. 145; *post*, p. 1048.
[7] See the general discussion in the Report of the Committee on Land Charges, 1956, Cmd. 9825; Law Commission Report 1969 (Law Com. No. 18).
[8] Except as regards local land charges: *post*, p. 1053.
[9] S.I. 1974, No. 1286.   [10] As required by L.C.A. 1972, s. 1.
[11] See (1974) 93 L.N. 243; 118 S.J. 692 (T. B. F. Ruoff).
[12] The new order is: land charges; pending actions; writs and orders; deeds of arrangement; and annuities.
[12a] L.C.A. 1972, ss. 3 (1), 5 (4); and see *post*, pp. 1041, 1045.

1. Pending actions. The register of pending actions contains pending land actions, and petitions in bankruptcy filed after 1925.[13] A " pending land action " (often called by its old name of *lis pendens*) is " any action or proceeding pending in court relating to land or any interest in or charge on land " [14]; but despite the width of this language, the term " pending land action " is confined to claims to some proprietary right in the land itself.[15] Thus it does not extend to a mere claim to prevent the land from being sold until some matter has been dealt with,[16] to a claim to a declaration that no contract affecting the land exists,[17] or even to a claim to a share in the proceeds of land held on trust for sale.[18] The court has a wide jurisdiction to order the removal of an unjustified entry.[19] Registration ensures that if the owner disposes of the land before the action is decided the new owner will be bound by the claim. For equitable claims, registration has the advantage of ensuring that third parties have notice, and for legal and equitable claims alike it avoids the penalties of non-registration.[20]

Registration lasts for five years; if the case has not then been decided, registration may be renewed for successive periods of five years.[21]

2. Annuities. This register, opened in 1855 for certain life annuities,[22] was closed in 1925,[23] since when the annuities concerned have been registrable as " general equitable charges," as explained below.[24] For the purposes of the old register an annuity was a rent-charge or annuity for a life or lives or for an estate determinable on a life or lives created after April 25, 1855, but before 1926 and not created by a marriage settlement or will.[25] These last words confined this class of annuities to a few cases only.

3. Writs and orders affecting land. This head does not include writs employed to commence an action relating to land; these come under the head of pending land actions. The register of writs and orders is for writs and orders *enforcing* judgments and orders of the court. The chief items are [26]—

---

[13] L.C.A. 1972, s. 5, replacing Judgments Act, 1839, ss. 4, 7, and later statutes.
[14] L.C.A. 1972, s. 17 (1).
[15] *Calgary and Edmonton Land Co Ltd.* v. *Dobinson* [1974] Ch. 102.
[16] *Ibid.*
[17] *Heywood* v. *B. D. C. Properties Ltd. (No. 2)* [1964] 1 W.L.R. 971.
[18] *Taylor* v. *Taylor* [1968] 1 W.L.R. 378.
[19] See *post*, p. 1053.
[20] See *post*, p. 1048.
[21] L.C.A. 1972, s. 8.
[22] Judgments Act, 1855, ss. 12, 14. There was an earlier register of annuities from 1777 to 1854.
[23] L.C.A. 1925, s. 4.
[24] *Post*, p. 1040. A few, however, are Class E land charges: *post*, p. 1044.
[25] L.C.A. 1972, s. 17 (1).
[26] *Ibid.*, s. 6, replacing Land Charges Registration and Searches Act, 1888 and later statutes.

(i) writs or orders affecting land made for the purpose of enforcing a judgment or recognisance, *e.g.*, an order of the court charging the land of a judgment debtor with payment of the money due [27] (in place of the old writ of elegit); a mere interest under a trust for sale is not an interest in " land " for this purpose [28];

(ii) an order appointing a receiver or sequestrator of land;

(iii) a receiving order in bankruptcy made after 1925.

Registration remains effective for five years, but may be renewed for successive periods of five years.[29]

4. Deeds of arrangement. The Deeds of Arrangement Act, 1914, elaborately defines deeds of arrangement, and the definition applies to this register.[30] For the present purpose a deed of arrangement may be taken as any document whereby control over a debtor's property is given for the benefit of his creditors generally, or, if he is insolvent, for the benefit of three or more of his creditors. A common example arises when a debtor, seeking to avoid bankruptcy, assigns all his property to a trustee for all his creditors.

Registration is effective for five years and may be renewed for successive periods of five years.[31] The registration may be effected by the trustee of the deed or by any creditor assenting to or taking the benefit of the deed.[32]

5. Land charges. This is the most important register. Land charges are divided into six classes, A, B, C, D, E and F.[33] The most important classes, C and D, are subdivided.

Class A consists of charges imposed on land by some statute, but which come into existence only when some person makes an application. Thus where a landlord who is not entitled to land for his own benefit has to pay compensation to an agricultural tenant, the landlord may apply to the Minister of Agriculture, Fisheries and Food for a charge on the land for the amount of compensation.[34]

---

27 Administration of Justice Act, 1956, ss. 34, 35, repealing provisions of L.P.A., 1925, s. 195, whereby judgments automatically created equitable charges. Until abolished, writs of elegit were registrable.
28 *Irani Finance Ltd.* v. *Singh* [1971] Ch. 59; contrast *National Westminster Bank Ltd.* v. *Allen* [1971] 2 Q.B. 718. In both cases the owners were joint tenants in law and in equity.
29 L.C.A. 1972, s. 8.
30 *Ibid.*, ss. 7, 17 (1), deriving from Land Charges Registration and Searches Act, 1888, ss. 7, 8.
31 L.C.A. 1972, s. 8.
32 *Ibid.*, s. 7 (1).
33 *Ibid.*, s. 2, deriving from Land Charges Registration and Searches Act, 1888, ss. 10, 14.
34 Agricultural Holdings Act, 1948, s. 82 (2), replacing Agricultural Holdings Act, 1923, s. 41.

A Class A charge is registrable whenever created. If it was created after 1888, it should be registered forthwith [35]; if it was created before 1889, it must be registered within a year of the first transfer of it made after 1888.[36]

Class B consists of charges which are similar to those in Class A except that they are not created on the application of any person, but are imposed automatically by statute.[37] Most charges thus imposed appear to be local land charges, and as these are registrable in a separate register, few charges are registrable in Class B. One example is a charge for money payable to redeem land tax,[38] and another is a charge on land recovered or preserved for an assisted litigant under the Legal Aid Act 1974 in respect of unpaid contributions to the legal aid fund.[39] Such a charge should be registered forthwith if it has been created after 1925,[40] or, if created before 1926, within one year of the first transfer after 1925.[41]

Class C land charges are divided into four categories.[42]

C (i): A PUISNE MORTGAGE. This is a legal mortgage not protected by a deposit of documents relating to the legal estate affected.[42a]

C (ii): A LIMITED OWNER'S CHARGE. This is an equitable charge which a tenant for life or statutory owner acquires under any statute by discharging death duties or other liabilities,[43] and to which the statute gives special priority. Thus on the death of a tenant for life of settled land, estate duty must be paid; if a succeeding tenant for life finds the money out of his own pocket instead of throwing the burden on the settled property itself, he is entitled to a charge on the land in the same way as if he had lent money to the estate on mortgage.[44] Such a charge arises automatically [45] and, being equitable,[46] is registrable in Class C (ii).

---

[35] L.C.A. 1972, s. 4 (2) deriving from Land Charges Registration and Searches Act, 1888, s. 12.

[36] L.C.A. 1972, s. 4 (3), deriving from Land Charges Registration and Searches Act, 1888, s. 13.

[37] L.C.A. 1972, s. 2 (3).

[38] Finance Act, 1949, s. 40 (4) (*a*).

[39] Legal Aid Act 1974, s. 9 (6); S.I. 1971 No. 62, r. 19 (3).

[40] L.C.A. 1972, s. 4 (5).   [41] *Ibid.*, s. 4 (7).

[42] *Ibid.*, s. 2 (4).

[42a] By L.C.A., 1925, s. 10 (1) no mortgage registered in a local deeds registry could be a puisne mortgage: but this was repealed by L.P.A. 1969, s. 17 (5).

[43] If a tenant for life pays off a mortgage on the settled property he may keep it alive and enforce his rights as mortgagee: *Lord Gifford* v. *Lord Fitzhardinge* [1899] 2 Ch. 32; see *ante*, p. 943.

[44] Finance Act, 1894, s. 9 (6).

[45] *Lord Advocate* v. *Countess of Moray* [1905] A.C. 531 at 539.

[46] L.P.A. 1925, s. 1 (3).

C (iii): A GENERAL EQUITABLE CHARGE. This is any equitable charge on land which—

(i) is not included in any other class of land charge;

(ii) is not secured by a deposit of documents relating to the legal estate affected [47]; and

(iii) does not arise, or affect an interest arising, under a trust for sale or settlement.

This is a residuary class which catches equitable charges not registrable elsewhere. It includes equitable annuities, *e.g.*, rentcharges for life, if created after 1925,[48] and equitable mortgages of a legal estate [49] if not protected by deposit of title deeds and if not limited owner's charges. It probably also includes an unpaid vendor's equitable lien.[50] It specifically excludes a charge given by way of indemnity against rents equitably apportioned or charged exclusively on land in exoneration of other land, and against the breach or non-observance of covenants or conditions.[51] Equitable mortgages of an equitable interest under a settlement or trust for sale (*e.g.*, a charge on an undivided share in land [52]) are excluded as they are overreached on a conveyance to a purchaser, and therefore no question of enforcing them against him can arise.[53] The same applies to other charges on the proceeds of sale of land, as opposed to charges on the land itself, such as an agreement to share the proceeds of sale,[54] or an estate agent's charge on them for commission.[55]

The abolition of this class, except as regards mortgages, has been suggested.[56]

C (iv): AN ESTATE CONTRACT. This is a "contract by an estate owner" (*i.e.*, the owner of a legal estate [57]) "or by a person entitled at the date of the contract to have a legal estate conveyed to him to convey or create a legal estate." The contract may be written or oral,[58] but it must amount to a binding and enforceable [59] contract, as distinct from mere negotiation [60] or a notice to treat served under a

---

[47] This excludes " protected " mortgages of a legal estate as explained *ante,* p. 969.

[48] See *ante,* p. 1037.

[49] Possibly equitable mortgages are registrable as estate contracts: see n. 65, *infra.*

[50] Wolst. & C. ii, 18. This lien is a charge: *ante,* p. 886. [51] L.P.(Am.)A., 1926, Sched.

[52] *Re Rayleigh Weir Stadium* [1954] 1 W.L.R. 786; for the co-ownership gives rise to a trust for sale: see *ante,* p. 410.

[53] *Ante,* pp. 372, 379, where it is also explained how a number of land charges (including general equitable charges) may be overreached even though created prior to the trust for sale or settlement.

[54] *Thomas* v. *Rose* [1968] 1 W.L.R. 1797.

[55] *Georgiades* v. *Edward Wolfe & Co. Ltd.* [1965] Ch. 487.

[56] Report of the Committee on Land Charges, 1956, Cmd. 9825, para. 13.

[57] L.C.A. 1972, s. 17 (1); L.P.A., 1925, s. 205 (1) (*v*); *ante,* p. 135.

[58] *Universal Permanent B.S.* v. *Cooke* [1952] Ch. 95 at 104.

[59] *Mens* v. *Wilson* (1973) 231 E.G. 843 (no evidence in writing: entry vacated); *Jones* v. *Morgan* (1973) 231 E.G. 1167.

[60] *Heywood* v. *B. D. C. Properties Ltd. (No. 1)* [1963] 1 W.L.R. 975.

compulsory purchase order.[61] The definition expressly includes "a contract conferring either expressly or by statutory implication a valid option of purchase, a right of pre-emption or any other like right." [62] The definition applies both to ordinary contracts for the sale, sub-sale,[63] lease [64] or mortgage [65] of a legal estate, and also to unilateral contracts such as an option to renew a lease [66] or to require a tenant to surrender his lease instead of assigning it [66a]; but it does not apply to such contracts at one remove (*e.g.*, a contract authorising an agent to make such a contract),[67] nor to a contract to sell an interest under a trust for sale,[68] nor to a boundary agreement unless it clearly involves the transfer of land.[68a]

If V contracts to sell land to P, who then contracts to sell it to Q, it is against V, the estate owner,[69] and not P, that Q must register his estate contract; registration against P will not be effective even if P later acquires the legal estate.[70] This is a trap for sub-purchasers, who often will not know that the sub-vendor is not an estate owner. But when a yearly tenant agreed that if he acquired the freehold he would grant his sub-tenant a lease for ten years, the contract was somewhat surprisingly held to be registrable as an estate contract because even though the tenant had only a hope of acquiring the freehold, his yearly tenancy made him an estate owner.[71]

It has also been held that a contract by a landowner with an agent to convey the land to such persons as the agent should direct is registrable.[72] Yet here it seems that the contract created no specifically enforceable rights in the land, for the agent's interest was merely financial, and damages would have been an adequate remedy.

A tenant's notice to purchase the freehold or take an extended lease under the Leasehold Reform Act 1967 is registrable as if it were an estate contract.[73]

[61] *Capital Investments Ltd.* v. *Wednesfield U. D. C.* [1965] Ch. 774.
[62] For options as interests in land see *ante*, p. 578.
[63] *i.e.*, a resale by a purchaser before the land has been conveyed to him.
[64] See *Blamires* v. *Bradford Corporation* [1964] Ch. 585, where a testamentary option to occupy land for life at a rent had been exercised.
[65] *Quaere* whether equitable mortgages are registrable as estate contracts: *ante*, p. 970.
[66] *Beesly* v. *Hallwood Estates Ltd.* [1960] 1 W.L.R. 549 (on appeal on another point [1961] Ch. 105).
[66a] *Greene* v. *Church Commissioners for England* [1974] Ch. 467.
[67] *Thomas* v. *Rose* [1968] 1 W.L.R. 1797.
[68] *Re Rayleigh Weir Stadium* [1954] 1 W.L.R. 786.
[68a] *Neilson* v. *Poole* (1969) 20 P. & C.R. 909.
[69] L.C.A. 1972, ss. 3 (1), 17 (1). Contrast s. 5 (4), which is not confined to estate owners: *ante*, p. 1036.
[70] *Barrett* v. *Hilton Developments Ltd.* [1974] 3 W.L.R. 545, a decision strengthened by the contrast mentioned in n. 69 above.
[71] *Sharp* v. *Coates* [1949] 1 K.B. 285. A legal estate in *other* land is of course irrelevant: see at p. 294. Such a contract should be registered against the freeholder: *ante*, p. 1036.
[72] *Turley* v. *Mackay* [1944] Ch. 37, questioned in *Thomas* v. *Rose, supra*; and see *Re Rayleigh Weir Stadium, supra*, at p. 791.
[73] Leasehold Reform Act 1967, s. 5 (5). See *post*, p. 1151.

Class D land charges are divided into three categories.[74]

D (i): DEATH DUTIES. This class consists of any charge for death duties arising on a death after 1925. Any such charge is of course statutory. Until August, 1949, there were three different kinds of death duties: estate duty, succession duty and legacy duty. Only estate duty now remains,[75] but charges for succession duty which attached before it was abolished may still be subsisting. The three kinds of duties may be briefly explained as follows:

(i) Estate duty is borne by all property, and varies according to the total value of the property passing on the death.[76]

(ii) Succession duty was borne by all property settled before the death of the deceased, and all land, whether settled or not.[77] This varied according to the relationship of the successor to the deceased, being 2 per cent. for spouses, ancestors or descendants, 10 per cent. for brothers and sisters or their descendants, and 20 per cent. for others.

(iii) Legacy duty was borne only by pure, unsettled personalty.[78] The rates for this were the same as for succession duty.

In the case of leaseholds estate duty is not a charge on the property, so there is nothing to register. But in the case of freeholds estate duty is a charge on the property [79] and consequently should be registered; in practice, this is rarely done.

D (ii): RESTRICTIVE COVENANTS. Under this head any covenant or agreement restrictive of the user of land may be registered provided it—

(i) was entered into after 1925, and

(ii) is not " between a lessor and a lessee."

Thus restrictive covenants in leases are never registrable, even where they relate not to the land demised but to adjoining land of the lessor [80]; the normal rules as to privity of contract and privity of estate apply and where there is neither of these the question is one of notice.[81] Similarly restrictive covenants made before 1926 still depend

---

[74] L.C.A. 1972, s. 2 (5).

[75] Succession duty and legacy duty were abolished by the Finance Act, 1949, s. 27.

[76] The principal statute is the Finance Act, 1894; it has been frequently amended.

[77] Succession Duty Act, 1853.

[78] Legacy Duty Act, 1796. The dates of the death duty statutes help to explain their pattern. At first only unsettled personalty was charged (legacy duty); then the charge was extended to settled property and to land (succession duty); then was added an overall duty computed without regard to relationship (estate duty).

[79] Finance Act, 1894, s. 9 (1).

[80] *Dartstone Ltd.* v. *Cleveland Petroleum Co. Ltd.* [1969] 1 W.L.R 1807.

[81] *Ante,* p. 720.

upon the doctrine of notice for their effect against purchasers, since they are enforceable against everyone except a purchaser for value of a legal estate without notice.

D (iii): EQUITABLE EASEMENTS. Any " easement, right or privilege over or affecting land " is registrable under this head, provided—

    (i) it is merely equitable, and

    (ii) it was created or arose after 1925.

An example would be an easement granted after 1925 merely by contract, or only for life.[82]

Much trouble has been caused both by the vagueness of this definition and by the injustice of applying it to informal arrangements, such as agreements between neighbours as to rights of way, which the dominant owner pardonably omits to register. These defects have caused the Court of Appeal to hold, at one extreme, that it does not include an equitable right of way arising by acquiescence or estoppel,[83] and, at the other extreme, that it includes the whole residue of equitable proprietary rights capable of binding a purchaser. The latter decision was reversed by the House of Lords, which held that the definition should be given " its plain prima facie meaning." [84] This meaning, though not precisely explained, is evidently narrow, being probably confined to rights in the nature of easements and profits.[85] Accordingly the House of Lords held that it does not extend to an equitable right of entry.[86] Nor does it extend to a right to remove fixtures at the end of a lease,[87] or to the interest of a public authority requisitioning land under Defence Regulations.[88]

The courts have therefore rejected the contention, discussed in an earlier chapter,[89] that the policy of 1925 was to require registration of all equitable interests in land which were not protected by deposit of title deeds and not overreachable.[90] Examples of unregistrable interests are bare trusts[91]; trusts for sale in so far as interests in land[92]; and licences specially protected in equity, if not in the nature

---

82 *Ante*, p. 827.
83 *E. R. Ives Investment Ltd.* v. *High* [1967] 2 Q.B. 379, holding that the equitable grounds on which the purchaser (with notice) was bound were unaffected by the Land Charges Act, 1925: see *ante*, p. 778; Another example of straining the law to avoid injustice where the right was not registered is *Johnstone* v. *Holdway* [1963] 1 Q.B. 601; *cf. Cordell* v. *Second Clanfield Properties Ltd.* [1969] 2 Ch. 9, *ante*, p. 830.
84 *Shiloh Spinners Ltd.* v. *Harding* [1973] A.C. 691 at 721, *per* Lord Wilberforce; and see *Poster* v. *Slough Estates Ltd.* [1968] 1 W.L.R. 1515 at 1520, 1521.
85 See (1937) 53 L.Q.R. 259 (C. V. Davidge); (1948) 12 Conv.(N.S.) 202 (J. F. Garner).
86 *Shiloh Spinners Ltd.* v. *Harding* [1973] A.C. 691.
87 *Poster* v. *Slough Estates Ltd., supra.*
88 *Lewisham Borough Council* v. *Maloney* [1948] 1 K.B. 50.
89 *Ante*, p. 383.
90 Contrast the policy for registered land: *post*, p. 1068.
91 *Ante*, p. 438.
92 *Ante*, pp. 287, 378.

of easements.[93] The defects of the legislation are now so obvious that the advantage lies in giving it the narrowest possible scope. It has indeed been suggested that the whole class of equitable easements might be abolished.[94] It was one of the mistakes of the reformers of 1925.[95]

Class E consists of annuities created before 1926 but not registered until after 1925. The definition is the same as for the old register of annuities, as explained above.[96]

Class F consists of charges affecting any land by virtue of the Matrimonial Homes Act 1967. This is the new class of spouses' statutory rights in the matrimonial home, which have already been explained.[97]

Companies. Most charges on land created by a company for securing money (including a charge created by a deposit of title deeds [98]) require registration within twenty-one days in the Companies Register maintained under the Companies Act, 1948. For floating charges this suffices in place of registration in the Land Charges Register, and has the same effect.[99] For other charges, this suffices if the charge was created before 1970, but otherwise the charge requires registration in both registers.[1]

II. EFFECTS OF REGISTRATION AND NON-REGISTRATION

1. Effect of registration

(*a*) *Actual notice.* By the Law of Property Act, 1925,[2] registration under the Land Charges Acts of any instrument or matter required or authorised to be registered under the Act [3] is deemed to constitute actual notice of the interest registered " to all persons and for all purposes [4] connected with the land affected. as from the date of registration or other prescribed date and so long as the registration continues in force." There are exceptions to this

---

93 See *ante,* p. 778.
94 Report of the Committee on Land Charges, 1956, Cmd. 9825, para. 16.
95 See *Poster* v. *Slough Estates Ltd., supra,* at p. 1521, *per* Cross J.; *cf. post,* p. 1045.
96 *Ante,* p. 1037.
97 *Ante,* p. 785.
98 *Re Wallis & Simmonds (Builders) Ltd.* [1974] 1 W.L.R. 391.
99 Companies Act, 1948, s. 95; L.C.A. 1972, s. 3 (7); see *Re Molton Finance Ltd.* [1968] Ch. 325.
1 L.P.A. 1969, s. 26; *cf. post,* p. 1073.
2 s. 198.
3 Thus registration of a covenant in a lease, or of any other non-registrable interest, is nugatory.
4 These words must probably be interpreted, in their context, to mean " for all purposes for which notice is material," or in other words " for all purposes

rule,[5] but in general it prevents any person claiming to be a purchaser without notice of a registered interest.

(b) *Names register.* Registration is effected against the name of the estate owner at the time.[6] An error in the name registered does not invalidate the registration if the name given may fairly be called a version of the true name (*e.g.,* " Frank " for " Francis "); but a person who makes an official search in the correct name is protected even if it fails to reveal the entry.[7]

This system of registration against names is seriously defective from the point of view of a purchaser. There is no map or plan enabling him to search against the land itself: he must search against the names of all previous owners of the land, as ascertained from the title deeds. The rights most likely to concern a purchaser, namely Classes C and D, only became registrable after 1925, but in the course of time the cost of searches may become considerable. It has been said that " this system will end in chaos if it is perpetuated,"[8] and that " it is obvious that such a register must in time sink under its own weight."[9] Trouble can be saved if each purchaser preserves the certificate of the search which he made when purchasing the land, handing the certificate on with the title deeds so that subsequent owners can rely upon it. But there is no means of enforcing this practice.

(c) *Names behind the root of title.* In 1955, when thirty years had elapsed since 1925, the time arrived when the names of persons against whom charges were registered might lie behind the root of title; and this possibility became much more serious in 1969 when the period for title was reduced to fifteen years.[10] A purchaser may be

connected with the enforcement of equitable interests against purchasers." " Notice " has a technical meaning and is probably not merely a synonym for " knowledge." Thus a purchaser of shares in a company was allowed to rescind the contract on account of misrepresentation in the prospectus, which did not disclose a registered land charge; the subscriber was in no sense a purchaser, and was unaffected by s. 198: *Coles* v. *White City (Manchester) Greyhound Association Ltd.* (1928) 45 T.L.R. 125 at 127, affirmed *ibid.,* 230. For the question whether statutory notice can affect the terms of a contract for sale, see *ante,* p. 584.

[5] *Ante,* pp. 926, 984.

[6] See L.C.A. 1972, ss. 3 (1), 17 (1); Land Charges (No. 2) Rules 1972, r. 5, Scheds. 1, 2; *ante,* p. 1036. For the machinery of search, see *post,* p. 1051.

[7] *Oak Co-operative B. S.* v. *Blackburn* [1968] Ch. 730; for searches, see *post,* p. 1051.

[8] (1940) 56 L.Q.R. 373 (D. W. Logan); and see Sir J. Stewart-Wallace, *Principles of Land Registration* (1937), 83–84.

[9] (1931) 75 S.J. 807. For an account of the mechanism, see *Oak Co-operative B. S.* v. *Blackburn, supra.*

[10] *Ante,* p. 579.

unable to discover the relevant names, but none the less he will be deemed to have actual notice of the charges because they are in fact registered. A problem of this kind had already arisen in the case of leases, owing to an intending tenant's inability to inspect the freehold title or a superior leasehold title.[11] These are grave difficulties, and a Committee [12] which studied them despaired of finding any satisfactory solution except by abandoning name registration and pressing on with the registration of title throughout the country. " We are the inheritors of a transitory system which was bound to disclose this defect after 30 years, and it seems too late to disclaim our inheritance." [13]

(*d*) *Compensation scheme.* In 1969 a palliative was provided in the form of financial compensation at public expense for purchasers affected by undiscoverable land charges.[14] The compensation is recoverable by action in the High Court against the Chief Land Registrar.[15] There are two main requirements. First, at the date of completion (which must be after 1969) neither the purchaser nor any agent of his, acting as such in the transaction, must have had any " actual knowledge " of the charge; and for this purpose, contrary to the general rule, registration is to be disregarded.[16] Secondly, the charge must be registered against the name of an owner of an estate in the land who was not, as such, a party to any transaction in the relevant title, or concerned in any event in it.[17] The " relevant title " means the full title as under an open contract, together with any additional title contracted to be shown; and if a document in the title expressly provided that it was to take effect subject to some registrable interest (*e.g.*, a restrictive covenant), the title includes the transaction creating that interest.[18] The scheme avoids the problem of leases by excluding grants and mortgages of leases derived out of the freehold; but, with no apparent logic, it extends to sub-leases,[19] and it extends generally to sales, exchanges, mortgages and compulsory purchases.

(*e*) *Transactions on the title.* Name registration is not only inherently defective: it has also been applied too widely. Its utility is greatest where it brings to a purchaser's notice, and so also protects,

---

11 This is explained *ante*, p. 705.
12 Report of the Committee on Land Charges, 1956 (Cmd. 9825), discussed in [1956] C.L.J. 215 (H.W.R.W.); and see *post*, p. 1165.
13 Report of the Committee on Land Charges, *supra*, at p. 8.
14 L.P.A. 1969, s. 25.   15 *Ibid.*, s. 25 (4), (6).
16 *Ibid.*, s. 25 (1), (2), (11).   17 *Ibid.*, s. 25 (1).
18 *Ibid.*, s. 25 (3), (10). Where compensation has been claimed, the registrar may make additions or alterations to the registers and index so as to facilitate disclosure: S.I. 1970, No. 136.
19 L.P.A. 1969, s. 25 (9). It appears that a sub-lessee can claim compensation for (*e.g.*) a registered restrictive covenant on the freehold title (the example discussed *ante*, p. 707) but that a lessee cannot. This discrimination seems inexplicable.

some equitable incumbrance which the purchaser might otherwise miss when investigating title, such as a prior contract for sale to another person (an estate contract).[20] But where the transaction normally appears or is mentioned in the title deeds, as for example does a restrictive covenant in a conveyance or an option in a lease, there is no risk of the purchaser overlooking it; yet there is a considerable risk of its owner failing to register it, so that it will be defeated by a purchase of a legal estate. To require registration in such cases merely creates insecurity of property. Accordingly it has been suggested that such covenants and options should cease to be registrable.[21] The difficulties in requiring registration of equitable easements have already been noted.[22]

2. Effect of non-registration

(a) *Persons affected.* It is only as against third parties, *i.e.*, successors in title, that non-registration may invalidate a registrable interest. Failure to register is immaterial as between the original parties to the transaction, *e.g.*, as between the vendor and the purchaser under an estate contract, or as between the covenantor and the covenantee in the case of a restrictive covenant. A registrable transaction, even though not registered, remains valid in every respect except as against certain purchasers.[23]

(b) *Categories of purchaser.* If a registrable incumbrance is not registered, the consequences fall into two main categories:

(i) The incumbrance may be void against a purchaser for value of any interest in the land; or

(ii) The incumbrance may be void against a purchaser for money or money's worth of a legal estate in the land.

One difference between (i) and (ii) is that a purchaser of an equitable interest is protected in case (i) but not in case (ii); and a purchaser of an equitable interest does not come within (ii) even if the legal estate which is subject to the incumbrance is specifically declared to be held in trust for him.[24] Another difference is that marriage

---

[20] Curiously enough, it is the practice of many solicitors not to register ordinary contracts of sale, though they are ideally suited for protection by a names register.

[21] Report of the Committee on Land Charges, *supra*, paras. 7, 15. See also Report of the Committee on Positive Covenants Affecting Land, 1965 (Cmnd. 2719), paras. 25, 27, preferring the old doctrine of notice to the defective system of land charge registration.

[22] *Ante*, p. 1043.

[23] Thus on a compulsory acquisition the statutory right to compensation is not prejudiced by non-registration: *Blamires* v. *Bradford Corporation* [1964] Ch. 585.

[24] *McCarthy & Stone Ltd.* v. *Julian S. Hodge & Co. Ltd.* [1971] 1 W.L.R. 1547. See *ante*, p 121.

is " value " but is not " money or money's worth " [25]; consequently
in the case of land settled by an ante-nuptial marriage settlement, the
spouses and issue will be protected in case (i) but not in case (ii).
In both cases " purchaser " has an extended meaning and includes a
lessee, mortgagee or other person taking an interest in land for
value.[26] The crucial time in every case is the completion of the transaction, *i.e.*, the actual transfer of the legal estate or the equitable
interest, as the case may be [27]; subsequent registration cannot impose
any burden on the purchaser.

(c) *Effect.* The effect of non-registration may be expressed as
follows.

   (i) In general, whichever register is concerned, non-registration
       of any registrable matter makes it void against a purchaser
       for value of any interest in the land.[28]

  (ii) But in the case of a post-1925 estate contract, restrictive
       covenant, equitable easement or charge for death duties [29]
       (*i.e.*, charges within Class C (iv) or Class D) non-registration
       makes it void only against a purchaser of a legal estate for
       money or money's worth.[30]

 (iii) Bankruptcy petitions (registrable as pending actions) and
       receiving orders (registrable as writs and orders) are void
       only against a bona fide purchaser of a legal estate for
       money or money's worth without notice of an available
       act of bankruptcy,[31] *i.e.*, an act of bankruptcy not more
       than three months old.[32]

  (iv) A pending land action is void against a purchaser for value
       of any interest in the land, unless he had express notice of it.[33]

(d) *Exclusion of the doctrine of notice.* It is very important
to observe that with the comparatively unimportant exceptions of
(iii) and (iv) above, the equitable doctrine of notice is wholly

---

[25] *Ante,* p. 116.
[26] L.C.A. 1972, s. 17 (1).
[27] L.C.A. 1972, s. 4, makes unregistered land charges void unless registered " before
    the completion of the purchase." The corresponding provisions for other registers
    are less specific, but " purchaser " means a person who " takes " an interest for
    value (s. 17 (1)), so that the moment of taking is presumably the critical moment.
[28] L.C.A. 1972, ss. 4–7.
[29] As to charges for death duties, see also L.P.A., 1925, s. 17, under which
    such a charge, if unregistered, and so void against a purchaser, is attached to
    the proceeds of sale, so that it is not destroyed, but overreached.
[30] L.C.A. 1972, s. 4 (6). As to a pre-1926 estate contract, see *infra.*
[31] L.C.A. 1972, ss. 5 (8), 6 (5).
[32] Bankruptcy Act, 1914, ss. 1, 4 (1) (*c*), 167.
[33] L.C.A. 1972, s. 5 (7). This does not prevent a fresh action being brought against
    the purchaser if there is some charge or interest which is enforceable against him.

excluded. The Law of Property Act, 1925,[34] provides (perhaps redundantly) that where an interest is void against a purchaser under the Land Charges Acts, he is not to be prejudicially affected by notice thereof. This is a sharp departure from the earlier law.[35] Where this new rule applies, it is quite immaterial that the purchaser was not diligent in investigating title,[1] or had actual knowledge of the interest,[2] or that the owner of the interest was in possession of the land[3]: the effect of registration and non-registration is automatic. It has even been held that where land is granted expressly subject to another person's interest, the grantee is not subject to that interest if it is registrable but unregistered.[4]

Practical convenience has thus been bought at the cost of some sacrifice of fairness. This sacrifice can hardly be said to be necessary, for the simultaneous legislation for registration of title preserved the more ethical doctrine in one important class of cases by providing that the rights of persons in possession must be respected.[5] A tenant in possession under an agreement for a lease, for example, may excusably fail to register it, and it seems indefensible to allow him to be ejected by a later purchaser with notice to whom the landlord may have been able to sell or let more profitably.

(e) *No duty to register.* Although in his own interests the owner of a registrable land charge obviously ought to register it, he is under no duty to anyone else to do so. This has a notable effect on the measure of damages for breach of contract. If V contracts to sell land to P, who fails to register the estate contract, and V conveys the land to X in breach of contract, P can recover full

---

[34] s. 199 (1) (i).

[35] *Ante*, p. 144; *post*, p. 1165.

[1] In *Sharp* v. *Coates* [1949] 1 K.B. 285 (*ante*, p. 1033), the owner of the defeated interest was in possession, so that the purchaser had at least constructive notice of it.

[2] *Coventry Permanent Economic B. S.* v. *Jones* [1951] 1 All E.R. 901 at 904 (disapproved on another point: see *ante*, p. 648); *Hollington Bros. Ltd.* v. *Rhodes* [1951] 2 T.L.R. 691 at 696; and see *ante*, p. 145. Registered land is similar: *post*, p. 1074.

[3] *Hollington Bros. Ltd.* v. *Rhodes, supra.* Despite *Bendall* v. *McWhirter* [1952] 2 Q.B. 466 at 483 it seems clear that L.P.A., 1925, s. 14, does not affect the new rule; for the operation of s. 14 is in terms confined to Part I of the Act (s. 1–39), and s. 199 is in Part XI: see (1952) 68 L.Q.R. at 384, 385 (R.E.M.); *Westminster Bank Ltd.* v. *Lee* [1956] Ch. 7 at 21; *ante*, p. 119. Contrast registered land, *post*, pp. 1067, 1068.

[4] *Hollington Bros. Ltd.* v. *Rhodes* [1951] 2 T.L.R. 691 (assignee of leasehold " subject to . . . such leases and tenancies as may affect the premises " held free from prior agreement for an underlease to another person who had taken possession but had not registered an estate contract).

[5] L.R.A., 1925, s. 70 (1) (g), for which see *post*, p. 1065.

damages from V (or the full amount paid by X to V [5a]), even though P, had he registered, could have enforced his equitable interest against X and so would have suffered no loss.[6]

3. Companies. If a charge registrable in the Companies Register [7] is not duly registered there within twenty-one days of its creation, it is, in addition to any consequences of not being registered in the Land Charges Register, void as a security as against the liquidator and all creditors of the company, and the money becomes immediately payable.[8]

4. Unregistrable interests. Unregistrable equitable interests, *e.g.*, pre-1926 restrictive covenants and pre-1926 equitable mortgages where there is either a deposit of title deeds or there has been no transfer since 1925, are still governed by the old doctrine of notice. And the same applies, by statute, to pre-1926 equitable mortgages which became legal mortgages by the operation of the transitional provisions of the Law of Property Act, 1925.[9] These provisions laid down that until such mortgages were registered they would gain no advantage by their conversion as against a bona fide purchaser for value without notice.[10] Thus only upon registration are such mortgages freed from their vulnerability to such a purchaser of a legal estate and translated to a status of validity against the whole world. But by an exception to the general rule such mortgages were made registrable before transfer,[11] so that advantage of their new status could be taken at once.

III.   DIFFERENCES BETWEEN CLASS C AND CLASS D LAND CHARGES

1. Date of creation. The main difference between Class C and Class D land charges is that a Class C land charge can be registered if it is either created or transferred after 1925, but a Class D land charge can be registered only if it is created after 1925.[12] Thus a Class D land charge arising before 1926 is never registrable, but a

---

[5a] *Lake* v. *Bayliss* [1974] 1 W.L.R. 1073 (since V is a qualified trustee for P: *ante*, p. 575).
[6] *Wright* v. *Dean* [1948] Ch. 686 (unregistered option for tenant to purchase freehold); *Hollington Bros. Ltd.* v. *Rhodes* [1951] 2 T.L.R. 691 (unregistered contract to grant underlease). See [1956] C.L.J. 227, n. 57 (H.W.R.W.).
[7] See *ante*, p. 1044.
[8] Companies Act, 1948, s. 95; *Capital Finance Co. Ltd.* v. *Stokes* [1969] 1 Ch. 261; but see *Re C. L. Nye Ltd.* [1971] Ch. 442 (delay in registration cured by registrar's certificate of registration).
[9] See *ante*, p. 894.
[10] L.P.A., 1925, 1st Sched., Pt. VII, para (6), Pt. VIII, para. (5). This is a statutory exception to the principle that notice of a legal estate is irrelevant to its enforceability against third parties.
[11] L.C.A. 1972, s. 3 (3).
[12] *Ibid.*, s. 4 (6), (7).

Class C land charge created before 1926 becomes registrable as soon as it (*i.e.*, the benefit of it, not the land upon which it is charged) is transferred after 1925. Failure to register a Class C land charge within a year of the first transfer of it after 1925 renders it void against a purchaser for value of any interest in the land.[13]

2. Non-registration. A further difference between Class C and Class D land charges is the effect of non-registration considered above.[14] This, however, is a qualified distinction, since estate contracts (Class C (iv)) created after 1925 fall into the same category for this purpose as Class D.[14a] But the two classes resemble each other in that there was no provision before 1926 for the registration of either.

IV. OPERATION OF THE REGISTER

1. Searches. The means by which an intending purchaser of land can discover registrable incumbrances is by a search. This may be made in person,[15] but it is advisable to obtain an official search.[16] An official certificate of search has three advantages.

(i) It is conclusive in favour of a purchaser or intending purchaser,[17] provided that his application correctly specified the persons [18] and land [1]; it therefore frees him from any liability in respect of rights which it fails to disclose.[2] The name in the title deeds will be presumed to be the correct name until the contrary is shown.[3]

(ii) It protects a solicitor or trustee who makes it from liability for any error in the certificate.[4]

(iii) It provides protection against incumbrances registered in the interval between search and completion.[5] If a purchaser completes his transaction before the expiration of the

---

[13] *Ibid.*, s. 4 (7).
[14] *Ante*, p. 1048.   [14a] *Ibid.*
[15] L.C.A. 1972, s. 9. " Anyone who nowadays is foolish enough to search personally deserves what he gets ": *Oak Co-operative B. S.* v. *Blackburn* [1968] Ch. 730 at 743, *per* Russell L.J.
[16] L.C.A. 1972, s. 10, providing also for inquiry by telephone. For the system of official searches by telephone through the computerised index, see *The Law Society's Gazette* (1970) Vol. 67, p. 545.
[17] L.C.A. 1972, s. 10 (4). *Cf. Re C. L. Nye Ltd.* [1971] Ch. 442.
[18] A trivial error may be fatal: *Oak Co-operative B. S.* v. *Blackburn* [1968] Ch. 730 (Francis Davis Blackburn specified by mistake for Francis David Blackburn: purchaser not protected); and see *ante*, p. 1045.
[1] *Du Sautoy* v. *Simes* [1967] Ch. 1146; the application must give " no reasonable scope for misunderstanding " in the Registry: see at p. 1168.
[2] See *Stock* v. *Wanstead and Woodford B. C.* [1962] 2 Q.B. 479.
[3] *Diligent Finance Co. Ltd.* v. *Alleyne* (1972) 23 P. & C.R. 346.
[4] L.C.A. 1972, s. 12.
[5] L.C.A. 1972, s. 11 (5), (6), replacing L.P.(Am.)A. 1926, s. 4.

fifteenth day [6] after the date of the certificate [7] (excluding days when the registry is not open to the public [8]), he is not affected by any entry made after the date of the certificate and before completion, unless it is made pursuant to a priority notice [9] entered on the register on or before the date of the certificate.

If the official certificate of search mistakenly fails to mention an incumbrance duly registered before the purchaser's search, the owner of the incumbrance is unjustly deprived of his rights over the land, since the certificate is conclusive. Parliament made no provision for compensation, but the court will award damages for negligence against the public authority responsible,[10] which in the case of the central register is the Crown. Registry employees are freed from personal liability of this kind except in case of fraud.[11]

A single search is effective for all divisions of all registers.

2. Priority notices. Special provision had to be made to provide for a rapid sequence of transactions, such as the creation of a restrictive covenant followed immediately by the creation of a mortgage before there has been time to register the covenant. Thus, if V is selling land to P, who is raising the purchase-money by means of a loan on mortgage from M, and is to enter into a restrictive covenant with V, the sequence of events will be—

    (i) conveyance from V to P, creating the restrictive covenant, followed a few moments later by

    (ii) mortgage by P to M, which enables P to pay V.

In such a case, V's restrictive covenant could not be registered in the few moments between its creation and the making of the mortgage, and so it will be void against M, a purchaser for money or money's worth of a legal estate, unless V has availed himself of the machinery of the priority notice. To do this he must give a priority notice to the registrar at least fifteen days before the creation of the restrictive covenant, and then, if he registers his charge within thirty days of the entry of the priority notice in the register, the registration dates back to the moment of the creation of the restrictive covenant, *i.e.*, to the execution of the

---

[6] Land Charges Rules 1972, r. 3. Originally only two days were allowed for completion, but the time was extended in 1940: S.R. & O., 1940, Nos. 1998, 2195.
[7] Defined by Land Charges (No. 2) Rules 1972, r. 17.
[8] L.C.A. 1972, s. 11 (6).   [9] See below.
[10] *Ministry of Housing and Local Government* v. *Sharp* [1970] 2 Q.B. 223 (damages awarded against local authority for overlooking entry on register of local land charges); *Coats Patons (Retail) Ltd.* v. *Birmingham Corporation* (1971) 69 L.G.R. 356 (exemption clause ineffective).
[11] L.C.A. 1972, s. 10 (6).

conveyance from V to P.[12] Days on which the registry is not open to the public are again excluded in the computation of these periods. The requirement of fifteen days' advance notice is to allow the expiry of the fifteen days' period of protection given to those who made official searches before the priority notice was lodged.[13] Priority notices are not, of course, confined to restrictive covenants, but apply to all charges governed by the Land Charges Act 1972.

Where another charge is created simultaneously with a charge which is protected by a priority notice, and that other charge is subject to or dependent on the protected charge, the other charge is deemed to have been created after the protected charge.[14] Thus time is notionally allowed for the priority notice to operate.

3. Vacation of registration. The court has a wide jurisdiction, both statutory[15] and inherent,[16] to order the vacation of any registration, *i.e.*, that it be removed from the register. The owner of the land affected thus has a means of clearing off an unjustified blot on his title, *e.g.*, where an estate contract is registered against him but the contract never existed,[17] or is unenforceable by action,[18] or has been terminated.[19] In a proper case this power will be exercised speedily on motion, and with a certain robustness,[20] without awaiting the trial of any action, thereby preventing the entry from improperly inhibiting dealings with the land. But of course a proper entry will not be disturbed.[21]

B. Local Land Charges Registers

1. The registers. In addition to the registers kept by the Land Charges Department of the Land Registry, registers of local land charges are kept, in London, by each London borough (or the City of London), and elsewhere by each district council.[22] These registers

---

[12] L.C.A. 1972, s. 11, replacing L.P.(Am.)A., 1926, s. 4 (1); Land Charges Rules 1972, r. 3. Originally periods of two and fourteen days respectively were prescribed, but these were extended in 1940: see n. 6, *supra*.   [13] See above.
[14] L.C.A. 1972, s. 11 (4). For an example, see Wolst & C. ii, 102.
[15] L.C.A. 1972, s. 1 (6).
[16] *Heywood* v. *B. D. C. Properties Ltd. (No. 2)* [1964] 1 W.L.R. 267; *Calgary and Edmonton Land Co. Ltd.* v. *Dobinson* [1974] Ch. 102; but see *Norman* v. *Hardy* [1974] 1 W.L.R. 1048.
[17] *Heywood* v. *B. D. C. Properties Ltd. (No. 2)*, *supra*; and see *Rawlplug Co. Ltd.* v. *Kamvale Properties Ltd.* (1968) 20 P. & C.R. 32 at 40.
[18] *Mens* v. *Wilson* (1973) 231 E.G. 843.
[19] *Hooker* v. *Wyle* [1974] 1 W.L.R. 235. See also *post*, p. 1071.
[20] *Rawlplug Co. Ltd.* v. *Kamvale Properties Ltd.*, *supra*.
[21] *Norman* v. *Hardy*, *supra* (pending action not likely to succeed but genuine).
[22] London Government Act 1963, s. 79; Local Government Act 1972, s. 212; L.C.A., 1925, s. 15 (amended but not replaced by L.C.A. 1972), as amended by L.P.(Am.) A., 1926; Local Land Charges Rules, 1966 (as amended by S.I. 1969, No. 1152, S.I. 1970, No. 1775, S.I. 1972, No. 690, S.I. 1973, No. 1862 and S.I. 1974, No. 424), replacing earlier rules. See generally Garner, *Local Land Charges*, 6th ed.; Report of the Committee on Local Land Charges, 1952 (Cmd. 8440); Report of Law Commission on Local Land Charges 1974 (Law Comn. No. 62).

have an important advantage over those kept at the Land Registry in that the charges are registered against the land itself and not against the owner of it. Thus a series of searches against successive owners is unnecessary, and there are no problems of discovering names. Since these registers are public, a purchaser can and normally does search them before contract.[23]

2. Rights registrable. Many widely differing matters are registrable, though in general they may be classified as being financial, restrictive or acquisitive; and they have the general nature of being imposed by or in favour of public authorities in nearly all cases,[24] whereas the land charges registers are essentially registers of private rights.[25] A few examples of local land charges are certain compulsory purchase orders [26]; charges for making up a road imposed in respect of land fronting the road, and charges for sanitary works; prohibitions or restrictions on the use of land, whether under planning law [27] or otherwise (*e.g.*, " building lines," preventing the erection of buildings nearer to a road than the prescribed line); and potential claims for repayment of compensation money paid on refusal of planning permission, in case permission should later be given.[28]

3. Non-registration. Failure to register a local land charge, whether created before or after 1925, renders it void against a purchaser for money or money's worth of a legal estate in the land affected who completes before the charge is registered.[29]

The provisions as to searches explained above apply in general to local land charges.[30]

Part 2

REGISTRATION OF TITLE

A. Introductory

1. Object. The prime object of registration of title is to substitute a single established title, guaranteed by the State, in place of the tradi-

---

[23] The trap represented by *Re Forsey and Hollebone's Contract* [1927] 2 Ch. 379 (*ante*, p. 584) does not then operate.
[24] For an exception, see *ante*, p. 864 (notice in lieu of obstruction of light).
[25] An exception is death duty charges: *ante*, p. 1042.
[26] See Garner, *op. cit.*, pp. 58, 75.
[27] See *post*, p. 1086.
[28] See *Ministry of Housing and Local Government* v. *Sharp* [1970] 2 Q.B. 223; *ante*, p. 1052.
[29] L.C.A., 1925, s. 15 (1).
[30] *Ibid.*, s. 16, as amended; L.C.A. 1972, ss. 10, 12. See Garner, *op. cit.*, pp. 14 *et seq.*

tional title which must be separately investigated on every purchase. In the case of unregistered land, a purchaser must satisfy himself from the abstract of title, the deeds, his requisitions on title, his searches and his inspection of the land that the vendor has power to sell the land and that it is subject to no undisclosed incumbrances; and this investigation must be repeated in full by every subsequent purchaser. This repetitive examination of the same title is eliminated in the case of registered land: the purchaser can discover from the mere inspection of the register whether the vendor has power to sell the land and about many important incumbrances; certain other incumbrances must be investigated in much the same way as in the case of unregistered land. The complexity of rights in land is such as to render it impossible to make the transfer of registered land as simple as the transfer of shares registered in the books of a company, but the present system of registration of title attempts to follow that analogy so far as is practicable.[31]

2. Extension. Registration of title is a great improvement on the old-fashioned system of private conveyancing, and is destined to supplant it in England as it has done in many other countries.[31a] The movement in favour of registration, and its relation to reform of the land law generally, is briefly described at the end of this book.[32] In these pages a short sketch will be given of the machinery. The policy is to extend this machinery as fast as the facilities of the Land Registry permit. It now covers many of the principal urban areas of England and a number of counties also. Nearly half the work of conveyancing is estimated to concern registered land, so that this is already a very important branch of the law.

3. Privacy. Unlike the land charges registers, the land register is not open to public inspection; in general, no person can inspect the register without the authority of the registered proprietor.[33] This restriction is intended to preserve the confidential character of conveyancing as established under the Statute of Uses, 1535,[34] though it is generally regarded as excessive for modern society.[35] It is carried to the point of absurdity by the rule which prevents intending lessees and chargees from inspecting the registered title.[36]

---

[31] On registration of title, see generally Ruoff & Roper (the most extensive work); Lewis & Holland, *Principles of Registered Land Conveyancing*; Hayton, *Registered Land*; (1969) 32 M.L.R. 61 (T. B. F. Ruoff); (1972) 88 L.Q.R. 93 (D. Jackson). Earlier works are Brickdale and Stewart-Wallace, *Land Registration Act, 1925*, 4th ed.; K. & E. iii, 1–355.

[31a] See Dowson & Sheppard, *Land Registration* (2nd ed. 1956), a comparative survey.

[32] *Post*, p. 1158.

[33] L.R.A., 1925, s. 112; L.R.R., 1925, rr. 12, 287, 288; and see *White* v. *Bijou Mansions Ltd*. [1937] Ch. 610 at 621 (on appeal [1938] Ch. 351).

[34] *Ante*, p. 163.

[35] See Law Commission Working Paper No. 32, Part D.

[36] *Post*, p. 1074.

There is, however, an Index Map and a Parcels Index which are open to public inspection, and can be searched.[37] These will show whether any particular parcel of land has been registered and so guard against any concealed registration; but they give none of the details of registration, such as the proprietor's name and address and the nature of his title.

4. Development. Registration of title has a long history.[38] The Land Registry Act, 1862 and the Land Transfer Act, 1875 provided for voluntary registration of title, but few titles were registered until the Land Transfer Act, 1897, made registration of title compulsory on dealings with land in the County of London. The present Acts are the Land Registration Acts, 1925, 1936 and 1966, and the Land Registration and Land Charges Act 1971. These are supplemented by the Land Registration Rules, 1925, as amended, and numerous other statutory rules.[39]

5. Character. Although the aim is simplicity, the scheme of the Land Registration Act, 1925, is complicated. Even its primary policy is far from clear. It is supposed to aim at improving the machinery of conveyancing and not at changing the substantive law.[40] In fact, it has made striking changes in the rights of owners, purchasers and incumbrancers, and its system of priorities is radically different. It abandons the fundamental principle that no one can pass a better title than he has (*nemo dat quod non habet*), and substitutes for it, though only by implication, the so-called principle of indefeasibility of the registered title.[41] On the technical plane the principles of the legislation are sometimes equally obscure, its definitions are often confusing, and by no means all its rules are meritorious. It can produce " difficulties and pitfalls in the way of comparatively simple transactions which would not have arisen with unregistered land." [42]

The legislation has received comparatively little judicial interpretation, and much therefore depends upon the practice of the Land Registry.[43] The Registry has to handle great numbers of transactions and at the same time provide a prompt and reliable service to the public. The system is therefore a branch of public administration as

---

[37] L.R.R., 1925, rr. 12, 286.
[38] *Post*, p. 1158. For the origin of land registration, see Ruoff & Roper, Chap. 1 and p. 99; (1939) 55 L.Q.R. 547 (R. R. A. Walker).
[39] See Ruoff & Roper, p. 973 *et seq.*
[40] Stewart-Wallace, *Principles of Land Registration*, 33; Law Commission Working Paper No. 32, para. 6.
[41] See *post*, p. 1079.
[42] *Re White Rose Cottage* [1965] Ch. 940 at 952, *per* Harman L.J.
[43] For this Ruoff & Roper, the work of three Land Registrars, is particularly authoritative. But registry practice does not make law: *Strand Securities Ltd.* v. *Caswell, infra,* at p. 977.

well as of property law. In view of the deficiencies of the Act, it is not surprising that the Registry does not always interpret it correctly.[44] Everyday conveyancing requires clear and rapid guidance, even where the clarity does not exist in the law. The Registry deserves credit for constructing a smooth-running machine out of inferior legislation.

Registration of title is a basically good system burdened with much more difficulty and technicality than seems necessary.[45] Its great merits are that it eliminates repetitive and unproductive work in conveyancing, and provides financial compensation in some cases where otherwise an innocent party would suffer loss.

B. Principles of Registration

1. Classification of rights. Three classes of rights in registered land must be distinguished.

(a) *Registered interests.*[46] These are rights in respect of which a title has been granted by the registrar. It is fundamental that the only estates in respect of which a proprietor can be registered are legal estates.[47] Thus a legal fee simple absolute in possession and (with certain exceptions[48]) a legal term of years absolute are registrable interests. All references to trusts are excluded from the register so far as possible.[49]

(b) *Overriding interests.* These are rights which will bind a purchaser whether or not disclosed by the register or otherwise, *e.g.*, rights being acquired under the Limitation Act, 1939, and most easements.

(c) *Minor interests.* These are rights which need to be protected by some entry on the register, *e.g.*, interests under a settlement or trust for sale, estate contracts and restrictive covenants.

Before dealing with these rights in detail, it should be made clear that if the title to land is registered, there is no question of registration in the Land Charges Registry, for entries on the Land Register take the place of this; but entries must still be made on the local land

---

[44] See *Strand Securities Ltd.* v. *Caswell* [1965] Ch. 958 (registry practice as to the registration of leasehold titles based on misunderstanding of the meaning of " the register," and inconsistent with the principle that a tenant cannot call for his landlord's title (*ante*, p. 705)); *Barclays Bank Ltd.* v. *Taylor, post*, p. 1078 (registry practice on mortgages contrary to the Act).

[45] The Law Commission has published three working papers (Nos. 32, 37 and 45) discussing possible improvements. This chapter will indicate many others.

[46] K. & E., iii, 18, has instead " registrable interests," but this seems unsound : see (1941) 57 L.Q.R. 566 (R.E.M.).

[47] L.R.A., 1925, s. 2. This specifies " estates capable of subsisting as " legal estates, but it is clear from s. 69 (1) that the words quoted are meaningless in this context.

[48] *Post*, p. 1059.

[49] L.R.A., 1925, s. 74.

charges registers.[50] Further, so far as possible, dealings with registered land must be carried out as provided by the Act and rules, and duly registered [51]; and the prescribed forms, adapted as necessary, must be used for such dealings.[52]

2. The register. The register itself is divided into three parts.[53]

    (a) *The property register.* This describes the land and the estate for which it is held, refers to a map or plan showing the land, and contains notes of interests held for the benefit of the land, such as easements and restrictive covenants of which the registered land is the dominant tenement.[54] Except where the register notes the boundaries shown on a map or plan as being " fixed," they are " general boundaries " only, so that the exact line of the boundary is left undetermined.[55] Fixing boundaries involves serving notice on neighbours and determining any disputes judicially, a process that is so contentious and expensive that it is scarcely ever used.[56]

    (b) *The proprietorship register.* This states the nature of the title (*i.e.*, whether it is absolute, good leasehold, qualified or possessory [57]), states the name, address and description of the registered proprietor, and sets out any cautions, inhibitions and restrictions [58] affecting his right of dealing with the land.[59]

    (c) *The charges register.* This contains entries relating to rights adverse to the land, such as mortgages or restrictive covenants, neighbours' easements over the land, and in general all notices [60] protecting rights over the land.[61]

The register is kept on the card index system at the Land Registry in London, and in District Registries at Lytham St. Annes, Nottingham, Tunbridge Wells, Harrow, Gloucester, Stevenage, Croydon, Durham, Plymouth and Swansea.[62] The three parts of the regis-

50 L.R.A., 1925, ss. 59, 110 (7), 135; and see s. 50 (1) (restrictive covenants).
51 L.R.A., 1925, ss. 39, 109; and see (1951) 15 Conv.(N.S.) 428 (F. W. Taylor).
52 L.R.R., 1925, rr. 74, 75; for the forms, see the Schedule to the Rules.
53 L.R.R., 1925, r. 2.
54 *Ibid.*, r. 3.
55 See *ibid.*, rr. 276–278; *Lee* v. *Barrey* [1957] Ch. 251.
56 Only nine cases are recorded since 1937: Law Commission Working Paper No. 45, para. 34.
57 See *post*, p. 1061.
58 See *post*, p. 1068.
59 L.R.R., 1925, r. 6.
60 *Post*, p. 1068.
61 L.R.R., 1925, r. 7.
62 S.I. 1974, No. 1304 (defining the areas); and see the map at (1974) 118 S.J. 731.

ter in respect of each property are usually filed on a single card. A copy of this, called a " Land Certificate," is given to each registered proprietor as his document of title; the old title deeds, stamped with a notice of registration,[63] are usually returned when the title is first registered. But the registered proprietor's proof of title is the register itself and not the Land Certificate; any Land Certificate may be out of date if entries have been made in the register since the certificate was last in the registry.[64]

3. Compulsory areas

(a) *The areas.* After a very slow start, the compulsory areas are now being steadily extended. An accelerated programme was undertaken in 1965, which aimed at including all urban areas with populations over 10,000 by 1973, and the rest of the country by 1980.[65] Although the speed of progress has been less than was intended, by the end of 1970 half the population of the country was in compulsory areas.[66]

(b) *Occasions for registration.* Land in a compulsory area does not have to be registered in any event. Registration is compulsory only on a conveyance on sale of the fee simple, or the creation or assignment on sale of certain leases.[67] Usually the sale or other transaction which makes registration requisite is completed in the ordinary way appropriate to unregistered land, and the new owner then effects first registration.

4. Leaseholds.
The position as to leaseholds, which is unnecessarily complicated,[68] may be summarised as follows.[69]

(a) *Registration prohibited.* The registration of a lease is prohibited, even if the land is in a compulsory area, if the lease—

(i) was granted for a term of twenty-one years or less [70] or

(ii) contains an absolute prohibition against assignment; or

(iii) is a mortgage term still subject to a right of redemption.[71]

---

[63] See L.R.A., 1925, s. 16.
[64] See *Strand Securities Ltd.* v. *Caswell* [1965] Ch. 958.
[65] See (1966) 110 S.J. 37. The procedure was simplified by L.R.A., 1966.
[66] S.I. 1974, No. 250 consolidates the Orders defining the compulsory areas, and S.I. 1974, No. 559 extends the areas.
[67] L.R.A., 1925, s. 123 (1). The Registrar has power to exclude areas where numerous small plots are sold as " souvenir land ": L.R. & L.C.A. 1971, s. 4; S.I. 1972, No. 985. Common land with registered ownership is subject to compulsory registration: Commons Registration Act 1965, s. 12; and see *post*, p. 1064.
[68] See Law Commission Working Paper No. 32, Part B.
[69] See Ruoff & Roper, 148 and Chap. 23 ; Hayton, *Registered Land*, 71.
[70] L.R.A., 1925, s. 19 (2) ; and see s. 8 (1), as construed in K. & E. iii, 115.
[71] L.R.A. 1925, s. 8 (1), (2).

(b) *Registration compulsory.* The registration of a lease not falling under any of the above heads is compulsory—

    (i) if the land is in a compulsory area and the transaction consists of the grant of a lease for forty years or more, or the assignment on sale of a lease with forty or more years unexpired [72]; or

    (ii) if the title to the freehold or leasehold out of which the lease is granted has been registered, and the transaction consists of the grant of a lease for more than twenty-one years, whether or not the land is in a compulsory area.[73] This rule springs from the requirement that dispositions by a registered proprietor must themselves be registered; for the grant of a lease is a " disposition." [74]

(c) *Registration optional.* The registration of any other lease is optional, *e.g.*, a lease for thirty years granted by a freeholder whose title is not registered, even if there is less than twenty-one years unexpired.[75]

(d) *Superior title.* In addition to being registered in its own right, a registrable lease will be noted on the charges register of the freehold or superior leasehold title, so as to give warning to all concerned.[76]

5. Effect of non-registration. When registration of title (freehold or leasehold) is compulsory because the land is in a compulsory area, and the transaction is one which calls for the first registration of the title, the transaction is void as to the legal estate unless application for registration is made within two months.[77] The result of default is, it seems, that the legal estate returns to the grantor, who holds it upon trust for the grantee.[78] Where registration is compulsory because the proprietor's title is registered, no legal estate passes until registration, but the time limit of two months does not appear to apply.[79]

6. Voluntary registration. Except where registration is prohibited (*e.g.*, in the case of a lease for twenty-one years or less), the owner of a legal estate may always apply for his title to be registered, whether or not any transaction is being effected and whether the land is in a compulsory area or not.[80] But the registrar can and does restrict registration in non-compulsory areas in order to concentrate resources on the extension of the compulsory areas.[81]

---

[72] *Ibid.*, s. 123 (1).
[74] *Ibid.*, s. 18 (1).
[73] *Ibid.*, s. 19 (2).
[75] See K. & E. iii, 115.
[76] L.R.R., 1925, r. 46. Any lease except an overriding interest may be noted thus: L.R.A., 1925, s. 48.
[77] L.R.A., 1925, s. 123 (1). " Souvenir land " may be excluded: *ante*, p. 1059, n. 67. For the problems of s. 123, see (1968) 32 Conv.(N.S.) 391 (D. G. Barnsley).
[78] See Barnsley, *Conveyancing Law and Practice*, 403. If in possession the grantee will have an overriding interest; otherwise a minor interest: *post*, pp. 1066, 1067.
[79] L.R.A., 1925, ss. 19 (1), (2), 22 (1). See preceding note.
[80] *Ibid.*, ss. 4, 8.
[81] L.R.A. 1966, s. 1 (2); Ruoff & Roper, 203.

7. Titles. There are four titles with which an applicant for registration may be registered.

(*a*) *Absolute.* In the case of freeholds, this vests the fee simple in possession in the first registered proprietor [82] subject only—

    (i) to entries on the register;

    (ii) to overriding interests, except so far as the register states that the land is free from them; and

    (iii) as between himself and those entitled to minor interests, to minor interests of which he has notice, if he is not entitled to the land for his own benefit; thus trustees for sale who are registered as proprietors will still hold subject to the claims of the beneficiaries.

In the case of leaseholds, registration with an absolute title vests the leasehold in the first registered proprietor [83] subject to the rights set out above and subject also—

    (iv) to all the implied and express covenants, obligations and liabilities incident to the leasehold.

An absolute title in the case of leaseholds guarantees not only that the registered proprietor is the owner of the lease but also that the lease was validly granted.

(*b*) *Qualified.* In the case of freeholds, this has the same effect as an absolute title except that the property is held subject to any estate, right or interest arising before a specified date, or under a specified instrument, or otherwise specified in the register.[84] This title is granted when an absolute title has been applied for but the registrar has been unable to grant it. A qualified title to leaseholds has the same effect as an absolute or good leasehold title, as the case may be, except for the specified defect.[85]

(*c*) *Possessory.* In the case of either freeholds or leaseholds, first registration with possessory title has the same effect as registration with an absolute title, save that the title is subject to all estates, rights and interests adverse to the first registered proprietor, and subsisting or capable of arising at the time of first registration.[86] In short, the title is guaranteed as far as all dealings after the date of registration are concerned, but no guarantee is

---

[82] L.R.A., 1925, s. 5, discussed at (1974) 38 Conv.(N.S.) 236 (S. N. L. Palk).
[83] L.R.A., 1925, s. 9, which in terms merely vests " the possession of the leasehold interest ": but the meaning appears to be as stated in the text.
[84] L.R.A., 1925, s. 7.
[85] *Ibid.*, s. 12.
[86] *Ibid.*, ss. 6, 11. See *Re King* [1962] 1 W.L.R. 632 (on appeal on other points, [1963] Ch. 459).

given as to the title prior to first registration, which must accordingly be investigated by a purchaser in the same way as if the land were not registered.

(*d*) *Good leasehold.* This is applicable only to leaseholds. It is the same as an absolute title, save that registration does not " affect or prejudice the enforcement of any estate, right or interest affecting or in derogation of the title of the lessor to grant the lease." [87] In short, the lessor's right to grant the lease is not guaranteed. Thus should it appear that the lessor was never entitled to grant the lease, the lessee is protected if he has an absolute title but unprotected if he has a good leasehold title. Since a lessee cannot investigate the freehold title unless he stipulates for this in his contract,[88] he usually cannot give the registrar evidence of the freehold title (unless it is registered), and so he can apply only for a good leasehold title.[89]

Application may be made for any of the above titles except a qualified title.[90]

8. Conversion of titles. When registration has taken place with certain of the above titles, conversion of the title may take place subsequently. There are two classes of case.

(*a*) *Compulsory conversion.* Provided he is satisfied that the proprietor is in possession of the land in question, the registrar is *bound* to convert the title [91]—

(i) to absolute, in the case of a freehold registered with possessory title for fifteen years; and

(ii) to good leasehold, in the case of a leasehold registered with possessory title for ten years.

(*b*) *Optional conversion.* The registrar *may* convert the title—

(i) to absolute or good leasehold if the land was registered with possessory title before 1926 [92];

(ii) to absolute or good leasehold, if the land is registered with qualified, possessory or good leasehold title and is transferred for value [93]; and

---

[87] L.R.A., 1925, ss. 8 (1), 10.
[88] *Ante*, p. 705; L.P.A., 1925, s. 44.
[89] For the procedure, see *Strand Securities Ltd.* v. *Caswell* [1965] Ch. 958; and see Ruoff & Roper, 87.
[90] See L.R.A., 1925, s. 7 (1).
[91] *Ibid.*, s. 77 (3).
[92] *Ibid.*, s. 77 (1).
[93] *Ibid.*, s. 77 (2).

(iii) to absolute, if the land has been registered with good lease-hold title for ten years and the registrar is satisfied that the owners of the lease have been in possession for that period [94]: this is the only head under which there can be no conversion unless the proprietor requests it.

9. Application for registration. With the exceptions set out above,[95] an application for registration may be made by an estate owner, including those holding the estate as a trustee. Further, anyone entitled to call for a legal estate to be vested in him (except a mortgagee or a mere purchaser under a contract) can apply for registration.[96] Thus if A holds land on a bare trust for B, B can apply for registration without first requiring a conveyance to be executed in his favour.

10. Ownership and dealings. It is fundamental to the system of registered title that the legal estate is vested in the registered proprietor for the time being.[97] This is a statutory title which is quite independent of legal ancestry or legitimacy: if a person is in fact registered as proprietor, he is owner of the land and all its appurtenances.[98] He may have obtained registration by fraud or by mistake, and according to the law of unregistered land he may have no title at all. None of this will prevent him from holding the legal estate if he is the registered proprietor,[99] though it may well provide grounds for rectifying the register against him.[1]

The registered proprietor's dealings with the legal estate have also been put on a statutory basis, for he may dispose of or deal with it only in the manner authorised by the Act,[2] which sets out the transactions permitted.[3] These include transfers generally, and grants of leases, mortgages and charges, rentcharges, easements and profits.[4]

C. *Classification of Interests*

I. REGISTERED INTERESTS

As mentioned above,[5] the only estates in respect of which a proprietor can be registered are " estates capable of subsisting as legal estates." [6]

---

[94] *Ibid.*, s. 77 (4).   [95] *Ante*, p. 1059.
[96] L.R.A., 1925, ss. 4, 8 (1).   [97] *Ibid.*, s. 69 (1).
[98] L.R.R., 1925, r. 251 provides that registration confers all the rights which would have been conferred by a conveyance at the time of registration (see *ante*, p. 836). But who is the hypothetical grantor? And is this rule authorised by s. 144 of the Act?
[99] See *post*, p. 1073.
[1] See *post*, p. 1080.   [2] L.R.A., 1925, s. 69 (4).
[3] ss. 18, 21.
[4] Statutory forms must sometimes be used: Ruoff & Roper, 291.
[5] See *ante*, p. 1057.
[6] L.R.A., 1925, s. 2 (1).

Thus a fee simple absolute in possession is registrable; and subject to the exceptions set out above,[7] so are terms of years absolute. The five classes of legal interests [8] are apparently likewise registrable,[9] but in practice they are not often registered; and there can be no registration of a right of common over land which is capable of being registered under the Commons Registration Act 1965.[10] It has indeed been suggested that a registered estate, whether a fee simple or a term of years, is a statutory estate, distinct from the fee simple or term of years at common law [11]; but this seems doubtful.[12]

II. OVERRIDING INTERESTS

1. Nature. Overriding interests bind the proprietor of registered land, even though he has no knowledge of them and no reference is made to them in the register.[13] In general, they are the kind of rights which a purchaser of unregistered land would not expect to discover from a mere examination of the abstract and title deeds, but for which he would make inquiries and inspect the land.[14] The principle is that the registered title is a substitute for the title deeds, not for the necessary inquiries and inspections.

Most overriding interests, though by no means all, are legal rights; but it must be emphasised that as far as incumbrances on registered land are concerned, the issue in deciding whether a purchaser is bound irrespective of any entry on the register is not whether the rights are legal or equitable but whether they are overriding interests or minor interests. The doctrine of notice has no part to play,[15] so that the difference between legal and equitable interests largely disappears.

Overriding interests are defined as the interests which are made overriding by the Act and are not entered on the register.[16] If so entered, as often they are,[17] they are protected as minor interests, as explained later.

---

7 *Ante*, p. 1059.
8 *Ante*, p. 141.
9 See L.R.A., 1925, ss. 2 (1), 3 (xi); L.P.A., 1925, s. 1 (4); but contrast the word " estates " with the words " estates interests and charges " in L.R.A., 1925, ss. 2 (1), 3 (xi). See also Ruoff & Roper, 151.
10 Commons Registration Act 1965, s. 1 (1). For the Act, see *ante*, p. 868.
11 (1947) 11 Conv.(N.S.) 184, 232 (R. C. Connell); (1949) 12 M.L.R. 205 (H. Potter).
12 (1949) 12 M.L.R. 139, 477 (A. D. Hargreaves). See also (1952) 16 Conv.(N.S.) 38 (A. K. R. Kiralfy).
13 L.R.A., 1925, s. 70 (1); and see ss. 5, 9, 20 (1), 23 (1). See also the definition in s. 3 (xvi).
14 See Ruoff & Roper, 98.
15 *Post*, p. 1067.
16 L.R.A., 1925, s. 3 (xvi).
17 *Post*, p. 1067.

2. Principal overriding interests. The full list of overriding interests is set out in section 70 (1) of the Act of 1925 in a series of unmethodical and overlapping definitions.[18] The most important items are as follows.

(i) " Rights of common, drainage rights, customary rights (until extinguished), public rights, profits à prendre, rights of sheepwalk, rights of way, watercourses, rights of water, and other easements not being equitable easements required to be protected by notice on the register." [19] Thus all easements and profits, except apparently equitable easements,[20] are overriding interests. Restrictive covenants are clearly not included.[21]

(ii) Liability to repair highways, chancels, embankments, and sea and river walls, and tenurial liabilities.

(iii) Land tax (now abolished [22]) and tithe redemption annuity.[23]

(iv) Rights acquired or being acquired under the Limitation Act, 1939.

(v) " The rights of every person in actual occupation of the land or in receipt of the rents and profits thereof," unless inquiry made of such person fails to disclose the right. This important provision is explained below.

(vi) Rights excepted from the effect of registration, such as rights existing at the time of first registration if only a possessory title is granted.

(vii) Local land charges, until protected by entry on the register. A purchaser should therefore always search the register of local land charges.

(viii) Fishing, sporting, seignorial and manorial rights and franchises.

(ix) Leases for not more than twenty-one years at a rent without a fine, including an agreement for a lease which actually creates a tenancy and is not merely a contract to grant one.[24]

---

[18] See Law Commission Working Paper No. 37, suggesting changes.

[19] See also L.R.R., 1925, r. 258, extending the definition to appurtenances and quasi-easements. This rule appears to be both redundant (in view of s. 20 of the Act) and *ultra vires* (as unauthorised by s. 144), despite the explanation in Law Commission Working Paper No. 37, para. 48.

[20] L.R.A., 1925, ss. 49 (1) (*c*), 59 (2), and L.R.R., 1925, r. 190 do not make their protection obligatory. But probably such easements are " required to be protected by notice " in that they will otherwise be overridden on a disposition: see ss. 20 (1), 23 (1), 59 (6); and compare *City Permanent B. S.* v. *Miller* [1952] Ch. 840 at 849, 850. See also Ruoff & Roper, 102, 760.

[21] See *Hodges* v. *Jones* [1935] Ch. 657 at 671; for these, see *post,* p. 1069.

[22] *Ante,* p. 142.

[23] Replacing tithe rentcharge: Tithe Act, 1936, ss. 1, 13 (11); and see *ante,* p. 804.

[24] See *City Permanent B. S.* v. *Miller* [1952] Ch. 840.

Nearly all leases, however, will take effect as overriding interests under head (v) above,[25] even if they are for more than twenty-one years.

3. Interests protected by occupation. Head (v) above is of special importance, since it safeguards equitable owners in possession even though they have not lodged cautions or other entries in the register[26]; and it can protect them even when their occupation is not obvious to a purchaser.[27] Residential occupation by a mere licensee may count as " actual occupation " by him,[28] whereas the nightly parking of a car on an undefined part of the land normally will not.[29]

The occupier's rights may be of any kind, *e.g.*, an option to purchase the freehold vested in the occupying lessee,[30] and an unpaid vendor's lien for the purchase price where he occupies as tenant under a lease-back transaction.[31] If he is in occupation when a later disposition takes place, he does not lose his priority over it by going out of occupation subsequently.[32] But the rights must be recognised proprietary rights which are capable of binding successors in title,[33] such as estate contracts and trusts.[34] A statutory exception is a spouse's right of occupation under the Matrimonial Homes Act 1967[35]: this is not an overriding interest, and requires protection by notice or caution,[36] as explained below.

Equitable owners in possession who omit to register their interests are thus much better protected in the case of registered land than in the case of unregistered land.[37] A tenant in possession of registered land under a mere agreement for a lease, for example, or who has an option to renew the lease or to purchase the freehold,[38] will be in no

---

25 See, *e.g.*, *Mornington Permanent B. S.* v. *Kenway* [1953] Ch. 382.
26 See *Woolwich Equitable B. S.* v. *Marshall* [1952] Ch. 1 ; *Mornington Permanent B. S.* v. *Kenway, supra*; *Bridges* v. *Mees* [1957] Ch. 475 ; *Grace Rymer Investments Ltd.* v. *Waite* [1958] Ch. 831.
27 *Hodgson* v. *Marks* [1971] Ch. 892 (occupier entitled under trust mistaken for vendor's wife).
28 *Strand Securities Ltd.* v. *Caswell* [1965] Ch. 958. It seems that the purchaser is at risk unless he investigates the rights of all persons in shared occupation ; but there are strong objections to requiring investigation as between husband and wife: *ante*, p. 447. See (1973) 36 M.L.R. 25 (R. H. Maudsley).
29 *Epps* v. *Esso Petroleum Co. Ltd.* [1973] 1 W.L.R. 1071.
30 *Webb* v. *Pollmount Ltd.* [1966] Ch. 584.
31 *London & Cheshire Insurance Co. Ltd.* v. *Laplagrene Property Co. Ltd.* [1971] Ch. 499. Minor interests, if supported by occupation, may therefore become overriding interests.
32 *London & Cheshire Insurance Co. Ltd.* v. *Laplagrene Property Co. Ltd., supra.*
33 *National Provincial Bank Ltd.* v. *Ainsworth* [1965] A.C. 1175 (see *ante*, p. 784); *Webb* v. *Pollmount Ltd., supra.*
34 *Hodgson* v. *Marks, supra.*
35 *Ante*, p. 785.
36 s. 2 (7). The registrar's practice of not notifying the owner affected was questioned in *Wroth* v. *Tyler* [1974] Ch. 30 at 39.
37 *Ante*, pp. 627, 1049; *post*, p. 1165.
38 *Webb* v. *Pollmount Ltd., supra.*

danger of losing his rights to a later purchaser if, as will often happen, he fails to protect his rights by entry on the register.[39] This is a much more satisfactory rule.[40] It equally protects tenants in occupation under registrable but unregistered leases.[41] "Fundamentally its object is to protect a person in actual occupation of land from having his rights lost in the welter of registration."[42] The extension to persons in receipt of rents and profits goes beyond the corresponding principle of the doctrine of notice.[43] But this provision is marred by a flaw in drafting: a tenant receiving rent from a sub-tenant is protected, but one who allows another to occupy the property rent-free is not.[44]

4. Entries on register. The registrar may make entries on the register stating that the land is free from or subject to certain over-riding interests.[45] This is a helpful practice since it brings third party rights on to the registered title, or clears them off, as the case may be. Dispositions by the registered proprietor, such as grants of easements, require to be completed by registration and noting on the register.[46] The registrar is also required to enter a notice of the existence of any easement, right, privilege or benefit created by an instrument (and not, for example, an easement acquired by prescription) which appears on the title at the time of first registration.[47]

III. MINOR INTERESTS

1. Definition. The Act defines minor interests elaborately and confusingly.[48] The essence of the definition is " all rights and interests which are not registered or protected on the register and are not overriding interests." This formula embraces the whole residue of interests in land [49] which require protection by some entry on the register. Registered interests are protected by the grant of the registered title; overriding interests need no protection; but all other interests fall into the class of minor interests and so need to be protected by an entry on the register, otherwise they will not bind

---

[39] See *post*, p. 1068.
[40] See [1956] C.L.J. at 227, 228 (H.W.R.W.) and *ante*, p. 1049. For a contrary view see Law Commission Working Paper No. 37, para. 20.
[41] *Strand Securities Ltd.* v. *Caswell* [1965] Ch. 958.
[42] *Ibid.*, at p. 979, *per* Lord Denning M.R.
[43] *Ante*, p. 122.
[44] *Strand Securities Ltd.* v. *Caswell, supra,* at p. 981.
[45] L.R.A., 1925, ss. 5, 9, 20 (1), 23 (1), 70 (3). See *Re Dances Way, West Town, Hayling Island* [1962] Ch. 490.
[46] L.R.A., 1925, s. 19 (2).
[47] *Ibid.*, s. 70 (3).
[48] *Ibid.*, s. 3 (xv).
[49] Understood as in the case of unregistered land: *Murray* v. *Two Strokes Ltd.* [1973] 1 W.L.R. 823 (on the actual decision, contrast (1973) 89 L.Q.R. 462 (M. J. Albery)). But interests under a trust for sale are interests in land for this purpose: *Elias* v. *Mitchell, infra.*

a purchaser for value under a registered disposition, *i.e.*, of a legal estate.[50] " A purchaser " means a purchaser in good faith[51]; but provided that the purchaser acts honestly, he is not affected merely by having notice of a minor interest.[52] Notice as such is immaterial.[53]

The policy of the Act, therefore, is that minor interests form a comprehensive residuary class, comprising all interests in land not otherwise provided for.[54] There is thus no room in the system for residuary interests or equities binding purchasers under the doctrine of notice. Every kind of interest other than an overriding interest must either be protected on the register, or else be defeasible by a purchaser. But there are some interests which it is unreasonable to expect their owners to register, and to which the doctrine of notice could more suitably give protection. Examples of these have been given elsewhere.[55] By forcing them into the mould of minor interests the Act has weakened their security.

Minor interests take effect in equity.[56] They fall into two classes:

(i) those which will be overreached on a proper sale, such as the equitable interests of beneficiaries under a settlement or trust for sale; and

(ii) those which will bind a purchaser provided they are protected by some entry on the register. These include estate contracts, restrictive covenants, and miscellaneous equities such as a vendor's lien.[57] Presumably they also include bare trusts, where the land is held for one beneficiary absolutely.

2. Protection of minor interests. A minor interest may be protected by a notice, a caution, an inhibition or a restriction.[58] There will sometimes be a choice among these devices[59]: an equitable charge by deposit of the land certificate, for example, may be protected by registering notice of the charge or notice of the deposit of the land

---

[50] *Miles* v. *Bull (No.* 2) [1969] 3 All E.R. 1585. *Contra* where the purchaser has only an equitable interest: *Barclays Bank Ltd.* v. *Taylor* [1974] Ch. 137; and see *post*, p. 1074.

[51] L.R.A., 1925, s. 3 (xxi).

[52] *Smith* v. *Morrison* [1974] 1 W.L.R. 659, rejecting the contrary doctrine of *Le Neve* v. *Le Neve* (1747) Amb. 436.

[53] L.R.A., 1925, s. 59 (6); see also s. 20 (1); *Parkash* v. *Irani Finance Ltd.* [1970] Ch. 101 ; *Smith* v. *Morrison, supra.*

[54] Contrast the policy of the L.C.A., 1925, as interpreted by the House of Lords: *ante*, p. 1043.

[55] See *ante*, p. 1043 and the cases there cited (*E. R. Ives Investment Ltd.* v. *High*; *Shiloh Spinners Ltd.* v. *Harding*; *Poster* v. *Slough Estates Ltd.*).

[56] L.R.A., 1925, s. 2. This provides a clearer concept than s. 3 (xv).

[57] For other examples, see *ante*, p. 1043.

[58] See Ruoff & Roper, 733.

[59] See the table in Ruoff & Roper, 740, 741.

certificate, or by lodging a caution.[60] A notice may be used, if it is available, in place of a caution, inhibition or restriction.[61]

(*a*) *Notices.* A notice is entered on the charges register.[62] Its effect is to ensure that any subsequent dealing with the land will take effect subject to the right protected by the notice, so far as it is valid and is not (apart from the Act) overridden by the disposition.[63] The notice also affects the registered proprietor and those claiming under him with notice of the claim as from the moment of entry.[64] It makes no difference that the person affected was unable to discover the notice, *e.g.*, if he was a lessee who had no right to inspect the registered freehold title,[65] under the rule criticised below.[66] This is, of course, a dangerous trap.[67]

The rights which can be protected by notice include leases where the term is not an overriding interest, all land charges under the Land Charges Act 1972 [68] (*e.g.*, estate contracts and restrictive covenants [69]), legal rentcharges, and the rights of creditors when a bankruptcy petition has been presented against the registered proprietor.[70] But the catalogue is open-ended, since it also includes " any other right, interest, or claim which it may be deemed expedient to protect by notice instead of by caution, inhibition, or restriction." [71]

A notice is the most efficient means of protecting a third party right. But it has the serious and apparently irrational defect that it can be entered only on production of the land certificate.[72] Consequently it is available only with the assistance of the owner or when the land certificate happens to be in the Registry.[73] There is no problem for a vendor entering notice of a restrictive covenant or

---

[60] See *Re White Rose Cottage* [1965] Ch. 940; *Elias* v. *Mitchell* [1972] Ch. 652 (interest under trust for sale: caution).
[61] L.R.A., 1925, s. 49 (1) (*f*).
[62] L.R.R., 1925, r. 7.
[63] L.R.A., 1925, s. 52.
[64] *Ibid.*, ss. 48 (1), 49 (1), 50 (2); L.R.R., 1925, r. 190.
[65] *White* v. *Bijou Mansions Ltd.* [1937] Ch. 610, affd. [1938] Ch. 351.
[66] *Post*, p. 1074.
[67] Especially if the doctrine of waiver in *Re Forsey and Hollebone's Contract* [1927] 2 Ch. 379 is followed: see *ante*, p. 584.
[68] See *City Permanent B. S.* v. *Miller* [1952] Ch. 840 at 849.
[69] L.R.A., 1925, s. 50 (1); (1937) 1 Conv.(N.S.) 326 (R. G. Page). See, *e.g.*, *Myton Ltd.* v. *Schwab-Morris* [1974] 1 W.L.R. 331 (conditional contract: condition broken). [70] L.R.A., 1925, ss. 48–51.
[71] L.R.A., 1925, s. 49 (1) (*f*). For a spouse's statutory right of occupation, see *ante*, p. 1066.
[72] L.R.A., 1925, s. 64 (1) (*c*), not applying to a creditor's notice, or notice of a lease at a rent and without a fine, nor to applications for first registration: *Strand Securities Ltd.* v. *Caswell* [1965] Ch. 958.
[73] It appears from *Smith* v. *Morrison* [1974] 1 W.L.R. 659 at 667 that priority was obtained by lodging notice of an estate contract without production of the land certificate; but the Land Registry's letters quoted at p. 668 suggest that the priority was only temporary pending production of the certificate. The registrar's power to compel production of certificates (ss. 64 (2), 128) is apparently not used for this purpose.

option. But for other purposes, *e.g.*, to protect an ordinary purchaser under an estate contract, the requirement of production of the land certificate may raise insuperable difficulty.

(*b*) *Cautions.* The essence of a caution is that it entitles the cautioner to notice of an intended transaction. There are two different types of caution, a caution against first registration and a caution against dealings: as the first relates to unregistered land and the second to registered land, the term " caution " *simpliciter*, when used in relation to registered land, means a caution against dealings. In each case the caution must be supported by a statutory declaration; and the usual length of notice to which the cautioner is entitled is fourteen days.[74] Abuse of the procedure is discouraged by provisions whereby any person who causes damage to another by lodging either form of caution without reasonable cause is liable to pay him compensation.[75]

(1) CAUTION AGAINST FIRST REGISTRATION. Any person who claims an interest in unregistered land which entitles him to object to any disposition of it being made without his consent may lodge a caution against first registration, and thereafter title to the land cannot be registered until notice has been served on the cautioner and has expired.[76] Thus a person who claims that he was tricked into executing a conveyance of his unregistered land may lodge a caution against first registration and so prevent the grantee from registering the title without his knowledge. Such cautions usually remain effective until after first registration is sought; they are not subject to the machinery for " warning off," explained below.[77]

(2) CAUTIONS AGAINST DEALINGS. Any person interested in registered land whose interest is not registered and is not protected by a notice or restriction may lodge a caution against any dealing with the land, and thereafter no entry of a dealing may be made on the register until notice has been served on the cautioner and has expired.[78] A person entitled to an interest under a trust for sale of the land is sufficiently " interested in " the land for this purpose.[79] The caution is entered in the proprietorship register.[80] A failure by the registry to give the cautioner due notice does not affect the protection con-

---

[74] L.R.A., 1925, ss. 53, 55; L.R.R., 1925, rr. 66, 67, 215, 218. For notices served by post, L.R.A., 1925, s. 79 in effect makes the 14 days 22: Ruoff & Roper, 773.

[75] L.R.A., 1925, s. 56 (3); and see *Clearbrook Property Holdings Ltd.* v. *Verrier* [1974] 1 W.L.R. 243. There is no corresponding provision for notices: see *Watts* v. *Waller* [1973] 1 Q.B. 153 at 169.

[76] L.R.A., 1925, s. 53; L.R.R., 1925, rr. 64–70.　　　　　　　[77] Ruoff & Roper, 275.

[78] L.R.A., 1925, ss. 54, 55; L.R.R., 1925, rr. 215–218; and see *Abigail* v. *Lapin* [1934] A.C. 491 at 500.

[79] *Elias* v. *Mitchell* [1972] Ch. 652; contrast Ruoff & Roper, 768–770; and see *Calgary & Edmonton Land Co. Ltd.* v. *Dobinson* [1974] Ch. 102. For a spouse's statutory right of occupation, see *ante*, p. 1066.

[80] L.R.R., 1925, r. 6.

ferred by the caution, since it is held to be implied in the Act that a purchaser takes subject to any interest properly so protected.[81] This inference makes the effect of a caution similar to that of a notice. But cautions do not otherwise affect priorities, except in special cases,[82] so that a caution will not give a later equitable interest priority over an earlier one.[83]

The registered proprietor need not wait until a dealing is about to take place, but may at any time " warn off " a caution by requiring notice to be given to the cautioner. Unless the cautioner successfully defends his claim, the caution then ceases to have effect.[84] Further, as with unregistered land,[85] the court has a wide jurisdiction, which in a proper case will be exercised on motion speedily and, if necessary, robustly, to order the vacation of cautions [86] and, no doubt, other entries as well. A caution may be vacated even where the cautioner can show a triable issue, but he may then be granted an interim injunction against dealings, subject to his giving an undertaking in damages so as to protect the registered owner, *e.g.*, if he loses a sale in the meantime.[87]

A caution is usually the only means of protection available to the owner of a minor interest who cannot obtain the land certificate and who cannot therefore make use of a notice. But the protection given is significantly weaker than that given by the registration of a land charge over unregistered land. The " warning off " procedure means that the cautioner may at any time be called upon to defend his interest and his caution will cease to have effect unless he responds within the few days prescribed.[88] It is true that a land charge over unregistered land may be speedily vacated in a proper case,[89] but the procedure is not so drastic as in the case of cautions.[90] Furthermore,

---

[81] *Parkash* v. *Irani Finance Ltd.* [1970] Ch. 101 (not discussed in *Barclays Bank Ltd.* v. *Taylor, infra*) making a converse deduction from L.R.A., 1925, s. 59 (6), notwithstanding s. 56 (2). No mention was made of s. 79 (4) (purchaser not to be affected by omission to send any notice or by non-receipt thereof), the effect of which is obscure.

[82] See L.R.A., 1925, s. 102 (2); *post*, p. 1079.

[83] *Barclays Bank Ltd.* v. *Taylor* [1974] Ch. 137 (contract for sale protected by caution held to be subject to earlier unprotected mortgage). *Cf.* (1971) 35 Conv.(N.S.) 100, 168 (S. Robinson).

[84] L.R.A., 1925, s. 55; L.R.R., 1925, r. 218. Contrast " mortgage cautions," *post*, p. 1077.   [85] See *ante*, p. 1053.

[86] *Rawlplug Co. Ltd.* v. *Kamvale Properties Ltd.* (1968) 20 P. & C.R. 32 ; *Calgary & Edmonton Land Co. Ltd.* v. *Discount Bank (Overseas) Ltd.* [1971] 1 W.L.R. 81 ; *Lester* v. *Burgess* (1973) 26 P. & C.R. 536 ; *Calgary & Edmonton Land Co. Ltd.* v. *Dobinson, supra* ; and see *Tiverton Estates Ltd.* v. *Wearwell Ltd.* [1974] 2 W.L.R. 176, where, however, jurisdiction seems to have been conceded : see at p. 195.

[87] *Clearbrook Property Holdings Ltd.* v. *Verrier* [1974] 1 W.L.R. 243 ; *Tiverton Estates Ltd.* v. *Wearwell, supra* ; contrast *Norman* v. *Hardy* [1974] 1 W.L.R. 1048.

[88] L.R.A., 1925, s. 55.

[89] *Ante*, p. 1053.

[90] If a warning-off notice is lost in the post, the cautioner would seem to have no protection under L.R.A., 1925, s. 79.

the registrar has substantial discretionary powers,[91] and it appears that he is unwilling to allow cautions to be indefinitely prolonged.[92] Yet continuous protection may be needed for such interests as options to purchase and equitable charges or easements. The court has tempered the rigour of the Act by protecting the cautioner against mistakes made in the registry,[93] but the legislation seems to be another instance of the policy of favouring clear titles and ease of transfer at the expense of third-party rights.

(c) *Inhibitions.* An inhibition is an order of the court or registrar which forbids any dealings with the land, either absolutely or until a certain time or event. The court or registrar may impose an inhibition on the application of any person, and annex to it such terms or conditions as the court or registrar thinks fit, and discharge or cancel the order, and generally act " in such manner as the justice of the case requires." [94] This is therefore a provision of last resort, intended for use only where there is no other way of protecting the claim. Nevertheless in a few cases it is used as a matter of routine; thus, where a receiving order in bankruptcy is registered as a land charge, a " bankruptcy inhibition " must be entered in the Land Register preventing the registered proprietor from disposing of the land.[95]

(d) *Restrictions.* A restriction is similar to an inhibition in that it prevents any dealing with the land until some condition has been complied with; it differs in that it is an entry usually made on the application of the registered proprietor himself.[96] Thus a restriction is usually a friendly entry, while inhibitions and cautions are hostile. Cases in which restrictions are appropriate include those where the registered proprietor is the tenant for life of settled land and restrictions are entered prohibiting the registration of any disposition not authorised by the Settled Land Act, 1925, or one in which capital money arises unless it is paid to the trustees, being at least two in number or a trust corporation, or into court. Similar restrictions are imposed in the case of trusts for sale. In practice, the registrar sees that suitable restrictions are framed; if the registered proprietor refuses to apply for their entry, any person interested may do so.[97]

It is vital for the security of trusts that they should be protected by a restriction or some other entry, since no one dealing with a

[91] See Ruoff & Roper, 774–775.
[92] *Ibid.*, 775.
[93] *Parkash* v. *Irani Finance Ltd., supra.*
[94] L.R.A., 1925, s. 57 (1), (2).
[95] *Ibid.*, s. 61 (3).
[96] *Ibid.*, s. 58 (1), (2); and see s. 58 (3) as to joint proprietors.
[97] L.R.A., 1925, s. 58 (5); L.R.R., 1925, r. 236.

registered estate or charge is to be affected with notice of any trust,[98] and minor interests not so protected do not bind a purchaser.[99] The registrar himself will enter the necessary restriction where the existence of the trust is shown by the title submitted for registration; and in the case of a transfer of registered land to, *e.g.*, trustees for sale, this will appear from the absence of purchase-money on the form of transfer, or from some reference to the trust deed.[1] But there are many cases where trusts arise without any obvious occasion for registration, as where land purchased by A and B with joint contributions is conveyed to A alone.[2] These trust interests are therefore inadequately protected, as also they are in the case of unregistered land where A and B are husband and wife.[3] But they may, of course, be protected as overriding interests by reason of the beneficiary being in actual occupation or in receipt of rents and profits.

3. Companies. Most charges on registered land created by a company for securing money require registration in the Companies Register in addition to protection by an entry on the Land Register.[4]

D. Certain Dealings with Registered Land

I. TRANSFER INTER VIVOS

1. Transfer. A freehold conveyance of registered land *inter vivos* is effected by a simple statutory form of transfer which must be lodged at the Land Registry together with the land certificate.[5] The disposition, when registered, confers the legal estate on the transferee.[6] It is immaterial that the transferor may have had no power to convey the land: it seems that even a forged transfer from an impostor will, if registered, make the transferee the legal owner.[7] Registration itself confers the legal title,[8] and there is no room for the principle *nemo*

---

[98] L.R.A., 1925, s. 74.
[99] See *infra*.
[1] See Ruoff & Roper, 404.
[2] *Ante*, p. 445.
[3] *Ibid*.
[4] Companies Act, 1948, s. 95: and see *Re Overseas Aviation Engineering (G. B.) Ltd.* [1963] Ch. 24; *Re Molton Finance Ltd.* [1968] Ch. 325; contrast *ante*, p. 1044; and see *ante*, p. 1050. For floating charges, see Ruoff & Roper, 533.
[5] L.R.R., 1925, rr. 74–138, Sched. Registration cures any irregularity in the form of transfer: L.R.R., 1925, r. 74; *Morelle Ltd.* v. *Wakeling* [1955] 2 Q.B. 379.
[6] L.R.A., 1925, s. 20. According to s. 20 (1), the legal estate is conferred by the "disposition . . . when registered". According to s. 69 (1) the proprietor is "deemed to have" the legal estate "vested in him without any conveyance". According to s. 19 (1) the transfer of the registered estate is completed by the registrar entering on the register the transferee, rather than the disposition. The obscure definition of "registered dispositions" in s. 3 (xxii) does not resolve the confusion.
[7] Ruoff & Roper, 68; for an example, see *post*, p. 1082. But see n. 16, *infra*.
[8] L.R.A., 1925, s. 69; *Morelle* v. *Wakeling, supra*, at p. 411.

dat quod non habet. The transferee acquires no legal estate until the transfer is registered.[9] The registrar makes the necessary entries on the register and the land certificate, and returns the latter to the proprietor. As with unregistered land, the land transferred passes with all its appurtenances, such as easements and quasi-easements.[10] The usual covenants for title[11] may be implied by conveying " as beneficial owner," or as the case may be.[12]

Leases, unlike conveyances, may be made in any form, provided that the land is identified by its title number and, where part only is let, by a plan.[13] The same applies to the grant and transfer of easements.[14]

2. Incumbrances. The transferee takes the land subject to all the interests which bound the transferor. But a purchaser for value takes free from minor interests other than those which bind him through being protected by an entry on the register.[15] Whether or not he has notice of them is immaterial.[16]

3. Searches. As the register is private, an intending purchaser cannot search it without the vendor's authority.[17] A vendor is bound, notwithstanding any stipulation to the contrary, to give the purchaser authority to inspect the register, so that he can confirm the accuracy of the copy of the entries on the register with which the vendor will have supplied him in lieu of an abstract of title.[18] The vendor must also, if required, furnish details of plans filed and documents noted on the register.

For no apparent reason these obligations do not apply in the case of a lessee or chargee.[19] A chargee will naturally refuse to advance money without a full disclosure of title. But a lessee is in a very weak position: unless he contracts for disclosure of the lessor's title he has no right to see it,[20] and consequently he has no means of

---

[9] L.R.A., 1925, ss. 19–23.　　　　　　[10] L.R.A., 1925, s. 20.
[11] See *ante*, p. 602.
[12] L.R.A., 1925, s. 38 (2); L.R.R., 1925, rr. 76, 77. For the contention that such covenants do not apply to overriding interests, see (1942) 58 L.Q.R. 356 (H. Potter); but the criticism of this view at (1941) 57 L.Q.R. 566 (R.E.M.) is accepted by K. & E. iii, 128; and see Ruoff & Roper, 312. But consider (1961) 105 S.J. 801.
[13] L.R.A., 1925, ss. 18 (1) (*e*), 21 (1) (*d*); L.R.R., 1925, r. 113.
[14] *Ibid.*
[15] L.R.A., 1925, ss. 20, 23; *Miles* v. *Bull* (*No.* 2) [1969] 3 All E.R. 1585.
[16] L.R.A., 1925, s. 59 (6); and see ss. 3 (xv), 74; *Hodges* v. *Jones* [1935] Ch. 657 at 671; *De Lusignan* v. *Johnson* (1973) 230 E.G. 499; *Smith* v. *Morrison* [1974] 1 W.L.R. 659. This is subject to the Act's provisions as to fraud and bankruptcy. A disposition which if unregistered would be fraudulent and void is equally void notwithstanding registration: s. 114. But fraudulent dispositions are voidable, not void (*ante*, p. 611), and in s. 114 " void " perhaps means " voidable." Conflict with s. 69 (*supra*) could thus be avoided.
[17] *Ante*, p. 1055.　　　　　　[18] L.R.A., 1925, s. 110 (1).
[19] *Ibid.*; Ruoff & Roper, 712.　　　　[20] See *ante*, p. 708, for the rules.

discovering restrictive covenants and other incumbrances on the register by which he will be bound.[21] There is no valid analogy with the restrictions on lessees' rights in unregistered conveyancing: for those are designed to save the elaborate old-fashioned procedure of proving title, whereas with a registered title all that the vendor need do is give authority to inspect the register. This is one of the Act's inexplicable deficiencies.[22]

If an official search is obtained by a purchaser in good faith (*i.e.*, one who acts honestly, even though he knows of a competing claim [23]), he may protect himself against entries on the register made during the " priority period," *i.e.*, the period between the opening of the appropriate office of the registry on the day when his application for an official search is delivered there and the opening of that office on the sixteenth day thereafter; on application, the period may be extended for a further fourteen days. If the purchaser's application to register his purchase is substantially [24] in order and is delivered to the appropriate office within the priority period, any entries on the register made during that period are postponed to the purchaser's application.[25]

II. TRANSFER ON DEATH

On the death of a sole registered proprietor, his personal representatives may either—

(i) apply for registration themselves, on producing to the registrar the grant of probate or letters of administration [26]; or

(ii) without being themselves registered, transfer the land direct either to a purchaser or to the person entitled under the will or intestacy; in this case, both the transfer or assent and the probate or letters of administration must be lodged with the application for registration.[27]

If one of two or more joint proprietors dies, his name will be removed from the register on proof of death, or production of probate or letters of administration, together with any further evidence required by the registrar.[28]

---

[21] *White* v. *Bijou Mansions Ltd.* [1937] Ch. 610 at 621 (affd. [1938] Ch. 351).
[22] The obvious reform is recommended by the Committee on Land Charges, Cmd. 9825 (1956) para. 42, and by the Law Commission, Working Paper No. 32 para. 54.
[23] *Smith* v. *Morrison* [1974] 1 W.L.R. 659.
[24] *Ibid.*
[25] L.R. (Official Searches) R. 1969.
[26] L.R.A., 1925, s. 41 (1); L.R.R., 1925, r. 168.
[27] L.R.A., 1925, s. 37 (1), (2); L.R.R., 1925, r. 170.
[28] L.R.R., 1925, r. 172.

III. SETTLEMENTS

In a settlement of registered land a vesting transfer in statutory form takes the place of a vesting deed,[29] but the trust instrument is made in ordinary form. In the vesting transfer the settlor or proprietor (normally the tenant for life) must apply for the entry of suitable restrictions to protect the beneficiaries against dealings not permitted by the Settled Land Act, 1925. Since that Act is subject to the Land Registration Act, 1925,[30] the principle that the registered title is paramount prevails over the normal rule that unauthorised dealings with settled land are void.[31] But in general the law of settled land applies to registered land without modification.

IV. TRANSFER ON BANKRUPTCY

The steps taken on bankruptcy, so far as they affect registered land, are briefly as follows.

(i) A bankruptcy petition is presented; this is protected by the entry of a creditor's notice, which prevents the registered proprietor from selling the land free from the claims of the creditors.[32]

(ii) A receiving order is made; this is protected by a bankruptcy inhibition, which prevents the registered proprietor from dealing with the land at all.[33]

(iii) The registered proprietor is adjudicated bankrupt. His trustee in bankruptcy (or, until a trustee is appointed, the official receiver) may be registered as proprietor in place of the bankrupt on production of an office copy of the adjudication and a certificate that the land is part of the bankrupt's property divisible among his creditors.[34]

V. MORTGAGES

There are three ways in which a mortgage of registered land may be effected.

1. By registered charge. A registered charge may be effected by any deed charging the land in a way making it identifiable without reference to any other document.[35] The charge must not refer to any other interest or charge which would have priority over it and is not registered or protected on the register, or which is not an overriding

---

[29] L.R.R., 1925, r. 99, prescribing forms.
[30] S.L.A., 1925, s. 119 (3).
[31] *Ante*, p. 313.
[32] *Ante*, p. 1069.
[33] *Ante*, p. 1072.
[34] L.R.A., 1925, s. 42 (1); L.R.R., 1925, rr. 174–177.
[35] L.R.A., 1925, s 25 (1), (2).

interest.[36] The deed must be registered, whereupon an entry is made in the Charges Register giving details of the charge.[37] A legal estate does not arise until the charge is registered.[38] The land certificate must be deposited at the registry for as long as a registered charge exists,[39] and a charge certificate is issued to the chargee as his document of title.[40]

A registered chargee has all the powers of a legal mortgagee, unless the register otherwise provides,[41] and any provision purporting to interfere with the registered chargee's power of transferring the charge by registered disposition is void.[42] The priority of registered charges is governed by the order of entry in the register, subject to any entry to the contrary.[43] As regards tacking, section 94 of the Law of Property Act, 1925,[44] does not apply to registered land; but further advances may be tacked only if (i) they are made by a chargee under an obligation to do so which has been entered on the register, or (ii) the charge was made for securing further advances, and the advance was made before notice of the intervening incumbrance (which the registrar must send to the chargee) ought to have reached the chargee in due course of post.[45] A right to consolidate may, it seems, be reserved as in the case of unregistered land.[46]

A sub-mortgage is made by means of a charge of the mortgage or charge by way of sub-charge.[47]

2. By unregistered mortgage. Unless the register otherwise indicates, registered land may be mortgaged in the same way as if it were unregistered [48]; and such a mortgage may be dealt with in the same way as if the land had not been registered.[49] Until it has been duly protected by the entry of a caution, such a mortgage takes effect only in equity as a minor interest [50]; and if the mortgage is made by deed, the caution is required to be in the special form of a " mortgage caution," which, unlike an ordinary caution, cannot be " warned off " the register.[51] But this procedure is so unsatisfactory

---

[36] *Ibid.*, s. 25 (2) (b).
[37] *Ibid.*, s. 26 (1).
[38] *Grace Rymer Investments Ltd.* v. *Waite* [1958] Ch. 831.
[39] L.R.A., 1925, s. 65.
[40] L.R.R., 1925, r. 262.
[41] L.R.A., 1925, ss. 27 (1), 34 (1).
[42] *Ibid.*, s. 25 (3).
[43] *Ibid.*, s. 29; *cf. ante*, p. 972.
[44] *Ante*, p. 983.
[45] L.R.A., 1925, s. 30 (1), (3), added by L.P.(Am.) Act, 1926, Sched. S. 30 (2) provides for compensation if any failure by the post office or registrar causes loss to the registered chargee in respect of a further advance.
[46] See (1950) 100 L.J.News. 353; (1952) 214 L.T.News. 305; Ruoff & Roper, 549.
[47] L.R.A., 1925, s. 6; L.R.R., 1925, rr. 163–166.
[48] L.R.A., 1925, s. 106 (1).
[49] *Ibid.*, s. 106 (1).
[50] *Ibid.*, s. 106 (2), (4).
[51] *Ibid.*, L.R.R. 1925, rr. 223, 225. For " warning off," see *ante*, p. 1071.

that it is never used,[52] and the usual practice, contrary to the terms of the Act,[53] is to protect the mortgage by a notice.[54] Law and practice are here thoroughly confused.

It is also possible to create an equitable charge, which is a minor interest, and can be protected by notice or caution.[55]

3. By deposit of the land certificate. The land certificate takes the place of the title deeds, and so, subject to overriding interests and registered interests, and to any entry on the register, a lien may be created by deposit of the land certificate with the lender.[56] A chargee can similarly create a lien on his charge by deposit of his charge certificate.[57] In such cases the lender may have a notice of the deposit or of the charge entered on the charges register of the interest affected, but by a paradoxical provision this is made to operate as a caution.[58] Alternatively a caution may be lodged.[59] It is common practice for a mortgagee to obtain a deposit of the land certificate and to lodge a notice [60]; but in order to exercise his power of sale he will be obliged to obtain registration of his charge, which will then take priority from the date of the notice.[61]

VI. LIMITATION AND PRESCRIPTION

A title to registered land may be acquired under the Limitation Act, 1939, by adverse possession in the same way as in the case of unregistered land. But in the case of registered land no legal title can vest in the adverse possessor until he has been registered as proprietor. In order to protect him in the meantime it is provided that the registered proprietor holds the land on trust for him.[62] This may be contrasted with unregistered land, where the former owner's estate is extinguished, and the adverse possessor obtains a wholly new estate.[63] But probably the statutory trust is a technicality

---

[52] Ruoff & Roper, 554, describe it as "expensive, cumbersome, inconvenient, relatively unsafe, and never now used in practice."

[53] L.R.A., 1925, s. 106 (2) provides that protection may be effected by mortgage caution "and in no other way": see *Barclays Bank Ltd.* v. *Taylor* [1974] Ch. 137.

[54] Thus presumably treating the charge as a mere lien (see next paragraph). In *Barclays Bank Ltd.* v. *Taylor* [1973] Ch. 63 the protection was held to be illusory, but the Court of Appeal (*supra*) did not deal with this question.

[55] K. & E. iii, 224.

[56] L.R.A., 1925, s. 66.

[57] *Ibid.*

[58] L.R.R., 1925, r. 239.

[59] See *Re White Rose Cottage* [1965] Ch. 940.

[60] This avoids the fees payable on registration of a charge.

[61] Ruoff & Roper, 674.

[62] L.R.A., 1925, s. 75 (1), (2); and see *London City & Midland Executor and Trustee Co. Ltd.* v. *Cave* [1925] W.N. 159; *Fairweather* v. *St. Marylebone Property Co. Ltd.* [1963] A.C. 510.

[63] See *ante*, pp. 1004 *et seq.*, 1028.

designed to fill the gap until the squatter registers an "independent possessory title."[64] His squatter's rights are an overriding interest,[65] so that no disposition by the registered proprietor can defeat them.

Registration of the squatter's title may be made with absolute, qualified, good leasehold or possessory title as the case may be; and this has the effect of first registration, though interests not extinguished by the adverse possession are not affected.[66]

Easements and profits may similarly be acquired by prescription against registered land in the same way as if it were not registered.[67]

VII. DEALINGS WITH MINOR INTERESTS

When beneficial interests under a settlement or trust for sale of unregistered land are assigned or mortgaged, the assignees or mortgagees preserve priority by giving written notice of their interests to the trustees under the rule in *Dearle* v. *Hall* as applied by the Law of Property Act, 1925.[68] In the case of registered land, priority is governed instead by the order in which the assignments or mortgages are protected by "Priority Inhibitions" or "Priority Cautions" entered in the "Index of Minor Interests".[69] The sole function of this index is to take the place of *Dearle* v. *Hall* notices. It is no part of the register. The inhibition is used for an absolute assignment, the caution for other cases. The rule that the order of entry governs priority appears to be absolute, so that a mortgagee may be postponed to a subsequent mortgagee who enters his inhibition or caution first, even though the subsequent mortgagee had notice of the prior mortgage when he advanced his money.[70]

It is generally agreed that the index is useless and, moreover, a source of anomalies and traps.[71] It is clear that the badly drafted provisions about it should be repealed, so that the rule in *Dearle* v. *Hall*, as applied by the Law of Property Act, 1925, can govern all cases without further formality.

E. *Indefeasibility*

1. The principle. One of the attractions of registration of title is the general principle (nowhere made explicit in the Act) that the registered proprietor has a title which is indefeasible without com-

---

[64] *Fairweather* v. *St. Marylebone Property Co. Ltd.*, *supra*, at p. 543, *per* Lord Radcliffe.
[65] *Ante*, p. 1065.
[66] L.R.A., 1925, s. 75 (3). See (1963) 27 Conv.(N.S.) 353 (T. B. F. Ruoff).
[67] L.R.R., 1925, r. 250.
[68] *Ante*, p. 976.
[69] L.R.A., 1925, s. 102 (2); L.R.R., 1925, rr. 11, 229.
[70] Contrast *ante*, p. 966.
[71] See Law Commission Working Paper No. 37, Part C.

pensation. In other words, there is a State guarantee of the title, so that the registered proprietor and those dealing with him may rely upon his title being as it appears in the register, and will normally be able to claim compensation if it is not. The principle, as it emerges from the Act, is rather a principle of partial compensation than of indefeasibility [72]; for there is wide jurisdiction to rectify the register, and the right to compensation is by no means automatic.

2. Rectification

(*a*) *Power to rectify.* Although the legal estate in registered land is vested in the registered proprietor,[73] the registrar or court has jurisdiction in certain circumstances to rectify the register.[74] This may be done, *inter alia*, where any entry has been obtained by fraud; where a legal estate has been registered in the name of a person who, if the land had not been registered, would not have been the estate owner; and where " by reason of any error or omission in the register . . . it may be deemed just to rectify the register." [75] Thus if a person is registered as proprietor of land to part of which a squatter has acquired title under the Limitation Acts, the register may be rectified so as to exclude the part from the registered proprietor's title.[76]

(*b*) *Registered proprietor in possession.* A registered proprietor who is in possession is protected against rectification except— [77]

(i) to give effect to an overriding interest, or

(ii) where he was party or privy, or by his act, neglect or default has caused or substantially contributed to the fraud, mistake or omission in consequence of which rectification is sought, or

(iii) where the immediate disposition to him was void (*i.e.*, wholly void, as where it was forged [78]), or the disposition to any person through whom he claims otherwise than for value [79] was void; or

(iv) where for any other reason it would be unjust not to rectify the register against him.[80]

---

[72] For criticism of the legislation and its interpretation, see (1968) 84 L.Q.R. 528 (S. Cretney and G. Dworkin).
[73] See *ante*, p. 1063.   [74] L.R.A., 1925, s. 82 (1); L.R.R., 1925, rr. 13, 14.
[75] L.R.A., 1925, s 82 (1); see, *e.g.*, *Chowood Ltd.* v. *Lyall* [1930] 2 Ch. 156 at 165, discussed in Ruoff & Roper, 839; and see *Re Dances Way, West Town, Hayling Island* [1962] Ch. 490 (dealing with the Registrar's jurisdiction).
[76] *Chowood Ltd.* v. *Lyall* [1930] 2 Ch. 156.   [77] L.R.A., 1925, s. 82 (3).
[78] See *Re 139 Deptford High Street* [1951] Ch. 884 at 892; and consider *Re Leighton's Conveyance* [1937] Ch. 149.
[79] Not including a nominal consideration : L.R.A., 1925, s. 3 (xxxi).
[80] See, *e.g.*, *Hodges* v. *Jones* [1935] Ch. 657 at 671; contrast *Re 139 Deptford High Street* [1951] Ch. 884 at 892 (proprietor's innocent expenditure of money on the land points against rectification); see Ruoff & Roper, 835–838, and (1955) 19 Conv.(N.S.) 350 (T. B. F. Ruoff).

It has been held that if any of the first three grounds exist the court ought to order rectification,[81] but the better view probably is that rectification is in all cases discretionary.[82]

The drafting of the second ground ("act, neglect or default") may deprive the proprietor of protection even though he has committed no fault. It would be more satisfactory if this ground were confined to cases of fraud or lack of proper care, as in the corresponding rule for compensation.[83] Under the present law, if X innocently obtains registration of his title by a description which appears to include other property which in fact is owned by Y, Y can obtain rectification, for by his application X substantially contributed to the mistake.[84] But if Y knowingly stood by and allowed X to carry out expensive work without intervening, the court might hold that rectification would not be just.[85] In assessing justice, the court will take account of the fact that rectification would entitle the losing party to indemnity, while non-rectification would not,[86] though rectification may still be refused if the indemnity will not be adequate compensation for loss of the land.

Proceedings for rectification are comparatively rare; but the statutory provision for rectification is important as an instance of the general principle that titles are relative, not absolute, and that no title is completely free from the danger that some better right to the land may be established.[87]

3. Compensation. In registered conveyancing, as in all conveyancing, ease of transfer can be bought only at some risk to titles and third parties' interests. An element of insurance is therefore provided in the form of monetary compensation for losses caused by the system; and these have been creditably small.[88] Formerly there was an insurance fund maintained from fees paid in the Land Registry.[89] This is now merged in the Consolidated Fund,[90] but the provisions for compensation remain. Both entitlement and amount are determinable by the court in proceedings against the Chief Land Registrar.[91] The provisions are as follows.

---

81 *Re 139 Deptford High Street, supra.*
82 See *Claridge* v. *Tingey* [1967] 1 W.L.R. 134; *Epps* v. *Esso Petroleum Co. Ltd.* [1973] 1 W.L.R. 1071.
83 *Post*, p. 1083. See Law Commission Working Paper No. 45, para. 81.
84 *Re 139 Deptford High Street, supra*; *Claridge* v. *Tingey, supra* (same land conveyed to two different purchasers).
85 *Claridge* v. *Tingey, supra.*
86 *Epps* v. *Esso Petroleum Co. Ltd., supra*; and see *post*, p. 1082.
87 See *ante*, p. 1006.
88 Ruoff & Roper, 10 (claims in over 50 years totalled £58,000).
89 L.R.A., 1925, s. 85; L.R.A., 1936, ss. 4, 5.
90 L.R. & L.C.A., 1971, s. 1.
91 *Ibid.*, s. 2.

(*a*) *Right to indemnity*. There are four main heads.

(1) RECTIFICATION. " Any person suffering loss by reason of any rectification of the register " under the Act is entitled to be indemnified out of the fund.[92] This protection is not so wide as it seems. If when a purchaser buys registered land part of it is in the possession of a squatter who has acquired title to it, the purchaser suffers no " loss " within this provision when the register is rectified to give effect to the squatter's title. For the registered title is in any case subject to the squatter's overriding interest[93]; the rectification is mere formal recognition of existing rights, and any " loss " occurred when the land was purchased.[94] Similarly, where a boundary is rectified in favour of an adjacent owner the registered proprietor suffers no " loss " as regards any part of the land which the adjacent owner actually occupied at the time of registration[95]; but the registered proprietor is entitled to indemnity in respect of any other land affected by the rectification, for it was subject to no overriding interest, and the registered title has proved bad.[96]

If the title of a proprietor claiming in good faith under a forged disposition is rectified, he is deemed to have suffered loss by reason of the rectification.[97]

(2) NON-RECTIFICATION. Where an error or omission has occurred in the register, but it is not rectified, any person suffering loss by reason of the error or omission is entitled to indemnity.[98] A classic example occurred when the murderer of a registered proprietor forged a transfer to himself, obtained registration, and sold the land to an innocent purchaser. Rectification was not available, for the purchaser was in possession, and so the victim's personal representative was indemnified for the loss to the estate.[99]

(3) CONVERSION OF TITLE. Anyone except the registered proprietor who suffers loss by reason of any entry made on the register on the conversion of a title into absolute or good leasehold is entitled to indemnity.[1]

(4) ERRORS. A person is entitled to indemnity if he suffers loss from any error in an official search,[2] or from any inaccuracy in an

[92] L.R.A., 1925, s. 83 (1): see generally Ruoff & Roper, Ch. 40.
[93] *Ante*, p. 1065.   [94] *Re Chowood's Registered Land* [1933] Ch. 574.
[95] *Re Boyle's Claim* [1961] 1 W.L.R. 339.
[96] *Ibid.*
[97] L.R.A., 1925, s. 83 (4).
[98] *Ibid.*, s. 83 (2). For examples, see Ruoff & Roper, 850.
[99] Related in Ruoff & Roper, 852 (the *Haigh*, or acid bath, case). *Cf. Frazer* v. *Walker* [1967] 1 A.C. 569.
[1] L.R.A., 1925, s. 77 (6).
[2] *Ibid.*, s. 83 (3), also applying to any loss or destruction of documents lodged at the registry.

office copy of the register or of any filed document or plan, or any extracts therefrom,[3] or from any error or omission in any filed abstract or copy of any document, or any extract therefrom, to which the register refers.[4]

(b) *Fraud and lack of care.* No indemnity is payable if the applicant (or a predecessor in title through whom he claims otherwise than by a registered disposition for value) " has caused or substantially contributed to the loss by fraud or lack of proper care." [5] This disqualification is now less severe than before [6] though it may cause hardship by depriving a claimant of all compensation where his lack of care was only a contributory factor.

(c) *Amount of indemnity.* The claimant is normally entitled to indemnity for the amount of his loss, together with reasonable costs and expenses properly incurred.[7] But an indemnity for rectification is limited to the value of the lost interest immediately before rectification; and an indemnity for non-rectification is limited to the value of the lost interest at the time when the mistake was made,[8] a restriction which may make the indemnity seriously inadequate.[9]

(d) *Time limit.* A liability to pay indemnity is deemed to be a simple contract debt, so that it is barred after six years; but time does not begin to run until the claimant knows of the existence of his claim, or but for his own default might have known.[10] Yet where the claim arises from the registration of an absolute or good leasehold title, time runs from the date of such registration, subject to exceptions in favour of infants, remaindermen, and certain covenantees and mortgagees.[11] The difference between this six-year period and the ordinary twelve-year period of limitation for the recovery of land is anomalous. Thus if six years ago a strip of O's land was mistakenly conveyed by V to P and P was registered with absolute title O, though still the true owner under the ordinary law, will normally be refused rectification if P is in possession,[12] and his claim to indemnity will be

---

[3] L.R.A., 1925, s. 113.
[4] *Ibid.*, s. 110 (4). For other cases, see s. 30 (2) (further advances under a registered charge: *ante*, p. 1077, n. 45); s. 61 (7) (trustee in bankruptcy: creditor's notice or bankruptcy inhibition).
[5] L.R.A., 1925, s. 83 (5), as amended by L.R. & L.C.A. 1971, s. 3; and see L.R.A., 1925, s. 83 (5) (b) (mines and minerals).
[6] L.T.A., 1897, s. 7 (3), extended to " act, neglect or default "; L.R.A., 1925, s. 83 (5) (a) cut this down to " fraud "; L.R.A. 1966, s. 1 (4), added " act, neglect or default."
[7] L.R.A., 1925, s. 83 (8), as replaced by L.R. & L.C.A. 1971, s. 2 (4); and see L.R.A., 1925, s. 83 (5) (c), as amended by L.R. & L.C.A. 1971, s. 2 (2).
[8] L.R.A., 1925, s. 83 (6).
[9] See *Epps* v. *Esso Petroleum Co. Ltd.* [1973] 1 W.L.R. 1071.
[10] L.R.A., 1925, s. 83 (11).   [11] *Ibid.*
[12] See *Epps* v. *Esso Petroleum Co. Ltd.* [1973] 1 W.L.R. 1071, where these events happened. See also Law Commission Working Paper No. 45, para. 110.

barred. In such cases, the claim to indemnity ought to be subject to the same limitation period as the claim to the land, *i.e.*, twelve years.

(*e*) *Comparison with unregistered land.* It will be evident from the above account that the compensation scheme provides a solution in some cases where otherwise one of two innocent parties would have to bear the loss, *e.g.*, where by forgery or fraud a false title has been marketed, or where by mere mistake there has been " double conveyancing " of the same piece of land to two different purchasers.[13] This is a notable advantage as compared with dealings in unregistered land, where in case of conflicting titles the weaker title merely fails.[14]

4. The limits of indefeasibility. The so-called principle of indefeasibility is by no means unqualified. The ultimate reality of the system is that the court has a wide discretion to rectify the register as may seem just. The " state guarantee of title," too, is far from comprehensive: there are a number of cases in which the true owner or an innocent purchaser may be left with neither the property nor compensation.[15] A purchaser may also fail to discover overriding interests which may seriously impair the value of this land, as where an occupier has some unexpected claim.[16] This emphasises the limited scope of registration of title: in general terms, the registered title takes the place of the title deeds, and greatly simplifies the purchaser's investigations. But it by no means fulfils the " mirror principle " by which, ideally, it should reflect every existing interest in the land. It cannot be expected to solve all the problems of reconciling security of ownership with ease of transfer, which must remain the central dilemma of the law of property.

13 See Ruoff & Roper, 851.
14 Subject to the possibility of compensation under L.P.A. 1969, s. 25: *ante*, p. 1046.
15 As in *Re Chowood's Registered Land, supra*; *Hodgson* v. *Marks* [1971] Ch. 892; *Epps* v. *Esso Petroleum Co. Ltd., supra*.
16 See *ante*, p. 1066.

CHAPTER 18

THE SOCIAL CONTROL OF LAND

DURING the twentieth century great changes have been made in the law governing the use and enjoyment of land. These changes are quite distinct from the property legislation of 1925, which concerned the ownership of estates and interests in land rather than the fruits of enjoyment. Further, they are piecemeal and unsystematic, whereas the 1925 legislation was unified. In addition to the changes in the law, the great increases in taxation, although for the most part not specifically aimed at land, have had a marked effect on the dispositions which landowners wish to make. The changes, which can here be considered only in outline, may be grouped under four main heads, namely—

1. Increased taxation.
2. Planning control.
3. Agricultural control.
4. The protection of tenants.

Sect. 1. Increased Taxation

1. Increased rates of taxation. In 1900 the standard rate of income tax was raised from eightpence to one shilling in the pound,[1] and surtax did not exist. An investment income of £10,000 a year bore approximately £500 in tax; in 1974 it bore over £5,000. The estate of a person who left property worth a million pounds was liable for estate duty of 7·5 per cent.; if he died in 1974, the estate duty would be nearly 70 per cent.[2] The cumulative effect of estate duty is especially apparent when it is realised that if property is settled on persons in succession, estate duty on the full capital value of the property is payable each time a tenant for life dies.[3]

2. Effect on settlements. In addition to leading to the break-up of large estates, these changes have transformed the types of settlement which are employed. A settlement in the old form, with successive interests to a long list of beneficiaries, attracts a disastrous

[1] Finance Act, 1899, s. 15; Finance Act, 1900, s. 15.
[2] Finance Act 1972, s. 120.
[3] Finance Act, 1894, s. 1.

burden of taxation. Instead, the tendency is towards discretionary trusts, where the death of a mere potential beneficiary formerly attracted no estate duty, and even now attracts less.[3a] Further, many parents now make substantial gifts of property to their children *inter vivos*, long before they die; for although most gifts made within seven years of death are liable to estate duty, those made more than seven years before death are not.[4] But in 1974 a capital transfer tax was proposed, to replace estate duty and to tax gifts made *inter vivos*. Again, the high rates of income tax (and surtax before it was abolished and replaced by the " unified system " of income taxation [5]) have made the maintenance of large estates difficult or impossible. The strict settlements of great estates so often made in the eighteenth and nineteenth centuries are rarely made today.

3. Mitigation of burdens. Perhaps the greatest change of all lies in the domination now exercised by taxation over the great majority of wills and settlements of large properties, and, indeed, over many other transactions. Seventy years ago the testator or settlor was primarily concerned with the beneficial interests, and paid little heed to matters of taxation. Today the effects of heavy taxation on the proposed dispositions are often predominant. Many transactions are entered into with little or no object other than mitigating the burden of taxation. Existing settlements, too, are often varied or terminated with the same object; this can be done with the concurrence of all the beneficiaries, actual or possible, and, if any of them are infants or unascertained, with the approval of the court on their behalf under the Variation of Trusts Act, 1958.[6]

Sect. 2. Planning Control

Town and country planning control will be considered under two main heads, control of development, and financial control; and the effect on the law of property will then be summarised.

A. *Control of Development*

I. GROWTH OF CONTROL

1. Control by schemes. At common law, any landowner was free to develop his land as he wished, provided he did not infringe the

---

[3a] See Finance Act 1969, ss. 36, 37.

[4] Customs and Inland Revenue Act, 1881, s. 38 (2) (a); Customs and Inland Revenue Act, 1889, s. 11 (1); Finance Act, 1894, s. 2 (1) (c); Finance (1909–10) Act, 1910, s. 59 (1); Finance Act, 1946, s. 47, 11th Sched., Pt. I, para. 1; Finance Act 1968, s. 35 (making progressive reductions for deaths in the last three of the seven years). Originally the period was three months, but it has been successively increased.

[5] By the Finance Act 1971, ss. 32–39.

[6] See Snell, *Equity*, 231–235.

rights of others. He could erect whatever buildings he wished, however unsuitable they might be, and however injurious to the amenities of the district. Not until the Housing, Town Planning, &c. Act, 1909, was enacted was there any general power for local authorities to control the development of land. Successive statutes strengthened and extended this control, culminating in the Town and Country Planning Act, 1932, which for the first time conferred planning powers over land in the country, as distinct from towns. The essence of this and the earlier Acts was the preparation of a scheme. Each local authority was empowered to prepare a scheme showing what development would be permitted in each part of its district; and there were powers of enforcement against those who carried out development contravening the scheme.

2. Interim development control

(a) *Control.* This system suffered from a number of defects. First, it was optional: there was no obligation for any local authority to prepare a scheme, and many did not. Secondly, there was the long period which usually elapsed between the decision of the local authority to prepare a scheme and the final approval of the scheme. During this period the land was subject to " interim development control." Under this, any landowner could develop his land at his own risk: if, when at last the scheme was made, the development accorded with the scheme, it was safe, whereas if it did not accord with it, the local authority could take enforcement action under the scheme and, for example, secure the removal of any offending buildings.[7]

(b) *Interim development permission.* To guard against this risk, an application for interim development permission could be made before carrying out the work. If this was given, the development was immune from enforcement action even if ultimately it was found to contravene the scheme.[8] But if development was carried out without interim development permission, there was no power to take enforcement action against it during the interim development period; and some speculative developers relied successfully on the probability that no scheme would come into force until they had been able to reap the profits of their development.

(c) *Ribbon development.* Only in one special respect was there a direct control of land irrespective of any scheme. After the 1914–18 war, it became increasingly frequent for houses to be built on each

---

[7] Town and Country Planning Act, 1932, s. 13.
[8] *Ibid.*, ss. 10, 53.

side of new roads constructed for traffic purposes; in this way, the builders saved the cost of making their own roads at the expense of the traffic and the safety of the occupants of the houses. The Restriction of Ribbon Development Act, 1935, dealt with this by prohibiting the making of any means of access to certain roads, or the erection of any building within a specified distance of the centre of those roads, unless the consent of the highway authority was obtained. The Act applied automatically to classified roads (the more important highways), and could be applied to other roads if the highway authority so resolved and the Minister of Transport approved; the specified distance was 220 feet in the former case, and not more than 80 feet in the latter.

3. The Act of 1943. This system continued until the Town and Country Planning (Interim Development) Act, 1943, was passed. At that time a mere 4 per cent. of England and Wales was subject to operative schemes; another 70 per cent. was subject to interim development control; and the remaining 26 per cent. was subject to no control. The Act imposed interim development control on all land in this last category, so that thenceforward the whole of the land in the country was under interim development control save for the 4 per cent. governed by schemes.[9] Secondly, the Act enabled local authorities to take enforcement proceedings against those who subsequently developed their land without obtaining interim development permission: unauthorised buildings could be demolished, and unauthorised uses penalised.[10]

These provisions transformed planning control. Formerly, over a quarter of the country was free from control, and all save some 4 per cent. of the rest was free from any control save the indefinite risk of a scheme ultimately being made which would be inconsistent with the development. After the Act of 1943, the whole of the country was subject to a system under which effective action could forthwith be taken against any future development carried out without permission.

II. THE TOWN AND COUNTRY PLANNING ACTS 1947–74

1. The Acts. The Town and Country Planning Act, 1947, was passed on August 6, 1947, and came into force on the "appointed day," July 1, 1948.[11] It transformed the subject by repealing virtually all the previous law and establishing a complex and far-reaching new

[9] s. 1.
[10] s. 5.
[11] S.I. 1948 No. 213.

system. This system has been amended in many important respects, but basically it remains in force today. There have been three main stages in the legislation. First, there was the Act of 1947, which was then extensively amended by the Town and Country Planning Acts, 1953, 1954 and 1959, and the Caravan Sites and Control of Development Act, 1960. Second, there was the Town and Country Planning Act, 1962, which repealed and consolidated most of the previous legislation, and then was itself amended by the Town and Country Planning Acts 1963 and 1968, and by the Control of Office and Industrial Development Act 1965. Third, there was again repeal and consolidation, this time by the Town and Country Planning Act 1971, which is now the principal Act; but this too has been amended, mainly by the Town and Country Planning (Amendment) Act 1972, the Land Compensation Act 1973 and the Town and Country Amenities Act 1974.[12] The central administration of these Acts is now under the Secretary of State for the Environment, in place of the Minister of Housing and Local Government and other Ministers with similar functions.

2. Development

(*a*) *Meaning.* A large part of planning control is based on the term " development." This is defined as meaning—

(i) " the carrying out of building, engineering, mining or other operations in, on, over or under land," or

(ii) " the making of any material change [13] in the use of any buildings or other land." [14]

Many of the expressions in the definition are themselves defined by the Act, though the only phrase which need be mentioned here is " engineering operations," which includes " the formation or laying out of means of access to highways." [15] This, coupled with the other provisions controlling development, made it possible to repeal the Restriction of Ribbon Development Act, 1935, and treat the control of ribbon development as an integral part of planning law instead of as a separate system. The Act makes it clear that it is development to begin using one dwelling-house as two or more separate dwelling-houses,[16] or to extend dumps of refuse or waste materials.

(*b*) *Exceptions.* On the other hand, " development " does not include improvements or alterations to a building which do not materially affect its external appearance, the use of any buildings or

[12] For planning purposes the Acts of 1971, 1972 and 1974 are cited as the Town and Country Planning Acts 1971 to 1974: Act of 1974, s. 13.
[13] See *Guildford R. D. C.* v. *Fortescue* [1959] 2 Q.B. 112 (intensification of use not a change). [14] Act of 1971, s. 22.
[15] *Ibid.*, s. 290. [16] See *Ealing Corporation* v. *Ryan* [1965] 2 Q.B. 486.

other land within the curtilage of a dwelling-house for any purpose incidental to the enjoyment of the dwelling-house as such, the use of any land for agricultural purposes, and any change from one use to another use within the same class in the eighteen classes of use set out in the Town and Country Planning (Use Classes) Order 1972,[17] *e.g.*, from one kind of shop to another (subject to certain exceptions), or from a theatre to a cinema. The Act further provides in effect that the definition does not include certain cases of reverting to a former use, including resuming the normal use where the land was subject to a temporary use on the appointed day, and reverting to the last use of the land before the appointed day in cases where the land was unoccupied on the appointed day.[18]

3. Planning permission

(*a*) *Permission required.* The general rule is that any person who proposes to develop land must first obtain planning permission from the local planning authority (*i.e.*, the appropriate county council or district council) or from the Secretary of State.[19] On an application for planning permission, the local planning authority must have regard to the development plan (mentioned below) and to any other material considerations, and may grant planning permission, either unconditionally or subject to " such conditions as they think fit," or may refuse planning permission.[20] In some cases permission may be granted even if the development is contrary to the provisions of the development plan.[21] Any conditions must fairly and reasonably relate to the development proposed,[22] and must not be wholly unreasonable; thus a condition may be *ultra vires* and so void if it requires the applicant to dedicate part of his land as a highway without compensation,[23] or if it takes away pre-existing rights of his without compensation,[24] or if it requires him to undertake some of the local authority's own housing obligations.[25] If a condition which is funda-

---

[17] Act of 1971, s. 22; S.I. 1972 No. 1385.
[18] Act of 1971, s. 23.
[19] Act of 1971, ss. 1, 23, 24; Local Government Act 1972, s. 182; *Att.-Gen.* v. *Smith* [1958] 2 Q.B. 173; but see *Francis* v. *Yiewsley and West Drayton U. D. C.* [1958] 1 Q.B. 478 as to retrospective permission.
[20] Act of 1971, s. 29.
[21] *Ibid.*, s. 31; S.I. 1973 No. 31, art. 12.
[22] *Fawcett Properties Ltd.* v. *Buckingham C. C.* [1961] A.C. 636, applying *Pyx Granite Co. Ltd.* v. *Ministry of Housing and Local Government* [1958] 1 Q.B. 554 (affirmed on other grounds [1960] A.C. 260); and see Act of 1971, s. 30 (conditions relating to other land).
[23] *Hall & Co. Ltd.* v. *Shoreham-by-Sea U. D. C.* [1964] 1 W.L.R. 240.
[24] *Minister of Housing and Local Government* v. *Hartnell* [1965] A.C. 1134 (reduction in number of caravans which could be put on the land; contrast *post*, p. 1093); but see *Kingston-upon-Thames L. B. C.* v. *Secretary of State for the Environment* [1973] 1 W.L.R. 1549.
[25] *R.* v. *Hillingdon L. B. C., ex p. Royco Homes Ltd.* [1974] Q.B. 720.

mental to the planning permission is void, the permission itself is also void.[26] Though a refusal of permission may be a very serious matter for the landowner, no compensation is payable except in a limited class of cases.[27]

(b) *Benefit of planning permission.* The benefit of a planning permission enures for the benefit of the land and all who are interested in it.[28] The precise terms of the permission (and in some cases the planning application) may be of great importance, and they sometimes give rise to difficult questions of construction; careful drafting is accordingly required.[29] Mutually inconsistent planning applications in respect of the same land may be made, but, if granted, the landowner may, by acting on one, make it impossible thereafter to act on the other.[30] Further, the local planning authority may by order revoke or modify a planning permission at any time before the building or other operations that it authorises have been completed or any change of use that it authorises has been made. Such an order, unless unopposed, requires confirmation by the Secretary of State; and compensation is usually payable.[31] Again, subject to confirmation by the Secretary of State, a local planning authority may order the discontinuance of any use of land or the alteration or removal of any building or works, even though fully authorised by a planning permission; but compensation is payable.[32]

(c) *General Development Order.* The Town and Country Planning General Development Order 1973 [33] grants the requisite planning permission to any development falling within the twenty-three classes specified in the Order, subject to certain conditions, *e.g.,* relating to the creation of traffic hazards. Thus the Order authorises development such as various enlargements and alterations of dwelling-houses (including the erection of a garage), certain temporary uses and the erection of certain temporary buildings, the installation or erection on industrial premises of certain industrial plant or erections, and the erection of various buildings and structures by various public authorities. In these cases, therefore, no application to the local planning authority for planning permission need be made.

(d) *Applications.* Applications for planning permission must be made to the local planning authority in the prescribed form.[34] An

---

[26] *Kent C. C.* v. *Kingsway Investments (Kent) Ltd.* [1971] A.C. 72.
[27] See *post,* p. 1102.   [28] Act of 1971, s. 33.
[29] See, *e.g., Crisp from the Fens* v. *Rutland C. C.* (1950) 1 P. & C.R. 48; *Miller-Mead* v. *Minister of Housing and Local Government* [1963] 2 Q.B. 196; *Wilson* v. *West Sussex C. C.* [1963] 2 Q.B. 764.
[30] *Pilkington* v. *Secretary of State for the Environment* [1973] 1 W.L.R. 1527.
[31] Act of 1971, ss. 45, 46; *post,* pp. 1103, 1104.   [32] *Ibid.,* s. 51; *post,* p. 1104.
[33] S.I. 1973 No. 31, as amended by No. 273 and 1974 No. 418 (replacing earlier Orders).
[34] Act of 1971, s. 24; S.I. 1973 No. 31, art. 5, as substituted by S.I. 1974 No. 418.

applicant who does not own the fee simple or a tenancy of the land must now usually give prior notice of any application to the owners and tenants [35]; and in certain cases of offensive development (*e.g.*, slaughter houses) any application must be advertised.[36] Each local planning authority must maintain a public register of planning applications and decisions [37]; this is distinct from the local land charges register. Nevertheless, planning permissions are often granted before neighbouring owners know that they have been applied for, so that they are unable to make representations against the grant of permission.[38] Sometimes, however, the Secretary of State calls in for decision by himself [39] an application thought likely to be controversial, and then holds a public inquiry before deciding the case.

A person who proposes to carry out any activity on land may seek and obtain from the local planning authority a determination whether planning permission must be obtained; and he may appeal to the Secretary of State and (on a point of law) to the High Court against an adverse decision.[40]

(*e*) *Industrial and office development.* In the case of much industrial and office development, there is an overriding requirement which must be satisfied before an application for planning permission can even be made. This requirement enables the Secretary of State to exercise a detailed control over the proper distribution of industry and of office employment.

(1) I.D.C. Before applying for planning permission to erect an industrial building or to change the use of a building to industrial use, an "industrial development certificate" ("I.D.C.") must be obtained from the Secretary of State.[41] This requirement applies in effect to such districts and such sizes and classes of industrial development as the Secretary of State prescribes. It now applies to all classes of industrial development [42]; but no certificate is required if the industrial floor space created by the development will not exceed 5,000 square feet in Greater London and the home counties, 15,000 square feet in certain specified industrial areas, or 10,000 square feet elsewhere in England and Wales,[43] or if, whatever the size, the

---

[35] Act of 1971, s. 27.   [36] *Ibid.*, s. 26; S.I. 1973 No. 31, art. 8.
[37] Act of 1971, s. 34; S.I. 1973 No. 31, art. 17, as substituted by S.I. 1974 No. 418.
[38] Nor have they any *locus standi* to seek a declaration that the permission is invalid: *Gregory* v. *Camden London Borough Council* [1966] 1 W.L.R. 899.
[39] Under Act of 1971, s. 35.
[40] Act of 1971, ss. 53, 247.
[41] *Ibid.*, ss. 66–72, 85, 86; Act of 1972, s. 5.
[42] Act of 1971, ss. 67, 68; S.I. 1966 No. 1034.
[43] Act of 1971, ss. 68, 69; S.I. 1974 No. 2028. What is to be said of an Order which specifies one group of these areas by means of a bare reference to three statutory instruments, two of which were not thought of sufficient importance even to be printed in the official annual bound volumes of statutory instruments?

development is in a development area,[44] where it is desired to encourage industry.

(2) O.D.P. Before applying for planning permission for the erection, extension or alteration of an office building, or for a change of use to office premises, an " office development permit " (" O.D.P. ") must be obtained from the Secretary of State.[45] This requirement applies in effect to such districts and sizes of office development as the Secretary of State prescribes. It now applies to the "metropolitan region " (which has a radius of some 30 or 35 miles from the centre of London) and also to the more densely populated areas of England and Wales [46]; but it does not apply where the office floor space to be created does not exceed 10,000 square feet.[47]

(f) *Caravan sites.* Caravan sites were notoriously hard to control under the general law of town and country planning, and so an additional system of control was imposed by the Caravan Sites and Control of Development Act, 1960.[48] Whereas the mere development of land without planning permission is no offence, the Act of 1960 makes it an offence in most cases to use land as a caravan site without a site licence granted by the local authority.[49] An applicant entitled to the benefit of planning permission to use land as a caravan site is entitled to have a site licence granted to him, though this may and usually will be subject to conditions imposed in the public interest.[50] Such conditions must fairly and reasonably relate to the physical use to be made of the caravan site, as by preventing overcrowding or poor sanitation, and so cannot, for example, impose a system of rent control [51]; but under this head [52] a condition which limits the number of caravans on the site is not bad merely because it takes away existing rights without compensation.[53]

(g) *Appeals.* If the local planning authority refuses planning permission, or grants it subject to conditions, the applicant may appeal to the Secretary of State [54]; there is no appeal against the grant of permission. The Secretary of State must give the appellant and

44 Act of 1971, s. 68; S.I. 1972 No. 904.
45 Act of 1971, ss. 73–86; Act of 1972, s. 5.
46 See S.I. 1965 No. 1564; 1966 No. 888; 1969 No. 173; 1970 No. 1823; 1974 No. 1054.
47 S.I. 1970 No. 1824.
48 See the account of the old law and the new in *Mixnam's Properties Ltd.* v. *Chertsey U. D. C.* [1964] 1 Q.B. 214 at 235 *et seq.,* per Diplock L.J.
49 Caravan Sites and Control of Development Act, 1960, ss. 1, 2, 1st Sched. Part I of the Act (ss. 1–30) was not included in the consolidating Acts of 1962 and 1971.
50 Caravan Sites and Control of Development Act, 1960, ss. 3, 5.
51 *Chertsey U. D. C.* v. *Mixnam's Properties Ltd.* [1965] A.C. 735.
52 Contrast *ante,* p. 1090.
53 *Esdell Caravan Parks Ltd.* v. *Hemel Hempstead R. D. C.* [1966] 1 Q.B. 895.
54 Act of 1971, s. 36.

the local planning authority an opportunity of being heard by a person appointed by him, and usually there is a public local inquiry at which any person who wishes will be heard.[55] Many of the less substantial types of appeal (*e.g.*, for permission to erect not more than 30 dwelling-houses) may instead be decided by a person appointed by the Secretary of State to hear the appeal,[56] usually an inspector. The Secretary of State (or the inspector) may decide the case as if the application had been made to him in the first place,[57] and so, *e.g.*, may even replace a conditional permission by a refusal.[58] The decision on appeal is final, except that any person aggrieved by the decision may apply to the High Court if (but only if) the decision is *ultra vires* or the applicant has been substantially prejudiced by a failure to comply with the Act.[59] A person who complains of the grant of planning permission to his neighbour is not a " person aggrieved " for this purpose.[60] For an *ultra vires* decision *certiorari* and *mandamus* also lie.[61]

Any person aggrieved by a condition attached to a caravan site licence may appeal to a magistrates' court, which may vary or cancel the condition if satisfied that it is " unduly burdensome." [62]

4. Development plans

(*a*) *The development plan.* Under the Act of 1947, each local planning authority was bound to survey its area and prepare a development plan for it by July 1, 1951, showing the proposed development of it.[63] After being approved by the Minister, these plans, with their detailed maps, were to be reconsidered every five years. They provided a prophecy of the planning permissions likely to be granted and those likely to be refused. Unlike planning schemes under the old law (which ceased to have effect) the plan itself does not authorise any development, and it is as necessary to obtain planning permission after the plan came into force as it was before. The whole country was thus covered by a uniform system of control which resembled the former interim development control in a strengthened form.

---

[55] For the procedure, see S.I. 1974 Nos. 419, 420.
[56] Act of 1971, s. 36, 9th Sched. ; S.I. 1972 No. 1652.
[57] Act of 1971, s. 36; and see *ante*, p. 1092.
[58] See, *e.g.*, James v. *Secretary of State for Wales* [1968] A.C. 409.
[59] Act of 1971, ss. 242, 245.
[60] *Buxton* v. *Minister of Housing and Local Government* [1961] 1 Q.B. 278.
[61] *R.* v. *Hillingdon L. B. C., ex p. Royco Homes Ltd.* [1974] Q.B. 720.
[62] Caravan Sites and Control of Development Act, 1960, s. 7. See *Esdell Caravan Parks Ltd.* v. *Hemel Hempstead R. D. C.* [1966] 1 Q.B. 895.
[63] Act of 1947, Part II (ss. 5–11) ; see now Act of 1971, 5th Sched.

(b) *Structure plans and local plans.* The preparation and quinquennial revision of development plans for the entire area of each
local planning authority, with the detailed maps and public inquiries
into objections, proved cumbersome and time-consuming, and so the
Act of 1968 [64] introduced a more flexible two-tier system, which is
now contained in the Act of 1971 [65] and applies to all local planning
authorities.[66] In place of a single detailed development plan for the
area, each local planning authority must now, after instituting a
survey of its area, prepare a " structure plan " for it. This in the
main consists of a written statement of the general proposals of
planning policy for the area, with diagrams and illustrations but no
map; and it requires approval by the Secretary of State, after considering any objections duly made to it.[67] In addition, the local
planning authority may prepare " local plans " for particular parts
of their area, and these will include a detailed map and a written statement. A local plan must be prepared for any area indicated as an
" action area " in the structure plan. Objections to a local plan will
be considered by the local planning authority and not the Secretary
of State.[68] Both structure plans and local plans may be altered from
time to time,[69] but there is no obligatory quinquennial review.[70] The
structure plan and any local plan, with their approvals and any
alterations, will, when in force, together constitute the development
plan, in place of the existing unitary development plan.[71]

5. Enforcement notices

(a) *The notice.* The local planning authority may serve an
enforcement notice in respect of any breach of planning control, *i.e.*,
the carrying out of any development without the requisite permission,
or any failure to comply with any conditions or limitations to
which a permission was subject. The notice must be served on the
owner and the occupier [72] of the land, and anyone else materially
affected. It must specify the matters complained of, the steps
required to be taken to remedy the breach (*e.g.*, to discontinue a use or
remove a structure [73]), and the period for compliance, calculated from
the date specified in the notice as being the date when it takes effect;
and this must be not less than twenty-eight days after service of

[64] Part I (ss. 1–14).
[65] Part II (ss. 6–21).
[66] Act of 1971, s. 21; S.I. 1974 Nos. 1069, 1070. There are modifications for
Greater London: see s. 19, 4th Sched.
[67] Act of 1971, ss. 6–9; and see Local Government Act 1972, ss. 182, 183.
[68] Act of 1971, ss. 11–14.
[69] *Ibid.*, ss. 10, 15.
[70] For the details of structure and local plans, see S.I. 1972 No. 1154.
[71] Act of 1971, s. 20.
[72] See *Stevens* v. *Bromley L.B.C.* [1972] Ch. 400 (permanent caravan occupation).
[73] See *Iddenden* v. *Secretary of State for the Environment* [1972] 1 W.L.R. 1433.

the notice.[79] A notice is a nullity unless it specifies both the period and the date.[80] The notice must also be served within four years of the breach of planning control, unless it consists of a change in the use, in which case there is no time limit.[81]

(b) *Appeal.* An appeal against an enforcement notice lies to the Secretary of State on a variety of grounds, and he has wide powers. He may quash the notice (*e.g.*, if planning permission was unnecessary or had in fact been granted, or the notice was not served in time), he may correct immaterial defects or errors in it, or vary it in favour of the appellant (as where its requirements are excessive or unreasonable), or he may grant planning permission.[82] A further appeal lies to the High Court, but only on a point of law.[83] A notice will be held void if it does not fairly comply with the statutory requirements.[84] But in many cases this point, like other objections, can be taken only on an appeal to the Secretary of State,[85] and in any case the courts now reject purely technical complaints and require merely that the notice should tell the landowner fairly what he has done wrong and what he must do to remedy it.[86] While an appeal is pending, the enforcement notice does not take effect.[87]

(c) *Non-compliance.* If a valid enforcement notice is not complied with, there is liability to prosecution and a fine of £400, with a further £50 a day for continued disobedience after conviction; and except where the notice requires discontinuance of a use, the local planning authority may also enter the land, take any steps required by the notice (*e.g.*, by removing offending structures), and recover the cost from the owner of the land.[88]

(d) *Stop notice.* A local planning authority which has served an enforcement notice which has not yet taken effect may also serve a " stop notice," prohibiting the carrying out of operations on the land (but not a mere change of use) in breach of planning control; and a breach of such a notice is an offence.[89] Compensation is usually

[79] Act of 1971, s. 87.   [80] *Burgess* v. *Jarvis* [1952] 2 Q.B. 41.
[81] Act of 1971, s. 87: but the four years' rule applies to a change to use as a single dwelling-house (*ibid.*).
[82] Act of 1971, s. 88; see, *e.g.*, *Miller-Mead* v. *Minister of Housing and Local Government* [1963] 2 Q.B. 196; *Howard* v. *Secretary of State for the Environment* [1974] 2 W.L.R. 459.
[83] Act of 1971, s. 246; see, *e.g.*, *East Barnet U. D. C.* v. *British Transport Commission* [1962] 2 Q.B. 484; *Bendles Motors Ltd.* v. *Bristol Corporation* [1963] 1 W.L.R. 247.
[84] *East Riding C. C.* v. *Park Estate (Bridlington) Ltd.* [1957] A.C. 223.
[85] Act of 1971, s. 243. See *Square Meals Frozen Foods Ltd.* v. *Dunstable Corporation* [1974] 1 W.L.R. 59 (declaration).
[86] *Munnich* v. *Godstone R. D. C.* [1966] 1 W.L.R. 427. But see *Bambury* v. *Hounslow London Borough Council* [1966] 2 Q.B. 204 (date essential).
[87] Act of 1971, s. 88.
[88] *Ibid.*, ss. 89, 91. On indictment, the fine is unlimited.
[89] Act of 1971, s. 90: the penalty is as for enforcement notices, *supra*.

payable if the stop notice proves to have been unjustified.[90] Further, where the statutory provisions provide an insufficient deterrent, the local planning authority may be able to persuade the Attorney-General to obtain an injunction.[91]

6. Additional controls. As well as regulating development, the Acts provide certain additional controls.[92]

(a) *Listed buildings.* The Secretary of State compiles lists of buildings of special architectural or historic interest, and it is an offence to demolish, alter or extend a listed building without a listed building consent, or to damage such a building.[93] The local planning authority may also serve a " building preservation notice " for any unlisted building of this nature, and for not more than six months this has the same effect as if the building had been listed.[94]

(b) *Trees.* The local planning authority may make a tree preservation order prohibiting the cutting of specified trees without consent.[95]

(c) *Conservation areas.* Any area of special architectural or historic interest with a character or appearance which ought to be preserved may be designated a " conservation area " by the local planning authority. No building in such an area may be demolished without consent, and trees in the area are protected as if they were subject to a tree preservation order.[96]

(d) *Waste land.* The local planning authority may serve a notice on the owner and occupier of any garden, vacant site or other open land which is in a condition that causes serious injury to amenity, requiring the abatement of the injury.[97]

(e) *Advertisements.* There is an elaborate system for controlling advertisements on land.[98]

B. Financial Control

Certain financial aspects of town and country planning now require explanation. The most important of these is the concept of " betterment," a term which has replaced " unearned increment." Before

---

[90] Act of 1971, s. 177.
[91] See, *e.g., Att.-Gen.* v. *Smith* [1958] 2 Q.B. 173.
[92] Compensation is payable in some cases: see *post,* p. 1103.
[93] Act of 1971, ss. 54–57; S.I. 1972 No. 1362, 1974 No. 1336.
[94] Act of 1971, s. 58.
[95] *Ibid.,* ss. 60–62. Breach of an order is an offence: s. 102. See also Act of 1974, s. 10.
[96] Act of 1974, ss. 1, 8; S.I. 1972 No. 1362, 1974 No. 1336.
[97] Act of 1971, s. 65; and see ss. 104–107 for penalties and rights of appeal. See also *Britt* v. *Buckinghamshire C. C.* [1964] 1 Q.B. 77.
[98] Act of 1971, ss. 63, 64, 109; S.I. 1969 No. 1532; 1972 No. 489; 1974 No. 185.

there was any effective planning control, Parliament recognised the principle that in a rise in land values, " there is an element which is due to the general progress of the community, and is independent of any labour or expenditure of the owner or his predecessors upon the land itself, and that this so-called ' unearned increment ' forms a proper subject for specific taxation." [99] Planning control added emphasis to this view; for the " betterment " to the value of land caused by the grant of planning permission results not from the endeavours of the landowner but from a decision made in the public interest on planning grounds. The concept of unearned increment gave rise (*inter alia* [1]) to " increment value duty," a tax at the rate of 20 per cent. on the " increment value " of land, imposed by the Finance (1909–10) Act, 1910 [2]; but the collection of this highly controversial tax proved uneconomic, and in 1920 it was repealed.[3] With the growth of planning control, the principle was revived and extended so as to form part of the planning system [4]; but the practical difficulties proved great, and there were strong divergences of social and political views.

The more recent legislation on the subject falls into three stages, each marked by a change of government. First, by the Town and Country Planning Act, 1947, an elaborate scheme was established whereby the development rights of landowners were in effect transferred to the State in return for compensation, and a " development charge " was imposed on future development of land. In 1952, after this system had operated for some four and a half years, the liability for development charges was abolished, and the right to compensation drastically changed. Second, by the Land Commission Act 1967 a " betterment levy " was imposed in respect of development; but after operating for some three and a half years, this was abolished in 1970. Third, the Finance Act 1974 imposed a " development gains tax," which is now in force. A common feature of all three systems is great complexity; only the broadest indications of their nature can be given here. The systems differ in many respects, not least in that what was initially a specialised and balanced system of compensation

---

[99] *Lumsden* v. *I.R.C.* [1914] A.C. 877 at 903, *per* Lord Moulton.
[1] *Ibid.*, at p. 904, referring to " undeveloped land duty," " reversion duty," and " mineral rights duty."
[2] Part I.
[3] Finance Act, 1920, s. 57, 4th Sched. See also the Finance Act, 1931, Part III, imposing a tax of one penny in the pound on land values; by the Finance Act, 1932, s. 27, this tax was suspended before it took effect, and by the Finance Act, 1934, ss. 27, 30, 4th Sched., it was abolished. But s. 28 of the Finance Act, 1931 (corresponding to the Finance (1909–10) Act, 1910, s. 4) still provides that conveyances of the fee simple and leases for 7 years or more (and assignments of such leases) are not properly stamped unless they bear a stamp denoting that the instrument has been produced to the Commissioners of Inland Revenue; and particulars of it must be delivered to them.
[4] See generally the Uthwatt Report (1942, Cmd. 6386).

and liabilities for landowners has now been replaced by what in essence is merely an addition to the ordinary system of taxing capital gains from land.

I. ACQUISITION OF DEVELOPMENT RIGHTS BY THE STATE

A major innovation of the Town and Country Planning Act, 1947, was that the State in effect expropriated nearly all the potential development rights of land in Great Britain, thus removing much of the financial incentive from speculative development. This was achieved mainly by subjecting most forms of development carried out after the appointed day to liability for a " development charge," *i.e.*, a sum of money payable to a new Government Department called the Central Land Board. In order to provide some compensation for the losses caused by the Act (and, in particular, by the new liability for development charges) a fund of £300 million was to be set aside and apportioned as between Scotland on the one hand and England and Wales on the other.[5] The two heads of development charges and compensation will be considered in turn, with certain exceptional cases under a third head. Although the first two heads roughly balanced each other, they differed in that development charges were payable every time new development was carried out, whereas compensation was to have been paid once for all time.

1. Development charges

(*a*) *The charge.* The general rule was that before carrying out any development for which planning permission was required, a development charge assessed by the Central Land Board had to be either paid or secured to the satisfaction of the Board.[6] The charge was equal to the increase in the value of the land caused by the planning permission in question. Thus if a plot of land was restricted to its existing agricultural use, it might be worth £100, whereas the grant of planning permission for the erection of houses on that land might increase its value to £1,000. In such a case, the development charge for the erection of those houses would have been £900.

(*b*) *Exemptions.* Many minor forms of development were exempted from liability to development charges, including many changes of use, and alterations to existing buildings which did not increase the cubic content by more than one-tenth.[7] Many of the exemptions were for cases in which no express planning permission

---

[5] Act of 1947, s. 58.
[6] *Ibid.*, s. 69.
[7] *Ibid.*, 3rd Sched. ; S.I. 1948 Nos. 955, 1188.

had to be obtained, but the two categories were by no means identical. Thus for the use of a single dwelling-house as two or more separate dwellings, planning permission was requisite, but no development charge was payable.

2. Compensation out of the funds

(a) *The funds.* In addition to the main fund of £300 million already mentioned, there was an unlimited fund to augment value payments under the War Damage Act, 1943 (*i.e.*, payments for the loss in value caused by war damage), in cases where the value payment had been assessed on the footing that the site was worth more than its value under the new system, *i.e.*, stripped of its development value; each fund was to be distributed by the Central Land Board in accordance with a Scheme to be made by the Treasury.[8]

(b) *Claims.* Claims on the £300 million fund, which could not be made after June 30, 1949, were based on the " development value " of the land in question. The development value of an interest in land was found by taking the " unrestricted " value of that interest (*i.e.*, the value under the law in force before the Act of 1947), and subtracting from it the " restricted " value of that interest, *i.e.*, the value of that interest on the footing that the only forms of development for which planning permission would ever be given were the eight minor forms of development set out in the Third Schedule to the Act.[9] And unless the development value so calculated exceeded both £20 an acre and one-tenth of the restricted value of the interest, no claim could be made.[10] The claims vested in those who owned a fee simple or leasehold interest on the appointed day; but subject to giving notice to the Central Land Board before 1953, the right to receive payment was transmissible as personal property.[11]

3. Special cases.

There were a number of special cases which were excepted both from liability for development charges and from the right to claim compensation out of the £300 million fund.[12] These cases included land which on July 1, 1948, was held by a local authority for its purposes or by a charity which used it in connection with its charitable purposes, and land which on July 1, 1948, was already fully ripe for development.

---

[8] Act of 1947, ss. 58, 59.
[9] *Ibid.*, s. 61.
[10] *Ibid.*, s. 63.
[11] *Ibid.*, ss. 60, 64; S.I. 1948 No. 902, r. 7; and see *Re Chance's W. T.* [1962] Ch. 593.
[12] Act of 1947, Part VIII (ss. 75–92).

4. Abolition of the system: Act of 1954

(*a*) *Defects in the Act of 1947.* However attractive in principle, the system of development charges imposed by the Act of 1947 did not work well in practice. In theory, if land had a value of £100 for its existing use and £1,000 for building purposes, the landowner should have been willing to accept £100 for it, and should have looked to the £300 million fund for the remaining £900; and the purchaser, faced with a development charge of £900, should have been unwilling to pay more than £100 for the land. In practice, such land might well change hands at a price of £700 or more, the purchaser recouping himself in the price of the houses which he built. And apart from these inflationary tendencies, there was the rebellion of human nature against paying large sums of money as development charges when the assessment of the correct amount was open to wide variations of expert opinion and yet there was no appeal from the official assessment. The Town and Country Planning Act, 1953, accordingly halted the existing system by abolishing the development charge system as from November 18, 1952, and repealing the provisions for making payments out of the £300 million fund, before any such payments had in fact been made. The Town and Country Planning Act, 1954, provided in detail for the consequences of these repeals, and those provisions of the Act which are still in force have now been consolidated in the Act of 1971.

(*b*) *Basis of the Act of 1954.* The Act of 1954, which was of great complexity, was concerned solely with the financial side of town and country planning. With few exceptions, the provisions of the Act were built round claims which had been duly made on the £300 million fund under the Act of 1947; if no such claim had been established, the Act in general provided no benefits. The main idea was to use as much as was necessary of each established claim as compensation to owners of a " claim holding " (*i.e.*, the benefit of an established claim against the £300 million fund) [13] who before 1955 had suffered certain forms of detriment from the Act of 1947, and then to attach the balance to the land concerned (under the title of " unexpended balance of established development value " [13a]), and use it as a fund for compensating the landowner for the time being for certain future planning losses. The claim thus provided a " ceiling " for payments under the Act, and once it has been exhausted, the Acts in general provide for no further payments.

(*c*) *Payments for past events.* The Act of 1954 [14] provided for

[13] Act of 1954, s. 2 ; Act of 1962, s. 91.
[13a] See now Act of 1971, ss. 135, 136.
[14] See Act of 1954 ss. 3–11, Part V.

payments out of claim holdings in respect of certain burdens borne by landowners under the Act of 1947. Thus development charges that had been paid were repaid, and payments were made to those whose land had been compulsorily acquired at prices which excluded its development value. Such claims must all have been dealt with long ago, and they are now of importance only in so far as they have reduced the "unexpended balance of established development value" which remains attached to the land.

5. Compensation for planning restrictions

(a) *Right to compensation.* The basic principle is that no compensation is payable to a landowner for the adverse effect of the planning statutes or decisions made under them. But this rule is subject to two important qualifications. These depend on a list of eight relatively minor forms of development set out in the Eighth Schedule to the Act of 1971. They include alterations to buildings which do not increase the cubic content by more than one-tenth (or, if greater, 1,750 cubic feet in the case of a dwelling-house), extending an existing use of part of land or a building to an additional part not exceeding one-tenth of the original part, and making a change of use to another use in the same general class of uses, as defined. Any form of development which is outside the narrow categories of this Schedule is known as "new development." [15] The general rule is that compensation for the refusal of planning permission for new development is payable only to the extent of any unexpended balance of established development value that the land has,[16] whereas any compensation that is payable for certain other development or other events is payable irrespective of any such unexpended balance.[17]

(b) *Unexpended balance: new development.* If planning permission for new development is refused (or is granted subject to conditions) compensation for any depreciation in the value of the land is payable by the Secretary of State up to the amount of the unexpended balance of established development value for the land.[18] But there are a number of important exceptions to this rule, and in any case the Secretary of State may review the planning decision and give a direction varying it so as to avoid or reduce the liability.[19] No compensation is payable in respect of a change of use, or if the application is premature because of priorities indicated in the development plan or deficiencies in water supply or sewerage, or if the land

---

[15] Act of 1971, s. 22.
[16] *Ibid.*, Part VII.
[17] *Ibid.*, Part VIII.
[18] *Ibid.*, ss. 134, 146; and see S.I. 1974 No. 1242.
[19] Act of 1971, ss. 38, 39, 155.

is liable to flooding or subsidence, or if the application is for the display of advertisements; nor is any compensation payable in respect of conditions as to density, lay-out, design or external appearance of buildings.[20] Compensation is also excluded if, despite the refusal, planning permission is available for other development consisting of the construction of residential, commercial or industrial buildings.[21] In cases where compensation is payable, planning applications are sometimes made in the hope that they will be refused, thereby making the unexpended balance payable. If " new development " is subsequently carried out on the land, the compensation will usually become repayable, and so when any compensation under this head is paid, a " compensation notice " will be registered in the local land charges register.[22]

(c) *Other compensation.* Whether or not there is any unexpended balance of established development value, compensation is payable by the local planning authority for the following six main classes of claim, provided the Secretary of State has made or confirmed the decision in question.

(1) PERMISSION REFUSED: for any reduction in the value of land if planning permission is refused (or granted subject to conditions) for any of the eight relatively minor forms of development set out in the Eighth Schedule to the Act of 1971 [23] except the first two, which relate mainly to making good war damage, and using a single dwelling-house as two or more separate dwellings.[24]

(2) LISTED BUILDING CONSENT REFUSED: for any reduction in value of a listed building if consent for any extension or alteration is refused (or granted subject to conditions) and the work is either not development or has planning permission under a development order.[25]

(3) TREE PRESERVATION ORDER CONSENT REFUSED: for any loss or damage resulting from the refusal (or grant subject to conditions) of any consent required under a tree preservation order, so far as the order provides for compensation.[26]

(4) REMOVAL OR DISCONTINUANCE: for any reduction in the value of land, and for disturbance, if an order is made for the alteration or

---

[20] *Ibid.,* s. 147.
[21] *Ibid.,* s. 148.
[22] *Ibid.,* ss. 158, 159. See, *e.g., Ministry of Housing and Local Government* v. *Sharp* [1970] 2 Q.B. 223.
[23] *See ante,* p. 1102.
[24] Act of 1971, s. 169.
[25] *Ibid.,* s. 171; and see s. 173 (building preservation notice). For listed buildings, see *ante,* p. 1097.
[26] Act of 1971, s. 174; *ante,* p. 1097.

removal of any authorised building, or for an authorised use of land to be discontinued or subjected to conditions.[27]

(5) REVOCATION OR MODIFICATION: for abortive expenditure (*e.g.*, in the preparation of plans) or other loss or damage if a planning permission or listed building consent is revoked or modified.[28]

(6) ADVERTISEMENTS: for expenses incurred in complying with a requirement to remove an advertisement, or discontinue the use of an advertisement site, if existing on August 1, 1948.[29]

6. Compensation on compulsory acquisition. One other manifestation of the Act of 1947 lay in the compensation payable on the compulsory acquisition of land. Under that Act, compensation was based on the " existing use " value of the land,[30] leaving the landowner with whatever claim he had against the £300 million fund. The Act of 1954 continued this basis, but added any unexpended balance of established development value to the compensation otherwise payable.[31] The Act of 1959 abolished these artificial provisions and reinstated the open market value of the land, as if sold by a willing seller, as the basis of compensation; and the Land Compensation Act, 1961, continues this basis.[32] The Act [33] makes detailed provision for the planning considerations to be taken into account for this purpose, *e.g.*, as to what grants of planning permission are to be assumed or expected. The complicated details of these provisions lie outside the scope of this book.

7. Compulsory acquisition in reverse. Although planning control often results in betterment increasing the value of land, it also often reduces the value of land, as where planning permission is refused. Apart from having the rights of compensation just considered, landowners who are adversely affected usually have no remedy: but there are two classes of case in which they can require their interests in such land to be purchased from them.

(*a*) *Useless land.* The first case is where an application for planning permission is refused (or granted subject to conditions) and the landowner can establish that the land " has become incapable of

27 *Ibid.*, s. 170; *ante*, p. 1091.
28 *Ibid.*, ss. 164, 165, 172; *ante*, p. 1091.
29 *Ibid.*, s. 176; *ante*, p. 1097.
30 See Act of 1947, s. 51; *Sampson's Executors* v. *Nottinghamshire C. C.* [1949] 2 K.B. 439.
31 Act of 1954, Part III.
32 Land Compensation Act, 1961, s. 5.
33 See also Land Compensation Act 1973, conferring, *inter alia*, wide rights to compensation on landowners injured by compulsory acquisitions or the execution of public works (*e.g.*, highway construction).

reasonably beneficial use in its existing state " [34] and cannot be rendered capable of such use by any development which has been or will be permitted by the local planning authority or the Secretary of State. He must serve a " purchase notice " on the local authority and, subject to confirmation by the Secretary of State if the local authority objects, this notice takes effect as if the local authority were acquiring the land compulsorily. Similar provisions apply where a listed building consent is refused (or granted subject to conditions), or where planning permission is revoked or modified, or where an order is made for the discontinuance of a use of land, or the alteration or removal of buildings.[35]

(b) *Blighted land*. The second case is one of " planning blight." Even before they became firm projects, planning proposals often cast a " blight " on the land affected, making it virtually unsaleable. This may occur when planning proposals in a development plan, structure plan, local plan or other document show land as being potentially required for some public authority, or a highway, or other purposes. If the owner-occupier of such land is unable to sell it except at a price substantially lower than its open market value in an unblighted state, he may serve a " blight notice " on the authority which under the planning proposal would acquire the land; and unless that authority abandons the proposal or postpones it for at least fifteen years, it must then acquire the land at its unblighted value.[36]

II. BETTERMENT LEVY

1. The levy. From November 18, 1952, to April 6, 1967, there was no development charge or any equivalent. But then the Land Commission Act 1967 set up a body known as the Land Commission to administer a " betterment levy," in place of the ordinary system of taxation, *e.g.*, of capital gains. Betterment levy was a charge or tax on any development value which was " realised " after April 6, 1967; and the six " chargeable acts or events " on which the development value was treated as being realised included selling the freehold or a leasehold interest, granting a tenancy, and commencing a project of material development.[37] Betterment levies differed from development charges in a number of respects, the most important being, first, that the rate of levy was not 100 per cent. but 40 per cent. of the develop-

---

[34] See *R. v. Minister of Housing and Local Government, ex p. Chichester R. D. C.* [1960] 1 W.L.R. 587.

[35] Act of 1971, ss. 180–191, replacing Act of 1962, ss. 129–137 and Act of 1968, s. 42.

[36] Act of 1971, ss. 192–208, replacing Act of 1962, ss. 138–152, as amended (mainly by the Act of 1968); Land Compensation Act 1973, Part V; Land Compensation Act, 1961, s. 9. The provisions are complex and subject to many qualifications.   [37] Land Commission Act 1967, s. 27.

ment value,[38] and, second, that the levy was payable by the person realising the development value,[39] who in many cases would be different from the person carrying out the development.

2. Amount of levy. In most cases the levy was charged on the " net development value," [40] ascertained by taking the open market value of the land and subtracting the " base value " and the value of any improvements to the land effected by the owner himself. Subject to many complexities, the " base value " was in essence either eleven-tenths of the current use value of the land, or, if higher, the price paid for the land by the owner, if he bought it after July 1, 1948 [41]; the extra one-tenth was intended to encourage the release of land for development. The " current use value " contrasted with the value of the land with the benefit of any planning permission that had been granted. As already mentioned, the levy was 40 per cent. of the net development value. Again, there were many exceptions and qualifications.[42]

3. Abolition of the levy. After operating for some three and a half years, betterment levy was abolished by the Land Commission (Dissolution) Act 1971 [43] in respect of any event occurring after July 22, 1970; and provision was made for the dissolution of the Land Commission and the transfer of its remaining functions to other bodies. Dealings in land once more became subject to the ordinary system of taxation, *e.g.*, for capital gains [44]; and as betterment levy was far more like a tax than the system of development charges under the Act of 1947 had been, with its claims against the £300 million fund, the transition was much less complicated.

III. DEVELOPMENT GAINS TAX

1. The tax. For some three and a half years after the abolition of betterment levy there was no special charge or tax on dealings in land. But then the Finance Act 1974 [45] imposed a new tax on disposals of land which is generally known as " development gains tax." Disposals of land were already subject to the ordinary capital gains tax at a flat rate of 30 per cent. under the Finance Act 1965, and this liability continues. Development gains tax, however, is imposed not at a flat rate but at graduated income tax rates which

---

[38] See *ibid.*, s. 28 ; S.I. 1967 No. 544.   [39] Land Commission Act 1967, s. 36.
[40] *Ibid.*, ss. 29–31.
[41] See *ibid.*, 4th, 5th and 6th Scheds.
[42] The Act occupied 191 pages of the statute book.
[43] s. 1.   [44] Finance Act 1971, s. 55, 9th Sched.
[45] Part III (ss. 38–48), and 3rd–10th Scheds.

increase with the amount; and the Finance Act 1974 subjects first lettings of buildings after development to both forms of tax. The Act applies to all disposals after December 17, 1973.[46]

2. Amount of tax. In broad terms, the amount which is liable to development gains tax is calculated by first taking the highest of three " base values." These base values consist of, first, the cost of acquiring and improving the land, plus 20 per cent.; second, the " current use value " of the land when it is disposed of, plus 10 per cent.; and, third, the cost of acquiring and improving the land plus the increase in its current use value since it was acquired (or since April 6, 1965, if it was acquired before then).[47] " Current use value " is much the same as " existing use value," *i.e.*, the value of the land without planning permission for any save minor forms of development, such as alterations of buildings not increasing the cubic content of the original buildings by more than 10 per cent.[48] The highest of these base values is then deducted from the price realised for the land. The result is the " development gain." On this, development gains tax must be paid at income tax rates,[49] though an individual who has held the land long enough may spread the gain over a period of up to four years.[50] If the development gain is less than the amount on which capital gains tax under the ordinary rules would be payable, capital gains tax is in addition payable on the difference. Both forms of tax are highly complex, and they are subject to many important qualifications and exceptions, *e.g.*, for an individual's principal or only private residence.[51]

C. *Effect on the Law of Property*

The Act of 1947 and its successors have made no change in the fundamentals of English land law. When the Act of 1947 was passed, it was even contended that the fee simple in land no longer existed, but instead the landowner merely had a fee simple in the existing or permitted use of land.[52] These contentions had no real basis, however, and although at first they persuaded some, it is now generally accepted that despite the great practical importance of planning control the fee simple in land remains the same fee simple as before.[53]

---

[46] Finance Act 1974, s. 38.
[47] *Ibid.*
[48] *Ibid.*, 3rd Sched.
[49] *Ibid.*, s. 38.
[50] *Ibid.*, 7th Sched.
[51] *Ibid.*, s. 38, in effect applying Finance Act 1965, s. 29.
[52] See (1948) 13 Conv.(N.S.) 36 (H. Potter).
[53] See 3rd edn. of this book, p. 1085.

" All that has happened is that the fruits of ownership have become less sweet; but that is nothing new in land law." [54]

Sect. 3. Agricultural Control

1. Control of farming. The Agriculture Act, 1947, put on the Statute-book a number of important provisions which had been enforced during the war of 1939–45 mainly by means of Defence Regulations. In so far as these provisions affected the law of land-lord and tenant, they were re-enacted in consolidated form by the Agricultural Holdings Act, 1948, which is considered later.[55] However, certain of the provisions affected all concerned with agricultural land, including owner-occupiers. Before the war there had been no direct control over the efficiency of farming operations; the community had no redress if valuable farming land was misused by a lazy owner-occupier, or by an incompetent tenant with a supine landlord. The legislation contained in the Act of 1947 was designed to safeguard the public interest and to ensure that the large subsidies given to agriculture were not wasted.

2. Former powers. To that end, the Act of 1947 put into the hands of the Minister of Agriculture, Fisheries and Food (who in practice acted in most of these matters through County Agricultural Executive Committees [56]) three main weapons to enforce the standards of good estate management for owners (especially in the provision and maintenance of fixed equipment) and of good husbandry for occupiers. These standards remain on the Statute-book, but by virtue of the Agriculture Act, 1958,[57] the weapons ceased to exist on August 1, 1958. The powers were, first, to make supervision orders; secondly, to give directions (*e.g.*, as to providing buildings, or as to methods of cropping the land), disobedience to which was punishable by fine; and thirdly, as a last resort, after a supervision order had been in force for at least a year, to dispossess the occupier.[58] These powers were subject to a number of safeguards.[59]

3. Present powers. The repeal of these disciplinary provisions means that the State once again relies mainly on social and economic

---

[54] Megarry, *Lectures on the Town and Country Planning Act, 1947* (1949), p. 104; see generally at pp. 102–109; *Belfast Corporation* v. *O.D. Cars Ltd.* [1960] A.C. 490; (1960) 76 L.Q.R. 198 (R.E.M.).

[55] See *post*, p. 1117.

[56] See (1952) 68 L.Q.R. 363 (R. M. Jackson) for a discussion of these bodies, now abolished: *post*, p. 1117.

[57] s. 1.

[58] Agriculture Act, 1947, ss. 12, 14, 16, 17.

[59] *Ibid.*, ss. 12, 15, 16, 17, 74.

factors (which are no less effective today than in 1939) to secure the efficient use of agricultural land. Under the Act of 1958 there is, however, a limited power for the Agricultural Land Tribunal to give a direction to the landlord of an agricultural holding to provide fixed equipment necessary to enable the tenant to comply with statutory requirements (*e.g.*, for producing clean milk); but disobedience to such a direction is now merely treated as a breach of the terms of the tenancy, and as empowering the tenant to do the work himself and recover the cost from the landlord.[60]

Sect. 4. Protection of Tenants

The modern tendency is to enact legislation designed to protect tenants against their landlords. At common law, the matter was in general one of contract: provided a landlord did not contravene the terms of his bargain, he might at will evict his tenant, or under the threat of eviction secure his agreement to pay an increased rent of whatever amount he could exact. Although a number of matters such as fixtures, emblements and the like are of importance, the two crucial matters in any scheme for protecting tenants are protection against eviction, and control of rent: and these subjects will be dealt with here.

Apart from recent general " rent freezes " imposed for economic reasons,[61] legislation has been piecemeal. There were some relatively mild provisions concerning agricultural land, beginning with the Agricultural Holdings (England) Act, 1875, but otherwise no real system of control existed until the first of the Rent Acts was enacted in 1915. There is little common design to be found in the systems established by the various statutes: as will be seen, protection against eviction is provided by a wide variety of devices, and so is control of rent. Each system will be summarised in turn.

A. Business Premises

Business premises were first protected [62] by Part I of the Landlord and Tenant Act, 1927. This gave the tenant the right to a new lease (or compensation in lieu thereof) provided he could establish that by reason of the carrying on by him or his predecessors in title at the premises of a trade or business for not less than five years, goodwill had become attached to the premises by reason whereof

---

[60] Agriculture Act, 1958, s. 4. For tenancies of agricultural holdings, see *post*, p. 1117.

[61] See *post*, p. 1154.

[62] Apart from nearly a year's protection under the Rent Acts: Act of 1920, s. 13.

they could be let at a higher rent than they otherwise would have realised.[63] The mere building up of goodwill was thus not enough, for often the tenant, on leaving, would carry much of it with him. What had to be shown was goodwill which remained adherent to the premises after the tenant had gone.[64] This was usually difficult to prove and, indeed, normally impossible except in the case of shops; and tenancies of professional premises were outside these provisions. The procedural requirements for making a valid claim under the Act were complicated, too, and many claims failed on purely technical grounds. These relatively ineffectual provisions were replaced by the far-reaching terms of the Landlord and Tenant Act, 1954, Part II,[65] which contains no requirement of adherent goodwill, and prohibits contracting out[66] except when authorised by the court.[67] The closely restricted right for business tenants to claim compensation for improvements, subject to certain conditions, continues in an amended form.[68]

1. Tenancies within Part II of the Act of 1954. Part II of the Landlord and Tenant Act, 1954, applies to " any tenancy where the property comprised in the tenancy is or includes premises which are occupied by the tenant and are so occupied for the purposes of a business carried on by him or for those and other purposes." [69] These terms have wide meanings. Thus " ' business ' includes a trade, profession or employment and includes any activity carried on by a body of persons, whether corporate or unincorporate," [70] so that, for example, shops, offices, factories, clubs,[71] hospitals,[72] surgeries, laboratories and schools [73] are all included; and " premises " can include bare land, *e.g.*, gallops for training racehorses.[74] Personal occupation is not required, so that the tenant may occupy premises by means of those who are genuinely his servants[75]; but the tenant

---

63 Landlord and Tenant Act, 1927, ss. 4, 5.
64 *Whiteman Smith Motor Co. Ltd.* v. *Chaplin* [1934] 2 K.B. 35 (goodwill analysed into dog, cat, rat and rabbit, with only the cat as " adherent ").
65 As amended by L.P.A. 1969.
66 See *Joseph* v. *Joseph* [1967] Ch. 78 (contract for future surrender).
67 L. & T.A., 1954, s. 38, as amended by L.P.A. 1969, s. 5. See, *e.g.*, *Tottenham Hotspur Football & Athletic Co. Ltd.* v. *Princegrove Publishers Ltd.* [1974] 1 W.L.R. 113.
68 *Post*, p. 1117.
69 L. & T.A., 1954, s. 23 (1).
70 *Ibid.*, s. 23 (2).
71 *Addiscombe Garden Estates Ltd.* v. *Crabbe* [1958] 1 Q.B. 513 (lawn tennis club).
72 See *Hills (Patents) Ltd.* v. *University College Hospital Board of Governors* [1956] 1 Q.B. 90.
73 But not a voluntary Sunday school carried on by an individual: *Abernethie* v. *A. M. & J. Kleiman Ltd.* [1970] 1 Q.B. 10.
74 *Bracey* v. *Read* [1963] Ch. 88.
75 *Teasdale* v. *Walker* [1958] 1 W.L.R. 1076.

of a block of flats who has sublet the flats does not thereby " occupy "
the premises for business purposes, unless the degree of his control
and provision of services suffices to constitute occupation.[76]
" Tenancy " is widely defined, and includes any tenancy created by a
tenancy agreement,[77] though other provisions of Part II of the Act
show that a tenancy at will is not included.[78]

2. Exceptions. Certain tenancies are expressly excluded from
Part II of the Act. They are as follows.[79]

(*a*) *Tenancies of agricultural holdings.*[80]

(*b*) *Mining leases.*

(*c*) *Rent Acts*: tenancies under which the Rent Acts protect the
tenant from eviction (or would do so, but for the rent being so low [81]).

(*d*) *Licensed premises*: tenancies of public-houses and similar
licensed premises, as distinct from bona fide hotels and restaurants
(the test being the proportion of the receipts attributable to alcoholic
beverages), and other places, such as theatres, where the licence is
merely ancillary.[82]

(*e*) *Service tenancies*: tenancies granted by reason of the tenant
holding an office, appointment or employment, and ending or terminable with it, provided the tenancy was granted before the commencement of the Act, or, if subsequently, was granted by written instrument
which expressed the purpose for which the tenancy was granted.

(*f*) *Short tenancies*: any tenancy granted for a term certain not
exceeding six months unless it contains provisions for renewing the
term or extending it beyond six months from the commencement,
or the tenant and any predecessor in his business have together been
in occupation for more than twelve months.[83]

3. Security of tenure. Security of tenure is given by the simple
provision that a tenancy within Part II " shall not come to an end
unless terminated in accordance with the provisions of this Part of
this Act." [84] An ordinary notice to quit given by the landlord thus

---

[76] Contrast *Bagettes Ltd.* v. *G. P. Estates Ltd.* [1956] Ch. 290 with *Lee-Verhulst
(Investments) Ltd.* v. *Harwood Trust* [1973] Q.B. 204.
[77] L. & T.A., 1954, s. 69 (1).
[78] *Wheeler* v. *Mercer* [1957] A.C. 416; *Mansfield & Sons Ltd.* v. *Botchin* [1970]
2 Q.B. 612.
[79] L. & T.A., 1954, s. 43.
[80] See Agricultural Holdings Act, 1948, s. 1; Agriculture Act, 1958, 1st Sched.,
para. 29.
[81] See *post*, p. 1128.
[82] Finance Act, 1959, s. 2, 2nd Sched., para. 5.
[83] L.P.A. 1969, s. 12.
[84] L. & T.A., 1954, s. 24 (1).

has no effect, and a tenancy for a fixed term will continue indefinitely after the expiration of the term.[85] A tenancy may still be determined by a notice to quit given by the *tenant*, or by surrender or forfeiture, or by the forfeiture of a superior tenancy[86]; but apart from cases such as these, the special machinery of the Act must be used. In operating this, it is to be noted that " landlord " is for these purposes defined as the next immediate reversioner who for the time being has either the fee simple or a tenancy which will not come to an end within fourteen months.[87]

The machinery falls under two heads.

(*a*) *Determination by landlord.* The landlord may determine the tenancy by giving not less than six nor more than twelve months' notice in the statutory form,[88] to expire not earlier than the date when, apart from the Act, the tenancy could have been determined by notice to quit, or would have expired.[89] The date of expiration thus need not be an anniversary or the end of a complete period of the tenancy; it merely must not be too early. On receiving such a notice, the tenant may claim a new tenancy if[90]—

(i) within two months he gives the landlord notice in writing that he is not willing to give up possession of the premises, and also

(ii) not less than[91] two nor more than four months after receiving the notice he applies to the county court (or Chancery Division, if the rateable value exceeds £5,000)[92] for a new tenancy.

(*b*) *Determination by tenant.* A tenant who wishes to leave the premises may determine the tenancy by an ordinary notice to quit, as at common law,[93] or, if the tenancy is for a fixed term, by three

---

85 Despite *Castle Laundry (London) Ltd.* v. *Read* [1955] 1 Q.B. 586, there seems to be no " business statutory tenancy " comparable to statutory tenancies under the Rent Acts (*post*, p. 1134), for the wording and machinery of the two sets of legislation are quite different: see (1955) 71 L.Q.R. 329 (R.E.M.). Compare *Weinbergs Weatherproofs Ltd.* v. *Radcliffe Paper Mill Co. Ltd.* [1958] Ch. 437 at 445. See also *Scholl Mfg. Co. Ltd.* v. *Clifton (Slim-Line) Ltd.* [1967] Ch. 41.

86 L. & T.A., 1954, s. 24 (2): but see L.P.A. 1969, s. 4 (notice to quit, or surrender, ineffective if during first month).

87 L. & T.A., 1954, s. 44; see *Piper* v. *Muggleton* [1956] 2 Q.B. 569; *Bowes-Lyon* v. *Green* [1963] A.C. 420. For special provisions for joint tenancies, see s. 41A, added by L.P.A. 1969, s. 9.

88 S.I. 1957 No. 1157; 1969 No. 1771; 1973 No. 792.

89 L. & T.A., 1954, s. 25 (1), (2), (3), (4). See *Sunrose Ltd.* v. *Gould* [1962] 1 W.L.R. 20.

90 L. & T.A., 1954, ss. 25 (5), 39 (2), (3).

91 The landlord may waive his right to object to an earlier notice: *Kammins Ballrooms Co. Ltd.* v. *Zenith Investments (Torquay) Ltd.* [1971] A.C. 850.

92 L. & T.A., 1954, s. 63 (2); Administration of Justice Act 1973, s. 6, Sched. 2; R.S.C., Ord. 97; C.C.R., Ord. 40. For criticisms of the machinery of the Act (some of which have since been met), see (1959) 75 L.Q.R. 180 (R.E.M.).

93 L. & T.A., 1954, s. 24 (2).

months' notice in writing to expire at the end of the term, or on any quarter day thereafter.[94] If, on the other hand, he wishes to have a new tenancy in place of his existing tenancy, he must serve on the landlord a request for a new tenancy in the statutory form.[95] This must specify a date for the commencement of the new tenancy not less than six nor more than twelve months ahead, and not earlier than the date on which the existing tenancy would expire or could be determined.[96] The tenant's application to the court for the new tenancy must also be made not less than two nor more than four months after he has made the request for a new tenancy.[97] But these provisions are confined to tenancies for a term certain exceeding a year, or for a term certain and thereafter from year to year[98]; a tenant under an ordinary periodic tenancy cannot make a request for a new tenancy, although he may claim a new tenancy if the landlord serves notice on him under the previous head.

4. Opposition to a new tenancy. The court is bound to grant a new tenancy unless the landlord establishes one or more of the seven statutory grounds of opposition; and the landlord is confined to such of the grounds as are stated or indicated[99] in the notice given by him or his predecessor in title[1] to determine the tenancy, or in a notice served on the tenant within two months of receiving his request for a new tenancy.[2] The seven grounds are as follow[3]—

(*a*) *Disrepair*: the tenant ought not to be granted a new tenancy in view of the state of repair of the " holding " (*i.e.*, the premises let, excluding any part not occupied by the tenant or a service tenant of his[4]) due to the tenant's failure to comply with his repairing obligations.

(*b*) *Rent unpaid*: the tenant ought not to be granted a new tenancy in view of his persistent delay in paying rent.

(*c*) *Breaches*: the tenant ought not to be granted a new tenancy in view of other substantial breaches by him of his obligations under the tenancy, or for any other reason connected with his use or management of the holding, including all his conduct *qua* tenant.[5]

---

[94] *Ibid.*, s. 27. But see L.P.A. 1969, s. 4: *supra*, n. 86.
[95] S.I. 1957 No. 1157; 1973 No. 792.
[96] L. & T.A., 1954, s. 26 (2).
[97] *Ibid.*, s. 29 (3).
[98] *Ibid.*, s. 26 (1).
[99] See *Bolton's (House Furnishers) Ltd.* v. *Oppenheim* [1959] 1 W.L.R. 913.
[1] *A. D. Wimbush & Son Ltd.* v. *Franmills Properties Ltd.* [1961] Ch. 419; *Marks* v. *British Waterways Board* [1963] 1 W.L.R. 1008; *Sevenarts Ltd.* v. *Busvine* [1968] 1 W.L.R. 1929.
[2] L. & T.A., 1954, ss. 25 (6), 26 (6), 30 (1).
[3] *Ibid.*, s. 30 (1).
[4] *Ibid.*, s. 23 (3).
[5] *Eichner* v. *Midland Bank Executor & Trustee Co. Ltd.* [1970] 1 W.L.R. 1120.

(*d*) *Alternative accommodation*: the landlord has offered and is willing to provide or secure the provision of suitable alternative accommodation on reasonable terms.

(*e*) *More valuable as a whole*: the premises are part of larger premises held by the landlord under a tenancy and the tenant ought not to be granted a new tenancy because the landlord could obtain a substantially greater rent for the property as a whole than for the parts separately.

(*f*) *Demolition or reconstruction*: " on the termination of the current tenancy the landlord intends to demolish or reconstruct [6] the premises comprised in the holding or a substantial part [7] of those premises [8] or to carry out substantial work of construction on the holding or part thereof and that he could not reasonably do so without obtaining possession of the holding." [9] The landlord cannot succeed on this ground of opposition if he has a contractual right to enter and do the intended work,[10] or if the tenant is willing to enable the landlord to carry out the intended work [11] without unduly inter-fering with the tenant's business by including such a right in the new tenancy or by accepting a new tenancy of only part of the holding.[12]

(*g*) *Own occupation*: " on the termination of the current tenancy the landlord intends to occupy the holding for the purposes, or partly for the purposes, of a business to be carried on by him therein, or as his residence." It suffices if the landlord will share occupation with another,[13] or if the occupier will be a company controlled by the landlord [14] or, where the landlord is a company, a company in the same group of companies.[15] But this head is not available to a land-lord whose interest [16] was purchased [17] or created 'less than five years before the termination of the current tenancy.[18]

---

[6] Compare *Percy E. Cadle Ltd.* v. *Jacmarch Properties Ltd.* [1957] 1 Q.B. 323 with *Joel* v. *Swaddle* [1957] 1 W.L.R. 1094.

[7] See *Bewlay (Tobacconists) Ltd.* v. *British Bata Shoe Co. Ltd.* [1959] 1 W.L.R. 45.

[8] *i.e.,* so much of the holding as is capable of being demolished: *Housleys Ltd.* v. *Bloomer-Holt Ltd.* [1966] 1 W.L.R. 1244.

[9] *i.e.,* as of right, and not merely by the tenant's permission: *Whittingham* v. *Davies* [1962] 1 W.L.R. 142.

[10] *Heath* v. *Drown* [1973] A.C. 498.

[11] See *Decca Navigator Co. Ltd.* v. *G. L. C.* [1974] 1 W.L.R. 748.

[12] L. & T.A., 1954, s. 31A, added by L.P.A. 1969, s. 7.

[13] *Willis* v. *Association of Universities of the British Commonwealth* [1965] 1 Q.B. 140; and see *Method Development Ltd.* v. *Jones* [1971] 1 W.L.R. 168 (absence of intention to use small part immaterial).

[14] L. & T.A., 1954, s. 30 (3), added by L.P.A. 1969, s. 6.

[15] L. & T.A., 1954, s. 42 (3).

[16] See *Artemiou* v. *Procopiou* [1966] 1 Q.B. 878.

[17] See *H. L. Bolton (Engineering) Co. Ltd.* v. *T. J. Graham & Sons Ltd.* [1957] 1 Q.B. 159.

[18] L. & T.A., 1954, s. 30 (2); see *Diploma Laundry Ltd.* v. *Surrey Timber Co. Ltd.* [1955] 2 Q.B. 604.

5. Intention. These last two heads both depend on what the land-lord " intends." It is now settled that what is required is that at the date of the hearing [19] there should be not a mere hope or aspiration, or an exploration of the possibilities, but a genuine, firm and settled intention, not likely to be changed, to do something which the land-lord has a reasonable prospect of bringing about.[20] If the landlord is a limited company, a formal resolution of the board of directors is neither essential [21] nor conclusive [22] as to the company's intention, which must be ascertained by considering all the relevant circum-stances; and similarly for a local authority.[23] But an undertaking to the court to take the requisite steps (*e.g.*, to demolish or reconstruct the premises, or occupy them for business purposes) will, if given by a responsible person or body, normally establish the necessary fixity of intention to take those steps.[24] A landlord who cannot rely upon the last head (own occupation) because of the five years' rule may still succeed on the previous head (demolition or reconstruction) if his intention is genuine and not merely colourable; for the existence of one ground does not exclude all others,[25] and " motive is something quite different from intention." [26] Provided the landlord retains control of the demolition or reconstruction, it matters not that it is carried out by some other person, *e.g.*, a contractor or a building lessee.[27]

6. Terms of new tenancy. When premises are first let to a business tenant there are no restrictions on the rent or other terms of the tenancy required by the landlord. But when the tenant succeeds in claiming a new tenancy under the Act, the rent and other terms are determined by the court. The rent is to be that at which the holding " might reasonably be expected to be let on the open market by a willing lessor " but disregarding any effect of the occupation of the holding by the tenant or his predecessors in title, any goodwill due to them, and any improvements made by any

---

[19] *Betty's Cafés Ltd.* v. *Phillips Furnishing Stores Ltd.* [1959] A.C. 20.
[20] *Reohorn* v. *Barry Corporation* [1956] 1 W.L.R. 845; *Gregson* v. *Cyril Lord Ltd.* [1963] 1 W.L.R. 41.
[21] *H. L. Bolton (Engineering) Co. Ltd.* v. *T. J. Graham & Sons Ltd., supra.*
[22] *Fleet Electrics Ltd.* v. *Jacey Investments Ltd.* [1956] 1 W.L.R. 1027.
[23] *Poppett's (Caterers) Ltd.* v. *Maidenhead Corporation* [1971] 1 W.L.R. 69.
[24] *Espresso Coffee Machine Co. Ltd.* v. *Guardian Assurance Co. Ltd.* [1959] 1 W.L.R. 250.
[25] *Fisher* v. *Taylors Furnishing Stores Ltd.* [1956] 2 Q.B. 78, giving effect to the criticism of *Atkinson* v. *Bettison* [1955] 1 W.L.R. 1127, expressed at (1956) 72 L.Q.R. 21 (R.E.M.); *Betty's Cafés Ltd.* v. *Phillips Furnishing Stores Ltd., supra*; and see *Craddock* v. *Hampshire County Council* [1958] 1 W.L.R. 202.
[26] *Espresso Coffee Machine Co. Ltd.* v. *Guardian Assurance Co. Ltd., supra*, at p. 254, *per* Lord Evershed M.R. Motive, indeed, may strengthen intention.
[27] *Gilmour Caterers Ltd.* v. *St. Bartholomew's Hospital Governors* [1956] 1 Q.B. 387.

tenant (otherwise than under an obligation to the landlord) within the previous twenty-one years if the holding has been continuously let under the Act since they were made; and provision may be made for rent revision.[28] The landlord may also apply to the court for an interim rent to be fixed for the period until the new tenancy begins.[29]

In default of agreement, the duration of the new tenancy is to be whatever the court considers reasonable in all the circumstances (not exceeding fourteen years),[30] and the other terms are to be such as the court may determine having regard to the terms of the current tenancy and to all relevant circumstances,[31] *e.g.*, as to including a " break " clause,[32] or the right to display advertising signs on neighbouring premises.[33] The property to be included in the new tenancy is to be the " holding," which means the whole of the premises let,[34] excluding any part not occupied by the tenant or a servant of his employed in the business[35] at the time when the order is made.[36] But if the holding is only part of the premises included in the current tenancy the landlord (but not the tenant) may require the whole of those premises to be included.[37]

These provisions give effect to what appears to be the basic principle of the Act, namely, that a business tenant has a prima facie right to continue his business[38] indefinitely in his premises on reasonable terms.

7. Compensation for eviction. Where the only grounds on which the landlord objects to the grant of a new tenancy are one or more of the last three grounds set out above[39] (all of which are for the landlord's own benefit), the tenant is entitled, on quitting the holding, to recover compensation from the landlord. This is equal to the rateable value of the premises, or twice that sum if the tenant and his predecessors in the particular business have between them

---

[28] L. & T.A., 1954, s. 34 as amended by L.P.A. 1969, ss. 1, 2. See, *e.g.*, *Harewood Hotels Ltd.* v. *Harris* [1958] 1 W.L.R. 108.

[29] L. & T.A., 1954, s. 24A, added by L.P.A. 1969, s. 3 (a difficult provision: see *English Exporters (London) Ltd.* v. *Eldonwall Ltd.* [1973] Ch. 415). The interim rent runs from the date of the application to fix it: *Stream Properties Ltd.* v. *Davis* [1972] 1 W.L.R. 645.

[30] L. & T.A., 1954, s. 33; consider *Upsons Ltd.* v. *E. Robins Ltd.* [1956] 1 Q.B. 131; *London and Provincial Millinery Stores Ltd.* v. *Barclays Bank Ltd.* [1962] 1 W.L.R. 510 (short term if redevelopment imminent).

[31] L. & T.A., 1954, s. 35. See, *e.g.*, *Cardshops Ltd.* v. *Davies* [1971] 1 W.L.R. 591.

[32] *McCombie* v. *Grand Junction Co. Ltd.* [1962] 1 W.L.R. 581.

[33] *Re No. 1 Albemarle Street* [1959] Ch. 531; contrast *G. Orlik (Meat Products) Ltd.* v. *Hastings & Thanet B. S.* (1974) 118 S.J. 811 (parking rights on other land).

[34] *Fernandez* v. *Walding* [1968] 2 Q.B. 606.

[35] L. & T.A., 1954, s. 23 (3). See, *e.g.*, *Nursey* v. *P. Currie (Dartford) Ltd.* [1959] 1 W.L.R. 273.

[36] See *I. & H. Caplan Ltd.* v. *Caplan* [1962] 1 W.L.R. 55.

[37] L. & T.A., 1954, s. 32; L.P.A. 1969, s. 8.

[38] See *Gold* v. *Brighton Corporation* [1956] 1 W.L.R. 1291.

[39] *Ante*, p. 1114.

occupied the premises for business purposes for the previous fourteen years.[40]

8. Compensation for improvements. Under the Landlord and Tenant Act, 1927,[41] if a tenant of premises used for a trade, business or profession carries out improvements to the premises which add to their letting value, the tenant may recover compensation from the landlord on leaving. But the tenant must satisfy a number of conditions; in addition to making his claim at the right time and in due form, he must give the landlord three months' notice of his intention to make the improvement. The landlord may then exclude the tenant's right to compensation if he successfully objects to the improvement, or carries it out himself in return for a reasonable increase of rent.

B. *Agricultural Holdings*

1. Introduction. Starting with the Agricultural Holdings (England) Act, 1875, Parliament has passed a long series of Acts regulating agricultural tenancies. The earlier Acts were mainly directed to securing proper compensation for the tenant, initially for improvements, and, latterly, also if his tenancy was determined without good cause.[42] But before the Agriculture Act, 1947, there were no general provisions giving agricultural tenants security of tenure or protection as to rent, although during the war some degree of security of tenure was secured under Defence Regulations. The provisions of the Act of 1947 were consolidated with those of the Agricultural Holdings Act, 1923, in the Agricultural Holdings Act, 1948, which, as modified by the Agriculture Act, 1958 and the Agriculture (Miscellaneous Provisions) Act 1963, is the principal Act.[43] The Acts confer a variety of powers on the Minister of Agriculture, Fisheries and Food, on Agricultural Land Tribunals, and on arbitrators. In general, the Act of 1958 transferred powers of determining disputes from the Minister and the former County Agricultural Executive Committees[44] to the Tribunals, which previously had mainly appellate functions. There is a Tribunal for each of the eight areas into which England and Wales is divided for this purpose, and each Tribunal is presided over by a legally qualified chairman

---

[40] L. & T.A., 1954, s. 37, as amended by L.P.A. 1969, s. 11 ; *Cramas Properties Ltd.* v. *Connaught Fur Trimmings Ltd.* [1965] 1 W.L.R. 892.
[41] ss. 1–3, as amended by the Landlord and Tenant Act, 1954, Part III.
[42] A.H.A., 1923, s. 12.
[43] See also *ante*, p. 1108.
[44] Abolished by Agriculture (Miscellaneous Provisions) Act 1972, s. 21.

appointed by the Lord Chancellor.[45] The arbitrators (unless appointed by agreement) and the Tribunals are under the supervision of the Council on Tribunals.[46]

2. Policy of the Act of 1948. Perhaps the most important provisions of the Act of 1948 are those which confer security of tenure on the tenant. The general scheme is as follows. First, the Act continues and strengthens the policy of the earlier Acts in making a year's notice to quit at the end of a year of the tenancy requisite for the determination of every agricultural tenancy, even if it is for a fixed term which has expired; and for this purpose certain licences and short tenancies are treated as yearly tenancies. Secondly, the Act [47] prevents any such notice to quit from operating at all except in certain specified cases. Agricultural tenancies accordingly now continue indefinitely until determined on one of the grounds permitted by the Act.

3. " Agricultural holding "

(*a*) *The definition.* " Agricultural holding " is defined as meaning " the aggregate of the agricultural land comprised in a contract of tenancy," other than a service tenancy.[48] " Agricultural land " is " land used for agriculture which is so used for the purposes of a trade or business " [49]; and " agriculture " has a wide definition which includes horticulture, fruit growing, seed growing, market gardening,[50] and even grazing the horses of a riding school.[51]

(*b*) *" Contract of tenancy."* The term " contract of tenancy " is restricted to " a letting of land, or agreement for letting land, for a term of years or from year to year." [52] But where any agreement for value [53] is made after February, 1948, whereby land is let (or a licence is granted " to occupy " the land [54]) for use as agricultural land for " an interest less than a tenancy from year to year " in circumstances which otherwise would make the land an agricultural

---

45 Agriculture Act, 1947, s. 73, 9th Sched.; Agriculture Act, 1958, ss. 8, 10, 1st & 2nd Scheds.; S.I. 1959 Nos. 81, 83, as amended; S.I. 1974 No. 66, revising the areas.
46 Tribunals and Inquiries Act 1971, s. 1, Sched. 1.
47 For the original provisions, replaced by the Act of 1948, see Agriculture Act, 1947, s. 31.
48 A.H.A., 1948, s. 1 (1).
49 *Ibid.*, s. 1 (2).
50 *Ibid.*, s. 94 (1).
51 *Rutherford* v. *Maurer* [1962] 1 Q.B. 16.
52 A.H.A., 1948, s. 94 (1).
53 *Goldsack* v. *Shore* [1950] 1 K.B. 708.
54 *Harrison-Broadley* v. *Smith* [1964] 1 W.L.R. 456 (mere licence to use, not to occupy); *Bahamas International Trust Co. Ltd.* v. *Threadgold* [1974] 1 W.L.R. 1514 (right of exclusive occupation requisite). Contrast *Holder* v. *Holder* [1966] 2 All E.R. 116, affirmed on this point [1968] Ch. 353.

holding, the agreement takes effect (with the necessary modifications) as if it were an agreement for a tenancy from year to year.[55] This extension applies to a tenancy for one year,[56] but by a *casus omissus* not to a tenancy for more than one year but less than two, which is thus outside the Act of 1948.[57] Nor does the extension apply to a letting or grant which had the prior approval of the Minister of Agriculture, Fisheries and Food,[58] nor to an agreement for the letting of land (or the grant of a licence to occupy it) made " in contemplation [59] of the use of the land only for grazing or mowing during some specified period of the year " [60]; and although 364 days may be such a " period," [61] one year cannot.[62]

(*c*) *Mixed lettings.* Where agricultural land is let with non-agricultural land (*e.g.,* where pasture land and an orchard are let with an inn [63]), the question is whether as a whole the tenancy is in substance a tenancy of agricultural land [64]; the Act either applies to the tenancy as a whole or not at all, and there is no segregation of the agricultural from the non-agricultural.[65] Even a cottage and garden let for use by a farm labourer employed by the tenant may constitute an agricultural holding.[66]

4. Determination of tenancies

(*a*) *Notice to quit.* The Act of 1948 provides a uniform code for the determination of agricultural tenancies by making a notice to quit requisite in every case, and by restricting the type of notice that will satisfy the Act. As has already been seen, certain short tenancies and licences are treated as yearly tenancies. Further, a tenancy for two years or upwards does not determine at the end of the term but is continued as a tenancy from year to year unless not less than one year nor more than two years before the date fixed for the expiration of the term either party has given to the other written notice of his intention to terminate the tenancy.[67] With some exceptions, the Act

---

[55] A.H.A., 1948, s. 2 (1). See, *e.g., Verrall* v. *Farnes* [1966] 1 W.L.R. 1254.
[56] *Bernays* v. *Prosser* [1963] 2 Q.B. 592.
[57] *Gladstone* v. *Bower* [1960] 2 Q.B. 384.
[58] A.H.A., 1948, s. 2 (1). See *Finbow* v. *Air Ministry* [1963] 1 W.L.R. 697.
[59] See *Scene Estate Ltd.* v. *Amos* [1957] 2 Q.B. 205 ; contrast *Rutherford* v. *Maurer* [1962] 1 Q.B. 16.
[60] A.H.A., 1948, s. 2 (1), proviso (also excepting a sub-tenancy or sub-licence granted by a person having less than a tenancy from year to year).
[61] *Reid* v. *Dawson* [1955] 1 Q.B. 214; see (1955) 71 L.Q.R. 19 (R.E.M.). Contrast *Lory* v. *Brent L. B. C.* [1971] 1 W.L.R. 823.
[62] *Rutherford* v. *Maurer, supra.*
[63] *Dunn* v. *Fidoe* [1950] 2 All E.R. 685.
[64] *Monson* v. *Bound* [1954] 1 W.L.R. 1321.
[65] *Howkins* v. *Jardine* [1951] 1 K.B. 614.
[66] *Blackmore* v. *Butler* [1954] 2 Q.B. 171.
[67] A.H.A., 1948, s. 3 (1), replacing Agriculture Act, 1920, s. 13, and A.H.A., 1923, s. 23.

also invalidates a notice to quit [68] an agricultural holding if it purports to terminate the tenancy before the expiration of twelve months from the end of the then current year of the tenancy [69]; and this is so even if the notice is given by the tenant.[70] A notice given before the tenancy began is bad, so that if the landlord and tenant replace the existing tenancy by a new tenancy, no notice to quit already given can determine the new tenancy.[71]

(b) *Statement of grounds.* As will shortly be seen, the tenant can often serve a counter-notice which will make the landlord's notice to quit ineffective. But if the notice to quit is given on certain specified grounds, the tenant cannot serve an effective counter-notice, provided the notice to quit makes plain the ground on which the landlord is relying.[72] If the landlord's notice purports to rely on one of these grounds [73] but is insufficiently explicit, the landlord cannot then claim that the notice does not depend on any of the grounds and that the tenant ought to have replied with a counter-notice.[74]

5. Security of tenure. Subject to the above rules, the landlord is still entitled to serve [75] a notice to quit. But, with important exceptions, within one month of receiving the notice to quit the tenant may serve on the landlord a counter-notice requiring section 24 (1) of the Act of 1948 to apply to the notice to quit.[76] If he does this, the notice to quit will not take effect unless the case is one in which the Agricultural Land Tribunal has power to consent to the notice taking effect, and does so on an application by the landlord made within one month.[77] Where the notice does take effect, it determines not only the tenancy but also any sub-tenancies, irrespective of any counter-notices served by the sub-tenants on the tenant; for no provision has been made to exclude the common law rule that a sub-tenancy falls with the tenancy out of which it was derived.[78]

---

[68] Including a notice exercising an option of termination contained in the tenancy agreement: *Edell* v. *Dulieu* [1924] A.C. 38.

[69] A.H.A., 1948, s. 23 (1), replacing Agriculture Act, 1920, s. 28, and A.H.A., 1923, s. 25.

[70] *Flather* v. *Hood* (1928) 44 T.L.R. 698.

[71] *Lower* v. *Sorrell* [1963] 1 Q.B. 959; see (1963) 79 L.Q.R. 178 (R.E.M.).

[72] A.H.A., 1948, s. 24 (2); see *Budge* v. *Hicks* [1951] 2 K.B. 335; *Magdalen College, Oxford* v. *Heritage* [1974] 1 W.L.R. 441. For the grounds, see *post*, p. 1121.

[73] *Secus* if it does not: *Hammon* v. *Fairbrother* [1956] 1 W.L.R. 490.

[74] *Cowan* v. *Wrayford* [1953] 1 W.L.R. 1340; *Mills* v. *Edwards* [1971] 1 Q.B. 379.

[75] See *Newborough (Lord)* v. *Jones* [1974] 3 W.L.R. 52 (notice pushed under door).

[76] See *Mountford* v. *Hodkinson* [1956] 1 W.L.R. 422 (abusive letter); *cf. Frankland* v. *Capstick* [1959] 1 W.L.R. 204.

[77] A.H.A., 1948, s. 24 (1); S.I. 1959 No. 81, Sched., r. 2. For the procedure, see S.I. 1959 Nos. 81, 359; 1964 No. 700; 1972 No. 1207.

[78] *Lord Sherwood* v. *Moody* [1952] 1 All E.R. 389; see *ante*, p. 661.

The tenant thus has security of tenure, and the landlord's notice to quit will not take effect, except in two categories of case.

(*a*) *No security.* A tenant has no security of tenure if he either fails to serve a counter-notice, or else the case is one where he has no right to serve a counter-notice. There are eight of these cases.[79]

(1) PRIOR CONSENT: the Tribunal has previously consented to the notice being given.

(2) PLANNING PERMISSION: the land is required [80] (even if not by the landlord [80a]) for some non-agricultural use for which planning permission has been given or (in certain cases [81]) is not required.

(3) BAD HUSBANDRY: on an application made within the previous six months the Tribunal has been satisfied that the tenant is not farming in accordance with the rules of good husbandry, and has so certified.

(4) UNREMEDIED BREACH: the tenant has committed a breach of any term of his tenancy (other than a term inconsistent with good husbandry) and has failed to comply fully [82] with a written notice by the landlord in the prescribed form requiring compliance within two months (in the case of rent) or (in other cases) a specified reasonable time, being not less than six months if works of repair, maintenance or replacement have to be done.[83]

(5) IRREPARABLE BREACH: the landlord's interest in the holding has been materially prejudiced by an irreparable breach by the tenant of a term of the tenancy (other than a term inconsistent with good husbandry).

(6) BANKRUPTCY: the tenant is bankrupt or has compounded with his creditors.

(7) DEATH: the notice is given within three months after the death of " the tenant with whom the contract of tenancy was made " or, in the case of original joint tenants, the death of the last survivor.[84]

---

[79] A.H.A., 1948, s. 24 (2), as amended by Agriculture Act, 1958, and Agriculture (Miscellaneous Provisions) Act 1963, s. 19; S.I. 1964 No. 706, art. 14. For a ninth case, see Agriculture Act 1967, s. 29 (4) (Minister's notice: reshaping holdings). [80] See *Jones* v. *Gates* [1954] 1 W.L.R. 222.

[80a] *Rugby Joint Water Board* v. *Foottit* [1973] A.C. 202.

[81] See, *e.g.*, *Ministry of Agriculture, Fisheries and Food* v. *Jenkins* [1963] 2 Q.B. 319.

[82] *Price* v. *Romilly* [1960] 1 W.L.R. 1360 (partial compliance not enough); *Stoneman* v. *Brown* [1973] 1 W.L.R. 459 (late payment no compliance).

[83] See, *e.g.*, *Lloyds Bank Ltd.* v. *Jones* [1955] 2 Q.B. 298 (personal residence); *Jones* v. *Lewis* (1973) 25 P. & C.R. 375 (notice to one of two joint tenants bad); and see *Wykes* v. *Davis* [1975] 2 W.L.R. 131. For forms and procedure, see S.I. 1964 Nos. 706, 707; 1972 No. 1207. For small holdings, see Agriculture Act 1970, 4th Sched.

[84] See Agriculture (Miscellaneous Provisions) Act, 1954, s. 7.

(8) NOTICE TO SUB-TENANT: the tenant has received notice to quit and has given his sub-tenant a notice to quit which states this; the notice to the sub-tenant takes effect only if the notice to the tenant does.

If the tenant wishes to contest the reasons stated in (2), (4) or (5) above, he must within one month serve notice on the landlord requiring the matter to be settled by arbitration; otherwise he cannot challenge them.[85]

It will be seen from this list that the death of the tenant provides the only normal occasion on which the landlord retains an unrestricted right to terminate the tenancy. But where the tenancy has once devolved on death, the drafting of the Act produces the inept result that the landlord has no such right on the death of the next succeeding tenant [86]; and where the tenancy has been assigned, the equally inept result is that the relevant death is that of the assignor, not that of the assignee.[87]

(b) *Security depending on reasonableness.* If the tenant has served a valid counter-notice, the Tribunal normally has no discretion in the matter, and must withhold consent to the landlord's notice to quit taking effect; the tenant is thus protected. But in certain cases the Tribunal must consent to the landlord's notice to quit taking effect unless it appears that in all the circumstances a fair and reasonable landlord would not insist on possession.[88] The cases in which the tenant's security of tenure thus depends on the reasonableness of his being evicted are as follows.

(1) GOOD HUSBANDRY: the landlord proposes to terminate the tenancy for a purpose that is desirable in the interests of good husbandry as respects the land to which the notice relates, treated as a separate unit.

(2) SOUND MANAGEMENT: the landlord proposes to terminate the tenancy for a purpose that is desirable in the interests of sound management of the land concerned (physically, and not merely financially for the landlord [89] or the tenant [90]) or of the estate of which it forms part.

---

[85] A.H.A., 1948, s. 26; Agriculture Act, 1958, 1st Sched., para. 10; S.I. 1964 No. 706, art. 9, amended by S.I. 1972 No. 1207, Sched.; *Att.-Gen. (Duchy of Lancaster)* v. *Simcock* [1966] Ch. 1; *Magdalen College, Oxford* v. *Heritage* [1974] 1 W.L.R. 441.

[86] *Costagliola* v. *Bunting* [1958] 1 W.L.R. 580; and see *Jenkin R. Lewis & Son Ltd.* v. *Kerman* [1971] Ch. 477.

[87] *Clarke* v. *Hall* [1961] 2 Q.B. 331.

[88] A.H.A., 1948, s. 25 (1); Agriculture Act, 1958, s. 3.

[89] *National Coal Board* v. *Naylor* [1972] 1 W.L.R. 908.

[90] *Evans* v. *Roper* [1960] 1 W.L.R. 814.

(3) RESEARCH: carrying out the purpose for which the landlord proposes to terminate the tenancy is desirable for the purposes of agricultural research, education, experiment or demonstration, or for the purposes of the statutes relating to smallholdings or allotments.

(4) GREATER HARDSHIP: considering all who might be affected,[91] greater hardship would be caused by withholding consent than by granting it.

(5) NON-AGRICULTURAL USE: the landlord proposes to terminate the tenancy for the purpose of the land being used for some non-agricultural use not falling within para. (2) of the foregoing list of eight cases.

Where consent is given to the operation of the notice to quit, the Tribunal may impose conditions to secure that the land is used for the purposes stated by the landlord; and the Tribunal may subsequently vary or revoke the conditions.[92]

6. Protection as to rent. When an agricultural tenancy is first granted, the parties are free to agree whatever rent they please. However, not more frequently than once in every three years, either party may require the amount of the rent to be submitted to arbitration by an arbitrator appointed either by agreement or in default by (usually) the Minister, on the basis of the open market rent.[93] Any increase or decrease awarded by the arbitrator takes effect as from the next day on which the tenancy could have been determined by a notice to quit given when the reference to arbitration was demanded,[94] provided the arbitrator has been duly appointed before that day.[95] Accordingly, no revision of rent is possible during a tenancy for a fixed term which is not determinable by notice to quit. In addition, the landlord may increase the rent in respect of certain improvements carried out by him.[96]

7. Compensation. The tenant's rights to compensation may be put under three main heads. None of them can be excluded by any agreement to the contrary[97]; and any provision which would even by implication exclude a claim for compensation (*e.g.*, a provision for

---

[91] *Purser* v. *Bailey* [1967] 2 Q.B. 500.
[92] A.H.A., 1948, s. 25 (5), (6), as amended by Agriculture Act, 1958; see, *e.g.*, *Martin-Smith* v. *Smale* [1954] 1 W.L.R. 247 (notice effective despite breach of condition).
[93] A.H.A., 1948, s. 8, as amended by Agriculture Act, 1958, s. 2.
[94] A.H.A., 1948, s. 8.
[95] *Sclater* v. *Horton* [1954] 2 Q.B. 1.
[96] A.H.A., 1948, s. 9.
[97] *Ibid.*, s. 65 (1); compare A.H.A., 1923, s. 50.

determination at such short notice as to leave no time to claim compensation) is void.[98]

(*a*) *Compensation for disturbance.* A tenant who quits the holding in consequence of a notice to quit given by the landlord (whether or not the notice is valid [99]) is entitled to compensation for disturbance of not more than two years' rent nor less than one.[1]

(*b*) *Compensation for improvements.* When an agricultural tenant quits his holding at the end of his tenancy, he is entitled to compensation for certain improvements carried out by him, provided he has observed the necessary conditions. Such improvements fall into three main categories. First, there are certain long-term improvements (*e.g.*, planting orchards) for which the landlord's consent is required. Secondly, there are other long-term improvements (*e.g.*, the erection of buildings) for which either the landlord's consent or the Tribunal's approval is necessary. Thirdly, there are some short-term improvements (*e.g.*, the chalking or liming of land) for which neither consent nor approval is needed. The measure of compensation is the increase in value of the holding, or, in the case of a short-term improvement, the value of the improvement to an incoming tenant.[2]

(*c*) *Other compensation.* Apart from compensation for improvements and for disturbance,[3] a tenant may claim compensation for any increase in the value of the holding due to his having adopted a more beneficial system of farming than that required by his tenancy agreement, or, if none, than that practised on comparable holdings.[4] The landlord is also entitled to recover from a tenant who has quitted the holding compensation in respect of dilapidation or deterioration of the holding, or damage to it caused by failure to farm in accordance with the rules of good husbandry,[5] having due regard to the landlord's contractual obligations [6] and the condition of the property when the tenancy was granted.[7]

C. Dwellings

1. The statutes. Some sixty years ago the Increase of Rent and Mortgage Interest (War Restrictions) Act, 1915, was passed. This

---

[98] *Coates* v. *Diment* [1951] 1 All E.R. 890.
[99] *Kestell* v. *Langmaid* [1950] 1 K.B. 233.
[1] A.H.A., 1948, s. 34, replacing Agriculture Act, 1920, s. 10, and A.H.A., 1923, s. 12.
[2] A.H.A., 1948, ss. 46–51, 3rd and 4th Sched., as amended by Agriculture Act, 1958.
[3] *Supra.*
[4] A.H.A., 1948, s. 56, replacing Agriculture Act, 1920, s. 16, and A.H.A., 1923, s. 9.
[5] A.H.A., 1948, ss. 57, 58, replacing Agriculture Act, 1920, s. 19, and A.H.A., 1923, s. 10.
[6] *Barrow Green Estate Co.* v. *Walker's Executors* [1954] 1 W.L.R. 231.
[7] *Evans* v. *Jones* [1955] 1 Q.B. 58.

short statute proved to be the forerunner of a complex mass of legislation mainly designed to protect tenants of houses, flats and other residential properties against their landlords. For a long time the main body of this legislation consisted of the Rent and Mortgage Interest Restrictions Acts, 1920 to 1939, but many amendments and additions to these Acts were made, principally by the Furnished Houses (Rent Control) Act, 1946, the Landlord and Tenant (Rent Control) Act, 1949, the Housing Repairs and Rents Act, 1954, and the Rent Acts, 1957 and 1965. The Rent Act 1968 consolidated these statutes, but that Act has now been successively amended by the Housing Act 1969, the Housing Finance Act 1972, the Counter-Inflation Act 1973, and the Rent Act 1974.[8] It is not possible to give here more than an outline of the principal provisions of this important but complicated and bulky legislation.

2. The two systems. There are two essentials for any system of protecting tenants. There must be, first, protection as to possession, securing the tenant against eviction without good cause, and, second, protection as to rent, preventing the landlord from requiring more than a proper rent. From the beginning, the Rent Acts conferred both forms of protection on tenants of unfurnished dwellings, operating mainly through the county courts. Not until the Furnished Houses (Rent Control) Act, 1946, was passed was there any effective protection for tenants of furnished accommodation. That Act established a separate system, operating mainly through rent tribunals; and with many modifications that system still remains in force. For want of better terms the two systems may thus be called " court protection " and " rent tribunal protection " respectively. The former broad division into the furnished and unfurnished systems is no longer accurate or helpful, for court protection now extends to many furnished tenancies, while rent tribunal protection applies to many unfurnished tenancies.

3. Nomenclature. A number of technical terms must be mentioned at the outset. Tenancies which receive rent tribunal protection are known as " Part VI contracts "; for the provisions of the Furnished Houses (Rent Control) Act, 1946, as amended, have now been replaced by Part VI of the Rent Act 1968. References to tenancies within the " Rent Acts," and the like, are references to tenancies within the main body of the Rent Acts (now represented by the Rent Act 1968, as amended) which receive court protection. Ordinary

[8] For a modern survey of the working of the Acts, see the Report of the Francis Committee (1971, Cmnd. 4609).

tenancies, recognised as such at common law or in equity, are called
" contractual tenancies," and, if they are within the Rent Acts, they
are called " protected tenancies." [9] These contrast with " statutory
tenancies," which consist of the rights which the Rent Acts give to
tenants to remain in possession as tenants after their protected
tenancies have ended. Both protected tenancies and statutory
tenancies may exist either as " controlled tenancies " or as " regulated
tenancies," [10] the main difference being in the method of ascertaining
the maximum permitted rent.

I. COURT PROTECTION : THE RENT ACTS

(1) Application of the Acts

1. " Controlled " and " regulated " tenancies. The main body of
the Rent Acts has undergone many changes over the past sixty years,
and it is unfortunately still sometimes necessary to know something
of the history of a dwelling in order to determine the rights of landlord and tenant. Today there are two main systems of protection
under the Rent Acts, closely similar on most matters except the
method of restricting the rent. First, there are " controlled tenancies,"
rapidly diminishing in number. They remain subject to the older
system whereby the maximum rent is fixed in relation to some objective criterion. Formerly this was the " standard rent," being the rent
at which the dwelling had been let on a particular date; but since the
Rent Act, 1957, it has been the " rent limit," based on double the
gross value of the dwelling for rating purposes in 1956. Second,
there are " regulated tenancies," introduced by the Rent Act 1965.
Under these, the existing rent remains the maximum rent until it is
replaced by a " registered rent," fixed as being a fair rent by a rent
officer, or, on appeal, by a rent assessment committee. Such committees, though technically " tribunals " (*e.g.*, for the purposes of the
Council on Tribunals [11]), are quite distinct from the rent tribunals
which have jurisdiction over Part VI contracts. Whether the tenancy
is controlled or regulated, it is court protection which confers security
of tenure for tenancies within the Rent Acts.

2. Conditions for application of the Acts. The Rent Acts apply
to every " dwelling-house " of an appropriate rateable value [12] which
satisfies certain conditions.

[9] Rent Act 1968, s. 1.
[10] See Rent Act 1968, s. 7; *post*, p. 1132.
[11] Tribunals and Inquiries Act 1971, 1st Sched.
[12] See *post*, p. 1130.

(*a*) " *Dwelling-house*." " Dwelling-house " means any house (or part of a house) which is " let as a separate dwelling." [13] Thus the existence of a tenancy is essential; this requirement excludes a mere licensee from the Acts, but not a tenant at will or at sufferance. Whether the premises are let " as " a dwelling depends on the use provided for or contemplated by the tenancy agreement, or, in default, by the *de facto* user at the time in question. [14] And the letting must be as " a " (*i.e.,* one) dwelling and not as two or more dwellings. [15]

(*b*) " *Separate dwelling*." The word " separate " formerly excluded lettings where the tenant was required to share living accommodation such as a kitchen. [16] However, the Act of 1949 modified the rule, so that where the sharing is with the landlord the tenant is protected under Part VI of the Rent Act 1968, [17] and where the sharing is with other tenants, the tenant is fully protected by the Rent Acts, subject to certain modifications. [18] Further, despite the requirement that the letting must be as a " dwelling," the use of some (or even the major part) of the premises for business purposes does not exclude the Acts, [19] provided the premises are let as a dwelling, as where the tenant uses most of the house for taking in paying guests but lives in the remainder. [20] Often what is structurally a single dwelling-house contains many " dwelling-houses " for the purposes of the Rent Acts, even if it has not been physically divided into self-contained flats; for one or two rooms, with a right to share the bathroom and lavatory, may for this purpose constitute a " dwelling-house."

3. Exceptions. Certain tenancies which would otherwise fall within the Acts are nevertheless excepted from them.

(*a*) *Personal*. In some cases, the exception is personal to the landlord. Thus the Crown is not bound by the Acts, [21] nor are local authorities, new town development corporations or certain housing associations or housing trusts, [22] though as regards rents these bodies are now subject to somewhat similar restrictions as to charging only

---

[13] Rent Act 1968, s. 1.
[14] *Wolfe* v. *Hogan* [1949] 2 K.B. 194; *British Land Co. Ltd.* v. *Herbert Silver (Menswear) Ltd.* [1958] 1 Q.B. 530.
[15] *Horford Investments Ltd.* v. *Lambert* [1973] 3 W.L.R. 872.
[16] *Neale* v. *Del Soto* [1945] K.B. 144; *Goodrich* v. *Paisner* [1957] A.C. 65; contrast *Fredco Estates Ltd.* v. *Bryant* [1961] 1 W.L.R. 76.
[17] Rent Act 1968, s. 101, replacing Act of 1949, s. 7; *post,* p. 1145.
[18] Rent Act 1968, s. 102, replacing Act of 1949, s. 8.
[19] Rent Act 1968, s. 9, replacing Act of 1920, s. 12 and Act of 1939, s. 3.
[20] *Vickery* v. *Martin* [1944] K.B. 679.
[21] Rent Act 1968, s. 4, replacing Crown Lessees (Protection of Sub-Tenants) Act, 1952.
[22] Rent Act 1968, s. 5, replacing Act of 1954, s. 33.

" fair rents." [23] For housing associations there are also complex provisions designed to give tenants the same protection as to possession
as if the Rent Acts applied.[24] Exemptions under this head do not
operate in favour of other persons concerned with the property, such
as sub-tenants or purchasers.

(b) *Nature of tenancy.* Other exceptions depend on the nature of
the tenancies. Thus the Acts do not apply where the letting is rent
free or the rent is less than two-thirds of the rateable value on March
23, 1965 (or, if not rated then, when first rated).[25] Long tenancies (*i.e.*,
tenancies for over twenty-one years) were excluded from the Acts
by the Rent Act, 1957,[26] though this exclusion ceased with the Leasehold Reform Act, 1967.[27] Again, the Acts are excluded if the tenancy
was granted in order to give the tenant the right to occupy the
dwelling for a holiday, or if the tenant is pursuing or intends to
pursue a course of study provided by a specified institution and the
tenancy was granted by that institution or by another specified
institution or body.[28] The Acts are also excluded if the rent includes
payments in respect of board or attendance; as will be seen below,
payments for furniture, which were formerly in this category, no
longer have this effect.

(c) *Nature of premises.* The third group of exceptions, however,
depends on the nature or status of the premises themselves. Thus for
diverse reasons, public-houses,[29] and parsonage houses of the Church
of England [30] (*e.g.*, the ordinary rectory or vicarage), are outside
the Acts, and so, prior to the Rent Act 1965, were premises erected
after August, 1954, and separate and self-contained premises produced by conversion after that date of other premises,[31] *e.g.*, flatlets
produced by sub-dividing a large house. Agricultural holdings
occupied by farmers are also outside the Acts, though, of course,
within the Agricultural Holdings Act, 1948.[32] Lastly, although in
general any land or premises " let together with " a dwelling-house
are treated as being part of the dwelling-house, if the dwelling-house
is let together with more than two acres of agricultural land, both

[23] See Housing Finance Act 1972, Parts V and VIII. For " fair rents," see *post*,
p. 1142.
[24] See Housing Act 1974, s. 18, 3rd Sched.
[25] Rent Act 1968, ss. 2, 6.
[26] s. 21 (1).
[27] See *post*, p. 1147, for such tenancies.
[28] Rent Act 1974, s. 2; S.I. 1974 No. 1366.
[29] Rent Act 1968, s. 9.
[30] *Bishop of Gloucester* v. *Cunnington* [1943] K.B. 101.
[31] Rent Act 1968, 2nd Sched., replacing Act of 1954, s. 35; *Higgins* v. *Silverston*
[1956] 2 Q.B. 525; and see *post*, p. 1132.
[32] Rent Act 1968, s. 2.

house and land are excluded from the Acts [33]; in the case of property subject to " old control " (dealt with below) the criterion is not two acres of agricultural land, but whether the land or premises, if let separately, would have at least one quarter of the original rateable value of the house.[34]

(d) *Furnished lettings.* What are commonly called furnished lettings require separate treatment. As already indicated, the Rent Acts have long been excluded when the rent includes payment in respect of board, attendance or the use of furniture, and (except in the case of board) the amount of rent attributable thereto, having regard to the value thereof to the tenant, " forms a substantial part of the whole rent." [35] The financial nature of this test meant that the Rent Acts might not be excluded even if a house was let fully furnished, if the furniture was cheap.[36] In the case of board or attendance, this provision continues to exclude the Rent Acts; but the Rent Act 1974 now prevents it from operating in most cases of furniture. Subject to an important exception, the general rule now is that the Acts are no longer excluded merely because the rent includes payments in respect of furniture; and all furnished tenancies thus brought within the Acts are regulated tenancies.[37] The exception arises in relation to resident landlords, considered below.

(e) *Resident landlords.* Special rules apply to tenancies granted by a "resident landlord." This term is used to denote a landlord where the dwelling that is let is part of a larger building which is not a purpose-built block of flats, and throughout the tenancy (with minor qualifications) the landlord for the time being has occupied another dwelling in the same building as a residence.[38] Where after August 13, 1974, any such landlord grants such a tenancy (whether furnished or unfurnished), the tenancy is outside the Rent Acts, and remains outside so long as the landlord continues to be resident, though it constitutes a Part VI contract, even if the rent includes no payment for furniture or services.[39] But such a tenancy is not excluded from the Rent Acts if it was granted to an existing tenant of the dwelling (or of another dwelling in the same building) holding under either a protected or statutory tenancy, or else an unprotected tenancy

---

[33] *Ibid.*, ss. 1, 2.
[34] *Ibid.*, 14th Sched.
[35] *Ibid.*, s. 2, replacing Act of 1920, s. 12 and subsequent provisions; *Palser* v. *Grinling* [1948] A.C. 291.
[36] See, *e.g.*, *Woodward* v. *Docherty* [1974] 1 W.L.R. 966; contrast *Goel* v. *Sagoo* [1970] 1 Q.B. 1.
[37] Rent Act 1974, s. 1. For these tenancies, see *post*, p. 1132.
[38] Rent Act 1968, s. 5A, inserted by Rent Act 1974, 2nd Sched., Pt. I.
[39] *Ibid.*; Rent Act 1968, s. 102A, inserted by Rent Act 1974, 2nd Sched., Pt. II. For Part VI contracts, see *post*, p. 1144.

for a fixed term.[40] Where the tenancy was granted before August 14, 1974, the rule is different. If the landlord was a resident landlord on that date (even if he had never been resident before) and the tenancy is unfurnished, it will remain within the Rent Acts, while if it is furnished, then as long as the landlord continues to be resident the tenancy will remain outside the Rent Acts but continue to be a Part VI contract.[41] The ordinary rules still apply if there is no resident landlord.

4. Rateable value. The Acts have a long history of changes in the circumstances and rateable values which have determined whether a tenancy fell within their scope. In some cases today the status of a tenancy still depends on the history of the dwelling and any former tenancies of it.

(*a*) *Acts of* 1920 *and* 1923. The Act of 1920 applied if either the rateable value or the recoverable rent of the dwelling-house did not exceed £105 in London or £78 elsewhere. Under the Act of 1923, a dwelling-house was decontrolled (*i.e.*, excluded from the Acts) as soon as the landlord obtained actual possession of it, or granted the tenant a lease of a specified length. Thus on a change of tenants, the position of the new tenant would depend on whether or not the landlord had decontrolled the house.

(*b*) *Acts of* 1933 *and* 1938. The Act of 1933 drastically modified this system of gradual decontrol. All houses not then within the Acts (*e.g.*, because they were not let) were forthwith excluded from the Acts. Those still within the Acts were divided into three classes. Class A houses, with a rateable value (or recoverable rent) in April, 1931, exceeding £45 in London and £35 elsewhere, were forthwith decontrolled. At the other extreme, Class C houses, with a rateable value in April, 1931, not exceeding £20 in London and £13 elsewhere, were made undecontrollable: even if the landlord obtained actual possession, future tenants would still be protected. The intermediate group of houses, Class B, continued within the Acts, and remained subject to decontrol, *e.g.*, by the landlord obtaining actual possession. The Act of 1938 carried this process further. It decontrolled all houses not then within the Acts, and also all Upper Class B houses, *i.e.*, those with a rateable value in April 1931, exceeding £35 in London and £20 elsewhere. The remaining Class B houses (" Lower Class B ") were rendered undecontrollable, like Class C houses. Any landlord of a Lower

---

[40] Rent Act 1968, s. 5A (5), inserted by Rent Act 1974, 2nd Sched., Pt. I; and see *post*, p. 1146.
[41] Rent Act 1974, 3rd Sched.; Rent Act 1968, s. 102A, *supra*.

Class B or a Class C house who claimed to have decontrolled the house before it became undecontrollable was obliged to preserve his claim to decontrol by registering it with the local authority.

(c) *Act of* 1939: *old control and new control.* The Act of 1939 left undisturbed those houses which were still subject to the Acts; they continued to be governed by the existing law, which is usually called " old control." The Act introduced a modified system of control, usually called " new control," and applied it to all dwelling-houses which were free from old control but had a rateable value in April, 1939, not exceeding £100 in London and £75 elsewhere.[42] Thus new control might apply not only to a large house in London with a rateable value of £95 which had never before been controlled, but also to a small house with a rateable value of £10, which, having formerly been controlled, had been decontrolled under the Act of 1923. In most respects old control and new control are similar or identical. Formerly there were some important differences, especially in relation to the standard rent; but now the surviving differences are small and unimportant.

(d) *Decontrol by Rent Act,* 1957. The Rent Act, 1957, decontrolled many houses forthwith and provided for the gradual decontrol of many others. First, all houses with a rateable value on November 7, 1956, which exceeded £40 in London and £30 elsewhere were decontrolled forthwith,[43] and provision was made whereby the Minister of Housing and Local Government could by order effect further decontrol.[44] Secondly, the Rent Acts ceased to apply to any tenancy created by a lease or agreement coming into operation after July 5, 1957,[45] however low the rateable value of the premises. This provision did not apply, however, where the new tenancy was granted to the sitting tenant and the premises comprised in the old tenancy and the new were the same, or had at least a part in common. But except in such cases, control attached to the tenancy existing on July 6, 1957, rather than to the premises; and as such tenancies were gradually replaced by others, so control came to an end. The impact of this decontrol was lessened by certain provisions giving some degree of temporary protection[46]; and decontrolled premises will now usually fall within

---

[42] Act of 1939, s. 3.
[43] Rent Act, 1957, s. 11. For a general summary of the Act, see Megarry, *The Rent Act, 1957.*
[44] Rent Act, 1957, s. 11, repealed by Act of 1965, 7th Sched. See now *post,* p. 1133.
[45] *Ibid.*
[46] See Rent Act, 1957, ss. 13, 14, 15, 4th Sched.; Landlord and Tenant (Temporary Provisions) Act, 1958.

the provisions of the Rent Act 1968 (replacing the Rent Act 1965) which relate to regulated tenancies.[47]

(e) *Recontrol by the Rent Act 1965*

(1) CONTROL, DECONTROL AND RECONTROL. The general pattern of earlier legislation was that rent control was imposed and expanded to meet war-time shortages, and then was gradually attenuated as days of peace brought relief. In the last decade, however, social and political pressures have intervened; and the pattern was changed by the Rent Act 1965. By 1965, many tenancies had escaped from the system of control described above, either because the rateable value was too high, or because the tenancy had been created after the Rent Act, 1957, had come into force, or because the premises had been erected or converted after the commencement of the Act of 1954.[48] Where these were the only reasons why the tenancy was outside the Acts, the Rent Act 1965 and subsequent Acts protected the tenancy, provided the rateable value did not exceed certain amounts.

(2) RATEABLE VALUE. The Rent Act 1965 conferred protection on a tenancy if the rateable value of the dwelling on March 23, 1965 (or when first rated, if later), did not exceed £400 in Greater London or £200 elsewhere; and this still applies.[49] Now, however, a dwelling is within the Acts, whether or not it had been previously excluded by the above limits, if its rateable value either on March 22, 1973 (or when first rated, if later), did not exceed £600 in Greater London or £300 elsewhere, or else on April 1, 1973 (or when first rated, if later), did not exceed £1,500 in Greater London or £750 elsewhere.[50] These changes not only allow for increased levels in rating assessments, many of which came into force on April 1, 1973, but also bring more dwellings within the Acts.[51]

5. " Control " and " regulation "

(a) *Regulated tenancies.* The protection conferred by the Rent Act 1965 was basically the same as that provided by the previous Acts, with the important difference that there was an entirely new system for ascertaining the maximum rent. Tenancies remaining subject to the former system are known as " controlled tenancies," and those brought within the new system are called " regulated

---

[47] See *post*, p. 1133.
[48] *Ante*, pp. 1128, 1131.
[49] Rent Act 1968, ss. 1, 6, replacing Rent Act 1965, ss. 1, 43 ; Counter-Inflation Act 1973, s. 14.
[50] Counter-Inflation Act 1973, s. 14.
[51] Allowing for changed levels of valuation, there is an increase of some 50 per cent. in the value of houses to which the Acts now apply, compared with the Rent Act 1968.

tenancies." The power of the Minister (now the Secretary of State for the Environment) to effect further decontrol by an Order approved by Parliament has been abolished,[52] but in any area or areas he may by such an Order release all regulated tenancies from regulation.[53]

(b) *Conversion of controlled tenancies into regulated tenancies.* Most controlled tenancies either have already been converted into regulated tenancies, or else soon will be. The Housing Finance Act 1972 makes two provisions for such conversions.

(1) RATEABLE VALUE. On April 29, 1973, all controlled tenancies of dwellings with a rateable value on March 31, 1972, of not less than £95 in Greater London and £60 elsewhere were automatically converted into regulated tenancies; and there is a similar conversion by stages for groups of dwellings with successively lower rateable values at six-monthly intervals from July 1, 1973, to July 1, 1975,[54] the intervals avoiding undue stress on rent officers and rent assessment committees. But these provisions do not apply to any dwelling which at the relevant date is subject to a notice or order declaring it to be unfit.

(2) QUALIFICATION CERTIFICATE. If the landlord obtains a " qualification certificate " for the house from the local authority, any controlled tenancy of it thereupon becomes a regulated tenancy.[55] Such a certificate certifies that the house is provided with all the " standard amenities " [56] (relating to washing and sanitary facilities), that it is in good repair (disregarding internal decorative repair), and that it is in all other respects fit for human habitation.[57]

(2) Protection as to Possession

The ordinary law sufficiently protects a tenant against eviction as long as his tenancy exists. But once it has ended, whether by notice to quit, effluxion of time or otherwise, he is liable to be evicted unless statute otherwise provides. The Rent Acts provide protection by prohibiting the court from making an order for possession except on

---

[52] Rent Act 1965, s. 11, 7th Sched., repealing Rent Act, 1957, s. 11; and see *ante*, p. 1131.
[53] Rent Act 1968, s. 100, replacing Rent Act 1965, s. 12.
[54] Housing Finance Act 1972, s. 35; S.I. 1973 No. 752. But after a limited postponement (see S.I. 1974 No. 615) there has now been a general postponement of all 1975 conversions until December 31, 1975: S.I. 1974 Nos. 1884, 1909 (for rateable values less than £70 in Greater London and £35 elsewhere).
[55] Housing Finance Act 1972, s. 27, replacing Housing Act 1969, s. 43.
[56] See Housing Act 1969, s. 7, 1st Sched., now replaced by Housing Act 1974, s. 58, 6th Sched.
[57] Housing Finance Act 1972, s. 27, replacing Housing Act 1969, s. 43. The detailed procedure is laid down in Part III of each Act. See also *post*, p. 1154.

specified grounds, and by giving the tenant the right to remain in possession despite the termination of his tenancy. The Acts thus bring into being what is usually called a " statutory tenancy," in contrast with the " contractual tenancy " which has come to an end.

1. Statutory tenancy. A statutory tenancy is the right of a tenant to remain in possession under the Rent Acts, despite the termination of his contractual tenancy, on all the terms of the contractual tenancy which are not inconsistent with the Acts, until the court makes an order for possession against him.[58] A statutory tenancy is not really a " tenancy " at all, in common law sense of the word: the tenant has no estate or interest in the land, but a mere personal right of occupation.[59] He cannot dispose of his statutory tenancy by assignment or by will, and it will not vest in his trustee in bankruptcy.[60] But he now has a limited statutory power, exercisable only with the landlord's consent, to substitute another tenant in his place without thereby creating a new contractual tenancy.[61] A statutory tenancy is always a regulated tenancy if the previous protected tenancy was regulated, whereas if it was controlled, the statutory tenancy will usually be controlled, but may be regulated.[62]

2. Determination. A statutory tenancy will cease to exist [63] if the tenant ceases to occupy the premises as his home,[64] or as one of his homes.[65] Mere temporary absences are immaterial; but once an absent tenant has lost either his *animus revertendi* (intention of returning) or his *corpus possessionis* (visible indication of his *animus*, such as the presence on the premises of some caretaker on his behalf), his statutory tenancy is at an end.[66] If a house is totally destroyed, any statutory tenancy perishes with the house, whereas a contractual tenancy would continue to exist in the ruins.[67] A statutory tenancy is thus an anomaly which fits into no recognised category of property law. If a protected or statutory tenant dies, his widow, if residing with him at his death, or otherwise any member [68] of his family who has resided with him for at least the previous six months,

---

58 Rent Act 1968, ss. 10, 12, replacing Act of 1920, s. 15, and Act of 1933, s. 3.
59 *Roe* v. *Russell* [1928] 2 K.B. 117 at 131.
60 *Sutton* v. *Dorf* [1932] 2 K.B. 304.
61 Rent Act 1968, s. 14, replacing Rent Act, 1957, s. 17.
62 See Rent Act 1968, s. 7, 2nd Sched.
63 *John M. Brown Ltd.* v. *Bestwick* [1951] 1 K.B. 21.
64 *Skinner* v. *Geary* [1931] 2 K.B. 546; contrast *Haines* v. *Herbert* [1963] 1 W.L.R. 1401.
65 *Hallwood Estates Ltd.* v. *Flack* (1950) 66 T.L.R. (Pt. 2) 368; and see *Herbert* v. *Byrne* [1964] 1 W.L.R. 519.
66 *Brown* v. *Brash* [1948] 2 K.B. 247.
67 *Ellis & Sons Amalgamated Properties Ltd.* v. *Sisman* [1948] 1 K.B. 653.
68 Not two or more members: *Dealex Properties Ltd.* v. *Brooks* [1966] 1 Q.B. 542.

becomes statutory tenant in his place [69]; any contractual tenancy vested in anyone else is suspended while the statutory tenancy lasts.[70] Formerly no second transmission could occur [71] but now this is permitted, and the tenancy is in every case a regulated tenancy even if formerly it was a controlled tenancy.[72]

3. Grounds for possession. The Rent Acts are restrictive, not enabling.[73] If a contractual tenancy still exists, the landlord must establish that he is entitled to possession under it, *e.g.*, by virtue of a forfeiture clause.[74] Where this is so, or where the tenancy is statutory, the Acts still prohibit the courts from making an order for possession against the tenant except in specified cases. There are two categories.[75] First, there are those cases, applicable to all tenancies within the Acts, in which an order for possession can be made only if the landlord satisfies the court that in all the circumstances of the case it is reasonable to do so. Some of these cases are based on misconduct by the tenant, while others look to the needs of the landlord or the existence of alternative accommodation. Second, there are those cases, applicable only to regulated tenancies, in which the court is bound to make an order for possession, irrespective of reasonableness. These cases, of more recent origin, are based on the landlord requiring possession for a particular purpose of which the tenant was given written warning before his tenancy began.

(*a*) *Cases dependent upon reasonableness.* An order for possession may be made in the following cases if the overriding requirement of reasonableness is satisfied.[76]

(1) BREACH: rent lawfully due has not been paid, or any other obligation of the tenancy [77] which is consistent with the Acts has been broken.

(2) NUISANCE: the tenant, his lodger or sub-tenant has been guilty of conduct which is a nuisance or annoyance to adjoining occupiers, or has been convicted of illegal or immoral user of the premises.[78]

---

[69] Rent Act 1968, 1st Sched., replacing Act of 1920, s. 12, as amended.
[70] *Moodie* v. *Hosegood* [1952] A.C. 61, a striking instance of judicial legislation: see (1951) 67 L.Q.R. 505 (R.E.M.).
[71] *Summers* v. *Donohue* [1945] K.B. 376; *Brown* v. *Conway* [1968] 1 Q.B. 222.
[72] Rent Act 1968, 1st Sched., 2nd Sched., para. 5, replacing Rent Act 1965, s. 13; *post*, p. 1141.
[73] For prohibitions against recovering possession except through the courts, see *ante*, pp. 657, 677, 683.
[74] *Whall* v. *Bulman* [1953] 2 Q.B. 198.
[75] Rent Act 1968, s. 10, replacing Act of 1933, s. 3.
[76] Rent Act 1968, s. 10, 3rd Sched., replacing Act of 1933, ss. 3, 4, 1st Sched.; Rent Act 1974, 1st Sched., Pt. I.
[77] *R. M. R. Housing Society, Ltd.* v. *Combs* [1951] 1 K.B. 486.
[78] See *Abrahams* v. *Wilson* [1971] 2 Q.B. 88 (drugs).

(3) DETERIORATION: the tenant or his lodger or sub-tenant is responsible for the deterioration of the premises or (if the tenancy is furnished) of the furniture.

(4) TENANT'S NOTICE TO QUIT: the tenant has given notice to quit and the landlord has acted on it so as to be seriously prejudiced if he could not obtain possession.

(5) ASSIGNMENT OR SUB-LETTING: the tenant, without the landlord's consent,[79] has assigned or sublet the whole of the premises, or has sublet part, the remainder being already sublet.[80]

(6) OFF-LICENCE IN JEOPARDY: the tenancy is a controlled tenancy and the tenant has committed certain acts which put in jeopardy an off-licence attached to the premises.

(7) REQUIRED FOR LANDLORD'S SERVANT: the premises are reasonably required as a residence for a person engaged (or with whom a conditional contract has been made) in the whole-time employment of the landlord, and the premises were let to the tenant in consequence of [81] his employment [82] by the landlord (or a former landlord), which has come to an end.

(8) REQUIRED FOR LANDLORD OR FAMILY: the landlord reasonably requires the premises for occupation as a residence for himself,[83] a child of his over 18 years old, or one of his parents (or parents-in-law, if the tenancy is a regulated tenancy). There are two exceptions to this head.

  (i) It is not available to a landlord who became landlord by purchasing [84] any interest in the premises after March 23, 1965, or, for controlled tenancies, November 7, 1956.[85] This prevents a landlord who has bought the premises subject to an existing tenancy from using this head to evict the sitting tenant [86]; but it does not affect a purchaser who buys with vacant possession and later grants a tenancy, for it was not " by purchasing " that he became landlord.[87]

[79] See *Hyde* v. *Pimley* [1952] 2 Q.B. 506.
[80] See *Finkle* v. *Strzelczyk* [1961] 1 W.L.R. 1201.
[81] *Braithwaite & Co. Ltd.* v. *Elliot* [1947] K.B. 177.
[82] *Duncan* v. *Hay* [1956] 1 W.L.R. 1329.
[83] See *Richter* v. *Wilson* [1963] 2 Q.B. 426.
[84] See *Powell* v. *Cleland* [1948] 1 K.B. 262, criticised at (1948) 64 L.Q.R. 17 (R.E.M.); *Thomas* v. *Fryer* [1970] 1 W.L.R. 845.
[85] See *Piper* v. *Harvey* [1958] 1 Q.B. 439. The dates under this and certain other heads are different for tenancies which are made regulated tenancies by the Counter-Inflation Act 1973, s. 14, 5th Sched. (see *ante*, p. 1132), and for regulated furnished tenancies under the Rent Act 1974, 1st Sched., Pt. I.
[86] See, *e.g.*, *Wright* v. *Walford* [1955] 1 Q.B. 363.
[87] *Epps* v. *Rothnie* [1945] K.B. 562.

(ii) This head does not apply if the tenant satisfies the court that in all the circumstances greater hardship would be caused by granting the order for possession than by refusing to grant it. In weighing the relative hardships, the court should consider not only the landlord and the tenant, but also all relatives, dependants, lodgers, guests and others likely to be affected, though with due regard to their status and proximity to the landlord or tenant, and to the extent to which hardship to them would be hardship to him.[88]

(9) EXCESSIVE RENT: the tenant has sublet part of the premises at an excessive rent.

(10) ALTERNATIVE ACCOMMODATION: Suitable alternative accommodation is available for the tenant, or will be available when the order for possession takes effect. The alternative accommodation must itself be protected by the Acts, or be let as a separate dwelling on terms affording a reasonably equivalent security of tenure; and in determining suitability, the court must consider proximity to the places of work of the tenant and his family, as well as their needs as regards extent and character,[89] and the tenant's means. But the accommodation need not be as good as the existing accommodation, and may even consist of part of it [90]; the question is whether it is " reasonably suitable," not " as suitable." [91]

(*b*) *Cases not dependent on reasonableness.* If a tenant has a regulated tenancy (and not otherwise), and apart from the Rent Acts the landlord would be entitled to possession, the court is bound to make an order for possession in eight cases.[92] In each case, the landlord must have given the tenant written notice of this liability before the contractual tenancy began, or, where statute has made an existing tenancy regulated, within six months of that statute coming into force. In the first two of these cases, however, the court may, if it seems just, dispense both with this requirement and with the further requirement that there should have been no previous letting without such a notice. The cases are as follows.

(1) OWNER-OCCUPIER: the landlord is a person who occupied the dwelling as his residence and let it on a regulated tenancy, and he

---

[88] *Harte* v. *Frampton* [1948] 1 K.B. 73.
[89] See *Redspring Ltd.* v. *Francis* [1973] 1 W.L.R. 134 (noise and smell).
[90] *Parmee* v. *Mitchell* [1950] 2 K.B. 199; *Mykolyshyn* v. *Noah* [1970] 1 W.L.R. 1271.
[91] *Warren* v. *Austen* [1947] 2 All E.R. 185 at 188.
[92] Rent Act 1968, s. 10, 3rd Sched., Pts. II, III, replacing Rent Act 1965, ss. 14–16 and Agriculture Act 1967, s. 38; Agriculture Act 1970, s. 100; Rent Act 1974, s. 3.

requires it as a residence for himself or a member of his family who resided with him when he last resided in the dwelling. But the landlord cannot rely on this head if after December 8, 1965 (when the Rent Act 1965 came into force [93]), the dwelling has been let on a protected tenancy without the tenant having been given the requisite written notice.

(2) RETIREMENT HOME: the landlord is a person who acquired the dwelling with a view to occupying it as his residence on retirement from regular employment, and either he has retired and requires the dwelling as a residence, or he has died and the dwelling is required as a residence for a member of his family who was residing with him at his death. But a landlord cannot rely on this head if after August 14, 1974 (when the Rent Act 1974 came into force), the dwelling has been let on a protected tenancy without the tenant having been given the requisite written notice.

(3) SHORT LETTING OF HOLIDAY HOME: the tenancy was granted for a fixed term of not more than eight months and during the previous twelve months the dwelling was occupied under a right to occupy it for a holiday. This encourages winter lettings of holiday accommodation.

(4) SHORT LETTING OF STUDENT RESIDENCE: the tenancy was granted for a fixed term of not more than twelve months, and during the previous twelve months the dwelling was subject to a tenancy granted by a specified institution or body of persons to a student at a specified [94] educational institution.

(5) MINISTER OF RELIGION: the dwelling is held for occupation by a minister of religion as a residence from which to perform his duties, and the dwelling is required for this purpose.

(6) AGRICULTURAL WORKER:

(7) FARMHOUSE REDUNDANT ON AMALGAMATION:

(8) OTHER REDUNDANT FARMHOUSES: The general purpose of the complicated provisions of these three heads is to enable a landlord to obtain possession of an agricultural dwelling for a farm worker of his from a tenant who lacks a sufficient agricultural justification for retaining it.

(3) Protection as to Rent

As already explained, there are now in force two distinct systems for ascertaining the maximum rent payable under every protected or

---

[93] Or, for regulated furnished tenancies, the Rent Act 1974, 1st Sched., Pt. I (August 14, 1974).

[94] See S.I. 1974 No. 1366; and see *ante*, p. 1128.

statutory tenancy, one for controlled tenancies, and the other for regulated tenancies. They are supplemented by provisions relating to premiums and mortgages.

1. Controlled tenancies

(*a*) *Standard rent.* Before the Rent Act, 1957, the system of controlling rent under the Rent Acts had always been based on the " standard rent " of the dwelling in question, *i.e.*, the rent at which the dwelling was let on August 3, 1914, in the case of old control, and September 1, 1939, in the case of new control, with further provisions for cases where the dwelling was not let on those dates. The standard rent was thus a permanent attribute of the dwelling, and affected all tenancies of it. In addition, there were certain " permitted increases " that could be made in respect of such matters as increases in any rates payable by the landlord, and 8 per cent. of any expenditure incurred by the landlord on the improvement or structural alteration of the dwelling; and the Housing Repairs and Rents Act, 1954, allowed a " repairs increase " to be made in respect of houses in good repair. The total of the standard rent and the permitted increases was known as the " recoverable rent." [95]

(*b*) *Abolition of standard rents.* This system was unsatisfactory in many respects. In particular, it was often both difficult to operate and capricious. Sometimes it was hard to ascertain exactly what rent was being paid on a particular date, perhaps forty years earlier; and in any case two houses of equal value might well have been let at very different rents on the relevant date. When the Local Government Act, 1948, Part III, transferred the responsibility for making valuation lists for rating purposes from local authorities to the Inland Revenue, and the first rating lists to be prepared on a uniform nation-wide basis came into force in August 1956, it was possible to adopt a new system of restricting rents by reference to rateable values; and this was done by the Rent Act, 1957. In place of the former "recoverable rent," there is now a "rent limit" which, unlike the former "standard rent," is an attribute not of the dwelling but of the particular tenancy in question. Notwithstanding any contrary agreement the landlord is not entitled to recover more than the rent limit.[96]

(*c*) *Rent limit.* The rent limit is ascertained by taking the gross value of the dwelling for rating purposes on November 7,

[95] See the 1st edition of this book, pp. 979, 981.
[96] Rent Act 1968, s. 52, replacing Rent Act, 1957, s. 1.

1956, and multiplying this by the "appropriate factor." [97] To this sum are added, where appropriate, certain sums for rates, services and furniture; and the total, converted into terms of the "rent period" (*e.g.*, a week for a weekly tenancy, a month for a monthly tenancy and so on), is the rent limit. [98] The appropriate factor is ascertained by examining the repairing responsibilities of the tenant under the tenancy in question. If apart from internal decorative repairs the tenant is responsible for all repairs, the factor is four-thirds; if he is responsible for none, it is two; and if his burden is partial, it is whatever intermediate figure the parties agree in writing or the county court determines. [99] If the landlord is responsible for internal decorative repairs, the factor is increased by an additional one-third. [1] Further, where during the "basic rental period" (*i.e.*, that which included July 6, 1957) the landlord bore any rates, the amount of those rates must be added. [2] Similarly, if during that period the landlord provided any services for the tenant, or the tenancy gave the tenant the right to use any furniture, there is an addition of whatever sum the parties agree in writing or the county court determines. [3] Finally, if the rent limit as thus ascertained is less than the rent recoverable for the basic rental period under the old law, the latter rent becomes the rent limit. [4]

(*d*) *Variation of rent limit.* The rent limit so ascertained is liable to subsequent variation in a number of ways. First, if the tenant successfully pursues the complex and lengthy process of obtaining an effective certificate of disrepair, [5] the main consequence is that the appropriate factor becomes four-thirds. [6] Secondly, if the landlord bears any rates, the rent limit rises and falls with any difference between the current rates and those for the basic rental period. [7] Thirdly, where in comparison with the basic rental period there is any relevant difference in the services or furniture, or in any circumstances relating to them, the rent limit is to be increased or decreased by an appropriate amount as agreed in writing by the parties or determined by the county court. [8] Lastly, the landlord may increase the rent limit by twelve and a half per cent. of his expenditure on any improvement or structural alteration [9] of the

---

[97] Rent Act 1968, s. 52, 8th and 9th Scheds., replacing Rent Act, 1957, s. 1, 1st and 5th Scheds.   [98] Rent Act 1968, s. 52, replacing Rent Act, 1957, s. 1.
[99] Rent Act 1968, s. 1, 9th Sched., replacing Rent Act, 1957, s. 1, 1st Sched.; and see *Regis Property Co. Ltd.* v. *Dudley* [1959] A.C. 370.
[1] Rent Act 1968, 9th Sched., para. 2, replacing Rent Act, 1957, 1st Sched., para. 2.
[2] Rent Act 1968, s. 52, replacing Rent Act, 1957, s. 1.
[3] *Ibid.*   [4] *Ibid.*
[5] Rent Act 1968, 9th Sched., Pt. II, replacing Rent Act, 1957, 1st Sched., Pt. II.
[6] *Ibid.*   [7] Rent Act 1968, s. 54, replacing Rent Act, 1957, s. 3.
[8] Rent Act 1968, s. 55, replacing Rent Act, 1957, s. 4.
[9] See *Morcom* v. *Campbell-Johnson* [1956] 1 Q.B. 106.

premises (including private street works, as in making up an unmade road outside the house) completed after July 6, 1957.[10]

(e) *Notice of increase.* No increase of rent, whether initial or on account of changed circumstances, can be made except by serving a proper notice of increase [11]; the one exception is an increase on account of changed circumstances relating to furniture or services, where the agreement between the parties or the decision of the court suffices to effect the increase.[12] In general, a three months' notice must be given, though increases for improvements may take place forthwith, and increases for rates may be retrospective for not more than six weeks.[13] Further, the Act gives no power to the landlord to make an increase in breach of the terms of the tenancy [14]; increases can be made only as against statutory tenants or contractual tenants whose tenancies permit increases to be made. But if a notice to quit given on the same date as a notice of increase could have determined the tenancy before the date on which the increase is to take effect, the notice of increase operates as a notice to quit, and converts the tenancy into a statutory tenancy as from that date.[15]

2. Regulated tenancies

(a) *Existing rent.* The general scheme for regulated tenancies is for the existing rent to continue until a " fair rent " has been fixed and registered. Accordingly, the rent recoverable under a regulated tenancy is limited to the last rent payable under the last previous regulated tenancy existing during the three years before the tenancy began, or, if none, the rent made payable under the regulated tenancy itself.[16] This concept has some similarity to that of " standard rents," [17] which the Rent Act, 1957, had supplanted. However, the rent under the last regulated tenancy must be adjusted so as to take account of any differences between the two tenancies as to liability for repairs, the provision or cost of services, the use of furniture, or rates; and if improvements are made, an extra twelve and a half per cent. of their cost may be added.[18]

(b) *Registered rent.* This general stand-still on rents may be ousted by obtaining a registered rent for the dwelling-house.[19]

---

[10] Rent Act 1968, ss. 56, 58, replacing Rent Act, 1957, ss. 5, 18, and Housing Act, 1961, s. 29.   [11] Rent Act 1968, s. 53, replacing Rent Act, 1957, s. 2.
[12] Rent Act 1968, s. 55, replacing Rent Act, 1957, s. 4.
[13] Rent Act 1968, ss. 53, 54, 56, replacing Rent Act, 1957, ss. 2, 3, 5.
[14] Rent Act 1968, s. 60, replacing Rent Act, 1957, s. 6.   [15] *Ibid.*
[16] Rent Act 1968, ss. 20, 22, replacing Rent Act 1965, ss. 3, 5.
[17] See *ante,* p. 1139.
[18] Rent Act 1968, ss. 21–25, replacing Rent Act 1965, ss. 4, 6.
[19] Rent Act 1968, s. 20, replacing Rent Act 1968, s. 3 ; and see S.I. 1973 Nos. 176, 1539.

Either the landlord or the tenant may apply to the rent officer for the area for the registration of a rent, and each is entitled to be heard; and the local authority may also apply.[20] The rent officer registers the rent, if he thinks it fair, or, if not, determines a fair rent and registers it; and within twenty-eight days of receiving notice of this, either landlord or tenant may make an objection requiring the matter to be referred to a rent assessment committee. After giving the parties an opportunity of being heard, the committee must either confirm the rent, or determine a fair rent which will be registered. Unless otherwise ordered, all registrations take effect from the date of application for registration; and for three years neither party can apply for the registration of a different rent unless there has been a change in the condition of the dwelling or in other circumstances which make the registered rent no longer a fair rent.[21] The registered rent constitutes the rent limit which must not be exceeded[22]; but it excludes any rates, even if borne by the landlord, and so if these increase he may, if otherwise entitled to do so, recover the increase from the tenant.[23] Other changes (*e.g.,* any improvements to the dwelling) can be dealt with on an application for reconsideration of the rent.

(c) *Fair rent.* In determining a fair rent, regard must be had " to all the circumstances (other than personal circumstances[24]) and in particular to the age, character, locality and state of repair of the dwelling-house," and the quantity, quality and condition of any furniture that is provided.[25] But the effect of local shortages of housing accommodation must be disregarded, and so must voluntary improvements carried out by the tenant or his predecessors in title, or disrepair or other defects due to his or their failure to comply with the terms of the tenancy.[26] Those who propose to provide a dwelling-house by erection or conversion, or to make improvements, or to let a dwelling-house when there is no registered rent or such rent is at least three years old, may apply to the rent officer for a certificate of fair rent, and the rent officer or, if necessary, the rent

---

20 Rent Act 1968, ss. 43, 44, 6th Sched., replacing Rent Act 1965, s. 26, 3rd Sched.; Housing Finance Act 1972, s. 39; S.I. 1972 No. 1307.
21 *Ibid.* But the landlord may apply within the last 3 months of the 3 years: Rent Act 1974, s. 4.
22 Rent Act 1968, ss. 20, 22, replacing Rent Act 1965, ss. 3, 5.
23 Rent Act 1968, s. 47, replacing Rent Act 1965, s. 28.
24 *Mason* v. *Skilling* [1974] 1 W.L.R. 1437 (occupation by tenant to be ignored); and see *Palmer* v. *Peabody Trust* [1974] 3 W.L.R. 575.
25 Rent Act 1968, s. 46, as amended by Rent Act 1974, 1st Sched., Pt. II, replacing Rent Act 1965, s. 27.
26 Rent Act 1968, s. 46, replacing Rent Act 1965, s. 27. On the process of determination generally, see *Metropolitan Properties Co. (F. G. C.) Ltd.* v. *Lannon* [1968] 1 W.L.R. 815 (reversed [1969] 1 Q.B. 577 on the issue of bias).

assessment committee, will determine it. Subject to confirmation that the work has been properly done, the rent so certified will become the registered rent.[27]

(*d*) *Conversion to regulated tenancy.* Where a controlled tenancy has been automatically converted into a regulated tenancy,[28] there are elaborate provisions for phasing any increase of rent up to the registered rent, *e.g.*, by three stages spread over two years.[29]

3. Premiums. For both controlled tenancies and regulated tenancies, there have long been wide provisions which prohibit any person from requiring a premium as a condition of the grant, renewal, continuance or assignment of any tenancy within the Acts, or in connection therewith, and also preventing a statutory tenant (who has no assignable interest) from asking or receiving any consideration from anyone except the landlord as a condition of giving up possession, or in connection therewith. Rent payable before the relevant rental period begins, and excessive prices for furniture, are treated as being premiums. It is an offence to require a premium; and, if paid, the money is recoverable.[30]

4. Mortgages

(*a*) *Classes of mortgage.* Where the Rent Acts restrict a landlord as against his tenant, it was long considered right that the landlord should correspondingly be protected against any legal mortgagee of his interest. The Rent Act 1965 changed this policy for the future, and mortgages of property within the Acts now fall into three categories. First, no mortgage created on or after December 8, 1965, is subject to any control or restriction under the Acts.[31] Second, there are regulated mortgages, where the court has a discretionary power to grant the mortgagor relief. Third, there are controlled mortgages, which are subject to defined restrictions on enforcement.

(*b*) *Regulated mortgages.* A mortgage is a regulated mortgage if, not being a controlled mortgage, it is a legal mortgage which includes a dwelling-house let on a regulated tenancy which has a rateable value of at least one-tenth of that of the whole of the land mortgaged, and the mortgagor is not in breach of covenant (apart from the covenant for repayment of principal).[32] The only protection given to

---

[27] Rent Act 1968, ss. 44, 45, 48, 6th Sched., replacing Rent Act 1965, 3rd and 4th Scheds.
[28] *Ante*, p. 1133.
[29] See Housing Finance Act 1972, s. 38, 6th Sched.
[30] Rent Act 1968, ss. 13, 15, Part VII, replacing various earlier provisions. See, *e.g.*, *Elmdene Estates Ltd.* v. *White* [1960] A.C. 528; *Zimmerman* v. *Grossman* [1972] 1 Q.B. 167.
[31] See Rent Act 1968, s. 93, replacing Rent Act 1965, s. 42.
[32] Rent Act 1968, s. 94, replacing Rent Act 1965, s. 42.

the mortgagor is the right to apply to the court within twenty-one days of the mortgagee increasing the rate of mortgage interest or taking any step to enforce his security, or of the registration of a rent for the tenancy lower than the existing rent. If by reason of such an event and the operation of the Rent Act 1968 the mortgagor would "suffer severe financial hardship," the court has a wide power to vary the terms of the mortgage or restrain the exercise of any remedies under it.[33]

(e) *Controlled mortgages.* A controlled mortgage is a legal [34] mortgage which, apart from the Rent Act 1968, would be controlled under the Acts of 1920 and 1939. Such mortgages are subject to prohibitions against enforcement of the security unless the mortgagor is in default, and against increases in the rate of interest above the "standard rate," *i.e.*, the rate payable in 1914 or 1939, subject to the court's power to vary the prohibitions if to maintain them would cause greater hardship than to vary them.[35]

II. TRIBUNAL PROTECTION: PART VI CONTRACTS

1. The system. The Furnished Houses (Rent Control) Act, 1946, set up a new system of control by means of rent tribunals for tenancies which previously had been unprotected by the Rent Acts because the dwelling had been let furnished or with services. The Act, as amended by the Landlord and Tenant (Rent Control) Act, 1949, formerly applied irrespective of the rateable value of the dwelling [36]; but the Rent Act, 1957 and subsequent Acts confined it to cases where the rateable value was low enough for the application of the main body of the Rent Acts, though latterly these values have been greatly increased.[37] The legislation is now contained in Part VI of the Rent Act 1968 (as amended), and, as already mentioned,[38] tenancies within Part VI are known as "Part VI contracts."

2. Application of Part VI. Part VI of the Rent Act 1968 is now capable of applying to any dwelling of which the rateable value on March 23, 1965, was £200 or less, or else on April 1, 1973,[39] was £750

---

[33] Rent Act 1968, s. 95, replacing Rent Act 1965, s. 42; and see Rent Act 1974, 1st Sched., Pt. II.

[34] See *London County and Westminster Bank Ltd.* v. *Tompkins* [1918] 1 K.B. 515.

[35] Rent Act 1968, s. 96, 12th Sched., Pt. II, replacing Act of 1920, s. 7, Act of 1939, 1st Sched., and Rent Act 1965, s. 42.

[36] See, *e.g.*, *Mauray* v. *Durley Chine (Investments) Ltd.* [1953] 2 Q.B. 433.

[37] Rent Act, 1957, s. 12; Rent Act 1965, s. 39; Rent Act 1968, s. 71; Rent Act 1974, s. 6; *ante*, p. 1132.

[38] *Ante*, p. 1125.

[39] Or after that, if not then rated.

or less, with double these figures for dwellings in Greater London.[40] Subject to the exceptions below, Part VI applies to any contract whereby a person has been granted the right to occupy as a residence [40a] a house or part of a house of this rateable value at a rent which includes payment for the use of furniture or for services,[40b] or on terms that he shares some of his living accommodation (*e.g.*, a kitchen) with his landlord.[41] It also applies to a number of tenancies which are excluded from the Rent Acts because they were granted by a " resident landlord." [42] But Part VI is excluded if a substantial proportion of the rent is for board, or if the right to occupy the dwelling is for a holiday, or if the contract creates a regulated tenancy under the main body of the Rent Acts.[43] This last exception prevents Part VI from applying to the many furnished tenancies now within the Rent Acts.[44]

3. Rent. A Part VI contract may be referred to the rent tribunal by either of the parties to the contract or by the local authority [45]; and after hearing the parties the tribunal may approve, reduce or increase the rent to the amount that the tribunal thinks reasonable.[46] The rent thus determined is then registered with the local authority, and thereafter it is an offence to require or receive more than the registered rent for the dwelling, or to charge any premium.[47] A registered rent may later be referred to the tribunal for reconsideration, but the tribunal cannot be required to hear such a reference within three years of its previous decision unless there has been such a change of circumstances as to make the registered rent no longer reasonable.[48] The jurisdiction of the tribunal is not ousted merely because the tenant quits the dwelling before his reference is heard.[49]

4. Security of tenure. If the statutory provisions as to rent stood alone, a landlord could deter his tenant from referring the contract to a rent tribunal by the threat of serving a notice to quit. Accord-

---

[40] Rent Act 1974, s. 6. Thus Part VI may apply to furnished lettings at £4,000 a year, or more.

[40a] See *Luganda* v. *Service Hotels Ltd.* [1969] 2 Ch. 209 (long term occupation of room in hotel suffices).

[40b] Whether or not charged separately: Rent Act 1968, s. 84. Most tenants of flats who pay substantial service charges now have a statutory right to a summary of the cost of providing the services, certified by a qualified accountant, whether or not they have Part VI contracts: Housing Finance Act 1972, ss. 90, 91 ; Housing Act 1974, 12th Sched.

[41] Rent Act 1968, ss. 70, 84, 101; *ante*, p. 1127.

[42] See *ante*, p. 1129.

[43] Rent Act 1968, s. 70. For regulated tenancies, see *ante*, p. 1132.

[44] See *ante*, p. 1129.

[45] See *R.* v. *Barnet and Camden R. T.*, *ex p. Frey Investments Ltd.* [1972] 2 Q.B. 342.   [46] Rent Act 1968, ss. 72, 73 ; Rent Act 1974, s. 7.

[47] Rent Act 1968, ss. 76, 87.   [48] *Ibid.*, ss. 73, 75 ; Rent Act 1974, s. 7

[49] *R.* v. *West London Rent Tribunal*, *ex p. Napper* [1967] 1 Q.B. 169.

ingly, two methods of obtaining security of tenure have been provided. Each depends upon a notice to quit being requisite, and so neither applies if the tenancy is for a fixed term and thus will determine without any notice to quit.[50] Further, unless the dwelling is part of a house in which the landlord resides, neither method applies where an owner-occupier, on letting the dwelling, gave written notice to the tenant that he was an owner-occupier, as defined, and the notice to quit is given because the dwelling is required for occupation by him or by a member of his family who was residing with him when he last resided in the dwelling.[51]

(a) *Automatic security.* Where a tenant or the local authority has referred a contract to the tribunal, either originally or for reconsideration, no notice to quit subsequently served on the tenant will take effect [52] before the expiration of six months after the decision of the tribunal. The tribunal may, however, substitute a shorter period for the statutory six months; and any period of security under this or the next head may subsequently be reduced by the tribunal if the tenant has broken the terms of the contract, or he or anyone residing or lodging with him has been guilty of misconduct, *e.g.*, in neglecting or maltreating the dwelling or the furniture.[53] This head, like the next, operates by preventing the contract of tenancy from being determined by notice to quit: under Part VI there is no equivalent of the statutory tenancy under the Rent Acts.[54]

(b) *Security on application.* Where a contract has been referred to a tribunal, and a notice to quit has been served (whether before or after making the reference), then at any time before the expiration of the period at the end of which the notice to quit will take effect, the tenant may apply to the tribunal for an extension of that period; and the tribunal may extend it by not more than six months.[55] Successive extensions may be granted, repeatedly postponing the operation of the notice to quit; and even if no notice to quit is served until, say, a year after the first reference to the tribunal, an application under this head may be made at any time before the notice expires.[56] But no application for an extension may be made once the period of security has been reduced by the tribunal for misconduct.[57]

[50] But, strangely, a renewal of such a tenancy may attract the protection of the Rent Acts: see *ante*, p. 1129.
[51] Rent Act 1968, s. 79.
[52] See *Francis Jackson Developments Ltd.* v. *Hall* [1951] 2 K.B. 488, and the criticism in Megarry's *Rent Acts* (10th ed. 1967) p. 534.
[53] Rent Act 1968, ss. 77, 80; Rent Act 1974, s. 8; and see s. 14 (powers of court).
[54] See *ante*, p. 1134.
[55] Rent Act 1968, s. 78; Rent Act 1974, s. 8.
[56] *Preston and Area Rent Tribunal* v. *Pickavance* [1953] A.C. 562.
[57] Rent Act 1968, s. 80.

D. Residential Long Tenancies

Building leases, mentioned in earlier chapters,[58] played a large part in the development of urban and suburban land. In a building lease the essence of the bargain is that the tenant takes a long lease, commonly for ninety-nine years, at a mere ground rent representing the undeveloped value of the land, and builds a house upon it at his own expense.[59] He and his successors then have a long period of enjoyment at this low rent; but at the expiry of the lease the house, being part of the land,[60] reverts with the land to the landlord or his successors. The landlord's object is long-term capital gain; and by imposing covenants for repair and residential use, and so forth, he can maintain the value of the property and control its use. Many landowners developed their land as building estates under this system, especially from the mid-nineteenth century onwards, and most houses held on long leases at ground rents have been freely bought and sold.

By the mid-twentieth century many of these leases were running out, leaving the tenants homeless unless they could afford to buy the house, or could obtain a new lease, at full market value. Such leases have always been outside the Rent Acts because the rent was less than two-thirds of the rateable value of the house and the land [61]; and, in addition, from 1957 to 1967 any " long tenancy " (*i.e.*, a tenancy granted [62] for a term exceeding twenty-one years [63]) was outside the Rent Acts, whatever the rent.[64] Parliament accordingly provided two forms of protection for long tenancies at a low rent; and these apply to all such tenancies, even if they are not building leases. A tenant under such a tenancy has, first, the right under Part I of the Landlord and Tenant Act, 1954, to a statutory tenancy under the Rent Acts, paying a reasonable rent for the house; and second, the right under the Leasehold Reform Act 1967 to " enfranchise " the property or extend the lease, obtaining either the freehold or else

---

[58] *e.g., ante*, pp. 334, 673, 681, 698.
[59] In practice the tenant would usually be given a licence under an agreement to build, coupled with the right to a lease for 99 years after building in accordance with the contract. Hence the use of 99-year leases for 100-year transactions. Further, there has long been a higher rate of Stamp Duty on leases for a term exceeding 100 years (see Stamp Act, 1870, Sched.; Stamp Act, 1891, 1st Sched.), and 99 years represents a margin for safety. Various statutes also provided an example by adopting 99 years as the maximum for building leases: see, *e.g.,* Crown Lands Act, 1829, s. 23 ; Ecclesiastical Leasing Act, 1842, s. 1.
[60] *Ante*, p. 711.
[61] See *ante*, p. 1128.
[62] See *Roberts* v. *Church Commissioners for England* [1972] 1 Q.B. 278 (10-year term subsequently extended by less than 21 years to over 21 years in all held insufficient).
[63] L. & T.A., 1954, s. 2 (4); Leasehold Reform Act 1967, s. 3 (1); Rent Act 1968, s. 113 (1).
[64] Rent Act, 1957, s. 21 (1); Leasehold Reform Act 1967, s. 39; and see *ante*, p. 1128.

a leasehold for fifty years, on paying a price or rent based on the value of the land alone, ignoring the house. The subjects are specialised, and the statutes complex, so that only a brief indication of their general effect will be given.

I. STATUTORY TENANCY: LANDLORD AND TENANT ACT, 1954, PART I

1. Tenancies protected. A tenant has the benefit of Part I of the Act of 1954 only if he has a long tenancy and, but for the lowness of the rent, he would be entitled under the Rent Act 1968 to retain possession of the premises when the tenancy ends.[65] Part I thus protects only occupying tenants of residential property [66] of a type and rateable value [67] which fall within the Rent Acts.

2. Protection. Part I of the Act of 1954 continues the expiring lease indefinitely at the same rent and on the same terms until it is terminated by notice under Part I.[68] The tenant may terminate it at any time by giving one month's notice, whereas the landlord must give not less than six nor more than twelve months' notice.[69] Two courses are open to the landlord. First, he may give a "landlord's notice to resume possession," and then apply to the court for possession on grounds similar to the grounds for possession under the Rent Acts.[70] Second, his notice may be a "landlord's notice proposing a statutory tenancy," in which case the terms of the statutory tenancy will be as agreed by the parties or, in default, as determined by the court.[71] The statutory tenancy is a regulated tenancy, and so the rent is subject to the provisions for assessment and registration of a fair rent which apply to such tenancies.[72]

3. Repairs. At the end of a long lease it is common for a house to be out of repair. There are accordingly special provisions for the landlord to carry out the initial repairs required to bring the house into good repair, and for the tenant to pay the landlord for those

---

[65] L. & T.A., 1954, ss. 1, 2.
[66] See *Haines* v. *Herbert* [1963] 1 W.L.R. 1401; *Herbert* v. *Byrne* [1964] 1 W.L.R. 519.
[67] See Counter-Inflation Act 1973, s. 14, 5th Sched., para. 11 (2), 6th Sched.; and see *Crown Lodge (Surbiton) Investments Ltd.* v. *Najecz* [1967] 1 W.L.R. 647.
[68] L. & T.A., 1954, s. 3.
[69] *Ibid.*, s. 4. For forms of notice, see S.I. 1957 No. 1157; 1967 No. 1831.
[70] L. & T.A., 1954, ss. 4, 12, 3rd Sched. For the grounds under the Rent Acts, see *ante*, p. 1135. Proposed redevelopment was formerly a ground, but the Leasehold Reform Act 1967, s. 38, confined this to "public bodies," for which see *post*, p. 1152.
[71] L. & T.A., 1954, ss. 4, 6–9.
[72] Leasehold Reform Act 1967, s. 39 (1), 5th Sched., paras. 3, 4; Rent Act 1968, 15th Sched.; *ante*, p. 1151

repairs for which the tenant is liable, either in a lump sum or by instalments which are recoverable as if they were rent.[73]

II. ENFRANCHISEMENT OR EXTENSION:
LEASEHOLD REFORM ACT 1967

1. Introduction. The Leasehold Reform Act 1967 is based on the " principle " announced in 1966, that under a building lease " the land belongs in equity to the landowner and the house belongs in equity to the occupying leaseholder." [74] Whatever political or social expediency there was in this " principle," it is difficult to perceive any equity in it, in any sense of that word.[75] For many years landlords and tenants had been dealing with ground leases and reversions on the footing that both house and land were the landlord's, subject to the lease. When the ground lease of a house needing repair neared its end, a purchaser could usually acquire it for little or nothing, yet the Act gave those who had done this the right to acquire the freehold for the price of the site at the expense of a reversioner who until then had a valuable and appreciating asset. The Landlord and Tenant Act, 1954, Part I, had respected the initial bargain between landlord and tenant at least to the extent of requiring the tenant to pay a rent based on the value of both house and land; but the Act of 1967 destroyed the major part of that bargain, and expropriated the reversioner without compensation.[76]

2. Qualifying tenancies. The Act of 1967 applies to any long tenancy [76a] at a low rent (*i.e.*, a rent less than two-thirds of the rateable value on March 23, 1965 [77]) which satisfies the statutory conditions. It applies equally to a sub-tenancy, and in that case there are elaborate provisions for extinguishing or adjusting intermediate tenancies and compensating their owners to the limited extent allowed by the Act.[78] The three statutory conditions [79] are as follows.

(*a*) *Rateable value*: the rateable value on the " appropriate day " must not have exceeded £400 in Greater London or £200 elsewhere.

---

[73] L. & T.A., 1954, ss. 8, 9, 1st Sched.
[74] White Paper on Leasehold Reform (1966, Cmnd. 2916), para. 14.
[75] All the more so because it does not apply to houses of a high value: see below.
[76] Since this was for the benefit of the tenant rather than for any public purpose, it may have been a breach of art. 1 of the First Protocol (1952) to the European Convention of Human Rights (1950), providing that " no one shall be deprived of his possessions except in the public interest."
[76a] See *ante*, p. 1147.
[77] Leasehold Reform Act 1967, ss. 1, 3, 4; and see *Gidlow-Jackson* v. *Middlegate Properties Ltd.* [1974] Q.B. 361.
[78] Leasehold Reform Act 1967, s. 5, 1st Sched.
[79] *Ibid.*, ss. 1, 2, as amended by Rent Act 1968, 15th Sched., and Housing Act 1974, s. 118.

The " appropriate day " is March 23, 1965, or if the valuation list then showed no rateable value for the premises, the first subsequent date when it did. But in some cases the figures are increased. If the appropriate day is on or after April 1, 1973, then if the tenancy was created after February 18, 1966, the figures are £1,000 and £500 respectively, and if the tenancy was created on or before that date they are £1,500 and £750 respectively.[80] If the appropriate day is before April 1, 1973, and the tenancy was created on or before February 18, 1966, the respective figures are again £1,500 and £750.

(*b*) *House*: the premises must consist of a house [81] (including semi-detached and terrace houses) and not be a flat or maisonette, though these remain protected under the Act of 1954. If the premises form part of a larger building, the division must in effect be vertical.[82]

(*c*) *Residence*: when the tenant gives his notice of enfranchisement or enlargement, he must have been occupying part [83] or all of the house under the tenancy as his only or main residence for the last five years, or for periods amounting to five years out of the last ten. It thus suffices if the house has been divided into flats and he has occupied one of them for five years; and it is immaterial if he also uses the house for other purposes. If the tenant dies and a member of his family succeeds him as tenant, the successor can, if the house was his main residence before the death, include in the period of five years his period of residence before the death.[84]

3. Claim. A tenant who wishes to claim either enfranchisement or extension must do so by serving on his landlord a written notice to this effect in a prescribed form.[85] He may do this at any time while his long tenancy exists under the lease itself or while it is being automatically continued on the original terms under the Act of 1954. But if under Part I of the Act of 1954 the landlord serves a notice seeking to terminate the tenancy, the tenant will lose his rights under the Act of 1967 unless he serves his notice within two months.[86] When served, the tenant's notice takes effect as a contract " freely

---

[80] The tenancy may have been granted some while before the house, after being erected or altered, acquired its rateable value.

[81] See, *e.g., Wolf* v. *Crutchley* [1971] 1 W.L.R. 100 (two interconnected houses held separate although run as one); *Lake* v. *Bennett* [1970] 1 Q.B. 663 (dwelling above, shop below: held " house ").

[82] The Act does not apply to a house " which is not structurally detached and of which a material part lies above or below a part of the structure not comprised in the house ": s. 2 (2). See *Parsons* v. *Viscount Gage* [1974] 1 W.L.R. 435.

[83] See *Haines* v. *Swick Securities Ltd.* [1969] 1 W.L.R. 1604.

[84] Leasehold Reform Act 1967, s. 7.

[85] *Ibid.,* s. 22, 3rd Sched., para. 6; S.I. 1967 No. 1768, 1969 No. 1481.

[86] Leasehold Reform Act 1967, 3rd Sched., para. 2. This applies to both forms of notice mentioned *ante*, p. 1148.

entered into " for the landlord to convey the freehold or grant the new tenancy, as the case may be; and it is registrable as if it were an estate contract or, in the case of registered land, it may be protected by a notice or caution similarly.[87] In default of agreement on the price or rent, these and the other terms will be determined by the Lands Tribunal[88]; otherwise the terms are a matter for the county court, which has general jurisdiction over claims under the Act.[89] For enfranchisement (but not for extension) there is a right for the tenant to withdraw within a month of the price being agreed or determined,[90] and also a special procedure where the landlord is unknown or cannot be found.[91]

4. Completion

(*a*) *Extension.* If the tenant's notice claims an extension of his tenancy, he is entitled to the grant of a tenancy for fifty years from the expiry of his existing lease, on corresponding terms.[92] The rent is to be a ground rent representing the letting value of the site when the new tenancy begins, disregarding the value of the buildings on it, though after twenty-five years the landlord may require the rent to be raised to the then current letting value of the site; and the tenant must pay the landlord's reasonable costs of the transaction.[93]

(*b*) *Enfranchisement.* If the tenant's notice claims enfranchisement, he is entitled to a conveyance in fee simple subject to his tenancy and any incumbrances on it, but otherwise free from incumbrances (*e.g.*, any mortgage or charge on the freehold).[94] The price is to be the amount which the house and land would fetch on the open market (excluding from that market the tenant and members of his family residing in the house), but on the assumption that the tenancy is to be extended under the Act.[95] The price to be paid by the tenant will therefore reflect the value of the house (as distinct from the site) only to the extent of the value of a right to the house in fifty years' time. But the assumption is different and the price will reflect more of the value of the house, if the house, after excluding the value of any tenant's improvements to it, has a rateable value on the appropriate day [95a] above £1,000 in Greater London or £500

[87] Leasehold Reform Act 1967, ss. 5, 8, 14.
[88] *Ibid.*, s. 21.
[89] *Ibid.*, s. 20.
[90] *Ibid.*, s. 9 (3).
[91] *Ibid.*, s. 27. See, *e.g.*, *Re Robertson's Application* [1969] 1 W.L.R. 109; *Re Frost's Application* [1970] 1 W.L.R. 1145; *Re Howell's Application* [1972] Ch. 509.
[92] Leasehold Reform Act 1967, ss. 14, 15.
[93] *Ibid.*
[94] *Ibid.*, s. 8.
[95] *Ibid.*, s. 9, as amended by Housing Act 1969, s. 82.
[95a] See *ante*, p. 1150.

elsewhere. In this case, the assumption is merely that the tenant has a right to remain in the house under Part I of the Landlord and Tenant Act, 1954, though without any liability for repairs, maintenance or redecoration; and the price is to be reduced to offset any improvements carried out by the tenant or his predecessors at their own expense.[96] In any case the tenant must also pay the landlord's reasonable costs of the transaction.[97]

5. Modifications. No contract can exclude or modify the tenant's right to enfranchisement, extension or compensation [98]; but the Act excludes or modifies the provisions for enfranchisement or extension in certain cases.

(a) *Required for landlord's residence.* A tenant's right to enfranchisement or extension will be defeated if the landlord obtains an order for possession on the ground that he reasonably requires possession of the house for occupation as the only or main residence for himself or for an adult member of his family; and there is a test of "greater hardship." [99] But a tenant whose claim is defeated in this way is entitled to compensation (determined by the Lands Tribunal in default of agreement) based on the open market value of a tenancy of the house as extended under the Act, though with nothing for the loss of his right of enfranchisement.[1]

(b) *Redevelopment.* If the landlord satisfies the court that for purposes of redevelopment he proposes to demolish or reconstruct the house or a substantial part of it, the court must declare that the landlord is entitled to possession and the tenant to compensation, as above. Such a declaration will defeat any claim to an extension, and will determine any extended tenancy that has been granted, though the tenant is entitled to compensation, as above.[2] But a claim to enfranchisement cannot normally be defeated on this ground.[3]

(c) *Development by public bodies.* If a Minister certifies that a public body will require the property within ten years for development for purposes of that body, a tenant cannot effectively claim either enfranchisement or extension under the Act; but if the tenancy has not been extended, his claim brings into play the provisions mentioned in the preceding paragraph, as if for redevelopment, and

[96] Housing Act 1974, s. 118, 8th Sched.
[97] Leasehold Reform Act 1967, s. 9, as amended by Housing Act 1969, s. 82.
[98] Leasehold Reform Act 1967, s. 23. For compensation, see below.
[99] *Ibid.*, s. 18.
[1] *Ibid.*, s. 21 (1), 2nd Sched., para. 5.
[2] *Ibid.*, s. 17.
[3] *Ibid*

the Minister's certificate is conclusive as to the required purposes.[4] Meanwhile the old tenancy continues indefinitely.[5] The term " public body " includes local authorities, New Town authorities, university bodies (including colleges), certain hospital authorities, nationalised industries, and certain other public bodies.[6]

(*d*) *The Crown.* A tenant holding directly from the Crown cannot claim either enfranchisement or extension under the Act,[7] though normally the Crown will as of grace agree to grant one or the other on the terms of the Act.

(*e*) *Management.* Where there is an area occupied by tenants under one landlord, the appropriate Minister could certify, on an application made to him before 1970, that in order to maintain standards it was in the general interest that the landlord should retain powers of management and control over the development and use of houses in the area. A scheme for this purpose (*e.g.,* regulating the redevelopment or use of enfranchised property, and providing for repairs) could then be submitted to the High Court and, if approved, take effect.[8] Although such schemes could regulate enfranchised property in many matters of detail, they do not prevent enfranchisement or extension. Application for a scheme could be made not only by a landlord but also by a tenants' association approved by the Minister, and the scheme could then confer on the association rights or powers which might have been conferred on the landlord.[9] Since the landlord's interest in the property was mostly expropriated, it was to tenants' associations that the provisions for management schemes were most useful.

E. Other Systems of Control

The systems of control that have been discussed are the main systems, but they do not exhaust the subject. There are other cases in which landlords have been restricted by statute. Examples may be briefly mentioned under two heads.

1. Special systems of control. Under the Reserve and Auxiliary Forces (Protection of Civil Interests) Act, 1951, a wide variety of statutory protection is given to service men and women, other than

---

[4] *Ibid.,* s. 28. as amended by Town and Country Planning Acts 1968, 9th Sched., para. 75, and 1971, 23rd Sched.
[5] *Ibid.*
[6] *Ibid*
[7] *Ibid.,* s. 33.
[8] *Ibid.,* s. 19.
[9] *Ibid.,* s. 19 (13). The landlord and the association could apply jointly, as in *Re Abbots Park Estate* [1972] 1 W.L.R. 598 ; *Re Abbots Park Estate (No. 2)* [1972] 1 W.L.R. 1597.

those in the regular services. In particular, Part II extends the protection of the Rent Acts and the powers of rent tribunals to a number of cases which otherwise would be outside their ambit. It also restricts to some extent the grounds on which possession can be obtained in cases within the Rent Acts or Agricultural Holdings Act, 1948. Again, the Housing Act, 1974 contains provisions (replacing and extending provisions in earlier statutes) for grants to be made by local authorities for the improvement, conversion and repair of dwellings, and the provision of " standard amenities " (relating to washing and sanitary facilities).[10] Where such grants are made, the dwelling becomes subject to certain conditions for five years, designed to ensure that the dwelling is available for residential occupation by the applicant and members of his household, or, after the first year, for this, or for letting to others as a residence (and not for a holiday) on a regulated tenancy or a Part VI contract,[11] with no premiums and a duly registered rent. Such conditions bind successors in title and are registrable as local land charges. If such a condition is broken, the whole of the grant becomes repayable to the local authority with compound interest.[12]

2. Counter-inflation measures. Wide overriding restrictions, intended to be temporary, have recently been imposed for economic reasons. By the Counter-Inflation (Temporary Provisions) Act 1972, and the Counter-Inflation Act 1973 that superseded it, wide powers were given to make statutory instruments which would, *inter alia*, restrict rents.[13] These powers have been exercised so as to impose a stand-still on agricultural [14] and business [15] rents and to supplement and extend the existing restrictions on residential rents.[16]

F. Status

1. Statutory protection. Today, most tenants in this country are protected by some statutory provision or other. The largest single class of tenants with unprotected tenure probably consists of residential tenants of houses owned by local authorities; but even they have some protection as to rent, since housing authorities are

---

[10] Housing Act 1974, Part VII, 6th Sched.; and see *ante*, p. 1133.

[11] For such contracts, see *ante*, p. 1144.

[12] Housing Act 1974, ss. 73–76.

[13] See Counter-Inflation (Temporary Provisions) Act 1972, s. 2; Counter-Inflation Act 1973, s. 11.

[14] See S.I. 1973 Nos. 682, 1717, 1741.

[15] See S.I. 1973 No. 741; S.I. 1974 Nos. 1030 (freezing rents not caught by the previous Orders), 1294 (making phased relaxations up to a " rent limit " based on the level of market rents on November 5, 1972). *No. 20 Cannon Street Ltd.* v. *Singer & Friedlander Ltd.* [1974] Ch. 229 illustrates the complexity that this legislation can achieve. S.I. 1975 No. 21 lifted this " freeze " on February 1, 1975, though for existing tenancies a " decontrol notice " must be given.

[16] See S.I. 1974 Nos. 184, 380, 381, 434, 1928.

required to charge " fair rents " determined under special procedure by " rent scrutiny boards." [17] Leasehold tenants, who in early law were regarded as holding mere contracts, and not until the sixteenth century became recognised as owners of estates,[18] have some claim now to have travelled from contract via estate to status: for their more important rights depend in large part not on the contracts which they have made but on the positive protection conferred on them by statute, overriding any contractual arrangements.

2. Rent. Nevertheless, the variations between the statutory provisions are so great that it is difficult to discern much common ground between the systems. Even though the premises have been let before, there may or may not be initial control as to rent (contrast business and agricultural lettings with the Rent Acts); control as to rent may attach only on a renewal of the tenancy (business), or at stated intervals (agriculture), or on application to a tribunal (Part VI contracts); and the rent may be fixed by the court (business, and statutory tenancies under the Act of 1967), the Lands Tribunal (50-year leases under the Act of 1954), an arbitrator (agriculture), or a tribunal (Part VI contracts and regulated tenancies). Further, in place of any tenancy at a rent there may be enfranchisement (Act of 1967).

3. Security of tenure. Security of tenure is equally varied. It may be provided by means of a restriction on determining the existing tenancy until the tenant has been able to apply to the court for a new tenancy (business), or the power of the tenant to paralyse a notice to quit by serving a counter-notice unless the landlord obtains permission from the Agricultural Land Tribunal for his notice to operate (agriculture), or the automatic suspension of a notice to quit for a limited period, with power for the tenant to apply to a tribunal for an extension (Part VI contracts), or the mere passive right for the tenant to remain, despite the termination of the contractual tenancy, until ordered to go by the court (the Rent Acts), or the right to compel the grant of a fifty years tenancy or a conveyance of the freehold (Act of 1967). There are also differences in whether or not the tenant need take any active steps to be protected, and whether or not tenants for fixed periods (as distinct from periodic tenants) are protected.

4. Protected tenant. The variations are thus great. Yet in the sense that on the major issues a tenant today will look more often

---

[17] Housing Finance Act 1972, Pt. V. The object of this " protection," however, was to raise these rents rather than to lower them. They are reviewable triennially: s. 59.
[18] *Ante*, pp. 11, 43, and *post*, p. 1170.

to the rights conferred on him by the Statute-book than to the terms of his tenancy, it is perhaps true to say that there is an ill-defined but nevertheless real status of protected tenant.

Sect. 5. Effect of Social Control of Land

Since 1939 there has been something of a silent revolution in the world of conveyancing. Formerly a conveyancer was concerned to see that his client obtained a good title to the land, and that his client's wishes as to any dispositions by will or settlement were carried out in as precise and suitable a way as was possible. Today those objects remain, but they tend to be overshadowed by two other objects. A good title to the land must still be obtained, but the conveyancer must also investigate whether his client will be able to use the land for the purposes he has in mind, or whether those purposes are liable to be frustrated by planning control or by the rights of protected tenants. Often " user " stands side by side with " title " as a matter for investigation, and often it overshadows it, especially if the land is registered land. Again, wills and settlements must carry out the client's intentions; yet often today the conveyancer must intervene to point out how serious the consequences of a particular proposal will be in the sphere of taxation. Both landowners and conveyancers have perforce become far more subservient than they were to the claims of the State and the public interest.

CHAPTER 19

THE LEGISLATION OF 1925

ANY attempt to take stock of the legislation of 1925 belongs to the end of this book rather than the beginning. The reforms were so many and so diverse that an account of them has little meaning until the whole field of their operation has been surveyed. They are without doubt the greatest single monument of legal wisdom, industry and ingenuity which the Statute-book can display. Perhaps the best tribute to the workmanship of their authors is the fact that in nearly fifty years the Acts have been litigated and amended so little. When introducing the Law of Property Bill, 1922, Sir Leslie Scott claimed [1] that it deserved the encomium (of a kind which falls but rarely from the bench) which Lord Macnaghten once bestowed upon another statute [2]: " Drawn with consummate skill it avoids all technical expressions, and yet there is not a single word misused or out of place, nor any expression which it would be easy to improve." Persons familiar with the weaker points of the final legislation of 1925 may feel that this praise is rather too high. Nevertheless the Acts as a whole have stood the test of time, and the benefits which they have conferred were not exaggerated by their sponsors. They are many and great.

A survey of the legislation may be divided into three parts: the historical background; a classification of the principal reforms; and some assessment of the possibility of further improvements.

Sect. 1. Historical Background

1. The nineteenth century. A long history lies behind some of the doctrines which became law in 1925.[3] It was plain enough in the later nineteenth century that the law of real property and conveyancing was antiquated and unnecessarily complex, despite the considerable reforms of the years from 1832 to 1845. But no root-and-branch amendment was attempted. Deeds became less lengthy and unintelligible when the Conveyancing Act, 1881 (which might

---

[1] 154 H.C.Deb. (5th ser.) 107 (1922).
[2] The Succession Duty Act, 1853.
[3] See Holdsworth, *Historical Introduction to the Land Law*, Chap. 4; J. H. Johnson, " Bibliography of the New Property Acts (Annotated), 1896–1925 " (1926) 42 L.Q.R. 67; (1931) 13 Jnl. of Comp. Legisln. (3rd ser.) 91; Sir Arthur Underhill (1935) 51 L.Q.R. 221; Prideaux, 22nd ed., Chap. 1.

have been called " The Solicitors (Drudgery Relief) Act " [4]), eliminated many lengthy common-form clauses,[5] while Parliament simultaneously removed the reproach that solicitors were paid " by the yard," according to the length of the documents they drew.[6] The Settled Land Acts, 1882–1890, carried out important social and legal reforms.[7] The Land Transfer Act, 1897, took one step towards the assimilation of real and personal property law by establishing the " real representative " [8]; yet this provision, sound in principle, was marred by bad drafting,[9] while the Act's scheme for compulsory registration of title, though better drafted, was unsound in principle. But it was out of the desire for registration of title that the proposals for a general reform of the law grew. It tends to be forgotten today that the object of those who first put forward the new ideas was to pave the way for the universal registration of title.

2. Registration of title. It became obvious that the practice of private conveyancing was wasteful and laborious, for the same title had to be fully investigated *de novo* upon every transaction. " Registration of title was invented, from the necessity of the case, when stocks and shares became an important form of property; it is a scientific system of conveyancing, based on common sense and modern requirements. The problem is how we are to engraft this system on our law of real property, which has been frequently described, by practical conveyancers, as a disgrace to a civilised community." [10] The Royal Commission on the Land Transfer Acts, which had to consider the defects of the Act of 1897, reported in 1911 that registration of title was greatly impeded by the state of the law, and by the differences between the rules for real and personal property.[11] It became the accepted truth that " to legislate for the registration of titles without, as a preliminary step, simplifying the titles to be registered is to begin at the wrong end." [12] A sound system of registration requires titles to be properly proved to the registrar in the first instance, and this enormous task must obviously be lightened in every way possible. Hence arose the cry for the simplification of conveyancing.

---

[4] See (1935) 51 L.Q.R. 222 (Sir Arthur Underhill).
[5] *Ante*, pp. 602, 829, 908.
[6] Scale fees were substituted by the Solicitors' Remuneration Act, 1881, and were replaced at the end of 1972 by a system of *quantum meruit* (" fair and reasonable "): S.I. 1972 No. 1139. See *Bates* v. *Lord Hailsham of St. Marylebone* [1972] 1 W.L.R. 1373.   [7] *Ante*, p. 288.
[8] *Ante*, p. 535.
[9] *Ante*, p. 544, n. 51.
[10] Charles Sweet (1912) 28 L.Q.R. 10.
[11] Cd. 5483 (1911), paras. 97, 101.
[12] A. Underhill, " The Line of Least Resistance," appendix to Cmd. 424 (1919), at p. 34, citing the Report of the Select Committee on Land Titles and Transfer of 1828.

3. The two systems. When the legislation came, its sponsors did not commit themselves to universal registration, perhaps because of the professional opposition which that subject was prone to arouse. They proposed an experimental period of ten years in which the merits of registered and unregistered conveyancing might again be compared.[13] There were two main schools of thought: " Some think that the present system of private conveyancing, which has been patched and repatched until the original material is hardly recognisable, only wants a little more patching to make it perfect. Others think that registration of title is inevitable, and resign themselves to their fate, without reflecting that there are good and bad systems of registration." [14] The Bills of 1922–25 were designed to win the support of both sides.

4. Reduction of legal estates. The foundation on which the legislation was built was the reduction in the number of legal estates. This had been advocated by Wolstenholme as early as 1862,[15] and his scheme for effecting it (and other improvements adopted in 1925) may be seen in his draft Conveyancing Bill of 1898.[16] Assimilation to personalty was the guiding policy. " In the case of stock, the entire interest must be transferred. Stock cannot be divided up into particular estates and remainders, which must be created only by way of trust. Accordingly the Bill prohibits the division of a fee simple into particular estates and remainders. This principle applied to land is not new; it already exists in the case of a term of years which cannot be conveyed to A for life with remainder to B. . . . The Bill provides against the necessity of vesting land in trustees by enabling the estate in the land to remain in the tenant for life . . . the limitations under the settlement will be equitable only." [17]

5. Earlier Bills. After the Royal Commission had reported in 1911, work on a general overhaul of the law was put in hand by Lord Haldane L.C., and Bills were produced in 1913, 1914 and 1915. After the war the work was resumed, first under the Minister of Reconstruction and then under Lord Birkenhead L.C., by a Committee over which Sir Leslie Scott presided. The fourth report of the Scott Committee [18] was the immediate cause of the Law of Property Act, 1922, drafted by Sir Benjamin Cherry. As Solicitor-General,

[13] Memorandum prefixed to Law of Property Bill, 1922; Sir Leslie Scott in 154 H.C.Deb. (5th ser.) 102, 103 (1922).
[14] Charles Sweet (1912) 28 L.Q.R. 24.
[15] Holdsworth, *Historical Introduction to the Land Law*, 313.
[16] Printed in Cherry and Marigold, *Land Transfer Acts* (1899), appendix, pp. 423 *et seq.*, with explanatory memorandum; in (1896) 40 S.J. 172, without memorandum.
[17] Memorandum cited in previous note, at p. 417.
[18] Cmd. 424 (1919).

Sir Leslie Scott presented it as " the biggest Bill ever introduced into Parliament," [19] and before it came into force it was amended and sub-divided into the Acts of 1925. Credit for much of the earlier work belongs to The Law Society, which commissioned the Wolstenholme Bill and other projects. But the immediate authors of the Acts of 1925 were Sir Benjamin Cherry, its principal draftsman, Sir Leslie Scott, and Lord Birkenhead L.C.,[19a] whose powers secured not only the passage of the Acts through the House of Lords but also the overwhelming support of the legal profession and of the public.

6. The Bill of 1922. Sir Leslie Scott's speech on the second reading of the Law of Property Bill, 1922,[20] gives a good general account of the intended legislation. " It is not revolution," he said, " it is evolution. . . . It is the slow and gradual product of half a century's work [21] by legal reformers, building on existing foundations." He stated that expert opinion was still sharply divided as to the merits of registration of title, and for that reason the ten-year trial period was proposed. Now that nearly half a century has passed, it may be added that the advantages of registered title are clearly appreciated, and that registration is at last proceeding as fast as the Land Registry can undertake it with the facilities and funds allowed. The initial work required by each extension of the system is heavy, but the speed of progress has nevertheless increased.

Sect. 2. The Reforms of 1925

Apart from many incidental reforms, the principal changes effected by the legislation of 1925 may be grouped under three heads of policy:

(a) The assimilation of the law of real property to that of personal property.

(b) The simplification of conveyancing.

(c) The abolition of anachronisms.

A. Assimilation of the Law of Real and Personal Property

The assimilation of the law of real property to that of personal property was the prime object of the reforms; but unless the old law

---

[19] 154 H.C.Deb. (5th ser.) 90 (1922). He yielded to the temptation to say that his Committee had decided " not to make several bites at the cherry ": *ibid.*, 105.
[19a] He thus fulfilled his ambition, formed when a law student, to abolish the rule in *Shelley's* case.
[20] 154 H.C.Deb. (5th ser.) 90 (1922).
[21] Contrast Holdsworth, *Historical Introduction to the Land Law*, 327: " it would be more true to say that some five centuries of law makers and law reformers have contributed to it."

of real property was to be abandoned altogether [22] assimilation could not be carried very far. The analogy with stocks and shares rapidly breaks down in practice owing to the wider range of transactions in land, and the number of charges, interests and incumbrances to which it can be subject. In the following list only the first two heads represent any substantial assimilation; but they are both of importance. It will be noticed that only under the third head has the rule for realty prevailed over that governing personalty.

1. Settlements : limited and future interests in land can now exist only in equity, and are kept off the title. Settlements of realty are in this way assimilated to settlements of pure personalty, where trusts have always had to be employed.

2. Intestacy : the heir-at-law and the old rules of inheritance have been abolished, so that the same person succeeds to the intestate's property, whether real or personal.[23] This was the only important social and economic reform made in 1925. It involved the abolition of primogeniture and of the preference of males in the descent of land, and the substitution of the principle of equal partibility, as had long been the law for personalty. It also put widows and widowers on an equal footing.

3. Entails of personalty: realty and personalty can now both be entailed, and so both can be settled on identical trusts.[24]

4. Settled chattels: chattels settled to devolve with land can now be sold in much the same way as the land.[25]

5. Words of limitation : the principle that the grantor's whole interest passes, unless a contrary intention appears, now applies also to grants of land.[26]

6. Mortgages : freeholds and leaseholds are now mortgaged by grant of terms of years,[27] and can be mortgaged together by legal charge.[28] The rule in *Dearle* v. *Hall* now governs the priority of mortgages of equitable interests in land as well as in pure personalty.[29]

---

[22] Sir Arthur Underhill was prepared to abandon it and substitute the law of chattels real: see "The Line of Least Resistance" (*ante*, n. 12) at p. 32; (1935) 51 L.Q.R. 228.
[23] *Ante*, p. 523.
[24] *Ante*, p. 94.
[25] *Ante*, p. 343.
[26] *Ante*, p. 56.
[27] *Ante*, p. 892.
[28] *Ante*, p. 897.
[29] *Ante*, p. 976.

B. *Simplification of Conveyancing*

This overlaps the preceding head, as well as the following one. A balance has to be struck between making investigation of title easier for purchasers and, on the other hand, preserving the security of incumbrances and other rights in or over land. The legislation has tilted this balance sharply in favour of purchasers, in particular by requiring the owners of many types of interests in land to register them. It is in the following reforms that the essence of the new system is to be found.

1. Legal estates and interests : the number of estates and interests which can exist at law, and so bind a purchaser irrespective of notice, has been reduced to a short list.[30] Although second and later mortgages may now more commonly exist at law, they must usually be registered.[31]

2. Overreaching : the technique of using the legal estate as a curtain to hide equitable interests which need not concern a purchaser has been extended wherever possible, notably in the new system of documents for settled land,[32] in concurrent interests,[33] and in transactions with personal representatives.[34]

3. Tenancy in common : a notorious complication of conveyancing has been removed by the abolition of legal tenancies in common, coupled with the application of the curtain principle to equitable tenancies in common.[35]

4. Registration of charges : by searching the central and local registers a purchaser can quickly and conclusively ascertain whether numerous rights and interests will bind him.[36]

5. Registration of title : an improved system has been enacted, and has now been put into force in many areas.[37]

6. Investigation of title: the minimum period was reduced to thirty years, and has since been further reduced to fifteen.[38]

---

[30] *Ante,* p. 135.
[31] *Ante,* p. 969.
[32] *Ante,* p. 298.
[33] *Ante,* p. 410.
[34] *Ante,* p. 540.
[35] *Ante,* pp. 408, 410.
[36] *Ante,* p. 1034.
[37] *Ante,* p. 1054.
[38] *Ante,* pp. 123, 579.

C. *Abolition of Anachronisms*

A remarkable number of useless and troublesome rules had survived the earlier reforms, and the incidental spring-cleaning carried out along with the major reforms of 1925 was in itself a great boon. The following may be instanced.

1. Abolition of copyhold, leaving socage the only tenure.[39]
2. Repeal of the Statute of Uses, 1535.[40]
3. Abolition of legal remainders and legal executory interests.[41]
4. Abolition of the rule in *Shelley's* case.[42]
5. Abolition of the rule in *Whitby* v. *Mitchell.*[43]
6. Abolition of *interesse termini* in leases.[44]
7. Abolition of the distinction between things *in posse* and things *in esse* in the rules for the running of covenants in leases.[45]
8. Abolition of the *tabula in naufragio* in mortgages.[46]

Sect. 3. Fifty Years On: A Brief Assessment

A full critique of the Acts would occupy much space, but some of their salient features may be noted in the perspective of half a century.[47] As already stated, the Acts as a whole are unquestionably a success, and fully justify the long and heavy work which prepared for them. Conveyancing is an art which tempts its skilled practitioners to strive for an unattainable perfection; yet the framers of the Acts of 1925, who knew the dangers better than any one, were bold enough to take calculated risks for the sake of their overriding object, practical simplicity. To a student in his early stages it can hardly seem that the legislation has much simplified the law. But in the routine work of conveyancing it has provided much more satisfactory machinery, and the time and trouble saved every day must be great.

Although the legislation of 1925 was intended to be followed by a ten-year experimental period, before making further decisions as to compulsory registration of title,[48] it was not until after the Second World War that registration came to be generally accepted as the

---

[39] *Ante*, p. 34.
[40] *Ante*, p. 171.
[41] *Ante*, p. 198.
[42] *Ante*, p. 65.
[43] *Ante*, p. 206.
[44] *Ante*, p. 633.
[45] *Ante*, p. 731.
[46] *Ante*, p. 983.
[47] For a survey after twenty years, see (1946) 62 L.Q.R. 167 (A. H. Withers).
[48] *Ante*, pp. 1158, 1160.

system of the future.[49] Even then the resources allotted to the Land Registry were inadequate for rapid progress. But the programme has now been accelerated, and compulsory registration of title is now already the prevailing system in urban areas. At last, therefore, there is a prospect that the hopes of the earlier reformers will be fulfilled. But at the same time practitioners are discovering that the system of registration is itself far from simple.[50] Certainly it is no easy avenue of escape from the complexities of English real property law, and it has added many complexities of its own.

If the paucity of litigation upon the Acts of 1925 is one of the clearest indications of their success, it is at the same time surprising that certain of their pitfalls (and some of them are serious) have not yet been before the courts. Against the apparently considerable dangers which appear in the catalogue below must be set the fact that they cause surprisingly little trouble in practice.

The following matters may be suggested for reconsideration.

1. Entails. Entails might well have been abolished in 1925, along with the old rules of inheritance. They are now little more than a nuisance, accompanied by much intricate law. It is true that entails played an important part in the old-fashioned type of strict settlement. But such settlements are out of favour today,[51] and were not of paramount importance even in 1925. Very similar results can be obtained, if indeed they are desired, by simpler forms of trust.

2. Settled land. The attempt to impose a rigid curtain has required a complicated system of documents, which are often artificial in their operation and involve considerable risks to purchasers.[52] The Settled Land Act curtain is far from satisfactory, and hardly justifies the complexity of the statutory machinery. All settlements of land might well take the form of trusts for sale,[53] with certain options as to vesting the powers (and the legal estate) in either the trustees or the tenant for life. The provisions as to overreaching could also be greatly simplified.

3. Legal estates and interests. It was perhaps a mistake to prohibit legal life (and other limited) interests in incorporeal hereditaments such as easements and rentcharges. The object of reducing the number of legal estates was to put limited interests behind trusts

---

[49] See the report by J. N. Gray, K.C. (H.M.S.O., 1951), on various objections to the extension of compulsory registration of title to Surrey (the only occasion on which an extension was formally contested.
[50] *Ante*, p. 1056.
[51] *Ante*, pp. 1085, 1086.
[52] *Ante*, p. 307.
[53] Consider the Kenya legislation on these lines: (1943) 59 L.Q.R. 24 (R.E.M.).

and to provide one indestructible legal estate as the basis of conveyancing. These arguments do not apply to third party rights, which come and go. In order to apply them it was necessary to provide for registration of limited interests in incorporeal rights as " general equitable charges " or " equitable easements." This system seems less satisfactory (partly for reasons given below) than allowing them to continue to exist as legal rights, like perpetual easements or rentcharges.

4. Tenant without notice of landlord's title. The remarkable provision whereby certain unregistrable incumbrances may be destroyed if the land is let to a tenant has already been criticised.[54] The Scott Committee recommended that the rule in *Patman* v. *Harland* should be reversed,[55] but the consequences of doing so do not seem to have been appreciated.

5. Tenancy in common. The beneficent provisions for abolishing legal tenancies in common were defectively drafted, for by attempting to deal in detail with every possible case they omitted several situations, for which there is now no proper provision.[56]

6. Mortgages. The subject of priorities, now fortunately little litigated, is beset by doubts whether the Law of Property Act, 1925, and the Land Charges Act 1972 conflict, and whether equitable mortgages protected by deeds are registrable.[57]

7. Purchase with notice. The rule that a registrable but unregistered land charge is void against a purchaser with actual notice is unreasonably severe. The advantages of simplicity are outweighed by the sense of injustice, and the courts are tempted to strain the law.[58]

8. Equitable owner in possession. Similarly, it is unreasonable to allow a purchaser to prevail over an equitable owner (*e.g.*, a prior tenant or purchaser by agreement) who is in possession and has failed to register an estate contract.[59] Actual possession should give effective protection in such cases, as it did under the doctrine of notice, and as it still does in the case of registered land.[60]

9. Registration of land charges. The scheme enacted by the Land Charges Act, 1925, is the one seriously weak part of the legislation.

[54] *Ante*, p. 707.
[55] Cmd. 424 (1919), para. 8.
[56] *Ante*, p. 411.
[57] *Ante*, pp. 971, 973.
[58] *Ante*, pp. 1043, 1050.
[59] *Ante*, pp. 627, 628.
[60] Rights of persons in possession are overriding interests: *ante*, p. 1066.

The shortcomings of the system of registration against owners' names are serious and incurable.[61] The rule that all persons have notice of registered rights which they are sometimes unable to discover is fundamentally unsound. Only registration of title can rescue the law from this defective machinery.[62] Meanwhile it has been necessary to insure purchasers at public expense against registered charges which they have no means of discovering.[63]

10. Registration of title. Although the Land Registration Act, 1925, may be said to be the only successful registration statute, it has become clear that it is far from satisfactory. It is indeed replete with obscurities, defective definitions, and unsuitable rules.[64] Though most of these are matters of detail, it is important that they should not become ingrained in the system which now governs so much of the conveyancing of the country. A thorough revision, rationalisation and simplification of the law is needed. The Law Commission has already criticised some of its broader features.[65]

The deficiencies listed above affect a great many common conveyancing transactions, and it certainly cannot be said that the legislation of 1925 left the system of conveyancing in no further need of reform. The last four items, it will be noticed, all derive from the inadequacy of statutory schemes of registration. Effort needs now to be concentrated on improving the machinery of registration of title, on which so many false starts have been made. Only then will our real property law fulfil the ideal which was before the eyes of the first advocates of reform more than a century ago.

---

61 *Ante,* pp. 584, 707, 1044.
62 *Ante,* p. 1044.
63 *Ante,* p. 1046.
64 *Ante,* p. 1056.
65 *Ante,* p. 1056.

ACTIONS FOR RECOVERY OF LAND

THE substantive law of real property has been deeply marked by the remedies which the law has provided, at various periods of history, for the recovery of land. The modern rules of procedure may be said to be the machinery for giving effect to the rules of law. But in earlier time the rules of law were themselves the product of the available remedies, so that it is hardly possible to understand some of the fundamental rules, particularly those relating to adverse possession, without some reference to the old forms of action. The purpose of this Appendix, therefore, is to give a short account of the way in which the rules of real property law, and the concept of title, have been influenced by the evolution of new forms of action in the past. Of no branch of our law can it be more truly said that it developed on the principle *ubi remedium, ibi jus*: rights result from remedies.

This short account of a curious chapter of legal history falls into three parts: the real actions, which were part of the old feudal land law; the action of ejectment, which replaced the real actions for most purposes in the sixteenth and seventeenth centuries; and the statutory reforms of modern times, which preserved the substantive law of the action of ejectment but greatly simplified its form.

Sect. 1. The Real Actions

1. The writ of right. The real actions were the original feudal remedies.[1] Foremost among them was the writ of right, which was the principal action for asserting title. Its feudal character appears from the rule that, though a royal writ, it was tried in the court of the lord of whom the land was held, and therefore not necessarily in the royal courts. Its primitive origins appear in the rule that trial was by battle.[2] But in or about 1179 Henry II introduced a new procedure, the Grand Assize, whereby the defendant had the option to claim trial in the royal court before a jury of twelve knights.

This ancient remedy was surrounded by much cumbersome procedure, and the pretexts which it offered for making essoins (excuses

---

[1] For the real actions, see Maitland, *Forms of Action*, 21; H.E.L. iii, 3; Booth, *Real Actions* (2nd ed., 1811).

[2] Battle was theoretically possible until its abolition by 59 Geo. 3, c. 46, 1819. For forms of writ of right, award of battle and grand assize, see Bl.Comm. iii, appendix No. I.

for non-appearance and other defaults) and other dilatory pleas meant that it was used only as a last resort.[3] Proceedings by writ of right bound only the parties to them, so that even at this early stage the question was which of the parties had the better right to possession, rather than who was the true owner of the land in an absolute sense.[4] The writ existed in various forms, including variants which could be used for claiming dower and incorporeal hereditaments.

2. The possessory assizes

(a) *Dispossession.* The possessory assizes were further remedies introduced by Henry II in order to bring litigation about land into the royal courts.[5] Seizure of land was a disturbance of the peace as well as a civil wrong, and the principle behind these remedies was that for the sake of public order the law should protect possession, whether rightful or wrongful, in order that the title might be tried peaceably. By a possessory assize, therefore, a man could recover land merely on the strength of having been dispossessed. It did not matter that the dispossessor might himself be the " true owner," *i.e.,* someone who could himself recover the land by resort to a writ of right. This partial protection of an interloper against the true owner illustrates the great importance of seisin in medieval law.

(b) *Types of assize.* The possessory assizes were principally of three kinds. *Novel disseisin* lay where the plaintiff had himself been disseised by the defendant or by the defendant's grantee; *mort d'ancestor* lay where the plaintiff claimed as heir but an interloper had taken possession; and *darrein presentment* lay for advowsons, showing how the ideas of seisin and disseisin were applied to incorporeal property.

(c) *Novel disseisin.* Novel disseisin, as its name implies, was intended at first to be a speedy remedy, which had to be sought within a short time. Limitation dates were prescribed from time to time, but this practice ceased after the Statute of Westminster I, 1275, which appointed the year 1242, at the same time as it appointed the year 1189 for the writ of right and other purposes.[6] There was then soon no effective time-limit, and the action lost its " novel " aspect; a mere possessory action thus tended to turn into a proprietary action, in a way characteristic of our legal history.

[3] H.E.L. iii, 8, 624.
[4] H.E.L. iii, 89; *ante,* p. 1005, n. 7.
[5] For the possessory assizes, see Maitland, *Forms of Action,* 27; H.E.L. iii, 8, 23, 24.
[6] H.E.L. iii, 8; *ante,* pp. 847, 848, 1010.

3. Writs of entry

(*a*) *Nature of writs.* The writs of entry were supplementary real actions which first appeared early in the thirteenth century, and which eventually covered many cases for which the older actions were not adapted.[7] Their common feature was that the plaintiff claiming the land averred that the defendant or his predecessor in title "had no entry" thereto save through some wrongful act or event. This put in issue that act or event alone, and not the whole title. There were many variants of the writ, which formed a "hopeless tangle."[8] The Statute of Marlbridge, 1267, allowed writs of entry "in the *post*," in which the defendant's wrongful title, if complicated, did not have to be pleaded precisely, but it was enough to claim that he came in after (*post*) the wrongful act or event.[9] This rounded off the system of the real actions, which would then meet any case. But their varieties were so numerous and their rules of procedure and pleading so unsatisfactory that better remedies were badly needed.[10] In the end recourse was had to fictions, with the courts' encouragement, so that freeholders could use the action of ejectment, which had in fact been devised for the benefit of leaseholders. In order to escape from the real actions, freeholders found means to fight their legal battles in the disguise of leaseholders. This they did until 1852, with important effects on the substance of the law.

(*b*) *Seisin and possession.* Except when used for claims to incorporeal property, the real actions were essentially demands for seisin, and thus would lie only against the person who was seised of the land at the time. Seisin essentially meant no more than possession,[11] but the term was so important in the old feudal land law that it acquired two of that law's limitations: it did not apply to the possession of leaseholders or to that of copyholders. In the case of a lease the landlord was seised, although the tenant was in possession; and in the case of copyholds the lord of the manor was seised, although possession was in the copyholder. This was because leases for years were always outside the law of freehold tenure on which the feudal system rested,[12] and in early times the rights of copyholders were not recognised by the royal courts.[13] In these cases, therefore, there was an artificial distinction between seisin and possession, although for other purposes they were virtually synonymous. For the same reasons leaseholders and copyholders were never able to use the real actions.

---

[7] For writs of entry, see Maitland, *Forms of Action*, 42; H.E.L. iii, 11.
[8] Maitland, *Forms of Action*, 43.
[9] *Ibid.*, 42. For the use of this writ in common recoveries for barring entails, see *ante*, p. 87, n. 51.
[10] H.E.L. iii, 624; vii, 5.
[11] *Ante*, p. 48; H.E.L. iii, 88.
[12] *Ante*, p. 43.
[13] *Ante*, p. 25.

Sect. 2. The Action of Ejectment

1. Origin. The action of ejectment [14] was originally invented for the protection of leaseholders, but was later allowed to copyholders also.[15] Since it was a species of the action of trespass (its proper title was "trespass in ejectment "), it belonged to a group of actions which were of later invention than the real actions, and were free from most of their archaisms. It was therefore pressed into service by freeholders as well, at a period when the real actions had become intolerable. But this could not be done directly, if only because the real actions were the recognised monopoly of the Court of Common Pleas. The other courts, however, encouraged a system of fictions whereby freeholders could use the action, while preserving a pretence that the plaintiff was a leaseholder. It was here that John Doe and Richard Roe came to the rescue. With their aid the real actions, with all their intricacies and pitfalls, were replaced by a single form of remedy which, if strange, was at least standardised and free from the relics of feudalism.

2. Recovery of leaseholds. Leases were at first regarded by the common law courts as personal contracts, outside the system of freehold tenures and estates, and not affecting seisin. They were classed as personal property, they could be left by will, and they were not subject to feudal incidents.[16] For these reasons they grew in popularity, and it became necessary to protect tenants by some better remedy than a mere action of trespass for damages. The action *Quaere ejecit infra terminum*, introduced about 1235, did allow a tenant to recover his land specifically, but it was held to be confined to actions against the lessor and his successors.[17] It was not until the second half of the fifteenth century that the common law courts, fearing competition from the specific remedies available in the Chancery, abandoned their scruples and allowed a leaseholder to recover his land specifically from any wrongful claimant.[18] This they did by awarding a writ of possession to a leaseholder, even though his action was an action of trespass. The result was the action of trespass in ejectment,[19] or for short " ejectment." Once the leaseholder was able to recover his land from all comers, it could no longer be denied that he had an estate in the land (a right *in rem*),

[14] For the action of ejectment, see H.E.L. vii, 4; Maitland, *Forms of Action*, 57; Bl.Comm. iii, 200, and appendix No. II.

[15] *Melwich* v. *Luter* (1588) 4 Co.Rep. 26a; H.E.L. iii, 209; vii, 9.

[16] *Ante*, pp. 43, 44.

[17] H.E.L. iii, 214.

[18] Bl.Comm. iii, 200; H.E.L. vii, 8, n. 7. Specific restitution in ejectment was finally allowed in 1499, after a period of uncertainty: H.E.L. iii, 216. The only remaining weakness in the leaseholder's position was that his estate was defeated if the landlord suffered a recovery (*cf. ante*, p. 86, n. 49). This was remedied by 21 Hen. 8, c. 15, 1529.

[19] Its Latin title was trespass *de ejectione firmae*.

or that he held it in tenure. At this point, therefore, leases became a branch of the land law, though retaining their anomalous classification as personalty. In such ways is substantive law created by the extension of remedies.

3. Procedure. By 1600, a century after the invention of ejectment, it was in common use by freeholders; and by about 1650 its form for this purpose had been perfected.[20] A full description need not be given, but the essence of the action was that the nominal plaintiff was John Doe, asserting that he was tenant of the true plaintiff and that he (Doe) had entered upon the land and had thence been ejected by Richard Roe. In the perfected form of the action Doe and Roe were imaginary characters, Roe being known as "the casual ejector." The first real step in the proceedings was that the plaintiff's solicitor sent to the defendant the declaration (or statement of claim) in Doe's action against Roe, under cover of a letter advising the defendant to apply for leave to defend the action in Roe's place and ending "otherwise I shall suffer judgment to be entered against me and you will be turned out of possession. Your loving friend, Richard Roe."[21] It was then essential for the true defendant to appear as such, but the court would allow him to do so only if he confessed the lease, entry and ouster: that is to say, if he undertook not to dispute any of the fictitious allegations. Thus, when the action came to trial, the only question left was whether Doe had a good claim to the land, and this was merely the question whether the plaintiff, as Doe's lessor, had a better title than the defendant. The action was then entitled *Doe* d. *A* v. *B*, meaning *Doe on the demise of A* v. *B*; and by this title an action of ejectment can be recognised.[22]

4. Limitations. This action, strange though it was, rapidly put the real actions out of business. But it did not supplant them completely. In the first place, ejectment was subject to a twenty-year period of limitation; but longer periods were appointed for the real actions, so that after twenty years a plaintiff might find that only a real action was open to him.[23] Secondly, ejectment was also barred if the plaintiff had lost his right of entry upon the land, for then he had no title to grant an effective lease in possession to Doe; and there were certain occasions when, for technical reasons derived from the medieval law, a right of entry was "tolled" (taken away), and all that remained was a right of action.[24] In those cases the plaintiff

---

[20] For details, see H.E.L. vii, 10.

[21] The common forms of these documents are printed in Sutton, *Personal Actions at Common Law*, 53, 54, and in Bl.Comm. iii, appendix, No. II.

[22] The plaintiff could, however, use any names he pleased, and sometimes the casual ejector was named as the defendant; thus cases were tendentiously entitled *Fairclaim* d. *Fowler* v. *Sham-title* (1762) 3 Burr. 1290 and *Goodtitle* d. *Pye* v. *Badtitle* (1800) 8 T.R. 638.

[23] H.E.L. vii, 20, 22.

[24] *Ibid.*; Lightwood, *Possession of Land*, 44; Co.Litt. 237a, 325a; and see *ante*, p. 193. The old law was very complex.

would be driven to fall back on the real actions, for although he had a title, he could not sue in ejectment. These cases, like novel disseisin in its early days, provide examples of a wrongful possessor being protected against the true owner. Thirdly, ejectment would not lie for incorporeal hereditaments such as advowsons, where the fictions of lease, entry and ouster broke down.[25]

5. Seisin and possession. It is important to remember that the action of ejectment was basically an action of trespass[26]: it lay to protect possession, and the question was whether, as against the defendant, the plaintiff had a good title to grant an effective lease. In breaking away from the real actions landowners also broke away from the dominance of seisin, which had been an essential ingredient in the real actions and which had produced a crop of technical peculiarities. Although seisin was often treated as being the root of title, it was in most respects synonymous with possession, except where the possession was clearly subject to some superior title, as was the possession of a tenant. It was the action of ejectment which shifted the basis of title from the feudal concept of seisin to the modern concept of adverse possession[27]; although, since there is so little difference between seisin and possession for most purposes, the same truth can be as well expressed by saying that ejectment offered a way of escape from some of the medieval refinements of seisin as well as from the real actions.

6. Titles relative. The theory that the action of ejectment introduced a new concept of " ownership " into English law, in the sense that a plaintiff had to prove a title that was absolutely good rather than one that was relatively better than the defendant's, has been criticised elsewhere.[28] The issue in ejectment was a purely relative one, and the relativity of all titles, which all depend in the last resort upon possession, has already been explained.[29] Far from requiring a plaintiff to prove absolute ownership, the action of ejectment preserved the conception of relative titles which had been part of English law from the time of the writ of right, while at the same time avoiding the difficulties which surrounded the real actions.

Sect. 3. Statutory Reforms

1. Abolition of real actions. The real actions were abolished by the Real Property Limitation Act, 1833[30]; the only exceptions were

---

25 H.E.L. vii, 21.
26 For the way in which it was " licked into the shape of a real action," by elimination of certain defects, see H.E.L. vii, 13–19.
27 See Lightwood, *Possession of Land*, 125, 146, 149. The process was completed by the abolition of the real actions by the Real Property Limitation Act, 1833.
28 *Ante*, p. 1006, n. 18. Holdsworth's theory of the growth of " ownership," and some of its corollaries, were discussed and criticised in *Allen* v. *Roughley* (1955) 94 C.L.R. 98, noted in [1956] C.L.J. 177 (H.W.R.W.).
29 *Ante*, p. 1006.
30 s. 36, naming the various actions, and taking effect on January 1, 1835.

the old actions for dower and advowsons, for which there were no satisfactory substitutes.[31] At the same time the old rules about "tolling" rights of entry were abolished.[32] Thus the action of ejectment was left without competitors. Curiously enough, the action itself underwent no reform, and Doe and Roe still had to play their old parts in actions by freeholders.

2. Abolition of forms of action. This continued until the Common Law Procedure Act, 1852, abolished the forms of action in general and ejectment in particular.[33] Thereafter a plaintiff merely had to institute his action for the recovery of land by pleading his claim to it in ordinary language. But this did not bring about any change in the substantive law: an action for the recovery of land would meet with the same success or failure as an action of ejectment would have done before the Act. Similarly, when new rules of court were introduced by the Judicature Acts, 1873–1875,[34] the new procedure made no change in the substantive law relating to titles. But the amalgamation of legal and equitable jurisdiction[35] meant that the same form of proceedings could be used to assert either a legal or an equitable title,[36] thus consummating a reform which Lord Mansfield had unsuccessfully attempted in the eighteenth century, when the action of ejectment was confined to claims at law.[37]

3. Modern law. The law of title to land therefore remains as it was in the latter days of the action of ejectment. An action for recovery of land is still in essence an action of trespass. Thus until 1962 an action to recover land, like other actions in tort, did not lie between husband and wife, except to protect her property.[38] The principle that possession itself confers a good title against all who cannot show a superior title[39] was reflected in the former rule of court that a defendant who was himself in possession need not plead his title unless he claimed under the plaintiff, or upon equitable grounds.[40] He needed to plead only that he was in possession, and leave it to the plaintiff to show a better title if he could.

---

[31] *Ibid.* The difficulty with dower was that ejectment would not lie until the dower land had been assigned (*ante*, p. 518). These exceptions were abolished by the Common Law Procedure Act, 1860, ss. 26, 27; this was the final disappearance of real actions.

[32] Real Property Limitation Act, 1833, s. 39.

[33] ss. 168–221.

[34] Judicature Act, 1873, Sched. The present rules are the R.S.C. (Revision) 1965, replacing R.S.C., 1883, as amended (particularly by R.S.C. (Revision) 1962), made under J.A., 1925, s. 99

[35] *Ante*, p. 128.

[36] See *General Finance Mortgage and Discount Co.* v. *Liberator Permanent Benefit Building Society* (1878) 10 Ch.D. 15 at 24; *Antrim County Land Building and Investment Co. Ltd.* v. *Stewart* [1904] 2 I.R. 357; *cf. ante*, p. 923.

[37] H.E.L. vii, 19, 23.

[38] See *ante*, p. 1006, n. 15.

[39] *Ante*, p. 1004.

[40] R.S.C., 1883, Ord. 21, r. 21, revoked and not replaced by R.S.C. (Revision), 1962.

A landowner now has a swift remedy against those who occupy his land without his consent. He may issue an originating summons claiming possession even if he cannot discover the names of the squatters, and seven clear days after it has been served the court may make an order for possession.[41] On proof of the case, the court must make the order; and there is no power to suspend its operation.[42]

---

[41] R.S.C., Ord. 113, added in 1970; see *Metropolitan Police Receiver* v. *Smith* (1974) 118 S.J. 583. The time may be shortened in cases of urgency. The corresponding provision in the county court is C.C.R., Ord. 26.

[42] *McPhail* v. *Persons, Names Unknown* [1973] Ch. 447; *Greater London Council* v. *Jenkins* [1975] 1 W.L.R. 155 (the procedure applies to expired licences).

INDEX

1175

FEE SIMPLE—*cont.*
  defeasible by condition subsequent,
    138, 316
  determinable, 74, 75
    distinguished from conditional, 76
  equitable, 130
  estate, 41, 42
  modified, nature of, 82
  nature of, 66–82
  owner, rights of, 68–74
  remainder after, is void, 184, 185
FEE TAIL: *see also* ENTAIL; ENTAILED
    INTERESTS,
  barrable by recovery or fine, 83–90
  conditional fee, development from,
    82, 83
  equitable interest after 1925...94
  estate, 42
  history of, 82–92
  words of limitation creating, 57–65
FENCING,
  rights of, 879, 880
FEOFFEE TO USES,
  breach of trust by, 153
FEOFFMENT—
  with livery of seisin, 163, 164, 166
    abolition of, 167
FEUDAL BURDENS,
  evasion of, 154
FEUDAL DUES,
  evasion of, 160
FEUDAL SYSTEM, 13
FIANCÉ,
  gift by will to, 485
  interest in matrimonial property,
    445, 446
FINE,
  capital money, is, 336
  definition of, 336, 697
  demanded for granting licence or
    consent, 697
  feudal incident payable on alien-
    ation, 25, 33, 37
FINE (ACTION),
  conveyance, used as, 163
  distinguished from recovery, 89
  entail, for barring, 87–90
FIRE,
  covenant to insure against, 703, 704
  insurance against, by mortgagee,
    926
FISHING RIGHTS, 72
FIXTURES,
  agricultural, 717
  chattels distinguished from, 712–715
  degree of annexation, 712, 713
  meaning of, 711, 712
  mortgage of land includes, 718, 925
  ornamental and domestic, 716, 717
  personal representatives cannot
    remove, 718
  purchaser's right to, 718
  purpose of annexation, 713–715

FIXTURES—*cont.*
  right—
    of third parties, 719
    to remove, 715–718
    to return to remove, 716
  statues, 714
  stone garden seats, 714
  tenant for life's right to remove,
    109, 717, 718
  tenant's right to remove, 715–717
  trade, 716
FLUCTUATING BODIES,
  rights of, 825–827: *see also*
    CUSTOMARY RIGHTS.
FORCIBLE ENTRY,
  premises, of, 683
FORECLOSURE,
  action, rights of parties to, 947, 948
  equitable mortgagee, primary
    remedy of, 922
  historical basis of, 889, 890
  opening the, 908
  parties to action for, 906, 907, 947,
    948
  precludes other remedies, 921, 922
  procedure in action for, 907
  right of, 905, 906
    waiver of, 906
  sale may be ordered instead of, 907,
    908
FORESHORE,
  ownership of, 69
FORFEITURE,
  assignee's right of, 737
  assignment does not prevent, 741
  breach of condition, for, 655, 656,
    662–667
  breach of covenant, for, 655, 662–
    667
    relief from, 664, 665
    service of statutory notice, 662–664
  breach of covenant not touching
    and concerning land, 740
  breach of repairing covenant, 702,
    703
  cases where relief not available,
    665, 666
  clause,
    inclusion of, 656
    operation of, 739–741
    precedent of, 710
  condition, for breach of, 655, 656
  conditions for, 659–667
  denial of title, for, 654, 655
  enforcement of, 656, 657
  irremediable breach of covenant,
    663
  lack of privity does not prevent,
    739, 740
  non-payment of rent, for, 659–662
  particular estate, of: *see* PARTICU-
    LAR ESTATE.